New Perspectives on

W9-BNT-204

Microsoft® Office Excel® 2007

Comprehensive

What is the Microsoft Business Certification Program?

The Microsoft Business Certification Program enables candidates to show that they have something exceptional to offer – proven expertise in Microsoft Office programs. The two certification tracks allow candidates to choose how they want to exhibit their skills, either through validating skills within a specific Microsoft product or taking their knowledge to the next level and combining Microsoft programs to show that they can apply multiple skill sets to complete more complex office tasks. Recognized by businesses and schools around the world, over 3 million certifications have been obtained in over 100 different countries. The Microsoft Business Certification Program is the only Microsoft-approved certification program of its kind.

What is the Microsoft Certified Application Specialist Certification?

The Microsoft Certified Application Specialist Certification exams focus on validating specific skill sets within each of the Microsoft® Office system programs. The candidate can choose which exam(s) they want to take according to which skills they want to validate. The available Application Specialist exams include:

- Using Windows Vista™
- Using Microsoft® Office Word 2007
- Using Microsoft® Office Excel® 2007
- Using Microsoft® Office PowerPoint® 2007
- Using Microsoft® Office Access 2007
- Using Microsoft® Office Outlook® 2007

What is the Microsoft Certified Application Professional Certification?

The Microsoft Certified Application Professional Certification exams focus on a candidate's ability to use the 2007 Microsoft® Office system to accomplish industry-agnostic functions, for example Budget Analysis and Forecasting, or Content Management and Collaboration. The available Application Professional exams currently include:

- Organizational Support
- Creating and Managing Presentations
- Content Management and Collaboration
- Budget Analysis and Forecasting

What do the Microsoft Business Certification Vendor of Approved Courseware logos represent?

The logos validate that the courseware has been approved by the Microsoft® Business Certification Vendor program and that these courses cover objectives that will be included in the relevant exam. It also means that after utilizing this courseware, you may be prepared to pass the exams required to become a Microsoft Certified Application Specialist or Microsoft Certified Application Professional.

For more information:

To learn more about Microsoft Certified Application Specialist or Professional exams, visit
www.microsoft.com/learning/msbc.
To learn about other Microsoft Certified Application Specialist approved courseware from Course Technology, visit
www.course.com.
*The availability of Microsoft Certified Application exams varies by Microsoft Office program, program version and language.
Visit www.microsoft.com/learning for exam availability.
Microsoft, the Office Logo, Outlook, and PowerPoint are either registered trademarks or trademarks of Microsoft Corporation in the United States and/or other countries. The Microsoft Certified Application Specialist and Microsoft Certified Application Professional Logos are used under license from Microsoft Corporation.

New Perspectives on

Microsoft® Office Excel® 2007

Comprehensive

June Jamrich Parsons

Dan Oja

Roy Ageloff

Patrick Carey

COURSE TECHNOLOGY
CENGAGE Learning™

Australia • Brazil • Japan • Korea • Mexico • Singapore • Spain • United Kingdom • United States

COURSE TECHNOLOGY
CENGAGE Learning™

**New Perspectives on Microsoft Office Excel
2007—Comprehensive**
Course Technology

Acquisitions Editor: Kristina Matthews

Senior Product Manager: Kathy Finnegan

Product Manager: Erik Herman

Associate Product Manager: Brandi Henson

Editorial Assistant: Leigh Robbins

Senior Marketing Manager: Joy Stark

Marketing Coordinator: Jennifer Hankin

Developmental Editor: Robin M. Romer

Content Project Managers: Daphne Barbas,
Danielle Chouhan

Composition: GEX Publishing Services

Text Designer: Steve Deschene

Cover Designer: Elizabeth Paquin

Cover Art: Bill Brown

© 2008 Course Technology, Cengage Learning

ALL RIGHTS RESERVED. No part of this work covered by the copyright herein may be reproduced, transmitted, stored or used in any form or by any means graphic, electronic, or mechanical, including but not limited to photocopying, recording, scanning, digitizing, taping, Web distribution, information networks, or information storage and retrieval systems, except as permitted under Section 107 or 108 of the 1976 United States Copyright Act, without the prior written permission of the publisher.

For product information and technology assistance, contact us at
Cengage Learning Customer & Sales Support, 1-800-354-9706

For permission to use material from this text or product, submit all
requests online at **cengage.com/permissions**
Further permissions questions can be emailed to
permissionrequest@cengage.com

ISBN-13: 978-1-4239-0585-1

ISBN-10: 1-4239-0585-7

Course Technology
25 Thomson Place
Boston, Massachusetts 02210
USA

Cengage Learning is a leading provider of customized learning solutions with office locations around the globe, including Singapore, the United Kingdom, Australia, Mexico, Brazil, and Japan. Locate your local office at:
international.cengage.com/region

Cengage Learning products are represented in Canada by Nelson
Education, Ltd.

For your lifelong learning solutions, visit **course.cengage.com**

Purchase any of our products at your local college store or at our preferred online store **www.ichapters.com**

Disclaimer: Any fictional data related to persons or companies or URLs used throughout this book is intended for instructional purposes only. At the time this book was printed, any such data was fictional and not belonging to any real persons or companies.

Microsoft and the Office logo are either registered trademarks or trademarks of Microsoft Corporation in the United States and/or other countries. Thomson Course Technology is an independent entity from the Microsoft Corporation, and not affiliated with Microsoft in any manner.

Printed in the United States of America
4 5 6 7 8 9 11 10 09 08

Preface

The New Perspectives Series' critical-thinking, problem-solving approach is the ideal way to prepare students to transcend point-and-click skills and take advantage of all that Microsoft Office 2007 has to offer.

In developing the New Perspectives Series for Microsoft Office 2007, our goal was to create books that give students the software concepts and practical skills they need to succeed beyond the classroom. We've updated our proven case-based pedagogy with more practical content to make learning skills more meaningful to students.

With the New Perspectives Series, students understand *why* they are learning *what* they are learning, and are fully prepared to apply their skills to real-life situations.

eally love the Margin s, which add 'tricks of the de' to students' skills ckage. In addition, the ality Check exercises pro- e for practical application students' knowledge. I n't wait to use them in the ssroom when we adopt ice 2007."

—Terry Morse Colucci nstitute of Technology, Inc.

About This Book

This book provides thorough, hands-on coverage of the new Microsoft Office Excel 2007 soft- ware, and includes the following:

- A new "Getting Started with Microsoft Office 2007" tutorial that familiarizes students with the new Office 2007 features and user interface
- Complete instruction on Excel 2007 basics, including creating and formatting a work- book, working with formulas and functions, and creating charts and graphics
- Expanded and in-depth coverage of higher level skills, including working with Excel tables, PivotTables, and PivotCharts; managing multiple worksheets and workbooks; using advanced functions and filtering; developing an Excel application; working with Excel's financial tools; importing data into Excel; and expanding Excel with Visual Basic for Applications
- A solid and thorough presentation of important spreadsheet concepts, including order of precedence, function syntax, absolute and relative cell references, what-if analysis, data validation, data tables, arrays, scenarios, and object-oriented programming
- Coverage of the exciting new features of Excel 2007, including table styles, design themes, Live Preview, SmartArt, Quick Styles, conditional formats, Trust Center, Document Inspector, Information Rights Management, and Compatibility Checker
- New business case scenarios throughout, which provide a rich and realistic context for students to apply the concepts and skills presented
- Certification requirements for the Microsoft Certified Application Specialist exam, "Using Microsoft® Office Excel® 2007"

System Requirements

This book assumes a typical installation of Microsoft Office Excel 2007 and Microsoft Windows Vista Ultimate with the Aero feature turned off (or Windows Vista Home Premium or Business edition). Note that you can also complete the tutorials in this book using Windows XP; you will notice only minor differences if you are using Windows XP. Refer to the tutorial "Getting Started with Microsoft Office 2007" for Tips noting these differences. The browser used in this book for any steps that require a browser is Internet Explorer 7.

The New Perspectives Approach

"I appreciate the real-world approach that the New Perspectives Series takes. It enables the transference of knowledge from step-by-step instructions to a far broader application of the software tools."

—Monique Sluymers
Kaplan University

Context

Each tutorial begins with a problem presented in a "real-world" case that is meaningful to students. The case sets the scene to help students understand what they will do in the tutorial.

Hands-on Approach

Each tutorial is divided into manageable sessions that combine reading and hands-on, step-by-step work. Colorful screenshots help guide students through the steps. **Trouble?** tips anticipate common mistakes or problems to help students stay on track and continue with the tutorial.

InSight

InSight Boxes

New for Office 2007! InSight boxes offer expert advice and best practices to help students better understand how to work with the software. With the information provided in the InSight boxes, students achieve a deeper understanding of the concepts behind the software features and skills.

Tip

Margin Tips

New for Office 2007! Margin Tips provide helpful hints and shortcuts for more efficient use of the software. The Tips appear in the margin at key points throughout each tutorial, giving students extra information when and where they need it.

Reality Check

Reality Checks

New for Office 2007! Comprehensive, open-ended Reality Check exercises give students the opportunity to practice skills by creating practical, real-world documents, such as resumes and budgets, which they are likely to use in their everyday lives at school, home, or work.

Review

In New Perspectives, retention is a key component to learning. At the end of each session, a series of Quick Check questions helps students test their understanding of the concepts before moving on. Each tutorial also contains an end-of-tutorial summary and a list of key terms for further reinforcement.

Apply

Assessment

Engaging and challenging Review Assignments and Case Problems have always been a hallmark feature of the New Perspectives Series. Colorful icons and brief descriptions accompany the exercises, making it easy to understand, at a glance, both the goal and level of challenge a particular assignment holds.

Reference Window

Task Reference

Reference

While contextual learning is excellent for retention, there are times when students will want a high-level understanding of how to accomplish a task. Within each tutorial, Reference Windows appear before a set of steps to provide a succinct summary and preview of how to perform a task. In addition, a complete Task Reference at the back of the book provides quick access to information on how to carry out common tasks. Finally, each book includes a combination Glossary/Index to promote easy reference of material.

Brief

Introductory

Comprehensive

Our Complete System of Instruction

Coverage To Meet Your Needs

Whether you're looking for just a small amount of coverage or enough to fill a semester-long class, we can provide you with a textbook that meets your needs.

- Brief books typically cover the essential skills in just 2 to 4 tutorials.
- Introductory books build and expand on those skills and contain an average of 5 to 8 tutorials.
- Comprehensive books are great for a full-semester class, and contain 9 to 12+ tutorials.

So if the book you're holding does not provide the right amount of coverage for you, there's probably another offering available. Visit our Web site or contact your Course Technology sales representative to find out what else we offer.

Student Online Companion

This book has an accompanying online companion Web site designed to enhance learning. This Web site, www.course.com/np/office2007, includes the following:

- Internet Assignments for selected tutorials
- Student Data Files
- PowerPoint presentations

CourseCasts – Learning on the Go. Always available…always relevant.

Want to keep up with the latest technology trends relevant to you? Visit our site to find a library of podcasts, CourseCasts, featuring a "CourseCast of the Week," and download them to your mp3 player at http://coursecasts.course.com.

Our fast-paced world is driven by technology. You know because you're an active participant—always on the go, always keeping up with technological trends, and always learning new ways to embrace technology to power your life.

Ken Baldauf, host of CourseCasts, is a faculty member of the Florida State University Computer Science Department where he is responsible for teaching technology classes to thousands of FSU students each year. Ken is an expert in the latest technology trends; he gathers and sorts through the most pertinent news and information for CourseCasts so your students can spend their time enjoying technology, rather than trying to figure it out. Open or close your lecture with a discussion based on the latest CourseCast.

Visit us at http://coursecasts.course.com to learn on the go!

Instructor Resources

We offer more than just a book. We have all the tools you need to enhance your lectures, check students' work, and generate exams in a new, easier-to-use and completely revised package. This book's Instructor's Manual, ExamView testbank, PowerPoint presentations, data files, solution files, figure files, and a sample syllabus are all available on a single CD-ROM or for downloading at www.course.com.

Blackboard

Skills Assessment and Training

SAM 2007 helps bridge the gap between the classroom and the real world by allowing students to train and test on important computer skills in an active, hands-on environment.

SAM 2007's easy-to-use system includes powerful interactive exams, training or projects on critical applications such as Word, Excel, Access, PowerPoint, Outlook, Windows, the Internet, and much more. SAM simulates the application environment, allowing students to demonstrate their knowledge and think through the skills by performing real-world tasks.

Designed to be used with the New Perspectives Series, SAM 2007 includes built-in page references so students can print helpful study guides that match the New Perspectives textbooks used in class. Powerful administrative options allow instructors to schedule exams and assignments, secure tests, and run reports with almost limitless flexibility.

Online Content

Blackboard is the leading distance learning solution provider and class-management platform today. Course Technology has partnered with Blackboard to bring you premium online content. Content for use with *New Perspectives on Microsoft Office Excel 2007, Comprehensive* is available in a Blackboard Course Cartridge and may include topic reviews, case projects, review questions, test banks, practice tests, custom syllabi, and more.

Course Technology also has solutions for several other learning management systems. Please visit http://www.course.com today to see what's available for this title.

Acknowledgments

We would like to thank the many people whose invaluable contributions made this book possible. First, sincere thanks go to our reviewers: Earl Belcher, Sinclair Community College; Alan Fisher, Walters State Community College; Ranida B. Harris, Indiana University Southeast; Brian Kovar, Kansas State University; Karleen Nordquist, Rasmussen College; Janet Reckmeyer, Glendale Community College; Kenneth J. Sousa, Bryant University; Martha Taylor, Sinclair Community College; and Cathy Van Landuyt, Missouri State University. At Course Technology we would like to thank Kristina Matthews, Acquisitions Editor; Kathy Finnegan, Senior Product Manager; Brandi Henson, Associate Product Manager; Leigh Robbins, Editorial Assistant; Daphne Barbas and Danielle Chouhan, Content Project Managers; Christian Kunciw, Manuscript Quality Assurance Project Leader; and John Freitas, Serge Palladino, Danielle Shaw, Marianne Snow, and Susan Whalen, MQA Testers. Special thanks to Robin Romer, Developmental Editor, for her exceptional efforts, keeping us focused and providing guidance and encouragement as we worked to complete this text.

–June Jamrich Parsons
–Dan Oja
–Roy Ageloff
–Patrick Carey

Brief Contents

File Managment

Managing Your Files . . . . .FM 1
Creating and Working with Files and Folders in Windows Vista

Office

Getting Started with Microsoft Office 2007 . . . . .OFF 1
Preparing a Meeting Agenda

Excel

Excel—Level I Tutorials

Excel—Level II Tutorials

Excel—Level III Tutorials

Table of Contents

Excel Level I Tutorials

Tutorial 1 Getting Started with Excel
Creating an Order Report . . . .*EX 1*

Tutorial 2 Formatting a Workbook
Formatting a Financial Report . . . . .EX 57

Tutorial 3 Working with Formulas and Functions
Developing a Budget . . . .*EX 113*

Tutorial 4 Working with Charts and Graphics
Charting Financial Data . . . .*EX 161*

Excel Level II Tutorials

Tutorial 5 Working with Excel Tables, PivotTables, and PivotCharts
Tracking Museum Art Objects . . . .*EX 217*

Tutorial 6 Managing Multiple Worksheets and Workbooks

Summarizing Ticket Sales . . . .*EX 281*

Tutorial 7 Using Advanced Functions, Conditional Formatting, and Filtering

Reviewing Employee Data ....*EX 337*

Excel Level III Tutorials

Tutorial 9 Developing a Financial Analysis
Working with Financial Tools and Functions . . . . . .*EX 457*

Tutorial 10 Performing What-If Analyses
Analyzing the Cost-Volume-Profit Relationship . . .EX 517

Tutorial 11 Connecting to External Data
Importing Financial Data from Several Sources . .EX 575

Appendix D Working with Enhanced Formatting Tools

Objectives

- Develop file management strategies
- Explore files and folders
- Create, name, copy, move, and delete folders
- Name, copy, move, and delete files
- Work with compressed files

Managing Your Files

Creating and Working with Files and Folders in Windows Vista

Case | Distance Learning Company

The Distance Learning Company specializes in distance-learning courses for people who want to participate in college-level classes to work toward a degree or for personal enrichment. Distance learning is formalized education that typically takes place using a computer and the Internet, replacing normal classroom interaction with modern communications technology. The company's goal is to help students gain new skills and stay competitive in the job market. The head of the Customer Service Department, Shannon Connell, interacts with the Distance Learning Company's clients on the phone and from her computer. Shannon, like all other employees, is required to learn the basics of managing files on her computer.

In this tutorial, you'll work with Shannon to devise a strategy for managing files. You'll learn how Windows Vista organizes files and folders, and you'll examine Windows Vista file management tools. You'll create folders and organize files within them. You'll also explore options for working with compressed files.

Starting Data Files

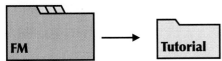

FM →

Tutorial	**Review**	**Case1**
Agenda.docx	Billing.xlsx	Inv Feb.xlsx
Holiday.bmp	Car Plan.xlsx	Inv Jan.xlsx
Members.htm	Commissions.xlsx	Inv March.xlsx
New Logo.bmp	Contracts.xlsx	Painting-Agenda.docx
Proposal.docx	Customers.xlsx	Painting-Eval.docx
Resume.docx	Loan.docx	Painting-Manual.docx
Stationery.bmp	Photos.pptx	Paris.jpg
Vinca.jpg	Speech.wav	Still Life.jpg
	Water lilies.jpg	

Organizing Files and Folders

Knowing how to save, locate, and organize computer files makes you more productive when you are working with a computer. A **file**, often referred to as a **document**, is a collection of data that has a name and is stored on a computer. After you create a file, you can open it, edit its contents, print it, and save it again—usually using the same program you used to create it. You organize files by storing them in **folders**, which are containers for your files. You need to organize files so that you can find them easily and work efficiently.

A file cabinet is a common metaphor for computer file organization. A computer is like a file cabinet that has two or more drawers—each drawer is a storage device, or **disk**. Each disk contains folders that hold documents, or files. To make it easy to retrieve files, you arrange them logically into folders. For example, one folder might contain financial data, another might contain your creative work, and another could contain information you're collecting for an upcoming vacation.

A computer can store folders and files on different types of disks, ranging from removable media—such as **USB drives** (also called USB flash drives), **compact discs (CDs)**, and **digital video discs (DVDs)**—to **hard disks**, or fixed disks, which are permanently stored on a computer. Hard disks are the most popular type of computer storage because they can contain many gigabytes of data and are economical.

To have your computer access a removable disk, you must insert the disk into a **drive**, which is a computer device that can retrieve and sometimes record data on a disk. See Figure 1. A hard disk is already contained in a drive, so you don't need to insert it each time you use the computer.

Figure 1 ▶ **Comparing drives and disks**

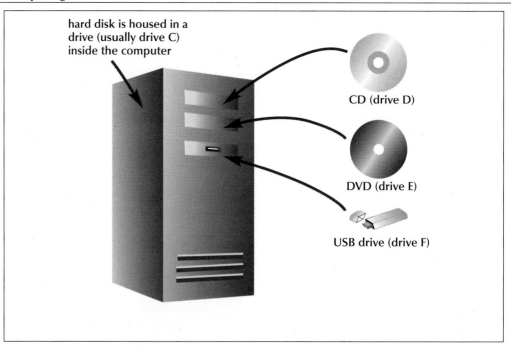

hard disk is housed in a
drive (usually drive C)
inside the computer

CD (drive D)

DVD (drive E)

USB drive (drive F)

A computer distinguishes one drive from another by assigning each a drive letter. The hard disk is usually assigned to drive C. The remaining drives can have any other letters, but are usually assigned in the order that the drives were installed on the computer—so your USB drive might be drive D or drive F. Most contemporary computers have ports for more than one USB drive.

Understanding the Need for Organizing Files and Folders

Windows Vista stores thousands of files in many folders on the hard disk of your computer. These are system files that Windows Vista needs to display the desktop, use drives, and perform other operating system tasks. To ensure system stability and find files quickly, Windows Vista organizes the folders and files in a hierarchy, or **file system**. At the top of the hierarchy, Windows Vista stores folders and important files that it needs when you turn on the computer. This location is called the **root directory**, and is usually drive C (the hard disk). The term "root" refers to another popular metaphor for visualizing a file system—an upside-down tree, which reflects the file hierarchy that Windows Vista uses. In Figure 2, the tree trunk corresponds to the root directory, the branches to the folders, and the leaves to the files.

Windows file hierarchy   Figure 2

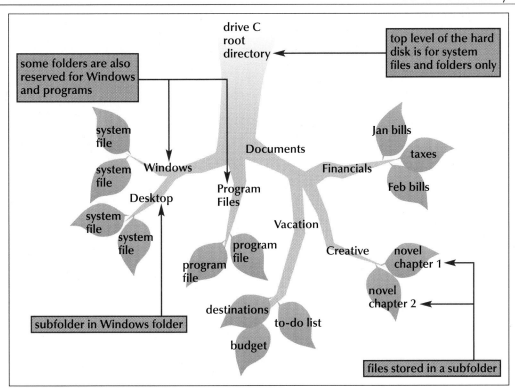

drive C
root
directory

top level of the hard disk is for system files and folders only

some folders are also reserved for Windows and programs

system file

system file   Windows

Desktop

system file

system file

subfolder in Windows folder

Documents

Program Files

Vacation

program file

program file

destinations

budget

to-do list

Jan bills

taxes

Financials

Feb bills

Creative   novel chapter 1

novel chapter 2

files stored in a subfolder

Note that some folders contain other folders. An effectively organized computer contains a few folders in the root directory, and those folders contain other folders, also called **subfolders**.

The root directory, or top level, of the hard disk is for system files and folders only—you should not store your own work here because it could interfere with Windows or a program. (If you are working in a computer lab, you might not be allowed to access the root directory.)

Do not delete or move any files or folders from the root directory of the hard disk—doing so could mean that you cannot run or start the computer. In fact, you should not reorganize or change any folder that contains installed software because Windows Vista expects to find the files for specific programs within certain folders. If you reorganize or change these folders, Windows Vista cannot locate and start the programs stored in that folder. Likewise, you should not make changes to the folder that contains the Windows Vista operating system (usually named Windows or Winnt).

Because the top level of the hard disk is off-limits for your files—the ones that you create, open, and save on the hard disk—you must store your files in subfolders. If you are working on your own computer, you should store your files within the Documents folder. If you are working in a computer lab, you will probably use a different location that your instructor specifies. If you simply store all your files in one folder, however, you will soon have trouble finding the files you want. Instead, you should create folders within a main folder to separate files in a way that makes sense for you.

Likewise, if you store most of your files on removable media, such as USB drives, you need to organize those files into folders and subfolders. Before you start creating folders, whether on a hard disk or removable disk, you should plan the organization you will use.

Developing Strategies for Organizing Files and Folders

The type of disk you use to store files determines how you organize those files. Figure 3 shows how you could organize your files on a hard disk if you were taking a full semester of distance-learning classes. To duplicate this organization, you would open the main folder for your documents, create four folders—one each for the Basic Accounting, Computer Concepts, Management Skills II, and Professional Writing courses—and then store the writing assignments you complete in the Professional Writing folder.

Figure 3 ▶ **Organizing folders and files on a hard disk**

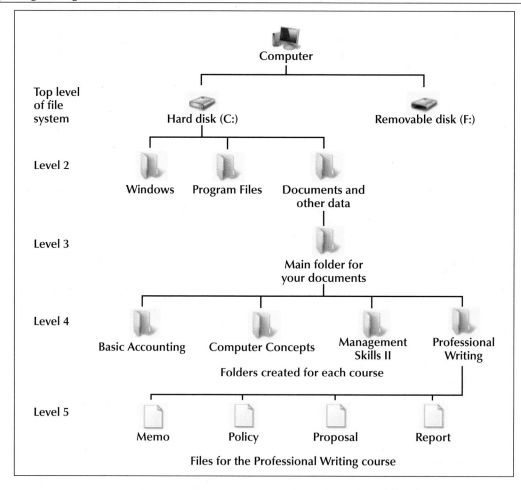

If you store your files on removable media, such as a USB drive or rewritable CD, you can use a simpler organization because you do not have to account for system files. In general, the larger the medium, the more levels of folders you should use because large media can store more files, and, therefore, need better organization. For example, you could organize your files on a 128-MB USB drive. In the top level of the USB drive, you could create folders for each general category of documents you store—one each for Courses, Creative, Financials, and Vacation. The Courses folder could then include one folder for each course, and each of those folders could contain the appropriate files.

If you work on two computers, such as one computer at an office or school and another computer at home, you can duplicate the folders you use on both computers to simplify transferring files from one computer to another. For example, if you have four folders in your Documents folder on your work computer, you would create these same four folders on your removable media as well as in the Documents folder of your home computer. If you change a file on the hard disk of your home computer, you can copy the most recent version of the file to the corresponding folder on your removable media so that it is available when you are at work. You also then have a **backup**, or duplicate copy, of important files that you need.

Planning Your Organization

Now that you've explored the basics of organizing files on a computer, you can plan the organization of your files for this book by writing in your answers to the following questions:

1. How do you obtain the files for this book (on a USB drive from your instructor, for example)?_____

2. On what drive do you store your files for this book (drive A, C, D, for example)? _____

3. Do you use a particular folder on this drive? If so, which folder do you use?_____
   _____

4. Is this folder contained within another folder? If so, what is the name of that main folder?_____

5. On what type of disk or drive do you save your files for this book (hard disk, USB drive, CD, or network drive, for example)?_____

   If you cannot answer any of these questions, ask your instructor for help.

Exploring Files and Folders

Windows Vista provides two tools for exploring the files and folders on your computer—Windows Explorer and the Computer window. Both display the contents of your computer, using icons to represent drives, folders, and files. However, by default, each presents a slightly different view of your computer. **Windows Explorer** shows the files, folders, and drives on your computer, making it easy to navigate, or move from one location to another within the file hierarchy. The **Computer** window shows the drives on your computer and makes it easy to perform system tasks, such as viewing system information. Most of the time, you use one of these tools to open a **folder window** that displays the files and subfolders in a folder.

The Windows Explorer and Computer windows are divided into two sections, called **panes**. The left pane is the **Navigation pane**. It contains a **Favorite Links list**, which can provide quick access to the folders you use often, and a **Folders list**, which shows the hierarchy of the folders and other locations on your computer. The right pane lists the contents of these folders and other locations. If you select a folder in the left pane, for example, the files stored in that folder appear in the right pane.

Tip

The term "folder window" refers to any window that displays the contents of a folder, including the Computer, Windows Explorer, and Recycle Bin windows. In all of these windows, you can use the same techniques to display folders and their contents, navigate your computer, and work with files.

If the Folders list showed all the folders on your computer at once, it could be a very long list. Instead, you open drives and folders only when you want to see what they contain. If a folder contains subfolders, an expand icon ▷ appears to the left of the folder icon. (The same is true for drives.) To view the folders contained in an object, you click the expand icon. A collapse icon ◢ then appears next to the folder icon; click the collapse icon to hide the folder's subfolders. To view the files contained in a folder, you click the folder icon, and the files appear in the right pane. See Figure 4.

Figure 4 **Viewing folder contents in Windows Explorer**

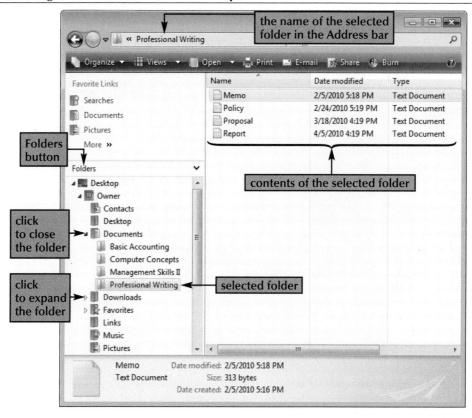

Tip

To display or hide the Folders list in a folder window, click the Folders button in the Navigation pane.

Using the Folders list helps you navigate your computer and orients you to your current location. As you move, copy, delete, and perform other tasks with the files in the right pane of a folder window, you can refer to the Folders list to see how your changes affect the overall organization.

Both Windows Explorer and the Computer window let you view, organize, and access the drives, folders, and files on your computer. In addition to using the Folders list, you can navigate your computer in other ways:

- **Opening drives and folders in the right pane**: To view the contents of a drive or folder, double-click the drive or folder icon in the right pane of a folder window.
- **Using the Address bar**: Use the Address bar to navigate to a different folder. The Address bar displays your current folder as a series of locations separated by arrows. Click a folder name or an arrow button to navigate to a different location.

- **Clicking the Back, Forward, and Recent Pages buttons**: Use the Back, Forward, and Recent Pages buttons to navigate to other folders you have already opened. After you change folders, use the Back button to return to the original folder or click the Recent Pages button to navigate to a location you've visited recently.
- **Using the Search box**: To find a file or folder stored in the current folder or its subfolders, type a word or phrase in the Search box. The search begins as soon as you start typing. Windows finds files based on text in the filename, text within the file, and other characteristics of the file, such as tags (descriptive words or phrases you add to your files) or the author.

These navigation controls are available in Windows Explorer, Computer, and other folder windows, including many dialog boxes. In fact, all of these folder windows share common tools. By default, when you first open Computer, it shows all the drives available on your computer, whereas Windows Explorer shows the folders on your computer. However, by changing a single setting, you can make the two windows interchangeable. If you open the Folders list in Computer, you have the same setup as Windows Explorer. Likewise, if you close the Folders list in the Windows Explorer window, you have the same setup as in the Computer window.

Shannon prefers to use Windows Explorer to manage her files. You'll use Windows Explorer to manage files in the rest of this tutorial.

Using Windows Explorer

Windows Vista also provides a folder for your documents—your **personal folder**, which is designed to store the files and folders you work with regularly and is labeled with the name you use to log on to Windows Vista, such as Shannon. On your own computer, this is where you can keep your data files—the memos, videos, graphics, music, and other files that you create, edit, and manipulate in a program. Windows Vista provides a few built-in folders in your personal folder, including Music (for songs and other music files), Pictures (for photos and other image files), and Documents (for text, spreadsheets, presentations, and other files you create). If you are working in a computer lab, you might not have a personal folder or be able to access the Documents folder, or you might have a personal folder or be able to store files there only temporarily because that folder is emptied every night. Instead, you might permanently store your Data Files on removable media or in a different folder on your computer or network.

When you start Windows Explorer from the All Programs menu, it opens to the Documents folder by default. If you cannot access the Documents folder, the screens you see as you perform the following steps will differ. However, you can still perform the steps accurately.

To examine the organization of your computer using Windows Explorer:

▶ **1.** Click the **Start** button ⊕ on the taskbar, click **All Programs**, click **Accessories**, and then click **Windows Explorer**. The Windows Explorer window opens.

▶ **2.** Scroll the Folders list, point to the **Folders list**, and then click the **expand** icon ▷ next to the Computer icon. The drives and other useful locations on your computer appear under the Computer icon, as shown in Figure 5. The contents of your computer will differ.

Figure 5 ▶ **Viewing the contents of your computer**

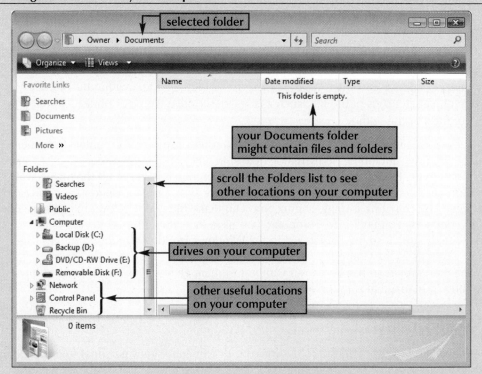

3. Click the **expand** icon ▷ next to the Local Disk (C:) icon. The contents of your hard disk appear under the Local Disk (C:) icon.

   Trouble? If you do not have permission to access drive C, skip Step 3 and read but do not perform the remaining steps.

   Documents is still the selected folder. To view the contents of an object in the right pane, you can click the object's icon in the Folders list.

4. If necessary, scroll up the list, and then click the **Public** folder in the Folders list. Its contents appear in the right pane. Public is a built-in Windows Vista folder that contains folders any user can access on this computer.

Navigating to Your Data Files

The **file path** is a notation that indicates a file's location on your computer. The file path leads you through the Windows file system to your file. For example, the Holiday file is stored in the Tutorial subfolder of the FM folder. If you are working on a USB drive, for example, the path to this file might be as follows:

F:\FM\Tutorial\Holiday.bmp

   This path has four parts, and each part is separated by a backslash (\ ):

- **F**: The drive name; for example, drive F might be the name for the USB drive. If this file were stored on the hard disk, the drive name would be C.
- **FM**: The top-level folder on drive F.
- **Tutorial**: A subfolder in the FM folder.
- **Holiday.bmp**: The full filename with the file extension.

If someone tells you to find the file F:\FM\Tutorial\Holiday.bmp, you know you must navigate to your USB drive, open the FM folder, and then open the Tutorial folder to find the Holiday file. By default, the Address bar includes arrow buttons instead of back-slashes when displaying a path. To navigate to a different folder in the FM folder, for example, you can click the arrow button to right of FM in the Address bar, and then click the folder name.

You can use Windows Explorer to navigate to the Data Files you need for the rest of this tutorial. Refer to the information you provided in the "Planning Your Organization" section and note the drive on your system that contains your Data Files. In the following steps, this is drive F, a USB drive. If necessary, substitute the appropriate drive on your system when you perform the steps.

To navigate to your Data Files:

▶ **1.** Make sure your computer can access your Data Files for this tutorial. For example, if you are using a USB drive, insert the drive into the USB port.

   Trouble? If you don't have the Data Files, you need to get them before you can proceed. Your instructor will either give you the Data Files or ask you to obtain them from a specified location (such as a network drive). In either case, be sure that you make a backup copy of your Data Files before you start using them, so that the original files will be available on your copied disk in case you need to start over because of an error or problem. If you have any questions about the Data Files, see your instructor or technical support person for assistance.

▶ **2.** In the Windows Explorer window, click the **expand** icon ▷ next to the drive containing your Data Files, such as Removable Disk (F:). A list of the folders on that drive appears.

▶ **3.** If the list of folders does not include the FM folder, continue clicking the **expand** icon ▷ to navigate to the folder that contains the FM folder.

▶ **4.** Click the **expand** icon ▷ next to the FM folder, and then click the **FM** folder. Its contents appear in the Folders list and in the right pane of the Windows Explorer window. The FM folder contains the Case1, Review, and Tutorial folders, as shown in Figure 6. The other folders on your system might vary.

Figure 6 ▶ Navigating to the FM folder

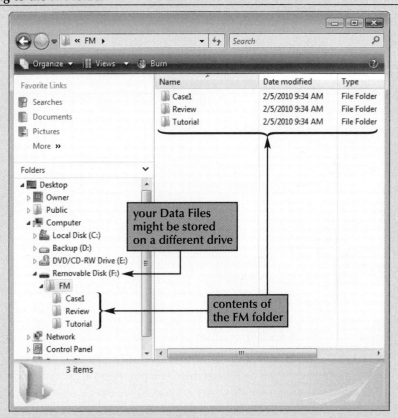

5. In the left pane, click the **Tutorial** folder. The files it contains appear in the right pane. You want to view them as a list.

6. Click the **Views button arrow** on the toolbar, and then click **List**. The files appear in List view in the Windows Explorer window. See Figure 7.

Figure 7 ▶ Files in the Tutorial folder in List view

The file icons in your window depend on the programs installed on your computer, so they might be different from the ones shown in Figure 7.

Working with Folders and Files

After you devise a plan for storing your files, you are ready to get organized by creating folders that will hold your files. For this tutorial, you create folders in the Tutorial folder. When you are working on your own computer, you usually create folders within the Documents folder in your personal folder.

Examine the files shown in Figure 7 again and determine which files seem to belong together. Holiday, New Logo, and Vinca are all graphics files containing pictures or photos. The Resume and Stationery files were created for a summer job hunt. The other files were created for a neighborhood association to update a playground.

One way to organize these files is to create three folders—one for graphics, one for the job hunt files, and another for the playground files. When you create a folder, you give it a name, preferably one that describes its contents. A folder name can have up to 255 characters, except / \ : * ? " < > or |. Considering these conventions, you could create three folders as follows:

- **Graphics folder**: Holiday, New Logo, and Vinca files
- **Job Hunt folder**: Resume and Stationery files
- **Playground folder**: Agenda, Proposal, and Members files

Guidelines for Creating Folders | InSight

- **Keep folder names short and familiar**: Long filenames can be cut off in a folder window, so use names that are short but clear. Choose names that will be meaningful later, such as project names or course numbers.
- **Develop standards for naming folders**: Use a consistent naming scheme that is clear to you, such as one that uses a project name as the name of the main folder, and includes step numbers in each subfolder name, such as 01Plan, 02Approvals, 03Prelim, and so on.
- **Create subfolders to organize files**: If a file listing in a folder window is so long that you must scroll the window, consider organizing those files into subfolders.

Creating Folders

You've already seen folder icons in the windows you've examined. Now, you'll create folders in the Tutorial folder using the Windows Explorer toolbar.

Creating a Folder | Reference Window

- In the left pane, click the drive or folder where you want to create a folder.
- Click the Organize button on the toolbar, and then click New Folder (*or* right-click a blank area in the folder window, point to New, and then click Folder).
- Type a name for the folder, and then press the Enter key.

Next you will create three folders in your Tutorial folder. The Windows Explorer window should show the contents of the Tutorial folder in List view.

To create folders in a folder window:

▶ **1.** Click the **Organize** button on the toolbar, and then click **New Folder**. A folder icon with the label "New Folder" appears in the right pane. See Figure 8.

Figure 8 Creating a folder in the Tutorial folder

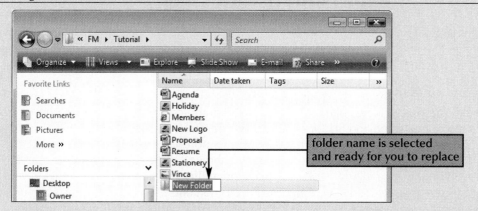

> **Trouble?** If the "New Folder" name is not selected, right-click the new folder, click Rename, and then continue with Step 2.

Windows Vista uses "New Folder" as a placeholder, and selects the text so that you can replace it with the name you want.

▶ **2.** Type **Graphics** as the folder name, and then press the **Enter** key. The new folder is named "Graphics" and is the selected item in the right pane.

You are ready to create a second folder. This time, you'll use a shortcut menu to create a folder.

▶ **3.** Right-click a blank area near the Graphics folder, point to **New** on the shortcut menu, and then click **Folder**. A folder icon with the label "New Folder" appears in the right pane with the "New Folder" text selected.

▶ **4.** Type **Job Hunt** as the name of the new folder, and then press the **Enter** key.

▶ **5.** Using the toolbar or the shortcut menu, create a folder named **Playground**. The Tutorial folder contains three new subfolders.

Moving and Copying Files and Folders

If you want to place a file into a folder from another location, you can either move the file or copy it. **Moving** a file removes it from its current location and places it in a new location you specify. **Copying** places the file in both locations. Windows Vista provides several techniques for moving and copying files. The same principles apply to folders—you can move and copy folders using a variety of methods.

Reference Window | **Moving a File or Folder**

- Right-click and drag the file or folder you want to move to the destination folder.
- Click Move Here on the shortcut menu.

or

- Right-click the file or folder you want to move, and then click Cut on the shortcut menu.
- Navigate to and right-click the destination folder, and then click Paste on the shortcut menu.

Next, you'll move the Agenda, Proposal, and Members files to the Playground folder.

To move a file using the right mouse button:

▶ **1.** Point to the **Agenda** file in the right pane, and then press and hold the *right* mouse button.

▶ **2.** With the right mouse button still pressed down, drag the **Agenda** file to the **Playground** folder. When a "Move to Playground" ScreenTip appears, release the button. A shortcut menu opens.

▶ **3.** With the left mouse button, click **Move Here** on the shortcut menu. The Agenda file is removed from the main Tutorial folder and stored in the Playground subfolder.

   Trouble? If you release the mouse button before dragging the Agenda file to the Playground folder, the shortcut menu opens, letting you move the file to a different folder. Press the Esc key to close the shortcut menu without moving the file, and then repeat Steps 1 through 3.

▶ **4.** In the right pane, double-click the **Playground** folder. The Agenda file is in the Playground folder.

▶ **5.** In the left pane, click the **Tutorial** folder to see its contents. The Tutorial folder no longer contains the Agenda file.

The advantage of moving a file or folder by dragging with the right mouse button is that you can efficiently complete your work with one action. However, this technique requires polished mouse skills so that you can drag the file comfortably. Another way to move files and folders is to use the **Clipboard**, a temporary storage area for files and information that you have copied or moved from one place and plan to use somewhere else. You can select a file and use the Cut or Copy commands to temporarily store the file on the Clipboard, and then use the Paste command to insert the file elsewhere. Although using the Clipboard takes more steps, some users find it easier than dragging with the right mouse button.

You'll move the Resume file to the Job Hunt folder next.

To move files using the Clipboard:

▶ **1.** Right-click the **Resume** file, and then click **Cut** on the shortcut menu. Although the file icon is still displayed in the folder window, Windows Vista removes the Resume file from the Tutorial folder and stores it on the Clipboard.

▶ **2.** In the Folders list, right-click the **Job Hunt** folder, and then click **Paste** on the shortcut menu. Windows Vista pastes the Resume file from the Clipboard to the Job Hunt folder. The Resume file icon no longer appears in the folder window.

▶ **3.** In the Folders list, click the **Job Hunt** folder to view its contents in the right pane. The Job Hunt folder now contains the Resume file.

   You'll move the Stationery file from the Tutorial folder to the Job Hunt folder.

▶ **4.** Click the **Back** button 🔙 on the Address bar to return to the Tutorial folder, right-click the **Stationery** file in the folder window, and then click **Cut** on the shortcut menu.

▶ **5.** Right-click the **Job Hunt** folder, and then click **Paste** on the shortcut menu.

▶ **6.** Click the **Back** button ⬅ on the Address bar to return to view the contents of the Job Hunt folder. It now contains the Resume and Stationery files. See Figure 9.

Figure 9 | **Moving files**

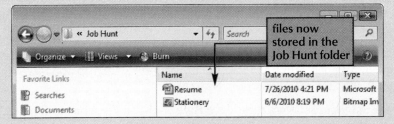

▶ **7.** Click the **Forward** button ➡ to return to the Tutorial folder.

Tip

To use keyboard shortcuts to move files, click the file you want to move, press Ctrl+X to cut the file, navigate to a new location, and then press Ctrl+V to paste the file.

You can also copy a file using the same techniques as when you move a file—by dragging with the right mouse button or by using the Clipboard. You can copy more than one file at the same time by selecting all the files you want to copy, and then clicking them as a group. To select files that are listed together in a window, click the first file in the list, hold down the Shift key, click the last file in the list, and then release the Shift key. To select files that are not listed together, click one file, hold down the Ctrl key, click the other files, and then release the Ctrl key.

Reference Window | **Copying a File or Folder**

- Right-click and drag the file or folder you want to copy to the destination folder.
- Click Copy Here on the shortcut menu.
or
- Right-click the file or folder you want to copy, and then click Copy on the shortcut menu.
- Navigate to the destination folder.
- Right-click a blank area of the destination folder window, and then click Paste on the shortcut menu.

You'll copy the three graphics files from the Tutorial folder to the Graphics folder now.

To copy files using the shortcut menu:

▶ **1.** In the Tutorial window, click the **Holiday** file.

▶ **2.** Hold down the **Ctrl** key, click the **New Logo** file, click the **Vinca** file, and then release the **Ctrl** key. Three files are selected in the Tutorial window.

Tip

It's easiest to select multiple files in List view or Details view.

▶ **3.** Right-click a selected file, and then click **Copy** on the shortcut menu.

▶ **4.** In the right pane, double-click the **Graphics** folder to open it.

▶ **5.** Right-click a blank area in the right pane, and then click **Paste** on the shortcut menu. Windows Vista copies the three files to the Graphics folder.

▶ **6.** Switch to List view, if necessary.

Now that you are familiar with two ways to copy files, you can use the technique you prefer to copy the Proposal and Members files to the Playground folder.

To copy the two files:

▶ **1.** In the Graphics folder window, click the **Back** button ⊙ on the toolbar to return to the Tutorial folder.

▶ **2.** Use any technique you've learned to copy the **Proposal** and **Members** files from the Tutorial folder to the Playground folder.

You can move and copy folders in the same way that you move and copy files. When you do, you move or copy all the files contained in the folder.

Naming and Renaming Files

As you work with files, pay attention to **filenames**—they provide important information about the file, including its contents and purpose. A filename such as Car Sales.docx has three parts:

• **Main part of the filename**: The name you provide when you create a file, and the name you associate with a file
• **Dot**: The period (.) that separates the main part of the filename from the file extension
• **File extension**: Usually three or four characters that follow the dot in the filename

The main part of a filename can have up to 260 characters—this gives you plenty of room to name your file accurately enough so that you'll know the contents of the file just by looking at the filename. You can use spaces and certain punctuation symbols in your filenames. Like folder names, however, filenames cannot contain the symbols \ / ? : * " < > | because these characters have special meaning in Windows Vista.

A filename might display an **extension**—three or more characters following a dot—that identifies the file's type and indicates the program in which the file was created. For example, in the filename Car Sales.docx, the extension "docx" identifies the file as one created by Microsoft Office Word 2007, a word-processing program. You might also have a file called Car Sales.xlsx—the "xlsx" extension identifies the file as one created in Microsoft Office Excel 2007, a spreadsheet program. Though the main parts of these filenames are identical, their extensions distinguish them as different files. You usually do not need to add extensions to your filenames because the program that you use to create the file adds the file extension automatically. Also, although Windows Vista keeps track of extensions, not all computers are set to display them.

Be sure to give your files and folders meaningful names that help you remember their purpose and contents. You can easily rename a file or folder by using the Rename command on the file's shortcut menu.

| **Guidelines for Naming Files** | | InSight |

The following are a few suggestions for naming your files:

• **Use common names**: Avoid cryptic names that might make sense now, but could cause confusion later, such as nonstandard abbreviations or imprecise names like Stuff08.
• **Don't change the file extension**: When renaming a file, don't change the file extension. If you do, Windows might not be able to find a program that can open it.
• **Find a comfortable balance between too short and too long**: Use filenames that are long enough to be meaningful, but short enough to read easily on the screen.

Next, you'll rename the Agenda file to give it a more descriptive name.

To rename the Agenda file:

▶ **1.** In the Tutorial folder window, double-click the **Playground** folder to open it.

▶ **2.** Right-click the **Agenda** file, and then click **Rename** on the shortcut menu. The file-name is highlighted and a box appears around it.

▶ **3.** Type **Meeting Agenda**, and then press the **Enter** key. The file now appears with the new name.

Trouble? If you make a mistake while typing and you haven't pressed the Enter key yet, press the Backspace key until you delete the mistake, and then complete Step 3. If you've already pressed the Enter key, repeat Steps 1 through 3 to rename the file again.

Trouble? If your computer is set to display file extensions, a message might appear asking if you are sure you want to change the file extension. Click the No button, right-click the Agenda file, click Rename on the shortcut menu, type "Meeting Agenda.docx", and then press the Enter key.

All the files in the Tutorial folder are now stored in appropriate subfolders. You can streamline the organization of the Tutorial folder by deleting the files you no longer need.

Deleting Files and Folders

Tip

To retrieve a deleted file from the hard disk, double-click the Recycle Bin, right-click the file you want to retrieve, and then click Restore.

You should periodically delete files and folders you no longer need so that your main folders and disks don't get cluttered. In the Computer window or Windows Explorer, you delete a file or folder by deleting its icon. Be careful when you delete a folder, because you also delete all the files it contains. When you delete a file from a hard disk, Windows Vista removes the filename from the folder, but stores the file contents in the Recycle Bin. The **Recycle Bin** is an area on your hard disk that holds deleted files until you remove them permanently; an icon on the desktop allows you easy access to the Recycle Bin. If you change your mind and want to retrieve a file deleted from your hard disk, you can use the Recycle Bin to recover it or return it to its original location. However, after you empty the Recycle Bin, you can no longer recover the files that were in it.

When you delete a file from removable media, it does not go into the Recycle Bin. Instead, it is deleted as soon as its icon disappears—and you cannot recover it.

Shannon reminds you that because you copied the Holiday, New Logo, Proposal, Members, and Vinca files to the Graphics and Playground folders, you can safely delete the original files in the Tutorial folder. As with moving, copying, and renaming files and folders, you can delete a file or folder in many ways, including using a shortcut menu.

To delete files in the Tutorial folder:

▶ **1.** Use any technique you've learned to navigate to and open the **Tutorial** folder.

▶ **2.** Click **Holiday** (the first file in the file list), hold down the **Shift** key, click **Vinca** (the last file in the file list), and then release the **Shift** key. All the files in the Tutorial folder are now selected. None of the subfolders should be selected.

▶ **3.** Right-click the selected files, and then click **Delete** on the shortcut menu. Windows Vista asks if you're sure you want to delete these files.

▶ **4.** Click the **Yes** button.

So far, you've moved, copied, renamed, and deleted files, but you haven't viewed any of their contents. To view file contents, you can preview or open the file. When you double-click a file in a folder window, Windows Vista starts the appropriate program and opens the file. To preview the file contents, you can select the file in a folder window, and then open the Preview pane by clicking the Organize button, pointing to Layout, and then clicking Preview Pane.

Working with Compressed Files

If you transfer files from one location to another, such as from your hard disk to a removable disk or vice versa, or from one computer to another via e-mail, you can store the files in a **compressed (zipped) folder** so that they take up less disk space. You can then transfer the files more quickly. When you create a compressed folder, Windows Vista displays a zipper on the folder icon.

You compress a folder so that the files it contains use less space on the disk. Compare two folders—a folder named Pictures that contains about 8.6 MB of files and a compressed folder containing the same files, but requiring only 6.5 MB of disk space. In this case, the compressed files use about 25 percent less disk space than the uncompressed files.

You can create a compressed folder using the Compressed (zipped) Folder command on the New submenu of the shortcut menu in a folder window. Then, you can compress files or other folders by dragging them into the compressed folder. You can open files directly from a compressed folder, although you cannot modify the file. To edit and save a compressed file, you must extract it first. When you **extract** a file, you create an uncompressed copy of the file and folder in a folder you specify. The original file remains in the compressed folder.

If a different compression program has been installed on your computer, such as WinZip or PKZIP, the Compressed (zipped) Folder command might not appear on the New submenu. Instead, it might be replaced by the name of your compression program. In this case, refer to your compression program's Help system for instructions on working with compressed files.

Shannon suggests you compress the files and folders in the Tutorial folder so that you can more quickly transfer them to another location.

To compress the folders and files in the Tutorial folder:

▶ 1. If necessary, navigate to the Tutorial folder.

▶ 2. Right-click a blank area of the right pane, point to **New** on the shortcut menu, and then click **Compressed (zipped) Folder**. A new compressed folder with a zipper icon appears in the Tutorial window. See Figure 10. Your window might appear in a different view.

Creating a compressed folder — **Figure 10**

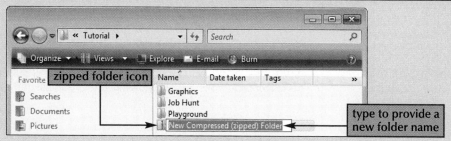

Trouble? If the Compressed (zipped) Folder command does not appear on the New submenu, a different compression program is probably installed on your computer. Click a blank area of the Tutorial window to close the shortcut menu, and then read but do not perform the remaining steps.

▶ 3. Type **Final Files**, and then press the **Enter** key. Windows Vista names the compressed folder in the Tutorial folder.

> **4.** Click the **Graphics** folder, hold down the **Shift** key, click the **Playground** folder in the right pane, and then release the **Shift** key. Three folders are selected in the Tutorial window.
>
> **5.** Drag the three folders to the **Final Files** compressed folder. Windows Vista copies the files to the folder, compressing them to save space.

You open a compressed folder by double-clicking it. You can then move and copy files and folders in a compressed folder, although you cannot rename them. When you extract files, Windows Vista uncompresses and copies them to a location that you specify, preserving the files in their folders as appropriate.

To extract the compressed files:

> **1.** Right-click the **Final Files** compressed folder, and then click **Extract All** on the shortcut menu. The Extract Compressed (Zipped) Folders dialog box opens.
>
> **2.** Press the **End** key to deselect the path in the text box, press the **Backspace** key as many times as necessary to delete "Final Files," and then type **Extracted**. The final three parts of the path in the text box should be "\FM\Tutorial\Extracted." See Figure 11.

Figure 11 | **Extracting compressed files**

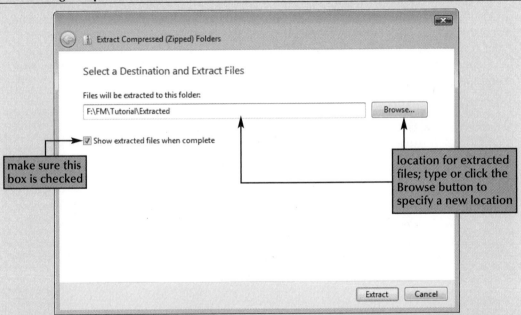

> **3.** Make sure the **Show extracted files when complete** check box is checked, and then click the **Extract** button. The Extracted folder opens, showing the Graphics, Job Hunt, and Playground folders.
>
> **4.** Open each folder to make sure it contains the files you worked with in this tutorial.
>
> **5.** Close all open windows.

Quick Check | Review

1. What do you call a named collection of data stored on a disk?
2. Name two types of removable media for storing files.
3. The letter C is typically used for the _____ drive of a computer.
4. What are the two tools that Windows Vista provides for exploring the files and folders on your computer?
5. What is the notation you can use to indicate a file's location on your computer?
6. True or False: The advantage of moving a file or folder by dragging with the right mouse button is that you can efficiently complete your work with one action.
7. What part of a filename indicates the file type and program that created it?
8. Is a file deleted from a compressed folder when you extract it?

Tutorial Summary | Review

In this tutorial, you examined Windows Vista file organization, noting that you need to organize files and folders to work efficiently. You learned about typical file management strategies, including how to organize files and folders by creating folders, moving and copying files, and renaming and deleting files. You also learned how to copy files to a compressed (zipped) folder, and then extract files from a compressed folder.

Key Terms

backup	extract	move
Clipboard	Favorite Links list	Navigation pane
compact disc (CD)	file	pane
compressed (zipped) folder	file path	personal folder
Computer	file system	Recycle Bin
copy	filename	root directory
disk	folder	subfolder
document	folder window	USB drive
drive	Folders list	Windows Explorer
extension	hard disk	

| Practice | **Review Assignments** |

Practice the skills you learned in the tutorial.

Data Files needed for the Review Assignments: Billing.xlsx, Car Plan.xlsx, Commissions.xlsx, Contracts.xlsx, Customers.xlsx, Loan.docx, Photos.pptx, Speech.wav, Water lilies.jpg

Complete the following steps, recording your answers to any questions:

1. Use the Computer window or Windows Explorer as necessary to record the following information:
   - Where are you supposed to store the files you use in the Review Assignments for this tutorial?
   - Describe the method you will use to navigate to the location where you save your files for this book.
   - Do you need to follow any special guidelines or conventions when naming the files you save for this book? For example, should all the filenames start with your course number or tutorial number? If so, describe the conventions.
   - When you are instructed to open a file for this book, what location are you supposed to use?
   - Describe the method you will use to navigate to this location.
2. Use the Computer window or Windows Explorer to navigate to and open the FM\Review folder provided with your Data Files.
3. Examine the nine files in the Review folder included with your Data Files, and then answer the following questions:
   - How will you organize these files?
   - What folders will you create?
   - Which files will you store in these folders?
   - Will you use any built-in Windows folders? If so, which ones? For which files?
4. In the Review folder, create three folders: Business, Finances, and Project.
5. Move the **Billing**, **Commissions**, **Contracts**, and **Customers** files from the Review folder to the Business folder.
6. Move the **Car Plan** and **Loan** files to the Finances folder.
7. Copy the remaining files to the Project folder.
8. Delete the files in the Review folder (do *not* delete any folders).
9. Rename the **Speech** file in the Project folder to **Ask Not**.
10. Create a compressed (zipped) folder in the Review folder named **Final Review** that contains all the files and folders in the Review folder.
11. Extract the contents of the Final Review files folder to a new folder named **Extracted**. (*Hint:* The file path will end with "\FM\Review\Extracted.")
12. Locate all copies of the **Loan** file in the subfolders of the Review folder. In which locations did you find this file?
13. Close all open windows.
14. Submit the results of the preceding steps to your instructor, either in printed or electronic form, as requested.

Apply | **Case Problem 1**

Use the skills you learned in the tutorial to manage files and folders for an arts organization.

Data Files needed for this Case Problem: Inv Feb.xlsx, Inv Jan.xlsx, Inv March.xlsx, Painting–Agenda.docx, Painting–Eval.docx, Painting–Manual.docx, Paris.jpg, Still Life.jpg

Jefferson Street Fine Arts Center Rae Wysnewski owns the Jefferson Street Fine Arts Center (JSFAC) in Pittsburgh, and offers classes and gallery, studio, and practice space for aspiring and fledgling artists, musicians, and dancers. Rae opened JSFAC two years ago, and this year the center has a record enrollment in its classes. She hires you to teach a painting class and to show her how to manage her files on her new Windows Vista computer. Complete the following steps:

1. In the FM\Case1 folder in your Data Files, create two folders: Invoices and Painting Class.
2. Move the **Inv Jan**, **Inv Feb**, and **Inv March** files from the Case1 folder to the Invoices folder.
3. Rename the three files in the Invoices folder to remove "Inv" from each name.
4. Move the three text documents from the Case1 folder to the Painting Class folder. Rename the three documents, using shorter but still descriptive names.
5. Copy the remaining files to the Painting Class folder.
6. Switch to Details view, if necessary, and then answer the following questions:
   a. What is the largest file in the Painting Class folder?
   b. How many files in the Painting Class folder are JPEG images?
7. Delete the **Paris** and **Still Life** files from the Case1 folder.
8. Open the Recycle Bin folder by double-clicking the Recycle Bin icon on the desktop. Do the Paris and Still Life files appear in the Recycle Bin folder? Explain why or why not. Close the Recycle Bin window.
9. Copy the Painting Class folder to the Case1 folder. The duplicate folder appears as "Painting Class – Copy." Rename the Painting Class – Copy folder as **Graphics**.
10. Delete the text files from the Graphics folder.
11. Delete the **Paris** and **Still Life** files from the Painting Class folder.
12. Close all open windows, and then submit the results of the preceding steps to your instructor, either in printed or electronic form, as requested.

Challenge | **Case Problem 2**

Extend what you've learned to discover other methods of managing files for a social service organization.

There are no Data Files needed for this Case Problem.

First Call Outreach Victor Crillo is the director of a social service organization named First Call Outreach in Toledo, Ohio. Its mission is to connect people who need help from local and state agencies to the appropriate service. Victor has a dedicated staff, but they are all relatively new to Windows Vista. In particular, they have trouble finding files that they have saved on their hard disks. He asks you to demonstrate how to find files in Windows Vista. Complete the following:

⊕ EXPLORE

1. Windows Vista Help and Support includes topics that explain how to search for files on a disk without looking through all the folders. Click the Start button, click Help and Support, and then use one of the following methods to locate topics on searching for files.
   • In the Windows Help and Support window, click the Windows Basics icon. Click the Working with files and folders link. In the "In this article" list, clicking Finding your files.

- In the Windows Help and Support window, click the Table of Contents icon. (If necessary, click the Home icon first, and then click the Table of Contents icon.) the Files and folders link, and then click Working with files and folders. In the "In this article" list, click Finding your files.
- In the Search Help box, type **searching for files**, and then press the Enter key. Click the Find a file or folder link. In the article, click the Show all link.

EXPLORE   2. Read the topic and click any See also or For more information links in the topic, if necessary, to provide the following information:

    a.   Where is the Search box located?

    b.   Do you need to type the entire filename to find the file?

    c.   Name three file characteristics you can use as search options.

EXPLORE   3. Use the Windows Vista Help and Support window to locate topics related to managing files and folders. Write out two procedures for working with files and folders that were not covered in the tutorial.

    4. Submit the results of the preceding steps to your instructor, either in printed or electronic form, as requested.

Assess | SAM Assessment and Training

SAM

If you have a SAM user profile, you may have access to hands-on instruction, practice, and assessment of the skills covered in this tutorial. Log in to your SAM account (**http://sam2007.course.com**) to launch any assigned training activities or exams that relate to the skills covered in this tutorial.

Review | Quick Check Answers

1. file
2. USB drives, CDs, and DVDs
3. hard disk
4. Windows Explorer and the Computer window
5. file path
6. True
7. extension
8. No

Ending Data Files

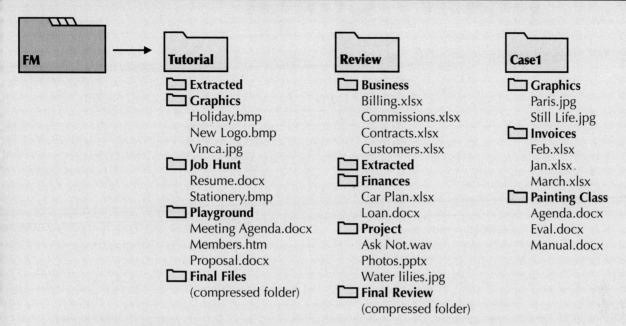

FM → **Tutorial**
- 📁 **Extracted**
- 📁 **Graphics**
  - Holiday.bmp
  - New Logo.bmp
  - Vinca.jpg
- 📁 **Job Hunt**
  - Resume.docx
  - Stationery.bmp
- 📁 **Playground**
  - Meeting Agenda.docx
  - Members.htm
  - Proposal.docx
- 📁 **Final Files**
  - (compressed folder)

Review
- 📁 **Business**
  - Billing.xlsx
  - Commissions.xlsx
  - Contracts.xlsx
  - Customers.xlsx
- 📁 **Extracted**
- 📁 **Finances**
  - Car Plan.xlsx
  - Loan.docx
- 📁 **Project**
  - Ask Not.wav
  - Photos.pptx
  - Water lilies.jpg
- 📁 **Final Review**
  - (compressed folder)

Case1
- 📁 **Graphics**
  - Paris.jpg
  - Still Life.jpg
- 📁 **Invoices**
  - Feb.xlsx
  - Jan.xlsx
  - March.xlsx
- 📁 **Painting Class**
  - Agenda.docx
  - Eval.docx
  - Manual.docx

Reality Check

Now that you have reviewed the fundamentals of managing files, organize the files and folders you use for course work or for other projects on your own computer. Be sure to follow the guidelines presented in this tutorial for developing an organization strategy, creating folders, naming files, and moving, copying, deleting, and compressing files. To manage your own files, complete the following tasks:

1. Use a program such as Word or Notepad to create a plan for organizing your files. List the types of files you work with, and then determine whether you want to store them on your hard disk or on removable media. Then sketch the folders and subfolders you will use to manage these files. If you choose a hard disk as your storage medium, make sure you plan to store your work files and folders in a subfolder of the Documents folder.

2. Use Windows Explorer or the Computer window to navigate to your files. Determine which tool you prefer for managing files, if you have a preference.

3. Create or rename the main folders you want to use for your files. Then create or rename the subfolders you will use.

4. Move and copy files to the appropriate folders according to your plan, and rename and delete files as necessary.

5. Create a backup copy of your work files by creating a compressed file and then copying the compressed file to a removable disk, such as a USB flash drive.

6. Submit your finished plan to your instructor, either in printed or electronic form, as requested.

Objectives

- Explore the programs that comprise Microsoft Office
- Start programs and switch between them
- Explore common window elements
- Minimize, maximize, and restore windows
- Use the Ribbon, tabs, and buttons
- Use the contextual tabs, Mini toolbar, and shortcut menus
- Save, close, and open a file
- Use the Help system
- Print a file
- Exit programs

Getting Started with Microsoft Office 2007

Preparing a Meeting Agenda

Case | Recycled Palette

Recycled Palette, a company in Oregon founded by Ean Nogella in 2006, sells 100 percent recycled latex paint to both individuals and businesses in the area. The high-quality recycled paint is filtered to industry standards and tested for performance and environmental safety. The paint is available in both 1 gallon cans and 5 gallon pails, and comes in colors ranging from white to shades of brown, blue, green, and red. The demand for affordable recycled paint has been growing each year. Ean and all his employees use Microsoft Office 2007, which provides everyone in the company with the power and flexibility to store a variety of information, create consistent files, and share data. In this tutorial, you'll review how the company's employees use Microsoft Office 2007.

Starting Data Files

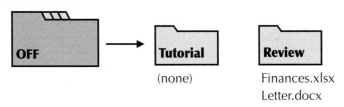

OFF → Tutorial (none)   Review Finances.xlsx Letter.docx

Exploring Microsoft Office 2007

Microsoft Office 2007, or **Office**, is a collection of Microsoft programs. Office is available in many suites, each of which contains a different combination of these programs. For example, the Professional suite includes Word, Excel, PowerPoint, Access, Outlook, and Publisher. Other suites are available and can include more or fewer programs (for additional information about the available suites, go to the Microsoft Web site). Each Office program contains valuable tools to help you accomplish many tasks, such as composing reports, analyzing data, preparing presentations, compiling information, sending e-mail, and planning schedules.

Microsoft Office Word 2007, or **Word**, is a computer program you use to enter, edit, and format text. The files you create in Word are called **documents**, although many people use the term *document* to refer to any file created on a computer. Word, often called a word processing program, offers many special features that help you compose and update all types of documents, ranging from letters and newsletters to reports, brochures, faxes, and even books—all in attractive and readable formats. You can also use Word to create, insert, and position figures, tables, and other graphics to enhance the look of your documents. For example, the Recycled Palette employees create business letters using Word.

Microsoft Office Excel 2007, or **Excel**, is a computer program you use to enter, calculate, analyze, and present numerical data. You can do some of this in Word with tables, but Excel provides many more tools for recording and formatting numbers as well as performing calculations. The graphics capabilities in Excel also enable you to display data visually. You might, for example, generate a pie chart or a bar chart to help people quickly see the significance of and the connections between information. The files you create in Excel are called **workbooks** (commonly referred to as spreadsheets), and Excel is often called a spreadsheet program. The Recycled Palette accounting department uses a line chart in an Excel workbook to visually track the company's financial performance.

Microsoft Office Access 2007, or **Access**, is a computer program used to enter, maintain, and retrieve related information (or data) in a format known as a database. The files you create in Access are called **databases**, and Access is often referred to as a database or relational database program. With Access, you can create forms to make data entry easier, and you can create professional reports to improve the readability of your data. The Recycled Palette operations department tracks the company's inventory in a table in an Access database.

Microsoft Office PowerPoint 2007, or **PowerPoint**, is a computer program you use to create a collection of slides that can contain text, charts, pictures, sound, movies, multimedia, and so on. The files you create in PowerPoint are called **presentations**, and PowerPoint is often called a presentation graphics program. You can show these presentations on your computer monitor, project them onto a screen as a slide show, print them, share them over the Internet, or display them on the World Wide Web. You can also use PowerPoint to generate presentation-related documents such as audience handouts, outlines, and speakers' notes. The Recycled Palette marketing department has created an effective slide presentation with PowerPoint to promote its paints to a wider audience.

Microsoft Office Outlook 2007, or **Outlook**, is a computer program you use to send, receive, and organize e-mail; plan your schedule; arrange meetings; organize contacts; create a to-do list; and jot down notes. You can also use Outlook to print schedules, task lists, phone directories, and other documents. Outlook is often referred to as an information management program. The Recycled Palette staff use Outlook to send and receive e-mail, plan their schedules, and create to-do lists.

Although each Office program individually is a strong tool, their potential is even greater when used together.

Integrating Office Programs

One of the main advantages of Office is **integration**, the ability to share information between programs. Integration ensures consistency and accuracy, and it saves time because you don't have to reenter the same information in several Office programs. The staff at Recycled Palette uses the integration features of Office daily, including the following examples:

- The accounting department created an Excel bar chart on the previous two years' fourth-quarter results, which they inserted into the quarterly financial report created in Word. They included a hyperlink in the Word report that employees can click to open the Excel workbook and view the original data.
- The operations department included an Excel pie chart of sales percentages by paint colors on a PowerPoint slide, which is part of a presentation to stockholders.
- The marketing department produced a mailing to promote its recycled paints to local contractors and designers by combining a form letter created in Word with an Access database that stores the names and addresses of these potential customers.
- A sales representative wrote a letter in Word about an upcoming promotion for new customers and merged the letter with an Outlook contact list containing the names and addresses of prospective customers.

These are just a few examples of how you can take information from one Office program and integrate it with another.

Starting Office Programs

You can start any Office program by clicking the Start button on the Windows taskbar, and then selecting the program you want from the All Programs menu. As soon as the program starts, you can immediately begin to create new files or work with existing ones. If an Office program appears in the most frequently used programs list on the left side of the Start menu, you can click the program name to start the program.

Starting Office Programs | Reference Window

- Click the Start button on the taskbar.
- Click All Programs.
- Click Microsoft Office.
- Click the name of the program you want to start.

or

- Click the name of the program you want to start in the most frequently used programs list on the left side of the Start menu.

You'll start Excel using the Start button.

To start Excel and open a new, blank workbook:

▶ **1.** Make sure your computer is on and the Windows desktop appears on your screen.

Trouble? If your screen varies slightly from those shown in the figures, your computer might be set up differently. The figures in this book were created while running Windows Vista with the Aero feature turned off, but how your screen looks depends on the version of Windows you are using, the background settings, and so forth.

Windows XP Tip

The Start button is the green button with the word "start" on it, located at the bottom left of the taskbar.

▶ **2.** Click the **Start** button 🔵 on the taskbar, and then click **All Programs** to display the All Programs menu.

▶ **3.** Click **Microsoft Office** on the All Programs list, and then point to **Microsoft Office Excel 2007**. Depending on how your computer is set up, your desktop and menu might contain different icons and commands.

Trouble? If you don't see Microsoft Office on the All Programs list, click Microsoft Office Excel 2007 on the All Programs list. If you still don't see Microsoft Office Excel 2007, ask your instructor or technical support person for help.

▶ **4.** Click **Microsoft Office Excel 2007**. Excel starts, and a new, blank workbook opens. See Figure 1.

| Figure 1 | New, blank Excel workbook |

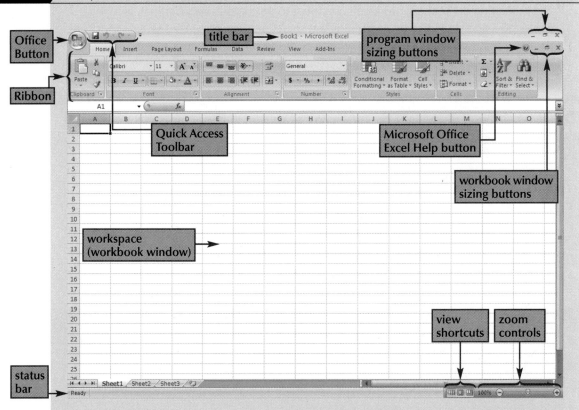

Trouble? If the Excel window doesn't fill your entire screen, the window is not maximized, or expanded to its full size. You'll maximize the window shortly.

You can have more than one Office program open at once. You'll use this same method to start Word and open a new, blank document.

To start Word and open a new, blank document:

▶ **1.** Click the **Start** button 🔵 on the taskbar, click **All Programs** to display the All Programs list, and then click **Microsoft Office**.

Trouble? If you don't see Microsoft Office on the All Programs list, click Microsoft Office Word 2007 on the All Programs list. If you still don't see Microsoft Office Word 2007, ask your instructor or technical support person for help.

▶ **2.** Click **Microsoft Office Word 2007**. Word starts, and a new, blank document opens. See Figure 2.

New, blank document in Word ◀ **Figure 2**

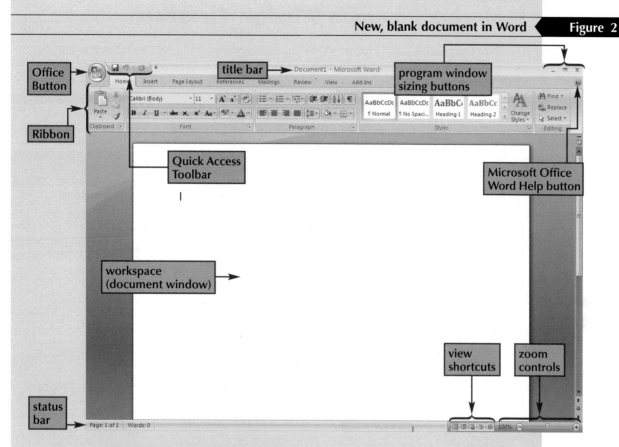

Trouble? If the Word window doesn't fill your entire screen, the window is not maximized. You'll maximize the window shortly.

Switching Between Open Programs and Files

Two programs are running at the same time—Excel and Word. The taskbar contains buttons for both programs. When you have two or more programs running or two files within the same program open, you can use the taskbar buttons to switch from one program or file to another. The button for the active program or file is darker. The employees at Recycled Palette often work in several programs at once.

To switch between Word and Excel files:

▶ **1.** Click the **Microsoft Excel – Book1** button on the taskbar. The active program switches from Word to Excel. See Figure 3.

Excel and Word programs opened simultaneously ◀ **Figure 3**

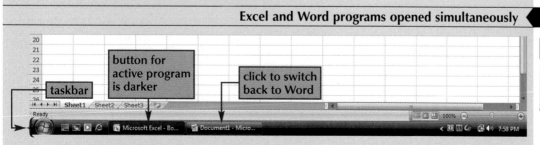

Tip

You can also press the Alt+Tab keys to switch between open files.

▶ **2.** Click the **Document1 – Microsoft Word** button on the taskbar to return to Word.

Exploring Common Window Elements

The Office programs consist of windows that have many similar features. As you can see in Figures 1 and 2, many of the elements in both the Excel program window and the Word program window are the same. In fact, all the Office programs have these same elements. Figure 4 describes some of the most common window elements.

Figure 4 ▶ Common window elements

Element	Description
Office Button	Provides access to document-level features and program settings
Quick Access Toolbar	Provides one-click access to commonly used commands, such as Save, Undo, and Repeat
Title bar	Contains the name of the open file, the program name, and the sizing buttons
Sizing buttons	Resize and close the program window or the workspace
Ribbon	Provides access to the main set of commands organized by task into tabs and groups
Microsoft Office Help button	Opens the Help window for that program
Workspace	Displays the file you are working on (Word document, Excel workbook, Access database, or PowerPoint slide)
Status bar	Provides information about the program, open file, or current task as well as the view shortcuts and zoom controls
View shortcuts	Change how a file is displayed in the workspace
Zoom controls	Magnify or shrink the content displayed in the workspace

Because these elements are the same in each program, after you've learned one program, it's easy to learn the others. The next sections explore these common features.

Resizing the Program Window and Workspace

There are three different sizing buttons. The Minimize button ▬ , which is the left button, hides a window so that only its program button is visible on the taskbar. The middle button changes name and function depending on the status of the window—the Maximize button ▢ expands the window to the full screen size or to the program window size, and the Restore Down button ◲ returns the window to a predefined size. The Close button ✕ , on the right, exits the program or closes the file. Excel has two sets of sizing buttons. The top set controls the program window and the lower set controls the workspace. The workspace sizing buttons look and function in exactly the same way as the program window sizing buttons, except the button names change to Minimize Window and Restore Window when the workspace is maximized.

Most often, you'll want to maximize the program window and workspace to take advantage of the full screen size you have available. If you have several files open, you might want to restore down their windows so that you can see more than one window at a time, or you might want to minimize programs or files you are not working on at the moment. You'll try minimizing, maximizing, and restoring down windows and workspaces now.

To resize windows and workspaces:

▶ **1.** Click the **Minimize** button ▭ on the Word title bar. The Word program window reduces to a taskbar button. The Excel program window is visible again.

▶ **2.** If necessary, click the **Maximize** button ▢ on the Excel title bar. The Excel program window expands to fill the screen.

▶ **3.** Click the **Restore Window** button ▢ in the lower set of Excel sizing buttons. The workspace is resized and is now smaller than the full program window. See Figure 5.

Resized Excel window and workspace ◀ **Figure** 5

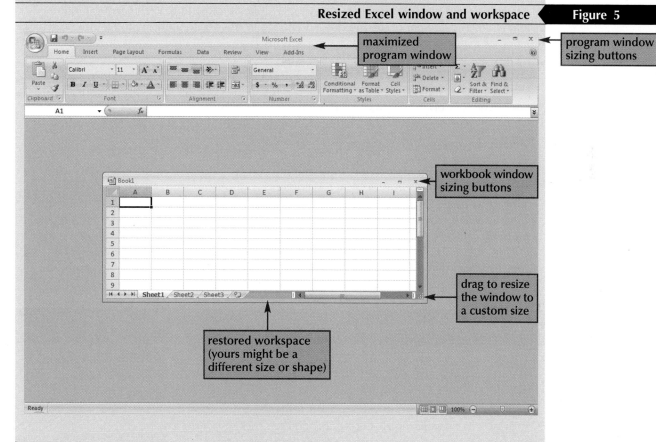

maximized program window

program window sizing buttons

workbook window sizing buttons

drag to resize the window to a custom size

restored workspace (yours might be a different size or shape)

▶ **4.** Click the **Maximize** button ▢ on the Excel workbook window title bar. The Excel workspace expands to fill the program window.

▶ **5.** Click the **Document1 - Microsoft Word** button on the taskbar. The Word program window returns to its previous size.

▶ **6.** If necessary, click the **Maximize** button ▢ on the Word title bar. The Word program window expands to fill the screen.

The sizing buttons give you the flexibility to arrange the program and file windows on your screen to best fit your needs.

Getting Information from the Status Bar

The **status bar** at the bottom of the program window provides information about the open file and current task or selection. It also has buttons and other controls for working with the file and its content. The status bar buttons and information displays are specific to the individual programs. For example, the Excel status bar displays summary information about a selected range of numbers (such as their sum or average), whereas the Word status bar shows the current page number and total number of words in a document. The right side of the status bar includes buttons that enable you to switch the workspace view in Word, Excel, PowerPoint, and Access as well as zoom the workspace in Word, Excel, and PowerPoint. You can customize the status bar to display other information or hide the **default** (original or preset) information.

Switching Views

Each program has a variety of views, or ways to display the file in the workspace. For example, Word has five views: Print Layout, Full Screen Reading, Web Layout, Outline, and Draft. The content of the file doesn't change from view to view, although the presentation of the content will. In Word, for example, Page Layout view shows how a document would appear as the printed page, whereas Web Layout view shows how the document would appear as a Web page. You can quickly switch between views using the shortcuts at the right side of the status bar. You can also change the view from the View tab on the Ribbon. You'll change views in later tutorials.

Zooming the Workspace

Zooming is a way to magnify or shrink the file content displayed in the workspace. You can zoom in to get a closer look at the content of an open document, worksheet, or slide, or you can zoom out to see more of the content at a smaller size. There are several ways to change the zoom percentage. You can use the Zoom slider at the right of the status bar to quickly change the zoom percentage. You can click the Zoom level button to the left of the Zoom slider in the status bar to open the Zoom dialog box and select a specific zoom percentage or size based on your file. You can also change the zoom settings using the Zoom group in the View tab on the Ribbon.

Reference Window | **Zooming the Workspace**

- Click the Zoom Out or Zoom In button on the status bar (or drag the Zoom slider button left or right) to the desired zoom percentage.

or

- Click the Zoom level button on the status bar.
- Select the appropriate zoom setting, and then click the OK button.

or

- Click the View tab on the Ribbon, and then in the Zoom group, click the zoom setting you want.

The figures shown in these tutorials are zoomed to enhance readability. You'll zoom the Word and Excel workspaces.

To zoom the Word and Excel workspaces:

▶ **1.** On the Zoom slider on the Word status bar, drag the **slider button** to the left until the Zoom percentage is **10%**. The document reduces to its smallest size, which makes the entire page visible but unreadable. See Figure 6.

Word document zoomed to 10% **Figure 6**

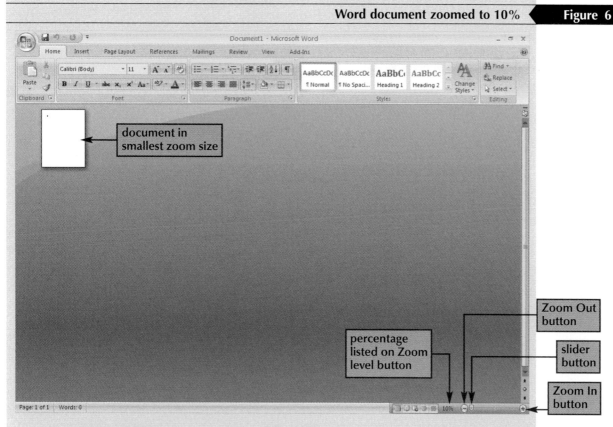

document in smallest zoom size

Zoom Out button

percentage listed on Zoom level button

slider button

Zoom In button

You'll zoom the document so its page width fills the workspace.

2. Click the **Zoom level** button `10%` on the Word status bar. The Zoom dialog box opens. See Figure 7.

Zoom dialog box **Figure 7**

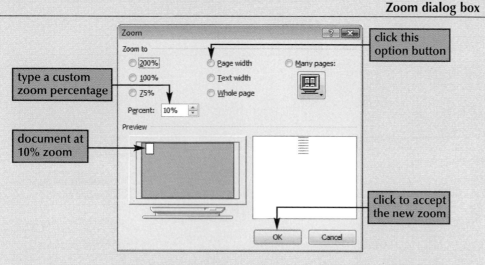

type a custom zoom percentage

click this option button

document at 10% zoom

click to accept the new zoom

3. Click the **Page width** option button, and then click the **OK** button. The Word document magnifies to its page width to match the rest of the Word figures shown in these tutorials.

Now, you'll zoom the workbook to 120%.

4. Click the **Microsoft Excel – Book1** button on the taskbar. The Excel program window is displayed.

5. Click the **Zoom In** button on the status bar two times. The workspace magnifies to 120%. This is the zoom percentage that matches the rest of the Excel figures shown in these tutorials.

6. Click the **Document1 – Microsoft Word** button on the taskbar. The Word program window is displayed.

Using the Ribbon

The **Ribbon** at the top of the program window just below the title bar is the main set of commands that you click to execute tasks. The Ribbon is organized into tabs. Each **tab** has commands related to particular activities. For example, in Word, the Insert tab on the Ribbon provides access to all the commands for adding objects such as shapes, pages, tables, illustrations, text, and symbols to a document. Although the tabs differ from program to program, the first tab in each program, called the Home tab, contains the commands for the most frequently performed activities, including cutting and pasting, changing fonts, and using editing tools. In addition, the Insert, Review, View, and Add-Ins tabs appear on the Ribbon in all the Office programs except Access, although the commands they include might differ from program to program. Other tabs are program specific, such as the Design tab in PowerPoint and the Datasheet tab in Access.

To use the Ribbon tabs:

1. In Word, point to the **Insert** tab on the Ribbon. The Insert tab is highlighted, though the Home tab with the options for using the Clipboard and formatting text remains visible.

2. Click the **Insert** tab. The Ribbon displays the Insert tab, which provides access to all the options for adding objects such as shapes, pages, tables, illustrations, text, and symbols to a document. See Figure 8.

Tip

To view more workspace, you can reduce the Ribbon to a single line by double-clicking any tab on the Ribbon. Double-click any tab again to redisplay the full Ribbon.

Figure 8   **Insert tab on the Ribbon**

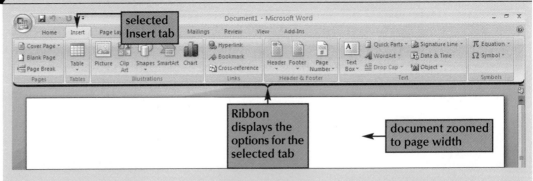

3. Click the **Home** tab on the Ribbon. The Ribbon displays the Home options.

Clicking Button Icons

Each **button**, or icon, on the tabs provides one-click access to a command. Most buttons are labeled so that you can easily find the command you need. For the most part, when you click a button, something happens in your file. If you want to repeat that action, you click the button again. Buttons for related commands are organized on a tab in **groups**. For example, the Clipboard group on the Home tab includes the Cut, Copy, Paste, and Format Painter buttons—the commands for moving or copying text, objects, and formatting.

Buttons can be toggle switches: one click turns on the feature and the next click turns off the feature. While the feature is on, the button remains colored or highlighted to remind you that it is active. For example, in Word, the Show/Hide button on the Home tab in the Paragraph group displays the nonprinting screen characters when toggled on and hides them when toggled off.

Some buttons have two parts: a button that accesses a command and an arrow that opens a menu of all the commands available for that task. For example, the Paste button on the Home tab includes the default Paste command and an arrow that opens the menu of all the Paste commands—Paste, Paste Special, and Paste as Hyperlink. To select a command on the menu, you click the button arrow and then click the command on the menu.

The buttons and groups change based on your monitor size, your screen resolution, and the size of the program window. With smaller monitors, lower screen resolutions, and reduced program windows, buttons can appear as icons without labels and a group can be condensed into a button that you click to display the group options. The figures in these tutorials were created using a screen resolution of 1024 × 768 and, unless otherwise specified, the program and workspace windows are maximized. If you are using a different screen resolution or window size, the button icons on the Ribbon might show more or fewer button names, and some groups might be condensed into buttons.

You'll type text in the Word document, and then use the buttons on the Ribbon.

To use buttons on the Ribbon:

1. Type **Recycled Palette**, and then press the **Enter** key. The text appears in the first line of the document and the insertion point moves to the second line.

   Trouble? If you make a typing error, press the Backspace key to delete the incorrect letters, and then retype the text.

2. In the Paragraph group on the Home tab, click the **Show/Hide** button ¶ . The nonprinting screen characters appear in the document, and the Show/Hide button remains toggled on. See Figure 9.

   Trouble? If the nonprinting characters are removed from your screen, the Show/Hide button ¶ was already selected. Repeat Step 2 to show the nonprinting screen characters.

Button toggled on | **Figure 9**

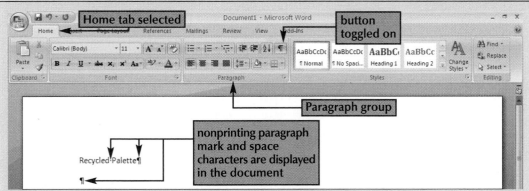

3. Drag to select all the text in the first line of the document (but not the paragraph mark).

4. In the Clipboard group on the Home tab, click the **Copy** button . The selected text is copied to the Clipboard.

5. Press the ↓ key. The text is deselected and the insertion point moves to the second line in the document.

6. In the Clipboard group on the Home tab, point to the top part of the **Paste** button. Both parts of the Paste button are highlighted, but the icon at top is darker to indicate it will be clicked if you press the mouse button.

7. Point to the **Paste button arrow**. The button arrow is now darker.

8. Click the **Paste button arrow**. A menu of paste commands opens. See Figure 10. To select one of the commands on the list, you click it.

Figure 10	Two-part Paste button

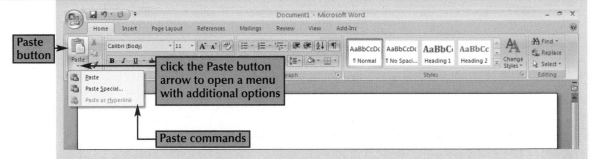

9. Click **Paste**. The menu closes, and the text is duplicated in the second line of the document.

As you can see, you can quickly access commands and turn features on and off with the buttons on the Ribbon.

InSight | **Using Keyboard Shortcuts and Key Tips**

Keyboard shortcuts can help you work faster and more efficiently. A **keyboard shortcut** is a key or combination of keys you press to access a tool or perform a command. To quickly access options on the Ribbon, the Quick Access Toolbar, and the Office Button without removing your hands from the keyboard:

1. Press the Alt key. Key Tips appear that list the keyboard shortcut for each Ribbon tab, each Quick Access Toolbar button, and the Office Button.
2. Press the key for the tab or button you want to use. An action is performed or Key Tips appear for the buttons on the selected tab or the commands for the selected button.
3. Continue to press the appropriate key listed in the Key Tip until the action you want is performed.

You can also use keyboard shortcuts to perform specific commands. For example, Ctrl+S is the keyboard shortcut for the Save command (you hold down the Ctrl key while you press the S key). This type of keyboard shortcut appears in ScreenTips next to the command's name. Not all commands have this type of keyboard shortcut. Identical commands in each Office program use the same keyboard shortcut.

Using Galleries and Live Preview

A button can also open a **gallery**, which is a grid or menu that shows a visual representation of the options available for that command. For example, the Bullet Library gallery in Word shows an icon of each bullet style you can select. Some galleries include a More button that you click to expand the gallery to see all the options in it. When you hover the pointer over an option in a gallery, **Live Preview** shows the results you would achieve in your file if you clicked that option. To continue the bullets example, when you hover over a bullet style in the Bullet Library gallery, the current paragraph or selected text previews that bullet style. By moving the pointer from option to option, you can quickly see the text set with different bullet styles; you can then select the style that works best for your needs.

To use a gallery and Live Preview:

▶ 1. In the Paragraph group on the Home tab, click the **Bullets button arrow** [≣ ▾]. The Bullet Library gallery opens.

▶ 2. Point to the **check mark bullet** style. Live Preview shows the selected bullet style in your document, so you can determine if you like that bullet style. See Figure 11.

Live Preview of bullet style   **Figure 11**

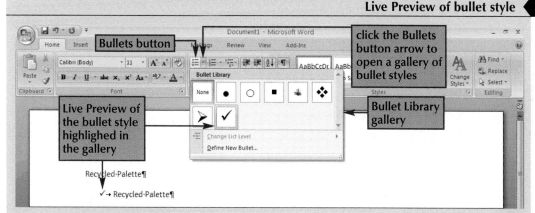

▶ 3. Place the pointer over each of the remaining bullet styles and preview them in your document.

You don't want to add bullets to your document right now, so you'll close the Bullet Library gallery and deselect the Bullets button.

▶ 4. Press the **Esc** key on the keyboard. The Bullet Library gallery closes and the Bullets button is deselected.

▶ 5. Press the **Backspace** key on the keyboard to delete the text "Recycled Palette" on the second line.

Galleries and Live Preview let you quickly see how your file will be affected by a selection.

Opening Dialog Boxes and Task Panes

The button to the right of the group names is the **Dialog Box Launcher**, which you click to open a task pane or dialog box that provides more advanced functionality for that group of tasks. A **task pane** is a window that helps you navigate through a complex task or feature. For example, the Clipboard task pane allows you to paste some or all of the items that have been cut or copied from any Office program during the current work session and the Research task pane allows you to search a variety of reference resources from within a file. A **dialog box** is a window from which you enter or choose settings for how you want to perform a task. For example, the Page Setup dialog box in Word contains options for how you want a document to look. Some dialog boxes organize related information into tabs, and related options and settings are organized into groups, just as they are on the Ribbon. You select settings in a dialog box using option buttons, check boxes, text boxes, lists, and other controls to collect information about how you want to perform a task.

In Excel, you'll use the Dialog Box Launcher for the Page Setup group to open the Page Setup dialog box.

To open the Page Setup dialog box using the Dialog Box Launcher:

▶ 1. Click the **Microsoft Excel – Book1** button on the taskbar to switch from Word to Excel.

▶ 2. Click the **Page Layout** tab on the Ribbon.

▶ 3. In the Page Setup group, click the **Dialog Box Launcher**, which is the small button to the right of the Page Setup group name. The Page Setup dialog box opens with the Page tab displayed. See Figure 12.

| Figure 12 | Page tab in the Page Setup dialog box |

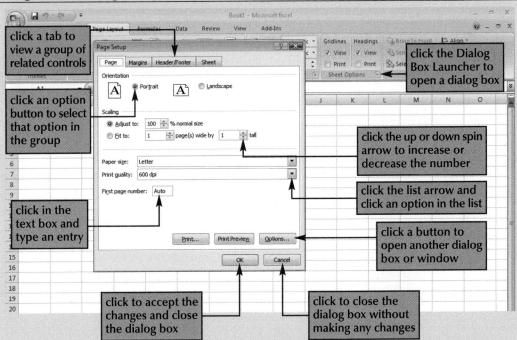

▶ 4. Click the **Landscape** option button. The workbook's page orientation changes to a page wider than it is long.

▶ 5. Click the **Sheet** tab. The dialog box displays options related to the worksheet. You can click a check box to turn an option on (checked) or off (unchecked). You can check more than one check box in a group, whereas you can select only one option button in a group.

▶ 6. In the Print group, click the **Gridlines** check box and the **Row and column headings** check box. Check marks appear in both check boxes, indicating that these options are selected.

You don't want to change the page setup right now, so you'll close the dialog box.

▶ 7. Click the **Cancel** button. The dialog box closes without making any changes to the page setup.

Using Contextual Tools

Some tabs, toolbars, and menus come into view as you work. Because these tools become available only as you might need them, the workspace on your screen remains more open and less cluttered. However, tools that appear and disappear as you work can be distracting and take some getting used to.

Displaying Contextual Tabs

Any object that you can select in a file has a related contextual tab. An **object** is anything that appears on your screen that can be selected and manipulated as a whole, such as a table, a picture, a text box, a shape, a chart, WordArt, an equation, a diagram, a header, or a footer. A **contextual tab** is a Ribbon tab that contains commands related to the selected object so you can manipulate, edit, and format that object. Contextual tabs appear to the right of the standard Ribbon tabs just below a title label. For example, Figure 13 shows the Table Tools contextual tabs that appear when you select a table in a Word document. Although the contextual tabs appear only when you select an object, they function in the same way as standard tabs on the Ribbon. Contextual tabs disappear when you click elsewhere on the screen and deselect the object. Contextual tabs can also appear as you switch views. You'll use contextual tabs in later tutorials.

Table Tools contextual tabs ◄ **Figure 13**

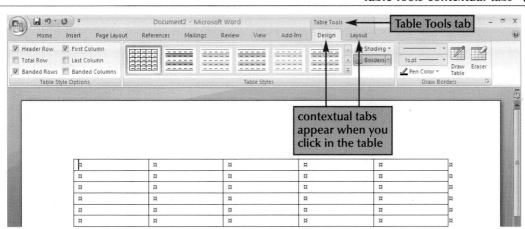

Accessing the Mini Toolbar

The **Mini toolbar** is a toolbar that appears next to the pointer whenever you select text, and it contains buttons for the most commonly used formatting commands, such as font, font size, styles, color, alignment, and indents that may appear in different groups or tabs on the Ribbon. The Mini toolbar buttons differ in each program. A transparent version of the Mini toolbar appears immediately after you select text. When you move the pointer over the Mini toolbar, it comes into full view so you can click the appropriate formatting button or buttons. The Mini toolbar disappears if you move the pointer away from the toolbar, press a key, or press a mouse button. The Mini toolbar can help you format your text faster, but initially you might find that the toolbar disappears unexpectedly. All the commands on the Mini toolbar are also available on the Ribbon. Be aware that Live Preview of selected styles does not work in the Mini toolbar.

You'll use the Mini toolbar to format text you enter in the workbook.

Tip

You can turn off the Mini toolbar and Live Preview in Word, Excel, and PowerPoint. Click the Office Button, click the Options button at the bottom of the Office menu, uncheck the first two check boxes in the Popular category, and then click the OK button.

To use the Mini toolbar to format text:

▶ 1. If necessary, click cell **A1** (the rectangle in the upper-left corner of the worksheet).

▶ 2. Type **Budget**. The text appears in the cell.

▶ 3. Press the **Enter** key. The text is entered in cell A1 and cell A2 is selected.

▶ 4. Type **2008**, and then press the **Enter** key. The year is entered in cell A2 and cell A3 is selected.

You'll use the Mini toolbar to make the word in cell A1 boldface.

▶ 5. Double-click cell **A1** to place the insertion point in the cell. Now you can select the text you typed.

▶ 6. Double-click **Budget** in cell A1. The selected text appears white in a black background, and the transparent Mini toolbar appears directly above the selected text. See Figure 14.

Figure 14 Transparent Mini toolbar

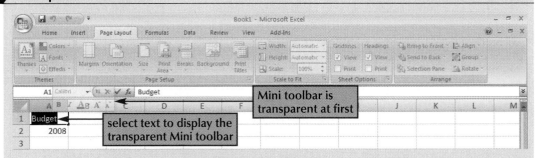

Tip

You can redisplay the Mini toolbar if it disappears by right-clicking the selected text.

▶ 7. Move the pointer over the Mini toolbar. The Mini toolbar is now completely visible, and you can click buttons.

Trouble? If the Mini toolbar disappears, you probably moved the pointer to another area of the worksheet. To redisplay the Mini toolbar, repeat Steps 5 through 7, being careful to move the pointer directly over the Mini toolbar in Step 7.

▶ 8. Click the **Bold** button B on the Mini toolbar. The text in cell A1 is bold and the Mini toolbar remains visible so you can continue formatting the selected text. See Figure 15.

Figure 15 Mini toolbar with the Bold button selected

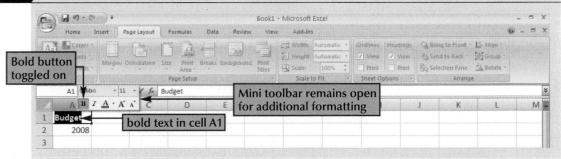

You don't want to make any other changes, so you'll close the Mini toolbar.

▶ 9. Press the **Enter** key. The Mini toolbar disappears and cell A2 is selected.

Opening Shortcut Menus

A **shortcut menu** is a list of commands related to a selection that opens when you click the right mouse button. Each shortcut menu provides access to the commands you'll most likely want to use with the object or selection you right-click. The shortcut menu includes commands that perform actions, commands that open dialog boxes, and galleries of options that provide Live Preview. The Mini toolbar also opens when you right-click. If you click a button on the Mini toolbar, the rest of the shortcut menu closes while the Mini toolbar remains open so you can continue formatting the selection. Using a shortcut menu provides quick access to the commands you need without having to access the tabs on the Ribbon. For example, you can right-click selected text to open a shortcut menu with a Mini toolbar, text-related commands, such as Cut, Copy, and Paste, as well as other program-specific commands.

You'll use a shortcut menu in Excel to delete the content you entered in cell A1.

To use a shortcut menu to delete content:

▶ 1. Right-click cell **A1**. A shortcut menu opens, listing commands related to common tasks you'd perform in a cell, along with a Mini toolbar. See Figure 16.

Shortcut menu with Mini toolbar ◄ Figure 16

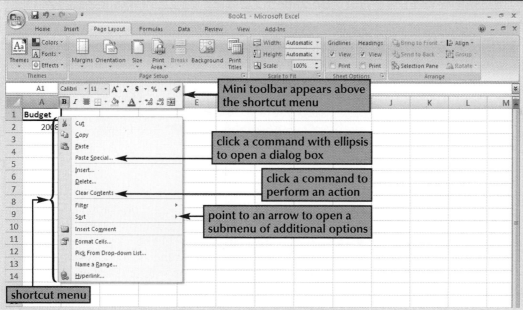

You'll use the Clear Contents command to delete the bold text from cell A1.

▶ 2. Click **Clear Contents** on the shortcut menu. The shortcut menu closes, the Mini toolbar disappears, and the formatted text is removed from cell A1.

You'll use the Clear Contents command again to delete the year from cell A2.

▶ 3. Right-click cell **A2**, and then click **Clear Contents** on the shortcut menu. The year is removed from cell A2.

Shortcut menus enable you to quickly access commands that you're most likely to need in the context of the task you're performing.

Tip

Press the Esc key to close an open menu, shortcut menu, list, gallery, and so forth without selecting an option.

Working with Files

The most common tasks you perform in any Office program are to create, open, save, and close files. The processes for these tasks are basically the same in all the Office programs. In addition, there are several methods for performing most tasks in Office. This flexibility enables you to use Office in a way that best fits how you like to work.

The **Office Button** provides access to document-level features, such as creating new files, opening existing files, saving files, printing files, and closing files, as well as the most common program options, called **application settings**. The **Quick Access Toolbar** is a collection of buttons that provide one-click access to commonly used commands, such as Save, Undo, and Repeat.

To begin working in a program, you need to create a new file or open an existing file. When you start Word, Excel, or PowerPoint, the program opens along with a blank file—ready for you to begin working on a new document, workbook, or presentation. When you start Access, the Getting Started with Microsoft Access window opens, displaying options for creating a new database or opening an existing one.

Ean has asked you to continue working on the agenda for the stockholder meeting. You already started typing in the document that opened when you started Word. Next, you will enter more text in the Word document.

Tip

You can add buttons you use frequently to the Quick Access Toolbar. Click the Customize Quick Access Toolbar button, and then click a button name on the menu.

To enter text in the Word document:

▶ 1. Click the **Document1 – Microsoft Word** button on the taskbar to activate the Word program window.

▶ 2. Type **Meeting Agenda** on the second line of the document, and then press the **Enter** key. The text you typed appears in the document.

   Trouble? If you make a typing error, press the Backspace key to delete the incorrect letters, and then retype the text.

Saving a File

As you create and modify Office files, your work is stored only in the computer's temporary memory, not on a hard disk. If you were to exit the programs without saving, turn off your computer, or experience a power failure, your work would be lost. To prevent losing work, save your file to a disk frequently—at least every 10 minutes. You can save files to the hard disk located inside your computer, a floppy disk, an external hard drive, a network storage drive, or a portable storage disk, such as a USB flash drive.

Reference Window | Saving a File

To save a file the first time or with a new name or location:
- Click the Office Button, and then click Save As (or for an unnamed file, click the Save button on the Quick Access Toolbar or click the Office Button, and then click Save).
- In the Save As dialog box, navigate to the location where you want to save the file.
- Type a descriptive title in the File name box, and then click the Save button.

To resave a named file to the same location:
- Click the Save button on the Quick Access Toolbar (or click the Office Button, and then click Save).

The first time you save a file, you need to name it. This **filename** includes a descriptive title you select and a file extension assigned by Office. You should choose a descriptive title that accurately reflects the content of the document, workbook, presentation, or database, such as "Shipping Options Letter" or "Fourth Quarter Financial Analysis." Your descriptive title can include uppercase and lowercase letters, numbers, hyphens, and spaces in any combination, but not the following special characters: ? " / \ < > * | and :. Each filename ends with a **file extension**, a period followed by several characters that Office adds to your descriptive title to identify the program in which that file was created. The default file extensions for Office 2007 are .docx for Word, .xlsx for Excel, .pptx for PowerPoint, and .accdb for Access. Filenames (the descriptive title and the file extension) can include a maximum of 255 characters. You might see file extensions depending on how Windows is set up on your computer. The figures in these tutorials do not show file extensions.

You also need to decide where to save the file—on which disk and in what folder. A **folder** is a container for your files. Just as you organize paper documents within folders stored in a filing cabinet, you can organize your files within folders stored on your computer's hard disk or a removable disk, such as a USB flash drive. Store each file in a logical location that you will remember whenever you want to use the file again. The default storage location for Office files is the Documents folder; you can create additional storage folders within that folder or navigate to a new storage location.

You can navigate the Save As dialog box by clicking a folder or location on your computer in the Navigation pane along the left side of the dialog box, and then double-clicking folders in the file list until you display the storage location you want. You can also navigate to a storage location with the Address bar, which displays the current file path. Each location in the file path has a corresponding arrow that you can click to quickly select a folder within that location. For example, you can click the Documents arrow in the Address bar to open a list of all the folders in the Documents folder, and then click the folder you want to open. If you want to return to a specific spot in the file hierarchy, you click that folder name in the Address bar. The Back and Forward buttons let you quickly move between folders.

Tip

Office adds the correct file extension when you save a file. Do not type one in the descriptive title, or you will create a duplicate (such as Meeting Agenda.docx.docx).

Windows XP Tip

The default storage location for Office files is the My Documents folder.

Saving and Using Files with Earlier Versions of Office | InSight

The default file types in Office 2007 are different from those used in earlier versions. This means that someone using Office 2003 or earlier cannot open files created in Office 2007. Files you want to share with earlier Office users must be saved in the earlier formats, which use the following extensions: .doc for Word, .xls for Excel, .mdb for Access, and .ppt for PowerPoint. To save a file in an earlier format, open the Save As dialog box, click the Save as type list arrow, and then click the appropriate 97-2003 format. A compatibility checker reports which Office 2007 features or elements are not supported by the earlier version of Office, and you can choose to remove them before saving. You can use Office 2007 to open and work with files created in earlier versions of Office. You can then save the file in its current format or update it to the Office 2007 format.

The lines of text you typed are not yet saved on disk. You'll do that now.

To save a file for the first time:

Windows XP Tip

To navigate to a location in the Save As dialog box, you use the Save in arrow.

1. Click the **Save** button 🔲 on the Quick Access Toolbar. The Save As dialog box opens because you have not yet saved the file and need to specify a storage location and filename. The default location is set to the Documents folder, and the first few words of the first line appear in the File name box as a suggested title.

2. In the Navigation pane, click the link for the location that contains your Data Files, if necessary.

   Trouble? If you don't have the starting Data Files, you need to get them before you can proceed. Your instructor will either give you the Data Files or ask you to obtain them from a specified location (such as a network drive). In either case, make a backup copy of the Data Files before you start so that you will have the original files available in case you need to start over. If you have any questions about the Data Files, see your instructor or technical support person for assistance.

3. Double-click the **OFF** folder in the file list, and then double-click the **Tutorial** folder. This is the location where you want to save the document.

   Next, you'll enter a more descriptive title for the filename.

4. Type **Meeting Agenda** in the File name box. See Figure 17.

| Figure 17 | Completed Save As dialog box |

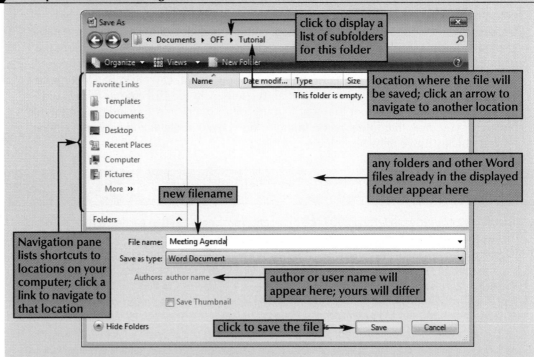

Trouble? If the .docx file extension appears after the filename, your computer is configured to show file extensions. Continue with Step 5.

5. Click the **Save** button. The Save As dialog box closes, and the name of your file appears in the title bar.

The saved file includes everything in the document at the time you last saved it. Any new edits or additions you make to the document exist only in the computer's memory and are not saved in the file on the disk. As you work, remember to save frequently so that the file is updated to reflect the latest content of the document.

Because you already named the document and selected a storage location, the Save As dialog box doesn't open whenever you save the document again. If you want to save a copy of the file with a different filename or to a different location, you reopen the Save As dialog box by clicking the Office Button, and then clicking Save As. The previous version of the file remains on your disk as well.

You need to add your name to the agenda. Then, you'll save your changes.

To modify and save the Word document:

▶ **1.** Type your name, and then press the **Enter** key. The text you typed appears on the next line.

▶ **2.** Click the **Save** button 🖫 on the Quick Access Toolbar to save your changes.

Closing a File

Although you can keep multiple files open at one time, you should close any file you are no longer working on to conserve system resources as well as to ensure that you don't inadvertently make changes to the file. You can close a file by clicking the Office Button and then clicking the Close command. If that's the only file open for the program, the program window remains open and no file appears in the window. You can also close a file by clicking the Close button in the upper-right corner of the title bar or double-clicking the Office Button. If that's the only file open for the program, the program also closes.

As a standard practice, you should save your file before closing it. However, Office has an added safeguard: If you attempt to close a file without saving your changes, a dialog box opens, asking whether you want to save the file. Click the Yes button to save the changes to the file before closing the file and program. Click the No button to close the file and program without saving changes. Click the Cancel button to return to the program window without saving changes or closing the file and program. This feature helps to ensure that you always save the most current version of any file.

You'll add the date to the agenda. Then, you'll attempt to close it without saving.

To modify and close the Word document:

▶ **1.** Type today's date, and then press the **Enter** key. The text you typed appears below your name in the document.

▶ **2.** In the upper-left corner of the program window, click the **Office Button** 🗐. A menu opens with commands for creating new files, opening existing files, saving files, printing files, and closing files.

▶ **3.** Click **Close**. A dialog box opens, asking whether you want to save the changes you made to the document.

▶ **4.** Click the **Yes** button. The current version of the document is saved to the file, and then the document closes. Word is still running.

After you have a program open, you can create additional new files for the open program or you can open previously created and saved files.

Opening a File

When you want to open a blank document, workbook, presentation, or database, you create a new file. When you want to work on a previously created file, you must first open it. Opening a file transfers a copy of the file from the storage disk (either a hard disk or a portable disk) to the computer's memory and displays it on your screen. The file is then in your computer's memory and on the disk.

Reference Window | **Opening an Existing File or Creating a New File**

- Click the Office Button, and then click Open.
- In the Open dialog box, navigate to the storage location of the file you want to open.
- Click the filename of the file you want to open.
- Click the Open button.

or

- Click the Office Button, and then click a filename in the Recent Documents list.

or

- Click the Office Button, and then click New.
- In the New dialog box, click Blank Document, Blank Workbook, Blank Presentation, or Blank Database (depending on the program).
- Click the Create button.

Ean asks you to print the agenda. To do that, you'll reopen the file.

To open the existing Word document:

1. Click the **Office Button** , and then click **Open**. The Open dialog box, which works similarly to the Save As dialog box, opens.

Windows XP Tip

To navigate to a location in the Open dialog box, you use the Look in arrow.

2. Use the Navigation pane or the Address bar to navigate to the **OFF\Tutorial** folder included with your Data Files. This is the location where you saved the agenda document.

3. Click **Meeting Agenda** in the file list. See Figure 18.

| Figure 18 | Open dialog box |

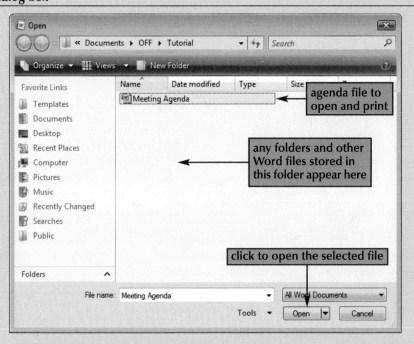

4. Click the **Open** button. The agenda file opens in the Word program window.

Next, you'll use Help to get information about printing files in Word.

Getting Help

If you don't know how to perform a task or want more information about a feature, you can turn to Office itself for information on how to use it. This information, referred to simply as **Help**, is like a huge encyclopedia available from your desktop. You can get Help in ScreenTips, from the Help window, and in Microsoft Office Online.

Viewing ScreenTips

ScreenTips are a fast and simple method you can use to get help about objects you see on the screen. A **ScreenTip** is a box with the button's name, its keyboard shortcut if it has one, a description of the command's function, and, in some cases, a link to more information. Just position the mouse pointer over a button or object to view its ScreenTip. If a link to more information appears in the ScreenTip, press the F1 key while the Screen-Tip is displayed to open the Help window with the appropriate topic displayed.

To view ScreenTips:

▶ 1. Point to the **Microsoft Office Word Help** button ⊚. The ScreenTip shows the button's name, its keyboard shortcut, and a brief explanation of the button. See Figure 19.

ScreenTip for the Help button ◀ Figure 19

▶ 2. Point to other buttons on the Ribbon to display their ScreenTips.

Using the Help Window

For more detailed information, you can use the **Help window** to access all the Help topics, templates, and training installed on your computer with Office and available on Microsoft Office Online. **Microsoft Office Online** is a Web site maintained by Microsoft that provides access to the latest information and additional Help resources. For example, you can access current Help topics, templates of predesigned files, and training for Office. To connect to Microsoft Office Online, you need Internet access on your computer. Otherwise, you see only those topics stored locally.

Reference Window | **Getting Help**

- Click the Microsoft Office Help button (the button name depends on the Office program).
- Type a keyword or phrase in the "Type words to search for" box, and then click the Search button.
- Click a Help topic in the search results list.
- Read the information in the Help window. For more information, click other topics or links.
- Click the Close button on the Help window title bar.

You open the Help window by clicking the Microsoft Office Help button 🔘 located below the sizing buttons in every Office program. Each program has its own Help window from which you can find information about all the Office commands and features as well as step-by-step instructions for using them. You can search for information in the Help window using the "Type words to search for" box and the Table of Contents pane.

The "Type words to search for" box enables you to search the Help system using key-words or phrases. You type a specific word or phrase about a task you want to perform or a topic you need help with, and then click the Search button to search the Help system. A list of Help topics related to the keyword or phrase you entered appears in the Help window. If your computer is connected to the Internet, your search results come from Microsoft Office Online rather than only the Help topics stored locally on your computer. You can click a link to open a Help topic with step-by-step instructions that will guide you through a specific procedure and/or provide explanations of difficult concepts in clear, easy-to-understand language. For example, if you type "format cell" in the Excel Help window, a list of Help topics related to the words you typed appears in the Help window. You can navigate through the topics you've viewed using the buttons on the Help window toolbar. These buttons—including Back, Forward, Stop, Refresh, Home, and Print—are the same as those in the Microsoft Internet Explorer Web browser.

You'll use the "Type words to search for" box in the Help window to obtain more information about printing a document in Word.

To use the "Type words to search for" box:

1. Click the **Microsoft Office Word Help** button 🔘 . The Word Help window opens.

2. Click the **Type words to search for** box, if necessary, and then type **print document**. You can set where you want to search.

3. Click the **Search button arrow**. The Search menu shows the online and local content available.

4. If your computer is connected to the Internet, click **All Word** in the Content from Office Online list. If your computer is not connected to the Internet, click **Word Help** in the Content from this computer list.

5. Click the **Search** button. The Help window displays a list of topics related to your keywords. See Figure 20.

Search results displaying Help topics   Figure 20

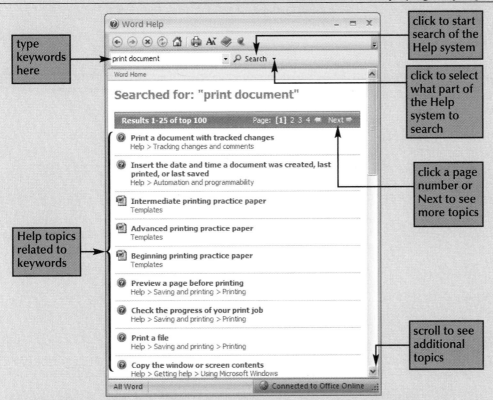

Trouble? If your search results list differs from the one shown in Figure 20, your computer is not connected to the Internet or Microsoft has updated the list of available Help topics since this book was published. Continue with Step 6.

6. Scroll through the list to review the Help topics.

7. Click **Print a file**. The Help topic is displayed in the Help window so you can learn more about how to print a document. See Figure 21.

Figure 21 **Print a file Help topic**

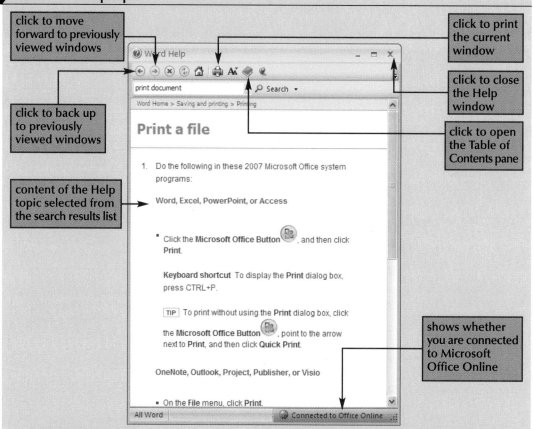

click to move forward to previously viewed windows

click to print the current window

click to close the Help window

click to back up to previously viewed windows

click to open the Table of Contents pane

content of the Help topic selected from the search results list

shows whether you are connected to Microsoft Office Online

Trouble? If you don't see the Print a file Help topic on page 1, its current location might be on another page. Click the Next link to move to the next page, and then scroll down to find the Print a file topic, repeating to search additional pages until you locate the topic.

▶ **8.** Read the information.

Another way to find information in the Help system is to use the Table of Contents pane. The Show Table of Contents button on the Help window toolbar opens a pane that displays a list of the Help system content organized by subjects and topics, similar to a book's table of contents. You click main subject links to display related topic links. You click a topic link to display that Help topic in the Help window. You'll use the Table of Contents to find information about getting help in Office.

To use the Help window table of contents:

▶ **1.** Click the **Show Table of Contents** button ◉ on the Help window toolbar. The Table of Contents pane opens on the left side of the Help window.

▶ **2.** Click **Getting help** in the Table of Contents pane, scrolling up if necessary. The Getting help "book" opens, listing the topics related to that subject.

▶ **3.** Click the **Work with the Help window** topic, and then click the **Maximize** button ▭ on the title bar. The Help topic is displayed in the maximized Help window, and you can read the text to learn more about the various ways to obtain help in Word. See Figure 22.

Table of Contents pane in the Help window ◄ **Figure 22**

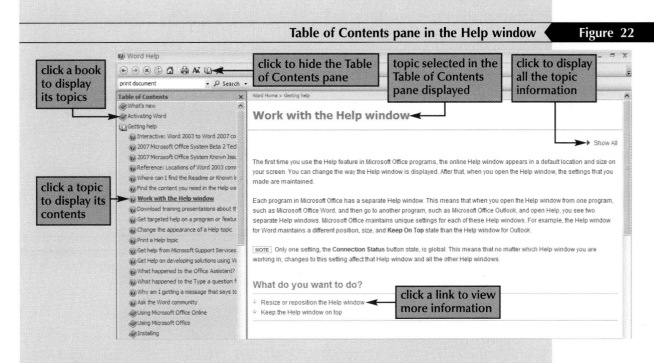

Trouble? If your search results list differs from the one shown in Figure 22, your computer is not connected to the Internet or Microsoft has updated the list of available Help topics since this book was published. Continue with Step 4.

▶ **4.** Click **Using Microsoft Office Online** in the Table of Contents pane, click the **Get online Help, templates, training, and additional content** topic to display information about that topic, and then read the information.

▶ **5.** Click the links within this topic and read the information.

▶ **6.** Click the **Close** button [X] on the Help window title bar to close the window.

Printing a File

At times, you'll want a paper copy of your Office file. The first time you print during each session at the computer, you should use the Print command to open the Print dialog box so you can verify or adjust the printing settings. You can select a printer, the number of copies to print, the portion of the file to print, and so forth; the printing settings vary slightly from program to program. If you want to use the same default settings for subsequent print jobs, you can use the Quick Print button to print without opening the dialog box.

Printing a File | Reference Window

- Click the Office Button, and then click Print.
- Verify the print settings in the Print dialog box.
- Click the OK button.
or
- Click the Office Button, point to Print, and then click Quick Print.

Now that you know how to print, you'll print the agenda for Ean.

To print the Word document:

▶ **1.** Make sure your printer is turned on and contains paper.

▶ **2.** Click the **Office Button** ⬤, and then click **Print**. The Print dialog box opens. See Figure 23.

Figure 23 Print dialog box

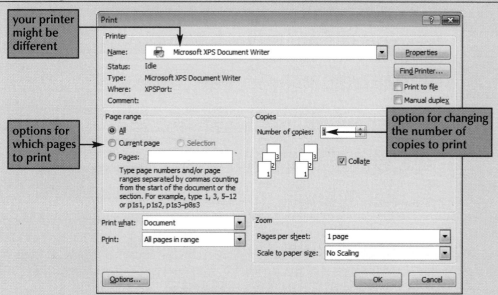

Trouble? If a menu of Print commands opens, you clicked the Print button arrow on the two-part Print button. Click Print on the menu to open the Print dialog box.

▶ **3.** Verify that the correct printer appears in the Name box in the Printer group. If necessary, click the **Name** arrow, and then click the correct printer from the list of available printers.

▶ **4.** Verify that **1** appears in the Number of copies box.

▶ **5.** Click the **OK** button to print the document.

Trouble? If the document does not print, see your instructor or technical support person for help.

Exiting Programs

When you finish working with a program, you should exit it. As with many other aspects of Office, you can exit programs with a button or a command. You'll use both methods to exit Word and Excel. You can use the Exit command to exit a program and close an open file in one step. If you haven't saved the final version of the open file, a dialog box opens, asking whether you want to save your changes. Clicking the Yes button saves the open file, closes the file, and then exits the program.

To exit the Word and Excel programs:

▶ **1.** Click the **Close** button ☒ on the Word title bar to exit Word. The Word document closes and the Word program exits. The Excel window is visible again.

Trouble? If a dialog box opens, asking if you want to save the document, you might have inadvertently made a change to the document. Click the No button.

▶ **2.** Click the **Office Button** 📄, and then click **Exit Excel**. A dialog box opens, asking whether you want to save the changes you made to the workbook. If you click the Yes button, the Save As dialog box opens and Excel exits after you finish saving the workbook. This time, you don't want to save the workbook.

▶ **3.** Click the **No** button. The workbook closes without saving a copy, and the Excel program exits.

Exiting programs after you are done using them keeps your Windows desktop uncluttered for the next person using the computer, frees up your system's resources, and prevents data from being lost accidentally.

Quick Check | Review

1. What Office program would be best to use to create a budget?
2. How do you start an Office program?
3. Explain the difference between Save and Save As.
4. How do you open an existing Office file?
5. What happens if you open a file, make edits, and then attempt to close the file or exit the program without saving the current version of the file?
6. What are two ways to get Help in Office?

Tutorial Summary | Review

You have learned how to use features common to all the programs included in Microsoft Office 2007, including starting and exiting programs; resizing windows; using the Ribbon, dialog boxes, shortcut menus, and the Mini toolbar; opening, closing, and printing files; and getting Help.

Key Terms

Access	Help window	Office Button
application settings	integration	Outlook
button	keyboard shortcut	PowerPoint
contextual tab	Live Preview	presentation
database	Microsoft Office 2007	Quick Access Toolbar
default	Microsoft Office Access 2007	Ribbon
dialog box	Microsoft Office Excel 2007	ScreenTip
Dialog Box Launcher	Microsoft Office Online	shortcut menu
document	Microsoft Office	status bar
Excel	Outlook 2007	tab
file extension	Microsoft Office	task pane
filename	PowerPoint 2007	Word
folder	Microsoft Office Word 2007	workbook
gallery	Mini toolbar	zoom
group	object	
Help	Office	

Practice		Review Assignments

*Practice the skills you
learned in the tutorial.*

Data Files needed for the Review Assignments: Finances.xlsx, Letter.docx

You need to prepare for an upcoming meeting at Recycled Palette. You'll open and print documents for the presentation. Complete the following:

1. Start PowerPoint.
2. Use the Help window to search Office Online for the PowerPoint demo "Demo: Up to Speed with PowerPoint 2007." (*Hint*: Use "demo" as the keyword to search for, and make sure you search All PowerPoint in the Content from Office Online list. If you are not connected to the Internet, continue with Step 3.) Open the Demo topic, and then click the Play Demo link to view it. Close Internet Explorer and the Help window when you're done.
3. Start Excel.
4. Switch to the PowerPoint window using the taskbar, and then close the presentation but leave open the PowerPoint program. (*Hint*: Click the Office Button and then click Close.)
5. Open a new, blank PowerPoint presentation from the New Presentation dialog box.
6. Close the PowerPoint presentation and program using the Close button on the PowerPoint title bar; do not save changes if asked.
7. Open the **Finances** workbook located in the OFF\Review folder included with your Data Files.
8. Use the Save As command to save the workbook as **Recycled Palette Finances** in the OFF\Review folder.
9. Type your name, press the Enter key to insert your name at the top of the worksheet, and then save the workbook.
10. Print one copy of the worksheet using the Print button on the Office Button menu.
11. Exit Excel using the Office Button.
12. Start Word, and then open the **Letter** document located in the OFF\Review folder included with your Data Files.
13. Use the Save As command to save the document with the filename **Recycled Palette Letter** in the OFF\Review folder.
14. Press and hold the Ctrl key, press the End key, and then release both keys to move the insertion point to the end of the letter, and then type your name.
15. Use the Save button on the Quick Access Toolbar to save the change to the Recycled Palette Letter document.
16. Print one copy of the document, and then close the document.
17. Exit the Word program using the Close button on the title bar.

Assess	SAM Assessment and Training

If you have a SAM user profile, you may have access to hands-on instruction, practice, and assessment of the skills covered in this tutorial. Log in to your SAM account (**http://sam2007.course.com**) to launch any assigned training activities or exams that relate to the skills covered in this tutorial.

Review	Quick Check Answers

1. Excel
2. Click the Start button on the taskbar, click All Programs, click Microsoft Office, and then click the name of the program you want to open.
3. Save updates a file to reflect its latest contents using its current filename and location. Save As enables you to change the filename and storage location of a file.
4. Click the Office Button, and then click Open.
5. A dialog box opens asking whether you want to save the changes to the file.
6. Two of the following: ScreenTips, Help window, Microsoft Office Online

Ending Data Files

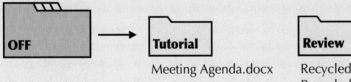

OFF → **Tutorial**
Meeting Agenda.docx

Review
Recycled Palette Finances.xlsx
Recycled Palette Letter.docx

Reality Check

At home, school, or work, you probably complete many types of tasks, such as writing letters and balancing a checkbook, on a regular basis. You can use Microsoft Office to streamline many of these tasks.

Note: Please be sure *not* to include any personal information of a sensitive nature in the documents you create to be submitted to your instructor for this exercise. Later on, you can update the documents with such information for your own personal use.

1. Start Word, and open a new document, if necessary.
2. In the document, type a list of all the personal, work, and/or school tasks you do on a regular basis.
3. For each task, identify the type of Office file (document, workbook, presentation, or database) you would create to complete that task. For example, you would create a Word document to write a letter.
4. For each file, identify the Office program you would use to create that file, and explain why you would use that program. For example, Word is the best program to use to create a document for a letter.
5. Save the document with an appropriate filename in an appropriate folder location.
6. Use a Web browser to visit the Microsoft Web site at *www.microsoft.com* and research the different Office 2007 suites available. Determine which suite includes all the programs you need to complete the tasks on your list.
7. At the end of the task list you created in your Word document, type which Office suite you decided on and a brief explanation of why you chose that suite. Then save the document.
8. Double-click the Home tab on the Ribbon to minimize the Ribbon to show only the tab names and extend the workspace area. At the end of the Word document, type your opinion of whether minimizing the Ribbon is a helpful feature. When you're done, double-click the Home tab to display the full Ribbon.
9. Print the finished document, and then submit it to your instructor.

Objectives

Session 1.1
- Understand the use of spreadsheets and Excel
- Learn the parts of the Excel window
- Scroll through a worksheet and navigate between worksheets
- Create and save a workbook file
- Enter text, numbers, and dates into a worksheet
- Resize, insert, and remove columns and rows

Session 1.2
- Select and move cell ranges
- Insert formulas and functions
- Insert, delete, move, and rename worksheets
- Work with editing tools
- Preview and print a workbook

Getting Started with Excel

Creating an Order Report

Case | RipCity Digital

When Amanda Dunn purchased a DVD burner a few years ago, one of her first tasks was to convert her home videos into DVDs. After she saw how simple it was, she upgraded her hardware and software and proceeded to create DVDs from home movies and slides for her parents and friends. Based on her success, Amanda decided to make a business out of her hobby and founded RipCity Digital, an online service specializing in creating DVDs from the home movies, photos, and slides sent to her from customers. Amanda wants to list the weekly orders from her customers, tracking the names and addresses of her clients, the number of DVDs that she creates, and finally the cost of creating and shipping the DVDs.

Amanda is so busy creating DVDs that she asks you to record her orders. You'll do this in **Microsoft Office Excel 2007** (or **Excel**), a computer program used to enter, analyze, and present quantitative data. You'll also enter the latest orders she received for her new business.

Starting Data Files

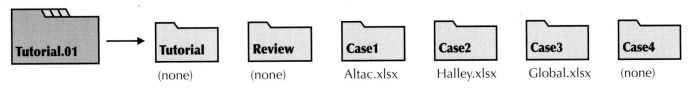

Tutorial.01 →	Tutorial	Review	Case1	Case2	Case3	Case4
	(none)	(none)	Altac.xlsx	Halley.xlsx	Global.xlsx	(none)

Session 1.1

Introducing Excel

Before you begin working in Excel, Amanda asks you to review some of the features, key terms, and concepts associated with spreadsheets. Understanding spreadsheets and how they work in Excel will help you as you enter RipCity Digital customer orders.

Understanding Spreadsheets

A **spreadsheet** is a collection of text and numbers laid out in a rectangular grid. Spreadsheets are often used in business for budgeting, inventory management, and decision making. They can also be used to manage personal budgets and track household assets. For example, the paper-based spreadsheet shown in Figure 1-1 shows a cash flow report. The spreadsheet records the estimated and actual cash flow for the month of January. Each line, or row, displays a different value, such as the starting cash balance or cash sales for the month. Each column displays the budgeted or actual numbers or text that describes those values. The total cash expenditures, net cash flow, and closing cash balance for the month are not entered directly, but calculated from other numbers in the spreadsheet. For example, the total cash expenditure is equal to the expenditures on advertising, wages, and supplies. For paper spreadsheets, these calculations are done using a hand calculator and then entered into the spreadsheet.

| Figure 1-1 | Sample paper spreadsheet |

Cash Flow Comparison Budgeted vs. Actual		Jan–10
	Budgeted	**Actual**
Cash balance (start of month)	$4,500.00	$4,500.00
Cash receipts		
Cash sales	12,600.00	14,688.00
Cash expenditures		
Advertising	1,200.00	1,425.00
Wages	7,200.00	7,850.00
Supplies	3,600.00	4,350.00
Total cash expenditures	12,000.00	13,625.00
Net cash flow	600.00	1,063.00
Cash balance (end of month)	$5,100.00	$5,563.00

Excel is a computer program used to create electronic versions of these paper spreadsheets. Figure 1-2 shows the data from Figure 1-1 as it might appear in Excel. As with paper spreadsheets, Excel uses a rectangular grid to lay out the financial information in rows and columns. As you'll see later, values such as total cash expenditures can be calculated automatically rather than entered manually into the spreadsheet. This allows you to use Excel to perform a **what-if analysis** in which you change one or more values in a spreadsheet and then assess the effect those changes have on the calculated values.

Spreadsheet data in Excel ◀ Figure 1-2

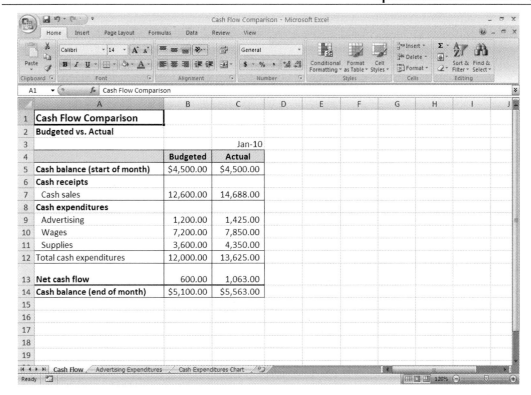

An Excel spreadsheet is more flexible than paper spreadsheets. In fact, it is no longer just an electronic substitute for paper spreadsheets. Excel is now often used for data storage, report generation, and as a tool to access data from the Internet.

Exploring the Excel Window

Before entering Amanda's data, you'll review the different parts of the Excel window. The Excel window contains many of the elements that you find in other Office 2007 programs, including a title bar, the Ribbon, scroll bars, and a status bar. The Excel window also contains features that are unique to Excel. You'll review these features after you start Excel.

To start Excel:

▶ **1.** Click the **Start** button 🙂 on the Windows taskbar, click **All Programs**, click **Microsoft Office**, and then point to **Microsoft Office Excel 2007**.

Trouble? If you don't see Microsoft Office Excel 2007 on the Microsoft Office submenu, look for it on a different submenu or on the All Programs menu. If you still cannot find Microsoft Office Excel 2007, ask your instructor or technical support person for help.

▶ **2.** Click **Microsoft Office Excel 2007**. The Excel window opens.

All the figures showing the Excel window in these tutorials are zoomed to 120% for better readability. If you want to zoom your Excel window to match the figures, complete Step 3. If you prefer to work in the default zoom of 100% or at another zoom level, continue with Step 4; you might see more or less of the worksheet on your screen, but this does not affect your work in the tutorials.

3. If you want your Excel window zoomed to match the figures, click the **Zoom In** button ⊕ on the status bar twice to increase the zoom magnification to **120%**. The worksheet is magnified to 120%, which increases the screen size of each cell, but reduces the number of worksheet cells visible in the workbook window.

4. If necessary, click the **Maximize** button ▢ on the Excel window title bar. The Excel window fills the screen, as shown in Figure 1-3. Depending on your installation of Excel and your monitor resolution, your Excel window might look different from the one shown in Figure 1-3.

Figure 1-3 ▶ **Parts of the Excel window**

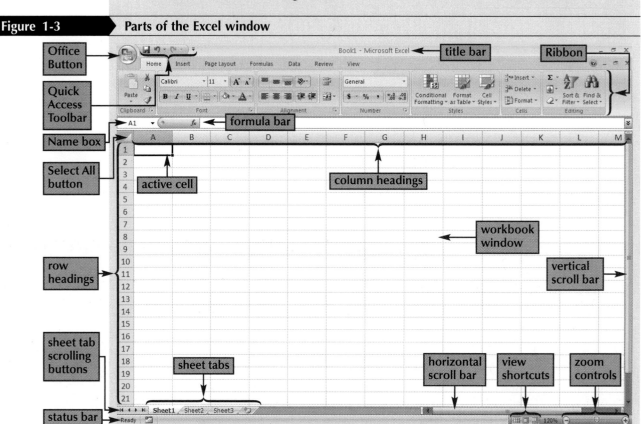

Trouble? If your screen varies slightly from those shown in the figures, your computer might be set up differently. The figures in this book were created while running Windows Vista in the Windows Vista Basic settings, but how your screen looks depends on a variety of things, including the version of Windows, background settings, and so forth.

Excel stores spreadsheets in files called **workbooks**. The contents of a workbook are shown in a **workbook window**. You can open more than one workbook window at a time to display the contents of different workbooks. You can also open multiple workbook windows for one workbook to display different views of the workbook's contents. The workbook that is currently being used is the **active workbook** and is displayed in the **active workbook window**. The name of the active workbook appears in the title bar of the Excel window. By default, Excel starts with a blank workbook named "Book1" in the workbook window, maximized to fill the entire Excel window.

Each workbook is made up of individual **sheets**, just as a notebook an accountant might use is made up of sheets of paper. Excel supports two kinds of sheets: worksheets and chart sheets. A **worksheet** contains data, laid out in rows and columns. A **chart sheet** contains an Excel chart that provides a visual representation of spreadsheet data. Charts can also be embedded within worksheets, allowing you to view both the data and charts in one sheet.

Each sheet is identified by a sheet name. The sheet names are displayed in **sheet tabs** located at the lower-left corner of the workbook window. The sheet currently displayed in the workbook window is the **active sheet**, and its sheet tab is white. In Figure 1-3, the active sheet is named "Sheet1." Other sheets included in the workbook shown in Figure 1-3, but not currently visible, are named "Sheet2" and "Sheet3." The sheet tabs for inactive sheets are gray and stacked behind the Sheet1 tab. An inactive sheet becomes active when you click its worksheet tab. By default, all new Excel workbooks are created with these three worksheets.

Each worksheet is laid out in rows and columns. **Row headings** identify each row by a different number. Row numbers range from 1 to 1,048,576. **Column headings** identify each column by a different letter. The first 26 column letters range in alphabetical order from A to Z. After Z, the next column headings are labeled AA, AB, AC, and so forth. Excel allows a maximum of 16,385 columns in a worksheet (the last column has the heading XFD).

Rows and columns intersect in a single **cell**; all the data entered in a worksheet is placed in different cells. You can have more than 17 billion cells in each worksheet. Each cell is identified by a **cell reference**, which indicates its column and row location. For example, the cell reference B6 indicates the cell located where column B intersects row 6. The column letter always appears before the row number in any cell reference. The cell in which you are working is the **active cell**. Excel distinguishes the active cell by outlining it with a thick border. In Figure 1-3, cell A1 is the active cell. The cell reference for the active cell appears in the **Name box** located in the upper-left corner of the worksheet.

Figure 1-4 describes the different parts of the Excel window, which are labeled in Figure 1-3.

Description of the Excel window elements ◄ **Figure 1-4**

Feature	Description
Office Button	A button that provides access to workbook-level features and program settings
Quick Access Toolbar	A collection of buttons that provide one-click access to commonly used commands, such as Save, Undo, and Repeat
Title bar	A bar that displays the name of the active workbook and the Excel program name
Ribbon	The main set of commands organized by task into tabs and groups
Column headings	The letters that appear along the top of the worksheet window to identify the different columns in the worksheet
Workbook window	A window that displays an Excel workbook
Vertical scroll bar	A scroll bar used to scroll vertically through the workbook window
Horizontal scroll bar	A scroll bar used to scroll horizontally through the workbook window
Zoom controls	Controls for magnifying and shrinking the content displayed in the active workbook window
View shortcuts	Buttons used to change how the worksheet content is displayed—Normal, Page Layout, or Page Break Preview view
Sheet tabs	Tabs that display the names of the worksheets in the workbook
Sheet tab scrolling buttons	Buttons to scroll the list of sheet tabs in the workbook
Row headings	The numbers that appear along the left of the worksheet window to identify the different rows in the worksheet
Select All button	A button used to select all of the cells in the active worksheet
Active cell	The cell currently selected in the active worksheet
Name box	A box that displays the cell reference of the active cell
Formula bar	A bar that displays the value or formula entered in the active cell

When Excel starts, it opens a blank workbook with Sheet1 as the active sheet and cell A1 as the active cell.

Navigating a Worksheet

Excel provides several ways to navigate a worksheet. You can use your mouse to click a cell to make it the active cell, or you can use the keyboard to move from one cell to another. Figure 1-5 describes some of the default keyboard shortcuts you can use to move between worksheet cells.

Figure 1-5 ▶ **Excel navigation keys**

Press	To move the active cell
↑, ↓, ←, →	Up, down, left, or right one cell
Home	To column A of the current row
Ctrl+Home	To cell A1
Ctrl+End	To the last cell in the worksheet that contains data
Enter	Down one row or to the start of the next row of data
Shift+Enter	Up one row
Tab	One column to the right
Shift+Tab	One column to the left
Page Up, Page Down	Up or down one screen
Ctrl+Page Up, Ctrl+Page Down	To the previous or next sheet in the workbook

You'll use both your mouse and keyboard to change the active cell in Sheet1.

To change the active cell:

► 1. Move your mouse pointer over cell **A5**, and then click the mouse button. The active cell moves from cell A1 to cell A5, and the cell reference in the Name box changes from A1 to A5. The column heading for column A and the row heading for row 5 are both highlighted.

► 2. Press the → key on your keyboard. The active cell moves one cell to the right to cell B5.

► 3. Press the **Page Down** key. The active cell moves down one full screen to cell B25.

Trouble? If the active cell in your workbook is not cell B25, your monitor size and screen resolution might be different from those used for the figures in these tutorials. Continue with Step 4.

► 4. Press the **Page Up** key. The active cell moves up one full screen back to cell B5.

► 5. Press the **Ctrl+Home** keys. The active cell returns to the first cell in the worksheet, cell A1.

The mouse and keyboard provide quick ways to navigate the active worksheet. For larger worksheets that span several screens, you can move directly to a specific cell using the Go To dialog box or by typing a cell reference in the Name box. You'll try both of these methods.

To use the Go To dialog box and Name box:

► 1. Click the **Home** tab on the Ribbon, if necessary. The button to open the Go To dialog box is in the Editing group.

2. In the Editing group, click the **Find & Select** button. A menu of options opens.

3. Click **Go To**. The Go To dialog box opens.

4. Type **C14** in the Reference text box.

5. Click the **OK** button. Cell C14 is the active cell and its cell reference appears in the Name box. You'll use the Name box to make a different cell active.

6. Click in the **Name** box, type **A1**, and then press the **Enter** key. Cell A1 is once again the active cell.

Tip

You can also open the Go To dialog box by pressing the Ctrl+G keys.

To view more of the active worksheet, you can use the horizontal and vertical scroll bars, located at the bottom and right side of the workbook window, respectively, to move through the worksheet horizontally and vertically. Scrolling through the worksheet does not change the location of the active cell.

To scroll the worksheet:

1. Click the **down arrow** on the vertical scroll bar three times. The worksheet scrolls down three rows, but the active cell remains cell A1.

2. Click the **right arrow** on the horizontal scroll bar twice. The worksheet scrolls two columns to the right. The active cell still remains cell A1, although that cell is scrolled out of view.

   You can scroll several rows and columns by dragging the vertical and horizontal scroll boxes.

3. Drag the vertical scroll box up until you can see the first row in the worksheet.

4. Drag the horizontal scroll box to the left until you can see the first column in the worksheet.

Navigating Between Worksheets

Recall that each workbook can contain multiple worksheets and chart sheets. This enables you to better organize data and focus each worksheet on one area of data. For example, a sales report workbook might have a different worksheet for each sales region and another worksheet that summarizes the results from all the regions. A chart sheet might contain a chart that graphically compares the sales results from all of the regions. To move from one sheet to another, you click the sheet tabs at the bottom of the workbook window.

Some workbooks contain so many worksheets and chart sheets that their sheet tabs cannot all be displayed at the same time in the workbook window. For these workbooks, you can scroll through the sheet tabs using the sheet tab scrolling buttons. Similar to the horizontal and vertical scroll bars and the active cell, scrolling through the sheet tabs does not change the active sheet in the workbook window. To change the active worksheet, you must click a sheet tab.

To change the active sheet:

1. Click the **Sheet2** sheet tab. The Sheet2 worksheet, which is also blank, becomes the active worksheet. The Sheet2 tab is white, indicating that this is the active worksheet.

▶ **2.** Click the **Sheet3** sheet tab. The Sheet3 worksheet becomes the active worksheet.

▶ **3.** Click the **Sheet1** sheet tab to return to the first worksheet.

Now that you've had some experience moving around a blank workbook, you are ready to start working on Amanda's workbook.

InSight		**Creating Effective Workbooks**

Effective workbooks are well planned and carefully designed. This helps you avoid errors and makes the workbook readable to others. A well-designed workbook should clearly identify its overall goal, and present information in a well-organized format. The process of developing a good workbook includes the following steps:

- Determine the workbook's purpose, content, and organization before you start entering data.
- Create a list of the sheets used in the workbook, making note of each sheet's purpose.
- Insert a documentation sheet into the workbook that describes the workbook's purpose and organization. Include the name of the workbook author, the date the workbook was created, and any additional information that will help others to track the workbook to its source.
- Enter all of the data in the workbook. Add text to indicate what the values represent and, if possible, where they originated. Other users might want to view the source of your data.
- Enter formulas for calculated items rather than entering the calculated values into the workbook. For more complicated calculations, provide documentation explaining them.
- Test the workbook with a variety of values to weed out any errors in your calculations. Edit the data and formulas to correct any errors.
- Save the workbook and create a backup copy when the project is completed. Print the workbook's contents if you need a hard-copy version for your files.

Planning a Workbook

Before you begin to enter data into a workbook, you should develop a plan. You can do this by using a **planning analysis sheet**, which includes a series of questions that help you think about the purpose of the workbook and how to achieve your desired results. In the planning analysis sheet, you answer the following questions:

- What problems do you want to solve? The answer defines the goal or purpose of the workbook.
- What data is needed to solve your problem? The answer defines the type of data that you have to collect and enter into the workbook.
- What calculations are required to solve your problem? The answer defines the formulas you need to apply to the data you've collected and entered.
- What form should the solution take? The answer defines the appearance of the workbook content and how it should be presented to others.

Amanda carefully considered these questions and developed the planning analysis sheet shown in Figure 1-6. You'll use this plan to create the workbook for Amanda.

Planning Analysis Sheet
Author: Amanda Dunn
Date: 4/1/2010

What problems do I want to solve?
• I need to have contact information for each RipCity Digital customer.
• I need to track how many DVDs I create for my customers.
• I need to record how much I charge my customers for my service.
• I need to determine how much revenue RipCity Digital is generating.

What data do I need?
• Each customer's name and contact information
• The date each customer order was placed
• The number of DVDs created for each customer
• The cost of creating each DVD

What calculations do I need to enter?
• The total charge for each order
• The total number of DVDs I create for all orders
• The total revenue generated from all orders

What form should my solution take?
• The customer orders should be placed in a grid with each row containing data on a different customer.
• Information about each customer should be placed in separate columns.
• The last column should contain the total charge for each customer.
• The last row should contain the total number of DVDs created and the total revenue from all customer orders.

Entering Text, Numbers, and Dates in Cells

Now that you have Amanda's plan for the workbook, your next step is to enter the data she's collected. You enter data by selecting a cell in the worksheet to make it the active cell, and then typing the content you want to enter in the active cell. When you finish typing, you can press the Enter key or the Tab key to complete the data entry and move to the next cell in the worksheet. As you enter data into the worksheet, the data entry appears in two locations: within the active cell and within the formula bar. The **formula bar** displays the content of the active cell and, as you'll see later, shows any formulas used to create calculated values.

In Excel, data falls into three general categories: text, numbers, and dates and times. **Text data** is a combination of letters, numbers, and some symbols that form words and sentences. Text data is often referred to as a **text string** because it contains a string of text characters. **Number data** is any numerical value that can be used in a mathematical calculation. **Date** and **time data** are commonly recognized formats for date and time values. For example, Excel interprets the cell entry "April 15, 2010" as a date and not as text. By default, text is left-aligned in cells, whereas numbers, dates, and times are right-aligned.

Entering Text

Tip

A documentation sheet reminds you why you created a workbook and what it contains and relays this information to others with whom you share the workbook.

Amanda wants you to enter some of the information from the planning analysis sheet into the first sheet of the workbook. The first sheet will document the purpose and content of the workbook and the sheets that follow. This documentation sheet will contain the name of the workbook, the workbook's author, the date the workbook was created, and a description of the workbook's purpose.

To enter the text for the documentation sheet:

1. Press the **Ctrl+Home** keys to make cell A1 the active cell on the Sheet1 worksheet, if necessary.

2. Type **RipCity Digital Customer Orders** in cell A1. As you type, the text appears both in cell A1 and in the formula bar.

3. Press the **Enter** key twice. Excel enters the text into cell A1 and moves the active cell down two cells to cell A3.

4. Type **Author** in cell A3, and then press the **Tab** key. The text is entered and the active cell moves one cell to the right to cell B3.

5. Type your name in cell B3, and then press the **Enter** key. The text is entered and the active cell moves one cell down and to the left to cell A4.

6. Type **Date** in cell A4, and then press the **Tab** key. The text is entered and the active cell moves one cell to the right to cell B4, where you would enter the date you created the worksheet. For now, you'll leave the cell for the date blank. You'll enter this date soon.

7. Click cell **A5** to make it the active cell, type **Purpose** in the cell, and then press the **Tab** key. The active cell moves one cell to the right to cell B5.

8. Type **To record orders from RipCity Digital customers** in cell B5, and then press the **Enter** key. Figure 1-7 shows the text entered in the Sheet1 worksheet.

Figure 1-7 | **Documentation sheet**

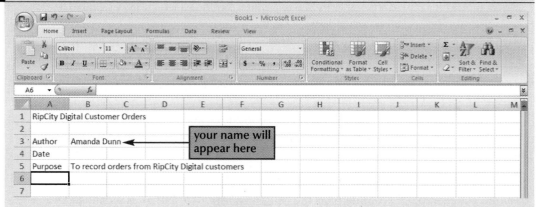

The text you entered in cell A1 is so long that it seems to overflow into cells B1 and C1. The same is true for the text you entered in cells B3 and B5. When you enter more text than can fit in a cell, Excel displays the additional text in the adjacent cells as long as they are empty. If the adjacent cells also contain data, Excel displays only as much text as fits into the cell, cutting off, or **truncating**, the rest of the text entry. The text itself is not affected. The complete text is still entered in the cell, it's just not displayed. To display all of the text, you must increase the cell's width, which you'll learn about in the next session.

Next, you'll enter the RipCity Digital customer orders. As shown in Figure 1-8, the orders will contain the name and address of each customer, the order date, the number of DVDs created from the customer's home videos, and the price per DVD. Amanda's price per DVD decreases for larger orders.

Customer orders **Figure 1-8**

Last	First	Address	Date	DVDs	Price per DVD
Dawes	Gregory	402 Elm St. Merrill, MI 48637	3/13/2010	7	$17.29
Garcia	Susan	1025 Drake Ave. Exeter, NH 03833	3/14/2010	25	$15.79
Torbet	Dr. Lilla	5 North Ln. Oswego, NY 13126	3/17/2010	32	$12.99
Rhoden	Tony	24 Mountain Dr. Auburn, ME 04210	3/24/2010	20	$15.79

You'll enter this data in the Sheet2 worksheet.

To enter the text labels and customer names:

1. Click the **Sheet2** sheet tab. Sheet2 becomes the active worksheet. You'll enter the column labels in cells A1, B1, C1, D1, E1, and F1.

2. Type **Last** in cell A1, and then press the **Tab** key. The label is entered in cell A1 and the active cell moves to cell B1.

3. Type **First** in cell B1, and then press the **Tab** key. The label is entered in cell B1 and the active cell moves to cell C1.

4. Type **Address** in cell C1, and then press the **Tab** key.

5. Type **Date** in cell D1, and then press the **Tab** key.

6. Type **DVDs** in cell E1, press the **Tab** key, and then type **Price per DVD** in cell F1. You've typed all the labels for the customer orders.

7. Press the **Enter** key. The active cell moves to cell A2, the start of the next row where you want to begin entering the customer data.

8. Type **Dawes** in cell A2, press the **Tab** key, type **Gregory** in cell B2, and then press the **Tab** key. You've entered the first customer's name and moved the active cell to cell C2. Figure 1-9 shows the text you've entered so far.

Text entered for the customer orders **Figure 1-9**

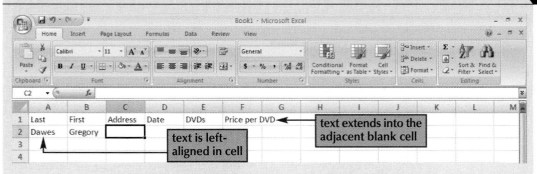

As you enter text in a worksheet, Excel tries to anticipate the text you are about to enter by displaying text that begins with the same letters as a previous entry in the same column. This feature, known as **AutoComplete**, helps make entering repetitive text easier. To accept the suggested text, press the Tab or Enter key. To override the suggested text, continue to type the text you want to enter in the cell. AutoComplete does not work with dates or numbers or when a blank cell is between the previous entry and the text you're typing.

Entering Multiple Lines of Text Within a Cell

The next cell in the Sheet2 worksheet contains the address of the first customer. Addresses are often entered on two or more separate lines. Amanda wants you to follow that convention with her customers' addresses. To place text on separate lines within the same cell, you press and hold the Alt key while you press the Enter key. This creates a line break within the cell.

Reference Window | **Entering Multiple Lines of Text Within a Cell**

- Click the cell in which you want to enter the text.
- Type the first line of text.
- For each additional line of text, press the Alt+Enter keys (that is, hold down the Alt key as you press the Enter key), and then type the text.

You'll enter the address for the first RipCity Digital customer, which will occupy two lines within the same cell.

To enter two lines of text within a cell:

1. Type **402 Elm St.** in cell C2, but do not press the Tab or Enter key. Instead, you'll insert a new line break.

2. Hold down the **Alt** key and press the **Enter** key, and then release both keys. The insertion point moves to a new line within cell C2.

3. Type **Merrill, MI 48637** on the new line, and then press the **Tab** key. The two lines of text are entered in cell C2, and cell D2 becomes the active cell. See Figure 1-10.

Figure 1-10 ▶ **Two lines of text entered within a cell**

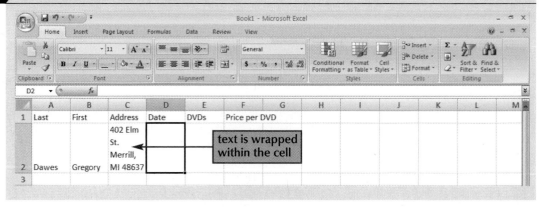

One impact of entering multiple lines of text within a cell is that it changes how text flows within the cell. Excel wraps the text within the cell, increasing the cell's height, if necessary, to show all of the text. As you can see, the text in cell C2 appears on four lines even though you entered the address on two lines. If the cell's width were increased, the text would then appear on two lines as Amanda wants. You'll do this in the next session.

Entering Dates

The next cell will contain the date of the order. You can enter dates in any of the standard formats. For example, you can enter the date April 6, 2010 in any of the following date formats (and many others) and Excel recognizes each format as representing the same date:

- 4/6/2010
- 4/6/10
- 4-6-2010
- April 6, 2010
- 6-Apr-10

In Excel, dates are actually numbers that are formatted to appear as text. This allows you to perform calculations with dates, such as determining the elapsed time between one date and another.

Sometimes Excel alters the date format you've chosen. For example, if you enter the date 4/6/10, Excel displays the date with the four-digit year value, 4/6/2010. Also, if you enter the text April 6, 2010, Excel converts the date format to 6-Apr-10. You'll enter the dates in the format *mm/dd/yyyy*, where *mm* is the month number, *dd* is the day number, and *yyyy* is the four-digit year number.

To enter the dates for the customer orders:

▶ **1.** Type **3/13/2010** in cell D2, and then press the **Tab** key to move to cell E2. The date of Gregory Dawes's order appears in cell D2 and cell E2 is the active cell.

You also need to enter the current date in the Sheet1 worksheet so you can document when you started working on this project.

▶ **2.** Click the **Sheet1** sheet tab. The Sheet1 worksheet is the active worksheet.

▶ **3.** Click cell **B4** to make it active, type today's date using the format *mm/dd/yyyy*, and then press the **Enter** key.

▶ **4.** Click the **Sheet2** sheet tab. The Sheet2 worksheet is the active worksheet, and cell E2 is still the active cell.

Entering Numbers

In the next two cells, you'll enter the number of DVDs that Amanda has created for Gregory Dawes and the price she will charge him for making each DVD. In both cases, you'll be entering numbers. In Excel, numbers can be integers such as 378, decimals such as 1.95, or negative such as −5.2. In the case of currency and percentages, you can include the currency symbol and percent sign when you enter the value. Excel treats a currency value such as $87.25 as the number 87.25 and a percentage such as 95% as the decimal number 0.95. Currency and percentages, like dates, are formatted in a convenient way for you to read. Excel right-aligns numbers within cells.

Tip

If a number exceeds its cell size, you see ###### for the truncated numeric value. You can display the entire number by increasing the column width.

You'll complete the information for Gregory Dawes's order by entering the number of DVDs Amanda created for him and the price she charged him for each DVD.

To enter the numbers for the first customer order:

▶ **1.** Type **7** in cell E2, and then press the **Tab** key. The order quantity for Gregory Dawes is entered and the active cell is cell F2.

▶ **2.** Type **$17.29** in cell F2, and then press the **Enter** key. The currency value is entered in cell F2, and the active cell moves to cell F3.

▶ **3.** Click cell **A3**, which is where you want to enter the information for the next customer. See Figure 1-11.

| Figure 1-11 | First customer order completed |

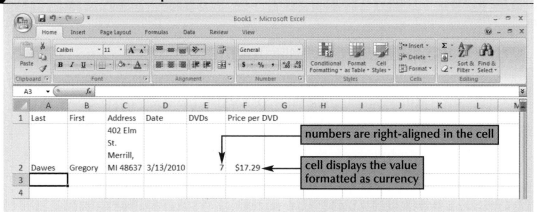

You've completed the data entry for Amanda's first customer. You still need to enter the data for three more customers into the worksheet. You'll use the same techniques you used to enter Gregory Dawes's order to enter their data.

To enter the remaining customer order data:

▶ **1.** Type **Garcia** in cell A3, press the **Tab** key, type **Susan** in cell B3, and then press the **Tab** key. The second customer name is entered.

▶ **2.** Type **1025 Drake Ave.** in cell C3, press the **Alt+Enter** keys, type **Exeter, NH 03833** on the next line, and then press the **Tab** key. The second customer's address is entered in the cell on two lines.

▶ **3.** Type **3/14/2010** in cell D3, press the **Tab** key, type **25** in cell E3, press the **Tab** key, type **$15.79** in cell F3, and then press the **Enter** key. The rest of the second customer's data is entered.

▶ **4.** Enter the following data for the remaining two customers in rows 4 and 5, making sure that you press the Alt+Enter keys to enter the addresses on two lines. See Figure 1-12.

Torbet, Dr. Lilla
5 North Ln.
Oswego, NY 13126
3/17/2010, 32, $12.99

Rhoden, Tony
24 Mountain Dr.
Auburn, ME 04210
3/24/2010, 20, $15.79

Customer data for RipCity Digital | Figure 1-12

	A	B	C	D	E	F	G	H	I	J	K	L	M
1	Last	First	Address	Date	DVDs	Price per DVD							
2	Dawes	Gregory	402 Elm St. Merrill, MI 48637	3/13/2010	7	$17.29							
3	Garcia	Susan	1025 Drake Ave. Exeter, NH	3/14/2010	25	$15.79							
4	Torbet	Dr. Lilla	5 North Ln. Oswego, NY 13126	3/17/2010	32	$12.99							
5	Rhoden	Tony	24 Mountain Dr. Auburn, ME	3/24/2010	20	$15.79							
6													
7													

Working with Columns and Rows

Amanda has reviewed the customer order data you entered in the worksheet. She asks you to modify the worksheet to make it easier to read and include more data. To do this, you'll need to change the column widths and row heights, insert columns and rows, and delete columns and rows.

Changing Column Width and Row Height

The default sizes of the columns and rows in a worksheet might not always accommodate the information you need to enter. For example, the addresses you entered in the worksheet on two lines wrapped within the cell to display all the text. Other times, long cell content might be truncated. To make the cell content easier to read or fully visible, you can resize the columns and rows in the worksheet.

New workbooks use the default sizes for column widths and row heights. Column widths are expressed either in terms of the number of characters the column can contain or the size of the column in pixels. A **pixel** is a single point on a computer monitor or printout. The default column width is 8.38 standard-sized characters. This means that, in general, you can type about 8 or 9 characters in a cell before that entry is either truncated or overlaps the adjacent cell. Of course, if you decrease the font size of characters, you can fit more text within a given cell. Row heights are expressed in points or pixels, where a **point** is 1/72 of an inch. The default row is 15.75 points high.

Setting Column Widths | InSight

You should set column widths based on the maximum number of characters you want to display in the cells rather than pixel size. Pixel size is related to screen resolution and a cell might be too narrow under a different resolution. This might come into play if you work on multiple computers or share your workbooks with others.

Reference Window | **Changing the Column Width or Row Height**

- Drag the right border of the column heading left to decrease the column width or right to increase the column width.
- Drag the bottom border of the row heading up to decrease the row height or down to increase the row height.

or

- Double-click the right border of a column heading or the bottom border of a row heading to AutoFit the column or row to the cell contents (or select one or more columns or rows, click the Home tab on the Ribbon, click the Format button in the Cells group, and then click AutoFit Column Width or AutoFit Row Height).

or

- Select one or more columns or rows.
- Click the Home tab on the Ribbon, click the Format button in the Cells group, and then click Column Width or Row Height.
- Enter the column width or row height you want, and then click the OK button.

Amanda suggests you increase the width of the Address column to allow the addresses to appear on two lines in the cells without additional line wrapping.

To increase the width of column C:

▶ **1.** Move the mouse pointer over the right border of the column C column heading until the pointer changes to ✛.

▶ **2.** Click and drag to the right until the width of the column heading reaches **20** characters, but do not release the mouse button. The ScreenTip shows the measurements of the new column width first as the numbers of characters and second in parentheses as pixels for the current screen resolution.

▶ **3.** Release the mouse button. The width of column C expands to 20 characters and all the addresses in column C fit on two lines with no extra line wrapping. See Figure 1-13.

Figure 1-13 ▶ **Increased column width**

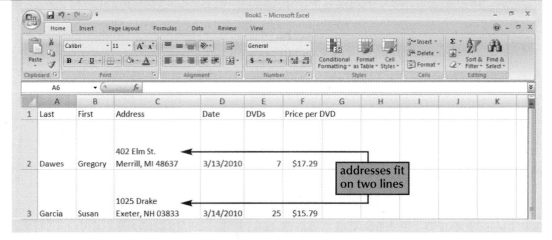

Amanda wants you to increase the widths of columns A and B to 15 characters to accommodate longer names. Rather than resizing each column separately, you can select both columns and adjust their widths at the same time. To select an entire column, you click its column heading. Likewise, to select an entire row, you click its row heading. You can drag across multiple column headings or row headings to select adjacent columns or rows. You can also press the Ctrl key as you click column or row headings to select non-adjacent columns or rows. You can select all the columns and rows in a worksheet by clicking the Select All button in the upper-left corner of the worksheet.

To increase the widths of columns A and B:

▶ **1.** Click the **column A** column heading. The entire column is selected.

▶ **2.** Hold down the **Ctrl** key, click the **column B** column heading, and then release the **Ctrl** key. Both columns A and B are selected.

▶ **3.** Move the mouse pointer to the right border of the column B column heading until the pointer changes to ✛.

▶ **4.** Drag to the right until the column width changes to **15** characters, and then release the mouse button. Both columns are wide enough to display longer names.

The text in cell F1, "Price per DVD," overflows the cell borders. This column would look better if you increased the width of column F to 12 characters. Rather than use the mouse, you can set the column width using the Format command on the Home tab. The Format command gives you precise control in setting column widths and row heights.

To set the width of column F to 12 characters:

▶ **1.** Click the **column F** column heading. The entire column is selected.

▶ **2.** In the Cells group on the Home tab, click the **Format** button, and then click **Column Width**. The Column Width dialog box opens.

▶ **3.** Type **12** in the Column width box, and then click the **OK** button. The width of column F changes to 12 characters, placing the text in cell F1 entirely within the borders of the cell.

The row heights didn't change after you resized the columns, which leaves a lot of blank space in the four rows of customer data. This extra blank space makes the data difficult to read and extends the content out of view. You'll reduce the heights of all these rows.

Row heights are set in the same way as column widths. You can drag the bottom border of the row or define a specific row height using the Format command on the Home tab. Another option is to autofit a column or row to its content. **Autofitting** eliminates any empty space by matching the column to the width of its longest cell entry or the row to the height of its tallest cell entry. If the column or row is blank, Excel restores the column or row to its default width or height. The simplest way to autofit a row or column is to double-click its border. You can also use the AutoFit commands.

Because you want to remove empty space from the four worksheet rows, you'll autofit the rows to their content rather than specify a particular row height.

To autofit row 2 to its content:

▶ **1.** Move the mouse pointer over the bottom border of the row 2 row heading until the pointer changes to ╪.

▶ **2.** Double-click the bottom border of row 2. The height of row 2 shrinks to match the content of cell C2, which is the tallest entry in the row with two lines of text.

You could continue to resize the remaining rows one at a time, but a quicker way is to select the rows you want to resize and then autofit all the selected rows simultaneously. Instead of double-clicking the row border, you'll use the AutoFit Row Height command.

To autofit the height of rows 3 through 5:

▶ **1.** Drag the pointer across the row headings for rows 3, 4, and 5. The contents of rows 3 through 5 are selected.

▶ **2.** In the Cells group on the Home tab, click the **Format** button. A menu of commands opens.

▶ **3.** Click **AutoFit Row Height**. The height of each of the three rows autofits to its contents, and all the empty space is removed.

▶ **4.** Click cell **A1** to make it the active cell. The other cells in the worksheet are deselected. Figure 1-14 shows the worksheet with the revised row heights.

Figure 1-14 ▶ **Autofitted row heights**

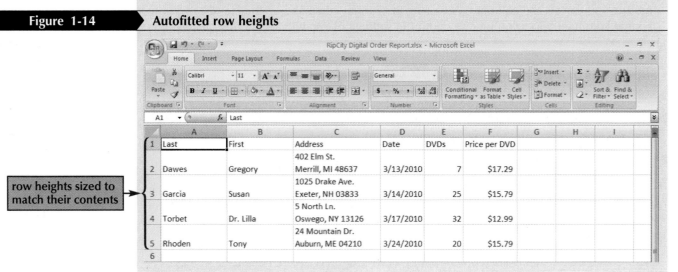

row heights sized to match their contents

Inserting a Column or Row

Amanda notices that the worksheet doesn't include a column containing customer phone numbers. She wants you to insert a column for the customer phone numbers between the Address column and the Date column.

You can insert a new column or row anywhere within a worksheet. When you insert a new column, the existing columns are shifted to the right and the new column has the same width as the column directly to its left. When you insert a new row, the existing rows are shifted down and the new row has the same height as the row above it.

Inserting a Column or Row | Reference Window

- Select the column(s) or row(s) where you want to insert the new column(s) or row(s); Excel will insert the same number of columns or rows as you select.
- In the Cells group on the Home tab, click the Insert button (or right-click a column or row heading or selected column and row headings, and then click Insert on the shortcut menu).

You'll insert a column and enter the customer phone numbers in the new column.

To insert a new column:

▶ **1.** Click the **column D** column heading to select the entire column.

▶ **2.** In the Cells group on the Home tab, click the **Insert** button. A new column D is inserted into the worksheet and the rest of the columns shift to the right. The new column has the same width as column C.

▶ **3.** Reduce the width of column D to **15** characters.

▶ **4.** Click cell **D1** to make it the active cell, type **Phone** as the label, and then press the **Enter** key. The new column label is entered in cell D1, and cell D2 becomes the active cell.

▶ **5.** Enter the phone numbers in cells D2, D3, D4, and D5, as shown in Figure 1-15, pressing the **Enter** key after each entry.

New column inserted in the worksheet | **Figure 1-15**

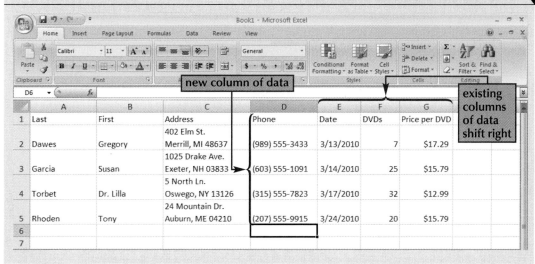

Amanda neglected to include a customer. Because the customer was RipCity Digital's first customer, he should be inserted at the top of the list. To add this new order, you need to insert a new row in the worksheet below the column labels.

To insert a new row:

▶ **1.** Click the **row 2** row heading. The entire second row is selected.

▶ **2.** In the Cells group on the Home tab, click the **Insert** button. A new row 2 is inserted, and the remaining rows shift down.

▶ **3.** Enter the new customer order shown in Figure 1-16 into row 2.

| Figure 1-16 | New row inserted in the worksheet |

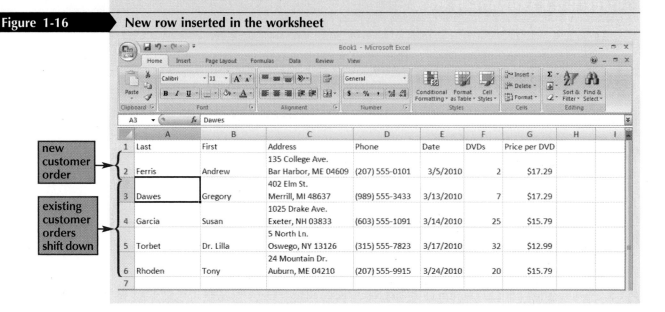

Deleting and Clearing a Row or Column

Adding new data to a workbook is common, as is removing old or erroneous data. Amanda just learned that her second customer, Gregory Dawes, canceled his order. She wants you to remove this order from the worksheet.

You can remove data in two ways: clearing and deleting. **Clearing** data from a worksheet removes the data but leaves the blank cells. **Deleting** data from the worksheet removes both the data and the cells. When you delete a column, the columns to the right shift left to fill the vacated space. Similarly, the rows below a deleted row shift up to fill the vacated space. Deleting a column or row has the opposite effect from inserting a column or row.

You'll first clear Gregory Dawes's data from the worksheet and then delete the row that contained the data. Usually, you would do this in one step by simply deleting the row, but this highlights the difference between clearing and deleting.

To clear and delete row 3:

▶ **1.** Click the **row 3** row heading. The entire row 3 with Gregory Dawes's order is selected.

▶ **2.** Right-click the **row 3** row heading, and then click **Clear Contents** on the shortcut menu. Excel clears the values in the third row, but leaves the blank row in that space.

▶ **3.** Verify that the third row is still selected.

▶ **4.** In the Cells group on the Home tab, click the **Delete** button. The third row is deleted, and the rows below it shift up. Only four customers remain in the worksheet.

Before proceeding, you'll save your workbook with the name "RipCity Digital Orders" in the default Excel workbook format.

To save the current workbook:

▸ **1.** Click the **Save** button 🔲 on the Quick Access Toolbar. Because this workbook has not yet been saved, the Save As dialog box opens.

▸ **2.** Navigate to the **Tutorial.01\Tutorial** folder included with your Data Files. You'll replace the default filename "Book1" with a more descriptive one.

    Trouble? If you don't have the starting Data Files, you need to get them before you can proceed. Your instructor will either give you the Data Files or ask you to obtain them from a specified location (such as a network drive). In either case, make a backup copy of the Data Files before you start so that you will have the original files available in case you need to start over. If you have any questions about the Data Files, see your instructor or technical support person for assistance.

▸ **3.** Select **Book1** in the File name box, and then type **RipCity Digital Orders**.

▸ **4.** Verify that **Excel Workbook** appears in the Save as type box.

▸ **5.** Click the **Save** button. The Save As dialog box closes and the workbook file is saved with its descriptive filename.

Tip

You can reopen the Save As dialog box to save a workbook with a new filename, to a different location, or in another file format; click the Office Button and then click Save As.

You've entered and saved the customer order data. In the process, you worked with rows and columns. In the next session, you'll learn how to work with individual cells and groups of cells. You will also add calculations to the worksheet to determine how much revenue Amanda will generate from these orders.

Session 1.1 Quick Check | Review

1. What are the two types of sheets used in a workbook?
2. List two ways of identifying the active cell in the worksheet.
3. What is the cell reference for the cell located in the third column and fifth row of a worksheet?
4. What keyboard shortcut moves the active cell to cell A1?
5. What is text data?
6. How do you enter two lines of text within a cell?
7. Cell A4 contains "May 3, 2010"; why doesn't Excel consider this entry a text string?
8. Explain the difference between clearing a row and deleting a row.

Session 1.2

Working with Cells and Cell Ranges

A group of cells is called a **cell range** or **range**. Ranges can be either adjacent or nonadjacent. An **adjacent range** is a single rectangular block of cells. For example, all the customer order data you've entered in cell A1 through cell G5 is an adjacent range because it forms one rectangular block of cells. A **nonadjacent range** consists of two or more distinct adjacent ranges. All the last names in cell A1 through cell A5 and all the numbers in cells F1 through G5 together are a nonadjacent range because they are two distinct blocks of cells. A nonadjacent range can include as many adjacent ranges as you want.

Just as a cell reference indicates the location of an individual worksheet cell, a **range reference** indicates the location and size of a cell range. For adjacent ranges, the range reference specifies the locations of the upper-left and lower-right cells in the rectangular block separated by a colon. For example, the range reference A1:G5 refers to all the cells from cell A1 through cell G5. The range reference for nonadjacent ranges separates each adjacent range reference by a semicolon. For example, A1:A5;F1:G5 is the range reference for cells A1 through A5 and cells F1 through G5.

Selecting a Cell Range

You select adjacent and nonadjacent ranges of cells with your mouse, just as you selected individual cells. Selecting a cell range enables you to work with all of the cells in the range as a group. This means you can do things like move the cells, delete them, or clear all their contents at the same time.

Reference Window | **Selecting Cell Ranges**

To select an adjacent range:
- Click the cell in the upper-left corner of the adjacent range, drag the pointer to the cell in the lower-right corner of the adjacent range, and then release the mouse button.
or
- Click the cell in the upper-left corner of the adjacent range, press the Shift key as you click the cell in the lower-right corner of the adjacent range, and then release the Shift key.

To select a nonadjacent range of cells:
- Select a cell or an adjacent range, press the Ctrl key as you select each additional cell or adjacent range, and then release the Ctrl key.

To select all the cells in a worksheet:
- Click the Select All button located at the intersection of the row and column headings (or press the Ctrl+A keys).

You'll use the mouse pointer to select the adjacent range A1:G5, which includes all the content you entered in the worksheet so far.

To select the adjacent range A1:G5:

1. If you took a break at the end of the previous session, make sure the RipCity Digital Orders workbook is open and the Sheet2 worksheet is active.

2. Click cell **A1** to select the cell in the upper-left corner of the range A1:G5.

3. Drag the pointer to cell **G5**, which is the cell in the lower-right corner of the range A1:G5.

4. Release the mouse button. As shown in Figure 1-17, all cells in the adjacent range A1:G5 are selected. The selected cells are highlighted with color and surrounded by a black border. The first cell you selected, cell A1, is still the active cell in the worksheet.

Adjacent range A1:G5 selected ◄ **Figure 1-17**

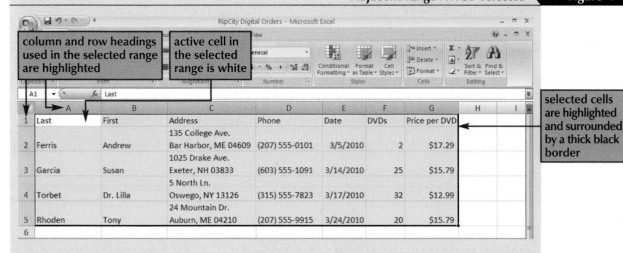

5. Click any cell in the worksheet to deselect the range.

Next, you'll select the nonadjacent range A1:A5;F1:G5.

To select the nonadjacent range A1:A5;F1:G5:

▶ **1.** Select the adjacent range **A1:A5**.

▶ **2.** Hold down the **Ctrl** key, and then select the adjacent range **F1:G5**.

▶ **3.** Release the **Ctrl** key. As shown in Figure 1-18, all the cells in the nonadjacent range A1:A5;F1:G5 are selected.

Nonadjacent range A1:A5;F1:G5 selected ◄ **Figure 1-18**

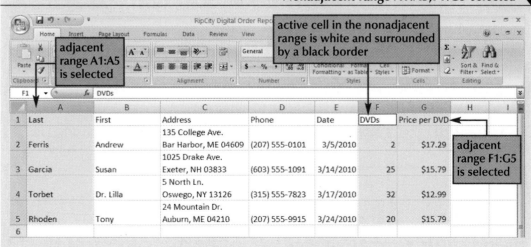

▶ **4.** Click any cell in the worksheet to deselect the range.

Moving and Copying a Cell Range

Amanda wants you to insert titles that describe the customer order data you've entered. Including the company name, a descriptive title, and the date is part of good worksheet design, enabling others to quickly see the *who*, *what*, and *when* of the data. The current worksheet has no space to add this information. You could insert several blank rows at the top of the worksheet for this information. Another option is to select and then move the customer data lower in the worksheet, freeing up the rows at the top for the new text.

Reference Window	**Moving or Copying a Cell or Range**

- Select the cell or range you want to move or copy.
- Move the mouse pointer over the border of the selection until the pointer changes shape.
- To move the range, click the border and drag the selection to a new location (or to copy the range, hold down the Ctrl key and drag the selection to a new location).

or

- Select the cell or range you want to move or copy.
- In the Clipboard group on the Home tab, click the Cut button or the Copy button (or right-click the selection, and then click Cut or Copy on the shortcut menu).
- Select the cell or upper-left cell of the range where you want to move or copy the content.
- In the Clipboard group, click the Paste button (or right-click the selection, and then click Paste on the shortcut menu).

Tip

You can drag and drop to a range not currently visible. Drag the selection to the edge of the worksheet in which you want to scroll. When the new location is visible, drop the selection.

One way to move a cell or range is to select it, position the mouse pointer over the bottom border of the selection, and then drag the selection to a new location. This technique is called **drag and drop** because you are dragging the range and dropping it in a new location. You can also use the drag-and-drop technique to copy cells by pressing the Ctrl key as you drag the selected range to its new location. A copy of the original range is placed in the new location without removing the original range from the worksheet.

You'll use the drag-and-drop method to move data.

To drag and drop the customer orders:

1. Select the range **A1:G5**.

2. Move the mouse pointer over the bottom border of the selected range so that the pointer changes to ⁺⇖.

3. Press and hold the mouse button to change the pointer to ⇖, and then drag the selection down four rows. Do not release the mouse button. A ScreenTip appears, indicating the new range reference of the selected cells. See Figure 1-19.

Selected range being moved | **Figure 1-19**

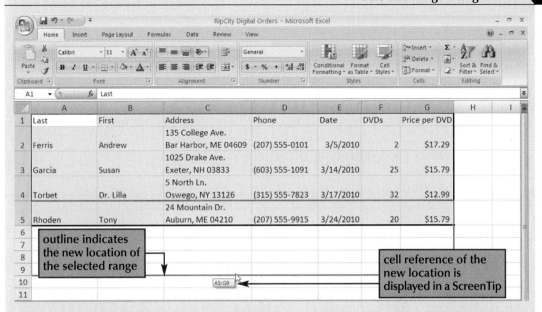

> **4.** When the ScreenTip displays the range A5:G9, release the mouse button. The selected cells move to their new location.

> **5.** Enter the title information shown in Figure 1-20 in the range A1:A3, pressing the **Enter** key after each entry.

Worksheet titles entered | **Figure 1-20**

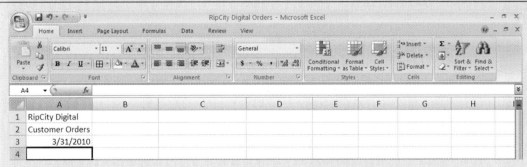

Some people find drag and drop a difficult and awkward way to move a selection, particularly if the worksheet is large and complex. In those situations, it's often more efficient to cut and paste the cell contents. **Cutting** places the cell contents into computer memory or on the Clipboard. The contents can then be pasted from the Clipboard into a new location in the worksheet. You'll cut and paste now.

To cut and paste cell contents:

> **1.** With the range **A5:G9** selected, in the Clipboard group on the Home tab, click the **Cut** button 🔏. The selected range is surrounded by a blinking border, which indicates that its contents are stored on the Clipboard.

> **2.** Click cell **A11**. This cell is the upper-left corner of the range where you want to paste the data.

3. In the Clipboard group, click the **Paste** button. Excel pastes the contents of the range A5:G9 into the new range A11:G15. The blinking border disappears as a visual clue that the Clipboard is now empty.

4. Select the range **A11:G15**, and then, in the Clipboard group, click the **Cut** button ✄.

5. Click cell **A5**, and then, in the Clipboard group, click the **Paste** button. The customer order data is pasted into its original location in the range A5:G9.

Inserting and Deleting a Cell Range

Another use of selecting a range is to insert or delete cells from within the worksheet. To insert a range, select the range where you want the new cells inserted, and then click the Insert button in the Cells group on the Home tab. The existing cells shift down when the selected range is wider than it is long, and they shift right when the selected range is longer than it is wide (as illustrated in Figure 1-21). The Insert Cells command located on the Insert button menu lets you specify whether you want to shift the existing cells right or down, or whether to insert an entire row or column into the new range.

Figure 1-21 ▶ **Cells inserted within a cell range**

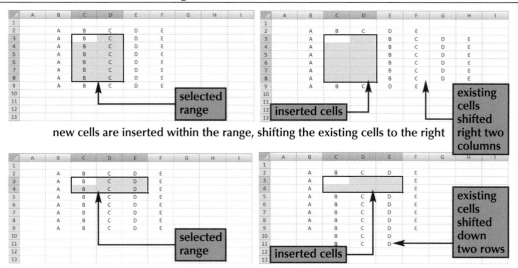

new cells are inserted within the range, shifting the existing cells to the right

new cells are inserted within the range, shifting the existing cells down

If you no longer need a specific cell or range in a worksheet, you can delete those cells and any content they contain. To delete a range, select the range, and then click the Delete button in the Cells group on the Home tab. As with deleting a row or column, cells adjacent to the deleted range either move up or left to fill in the vacancy left by the deleted cells. The Delete Cells command located on the Delete button menu lets you specify whether you want to shift the adjacent cells left or up, or whether to delete the entire column or row.

Inserting or Deleting a Cell Range | Reference Window

- Select a range that matches the range you want to insert or delete.
- In the Cells group on the Home tab, click the Insert button or the Delete button.

or

- Select the range that matches the range you want to insert or delete.
- In the Cells group, click the Insert button arrow and then click the Insert Cells button or click the Delete button arrow and then click the Delete Cells command (or right-click the selected range, and then click Insert or Delete on the shortcut menu).
- Click the option button for the direction in which you want to shift the cells, columns, or rows.
- Click the OK button.

You do not need to insert or delete any cells in the worksheet at this time.

Working with Formulas

Up to now you have entered only text, numbers, and dates in the worksheet. However, the main reason for using Excel is to perform calculations on data. Amanda wants the workbook to determine the number of DVDs she has to create for her customers and how much revenue will be generated by completing these orders. Such calculations are added to a worksheet using formulas and functions.

Entering a Formula

A **formula** is an expression that returns a value. In most cases, this is a number. You can also create formulas in Excel that return text strings. Every Excel formula begins with an equal sign (=) followed by an expression that describes the operation to be done. A formula is written using **operators** that combine different values, returning a single value that is then displayed in the cell. The most commonly used operators are **arithmetic operators** that perform addition, subtraction, multiplication, division, and exponentiation. For example, the following formula adds 5 and 7, returning a value of 12.

```
=5+7
```

However, formulas in Excel most often use numbers stored within cells. For example, the following formula returns the result of adding the values in cells A1 and B2.

```
=A1+B2
```

So, if the value 5 is stored in cell A1 and the value 7 is stored in cell B2, this formula would also return a value of 12. Figure 1-22 describes the different arithmetic operators and provides examples of formulas.

Figure 1-22 ▷ **Arithmetic operators**

Operation	Arithmetic Operator	Example	Description
Addition	+	=10+A1 =B1+B2+B3	Adds 10 to the value in cell A1 Adds the values in cells B1, B2, and B3
Subtraction	–	=C9–B2 =1–D2	Subtracts the value in cell B2 from the value in cell C9 Subtracts the value in cell D2 from 1
Multiplication	*	=C9*B9 =E5*0.06	Multiplies the values in cells C9 and B9 Multiplies the value in cell E5 by 0.06
Division	/	=C9/B9 =D15/12	Divides the value in cell C9 by the value in cell B9 Divides the value in cell D15 by 12
Exponentiation	^	=B5^3 =3^B5	Raises the value of cell B5 to the third power Raises 3 to the value in cell B5

If a formula contains more than one arithmetic operator, Excel performs the calculation using the same order of precedence you might have already seen in math classes. The **order of precedence** is a set of predefined rules used to determine the sequence in which operators are applied in a calculation—first exponentiation (^), second multiplication (*) and division (/), and third addition (+) and subtraction (–). For example, consider the formula below:

`=3+4*5`

This formula returns the value 23 because multiplication (4*5) takes precedence over addition. If a formula contains two or more operators with the same level of precedence, the operators are applied in order from left to right. Note the formula below:

`=4*10/8`

This formula first calculates the leftmost operation (4*10) and then divides that result of 40 by 8 to return the value 5.

To change the order of operations, you can enclose parts of the formula within parentheses. Any expression within a set of parentheses is calculated before the rest of the formula. Note the following formula:

`=(3+4)*5`

This formula first calculates the value of the expression (3+4) and then multiplies that total of 7 by 5 to return the value 35. Figure 1-23 shows how slight changes in a formula affect the order of precedence and the result of the formula.

Figure 1-23 ▷ **Order of precedence rules**

Formula (A1=50, B1=10, C1=5)	Order of Precedence Rule	Result
=A1+B1*C1	Multiplication before addition	100
=(A1+B1)*C1	Expression inside parentheses executed before expression outside	300
=A1/B1–C1	Division before subtraction	0
=A1/(B1–C1)	Expression inside parentheses executed before expression outside	10
=A1/B1*C1	Two operators at same precedence level, leftmost operator evaluated first	25
=A1/(B1*C1)	Expression inside parentheses executed before expression outside	1

Entering a Formula | Reference Window

- Click the cell in which you want the formula results to appear.
- Type = and an expression that calculates a value using cell references and arithmetic operators.
- Press the Enter key or press the Tab key to complete the formula.

Amanda wants the worksheet to include the total amount she charged for creating each customer's DVDs. The charge is equal to the number of DVDs created multiplied by the price per DVD. You've already entered this information for each customer in columns F and G. You'll enter a formula to calculate the charge for each customer in column H.

To enter the formula in column H:

▶ **1.** Click cell **H5** to make it the active cell, type **Charge** for the column label, and then press the **Enter** key. The column label is entered in cell H5. Cell H6, where you want to enter the formula, is the active cell.

▶ **2.** Type **=F6*G6** (the number of DVDs created multiplied by the price per DVD). As you type the formula, a list of Excel function names appears in a ScreenTip, which provides a quick method for entering functions. The list will close when you complete the formula. You'll learn more about Excel functions shortly.

▶ **3.** Press the **Enter** key. The formula is entered in cell H6, which displays the value $34.58. The result is displayed as currency because cell G6 referenced in the formula contains a currency value.

After a formula has been entered into a cell, the cell displays the results of the formula and not the formula itself. If the results are not what you expect, you might have entered the formula incorrectly. You can view the formula by selecting the cell and reviewing the expression displayed in the formula bar. One challenge with formulas, particularly long formulas, is interpreting the cell references. Excel makes this simpler by color coding each cell reference in the formula and its corresponding cell in the worksheet. You'll see this when you view the formula you just entered.

To view the formula:

▶ **1.** Click cell **H6** to make it the active cell. The formula you entered appears in the formula bar, whereas the value returned by the formula appears in the cell.

▶ **2.** Click in the formula bar. As shown in Figure 1-24, each cell used in the formula has a different colored border that matches the color of its cell reference in the formula. This provides a visual cue to the formula, enabling you to quickly match cell references with their locations in the worksheet.

Figure 1-24   **Formula references color coded**

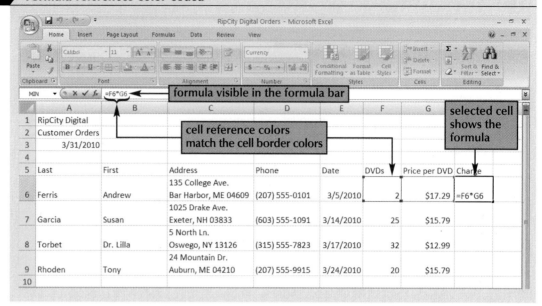

For Amanda's first customer, you entered the formula by typing each cell reference. You can also enter a cell reference by clicking the cell as you enter the formula. This technique reduces the possibility of error caused by typing an incorrect cell reference. You'll use this method to enter the formula to calculate the charge for the second customer.

To enter a cell reference in the formula using the mouse:

1. Click cell **H7** to make it the active cell, and then type **=**. When you type the equal sign, Excel knows that you're entering a formula. Any cell that you click from now on causes Excel to insert the cell reference of the selected cell into the formula until you complete the formula by pressing the Enter or Tab key.

2. Click cell **F7**. The cell reference is inserted into the formula on the formula bar. At this point, any cell you click changes the cell reference used in the formula. The cell reference isn't "locked" until you type an operator.

3. Type ***** to enter the multiplication operator. The cell reference for cell F7 is "locked" in the formula, and the next cell you click will be inserted after the operator.

4. Click cell **G7** to enter its cell reference in the formula, and then press the **Enter** key. Cell H7 displays the value $394.75, which is the total charge for the second customer.

Copying and Pasting Formulas

Sometimes, you'll need to repeat the same formula for several rows of data. Rather than retyping the formula, you can copy the formula and then paste it into the remaining rows. You'll copy the formula you just entered in cell H7 to cells H8 and H9 to calculate the charges for Amanda's two remaining customers.

To copy the formula in cell H7:

1. Click cell **H7** to select the cell that contains the formula you want to copy.

▶ **2.** In the Clipboard group on the Home tab, click the **Copy** button 🗎 . The formula is copied to the Clipboard.

▶ **3.** Select the range **H8:H9**, the cells in which you want to paste the formula.

▶ **4.** In the Clipboard group, click the **Paste** button. Excel pastes the formula into the selected range. See Figure 1-25.

Formula copied and pasted ◀ **Figure 1-25**

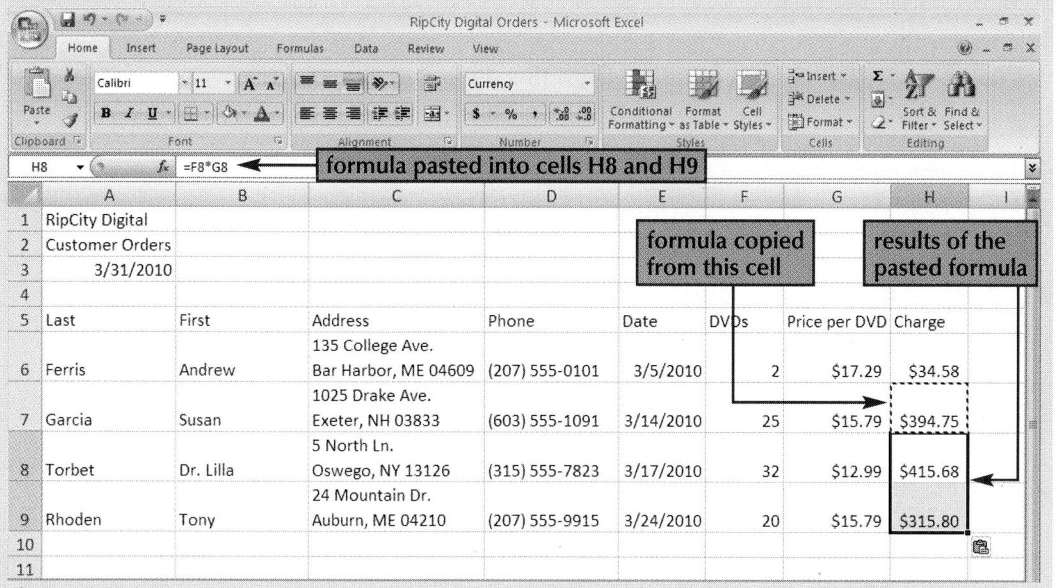

▶ **5.** Click cell **H8** and verify that the formula =F8*G8 appears in the formula bar, and then click cell **H9** and verify that the formula =F9*G9 appears in the formula bar.

Pasting a formula is different from pasting a value. With the customer order data, Excel pasted the same values in a new location. With formulas, Excel adjusts the formula's cell references to reflect the new location of the formula in the worksheet. This is because you want to replicate the actions of a formula rather than duplicate the specific value the formula generates. In this case, the formula's action is to multiply the number of DVDs Amanda created for the customer by the price she charged for creating each DVD. By copying and pasting that formula, that action is replicated for every customer in the worksheet.

Introducing Functions

In addition to cell references and operators, formulas can also contain functions. A **function** is a named operation that returns a value. Functions are used to simplify formulas, reducing what might be a long expression into a compact statement. For example, to add the values in the range A1:A10, you could enter the following long formula:

=A1+A2+A3+A4+A5+A6+A7+A8+A9+A10

Or, you could use the SUM function to accomplish the same thing:

=SUM(A1:A10)

In both cases, Excel adds the values in cells A1 through A10, but the SUM function is faster and simpler to enter and less prone to a typing error. You should always use a function, if one is available, in place of a long, complex formula.

Excel supports over 300 different functions from the fields of finance, business, science, and engineering. Functions are not limited to numbers. Excel also provides functions that work with text and dates.

Entering a Function

Amanda wants to calculate the total number of DVDs she needs to create for her customers. To do that, you'll use the SUM function to add the values in the range F6:F9.

To enter the SUM function:

1. Click cell **E10**, type **TOTAL** as the label, and then press the **Tab** key. The label is entered in cell E10, and cell F10 is the active cell.

2. Type **=SUM(F6:F9** in cell F10. As you begin to type the SUM function, a ScreenTip lists the names of all functions that start with the letter "S." When you type the cell references, Excel highlights all the cells in the specified range to provide a visual reminder of exactly which cells the SUM function is using. See Figure 1-26.

Tip

You can also insert a range reference into a function by selecting the range with your mouse.

Figure 1-26 | SUM function being entered

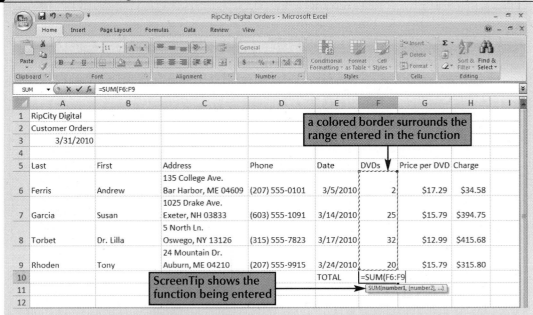

3. Type **)** to complete the function, and then press the **Tab** key. The value of the SUM function appears in cell F10, indicating that Amanda has to create 79 DVDs to meet all of her current orders.

Entering Functions with AutoSum

A fast and convenient way to enter the SUM function is with the Sum button in the Editing group on the Home tab. The **Sum** button (also referred to as the **AutoSum** feature) quickly inserts Excel functions that summarize all the values in a column or row using a single statistic. With the Sum button, you can insert the SUM, AVERAGE, COUNT, MIN, and MAX functions to generate the following:

- Sum of the values in the column or row
- Average value in the column or row
- Total count of numeric values in the column or row
- Minimum value in the column or row
- Maximum value in the column or row

The Sum button inserts both the name of the function and the range reference to the row or column of data to which the summary function is being applied. Excel determines the range reference by examining the layout of the data and choosing what seems to be the most likely cell range. For example, if you use the Sum button in a cell that is below a column of numbers, Excel assumes that you want to summarize the values in the column. Similarly, if you use the Sum button in a cell to the right of a row of values, Excel summarizes the values in that row. When you use the Sum button, Excel highlights the range it "thinks" you want to use. You can change that range by typing a different range reference or selecting a different range with your mouse.

Understanding How the AutoSum Feature Works		InSight

Make sure to always verify the range selected by AutoSum, especially when a worksheet's column or row titles contain numbers. AutoSum cannot differentiate between numbers used as titles (such as years) and numbers used as data for the calculation.

Amanda wants to calculate the total revenue she'll generate by fulfilling her customer orders. You'll use the AutoSum feature to enter the SUM function.

To use AutoSum to calculate the total revenue:

▶ 1. Click cell **H10** to make it the active cell.

▶ 2. In the Editing group on the Home tab, click the **Sum button arrow** Σ ▾ . The button's menu opens and displays five common summary functions: Sum, Average, Count Numbers, Max (for maximum), and Min (for minimum).

▶ 3. Click **Sum** to enter the SUM function. See Figure 1-27.

> **Figure 1-27** **SUM function entered with AutoSum**

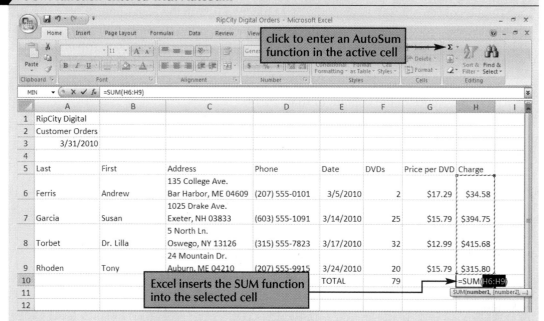

4. Verify that the range H6:H9 appears in the SUM function and is highlighted with a dotted border. The dotted border provides a visual reminder that this is where the SUM function will be applied.

5. Press the **Enter** key to accept the automatically generated formula. The total charge for all of Amanda's customers, shown in cell H10, is $1,160.81.

InSight | Creating Effective Formulas

You can use formulas to quickly perform calculations on business, science, and engineering data. To use formulas effectively:

- Do not place important data in a formula because the worksheet displays the formula result rather than the actual formula. For example, the formula =0.05*A5 calculates a 5% sales tax on a price in cell A5, but hides the 5% tax rate. Instead, enter the tax rate in another cell, such as cell A4, with an appropriate label and use the formula =A4*A5 to calculate the sales tax. Readers can see the tax rate as well as the resulting sales tax.

- Keep formulas simple. Use functions in place of long, complex formulas whenever possible. For example, use the SUM function instead of entering a formula that adds individual cells.

- Break up formulas to show intermediate results. For example, the formula =SUM(A1:A10)/SUM(B1:B10) calculates the ratio of two sums, but hides the two sum values. Instead, enter each SUM function in a separate cell, such as cells A11 and B11, and use the formula =A11/B11 to calculate the ratio. Readers can see both sums and the value of their ratio in the worksheet.

Working with Worksheets

Recall that new workbooks contain three worksheets labeled Sheet1, Sheet2, and Sheet3. You can add new worksheets to the workbook and remove unneeded ones. You can also give worksheets more descriptive and meaningful names. For Amanda's workbook, you'll remove unused worksheets from the workbook, and you'll rename the two worksheets in which you entered data.

Inserting and Deleting a Worksheet

Although each workbook includes three worksheets to start, sometimes you'll need more or fewer worksheets. You can add worksheets or delete unneeded ones. To insert a new worksheet into the workbook, right-click a sheet tab, click Insert on the shortcut menu, select a sheet type, and then click the OK button. Excel inserts the new sheet directly to the left of the active sheet. You can insert a new worksheet at the end of the workbook by clicking the Insert Worksheet tab located to the right of the last sheet tab in the workbook. The new worksheet is named with the next consecutive sheet number, such as Sheet4. You'll insert a new, blank worksheet at the end of your workbook.

To insert a new worksheet:

▶ **1.** Click the **Insert Worksheet** tab 🗐 to the right of the Sheet3 sheet tab. Excel inserts a new worksheet named "Sheet4" at the end of the workbook.

The workbook now includes two empty worksheets: Sheet3 and Sheet4. Because you don't plan to use these sheets, it's a good idea to remove them. You can delete a worksheet from a workbook in two ways. You can right-click the sheet tab of the worksheet you want to delete, and then click Delete on the shortcut menu. You can also click the Delete button arrow in the Cells group on the Home tab, and then click Delete Sheet. You'll use both of these methods to delete the Sheet3 and Sheet4 worksheets.

To delete the Sheet3 and Sheet4 worksheets:

▶ **1.** Right-click the **Sheet3** sheet tab, and then click **Delete** on the shortcut menu. Excel removes the Sheet3 worksheet.

▶ **2.** If necessary, click the **Sheet4** sheet tab to make it the active sheet.

▶ **3.** In the Cells group on the Home tab, click the **Delete button arrow**, and then click **Delete Sheet**. Excel removes Sheet4 from the workbook.

Renaming a Worksheet

The remaining worksheet names, Sheet1 and Sheet2, are not very descriptive. Amanda suggests that you rename Sheet1 as "Documentation" and rename Sheet2 as "Customer Orders." To rename a worksheet, you double-click the sheet tab to select the sheet name, type a new name for the sheet, and then press the Enter key. Sheet names cannot exceed 31 characters in length, including blank spaces. The width of the sheet tab adjusts to the length of the name you enter.

To rename the two worksheets:

▶ **1.** Double-click the **Sheet2** sheet tab. The sheet name is selected in the sheet tab.

▶ **2.** Type **Customer Orders**, and then press the **Enter** key. The width of the sheet tab expands to match the longer sheet name.

▶ **3.** Double-click the **Sheet1** sheet tab, type **Documentation**, and then press the **Enter** key. Both sheets are renamed.

Moving and Copying a Worksheet

You can change the placement of the worksheets in a workbook. A good practice is to place the most important worksheets at the beginning of the workbook (the leftmost sheet tabs), and less important worksheets toward the end (the rightmost tabs). To reposition a worksheet, you click and drag the sheet tab to a new location relative to other worksheets in the workbook. You can use a similar method to copy a worksheet. Just press the Ctrl key as you drag and drop the sheet tab. The new copy appears where you drop the sheet tab, while the original worksheet remains in its initial position. You'll move the Documentation sheet to the end of the workbook and then return it to the beginning.

To move the Documentation worksheet:

▶ **1.** If necessary, click the **Documentation** sheet tab to make that worksheet active.

▶ **2.** Press and hold the mouse button so the pointer changes to ⯈ and a small triangle appears in the upper-left corner of the tab.

▶ **3.** Drag the pointer to the right of the Customer Orders sheet tab, and then release the mouse button. The Documentation sheet is now the second sheet in the workbook.

▶ **4.** Drag the Documentation sheet back to be the first sheet in the workbook.

Editing Your Work

As you work, you might make mistakes that you want to correct or undo, or you might need to replace a value based on more current information. Amanda realizes that the price per DVD for Andrew Ferris's order should be $18.29 not $17.29 as entered in cell G6. You could simply clear the value in the cell and then type the correct value. However, sometimes you need to edit only a portion of an entry rather than change the entire contents of a cell, especially if the cell contains a large block of text or a complex formula. To edit the cell contents, you can work in **editing mode**.

You can enter editing mode in several ways: (1) double-clicking the cell, (2) selecting the cell and pressing the F2 key, or (3) selecting the cell and clicking anywhere within the formula bar. When you work in editing mode, some of the keyboard shortcuts you've been using work differently because now they apply only to the text within the selected cell. For example, the Home, End, Backspace, Delete, and arrow keys now move the insertion point to different locations within the cell. The Home key moves the insertion point to the beginning of the cell's content. The End key moves the insertion point to the end of the cell's content. The left and right arrow keys move the insertion point backward and forward through the cell's content. The Backspace key deletes the character immediately to the left of the insertion point, and the Delete key deletes the character to the right of the insertion point. To exit editing mode and accept the changes you made, press the Enter key.

Tip

If you make a mistake as you type in editing mode, you can press the Esc key or click the Cancel button on the formula bar to cancel all of the changes you made while in editing mode.

You'll see how keyboard commands differ when you're in editing mode as you change one digit of the value in cell G6.

To edit the value in cell G6:

▶ **1.** Click the **Customer Orders** sheet tab.

▶ **2.** Double-click cell **G6**. The mode indicator in the status bar switches from Ready to Edit to indicate that you are in editing mode.

▶ **3.** Press the **End** key. The insertion point moves to the end of the cell.

▶ **4.** Press the ← key three times. The insertion point moves to the right of the 7.

▶ **5.** Press the **Backspace** key to delete the 7, and then type **8**. The value in cell G6 changes to 18.29. See Figure 1-28.

Working in editing mode ◀ **Figure 1-28**

	A	B	C	D	E	F	G	H	I
1	RipCity Digital								
2	Customer Orders								
3	3/31/2010								
4									
5	Last	First	Address	Phone	Date	DVDs	Price per DVD	Charge	
6	Ferris	Andrew	135 College Ave. Bar Harbor, ME 04609	(207) 555-0101	3/5/2010	2	18.29	$34.58	
7	Garcia	Susan	1025 Drake Ave. Exeter, NH 03833	(603) 555-1091	3/14/2010	25	$15.79	$394.75	
8	Torbet	Dr. Lilla	5 North Ln. Oswego, NY 13126	(315) 555-7823	3/17/2010	32	$12.99	$415.68	
9	Rhoden	Tony	24 Mountain Dr. Auburn, ME 04210	(207) 555-9915	3/24/2010	20	$15.79	$315.80	
10					TOTAL	79		$1,160.81	

insertion point to edit the text within the cell

status bar indicates Excel is in editing mode

▶ **6.** Press the **Enter** key to accept the edit in cell G6. The value $18.29 appears in cell G6, the active cell is cell G7, and the mode indicator in the status bar changes from Edit to Ready to indicate that you are no longer in editing mode.

Undoing and Redoing an Action

As you revise a workbook, you might find that you need to undo one of your previous actions. To undo an action, click the Undo button on the Quick Access Toolbar. As you work, Excel maintains a list of your actions, so you can undo most of the actions you perform in a workbook during the current session. To reverse more than one action, click the Undo button arrow and click the earliest action you want to undo from the list. All actions subsequent to that action will also be undone.

You'll undo the action you just performed, removing the edit to cell G6.

To undo your last action:

▶ **1.** On the Quick Access Toolbar, click the **Undo** button .

▶ **2.** Verify that $17.29 appears again in cell G6, indicating that your last action—editing the value of this cell—has been undone.

If you find that you have gone too far in undoing previous actions, you can go forward in the action list and redo those actions. To redo an action, you click the Redo button on the Quick Access Toolbar. As with the Undo button, you can click the Redo button arrow to redo more than one action at a time. You'll use Redo to restore the value of cell G6.

To redo your last action:

▶ **1.** On the Quick Access Toolbar, click the **Redo** button .

▶ **2.** Verify that the value in cell G6 returns to $18.29.

Using Find and Replace

Amanda wants to you to replace all the street title abbreviations with their full names. Specifically, she wants you to use "Avenue" in place of "Ave.", "Lane" in place of "Ln.", and "Drive" in place of "Dr." Although you could read through the worksheet to locate each occurrence, this becomes a cumbersome process with larger workbooks. For greater speed and accuracy, you can use the **Find** command to locate numbers and text in the workbook and the **Replace** command to overwrite them. You'll replace each occurrence of a street title abbreviation.

To use the Find and Replace commands:

▶ **1.** In the Editing group on the Home tab, click the **Find & Select** button, and then click **Replace**. The Find and Replace dialog box opens.

▶ **2.** Type **Ave.** in the Find what box, press the **Tab** key, and then type **Avenue** in the Replace with box.

You can limit the search to the current worksheet or search the entire workbook. You can specify whether to match the capitalization in the Find what box and whether the search text should match the entire cell contents or part of the cell contents.

▶ **3.** Click the **Options** button to display additional Find and Replace options. See Figure 1-29.

| Figure 1-29 | Find and Replace dialog box |

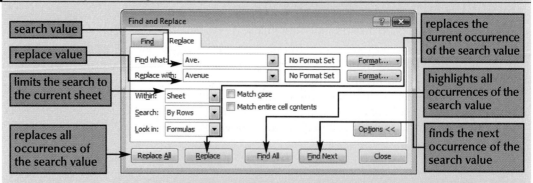

You can choose to review each occurrence of the search value and decide whether to replace it, or you can click the Replace All button to replace all occurrences at once.

▶ **4.** Click the **Replace All** button. A dialog box opens, indicating that Excel has completed its search and made two replacements.

▶ **5.** Click the **OK** button to close the dialog box.

▶ **6.** Type **Ln.** in the Find what box, press the **Tab** key, type **Lane** in the Replace with box, click the **Replace All** button, and then click the **OK** button to close the dialog box that indicates Excel has completed its search and made one replacement.

Next, you want to replace the street abbreviation "Dr." with "Drive." Because "Dr." is also used as the abbreviation for "Doctor" for one customer, you must review each "Dr." abbreviation and make the replacement only in the addresses.

▶ **7.** Type **Dr.** in the Find what box, press the **Tab** key, type **Drive** in the Replace with box, and then click the **Find Next** button. The next occurrence of "Dr." in the worksheet occurs in cell B8 with the text, "Dr. Lilla."

▶ **8.** Click the **Find Next** button to ignore this occurrence. The next occurrence of "Dr." is in the mailing address for Tony Rhoden.

▶ **9.** Click the **Replace** button to replace this text. You've finished finding and replacing text in the worksheet.

▶ **10.** Click the **Close** button to close the Find and Replace dialog box. See Figure 1-30.

Revised customer orders **Figure 1-30**

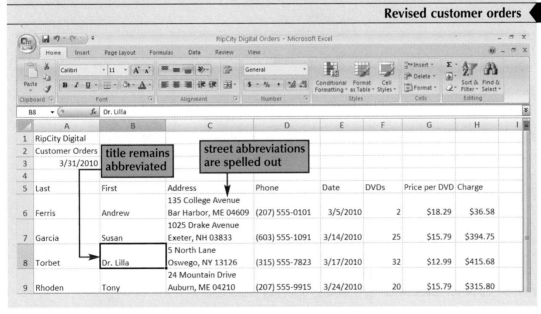

Using the Spelling Checker

Another editing tool is the spelling checker. The **spelling checker** verifies the words in the active worksheet against the program's dictionary. Although the spelling checker's dictionary includes a large number of words, as well as common first and last names and places, many words you use in workbooks might not be included. If the spelling checker finds a word not in its dictionary, the word appears in a dialog box along with a list of suggested replacements. You can replace the word with one from the list, or you can ignore the word and go to the next possible misspelling. You can also add words to the dictionary to prevent them from being flagged as misspellings in the future. Note that the spelling checker will not find a correctly spelled word used incorrectly, such as "there" instead of "their" or "your" instead of "you're." The best way to catch these types of errors is to proofread your worksheets.

Before giving the customer orders workbook to Amanda, you'll check the spelling.

To check the spelling in the worksheet:

▶ 1. Click cell **A1**, click the **Review** tab on the Ribbon, and then, in the Proofing group, click the **Spelling** button. The Spelling dialog box opens and flags "RipCity" as a possible spelling error. Excel suggests two alternatives. See Figure 1-31.

Figure 1-31 ▶ Spelling dialog box

Because RipCity is the name of Amanda's company, you'll ignore all the occurrences of this spelling.

▶ 2. Click the **Ignore All** button. The spelling checker flags "Torbet," a last name that is not in the program's dictionary.

▶ 3. Click the **Ignore All** button to ignore the spelling of this name. The next potential spelling error is the name "Lilla" in cell B8. Amanda tells you the name should have been entered as "Lila," a first name that the spelling checker recognizes.

▶ 4. Click **Lila** in the list of suggestions, if necessary, and then click the **Change** button. The text is changed within the cell. The spelling checker doesn't find any other errors.

Trouble? If the spelling checker finds another error, you might have another typing error in your worksheet. Use the spelling checker to find and correct any other errors in your workbook, and then continue with Step 5.

▶ 5. Click the **OK** button to close the Spelling dialog box.

▶ 6. Proofread the worksheet and correct any other spelling errors you find. You do not have to check the spelling in the Documentation worksheet.

Previewing and Printing a Worksheet

Now that you have finished the final edit of the workbook, you are ready to print a hard copy of the customer orders list for Amanda. However, before you print the workbook, you should preview it to ensure that it will print correctly.

Changing Worksheet Views

You can view a worksheet in three ways. **Normal view**, which you've been using throughout this tutorial, simply shows the contents of the worksheet. **Page Layout view** shows how the worksheet will appear on the page or pages sent to the printer. **Page Break Preview** displays the location of the different page breaks within the worksheet. This is particularly useful when a worksheet will span several printed pages.

You'll switch between these views to see how the Customer Orders worksheet will appear on printed pages.

To switch the worksheet views:

▶ **1.** Click the **Page Layout** button 🔳 on the status bar. Excel displays the page layout of the worksheet. You want to see the rest of the data, which extends to a second page.

▶ **2.** Reduce the zoom level to **60%**. See Figure 1-32.

Worksheet displayed in Page Layout view ◀ **Figure 1-32**

Tip

You can view the workbook in the full screen space (which hides the Ribbon); in the Workbook Views group on the View tab, click Full Screen.

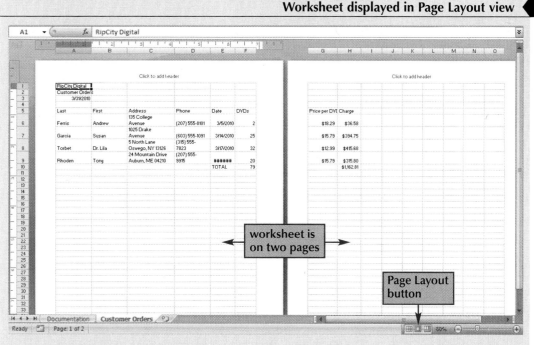

▶ **3.** Click the **Page Break Preview** button 🔳 on the status bar. The view switches to Page Break Preview, which shows only those parts of the current worksheet that will print. A dotted blue border separates one page from another.

Trouble? If the Welcome to Page Break Preview dialog box opens, this is the first time you've switched to Page Break Preview. Click the OK button to close the dialog box and continue with Step 4.

▶ **4.** Zoom the worksheet to **120%** so that you can more easily read the contents of the worksheet. See Figure 1-33.

| Figure 1-33 | Worksheet displayed in Page Break Preview |

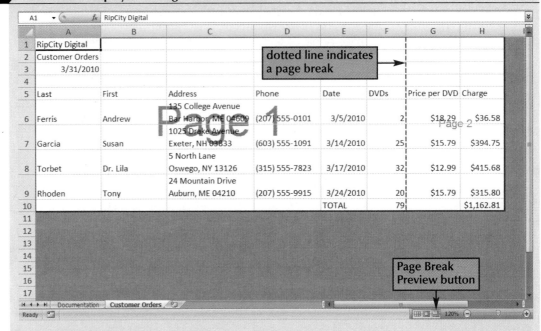

5. Click the **Normal** button ▦ on the status bar. The worksheet returns to Normal view. A dotted black line indicates where the page break will be placed when the worksheet is printed.

Working with Portrait and Landscape Orientation

As you saw in Page Layout view and Page Break Preview, the Customer Orders worksheet will print on two pages—columns A through F will print on one page and columns G and H will print on a second page. Amanda wants the entire worksheet printed on a single page. The simplest way to accomplish this is to change the page orientation. In **portrait orientation**, the page is taller than it is wide. In **landscape orientation**, the page is wider than it is tall. By default, Excel displays pages in portrait orientation. In many cases, however, you will want to print the page in landscape orientation.

You'll change the orientation of the Customer Orders worksheet.

To change the page orientation:

1. Click the **Page Layout** tab on the Ribbon.

2. In the Page Setup group, click the **Orientation** button, and then click **Landscape**. The page orientation switches to landscape, and the Customer Orders worksheet contents fit on one page.

3. Click the **Page Layout** button ▣ on the status bar, and then verify that all the worksheet contents fit on one page.

Changing the page orientation affects only the active worksheet. The Documentation sheet remains in portrait orientation.

▶ **4.** Click the **Documentation** sheet tab, and then click the **Page Layout** button 🔲. The entire contents of the Documentation worksheet fit on one page in portrait orientation.

Printing the Workbook

You can print the contents of your workbook by using the Print command on the Office Button. The Print command provides three options. You can open the Print dialog box from which you can specify the printer settings, including which printer to use, which worksheets to include in the printout, and the number of copies to print. You can perform a Quick Print using the print options currently set in the Print dialog box. Finally, you can preview the workbook before you send it to the printer to see exactly how the worksheet will look on the printer you selected with the print settings you've chosen. In general, you should always preview the printout before sending it to the printer.

You'll preview and print Amanda's workbook now.

To preview and print the workbook:

▶ **1.** Click the **Office Button** 🔘, point to **Print**, and then click **Print**. The Print dialog box opens.

▶ **2.** Click the **Name** box, and then click the printer to which you want to print if it is not already selected.

Next, you need to select what to print. You can choose to print only the selected cells, the active sheet (or sheets), or all the worksheets in the workbook that contain data.

▶ **3.** If necessary, click the **Entire workbook** option button to print both of the worksheets in the workbook.

▶ **4.** Make sure **1** appears in the Number of copies box because you only need to print one copy of the workbook. Next, you'll preview how the worksheet will appear on the printed page with these settings.

▶ **5.** Click the **Preview** button. Print Preview displays a preview of the full first page of the printout—the Documentation sheet printed in portrait orientation. The status bar shows that this is the first of two pages that will print.

▶ **6.** In the Preview group on the Print Preview tab, click the **Next Page** button. Print Preview shows the second page of the printout.

The printout will include only the data in the worksheet. The other elements in the worksheet, such as the row and column headings and the gridlines around the worksheet cells, will not print.

▶ **7.** In the Print group, click the **Print** button. The workbook is sent to the printer and Print Preview closes.

Viewing and Printing Worksheet Formulas

Amanda notices that the printout displays only the worksheet values and none of the formulas. Most of the time, you will be interested in only the final results of the worksheet, not the formulas used to calculate those results. In some cases, you might want to view the formulas used to develop the workbook. This is particularly useful when you encounter unexpected results and you want to examine the underlying formulas. You can view the formulas in a workbook by switching to **formula view**, a view of the workbook contents that displays formulas instead of the resulting values. You'll switch to formula view now.

To view the worksheet formulas:

Tip

To toggle in and out of formula view, press the Ctrl+` keys. The ` grave accent symbol is usually located above the Tab key on your keyboard.

1. Click the **Customer Orders** sheet tab, if necessary, and then click the **Normal** button ⊞ on the status bar. The Customer Orders worksheet is active and displayed in Normal view.

2. Press the **Ctrl+`** keys. The worksheet changes to formula view.

3. Scroll the worksheet to the right to view the formulas in columns F and H. The column widths are wider to display the entire formula in each cell. As long as you don't resize the column widths while in formula view, they remain unchanged in other views. See Figure 1-34.

| Figure 1-34 | Worksheet in formula view |

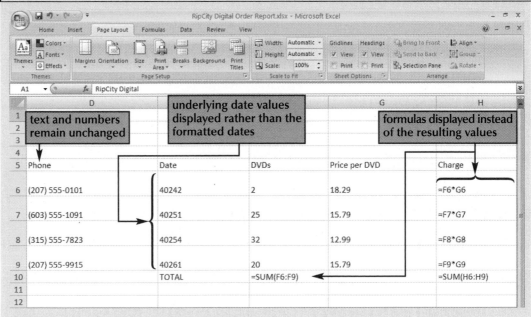

Amanda wants a printout of the formula view. The Customer Orders worksheet will not fit on one page because of the expanded column widths. You can scale the worksheet to force the contents to fit on a single page. **Scaling** a printout reduces the width and the height of the printout to fit the number of pages you specify by shrinking the text size as needed. You can also scale a printout proportionally to a percentage of its actual size. You'll scale the Customer Orders worksheet to a width and height of one page.

To scale the worksheet formulas to print on one page:

▶ **1.** In the Scale to Fit group on the Page Layout tab, click the **Width arrow**, and then click **1 page**.

▶ **2.** In the Scale to Fit group, click the **Height arrow**, and then click **1 page**. You'll verify that the worksheet formula view fits on a single page.

▶ **3.** Click the **Page Layout** button 🔲 on the status bar, and then zoom the worksheet to **50%**. The formula view of the worksheet fits on one page. See Figure 1-35.

Printout scaled to one page   **Figure 1-35**

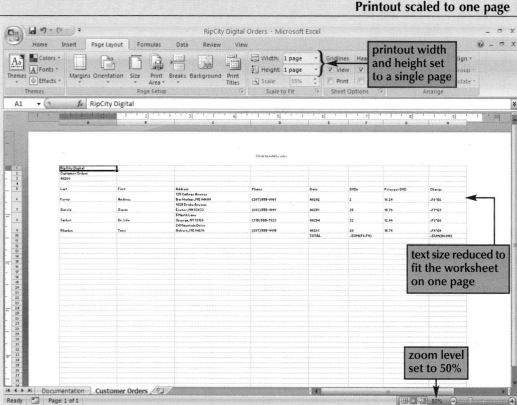

▶ **4.** Click the **Office Button** , point to **Print**, and then click **Print**. The Print dialog box opens. You'll specify that only the active worksheet will be printed.

▶ **5.** Click the **Active sheet(s)** option button to print only the Customer Orders worksheet.

▶ **6.** Click the **Preview** button. Print Preview displays a preview of the one-page printout of the Customer Orders worksheet in formula view.

▶ **7.** In the Print group on the Print Preview tab, click the **Print** button. The workbook is sent to the printer and Print Preview closes.

At this point, you've completed your work for Amanda. Before closing the workbook, you'll change the view of the workbook contents back to Normal view.

To save and close the workbook:

▶ **1.** Press the **Ctrl+`** keys to switch the worksheet back to Normal view.

▶ **2.** Save your changes to the workbook, and then close it.

Amanda is pleased with the job you've done for her. She will review the workbook you've created and let you know if she has any changes that she wants you to make.

Review | Session 1.2 Quick Check

1. Describe the two types of cell ranges in Excel.

2. What is the range reference for the block of cells from A3 through G5 and J3 through M5?

3. What formula would you enter to add the values in cells B4, B5, and B6? What function would you enter to achieve the same result?

4. How do you rename a worksheet?

5. Describe four ways of viewing the content of an Excel workbook.

6. Why would you scale a worksheet?

7. How do you display the formulas used in a worksheet?

8. How are page breaks indicated in Page Break Preview?

Review | Tutorial Summary

In this tutorial, you learned the basics of spreadsheets and Excel. After reviewing the major components of the Excel window, you navigated between and within worksheets. You entered text, dates, values, and formulas, and used the AutoSum feature to quickly insert the SUM function. You inserted and deleted rows, columns, and worksheet cells. You selected cell ranges and moved cell contents using drag and drop or cut and paste. You also created new worksheets, renamed worksheets, and moved worksheets within the workbook. You edited your work by using editing mode, finding and replacing text, and using the spelling checker to correct errors. Finally, you previewed and then printed the contents of the workbook.

Key Terms

active cell	editing mode	point
active sheet	Excel	portrait orientation
active workbook	Find	range
active workbook window	formula	range reference
adjacent range	formula bar	Replace
arithmetic operator	formula view	row heading
AutoComplete	function	scale
autofit	landscape orientation	sheet
AutoSum	Microsoft Office Excel 2007	sheet tab
cell	Name box	spelling checker
cell range	nonadjacent range	spreadsheet
cell reference	Normal view	text data
chart sheet	number data	text string
clear	operator	time data
column heading	order of precedence	truncate
cut	Page Break Preview	what-if analysis
date data	Page Layout view	workbook
delete	pixel	workbook window
drag and drop	planning analysis sheet	worksheet

Practice		Review Assignments

Practice the skills you learned in the tutorial using the same case scenario.

There are no Data Files needed for the Review Assignments.

Amanda reviewed your work on the Customer Orders worksheet, and has another set of orders she wants you to enter. The data for the new customer orders is shown in Figure 1-36. In addition to calculating the charge for creating the DVDs, Amanda also wants to include the cost of shipping in the total charged to each customer.

Figure 1-36

Date	Last	First	Address	Phone	DVDs	Price per DVD	Shipping Charge
3/27/2010	Fleming	Doris	25 Lee St. Bedford, VA 24523	(540) 555-5681	7	$18.29	$7.49
4/4/2010	Ortiz	Thomas	28 Ridge Ln. Newfane, VT 05345	(802) 555-7710	13	$16.55	$9.89
4/8/2010	Dexter	Kay	150 Main St. Greenbelt, MD 20770	(301) 555-8823	25	$15.79	$7.23
4/9/2010	Sisk	Norman	250 East Maple Ln. Cranston, RI 02910	(401) 555-3350	15	$16.55	$10.55
4/17/2010	Romano	June	207 Jackston Ave. Westport, IN 47283	(812) 555-2681	22	$15.79	$13.95

Complete the following:

1. Open a blank workbook, and then save the workbook as **Order Report** in the Tutorial.01\Review folder.
2. Rename Sheet1 as **Documentation**, and then enter the following data into the worksheet:

Cell	Data	Cell	Data
A1	**RipCity Digital**		
A3	**Author**	B3	*your name*
A4	**Date**	B4	*the current date*
A5	**Purpose**	B5	**To track customer orders for RipCity Digital**

3. Rename Sheet2 as **Customer Orders**.
4. Delete Sheet3.
5. On the Customer Orders worksheet, in cell A1, enter **RipCity Digital**. In cell A3, enter **Customer Orders Report**. In cell A4, enter **March 27 to April 17, 2010**.
6. In cells A5 through H10, enter the data from Figure 1-36. In column D, enter the address text on two lines within each cell.
7. Set the width of column A to 10 characters, columns B and C to 12 characters, column D to 20 characters, and columns E, G, and H to 16 characters.
8. Autofit all of the rows in the worksheet to the cell contents.
9. In cell I5, enter **Total**. In cell I6, insert a formula that calculates the total charge for the first customer (the number of DVDs created multiplied by the price per DVD and then added to the shipping charge). Increase the width of column I to 11 characters.
10. Copy the formula in cell I6 and paste it into the cell range I7:I10.

11. In cell E11, enter **Total**. In cell F11, use the SUM function to calculate the total number of DVDs created for all customers. In cell I11, use AutoSum to insert the SUM function to calculate the total charges for all of the customer orders.

12. Use editing mode to make the following corrections:
    - In cell D6, change the street address from 25 Lee St. to **2500 Lee St.**
    - In cell F9, change the number of DVDs from 15 to **17**.
    - In cell H8, change the shipping charge from $7.23 to **$8.23**.

13. Use the Find and Replace commands to replace all occurrences of St. with **Street**, Ln. with **Lane**, and Ave. with **Avenue**.

14. Change the page layout of the Customer Orders worksheet to print in landscape orientation on a single page.

15. Preview and print the contents of the entire workbook.

16. Change the Customer Orders worksheet to formula view, landscape orientation, and scaled to fit on a single page. Preview and print the Customer Orders worksheet.

17. Return the view of the Customer Orders worksheet to Normal view, save your changes to the Order Report workbook, and then save the current workbook as **Revised Report** in the Tutorial.01\Review folder. (*Hint:* Use the Save As command on the Office Button to save the existing workbook with a new name.)

18. Kay Dexter has canceled her order with RipCity Digital. Remove her order from the Customer Orders worksheet.

19. Add the following order directly after the order placed by June Romano: date **4/22/2010**; name **Patrick Crawford**; address **200 Valley View Road, Rome, GA 30161**; phone **(706) 555-0998**; DVDs **14**; price per DVD **$16.55**; shipping charge **$12.45**

20. Verify that Excel automatically updates the formulas and functions used in the workbook so they properly calculate the total charge for this order and for all the orders.

21. Edit the title in cell A4, changing the ending date of the report from April 17 to **April 22**.

22. Save the workbook, preview and print the contents and formulas of the revised Customer Orders worksheet, close the workbook, and then submit the finished workbook and printouts to your instructor.

| Apply | **Case Problem 1** |

Use the skills you learned to complete an income statement for a bicycle company.

Data File needed for this Case Problem: Altac.xlsx

Altac Bicycles   Deborah York is a financial consultant for Altac Bicycles, an online seller of bicycles and bicycle equipment based in Silver City, New Mexico. She has entered some financial information in an Excel workbook for an income statement she is preparing for the company. She asks you to enter the remaining data and formulas.

Complete the following:

1. Open the **Altac** workbook located in the Tutorial.01\Case1 folder, and then save the workbook as **Altac Bicycles** in the same folder.

2. Insert three new rows at the top of the Sheet1 worksheet, and then enter the following text on two lines within cell A1:
   Altac Bicycles
   Income Statement*

3. In cell A2, enter **For the Years Ended December 31, 2007 through December 31, 2009**.

4. In the range C6:E7, enter the following net sales and cost of sales figures:

	2009	2008	2007
Net Sales	**12,510**	**10,981**	**9,004**
Cost of Sales	**4,140**	**3,810**	**3,011**

5. In the range C11:E14, enter the following expense figures:

	2009	2008	2007
Salaries and Wages	**1,602**	**1,481**	**1,392**
Sales and Marketing	**2,631**	**2,012**	**1,840**
Administrative	**521**	**410**	**324**
Research and Development	**491**	**404**	**281**

6. Select the nonadjacent range C18:E18;C20:E20;C24:E24, and then enter the following values for Other Income, Income Taxes, and Shares, pressing the Enter or Tab key to navigate from cell to cell in the selected range:

	2009	2008	2007
Other Income	341	302	239
Income Taxes	**1,225**	**1,008**	781
Shares	**3,581**	**3,001**	**2,844**

7. In the range C8:E8, enter a formula to calculate the gross margin for each year, where the gross margin is equal to the net sales minus the cost of sales.

8. In the range C15:E15, enter the SUM function to calculate the total operating expenses for each year, where the total operating expenses is the sum of the four expense categories.

9. In the range C17:E17, enter a formula to calculate the operating income for each year, where operating income is equal to the gross margin minus the total operating expenses.

10. In the range C19:E19, enter a formula to calculate the pretax income for each year, where pretax income is equal to the operating income plus other income.

11. In the range C22:E22, enter a formula to calculate the company's net income for each year, where net income is equal to the pretax income minus income taxes.

12. In the range C25:E25, enter a formula to calculate the earnings per share for each year, where earnings per share is equal to the net income divided by the number of shares outstanding.

13. Use the spelling checker to correct and replace any spelling errors in the worksheet. Ignore the spelling of Altac.

14. In cell A18, use editing mode to capitalize the word *income*.

15. Increase the width of column A to 18 characters and increase the width of column B to 25 characters. Autofit the height of row 1.

16. Rename Sheet1 as **Income Statement**; rename Sheet2 as **Documentation** and move it to the beginning of the workbook; and then delete the Sheet3 worksheet.

17. In the Documentation worksheet, enter the following text and values:

Cell	Data	Cell	Data
A1	**Altac Bicycles**		
A3	**Author**	B3	*your name*
A4	**Date**	B4	*the current date*
A5	**Purpose**	B5	**Income statement for Altac Bicycles for 2007 through 2009**

18. Save the workbook, preview the workbook and make sure each worksheet in portrait orientation fits on one page in the printout, and then print the entire workbook. Close the workbook, and then submit the finished workbook and printouts to your instructor.

Apply | **Case Problem 2**

Use the skills you learned to complete a balance sheet for a food retailer.

Data File needed for this Case Problem: Halley.xlsx

Halley Foods Michael Li is working on the annual financial report for Halley Foods of Norman, Oklahoma. One part of the financial report will be the company's balance sheet for the previous three years. Michael has entered some of the labels for the balance sheet but wants you to finish the job by entering the actual values and formulas.

Complete the following:

1. Open the **Halley** workbook located in the Tutorial.01\Case2 folder, and then save the workbook as **Halley Foods** in the same folder.
2. Rename the Sheet1 worksheet as **Balance Sheet**, and then delete the Sheet2 and Sheet3 worksheets.
3. Insert three new rows at the top of the sheet, and then enter the following text on four lines within cell A1:
   Halley Foods
   Balance Sheet
   As of December 31
   For the Years 2007 through 2009
4. Change the width of column A to 30 characters, the width of column B to 20 characters, and the width of column C to 26 characters. Autofit the height of row 1.
5. Enter the assets and liability values shown in Figure 1-37 into the corresponding cells in the Balance Sheet worksheet for each of the last three years.

Figure 1-37

		2009	2008	2007
Current Assets	Cash and equivalents	796	589	423
	Short-term investments	1,194	1,029	738
	Accounts receivable	1,283	1,151	847
	Net inventories	683	563	463
	Deferred taxes	510	366	332
	Other current assets	162	137	103
Other Assets	Investments	7,077	5,811	4,330
	Restricted investments	910	797	681
	Property and equipment	779	696	420
	Other assets	1,178	484	485
Current Liabilities	Accounts payable	350	293	182
	Income taxes payable	608	442	342
	Accrued payroll	661	564	384
	Other accrued liabilities	1,397	1,250	775
Minority Interest		44	43	36
Shareholders' Equity	Preferred and common stock	5,557	4,821	3,515
	Retained earnings	5,666	4,007	3,401
	Other comprehensive income	289	203	187

6. Use AutoSum to calculate the total current assets, other assets, current liabilities, and shareholders' equity in the ranges D11:F11, D17:F17, D25:F25, and D33:F33, respectively, for each of the previous three years.

7. Insert a formula in the range D19:F19 to calculate the total assets (current plus other) for each year.

8. Insert a formula in the range D36:F36 to calculate the value of the total current liabilities plus the minority interest plus the total shareholders' equity for each year.

9. Use the spelling checker to correct any spelling mistakes in the Balance Sheet worksheet, and then proofread the worksheet.

10. Change the zoom level of the Balance Sheet worksheet to 70% in Normal view to view the entire contents of the sheet in the workbook window.

11. View the Balance Sheet worksheet in Page Layout view zoomed to 80%, and then scale the height and width of the worksheet to fit on one page.

12. Insert a new worksheet named **Documentation** at the beginning of the workbook.

13. In the Documentation worksheet, enter the following data:

Cell	Data	Cell	Data
A1	**Halley Foods**		
A3	**Author**	B3	*your name*
A4	**Date**	B4	*the current date*
A5	**Purpose**	B5	**Balance sheet for Halley Foods for 2007 through 2009**

14. Save, preview, and then print the entire Halley Foods Balance Sheet workbook.

15. Print the formula view of the Balance Sheet worksheet on two pages in landscape orientation. Return the Balance Sheet worksheet to Page Layout view when you're finished.

16. Save and close the workbook, and then submit the finished workbook and printouts to your instructor.

| Challenge | **Case Problem 3** |

Explore using Auto-Sum to calculate production statistics.

Data File needed for this Case Problem: Global.xlsx

Global Site GPS   Kevin Hodge is a production assistant at Global Site GPS, a leading manufacturer of GPS devices located in Crestwood, Missouri. One of Kevin's jobs is to monitor output at the company's five regional plants. He wants to create an Excel workbook that reports the monthly production at the five sites, including the monthly average, minimum, and maximum production and total production for the previous year. He asks you to create the workbook that reports these statistics.

Complete the following:

1. Open the **Global** workbook located in the Tutorial.01\Case3 folder, and then save the workbook as **Global Site** in the same folder.

2. Rename the Sheet1 worksheet as **Production History**, and then insert 12 new rows at the top of the worksheet.

3. Increase the width of column A to 23 characters and the width of columns B through F to 14 characters.

4. In the range B7:F7, enter the titles **Plant1**, **Plant2**, **Plant3**, **Plant4**, and **Plant5**, respectively.

5. In the range A8:A11, enter **Total Units Produced**, **Average per Month**, **Maximum**, and **Minimum**, respectively.

✦ EXPLORE
6. Select the range B26:F26, use AutoSum to calculate the sum of the production values for each of the five plants, and then drag and drop the selected cells to the range B8:F8.

✦ EXPLORE
7. Select the range B26:F26, use AutoSum to calculate the average of the production values for each of the five plants, and then drag and drop the selected cells to the range B9:F9.

✦ EXPLORE
8. Repeat Step 7 to calculate the maximum values for each of the five plants and then move those calculated values to the range B10:F10, and then repeat to calculate the minimum production values and drag and drop those calculated values to the range B11:F11.

9. In the Production History worksheet, enter the following data:

Cell	Data	Cell	Data
A1	**Global Site GPS**		
A2	**Production Report**		
A3	**Model**	B3	**MapTracker 201**
A4	**Year**	B4	**2010**
A5	**Total Units Produced**		

10. In cell B5, use the SUM function to add the values in the range B8:F8.

11. Insert a new worksheet named **Plant Directory** as the first worksheet in the workbook.

12. In cells A1 and A2, enter **Global Site GPS** and **Plant Directory**, respectively, and then enter the text shown in Figure 1-38 in the range A4:D9, making sure that the address is entered on two lines within the cell.

Figure 1-38

Plant	Plant Manager	Address	Phone
1	Karen Brookers	300 Commerce Avenue Crestwood, MO 63126	(314) 555-3881
2	Daniel Gomez	15 North Main Street Edison, NJ 08837	(732) 555-0012
3	Jody Hetrick	3572 Howard Lane Weston, FL 33326	(954) 555-4817
4	Yong Jo	900 South Street Kirkland, WA 98033	(425) 555-8775
5	Sandy Nisbett	3771 Water Street Helena, MT 59623	(406) 555-4114

13. Set the width of column B to 15 characters, the width of column C to 30 characters, and the width of column D to 16 characters. Autofit the height of each row to its content.

14. Insert a new worksheet named **Documentation** as the first worksheet in the workbook, and then enter the following data:

Cell	Data	Cell	Data
A1	**Global Site GPS**		
A3	**Author**	B3	*your name*
A4	**Date**	B4	*the current date*
A5	**Purpose**	B5	**Production report for Global Site GPS**

15. Switch the Production History worksheet to Page Layout view, change the orientation to landscape, and then verify that the worksheet fits on a single page.

16. Save your workbook, preview and print the workbook, close the workbook, and then submit the finished workbook and printouts to your instructor.

| Create | Case Problem 4 |

Create an Excel workbook to record service calls for a lawn service agency.

There are no Data Files needed for this Case Problem.

Green Lawns Green Lawns provides yard service and maintenance for homes in and around Mount Vernon, Ohio. Gary Taylor manages the accounts for Green Lawns and wants to use Excel to record weekly service calls made by the company. He asks you to create the workbook for him. Gary provides you the list of service calls made in the first week of August shown in Figure 1-39.

Figure 1-39

Customer	Address	Phone	Last Service	Hours	Base Fee	Hourly Rate
David Lane	391 Country Drive Mount Vernon, OH 43050	(740) 555-4439	8/2/2010	3	$35	$15.50
Robert Gomez	151 Apple Lane Mount Vernon, OH 43051	(740) 555-0988	8/2/2010	3.5	$35	$15.50
Sandra Lee	112 Main Street Mount Vernon, OH 43050	(740) 555-3773	8/3/2010	1.5	$20	$12.50
Gregory Sands	305 Country Drive Mount Vernon, OH 43050	(740) 555-4189	8/3/2010	4	$35	$17.50
Betty Oaks	205 Second Street Mount Vernon, OH 43049	(740) 555-0088	8/3/2010	1	$20	$12.50

Complete the following:

1. Open a blank workbook, and then save it as **Green Lawns** in the Tutorial.01\Case4 folder included with your Data Files.

2. Rename Sheet1 as **Documentation**, and then enter information documenting the workbook. Include the name of the company, your name, the current date, and a brief description of the purpose of the workbook. The layout and appearance of the worksheet is up to you.

3. In Sheet2, enter the service calls shown in Figure 1-39, and then enter appropriate formulas and functions to calculate the service charge for each customer. Green Lawns charges each customer a base fee plus a working fee that is equal to the hourly rate multiplied by the number of hours worked. Also, enter a formula to calculate the total charges for all customer calls. The layout and appearance of the page is up to you.

4. Rename Sheet2 as **Service Calls**, and then delete any unused sheets in the workbook.

5. Check the spelling in the workbook, correcting any spelling errors, and then proofread the workbook.

6. Save your workbook, preview the worksheets to ensure that each fits onto a single page, and then print the entire workbook. Close the workbook, and then submit the finished workbook and printouts to your instructor.

Research | **Internet Assignments**

Use the Internet to find and work with data related to the topics presented in this tutorial.

The purpose of the Internet Assignments is to challenge you to find information on the Internet that you can use to work effectively with this software. The actual assignments are updated and maintained on the Course Technology Web site. Log on to the Internet and use your Web browser to go to the Student Online Companion for New Perspectives Office 2007 at **www.course.com/np/office2007**. Then navigate to the Internet Assignments for this tutorial.

Assess | **SAM Assessment and Training**

If you have a SAM user profile, you may have access to hands-on instruction, practice, and assessment of the skills covered in this tutorial. Log in to your SAM account (**http://sam2007.course.com**) to launch any assigned training activities or exams that relate to the skills covered in this tutorial.

Review | **Quick Check Answers**

Session 1.1

1. chart sheets and worksheets
2. The active cell is surrounded by a thick border and its cell reference appears in the Name box.
3. C5
4. the Ctrl+Home keys
5. a combination of alphanumerical characters that form words and sentences (called a text string)
6. Enter the first line of text, press the Alt+Enter keys, and then type the second line of text.
7. Because it's a date; all dates are numbers formatted to appear in standard date formats.
8. Clearing a row removes only the contents of the row, deleting a row removes the contents and the row.

Session 1.2

1. Adjacent cell ranges contain a rectangular block of cells; nonadjacent cell ranges contain a collection of adjacent cell ranges.
2. A3:G5;J3:M5
3. =B4+B5+B6; =SUM(B4:B6)
4. Double-click the sheet tab, and then type a new name on the sheet tab.
5. Normal view shows the columns and rows of the worksheet. Page Layout view shows the layout of the worksheet as it appears on a page. Page Break Preview shows the page breaks within the worksheet. Formula view shows formulas rather than the values returned by the formulas.
6. to force a worksheet to print on one page
7. Press the Ctrl+` keys to switch to formula view.
8. as dotted lines

Ending Data Files

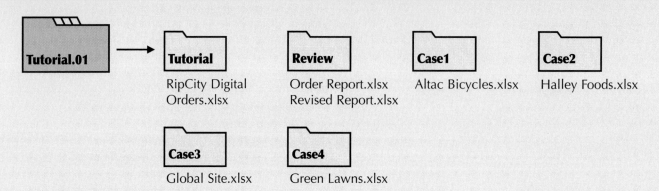

Tutorial.01 → Tutorial
RipCity Digital
Orders.xlsx

Review
Order Report.xlsx
Revised Report.xlsx

Case1
Altac Bicycles.xlsx

Case2
Halley Foods.xlsx

Case3
Global Site.xlsx

Case4
Green Lawns.xlsx

Objectives

Session 2.1
- Format text, numbers, and dates
- Change font colors and fill colors
- Merge a range into a single cell
- Apply a built-in cell style
- Select a different theme

Session 2.2
- Apply a built-in table style
- Add conditional formats to tables with highlight rules and data bars
- Hide worksheet rows
- Insert print titles, set print areas, and insert page breaks
- Enter headers and footers

Formatting a Workbook

Formatting a Financial Report

Case | ExerComp Exercise Equipment

ExerComp, based in Mason, Ohio, manufactures electronic and computer components for fitness machines and sporting goods. At the upcoming annual sales meeting, sales managers will present reports that detail the sales history of different ExerComp products. Sales manager Tom Uhen will report on the recent sales history of the X310 heart rate monitor.

Tom has already created a workbook and entered the sales figures for the past two years. He wants you to make that data more readable and informative. To do this, you will work with formatting tools to modify the appearance of the data in each cell, the cell itself, and the entire worksheet. Because much of Tom's data has been stored in tables, you will also use some special formatting tools designed for tables.

Starting Data Files

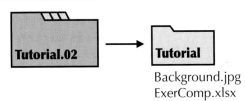

Tutorial.02 →

Tutorial

Background.jpg
ExerComp.xlsx

Review

Paper.jpg
X410.xlsx

Case1

Frosti.xlsx

Case2

GrillRite.xlsx

Case3

Iowa.xlsx

Case4

Life.xlsx

Session 2.1

Formatting Workbooks

Tom already entered the data and some formulas in the worksheets, but the workbook is only a rough draft of what he wants to submit to the company. Tom's workbook has three worksheets. The Documentation sheet describes the workbook's purpose and content. The Yearly Sales sheet records the total sales of the X310 heart rate monitor for 2008 and 2009, including the total number of units sold per sales region (labeled R01 through R08) and the total revenue generated by those sales. The Monthly Sales sheet reports the number of X310 units sold in 2008 and 2009 by region and month as well as the corresponding increase in sales. You'll open the workbook and review its content.

To open the workbook:

▶ **1.** Open the **ExerComp** workbook located in the **Tutorial.02\Tutorial** folder included with your Data Files, and then save the workbook as **ExerComp Sales Report** in the same folder.

▶ **2.** In the Documentation sheet, enter your name in cell B4 and the current date in cell B5.

▶ **3.** Review the contents in the three worksheets.

In its current form, the data is difficult to read and interpret. Tom wants you to format the workbook contents to improve its readability and visual appeal. **Formatting** is the process of changing a workbook's appearance by defining the fonts, styles, colors, and decorative features. Formatting changes only the appearance of data—it does not affect the data itself.

| InSight | **Formatting Workbooks Effectively** |

A well-formatted workbook can be easier to read, establish a sense of professionalism, help draw attention to the points you want to make, and provide continuity between the worksheets. Too little formatting can make the data hard to understand, whereas too much formatting can overwhelm the data. Proper formatting is a balance between these two extremes. Always remember, the goal of formatting is not simply to make a "pretty workbook," but also to accentuate important trends and relationships in the data.

One goal of formatting is to maintain a consistent look within a workbook. Excel, along with all the Office 2007 programs, uses themes to do this. A **theme** is a collection of formatting that specifies the fonts, colors, and graphical effects used throughout the workbook. The Office theme is the default, although you can choose others or create your own. You can also use fonts and colors that are not part of the current theme.

As you work, **Live Preview** shows the effects of formatting options on the workbook's appearance before you apply them. This lets you see and evaluate different formats as you develop your workbook.

Formatting Text

Tom suggests that you first modify the title in the Documentation sheet. The appearance of text is determined by its **typeface**, which is the specific design used for the characters, including letters, numbers, punctuation marks, and symbols. Typefaces are organized into fonts; a **font** is a set of characters that employ the same typeface. Some commonly used fonts are Arial, Times New Roman, and Courier. **Serif fonts**, such as Times New Roman, have extra decorative strokes at the end of each character. **Sans serif fonts**, such as Arial, do not include these decorative strokes. Other fonts are purely decorative, such as a font used for specialized logos.

Fonts are organized into theme and non-theme fonts. A **theme font** is associated with a particular theme and used for headings and body text in the workbook. The Office theme uses the theme font Cambria for headings and the theme font Calibri for body text. When you don't want to associate a font with a particular design, you use a **non-theme font**. Text formatted with a non-theme font retains its appearance no matter what theme is used with the workbook.

Every font can be further formatted with a **font style**, such as *italic*, **bold**, or ***bold italic***, and special effects, such as underline, ~~strikethrough~~, and color to text. Finally, you can set the **font size** to increase or decrease the size of the text. Font sizes are measured in **points** where one point is approximately ¹/₇₂ of an inch.

You'll format the company name displayed at the top of each worksheet to appear in large, bold letters using the default heading font from the Office theme. Tom wants the slogan "the Intelligent path to Fitness" displayed below the company name to appear in the heading font, but in smaller, italicized letters.

To format text in the Documentation sheet:

1. Click the **Documentation** sheet tab to make that worksheet active, and then click cell **A1** to make it active.

2. In the Font group on the Home tab, click the **Font arrow** to display a list of fonts available on your computer. The first two fonts are the theme fonts for headings and body text—Cambria and Calibri. See Figure 2-1.

Font list | **Figure 2-1**

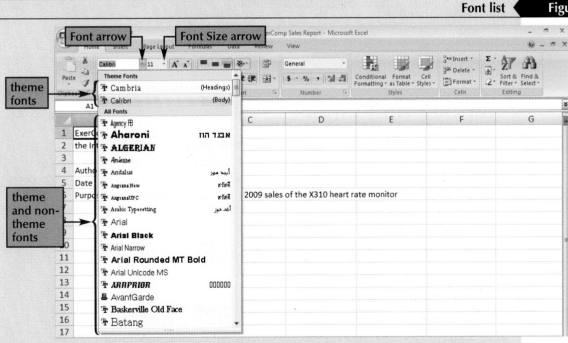

Trouble? If your screen displays more or less of the worksheet, your worksheet is at a different zoom level. If you want your worksheet zoomed to match the figures, click the Zoom In button on the status bar twice to increase the zoom magnification to 120%.

3. Click **Cambria**. The company name in cell A1 changes to the Cambria font, the default headings font in the current theme.

4. In the Font group, click the **Font Size arrow** to display a list of font sizes, and then click **26**. The company name changes to 26 points.

5. In the Font group, click the **Bold** button B. The company name is boldfaced. Next, you'll format the company slogan.

6. Click cell **A2** to make it active. The slogan text is selected.

7. In the Font group, click the **Font arrow**, and then click **Cambria**. The slogan text changes to the Cambria font.

8. In the Font group, click the **Font Size arrow**, and then click **10**. The slogan text changes to 10 points.

9. In the Font group, click the **Italic** button I. The slogan is italicized.

10. Select the range **A4:A6**, click the **Bold** button B in the Font group, and then click cell **A7**. The column labels are bolded. See Figure 2-2.

Tip

You can change the font size one point at a time. In the Font group on the Home tab, click the Increase Font Size or Decrease Font Size button.

Figure 2-2   Formatted worksheet text

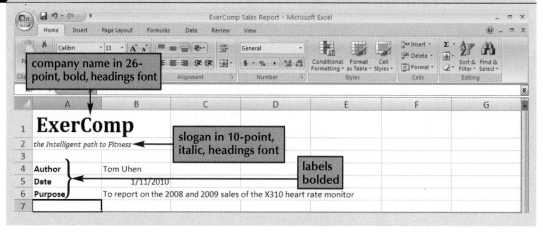

Working with Color

Color can transform a plain workbook filled with numbers and text into a powerful presentation that captures attention and adds visual emphasis to the points you want to make. By default, text is black and cells have no background fill color. You can add color to both the text and the cell background.

Colors are organized into two main categories. **Theme colors** are the 12 colors that belong to the workbook's theme. Four colors are designated for text and backgrounds, six colors are used for accents and highlights, and two colors are used for hyperlinks (followed and not followed links). These 12 colors are designed to work well together and to remain readable in all color combinations.

Ten **standard colors**—dark red, red, orange, yellow, light green, green, light blue, blue, dark blue, and purple—are always available regardless of the workbook's theme. You can also open an extended palette of 134 standard colors. In addition, you can create a **custom color** by specifying a mixture of red, blue, and green color values, making available 16.7 million custom colors—more colors than the human eye can distinguish. Some dialog boxes have an **automatic color** option that uses your Windows default text and background color values, usually black text on a white background.

Applying Font Color and Fill Color

Tom wants the labels in the Documentation sheet to stand out. You will change the ExerComp title and slogan to blue, and then you'll format the other labels in the worksheet with a blue background fill and a white font color.

Tip

You can add a fill color to a sheet tab. In the Cells group on the Home tab, click the Format button, point to Tab Color, and then click a color.

To change the title and slogan font color and fill color:

▶ **1.** Select the range **A1:A2**.

▶ **2.** In the Font group on the Home tab, click the **Font Color button arrow** ![A] to display the available theme and standard colors. There are 10 theme colors (the two colors for hyperlinked text are not shown), and each theme color has five variations, or **accents**, in which a different tint or shading is applied to the theme color.

▶ **3.** Point to the **Blue** color (the eighth color) in the Standard Colors section. The color name appears in a ScreenTip. See Figure 2-3.

Font colors ◀ Figure 2-3

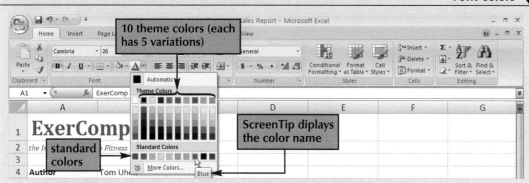

▶ **4.** Click the **Blue** color. The company name and slogan change to blue.

▶ **5.** Select the range **A4:A6**. You'll change both the fill and the font colors of these cells.

▶ **6.** In the Font group, click the **Fill Color button arrow** ![fill], and then click the **Blue** color in the Standard Colors section. The cell backgrounds change to blue.

▶ **7.** In the Font group, click the **Font Color button arrow** ![A], and then click the **white** color (ScreenTip is White, Background1) in the Theme Colors section. The font color changes to white.

▶ **8.** Click cell **A7** to deselect the range. The white text on a blue background is visible. See Figure 2-4.

Figure 2-4 | Font colors and fill colors applied

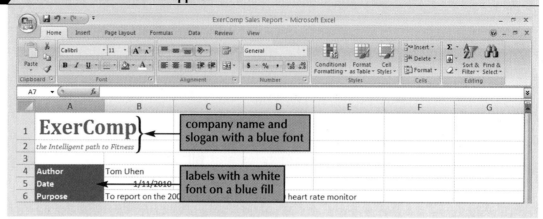

Formatting Text Selections

The ExerComp logo usually appears in two colors—"Exer" in blue and "Comp" in red. Tom asks you to make this change to the text in cell A1. You'll need to format part of the cell content one way and the rest a different way. To do this, you first select the text you want to format in editing mode, and then apply the formatting to the selection. The **Mini toolbar** appears when you select text and contains buttons for commonly used text formats. You'll use the Mini toolbar to format "Comp" in a red font.

To format the "Comp" text selection:

▶ 1. Double-click cell **A1** to select the cell and go into editing mode, and then select **Comp**. A transparent version of the Mini toolbar appears.

▶ 2. Click the **Font Color button arrow** ![A] on the Mini toolbar, and then click the **Red** color (the second color) in the Standard Colors section. The text color changes and the Mini toolbar remains open for additional formatting. See Figure 2-5.

Figure 2-5 | Mini toolbar used to format text

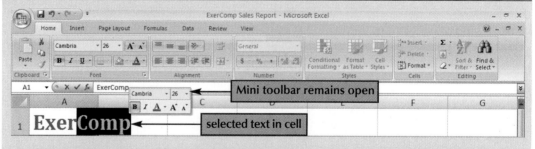

Trouble? If the Mini toolbar disappears before you can click the Font Color button arrow, you probably moved the pointer away from the Mini toolbar, pressed a key, or pressed a mouse button. Right-click the selected text to redisplay the Mini toolbar above a shortcut menu, immediately move your pointer to the Mini toolbar, and then repeat Step 2.

▶ 3. Click cell **A7** to deselect the cell. The text "ExerComp" in cell A1 is blue and red.

Setting a Background Image

You can use a picture or image as the background for all the cells in a worksheet. An image can give the worksheet a textured appearance, like that of granite, wood, or fibered paper. The image is inserted until it fills the entire worksheet. The background image does not affect any cell's format or content. Any cells with a background color display the color on top, hiding that portion of the image. Background images do not print.

Tom has an image that resembles fibered paper that you will use as the background for the Documentation sheet.

To add a background image to the Documentation sheet:

▶ **1.** Click the **Page Layout** tab on the Ribbon. The page layout options appear on the Ribbon.

▶ **2.** In the Page Setup group, click the **Background** button. The Sheet Background dialog box opens.

▶ **3.** Navigate to the **Tutorial.02\Tutorial** folder included with your Data Files, click the **Background.jpg** image file, and then click the **Insert** button. The image file is added to the background of the Documentation sheet.

Next, you'll change the fill color of the cells with the author's name, the date, and the workbook's purpose to white to highlight them in the worksheet.

▶ **4.** Select the range **B4:B6**, and then click the **Home** tab on the Ribbon.

▶ **5.** In the Font group, click the **Fill Color button arrow** , and then click the **white** color in the Theme Colors section.

▶ **6.** Increase the width of column B to **55** characters, and then click cell **A7** to deselect the range. See Figure 2-6.

Background image added to the Documentation sheet ◀ **Figure 2-6**

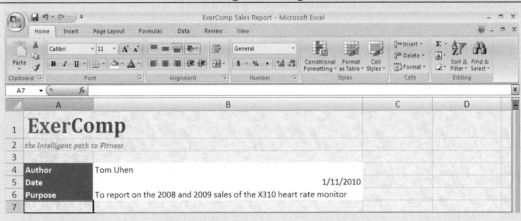

InSight | **Enhancing Workbooks with Color**

Color, used wisely, can enhance any workbook. Too much color can be just as bad as "not enough" color. An overuse of color can cause readers' eyes to wander around the workbook without focusing on a central point. As you format a workbook, keep in mind the following tips:

- Use colors from the same theme within a workbook to maintain a consistent look and feel across the worksheets. If the built-in themes do not fit your needs, you can create a custom theme.
- Use colors to differentiate types of cell content and to direct users where to enter data. For example, format a worksheet so formula results appear in cells without a fill color and users enter data in cells with a light gray fill color.
- Avoid garish color combinations that can annoy the reader and be difficult to read.
- Print on color and black-and-white printers to ensure that the output is readable in both versions.
- Understand your printer's limitations and features. Colors that look good on your monitor might not print well.
- Be sensitive to your audience. About 8% of all men and 0.5% of all women have some type of color blindness and might not be able to see the text with certain color combinations. Red-green color blindness is the most common color blindness, so avoid using red text on a green background or green text on a red background.

Formatting Data

The Yearly Sales worksheet contains the annual sales figures from 2008 and 2009 for the X310 heart rate monitor. The top of the worksheet displays the number of units sold in each sales region per year, and the bottom displays the sales revenue generated by region per year. You'll add formulas to calculate the total sales for each year as well as the difference and percentage difference in sales from one year to another.

To enter formulas in the Yearly Sales worksheet:

1. Click the **Yearly Sales** sheet tab. The Yearly Sales worksheet becomes active.

2. In cells B15 and B26, enter **Total**; in cells E6 and E17, enter **Increase**; in cells F6 and F17, enter **% Increase**; and then select cell **C15**.

3. In the Editing group on the Home tab, click the **Sum** button Σ, and then press the **Enter** key. The formula =SUM(C7:C14) is entered in the cell, adding the numbers in the range C7:C14.

4. Select cell **C15**, and then, in the Clipboard group, click the **Copy** button. The formula is copied to the Clipboard.

   Next, you'll paste the formula into a nonadjacent range. Remember, to select a nonadjacent range, select the first cell or range, press and hold the Ctrl key as you select other cells or ranges, and then release the Ctrl key.

5. Select the range **D15;C26:D26**, and then, in the Clipboard group, click the **Paste** button. The formula is pasted into cells D15, C26, and D26, adding the values in each column.

6. Select cell **E7**, and then enter the formula **=D7–C7** to calculate the increase in sales from 2008 to 2009 for region R01.

7. Select cell **F7**, and then enter the formula **=E7/C7** to calculate the percentage increase from 2008 to 2009.

▶ **8.** Select the range **E7:F7**, and then, in the Clipboard group, click the **Copy** button 🔳.

▶ **9.** Select the range **E8:F15;E18:F26**, and then, in the Clipboard group, click the **Paste** button. The formulas are copied into the selected cells.

▶ **10.** Click cell **A6** to deselect the range. See Figure 2-7.

Formulas added to the Yearly Sales sheet ◀ **Figure 2-7**

The sales figures are hard to read, making them difficult to interpret and understand. By default, values appear in the **General number format**, which, for the most part, displays numbers exactly as you enter them. Calculated values show as many digits after the decimal point as will fit in the cell and the last displayed digit is rounded, as you can see with the percentage increase values in column F. Only the displayed number is rounded; the actual value stored in the cell is not. Calculated values too large to fit into the cell are displayed in scientific notation.

Formatting Numbers

The Number group on the Home tab has buttons for formatting the appearance of numbers. You can select a number format, apply accounting or other currency formats, change a number to a percentage, insert a comma as a thousands separator, and increase or decrease the number of digits displayed to the right of the decimal point.

You'll add a thousands separator to the sales values to make them easier to read and remove the digits shown to the right of the decimal point because the data values for units sold will always be whole numbers. You'll format the percentage difference values as percentages with two decimal places. Tom also wants you to format the revenue values in the range C18:E26 as currency by adding dollar signs. Because applying dollar signs to large columns of numbers often makes them unreadable, standard accounting practice displays currency symbols only in the first and last rows of the range.

To format the units sold, percentage differences, and revenue numbers:

▶ **1.** Select the range **C7:E15;C18:E26**, and then, in the Number group on the Home tab, click the **Comma Style** button 🔹. The numbers include a thousands separator, but still display two digits to the right of the decimal point.

> **2.** Select the range **C7:E15**, and then, in the Number group, click the **Decrease Decimal** button twice. The two extra digits are removed.

> **3.** Select the range **F7:F15;F18:F26**, and then, in the Number group, click the **Percent Style** button %. The values now include the percentage symbol.

> **4.** In the Number group, click the **Increase Decimal** button twice. Two digits are added to the right of the decimal point.

> **5.** Select the range **C18:E18;C26:E26**, and then, in the Number group, click the **Accounting Number Format** button $. The first row and the Total row display the currency symbol.

> **6.** Click cell **A6** to deselect the range. See Figure 2-8.

Figure 2-8	Worksheet after formatting numbers

	A	B	C	D	E	F	G
6	Units Sold	Region	2008 Sales	2009 Sales	Increase	% Increase	
7		R01	3,605	3,853	248	6.88%	
8		R02	3,966	3,842	(124)	-3.13%	
		R03	3,760	4,035	275	7.31%	
		R04	3,777	4,063	286	7.57%	
		R05	3,974	3,725	(249)	-6.27%	
		R06	3,656	3,937	281	7.69%	
13		R07	3,554	3,875	321	9.03%	
14		R08	3,844	3,844	-	0.00%	
15		Total	30,136	31,174	1,038	3.44%	
16							
17	Revenue	Region	2008 Sales	2009 Sales	Increase	% Increase	
18		R01	$ 104,364.75	$ 115,397.35	$ 11,032.60	10.57%	
19		R02	114,815.70	115,067.90	252.20	0.22%	
		R03	108,852.00	120,848.25	11,996.25	11.02%	
		R04	109,344.15	121,686.85	12,342.70	11.29%	
		R05	115,047.30	111,563.75	(3,483.55)	-3.03%	
		R06	105,841.20	117,913.15	12,071.95	11.41%	
		R07	102,888.30	116,056.25	13,167.95	12.80%	
25		R08	111,283.80	115,127.80	3,844.00	3.45%	
26		Total	$ 872,437.20	$ 933,661.30	$ 61,224.10	7.02%	

units include commas and no decimal places

percentages include two decimal places and symbol

first and last rows display the currency symbol

revenues include commas and two decimal places

Tom examines this reformatted data and notes that the company sold 1,038 more units in 2009 than in 2008—an increase of 3.44%, which increased revenue by $61,224.10, or 7.02%. This was not uniform across all sales regions. Total sales and revenue for Region R05, for example, decreased from 2008 to 2009.

Formatting Dates and Times

Although dates and times in Excel appear as text, they are actually numbers that measure the interval between the specified date and time and January 1, 1900 at 12:00 a.m. You can then calculate date and time intervals, and you can format a date or time value. For example, you can apply a date format that displays the day of the week for any date value stored in your worksheet.

The date in the Documentation sheet is an abbreviated format, *mm/dd/yyyy*. Tom wants you to use an extended format that includes the day of the week, the full month name, the day, and the year. This Long Date format is a built-in date format.

To format the date in the Long Date format:

1. Click the **Documentation** sheet tab to make that worksheet active, and then select cell **B5**.

2. In the Number group on the Home tab, click the **Number Format arrow** to open a list of built-in number formats.

3. Click **Long Date**. The date format changes to show the weekday name, month name, day, and year. See Figure 2-9.

Formatted date | **Figure 2-9**

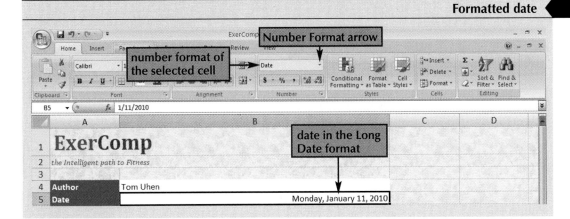

Formatting Dates for International Audiences | InSight

When your workbooks are intended for international audiences, be sure to use a date format that will be clear to everyone, such as November 10, 2010 or 10 November 2010. Many countries use a day/month/year format for dates rather than the month/day/year format commonly used in the United States. For example, the date 10/11/2010 is read as October 11, 2010 by people in the United States but as November 10, 2010 by people in most other countries.

Formatting Worksheet Cells

The date in the Documentation worksheet is formatted to display as text. Because all dates are actually numbers, they are right-aligned in the cell by default, regardless of their date format. Tom asks you to left-align the date to make it easier to read.

Aligning Cell Content

In addition to left and right alignments, you can change the vertical and horizontal alignments of cell content to make a worksheet more readable. You can also increase or decrease the space between the cell content and the cell border. In general, you should center column titles, left-align text, and right-align numbers to keep their decimal places lined up within the column. Figure 2-10 describes the alignment buttons located in the Alignment group on the Home tab.

Figure 2-10 **Alignment buttons**

Button	Description
▤	Aligns the cell content with the cell's top edge
▤	Vertically centers the cell content within the cell
▤	Aligns the cell content with the cell's bottom edge
▤	Aligns the cell content with the cell's left edge
▤	Horizontally centers the cell content within the cell
▤	Aligns the cell content with the cell's right edge
帚	Decreases the size of the indentation used in the cell
帚	Increases the size of the indentation used in the cell
▦	Rotates the cell content to an angle within the cell
▤	Forces the cell text to wrap within the cell borders
▦	Merges the selected cells into a single cell

You'll left-align the date in the Documentation worksheet and center the column titles in the Yearly Sales worksheet.

To left-align the date and center the column titles:

1. If necessary, select cell **B5**.

2. In the Alignment group on the Home tab, click the **Align Text Left** button ▤. The date shifts to the left edge of the cell.

3. Click the **Yearly Sales** sheet tab to make that worksheet active, and then select the range **C6:F6;C17:F17**.

4. In the Alignment group, click the **Center** button ▤. The column titles in columns C, D, E, and F are centered.

Indenting Cell Content

Sometimes, you want a cell's content moved a few spaces from the cell edge. This is particularly useful for entries that are considered subsections of a worksheet. For example, Tom recorded sales for eight regions and then added the totals. Each region can be considered a subsection, and Tom thinks it would look better if the region labels were indented a few spaces. You increase the indentation by roughly one character each time you click the Increase Indent button in the Alignment group on the Home tab. To decrease or remove an indentation, click the Decrease Indent button. You'll increase the indent for the region labels.

To indent the region labels:

1. Select the range **B7:B14;B18:B25**.

2. In the Alignment group on the Home tab, click the **Increase Indent** button ▤. Each region label indents one space.

3. Click cell **A6** to deselect the range. See Figure 2-11.

Centered and indented text | **Figure 2-11**

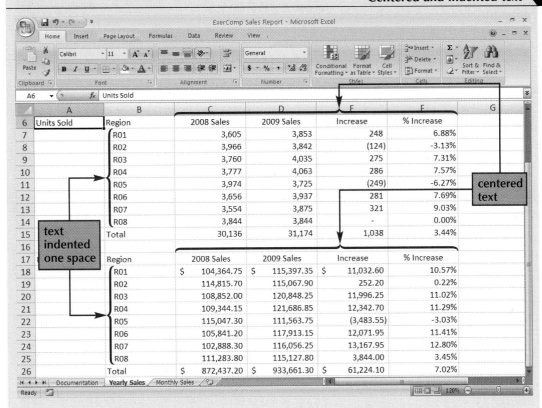

You can make all text visible within a cell rather than extending the text into an adjacent empty cell or truncating it. Just click the Wrap Text button 📑 in the Alignment group on the Home tab. The row height increases as needed to wrap all the text within the cell.

Merging Cells

In the Yearly Sales worksheet, Tom wants the title "X310 Yearly Sales Analysis" in cell A4 centered over columns A through F. So far, you've aligned text only *within* a cell. One way to align text over several columns or rows is to **merge**, or combine, several cells into one cell. When you merge cells, only the content from the upper-left cell in the range is retained and the upper-left cell becomes the merged cell reference.

After you merge a range into a single cell, you can realign its content. The Merge button in the Alignment group on the Home tab includes a variety of merge options. Merge & Center merges the range into one cell and horizontally centers the content. Merge Across merges each of the rows in the selected range across the columns in the range. Merge Cells merges the range into a single cell, but does not horizontally center the cell content. Unmerge Cells reverses a merge, returning the merged cell back into a range of individual cells.

Tom wants you to merge and center the title in cell A4 across the range A4:F4.

To merge and center the range with the title:

▶ **1.** Select the range **A4:F4**.

▶ **2.** In the Alignment group on the Home tab, click the **Merge & Center** button. The range A4:F4 merges into one cell with a cell reference of A4 and the text is centered within the cell. See Figure 2-12.

Figure 2-12 ▶ **Merged range with centered text**

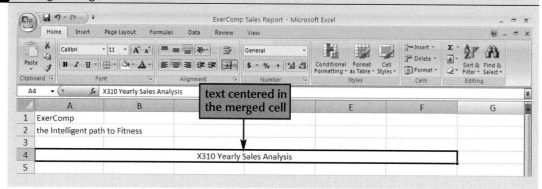

Rotating Cell Content

Text and numbers are oriented within a cell horizontally from left to right. To save space or to provide visual interest to a worksheet, you can rotate the cell contents so that they appear at any angle or orientation. These options are available on the Orientation button in the Alignment group on the Home tab.

Tom wants you to merge and center the ranges with the labels, and then rotate the labels in the merged cells A6 and A17 so they look better and take up less room.

To rotate the labels:

▶ **1.** Select the range **A6:A15**.

▶ **2.** In the Alignment group on the Home tab, click the **Merge & Center** button. The text from cell A6 is centered in the merged cell.

▶ **3.** In the Alignment group, click the **Orientation** button, and then click **Rotate Text Up**. The cell text rotates 90 degrees counterclockwise.

▶ **4.** In the Alignment group, click the **Middle Align** button. The rotated text vertically aligns within the merged cell.

▶ **5.** Select the range **A17:A26**, and then repeat Steps 2 through 4 to merge and center, rotate, and align the text.

▶ **6.** Reduce the width of column A to **5** characters. See Figure 2-13.

Merged and rotated cell text ◄ **Figure 2-13**

	A	B	C	D	E	F	G	H
6		Region	2008 Sales	2009 Sales	Increase	% Increase		
7		R01	3,605	3,853	248	6.88%		
8		R02	3,966	3,842	(124)	-3.13%		
9		R03	3,760	4,035	275	7.31%		
10	Units Sold	R04	3,777	4,063	286	7.57%		
11		R05	3,974	3,725	(249)	-6.27%		
12		R06	3,656	3,937	281	7.69%		
13		R07	3,554	3,875	321	9.03%		
14		R08	3,844	3,844	-	0.00%		
15		Total	30,136	31,174	1,038	3.44%		
16								
17		Region	Sales	2009 Sales	Increase	% Increase		
18		R01	$ 104,364.75	$ 115,397.35	$ 11,032.60	10.57%		
19		R02	114,815.70	115,067.90	252.20	0.22%		
20		R03	108,852.00	120,848.25	11,996.25	11.02%		
21	Revenue	R04	109,344.15	121,686.85	12,342.70	11.29%		
22		R05	115,047.30	111,563.75	(3,483.55)	-3.03%		
23		R06	105,841.20	117,913.15	12,071.95	11.41%		
24		R07	102,888.30	116,056.25	13,167.95	12.80%		
25		R08	111,283.80	115,127.80	3,844.00	3.45%		
26		Total	$ 872,437.20	$ 933,661.30	$ 61,224.10	7.02%		

rotated labels take up less space in the merged cells

Documentation | **Yearly Sales** | Monthly Sales

Ready   120%

Adding Cell Borders

When a worksheet is printed, the gridlines that surround the cells are not printed by default. Sometimes you will want to include such lines to enhance the readability of the rows and columns of data. One way to do this is by adding a line, or **border**, around a cell or range. You can add borders to the left, top, right, or bottom of a cell or range, around an entire cell, or around the outside edges of a range. You can also specify the thickness of and the number of lines in the border. To create a border, use the Border button located in the Font group on the Home tab.

Tom wants you to add borders to the column titles and Total rows. Standard accounting practice is to add a single top border and a double bottom border to the Total row to clearly identify a summary row from financial data.

To add cell borders to the column labels and Total rows:

▶ **1.** Select the range **B6:F6;B17:F17**. You'll add a bottom border to these column labels.

▶ **2.** In the Font group on the Home tab, click the **Border button arrow** , and then click **Bottom Border**. A bottom border is added to the selected cells.

▶ **3.** Select the range **B15:F15;B26:F26**. You'll add top and bottom borders to these Total rows.

▶ **4.** In the Font group, click the **Border button arrow** , and then click **Top and Double Bottom Border**. The Total rows both have a single top border and a double bottom border, which is standard accounting practice.

▶ **5.** Click cell **A5** to deselect the range. See Figure 2-14.

Figure 2-14 Borders added to cells

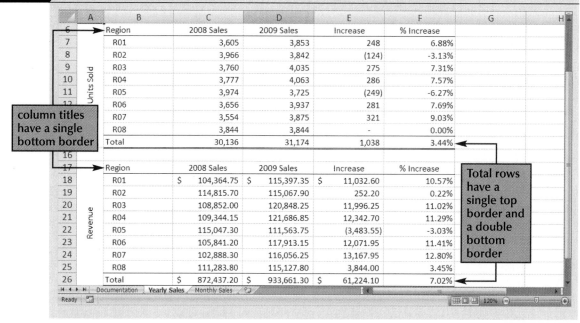

Working with the Format Cells Dialog Box

The buttons on the Home tab provide quick access to the most common formatting choices. For more options, you can use the Format Cells dialog box. For example, the numbers in cells E8 and E10 are displayed in parentheses to indicate that they are negative. Although parentheses are common in accounting to indicate negative currency values, Tom wants you to reformat the units sold numbers to display negative numbers with a minus symbol. You can do this in the Format Cells dialog box.

Tip

You can also open the Format Cells dialog box by right-clicking a cell or selected range, and then clicking Format Cells on the shortcut menu.

To open the Format Cells dialog box:

1. Select the range **C7:E15**.

2. In the Number group on the Home tab, click the **Dialog Box Launcher**. The Format Cells dialog box opens with the Number tab active.

The Format Cells dialog box has six tabs, each focusing on a different set of formatting options. You can apply the formats in this dialog box to selected worksheet cells. The six tabs are as follows:

- **Number**: Provides options for formatting the appearance of numbers, including dates and numbers treated as text (for example, telephone or Social Security numbers)
- **Alignment**: Provides options for how data is aligned within a cell
- **Font**: Provides options for selecting font types, sizes, styles, and other formatting attributes such as underlining and font colors
- **Border**: Provides options for adding cell borders
- **Fill**: Provides options for creating and applying background colors and patterns to cells
- **Protection**: Provides options for locking or hiding cells to prevent other users from modifying their contents

Although you've applied many of these formats from the Home tab, the Format Cells dialog box presents them in a different way and provides more options. You'll use the Number tab to change the number format for the selected cells. Remember, modifying the number format does not affect the value stored in the workbook.

To set the format for negative numbers of units:

▶ **1.** In the Category list on the left side of the Format Cells dialog box, click **Number**.

▶ **2.** Verify that **0** (zero) appears in the Decimal places box.

▶ **3.** Verify that the **Use 1000 Separator (,)** check box contains a check mark.

▶ **4.** In the Negative numbers list, verify that **−1,234** (the first option) is selected. See Figure 2-15.

Number tab in the Format Cells dialog box ◀ **Figure 2-15**

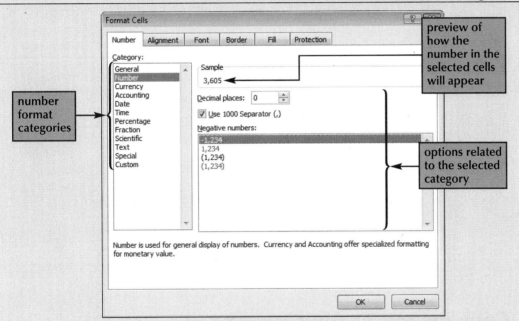

▶ **5.** Click the **OK** button. The Format Cells dialog box closes and the negative numbers in the range C7:E15 appear with minus symbols, a comma as the thousands separator, and no decimal places.

Tom wants the bottom border color used for the column titles changed from black to green. You'll use the Border tab in the Format Cells dialog box to make this change.

To set the border color for the column title cells:

▶ **1.** Select the range **B6:F6;B17:F17**.

▶ **2.** In the Font group on the Home tab, click the **Borders button arrow** [image], and then click **More Borders**. The Format Cells dialog box opens with the Border tab active.

In the Border tab, you can select a line style ranging from thick to thin, choose double to dotted lines, and place these lines anywhere around the cells in the selected range. Right now, you only want to set the border line color.

3. In the Line group, click the **Color** arrow to display the color palette, and then click **Green** (the sixth color) in the Standard Colors section.

4. Click the bottom border of the border preview. A green bottom border is added to the preview. See Figure 2-16.

Figure 2-16 | **Border tab in the Format Cells dialog box**

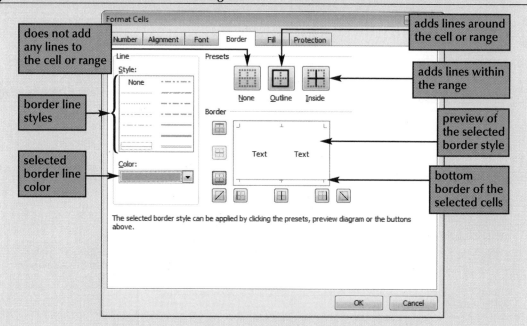

5. Click the **OK** button. The dialog box closes and the cells with column titles have a green bottom border.

Copying and Pasting Formats

You have not yet formatted the titles in cells A1 and A2 of the Yearly Sales worksheet to match the Documentation sheet. You could repeat the same steps to format these cells, but a quicker method is to copy the formats from the Documentation worksheet into the Yearly Sales worksheet.

Copying Formats with the Format Painter

The **Format Painter** copies the formatting from one cell or range to another cell or range, without duplicating any of the data. Using the Format Painter is a fast and efficient way of maintaining a consistent look and feel throughout a workbook.

You'll use the Format Painter to copy the cell formats from the range A1:A2 in the Documentation sheet into the same range in the Yearly Sales worksheet.

To copy and paste the format:

▶ **1.** Click the **Documentation** sheet tab to make that worksheet active, and then select the range **A1:A2**.

▶ **2.** In the Clipboard group on the Home tab, click the **Format Painter** button 🖋. The formats from the selected cells are copied to the Clipboard.

▶ **3.** Click the **Yearly Sales** sheet tab to make that worksheet active, and then select the range **A1:A2**. The formatting from the Documentation sheet is removed from the Clipboard and applied to the selected cells except for the red color you applied to "Comp." Format Painter does not copy formatting applied to text selections.

▶ **4.** Double-click cell **A1** to go into editing mode, and then select **Comp** in the text string.

▶ **5.** Click the **Font Color button arrow** 🅰 on the Mini toolbar, and then click **Red** (the second color) in the Standard Colors section. The selected text changes to red.

▶ **6.** Press the **Enter** key to exit editing mode.

▶ **7.** Select the range **A1:A2** in the Yearly Sales worksheet, and then repeat Steps 2 through 6 to copy the formatting to the range A1:A2 in the Monthly Sales worksheet.

Tip

To paste a format to multiple selections, double-click the Format Painter button, select each cell or range to format, and then click the Format Painter button again to turn it off.

Copying Formats with the Paste Options Button

The Format Painter copies and pastes only formatting. When you copy and paste, you can also use the Paste Options button 📋, which lets you choose whether to paste the formatting from a copied range along with its contents. As shown in Figure 2-17, each time you paste, the Paste Options button appears in the lower-right corner of the pasted cell or range. When you click the Paste Options button, you can choose from a list of pasting options, such as pasting only the values or only the formatting.

Using the Paste Options button ◀ **Figure 2-17**

	A	B	C	D	E	F	G	H	I	J
1										
2		2008 Sales	Model	R01	R02	R03	Total			
3			X310	3,605	3,996	3,760	11,361		pastes only the formats	
4			X410	1,875	1,924	2,112	5,911			
5			X510	850	912	750	2,512			
6			Total	6,330	6,832	6,622	19,784	○ Keep Source Formatting		
7								○ Use Destination Theme		
8								○ Match Destination Formatting		
9		2009 Sales	Model	R01	R02	R03	Total	○ Values Only		
10			X310	3,853	3,842	4,035	11,730	○ Values and Number Formatting		
11			X410	2,112	1,801	2,304	6,217	○ Values and Source Formatting		
12			X510	1025	1,115	912	3,052	○ Keep Source Column Widths		
13			Total	6,990	6,758	7,251	20,999	◉ Formatting Only		
14					**Paste Options button** → 📋			○ Link Cells		
15										

Copying Formats with Paste Special

The Paste Special command is another way to control what you paste from the Clipboard. To use Paste Special, select and copy a range, select the range where you want to paste the Clipboard contents, click the Paste button arrow in the Clipboard group on the Home tab, and then click Paste Special to open the dialog box shown in Figure 2-18. From the Paste Special dialog box, you can specify exactly what you want to paste.

Figure 2-18	**Paste Special dialog box**

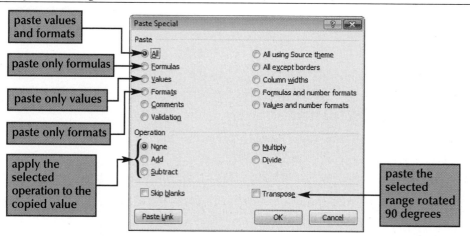

You can use the Transpose option in the Paste Special dialog box to paste a range of numbers cut from a row into a column. You can also use Paste Special to quickly modify all the values in a range. For example, you can copy the value 5 from a cell, select the range, open the Paste Special dialog box, click the Add option button in the Operation group, and then click the OK button. Excel adds 5 to every value in the selected range.

Applying Styles

A workbook often contains several cells that store the same type of data. For example, each worksheet might have a cell displaying the sheet title, or a range of financial data might have several cells containing summary totals. Using the same format on cells storing the same type of data gives your workbook a consistent look. You can do this using the Format Painter or by copying and pasting a format from one cell to another.

The Format Painter is effective, but it can also be time consuming if you have to copy the same format to many cells. Moreover, if you decide to modify the format, you must copy and paste the revised format all over again. Another way to ensure that cells displaying the same type of data use the same format is with styles. A **style** is a collection of formatting. For example, you can create a style to display sheet titles in a bold, white, 20-point Calibri font on a blue background. You can then apply that style to any sheet title in a workbook. If you later revise the style, the appearance of any cell formatted with that style is updated automatically. This saves you the time and effort of reformatting each cell individually.

Excel has a variety of built-in styles to format worksheet titles, column and row totals, and cells with emphasis. You used the built-in Currency and Percent styles when you formatted data in the Yearly Sales worksheet as currency and percentages. Some styles are connected to the workbook's current theme.

Applying Styles
| Reference Window

- Select the cell or range to which you want to apply a style.
- In the Styles group on the Home tab, click the Cell Styles button.
- Point to each style in the Cell Styles gallery to see a Live Preview of that style on the selected cell or range.
- Click the style you want to apply to the selected cell or range.

Tom asks you to use some of the built-in styles to add more color and visual interest to the Yearly Sales worksheet.

To apply built-in styles to the Yearly Sales sheet:

1. Click the **Yearly Sales** sheet tab to make that worksheet active, and then select the merged cell **A4**.

2. In the Styles group on the Home tab, click the **Cell Styles** button. The Cell Styles gallery opens.

3. Point to the **Heading 1** style in the Titles and Headings section. Live Preview shows cell A4 in a 15-point, bold font with a solid blue bottom border. See Figure 2-19.

Cell Styles gallery ◀ **Figure 2-19**

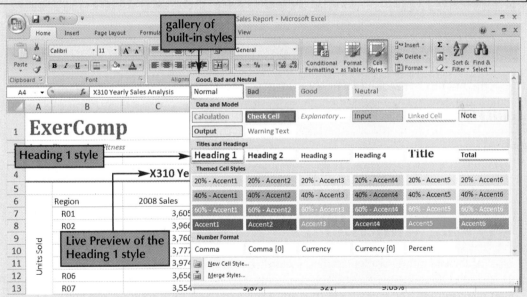

4. Move the pointer over different styles in the Cell Styles gallery to preview cell A4 with each style, and then click the **Heading 1** style. The style is applied to cell A4.

5. Select the range **B6:F6;B17:F17**, click the **Cell Styles** button, and then click the **Accent1** style in the Themed Cell Styles section. Each of the column headings is formatted.

6. Select the range **E7:F15;E18:F26**, click the **Cell Styles** button, and then click the **20% – Accent1** style in the Themed Cell Styles section. The calculated values are formatted differently from the data.

7. Click cell **F1** to deselect the range, and then zoom the worksheet to **90%**. See Figure 2-20.

Figure 2-20 Formatted yearly sales data

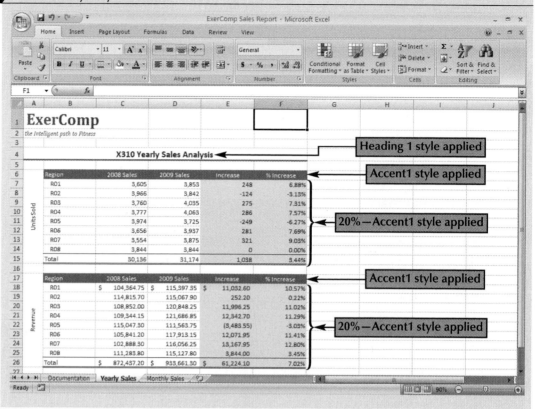

If the built-in styles don't meet your needs, you can modify an existing style or create a new one. To modify a style, right-click the style in the Cell Styles gallery, click Modify on the shortcut menu to open the Style dialog box, and then click the Format button to change the formatting for that style. Any cells formatted with that style are automatically updated. To create a new style, click New Cell Style in the Cell Styles gallery to open the Style dialog box, type a name in the Style name box, and then click the Format button to select the formatting for that style. The new cell style is added to the Cell Styles gallery.

Working with Themes

Most of the formatting you've applied so far is based on the workbook's current theme—the default Office theme. As you've seen, fonts, colors, and cell styles are organized in theme and non-theme categories. The appearance of these fonts, colors, and cell styles depends on the workbook's current theme. If you change the theme, the formatting of these elements also changes.

You'll change the workbook's theme to see its effect on the workbook's appearance.

To change the workbook's theme:

1. Click the **Page Layout** tab on the Ribbon, and then, in the Themes group, click the **Themes** button. The Themes gallery opens. Office—the current theme—is the default.

2. Point to each theme in the Themes gallery. Live Preview shows the impact of each theme on the appearance of the Yearly Sales worksheet.

3. Click the **Aspect** theme. The Aspect theme is applied to the workbook. See Figure 2-21.

Yearly Sales data with the Aspect theme applied **Figure 2-21**

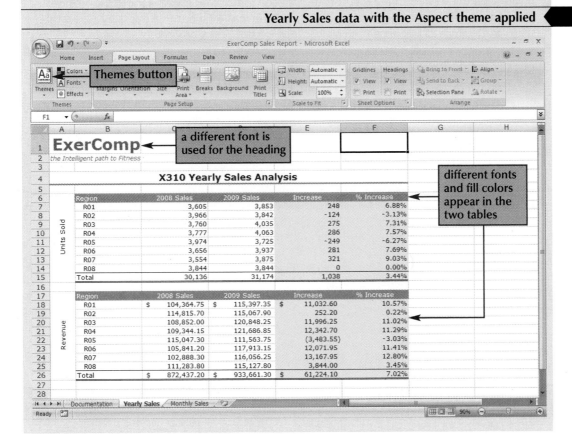

Changing the theme has made a significant difference in the worksheet's appearance. The most obvious changes are the fill colors and the fonts. Only elements directly tied to a theme change when you select a different theme. The cells you formatted with the Accent1 cell style changed because the Accent1 color is blue in the Office theme and orange in the Aspect theme. The Heading 1 style you used for the titles in cells A1 and A2 uses the Cambria typeface in the Office theme and the Verdana typeface in the Aspect theme. The Aspect theme also uses a different font for body text, which is why the rest of the text changed size and appearance.

The logo colors in cell A1 did not change because you used two standard colors, blue and red, which are not part of a theme. Changing the theme does not affect these colors.

Tom prefers the default Office theme, so you'll switch back to that theme and then save the workbook.

To select the Office theme and save the workbook:

1. In the Themes group on the Page Layout tab, click the **Themes** button, and then click the **Office** theme.

2. Save your changes to the workbook.

InSight	**Sharing Styles and Themes**

If you're part of a team creating files with Microsoft Office, you might want to use a common style and design theme for all your projects. The easiest way to do this is by saving the styles and themes as permanent files other members of your workgroup can use.

To copy a style from one workbook to another, open the workbook with the styles you want to copy, and then open the workbook in which you want to copy those styles. In the Styles group on the Home tab, click the Cell Styles button, and then click Merge Styles. The Merge Styles dialog box opens, listing the currently open workbooks. Select the workbook with the styles you want to copy, and then click the OK button to copy those styles into the current workbook. If you modify any styles, you must copy the styles to the other workbook; Excel does not update styles between workbooks.

You can save a workbook's theme as a file that can be used in other workbooks or Office files. Microsoft Excel, Word, and PowerPoint use the same file format for their theme files. To save a theme, in the Themes group on the Page Layout tab, click the Themes button, and then click Save Current Theme. The Save Current Theme dialog box opens. Select a save location (in a default Theme folder on your computer or another folder), type a descriptive name in the File name box, and then click the Save button. A Theme file saved in a default Theme folder appears in the Themes gallery, and any changes made to the theme are reflected in any Office file that uses that theme.

You've completed some formatting of Tom's workbook. In the process, you've formatted cells and ranges, applied built-in styles, and applied a new theme. In the next session, you'll work with table styles, conditional formatting, and page layout tools.

Review	**Session 2.1 Quick Check**

1. What is the difference between a serif font and a sans serif font?
2. What is the difference between a standard color and a theme color?
3. What is the General number format?
4. Why are dates right-aligned within a worksheet cell by default?
5. The range A1:C5 is merged into a single cell. What is the cell reference of this merged cell?
6. Where can you access all the formatting options for worksheet cells?
7. You want the range A1:A3 on all the worksheets in your workbook to be formatted the same way. Discuss two methods of applying the same format to different ranges.

Session 2.2

Formatting the Monthly Sales Worksheet

The Monthly Sales worksheet contains the sales results by month for the eight sales regions in 2008 and 2009. Tom's main goal for this data is to identify trends. He's more interested in the "big picture" than in specific numbers. He wants to know which sales regions are performing well, which are underperforming, and, in general, how the sales change throughout the year.

The top of the worksheet contains sales for 2008 and 2009. The bottom of the worksheet displays the increase in sales from 2008 to 2009 for each region and month. You need to calculate the monthly totals and do some basic formatting.

To calculate the monthly totals:

▶ 1. If you took a break after the previous session, open the ExerComp Sales Report workbook located in the Tutorial.02\Tutorial folder included with your Data Files.

▶ 2. Click the **Monthly Sales** sheet tab to make the worksheet active, and then, in cells B19, B34, B49, K6, K21, and K36, enter **Total**.

▶ 3. Select the range **K7:K18;K22:K33;K37:K48**, and then click the **Home** tab on the Ribbon.

▶ 4. In the Editing group, click the **Sum** button Σ to add the total of each row.

▶ 5. Select the range **C19:K19;C34:K34;C49:K49**, and then, in the Editing group, click the **Sum** button Σ to add the total of each column.

Next, you'll format the row and column titles.

To format the titles:

▶ 1. Select the range **A4:K4**, and then, in the Alignment group on the Home tab, click the **Merge & Center** button. The title is centered in the merged cell.

▶ 2. In the Styles group, click the **Cell Styles** button, and then click the **Heading 1** style. The Heading 1 style is applied to the title.

▶ 3. Select the range **A6:A19;A21:A34;A36:A49**, and then, in the Alignment group, click the **Merge & Center** button. The labels are centered in the merged cells.

▶ 4. In the Alignment group, click the **Orientation** button, and then click **Rotate Text Up**. The text in the three cells rotates 90 degrees.

▶ 5. In the Alignment group, click the **Middle Align** button. The text is centered both horizontally and vertically in the cells.

▶ 6. Reduce the width of column A to **5** characters.

▶ 7. Select the range **C7:K19;C22:K34;C37:K49**, and then, in the Number group, click the **Dialog Box Launcher**. The Format Cells dialog box opens with the Number tab displayed.

▶ 8. Click **Number** in the Category list, type **0** (a zero) in the Decimal places box, click the **Use 1000 Separator (,)** check box to insert a check mark, verify that the **−1,234** option is selected, and then click the **OK** button. The numbers display a thousands separator and use a minus symbol for negatives.

▶ 9. Click cell **A1** to deselect the cells. Figure 2-22 shows the formatted Monthly Sales worksheet for the first range. The other ranges are formatted similarly.

Figure 2-22 **Monthly Sales worksheet with formulas and formatting**

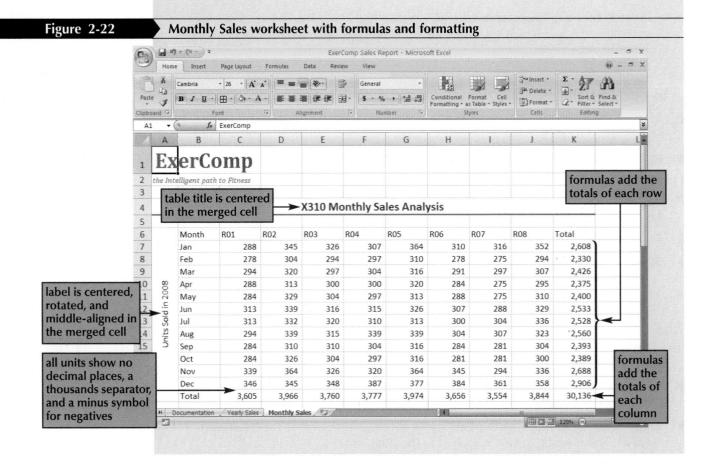

Working with Table Styles

You can treat a range of data as a distinct object in a worksheet known as an **Excel table**. After you identify a range as an Excel table, you can apply a **table style** that formats the entire table as a single unit. Excel tables can include some common elements, such as a header row that contains titles for the different columns in the table and a total row that contains formulas summarizing the values in the table's data. A table style specifies formats for each of these elements, such as font color, fill color, and so forth. Formatting an entire table with a table style is more efficient than formatting individual cells in the range.

Reference Window | **Applying a Table Style to an Existing Table**

- Select the range to which you want to apply the table style.
- In the Styles group on the Home tab, click the Format as Table button.
- Click a table style in the Table Style gallery.

A table style will update the table's formatting to reflect changes you make to the table, such as adding or deleting table rows or columns. For example, many tables display alternate rows with different fill colors. This effect, known as **banded rows**, makes the text easier to read, especially in large tables with many rows. You could create the banded rows effect by applying a cell style with a background fill to every other row in the table, but then, if you add or delete a row from the table, the banded rows effect might be lost. A table style, on the other hand, applies alternating row colors to the entire Excel table and adjusts the banded rows effect as needed if you add or delete rows. This is because a table style treats the table as a single object rather than a collection of cells. Figure 2-23 shows the banded rows effect applied both manually and with a table style.

Banded rows effect applied manually and with a table style ◄ **Figure 2-23**

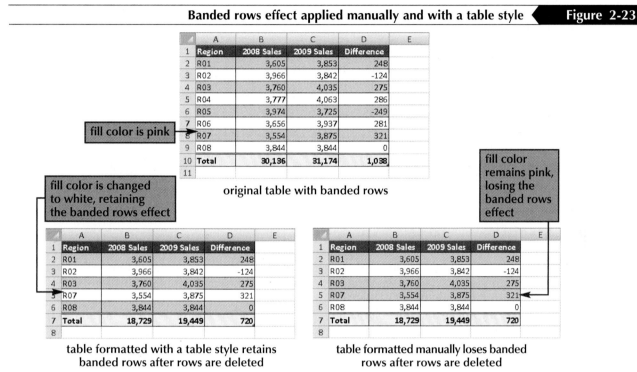

original table with banded rows

table formatted with a table style retains banded rows after rows are deleted

table formatted manually loses banded rows after rows are deleted

Tom wants you to format the 2008, 2009, and sales increase data in the Monthly Sales worksheet as Excel tables. First, you'll apply a table style to the units sold in 2008 data.

To apply a table style to the units sold in 2008 data:

1. Select the range **B6:K19**.

2. In the Styles group on the Home tab, click the **Format as Table** button, and then click **Table Style Medium 2** (the second style in the first row in the Medium section). The Format as Table dialog box opens, confirming the range you selected for the table and whether the table includes header rows.

3. Verify that the range is **=$B$6:$K$19**, verify that the **My table has headers** check box contains a check mark, and then click the **OK** button. The table style is applied.

4. Click cell **A5** to deselect the range. See Figure 2-24.

Figure 2-24 **Data formatted with a table style**

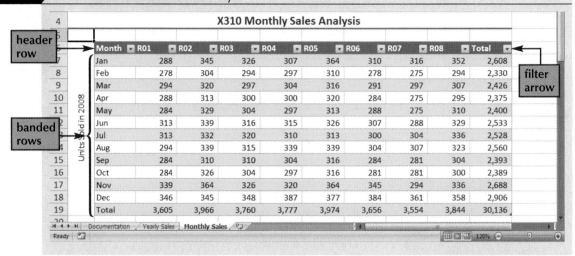

The table style treated the range as a single unit and modified its overall appearance. In this case, Table Style Medium 2 formatted the range so the header row appears in a white font on a blue fill and the remaining rows are formatted as banded rows.

Applying a table style also marks the range as a table, making available tools designed for analyzing tabular data, such as the ability to sort data, transfer data to and from an external file, and filter the data to show only those rows that match specified criteria. The filter arrows next to the column titles in the header row are used for filtering and sorting the table. Tom doesn't want to filter or sort the data right now; he asks you to remove the arrows so he can focus on the table data.

To remove the filter arrows from the table:

▶ **1.** Click cell **B6** to make the table active, and then click the **Data** tab on the Ribbon.

▶ **2.** In the Sort & Filter group, click the **Filter** button. The filter arrows disappear from the header row.

Selecting Table Style Options

After you apply a table style, you can choose which table elements you want included in the style. Table styles have six elements that can be turned on or off: (1) Header Row, which formats the first row of the table; (2) Total Row, which inserts a new row at the bottom of the table that adds the column values; (3) First Column, which formats the first column of the table; (4) Last Column, which formats the last column of the table; (5) Banded Rows, which formats alternating rows in different colors; and (6) Banded Columns, which formats alternating columns in different colors. For example, if you turn on the Header Row option, you can specify a format for the table's first row, which usually contains text that describes the contents of each table column. If you insert a new row at the top of the table, the new row becomes the header row and is formatted with the table style.

In the table style you just used, only the Header Row and Banded Rows options are turned on. Although the other elements are still part of the table structure, the current style does not format them. Tom wants you to format the table's last column and the header row and remove the banded rows effect.

To select the table style options:

▶ **1.** If necessary, click cell **B6** to make the table active.

▶ **2.** Click the **Design** tab on the Ribbon. The table design options appear on the Ribbon.

▶ **3.** In the Table Style Options group, click the **Last Column** check box to insert a check mark. The last column is formatted.

▶ **4.** In the Table Style Options group, click the **Banded Rows** check box to remove the check mark. The banded rows are removed from the table.

Only the Header Row and Last Column elements appear in the table. You'll use a built-in table style to format them.

▶ **5.** In the Table Styles group, click the **More** button to open the Table Styles gallery, and then, in the Medium section, click **Table Style Medium 20** (the third table style in the sixth column). The table styles in the gallery show the formatting applied to the current table elements. See Figure 2-25.

Tip

To select a table style option, you can click in the table to make it active. You do not need to select the entire table.

Revised table style | Figure 2-25

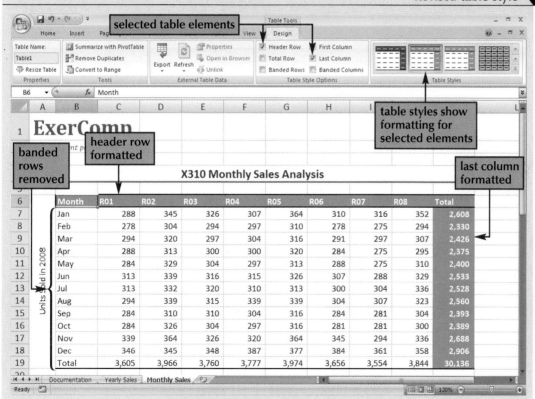

A table style might not format a table exactly the way you want. For example, Tom wants the column titles in the header row to be centered and the Total row to have a single top border and a double bottom border. Because the table style you used does not include either of these formats, you'll add these formats to the table cells. You can use cell styles and the formatting tools you've used with individual cells and ranges to format Excel tables.

To format the header row and the Total row:

▶ 1. Select the range **C6:K6**, click the **Home** tab on the Ribbon, and then, in the Alignment group, click the **Center** button ▤. The column titles are centered.

▶ 2. Select the range **B19:K19**.

▶ 3. In the Styles group, click the **Cell Styles** button, and then, in the Titles and Headings section, click **Total** (the sixth cell style).

▶ 4. Click cell **A5** to deselect the range. The Total row is formatted in bold with a single top border and a double bottom border.

Tom likes the formatting of the first table, and wants you to format the other two tables similarly. You cannot use the Format Painter to copy table formats, and you must format each range as a table separately.

To format the other two tables:

▶ 1. Select the range **B21:K34**.

▶ 2. In the Styles group on the Home tab, click the **Format as Table** button, click **Table Style Medium 6** (the sixth table style in the first row of the Medium section), and then click the **OK** button in the Format as Table dialog box.

▶ 3. Click the **Data** tab on the Ribbon, and then, in the Sort & Filter group, click the **Filter** button to turn off the filter arrows.

▶ 4. Click the **Design** tab on the Ribbon, and then, in the Table Style Options group, click the **Banded Rows** check box to remove the check mark and click the **Last Column** check box to insert a check mark.

▶ 5. In the Table Styles group, click the **More** button, and then click **Table Style Medium 20** (the sixth table style in the third row of the Medium section).

▶ 6. Select the range **C21:K21**, click the **Home** tab on the Ribbon, and then, in the Alignment group, click the **Center** button ▤.

▶ 7. Select the range **B34:K34**. You'll apply the Total cell style to this range.

▶ 8. In the Styles group, click the **Cell Styles** button, and then click **Total** (the sixth cell style in the Titles and Headings section).

▶ 9. Select the range **B36:K49** and repeat Steps 2 through 5, select the range **C36:K36** and repeat Step 6, and then select the range **B49:K49** and repeat Step 8.

Introducing Conditional Formats

So far, you have used formatting to make the workbook more readable or visually interesting. Formatting can also help you analyze data by highlighting significant numbers or trends in the data. Tom wants the sales report to highlight sales regions that have performed particularly well or done poorly in the past two years. Tom also wants to show how sales of the X310 heart rate monitor changed during the year. This information can help him plan inventory for the next year as well as project future sales and revenue.

To prepare this kind of report, you can use conditional formatting. A **conditional format** applies formatting only when a cell's value meets a specified condition. For example, a conditional format can make negative numbers red and positive numbers black. Conditional formats are dynamic, so a cell's appearance will change to reflect its current value.

Excel has four conditional formats—data bars, highlighting, color scales, and icon sets. This tutorial looks at data bars and cell highlighting.

Applying Conditional Formats (Data Bars and Highlights) | Reference Window

- Select the range or ranges to which you want to add data bars.
- In the Styles group on the Home tab, click the Conditional Formatting button, point to Data Bars, and then click a data bar color.

or

- Select the range in which you want to highlight cells that match a specified rule.
- In the Styles group, click the Conditional Formatting button, point to Highlight Cells Rules or Top/Bottom Rules, and then click the appropriate rule.
- Select the appropriate options in the dialog box, and then click the OK button.

Adding Data Bars

A **data bar** is a horizontal bar added to the background of a cell to provide a visual indicator of the cell's value. Larger values are associated with longer data bars; smaller values are associated with shorter data bars. Data bars will help Tom see how the 2008 and 2009 sales totals vary throughout the year.

To format the 2008 monthly sales with data bars:

▶ 1. Select the range **K7:K18**.

▶ 2. In the Styles group on the Home tab, click the **Conditional Formatting** button, point to **Data Bars** to open the Data Bars gallery, and then click **Purple Data Bar** (the third data bar in the second row of the Data Bars gallery). Data bars appear for the 2008 monthly sales.

▶ 3. Click cell **A3** to deselect the range. See Figure 2-26.

Data bars added to the 2008 monthly sales ◀ Figure 2-26

Month	R01	R02	R03	R04	R05	R06	R07	R08	Total
Jan	288	345	326	307	364	310	316	352	2,608
Feb	278	304	294	297	310	278	275	294	2,330
Mar	294	320	297	304	316	291	297	307	2,426
Apr	288	313	300	300	320	284	275	295	2,375
May	284	329	304	297	313	288	275	310	2,400
Jun	313	339	316	315	326	307	288	329	2,533
Jul	313	332	320	310	313	300	304	336	2,528
Aug	294	339	315	339	339	304	307	323	2,560
Sep	284	310	310	304	316	284	281	304	2,393
Oct	284	326	304	297	316	281	281	300	2,389
Nov	339	364	326	320	364	345	294	336	2,688
Dec	346	345	348	387	377	384	361	358	2,906
Total	**3,605**	**3,966**	**3,760**	**3,777**	**3,974**	**3,656**	**3,554**	**3,844**	30,136

Units Sold in 2008

data bar length is based on the cell value

Month	R01	R02	R03	R04	R05	R06	R07		
Jan	352	364	345	352	336	361			
Feb	297	326	310	313	288	300			

Documentation   Yearly Sales   Monthly Sales

Ready

The data bars highlight several important facts that might not be immediately apparent from viewing the cell values. First, the highest sales occurred during the months of November, December, and January—a reflection of heavy shopping during the holiday season. Second, an increase in sales occurred during the summer months. Again, this is expected because customers are more physically active during those months and likely to purchase a heart rate monitor. Third, the periods of lowest sales occurred in the spring and fall. To find out if all of the sales regions reflect this seasonal trend, you'll add data bars to the individual sales region figures.

To add data bars for all sales regions:

▶ **1.** Select the range **C7:J18**.

▶ **2.** In the Styles group on the Home tab, click the **Conditional Formatting** button, point to **Data Bars**, and then click **Light Blue Data Bar** (the second data bar in the second row of the Data Bars gallery). Monthly data bars appear for all the sales regions in 2008.

▶ **3.** Click cell **A3** to deselect the range. See Figure 2-27.

| Figure 2-27 | Data bars added to the regional monthly sales data |

January sales for the R01 region are lower than expected

For the most part, the seasonal trend is reflected in all the sales regions, with some exceptions. For example, the R01 region had lower-than-expected sales during January 2008. Tom discovers that a distribution problem prevented several stores in the R01 region from receiving its stock of ExerComp heart rate monitors until near the end of January, causing the decreased sales totals. Data bars highlight this important piece of information.

Data bar lengths depend on the values in the selected range. The largest value in the range has the longest data bar; the smallest value has the shortest data bar. For example, in the Total column, the shortest data bar represents the February total of 2,330 and the longest data bar represents the December total of 2,906. You should use different colored data bars to distinguish data bars for different ranges. For example, you used blue data bars for the regional sales and purple data bars for the totals.

Because data bar lengths are based on the values in the range, changing the value of one cell in the range can affect the size of all the other cells' data bars. You'll change the units sold value in cell C7 and see how this affects the data bars.

To see the effect on data bars of changing a units sold value:

▶ **1.** In cell C7, enter **588**. The lengths of all the data bars in the 2008 sales table change to reflect this increased value.

▶ **2.** On the Quick Access Toolbar, click the **Undo** button 🔄 . The value in cell C7 returns to 288, its original value.

Clearing a Conditional Format

Tom wants you to add data bars to the 2009 sales table. You can base the data bars on the values in only the 2009 sales table, or you can base them on the values in both the 2008 and 2009 sales tables. Both approaches have advantages. Basing the data bars on only the 2009 sales allows you to focus on that data and see more detail on the seasonal and regional trends within that year. However, basing the data bars on sales results from both years makes it easier to compare sales trends from one year to another. Tom wants you to base the length of the data bars on the values from both years. First, you need to remove the data bars you created for the 2008 sales table. Then, you can add a new set of data bars based on a different selection of cells.

To clear the data bars from the 2008 sales table:

▶ **1.** If necessary, click cell **C7** to select it and make the table active.

▶ **2.** In the Styles group on the Home tab, click the **Conditional Formatting** button, point to **Clear Rules**, and then click **Clear Rules from This Table**. Both sets of data bars are removed from the 2008 sales table.

Next, you'll add data bars for the sales data in both the 2008 and 2009 sales tables.

> **Tip**
>
> To remove all conditional formatting from a worksheet, click Clear Rules from Entire Sheet. To remove it from the selected range, click Clear Rules from Selected Cells.

To add data bars to both the 2008 and 2009 sales tables:

▶ **1.** Select the range **K7:K18;K22:K33**. This selects the 2008 and 2009 monthly sales totals.

▶ **2.** In the Styles group on the Home tab, click the **Conditional Formatting** button, point to **Data Bars**, and then click **Purple Data Bar** (the third data bar in the second row of the Data Bars gallery).

▶ **3.** Select the range **C7:J18;C22:J33**. This selects the 2008 and 2009 monthly sales for each region.

▶ **4.** In the Styles group, click the **Conditional Formatting** button, point to **Data Bars**, and then click **Light Blue Data Bar** (the second data bar in the second row of the Data Bars gallery).

▶ **5.** Click cell **A20** to deselect the range. See Figure 2-28.

Figure 2-28 | **Data bars added to the 2008 and 2009 sales tables**

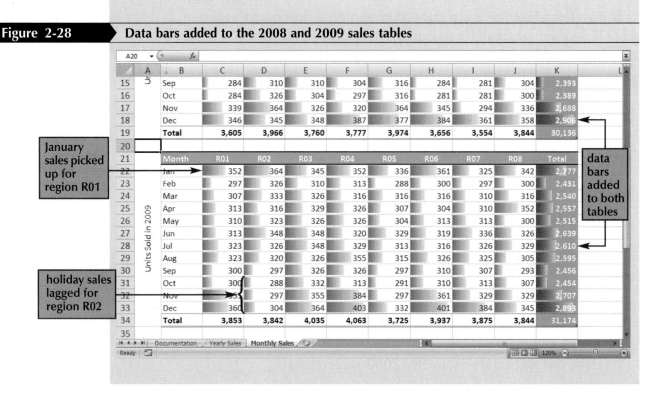

January sales picked up for region R01

holiday sales lagged for region R02

data bars added to both tables

Tom sees some of the same seasonal trends in 2009 as he saw for 2008. He notes that sales in the R01 region did not lag as they did in 2008, but sales in the R02 region were lower than expected during the holiday season. Other than that, it's hard to compare the regional and monthly sales to determine any trends from 2008 to 2009. He knows that, overall, the number of heart rate monitors sold increased in 2009, but he doesn't know if this is true for all regions and for all months. Tom wants to highlight those sales regions and months in which sales increased from 2008 to 2009.

Highlighting Cells

The third table shows the increase in sales from 2008 to 2009, which is the data that Tom wants to analyze. Because Tom wants to highlight those regions and months in 2008 in which the sales increased, you'll highlight only those cells that contain positive values. Highlighting cells based on their values is another type of conditional format. Figure 2-29 describes some of the ways that cells can be highlighted.

Figure 2-29 | **Highlighting rules**

Rule	Highlights
Greater Than	Cells that are greater than a specified number
Less Than	Cells that are less than a specified number
Between	Cells that are between two specified numbers
Equal To	Cells that are equal to a specified number
Text That Contains	Cells that contain specified text
A Date Occurring	Cells that contain a specified date
Duplicate Values	Cells that contain duplicate or unique values

Tom wants you to highlight all the positive numbers in the third table to show those months and sales regions that increased sales from 2008 to 2009.

To highlight the positive sales numbers:

▶ 1. Select the range **C37:J48**. This selects the difference in sales by region and month for 2008 and 2009.

▶ 2. In the Styles group on the Home tab, click the **Conditional Formatting** button, point to **Highlight Cells Rules**, and then click **Greater Than**. The Greater Than dialog box opens. You want to highlight positive sales numbers, which are numbers greater than zero.

▶ 3. Type **0** (a zero) in the Format cells that are GREATER THAN box, click the **with** arrow, and then click **Green Fill with Dark Green Text**.

▶ 4. Click the **OK** button to apply the highlight rule.

▶ 5. Click cell **A35** to deselect the range. Cells with positive numbers are highlighted in green. See Figure 2-30.

Positive cells highlighted ◀ **Figure 2-30**

Month	R01	R02	R03	R04	R05	R06	R07	R08	Total
Jan	64	19	19	45	-28	51	9	-10	169
Feb	19	22	16	16	-22	22	22	6	101
Mar	13	13	29	12	0	25	13	9	114
Apr	25	3	29	26	-13	20	35	57	182
May	26	-6	22	29	-9	25	38	-10	115
Jun	0	9	32	5	3	12	48	-3	106
Jul	10	-6	28	19	0	16	22	-7	82
Aug	29	-19	11	16	-24	22	18	-18	35
Sep	16	-13	16	22	-19	26	26	-11	63
Oct	16	-38	28	16	-25	29	32	7	65
Nov	16	-67	29	64	-67	16	35	-7	19
Dec	14	-41	16	16	-45	17	23	-13	-13
Total	248	-124	275	286	-249	281	321	0	1,038

Net Increase from 2008 to 2009

green cells indicate an increase in sales from 2008 to 2009

Documentation / Yearly Sales / **Monthly Sales**

Ready   120%

From the highlighting, you can tell that most regions and months had increased sales in 2009. Most of the declines occurred in regions R02, R05, and R08. Tom wonders if some months or regions had particularly strong sales increases. You'll remove the current highlighting, and then highlight the top 10% in sales increases.

To highlight the top 10 percent in sales increases:

▶ 1. Select the range **C37:J48**.

▶ 2. In the Styles group on the Home tab, click the **Conditional Formatting** button, point to **Clear Rules**, and then click **Clear Rules from Selected Cells**. The current highlighting is removed.

▶ 3. In the Styles group, click the **Conditional Formatting** button, point to **Top/Bottom Rules**, and then click **Top 10 %**. The Top 10% dialog box opens.

▶ 4. Verify that **10** is entered in the % box, click the **with** arrow, and then click **Green Fill with Dark Green Text**.

▶ 5. Click the **OK** button. Cells whose sales increases for 2008 and 2009 were in the top 10% are highlighted in green.

▶ 6. Click cell **A35** to deselect the range. See Figure 2-31.

| Figure 2-31 | Top 10% sales increases highlighted |

green cells indicate sales increases that were in the top 10%

Month	R01	R02	R03	R04	R05	R06	R07	R08	Total
Jan	64	19	19	45	-28	51	9	-10	169
Feb	19	22	16	16	-22	22	22	6	101
Mar	13	13	29	12	0	25	13	9	114
Apr	25	3	29	26	-13	20	35	57	182
May	26	-6	22	29	-9	25	38	-10	115
Jun	0	9	32	5	3	12	48	-3	106
Jul	10	-6	28	19	0	16	22	-7	82
Aug	29	-19	11	16	-24	22	18	-18	35
Sep	16	-13	16	22	-19	26	26	-11	63
Oct	16	-38	28	16	-25	29	32	7	65
Nov	16	-67	29	64	-67	16	35	-7	19
Dec	14	-41	16	16	-45	17	23	-13	-13
Total	248	-124	275	286	-249	281	321	0	1,038

Net Increase from 2008 to 2009

Documentation / Yearly Sales / **Monthly Sales**

The results provide Tom with some interesting information. For example, region R08, which underperformed for most of the year, had one of the largest sales increases during April (cell J40). In fact, the increase in sales during that one month compensated for the sales declines in other months, so that by the end of the year, region R08 showed no overall decline in sales. Also, region R01 had a large increase in sales during January 2009, indicating that this region fixed the distribution problems that occurred in 2008. Finally, of the nine cells highlighted in the table, four of them come from region R07, three of those occurring during the usually slow spring months.

Tom wonders what insights he could gain from highlighting the bottom 10% of the table—the regions and months that showed the lowest sales increases in 2009.

To highlight the bottom 10 percent in sales increases:

1. Select the range **C37:J48**.

2. In the Styles group on the Home tab, click the **Conditional Formatting** button, point to **Top/Bottom Rules**, and then click **Bottom 10 %**. The Bottom 10% dialog box opens.

3. Verify that **10** is entered in the % box and **Light Red Fill with Dark Red Text** is selected in the with box, and then click the **OK** button. Red cells highlight the regions and months that placed in the bottom 10% for sales increases from 2008 to 2009.

4. Click cell **A35** to deselect the range. See Figure 2-32.

Bottom 10% of sales increases highlighted ◄ Figure 2-32

Month	R01	R02	R03	R04	R05	R06	R07	R08	Total
Jan	64	19	19	45	-28	51	9	-10	169
Feb	19	22	16	16	-22	22	22	6	101
Mar	13	13	29	12	0	25	13	9	114
Apr	25	3	29	26	-13	20	35	57	182
May	26	-6	22	29	-9	25	38	-10	115
Jun	0	9	32	5	3	12	48	-3	106
Jul	10	-6	28	19	0	16	22	-7	82
Aug	29	-19	11	16	-24	22	18	-18	35
Sep	16	-13	16	22	-19	26	26	-11	63
Oct	16	-38	28	16	-25	29	32	7	65
Nov	16	-67	29	64	-67	16	35	-7	19
Dec	14	-41	16	16	-45	17	23	-13	-13
Total	248	-124	275	286	-249	281	321	0	1,038

Net Increase from 2008 to 2009

red cells indicate sales increases were in the bottom 10%

Documentation / Yearly Sales / Monthly Sales /
Ready   120%

Tom immediately sees that the bottom 10% come from only regions R02 and R05, and that six of the nine cells highlighted occurred in the most recent months: October, November, and December. Conditional formatting has helped Tom isolate and highlight potential problem areas, which he can investigate further.

When you use conditional formatting to highlight cells in a worksheet, you should always include a **legend**, which is a key that shows each color used in the worksheet and what it means, so others know why certain cells are highlighted. Tom asks you to add a legend to the Monthly Sales worksheet.

To create a conditional formatting legend:

▶ 1. In cell D51, enter **light red**, and then click cell **D51** to select it. You'll use a highlight rule to fill this cell with the light red color used for the bottom 10% sales increases.

▶ 2. In the Styles group on the Home tab, click the **Conditional Formatting** button, point to **Highlight Cells Rules**, and then click **Text that Contains**. The Text That Contains dialog box opens.

▶ 3. Verify that **light red** appears in the Format cells that contain the text box, select **Light Red Fill with Dark Red Text** in the with box, and then click the **OK** button. Cell D51 is filled with the same light red fill color used for the bottom 10% values.

▶ 4. In cell D52, enter **light green**, and then click cell **D52** to select it. You'll use a highlight rule to fill this cell with the green color used for the top 10% sales increases.

▶ 5. In the Styles group on the Home tab, click the **Conditional Formatting** button, point to **Hightlight Cells Rules**, and then click **Text that Contains**. The Text That Contains dialog box opens.

▶ 6. Verify that **light green** appears in the Format cells that contain the text box, select **Green Fill with Dark Green Text** in the with box, and then click the **OK** button. Cell D52 is filled with the same light green fill color used for the top 10% values.

▶ 7. In cell E51, enter **Bottom 10% in terms of sales increase**, and then, in cell E52, enter **Top 10% in terms of sales increase**.

▶ **8.** Select the range **E51:E52**. You'll format these cells with a cell style to distinguish them from the rest of the text in the worksheet.

▶ **9.** In the Styles group, click the **Cell Styles** button, and then, in the Date and Model group, click **Explanatory** (the third cell style in the first row).

▶ **10.** Click cell **A35** to deselect the range. See Figure 2-33.

| Figure 2-33 | Cell highlighting legend |

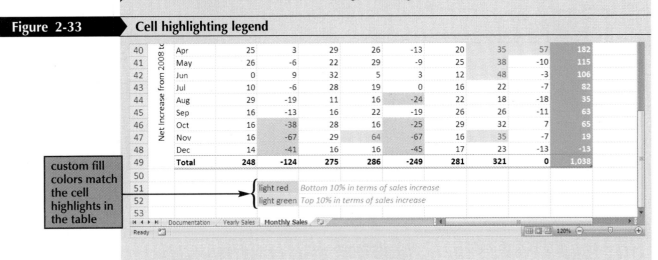

custom fill colors match the cell highlights in the table

The conditional formatting in the Monthly Sales worksheet helps Tom understand how sales of the X310 heart rate monitor changed over the past two years and helps him focus on particular sales regions for additional analysis.

| InSight | **Using Conditional Formatting Effectively** |

Conditional formatting is an excellent way to point out trends and highlight key data values, but it should be used judiciously. An overuse of conditional formatting can sometimes obscure the very data values you want to emphasize. Keep in mind the following tips:

- Document the conditional formats you use. If a bold, green font means that a sales number is in the top 10% of all sales, include that information in a legend in the worksheet.
- Don't clutter data with too much highlighting. Limit highlight rules to one or two per data set. Highlights are designed to draw attention to points of interest. If you use too many, you'll end up highlighting everything—and, therefore, nothing.
- Use color sparingly in worksheets with highlights. It's difficult to tell a highlight color from a regular fill color, especially when fill colors are used in every cell.
- Consider alternatives to conditional formats. If you want to highlight the top 10 sales regions, it might be more effective to simply sort the data with the best-selling regions at the top of the list.
- Don't let data bars overwhelm cell text. Use data bars when you're more interested in the "big picture" rather than specific cell values. If you want to show both, use a chart.

Hiding Worksheet Data

The Monthly Sales worksheet contains too much data to fit into the worksheet window without drastically reducing the zoom level. This would make the contents too small to read easily. Another way to view a large worksheet is by selectively hiding rows or columns (or even entire worksheets in a workbook). Hiding rows, columns, and worksheets is an excellent way to conceal extraneous or distracting information; but you should never hide data that is crucial to understanding a workbook.

Tom wants to view only the third table, which shows the difference in sales between 2008 and 2009, but not the other tables. You'll hide the rows that contain the first two tables and then unhide those rows after Tom has looked at the third table.

To hide and unhide worksheet rows:

▶ **1.** Select row **6** through row **35** in the Monthly Sales worksheet.

▶ **2.** In the Cells group on the Home tab, click the **Format** button, point to **Hide & Unhide**, and then click **Hide Rows**. Rows 6 to 35 are hidden, and the row numbers in the worksheet jump from row 5 to row 36. The data in the third table hasn't changed even though its formulas use data from the hidden tables.

▶ **3.** Select row **5** and row **36**, which are the rows before and after the hidden rows.

▶ **4.** In the Cells group, click the **Format** button, point to **Hide & Unhide**, and then click **Unhide Rows**. The hidden rows 6 through 35 reappear.

Formatting the Worksheet for Printing

Tom wants you to print this analysis of the monthly sales figures. In preparing the worksheet for the printer, you can select the position of the report on the page, the orientation of the page, and whether the page will include headers or footers. First, you'll look at the Monthly Sales worksheet in Page Layout view to see how it would currently print.

To view the Monthly Sales worksheet in Page Layout view:

▶ **1.** Click the **Page Layout** button 🔳 on the status bar. The worksheet switches to Page Layout view.

▶ **2.** Zoom the worksheet to **60%** to view more of the page layout. See Figure 2-34.

Page Layout view of the Monthly Sales worksheet ◀ **Figure 2-34**

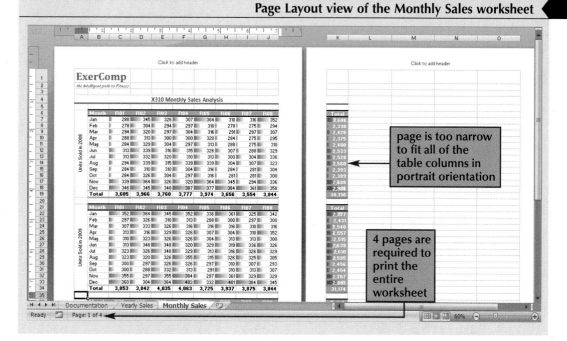

In the worksheet's current orientation, its contents do not fit on a single page and the tables break across pages. You'll change the orientation from portrait to landscape so that the page is wide enough to fit all the table columns on one page.

To change the page orientation to landscape:

▶ **1.** Click the **Page Layout** tab on the Ribbon.

▶ **2.** In the Page Setup group, click the **Orientation** button, and then click **Landscape**. The page orientation changes to landscape, making each page wide enough to display all of the columns of each table.

Defining the Print Area

By default, all parts of the active worksheet containing text, formulas, or values are printed. You can also select the cells you want to print, and then define them as a **print area**. A print area can cover an adjacent or nonadjacent range.

For his report, Tom wants to print only the first table. You'll set the print area to cover only those cells. It's generally easier to work with the print area in Page Break Preview.

To switch to Page Break Preview and define the print area:

▶ **1.** Click the **Page Break Preview** button 🔳 on the status bar, and then zoom the worksheet to **70%**.

   Trouble? If the Welcome to Page Break Preview dialog box opens, click the OK button.

▶ **2.** Select the range **A1:K19**, which is the range of the first table.

▶ **3.** In the Page Setup group on the Page Layout tab, click the **Print Area** button, and then click **Set Print Area**. The print area changes to cover only the range A1:K19. The rest of the worksheet content is shaded to indicate that it will not be part of the printout.

   Tom decides that he wants you to print all the content in the worksheet, so you'll clear the print area you just defined, resetting the print area to the default.

▶ **4.** In the Page Setup group, click the **Print Area** button, and then click **Clear Print Area**. The print area again covers the entire contents of the worksheet.

Inserting Page Breaks

Large worksheets often do not fit onto one page unless you scale the printout to fit, but that usually results in text that is too small to read comfortably. When a printout extends to multiple pages, Excel prints as much as fits on a page and then inserts a **page break** to continue printing the remaining worksheet content on the next page. This can result in page breaks that split worksheet content in awkward places, such as within a table.

Instead, you can insert **manual page breaks** that specify exactly where the page breaks occur. A page break is inserted directly above and to the left of a selected cell, directly above a selected row, or to the left of a selected column.

Setting and Removing Page Breaks | Reference Window

To set a page break:

- Select the first cell below the row where you want to insert a page break.
- In the Page Setup group on the Page Layout tab, click the Breaks button, and then click Insert Page Break.

To remove a page break:

- Select any cell below or to the right of the page break you want to remove.
- In the Page Setup group on the Page Layout tab, click the Breaks button, and then click Remove Page Break (or click Reset All Page Breaks to remove all the page breaks from the worksheet).

Tom wants the three tables in the Monthly Sales worksheet to print on separate pages. You'll insert page breaks to accomplish this.

To insert page breaks between the tables:

▶ 1. Click cell **A20**.

▶ 2. In the Page Setup group on the Page Layout tab, click the **Breaks** button, and then click **Insert Page Break**. A page break separates row 19 from row 20.

▶ 3. Click cell **A35**, and then repeat Step 2 to insert a second page break that splits the second table from the third. The printout is now three pages. See Figure 2-35.

Worksheet in Page Break Preview ◣ **Figure 2-35**

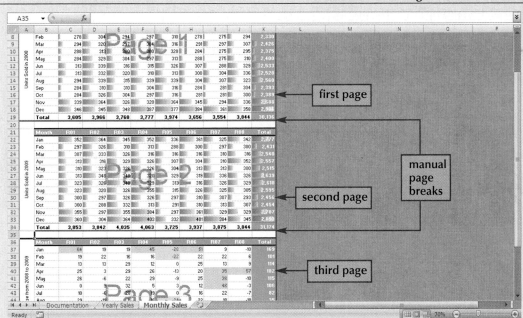

Tip

In Page Break Preview, a dashed blue line indicates an automatic page break and a solid blue line indicates a manual page break.

▶ 4. Click the **Page Layout** button 🔲 on the status bar, and then verify that each table appears on a separate page.

Adding Print Titles

The company name, the slogan, and the worksheet title all appear on the first page of the printout, but do not appear on the other two pages. This is because the range that includes that text is limited to the first page of the printout. It's a good practice to include the company name, logo, and worksheet title on each page of a printout in case a page becomes separated from the other pages. You can repeat information, such as the company name, by specifying which rows or columns in the worksheet act as **print titles**, information that prints on each page.

Tom wants the first four rows of the Monthly Sales worksheet printed on each page.

To define the print titles for the pages:

▶ 1. In the Page Setup group on the Page Layout tab, click the **Print Titles** button. The Page Setup dialog box opens with the Sheet tab displayed.

▶ 2. Click the **Rows to repeat at top** box, move your pointer over the worksheet, and then select the range **A1:A4**. A flashing border appears around the first four rows of the worksheet as a visual indicator that the contents of the first four rows will be repeated on each page of the printout. The cell reference $1:$4 appears in the Rows to repeat at top box.

▶ 3. Click the **OK** button.

▶ 4. Click the **Page Layout** button 🔲 on the status bar, and then scroll through the second and third pages of the printout in Page Layout view to verify that the company name, slogan, and worksheet title appear on each page. See Figure 2-36.

| Figure 2-36 | Second page of the printout |

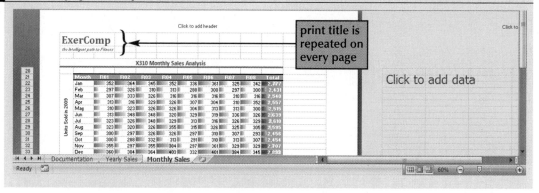

The Sheet tab in the Page Setup dialog box provides other print options, such as printing the gridlines or row and column headings. You can also print the worksheet in black and white or in draft quality. For a multiple page printout, you can specify whether the pages are ordered by first going down the worksheet and then across or across first and then down.

Adding Headers and Footers

Another way to repeat information on each page of a printout is with headers and footers. A **header** is the text printed in the top margin of each page. A **footer** is the text printed in the bottom margin of each page. A **margin** is the space between the page content and the edges of the page. Headers and footers can be used to add information to the printed page that is not found in the worksheet cells, such as the workbook's author, the date the page was printed, or the workbook filename. If the printout covers multiple pages, you can add a footer that displays the page number and the total number of pages in the printout to help ensure you and others have the entire printout.

The header and footer have three sections: a left section, a center section, and a right section. Within each section, you type the text you want to appear or insert elements such as the worksheet name or current date and time. These header and footer elements are dynamic; if you rename the worksheet, for example, the name is automatically updated in the header or footer.

Tom wants his printouts to display the workbook's filename in the header's left section and the current date in the header's right section. He wants the center footer to display the page number and the total number of pages in the printout, and the right footer to display your name as the workbook's author.

To insert the header and footer text:

▶ **1.** Zoom the worksheet to **90%** in Page Layout view.

▶ **2.** Scroll to the top of the worksheet, and then click the left section of the header directly above cell A1. The Header & Footer Tools contextual tab appears on the Ribbon.

▶ **3.** Type **Filename:** in the left section of the header, press the **spacebar**, and then, in the Header & Footer Elements group on the Header & Footer Tools Design tab, click the **File Name** button. The code &[File], which displays the filename of the current workbook, is added into the left section of the header.

▶ **4.** Press the **Tab** key twice to move to the right section of the header, and then, in the Header & Footer Elements group, click the **Current Date** button. The code &[Date] is added into the right section of the header. See Figure 2-37.

Page header ◀ **Figure 2-37**

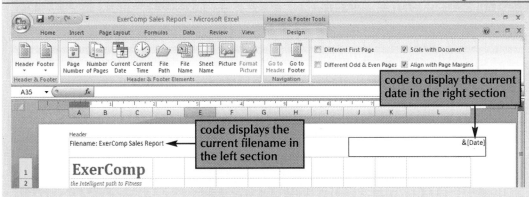

▶ **5.** In the Navigation group, click the **Go to Footer** button. The right section of the footer is selected.

▶ **6.** Click the center section of the footer, type **Page**, press the **spacebar**, and then, in the Header & Footer Elements group, click the **Page Number** button.

▶ **7.** Press the **spacebar**, type **of**, press the **spacebar**, and then, in the Header & Footer Elements group, click the **Number of Pages** button. The text, "Page &[Page] of &[Pages]" appears in the center section of the footer.

▶ **8.** Press the **Tab** key to move to the right section of the footer, type **Prepared by:**, press the **spacebar**, and then type your name. See Figure 2-38.

Figure 2-38 ▷ **Page footer**

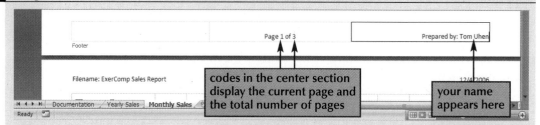

9. Click cell **A1**, and then scroll through the other two pages of the worksheet to verify that the same header appears for each page and the center section of the footer displays the correct page number and total number of pages.

Adjusting Margins

Tom wants you to try different margins to see the effect on the Monthly Sales worksheet and how it will print. You can use the preset Normal margins, Wide margins, or Narrow margins. Or, you can enter custom settings for each margin in the Page Setup dialog box.

To adjust the worksheet's margins:

1. In the Page Setup group on the Page Layout tab, click the **Margins** button. The Margins menu opens. The default margin setting, Normal, is selected.

2. Click **Custom Margins**. The Page Setup dialog box opens, and the Margins tab is active. You can enter the exact margin setting you want in each box. The preview image changes to show the new margins.

3. Select the text in the Top box, type **2** (you do not need to type the inches symbol), press the **Tab** key to select the text in the Bottom box, and then type **3**.

4. Press the **Tab** key to select the text in the Left box, type **1**, press the **Tab** key to select the text in the Right box, and then type **1**. The preview image shows the new margins.

5. Click the **OK** button. The worksheet reflects the new margins.

   Tom prefers the default margin settings, so you'll return the margins to their original settings.

6. In the Page Setup group on the Page Layout tab, click the **Margins** button, and then click **Normal**. The margins change back to their default settings.

> **Tip**
>
> The settings most recently selected in the Page Setup dialog box appear as the Last Custom Setting option in the Margins menu.

The worksheet is formatted for printing. Tom asks you to save and print the Monthly Sales worksheet.

To save the workbook and print the worksheet:

1. Click the **Normal** button ⊞ on the status bar to return the Monthly Sales worksheet to Normal view.

2. Save your changes to the workbook.

> **3.** Print the contents of the Monthly Sales worksheet, and then close the workbook. Each table is printed on a separate page and the headers and footers display the filename, current date, page number and total number of pages, and your name.

Tom will analyze the finished report, and distribute it during the upcoming sales meeting.

Session 2.2 Quick Check | Review

1. What is a table style?
2. What are the six table style options you can turn on and off?
3. What is conditional formatting?
4. How is the length of a data bar determined by default?
5. How would you highlight the top five values in the range A1:C20?
6. What are print titles?
7. How do you insert a page break into your worksheet?

Tutorial Summary | Review

In this tutorial, you used formatting tools to create visually appealing and informative workbooks. You formatted text, backgrounds, borders, numbers, and dates, and copied formats from one range into another. You applied built-in styles and themes to the workbook. Next, you looked at how formatting can be helpful for analyzing and interpreting data. You applied a table style to format an Excel table. Then, you used two types of conditional formatting—data bars and highlighting rules—to better understand the data entered into the workbook. Finally, you formatted the worksheet for printing by setting page breaks and page titles, and inserting headers and footers.

Key Terms

accent	Format Painter	points
automatic color	formatting	print area
banded rows	General number format	print title
border	header	sans serif font
conditional format	legend	serif font
custom color	Live Preview	standard color
data bar	manual page break	style
Excel table	margin	table style
font	merge	theme
font size	Mini toolbar	theme color
font style	non-theme font	theme font
footer	page break	typeface

| Practice | **Review Assignments** |

Practice the skills you learned in the tutorial using the same case scenario.

Data Files needed for the Review Assignments: X410.xlsx, Paper.jpg

ExerComp introduced another heart rate monitor, the X410, two years ago. Tom wants you to format a workbook that compares the sales of the X310 and X410 models during that time. The workbook has a Documentation sheet, a Model Comparison sheet comparing the total units sold for each model in the eight sales regions, and a Monthly Sales sheet reporting the number of units sold per month.

In the Model Comparison sheet, Tom wants you to highlight the sales regions that showed the greatest sales increases from 2008 to 2009. Figure 2-39 shows a preview of the formatted Model Comparison sheet.

Figure 2-39

		A	B	C	D	E	F
1		ExerComp					
2		*the Intelligent path to Fitness*					
3					highest	Highest increase in units sold	
4					highest	Highest % increase in units sold	
5							
6			Region	Units Sold (2008)	Units Sold (2009)	Increase	% Increase
7			R01	3,605	3,853	248	6.88%
8	X		R02	3,966	3,842	-124	-3.13%
9			R03	3,760	4,035	275	7.31%
10	3		R04	3,777	4,063	286	7.57%
11	1		R05	3,974	3,725	-249	-6.27%
12			R06	3,656	3,937	281	7.69%
13	0		R07	3,554	3,875	321	9.03%
14			R08	3,844	3,844	0	0.00%
15			Total	30,136	31,174	1,038	3.44%
16							
17			Region	Units Sold (2008)	Units Sold (2009)	Increase	% Increase
18			R01	2,488	4,156	1,668	67.04%
19	X		R02	2,531	4,293	1,762	69.62%
20			R03	2,231	4,292	2,061	92.38%
21	4		R04	2,613	4,851	2,238	85.65%
22			R05	2,512	4,308	1,796	71.50%
23	1		R06	2,824	4,689	1,865	66.04%
24	0		R07	2,355	4,529	2,174	92.31%
25			R08	2,412	4,140	1,728	71.64%
26			Total	19,966	35,258	15,292	76.59%

In the Monthly Sales sheet, Tom wants you to include data bars that show the monthly sales totals for both models during 2008 and 2009. Figure 2-40 shows a preview of the completed Monthly Sales sheet.

Figure 2-40

	A	B	C	D	E	F	G	H	I
1	ExerComp								
2	*the Intelligent path to Fitness*								
3									
4		**2008 Sales (Units Sold)**					**2009 Sales (Units Sold)**		
5	**Month**	**X310**	**X410**	**All Models**		**Month**	**X310**	**X410**	**All Models**
6	Jan	2,608	-	2,608		Jan	2,777	3,223	6,000
7	Feb	2,330	-	2,330		Feb	2,431	2,612	5,043
8	Mar	2,426	25	2,451		Mar	2,540	2,714	5,254
9	Apr	2,375	75	2,450		Apr	2,557	2,877	5,434
10	May	2,400	1,500	3,900		May	2,515	2,749	5,264
11	Jun	2,533	1,750	4,283		Jun	2,639	2,955	5,594
12	Jul	2,528	2,135	4,663		Jul	2,610	2,839	5,449
13	Aug	2,560	2,620	5,180		Aug	2,595	2,875	5,470
14	Sep	2,393	2,714	5,107		Sep	2,456	2,823	5,279
15	Oct	2,389	2,689	5,078		Oct	2,454	2,791	5,245
16	Nov	2,688	3,144	5,832		Nov	2,707	3,278	5,985
17	Dec	2,906	3,314	6,220		Dec	2,893	3,522	6,415
18	Total	30,136	19,966	50,102		Total	31,174	35,258	66,432

Complete the following. (*Note:* Text you need to enter is shown in bold for ease of reference only; do not bold the text unless otherwise instructed.)

1. Open the **X410** workbook located in the Tutorial.02\Review folder included with your Data Files, and then save the workbook as **X410 Sales Comparison** in the same folder. In the Documentation sheet, enter your name in cell B4 and the current date in cell B5 in the format *mm/dd/yyyy*.

2. In the Documentation sheet, set the font color of cells A1 and A2 to blue, format the text in cell A1 in a 26-point Times New Roman font, and then format the text in cell A2 in a 10-point italicized Times New Roman font. In cell A1, change the font color of the text string "Comp" to red.

3. In the range A4:A6, set the font color to white and set the fill color to blue. In the range B4:B6, set the fill color to white. In the range A4:B6, add border lines around all of the cells.

4. In cell B5, display the date with the Long Date format and left-aligned within the cell.

5. In the Documentation sheet, insert a background image, using the **Paper.jpg** image file located in the Tutorial.02\Review folder included with your Data Files.

6. Use the Format Painter to copy the format from the range A1:A2 in the Documentation sheet to the range A1:A2 in the other two sheets. In cell A1, change the font color of the text string "Comp" to red.

7. In the Model Comparison sheet, merge and center the range A6:A15, center the text vertically, and then rotate the text to a vertical orientation. (*Hint:* In the Alignment group on the Home tab, click the Orientation button, and then click Vertical Text.) Center the text in the range C6:F6, and then indent the region labels in the range B7:B14 one character.

8. In the range C7:E15, format the numbers in a Number format using a thousands separator, no decimal places, and negative numbers displayed with a minus symbol. In the range F7:F15, format the numbers in a Percentage format with two decimal places.

9. Apply the Accent1 cell style to the range B6:F6. Apply the Accent1 cell style to the merged cell A6, and then increase that cell's font size to 18 points and bold. Apply the Total cell style to the range B15:F15.

10. In the range E7:E14, apply a conditional format that adds a Top/Bottom Rule to display the highest number in the range in dark green text with a green fill. In the range F7:F14, apply a conditional format that adds a Top/Bottom Rule to display the highest number in the range in dark red text with a light red fill.

11. Use the Format Painter to copy all of the formats from the range A6:F15 to the range A17:F26.

12. In cell D3, enter **highest**, and then apply a conditional format to cell D3 that adds a Highlight Cells Rule to format the cell that contains the text "highest" with Green Fill with Dark Green Text. In cell D4, enter **highest**, and then apply a conditional format to cell D3 that adds a Highlight Cells Rule to format the cell that contains the text "highest" with Light Red Fill with Dark Red Text.

13. In cell E3, enter **Highest increase in units sold**. In cell E4, enter **Highest % increase in units sold**. Format both cells with the Explanatory Text cell style.

14. In the Monthly Sales sheet, merge and center the range A4:D4, merge and center the range F4:I4, and then apply the Heading 1 style to both merged cells. In the range B5:D5;G5:I5, center the text.

15. In the range B6:D18;G6:I18, format the numbers to show a thousands separator (,) with no decimal places to the right of the decimal point.

16. Select the range A5:D18, and then apply Table Style Light 8 (the second table style in the second row of the Light section in the Table Styles gallery). Turn off the filter arrows, and then turn on only the header row, first column, and last column table style options. In the range A18:D18, apply the Total cell style.

17. Select the range F5:I18, and then repeat Step 16, applying the Total cell style to the range F18:I18.

18. In the range D6:D17, add green data bars. In the range I6:I17, add purple data bars.

19. For the Model Comparison and Monthly Sales worksheets, set the page orientations to landscape, display your name in the center section of the header, display the sheet name in the left section of the footer, display the workbook filename in the center section of the footer, and then display the current date in the right section of the footer.

20. Save and close your workbook. Submit the finished workbook to your instructor, either in printed or electronic form, as requested.

| Apply | **Case Problem 1** |

Use the skills you learned to create a sales report for a winter clothing company.

Data File needed for this Case Problem: Frosti.xlsx

FrostiWear Linda Young is a sales manager for FrostiWear, a successful new store based in Hillsboro, Oregon. She's tracking the sales figures for FrostiWear's line of gloves. She created a workbook that contains the sales figures from the past year for three glove models. She wants you to help format the sales report. Figure 2-41 shows a preview of the formatted report.

Figure 2-41

	Month	Region 1	Region 2	Region 3	Region 4	Region 5	Total	
				FrostiWear				
				2009 Sales Report				
PolyFleece Mitts	Month	Region 1	Region 2	Region 3	Region 4	Region 5	Total	
	Jan	1,150	1,690	930	2,850	1,210		7,830
	Feb	1,100	2,200	680	2,340	1,100		7,420
	Mar	1,070	1,290	960	2,740	1,180		7,240
	Apr	780	1,520	720	2,170	1,180		6,370
	May	1,070	1,370	700	1,940	1,210		6,290
	Jun	670	1,300	780	3,430	1,170		7,350
	Jul	1,390	1,590	1,240	2,230	1,430		7,880
	Aug	1,310	1,730	610	2,560	960		7,170
	Sep	1,100	1,820	370	3,040	1,100		7,430
	Oct	1,350	2,010	750	2,430	1,230		7,770
	Nov	680	1,620	780	3,210	1,230		7,520
	Dec	1,120	1,170	670	1,920	1,310		6,190
	Total	12,790	19,310	9,190	30,860	14,310		86,460
ArcticBlast Gloves	Month	Region 1	Region 2	Region 3	Region 4	Region 5	Total	
	Jan	790	1,160	620	2,590	760		5,920
	Feb	1,010	1,170	610	1,950	1,010		5,750
	Mar	710	1,270	600	2,050	930		5,560
	Apr	890	1,190	750	2,030	980		5,840
	May	990	1,340	660	2,670	1,040		6,700
	Jun	990	1,280	620	2,330	800		6,020
	Jul	780	1,180	690	2,260	920		5,830
	Aug	800	1,220	560	2,460	900		5,940
	Sep	810	1,150	670	2,500	970		6,100
	Oct	760	1,070	630	2,350	1,040		5,850
	Nov	770	1,140	630	2,540	1,080		6,160
	Dec	850	1,370	590	2,490	1,060		6,360
	Total	10,150	14,540	7,630	28,220	11,490		72,030
Glomitts	Month	Region 1	Region 2	Region 3	Region 4	Region 5	Total	
	Jan	340	780	280	1,670	600		3,670
	Feb	460	810	280	1,770	480		3,800
	Mar	410	820	310	1,490	460		3,490
	Apr	490	890	330	1,610	650		3,970
	May	470	960	290	1,580	540		3,840
	Jun	480	740	340	1,780	640		3,980
	Jul	470	760	320	1,500	640		3,690
	Aug	490	690	340	1,610	600		3,730
	Sep	420	780	340	1,660	680		3,880
	Oct	460	820	350	1,800	660		4,090
	Nov	550	830	440	1,250	590		3,660
	Dec	400	790	220	1,620	540		3,570
	Total	5,440	9,670	3,840	19,340	7,080		45,370

Complete the following. (*Note:* Text you need to enter is shown in bold for ease of reference only; do not bold the text unless otherwise instructed.)

1. Open the **Frosti** workbook located in the Tutorial.02\Case1 folder included with your Data Files, and then save the workbook as **FrostiWear Sales Report** in the same folder.

2. In the Documentation sheet, enter your name in cell B3 and the date in cell B4. Set the background color for all the cells in the worksheet to standard blue, and then set the background color for the range B3:B5 to white. Add a border line around each cell in the range B3:B5.

3. Change the font of cell A1 to the Headings font of the current theme, change the font size to 36 points, change the font color to white, and then bold the text. Change the font size of the range A3:A5 to 16 points, change the font color to white, and then bold the text.

4. In the Glove Sales worksheet, merge and center the range A1:H1, apply the Title cell style, and then increase the font size to 26 points. Merge and center the range A2:H2, apply the Heading 4 cell style, and then increase the font size to 16 points.

5. Merge and center the range A3:A16, set the alignment to Middle Align, rotate the text 90° counterclockwise, apply the Accent1 cell style, increase the font size to 18 points, and then bold the text.

6. Use the Format Painter to copy the format of merged cell A3 into the range A18:A31;A33:A46.

7. Center the text in the range C3:H3. Format the range C4:H16 to include thousands separators (,) and no decimal places. Use the Format Painter to copy the formats in the range C3:H16 to the range C18:H31;C33:H46.

8. In the range B3:H16, apply the Table Style Medium 2 table style. Turn off the filter arrows, and then display the header row, first column, last column, and banded rows. In the range B16:H16, change the fill color of the Total row to standard yellow. In the range H4:H15, change the fill color of the Total column to white.

9. Repeat Step 8 for the other two tables in the worksheet.

10. Increase the width of column H to 25 characters.

11. Add blue data bars to the range H4:H15. Also add blue data bars to the ranges H19:H30 and H34:H45.

12. In the Glove Sales worksheet, set the page orientation to landscape, insert manual page breaks at cells A18 and A33, and then repeat the first two rows of the worksheet on every printed page.

13. Display your name in the center header, display the filename in the left footer, display **Page** *page number* **of** *number of pages* in the center footer, and then display the current date in the right footer.

14. Save and close your workbook. Submit the finished workbook to your instructor, either in printed or electronic form, as requested.

Create	**Case Problem 2**

Create and format a worksheet as a packing slip for GrillRite Grills.

Data File needed for this Case Problem: GrillRite.xlsx

GrillRite Grills Brian Simpko is a shipping manager at GrillRite Grills in Hammond, Indiana. He uses an Excel workbook to provide shipping and order information for customer orders and deliveries. He asks you to help create and format a worksheet that he can use to enter information for packing slips. Figure 2-42 shows the worksheet you'll create for Brian.

Figure 2-42

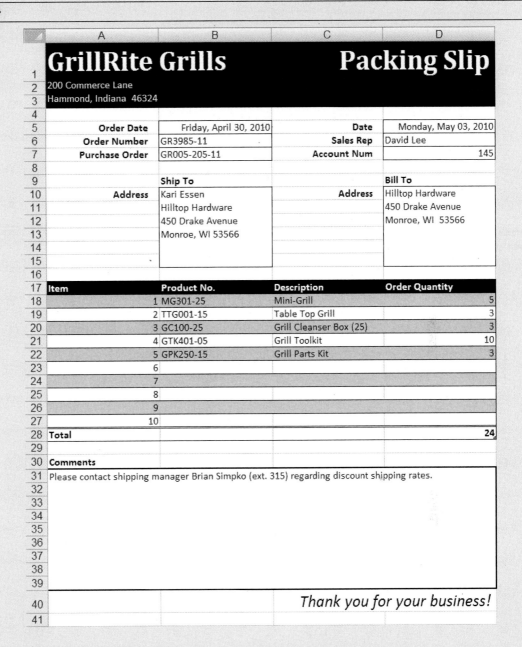

Complete the following. (*Note:* Text you need to enter is shown in bold for ease of reference only; do not bold the text unless otherwise instructed.)

1. Open the **GrillRite** workbook located in the Tutorial.02\Case2 folder included with your Data Files, and then save the workbook as **GrillRite Grills Packing Slip** in the same folder. In the Documentation sheet, enter your name in cell B3 and the date in cell B4.

2. Insert a new worksheet at the end of the document named **Packing Slip**.

3. In the Packing Slip worksheet, select all of the cells in the worksheet. (*Hint:* Click the Select All button at the intersection of the row and column headings.) Change the font to the Body font of the current theme. For the range A1:D3, set the fill color to black and the font color to white.

4. Set the width of columns A through D to 20 characters. Set the height of the first row to 36.

5. Merge the range A1:B3, merge the range C1:D3, and then left- and top-align both merged cells.

6. In cell A1, enter the following three lines of text, and then format the first line in a 26-point bold font using the Headings font of the current theme:

   GrillRite Grills

   200 Commerce Lane

   Hammond, Indiana 46324

7. In cell C1, enter **Packing Slip**, format the text in a 26-point bold font using the Headings font of the current theme, and then right-align the text.

8. In the range A5:A7, enter the following three lines of text in a bold font, and then right-align the text and indent the text one character:

   Order Date

   Order Number

   Purchase Order

9. Format cell B5 in the Long Date format. Insert border lines around each of the cells in the range B5:B7.

10. In the range C5:C7, enter the following three lines of text, and then use the Format Painter to copy the formats from the range A5:B7 to the range C5:D7:

    Date

    Sales Rep

    Account Num

11. In cell B9, enter **Ship To** and in cell D9, enter **Bill To** and then format both in a bold font.

12. In cell A10, enter **Address** in a bold font, right-align the text, and then indent it one character.

13. Merge the cells in the range B10:B15, left- and top-align the cell contents, and then insert a border around the merged cell.

14. In cell C10, enter **Address**. Copy the format from the range A10:B15 into the range C10:D15.

15. Enter the following data into the worksheet:

Cell	Data
A17	**Item**
B17	**Product No.**
C17	**Description**
D17	**Order Quantity**
A18:A27	*the numbers from 1 to 10*

⊕ EXPLORE

16. For the range A17:D27, apply Table Style Medium 1, turn off the filter arrows, and display the header row, total row, and banded rows. In cell D28, select the SUM function from the list.

17. In cell A30, enter **Comments** in a bold font.

18. Merge the range A31:D39, left- and top-align the cell contents, and then add a thick box border around the merged cell.

19. In cell D40, enter **Thank you for your business!** in an italic, 16-point font, and then right-align the cell contents.

20. Enter the packing slip data shown in Figure 2-42.

21. Make sure the worksheet's page orientation is set to portrait, and then add a footer that displays your name in the left section, the filename in the center section, and the current date in the right section.

22. Save and close your workbook. Submit the finished workbook to your instructor, either in printed or electronic form, as requested.

Challenge | **Case Problem 3**

Explore how to use different Excel formatting features to create an election report.

Data File needed for this Case Problem: Iowa.xlsx

Lewis Reports Kay Lewis is a political columnist, commentator, and blogger. Her Web site, *Lewis Reports*, contains historical information on campaigns and elections. Recently, Kay compiled state-by-state and county-by-county voting totals for the past 15 presidential elections. She wants this information in an Excel workbook so she can analyze voting preferences and trends. Kay has created a workbook that contains the election results from the 2004 presidential election in Iowa. She asks you to format the workbook. She wants formats that quickly show which candidates won at the state and county levels as well as the margin of victory. Counties that went heavily Democratic or Republican should have formats that reflect this fact. Figure 2-43 shows a preview of the worksheet you'll format for Kay.

Figure 2-43

	A	B	C	D	E	F
1	**2004 Presidential Election**					
2						
3	**Iowa Vote Totals**					
4	State	Counties	Candidate	Votes		%
5	Iowa	99	George W. Bush (Rep)	746,600		50.46%
6			John F. Kerry (Dem)	733,102		49.54%
7			Total	1,479,702		
8						
9	**County-by-County Totals**					
10	County	Precincts	Candidate	Votes		%
11	Adair	10	Bush	2,393		56.63%
12			Kerry	1,833		43.37%
13			Total	4,226		
14	Adams	12	Bush	1,313		57.44%
15			Kerry	973		42.56%
16			Total	2,286		
17	Allamakee	23	Bush	3,523		50.62%
18			Kerry	3,437		49.38%
19			Total	6,960		

Complete the following. (*Note:* Text you need to enter is shown in bold for ease of reference only; do not bold the text unless otherwise instructed.)

1. Open the **Iowa** workbook located in the Tutorial.02\Case3 folder included with your Data Files, and then save the workbook as **Iowa Election Results** in the same folder. In the Documentation sheet, enter your name in cell B3 and the date in cell B4.

2. In the Iowa worksheet, apply the Title style to cell A1, and then apply the Heading 1 style to cells A3 and A9.

3. Apply the Accent3 style to the range A4:F4, and then center the heading text in cells D4:F4.

4. In the range D5:D7, format the numbers with a thousands separator (,) and no decimal places. In the range F5:F7, format the numbers as percentages with two decimal places.

5. Merge the range A5:A7, and then left- and top-align the cell contents. Merge the range B5:B7, and then right- and top-align the cell contents. Merge the range E5:E7.

6. Add border lines around each cell in the range A4:F7.

7. Format the range C5:D5 as white text on a standard red background. Format the range C6:D6 as white text on a standard light blue background.

8. Copy the format in the range A4:F7 to the range A10:F13.

⊕ **EXPLORE** 9. Add a double bottom border to the range A11:F13, and then copy the format in the range A11:F13 to the larger range A14:F307. Excel repeats the format until it fills up the larger range.

⊕ **EXPLORE** 10. Select the range E5;E11:E307, which shows the difference in votes between the Republican and Democratic candidates. Create a highlight rule to format cells with values greater than zero (indicating a Republican winner) in red text on a red background (thus, obscuring the text). (*Hint:* In the Greater Than dialog box, click Custom Format in the with list to open the Format Cells dialog box, and then use the Font tab and the Fill tab to select the colors.) Create a second highlight rule to format cells with values less than zero (indicating a Democratic winner) in light blue text on a light blue background. Reduce the width of column E to 3 characters.

11. Select the range F5:F7;F11:F307, which shows the vote percentages for each candidate. Apply green data bars, left-align the cells, and then increase the width of column F to 23 characters.

12. Verify the conditional formatting by entering different totals in column D and checking that the highlights and data bars are changed accurately. Restore the original values to the worksheet.

13. For the Iowa worksheet, make sure the page orientation is set to portrait, and then scale the page so that the width of the printout is one page and the height is automatic. (*Hint:* Use the buttons in the Scale To Fit group on the Page Layout tab.)

⊕ **EXPLORE** 14. Format the printout of the Iowa worksheet to repeat the first 10 rows of the worksheet on every page of the printout. Insert manual page breaks into the rest of the table to keep each county's vote from splitting between two pages.

15. Display your name in the center section of the header, and then display the filename in the left section of the footer, **Page** *page number* **of** *number of pages* in the center section of the footer, and the current date in the right section of the footer.

16. Save and close your workbook. Submit the finished workbook to your instructor, either in printed or electronic form, as requested.

| Create | **Case Problem 4** |

Use your creativity to format a meal-planning worksheet that highlights foods with high calorie counts and fat contents.

Data File needed for this Case Problem: Life.xlsx

Life Managers   Kate Dee is a dietician at *Life Managers*, a company in Kleinville, Michigan, that specializes in personal improvement, particularly in areas of health and fitness. Kate wants to create a meal-planning workbook for her clients who want to lose weight and improve their health. One goal of meal planning is to decrease the percentage of fat in the diet. Kate thinks it would be helpful to highlight foods that have a high percentage of fat as well as list their total fat calories. She already created an Excel workbook that contains a few sample food items and lists the number of calories and grams of fat in each item. She wants you to format this workbook.

Complete the following:

1. Open the **Life** workbook located in the Tutorial.02\Case4 folder included with your Data Files, and then save the workbook as **Life Managers Nutrition Table** in the same folder. In the Documentation sheet, enter your name in cell B3 and the date in cell B4.

2. Fat contains nine calories per gram. In the Meal Planner worksheet, add a column that calculates the calories from fat for each food item. The percentage of fat is calculated by dividing the calories from fat by the total number of calories. Enter this calculated value to the table for each food item.

3. Display all calories and grams of fat values with one decimal place. Display the fat percentages as percentages with one decimal place.

4. Design the rest of the Meal Planner worksheet as you'd like, but be sure to include at least one example of each of the following design elements:
   - A range merged into a single cell
   - Text centered and rotated within a cell
   - Cell styles applied to one or more elements
   - Border line styles applied to one or more elements

5. The FDA recommends for good health that the fat percentage should not exceed 30% of the total calories. Apply a rule to the fat percentages to highlight those food items that exceed the FDA recommendations. Include a legend to document the highlighting color you used.

6. Add data bars to the display of calories from fat values to graphically show the relative amounts of fat calories for different food items.

7. Add descriptive headers and footers to the printed document. Also insert page breaks and print titles to ensure that the printout is easily read and interpreted.

8. Save and close your workbook. Submit the finished workbook to your instructor, either in printed or electronic form, as requested.

Research | Internet Assignments

Use the Internet to find and work with data related to the topics presented in this tutorial.

The purpose of the Internet Assignments is to challenge you to find information on the Internet that you can use to work effectively with this software. The actual assignments are updated and maintained on the Course Technology Web site. Log on to the Internet and use your Web browser to go to the Student Online Companion for New Perspectives Office 2007 at **www.course.com/np/office2007**. Then navigate to the Internet Assignments for this tutorial.

Assess | SAM Assessment and Training

If you have a SAM user profile, you may have access to hands-on instruction, practice, and assessment of the skills covered in this tutorial. Log in to your SAM account (**http://sam2007.course.com**) to launch any assigned training activities or exams that relate to the skills covered in this tutorial.

Review | Quick Check Answers

Session 2.1

1. Serif fonts have extra decorative strokes at the end of each character. Sans serif fonts do not include these decorative strokes.

2. Theme colors are the colors that belong to a workbook's basic design, giving the elements in the workbook a uniform appearance. A standard color is always available to every workbook regardless of which themes might be in use.

3. the default Excel number format that displays numbers just as they're entered

4. Dates are formatted numeric values and, as such, are right-aligned in cells.

5. A1

6. Open the Format Cells dialog box.

7. You can use the Format Painter to copy and paste the format from one range into another, or you can define a style for the different ranges.

Session 2.2

1. A style applied to a table allows you to turn on table style options.

2. header row, total row, first column, last column, banded rows, and banded columns

3. A conditional format depends on the cell's value.

4. by the cell's value relative to other cells in the range for which the data bars have been defined

5. Select the range A1:C20, click the Conditional Formatting button in the Styles group on the Home tab, point to Top/Bottom Rules, and then click Top 10%. In the dialog box, enter 5 for the top items to show, and then click the OK button.

6. titles taken from worksheet rows or columns that are repeated on every page of the printed sheet

7. Select the first cell below the row at which you want to insert the page break, click the Breaks button in the Page Setup group on the Page Layout tab, and then click Insert Break.

Ending Data Files

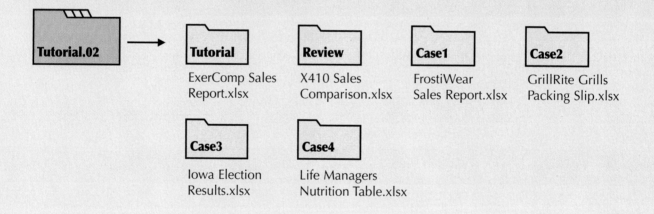

Tutorial.02 →

Tutorial
ExerComp Sales
Report.xlsx

Review
X410 Sales
Comparison.xlsx

Case1
FrostiWear
Sales Report.xlsx

Case2
GrillRite Grills
Packing Slip.xlsx

Case3
Iowa Election
Results.xlsx

Case4
Life Managers
Nutrition Table.xlsx

Objectives

Session 3.1
- Copy formulas
- Build formulas containing relative, absolute, and mixed references
- Review function syntax
- Insert a function with the Insert Function dialog box
- Search for a function
- Type a function directly in a cell

Session 3.2
- Use AutoFill to fill in a formula and complete a series
- Enter the IF logical function
- Insert the date with the TODAY function
- Calculate monthly mortgage payments with the PMT financial function

Working with Formulas and Functions

Developing a Budget

Case | Drake Family Budget

Diane and Glenn Drake, newly married, are trying to balance career, school, and family life. Diane works full-time as a legal assistant, and Glenn is in a graduate program at a nearby university where he recently was hired as a lab assistant. In the summer, he does other work that brings additional income to the family. The couple just moved into a new apartment. Although Glenn and Diane's salaries have grown in the past years, the couple seems to have less cash on hand. This financial shortage has prompted them to take a closer look at their finances and figure out how to best manage them.

Diane has set up an Excel workbook and entered the take-home pay from their two jobs. She has identified and entered expenses the family pays on a monthly basis, such as the rent and grocery bill, as well as other expenses that occur only a few times a year, such as Glenn's tuition and vacations. She wants to calculate how much money they are bringing in and how much money they are spending. She also wants to come up with a savings plan for the down payment on a house they hope to buy in a few years.

You'll help Diane complete the workbook. Diane wants you to enter formulas to perform the calculations she needs to get a better overall picture of the family's finances, which, in turn, should help the couple manage their money more effectively.

Starting Data Files

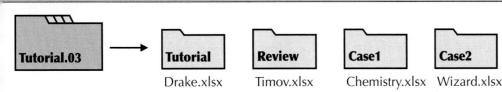

| Tutorial.03 | → | Tutorial | Review | Case1 | Case2 | Case3 | Case4 |
| | | Drake.xlsx | Timov.xlsx | Chemistry.xlsx | Wizard.xlsx | Loan.xlsx | V6.xlsx |

Session 3.1

Understanding Cell References When Copying Formulas

Diane has already done a lot of the work on her family budget. She used data from the past year to estimate the couple's monthly expenses for the upcoming year and she knows their monthly take-home pay. She already entered this data into an Excel workbook. You'll open this workbook now.

To open Diane's workbook:

▶ **1.** Open the **Drake** workbook located in the **Tutorial.03\Tutorial** folder included with your Data Files, and then save the workbook as **Drake Family Budget** in the same folder.

▶ **2.** In the Documentation sheet, enter your name in cell B3 and the date in cell B4.

▶ **3.** Review the contents of the **2010 Proposed Budget** worksheet.

Diane organized the worksheet so the top displays the values that she'll use throughout her budget, such as the family's monthly take-home pay. One of the advantages of placing these values in their own cells in one location is that you can reference them in formulas throughout the worksheets. Then, rather than changing the same value in several locations, you can change it once and any formulas based on that cell are automatically updated to reflect the new value. The top of the worksheet will also include some summary calculations, such as the total take-home pay and expenses for the upcoming year as well as what Diane can expect to earn and spend on average each month. Below that section is a grid in which Diane wants to record how the family's take-home pay and expenses change month by month.

Diane points out a few things about her data. First, she has two possible values for the couple's take-home pay: one for months during the school year and one for months during the summer. Because Glenn works only part-time during the school year as a lab assistant, he earns less during that time than during the summer months. On the other hand, Diane earns the same amount throughout the year. The couple's expenses also vary throughout the year. January and August are particularly expensive months because Glenn has to pay for tuition and books for the upcoming semester. The couple is planning a trip next summer for a family reunion and expenses always seem to add up during the holiday season. With all of these factors in mind, Diane wants to make sure that they will not be caught short in any month. Glenn and Diane hope to purchase a house in about three years, so they need to follow a well-planned budget.

In the range D19:O20, Diane reserved space for entering the couple's monthly take-home pay. You'll enter their projected take-home pay for January through May, using the values at the top of the worksheet.

To insert the monthly take-home pay for January through May:

▶ **1.** Click cell **D19**, type **=E5**, and then press the **Enter** key. The value 2,000, Diane's take-home pay for January, appears in cell D19.

▶ **2.** In cell D20, enter the formula **=E6**. The value 950, Glenn's take-home pay for January, appears in cell D20.

> **3.** In cell D21, enter the formula **=D19+D20**. This formula calculates the total take-home pay for the couple in the month of January.
>
> The couple will have the same take-home pay for the next four months as they did in January, so you can copy the formulas from January into February through May.
>
> **4.** Select the range **D19:D21**, and then, in the Clipboard group on the Home tab, click the **Copy** button.
>
> **5.** Select the range **E19:H21**, and then, in the Clipboard group, click the **Paste** button. Figure 3-1 shows the couple's take-home pay for January through May.

Tip

You can also use the SUM function to calculate the total take-home pay by clicking the Sum button in the Editing group on the Home tab.

Take-home pay values copied through May | **Figure 3-1**

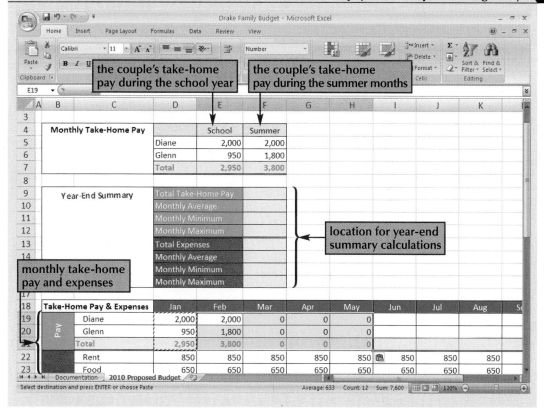

Notice that the formulas you copied and pasted from January resulted in incorrect values for February, March, April, and May. Diane's take-home pay of $2,000 is correct for January and February, but incorrectly changed to 0 for March, April, and May. Likewise, Glenn's take-home pay of $950 is correct for January, but incorrectly changed to $1,800 for February and 0 for March, April, and May. You need to investigate why you didn't get the results you expected. You'll examine how formulas change when copied to new locations in the workbook.

Using Relative References

When you enter a formula into a cell, Excel interprets cell references in the formula in relation to the cell's location. For example, the formula =A1 entered into cell A3 tells Excel to insert the value from the cell two rows above cell A3. When you copy the formula into other cells, Excel applies the same interpretation to the formula's new location, always displaying the value from the cell two rows above. Such cell references are called **relative references** because they are always interpreted in relation, or relative, to the location of the cell containing the formula. Figure 3-2 illustrates how a relative reference in a formula changes when the formula is copied to another range.

Figure 3-2 **Formula using a relative reference**

original formula with a relative reference

	A	B	C	D
1	10	20	30	
2				
3	=A1			
4				
5				

formula copied to a new range (column and row references shift based on cell location)

	A	B	C	D
1	10	20	30	
2				
3	=A1	=B1	=C1	
4				
5				

formula results

	A	B	C	D
1	10	20	30	
2				
3	10	20	30	
4				
5				

In this figure, the formula =A1 entered in cell A3 produced the result of 10, which is the value in cell A1. After the formula in cell A3 was copied to cell B3, the copied formula changed to =B1 and produced the result of 20, which is the value in cell B1. As you can see, when the formula was copied one cell to the right, the relative reference in the original formula (A1) adjusted one cell to the right to become B1. Similarly, when the formula in cell A3 was copied two cells to the right to cell C3, the copied formula changed to =C1 and produced the result of 30, which is the value in cell C1. In each instance, the formula references the cell two rows above the cell that contains the formula.

In Diane's worksheet, when you copied the formulas in the range D19:D21 into a new range, the cell references in those formulas adjusted to their new cell location. For example, the formula in cell E19 is =F5, the formula in cell F19 is =G5, and so forth. In each case, Excel references the cell that is 14 rows up and one column to the right of the current location.

The advantage of relative references is that you can create a "general" formula that you can use again and again in your worksheet. Relative references free you from having to rewrite a formula each time you copy it to a new location. For example, you can write a formula to add the values in a column of data, and then copy that formula to other columns to quickly add their values. You used this technique in the previous set of steps to calculate the couple's total take-home pay for each of the months from January to May.

Using Absolute References

Sometimes, you want references that are fixed on specific cells in the worksheet. This usually occurs when the referenced cell contains a value that needs to be repeated in different formulas throughout the workbook. In Diane's worksheet, any formulas involving take-home pay should be fixed on those cells that contain those values, which are the range E5:E6 for the school months and the range F5:F6 for the summer months.

References that are fixed are called **absolute references**. In Excel, absolute references are marked with a $ (dollar sign) before each column and row designation. For example, B8 is a relative reference to cell B8, whereas $B$8 is an absolute reference to cell B8. When you copy a formula that contains an absolute reference to a new location, the reference does not change. Figure 3-3 shows an example of how copying a formula with an absolute reference does not change the cell reference.

Formula using an absolute reference ◄ **Figure 3-3**

original formula with an absolute reference

formula copied into a new range (column and row references fixed regardless of cell location)

formula results

In this figure, the formula =$A$1 entered in cell A3 produced the result of 10, which is the value in cell A1. After the formula in cell A3 was copied to cell B3, the copied formula remained unchanged and produced the result of 10, which is the value in cell A1. As you can see, when the formula was copied one cell to the right, the absolute reference in the original formula (A1) did not change. Similarly, when the formula in cell A3 was copied two cells to the right to cell C3, the copied formula and the results did not change. In each instance, the formula references the cell A1.

You'll see how absolute references work when you fix the formulas in cells D19 and D20, and then recopy the formulas.

To use absolute references in the take-home pay formulas:

1. In cell D19, enter **=$E$5**. This formula contains an absolute reference to cell E5, which contains Diane's take-home pay during the school months.

2. In cell D20, enter **=$E$6**. This formula contains an absolute reference to cell E6, which contains Glenn's take-home pay during the school months.

3. Copy the corrected formulas in the range **D19:D20**, and then paste them in the range **E19:H20**. As shown in Figure 3-4, the months of February through May now correctly show the take-home pay values that Diane has specified for the school months.

| Figure 3-4 | Results of formulas with absolute references |

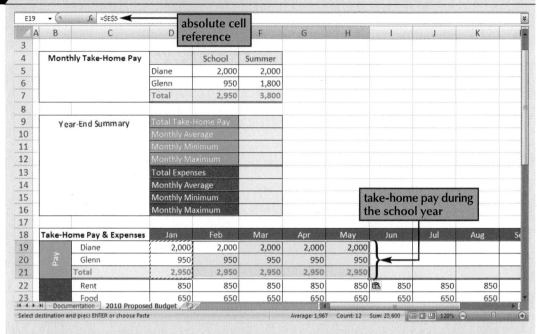

4. Click each cell in the range E19:H20 to verify that the formulas =$E$5 and =$E$6 were copied into the appropriate cells.

InSight | **Understanding Relative and Absolute References**

Part of writing effective formulas is knowing when to use relative and absolute references. Use relative references when you want to repeat the same formula with different cells. For example, in a customer order worksheet, you might need to calculate the cost of an item multiplied by the quantity being purchased. To repeat this formula for all of the items in an order, you would use relative references for the item cost and item quantity. Use absolute references when you want different formulas to refer to the same cell. For example, in a customer order worksheet, you might need to apply the same sales tax percentage to each order. You could store the sales tax percentage in a worksheet cell, and then use an absolute reference to that cell in the formula that multiples the order total with the sales tax percentage.

Using Mixed References

A formula can also contain mixed references. A **mixed reference** contains both relative and absolute references. For example, a mixed reference for cell A2 can be either $A2 or A$2. In the mixed reference $A2, the column reference is fixed on column A and the reference to row 2 is relative. In the mixed reference A$2, the column reference is relative and the row reference is fixed. In other words, a mixed reference "locks" one part of the cell reference while the other part can change. When you copy and paste a formula with a mixed reference to a new location, the absolute portion of the cell reference remains fixed and the relative portion shifts. For example, the mixed reference in the formula =$A2 in cell B2 becomes =$A3 when copied to cell B3, and the mixed reference in the formula =B$1 in cell B2 becomes =C$1 when copied to cell C2.

Figure 3-5 shows an example of using a formula with a mixed reference in which the column is relative and the row is fixed. When you copy and paste the formula from cell A3 into cells A4 and A5, the row reference remains fixed on row 1. In this instance, the column reference, which is relative, doesn't change either, because the formula was copied to the same column. However, when you copy the formula to other columns, the column reference, which is relative, shifts to reflect the new column location. The row reference remains fixed on row 1 and doesn't change no matter where you copy the formula.

Formulas using mixed references ◄ **Figure 3-5**

	A	B	C	D
1	10	20	30	
2				
3	=A$1			
4				
5				

original formula with a mixed reference

	A	B	C	D
1	10	20	30	
2				
3	=A$1	=B$1	=C$1	
4	=A$1	=B$1	=C$1	
5	=A$1	=B$1	=C$1	

formula copied to a new range (row reference fixed on row 1, column reference shifts based on the cell location)

	A	B	C	D
1	10	20	30	
2				
3	10	20	30	
4	10	20	30	
5	10	20	30	

formula results

As you develop formulas, you might want to switch a cell reference from relative to absolute or mixed. Rather than retyping the formula, you can switch the reference in editing mode by selecting the cell reference and pressing the **F4 key**. As you press the function key, Excel cycles through the different reference types, starting by changing a relative reference to an absolute reference, then to a mixed reference with the row absolute, then to a mixed reference with the column absolute, and then finally back to a relative reference.

Entering Relative, Absolute, and Mixed References | Reference Window

- To enter a relative reference, type the cell reference as it appears in the worksheet. For example, enter B2 for cell B2.
- To enter an absolute reference, type $ (a dollar sign) before both the row and column references. For example, enter $B$2.
- To enter a mixed reference, type $ before either the row or column reference. For example, enter $B2 or B$2.

or

- Select the cell reference you want to change.
- Press the F4 key to cycle the reference from relative to absolute to mixed and then back to relative.

You'll use the F4 key to cycle through the different types of references as you enter the remaining formulas with the take-home pay for the summer months.

To insert the remaining take-home pay formulas:

▶ **1.** Click cell **I19**, type **=**, and then click cell **F5**. The formula =F5 appears in the cell, which remains in editing mode. This formula enters Diane's summer take-home pay for June.

▶ **2.** Select the cell reference **F5** in the formula, and then press the **F4** key. The formula changes to =$F$5, which is an absolute reference.

▶ **3.** Press the **F4** key again. The formula changes to =F$5, which is a mixed reference with a relative column reference and an absolute row reference.

▶ **4.** Press the **F4** key again to change to formula to =$F5, which is a mixed cell reference with an absolute column reference and a relative row reference.

▶ **5.** Press the **F4** key again to return to the formula to =F5, which is a relative reference.

▶ **6.** Press the **F4** key one more time to change the formula back to =$F$5, and then press the **Enter** key to exit editing mode. You want an absolute reference to cell F5 so that the formula always references Diane's summer take-home pay.

▶ **7.** In cell I20, enter the formula **=$F$6**. This formula uses an absolute reference to enter Glenn's summer take-home pay for June, and won't change when copied to the rest of the months.

▶ **8.** In cell I21, enter the formula **=I19+I20**. This formula adds Diane and Glenn's take-home pay for June.

▶ **9.** Copy the range **I19:I21**, and then paste the copied formulas into the range **J19:K21**. The summer take-home pay values appear for the months of June through August.

You'll complete the take-home pay values for the remaining school months.

▶ **10.** Copy the range **D19:D21**, and then paste it into the range **L19:O21**. The take-home pay for the couple is entered for all twelve months of the year.

Now that you've calculated the monthly take-home pay and expenses for Diane and Glenn, you'll summarize these for the entire year. Diane wants to compare the couple's annual take-home pay to their annual expenses. She also wants to know the average take-home pay and average expenses for a typical month.

Working with Functions

The month-by-month data is too large to see in the workbook window unless you reduce the zoom level, but then the resulting text would be too small to read. Rather than adding another column to this large collection of data, Diane wants to summarize the data at the top of the worksheet. You'll use Excel functions to do these summary calculations.

Summarizing Data | InSight

Statisticians, scientists, and economists often want to reduce a large sample of data into a few easy-to-use statistics. How do they best summarize the data? The most common approach is to average the sample data. You can calculate the average in Excel with the AVERAGE function. However, this is not always the best choice. Averages are susceptible to extremely large or small data values. Imagine calculating the average price of houses on a block that has one mansion and several small homes. The average value is heavily affected by the mansion. When the data includes a few extremely large or extremely small values, it might be best to use the **median**, or middle, value from the sample. You can calculate the median in Excel with the MEDIAN function.

Another approach is to calculate the most common value in the data, otherwise known as the **mode**. The mode is most often used with data that has only a few possible values, such as the number of bedrooms in a house. The most common number of bedrooms per house might provide more relevant information than the average number of bedrooms. You can calculate the mode in Excel using the MODE function.

Understanding Function Syntax

Recall from Tutorial 1 that a function is a named operation that returns a value. Every function has to follow a set of rules, or **syntax**, which specifies how the function should be written. The general syntax of all functions is as follows:

FUNCTION(argument1, argument2, ...)

In this syntax, *FUNCTION* is the name of the function and *argument1*, *argument2*, and so forth are **arguments**, which are the numbers, text, or cell references used by the function to return a value. Arguments are always separated by a comma.

Not all functions have arguments, and some functions have **optional arguments**, which are not required for the function to return a value, but can be included to provide more control over the returned value. If an optional argument is not included, Excel assumes a default value for it. These tutorials show optional arguments within square brackets along with the argument's default value, as follows:

> **Tip**
>
> Optional arguments are always placed last in the argument list.

FUNCTION(argument1, [argument2=value2, ...])

In this function, *argument2* is an optional argument and *value2* is the default value used for this argument. As you learn more about individual functions, you will learn which arguments are required and which are optional, and the default values used for optional arguments.

There are hundreds of Excel functions, which are organized into 11 categories. Figure 3-6 describes these different categories.

Figure 3-6 ▸ **Categories of Excel functions**

Category	Contains functions that
Cube	Retrieve data from multidimensional databases involving online analytical processing or OLAP
Database	Retrieve and analyze data stored in databases
Date & Time	Analyze or create date and time values and time intervals
Engineering	Analyze engineering problems
Financial	Have financial applications
Information	Return information about the format, location, or contents of worksheet cells
Logical	Return logical (true-false) values
Lookup & Reference	Look up and return data matching a set of specified conditions from a range
Math & Trig	Have math and trigonometry applications
Statistical	Provide statistical analyses of a set of data
Text	Return text values or evaluate text

You can learn about each function using the Help system. Figure 3-7 describes some of the more common Math, Trig, and Statistical functions that you might often use in your workbooks.

Figure 3-7 ▸ **Math, Trig, and Statistical functions**

Function	Category	Description
AVERAGE(*number1* [, *number2*, *number3*, ...])	Statistical	Calculates the average of a collection of numbers, where *number1*, *number2*, and so forth are either numbers or cell references. Only *number1* is required. For more than one cell reference or to enter numbers directly into the function, use the optional arguments *number2*, *number3*, and so forth.
COUNT(*value1* [, *value2*, *value3*, ...])	Statistical	Counts how many cells in a range contain numbers, where *value1*, *value2*, and so forth are text, numbers, or cell references. Only *value1* is required. For more than one cell reference or to enter numbers directly into the function, use the optional arguments *value2*, *value3*, and so forth.
COUNTA(*value1* [, *value2*, *value3*, ...])	Statistical	Counts how many cells are not empty in ranges *value1*, *value2*, and so forth, or how many numbers are listed within *value1*, *value2*, and so forth.
INT(*number*)	Math & Trig	Displays the integer portion of a number, *number*.
MAX(*number1* [, *number2*, *number3*, ...])	Statistical	Calculates the maximum value of a collection of numbers, where *number1*, *number2*, and so forth are either numbers or cell references.
MEDIAN(*number1* [, *number2*, *number3*, ...])	Statistical	Calculates the median, or middle, value of a collection of numbers, where *number1*, *number2*, and so forth are either numbers or cell references.
MIN(*number1* [, *number2*, *number3*, ...])	Statistical	Calculates the minimum value of a collection of numbers, where *number1*, *number2*, and so forth are either numbers or cell references.
RAND()	Math & Trig	Returns a random number between 0 and 1.
ROUND(*number, num_digits*)	Math & Trig	Rounds a number to a specified number of digits, where *number* is the number you want to round and *num_digits* specifies how many digits to which you want to round the number.
SUM(*number1* [, *number2*, *number3*, ...])	Math & Trig	Adds a collection of numbers, where *number1*, *number2*, and so forth are either numbers or cell references.

For example, the AVERAGE function calculates the average value from a collection of numbers. The syntax of the AVERAGE function is as follows:

```
AVERAGE(number1, [number2, number3, ...])
```

In this function, *number1, number2, number3,* and so forth are either numbers or cell references to numbers. For example, the following function calculates the average of 1, 2, 5, and 8:

```
AVERAGE(1, 2, 5, 8)
```

This function returns the value 4. However, you usually reference values entered in the worksheet. So, if the range A1:A4 contains the values 1, 2, 5, and 8, the following function also returns a value of 4:

```
AVERAGE(A1:A4)
```

Functions can be incorporated as part of larger formulas. For example, consider the following formula:

```
=MAX(A1:A100)/100
```

This formula returns the maximum value from the range A1:A100, and then divides that value by 100. Functions can also be placed inside another function, or **nested**. If a formula contains several functions, Excel starts with the innermost function and then moves outward. For example, the following formula first calculates the average of the values in the range A1:A100 using the AVERAGE function, and then extracts the integer portion of that value using the INT function.

```
=INT(AVERAGE(A1:A100))
```

One challenge of nesting functions is to make sure that you include all of the parentheses. You can check this by counting the number of left parentheses, and making sure that number matches the number of right parentheses. If the numbers don't match, Excel will not accept the formula and offers a suggestion for rewriting the formula so the left and right parentheses do match.

Inserting a Function

Functions are organized in the Function Library group in the Formulas tab on the Ribbon. In the Function Library, you can select a function from a function category or you can open the Insert Function dialog box to search for a particular function.

Inserting a Function | Reference Window

- Click the Formulas tab on the Ribbon.
- To insert a function from a specific category, click the appropriate category button in the Function Library group. To search for a function, click the Insert Function button in the Function Library group, enter a description of the function, and then click the Go button.
- Select the appropriate function from the list of functions.
- Enter the argument values in the Function Arguments dialog box, and then click the OK button.

You'll use the SUM function to add the total take-home pay for the entire year in Diane's proposed budget.

To insert the SUM function:

▶ 1. Click cell **F9** to select it.

▶ 2. Click the **Formulas** tab on the Ribbon.

▶ 3. In the Function Library group on the Formulas tab, click the **Math & Trig** button. A list displays all of the math and trigonometry functions arranged in alphabetical order.

▶ 4. Scroll down the list, and then click **SUM**. The Function Arguments dialog box opens.

The Function Arguments dialog box lists all of the arguments associated with the SUM function. Required arguments are in bold type; optional arguments are in normal type. Excel tries to "anticipate" the values for the different arguments based on the location of the cell containing the formula and the data contained in other cells of the worksheet. In this case, the range reference F5:F8, which is the range that contains the couple's take-home pay for the summer months and is the range of numbers closest to the cell in which you are entering the SUM function, already appears for the first argument. Because you want to calculate the total take-home pay for the year, you'll replace this range reference with the reference D21:O21.

To enter the argument for the SUM function:

▶ 1. Click in the worksheet, and then select the range **D21:O21**. The range reference appears as the value of the Number1 argument. See Figure 3-8.

Figure 3-8	Function Arguments dialog box

Tip

You can click the Collapse Dialog Box button to shrink the Function Arguments dialog box to see more of the worksheet, select the range, and then click the Expand Dialog Box button to restore the dialog box.

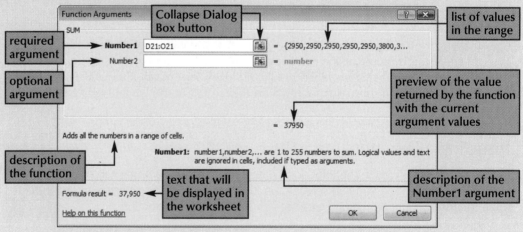

▶ 2. Click the **OK** button. The formula =SUM(D21:O21) is inserted into cell F9, which displays the value 37,950. This represents the total take-home pay for the year from both Diane and Glenn.

Diane also wants to know how this value compares to the total expenses for the year.

▶ 3. Click cell **F13**. This is where you want to enter the second SUM function.

▶ 4. In the Function Library group on the Formulas tab, click the **Math & Trig** button, and then click **SUM**. The Function Arguments dialog box opens. You'll enter the monthly expenses stored in the range D32:O32 for the argument.

> **5.** Select the range **D32:O32** in the worksheet, and then click the **OK** button in the Function Arguments dialog box. The formula =SUM(D32:O32) is inserted in cell F13, which displays the value 35,840. This represents the total projected expenses for the upcoming year. See Figure 3-9.

SUM functions entered ◄ **Figure 3-9**

Diane projects that she and Glenn will earn roughly $2,000 more than they will spend throughout the year. It's easier for Diane to plan her budget if she knows how much, on average, the couple takes home and spends each month. You can use the AVERAGE function to do this calculation using the same method you used for the SUM function; but what if you weren't sure of the function's name or its function category? You can use the Insert Function dialog box. The **Insert Function dialog box** organizes all of the functions by category and allows you to search for functions that perform particular calculations.

To insert the AVERAGE function to calculate the average take-home pay:

> **1.** Click cell **F10**.

> **2.** In the Function Library group on the Formulas tab, click the **Insert Function** button. The Insert Function dialog box opens.

> **3.** Type **Calculate an average value** in the Search for a function box, and then click the **Go** button. Functions for calculating an average appear in the Select a function box. See Figure 3-10.

Figure 3-10	**Insert Function dialog box**

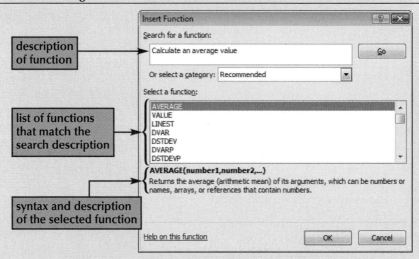

Tip

You can also open the Insert Function dialog box by clicking the Insert Function button on the formula bar.

▶ **4.** Verify that **AVERAGE** is selected in the Select a function box, and then click the **OK** button. The Function Arguments dialog box opens with the arguments for the AVERAGE function. As before, a range reference for cells directly above this cell already appears for the Number1 argument.

▶ **5.** Select the range reference in the Number1 argument box, and then select the range **D21:O21** in the worksheet.

▶ **6.** Click the **OK** button. The dialog box closes, and the formula =AVERAGE(D21:O21) is entered in cell F10, displaying the value 3,163, the average take-home pay.

Although the exact average take-home pay is 3,162.50, you see the value 3,163 in the cell because Diane formatted the worksheet to display currency values to the nearest dollar.

How does the couple's average take-home pay compare to their average expenses? To find out, you'll use the AVERAGE function again. Because the function has already been used in your workbook, you can select it from a list of recently used functions.

To calculate the average monthly expenses:

▶ **1.** Click cell **F14**, and then click the **Insert Function** button fx on the formula bar. The Insert Function dialog box opens.

▶ **2.** If necessary, click the **Or select a category** arrow, and then click **Most Recently Used**. The most recently used functions, sorted in order of recent use, appear in the Select a function box. The AVERAGE function is at the top followed by the SUM function.

▶ **3.** Verify that **AVERAGE** is selected in the Select a function box, and then click the **OK** button.

▶ **4.** Select the range **D32:O32** to insert the range reference D32:O32 in the Number1 box.

▶ **5.** Click the **OK** button. The formula =AVERAGE(D32:O32) is inserted into cell F14, displaying the value 2,987. This represents the average expenses per month under Diane's budget. See Figure 3-11.

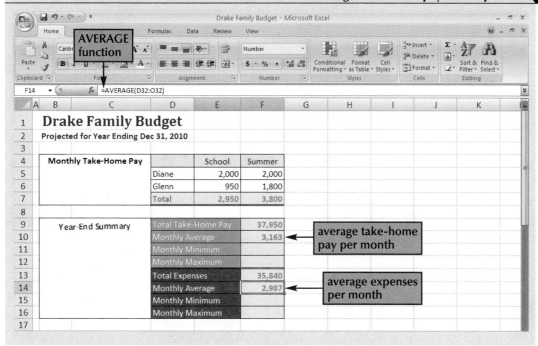

Average take-home pay and expenses | Figure 3-11

From the two averages, Diane sees that the couple will bring in about $200 more than they spend each month. That is not much, so Diane wants to know how much variation is in the budget. What is the most money she could expect to take home during a single month in the upcoming year? What is the least? And what are the largest and smallest values for the monthly expenses? You'll use the MAX and MIN functions to calculate those values.

Typing a Function

After you become more familiar with functions, it is often faster to type the functions directly in cells rather than using the Insert Function dialog box or the Function Library. As you begin to type a function name within a formula, a list of functions that begin with the letters you typed appears. For example, when you type *S*, the list shows all of the functions starting with the letter *S*; when you type *SU,* the list shows only those functions starting with the letters *SU*, and so forth. This helps to ensure that you're entering a legitimate Excel function name.

You'll type the formulas to calculate the minimum monthly take-home pay and expenses under Diane's proposed budget.

To calculate the minimum values for monthly take-home pay and expenses:

▶ **1.** Click cell **F11**. This is the cell in which you want to enter the minimum take-home pay.

▶ **2.** Type **=M**. As you type a formula, a list with function names starting with *M* opens.

▶ **3.** Type **I**. The list shows only those functions starting with *MI*. See Figure 3-12. As soon as the function you want appears in the list, you can double-click its name to enter it in the cell without typing the rest of its name.

Figure 3-12 ▶ **Typing a function**

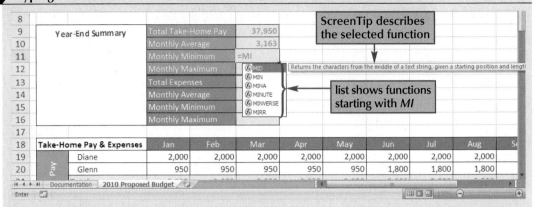

4. Double-click **MIN** in the list box. The MIN function with its opening parenthesis is inserted into cell F11 and a ScreenTip shows the syntax for the function. At this point, you can either type in the range reference or select the range with your mouse. To avoid typing errors, it's often better to use your mouse to enter range references.

5. Select the range **D21:O21**, type **)**, and then press the **Enter** key. The formula =MIN(D21:O21) is inserted in cell F11, displaying the value 2,950. This is the minimum amount that Diane expects the couple to bring home in a single month for the upcoming year.

   Next, you'll calculate the minimum monthly expense projected for the year.

6. Click cell **F15**, and then follow Steps 2 through 5 to enter the formula **=MIN(D32:O32)** in cell F15. The cell displays the value 2,265, which is the least amount that Diane expects to spend in a single month in the upcoming year.

The final piece of the year-end summary is the maximum monthly value for both take-home pay and expenses. Maximum values are calculated using the MAX function.

To calculate the maximum values for monthly take-home pay and expenses:

1. Click cell **F12**, and then enter the formula **=MAX(D21:O21)**. The value 3,800 appears in cell F12, indicating that the maximum take-home pay the couple can expect in a single month is $3,800.

   Trouble? If #NAME? appears in the cell, you probably mistyped the function name. Edit the formula to correct the misspelling.

2. Click cell **F16**, and then enter the formula **=MAX(D32:O32)**. The value 5,170 appears in cell F16, indicating that the maximum expenses for a single month are projected to be $5,170. See Figure 3-13.

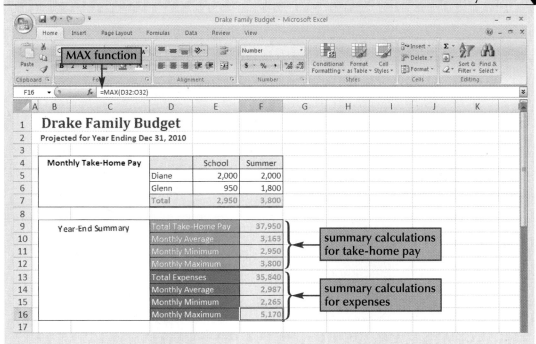

Year-end summary values | Figure 3-13

Based on the year-end summary, Diane and Glenn's monthly take-home pay will range from a minimum of $2,950 to a maximum of $3,800 with an average of about $3,163. Monthly expenses, on the other hand, range from a minimum of $2,265 to a maximum of $5,170 with an average of $2,987. Clearly, the Drake family budget does not have a lot of wiggle room.

Diane has just been promoted at work. Her take-home pay will increase from $2,000 per month to $2,500 per month. She wants to know how this affects the year-end summary.

To modify Diane's estimates of her take-home pay:

▶ **1.** In cell E5, enter the value **2500**.

▶ **2.** In cell F5, enter the value **2500**. Figure 3-14 shows the updated calculations for the couple's take-home pay for the entire year as well as the monthly average, minimum, and maximum values.

| Figure 3-14 | Revised salary values |

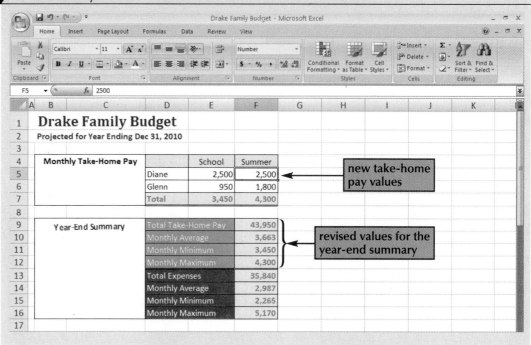

With Diane's new position, the couple's annual take-home pay increases from $37,950 to $43,950 and the monthly average increases from $3,163 to $3,663. The couple's take-home pay should exceed their expenses by an average of $700 per month. The monthly take-home pay now ranges from a minimum of $3,450 up to a maximum of $4,300. The raise has brightened the couple's financial picture quite a bit.

Diane now has a better picture of the family's finances for the upcoming year, and she's more confident about how to manage the couple's budget. She and Glenn hope to save enough for a down payment on a house in a few years. With the promotion, this seems like a real possibility. In the next session, you'll help Diane explore the couple's options in planning for a purchase of a house.

Review | Session 3.1 Quick Check

1. What is the absolute cell reference for cell B21? What are the two mixed references?
2. Cell B10 contains the formula =B1+B2. What formula is entered if this formula is copied and pasted into cell C20?
3. Cell B10 contains the formula =$B1+B$2. What formula is entered if this formula is copied and pasted into cell C20?
4. Cell B10 contains the formula =AVERAGE($A1:$A5). What formula is entered if this formula is copied and pasted into cell C20?
5. What are optional arguments? What happens if you do not include an optional argument in a function?
6. What formula should you enter to add the numbers in the range B1:B10?
7. The range of a set of values is defined as the maximum value minus the minimum value. What formula would you enter to calculate the range of the values in B1:B10?
8. What formula would you enter to calculate the ratio of the maximum value in the range B1:B10 to the minimum value?

Session 3.2

Working with AutoFill

Diane and Glenn hope to purchase a home in the next three years. Currently, the couple has $4,000 in their savings account, and they plan to start putting money into a home savings account. Diane wants to see what impact her proposed budget will have on their savings. To do that, you'll enter the current account information at the top of the worksheet. You'll include the current savings balance and the expected balance at the end of the next year under Diane's proposed budget.

To produce the results Diane wants, you will use a feature known as **AutoFill**, which copies content and formats from a cell or range into an adjacent cell or range. You'll begin by copying the formatting from the Monthly Take-Home Pay section to the range where you'll enter this new Savings section.

To format the range and insert data about the couple's savings account:

▶ **1.** If you took a break after the previous session, make sure the Drake Family Budget workbook is open and the 2010 Proposed Budget worksheet is active.

▶ **2.** Select the range **B4:F7**, and then, in the Clipboard group on the Home tab, click the **Format Painter** button 🖋 to copy the formatting for the new section.

▶ **3.** Select the range **H4:L7** to paste the selected format to this range.

▶ **4.** Referring to Figure 3-15, enter the labels and data shown in the range H4:L7. In cell K7, enter a formula to add the values in the range K5:K6. In cell L7, enter a formula to add the values in the range L5:L6.

Initial savings data ◀ **Figure 3-15**

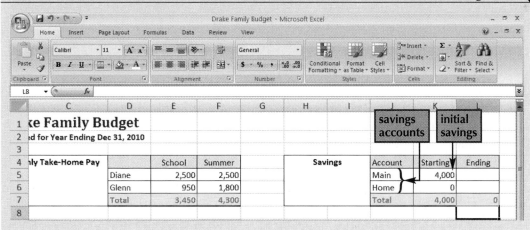

Diane wants to learn how much the couple could save each month. To find out, you must first determine the couple's monthly net cash flow, which is equal to their take-home pay minus their expenses. You'll start by formatting the cells where you'll enter this data and calculating the net cash flow during the month of January.

To format the range and calculate the net cash flow for January:

▶ **1.** Click cell **B18**, and then, in the Clipboard group on the Home tab, click the **Format Painter** button 🖋.

▶ **2.** Select the range **B33:C33**. The formatting from cell B18 is pasted into the range, merging the two cells.

> 3. In cell B33, type **Net Cash Flow**, and then right-align the contents of the cell.

> 4. In cell D33, enter the formula **=D21–D32**. This formula subtracts total expenses from total take-home pay for the month of January. The value –1,590 is displayed, indicating a projected shortfall of $1,590 for the month of January. Next, you'll format cell D33 to distinguish net cash flow amount from the other values.

> 5. Click cell **D33**.

> 6. In the Styles group, click the **Cell Styles** button, and then click the **60% – Accent6** style. See Figure 3-16.

Figure 3-16	January net cash flow

		Jan	Feb	Mar	Apr	May	Jun	Jul	Aug	S
17										
18	Take-Home Pay & Expenses	Jan	Feb	Mar	Apr	May	Jun	Jul	Aug	S
19	Diane	2,500	2,500	2,500	2,500	2,500	2,500	2,500	2,500	
20	Glenn	950	950	950	950	950	1,800	1,800	1,800	
21	Total	3,450	3,450	3,450	3,450	3,450	4,300	4,300	4,300	
22	Rent	850	850	850	850	850	850	850	850	
23	Food	650	650	650	650	650	650	650	650	
24	Utilities	225	210	175	165	120	135	145	145	
25	Phone	75	75	75	75	75	75	75	75	
26	Car Payments	175	175	175	175	175	175	175	175	
27	Insurance	125	125	125	125	125	125	125	125	
28	Tuition	1,900	0	0	0	0	900	0	1,900	
29	Books	700	0	0	0	0	300	0	700	
30	Travel	190	120	150	450	120	180	720	400	
31	Miscellaneous	150	150	150	150	150	150	150	150	
32	Total	5,040	2,355	2,350	2,640	2,265	3,540	2,890	5,170	
33	Net Cash Flow	-1,590								
34										
35	Monthly Savings									
36	Starting Balance									

January shows a negative net cash flow

Documentation | 2010 Proposed Budget

Ready

AutoFilling a Formula

You could copy and paste the formula and format from cell D33 into the rest of the row to calculate the net cash flow for the other months, as you've done before, but AutoFill is faster. The small black square in the lower-right corner of a selected cell or range is called the **fill handle**. When you drag the fill handle over an adjacent range, Excel copies the formulas and formats from the original cell into the adjacent range. This process is more efficient than the two-step process of copying and pasting.

Reference Window	**Copying Formulas and Formats with AutoFill**

- Select the cell or range that contains the formula or formulas you want to copy.
- Drag the fill handle in the direction you want to copy the formula(s) and then release the mouse button.
- To copy only the formats or only the formulas, click the AutoFill Options button and select the appropriate option.

or

- Select the cell or range that contains the formula or formulas you want to copy.
- In the Editing group on the Home tab, click the Fill button.
- Select the appropriate fill direction and fill type (or click Series, enter the desired fill series options, and then click the OK button).

You'll use AutoFill to fill in the cash flow values for the remaining months of the year.

To copy the formulas and formats using AutoFill:

▶ **1.** Click cell **D33**, if necessary. The fill handle appears in the lower-right corner of the cell.

▶ **2.** Position the pointer over the fill handle until the pointer changes to **+**.

▶ **3.** Drag the fill handle over the range **E33:O33**. A solid outline appears around the selected range as you move the pointer.

▶ **4.** Release the mouse button. The selected range is filled in with the formula and format from cell D33, and the AutoFill Options button appears in the lower-right corner of the selected cells. See Figure 3-17.

Tip

With AutoFill, it's easy to copy formulas into the wrong range; if that happens, click the Undo button and try again.

Formulas and formats copied with AutoFill ◀ **Figure 3-17**

	Mar	Apr	May	Jun	Jul	Aug	Sep	Oct	Nov	Dec	
18	Mar	Apr	May	Jun	Jul	Aug	Sep	Oct	Nov	Dec	
19	2,500	2,500	2,500	2,500	2,500	2,500	2,500	2,500	2,500	2,500	
20	950	950	950	1,800	1,800	1,800	950	950	950	950	
21	3,450	3,450	3,450	4,300	4,300	4,300	3,450	3,450	3,450	3,450	
22	850	850	850	850	850	850	850	850	850	850	
23	650	650	650	650	650	650	650	650	650	650	
24	175	165	120	135	145	145	140	140	170	210	
25	75	75	75	75	75	75	75	75	75	75	
26	175	175	175	175	175	175	175	175	175	175	
27	125	125	125	125	125	125	125	125	125	125	
28	0	0	0	900	0	1,900	0	0	0	0	
29	0	0	0	300	0	700	0	0	0	0	
30	150	450	120	180	720	400	130	150	250	300	AutoFill Options button
31	150	150	150	150	150	150	150	150	150	150	
32	2,350	2,640	2,265	3,540	2,890	5,170	2,295	2,315	2,445	2,535	
33	1,100	810	1,185	760	1,410	870	1,155	1,135	1,005	915	

formula and formats copied to the selected range

fill handle

Ready | Average: 676 Count: 12 Sum: 8,110 120%

▶ **5.** Review the monthly net cash flows to confirm that AutoFill correctly copied the formula into the selected range.

These calculations provide Diane with a better picture of how the couple's net cash flow varies from month to month. Only in January and August do the couple's expenses exceed their take-home pay. In most months, their take-home pay exceeds expenses by at least $1,000, and in July, it exceeds expenses by $1,410.

Using the AutoFill Options Button

By default, AutoFill copies both the formulas and the formats of the original range to the selected range. However, sometimes you might want to copy only the formulas or only the formatting. You can specify what is copied by using the AutoFill Options button that appears after you release the mouse button. As shown in Figure 3-18, clicking this button provides a list of AutoFill options. The Copy Cells option, which is the default, copies both the formulas and the formatting. The Fill Formatting Only option copies the formatting into the selected cells but not any formulas. The Fill Without Formatting option copies the formulas but not the formatting.

AutoFill options ◀ **Figure 3-18**

copies only the formats → Fill Formatting Only

copies the cells, filling in both formats and formulas → Copy Cells

copies only the formulas → Fill Without Formatting

Filling a Series

AutoFill can also be used to create a series of numbers, dates, or text based on a pattern. To create a series of numbers, you enter the initial values in the series in a selected range and then use AutoFill to complete the series. Figure 3-19 shows how AutoFill can be used to insert the numbers from 1 to 10 in a selected range. You enter the first few numbers in the range A1:A3 to establish the pattern for AutoFill to use. Then, you select the range and drag the fill handle over the cells where you want the pattern continued. In Figure 3-19, the fill handle is dragged over the range A4:A10 and the rest of the series is filled in.

Figure 3-19 ▶ **AutoFill extends a numeric sequence**

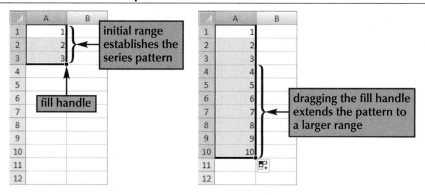

AutoFill can fill in a wide variety of series, including dates and times and text. Figure 3-20 shows examples of some series that AutoFill can generate. In each case, you must provide enough information for AutoFill to identify the pattern. AutoFill can recognize some patterns from only a single value, such as Jan or January to create a series of month abbreviations or names, or Mon or Monday to create a series of the days of the week.

Figure 3-20 ▶ **AutoFill applied to different series**

Type	Initial Entry	Extended Series
Values	1, 2, 3	4, 5, 6, ...
	2, 4, 6	8, 10, 12, ...
Dates and Times	Jan	Feb, Mar, Apr, ...
	January	February, March, April, ...
	15-Jan, 15-Feb	15-Mar, 15-Apr, 15-May, ...
	12/30/2010	12/31/2010, 1/1/2011, 1/2/2011, ...
	12/31/2010, 1/31/2011	2/28/2011, 3/31/2011, 4/30/2011, ...
	Mon	Tue, Wed, Thu, ...
	Monday	Tuesday, Wednesday, Thursday, ...
	11:00AM	12:00PM, 1:00PM, 2:00PM, ...
Patterned Text	1st period	2nd period, 3rd period, 4th period, ...
	Region 1	Region 2, Region 3, Region 4, ...
	Quarter 3	Quarter 4, Quarter 1, Quarter 2, ...
	Qtr3	Qtr4, Qtr1, Qtr2, ...

For more complex patterns, you can use the Series dialog box. Enter the first value of the series in a worksheet cell, select the entire range that will contain the series, click the Fill button in the Editing group on the Home tab, and then click Series. The Series dialog box opens. You then choose how a series grows, set how fast the series grows and its stopping value, and decide whether to use existing values in the selected range as the basis for the series trend.

Creating a Series with AutoFill | Reference Window

- Enter the first few values of the series into a range.
- Select the range, and then drag the fill handle of the selected range over the cells you want to fill.

or

- Enter the first few values of the series into a range.
- Select the entire range into which you want to extend the series.
- In the Editing group on the Home tab, click the Fill button, and then click Down, Right, Up, Left, Series, or Justify to set the direction you want to extend the series.

Diane wants to see how the monthly balances in her savings account are affected by the couple's changing expenses and take-home pay. She wants to make sure that the balance doesn't drop too low after months with particularly high expenses—such as January and August when Glenn's tuition payments are due. You'll add data to the worksheet to display the monthly savings balance. Diane already entered titles for the couple's different savings accounts. You'll use AutoFill to enter the month titles.

To use AutoFill to enter a series of months:

1. In cell D35, enter **Jan**. This is the first value in the series. Because Jan is a common abbreviation for January, Excel recognizes it as a month and you don't need to type Feb for the next month in the series.

2. Click cell **D35**, center the text, format it using the **Accent1** cell style, and then add a single border around the cell. This is the formatting you want to use for all the month abbreviations.

3. Position the pointer over the fill handle in cell D35 until the pointer changes to **+**.

4. Drag the fill handle over the range **E35:O35**. As you drag the fill handle, Screen-Tips show the month abbreviations. When you release the mouse button, AutoFill enters the remaining three-letter abbreviations for each month of the year with the formatting you applied to cell D35. See Figure 3-21.

Formatted month titles ◄ **Figure 3-21**

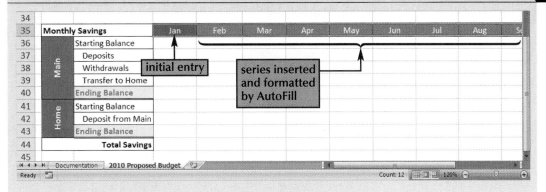

Next, you'll enter formulas to calculate the changing balance in the couple's main savings account and their home savings account. The main savings account balance is determined by four factors: the initial balance, the amount of money they deposit, the amount of money they withdraw, and the amount of money they transfer into their home savings account. The amount Diane and Glenn deposit will always equal their take-home pay, and the amount they withdraw will always equal their expenses. For now, you'll assume that the couple won't transfer any money from their main savings account into their home savings account.

To calculate the initial balances in the savings accounts:

1. In cell D36, enter the formula **=$K$5**. The formula uses an absolute reference to set the starting balance in the main savings account (cell D36) equal to the starting balance for the year (cell K5), which is already entered at the top of the worksheet. The absolute reference ensures that the copied formula always refers to the correct cell.

2. In cell D37, enter **=D21** to retrieve the couple's take-home pay for January.

3. In cell D38, enter **=D32** to retrieve the January expenses. You'll leave cell D39 blank because, at this point, you won't assume that any money will be transferred from the main savings account to the home savings account.

4. In cell D40, enter **=D36+D37–D38–D39**. This formula calculates the ending balance for the main savings account, which is equal to the starting balance plus any deposits minus the withdrawals and transfers. Cell D40 displays the value 2,410, representing the balance in the main savings account at the end of January.

5. In cell D41, enter the formula **=$K$6**. The formula sets the starting balance for the home savings account equal to the starting balance for the year. Again, you used an absolute reference to ensure that the formula won't change when copied.

6. In cell D42, enter the formula **=D39**. Any deposits in the home savings account will be the result of transfers from the main savings account.

7. In cell D43, enter the formula **=D41+D42**. The ending balance in the home savings account will be equal to the starting balance plus any deposits.

8. In cell D44, enter the formula **=D40+D43**. The total savings is equal to the amount in both accounts at the end of the month.

9. Add borders around the cells in the range D36:D43.

10. Use the Format Painter to copy the formats from cell D32 into cells D40 and D43, and then use the Format Painter to copy the formats from cell D33 into cell D44. See Figure 3-22.

| Figure 3-22 | Formatted savings account values for January |

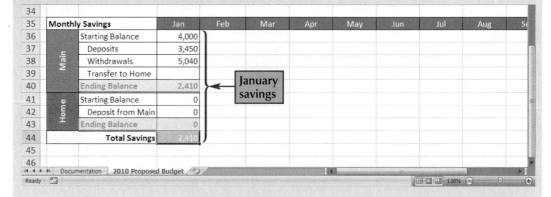

At this point, the couple's projected savings at the end of January will be $2,410, which is $1,590 less than their starting balance of $4,000 at the beginning of the year. The savings formulas for the remaining months are the same as for January except that their starting balances are based on the ending balance of the previous month.

To calculate the remaining balances in the savings accounts:

▶ **1.** Copy the range **D36:D44**, and then paste it into the range **E36:E44**.

▶ **2.** Change the formula in cell E36 to **=D40** so that the February starting balance for the main savings account equals the January ending balance.

▶ **3.** Change the formula in cell E41 to **=D43** so that the starting February balance in the home savings account is equal to the ending January balance.

Next, you'll use AutoFill to copy the February formulas into the remaining months of the year.

▶ **4.** Select the range **E36:E44**, and then drag the fill handle over the range **F36:O44**. All of the formulas and formatting for the rest of the year are filled in. See Figure 3-23.

Savings values for the remaining months ◀ Figure 3-23

		Jan	Feb	Mar	Apr	May	Jun	Jul	Aug	S
35	**Monthly Savings**									
36	Starting Balance	4,000	2,410	3,505	4,605	5,415	6,600	7,360	8,770	
37	Deposits	3,450	3,450	3,450	3,450	3,450	4,300	4,300	4,300	
38	Withdrawals	5,040	2,355	2,350	2,640	2,265	3,540	2,890	5,170	
39	Transfer to Home									
40	Ending Balance	2,410	3,505	4,605	5,415	6,600	7,360	8,770	7,900	
41	Starting Balance	0	0	0	0	0	0	0	0	
42	Deposit from Main	0	0	0	0	0	0	0	0	
43	Ending Balance	0	0	0	0	0	0	0	0	
44	**Total Savings**	2,410	3,505	4,605	5,415	6,600	7,360	8,770	7,900	

Documentation   2010 Proposed Budget

Ready   Average: 3,656   Count: 88   Sum: 321,715   120%

Diane wants to see the ending balances for the two savings accounts without scrolling, so you'll add the ending balances at the top of the worksheet.

▶ **5.** In cell L5, enter the formula **=$O$40**. You used an absolute reference so that the formula won't change if you later copy it to another cell. The ending balance of the main savings account in December—12,110—appears in cell L5.

▶ **6.** In cell L6, enter the formula **=$O$43**. Again, you used an absolute reference to ensure the formula won't change if you later copy it to another cell. The ending balance of the home savings account in December—0—appears in cell L6.

Developing a Savings Plan

Under her current budget projections, Diane expects to have $12,110 in the main savings account at the end of the next year but nothing in the home savings account. Diane wants to transfer some money into the home savings account each month. Because the home savings account is used for longer-term savings, Diane cannot withdraw money from it without penalty. So, she wants to make sure the main savings account always has enough money to meet monthly expenses and any unexpected bills without relying on money from the home savings account.

Diane needs to balance two things in her savings plan: a desire to keep a reasonable amount in the main savings account and the desire to save enough for a future down payment on a home mortgage. To achieve this balance, she needs to determine her overall savings goal and how soon she and Glenn want to meet that goal.

To help Diane determine an overall savings goal, you'll create a new worksheet with calculations for different savings plans. Diane wants to know how much money the couple can save if they put $500 to $1,000 into the home savings account each month for the next three years. You'll create a worksheet that shows the total amount saved in one, two, and three years from deposits starting at $500 that increase in $100 increments through $1,000.

To create the savings plan:

▶ 1. Insert a new worksheet named **Home Savings Plan** at the end of the workbook.

▶ 2. In cell A1, enter **Home Savings Projections**, and then format the title using the **Title** cell style.

▶ 3. Merge and center the range **B3:G3**, enter **Savings Deposit per Month** in the merged cell, and then format the merged cell using the **Heading 2** cell style.

▶ 4. In cell A4, enter **Months**, format the cell in bold.

▶ 5. In cell B4, enter **500**; in cell C4, enter **600**; select the range **B4:C4**; and then drag the fill handle to cell **G4**. The values entered in the series—500, 600, 700, 800, 900, and 1,000—are the different amounts the couple might transfer into their home savings account each month.

▶ 6. In the range A5:A7, enter the values **12**, **24**, and **36**. These monthly values are equal to one year, two years, and three years, respectively. You entered the years in months because Diane and Glenn plan to deposit money into their home savings account each month. So, they would make 12 deposits in one year, they would make 24 deposits in two years, and they would make 36 deposits in three years.

▶ 7. Format the range B4:G4;A5:A7 with the **Input** cell style.

Next, you'll use mixed cell references to calculate the amount of money saved under each plan. The amount saved is equal to the number of months of savings multiplied by the deposit per month.

▶ 8. In cell B5, enter **=$A5*B$4**. This formula uses mixed references to calculate the amount of savings generated by saving $500 per month for 12 months. The first mixed reference in the formula, $A5, has a fixed column reference and a relative row reference. When you copy the formula across row 5, the reference to cell A5 remains unchanged. When you copy the formula down column B, the reference to cell A5 changes to cell A6 in row 6 and cell A7 in row 7, which references the correct number of months of savings in the formula. The second mixed cell reference, B$4, has a relative column reference and a fixed row reference. When you copy the formula down column B, the reference to cell B4 remains unchanged. When you copy the formula across row 5, the reference to cell B4 changes to cell C4 in column C, cell D4 in column D, and so forth, which references the correct deposit per month in the formula.

▶ 9. Copy cell **B5** and paste the formula into the range **B5:G7**. The formula results show the projected savings based on different combinations of monthly deposits and lengths of time. Notice that the mixed references in each cell always reference a monthly deposit value from the range B4:G4 and a time length from the range A5:A7. The mixed references enable you to copy and paste the correct formulas quickly.

▶ 10. Format the values in the range B5:G7 using a thousands separator with no digits to the right of the decimal point, and add a single border around each cell in the range. Figure 3-24 shows the completed and formatted values.

Savings from monthly deposits ◀ Figure 3-24

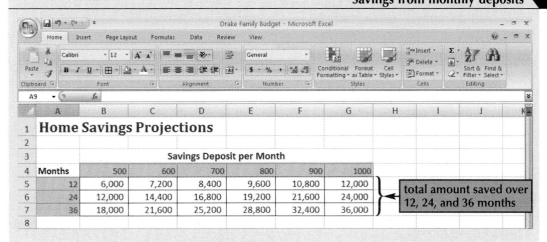

The data shows how increasing the amount that Diane and Glenn save toward their home each month quickly adds up. For example, if they save $800 per month, at the end of three years (36 months), they would have saved $28,800. This is just a little less than the $30,000 they want to save for the down payment. Diane asks you to enter in the budget projections the transfer of $800 from the main savings account to the home savings account each month.

To enter and format the home savings plan section:

1. Switch to the **2010 Proposed Budget** worksheet.

2. In cell H9, enter **Home Savings Plan**, and then format the cell in bold.

3. In cell H10, enter **Monthly Transfer to Home Acct**, and then, in cell K10, enter **800**.

4. Merge the range **H10:J10**, left-align the merged cell, and then format the cell using the **20% – Accent6** cell style.

5. Add a border around cell H10 and cell K10. See Figure 3-25.

Formatted savings plan ◀ Figure 3-25

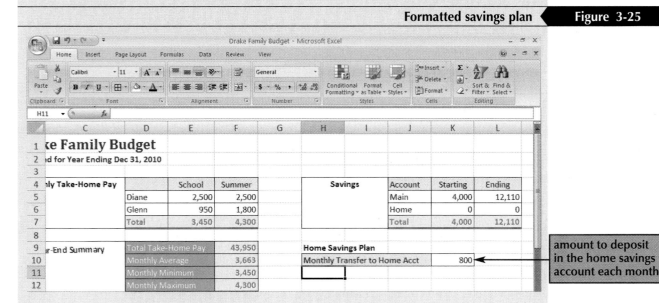

Next, you'll apply this $800 per month deposit value to the monthly transfer of funds from the main savings account to the home savings account.

To project the new savings account balances:

▶ 1. In cell D39, enter the formula **=$K$10**. You used an absolute value in this formula because the amount to transfer to the home savings account each month is always in cell K10 and you don't want the cell reference to change when you copy the formula to the rest of the months. The value 800 is displayed in the cell, indicating that for the month of January, $800 will be transferred from the couple's main savings account into the home savings account. The ending balance of the home savings account is now $800.

▶ 2. Copy cell **D39** and paste it into the range **E39:O39**. The value 800 is pasted into the rest of the row, indicating that each month the couple will transfer $800 into the home savings account. See Figure 3-26.

Figure 3-26   Monthly savings balance

		Jan	Feb	Mar	Apr	May	Jun	Jul	Aug	Se
35	**Monthly Savings**									
36	Starting Balance	4,000	1,610	1,905	2,205	2,215	2,600	2,560	3,170	
37	Deposits	3,450	3,450	3,450	3,450	3,450	4,300	4,300	4,300	
38	Withdrawals	5,040	2,355	2,350	2,640	2,265	3,540	2,890	5,170	
39	Transfer to Home	800	800	800	800	800	800	800	800	
40	Ending Balance	1,610	1,905	2,205	2,215	2,600	2,560	3,170	1,500	
41	Starting Balance	0	800	1,600	2,400	3,200	4,000	4,800	5,600	
42	Deposit from Main	800	800	800	800	800	800	800	800	
43	Ending Balance	800	1,600	2,400	3,200	4,000	4,800	5,600	6,400	
44	**Total Savings**	2,410	3,505	4,605	5,415	6,600	7,360	8,770	7,900	

amount transferred to the home savings account each month

balance in the home savings account

Average: 800   Count: 11

▶ 3. Examine the monthly balance in both the main savings account and the home savings account under Diane's proposed savings plan. Notice that the ending balance in the main savings account falls below $2,000 some months.

▶ 4. Scroll to the top of the worksheet and verify that the value displayed in cell L5 is 2,510 and the value displayed in cell L6 is 9,600.

Under this savings plan, Diane and Glenn will have deposited $9,600 into the home savings account by the end of the year and the balance in their main savings account will be down to $2,510. Although Diane is pleased that $9,600 will be moved into the home savings account in the next year, she's concerned about the amount of money left in the main savings account. Even more troubling are the month-to-month balances in that account. For example, the balance in the main savings account will be $1,500 at the end of August and will remain below $2,000 for several months of the year. Recall that Diane does not want to have a savings plan that will leave the couple with insufficient funds in the main savings account to handle unforeseen expenses.

Part of the problem is that the couple's net cash flow is negative during several months of the year. If they continue to transfer $800 into the home savings account during those months, the main savings account might fall below an acceptable level. Diane wants to modify her savings plan so that money is not transferred into the home savings account during months of negative cash flow. You need a formula that can "choose" whether to transfer the funds. You can build this kind of decision-making capability into a formula through the use of a logical function.

Working with Logical Functions

A **logical function** is a function that works with values that are either true or false. If it seems strange to think of a value as being true or false, consider a statement such as "Today is Monday." If today is Monday, that statement is true or has a true value. If today isn't Monday, the statement has a value of false. In Excel, you usually will not work with statements regarding days of the week (unless you're creating a calendar application), but instead you'll examine statements such as "Is cell A5 equal to 3?" or "Is cell B10 greater than cell C10?"

Using the IF Function

You can use the IF function to evaluate a statement such as "Is cell A5 equal to 3?" The **IF function** is a logical function that returns one value if the statement is true and returns a different value if the statement is false. The syntax of the IF function is as follows:

IF(*logical_test, value_if_true,* [*value_if_false*])

In this function, *logical_test* is a statement that is either true or false, *value_if_true* is the value returned by the IF function if the statement is true, and *value_if_false* is the value returned by the function if the statement is false. Although the *value_if_false* argument is optional, you should usually include this argument so that the IF function covers both possibilities.

The statement in the *logical_test* argument of the IF function always includes a comparison operator. A **comparison operator** is a symbol that indicates the relationship between two values. Figure 3-27 describes the different comparison operators. The most common comparison operator is the equal sign.

Comparison operators ◀ Figure 3-27

Operator	Statement	Tests whether
=	A1 = B1	the value in cell A1 *is equal to* the value in cell B1
>	A1 > B1	the value in cell A1 *is greater than* the value in cell B1
<	A1 < B1	the value in cell A1 *is less than* the value in cell B1
>=	A1 >= B1	the value in cell A1 *is greater than or equal to* the value in cell B1
<=	A1 <= B1	the value in cell A1 *is less than or equal to* the value in cell B1
<>	A1 <> B1	the value in cell A1 *is not equal to* the value in cell B1

For example, you might want a formula that compares the values in cells A1 and B1. If they're equal, you want to return a value of 100; if they're not equal, you want to return a value of 50. The IF function to perform this test is as follows:

=IF(A1=B1, 100, 50)

In many cases, however, you will not use values directly in the IF function. The following formula uses cell references, returning the value of cell C1 if A1 equals B1; otherwise, it returns the value of cell C2.

=IF(A1=B1, C1, C2)

The IF function also works with text. For example, consider the following formula:

```
=IF(A1="YES", "DONE", "RESTART")
```

This formula tests whether the value of cell A1 is equal to YES. If it is, the formula returns the text DONE; otherwise, it returns the text RESTART. Also, you can nest other functions inside an IF statement. Consider the following formula:

```
=IF(A1="MAXIMUM", MAX(B1:B10), MIN(B1:B10))
```

This function first tests whether cell A1 contains the text MAXIMUM. If it does, the formula uses the MAX function to return the maximum of the values in the range B1:B10. If it doesn't, the formula uses the MIN function to return the minimum of the values in that range.

Diane wants the IF function to test whether the net cash flow for the current month is greater than zero. If it is, the couple has increased their savings and she wants to transfer some of it into the home savings account. On the other hand, if the net cash flow is negative, the couple has not saved any money and Diane doesn't want to transfer any funds to the home savings account. For the month of January, the formula to determine how much money is transferred is as follows:

```
=IF(D33>0, $K$10, 0)
```

Recall that cell D33 contains the net cash flow for the month of January and cell K10 contains the amount of money that Diane wants to transfer when she can. So, this function tests whether the net cash flow for the month of January (cell D33) is positive (greater than zero). If it is, the formula returns $800 (the value in cell K10) as the amount to transfer from the main savings account into the home savings account; otherwise, it returns 0 and no money will be transferred that month. You'll delete the formula currently in cell D39, and then insert this function.

To insert the IF function:

▶ 1. Right-click cell **D39**, and then click **Clear Contents** on the shortcut menu. The cell's contents are erased.

▶ 2. In the Function Library group on the Formulas tab, click the **Logical** button, and then click **IF** in the list of logical functions. The Function Arguments dialog box opens.

▶ 3. Enter **D33>0** in the Logical_test argument box. This tests whether the net cash flow for January is positive (greater than zero).

▶ 4. Enter **$K$10** in the Value_if_true argument box. If the value in cell D33 is greater than zero (the net cash flow for the month is positive), then the formula returns the value in cell K10, which is the amount of money to transfer from the main savings account into the home savings account. You used an absolute reference because you don't want the cell reference to change when you copy the formula to the other months.

▶ 5. Enter the value **0** in the Value_if_false argument box. If the value in cell D33 is less than zero (the net cash flow for the month is negative), the formula returns the value 0 and no money will be transferred from the main savings account into the home savings account that month. See Figure 3-28.

Function arguments for the IF function ◀ **Figure 3-28**

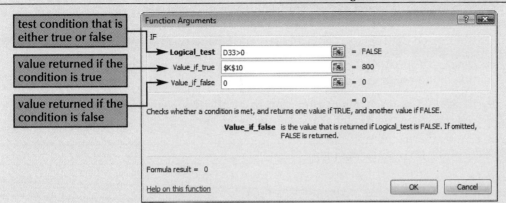

> **6.** Click the **OK** button. A value of 0 is displayed in cell D39. Because the net cash flow for January is –1,590, no money will be transferred from the main savings account into the home savings account. You'll copy this formula into the remaining months of Diane's proposed budget.

> **7.** Click cell **D39**, and then drag the fill handle over the range **E39:O39**. The remaining values are filled in, as shown in Figure 3-29. Examine the monthly balance in both savings accounts.

Amount to transfer to the home savings account each month ◀ **Figure 3-29**

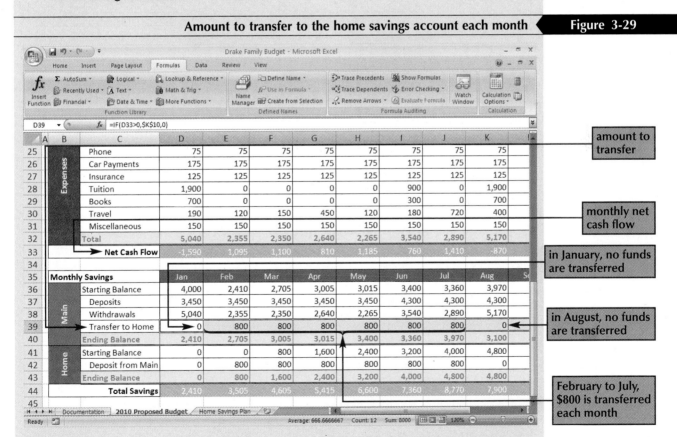

The monthly ending balance in the main savings account remains above $3,000 for most of the year, and $800 is transferred from the main savings account into the home savings account in ten months of the year. Diane wants you to document what the formula results are showing. You'll enter text that clarifies when funds are transferred between accounts in the Home Savings Plan section.

► **8.** Double-click cell **H10** to enter editing mode, type an asterisk (*****) at the end of the text in the cell, and then press the **Enter** key.

► **9.** In cell H11, enter ***Only during months of positive cash flow**, and then format cell H11 using the **Explanatory** cell style. See Figure 3-30.

| Figure 3-30 | **Results of the revised savings plan** |

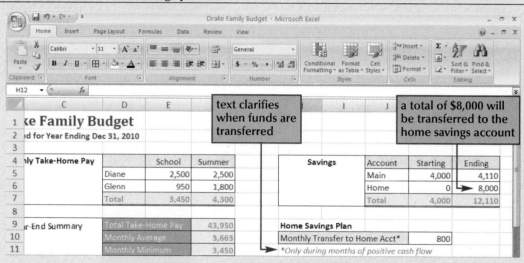

Based on this savings plan, Diane can transfer $800 from the main savings account to the home savings account in all but two months of the year, depositing a total of $8,000 into the home savings account by the end of the year. The main savings account balance stays above $3,000 for most of the year. Diane feels this is adequate, but wants to explore what would happen if she increases the monthly transfer from $800 to $1,000. How would that affect the monthly balance of the main savings account?

To change the amount transferred per month:

► **1.** Change the value in cell K10 to **1000**. The total in the home savings account at the end of the year increases to $10,000.

► **2.** Scroll down the worksheet and examine how the monthly balance in the main savings account changes throughout the year. Under this scenario, the balance in the main savings account drops to $1,900 in the month of August. This is a little too low for Diane.

► **3.** Change the value in cell K10 to **900**. With this savings plan, the couple will save $9,000 toward the purchase of a home.

► **4.** Scroll through the worksheet, examining the monthly balances of the two savings accounts. The balance in their savings account stays above $2,500 for most of the year. This seems like a good compromise to Diane, and she decides to adopt it as a model budget for the upcoming year.

Working with Date Functions

Diane's budget is just the start of her financial planning. To be effective, budgets need to be monitored and updated as conditions change. In the upcoming year, Diane plans to use this workbook to enter the actual salaries, expenses, and savings. This will enable her to track how well her projected values match the actual values. Because Diane will be updating the workbook throughout the year, she wants the worksheet to always display the current date so she can tell how far she is into her budget projections. You can accomplish this using a **date function**. Seven of the date functions supported by Excel are described in Figure 3-31. You can use these functions to help with scheduling or to determine on what days of the week certain dates occur.

Date functions ◀ Figure 3-31

Function	Description
DATE(year, month, day)	Creates a date value for the date represented by the year, month, and day arguments
DAY(date)	Extracts the day of the month from the date value
MONTH(date)	Extracts the month number from the date value where 1=January, 2=February, and so forth
YEAR(date)	Extracts the year number from the date value
WEEKDAY(date, [return_type])	Calculates the day of the week from the date value, where 1=Sunday, 2=Monday, and so forth; to choose a different numbering scheme, set the optional return_type value to "1" (1=Sunday, 2=Monday, ...), "2" (1=Monday, 2=Tuesday, ...), or "3" (0=Monday, 1=Tuesday, ...)
NOW()	Displays the current date and time
TODAY()	Displays the current date

Perhaps the most commonly used date function is the TODAY function, which returns the current date. The syntax of the TODAY function is as follows:

`=TODAY()`

The TODAY function doesn't have any arguments. Neither does the NOW function, which returns both the current date and current time. The values returned by the TODAY and NOW functions are updated automatically whenever you reopen the workbook or enter a new calculation. If you don't want the date and time to change, you must enter the date and time value directly in the cell.

Diane wants the 2010 Proposed Budget workbook to display the current date.

To enter the TODAY function to display the current date:

▶ **1.** In cell J1, enter **Current Date**.

▶ **2.** Merge cells **J1** and **K1**, right-align the merged cell, and then apply the **20% – Accent6** cell style.

▶ **3.** Click cell **L1**. You'll enter the TODAY function in this cell.

▶ **4.** In the Function Library group on the Formulas tab, click the **Date & Time** button, and then click **TODAY** in the date functions list. The Function Arguments dialog box opens, but there are no arguments for the TODAY function.

▶ **5.** Click the **OK** button. The Function Arguments dialog box closes, and the current date appears in cell L1. See Figure 3-32.

Figure 3-32 **TODAY function displays the current date**

You can also enter the TODAY function by typing =TODAY() directly in a cell.

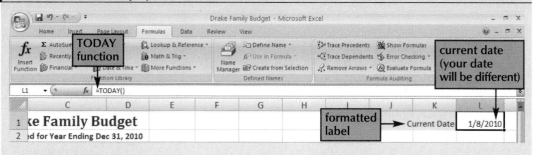

Working with Financial Functions

Diane wants to estimate how much monthly mortgage payments for a house might be. You can use the **PMT function** to calculate the payments for any type of loan.

The PMT function is one of many **financial functions** in Excel that calculate values from loans and investments. Figure 3-33 describes this and some of the other financial functions often used to develop budgets. These financial functions are the same as those widely used in business and accounting to perform various financial calculations, such as depreciation of an asset, the amount of interest paid on an investment, and the present value of an investment.

Figure 3-33 **Financial functions for loans and investments**

Function	Description
FV(rate, nper, pmt, [pv=0] [,type=0])	Returns the future value of an investment, where rate is the interest rate per period, nper is the total number of periods, pmt is the payment in each period, pv is the present value of the investment, and type indicates whether payments should be made at the end of the period (0) or the beginning of the period (1)
PMT(rate, nper, pv, [fv=0] [,type=0])	Calculates the payments required each period on a loan or investment
IPMT(rate, per, nper, pv, [fv=0] [,type=0])	Calculates the amount of a loan payment devoted to paying the loan interest, where per is the number of the payment period
PPMT(rate, per, nper, pv, [fv=0] [,type=0])	Calculates the amount of a loan payment devoted to paying off the principal of a loan, where per is the number of the payment period
PV(rate, nper, pmt, [fv=0] [,type=0])	Calculates the present value of a loan or investment based on periodic, constant payments
NPER(rate, pmt, pv, [fv=0] [,type=0])	Calculates the number of periods required to pay off a loan or investment
RATE(nper, pmt, pv, [fv=0] [,type=0])	Calculates the interest rate of a loan or investment based on periodic, constant payments

For expensive items, such as cars and houses, people often borrow money from a bank to make the purchase. Every loan has two main components: the principal and the interest. **Principal** is the amount of money being loaned, and **interest** is the amount charged for lending the money. You can think of interest as a kind of "user fee" because the borrower is paying for the right to use the lender's money for a period of time. The more money borrowed and the longer time for which it's borrowed, the higher the user fee. A few years ago, Diane and Glenn borrowed money to buy a second car and are still repaying the principal and interest on that loan.

Interest is calculated either as simple interest or as compound interest. In **simple interest**, the interest paid is equal to a percentage of principal for each period that the money has been lent. For example, if Diane and Glenn deposit $1,000 in an account that pays simple interest at a rate of 5% per year, they'll receive $50 in interest each year that the money is deposited. More often, interest is calculated as **compound interest** in which the interest paid is calculated on the principal and any previous interest payments that have been added to that principal. For example, the interest payment for a $1,000 deposit at a 5% interest that is compounded every year is $50. If the interest is left in the account, the interest payment for the second year is calculated on $1,050 (the original principal plus the previous year's interest), resulting in an interest payment for the second year of $52.50. With compound interest, the borrower always pays more money to the lender the following year. Most banks and financial institutions use compound interest in their financial transactions.

Using Functions to Manage Personal Finances | InSight

Excel has many financial functions you can use to manage your personal finances. The following list can help you determine which function to use for the most common personal finance problems:

- To determine how much an investment will be worth after a series of monthly payments at some future time, use the FV (future value) function.
- To determine how much you have to spend each month to repay a loan or mortgage within a set period of time, use the PMT (payment) function.
- To determine how much of your monthly loan payment is used to pay the interest, use the IPMT (interest payment) function.
- To determine how much of your monthly loan payment is used for repaying the principal, use the PPMT (principal payment) function.
- To determine the largest loan or mortgage you can afford at present, given a set monthly payment, use the PV (present value) function.
- To determine how long it will take to pay off a loan with constant monthly payments, use the NPER (number of periods) function.

In each case, you usually need to enter the annual interest rate divided by the number of times the interest is compounded during the year. If interest is compounded monthly, divide the annual interest rate by 12; if interest is compounded quarterly, divide the annual rate by 4. You must also convert the length of the loan or investment to the number of interest payments per year. If you will make payments monthly, multiply the number of years of the loan or investment by 12.

Using the PMT Function to Determine a Monthly Loan Payment

You'll use the PMT function to calculate the potential monthly loan payment for Diane and Glenn. For loan or investment calculations, you need to know the following information:

- The annual interest rate
- The payment period, or how often payments are due and interest is compounded (usually monthly for mortgages)

- The length of the loan in terms of the number of payment periods
- The amount being borrowed or invested

In Diane and Glenn's neighborhood, starter homes are selling for about $200,000. If Diane and Glenn can keep to their savings plan, they will have saved $9,000 by the end of the year (as shown in cell L6 in the Proposed Budget 2010 worksheet). If they save this same amount for the next three years, they will have at least $27,000 in their home savings account to put toward the down payment. Based on this, Diane estimates that she and Glenn will need a home loan of about $170,000. To calculate how much it would cost to repay such a loan, you can use the PMT (payment) function. The PMT function has the following syntax:

```
PMT(rate, nper, pv, [fv=0] [type=0])
```

In this function, *rate* is the interest rate for each payment period, *nper* is the total number of payment periods required to pay off the loan, and *pv* is the present value of the loan or the amount that needs to be borrowed. For Diane and Glenn, the present value of the loan is $170,000.

The PMT function has two optional arguments: *fv* and *type*. The *fv* argument is the future value of the loan. Because the intent with most loans is to pay them off completely, the future value is equal to 0 by default. The *type* argument specifies when the interest is charged on the loan, either at the end of the period (*type*=0), which is the default, or at the beginning of the period (*type*=1).

For most loans, the payment period is one month. This means that Diane and Glenn must make a payment on the loan every month, and interest on the loan is compounded every month. The annual interest rate on home loans in Diane and Glenn's area is 6.5%. To determine the interest rate per month, you divide the annual interest rate by 12. For Diane and Glenn, the interest rate each month or payment period is 6.5% divided by 12, or about 0.541% per month.

Diane and Glenn want to pay off their home loan in 20 years, which is a payment period of 240 months (20 years multiplied by 12 payment periods each year). Putting all of this information together, you can calculate the monthly payment for the couple's home loan with the following formula:

```
=PMT(0.065/12, 20*12, 170000)
```

This formula returns a value of −$1,267.47. The value is negative because the payment is considered an expense, or a negative cash flow. If you want to display this value as a positive number in a worksheet, enter a minus symbol directly before the PMT function as follows:

```
=-PMT(0.065/12, 20*12, 170000)
```

Based on these calculations, Diane and Glenn would have to pay the bank $1,267.47 every month for 20 years before the loan and the interest are completely paid. Right now, the couple is spending about $850 per month on rent. So this home loan is a significant increase over their current expenses. Diane asks you to calculate the monthly payment for a home loan of $160,000. You'll make that calculation in another worksheet.

To set up the monthly loan payment calculation:

▶ **1.** Insert a new worksheet named **Loan Analysis** at the end of the workbook.

▶ **2.** In cell A1, enter **Home Loan**, format cell A1 using the **Title** cell style, and then increase the width of column A to **25** characters.

▶ **3.** In the range A3:A9;B3:B8, enter the labels and components of the home loan shown in Figure 3-34. In cell B5, enter **=B3/B4** to calculate the interest rate per period by dividing the annual interest rate by the number of payments per year. In cell B7, enter **=B4*B6** to calculate the number of loan payments per year by multiplying the number of payments per year (12) by the number of years of the loan (20).

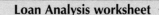

Loan Analysis worksheet ◄ Figure 3-34

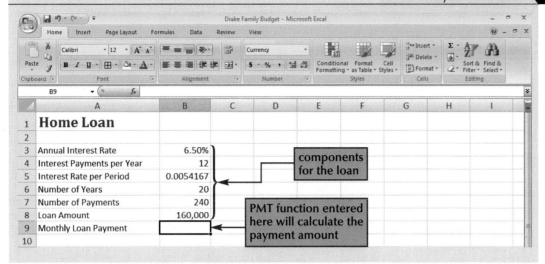

Next, you'll enter the PMT function to calculate the monthly payment for the $160,000 home loan.

To enter the PMT function to calculate the monthly payment:

▶ 1. Apply the **Calculation** cell style to cell B9 to distingish the monthly loan payment amount from the loan components.

▶ 2. In the Function Library group on the Formulas tab, click the **Financial** button, and then click **PMT** in the list of financial functions. The Function Arguments dialog box opens.

▶ 3. For the Rate argument, enter the cell reference **B5**, which is the cell with the interest rate per payment period.

▶ 4. For the Nper argument, enter the cell reference **B7**, which is the cell with the total number of payments.

▶ 5. For the Pv argument enter the cell reference **B8**, which is the cell with the present value of the loan. See Figure 3-35.

Function Arguments dialog box for the PMT function ◄ Figure 3-35

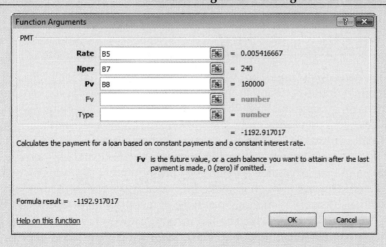

▶ 6. Click the **OK** button. The value $1,192.92 is displayed in parentheses in cell B9 to indicate a negative currency value.

> **7.** Double-click cell **B9**, type **–** (minus symbol) between = and PMT, and then press the **Enter** key. The value $1,192.92 is displayed as a positive currency value. See Figure 3-36.

Figure 3-36 ▶ **Monthly payment for a $160,000 loan**

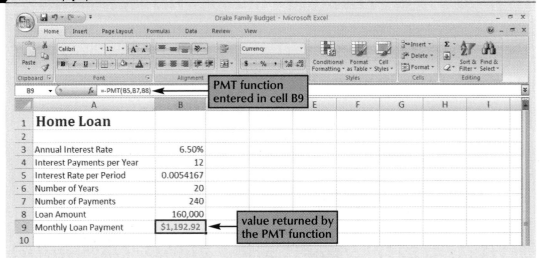

Diane and Glenn would have to pay about $1,193 per month for 20 years to repay a $160,000 loan at 6.5% interest. Diane is interested in other loan possibilities. Because you already set up the worksheet, you can quickly try other scenarios without having to reenter any formulas. Diane wonders whether extending the length of the loan would reduce the monthly payment by a sizeable margin. She asks you to calculate the monthly payment for a 30-year loan.

To calculate other loan options:

> **1.** In cell B6, change the value to **30**. The amount of the monthly payment drops to $1,011.31, which is $180 less per month. Next, Diane wants to see the monthly payments for a $150,000 loan with these same conditions.

> **2.** In cell B8, change the value to **150,000**. For this smaller home loan, the monthly payment drops even further to $948.10 per month. This is only about $100 more than the couple is currently paying in rent.

> **3.** Save your changes to the workbook, and then close it.

You've completed your work on Diane and Glenn's budget. Based on your analysis, Diane has learned several important things. She's discovered that the projected budget allows the couple to transfer enough money to the home savings account to make a down payment on a home in about three years. The savings plan seems reasonable to Diane and leaves enough funds in the main savings account to cover their monthly expenses. Finally, by analyzing some of the possible loan options they might encounter when they buy a home, Diane realizes that the monthly mortgage payments will not be substantially more than what they are currently paying in rent. So, not only will Diane and Glenn be able to save enough to make the initial down payment, their monthly income should also cover the monthly payments. Of course, all budgets must be revised periodically to meet changing expenses and income. However, your work has given Diane and Glenn enough information to make informed choices about their immediate financial future.

Session 3.2 Quick Check | Review

1. How do you use AutoFill to copy a set of cell values, but not the formatting?
2. The first three selected values in a series are 3, 6, and 9. What are the next three values that will be inserted using AutoFill?
3. Cell A5 contains the text Mon. If you select the cell and drag the fill handle over the range A6:A8, what text will be entered into those cells?
4. If cell A3 is greater than cell A4, you want to display the text "OK"; otherwise, you want to display the text string "RETRY". What formula accomplishes this?
5. What formula do you use to display the current date?
6. What formula do you use to display the current date and time?
7. You want to take out a loan for $130,000. The interest on the loan is 5% compounded monthly. You intend to pay back the loan in 20 years. What formula do you enter to calculate the monthly payment required to pay off the loan under those conditions?
8. What financial function do you use to determine how payment periods are required to pay off a loan?

Tutorial Summary | Review

In this tutorial, you learned how to work with Excel functions and formulas. First, you learned about relative, absolute, and mixed cell references and under what conditions you would use each. Then, you looked at function syntax, entered a function using the Insert Function dialog box, and then you entered a function directly into the worksheet to calculate sums, counts, averages, maximums, and minimums. You also searched for a function that matched search criteria. Next, you used AutoFill to quickly copy formulas and formatting and to extend a series of numbers, text, or dates. Then, you used logical functions to return different values based on conditions in the worksheet, and then you entered a date function. Finally, you examined financial functions and used the PMT function to calculate the monthly payments to repay a loan within a set interval of time.

Key Terms

absolute reference	financial function	nested
argument	IF function	optional argument
AutoFill	Insert Function dialog box	PMT function
comparison operator	interest	principal
compound interest	logical function	relative reference
date function	median	simple interest
F4 key	mixed reference	syntax
fill handle	mode	

| Practice | **Review Assignments** |

Practice the skills you learned in the tutorial using the same case scenario.

Data File needed for the Review Assignments: Timov.xlsx

Diane and Glenn appreciate the work you did on their budget. Their friends, Sergei and Ava Timov, ask you to create a similar workbook for their family budget. The Timovs want to purchase a new home. They are considering two houses with different mortgages. They want the budget worksheet you create to display the impact of monthly mortgage payments on the couple's cash flow. The couple has already designed the workbook and entered estimates of their take-home pay and expenses for the upcoming year. They want you to set up the formulas.

Complete the following:

1. Open the **Timov** workbook located in the Tutorial.03\Review folder included with your Data Files, and then save the workbook as **Timov Family Budget** in the same folder.
2. In the Documentation sheet, enter your name in cell B3 and the date in cell B4.
3. In the Family Budget worksheet, in the range C17:N17, use AutoFill to enter the month names **January** through **December**.
4. In the range C20:N20, calculate the family's take-home pay. In the range C26:N26, calculate the monthly expenses. In the range C27:N27, calculate the monthly net cash flow (equal to the monthly take-home pay minus the expenses).
5. In cell C6, enter a formula to calculate the sum of Sergei's monthly salary for the entire year. In cell D6, calculate Sergei's average take-home pay each month. In cell E6, calculate Sergei's maximum monthly take-home pay. In cell F6, calculate Sergei's minimum monthly take-home pay.
6. Select the range C6:F6, and then use AutoFill to copy the formula in the C6:F6 range into the C7:F15 range. Use the AutoFill Options button to copy only the formulas into the selected range and not both the formulas and formats. (*Hint:* Because you haven't yet entered any mortgage payment values, cell D13 will show the value #DIV/0!, indicating that Excel cannot calculate the average mortgage payment. You'll correct that problem shortly.)
7. In the range J5:J12, enter the following loan and loan conditions of the first mortgage:
   • The loan amount (or value of the principal) is **$315,000**.
   • The annual interest rate is **6.7%**.
   • The interest rate is compounded **12** times a year (or monthly).
   • The mortgage will last **30** years.
   The monthly rate is equal to the annual interest rate divided by how often the interest rate is compounded. The number of payments is equal to the number of years the mortgage will last multiplied by 12.
8. In cell J11, enter the PMT function to calculate the monthly payment required to repay this loan. The *rate* argument is equal to the monthly rate, the *nper* argument is equal to the number of payments, and the *pv* argument is equal to the value of the principal.
9. In cell J11, enter a minus symbol between = and PMT to make the value positive.
10. In the range N5:N12, enter the following loan and loan conditions of the second mortgage:
   • The loan amount (or value of the principal) is **$218,000**.
   • The annual interest rate is **6.7%**.
   • The interest rate is compounded **12** times a year (or monthly).
   • The mortgage will last **20** years.

11. In cell N11, enter the PMT function to calculate the monthly payment needed to pay off this loan, and then make the PMT value positive.

12. Sergei and Ava want to be able to view their monthly cash flow under both mortgage possibilities. The mortgage being applied to the budget will be determined by whether 1 or 2 is entered into cell C3. To switch from one mortgage to another, do the following:

    • In cell C25, enter an IF function that tests whether cell C3 equals 1. If it does, display the value from cell J11; otherwise, display the value from cell N11. Use absolute cell references in the formula.

    • Use AutoFill to copy the formula in cell C25 into the range D25:N25.

    • Verify that the values in the range C25:N25 match the monthly payment for the first mortgage condition.

13. In cell C3, edit the value from 1 to **2**. Verify that the monthly payment for the second mortgage appears in the range C25:N25.

14. Sergei and Ava want to maintain an average net cash flow of at least $1,000 per month. Under which mortgage is this achieved?

15. Save and close the workbook, and then submit the finished workbook to your instructor, either in printed or electronic form, as requested.

Apply	**Case Problem 1**

Use the skills you learned to create a grading sheet for a chemistry course.

Data File needed for this Case Problem: Chemistry.xlsx

Chemistry 303   Karen Raul is a professor of chemistry at a community college in Shawnee, Kansas. She has started using Excel to calculate the final grade for students in her Chemistry 303 course. The final score is a weighted average of the scores given for three exams and the final exam. Karen wants your help in creating the formulas to calculate the final score and to summarize the class scores on all exams. One way to calculate a weighted average is by multiplying each student's exam score by the weight given to the exam, and then totaling the results. For example, consider the following four exam scores:

• Exam 1 = 84

• Exam 2 = 80

• Exam 3 = 83

• Final Exam = 72

If the first three exams are each given a weight of 20% and the final exam is given a weight of 40%, the weighted average of the four scores is:

84*0.2 + 80*0.2 + 83*0.2 + 72*0.4 = 78.2

Karen already entered the scores for her students and formatted much of the workbook. She wants you to enter the final formulas and highlight the top 10 overall scores in her class. Figure 3-37 shows the worksheet you'll create.

Figure 3-37

	A	B	C	D	E	F	G	H
1	**Chemistry 303**							
2	First Semester Scores							
3	Posted 12/20/2010							
4								
5	Students	36						
6								
7		Exam	Weight	Median	Maximum	Minimum	Range	
8		Exam 1	20%	86.0	99.0	52.0	47.0	
9		Exam 2	20%	80.0	99.0	53.0	46.0	
10		Exam 3	20%	83.0	98.0	50.0	48.0	
11		Final Exam	40%	81.5	99.0	51.0	48.0	
12		Overall	100%	80.5	96.8	55.8	41.0	
13								
14								
15	Student Scores				Top Ten Overall Scores			
16	Student ID	Exam 1	Exam 2	Exam 3	Final Exam	Overall		
17	390-120-2	84.0	80.0	83.0	72.0	78.2		
18	390-267-4	98.0	92.0	91.0	99.0	95.8		
19	390-299-8	54.0	56.0	51.0	65.0	58.2		
20	390-354-3	98.0	95.0	90.0	94.0	94.2		

(Column A rows 7–12 contain the vertical label "Class Summary")

Complete the following:

1. Open the **Chemistry** workbook located in the Tutorial.03\Case1 folder included with your Data Files, and then save the workbook as **Chemistry 303 Final Scores** in the same folder.

2. In the Documentation sheet, enter your name in cell B3 and enter the date in cell B4.

3. In the First Semester Scores worksheet, in cell F17, enter a formula to calculate the weighted average of the first student's four exams. Use the weights found in the range C8:C11, matching each weight with the corresponding exam score. Use absolute cell references for the four weights.

4. Use AutoFill to copy the formula in cell F17 into the range F18:F52.

5. In cell B5, enter a formula to count the number of final scores in the range F17:F52.

 EXPLORE

6. In cell D8, use the MEDIAN function to calculate the median or middle score for the first exam.

7. In cell E8, calculate the maximum score for the first exam.

8. In cell F8, calculate the minimum score for the first exam.

9. In cell G8, calculate the range of scores for the first exam, which is equal to the difference between the maximum and minimum score.

10. Repeat Steps 6 through 9 for each of the other two exams, the final exam, and the overall weighted score.

11. Use conditional formatting to highlight the top 10 scores in the range F17:F52 in a light red fill with dark red text.

12. Insert a page break at cell A14, repeat the first three rows of the worksheet in any printout, and verify that the worksheet is in portrait orientation.

13. Save and close the workbook, and then submit the finished workbook to your instructor, either in printed or electronic form, as requested.

Apply | Case Problem 2

Use the skills you learned to create an order form for a fireworks company.

Data File needed for this Case Problem: Wizard.xlsx

WizardWorks Andrew Howe owns and operates WizardWorks, an online seller of fireworks based in Franklin, Tennessee. Andrew wants you to help him use Excel to develop an order form for his business. The form needs to contain formulas to calculate the charge for each order. The total charge is based on the quantity and type of items ordered plus the shipping charge and the 5% sales tax. Orders can be shipped using standard 3 to 5 day shipping for $4.99 or overnight for $12.99. Andrew is also offering a 3% discount for orders that exceed $200. Both the shipping option and the discount need to be calculated using formulas based on values entered into the worksheet. Figure 3-38 shows a preview of a sample order.

Figure 3-38

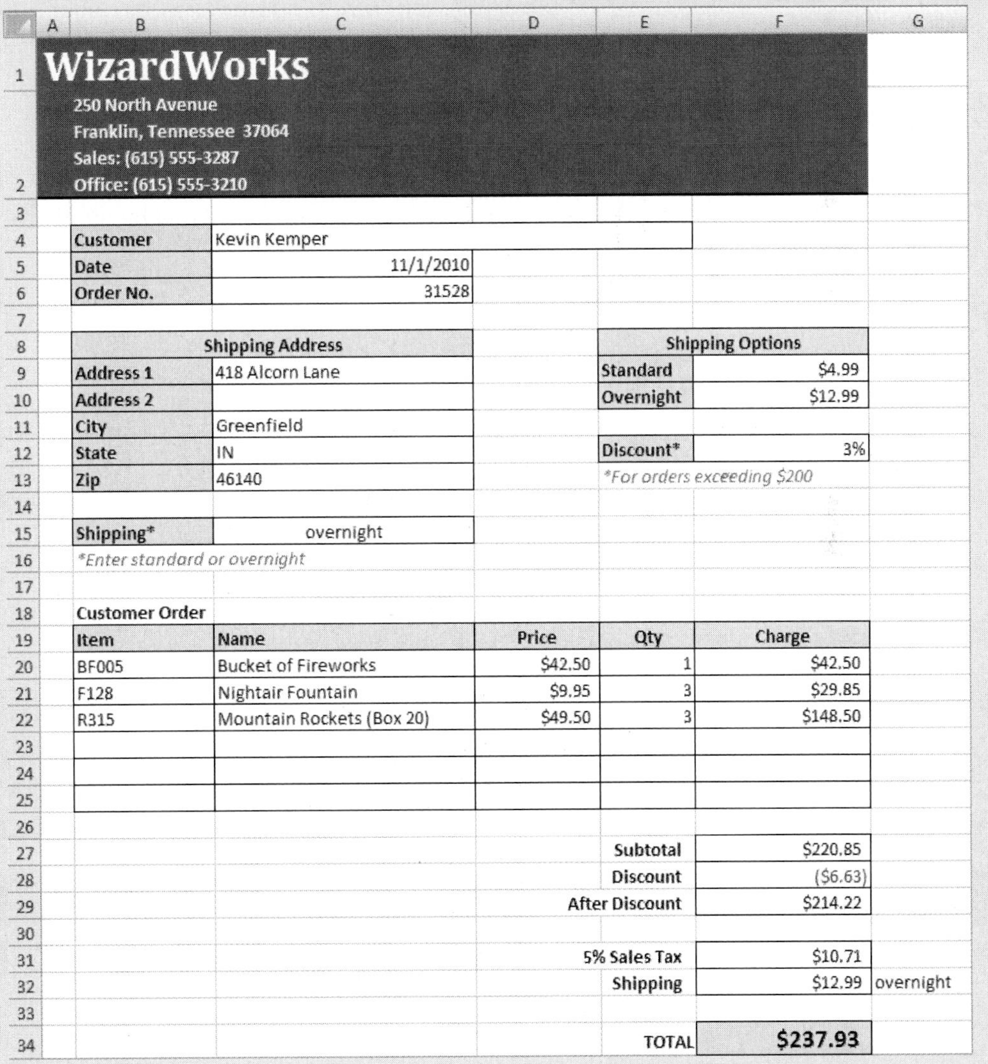

	A	B	C	D	E	F	G
1	WizardWorks						
2		250 North Avenue Franklin, Tennessee 37064 Sales: (615) 555-3287 Office: (615) 555-3210					
3							
4		Customer	Kevin Kemper				
5		Date	11/1/2010				
6		Order No.	31528				
7							
8		Shipping Address			Shipping Options		
9		Address 1	418 Alcorn Lane		Standard	$4.99	
10		Address 2			Overnight	$12.99	
11		City	Greenfield				
12		State	IN		Discount*	3%	
13		Zip	46140		*For orders exceeding $200		
14							
15		Shipping*	overnight				
16		*Enter standard or overnight					
17							
18		Customer Order					
19		Item	Name	Price	Qty	Charge	
20		BF005	Bucket of Fireworks	$42.50	1	$42.50	
21		F128	Nightair Fountain	$9.95	3	$29.85	
22		R315	Mountain Rockets (Box 20)	$49.50	3	$148.50	
23							
24							
25							
26							
27					Subtotal	$220.85	
28					Discount	($6.63)	
29					After Discount	$214.22	
30							
31					5% Sales Tax	$10.71	
32					Shipping	$12.99	overnight
33							
34					TOTAL	$237.93	

Complete the following:

1. Open the **Wizard** workbook located in the Tutorial.03\Case2 folder included with your Data Files, and then save the workbook as **WizardWorks Order Form** in the same folder.
2. In the Documentation sheet, enter your name in cell B3 and enter the date in cell B4.

3. In the Order Form worksheet, in cell C4, enter the customer name, **Kevin Kemper**. In cell C6, enter the order number, **31528**. In the range C9:C13, enter the following address:

Address 1:   **418 Alcorn Lane**

City: **Greenfield**

State: **IN**

Zip: **46140**

⊕ **EXPLORE**   4. In cell C5, enter a function that displays the current date.

5. In the range B20:E22, enter the following orders:

Item	Name	Price	Qty
BF005	**Bucket of Fireworks**	**$42.50**	**1**
F128	**Nightair Fountain**	**$9.95**	**3**
R315	**Mountain Rockets (Box 20)**	**$49.50**	**3**

6. In cell C15, enter **overnight** to ship this order overnight.

⊕ **EXPLORE**   7. In cell F20, enter an IF function that tests whether the order quantity in cell E20 is greater than 0 (zero). If it is, return the value of E20 multiplied by D20; otherwise, return no text by entering "". AutoFill this formula into the range F21:F25.

8. In cell F27, calculate the sum of the values in the range F20:F25.

9. In cell F28, enter an IF function that tests whether cell F27 is greater than 200. If it is, return the negative value of F27 multiplied by the discount percentage in cell F12; otherwise, return the value 0 (zero).

10. In cell F29, add the subtotal from cell F27 and the discount value from cell F28.

11. In cell F31, calculate the sales tax by multiplying the after discount value in cell F29 by the sales tax percentage, 0.05.

12. In cell F32, determine the shipping charge by entering an IF function that tests whether cell C15 equals "standard". If it does, return the value in cell F9; otherwise, return the value in cell F10.

13. In cell G32, display the value of cell C15.

14. In cell F34, calculate the total of the after discount value, the sales tax, and the shipping fee.

15. Scale the order form so that it will print on a single page.

16. Reduce the quantity of Mountain Rockets boxes from 3 to **2**, and then verify that the discount is changed to 0 for the order. Change the shipping option from overnight to **standard**, and then verify that the shipping fee is changed to the fee for standard shipping.

17. Save and close the workbook, and then submit the finished workbook to your instructor, either in printed or electronic form, as requested.

Challenge | **Case Problem 3**

Explore how to use relative and absolute references and the PMT function to create a loan table.

Data File needed for this Case Problem: Loan.xlsx

Eason Financial Services Jesse Buchmann is a finance officer at Eason Financial Services in Meridian, Idaho. She works with people who are looking for home mortgages. Most clients want mortgages they can afford, and affordability is determined by the size of the monthly payment. The monthly payment is determined by the interest rate, the total number of payments, and the size of the home loan. Jesse can't change the interest rate, but homebuyers can reduce their monthly payments by increasing the number of years to repay the loan. Jesse wants to give her clients a grid that displays combinations of loan amounts and payment periods so that they can select a loan that best meets their needs and budget. Figure 3-39 shows a preview of the grid that Jesse has in mind.

Figure 3-39

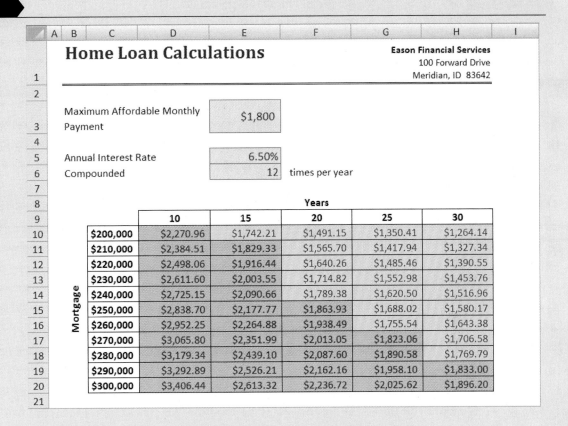

Home Loan Calculations						Eason Financial Services

Eason Financial Services
100 Forward Drive
Meridian, ID 83642

Maximum Affordable Monthly Payment	$1,800					
Annual Interest Rate	6.50%					
Compounded	12	times per year				

		Years				
Mortgage		**10**	**15**	**20**	**25**	**30**
	$200,000	$2,270.96	$1,742.21	$1,491.15	$1,350.41	$1,264.14
	$210,000	$2,384.51	$1,829.33	$1,565.70	$1,417.94	$1,327.34
	$220,000	$2,498.06	$1,916.44	$1,640.26	$1,485.46	$1,390.55
	$230,000	$2,611.60	$2,003.55	$1,714.82	$1,552.98	$1,453.76
	$240,000	$2,725.15	$2,090.66	$1,789.38	$1,620.50	$1,516.96
	$250,000	$2,838.70	$2,177.77	$1,863.93	$1,688.02	$1,580.17
	$260,000	$2,952.25	$2,264.88	$1,938.49	$1,755.54	$1,643.38
	$270,000	$3,065.80	$2,351.99	$2,013.05	$1,823.06	$1,706.58
	$280,000	$3,179.34	$2,439.10	$2,087.60	$1,890.58	$1,769.79
	$290,000	$3,292.89	$2,526.21	$2,162.16	$1,958.10	$1,833.00
	$300,000	$3,406.44	$2,613.32	$2,236.72	$2,025.62	$1,896.20

Jesse already entered much of the layout and formatting for the worksheet containing the loan payment grid. She needs your help in entering the PMT function.

Complete the following:

1. Open the **Loan** workbook located in the Tutorial.03\Case3 folder included with your Data Files, and then save the workbook as **Loan Grid** in the same folder.
2. In the Documentation sheet, enter your name and the date.
3. In the Loan Calculation worksheet, in cell E3, enter a monthly payment of **$2,200**.
4. In cell E5, enter the annual interest rate of **6.5%**. In cell E6, enter **12** to indicate that the interest payment is compounded 12 times a year, or monthly.
5. In the range C10:C20, use AutoFill to enter the currency values **$200,000** through **$300,000** in increments of $10,000. In the range D9:H9, use AutoFill to enter the year values **10** through **30** in increments of 5 years.

⊕ EXPLORE 6. In cell D10, use the PMT function to calculate the monthly payment required to repay a **$200,000** loan in **10** years at **6.5%** interest compounded monthly. Use absolute references to cells E5 and E6 to enter the annual interest rate and number of payments per year. Use the mixed references D$9 and $C10 to cells D9 and C10, respectively, to reference the number of years to repay the loan and the loan amount. Place a minus symbol before the PMT function so that the value returned by the function is positive rather than negative.

⊕ EXPLORE 7. Using AutoFill, copy the formula in cell D10 into the range D11:H10, and then copy that range of formulas into the range D11:H20. Verify that the values entered in those cells match the values shown in Figure 3-39.

⊕ EXPLORE   8. Conditionally format the range D10:H20 to highlight all of the values in the range that are less than the value in cell E3 in a dark green font on a green fill.

9. Add a second conditional format to the range D10:H20 to highlight all of the values in the range that are greater than the value in cell E3 in a dark red font on a red fill.

⊕ EXPLORE   10. Change the value in cell E3 from $2,200 to **$1,800**. If this represents the maximum affordable monthly payment, use the values in the grid to determine the largest mortgage for payment schedules lasting 15 through 30 years. Can any of the home loan values displayed in the grid be repaid in 10 years at $1,800 per month?

11. Save and close the workbook, and then submit the finished workbook to your instructor, either in printed or electronic form, as requested.

Create | **Case Problem 4**

Create a workbook that automatically grades a driving exam.

Data File needed for this Case Problem: V6.xlsx

V-6 Driving Academy   Sebastian Villanueva owns and operates the V-6 Driving Academy, a driving school located in Pine Hills, Florida. In addition to driving, students must take multiple-choice tests offered by the Florida Department of Motor Vehicles. Students must answer at least 80% of the questions correctly to pass each test. Sebastian has to grade these tests himself. Sebastian realizes that he can save a lot of time if the test questions were in a workbook and Excel totaled the test results. He asks you to help create the workbook.

Sebastian already entered a 20-question test into a workbook. He needs you to format this workbook and insert the necessary functions and formulas to grade a student's answers.

Complete the following:

1. Open the **V6** workbook located in the Tutorial.03\Case4 folder included with your Data Files, and then save the workbook as **V6 Driving Test** in the same folder.

2. In the Documentation sheet, enter your name in cell B3 and enter the date in cell B4.

3. In the Exam1 worksheet, format the questions and possible answers so that the worksheet is easy to read. The format is up to you. At the top of the worksheet, enter a title that describes the exam and then enter a function that returns the current date.

4. Add a section somewhere on the Exam1 worksheet where Sebastian can enter the student's name and answers to each question.

⊕ EXPLORE   5. The answers for the 20 questions are listed below. Use this information to write functions that will grade each answer, giving 1 point for a correct answer and 0 otherwise. Assume that all answers are in lowercase letters; therefore, the function that tests the answer to the first question should check for a "c" rather than a "C".

Question	Answer	Question	Answer	Question	Answer
1	c	8	a	15	b
2	a	9	c	16	b
3	b	10	b	17	b
4	a	11	c	18	b
5	c	12	b	19	b
6	b	13	b	20	c
7	c	14	a		

6. At the top of the worksheet, insert a formula to calculate the total number of correct answers.

7. Insert another formula that divides the total number of correct answers by the total number of exam questions on the worksheet. Display this value as a percentage.

8. Enter a logical function that displays the message "PASS" on the exam if the percentage of correct answers is greater than or equal to 80%; otherwise, the logical function displays the message "FAIL".

Test your worksheet on the following student exams. Which students passed and which failed? What score did each student receive on the exam?

Juan Marquez

Question	Answer	Question	Answer	Question	Answer
1	b	8	a	15	b
2	a	9	c	16	b
3	b	10	b	17	a
4	a	11	c	18	b
5	c	12	c	19	b
6	b	13	b	20	a
7	c	14	a		

Kurt Bessette

Question	Answer	Question	Answer	Question	Answer
1	c	8	b	15	c
2	c	9	c	16	b
3	b	10	b	17	a
4	a	11	c	18	b
5	c	12	a	19	b
6	b	13	b	20	b
7	c	14	a		

Rebecca Pena

Question	Answer	Question	Answer	Question	Answer
1	c	8	a	15	b
2	a	9	c	16	c
3	b	10	a	17	b
4	a	11	c	18	b
5	c	12	b	19	b
6	b	13	b	20	c
7	c	14	a		

9. Save and close the workbook, and then submit the finished workbook to your instructor, either in printed or electronic form, as requested.

Research | **Internet Assignments**

Use the Internet to find and work with data related to the topics presented in this tutorial.

The purpose of the Internet Assignments is to challenge you to find information on the Internet that you can use to work effectively with this software. The actual assignments are updated and maintained on the Course Technology Web site. Log on to the Internet and use your Web browser to go to the Student Online Companion for New Perspectives Office 2007 at **www.course.com/np/office2007**. Then navigate to the Internet Assignments for this tutorial.

Assess | **SAM Assessment and Training**

If you have a SAM user profile, you may have access to hands-on instruction, practice, and assessment of the skills covered in this tutorial. Log in to your SAM account (**http://sam2007.course.com**) to launch any assigned training activities or exams that relate to the skills covered in this tutorial.

Review | **Quick Check Answers**

Session 3.1

1. Absolute cell reference is \$B\$21. Mixed cell references are \$B21 and B\$21.
2. =C11+C12
3. =\$B11+C\$2
4. =AVERAGE(\$A11:\$A15)
5. Optional arguments are not required in a function. If not included, Excel assumes a default value for the argument.
6. =SUM(B1:B10)
7. =MAX(B1:B10)–MIN(B1:B10)
8. =MAX(B1:B10)/MIN(B1:B10)

Session 3.2

1. Drag the fill handle over the selected range, click the AutoFill Options button, and then click Fill Without Formatting.
2. 12, 15, 18
3. Cell A6 displays the text Tue, cell A7 displays Wed, and cell A8 displays Thu.
4. =IF(A3 > A4, "OK", "RETRY")
5. =TODAY()
6. =NOW()
7. =PMT(0.05/12, 12*20, 130000)
8. NPER

Ending Data Files

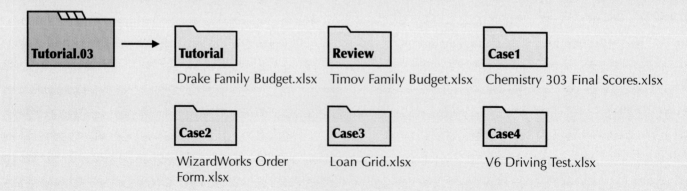

Tutorial.03 → Tutorial — Drake Family Budget.xlsx

Review — Timov Family Budget.xlsx

Case1 — Chemistry 303 Final Scores.xlsx

Case2 — WizardWorks Order Form.xlsx

Case3 — Loan Grid.xlsx

Case4 — V6 Driving Test.xlsx

Objectives

Session 4.1
- Create an embedded chart
- Work with chart titles and legends
- Create and format a pie chart
- Work with 3D charts
- Create and format a column chart

Session 4.2
- Create and format a line chart
- Use custom formatting with chart axes
- Work with tick marks and scale values
- Create and format a combined chart
- Insert and format a graphic shape
- Create a chart sheet

Working with Charts and Graphics

Charting Financial Data

Case | Seaborg Group

Ajita Jindal is a financial assistant for the Seaborg Group, a financial consulting agency located in Providence, Rhode Island. One of her duties is to prepare financial reports on the investments the Seaborg Group makes for its clients. These reports go into a binder containing the financial status of the client's different investments. The client receives the binder at annual meetings with his or her financial advisor, and receives updates on the status of the investments periodically throughout the year.

Many of the company's clients invest in the New Century Fund, a large growth/large risk mutual fund that has been operating for the past 10 years. Ajita needs to create a one-page report that summarizes the fund's financial holdings as well as its 10-year performance record. She already entered the financial data into an Excel workbook, but needs some help in finishing the report. Because many clients are overwhelmed by tables of numbers, Ajita wants to include charts and graphs in the report that display the current and past performance of the New Century Fund. She asks you to help create these charts.

Starting Data Files

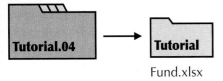

Tutorial.04

Tutorial

Fund.xlsx

Review

Crockett.xlsx

Case1

Kenai.xlsx

Case2

Cloud.jpg
Tornado.xlsx

Case3

Mitchell.xlsx

Case4

Basketball.xlsx

Session 4.1

Creating Charts

Ajita already created a workbook in which she entered and formatted data that describes the New Century Fund. You'll begin by opening this workbook.

> **To open Ajita's workbook:**
>
> ▶ **1.** Open the **Fund** workbook located in the **Tutorial.04\Tutorial** folder included with your Data Files, and then save the workbook as **New Century Fund** in the same folder.
>
> ▶ **2.** In the Documentation sheet, enter your name in cell B3 and the date in cell B4.
>
> ▶ **3.** Review the contents of the workbook.

Ajita's workbook contains the following four worksheets in addition to the Documentation sheet:

- The Summary Report worksheet includes summary data and facts about the New Century Fund.
- The Assets worksheet lists the assets of the New Century Fund grouped by investment categories.
- The Sector Weightings worksheet shows the economic sectors in which the New Century Fund invests.
- The Performance History worksheet provides a table that shows how well the New Century Fund performed over the past 10 years compared to two similar funds.

Ajita wants financial data from the Assets, Sector Weightings, and Performance History worksheets placed in the Summary Report worksheet as charts, or graphs. A **chart**, or **graph**, is a visual representation of a set of data. Charts show trends or relationships in data that are more difficult to see by simply looking at numbers, such as the range of months in which the New Century Fund performed exceptionally well.

Figure 4-1 shows Ajita's sketch of how she wants the final Summary Report worksheet to look. In the summary report, she wants one chart that shows the performance of the New Century Fund compared to two similar funds, and she wants two charts that show how money in the New Century Fund is currently invested. The final Summary Report worksheet will be a single page that includes all of the information Ajita wants her clients to see.

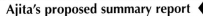

Ajita's proposed summary report | Figure 4-1

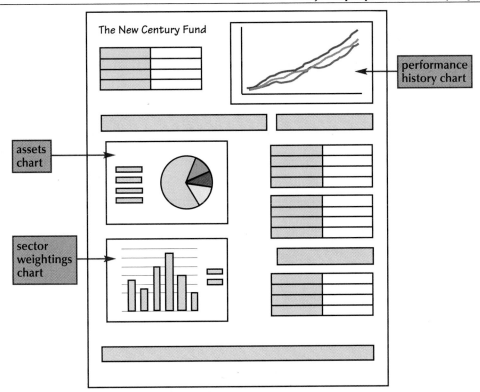

Inserting a Chart | Reference Window

- Select the data source with the range of data you want to chart.
- In the Charts group on the Insert tab, click a chart type, and then click a chart subtype in the Chart gallery.
- In the Location group on the Chart Tools Design tab, click the Move Chart button to place the chart in a chart sheet or embed it into a worksheet.

Selecting a Data Source

Each chart must have a data source. The **data source** is the range that contains the data you want to display in the chart. Each data source is a collection of one or more data series, where each **data series** is a range of values that is plotted as a single unit on the chart. Each data series has three components: the **series name** identifies the data series, the **series values** are the actual data displayed in the chart, and the **category values** are the groups or categories that the series values belong to. After you select the data source, Excel determines the series name, series values, and category values based on that data source. Sometimes, you might need to edit the data series Excel selects.

You'll select the data source for the chart that shows how the money in the New Century Fund is divided among investment categories. This data is located on the Assets worksheet.

To select the data source for the assets chart:

► 1. Click the **Assets** sheet tab to make the Assets worksheet active. You'll select one data series that shows the assets for five investment categories.

► 2. Select the range **A3:B8**. See Figure 4-2.

Figure 4-2 ▶ Data source selected for the assets chart

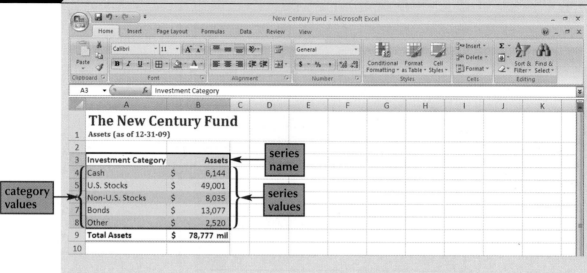

The range you selected for the data source, A3:B8, has a single data series. Excel uses the first row of the selected range as the series name, the first column as the category values, and the remaining columns as the series values. This data source has only one data series, the Assets data series. Its category values in the range A4:A8 list the different asset categories, and its series values in the range B4:B8 contain the data.

If the data source is organized in rows rather than in columns, the first row contains the category values, the remaining rows contain the data values for each data series, and the first column of each series row contains the series names. If your data is organized differently, you can specify a layout for the data source. You'll look at the tools to do this later in this tutorial.

Selecting a Chart Type

Next, you select the type of chart you want to create. Excel supports 73 built-in charts organized into 11 categories. Figure 4-3 describes the different chart type categories. You can also create custom chart types based on the built-in charts.

Chart Type	Description
Column	Compares values from different categories. Values are indicated by the height of the columns.
Line	Compares values from different categories. Values are indicated by the height of the line. Often used to show trends and changes over time.
Pie	Compares relative values of different categories to the whole. Values are indicated by the areas of the pie slices.
Bar	Compares values from different categories. Values are indicated by the length of the bars.
Area	Compares values from different categories. Similar to the line chart except that areas under the lines contain a fill color.
XY (Scatter)	Shows the patterns or relationship between two or more sets of values. Often used in scientific studies and statistical analyses.
Stock	Displays stock market data, including the high, low, opening, and closing prices of a stock.
Surface	Compares three sets of values in a three-dimensional chart.
Doughnut	Compares relative values of different categories to the whole. Similar to the pie chart except that it can display multiple sets of data.
Bubble	Shows the patterns or relationship between two or more sets of values. Similar to the XY (Scatter) chart except the size of the data marker is determined by a third value.
Radar	Compares a collection of values from several different data sets.

Ajita wants you to create a pie chart of the assets data. A **pie chart** is a chart in the shape of a circle (like a pie) that shows data values as a percentage of the whole. Each value in the data series represents a slice of the pie. The larger the value, the larger the pie slice. For the assets data, each slice will represent the percentage of the total assets from each investment category in the New Century Fund.

Pie charts are most effective with six or fewer slices, and when each slice is large enough to view. The pie chart you are creating for Ajita has five large slices, representing each of the five asset categories—Cash, U.S. Stocks, Non-U.S. Stocks, Bonds, and Other. Notice in Figure 4-2 that you did not select the Total Assets row. The Total Assets row is not an asset category and should not be included in a pie chart.

Tip

Do not include a totals row or column in the data source for a pie chart. Only select the rows or columns that contain the data values and the individual categories.

To insert a pie chart:

▶ **1.** Click the **Insert** tab on the Ribbon. The Ribbon displays the insert options.

▶ **2.** In the Charts group, click the **Pie** button to open the Charts gallery, and then click **Pie** (the first pie chart) in the 2-D Pie section. The pie chart is inserted in the Assets sheet, and three new tabs appear on the Ribbon with a label identifying them as Chart Tools contextual tabs. See Figure 4-4.

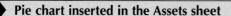

Figure 4-4 ▶ Pie chart inserted in the Assets sheet

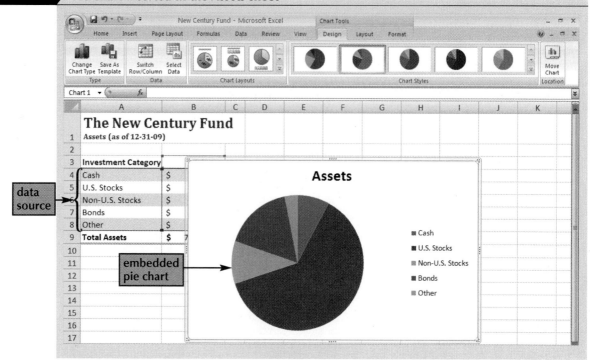

Each slice in the pie chart you just created is a different size based on its value in the data series. The biggest slice of the pie represents the U.S. stocks, because that category has the largest value in the data series. The smallest slice of pie represents the Other category, which has the smallest value in the data series.

When you create or select a chart, three Chart Tools contextual tabs appear on the Ribbon. The Design, Layout, and Format tabs provide additional commands to work with the chart's content and appearance. On the Design tab, you set the chart's overall design. On the Layout tab, you work with individual elements of the chart, such as the chart's title. On the Format tab, you format graphic shapes found in the chart, such as the chart's border or markers placed in the chart. When you select a worksheet cell or another object that is not a chart, the Chart Tools contextual tabs disappear until you reselect the chart.

Moving and Resizing Charts

By default, a chart is inserted as an **embedded chart**, which means the chart is placed in a worksheet next to its data source. The advantage of an embedded chart is that you can display the chart alongside any text or figures that can explain the chart's meaning and purpose. An embedded chart covers worksheet cells, which might contain data and formulas.

You can also place a chart in a **chart sheet**, so that the entire sheet contains only the chart and no worksheet cells. Chart sheets are helpful for detailed charts that need more space to be seen clearly or when you want to show a chart without any worksheet text or data. For now, you'll leave Ajita's pie chart as an embedded chart. You'll work with chart sheets later in this tutorial.

Right now, the pie chart is embedded in the Assets worksheet. However, Ajita wants the chart embedded in the Summary Report worksheet. You can move an embedded chart to a different worksheet in the workbook or you can move it into a chart sheet. Likewise, you can move a chart from a chart sheet and embed it in any worksheet you select. The Move Chart dialog box provides options for moving charts between worksheets and chart sheets. You can also cut and paste a chart to a new location in the workbook.

To move the embedded pie chart to the Summary Report worksheet:

▶ **1.** In the Location group on the Chart Tools Design tab, click the **Move Chart** button. The Move Chart dialog box opens.

Trouble? If you don't see the Chart Tools Design tab on the Ribbon, the chart is probably not selected. Click the chart in the Assets sheet to select it, and then repeat Step 1.

▶ **2.** Click the **Object in** arrow to display a list of worksheets in the active workbook, and then click **Summary Report**. See Figure 4-5.

Move Chart dialog box ◀ **Figure 4-5**

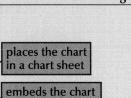

3. Click the **OK** button. The embedded pie chart moves from the Assets worksheet to the Summary Report worksheet, and remains selected.

The pie chart is now in the correct worksheet, but its location and size obscures other content in the Summary Report worksheet. You move or resize an embedded chart by first selecting the chart, which displays a **selection box** around the chart, and then dragging the selection box to a new location in the worksheet. You can also drag a **resizing handle** on the selection box to change the chart's width and height.

To move and resize the pie chart:

▶ **1.** Move the pointer over an empty area of the selected chart until the pointer changes to ⬚ and you see the ScreenTip "Chart Area."

▶ **2.** Drag the chart so its upper-left corner is within cell **A13**, and then release the mouse button. The chart's upper-left corner is in cell A13, but it still overlaps some data.

Trouble? If the pie chart resizes or does not move to the new location, you probably didn't drag the chart from the chart area. Press the Ctrl+Z keys to undo your last action, and then repeat Steps 1 and 2, being sure to drag the pie chart from the chart area.

▶ **3.** Move the pointer over the resizing handle in the lower-right corner of the chart until the pointer changes to ⬚, and then drag the resizing handle up to cell **E21**. The chart resizes to cover the range A13:E21 and remains selected. See Figure 4-6.

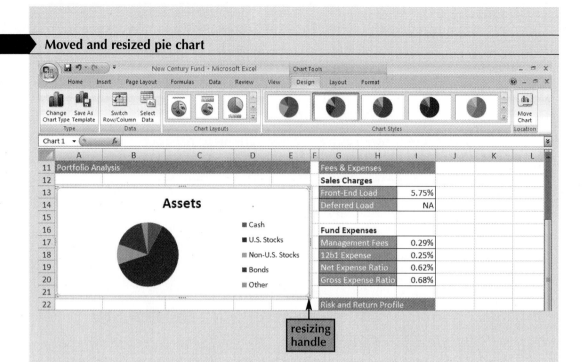

Figure 4-6 ▶ **Moved and resized pie chart**

Working on Chart Design

The assets pie chart you have just resized includes a lot of empty space. Also, it's unclear how the different asset categories are related. For example, you can easily see that the largest slice represents the U.S. Stocks category, but it's difficult to tell whether the non-U.S. stocks slice is bigger than the Cash slice. To clarify the relationship between the pie slices, Ajita wants each slice to display its percentage of the whole. She also wants less empty space within the chart.

Selecting Chart Elements

Pie charts have five elements that are common to most charts. The **chart area** is the rectangular box containing the chart and all of the other chart elements. The **chart title** is a descriptive label or name for the chart, and usually appears at the top of the chart area. The **plot area** is the part of the chart that contains the graphical representation of all the data series in the chart. Each data value or data series is represented by a **data marker**. For pie charts, the data markers are the individual pie slices, which represent the data values. The **legend** is a rectangular area that labels the markers or symbols used in the chart. If the chart contains several data series, the legend identifies the markers used for each series. Pie charts, having only one data series, use the legend to identify the different pie slices. Figure 4-7 identifies each of these elements on the pie chart you just created for the assets data.

Common chart elements **Figure 4-7**

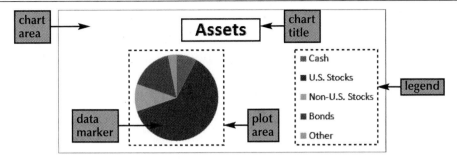

You can select and format any chart element individually or you can apply a built-in style or chart layout to format all of these elements at once. To select a chart element, you click that element or select it from a list of chart elements on the Chart Tools Layout tab. As you move your pointer over a chart element, its name appears in a ScreenTip. When you click that element, its name appears in the Chart Elements button in the Current Selection group on the Chart Tools Layout tab.

To select elements of the pie chart:

▶ 1. Move your pointer over the chart title until you see the ScreenTip "Chart Title," and then click the chart title. A selection box appears around the chart title.

▶ 2. Click the **Chart Tools Layout** tab on the Ribbon. The Ribbon displays the layout options for charts.

▶ 3. In the Current Selection group, click the **Chart Elements arrow** to display an alphabetical list of all the chart elements in the active chart. In this case, the Chart Elements box shows "Chart Title," indicating that this element is currently selected.

▶ 4. Click **Legend**. The legend is selected in the chart.

▶ 5. In the Current Selection group, click the **Chart Elements arrow**, and then click **Plot Area**. The chart's plot area is selected.

▶ 6. Click the chart area in the chart. The chart area is selected.

Choosing a Chart Style and Layout

The assets pie chart uses the default style for the different slices. A chart style is similar to a cell style or a table style in that it formats several chart elements at one time. You can change the color and appearance of the slices by selecting a different chart style from the Chart Styles gallery on the Chart Tools Design tab. Ajita wants a chart style that gives the slices a rounded, shaded look.

To apply a different chart style to the assets pie chart:

▶ 1. Click the **Chart Tools Design** tab on the Ribbon. The Ribbon displays the design options for charts.

▶ 2. In the Chart Styles group, click the **More** button to open the Chart Styles gallery, and then click **Style 26** (the fourth row, second column). Each pie slice now has a rounded, raised look. See Figure 4-8.

Figure 4-8 ▶ **Style 26 chart style applied**

Trouble? If a dialog box opens, indicating that complex formatting applied to the selected chart may take awhile to display, click the Yes button to continue using the formatting.

You can also use a chart layout to choose which chart elements are displayed and how they are formatted. The chart layouts include some of the most common ways of displaying different charts. Each chart type has its own collection of layouts. Figure 4-9 shows the available layouts for pie charts. Depending on the pie chart layout you choose, you can hide or display the chart title, display a chart legend or place legend labels in the pie slices, and add percentages to the pie slices.

Figure 4-9 ▶ **Pie chart layouts**

Layout	Name	Pie chart with
	Layout 1	Chart title, labels, and percentages
	Layout 2	Chart title, percentages, and legend above the pie
	Layout 3	Legend below the pie
	Layout 4	Labels in pie slices
	Layout 5	Chart title and labels in pie slices
	Layout 6	Chart title, percentages, and legend to the right of the pie
	Layout 7	Legend to the right of the pie

Ajita wants you to apply a layout that shows percentages for the pie slices so her clients can tell exactly how large each asset category is relative to the whole. She also wants to the chart title to remain displayed above the chart and the legend to remain displayed to the side of the chart. Layout 6 does all of these things.

To apply Layout 6 to the assets pie chart:

▶ **1.** In the Chart Layouts group on the Chart Tools Design tab, click the **More** button to open the Chart Layouts gallery.

▶ **2.** Click **Layout 6** in the second row, third column. Percentages appear on or next to the slices in the pie chart. See Figure 4-10.

Layout 6 chart layout applied ◀ **Figure 4-10**

percentages added to the pie slices

Tip

Percentages appear on pie slices large enough to fit the number; otherwise, percentages appear next to the slices in the chart area.

Trouble? Depending on your monitor size and resolution, your chart might look different from that shown in Figure 4-10. This does not affect your work with the pie chart.

The percentages on the pie chart will enable clients to quickly see how the assets of the New Century Fund are allocated. For example, 62% of the New Century Fund is invested in U.S. stocks and 10% in non-U.S. stocks. To fit the percentages, Excel reduced the size of the pie chart in the plot area. Ajita wants the pie chart larger, so you'll format some of the other chart elements smaller to make more space for the pie.

Working with the Chart Title

Ajita thinks that the chart title is too large and not descriptive enough. The chart title uses the heading from the column of asset values in the Assets worksheet. You'll change the title to "Allocation of Assets" and reduce its font size to 12 points.

To format the chart title:

▶ **1.** Click the chart title to select it. A selection box appears around the chart title.

▶ **2.** Type **Allocation of Assets**, and then press the **Enter** key. The chart title is updated with your typed entry, and remains selected.

▶ **3.** Click the **Home** tab on the Ribbon.

Tip

You can revise the title text rather than replace it by double-clicking the chart title to place the insertion point in the text, and then editing the text as needed.

> **4.** In the Font group, click the **Font Size arrow**, and then click **12**. The chart title shrinks from 18 points to 12 points, and the pie chart increases in size to fill in the extra space. See Figure 4-11.

Figure 4-11 ▶ **Chart title updated and formatted**

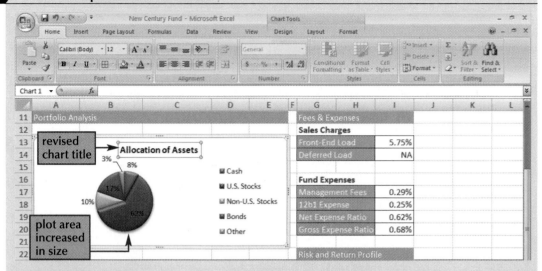

Trouble? Depending on your monitor size and resolution, your chart might look slightly different from that shown in Figure 4-11. This does not affect your work with the pie chart.

Working with the Chart Legend

Ajita wants the legend moved to the left side of the chart and an orange border added around the legend text to distinguish it from the rest of the chart. You'll use the tools on the Chart Tools Layout tab to format the legend.

To format the chart legend:

> **1.** Click the **Chart Tools Layout** tab on the Ribbon.

> **2.** In the Labels group, click the **Legend** button, and then click **Show Legend at Left**. The legend moves to the left side of the chart.

> **3.** In the Labels group, click the **Legend** button, and then click **More Legend Options**. The Format Legend dialog box opens. Every chart element has a corresponding dialog box from which you can select more advanced options to format the element's appearance.

> **4.** Click **Border Color** in the list on the left side of the dialog box. The Border Color options appear on the right side of the dialog box.

> **5.** Click the **Solid line** option button. Two more options related to border colors appear.

> **6.** Click the **Color** button [🎨 ▾] to open the color palette, and then click **Orange, Accent 6, Lighter 40%** (the fourth row, last column) in the Theme Colors section. See Figure 4-12.

Border Color options set in the Format Legend dialog box ◣ **Figure 4-12**

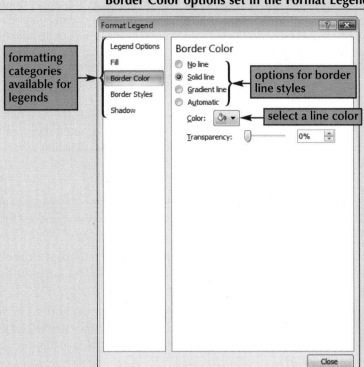

7. Click the **Close** button, and then click cell **A23** to deselect the chart. The legend now has a light orange border. See Figure 4-13.

Chart legend moved and formatted ◣ **Figure 4-13**

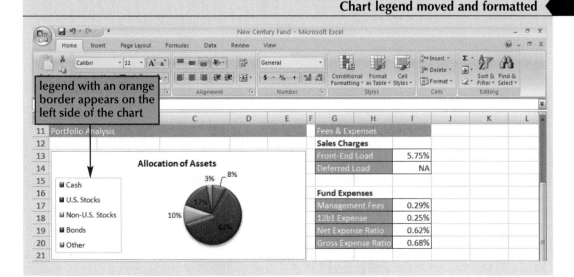

Formatting a Pie Chart

Chart titles and legends are common to almost all types of charts. Another common element is a **data label**, which is text associated with a data value. In pie charts, data labels are added to the slices. You already created data labels for the assets chart when you selected Layout 6 to add percentages to the slices. These labels were placed where they best fit in relation to the pie slices. For some asset categories, the label appears within the pie slice; for others, the label appears alongside the slice. Labels placed outside of the pie might appear farther from their slices than is easily read due to space limitations. In those cases, **leader lines** might be added to the labels to connect them to their corresponding slices. For example, a leader line connects the Cash slice and its label in Figure 4-13. Note that a leader line will disappear when enough space exists in the pie chart to place a label next to its slice.

For consistency, Ajita wants all the data labels to appear outside the pie chart. This will make the text for the dark blue and red pie slices easier to read. You'll show leader lines for the labels, which means the leader lines will appear only when the chart area does not have enough space for the labels to appear close to their pie slices.

To format the pie chart's data labels:

1. Click the chart to select it.

2. In the Labels group on the Chart Tools Layout tab, click the **Data Labels** button, and then click **More Data Label Options**. The Format Data Labels dialog box opens with the the Label Options displayed.

3. In the Label Position section, click the **Outside End** option button. In the Label Contains section, the Percentage check box and the Show Leader Lines check box are already checked because these were included in the chart layout you applied earlier. See Figure 4-14.

| Figure 4-14 | Label Options in the Format Data Labels dialog box |

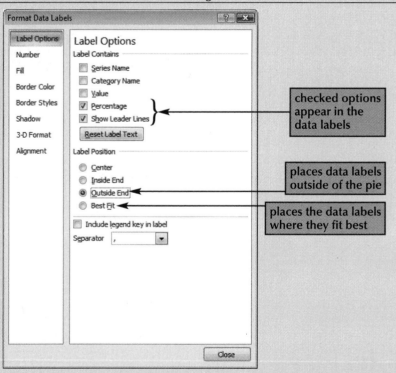

These options set the data labels to display percentages outside the pie chart and use leader lines when needed to connect the labels with their corresponding pie slices. Next, you'll change the percentage values to show two decimal places for more accuracy.

4. Click **Number** in the list on the left side of the dialog box.

5. Click **Percentage** in the Category list, and then verify that **2** appears in the Decimal places box.

6. Click the **Close** button to close the Format Data Labels dialog box, and then click cell **A23** to deselect the chart. See Figure 4-15. Leader lines don't appear in the pie chart shown in Figure 4-15 because the chart area has enough space to place the labels close to their slices.

Pie chart data labels formatted   **Figure 4-15**

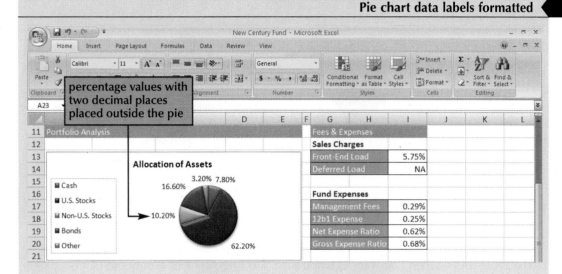

Setting the Pie Slice Colors

The pie slices for Cash, Bonds, and Other have similar colors. Depending on the printer quality or the monitor resolution, these slices might be difficult to distinguish in the final report. In pie charts with legends, it's best to make the slice colors as distinct as possible to avoid confusion, especially slices adjacent to each other in the pie. You'll change the fill color of the Other slice to yellow and the Cash slice to light blue. Because each slice represents a different value in the series, you must format each slice rather than the entire data series.

To select and format pie slices in the assets pie chart:

1. Click the pie to select the entire data series.

2. Click the light blue **Other** slice, which represents 3.20% of the pie. Only that value, or slice, is selected.

3. Click the **Home** tab on the Ribbon.

4. In the Font group, click the **Fill Color button arrow** ⬚▾, and then click **Yellow**, the fourth color in the Standard Colors section. The Other slice and legend marker change to yellow.

5. Click the dark blue **Cash** slice, which covers 7.80% of the pie.

6. In the Font group, click the **Fill Color button arrow** ⬚▾, and then click **Light Blue**, the seventh color in the Standard Colors section. The Cash slice and legend marker change to light blue. Each slice of the pie is now a distinct color. See Figure 4-16.

Figure 4-16 ▶ **Pie slices with new colors**

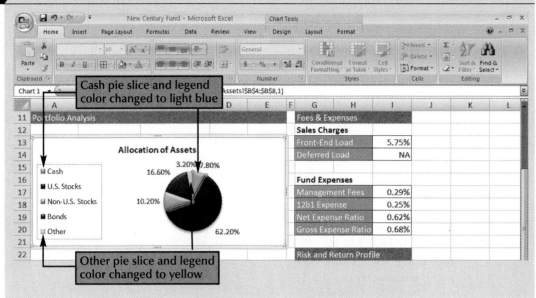

Pie slices do not need to be fixed in place. An **exploded pie chart** moves one slice away from the pie as if someone were taking the piece out of the pie. To explode a pie slice, select that slice and then drag it away from the pie. To explode all of the slices, select the entire pie and drag the pointer away from the center of the pie. Exploded pie charts are useful when you want to emphasize one category above all of the others. Although you can explode more than one slice, the resulting pie chart is rarely effective.

Creating a 3D Pie Chart

Ajita thinks the pie chart will look better as a three-dimensional (3D) figure. Although 3D charts are visually attractive, they can obscure the relationship between the values in the chart. For example, it is unclear which slice—red or yellow—is bigger in the pie chart shown in Figure 4-17. Actually, they are the same size, each representing 20% of the whole. The yellow slice appears bigger because the 3D effect brings that slice closer to the viewer.

Figure 4-17 ▶ **Misleading 3D pie chart**

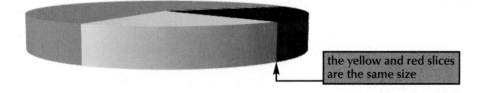

the yellow and red slices are the same size

Because you already added data labels to the assets pie chart, Ajita thinks her clients will not misinterpret a 3D pie chart. She thinks that making the assets pie chart 3D will provide visual interest to the report while maintaining the pie chart's effectiveness.

To change the assets pie chart to 3D:

▶ **1.** Click the chart area to select the chart, and then click the **Chart Tools Design** tab on the Ribbon.

▶ **2.** In the Type group, click the **Change Chart Type** button. The Change Chart Type dialog box opens.

▶ **3.** Click **Pie in 3-D** (the second chart type in the Pie section).

▶ **4.** Click the **OK** button. The pie chart is now a 3D chart.

Creating Effective 3D Charts | InSight

Because of the visual distortion that can result with 3D representations, you should include data labels with all 3D charts. Also, try to avoid extreme viewing angles that elongate the chart and misrepresent the data. Although 3D charts can be eye-catching, do not use this effect if it overrides the main purpose of a chart, which is data interpretation.

Working with 3D Options

The 3D pie chart does not look very different from the 2D version because you are look-ing straight down on the chart from "above." To increase the 3D effect, you need to rotate the chart. You can rotate the chart in two directions: horizontally along the x-axis and vertically along the y-axis. Increasing the rotation along the x-axis spins the chart clockwise. Increasing the rotation along the y-axis raises the viewpoint higher above the chart. All 3D charts have a third axis that corresponds to the depth of the chart. Depth values can range from 0 to 2000. The larger the value, the thicker the chart appears. You can also change the chart's **perspective**, which controls how fast the chart appears to recede from the viewer's eye. Perspective values range from 0° to 90°. A 90° perspective value exaggerates the 3D effect, making distant objects appear very small, whereas per-spective values near 0° minimize this effect. Try different values for depth and perspective to determine which work best for your chart.

You'll orient the pie chart so that the viewer's eye level is slightly above the chart. You'll also rotate the chart along the horizontal axis so that the largest slice is on the left side of the pie. Often you'll need to experiment to find the right angles for a 3D chart by rotating the chart in different directions until it looks correct without distorting the data. In this case, you'll rotate the chart 90° along the horizontal axis and place the viewer's eye at an angle of 20° above the chart. You will not change the chart's perspective or depth.

To rotate the 3D pie chart:

▶ **1.** Click the **Chart Tools Layout** tab on the Ribbon, and then, in the Background group, click the **3-D Rotation** button. The Format Chart Area dialog box opens with the 3-D Rotation options displayed.

▶ **2.** In the Rotation section, type **90** in the X box and type **20** in the Y box. See Figure 4-18.

Figure 4-18 | **Format Chart Area dialog box**

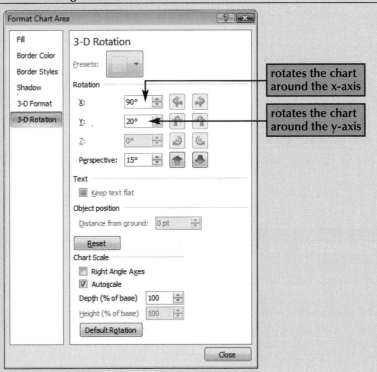

3. Click the **Close** button. The pie chart rotates based on the new x-axis and y-axis values. See Figure 4-19.

Figure 4-19 | **3D assets pie chart**

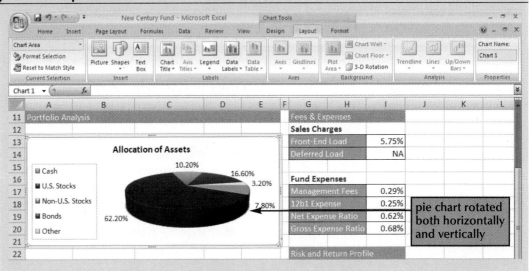

The new x-axis and y-axis values have a significant impact on the way the chart looks. The new x-axis value shifted the pie chart clockwise one quarter of the way around the circle so the largest slice, the red U.S Stocks slice, is in the front. The new y-axis value turned the pie chart so the viewer is looking down on the chart. Ajita is pleased with the 3D effect you added.

The Format Chart Area dialog box shown in Figure 4-18 also includes options to change the 3-D Format of the chart. These options allow you to add drop shadows, raised or beveled corners, and textured surfaces that give the illusion of light reflecting off the chart elements. You saw an example of such a surface in Figure 4-13 when you added a shaded, rounded chart style to the pie chart. You will not use the 3-D Format options for the assets pie chart.

Editing Chart Data

Charts remain linked or connected to their data sources, even if they appear in different worksheets. If you change any values or labels in the data source, the chart is automatically updated to show the new content. For example, if the Other assets increase from $2,520 to $4,520 and the remaining assets are unchanged, the Other slice becomes bigger to reflect its larger percentage of the whole and the remaining slices shrink to reflect their smaller percentage of the whole.

Ajita wants you to edit the data source for the assets pie chart. She thinks the Other category would be better titled as Other Assets and she wants you to correct the assets value for that category. You'll make both of these changes to the data in the Assets worksheet.

To edit the data source for the assets pie chart:

▶ **1.** Click the **Assets** sheet tab to make it the active worksheet.

▶ **2.** Edit the text in cell A8 to **Other Assets**, and then change the value in cell B8 to **4520**.

▶ **3.** Click the **Summary Report** sheet tab, and then verify that the pie chart was updated with the new data value and category name. See Figure 4-20. Note that the percentage values for each category are recalculated based on the new data. As a result, the Other Assets slice increased in size to reflect its larger percentage of the whole, and the remaining slices decreased in size.

Updated pie chart based on revised data | Figure 4-20

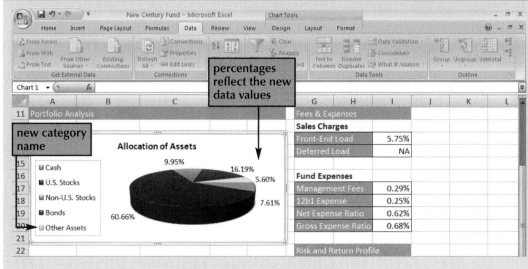

Occasionally, you will not want a chart to reflect new values in the data source, such as when a chart shows a "snapshot" of the data at a certain time. You can do this by copying and pasting the chart as a picture. Select the chart, copy it as usual, click the Paste button arrow, point to As Picture, and then click Paste as Picture. The chart is pasted as a picture without any connection to its data source and cannot be edited or formatted in any way.

Working with Column Charts

The pie chart in the summary report clearly shows that most assets of the New Century Fund are allocated toward U.S. stocks. The next part of the summary report lists the type of stocks being purchased by the fund. Each mutual fund invests in different kinds of stocks. Some funds are heavily invested in information technology, others in the service industry, and still others in manufacturing. Diversification (the distribution of investments among a variety of companies or sectors to limit losses in the event one company or sector has an economic downturn) is important, so all funds are invested to some degree in multiple economic sectors. The New Century Fund is invested in 12 different economic sectors, organized into categories of information, services, and manufacturing.

Creating a Column Chart

Twelve categories are too many for an effective pie chart, so Ajita wants you to create a column chart to display this economic sector data. A **column chart** displays values in different categories as columns; the height of each column is based on its value. Related to the column chart is the **bar chart**, which is a column chart turned on its side, so each bar length is based on its value.

Column and bar charts are superior to pie charts when the number of categories is large or the categories are close in value. It is easier to compare height or length than area. Figure 4-21 displays the same data as a pie chart and a column chart. As you can see, it's difficult to determine which pie slice has the largest area and by how much. This is much simpler to determine in the column chart.

| Figure 4-21 | Same data displayed as a pie chart and a column chart |

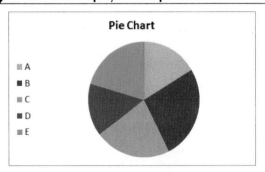
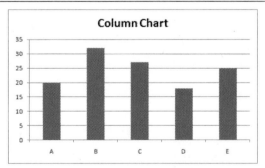

Column and bar charts can also be applied to a wider range of data than pie charts. For example, you can demonstrate how a set of values changes over time, such as the value of the New Century Fund over several years. You can also include several data series in a column or bar chart, such as the value of three funds over several years. The values from different data series are displayed in columns side by side. Pie charts usually show only one data series.

Ajita wants you to create a column chart that shows how the the New Century Fund is distributed among the 12 sectors in which it is invested. The columns will represent only one data series, so you'll use the 2D Clustered Columns chart type. A clustered columns chart uses vertical rectangles to compare values across categories.

To create a column chart from the sector data:

▶ **1.** Click the **Sector Weightings** sheet tab, and then select the range **A3:C15**.

▶ **2.** Click the **Insert** tab on the Ribbon.

▶ **3.** In the Charts group, click the **Column** button, and then click the **Clustered Column** chart, the first chart in the 2-D Column section. The column chart is inserted in the Sector Weightings worksheet, and the Chart Tools Design tab on the Ribbon is selected.

▶ **4.** In the Location group on the Chart Tools Design tab, click the **Move Chart** button. The Move Chart dialog box opens. You'll move the chart to the Summary Report worksheet.

▶ **5.** Click the **Object in** arrow, click **Summary Report**, and then click the **OK** button. The column chart moves to the Summary Report worksheet.

▶ **6.** In the Summary Report worksheet, click a blank spot in the chart area of the column chart, and then drag the chart down so its upper-left corner is in cell **A23**.

▶ **7.** Drag the resizing handle in the lower-right corner of the chart until the chart covers the range **A23:E37**. See Figure 4-22.

Column chart moved and resized in the Summary Report worksheet ◀ Figure 4-22

The column chart shows that the New Century Fund is most heavily invested in health care and consumer services, hardware information technology, and energy manufacturing. On the other hand, the fund does not invest much in telecommunications, software, and media.

Formatting Column Chart Elements

Similar to the pie chart, the column chart has a chart title and a legend that identifies different data series rather than values within a data series. Because this column chart contains only one data series, the sector weightings of the New Century Fund, the legend has only one entry. The column chart also has a few new elements, which are identified in Figure 4-23.

Figure 4-23 ▷ **Elements of the column chart**

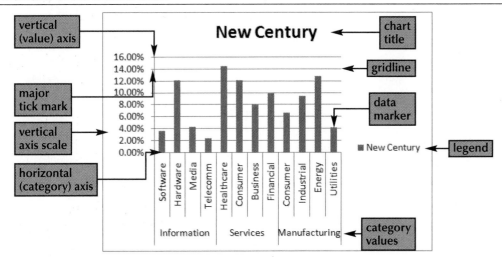

The **vertical**, or **value, axis** displays the values associated with the heights of each column. You can use two value axes to plot different types of data on a chart, such as the number of units sold and the revenue generated from the sale of a group of products. One axis (usually the axis on the left) is called the **primary value axis**, and the other axis is called the **secondary value axis**. The chart shown in Figure 4-23 has a primary value axis but not the optional secondary value axis.

Excel selects the scale that best displays the values in the chart. A **scale** is a range of values that spans the vertical axis, which is 0% to 16% in Figure 4-23. Each value has a **major tick mark** that acts like the lines on a ruler, making it easier to read the scale. In Figure 4-23, major tick marks appear every 2% along the scale. Some axes also use **minor tick marks** to further divide the space between the major tick marks. Figure 4-23 does not display minor tick marks.

Many charts use **gridlines** to extend the tick marks across the plot area. As you can see in Figure 4-23, gridlines make it easier to determine the value of a column. For example, little more than 14% of the stocks from the New Century Fund are invested in healthcare services. A chart can also have vertical gridlines, though none are shown here.

The **horizontal**, or **category**, **axis** displays the categories associated with each data value. This column chart has two levels of category values: one for the sector category and one for the sector name. You can include as many levels as you need to clearly define the category values; Excel will fit as many as possible below the category axis. In this chart, Excel rotated the sector names to fit them in the space. You can format the axes text, rotate and align the text entries, or select which entries to display in the chart.

The data markers in the column chart are the individual columns. The same data marker (a column) is used for an entire data series; only the columns' heights differ from one data value to another. When a chart has only one data series—such as the column chart you just created—the chart title and legend are redundant. Ajita asks you to remove the legend, and then edit and format the chart title.

To format the legend and chart title of the column chart:

▶ **1.** Click the **Chart Tools Layout** tab on the Ribbon.

▶ **2.** In the Labels group, click the **Legend** button, and then click **None**. The chart legend no longer appears in the chart, and the column chart is resized to fill the available space.

▶ **3.** Click the chart title to select it, and then click the **Home** tab on the Ribbon.

▶ **4.** In the Font group, click the **Font Size arrow**, and then click **12**. The chart title is reduced to 12 points, and remains selected.

▶ **5.** Type **Sector Weightings** as the new chart title, and then press the **Enter** key.

Formatting the Chart Axes

Ajita thinks that the font used in both the value axis and the category axis is too large, and that the value axis scale looks crowded. She asks you to reduce the font size of the axes, place the major tick marks at 5% intervals, and display the percentages without any decimal places.

To format the chart axes:

▶ **1.** Click the **category axis** to select it.

▶ **2.** In the Font group on the Home tab, click the **Font Size arrow**, and then click **8**. The category axis labels are smaller.

▶ **3.** Click the **value axis** to select it, and repeat Step 2 to change the axis font size to **8** points.

▶ **4.** Click the **Chart Tools Layout** tab on the Ribbon.

▶ **5.** In the Axes group, click the **Axes** button, point to **Primary Vertical Axis**, and then click **More Primary Vertical Axis Options**. The Format Axis dialog box opens with the Axis Options displayed. The value axis options are set to Auto, which tells Excel to set the values. You'll modify these so that the major tick marks appear at 5% intervals on the vertical axis to make the chart less cluttered and easier to read.

▶ **6.** Click the **Major unit Fixed** option button, press the **Tab** key, and then type **0.05** for the size of the major tick mark. Major tick marks will now appear on the value axis in 5% increments. See Figure 4-24.

Axis Options in the Format Axis dialog box | **Figure 4-24**

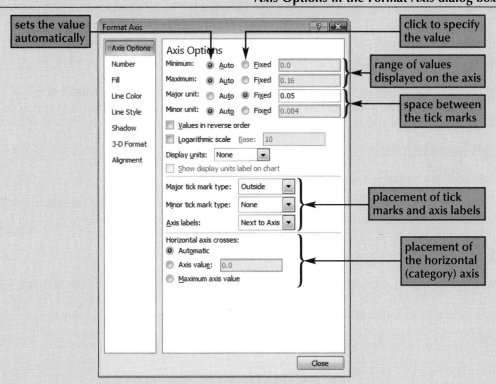

▶ **7.** Click **Number** on the left side of the dialog box, type **0** in the Decimal places box, and then click the **Close** button. The percentages on the value axis show no decimal places. See Figure 4-25.

Figure 4-25 ▶ **Formatted chart axes**

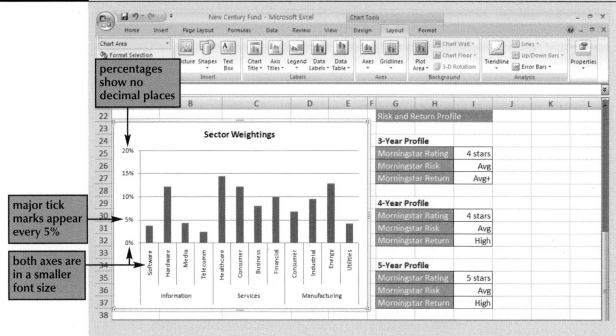

The value axis now ranges from 0% to 20% rather than 16%, and the percentages no longer show any decimal places. These changes make the value axis easier to read. Also, the smaller font size used for the value and category axes left more room for the data series. No titles appear next to the value and category axes. This isn't a problem for the category axis because the chart title and the axis labels are self-explanatory. Ajita wants you to add the title "Stock Percentages" to the value axis and rotate it to save space.

To add a rotated title to the value axis:

▶ **1.** In the Labels group on the Chart Tools Layout tab, click the **Axis Titles** button, point to **Primary Vertical Axis Title**, and then click **Rotated Title**. The text "Axis Title" appears rotated to the left of the vertical axis in a selection box.

▶ **2.** Type **Stock Percentages**, and then press the **Enter** key. The title is added to the vertical axis.

As with other chart text in the chart, you can format an axis title. Ajita is pleased with the current format of the vertical axis title, so no further changes are needed.

Formatting the Chart Columns

Ajita thinks that the columns are spaced too widely and wants you to reduce the gap between them. Also, she wants you to change the fill color of the columns to a lighter blue and add a shaded appearance to make the columns stand out. To modify the appearance of a data series, you first select the data markers for that series and then apply formatting to selected markers.

To format the chart columns:

▶ **1.** Click any column in the Sector Weightings chart. A selection box surrounds each column in the chart, indicating that the entire series is selected.

Trouble? If only the column you clicked is selected, you selected only a single data value rather than the entire data series. Click a blank spot in the chart area, and then repeat Step 1 to select the entire series.

▶ **2.** In the Current Selection group on the Chart Tools Layout tab, click **Format Selection**. The Format Data Series dialog box opens with the Series Options displayed.

▶ **3.** Drag the Gap width slider to **50%** to reduce the gap between adjacent columns. The columns become wider to fill the space.

Trouble? If you cannot drag the Gap width slider to exactly 50%, type the value 50 in the Gap width box below the slider.

▶ **4.** Click **Fill** on the left side of the dialog box, and then click the **Gradient fill** option button to fill the columns with a gradually changing mix of colors.

▶ **5.** Click the **Direction** button ▨ ▾ to open a gallery of fill directions, and then click **Linear Right** (the fourth fill direction in the first row). The columns have a gradient fill that blends to the right. See Figure 4-26.

Tip

You can also highlight a data value by formatting one column in a column chart; select the data series and then click the column you want to format. Any formatting applies only to that data marker.

Fill options set in the Format Data Series dialog box ◀ **Figure 4-26**

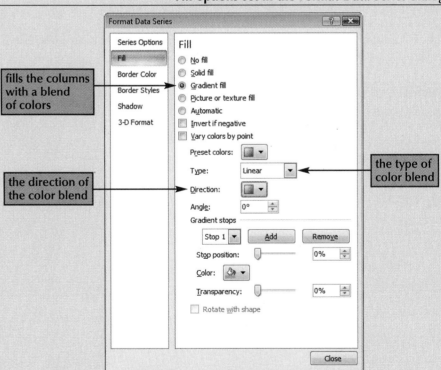

▶ **6.** Click the **Close** button, and then click cell **A38** to deselect the chart. See Figure 4-27.

Figure 4-27 | Formatted chart columns

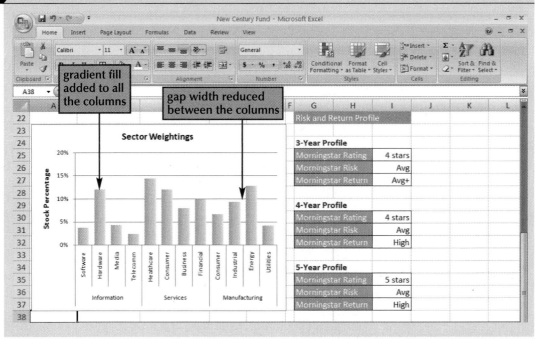

Ajita is pleased with the two charts you've created for the Summary Report worksheet. In the next session, you'll add a chart that describes the performance of the New Century Fund over the past 10 years and work with drawing objects.

InSight | Designing Effective Charts

A well-designed chart can illuminate facts that might be hidden by viewing only the numbers. However, poorly designed charts can mislead readers and make it more difficult to interpret data. Keep in mind the following tips for creating more effective and useful charts:

- Keep it simple. Do not clutter a chart with too many graphic elements. Focus attention on the data rather than on decorative elements that do not inform.
- Limit the number of data series used in the chart. Line charts and column charts should display no more than three or four data series. Pie charts should have no more than six slices.
- Use gridlines in moderation. Gridlines should be used to provide only approximate values for the data markers. Too many gridlines can obscure the data being graphed.
- Choose colors carefully. Display different data series in contrasting colors to make it easier to distinguish one series from another. Do not always accept the default color choices. When printing charts, make sure the colors are distinct in the printed copy.
- Limit the use of different text styles to no more than two. Too many text styles in one chart can distract attention from the data.
- Analyze whether you need a chart in the first place. Remember, not all data is meant to be charted. Some data is presented more effectively in a table or as part of a narrative.

1. What are the three components of a data series?
2. In what two locations can a chart be placed?
3. What is the difference between the chart area and the plot area?
4. A data series contains values divided into 10 categories. Which chart would be better for displaying this data: a pie chart or a column chart? Why?
5. Explain how 3D charts can lead to a false interpretation of the data. What can you do to correct this problem?
6. What are major tick marks, minor tick marks, and gridlines?
7. What is a bar chart?
8. How do you rescale a chart axis?

Session 4.2

Creating a Line Chart

Ajita will include the performance history of the New Century Fund in the summary report because her clients always want to know how well their investments are doing. Clients also want to compare different investments, so Ajita has other data that provides a standard of comparison, or benchmark, to the performance of the New Century Fund. One benchmark is the average performance of other large growth funds, and the other benchmark is the S&P 500 (or Standard and Poor's 500, which is an index of 500 blue chip stocks that is commonly used to measure the performance of stocks and funds).

Ajita entered this data in the Performance History worksheet. She calculated the quarterly returns for the past 10 years from an initial investment of $10,000. Because there are 40 data points for each of the three data series, you'll create a line chart. A **line chart** compares values from several categories with a sequential order, such as dates and times that occur at evenly spaced intervals. The values are indicated by the height of the line. In this case, you'll plot the quarterly value of each investment on the vertical axis and the date on the horizontal axis.

To create the line chart:

▶ 1. If you took a break after the previous session, make sure the New Century Fund workbook located in the Tutorial.04\Tutorial folder is open.

▶ 2. Click the **Performance History** sheet tab to make it the active worksheet, and then select the range **A4:D44**. This range contains the data for the value of the New Century Fund, the average value of large growth funds, and the value of the S&P 500 for each quarter of 2000 through 2009.

▶ 3. Click the **Insert** tab on the Ribbon.

▶ 4. In the Charts group, click the **Line** button, and then click the **Line** chart (the first chart in the 2-D Line section). A line chart is embedded in the Performance History worksheet.

▶ 5. In the Location group on the Chart Tools Design tab, click the **Move Chart** button to open the Move Chart dialog box, click **Summary Report** in the Object in list, and then click the **OK** button. The line chart moves to the Summary Report worksheet.

▶ 6. Move and resize the chart to cover the range **D1:I9**. See Figure 4-28.

Figure 4-28 ▶ **Moved and resized line chart**

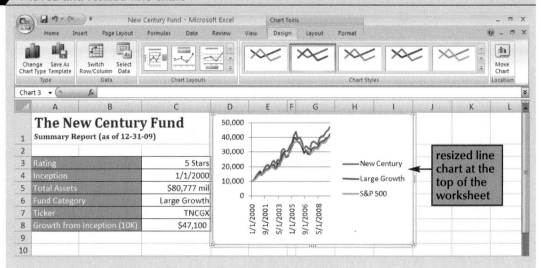

This chart includes three data series—the New Century Fund, the average of large growth funds, and the S&P 500. Each series has a different line color, which is identified in the legend on the right side of the chart area. However, the line chart has little blank space in the chart area and seems crowded by the legend and the date labels on the category axis. You'll reduce the font size of the axis and legend labels, and then add a chart title that clearly identifies the chart's content—the growth of $10,000 for the New Century Fund and the two benchmarks.

To edit the line chart:

▶ **1.** Click the **Chart Tools Layout** tab on the Ribbon.

▶ **2.** In the Labels group, click the **Chart Title** button, and then click **Above Chart**. A chart title appears above the line chart surrounded by a selection box.

▶ **3.** Type **Growth of $10,000** and then press the **Enter** key. The new, descriptive title appears above the chart.

▶ **4.** Click the **Home** tab on the Ribbon.

▶ **5.** In the Font group, click the **Font Size arrow**, and then click **10**. The chart title is reduced to 10 points.

▶ **6.** Click the **value axis** to select it, and then set its font size to **8** points.

▶ **7.** Click the **category axis** to select it, and then set its font size to **8** points.

▶ **8.** Click the **chart legend** to select it, and then set its font size to **8** points. The line chart resizes to fill the space left by the smaller chart titles, axes, and chart legend.

Formatting Date Labels

Reducing the font size of the different chart elements helps the layout, but the chart still needs work. The most awkward part of the chart is the list of dates. Ajita is more interested in the general trend from year to year, than the exact date on which the different fund values were calculated. She wants the labels to show only years. You can save space by showing the labels only every other year. To do this, you have to set the major tick marks to appear at two-year intervals. You'll also set the minor tick marks to appear at one-year intervals, even though you won't display the minor tick marks on the chart until later.

To format the category axis labels:

▶ **1.** Click the **Chart Tools Layout** tab on the Ribbon.

▶ **2.** In the Axes group, click the **Axes** button, point to **Primary Horizontal Axis**, and then click **More Primary Horizontal Axis Options**. The Format Axis dialog box opens with the Axis Options displayed.

Because the horizontal axis contains date values, its scale is based on dates rather than on numbers. This means you can set the tick mark intervals in terms of months and years. You'll display the major tick marks (and their labels) every two years. You'll set the interval for minor tick marks to one year.

▶ **3.** Click the **Major unit Fixed** option button, type **2** in the box, press the **Tab** key, select **Years** in the list. The major tick marks are set to every two years.

▶ **4.** Click the **Minor unit Fixed** option button, verify that **1** is entered in the box, select **Years** in the list, and then press the **Tab** key. The minor tick marks are set to every year. See Figure 4-29.

Date intervals for tick marks ◀ **Figure 4-29**

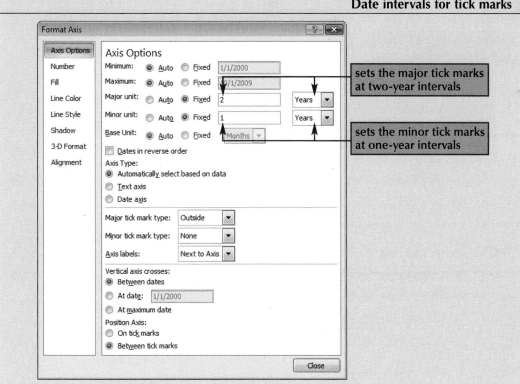

Next, you'll format the category labels to show the four-digit year value rather than the complete date. Excel does not have a built-in format to display four-digit year values, but you can create a custom format. Custom date formats use combinations of the letters *m*, *d*, and *y* for months, days, and years. The number of each letter controls how Excel displays the date. Use *m* or *mm* to display the month number, *mmm* to display the month's three-letter abbreviation, and *mmmm* to display the month's full name. For days, use *dd* to display a two-digit day value and *dddd* to display the day's full name. For example, a custom format of *mmm-dd* shows a three-letter month abbreviation followed by a hyphen and a two-digit day number (such as Apr-05). If you don't want to display the month or day but only the year, use the custom format *yy* for a two-digit year or *yyyy* for a four-digit year.

To create a custom format for the four-digit year:

▶ **1.** Click **Number** on the left side of the Format Axis dialog box.

▶ **2.** Type **yyyy** in the Format Code box, which is the code for displaying only years. See Figure 4-30.

Figure 4-30 ▶ Number options

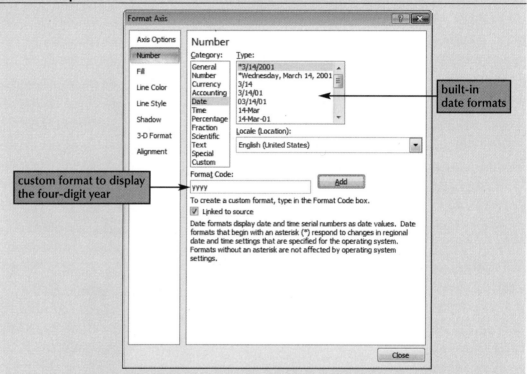

▶ **3.** Click the **Add** button. This format code is added to the list of custom formats.

▶ **4.** Click the **Close** button. The Format Axis dialog box closes and the category axis labels show values for every other year on the major tick marks. See Figure 4-31.

Formatted date labels | **Figure 4-31**

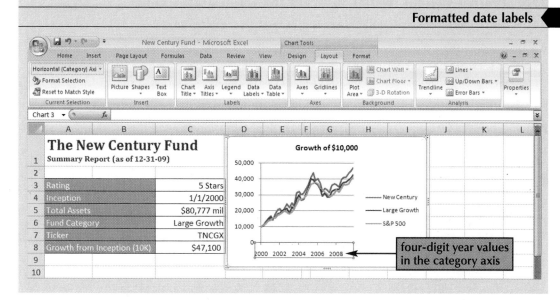

The category axis shows four-digit year values for 2000, 2002, 2004, 2006, and 2008. Because fewer years are included on the axis, there is enough room to display the labels horizontally instead of rotated.

Setting Label Units

Changing the format and tick mark intervals for the category axis has made the text easier to read. Ajita wants you to do something similar for value axis labels. Rather than displaying a large value such as "20,000," she wants to save space by displaying numbers in units of one thousand.

To format the value axis labels:

1. In the Axes group on the Chart Tools Layout tab, click the **Axes** button, point to **Primary Vertical Axis**, and then click **More Primary Vertical Axis Options**. The Format Axis dialog box opens, displaying the Axis Options.

2. Click the **Display units** arrow, click **Thousands**, and then move the dialog box so you can see the chart. The scale of the value axis changes from 10,000 to 50,000 in intervals of 10,000 to 0 through 50 in intervals of 10. The title "Thousands" is added to the axis to indicate that the values are expressed in units of one thousand. To save space, you'll remove this title from the chart.

3. Click the **Show display units label on chart** check box to remove the check mark.

Without the Thousands title, there is no indication what the numbers of the value axis mean. Ajita suggests you add the letter k to each number, displaying the numbers as 10k, 20k, and so forth. To do this, you need to create another custom format. In this custom format, you specify the text you want to appear at the end of number. The text must be placed in quotation marks. So, to display the letter k after the number you use the custom format #,##0"k". The first part of the custom format specifies that the number should include a thousands separator, and the second part indicates that the number should be followed by the the letter k. Next, you'll create the custom format to add the letter k after the number.

To create a custom format showing the thousandths unit:

▶ 1. Click **Number** on the left side of the Format Axis dialog box.

▶ 2. Click in the Format Code box after the number format, and then type **"k"** to make the format code #,##0"k". The quotation marks surround the text you want to add after the number, which, in this case, is the letter *k*.

▶ 3. Click the **Add** button. This format code is added to the list of custom formats.

▶ 4. Click the **Close** button. The Format Axis dialog box closes, and the value axis labels are revised. See Figure 4-32.

| Figure 4-32 | Formatted labels in the vertical axis |

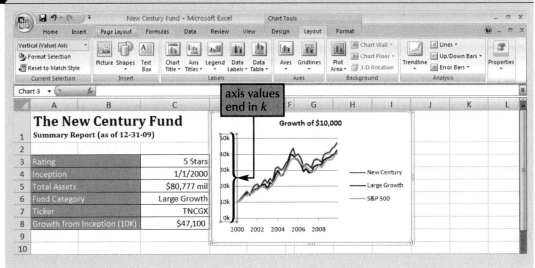

Overlaying a Legend

Tip

You can also resize a chart legend by selecting the legend, and then dragging a resizing handle.

The modified value axis labels freed space in the chart area. The only other place where you can save space is the chart legend. Rather than displaying the chart legend on the right, you can overlay the legend. There seems to be enough space in the lower-right corner for a legend that will not obscure any of the data lines in the chart.

You can also overlay chart titles on surrounding chart elements to save space, but be aware that overlapping elements might obscure some of the chart content.

To format and overlay the chart legend:

▶ 1. In the Labels group on the Chart Tools Layout tab, click the **Legend** button, and then click **More Legend Options**. The Format Legend dialog box opens, displaying Legend Options.

▶ 2. Click the **Show the legend without overlapping the chart** check box to remove the check mark. The legend moves left, overlaying the chart. Because the plot and the legend now intersect, you'll add a fill color and border to the legend to make it easier to read.

▶ 3. Click **Fill** on the left side of the Format Legend dialog box, and then click the **Solid fill** option button.

▶ 4. Click the **Color** button [🎨▾], and then click **white** (the first color) in the Theme Colors section.

5. Click **Border Color** on the left side of the Format Legend dialog box, and then click the **Solid line** option button.

6. Click the **Color** button ⬛▾ , and then click **Blue** (the eighth color) in the Standard Colors section.

7. Click the **Close** button. The Format Legend dialog box closes, and the reformatted legend overlays the chart.

An overlaid chart element floats in the chart area and is not fixed to a particular position. This means you can drag the chart element to a new location. You'll drag the overlaid legend down a bit so it doesn't obscure any of the data in the line chart.

To move the chart legend:

1. Position the pointer over a blank spot in the chart legend so the pointer changes to ⬚ and "Legend" appears in a ScreenTip.

2. Drag the legend to the lower-right corner of the plot area so the bottom of the legend is on the horizontal axis. The legend no longer covers the data lines.

   The chart has many horizontal lines from the horizontal gridlines and the chart legend; the chart would look better with vertical gridlines at each minor tick mark.

3. In the Axes group on the Chart Tools Layout tab, click the **Gridlines** button, point to **Primary Vertical Gridlines**, and then click **Minor Gridlines**. Vertical gridlines appear on the chart at each minor tick mark (recall that minor tick marks appear every year).

4. Click cell **J2** to deselect the chart. See Figure 4-33.

Final line chart ◀ **Figure 4-33**

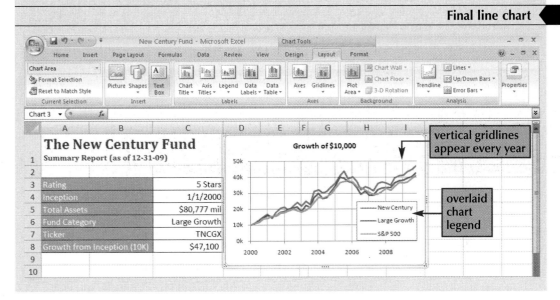

Ajita is pleased with the final version of the line chart. It's easier to read than the unformatted version, and it highlights how well the New Century Fund has performed in the past 10 years compared to the two benchmarks.

Adding a Data Series to an Existing Chart

Ajita wonders how the distribution of stocks owned by the New Century Fund compares to the S&P 500. For example, does the New Century Fund invest more in the information sector, and is that why it outperformed the S&P 500 for the past 10 years? Ajita researched the sector weightings for the S&P 500. She wants you to enter this data in the Sector Weightings worksheet and then add it to the Sector Weightings column chart you already created.

To enter data on the S&P 500 to the Sector Weightings worksheet:

1. Click the **Sector Weightings** sheet tab to make that the active worksheet, and then select the range **C3:C15**. You'll copy these formats from the New Century Fund data and paste them in column D for the S&P 500 data.

2. Click the **Home** tab on the Ribbon, and then, in the Clipboard group, click the **Format Painter** button ✍.

3. Select the range **D3:D15** to paste the formats. Now, you'll enter the S&P data in the range you just formatted.

4. In the range **D3:D15**, enter the data shown in Figure 4-34.

Figure 4-34	Sector weightings for the S&P 500

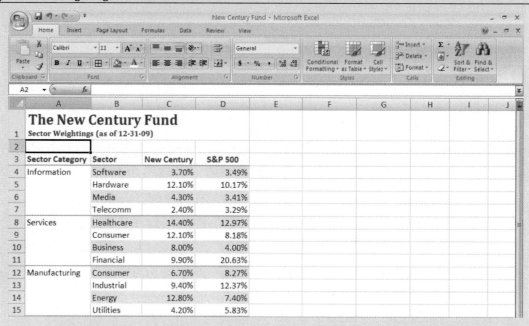

Adding the data to the table in the Sector Weightings worksheet does not add the data to the chart you already created. You must explicitly add the new data series to the chart. A new data series will have the same style and format as the existing data series in the chart.

Adding a Data Series to a Chart | Reference Window

- Select the chart to which you want to add a data series.
- In the Data group on the Chart Tools Design tab, click the Select Data button.
- Click the Add button in the Select Data Source dialog box.
- Select the range with the series name and series values you want for the new data series.
- Click the OK button in each dialog box.

You'll add the sector weightings data for the S&P 500 to the column chart in the Summary Report worksheet.

To add a data series to the existing column chart:

▶ 1. Click the **Summary Report** sheet tab, and then click the chart area of the column chart to select it.

▶ 2. Click the **Chart Tools Design** tab on the Ribbon, and then, in the Data group, click the **Select Data** button. The Select Data Source dialog box opens. The left side lists all of the data series displayed in the chart. The right side lists the category axis labels associated with each data series. You can add, edit, or remove any of these data series from the chart.

▶ 3. Click the **Add** button. The Edit Series dialog box opens. In this dialog box, you specify the name of the new data series and its range of data values.

▶ 4. With the insertion point in the Series name box, click the **Sector Weightings** sheet tab, click cell **D3**, and then press the **Tab** key. The cell with the series name is entered and the insertion point is in the Series values box.

▶ 5. Click the **Sector Weightings** sheet tab, and then select the range **D4:D15**. See Figure 4-35.

Edit Series dialog box ◀ **Figure 4-35**

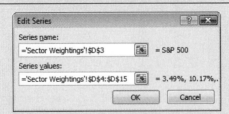

▶ 6. Click the **OK** button. In the Select Data Source dialog box, you can see that the S&P 500 data is added to the list of data series in the chart. See Figure 4-36.

Figure 4-36 ▸ **Select Data Source dialog box**

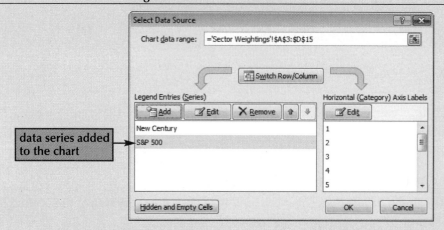

data series added to the chart

7. Click the **OK** button. The S&P 500 sector values appear as red columns in the chart. See Figure 4-37.

Figure 4-37 ▸ **Column chart with added series**

S&P 500 values are shown in the red columns

With so many columns, the data is difficult to read and interpret. Ajita suggests you separate the S&P 500 values from the New Century Fund values by plotting them as lines rather than columns.

Creating a Combination Chart

Tip

Combination charts can only be two-dimensional. You cannot create 3-D combination charts.

The type of chart that Ajita wants you to create is a **combination chart**, which is a chart that combines two or more chart types in a single graph. To create a combination chart, you select a data series in an existing chart, and then apply a new chart type to that series, leaving the other data series in its original format.

Creating a Combination Chart

- Select a data series in an existing chart that you want to appear as another chart type.
- In the Type group on the Chart Tools Design tab, click the Change Chart Type button, and then click the chart type you want.
- Click the OK button.

You'll display the S&P 500 values as a line chart so that it's easier to distinguish between the two data series.

To apply the line chart type to a data series:

1. Click any red column to select the entire S&P 500 data series.

2. In the Type group on the Chart Tools Design tab, click the **Change Chart Type** button. The Change Chart Type dialog box opens.

3. In the Line section, click **Line with Markers** (the fourth Line chart type).

4. Click the **OK** button. The S&P 500 values change to a line chart with markers. See Figure 4-38.

Combination chart   Figure 4-38

As noted earlier, line charts are best for categories that follow some sequential order, such as the performance history chart in which the categories represented dates. In this case, the sector categories do not have a sequential order and the lines between sectors have no meaning. You'll remove these lines from the chart to avoid confusing Ajita's clients. Also, you'll change the square markers to horizontal line markers at each data point.

To remove the lines and edit the markers in the line chart:

▶ **1.** Click the red line in the S&P 500 line chart to select it.

▶ **2.** Click the **Chart Tools Layout** tab on the Ribbon, and then, in the Current Selection group, click **Format Selection**. The Format Data Series dialog box opens.

▶ **3.** Click **Line Color** on the left side of the dialog box, and then click the **No line** option button to remove the line from the line chart.

▶ **4.** Click **Marker Options** on the left side of the dialog box, and then click the **Built-in** option button.

▶ **5.** Click the **Type** arrow and click the horizontal line marker (the seventh marker in the list), and then click the **Size** up arrow until **10** appears in the box. See Figure 4-39.

Figure 4-39 ▶ Marker Options in the Format Data Series dialog box

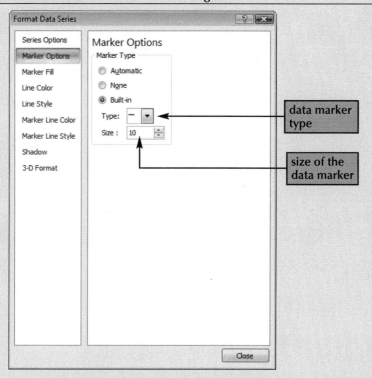

▶ **6.** Click the **Close** button. The S&P 500 values appear only as data markers.

Because the chart now has two data series, you'll add a legend to the top of the chart to identify them.

▶ **7.** In the Labels group, click the **Legend** button, and then click **Show Legend at Top**. The legend appears above the chart.

▶ **8.** Click the **legend** to select it, click the **Home** tab on the Ribbon, and then reduce the font size of the legend to **8** points.

▶ **9.** Click cell **A38** to deselect the chart. See Figure 4-40.

Completed combination chart ◁ Figure 4-40

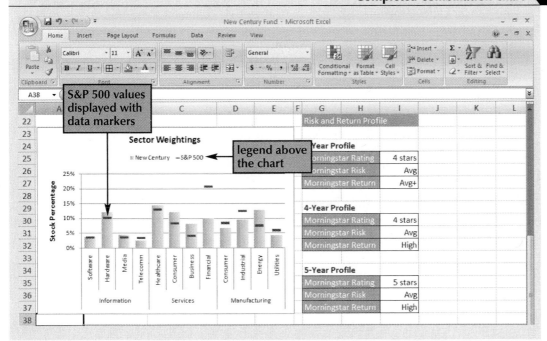

The combination chart effectively shows that the New Century Fund invests less than the S&P 500 in sectors from the financial service industry, and invests more in other sectors such as energy, consumer services, and hardware. This might account for the higher performance of the New Century Fund.

| **Choosing the Right Type of Chart** | InSight |

How do you know which type of chart to use with your data? In general, pie charts should be used only when the number of categories is small and the relative sizes of the different slices can be easily determined. If you have several categories, use a column or bar chart.

Line charts are best for categories that follow a sequential order. Be aware, however, that the time intervals must be a constant length if used in a line chart. Line charts will distort data that occurs in irregular time intervals, making it appear that the data values occurred at regular intervals when they did not.

Pie, column, bar, and line charts assume that numbers are plotted against categories. In science and engineering applications, you will often want to plot two numeric values against one another. For that data, use **XY scatter charts**, which show the patterns or relationship between two or more sets of values. XY scatter charts are also good for data recorded at irregular time intervals.

If you still can't find the right chart to meet your needs, you can create a custom chart based on the built-in chart types. Third-party vendors also sell software to allow Excel to create charts not built into the software.

Working with Shapes

Financial analysts give the New Century Fund a five-star rating based on its performance history. In cell C3, Ajita entered this rating as text. She wants you to replace the text with five stars.

Inserting a Shape

Tip

You can add text to a shape by selecting the shape, and then typing the text you want to insert.

Excel, like all Office programs, includes a gallery of 160 different shapes organized into eight categories. These shapes range from simple squares and circles to more complex objects such as flowchart symbols, block arrows, and banners. After you insert a shape into a chart or worksheet, you can resize and move it, set its fill color and border color, and apply 3D effects to make it stand out on the page.

You'll add the first star shape to the Summary Report worksheet.

To insert a star shape in cell C3:

1. Right-click cell **C3**, and then click **Clear Contents** on the shortcut menu. The text "5 Stars" is erased from the cell.

2. Click the **Insert** tab on the Ribbon.

3. In the Illustrations group, click the **Shapes** button to display the Shapes gallery, and then click **5-Point Star** (the fourth star) in the Stars and Banners section. The pointer changes to **+**.

4. Drag the pointer over cell C3 to create a star shape. The embedded star shape is selected and the Format tab appears on the Ribbon with a label identifying it as Drawing Tools. The Drawing Tools Format tab appears whenever you select a shape. See Figure 4-41.

Figure 4-41 | **Star shape embedded in cell C3**

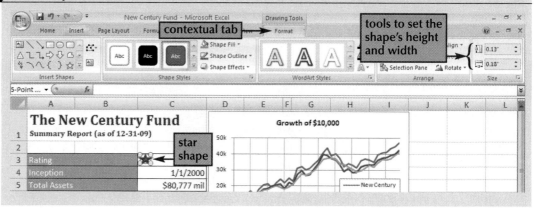

Resizing, Moving, and Copying a Shape

Shapes, like embedded charts, are objects you can move and resize. To set a shape's size more exactly, you enter the width and height you want in the Size group on the Drawing Tools Format tab. You'll match the star's height and width to the cell's height and width so it fills the cell.

Tip

You can move an embedded shape more precisely by selecting the shape, and then pressing the arrow keys on your keyboard in the direction you want the shape to move.

To resize the star shape:

1. In the Size group on the Drawing Tools Format tab, click the **Shape Height** down arrow to set the height to **0.1"**.

2. In the Size group, click the **Shape Width** down arrow to set the width to **0.1"**.

3. Drag the star to the left edge of cell C3 and center it within the height of the cell.

The first star is embedded and positioned in cell C3. Next, you'll copy the star shape and paste four copies into cell C3 so that the contains a total of five stars.

To copy and paste the star shape:

▶ **1.** With the star selected, click the **Home** tab on the Ribbon, and then, in the Clipboard group, click the **Copy** button 🖺.

▶ **2.** In the Clipboard group, click the **Paste** button to paste the star shape. The new star shape is pasted to the lower-right of the first star.

▶ **3.** Drag the star to the right of the star already in cell C3.

▶ **4.** Repeat Steps 2 and 3 until you have five stars next to each other in cell C3. The stars do not have to align exactly. You'll align them next.

Aligning and Grouping Shapes

Placing shapes by dragging is inexact and can be frustrating. Instead of dragging and dropping shapes, you can line them up neatly using the tools on the Drawing Tools Format tab. You can horizontally align selected shapes in several ways: by their tops, by their bottoms, or by their middles. If you're aligning the shapes vertically, you can align them along their left edges, their right edges, or their centers. In this case, you'll line up the stars by their middles, and then distribute them horizontally so that they are evenly spaced from each other.

To horizontally and vertically align the five star shapes:

▶ **1.** Click the first star in cell C3 to select it.

▶ **2.** Hold down the **Shift** key, click each of the four remaining stars, and then release the **Shift** key. Each star you click is added to the selected shapes.

▶ **3.** Click the **Drawing Tools Format** tab on the Ribbon.

▶ **4.** In the Arrange group, click the **Align** button, and then click **Align Middle**. The stars align along their middles. You also want the stars evenly spaced in the cell.

▶ **5.** In the Arrange group, click the **Align** button and then click **Distribute Horizontally**. The five stars are evenly spaced within the cell.

When you have several shapes that you want to treat as one unit, you can **group** them. You can move and resize grouped shapes as one, which makes it easier to develop interesting graphical shapes composed of several smaller parts. It also frees you from having to realign and redistribute the shapes if you move or copy them to a new location in the worksheet. You'll group the five stars in cell C3 so that they always remain together and aligned properly.

To group several shapes into a single unit:

▶ **1.** With all five stars selected, in the Arrange group on the Drawing Tools Format tab, click the **Group** button, and then click **Group**. A single selection box surrounds the five stars, indicating that they are grouped. The grouped stars can be moved together if needed without losing their relative alignment.

▶ **2.** Click cell **A2** to deselect the group of stars. See Figure 4-42.

Figure 4-42 **Grouped and aligned star shapes**

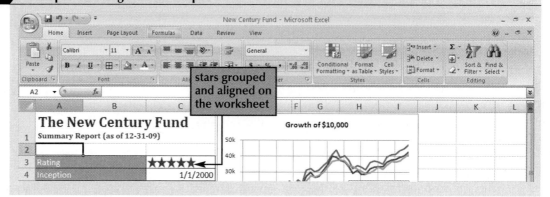

Creating a Chart Sheet

Tip

A chart sheet can contain embedded charts, enabling you to display several charts at once within a single sheet.

Ajita asks you to create a cover sheet for the workbook that shows a 3D image of the performance of the New Century Fund over the past 10 years. Because this chart is purely decorative, you can make a visually interesting chart without concern about easily reading its data. The cover sheet will contain only the chart and no other data or text, so you'll create a chart sheet. Recall that chart sheets show only charts and no worksheet data.

To create a chart sheet:

▶ 1. Click the **Performance History** sheet tab, and then select the range **A4:B44**, if necessary. This range contains the data you want to use in the chart.

▶ 2. Click the **Insert** tab on the Ribbon.

▶ 3. In the Charts group, click the **Line** button, and then click the **3-D Line** chart type. The 3D line chart is embedded in the Performance History worksheet. You'll move this chart to its own chart sheet.

▶ 4. In the Location group on the Chart Tools Design tab, click the **Move Chart** button. The Move Chart dialog box opens.

▶ 5. Click the **New sheet** option button, type **Cover Sheet** in the box, and then click the **OK** button. A chart sheet named "Cover Sheet" that contains the 3D line chart is inserted in the workbook.

▶ 6. Drag the **Cover Sheet** sheet tab to the right of the Documentation sheet tab. See Figure 4-43.

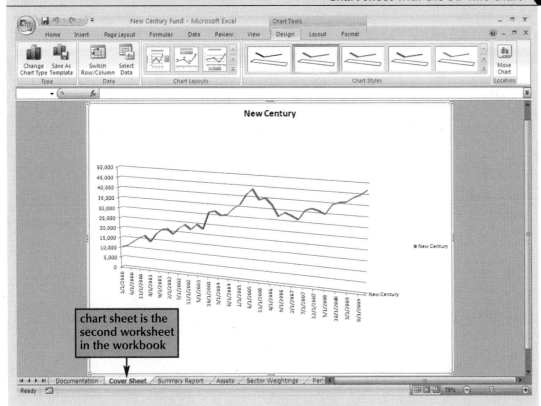

The Cover Sheet appears before Summary Report worksheet and the worksheets that contain the detailed data used to create the summary report. Next, you'll remove the axes labels and legend from the chart and rotate the chart in three dimensions. To increase the 3D effect, you'll widen the chart's base from 100 to 1000 points.

To format the chart sheet:

▶ **1.** If necessary, click the chart area to select it.

▶ **2.** In the Chart Styles group on the Chart Tools Design tab, click the **More** button, and then click **Style 40** (the fifth row, last column) of the Chart Styles gallery.

▶ **3.** Click the **Chart Tools Layout** tab on the Ribbon.

▶ **4.** In the Labels group, click the **Legend** button, and then click **None** to turn off the legend.

▶ **5.** In the Axes group, click the **Axes** button, point to **Primary Horizontal Axis**, and then click **None** to remove the horizontal axis.

▶ **6.** In the Axes group, click the **Axes** button, point to **Primary Vertical Axis**, and then click **None** to remove the vertical axis from the chart.

▶ **7.** In the Axes group, click the **Axes** button, point to **Depth Axis**, and then click **None** to remove the depth axis.

▶ **8.** In the Background section, click the **3-D Rotation** button. The Format Chart Area dialog box opens, displaying the 3-D Rotation options.

▶ **9.** In the Rotation section, set X to **60°**, Y to **20°**, and Perspective to **80°**, and then, in the Chart Scale section, set the Depth (% of base) to **1000**.

These settings rotate the chart, exaggerate the 3D effect, and make the chart appear thicker. Next, you'll change the background color of the chart area to a gradient fill.

▶ **10.** Click **Fill** on the left side of the dialog box, and then click the **Gradient fill** option button.

▶ **11.** Click the **Preset colors** button, and then click **Daybreak**, the fourth color in the first row.

▶ **12.** Click the **Direction** button, and then click **Linear Down**, the second direction in the first row.

▶ **13.** Click the **Close** button. See Figure 4-44.

Figure 4-44 ▶ **Formatted chart sheet**

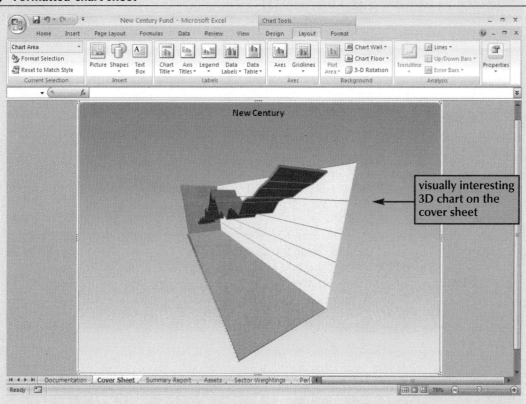

To complete the chart sheet, you'll overlay the chart title "The New Century Fund," and format it in a 48-point white font.

To overlay and format the chart title:

▶ **1.** In the Labels group on the Chart Tools Layout tab, click the **Chart Title** button, and then click **Centered Overlay Title**. The chart title is overlaid above the chart.

▶ **2.** Type **The New Century Fund**, and then press the **Enter** key. The new title is entered.

▶ **3.** Click the **Home** tab on the Ribbon, and then set the font size to **48** points and the font color to **white**.

▶ **4.** Click outside of the chart to deselect it. The cover sheet is final. See Figure 4-45.

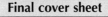

Final cover sheet | **Figure 4-45**

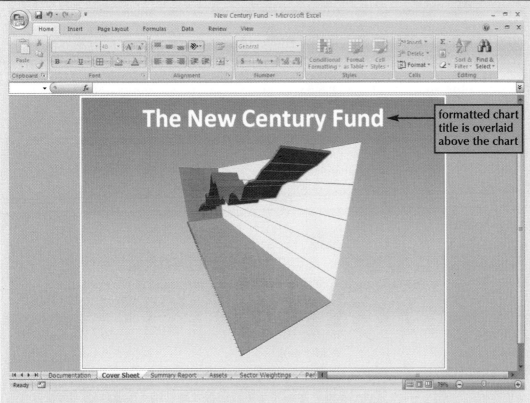

formatted chart title is overlaid above the chart

5. Save your changes to the workbook, and then close it.

You show the final version of the cover sheet and the workbook to Ajita. She is pleased with the work you've done adding charts and graphics to the workbook. Ajita will present the Summary Report worksheet, with the embedded charts, to her clients to provide them a concise report on the performance of the New Century Fund. The cover sheet you've created adds visual interest to the report.

Session 4.2 Quick Check | Review

1. When should you use a line chart in place of a column chart?
2. How do you overlay a chart legend?
3. How do you add a data series to an already existing chart?
4. What is a combination chart? Describe how you create a combination chart.
5. How do you insert a shape into a worksheet?
6. Describe how to set the exact height and width of a shape.
7. Describe how to horizontally align the tops of three shapes in Excel.
8. How do you create a chart sheet?

In this tutorial, you learned how to work with charts and graphics. You reviewed the different parts of a chart and the relationship between charts and data sources. Then, you inserted an embedded chart and reviewed the different types of chart, chart layouts, and chart styles supported by Excel. The first chart you created was a pie chart. You worked with the pie chart legend and formatted individual slices. Next, you made the pie chart a 3D chart and learned about some limitations of 3D charts. The second chart you created and formatted was a column chart. The third chart you created and formatted was a line chart. You also learned when line charts are preferable to column charts. The fourth chart you created was a combination chart that combined the column and line charts. You then inserted shapes into a worksheet, and aligned and grouped them. Finally, you created a chart sheet as a cover sheet for the entire workbook.

Key Terms

bar chart

category values

chart

chart area

chart sheet

chart title

column chart

combination chart

data label

data marker

data series

data source

embedded chart

exploded pie chart

graph

gridlines

group

horizontal (category) axis

leader line

legend

line chart

major tick mark

minor tick mark

perspective

pie chart

plot area

primary value axis

resizing handle

scale

secondary value axis

selection box

series name

series values

vertical (value) axis

XY scatter chart

| Practice | **Review Assignments** |

Practice the skills you learned in the tutorial using the same case scenario.

Data File needed for the Review Assignments: Crockett.xlsx

Ajita asks you to help on a new project. She has to create a report on the investment portfolio for Brian and Tammy Crockett. She wants to add charts that display where the couple's money is currently being invested and how their portfolio has performed in recent years. She's already entered the data. She needs you to complete the report by adding the charts and a decorative cover sheet.

Complete the following:

1. Open the **Crockett** workbook located in the Tutorial.04\Review folder included with your Data Files, and then save the workbook as **Crockett Portfolio** in the same folder. In the Documentation sheet, enter your name in cell B3 and the date in cell B4.

2. In the Composition worksheet, select the range A3:B8, and then insert a 2D pie chart. Move and resize the embedded pie chart to cover the range D1:G9 in the Portfolio Report worksheet.

3. Move the legend to the left side of the chart area. Change the chart title to **Composition** and set its font size to 12 points. Change the fill color of the Cash slice to yellow. Add data labels that show the percentage of each pie slice to two decimal places outside of the pie chart, and then set the font size of the labels to 8 points.

4. Change the pie chart to a 3D pie chart and set the 3D rotation of the x-axis to 230° and the y-axis to 40°.

5. In the Sector Weightings worksheet, select the range A3:D15, and then insert a 2D clustered column chart. Move and resize the embedded chart to cover the range A12:D25 in the Portfolio Report worksheet.

6. Change the font size of the axis labels and legend to 8 points. Insert the chart title **Sector Weightings** over the plot and set its font size to 12 points. Change the format of the percentages in the vertical axis to display no decimal places. Overlay the legend at the top of the chart, and then change its fill color to white and insert a solid border around the legend.

7. Change the chart type of the S&P 500 series to a line chart, remove the line connecting the markers in the chart, and then change the marker type to a solid horizontal line of size 10.

8. Change the fill color of the columns for the Portfolio data series to the theme color Purple, Accent 4, Lighter 60%. Set the gap width of the columns in the Portfolio data series to 30%.

9. In the Portfolio Value worksheet, select the range A3:B127, and then insert a 2D area chart. Move and resize the chart to cover the range D28:G42 in the Portfolio Report worksheet. (*Hint:* You will need to scroll down the Portfolio Report worksheet to locate the chart when you move it from the Portfolio Value worksheet.)

10. Remove the chart legend. Set the font size of the chart title to 11 points, and then set the font size of the axis labels to 8 points. Change the fill color of the data series to the theme color Purple, Accent 4, Lighter 60%.

11. Modify the category axis so that the vertical axis crosses the maximum date. (*Hint:* Use the Axis Options in the Format Axis dialog box.)

12. Set the major tick mark interval at two years and the minor tick mark interval at one year. Use a custom format that displays the category axis date values as four-digit year values. Insert vertical gridlines for the minor tick marks.

13. In the Portfolio Value worksheet, select the range A3:B127, and insert a 3D area chart. Move the embedded chart into a new chart sheet named **Cover Sheet**. Move the Cover Sheet worksheet directly after the Documentation sheet.

14. Change the chart style to Style 34, located in the fifth row and second column of the Chart Styles gallery. Remove the display of the horizontal, vertical, and depth axes. Remove the chart legend.

15. For the 3D rotation, set the x-axis to 60°, the y-axis to 10°, the perspective to 40°, and the depth of the base to 2000.

16. Change the chart title to **Crockett Family Portfolio**. Set the font size of the chart title to 40 points.

17. Insert two 5-pointed stars, one directly to the left and the other directly to the right of the chart title. Set the height and width of each star to 0.3". Align the middle of the two stars and then group them into a single object.

18. Save and close your workbook, and then submit the finished workbook to your instructor, either in printed or electronic form, as requested.

| Apply | Case Problem 1 |

Use the skills you learned to create 3D charts of usage data for a national park.

Data File needed for this Case Problem: Kenai.xlsx

Kenai Fjords National Park Maria Sanford is the chief of interpretation at Kenai Fjords National Park. Part of her job is to report on park usage at each visitor center and all visitor centers. She has recorded last year's usage data in an Excel workbook. She asks you to present this data in a 3D column chart for an upcoming meeting with her supervisor. She wants the chart to show the monthly usage totals organized by visitor center. Figure 4-46 shows a preview of the 3D column chart you'll create for Maria.

Figure 4-46

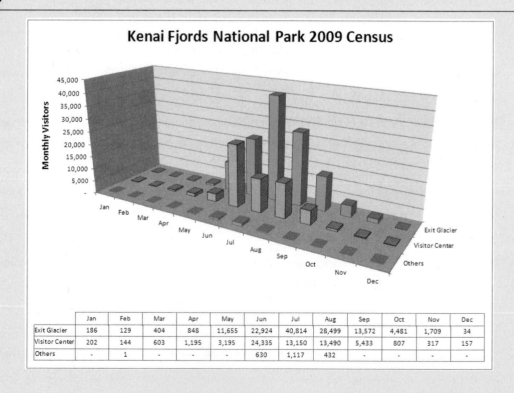

	Jan	Feb	Mar	Apr	May	Jun	Jul	Aug	Sep	Oct	Nov	Dec
Exit Glacier	186	129	404	848	11,655	22,924	40,814	28,499	13,572	4,481	1,709	34
Visitor Center	202	144	603	1,195	3,195	24,335	13,150	13,490	5,433	807	317	157
Others	-	1	-	-	-	630	1,117	432	-	-	-	-

Complete the following:

1. Open the **Kenai** workbook located in the Tutorial.04\Case1 folder included with your Data Files, and then save the workbook as **Kenai Fjords Park** in the folder. In the Documentation sheet, enter your name in cell B3 and the date in cell B4.

2. In the Park Usage Data worksheet, select the range A4:D16, and then insert the 3-D Column chart (the last chart in the 3-D Column section in the Charts gallery).

3. Move the chart to a chart sheet named **Monthly Visits**. Place the Monthly Visits chart sheet directly after the Documentation sheet.

4. Change the style of the chart to Style 34 (the fifth style in the second column in the Chart Styles gallery).

5. Insert the chart title **Kenai Fjords National Park 2009 Census** at the top of the chart area, and then set its font size to 24 points. Remove the legend from the chart.

6. Add the title **Monthly Visitors** to the vertical axis. Rotate the title 90° and set the font size to 14 points.

7. Rotate the 3D chart using the following parameters: x-axis rotation 30°, y-axis rotation 20°, perspective 25°, and base width 130. Modify the depth axis so that the values are displayed in reverse order.

⊕ **EXPLORE**

8. Insert a data table without legend keys below the 3-D chart to provide data values so that the reader is not confused about the relative sizes of the different columns. (*Hint:* Use the Data Table button in the Labels group on the Chart Tools Layout tab.)

9. Change the fill color of the Exit Glacier series to light blue. Change the fill color of the Visitor Center series to orange.

10. In the Park Usage Data worksheet, select the range B4:D4;B17:D17, and then insert a 3D pie chart. Move the embedded chart to a chart sheet named **Center Visits**. Place the Center Visits sheet directly after the Monthly Visits chart sheet.

11. Insert the chart title **Kenai Fjords National Park: Visits by Center** above the pie chart, and set its font size to 24 points.

12. Move the chart legend below the pie chart, and change its font size to 18 points.

13. Change the fill color of the Exit Glacier slice to light blue. Change the fill color of the Visitor Center slice to orange.

14. Add data labels to the outside end of the pie chart showing the values (not percentages) of each slice. Set the font size of the labels to 18 points.

15. Save and close your workbook, and then submit the finished workbook to your instructor, either in printed or electronic form, as requested.

| Apply | **Case Problem 2** |

Use the skills you learned to create a combination chart describing the occurrence of tornados in the twentieth century.

Data Files needed for this Case Problem: Cloud.jpg, Tornado.xlsx

Midwest Tornado Institute Joyce Bishop is a meteorologist at the Midwest Tornado Institute located in Decatur, Illinois. Joyce is preparing for a talk she is giving to a local civic group on the possible effects of global warming on tornados. She's collected data on minor, moderate, and major tornado sightings in five-year periods during the second half of the twentieth century and wants to create a graph for her talk showing her data. She's already entered her data into an Excel workbook; she needs your help in creating the chart. Figure 4-47 shows a preview of the chart you'll create for Joyce.

Figure 4-47

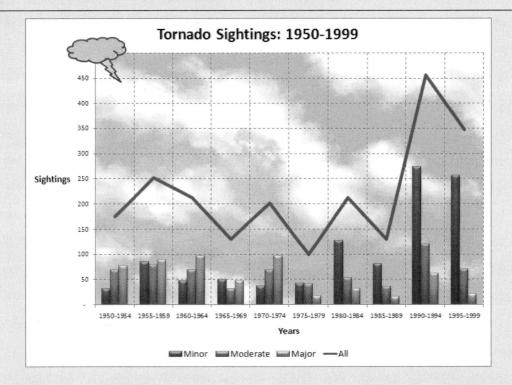

Complete the following:

1. Open the **Tornado** workbook located in the Tutorial.04\Case2 folder included with your Data Files, and then save the workbook as **Tornado Sightings** in the same folder. In the Documentation sheet, enter your name in cell B3 and the date in cell B4.

2. In the Sightings History worksheet, select the range A3:E13, and then insert a 2D clustered column chart. Move the embedded chart to a chart sheet named **Sightings Chart**.

3. Change the chart style to Style 32 (the last chart style in the fourth row of the Chart Styles gallery).

4. Insert the chart title **Tornado Sightings: 1950 – 1999** at the top of the chart in a 24-point font.

5. Add the vertical axis title **Sightings** in a 14-point font with horizontal orientation. Add the horizontal axis title **Years** in a 14-point font.

6. Move the legend to the bottom of the chart, and then set its font size to 14 points.

 EXPLORE

7. Change the line style of the horizontal gridline from a solid line to a dashed line. (*Hint:* Use the Dash type list in the Line Style group in the Format Major Gridlines dialog box.)

8. Add vertical gridlines to the major tick marks in the chart. Display the gridlines as dashed lines.

9. Change the chart type of the All data series from a column chart to a 2D line chart. Change the color of the line to a standard blue.

10. In the upper-left corner of the chart, insert a cloud shape. Set the width of the cloud to 1.2". Set the height to 0.5". Set the fill color of the cloud shape to a light gray.

11. Adjacent to the cloud shape, insert a lightning bolt shape with a height of 0.48" and a width of 0.42". Set the fill color of the shape to yellow.

12. Group the cloud and lightning bolt shapes.

⊕ **EXPLORE**   13. Select the plot area and change the fill to a picture fill, using the **Cloud.jpg** file located in the Tutorial.04\Case2 folder included with your Data Files. (*Hint:* Click the Shape Fill button in the Shape Styles group on the Drawing Tools Format tab, click Picture, and then locate and select the picture file.)

14. Save and close your workbook, and then submit the finished workbook to your instructor, either in printed or electronic form, as requested.

Challenge | Case Problem 3

Explore how to use Excel to chart stock market data.

Data File needed for this Case Problem: Mitchell.xlsx

Hardin Financial   Kurt Lee is a financial analyst for Hardin Financial, a consulting firm in Owatonna, Minnesota. As part of his job, he records stock market activity in Excel workbooks. One of his workbooks contains the recent stock market activity of Mitchell Oil. He wants your help in creating a chart displaying the stock values. The chart should display the stock's opening, high, low, and closing values and number of shares traded for each day of the past few weeks. The volume of shares traded should be expressed in terms of millions of shares.

Excel includes several chart types specially designed for displaying stock market activity. A preview of the chart you'll create for Kurt is shown in Figure 4-48.

Figure 4-48

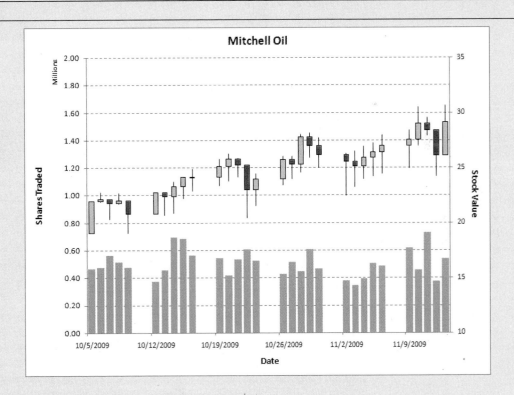

Complete the following:

1. Open the **Mitchell** workbook located in the Tutorial.04\Case3 folder included with your Data Files, and then save the workbook as **Mitchell Oil** in the same folder. In the Documentation sheet, enter your name and the date.

⊕ **EXPLORE** 2. In the Stock Values worksheet, select the range A3:F33, and then insert a Volume-Open-High-Low-Close stock chart. Move the embedded chart to the chart sheet named **Stock History**.

3. Insert the chart title **Mitchell Oil** above the plot area. Remove the chart legend.

4. Add the title **Date** to the primary horizontal axis, and then set its font size to 14 points. Add the title **Shares Traded** to the primary vertical axis, set its font size to 14 points, and then rotate the title 270°, as shown in Figure 4-48.

⊕ **EXPLORE** 5. Add the title **Stock Value** to the secondary vertical axis, set its font size to 14 points, and rotate the title 90°, as shown in Figure 4-48. (*Hint:* Open the Format Axis Title dialog box for the secondary vertical axis and use the Text Direction button found in the Alignment category.)

6. Set the font size of all of the axes values to 12 points.

7. Display the horizontal gridlines using a dashed line style. Set the interval between major tick marks on the primary horizontal axis to 7 days.

8. For the primary vertical axis, display the values in units of one million, change the number format to two decimal place accuracy, and then set the maximum value of the axis scale to 2,000,000.

9. For the secondary vertical axis, set the minimum value of the scale to 10.

10. Decrease the gap width between the columns in the plot to 30% and change the fill color to light blue.

⊕ **EXPLORE** 11. In a stock market chart, the daily chart values will either show an increase or a decrease from the previous day. Increases are shown with an up bar displayed in white and decreases are shown in a down bar displayed in black. Select the data series for the up bars and change their fill colors to light green. Select the data series for the down bars and change their fill colors to red.

12. Save and close your workbook, and then submit the finished workbook to your instructor, either in printed or electronic form, as requested.

Create | **Case Problem 4**

Create an Excel workbook to provide a graphical report on a sporting event.

Data File needed for this Case Problem: Basketball.xlsx

Blowout Sports Steve Eagan is the owner and operator of Blowout Sports, a sports information and scouting company located in Lexington, Kentucky. One of Steve's jobs is to provide detailed graphical reports and analysis of college basketball games for the media, coaches, and interested fans. Steve has been placing box score data and game logs into an Excel workbook. He wants to summarize this data in one worksheet using charts and graphs. He's asked you to help develop the workbook. Steve has a sample workbook containing the results of a recent basketball game for you to work on.

Complete the following:

1. Open the **Basketball** workbook located in the Tutorial.04\Case4 folder included with your Data Files, and then save the workbook as **Basketball Report** in the same folder. In the Documentation sheet, enter your name and the date.

2. The Game Report worksheet contains some basic information about a recent basketball game. Supplement this information with charts and graphs. The final format of the sheet is up to you and you may insert additional information if you desire.

3. The Game Log worksheet contains the minute-by-minute score of the game. Use the data in this worksheet to create a line chart describing the ebb and flow of the game that is embedded in the Game Report worksheet. The format of the chart is up to you, but should include titles for the chart and the axes, a chart legend overlay, vertical gridlines spaced at 4-minute intervals, and horizontal gridlines at 5-point intervals. (*Hint:* To display vertical gridlines at 4-minute intervals, you must turn off the multi-level category labels.)

4. The Box Score worksheet contains statistical summaries of the game. Use the data in this worksheet to create two column charts describing the points scored by each player on the two teams. Embed the charts in the Game Report worksheet. The format of the charts is up to you, but should include titles for the chart and axes and fill colors for the columns that employ a fill gradient.

5. The Box Score worksheet also contains team statistics. Use this data to create several pie charts that compare the two teams. Embed the pie charts in the Game Report worksheet. The final pie charts should include data labels for the pie slices and slice colors that match the team's colors (red for Wisconsin, gold for Iowa).

6. Create a chart sheet for the report that will be a cover sheet. The cover sheet should include a 3D chart from some of the data in the workbook. The format of the chart and chart sheet is up to you.

7. Save and close your workbook, and then submit the finished workbook to your instructor, either in printed or electronic form, as requested.

Research | Internet Assignments

Use the Internet to find and work with data related to the topics presented in this tutorial.

The purpose of the Internet Assignments is to challenge you to find information on the Internet that you can use to work effectively with this software. The actual assignments are updated and maintained on the Course Technology Web site. Log on to the Internet and use your Web browser to go to the Student Online Companion for New Perspectives Office 2007 at **www.course.com/np/office2007**. Then navigate to the Internet Assignments for this tutorial.

Assess | SAM Assessment and Training

If you have a SAM user profile, you may have access to hands-on instruction, practice, and assessment of the skills covered in this tutorial. Log in to your SAM account (**http://sam2007.course.com**) to launch any assigned training activities or exams that relate to the skills covered in this tutorial.

Review | Quick Check Answers

Session 4.1

1. the series name, series values, and category values
2. in a chart sheet or embedded in a worksheet
3. The chart area contains the entire chart, including the plot area. The plot area contains the region of the chart in which the data values are plotted.
4. A column chart is more appropriate because there are so many categories; pie charts make it difficult to compare one category to another.

5. Objects that are rendered as more distant from the eye will appear smaller, reducing their significance in the chart. To avoid confusion, 3D charts should include data labels explicitly identifying the values associated with different data markers.

6. A major tick mark matches each entry on the chart axis. Minor tick marks further divide the space between the major tick marks. Gridlines extend the tick marks into the plot area.

7. A bar chart is similar to a column chart except that the length of the bars, rather than the height of the columns, is used to indicate the data value.

8. Click the Axes button in the Axes group on the Chart Tools Layout tab, select the axis you want to rescale, and then click the More Options button. Enter the new axis scale in the Axis Options of the Format Axis dialog box, specifying the minimum and maximum value of the new scale and the space between the minor and major tick marks.

Session 4.2

1. Use line charts in place of column charts when the number of categories is so large that the columns will be forced to be too small to read, and the categories have a natural, sequential order (such as time and dates) that you want to show in the chart.

2. Click the Legend button in the Labels group on the Chart Tools Layout tab and select one of the overlay options, or open the Format Legend dialog box and deselect the check box to show the legend without overlaying the chart.

3. Click the Select Date button in the Date group on the Data tab. Click the Add button in the Select Data Source dialog box and select the range with the new data series.

4. A combination chart combines two or more of the Excel chart types. To create a combination chart, select a data series from the chart and apply a chart type to that series.

5. Click the Shapes button in the Illustrations group on the Insert tab, and then select a shape from the gallery.

6. Select the shape, and then enter the exact height and width in the Shape Height and Shape Width boxes in the Size group on the Drawing Tools Format tab.

7. Select all of the shapes by holding down the Shift key and clicking each of the shapes. Click the Align button in the Arrange group on the Drawing Tools Format tab, and then click Align Top.

8. Select a chart, and then click the Move Chart button in the Location group on the Chart Tools Design tab. Specify the name of the chart sheet in the Move Chart dialog box.

Ending Data Files

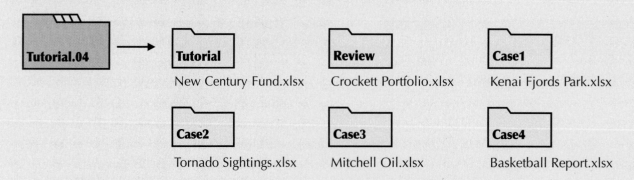

Tutorial.04 → Tutorial
New Century Fund.xlsx

Review
Crockett Portfolio.xlsx

Case1
Kenai Fjords Park.xlsx

Case2
Tornado Sightings.xlsx

Case3
Mitchell Oil.xlsx

Case4
Basketball Report.xlsx

Reality Check

Excel is valuable to a wide audience of users: from accountants of *Fortune 500* companies to homeowners managing their budgets. An Excel workbook can be complex, recording data from thousands of financial transactions, or it can simply track a few monthly expenses. Everyone who has to balance a budget, track expenses, or project future income can make use of the financial tools in Excel. In this exercise, you'll use Excel to create a sample budget workbook that will contain information of your choice, using Excel skills and features presented in Tutorials 1 through 4. Use the following steps as a guide to completing your workbook.

Note: Please be sure *not* to include any personal information of a sensitive nature in any workbooks you create to be submitted to your instructor for this exercise. Later, you can update the workbooks with such information for your personal use.

1. Create a new workbook for the sample financial data. Use the first worksheet as a documentation sheet that includes your name, the date on which you start creating the workbook, and a brief description of the workbook's purpose.
2. In a second worksheet, enter realistic monthly earnings for each month of the year. Use formulas to calculate the total earnings each month, the average monthly earnings, and the total earnings for the entire year.
3. On the same worksheet, enter realistic personal expenses for each month. Divide the expenses into at least three categories, providing subtotals for each category and a grand total of all the monthly expenses. Calculate the average monthly expenses and total expenses for the year.
4. Calculate the monthly net cash flow (the value of total income minus total expenses).
5. Use the cash flow values to track the savings throughout the year. Use a realistic amount for savings at the beginning of the year. Use the monthly net cash flow values to add or subtract from this value. Project the end-of-year balance in the savings account under your proposed budget.
6. Format the worksheet's contents using appropriate text and number formats. Add colors and line borders to make the content easier to read and interpret. Use cell styles and themes to provide your worksheet with a uniform appearance.
7. Use conditional formatting to automatically highlight negative net cash flow calculated in Step 4.
8. Insert a pie chart that compares the monthly expenses for the categories.
9. Insert a column chart that charts all of the monthly expenses regardless of the category.
10. Insert a line chart that shows the change in the savings balance throughout the 12 months of the year.
11. Insert new rows at the top of the worksheet and enter titles that describe the worksheet's contents.

12. Think of a major purchase you might want to make—for example, a car. Determine the amount of the purchase and the current annual interest rate charged by your local bank. Provide a reasonable length of time to repay the loan, such as five years for a car loan or 20 to 30 years for a home loan. Use the PMT function to determine how much you would have to spend each month on the payments for your purchase. Add this information to your monthly budget. If the payment exceeds your budget, reduce the estimated price of the item you're thinking of purchasing until you determine the monthly payment you can afford under the conditions of the loan.

13. Format the worksheets for your printer. Include headers and footers that display the filename of your workbook, the workbook's author, and the date on which the report is printed. If the report extends across several pages, repeat appropriate print titles on all of the pages and include page numbers and the total number of pages on every printed page.

14. Save and close your workbook, and then submit the completed workbook to your instructor, in printed or electronic form, as requested.

Objectives

Session 5.1
- Explore a structured range of data
- Freeze rows and columns
- Plan and create an Excel table
- Rename and format an Excel table
- Add, edit, and delete records in an Excel table
- Sort data

Session 5.2
- Filter data
- Insert a Total row to summarize an Excel table
- Insert subtotals into a range of data
- Use the Outline buttons to show or hide details

Session 5.3
- Create and modify a PivotTable
- Apply PivotTable styles and formatting
- Filter and sort a PivotTable
- Group PivotTable items
- Create a PivotChart

Working with Excel Tables, PivotTables, and PivotCharts

Tracking Museum Art Objects

Case | LaFouch Museum

Henry LaFouch, a rancher in Missoula, Montana, amassed a huge collection of North American art, particularly art of the West. Henry was a well-respected, active member of the community, and he often donated art to the town. Similarly, he loaned the town artwork to place in public locations and community centers. Upon his death, Henry donated his art collection to the town of Missoula and its people. They established an art museum in his name.

Mary Littlefield was recently hired as the curator and director of the LaFouch Museum. She is responsible for assessing the current holdings and using the endowment set aside by Henry to purchase additional art in keeping with his vision for the collection. One of Mary's first tasks was to establish an accurate inventory of the museum's holdings. For each piece of artwork, she identified the title, the artist, the date acquired, the type of art, and other pertinent facts such as its location in the museum, its condition, and its appraised value. Then, she entered all this data in an Excel worksheet.

Mary asks you to help her maintain this data so she can provide current and accurate information to the administration and board of directors about the art objects. You'll work with the data using Excel table features. You will sort the data and add, modify, and delete the data to ensure it is current. You'll also filter the information to display only data that meets certain criteria. Finally, you'll summarize the data using a PivotTable and a PivotChart.

Starting Data Files

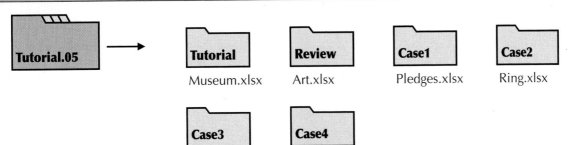

Tutorial.05 →

Tutorial
Museum.xlsx

Review
Art.xlsx

Case1
Pledges.xlsx

Case2
Ring.xlsx

Case3
CustLoans.xlsx

Case4
Bowls.xlsx

Session 5.1

Planning a Structured Range of Data

One of the more common uses of a worksheet is to manage data, such as lists of clients, products, and transactions. Using Excel, you can store and update data, sort data, search for and retrieve subsets of data, summarize data, and create reports. In Excel, a collection of similar data can be structured in a range of rows and columns. Each column in the range represents a **field** that describes some attribute or characteristic of a person, place, or thing, such as a last name, address, city, or state. Each row in the range represents a **record**, or a collection of related fields that are grouped together. The first row of the range contains column headers that describe the data fields in each column. Figure 5-1 shows a portion of the data Mary compiled for the LaFouch Museum's art objects. In this data, the ArtID, Artist, and Title columns are the first three fields. Each row is a record that stores the data for each art object—art ID, artist name, title, date acquired, category, condition, location, and appraised value. All the art object records make up the structured range of data. A structured range of data is commonly referred to as a list or table.

Figure 5-1   LaFouch Museum art objects data

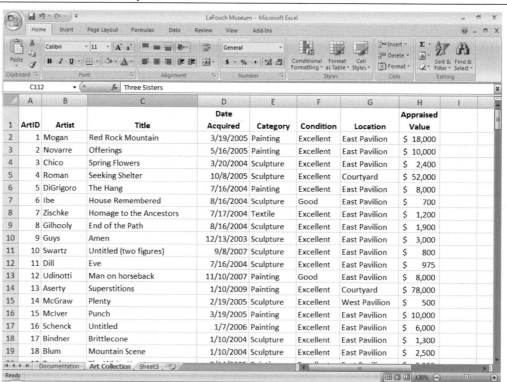

The Importance of Planning | InSight

Before you create a structured range of data, you should do some planning. Spend time thinking about how you will use the data. Consider what reports you want to create for different audiences (supervisors, customers, directors, and so forth) and the fields needed to produce those reports. Also consider the various questions, or queries, you want answered and the fields needed to create these results. The end results you want to achieve will help you determine the kind of data to include in each record and how to divide that data into fields. Careful and thorough planning will help to prevent having to redesign a structured range of data later on.

Before creating the list of art objects, Mary carefully planned what information she needs and how she wants to use it. Mary plans to use the data to track where each art object is located in the museum, its condition, the date it was acquired, its art category, and its appraised value. She wants to be able to create reports that show specific lists of art objects, such as all the objects by a specific artist or all the objects that are paintings. Based on her needs, Mary developed a **data definition table**, which is documentation that lists the fields to be maintained for each record (in this case, each art object) and a description of the information each field will include. Figure 5-2 shows Mary's completed data definition table.

Data definition table for the art objects ◀ Figure 5-2

Field	Description
ArtID	Unique number
Artist	Name of artist
Title	Title of art object
Date Acquired	Date of purchase or donation of art object
Category	Painting, Sculpture, Installation, Textile
Condition	Excellent, Good, Fair, Poor
Location	Location of art object
Appraised Value	Appraised value of art object

After you determine the fields and records you need, you can enter the data in a blank worksheet or use a range of data that is already entered in a worksheet. You can then work with the data in many ways. The following is a list of common operations you can perform on a structured range of data:

- Add, edit, and delete data in the range
- Sort the data range
- Filter to display only rows that meet specified criteria
- Insert formulas to calculate subtotals
- Create summary tables based on the data in the range (usually with PivotTables)
- Add data validation to ensure the integrity of the data
- Apply conditional formatting

You'll perform many of these operations on the art objects data.

InSight	**Creating an Effective Structured Range of Data**

For a range of data to be used effectively, it must have the same structure throughout. Keep in mind the following guidelines:

- Enter field names in the top row of the range. A **field name** (also called a **column header**) is a unique label that describes the contents of the data in that column. The row of field names is called the **header row**. Although the header row often is row 1, it can be any row.
- Use short, descriptive field names. Shorter field names are easier to remember and enable more fields to appear in the workbook window at once.
- Format field names to distinguish the header row from the data. For example, apply bold, color, and a different font size.
- Enter the same kind of data for a field in each record.
- Separate the data from other information in the worksheet by at *least* one blank row and one blank column. The blank row and column enable Excel to accurately determine the range of the data.

You'll open the workbook in which Mary entered the art objects data according to the data definition table.

To open and review the Museum workbook:

1. Open the **Museum** workbook located in the **Tutorial.05\Tutorial** folder included with your Data Files, and then save the workbook as **LaFouch Museum** in the same folder.

2. In the Documentation worksheet, enter your name in cell B3 and the current date in cell B4.

3. Switch to the **Art Collection** worksheet. This worksheet (which is shown in Figure 5-1) contains data about the museum's art objects. Currently, the worksheet lists 115 art objects. Each art object record is a separate row (rows 2 through 116) and contains eight fields (columns A through H). The top row, the header row, contains labels that describe the data in each column. The field names are boldface to make it easier to distinguish them from the data.

4. Scroll the worksheet to row 116, the last record. The column headers, in the top row, are no longer visible.

5. Press the **Ctrl+Home** keys to return to cell A1.

Freezing Rows and Columns

You want to see the column headers as you scroll the art objects data. Without the column headers visible, it is difficult to know what the data entered in each column represents. You can select rows and columns to remain visible in the workbook window as you scroll around the worksheet. **Freezing** a row or column lets you keep headings visible as you work with the data in a large worksheet. To freeze a row or column, you select the cell immediately below the row(s) and to the right of the column(s) you want to freeze. For example, if you want to keep only the column headers in the top row displayed on the screen, you click cell A2 (first column, second row), and then freeze the panes. As you scroll the data, the first row remains on the screen so the column headers are visible, making it easier to identify the data in each record.

You'll freeze the first row, which contains the column headers, so that they remain on the screen as you scroll the data.

To freeze the top row in the worksheet:

▶ **1.** Click the **View** tab on the Ribbon. The Ribbon changes to display the View options.

▶ **2.** In the Window group, click the **Freeze Panes** button, and then click **Freeze Top Row**. A dark, horizontal line appears below the column headers to indicate which row is frozen.

▶ **3.** Scroll the worksheet to row 116. This time, the column headers remain visible as you scroll. See Figure 5-3.

Freezing the top row of the worksheet | **Figure 5-3**

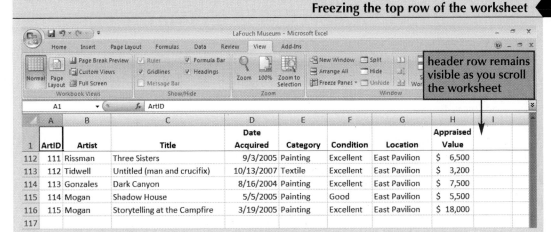

▶ **4.** Press the **Ctrl+Home** keys to return to cell A2, the cell directly below the frozen row.

After you freeze panes, the first option on the Freeze Panes menu changes to Unfreeze Panes. This option unlocks all the rows and columns so you can scroll the entire worksheet. You will use a different method to keep the column headers visible, so you will unfreeze the top row of the worksheet.

To unfreeze the top row of the worksheet:

▶ **1.** In the Window group on the View tab, click the **Freeze Panes** button. The first Freeze Panes option is now Unfreeze Panes.

▶ **2.** Click **Unfreeze Panes**. The dark, horizontal line below the column headers is removed, and you can scroll all the rows and columns in the worksheet.

Creating an Excel Table

You can convert a structured range of data, such as the art objects data in the range A1:H116, to an Excel table. Recall that an Excel table is a range of related data that is managed independently from the data in other rows and columns in the worksheet. An Excel table uses features designed to make it easier to identify, manage, and analyze the groups of related data. You can create more than one Excel table in a worksheet.

InSight	**Saving Time with Excel Table Features**

Excel tables provide many advantages to structured ranges of data. When you create an Excel table, you can perform the same operations as you can for a structured range of data. In addition, you can do the following:

- Format the Excel table quickly using a table style.
- Add new rows and columns to the Excel table that automatically expand the range.
- Add a Total row to calculate the summary function you select, such as SUM, AVERAGE, COUNT, MIN, and MAX.
- Enter a formula in one table cell that is automatically copied to all other cells in that table column.
- Create formulas that reference cells in a table by using table and column names instead of cell addresses.

These Excel table features let you focus on analyzing and understanding the data, letting the program perform the more time-consuming tasks. You will use these Excel table features in this and other tutorials.

Next, you'll create an Excel table from the art objects data in the Art Collection worksheet. By doing so, you'll be able to take advantage of the many features and tools for working with Excel tables to analyze data effectively.

Tip

If your data does not contain column headers, Excel adds headers with the default names Column1, Column2, and so forth to the table.

To create an Excel table from the art objects data:

1. Verify that the active cell is cell **A2**, which is in the range of art objects data.

2. Click the **Insert** tab on the Ribbon, and then, in the Tables group, click the **Table** button. The Create Table dialog box opens. The range of data for the table is entered in the dialog box. See Figure 5-4.

Figure 5-4	Create Table dialog box

range reference for the art objects table data

option checked because the art objects table includes column headers

3. Click the **OK** button. The dialog box closes, and the range of data is converted to an Excel table. Filter arrows appear in the header row, the table is formatted with a predefined table style, and the Table Tools Design contextual tab appears on the Ribbon. See Figure 5-5.

Excel table created for the art objects data ◄ **Figure 5-5**

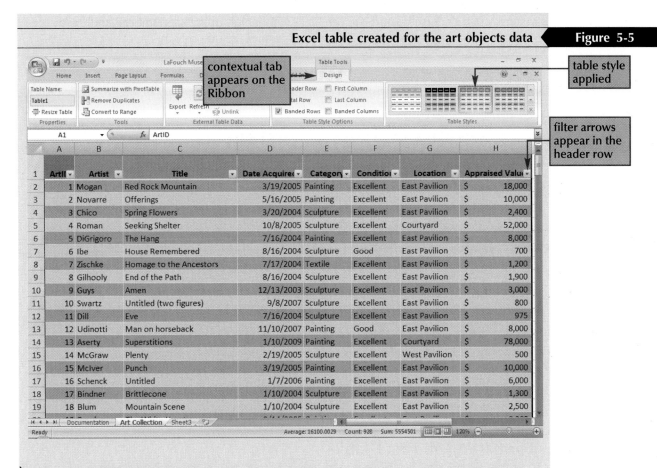

4. Scroll the table down. The text of the header row replaces the standard lettered column headings (A, B, C, and so on) as you scroll so that you don't need to freeze panes to keep the header row visible. See Figure 5-6.

Art objects table scrolled ◄ **Figure 5-6**

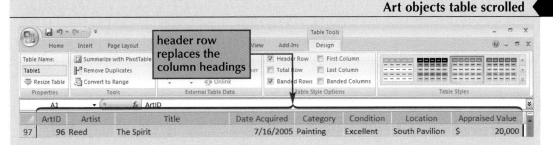

5. Press the **Ctrl+Home** keys to make cell A1 active. The column headings return to the standard display, and the header row scrolls back into view as row 1.

Renaming an Excel Table

Excel assigns the name Table1 to the first Excel table created in a workbook. Any additional Excel tables you create in the workbook are named consecutively, Table2, Table3, and so forth. You can assign a more descriptive name to a table, which makes it easier to identify a particular table by its content. Descriptive names are especially useful when you create more than one Excel table in the same workbook. Table names must start with a letter or an underscore and can use any combination of letters, numbers, and underscores for the rest of the name. Table names cannot include spaces.

Mary asks you to change the name of the Excel table you just created from the art objects data to ArtObjects.

To rename the Table1 table:

▶ **1.** In the Properties group on the Table Tools Design tab, select **Table1** in the Table Name box. See Figure 5-7.

Figure 5-7 Table Name box

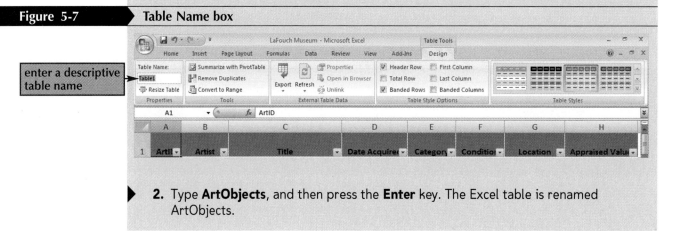

enter a descriptive table name

▶ **2.** Type **ArtObjects**, and then press the **Enter** key. The Excel table is renamed ArtObjects.

Formatting an Excel Table

Refer to Figure 5-7 and note the check boxes in the Table Style Options group on the Table Tools Design tab. These check boxes enable you to quickly and easily add or remove table elements or change the format of the table elements. For example, you can choose to remove the header row in a table by deselecting the Header Row check box; you can easily toggle back to display the header row by clicking to select this check box. Similarly, you can change the appearance of a table from banded rows to banded columns by deselecting the Banded Rows check box and then clicking to select the Banded Columns check box. With these options readily available on the Table Tools Design tab, it's easy to achieve the exact content and look for a table.

Mary likes the default table style applied to the Excel table, but asks you to make a few modifications to improve the table's appearance. She wants the ArtID values in the first column of the table highlighted for emphasis. She also wants the width in the Date Acquired and Appraised Value columns reduced to better fit the values.

To format the ArtObjects table:

▶ **1.** In the Table Style Options group on the Table Tools Design tab, click the **First Column** check box to insert a check mark. The text in the ArtID column is bold, and the fill color is the same as the header row.

▶ **2.** Change the width of column D to **12**. The Date Acquired column width better fits the dates.

▶ **3.** Change the width of column H to **12**. The Appraised Value column better fits the monetary values.

▶ **4.** Click cell **A1**, if necessary.

Maintaining an Excel Table

Mary has several changes that need to be reflected in the ArtObjects table. First, the museum acquired a new painting and received a sculpture from an anonymous donor; both art objects need to be added to the table. Second, Mary just learned that the Moonlight painting needs to be repaired as its condition has deteriorated; the condition of this art object needs to be changed from Fair to Poor. Finally, one of the paintings has been sold to raise money for new acquisitions; the record for this art object needs to be deleted from the table. Mary asks you to update the ArtObjects table to reflect these changes.

Adding Records

As you maintain an Excel table, you often need to add new records. You add a record to an Excel table in a blank row. The simplest and most convenient way to add a record to an Excel table is to enter the data in the first blank row below the last record. You can then sort the data to arrange the table in the order you want. You can also insert a row within the table for the new record, if you want the record in a specific location.

Adding a Record to an Excel Table | Reference Window

- Click in the row below the last row of the Excel table.
- Type the values for the new record, pressing the Tab key to move from field to field.
- Press the Tab key to create another new record, or press the Enter key if this is the last record.

Next, you'll add records for the new painting and sculpture to the ArtObjects table.

To add two records to the ArtObjects table:

▶ 1. Press the **End+↓** keys to make cell A116 the active cell. This cell is in the last row of the table.

▶ 2. Press the **↓** key to move the active cell to cell A117. This is the first blank row below the table.

▶ 3. Type **116** in cell A117, and then press the **Tab** key. Cell B117 in the Artist column becomes the active cell. The table expands to include a new row in the table structure with the same formatting as the rest of the table. The AutoCorrect Options button appears so you can undo the table formatting if you hadn't intended the new data to be part of the existing table. The sizing handle in the lower-right corner of the table indicates the last row and column in the table. You can use the sizing handle to add columns or rows to the Excel table to expand it or remove them to make the table smaller. See Figure 5-8.

New row added to the ArtObjects table | Figure 5-8

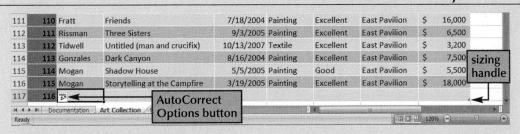

Trouble? If cell A118 is the active cell, you probably pressed the Enter key instead of the Tab key. Click cell B117 and then continue entering the data in Step 4.

4. In the range B117:H117, enter **Giama**, **Starry Night**, **4/3/2010**, **Painting**, **Excellent**, **South Pavilion**, and **8500** for the Artist, Title, Date Acquired, Category, Condition, Location, and Appraised Value fields, pressing the **Tab** key to move from cell to cell, and pressing the **Tab** key after you enter all the data for the record. Cell A118 becomes the active cell and the table expands to incorporate row 118.

Next, you'll enter the second record.

5. In the range A118:H118, enter **117**, **Higgins**, **Apache Warrior**, **4/5/2010**, **Sculpture**, **Excellent**, **Garden**, and **23000**, and then click cell **A119** after the last entry. The record for the sculpture is added to the table. See Figure 5-9.

> **Tip**
>
> As you type in a cell, Auto-Complete displays any existing entry in the column that matches the characters you typed. Press the Tab key to accept the entry or continue typing to replace it.

Figure 5-9   **Two records added to the ArtObjects table**

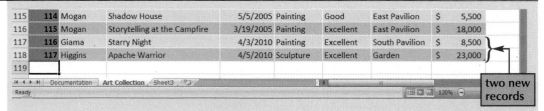

115	114	Mogan	Shadow House	5/5/2005	Painting	Good	East Pavilion	$	5,500
116	115	Mogan	Storytelling at the Campfire	3/19/2005	Painting	Excellent	East Pavilion	$	18,000
117	116	Giama	Starry Night	4/3/2010	Painting	Excellent	South Pavilion	$	8,500
118	117	Higgins	Apache Warrior	4/5/2010	Sculpture	Excellent	Garden	$	23,000
119									

two new records

Trouble? If a new row is added to the table, you probably pressed the Tab key instead of the Enter key after the last entry in the record. On the Quick Access Toolbar, click the Undo button 🔄 to remove the extra row.

Finding and Editing Records

You need to update the condition for the art object with the title Moonlight. Although you can manually scroll through the table to find a specific record, a quicker and more accurate way to locate a record is to use the Find command. You edit the data in a field the same way as you edit data in a worksheet cell. You'll use the Find command to locate the record for the Moonlight painting, which has deteriorated to poor condition. Then, you'll edit the record in the table to change the condition to "Poor."

To find and edit the record for the Moonlight painting:

1. Press the **Ctrl+Home** keys to move to the top of the worksheet, and then click cell **C2** to make it the active cell.

2. In the Editing group on the Home tab, click the **Find & Select** button, and then click **Find**. The Find and Replace dialog box opens.

3. Type **Moonlight** in the Find what box, and then click the **Find Next** button. Cell C69, which contains the title Moonlight, is selected. This is the record you want. If it weren't, you would click the Find Next button again to display the next record that meets the search criteria.

4. Click the **Close** button. The Find and Replace dialog box closes.

5. Press the **Tab** key three times to move the active cell to the Condition column, and then type **P**. AutoComplete displays Poor in the cell, which is the condition text you want to enter.

▶ **6.** Press the **Tab** key to enter the AutoComplete entry. The painting's condition is changed in the table.

▶ **7.** Press the **Ctrl+Home** keys to make cell A1 active.

Deleting a Record

The final update you need to make to the ArtObjects table is to delete the record for the Trappers painting (art ID 90), which is the art object that was sold. You'll use the Find command to locate the painting's record. Then, you'll delete the record from the table.

To find and delete the Trappers painting record:

▶ **1.** In the Editing group on the Home tab, click the **Find & Select** button, and then click **Find**. The Find and Replace dialog box opens.

▶ **2.** Type **90** in the Find what box, and then click the **Find Next** button. Because Excel searches the entire worksheet (not just the current column), and because it finds the search value even if it is part of another value, the appraised value $1,900 is selected. This is not the record you want to delete.

▶ **3.** Click the **Find Next** button to highlight the appraised value $1,900 for a different record, and then click the **Find Next** button again to highlight the value 90 in the ArtID column. This is the record you need to delete.

▶ **4.** Click the **Close** button. The Find and Replace dialog box closes.

Next, you'll delete the record for the Trappers painting.

▶ **5.** In the Cells group on the Home tab, click the **Delete button arrow**, and then click **Delete Table Rows**. The record for the Trappers painting is deleted from the table.

Trouble? If a different record was deleted, the active cell was not in the record for the Trappers painting. On the Quick Access Toolbar, click the Undo button 🔄 to restore the record, and then repeat Steps 1 through 5.

▶ **6.** Press the **Ctrl+Home** keys to make cell A1 active.

Tip

You can find fields whose contents match a value (such as 90) exactly by clicking the Options button in the Find & Replace dialog box, and checking the Match entire cell contents check box.

Tip

Be sure to verify that you select the correct record to delete, because a dialog box does not open for you to confirm the delete operation.

Sorting Data

The records in the ArtObjects table appear in the order that Mary entered them. As you work with tables, however, you'll want to view the same records in a different order, such as by the artist name or by the art object's location in the museum. You can rearrange, or **sort**, the records in a table or range based on the data in one or more fields. The fields you use to order the data are called **sort fields**. For example, to arrange the art objects by artist name, you can sort the data using the Artist column as the sort field.

You can sort data in ascending or descending order. **Ascending order** arranges text alphabetically from A to Z, numbers from smallest to largest, and dates from oldest to newest. **Descending order** arranges text in reverse alphabetical order from Z to A, numbers from largest to smallest, and dates from newest to oldest. In both ascending and descending order, blank fields are placed at the end of the table.

Sorting One Column Using the Sort Buttons

The simplest way to sort data with one sort field is to use the ⬇ or ⬆ button. Mary wants you to sort the art objects in ascending order by the artist. This will rearrange the table data so that the records appear in alphabetical order by the artist name.

To sort the art objects table in ascending order by the artist name:

1. Click any cell in the Artist column. You do not need to select the entire ArtObjects table, which consists of the range A1:H117. Excel determines the table's range when you click any cell in the table.

2. Click the **Data** tab on the Ribbon, and then, in the Sort & Filter group, click the **Sort A to Z** button ⬇. The data is sorted in ascending order by Artist. The Artist filter arrow indicates the data is sorted by that column. See Figure 5-10.

Tip

You can also access the Sort buttons in the Editing group on the Home tab by clicking the Sort & Filter button and clicking a sort option.

Figure 5-10 ArtObjects table sorted by Artist

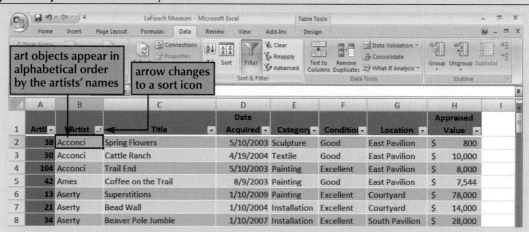

Trouble? If the data is sorted in the wrong order, you might have clicked in a different column than the Artist column. Repeat Steps 1 and 2.

Sorting Multiple Columns Using the Sort Dialog Box

Sometimes, sorting by one sort field is not adequate for your needs. For example, Mary wants you to arrange the ArtObjects table so that all the art objects in each location are together, and then all the objects for each artist within each location are together, and then each artist's work is arranged by the date acquired. You must sort on more than one column to accomplish this. The first sort field is called the **primary sort field**, the second sort field is called the **secondary sort field**, and so forth. You can use up to 64 sort fields in a single sort. In this case, the Location field is the primary sort field, the Artist field is the secondary sort field, and the Date Acquired field is the tertiary sort field. When you have more than one sort field, you should use the Sort dialog box to specify the sort criteria.

Sorting Data Using Multiple Sort Fields | Reference Window

- Click any cell in a table or range.
- In the Sort & Filter group on the Data tab, click the Sort button to open the Sort dialog box.
- If the Sort by row exists, modify the primary sort by selections; otherwise, click the Add Level button to insert the Sort by row.
- Click the Sort by arrow, select the column heading that you want to specify as the primary sort field, click the Sort On arrow to select the type of data, and then click the Order arrow to select the sort order.
- To sort by a second column, click the Add Level button to add the first Then by row. Click the Sort by arrow, select the column heading that you want to specify as the secondary sort field, click the Sort On arrow to select the type of data, and then click the Order arrow to select the sort order.
- To sort by additional columns, click the Add Level button and select appropriate Then by, Sort On, and Order values.
- Click the OK button.

Mary wants you to sort the art objects by location, and then within location by artist, and then within artist by date acquired with the most recently acquired objects for the artist appearing before the older ones. This will make it faster for her to find information about the location and the creator of the art objects in each location.

To sort the art objects table by location, then by artist, and then by date acquired:

▶ **1.** Click cell **A1** in the ArtObjects table. Cell A1 is the active cell, although you can click any cell in the table to sort the table data.

▶ **2.** In the Sort & Filter group on the Data tab, click the **Sort** button. The Sort dialog box opens. Any sort specifications (sort field, type of data sorted on, and sort order) from the last sort appear in the dialog box.

You'll set the primary sort field—Location.

▶ **3.** Click the **Sort by** arrow to display the list of the column headers in the ArtObjects table, and then click **Location**.

▶ **4.** If necessary, click the **Sort On** arrow to display the type of sort, and then click **Values**. Typically, you want to sort by the numbers, text, or dates stored in the cells, which are all values. However, you can also sort by formats, such as cell color, font color, and cell icon (a graphic that appears in a cell as a result of applying a conditional format).

▶ **5.** If necessary, click the **Order** arrow to display sort order options, and then click **A to Z**. The sort order is set to ascending.

The specification for the primary sort field are complete. Next, you will specify the secondary sort field—Artist. First, you need to insert a blank sort level.

▶ **6.** Click the **Add Level** button. A Then by row is added below the primary sort field.

▶ **7.** Click the **Then by** arrow and click **Artist**, and then verify that **Values** appears in the Sort On box and **A to Z** appears in the Order box.

The second sort field is specified. You'll add the third sort field—Date Acquired.

▶ **8.** Click the **Add Level** button to add a second Then by row.

9. Click the second **Then by** arrow and click **Date Acquired**, verify that **Values** appears in the Sort On box, click the **Order** arrow, and then click **Newest to Oldest** to specify a descending sort order for the Date Acquired values. See Figure 5-11.

Figure 5-11 | **Sort dialog box with complete sort specifications**

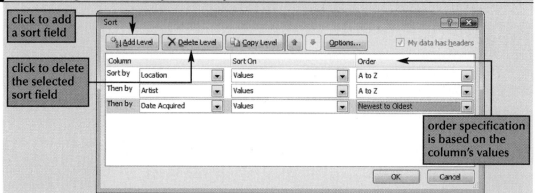

10. Click the **OK** button. Excel sorts the table records first in ascending order by Location, then within each location by Artist (again, in ascending order), and then within each artist by Date Acquired. For example, notice the three works by Acconci located in the East Pavilion; the works are arranged in descending order by the value in the Date Acquired column, so that the newer works appear before the older works. See Figure 5-12.

Figure 5-12 | **Art objects sorted by Location, then by Artist, and then by Date Acquired**

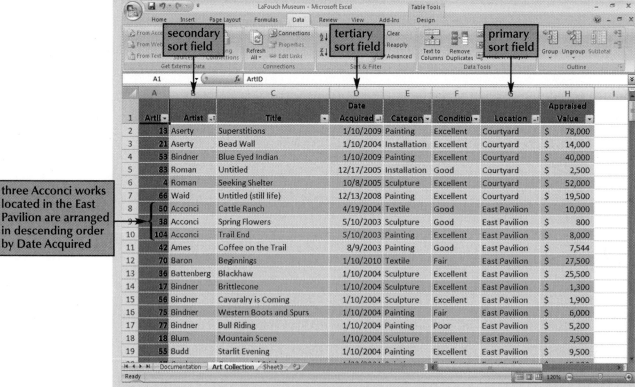

11. Scroll the table to view the sorted table data.

Mary wants to review the condition of each art object to determine how many objects need repairs. To do this more easily, she asks you to sort the objects by Condition. Because she wants to sort by only one field, you'll use the Sort A to Z button.

To sort the table by condition:

▶ **1.** Click any cell in the **Condition** column.

▶ **2.** In the Sort & Filter group on the Data tab, click the **Sort A to Z** button ⬛. The previous sort is removed and the art objects are now sorted in ascending order by Condition.

▶ **3.** Scroll the table to see the reordered art objects.

As Mary reviews the sorted table, she realizes that the data is sorted in alphabetical order by the condition of the art objects: Excellent, Fair, Good, and Poor. This default sort order for fields with text values is not appropriate for the condition ratings. Instead, Mary wants you to base the sort on quality ranking rather than alphabetical. You'll use a custom sort list to set up the sort order Mary wants.

Sorting Using a Custom List

Text is sorted in ascending or descending alphabetical order unless you specify a different order using a custom list. A **custom list** indicates the sequence in which you want data ordered. Excel provides four predefined custom sort lists. Two days-of-the-week custom lists (Sun, Mon, Tues, ... and Sunday, Monday, Tuesday, ...) and two months-of-the-year custom lists (Jan, Feb, Mar, Apr, ... and January, February, March, April, ...). If a column consists of day or month labels, you can sort them in their correct chronological order using one of these predefined custom lists. You can also create custom lists to sort records in a sequence you define. In this case, you want to create a custom list to arrange the art objects based on their condition, with the top-quality condition appearing first, as follows: Excellent, Good, Fair, Poor.

Creating a Custom List	Reference Window

- In the Sort & Filter group on the Data tab, click the Sort button.
- Click the Order arrow, and then click Custom List.
- In the List entries box, type each entry for the custom list, pressing the Enter key after each entry.
- Click the Add button.
- Click the OK button.

You'll create a custom list that Mary can use to sort the records by the Condition field.

To create the custom list based on the Condition field:

▶ **1.** Make sure the active cell is in the table, and then, in the Sort & Filter group on the Data tab, click the **Sort** button. The Sort dialog box opens, showing the sort specifications from the previous sort.

▶ **2.** Click the **Sort by** arrow, click **Condition** to select the sort field (if necessary), and then verify that **Values** appears in the Sort On box.

▶ **3.** Click the **Order** arrow to display the sort order options, and then click **Custom List**. The Custom Lists dialog box opens.

▶ **4.** Click **NEW LIST** in the Custom lists box to place the insertion point in the List entries box.

Next, you'll enter the condition values in the order you want them sorted. You must press the Enter key after each entry.

▶ **5.** Type **Excellent**, press the **Enter** key to move the insertion point to the next line, type **Good**, press the **Enter** key, type **Fair**, press the **Enter** key, type **Poor**, and then press the **Enter** key. The four items appear in the List entries box.

▶ **6.** Click the **Add** button. The custom list entries are added to the Custom lists box. See Figure 5-13.

Figure 5-13	Custom Lists dialog box with custom list defined

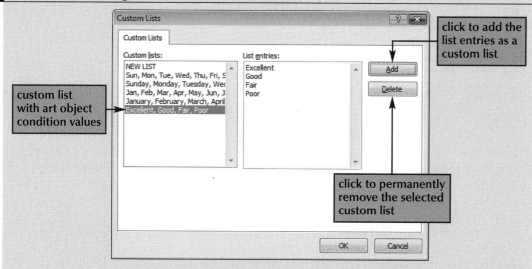

custom list with art object condition values

click to add the list entries as a custom list

click to permanently remove the selected custom list

▶ **7.** Click the **OK** button to return to the Sort dialog box. The custom sort list—Excellent, Good, Fair, Poor—appears in the Order box.

▶ **8.** Click the **OK** button. The table is sorted based on the custom list.

▶ **9.** Scroll the sorted table to verify that the art objects are sorted by their condition rankings: Excellent, Good, Fair, and Poor. Note that there are six art objects in poor condition.

In this session, you created an Excel table for the art objects, and then named and formatted the table. Next, you updated the table by adding records, editing a record, and deleting a record. You sorted the records by one field and then by three fields. Finally, you created a custom list to sort the Condition field by its quality ratings. In the next session, you will filter the ArtObjects table to retrieve specific information on some of the art objects.

Review | **Session 5.1 Quick Check**

1. What is the purpose of the Freeze Panes button in the Window group on the View tab? Why is this feature helpful?

2. What three elements indicate an Excel table has been created in the worksheet?

3. What fields do you use to order data?
4. An Excel table of college students tracks each student's first name, last name, major, and year of graduation. How can you order the table so students graduating the same year appear together in alphabetical order by the student's last name?
5. How do you enter a new record in an Excel table?
6. An Excel table of faculty data includes the Rank field with the values Full, Associate, Assistant, and Instructor. How can you sort the data by rank in the following order: Full, Associate, Assistant, and Instructor?
7. If you sort table data from the most recent purchase date to the oldest purchase date, in what order have you sorted the data?

Session 5.2

Filtering Data

Mary is working on her budget for the upcoming year. She needs to determine which art objects the museum can afford to repair this year. She asks you to prepare a list of all paintings in poor condition. Mary will then examine these paintings, estimate the repair costs, and decide which ones to place on the upcoming year's repairs list.

Although you could sort the list of paintings by condition to group those in poor condition, you are still working with the entire table. A better solution is to display only the specific records you want. The process of displaying a subset of rows in the table that meets the criteria you specify is called **filtering**. Filtering, rather than rearranging the data as sorting does, temporarily hides any records that do not meet the specified criteria. After data is filtered, you can sort, copy, format, chart, and print it.

Filtering Using One Column

When you create an Excel table, filter arrows appear in each of the column headers. You can see these filter arrows in the ArtObjects table you created for Mary. You click a filter arrow to open the Filter menu for that field. You can use options on the Filter menu to create three types of filters. You can filter a column of data by its cell colors or font colors; by a specific text, number, or date filter, although the specific choices depend on the type of data in the column; or by selecting one or more of the exact values by which you want to filter in the column. After you filter a column, the Clear Filter command becomes available so you can remove the filter and redisplay all the records.

Mary wants to see only paintings in poor condition. First, you need to filter the ArtObjects table to show only those records with the value "Paintings" in the Category column. Remember, filtering the data only hides some of the records.

> **Tip**
>
> You can display or hide filter arrows for an Excel table or a range of data by using the Filter button in the Sort & Filter group on the Data tab.

To filter the ArtObjects table to show only paintings:

▶ 1. If you took a break after the previous session, make sure the LaFouch Museum workbook is open, the Art Collection worksheet is active, and the ArtObjects table is active.

▶ 2. Click the **Category filter arrow**. The Filter menu opens, as shown in Figure 5-14, listing the unique entries in the Category column: Installation, Painting, Sculpture, and Textile. Initially, all the items are selected, but you can select which items you want to use to filter the data. In this case, you want to select the Painting item.

Figure 5-14 **Filter menu for the Category column**

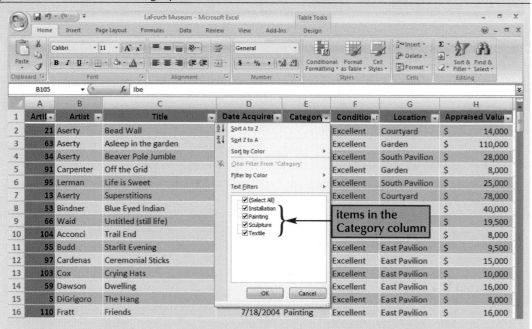

Notice the **Sort by Color** and **Filter by Color** options in the filter menu. These options enable you to filter and sort data using color, one of many cell attributes. Suppose that Mary used specific cell background colors for certain works of art in the ArtObjects table. For example, she might want to highlight those works given to the museum by its two most generous donors, using yellow for one and red for the other. So, the cells in the Title column for the two donors would be formatted with these colors. You could then click the Sort by Color option in the filter menu to display a list of available colors by which to sort, and then click the specific color so that all the records for the first donor (formatted with yellow) would appear together, and all the records for the second donor (formatted with red) would appear together. Similarly, you could click the Filter by Color option to display a submenu with the available colors by which to filter, and then click a color. In this example, if you selected yellow, only the records for the first donor would be displayed in the table, allowing you to focus on just those records.

▶ 3. Click the **(Select All)** check box to remove the check marks from all the Category items, and then click the **Painting** check box to insert a check mark. The filter will show only those records that match the checked item and hide records that contain the unchecked items.

▶ 4. Click the **OK** button. The filter is applied. The status bar lists the number of paintings found in the entire table. Fifty-seven of the 116 records in the table are displayed. See Figure 5-15.

ArtObjects table filtered to show only paintings **Figure 5-15**

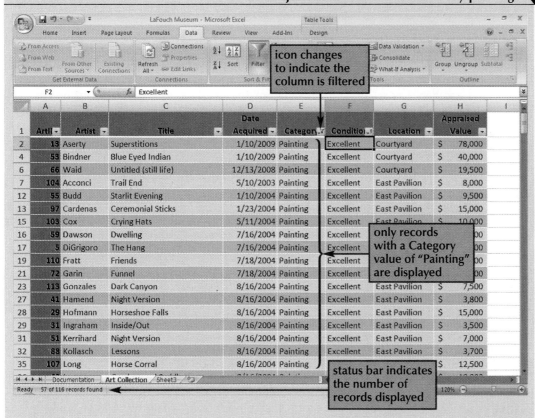

5. Review the records to verify that only records with a value equal to Painting in the Category column are visible. All records that do not have the value Painting in this column are hidden. Notice the gaps in the row numbers in the worksheet. As a reminder that the records are filtered, the row numbers of the filtered records are blue and the Category filter arrow changes to indicate that this column is being used to filter the table.

6. Point to the **Category filter arrow**. A ScreenTip—Category: Equals "Painting"—describes the filter applied to the column.

InSight | **Exploring Text Filters**

You can use different text filters to display the records you want. If you know only part of a text value or want to match a certain pattern, you can use the Begins With, Ends With, and Contains operators to filter a text field to match the pattern you specify.

The following examples are based on a student directory table that includes First Name, Last Name, Address, City, State, and Zip fields:

- To find a student named Smith, Smithe, or Smythe, create a text filter using the Begins With operator. In this example, use Begins With *Sm* to display all records that have *Sm* at the beginning of the text value.
- To Find anyone whose Last Name ends in "son" (such as Robertson, Anderson, Dawson, Gibson, and so forth), create a text filter using the Ends With operator. In this example, use Ends With *son* to display all records that have *son* as the last characters in the text value.
- To find anyone whose street address includes *Central* (such as 101 Central Ave, 1024 Central Road, or 457 Avenue De Central), create a text filter using the Contains operator. In this example, use Contains *Central* to display all records that have *Central* anywhere in the text value.

When you create a text filter, think about the results you want. Then, consider what text filter you can use to best achieve those results.

Filtering Using Multiple Columns

If you need to further restrict the records that appear in a filtered table, you can filter by one or more of the other columns. Each additional filter is applied to the currently filtered data and further reduces the records that are displayed. Mary wants to see only paintings that are in poor condition, rather than all the paintings in the ArtObjects table. To do this, you need to filter the paintings records to display only those with the value "Poor" in the Condition column. You'll use the filter arrow in the Condition column to add this second filter criterion to the filtered data.

To filter the painting records to show only those in poor condition:

▶ 1. Click the **Condition filter arrow**. The Filter menu opens.

▶ 2. Click the **Excellent**, **Good**, and **Fair** check boxes to remove the check marks. The Poor check box remains checked, so only paintings in poor condition will be displayed.

▶ 3. Click the **OK** button. The ArtObjects table is further filtered and shows the three paintings that are in poor condition. See Figure 5-16.

ArtObjects table filtered to show only paintings in poor condition   Figure 5-16

three paintings are in poor condition

Clearing Filters

When you want to see all the data in a filtered table, you can **clear** (or remove) the filters. When you clear a filter from a column, any other filters are still applied. For example, in the ArtObjects table, you would see all the paintings in the table if you cleared the filter from the Condition field, or you would see all the art objects in poor condition if you cleared the filter from the Category field. To redisplay all the art objects in the table, you need to clear both the Condition filter and the Category filter. You will do this now to restore the entire table of art objects.

To clear the filters to show all the records in the ArtObjects table:

▶ 1. Click the **Condition filter arrow**, and then click **Clear Filter From "Condition"**. The Condition filter is removed from the table. The table shows only paintings because the Category filter is still in effect.

▶ 2. Click the **Category filter arrow**, and then click **Clear Filter From "Category"**. The Category condition is removed, and all the records in the ArtObjects table are displayed again.

Selecting Multiple Filter Items

You can often find the information you need by selecting a single filter item from a list of filter items. Sometimes, however, you need to specify a more complex set of criteria to find the records you want. Earlier, you selected one filter item for the Category column and one filter item for the Condition column to display the records whose Category field value equals Painting AND whose Condition field value equals Poor. The records had to have both values to be displayed. The AND condition requires that all of the selected criteria be true for the record to be displayed. Now you want to select two filter items for the Category column to display records whose Category field value equals Installation OR whose Category field value equals Sculpture. The records must have at least one of these values to be displayed. A filter that selects more than one item from the list of items uses the OR condition, which requires that only one of the selected criteria be true for a record to be displayed. For example, if you check the Installation and Sculpture check boxes in the Category filter items, you create the filter condition "*Category equal to installation*" OR "*Category equal to sculpture.*"

The museum's board of directors wants a list of all installations or sculptures valued above $20,000. Mary asks you to create a list of these holdings.

To select multiple filter items:

▶ **1.** Click the **Category filter arrow**, and then click the **Painting** and **Textile** check boxes to remove the check marks.

▶ **2.** Verify that the **Installation** and **Sculpture** check boxes remain checked. When you select more than one item, you create a multiselect filter.

▶ **3.** Click the **OK** button. The ArtObjects table is filtered, and the status bar indicates that 51 out of 116 records are either an installation or a sculpture.

Creating Criteria Filters to Specify More Complex Criteria

Filter items enable you to filter a range of data or an Excel table based on exact values in a column. However, many times you need broader criteria. **Criteria filters** enable you to specify various conditions in addition to those that are based on an "equals" criterion. For example, you might want to find all art objects with an appraised value greater than $20,000 or acquired after 7/1/2009. You use criteria filters to create these conditions.

The type of criteria filters available change depending on whether the data in a column contains text, numbers, or dates. Figure 5-17 shows some of the options for text, number, and date criteria filters.

Figure 5-17 ▶ **Options for text, number, and date criteria filters**

Filter	Criteria	Records displayed
Text	Equals	Exactly match the specified text string
	Does Not Equal	Do not exactly match the specified text string
	Begins With	Begin with the specified text spring
	Ends With	End with the specified text string
	Contains	Have the specified text string anywhere
	Does Not Contain	Do not have the specified text string anywhere
Number	Equals	Exactly match the specified number
	Greater Than or Equal to	Are greater than or equal to the specified number
	Less Than	Are less than the specified number
	Between	Are greater than or equal to *and* less than or equal to the specified numbers
	Top 10	Are the top or bottom 10 (or the specified number)
	Above Average	Are greater than the average
Date	Today	Have the current date
	Last Week	Are in the prior week
	Next Month	Are in the month following the current month
	Last Quarter	Are in the previous quarter of the year (quarters defined Jan, Feb, Mar; Apr, May, June; and so on)
	Year to Date	Are since January 1 of the current year to the current date
	Last Year	Are in the previous year (based on the current date)

You will modify the filtered ArtObjects table to add a criteria filter that includes only objects valued greater than $20,000.

To create a number criteria filter:

▶ 1. Click the **Appraised Value filter arrow**, and then point to **Number Filters**. A menu opens displaying the comparison operators available for columns of numbers.

▶ 2. Click **Greater Than**. The Custom AutoFilter dialog box opens. The upper-left box lists *is greater than*, the comparison operator you want to use to filter the Appraised Value column. You enter the value you want to use for the filter criteria in the upper-right box, which, in this case, is 20,000.

▶ 3. Type **20000** in the upper-right box. See Figure 5-18. You use the lower set of boxes if you want the filter to meet a second condition. You click the And option button to display rows that meet both criteria. You click the Or option button to display rows that meet either of the two criteria. You only want to set one criteria for this filter, so you'll leave the lower boxes empty.

Custom AutoFilter dialog box | **Figure 5-18**

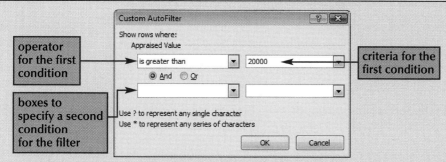

▶ 4. Click the **OK** button. The status bar indicates that 7 of 116 records were found. The seven records that appear in the ArtObjects table are either installations or sculptures and have an appraised value greater than $20,000.

Before Mary sends this list to the board of directors, you'll sort the filtered data to show the largest appraised value first. Although you can sort the data using Sort buttons, as you did earlier, these sort options are also available on the Filter menu for your convenience. If you want to perform a more complex sort, you still need to use the Sort dialog box.

To sort the filtered table data:

▶ 1. Click the **Appraised Value filter arrow**. The Filter menu opens. The sort options are at the top of the menu.

▶ 2. Click **Sort Largest to Smallest**. The filtered table now displays installations and sculptures with an appraised valued above $20,000 sorted in descending order. See Figure 5-19.

Figure 5-19 ▸ **Filtered ArtObjects table**

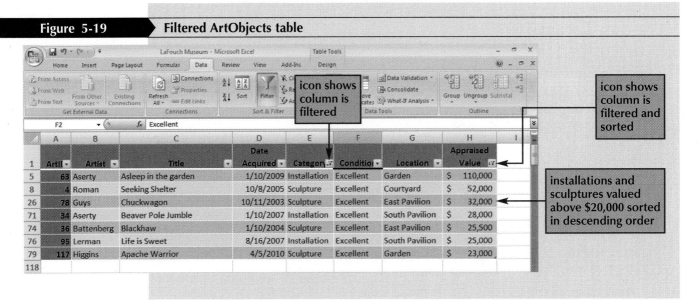

Mary will send this list to the board of directors. You need to restore the entire table of art objects, which you can do by clearing all the filters at one time.

To clear all the filters from the ArtObjects table:

▸ **1.** Click the **Data** tab on the Ribbon, if necessary.

▸ **2.** In the Sort & Filter group, click the **Clear** button. All the records appear in the table.

Using the Total Row to Calculate Summary Statistics

You can calculate summary statistics (including sum, average, count, maximum, and minimum) on all the columns in an Excel table or on a filtered table in a Total row. A **Total row**, which you can display at the end of the table, is used to calculate summary statistics for the columns in an Excel table. When you click in each cell in the Total row, an arrow appears that you can click to open a list of the most commonly used functions.

Mary is creating a brochure for an upcoming fund-raising event, and wants to know the number and value of the items in the current museum collection, excluding art objects in poor condition. She asks you to filter the table to display art objects that are in excellent, good, and fair condition. Then, you will display the Total row for the ArtObjects table to count the number of art objects and add their total appraised value.

To add a Total row and select summary statistics:

▸ **1.** Click the **Condition filter arrow**, click the **Poor** check box to remove the check mark, and then click the **OK** button. The ArtObjects table displays objects that are in excellent, good, or fair condition. The status bar indicates that 110 of 116 records remain in the filtered table.

Next, you will display the Total row.

▸ **2.** Click the **Table Tools Design** tab on the Ribbon, and then, in the Table Style Options group, click the **Total Row** check box to insert a check mark.

3. Scroll to the end of the table. The Total row is the last row of the table, the word "Total" appears in the leftmost cell, and the total appraised value $1,118,723 appears in the rightmost cell. By default, the Total row adds the numbers in the last column of the Excel table or counts the number of records if the data in the last column contains text. See Figure 5-20.

Total row added to the ArtObjects table   **Figure 5-20**

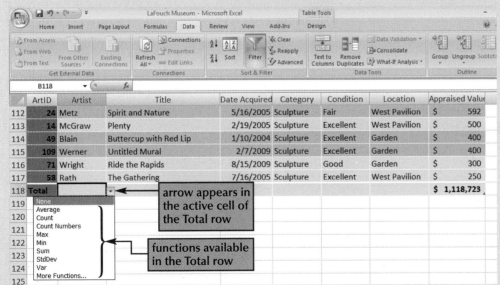

In the Artist cell of the Total row, you want to count the number of records whose Appraised Values were added in the last column.

4. Click cell **B118** (the Artist cell in the Total row), and then click the **arrow button** to display a list of functions. None is the default function in all columns except the last column. See Figure 5-21.

Total row functions   **Figure 5-21**

Tip

You can click the More Functions command to open the Insert Function dialog box and select any available function.

5. Click **Count**. The number 110 appears in the cell, which is the number of records in the filtered ArtObjects table. See Figure 5-22.

Figure 5-22 ▶ **Count of records in the filtered table**

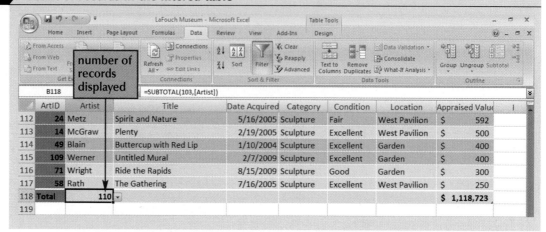

Mary will include this information in her fund-raising brochure. You will remove the Total row and clear the filter.

Tip

If you redisplay the Total row, the functions you last used will appear even after you save, close, and then reopen the file.

To remove the Total row and clear the filter from the ArtObjects table:

▶ **1.** In the Table Style Options group on the Table Tools Design tab, click the **Total Row** check box to remove the check mark. The Total row is no longer visible.

▶ **2.** Scroll to the top of the table, click the **Condition filter arrow**, and then click **Clear Filter From "Condition"**. The ArtObjects table displays all the art objects.

The board of directors asked Mary to create a report that shows all the museum's art objects sorted by Category with the total appraised value of the art objects in each category. The board also wants to see the total appraised value for each category after the last item of that category. Although you could use the Total row in the Excel table to calculate the results, you would need to filter, total, and print the data for each category separately. A faster way to provide the information Mary needs is to use the Subtotal command.

Inserting Subtotals

You can summarize data in a range of data by inserting subtotals. The Subtotal command offers many kinds of summary information, including counts, sums, averages, minimums, and maximums. The Subtotal command inserts a subtotal row into the range for each group of data and adds a grand total row below the last row of data. Because Excel inserts subtotals whenever the value in a specified field changes, you need to sort the data so that records with the same value in a specified field are grouped together *before* you use the Subtotal command. The Subtotal command cannot be used in an Excel table, so you must first convert the Excel table to a range.

| **Calculating Subtotals for a Range of Data** | | Reference Window |

- Sort the data by the column for which you want a subtotal.
- If the data is in an Excel table, in the Tools group on the Table Tools Design tab, click the Convert to Range button, and then click the Yes button to convert the Excel table to a range.
- In the Outline group on the Data tab, click the Subtotal button.
- Click the At each change in arrow, and then click the column that contains the group you want to subtotal.
- Click the Use function arrow, and then click the function you want to use to summarize the data.
- In the Add subtotal to box, click the check box for each column that contains the values you want to summarize.
- To calculate another category of subtotals, click the Replace current subtotals check box to remove the check mark, and then repeat the previous three steps.
- Click the OK button.

To produce the results Mary needs, you will sort the art objects by category and calculate subtotals in the Appraised Value column for each category grouping.

To calculate appraised values subtotals for each category of art object:

▶ **1.** Click the **Category filter** arrow, and then click **Sort A to Z** on the Filter menu. The ArtObjects table is sorted in ascending order by the Category field. This ensures one subtotal is created for each category.

▶ **2.** In the Tools group on the Table Tools Design tab, click the **Convert to Range** button. A dialog box opens, asking if you want to convert the table to a normal range.

▶ **3.** Click the **Yes** button. The Excel table is converted to a range. You can tell this because the filter arrows and the Table Tools Design tab disappear, and the Home tab on the Ribbon is selected.

Next, you'll calculate the subtotals. The active cell needs to be in the header row so you can select the correct column.

▶ **4.** Press the **Ctrl+Home** keys to make cell A1 the active cell, click the **Data** tab on the Ribbon, and then, in the Outline group, click the **Subtotal** button. The Subtotal dialog box opens. See Figure 5-23.

| Subtotal dialog box | Figure 5-23 |

▶ **5.** Click the **At each change in** arrow, and then click **Category**. This is the column you want Excel to use to determine where to insert the subtotals; it's the column you sorted. A subtotal will be calculated at every change in the Category value.

▶ **6.** If necessary, click the **Use function** arrow, and then click **Sum**. The Use function list provides several options for subtotaling data, including counts, averages, minimums, maximums, and products.

▶ **7.** In the Add subtotal to list box, make sure only the **Appraised Value** check box is checked. This specifies the Appraised Value field as the field to be subtotaled. If the data already included subtotals, you would check the Replace current subtotals check box to replace the existing subtotals or uncheck the option to display the new subtotals on separate rows above the existing subtotals. Because the data has no subtotals, it makes no difference whether you select this option.

▶ **8.** Make sure the **Summary below data** check box is checked. This option places the subtotals below each group of data, instead of above the first entry in each group, and places the grand total at the end of the data, instead of at the top of the column just below the row of column headings.

▶ **9.** Click the **OK** button to insert subtotals into the data. Excel inserts rows below each category group and displays the subtotals for the appraised value of each art category. A series of Outline buttons appears to the left of the worksheet so you can display or hide the detail rows within each subtotal.

   Trouble? If each item has a subtotal following it, you probably forgot to sort the data by Category. Repeat Steps 1 through 9.

▶ **10.** Scroll through the data to see the subtotals below each category and the grand total at the end of the data. See Figure 5-24.

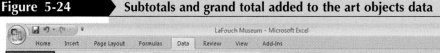

Figure 5-24 ▶ **Subtotals and grand total added to the art objects data**

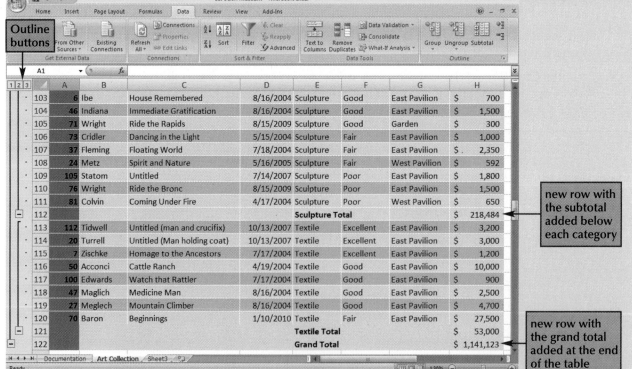

> **Trouble?** If necessary, increase the column width so you can view the subtotal values.

Using the Subtotal Outline View

In addition to displaying subtotals, the Subtotal feature "outlines" your worksheet so you can control the level of detail that is displayed. The three Outline buttons at the top of the outline area, as shown in Figure 5-24, allow you to show or hide different levels of detail in the worksheet. By default, the highest level is active, in this case, Level 3. Level 3 displays the most detail—the individual art object records, the subtotals, and the grand total. Level 2 displays the subtotals and the grand total, but not the individual records. Level 1 displays only the grand total.

The subtotals are useful, but Mary wants you to isolate the different subtotal sections so that she can focus on them individually. You will use the Outline buttons to prepare a report for Mary that includes only subtotals and the grand total.

To use the Outline buttons to hide records:

▶ **1.** Click the **Level 2 Outline** button. The individual art object records are hidden, and you see only the subtotals for each category and the grand total. See Figure 5-25.

Table displaying only subtotals and grand total | **Figure 5-25**

> **Trouble?** If necessary, scroll the worksheet up to see the complete Level 2 list.

▶ **2.** Click the **Level 1 Outline** button. The individual art object records and the subtotals for each category are hidden. Only the grand total remains visible.

▶ **3.** Click the **Level 3 Outline** button. All the records along with the subtotals and the grand total are visible.

Mary has all the information she needs for her meeting with the board to review financial plans for the next fiscal cycle. So you can remove the subtotals from the data.

To remove the subtotals from the art objects data:

▶ 1. In the Outline group on the Data tab, click the **Subtotal** button. The Subtotal dialog box opens.

▶ 2. Click the **Remove All** button to remove the subtotals from the data. Only the records appear in the worksheet.

You'll reset the art objects data as an Excel table.

▶ 3. Make sure the active cell is a cell within the structured range of data.

▶ 4. Click the **Insert** tab on the Ribbon, and then, in the Tables group, click the **Table** button. The Create Table dialog box opens.

▶ 5. Click the **OK** button to create the Excel table, and then click any cell in the table. The table structure is active.

You need to rename the table as ArtObjects.

▶ 6. In the Properties group on the Table Tools Design tab, type **ArtObjects** in the Table Name box, and then press the **Enter** key. The Excel table is again named ArtObjects.

Mary needs to generate some information for a meeting with the budget director to review financial plans for the next fiscal cycle. You will work with the art objects data in the next session to gather the information she needs for that meeting.

Review | **Session 5.2 Quick Check**

1. Explain the relationship between the Sort and Subtotal commands.
2. An Excel table includes records for 500 employees. What can you use to calculate the average salary of employees in the finance department?
3. How can you display a list of marketing majors with a GPA of 3.0 or greater from an Excel table with records for 300 students?
4. After you display subtotals, how can you change the amount of detail displayed?
5. True or False: The Count function is a valid subtotal function when using the Subtotal command.
6. An Excel table of major league baseball players includes the column Position (pitchers, catchers, infielders, outfielders, and so forth). What feature can you use to display only pitchers and catchers in the table?
7. If you have a list of employees that includes fields for gender and salary, among others, how can you determine the average salary for females using the Total row feature?

Session 5.3

Analyzing Data with PivotTables

An Excel table can contain a wealth of information, but the large amounts of detailed data often make it difficult to form a clear, overall view of that information. You can use a PivotTable to help organize the data into a meaningful summary. A **PivotTable** is an interactive table that enables you to group and summarize either a range of data or an Excel table into a concise, tabular format for easier reporting and analysis. A PivotTable summarizes data into categories using functions such as COUNT, SUM, AVERAGE, MAX, and MIN. For example, Mary is preparing a presentation for the museum's board of directors that will include a report of the appraised value of the museum's art objects by location, category, and condition. A PivotTable can generate the information she needs.

To create a PivotTable report, you need to specify which fields in your data source you want to summarize. In the ArtObjects table, the Appraised Value field is the most likely field to summarize. In other applications, fields such as salaries, sales, and costs are frequently summarized fields for PivotTables. In PivotTable terminology, the fields that contain summary data are known as **value fields**. **Category fields** group the values in a PivotTable by fields, such as condition, location, and year acquired. Category fields appear in PivotTables as row labels, column labels, and report filters, which allows you to focus on a subset of the PivotTable by displaying one, several, or all items. Figure 5-26 shows the PivotTable you will create.

Sample PivotTable   **Figure 5-26**

	A	B	C	D	E	F
1	Location	(All)				
2						
3	Sum of Appraised Value	Column Labels				
4	Row Labels	Excellent	Good	Fair	Poor	Grand Total
5	Installation	$185,000	$2,500			$187,500
6	Painting	$611,520	$41,669	$10,500	$18,450	$682,139
7	Sculpture	$194,292	$16,300	$3,942	$3,950	$218,484
8	Textile	$7,400	$18,100	$27,500		$53,000
9	Grand Total	$998,212	$78,569	$41,942	$22,400	$1,141,123

You can easily rearrange, hide, and display different category fields in the PivotTable to provide alternative views of the data. This ability to "pivot" the table—for example, change row headings to column positions and vice versa—gives the PivotTable its name and makes it a powerful analytical tool. The PivotTable in Figure 5-26 could be rearranged so that the Condition items appear as row labels and the Category items appear as column labels.

To conceptualize the layout of a PivotTable and convey your ideas to others who might implement them, a useful first step in creating a PivotTable is to sketch its layout. Mary's sketch, shown in Figure 5-27, illustrates the PivotTable you will create to show the appraised value of the art objects organized by location, category, and condition.

PivotTable sketch   **Figure 5-27**

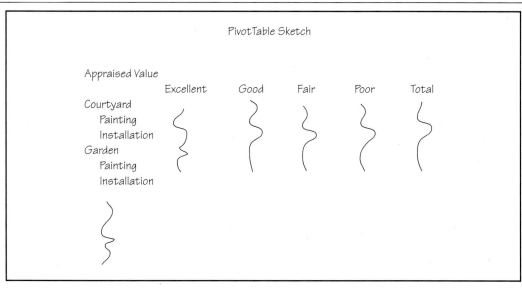

You are ready to create a PivotTable summarizing the total appraised value of art objects by location, category, and condition.

InSight | **Creating a Professional Report with PivotTables**

PivotTables are a great way to summarize data in a professional looking report when you do not want to see detailed data and you have many variables you want to summarize.

Although PivotTables most frequently show results using the SUM function, you can use many other functions to summarize the data, including COUNT, AVERAGE, MIN, MAX, PRODUCT, COUNT NUMBERS, STDEV, STDEVP, VAR, and VARP.

You can also display the values of a PivotTable in different views. If you want to compare one item to another item in the PivotTable, you can show the values as a percentage of a total. You can display the data in each row as a percentage of the total for the row. You can display the data in each column as a percentage of the total for the column. You can display the data as a percentage of the grand total of all the data in the PivotTable. Viewing data as a percentage of total is useful for analyses such as comparing product sales with total sales within a region or expense categories compared to total expenses for the year.

Creating a PivotTable

To create the PivotTable that will provide Mary with the information she needs, you will use the PivotTable dialog box to select the data to analyze and the location of the Pivot-Table report. Often when creating a PivotTable, you begin with data stored in a worksheet, although a PivotTable can also be created using data stored in an external database file, such as one in Access. In this case, you will use the ArtObjects table to create the PivotTable and place the PivotTable in a new worksheet.

Reference Window | **Creating a PivotTable**

- Click in the Excel table or select the range of data for the PivotTable.
- In the Tables group on the Insert tab, click the PivotTable button.
- Click the Select a table or range option button and verify the reference in the Table/ Range box.
- Click the New Worksheet option button or click the Existing Worksheet option button and specify a cell.
- Click the OK button.
- Click the check boxes for the fields you want to add to the PivotTable (or drag fields to the appropriate box in the layout section).
- If needed, drag fields to different boxes in the layout section.

Adding Fields to a PivotTable

You need to calculate the total appraised value of art objects by location, within location by category, and within category by condition. In the PivotTable, you'll begin by adding the Location, Category, and Condition fields to appear as row labels, and the data in the Appraised Value field to be summarized. First, you will create a PivotTable summarizing Appraised Value by Location. Then, you'll expand the PivotTable report by adding the Category and Condition fields.

To add fields to the PivotTable:

▶ **1.** In the PivotTable Field List, click the **Location** check box. The Location field is added to the Row Labels box and the unique values in the Location field—Courtyard, East Pavilion, Garden, South Pavilion, and West Pavilion—appear in the PivotTable report area. See Figure 5-31.

PivotTable with the Location field items as row labels ◀ **Figure 5-31**

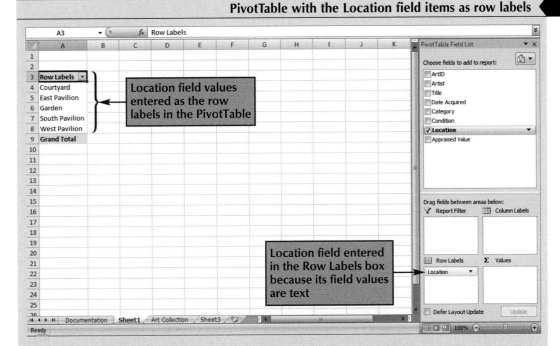

▶ **2.** Click the **Appraised Value** check box in the PivotTable Field List. The Sum of Appraised Value button appears in the Values box. The PivotTable groups the items from the ArtObjects table by Location, and calculates the total appraised value for each location. The grand total appears at the bottom of the PivotTable. See Figure 5-32.

Figure 5-32 PivotTable of the appraised value of art objects by location

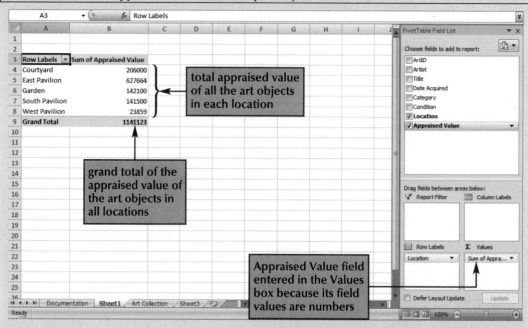

3. Rename the worksheet as **Appraised Value Summary**.

By default, the PivotTable report uses the SUM function for numbers in the Values area and the COUNT function for text and other nonnumeric values. If you want a different summary function, such as average, maximum, or minimum, click the appropriate button in the Values box (in this case, the button is called Sum of Appraised Value) in the Pivot-Table Field List, and then click Value Field Settings. The Value Field Settings dialog box opens. You can then select the type of calculation you want from the list of available functions, and then click the OK button.

Next, you'll add the Category and Condition fields to the PivotTable.

To add the Category and Condition fields to the PivotTable:

1. In the PivotTable Field List, click the **Category** check box. The Category field appears in the Row Labels box below the Location field and the unique items in the Category field are indented below each location field item in the PivotTable.

2. In the PivotTable Field List, click the **Condition** check box. The Condition field appears in the Row Labels box below the Category field and its unique items are indented below the Location and Category fields already in the PivotTable. See Figure 5-33.

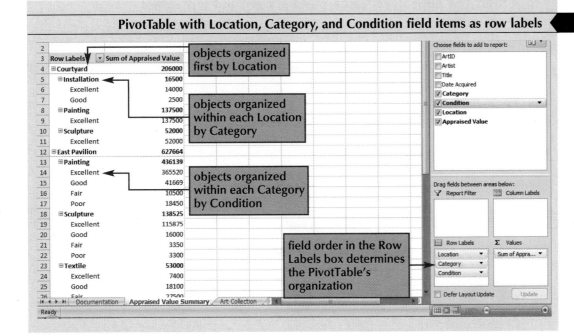

Applying PivotTable Styles

As with worksheet cells and Excel tables, you can quickly format a PivotTable report using a preset style. You can choose from a gallery of PivotTable styles similar to Table styles. Remember that you can point to any style in the gallery to see a Live Preview of the PivotTable with that style applied. You also can modify the appearance of PivotTables using PivotTable Style Options by adding or removing Banded Rows, Banded Columns, Row Headers, and Column Headers.

Mary wants you to apply the Medium 3 Style, which makes each group in the Pivot-Table stand out and subtotals in the report easier to find.

To apply a PivotTable style to the PivotTable report:

▶ **1.** Make sure the active cell is in the PivotTable, and then click the **PivotTable Tools Design** tab on the Ribbon.

▶ **2.** In the PivotTable Styles group, click the **More** button to open the PivotTable Styles gallery.

▶ **3.** Move the pointer over each style to preview the PivotTable report with that style.

▶ **4.** Click the **Pivot Style Medium 3** style (the third style in the Medium section). The style is applied to the PivotTable.

Formatting PivotTable Value Fields

Applying PivotTable styles does not change the numeric formatting in the PivotTable. Mary wants the numbers in the PivotTable to be quickly recognized as currency. You can format cells in a PivotTable the same way as you do cells in the worksheet. You'll change the total appraised values in the PivotTable to Currency style.

To format the appraised value numbers in the PivotTable:

▶ **1.** Click any cell in the **Sum of Appraised Value** column of the PivotTable report.

▶ **2.** Click the **PivotTable Tools Options** tab on the Ribbon, and then, in the Active Field group, click the **Field Settings** button. The Value Field Settings dialog box opens. See Figure 5-34.

Figure 5-34 ▶ | **Value Field Settings dialog box**

Tip

You can use the Summarize by tab to change the SUM function to a different summary function, such as AVERAGE. The name in the PivotTable is updated to reflect your selection.

settings affect this component of the PivotTable

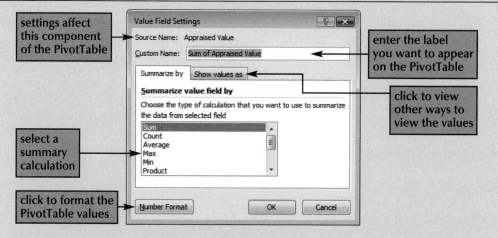

enter the label you want to appear on the PivotTable

click to view other ways to view the values

select a summary calculation

click to format the PivotTable values

If you want to change "Sum of Appraised Value" (cell B3), the name used to describe the calculations in the PivotTable report, use the Custom Name box in the Value Field Settings dialog box.

▶ **3.** Click the **Number Format** button. The Format Cells dialog box opens. This is the same dialog box you've used before to format numbers in worksheet cells.

▶ **4.** Click **Currency** in the Category list, and then type **0** in the Decimal places box.

▶ **5.** Click the **OK** button in each dialog box. The numbers in the PivotTable are formatted as currency with no decimal places.

With the style applied and the numbers formatted as currency, the data in the Pivot-Table is much easier to interpret.

Rearranging a PivotTable

Although you cannot change the values within a PivotTable, you can add, remove, and rearrange fields to change the PivotTable's layout. Recall that the benefit of a PivotTable is that it summarizes large amounts of data into a readable format. After you create a PivotTable, you can view the same data in different ways. The PivotTable Field List enables you to change, or pivot, the view of the data in the PivotTable by dragging the field buttons to different areas in the layout section.

Refer back to Mary's PivotTable sketch in Figure 5-27. As illustrated in the sketch, the Condition field items should be positioned as column labels instead of row labels in the PivotTable. You'll move the Condition field now to produce the format Mary wants.

To move the Condition field:

▶ 1. In the layout section of the PivotTable Field List, drag the **Condition** field button from the Row Labels box to the Column Labels box. The PivotTable is rearranged so that the Condition field is a column label instead of a row label. See Figure 5-35. Each time you make a change in the PivotTable Field List, the PivotTable layout is rearranged.

PivotTable rearranged with Condition as a column label | **Figure 5-35**

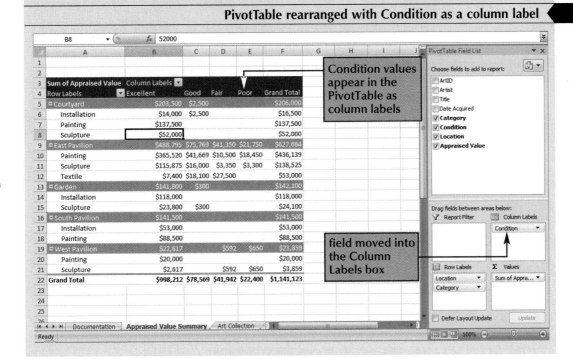

Changing the PivotTable Report Layout Options

The Compact report layout, shown in Figure 5-35, places all fields from the row area in a single column and indents the items from each field below the outer fields. This is the default layout for PivotTable reports. You can choose two other layouts. In the Outline report layout, each field in the row area takes a column in the PivotTable. By default, the outline form shows the subtotals for each group at the top of every group. The Tabular report layout displays one column for each field and leaves space for column headers. A total for each group appears at the bottom of each group. You can find these report layout options on the PivotTable Tools Design tab in the Layout group. Mary asks you to show her how the PivotTable looks in these alternative layouts so she can select the one she prefers.

To display the PivotTable in Outline and Tabular layouts:

▶ 1. Click the **PivotTable Tools Design** tab on the Ribbon.

▶ 2. In the Layout group, click the **Report Layout** button, and then click **Show in Outline Form**. The PivotTable layout changes. See Figure 5-36.

Figure 5-36 Outline PivotTable report layout

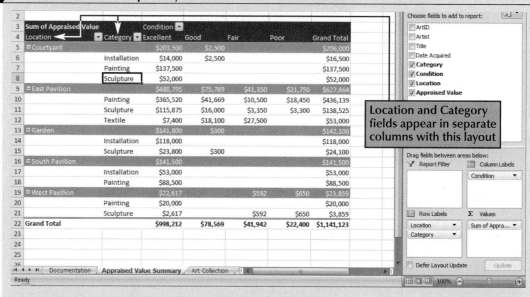

Next, you'll review the Tabular report layout.

▶ **3.** In the Layout group, click the **Report Layout** button, and then click **Show in Tabular Form**. The PivotTable layout changes. See Figure 5-37.

Figure 5-37 Tabular PivotTable report layout

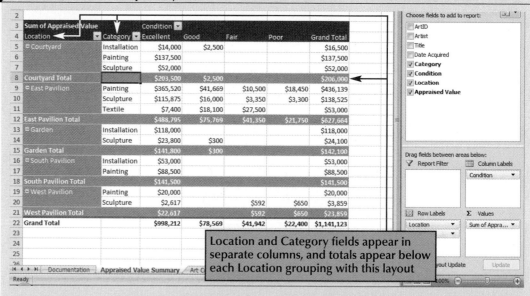

Mary prefers the original layout, the Compact form.

▶ **4.** In the Layout group, click the **Report Layout** button, and then click **Show in Compact Form**.

Adding a Report Filter to a PivotTable

You can drag a field to the Report Filter area to create a filtered view of the PivotTable report. A **report filter** allows you to filter the PivotTable to display summarized data for one or more field items or all field items in the Report Filter area. For example, creating a report filter for the Location field allows you to view or print the total appraised value for all locations or for specific locations such as the Courtyard.

You will add a report filter for the Location field to see if displaying the information in this way adds value to the report.

To add a report filter for the Location field:

▶ **1.** Drag the **Location** button from the Row Labels box to the Report Filter box. The Report Filter field item shows All to indicate that the PivotTable report displays all the summarized data associated with the Location field. See Figure 5-38.

PivotTable with the Location report filter applied ◀ Figure 5-38

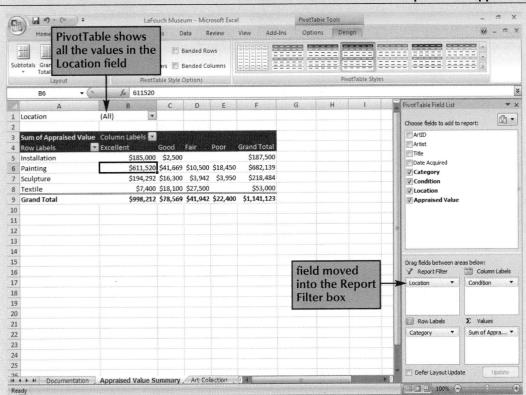

Next, you'll change the summarized report to show only art objects in the East Pavilion.

Tip

If you want to filter more than one location at a time, you can click the Select Multiple Items check box to add a check box next to each item. You could then choose multiple items from the list.

2. Click the **report filter arrow** in cell B1. A filter menu opens, showing the field items displayed.

Mary wants you to filter by a single item.

3. Click **East Pavilion** in the filter menu, and then click the **OK** button. The Pivot-Table displays the total appraised value of art objects located in the East Pavilion only. The report filter arrow changes to an icon to indicate the PivotTable is currently filtered. See Figure 5-39.

| Figure 5-39 | Report filter view for art objects in the East Pavilion |

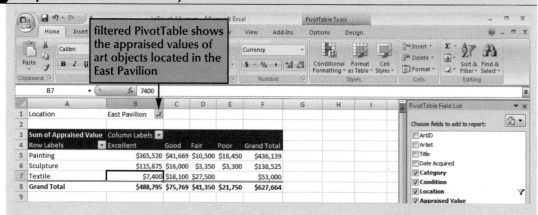

After reviewing the PivotTable, Mary decides she prefers the previous layout.

4. In the PivotTable Field List, drag the **Location** button from the Report Filter box to the top of the Row Labels box. The Location field is positioned above the Category field, and the PivotTable returns to its previous layout.

Trouble? If the PivotTable report is arranged differently, the Location field is not the top field in the Row Labels box. Drag the Location button in the Row Labels box above the Category button.

Filtering PivotTable Fields

Filtering a field lets you focus on a subset of items in that field. You can filter field items in the PivotTable by clicking the field arrow button in the PivotTable that represents the data you want to hide and then uncheck the check box for each item you want to hide. To show hidden items, you click the field arrow button and check the check box for the item you want to show.

Mary wants to focus her analysis on art objects in excellent, good, and fair condition. She asks you to remove art objects in poor condition from the PivotTable. You will hide the art objects in poor condition from the PivotTable report.

To filter the Condition field items from the PivotTable:

1. In the PivotTable, click the **Column Labels filter arrow**. The Filter menu displays the list of items in the Condition field.

2. Click the **Poor** check box to remove the check mark. The Select All check box is deselected as well.

3. Click the **OK** button. The Poor column is removed from the PivotTable. The PivotTable includes only art objects in excellent, good, and fair condition. See Figure 5-40.

PivotTable report filtered by Condition ◄ **Figure 5-40**

The report contains the art objects data Mary wants to review. Although the art objects in poor condition are hidden, you can show them again by clicking the Column Labels arrow and checking the Poor check box.

Collapsing and Expanding Items

You can expand and collapse items in the row labels of the PivotTable to view fields at different levels of detail. The Expand and Collapse buttons identify where more details exist. The Expand button indicates you can show more details for that item, and the Collapse button indicates you can hide details for that item. The lowest level of the hierarchy does not have Expand and Collapse buttons because there is no data to expand or collapse. These buttons are helpful when you have complex PivotTables where you want to switch quickly between a detailed view and an overview.

Mary wants to see the total appraised value for each location without the Category items in the PivotTable. She asks you to collapse the level of detail so that only the Location items are showing. Currently, all items are expanded.

To collapse the Courtyard items in the PivotTable:

▶ 1. Point to the **Collapse** button ⊟ next to Courtyard until the pointer changes to ⬚, and then click the **Collapse** button ⊟ next to Courtyard. The detail items below Courtyard are hidden, and the Collapse button changes to an Expand button.

▶ 2. Click the **Collapse** button ⊟ next to East Pavilion, Garden, South Pavilion, and West Pavilion. The details for these four locations are hidden, and only the Location items are displayed. The PivotTable provides a higher level summary without displaying the Category details. See Figure 5-41.

Figure 5-41 **PivotTable with all locations collapsed and categories hidden**

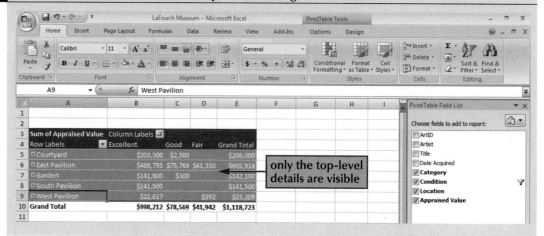

You can collapse or expand all level of detail in a PivotTable at one time. You'll do this to return to the original level of detail.

To expand all items in the PivotTable:

▶ **1.** Click the **PivotTable Tools Options** tab on the Ribbon. The Active Field group has buttons for expanding or collapsing all the details at one time.

▶ **2.** In the Active Field group, click the **Expand Entire Field** button. The detail items for all levels reappear. The lowest level of the hierarchy does not have Expand and Collapse buttons.

Sorting PivotTable Fields

Mary thinks the PivotTable would be more informative if the appraised values in each location were sorted in descending order. You can sort a PivotTable field either by its own items, for example alphabetizing fields such as Location and Category, or on the values in the body of the PivotTable. To sort a PivotTable field, you can use any of the Sort buttons on the Options tab to sort the information in a PivotTable report. These options are similar to the sort options you used earlier in the tutorial.

Mary wants you to sort the PivotTable so that the location with the highest total appraised value is displayed first. You need to sort the PivotTable values in descending order.

To sort the PivotTable to display the Location values in descending order based on their total appraised value amounts:

▶ **1.** Click cell **E5**, which contains the Grand Total for Courtyard. This is the field total you want to sort.

▶ **2.** In the Sort group on the PivotTable Tools Options tab, click the **Sort Largest to Smallest** button 🔽. The Location field is sorted based on the total appraised value for each location. Note, for example, that the East Pavilion location appears first in the PivotTable because it has the highest total appraised value, $605,914. The Courtyard location appears next because it has the second highest total appraised value, $206,000, and so on. See Figure 5-42.

PivotTable results sorted by Location ◀ | **Figure 5-42**

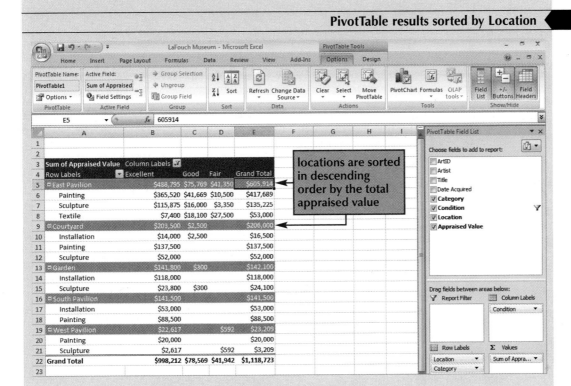

Adding a Second Value Field to a PivotTable

You can expand a PivotTable to create a more informative table by adding fields to the Values layout area. For example, Mary believes that a more accurate presentation of the art objects would include the number of objects corresponding to the total value in each cell of the PivotTable. Adding the Title field to the Values box would count the number of art objects in each location-category-condition combination (because the title is a nonnumeric field). Mary thinks the additional information will be useful during her meeting with the board of directors. You will add the Title field to the PivotTable.

To drag and drop the Title field to the Values box:

▶ **1.** In the PivotTable Field List, drag **Title** from the field list to immediately below the Sum of Appraised Value button in the Values box. The PivotTable displays the number of art objects as well as the total appraised value. The Values box in the layout area includes a second button, Count of Title, and fields from the Values box are added to the Column Labels box. See Figure 5-43.

Figure 5-43 | **Count of art objects added to the PivotTable**

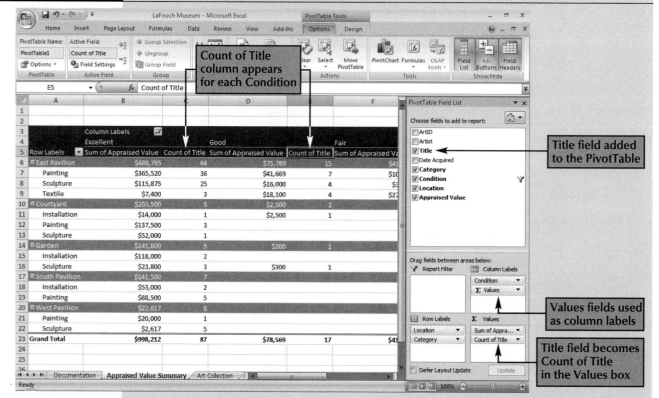

Part of the PivotTable is hidden behind the PivotTable Field List. You'll hide the Pivot-Table Field List so you can view more of the PivotTable.

▶ **2.** In the Show/Hide group on the PivotTable Tools Options tab, click the **Field List** button. The PivotTable Field List disappears.

Next, you'll change the "Count of Title" label to "Count."

▶ **3.** In the PivotTable, click any of the **Count of Title** labels.

▶ **4.** In the Active Field group on the PivotTable Tools Options tab, click the **Field Settings** button. The Value Field Settings dialog box opens.

▶ **5.** In the Custom Name box, type **Count**, and then click the **OK** button. The Count label appears in the PivotTable instead of Count of Title.

Tip

You can also rename a value label by typing the new text directly in any cell where the value label appears in the PivotTable.

Removing a Field from a PivotTable

The PivotTable report with the Count looks cluttered and is difficult to read. Mary asks you to remove the Count field. If you want to remove a field from a PivotTable, you click the field's check box in the PivotTable Field List. Removing a field from the PivotTable has no effect on the underlying Excel table. You will remove the Title field from the PivotTable.

To remove the Title field from the PivotTable:

▶ **1.** In the Show/Hide Group on the PivotTable Tools Options tab, click the **Field List** button. The PivotTable Field List is displayed.

▶ **2.** Click the **Title** check box in the field area. The Count column is removed from the PivotTable, which returns to its previous layout. The Title field is still in the ArtObjects table.

The PivotTable is almost complete. Mary asks you to improve the appearance of the PivotTable by removing the field headers (Row Labels and Column Labels) and hiding the Expand/Collapse buttons.

To hide field headers and the Expand/Collapse buttons from the PivotTable:

▶ **1.** In the Show/Hide group on the PivotTable Tools Options tab, click the **+/- Buttons** button. The Expand/Collapse buttons disappear from the PivotTable.

▶ **2.** In the Show/Hide group, click the **Field Headers** button. The headers Column Labels and Row Labels are hidden. See Figure 5-44.

PivotTable without field headers and Expand/Collapse buttons ◀ **Figure 5-44**

Refreshing a PivotTable

Mary just learned that the art object Dancing in the Light by Cridler has been reappraised and its value is now $4,000 (its value is currently listed as $1,000). You cannot change the data directly in the PivotTable. Instead, you must edit the Excel table, and then **refresh**, or update, the PivotTable to reflect the current state of the art objects list.

You'll edit the record for Dancing in the Light in the ArtObjects table. This sculpture is located in the East Pavilion and is in fair condition. This one change will affect the Pivot-Table in several locations. For example, currently the Total value of objects in the East Pavilion is $605,914; the sculptures in the East Pavilion are valued at $135,225; and sculptures in the East Pavilion in fair condition are valued at $3,350. After you update the appraised value of this art object in the Excel table, all these values in the PivotTable will increase by $3,000.

To update the ArtObjects table:

▶ 1. Switch to the **Art Collection** worksheet, and then find **Cridler, Dancing in the Light** (ArtID 73).

▶ 2. Click the record's Appraised Value cell, and then enter **4000**. The sculpture's value is updated in the table. You'll return to the PivotTable report to see the effect of this change on its values.

▶ 3. Switch to the **Appraised Value Summary** worksheet. The appraised value totals for the East Pavilion are still $605,914, $135,225, and $3,350, respectively.

The PivotTable is not updated when the data in its source table is updated, so you need to refresh the PivotTable manually.

▶ 4. Click any cell in the PivotTable.

▶ 5. Click the **PivotTable Tools Options** tab on the Ribbon, and then, in the Data group, click the **Refresh** button. The PivotTable report is updated. The appraised value totals are now $608,914, $138,225, and $6,350. See Figure 5-45.

Figure 5-45 **Refreshed PivotTable**

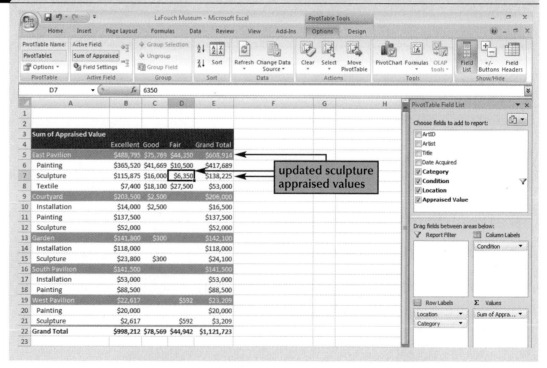

Mary is satisfied with the final version of the PivotTable report.

Grouping PivotTable Items

When a field contains numbers, dates, or times, you can combine items in the rows of a PivotTable and combine them into groups automatically. Mary thinks another PivotTable, one displaying the number of objects acquired each year, would be of interest to the board of directors. This report involves using the Date Acquired field as a row label and ArtID (or other field) as the value field. When using a date field as a row label in a Pivot-Table, each date initially appears as a separate item. Typically, you want to analyze date data by month, quarter, or year. To do that, you need to group the data in the Date Acquired field. Grouping items combines dates into larger groups such as months, quarters, or years, so that the PivotTable can include the desired level of summarization. You can also group numeric items, typically into equal ranges. For example, you can calculate the number of art objects in appraised value groups based on increments of any amount you specify (for example, 1–25,000, 25,001–50,000, and so on).

You'll add a second PivotTable in a new worksheet.

To create the PivotTable based on the Date Acquired field:

▶ 1. Switch to the **Art Collection** worksheet, and then click any cell in the Excel table. The table is active.

▶ 2. Click the **Insert** tab on the Ribbon, and then, in the Tables group, click the **PivotTable** button. The Create PivotTable dialog box opens.

▶ 3. Verify that the Table/Range box shows **ArtObjects** and the **New Worksheet** option button is selected, and then click the **OK** button. The PivotTable report area and PivotTable Field List appear in a new worksheet.

▶ 4. In the PivotTable Field List, click the **Date Acquired** check box. The Date Acquired field appears in the Row Labels box. Each unique date appears in the PivotTable report area. Mary wants each year to appear as a row label. You will correct that shortly.

Next, you'll add the ArtID field to the PivotTable.

▶ 5. Click the **ArtID** check box in the PivotTable Field List. The Sum of ArtID appears in the Values box in the layout area, because the ArtID field contains numeric data. See Figure 5-46.

| Figure 5-46 | PivotTable with Sum of ArtID for each date |

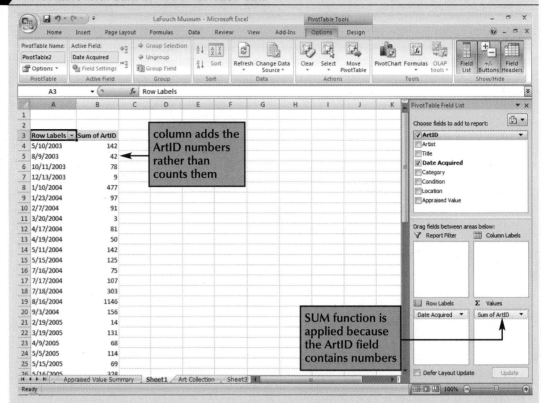

The PivotTable includes the sum of ArtIDs instead of a count of art objects, as Mary requested. This occurs because fields that contain numbers placed in the Values area are summed. Adding all the ArtIDs together to get a total is meaningless; you need to count the number of ArtIDs in each year. To do this, you need to change the SUM function to the COUNT function so Excel will *count* the number of objects in each group.

▶ 6. Click any value in the **Sum of ArtID** column, and then, in the Active Field group on the PivotTable Tools Options tab, click the **Field Settings** button. The Value Field Settings dialog box opens.

▶ 7. Click **Count** in the Summarize value field by box, and then type **Count** in the Custom Name box. The label indicating the type of summary in the PivotTable will be changed to Count.

▶ 8. Click the **OK** button. The dialog box closes and the PivotTable report displays the number of art objects acquired by date. See Figure 5-47.

PivotTable report with count | **Figure 5-47**

	A	B	C	D	E	F	G	H	I	J	K
1											
2											
3	Row Labels	Count									
4	5/10/2003	2									
5	8/9/2003	1									
6	10/11/2003	1									
7	12/13/2003	1									
8	1/10/2004	11									
9	1/23/2004	1									
10	2/7/2004	1									
11	3/20/2004	1									
12	4/17/2004	1									
13	4/19/2004	1									
14	5/11/2004	2									
15	5/15/2004	2									
16	7/16/2004	3									
17	7/17/2004	2									
18	7/18/2004	4									
19	8/16/2004	21									
20	9/3/2004	3									
21	2/19/2005	1									
22	3/19/2005	3									
23	4/9/2005	1									
24	5/5/2005	1									
25	5/15/2005	1									
26	5/16/2005	7									

the number of art objects acquired by date

PivotTable Field List

Choose fields to add to report:
- ☑ ArtID
- ☐ Artist
- ☐ Title
- ☑ Date Acquired
- ☐ Category
- ☐ Condition
- ☐ Location
- ☐ Appraised Value

Drag fields between areas below:

▼ Report Filter	🎚 Column Labels

🎚 Row Labels	Σ Values
Date Acquired ▼	Count ▼

☐ Defer Layout Update   Update

Sheets: Appraised Value Summary, Sheet1, Art Collection, Sheet3

Ready   100%

Grouping Date Fields

The layout of this PivotTable is not what Mary would like. Mary wants a count of acquisitions by year, not by date. You can group a range of dates into periods such as months, quarters, or years using the Group Fields command. Mary wants to group the Date Acquired dates by year.

To group Date Acquired by year:

▶ **1.** Click any date value in the Row Labels column of the PivotTable, and then, in the Group group on the PivotTable Tools Options tab, click the **Group Field** button. The Grouping dialog box opens.

▶ **2.** Click **Months** to deselect it, and then click **Years** to select it. See Figure 5-48.

Grouping dialog box | **Figure 5-48**

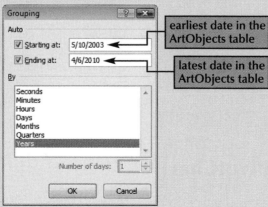

Grouping

Auto
☑ Starting at: 5/10/2003 ← earliest date in the ArtObjects table
☑ Ending at: 4/6/2010 ← latest date in the ArtObjects table

By
- Seconds
- Minutes
- Hours
- Days
- Months
- Quarters
- Years

Number of days: 1

OK   Cancel

> **3.** Click the **OK** button. The PivotTable report is grouped by year, displaying the number of art acquisitions in each year. See Figure 5-49.

Figure 5-49 **PivotTable report of annual acquisitions**

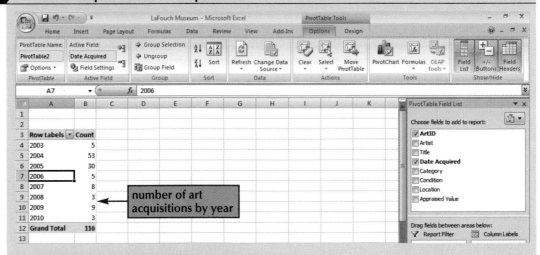

> **4.** Rename the worksheet as **Acquired By Year**.

InSight | **Creating Different Types of PivotTable Reports**

This tutorial only touched the surface of the variety of PivotTable reports you can create. Here are a few more examples:

- Most PivotTable summaries are based on numeric data, but PivotTables can also contain only nonnumeric data. You cannot add nonnumeric data, so you must use the COUNT function to produce summaries. For example, you could count the number of art objects by Location and Category.
- You can use PivotTables to combine items into groups. Items that appear as row labels or column labels can be grouped. If items are numbers or dates, they can be grouped automatically using the Grouping dialog box or manually using the Ctrl key to select items in a group and choosing Group from the shortcut menu. For example, you can manually combine the Courtyard and Garden locations into an Outdoor group and combine the three pavilion locations into an Indoor group and then provide counts or total appraised values by these groups within the PivotTable. Being able to combine categories that aren't part of your original data with the grouping feature gives you flexibility to summarize your PivotTables in a way that meets your analysis requirements.
- You can develop PivotTables using the value filter, which allows you to filter one of your row or column fields in the PivotTable based on numbers that appear in the Values area of the PivotTable. For example, a PivotTable can show the total value of art objects for each artist and be filtered to display only artists whose total is greater than $25,000. Filtering provides you with a more precise way to view the PivotTable results by enabling you to include or remove data from the report.

Creating a PivotChart

Now that the PivotTable is complete, Mary asks you to add a PivotChart next to the PivotTable. A **PivotChart** is a graphical representation of the data in a PivotTable. A

PivotChart allows you to interactively add, remove, filter, and refresh data fields in the PivotChart similar to working with a PivotTable. PivotCharts can have all the same formatting as other charts, including layouts and styles. You can move and resize chart elements, or change formatting of individual data points.

Mary asks you to prepare a clustered column chart next to the new PivotTable report. You can create a PivotChart from the PivotTable.

To create the PivotChart:

▶ **1.** Click any cell in the PivotTable, and then, in the Tools group on the PivotTable Tools Options tab, click the **PivotChart** button. The Insert Chart dialog box opens.

▶ **2.** Click the **Clustered Column** chart (the first chart in the first row of the Column section), if necessary, and then click the **OK** button. A PivotChart appears next to the PivotTable along with the PivotChart Filter Pane, which you use to filter the data shown in the PivotChart.

▶ **3.** Close the PivotTable Field List, and then move the PivotChart Filter Pane to the right of the PivotChart.

Because the PivotChart has only one series, you do not need a legend.

▶ **4.** In the PivotChart, click the **legend** to select it, and then press the **Delete** key. The legend is removed from the PivotChart.

Next, you'll modify the chart title.

▶ **5.** Right-click the **chart title**, and then click **Edit Text**. The insertion point appears in the title so you can edit it.

▶ **6.** Select the title, type **Number Acquired By Year** as the new title, and then click the **chart area** to deselect the title.

▶ **7.** Move the PivotChart so its upper-left corner is in cell D3. The PivotChart is aligned with the PivotTable. See Figure 5-50.

Tip

You can also create a Pivot-Chart based directly on the Excel table, in which case both a PivotTable and a PivotChart are created.

PivotChart added to the PivotTable report | **Figure 5-50**

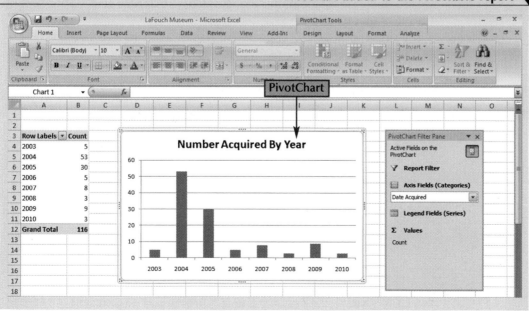

The PivotChart Tools contextual tabs enable you to manipulate and format the selected PivotChart the same way as an ordinary chart. A PivotChart and its associated PivotTable are linked. When you modify one, the other also changes. Mary asks you to display only art acquisitions after 2004.

To filter items in the PivotChart:

▶ **1.** Make sure the PivotChart is selected, and then, in the PivotChart Filter Pane, click the **Axis Fields (Categories) filter arrow**. The filter menu opens.

▶ **2.** Click the **<5/10/2003**, **2003**, and **2004** check boxes to remove the check marks.

▶ **3.** Click the **OK** button. The PivotChart displays only art objects acquired after 2004. The PivotTable is also filtered to display the same results.

You have completed your work on the LaFouch Museum workbook.

▶ **4.** Save your changes to the workbook, and then close it.

Mary is pleased with the PivotTable and PivotChart. Both show the number of art objects acquired by year, which will be important information for her upcoming board meeting.

Review | **Session 5.3 Quick Check**

---

1. What is the default summary function for numeric data in a PivotTable?

2. When creating a PivotTable, what do you use to lay out the fields in the PivotTable report?

3. After you update data in an Excel table, what must you do to a PivotTable based on that table?

4. Fields such as region, state, and country are most likely to appear as _____ in a PivotTable.

5. Fields such as revenue, costs, and profits are most likely to appear as _____ in a PivotTable.

6. A list of college students includes a code to indicate the student's gender (male or female) and a field to identify the student's major. Which tool, Filter or PivotTable, would you use to (a) create a list of all females majoring in history, and (b) count the number of males and females in each major?

In this tutorial, you learned how to create an Excel table, enter, edit, and delete data in the table, and then sort data. You filtered the Excel table to display only data that meets certain criteria. You used the Total row to display detailed rows along with summary results for a filtered table. You inserted subtotals into a structured range of data. Finally, you summarized a table using a PivotTable and PivotChart.

Key Terms

ascending order	field	record
category field	field name	refresh
clear	filter	report filter
column header	freeze	secondary sort field
criteria filter	header row	sort
custom list	PivotChart	sort field
data definition table	PivotTable	Total row
descending order	primary sort field	value field

Practice	Review Assignments

Practice the skills you learned in the tutorial using the same case scenario.

Data File needed for the Review Assignments: Art.xlsx

Mary has another art object that needs to be entered in the art objects list. To further understand the information in the workbook, she wants to sort the data by date acquired. She wants to filter data to retrieve all art with the word *cowboy* in the title. She wants to use a PivotTable to determine the average value of artwork for each artist. Mary has asked you to gather the information she needs for further analysis of the museum's art objects.

Complete the following:

1. Open the **Art** workbook located in the Tutorial.05\Review folder included with your Data Files, and then save the workbook as **Art Museum** in the same folder.
2. In the Documentation sheet, enter your name and the date, and then switch to the Art Collection worksheet.
3. Create an Excel table for the art objects data. Change the table style to Medium 25.
4. Rename the Excel table as **Collection**.
5. Sort the art objects by Date Acquired to display the newest objects first. Make a copy of the Art Collection worksheet, rename the copied worksheet as **Q5** (for "Question 5"), and then return to the Art Collection worksheet. (*Hint*: Ctrl + drag the sheet tab to make a copy of the worksheet.)
6. Sort art objects by Category (Z to A), Location (A to Z), Artist (A to Z) in ascending order, and by Date Acquired (showing the oldest first). Make a copy of the Art Collection worksheet, rename the copied worksheet as **Q6** (for "Question 6"), and then return to the Art Collection worksheet.
7. Filter the Collection table to produce a list of art objects with the word *Cowboy* in the title, and then redisplay all the art objects. Make a copy of the Art Collection worksheet, rename the copied worksheet as **Q7**, and then return to the Art Collection worksheet. Display all records.
8. Use the Total row to calculate the average value of objects acquired between 2006 and 2010. Change the label in the Total row from Total to **Average**. Make a copy of the Art Collection worksheet, rename the copied worksheet as **Q8**, and then return to the Art Collection worksheet. Remove the Total row.
9. Use the Subtotal command to count how many art objects there are in each Location, displaying the count in the ArtID column. Make a copy of the Art Collection worksheet, rename the copied worksheet as **Q9**, and then return to the Art Collection worksheet. Remove the subtotals.
10. Create a PivotTable to show the average value of art objects by artist. Format the Value column.
11. Sort the PivotTable showing the artist with highest average value first.
12. Rename the PivotTable sheet as **Q10-15 Artist Summary**.
13. Modify the PivotTable to include Category as a Report filter field, and then filter the report so the average by Artist is based on Paintings.
14. Insert a new record in the Collection Excel table, and then enter the following data:
    ArtID #: **118**   Category: **Painting**
    Artist: **Abonti**   Condition: **Excellent**
    Title: **Trouble Ahead**   Location: **Garden**
    Date Acquired: **4/15/2010**   Appraised Value: **1200**
15. Refresh the PivotTable.
16. Save and close the workbook. Submit the finished workbook to your instructor, either in printed or electronic form, as requested.

| Apply | | Case Problem 1 |

Use the skills you learned to analyze and summarize donation data for a zoo.

Data File needed for this Case Problem: Pledges.xlsx

Hewart Zoo   Marvis Chennard is the director of fund-raising for the Hewart Zoo. The zoo relies on donations to fund operations, temporary exhibits, and special programs. Marvis created an Excel table to track information about donors and their pledges. Marvis asks you to analyze the data in the list.

Complete the following:

1. Open the **Pledges** workbook located in the Tutorial.05\Case1 folder included with your Data Files, and then save the workbook as **Zoo Pledges** in the same folder.

2. In the Documentation worksheet, enter the date and your name, and then switch to the Pledges worksheet.

3. Create an Excel table, and then rename the table as **PledgeData**.

4. Sort the data in ascending order by Donor Type and Fund Name, and in descending order by Amt Pledged (largest first). Make a copy of the Pledges worksheet, rename the copied worksheet as **Q4** (for "Question 4"), and then return to the Pledges worksheet. (*Hint*: Ctrl + drag the sheet tab to make a copy of the worksheet.)

5. Filter the data to display Individual donors whose Amt Owed is over zero. Sort the filtered data by Pledge Date, with the oldest date displayed first. Make a copy of the Pledges worksheet, rename the copied worksheet as **Q5** (for "Question 5"), and then return to the Pledges worksheet. Display all records.

6. Filter the data to display records that have a Pledge Date in October through December. Sort the filtered data by Amt Pledged (largest first). Make a copy of the Pledges worksheet, rename the copied worksheet as **Q6**, and then return to the Pledges worksheet. Display all records.

7. Filter the data to display only records with Amt Received greater than zero. Then use the Subtotal command (SUM) to display the total Amt Received by Fund Name. Make a copy of the Pledges worksheet, rename the copied worksheet as **Q7**, and then return to the Pledges worksheet. Remove the subtotals.

8. Create a PivotTable that displays the total and average Amt Owed by each Donor Type and Fund Name. Place the PivotTable in a new worksheet. Select an appropriate report layout and format, and rename the worksheet with a descriptive name.

9. Using Figure 5-51 as a guide, create a PivotTable on a new worksheet that shows the Amt Pledged by month and Fund Name. Format the PivotTable appropriately, and then rename the worksheet with a descriptive name. Print the PivotTable report.

Figure 5-51

	A	B	C	D	E	F
1						
2						
3	Sum of Amt Pledged	Column Labels				
4	Row Labels	Bird Sanctuary	General Support	Kids Zoo	ZooMobile	Grand Total
5	Jan		$1,000	$100		$1,100
6	Feb			$1,100	$150	$1,250
7	Mar			$100	$1,000	$1,100
8	Apr	$75	$500	$425		$1,000
9	Jun			$1,000	$50	$1,050
10	Jul	$1,000	$1,000			$2,000
11	Sep	$100	$25	$250	$150	$525
12	Oct	$200	$200			$400
13	Nov		$250			$250
14	Dec			$150	$750	$900
15	Grand Total	$1,375	$2,975	$3,125	$2,100	$9,575

10. Add the following data to the Pledge table, and then update the PivotTable you created in Step 9.

Pledge #	Donor Name	Donor Type	Fund Name	Pledge Date	Amt Pledged
2129	Elliot Anderson	Individual	Kids Zoo	12/31/2010	1000

11. Save and close the workbook. Submit the finished workbook to your instructor, either in printed or electronic form, as requested.

Apply		Case Problem 2

Use the skills you learned to analyze and summarize expenditure data for a farm.

Data File needed for this Case Problem: Ring.xlsx

Ring Family Farm Fred and Alesia Ring own a small family farm just outside Abita Springs, Louisiana. The couple wants to better organize their financial records for their accountant. They created an Excel workbook to record the various expenses associated with farming. Typical expenses include those associated with hay production (seed, fertilizer, and irrigation), animal husbandry, fence maintenance, veterinary services, self-administered medicines, vehicles and maintenance, and so forth. The workbook includes categories associated with these expenses as well as an area to record how much is spent, the purpose of the expenditure, the check number, and the date paid.

Complete the following:

1. Open the **Ring** workbook located in the Tutorial.05\Case2 folder included with your Data Files, and then save the workbook as **Ring Farm** in the same folder.
2. Insert a new worksheet. Enter the company name, your name, the date, and a purpose statement in the worksheet, and then rename the worksheet as **Documentation**.
3. Create an Excel table in the Expenditures worksheet, and then rename the table as **Checkbook**.
4. Replace the Category code Farm in each record with the more descriptive Category code **Payroll**.
5. Sort the Checkbook table in ascending order by Category, then by Description, and then by Date Paid (newest first). Make a copy of the Expenditures worksheet, rename the copied worksheet as **Q5** (for "Question 5"), and then return to the Expenditures worksheet. (*Hint*: Ctrl + drag the sheet tab to make a copy of the worksheet.)
6. Filter the Checkbook table to display all expenditures for Equipment and Repairs in December, and then sort by Amount (smallest first). Make a copy of the Expenditures worksheet, rename the copied worksheet as **Q6** (for "Question 6"), and then return to the Expenditures worksheet. Display all records.
7. Filter the Checkbook table to display all checks that include the word **vet** in the description. Include the total Amount at the bottom of the table. Make a copy of the Expenditures worksheet, rename the copied worksheet as **Q7**, and then return to the Expenditures worksheet. Remove the filter and totals.
8. Use conditional formatting to apply a Yellow Fill with Dark Yellow text to all Outstanding checks. (*Hint:* "Yes" appears in the Outstanding column.) Make a copy of the Expenditures worksheet, rename the copied worksheet as **Q8**, and then return to the Expenditures worksheet.
9. Use the Subtotal command to display total Amount for each Category, displaying the subtotal in the Amount column. Make a copy of the Expenditures worksheet, rename the copied worksheet as **Q9**, and then return to the Expenditures worksheet. Remove all subtotals.

10. Create a PivotTable that summarizes expenditures by Category and month. Place the PivotTable in a new worksheet. Format the PivotTable appropriately, choose a layout, and then rename the worksheet with a descriptive name.

11. Insert a PivotChart with the Clustered Column chart type on the same sheet as the PivotTable.

⊕ EXPLORE 12. Create the PivotTable shown in Figure 5-52 in a new worksheet. Sort the Amount column in descending order. (*Hint:* Check the Show values as tab in the Value Field Setting dialog box to calculate percent of total.)

Figure 5-52

	A	B	C
1			
2			
3		**Values**	
4	Row Labels ▾	Sum of Amount	Pct of Total
5	Equipment	$6,575.00	37.0%
6	Payroll	$2,638.27	14.9%
7	Vet	$2,320.57	13.1%
8	Repairs	$2,003.44	11.3%
9	Feed	$2,002.24	11.3%
10	Medicine	$1,249.32	7.0%
11	Administration	$958.09	5.4%
12	Grand Total	$17,746.93	100.0%

13. Save and close the workbook. Submit the finished workbook to your instructor, either in printed or electronic form, as requested.

Apply | Case Problem 3

Use the skills you learned to analyze and summarize loan data for a bank.

Data File needed for this Case Problem: CustLoans.xlsx

High Desert Bank Eleanor Chimayo, loan manager for High Desert Bank, is getting ready for the bank's quarterly meeting. Eleanor is expected to present data on the status of different types of loans within three New Mexican cities. Eleanor asks you to summarize and analyze the data for her presentation.

Complete the following:

1. Open the **CustLoans** workbook located in the Tutorial.05\Case3 folder included with your Data Files, and then save the workbook as **High Desert Bank** in the same folder.

2. In the Documentation sheet, enter the date and your name.

3. In the Loans worksheet, create an Excel table, and then rename the table as **LoanData**.

4. Format the Amount and Interest Rate fields so it is clear that these fields contain dollars and percentages.

5. Change the table style to one of your choice.

⊕ EXPLORE 6. To the right of the Type column, insert a new column named **Monthly Payment**. Use the PMT function to calculate the monthly payment for each loan. Adjust the formula so each loan is displayed as a positive amount and improve the formatting.

7. Sort the loan data in ascending order by Type, within Type by City, and within City by Last Name.

8. Use conditional formatting to display loans above average using a format that highlights these loans. Make a copy of the Loans worksheet, rename the copied worksheet as **Q3–8**, for ("Question 3–8"), and then return to the Loans worksheet. (*Hint:* Ctrl + drag the sheet tab to make a copy of the worksheet.)

9. Filter the LoanData table to display loans made during March and April of 2010. Include the number of loans, total amount of loans, and average monthly payment for the filtered data at the bottom of the table. Make a copy of the Loans worksheet, rename the copied worksheet as **Q9**, for ("Question 9"), and then return to the Loans worksheet. Then remove the total loans and show all records.

10. Sort the loans in ascending order by City; then by Type of loan; and then by Amount of loan (largest loan first). Insert subtotals (Average) for loan Amount and Monthly Payment by City. Include your name in a custom footer. Make a copy of the Loans worksheet, rename the copied worksheet as **Q10**, and then return to the Loans worksheet. Remove the subtotals.

11. Create a PivotTable that displays the number (Count) and average loan by Type and City. Place the PivotTable in a new worksheet. Remove the Other loan type from the PivotTable. Format the PivotTable appropriately. Rename the PivotTable worksheet as **Q11 Loans-Type And City**.

⊕ EXPLORE 12. Create a second PivotTable, shown in Figure 5-53, in a new worksheet. The PivotTable shows three calculations: Number of Loans, total loans (Loan Amount), and total monthly payments (Payment) categorized by Type of loan. Insert a report filter based on Loan Date, grouped so you can filter by month. Filter the PivotTable report for March and April. Rename the PivotTable worksheet as **Q12 Loans-Type and Loan Date**.

Figure 5-53

	A	B	C	D
1	Loan Date	(Multiple Items) ▼		
2				
3		Number of Loans	Loan Amount	Payment
4	Car	5	$157,000	$3,681.77
5	Mortgage	5	$929,000	$7,890.77
6	Other	2	$35,000	$860.49
7	Grand Total	12	$1,121,000	$12,433.03

13. Save and close the workbook. Submit the finished workbook to your instructor, either in printed or electronic form, as requested.

Challenge | Case Problem 4

Explore how to summarize data from a department store by creating more complex subtotals, PivotTables, and PivotCharts.

Data File needed for this Case Problem: Bowls.xlsx

Bowls Department Stores   Bowls Department Stores, with corporate headquarters in Portland, Oregon, operates department stores in midsize towns in selected northwestern areas. Although the organization maintains a large computer system for its accounting operations, the sales department often downloads data to complete additional analysis of its operations. Daniel Partner, analyst for the corporate sales department, regularly downloads data by territories and product areas including automotive, electronics, garden centers, and sporting goods. He often presents reports based on his analysis of sales by product areas and territory, best and worst performing product group-periods, and total sales for certain regions and product groups. He asks you to help him compile and summarize the data.

Complete the following:

1. Open the **Bowls** workbook located in the Tutorial.05\Case4 folder included with your Data Files, and then save the workbook as **Bowls Stores** in the same folder.

2. In the Documentation sheet, enter the date and your name and an appropriate purpose statement.

3. In the SalesData worksheet, create an Excel table. Rename the table as **ProductSales**. Format the Sales column in the Currency number format with no decimal places.

4. Sort the table in ascending order by Territories, then by Product Group, then by Year, and then by Month. Month should be sorted in Jan, Feb, Mar, ... order, not alphabetically. Make a copy of the SalesData worksheet, rename the copied worksheet as **Q4**, for ("Question 4"), and then return to the SalesData worksheet. (*Hint:* Ctrl + drag the sheet tab to make a copy of the worksheet.)

⊕ EXPLORE 5. Display records for Automotive and Electronic products in 2010, excluding sales in Vancouver. Sort this data by Sales in descending order. Add a Total row and calculate the average sales for the filtered data. Change the label in the Total row to **Average**. Insert a new worksheet and copy this filtered data to the new worksheet. Split the worksheet into two panes. The top pane displays all the rows but the last row on your screen. The bottom pane displays the Total row. (*Hint:* Click the Split button in the Window group on the View tab.) Rename the new worksheet as **Q5 Auto Electronic**. Return to the SalesData worksheet, remove the Total row, and display all the records.

⊕ EXPLORE 6. Display subtotals for sales (Sum) by Year, Month (Jan, Feb, Mar, ...), and Territory. Make a copy of the SalesData worksheet, rename the copied worksheet as **Q6**, for ("Question 6"), and then return to the SalesData worksheet. Remove the subtotals.

7. Display the five lowest periods based on sales. Assume each row represents a period. Sort the Sales so lowest sales appears first. Insert a new worksheet and copy this filtered data to the new worksheet. Rename the new worksheet as **Q7 Lowest Periods**. Return to the SalesData worksheet, and then display all the records.

⊕ EXPLORE 8. Create a PivotTable similar to the one shown in Figure 5-54, displaying percentage of sales by Product Group, Territories, and Year. Omit the columnar grand totals. Use a tabular layout, inserting subtotals at the bottom of each Product Group and excluding the Sporting product group. Rename the worksheet as **Q8 Percent of Sales**.

Figure 5-54

	A	B	C	D
1				
2				
3	Pct of Sales		Year	
4	Product Group	Territories	2009	2010
5	⊟Automotive	Oregon	10.05%	8.85%
6		Vancouver	7.32%	9.71%
7		Washington	6.88%	9.94%
8	Automotive Total		24.25%	28.50%
9	⊟Electronics	Oregon	7.53%	8.67%
10		Vancouver	7.61%	6.88%
11		Washington	8.05%	9.22%
12	Electronics Total		23.20%	24.78%
13	⊟Gardening	Oregon	8.19%	6.85%
14		Vancouver	8.46%	5.89%
15		Washington	9.77%	9.91%
16	Gardening Total		26.42%	22.66%
17	⊟Houseware	Oregon	6.86%	5.01%
18		Vancouver	8.20%	7.67%
19		Washington	11.07%	11.39%
20	Houseware Total		26.14%	24.07%
21	Grand Total		100.00%	100.00%

EXPLORE 9. Using Figure 5-55 as a guide, create a PivotChart of total Sales By Product Group. Create a second PivotChart of total Sales By Territory in the same worksheet. Include only the PivotCharts in the worksheet. Rename the worksheet as **Q9 PivotCharts**.

Figure 5-55

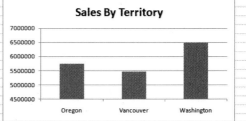

10. Using Figure 5-56 as a guide, create a PivotTable to show four calculations: minimum, maximum, average, and total Sales categorized by Territories and Product Group and filtered by Year. Display the results for 2010. Rename the worksheet as **Q10 Statistical Summary**.

Figure 5-56

	A	B	C	D	E	F
1	Year	2010				
2						
3			**Values**			
4	Territories	Product Group	Average	Sum	Minimum	Maximum
5	⊟Oregon	Automotive	$ 50,196	$ 602,354	$ 1,825	$ 98,358
6		Electronics	$ 49,175	$ 590,099	$ 7,164	$ 95,985
7		Gardening	$ 38,859	$ 466,305	$ 5,396	$ 95,795
8		Houseware	$ 28,428	$ 341,139	$ 3,374	$ 64,982
9		Sporting	$ 70,243	$ 842,910	$ 26,643	$ 91,786
10	Oregon Total		$ 47,380	$2,842,807	$ 1,825	$ 98,358
11	⊟Vancouver	Automotive	$ 55,074	$ 660,886	$ 865	$ 99,526
12		Electronics	$ 39,033	$ 468,391	$ 2,141	$ 98,044
13		Gardening	$ 33,419	$ 401,027	$ 467	$ 97,793
14		Houseware	$ 43,473	$ 521,678	$ 4,046	$ 80,035
15		Sporting	$ 60,199	$ 722,385	$ 29,824	$ 94,129
16	Vancouver Total		$ 46,239	$2,774,367	$ 467	$ 99,526
17	⊟Washington	Automotive	$ 56,359	$ 676,304	$ 3,893	$ 99,258
18		Electronics	$ 52,307	$ 627,680	$ 15,485	$ 84,624
19		Gardening	$ 56,206	$ 674,471	$ 5,507	$ 94,166
20		Houseware	$ 64,579	$ 774,942	$ 27,164	$ 94,725
21		Sporting	$ 63,189	$ 758,272	$ 17,919	$ 90,879
22	Washington Total		$ 58,528	$3,511,669	$ 3,893	$ 99,258
23	Grand Total		$ 50,716	$9,128,843	$ 467	$ 99,526

11. Save and close the workbook. Submit the finished workbook to your instructor, either in printed or electronic form, as requested.

Research | Internet Assignments

Use the Internet to find and work with data related to the topics presented in this tutorial.

The purpose of the Internet Assignments is to challenge you to find information on the Internet that you can use to work effectively with this software. The actual assignments are updated and maintained on the Course Technology Web site. Log on to the Internet and use your Web browser to go to the Student Online Companion for New Perspectives Office 2007 at **www.course.com/np/office2007**. Then navigate to the Internet Assignments for this tutorial.

Assess | SAM Assessment and Training

If you have a SAM user profile, you may have access to hands-on instruction, practice, and assessment of the skills covered in this tutorial. Log in to your SAM account (**http://sam2007.course.com**) to launch any assigned training activities or exams that relate to the skills covered in this tutorial.

Review | Quick Check Answers

Session 5.1

1. To keep, or freeze, rows and columns so that they don't scroll out of view as you move around the worksheet. Freezing the rows and columns that contain headings makes understanding the data in each record easier.
2. Filter arrows appear in the column headers, a table style format is applied to the table, and the Table Tools Design contextual tab appears on the Ribbon.
3. sort fields
4. Sort by year of graduation and then by last name.
5. Enter the data for the new record in the row immediately following the last row of data in the table.
6. Create a custom list.
7. descending (Newest to Oldest)

Session 5.2

1. You must first sort the data for which you want to calculate subtotals, because subtotals are inserted whenever the value in the specified field changes.
2. Filter the table to show only the finance department, and then use the AVERAGE function in the Total row.
3. Click the Major filter arrow, and then check only the Accounting and Finance check boxes. Click the GPA filter arrow, point to Number Filters, click Greater Than, and then enter the value 3.0 in the Greater Than dialog box to specify the condition for a GPA greater than 3.0.

4. Click the Level Outline buttons.
5. True
6. Multiselect
7. Click the Gender filter arrow, and check only the Female check box. Insert the Total row, click the arrow that appears to the right of the total for the Salary column, and then click Average in the list of functions.

Session 5.3

1. SUM
2. PivotTable Field List box
3. refresh the PivotTable
4. rows labels, column labels, or report filters
5. values
6. (a) Filter; (b) PivotTable

Ending Data Files

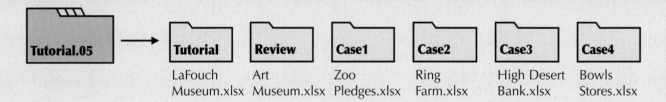

Tutorial.05 →

Tutorial	Review	Case1	Case2	Case3	Case4
LaFouch Museum.xlsx	Art Museum.xlsx	Zoo Pledges.xlsx	Ring Farm.xlsx	High Desert Bank.xlsx	Bowls Stores.xlsx

Objectives

Session 6.1
- Format and edit multiple worksheets at once
- Create cell references to other worksheets
- Consolidate information from multiple worksheets using 3-D references
- Create and print a worksheet group

Session 6.2
- Create a link to data in another workbook
- Create a workbook reference
- Learn how to edit links
- Create and use an Excel workspace

Session 6.3
- Insert a hyperlink in a cell
- Create a custom template
- Create a Web page

Managing Multiple Worksheets and Workbooks

Summarizing Ticket Sales

Case | Global Travel

Global Travel, a member-owned organization, provides a variety of services ranging from travel assistance to insurance programs to discounted vacation packages. Global Travel also offers special services and discounts to one-time entertainment events. Global Travel purchases tickets to selected theme and amusement parks to resell to its members, particularly those with families. Each local office of Global Travel markets and sells these tickets to its members. Theme and amusement park sales account for more than 10 percent of Global Travel's sales. Rhohit Gupta, accountant for Global Travel in New Mexico, is responsible for tracking ticket sales within the state and preparing an analysis for the corporate controller. Rhohit asks you to create a summary report that shows the quarterly sales in New Mexico for the past year. He already entered each quarter's values in separate worksheets, but wants you to "roll up" all the information in the four quarterly worksheets into one summary worksheet.

Rhohit reports to Alvin Alton, controller for Global Travel. Alvin already received workbooks from Colorado and Utah. After Alvin receives the New Mexico workbook, he will create a workbook that summarizes the annual totals from each state workbook in the Southwest region. He asks for your help with this.

Starting Data Files

Tutorial.06 →

Tutorial
Colorado.xlsx
NM.xlsx
Sales 2010.docx
TravelTotals.xlsx
Utah.xlsx

Review
Idaho.xlsx
NW Totals 2010.xlsx
NW Travel.xltx
OR.xlsx
Washington.xlsx

Case1
Cafe.xlsx

Case2
Carson.xlsx
Reno.xlsx
Vegas.xlsx

Case3
InBurger.xlsx

Case4
Europe.xlsx
North America.xlsx
Pluto Template.xltx
South America.xlsx

Session 6.1

Using Multiple Worksheets

Workbook data is often placed in several worksheets. Using multiple worksheets makes it easier to group and summarize data. For example, a company such as Global Travel with branches in different geographic regions can place sales information for each region in separate worksheets. Rather than scrolling through one large and complex worksheet that contains data for all regions, users can access sales information for a specific region simply by clicking a sheet tab in the workbook.

Multiple worksheets enable you to place summarized data first. Managers interested only in an overall picture can view the first worksheet of summary data without looking at the details available in the other worksheets. Others, of course, might want to view the supporting data in the individual worksheets that follow the summary worksheet. In the case of Global Travel, Rhohit used separate worksheets to summarize the number of tickets sold and sales in dollars for the New Mexico branch offices for each quarter of the 2010 fiscal year. You will open Rhohit's workbook and review the current information.

To open and review the Global Travel workbook:

1. Open the **NM** workbook located in the **Tutorial.06\Tutorial** folder included with your Data Files, and then save the workbook as **New Mexico** in the same folder.

2. In the **Documentation** worksheet, enter your name and the current date.

3. Switch to the **Quarter 1** worksheet, and then view the number of tickets sold and sales for the first quarter of the year. See Figure 6-1.

| Figure 6-1 | Quarter 1 worksheet for Global Travel—New Mexico |

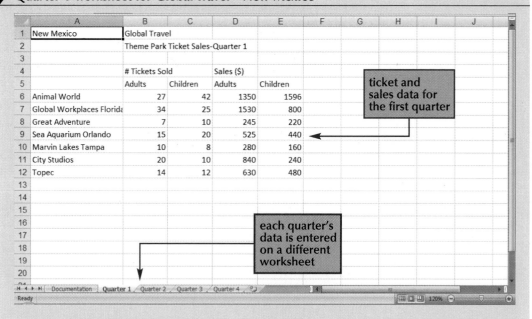

4. Review the **Quarter 2**, **Quarter 3**, and **Quarter 4** worksheets. The layout for all four worksheets is identical.

Grouping Worksheets

Rhohit didn't enter any formulas in the workbook. You need to enter formulas to calculate the total number of tickets and sales for each column (B through E) in all four worksheets. Rather than retyping the formulas in each worksheet, you can enter them all at once by creating a worksheet group. A **worksheet group** is a collection of two or more selected worksheets. When worksheets are grouped, everything you do to the active worksheet also affects the other worksheets in the group. For example, you can:

Tip

If a worksheet group includes all the worksheets in a workbook, you can edit only the active worksheet.

- Enter data and formulas in cells in one worksheet to enter the data and formulas in the same cells in all the worksheets in the group.
- Apply formatting to the active worksheet to format all the worksheets in the group, including changing row heights or column widths and applying conditional formatting.
- Edit data or formulas in one worksheet to edit the data and formulas in the same cells in all the worksheets in the group. Commands such as insert rows and columns, delete rows and columns, and find and replace can also be used with a worksheet group.
- Set the page layout options in one worksheet to apply the settings to all the worksheets in the group, such as orientation, scaling to fit, and inserting headers and footers.
- Apply view options such as zooming, showing and hiding worksheets, and so forth to all worksheets in the group.
- Print all the worksheets in the worksheet group at the same time.

Worksheet groups save you time because you can perform an action once, yet affect multiple worksheets. A worksheet group, like a range, can contain adjacent or nonadjacent worksheets.

Grouping and Ungrouping Worksheets | Reference Window

- To select an adjacent group, click the sheet tab of the first worksheet in the group, press and hold the Shift key, and then click the sheet tab of the last worksheet in the group.
- To select a nonadjacent group, click the sheet tab of one worksheet in the group, press and hold the Ctrl key, and then click the sheet tabs of the remaining worksheets in the group.
- To ungroup the worksheets, click the sheet tab of a worksheet not in the group (or right-click the sheet tab of one worksheet in the group, and then click Ungroup Sheets on the shortcut menu).

Entering Formulas in a Worksheet Group

In the travel workbook, you'll select an adjacent range of worksheets: the Quarter 1 worksheet through the Quarter 4 worksheet.

To group the quarterly worksheets:

▶ 1. Click the **Quarter 1** sheet tab to make the worksheet active. This is the first worksheet you want to include in the group.

▶ 2. Press and hold the **Shift** key, and then click the **Quarter 4** sheet tab. This is the last worksheet you want to include in the group.

▶ 3. Release the **Shift** key. The sheet tabs for Quarter 1 through Quarter 4 are white, indicating they are all selected. The text *[Group]* appears in the title bar to remind you that a worksheet group is selected in the workbook. See Figure 6-2.

Tip

If you cannot see the sheet tab of a worksheet you want to include in a group, use the sheet navigation controls to display it.

Figure 6-2 **Grouped worksheets**

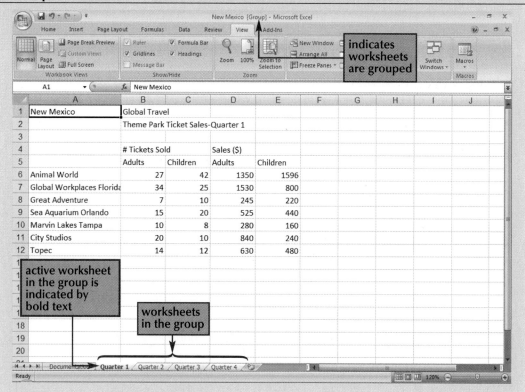

With the quarterly sheets grouped, you can enter the formulas to calculate the total number of tickets sold and total sales. When you enter a formula in the active worksheet (in this case, the Quarter 1 worksheet), the formula is entered in the same cells in all the worksheets in the group. The grouped worksheets must have the exact same organization and layout (rows and columns) for this to work. Otherwise, any formulas you enter in the active sheet will be incorrect in the other worksheets in the group and could overwrite existing data.

To enter the same formulas in all the worksheets in the group:

1. Click cell **B13**. You want to enter the formula in cell B13 in each of the four grouped worksheets.

2. In the Editing group on the Home tab, click the **Sum** button Σ, and then press the **Enter** key. The formula =SUM(B6:B12) is entered in the cell and adds the total number of adult tickets sold in the quarter, which is 127.

   You will copy the formula to add the total number of children's tickets sold, the total adult ticket sales, and the total children's ticket sales.

3. Copy the formula in cell B13 to the range **C13:E13**.

4. In cell A13, enter **Totals**, and then, in the Alignment group on the Home tab, click the **Increase Indent** button. The label shifts to the right.

   The formulas and label you entered in the Quarter 1 worksheet were entered in the Quarter 2, 3, and 4 worksheets at the same time.

5. Click the **Quarter 2** sheet tab, and then click cell **B13**. The value 174 appears in the cell and the formula =SUM(B6:B12), which adds the number of adult tickets sold in Quarter 2, appears in the formula bar.

6. Click the **Quarter 4** sheet tab, and then click cell **B13**. The value 177 appears in the cell, and the same formula used in cell B13 in the Quarter 1 and Quarter 2 worksheets appears in the formula bar. See Figure 6-3.

Formulas entered in all worksheets in the group | Figure 6-3

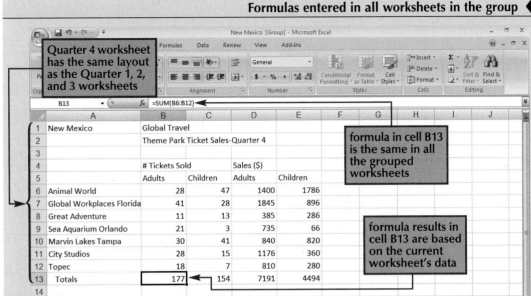

7. Click the **Quarter 1** sheet tab to redisplay the Quarter 1 results.

Editing Grouped Worksheets | InSight

When you enter, edit, or format cells in a worksheet group, the changes you make to one worksheet are automatically applied to the other worksheets in the group. For example, if you delete a value from one cell, the value in that cell in all the worksheets in the group is also deleted. Be cautious when editing the contents of a worksheet when it is part of a group. Also, remember to ungroup the worksheet group after you finish entering data, formulas, and formatting. Otherwise, changes you intend to make to a cell or range in one worksheet will be made to all the worksheets in the worksheet group, potentially producing incorrect results.

Formatting a Worksheet Group

Now that you've applied a common set of formulas to the quarterly worksheets, you can format them. As with inserting formulas and text, any formatting changes you make to a single sheet in a group are applied to all sheets.

To apply the same formatting to all the worksheets in the group:

1. Bold the text in the nonadjacent range **A1:B2;A6:A13;B4:E5**.

2. Increase the width of column A to **24**.

3. Merge and center each of the ranges **B1:E1**, **B2:E2**, **B4:C4**, and **D4:E4**.

4. Center the text in the range **B5:E5**.

5. Apply the **Comma Style** number format with no decimal places to the range B6:C13. No change is visible because all the numbers are less than 1000.

6. Apply the **Accounting** number format with no decimal places to the range D6:E13 so the values appear with a dollar sign and no decimal places.

7. Add a bottom border to the ranges **B5:E5** and **B12:E12**.

8. Click cell **A1**. All the worksheets in the group are formatted. See Figure 6-4.

Figure 6-4 | **Formatting applied to the worksheet group**

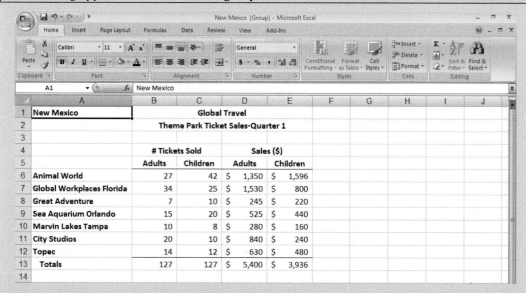

9. Click each sheet tab in the worksheet group to view the formatting changes, and then click the **Quarter 1** sheet tab.

Ungrouping Worksheets

You can ungroup the quarterly worksheets so you can work in each worksheet separately. When you ungroup the worksheets, each worksheet functions independently again. If you forget to ungroup the worksheets, any changes you make in one worksheet will be applied to all the worksheets in the group.

To ungroup the quarterly worksheets:

1. Click the **Documentation** sheet tab. The worksheets are ungrouped and the text *[Group]* is removed from the Excel title bar.

2. Verify that the worksheets are ungrouped and the word *[Group]* no longer appears in the title bar.

Tip

To ungroup worksheets, you can also right-click any sheet tab in the worksheet group, and then click Ungroup Sheets on the shortcut menu.

Copying Worksheets

Next, you'll create the Summary worksheet to provide an overall picture of the data included in the detailed quarterly worksheets. The Summary worksheet needs the same formatting and structure as the quarterly worksheets. To ensure consistency among worksheets, you will copy the Quarter 1 worksheet, and then modify its contents. The fastest way to copy an entire worksheet or worksheet group is to press and hold the Ctrl key as you drag and drop the sheet tab to another location in the workbook. A number in parentheses is added to the copy's sheet tab to distinguish it from the original worksheet. You will use this method to create the Summary worksheet.

Tip

To move a worksheet or worksheet group to another location in the same workbook, select the worksheets and then drag and drop them by the selected sheet tabs.

Copying Worksheets to Another Workbook | Reference Window

- Select the sheet tabs of the worksheets you want to copy.
- Right-click the sheet tabs, and then click Move or Copy on the shortcut menu.
- In the Move or Copy dialog box, select the worksheets you want to move or copy to another workbook.
- Click the To book arrow, and then click an existing workbook name or (new book) to create a new workbook for the worksheets.
- Click the Create a copy check box to insert a check mark if you want to copy the worksheets to another workbook, leaving the originals in the current workbook; uncheck the Create a copy check box to move the worksheets.
- Click the OK button.

You'll copy the Quarter 1 worksheet to the beginning of the workbook, and then modify the new copy to create the Summary worksheet.

To copy the Quarter 1 worksheet and create the Summary worksheet:

▶ **1.** Click the **Quarter 1** sheet tab, press and hold the **Ctrl** key, drag the worksheet to the left of the Documentation sheet, and then release the **Ctrl** key. An identical copy of the Quarter 1 worksheet appears in the new location. The sheet tab shows *Quarter 1 (2)* to indicate that this is the copied sheet.

▶ **2.** Rename the copied worksheet as **Summary**.

▶ **3.** Move the Summary worksheet between the Documentation worksheet and the Quarter 1 worksheet.

You will modify the Summary worksheet.

▶ **4.** In cell A2, enter **2010**. This is the year to which the summary refers.

▶ **5.** In cell B2, enter **Theme Park Ticket Sales-Total**. The new title reflects this worksheet's content.

The range B6:E12 should add the results for the entire year. You need to delete the Quarter 1 sales, which were copied from the Quarter 1 worksheet.

▶ **6.** Select the range **B6:E12**, and then press the **Delete** key. The Quarter 1 sales data is removed, but the formatting remains intact and will apply to the sales data for all four quarters that you will enter shortly.

Referencing Cells and Ranges in Other Worksheets

The Summary worksheet will show the total sales for all four quarters, which are stored in separate worksheets. When you use multiple worksheets to organize related data, you can reference a cell or range in another worksheet in the same workbook. You'll do this to create the sales totals for the entire year.

To reference a cell or range in a different worksheet, you precede the cell or range reference with the worksheet name followed by an exclamation mark. The syntax is as follows:

```
=SheetName!CellRange
```

In this formula, *SheetName* is the worksheet's name as listed on the sheet tab and *CellRange* is the reference for the cell or range in that worksheet. An exclamation mark (!) separates the worksheet reference from the cell or range reference. For example, to enter a formula in the Summary worksheet that references cell D10 in the Quarter1 worksheet, you would enter the following formula:

```
=Quarter1!D10
```

If the worksheet name contains spaces, you must enclose the sheet name in single quotation marks. For example, the reference for the *Quarter 1* worksheet is *'Quarter 1'!D10*. You can use these references to create formulas that reference cells in different locations in different worksheets. For example, to add sales from two worksheets—cell E12 in the Quarter 1 worksheet and cell D12 in the Quarter 2 worksheet—you would enter the following formula:

```
='Quarter 1'!E12+'Quarter 2'!D12
```

Reference Window | **Entering a Formula That References Another Worksheet**

- Click the cell where you want to enter the formula.
- Type = and enter the formula. To insert a reference from another worksheet, click the sheet tab for the worksheet, and then click the cell or select the range you want to reference.
- When the formula is complete, press the Enter key.

Rhohit wants you to enter a formula in cell A2 in each quarterly worksheet that displays the fiscal year from cell A2 in the Summary worksheet. All four quarterly worksheets will use the formula =*Summary!A2* to reference the fiscal year in cell A2 of the Summary sheet. You could type the formula directly in the cell, but it is faster and more accurate to use the point-and-click method to enter references to other worksheets.

To enter a formula in the quarterly worksheets that references the Summary worksheet:

1. Click the **Quarter 1** sheet tab, press and hold the **Shift** key, and then click the **Quarter 4** worksheet. The Quarter 1 through Quarter 4 worksheets are grouped.

2. Click cell **A2**. This is the cell in which you want to enter the formula to display the fiscal year.

3. Type **=** to begin the formula, click the **Summary** sheet tab, click cell **A2**, and then press the **Enter** key. The reference to cell A2 in the Summary worksheet is entered in the formula in the grouped worksheets.

4. In the Quarter 1 worksheet, click cell **A2**. The formula =*Summary!A2* appears in the formula bar and 2010 appears in the cell. See Figure 6-5.

Formula with a worksheet reference ◄ **Figure 6-5**

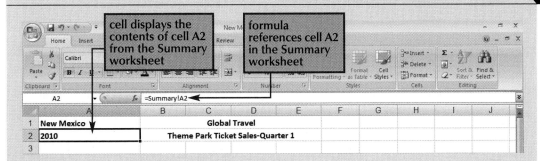

5. In each worksheet, verify that the formula =*Summary!A2* appears in the formula bar and 2010 appears in cell A2.

   Rhohit wants to use a more descriptive label in cell A2.

6. Switch to the **Summary** worksheet. The quarterly worksheets are ungrouped.

7. In cell A2, enter **Fiscal Year - 2010**.

8. Verify that the label in cell A2 changed in the Quarter 1 through Quarter 4 worksheets.

Using 3-D References to Add Values Across Worksheets

You need to calculate the number of tickets sold and the total sales for each theme park for the year and display the totals for the fiscal year in the Summary worksheet. To calculate the totals for the year, you can add the results from each quarterly worksheet and place the sum in the Summary worksheet. For example, in cell B6 of the Summary worksheet, you can enter the formula:

```
='Quarter 1'!B6+'Quarter 2'!B6+'Quarter 3'!B6+'Quarter 4'!B6
```

This formula calculates the number of Adult tickets sold to Animal World by adding the values in cell B6 in each of the quarterly worksheets. Continuing this approach for the entire worksheet is time consuming and error prone. There is an easier way.

When two or more worksheets have *identical* row and column layouts, as do the quarterly worksheets in the New Mexico workbook, you can enter formulas with 3-D references to summarize those worksheets in another worksheet. A **3-D reference** refers to the *same* cell or range in multiple worksheets in the same workbook. The reference specifies not only the range of rows and columns, but also the range of worksheet names in which the cells appear. The general syntax of a 3-D cell reference is as follows:

WorksheetRange!CellRange

WorksheetRange is the range of worksheets you want to reference and is entered as *FirstSheetName:LastSheetName* with a colon separating the first and last worksheets in the worksheet range. *CellRange* is the same cell or range in each of those worksheets that you want to reference. An exclamation mark (!) separates the worksheet range from the cell or range.

For example, the formula =*SUM(Quarter1:Quarter4!E13)* adds the values in cell E13 in the worksheets between Quarter1 and Quarter4, including Quarter1 and Quarter4. If worksheets named *Quarter1, Quarter2, Quarter3,* and *Quarter4* are included in the workbook, the worksheet range *Quarter1:Quarter4* references all four worksheets. Although *Quarter2* and *Quarter3* aren't specifically mentioned in this 3-D reference, all worksheets positioned within the starting and ending names are included in the calculations.

InSight	**Managing 3-D References**

The results of a formula using a 3-D reference reflect the current worksheets in the worksheet range. If you move a worksheet outside the referenced worksheet range or remove a worksheet from the workbook, the formula results will change. For example, consider a workbook with four worksheets named *Quarter1, Quarter2, Quarter3, and Quarter4*. If you move the Quarter3 worksheet after the Quarter4 worksheet, the worksheet range *Quarter1:Quarter4* includes only the Quarter1, Quarter2, and Quarter4 worksheets. Similarly, if you insert a new worksheet or move an existing worksheet within the worksheet range, the formula results reflect the change. To continue the example, if you insert a Quarter5 worksheet before the Quarter4 worksheet, the 3-D reference *Quarter1:Quarter4* includes the Quarter5 worksheet.

When you create a formula, make sure that the 3-D cell reference reflects the appropriate worksheets. Also, if you later insert or delete a worksheet within the 3-D reference, be aware of how doing so will affect the formula results.

3-D references are used in formulas that contain Excel functions, including SUM, AVERAGE, COUNT, MAX, MIN, STD, and VAR. You enter a 3-D reference either by typing the reference directly in the cell or by using your mouse to select first the sheet range, and then the cell or cell range.

Reference Window	**Entering a Function That Contains a 3-D Reference**

- Click the cell where you want to enter the formula.
- Type = to begin the formula, type the name of the function, and then type (to indicate the beginning of the argument.
- Click the sheet tab for the first worksheet in the worksheet range, press and hold the Shift key, and then click the tab for the last worksheet in the worksheet range.
- Select the cell or range to reference, and then press the Enter key.

In the New Mexico workbook, you'll use 3-D references in the Summary worksheet to add the total number of tickets sold and sales for the year.

You will begin by entering a formula to add the number of tickets sold to adults for the Animal World theme park in all four quarters of the year. Then, you'll copy this formula to calculate the tickets sold to adults and children for each theme park as well as the sales generated.

To enter a formula with the 3-D reference to the quarterly worksheets:

1. In the Summary sheet, click cell **B6**, and then type **=SUM(** to begin the formula. A ScreenTip shows the SUM function syntax.

   You'll enter a 3-D reference to cell B6 in the four quarterly worksheets.

2. Click the **Quarter 1** sheet tab, press and hold the **Shift** key, click the **Quarter 4** sheet tab, and then release the **Shift** key. The worksheet range is selected and added to the SUM function as '*Quarter 1:Quarter 4*'. Single quotation marks appear around the worksheet range because the worksheet names include spaces.

3. In the Quarter 1 worksheet, click cell **B6**. The cell is selected and added to the function. See Figure 6-6.

3-D reference added to the SUM function | Figure 6-6

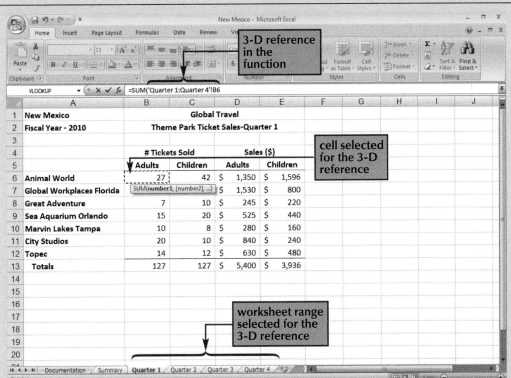

4. Press the **Enter** key to complete the formula, and then, in the Summary worksheet, click cell **B6**. The completed formula =SUM('Quarter 1:Quarter 4'!B6) appears in the formula bar, and 116—the total number of tickets for Animal World sold to adults in 2010—appears in cell B6.

You'll repeat the process to enter a 3-D reference in cell C6 that adds the total number of tickets sold to children for Animal World in 2010.

5. In the Summary worksheet, click cell **C6**, and then type **=SUM(** to begin the formula.

6. Click the **Quarter 1** sheet tab, press and hold the **Shift** key, click the **Quarter 4** sheet tab, and then release the **Shift** key. The quarterly worksheets are grouped.

7. In the Quarter 1 worksheet, click cell **C6** to select the cell, and then press the **Enter** key to complete the formula and return to the Summary worksheet.

8. In the Summary worksheet, click cell **C6**. The following formula appears in the formula bar: =SUM('Quarter 1:Quarter 4'!C6). Also, the value 175—the total number of tickets sold to children for Animal World in 2010—appears in cell C6.

In cells D6 and E6, you'll enter the SUM function with a 3-D reference to calculate the total revenue from tickets sales for Animal World.

9. In the Summary worksheet, click cell **D6**, type **=SUM(** to begin the formula, group the **Quarter 1** through **Quarter 4** worksheets, click cell **D6**, and then press the **Enter** key. The SUM function with a 3-D reference to cell D6 in the quarterly worksheets is entered. The completed formula is =SUM('Quarter 1:Quarter 4'!D6) and the total revenue from ticket sales to adults for Animal World in 2010 is $5,800.

> **10.** In the Summary worksheet, click cell **E6**, then enter the SUM function formula with a 3-D reference to cell **E6** in the quarterly worksheets. The completed formula is =SUM('Quarter 1:Quarter 4'!E6) and the total revenue from ticket sales to children for Animal World in 2010 is $6,650.

Instead of entering the SUM function to create the totals for the remaining theme parks, you can copy the formulas to the rest of the range. You copy formulas with 3-D references the same way you copy other formulas—using copy and paste or AutoFill. You'll copy the formulas in the range B6:E6 to the range B7:E12 so you can calculate the total ticket sales and revenue in 2010 for the remaining theme parks.

To copy the formulas with 3-D cell references:

> **1.** Select the range **B6:E6**. This range contains the SUM functions with the 3-D references you already entered.

> **2.** Drag the fill handle down over the range **B7:E12**. The formulas are copied for the rest of the theme park rows. The Auto Fill Options button appears below the copied range.

> **3.** Below cell E12, click the **Auto Fill Options** button 🔳, and then click the **Fill Without Formatting** option button. You don't want to copy the formatting in this case because you want to keep the bottom border formatting in the range B12: E12. The total values for the year appear in the range.

> **4.** Click cell **B6** to deselect the range. See Figure 6-7.

| Figure 6-7 | Summary worksheet with all the 3-D reference formulas |

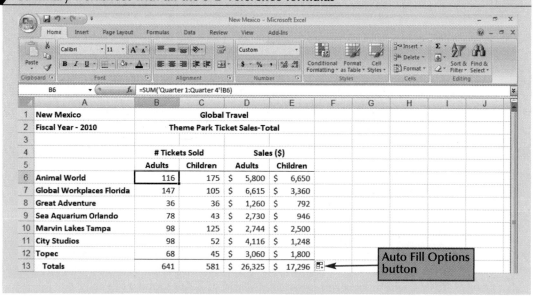

The Summary worksheet now shows the totals for the year 2010 in New Mexico for each theme park as well as statewide totals.

Rhohit discovered an error in the ticket sales data. Sea Aquarium Orlando sold 17 adult tickets in Quarter 1, not 15. One benefit of summarizing data using 3-D reference formulas, like any other formula, is that if you change the value in one worksheet, the results of formulas that reference that cell reflect the change. You will correct the number of tickets sold for Sea Aquarium Orlando in Quarter 1.

To change a value in the Quarter 1 worksheet:

1. In the Summary worksheet, note that 78 adult tickets were sold for Sea Aquarium Orlando in 2010 and 641 total adult tickets were sold.

2. Switch to the **Quarter 1** worksheet, and then, in cell B9, enter **17**. The total adult tickets sold in Quarter 1 is now 129.

    The results in the Summary worksheet are also updated because of the 3-D references in the formulas.

3. Switch to the **Summary** worksheet. The total number of tickets sold to adults for Sea Aquarium Orlando in 2010 is now 80, and the total number of tickets sold to adults for all theme parks in 2010 is now 643. See Figure 6-8.

Summary worksheet with updated ticket data   Figure 6-8

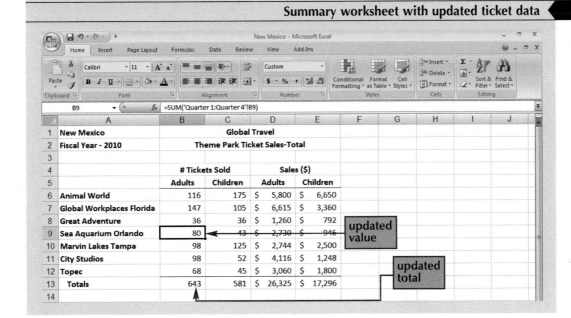

Printing a Worksheet Group

The Summary worksheet is complete and accurate. Rhohit asks you to print the five Ticket Sales worksheets to include in his report. He wants the same setup on each page. Recall that you set up the page layout and print area separately for each worksheet using the Page Layout tab on the Ribbon. Because the layout will be the same for all the quarterly worksheets in the New Mexico workbook, you can speed the page layout setup by creating a worksheet group before using the Page Setup dialog box. You will set up the worksheet group to print the report centered horizontally on the page with the name of the worksheet in the header and your name and the date in the footer.

To print the Summary and quarterly worksheets with a custom header and footer:

1. Select the **Summary** worksheet through the **Quarter 4** worksheet. The five worksheets are grouped.

2. Click the **Page Layout** tab on the Ribbon, and then, in the Page Setup group, click the Dialog Box Launcher. The Page Setup dialog box opens with the Page tab active.

▶ **3.** Click the **Margins** tab, and then click the **Horizontally** check box to insert a check mark. The printed content will be centered horizontally on the page.

▶ **4.** Click the **Header/Footer** tab, click the **Custom Header** button to open the Header dialog box, click in the **Center section** box, click the **Insert Sheet Name** button 🗐 to add the code *&[Tab]* in the section box to insert the sheet tab name in the center section of the header, and then click the **OK** button. A preview of the header appears in the upper portion of the dialog box.

▶ **5.** Click the **Custom Footer** button to open the Footer dialog box, type your name in the Left section box, click in the Right section box, click the **Insert Date** button 🗐 to add the code *&[Date]* in the section box to insert the current date in the right section of the footer, and then click the **OK** button.

▶ **6.** Click the **Print Preview** button. The Summary worksheet, the first worksheet in the group, appears in Print Preview. See Figure 6-9.

Figure 6-9	Print Preview of the worksheet group

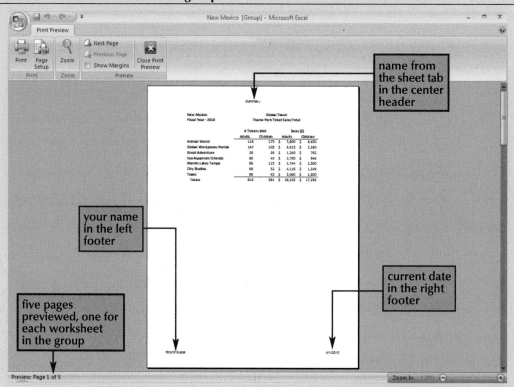

▶ **7.** In the Preview group on the Print Preview tab, click the **Next Page** button four times to view the other four worksheets in the group. Each page has the same page layout but the header shows the sheet tab names.

Trouble? If only one page appears in the Print Preview window, the worksheets are not grouped. Close the Print Preview window and repeat Steps 1 through 7.

▶ **8.** In the Preview group on the Print Preview tab, click the **Close Print Preview** button to close the Print Preview window without printing the worksheet group, unless you are instructed to print. In that case, in the Print group on the Print Preview tab, click the **Print** button.

▶ **9.** Switch to the **Documentation** sheet to ungroup the worksheets, and then switch to the **Summary** worksheet.

You have consolidated the data in Global Travel's New Mexico workbook in a Summary sheet, which will help Rhohit and the corporate controller to quickly see the totals for the theme park sales. Next, you will help the corporate controller to determine the annual totals for all of Global Travel's southwest locations—New Mexico, Utah, and Colorado.

Session 6.1 Quick Check | Review

1. What is a worksheet group?
2. How do you select an adjacent worksheet group? How do you select a nonadjacent worksheet group? How do you deselect a worksheet group?
3. What formula would you enter in the Summary worksheet to reference cell A10 in the Quarter 2 worksheet?
4. What is the 3-D cell reference to cell A10 in the adjacent Summary 1, Summary 2, and Summary 3 worksheets?
5. Explain what the formula *MAX(Sheet1:Sheet4!B1)* calculates.
6. If you insert a new worksheet (named *Sheet5*) after Sheet4, how would you change the formula in Question 5 to include Sheet5 in the calculation? How would you change the formula in Question 5 to include Sheet5 in the calculation if Sheet5 were positioned before Sheet4?
7. How do you apply the same printing page layout to all the worksheets in a workbook?

Session 6.2

Linking Workbooks

Alvin Alton, controller for Global Travel, has workbooks from the Colorado and Utah accountants similar to the one that you helped Rhohit prepare. Alvin now has three travel workbooks (named New Mexico, Colorado, and Utah), which contain the number of tickets sold and sales for the year 2010. Alvin wants to create a company-wide workbook that summarizes the annual totals from each state workbook.

If while creating formulas in one workbook you need to reference data located in one or more other workbooks, you must create a link between the workbooks. A **link** is a connection between the files that allows data to be transferred from one file to the other. When two files are linked, the **source file** is the workbook that contains the data, and the **destination file** (sometimes referred to as the *dependent* file) is the workbook that receives the data. In this case, as illustrated in Figure 6-10, the New Mexico, Utah, and Colorado workbooks are the *source* files because they contain the data from the three states. The Totals 2010 workbook is the *destination* file because it receives the data from the three state workbooks to calculate the company totals for 2010. Creating a link in the Totals 2010 workbook to the three state workbooks means the Totals 2010 workbook will always have access to the most recent information in the state workbooks, because it can be updated whenever any of the state workbook values change.

Figure 6-10   Source and destination files

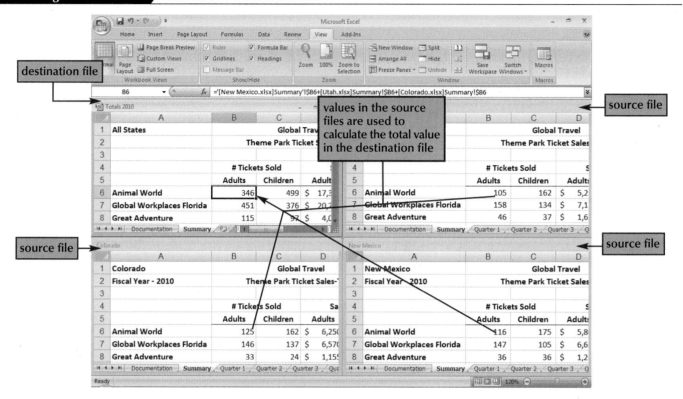

To create the link between destination and source files, you need to insert a formula in the Totals 2010 workbook that references a specific cell or range in the three state workbooks. Because the formula will contain a reference to a cell or range in a worksheet in another workbook, that reference is called an **external reference**. The syntax of an external reference is the following:

[WorkbookName]WorksheetName!CellRange

WorkbookName is the filename of the workbook (including the file extension) enclosed in square brackets. *WorksheetName* is the name of the worksheet that contains the data followed by an exclamation mark. *CellRange* is the cell or range that contains the data. For example, if you were to create a formula in one workbook to reference cell B6 in the Summary worksheet of the Colorado.xlsx workbook, you would enter the following formula:

`=[Colorado.xlsx]Summary!B6`

If the workbook name or the worksheet name contains one or more spaces, you must enclose the entire workbook name and worksheet name in single quotation marks. For example, to reference cell B6 in the Summary worksheet of the New Mexico.xlsx workbook, you would enter the following formula:

`='[New Mexico.xlsx]Summary'!B6`

When the source and destination workbooks are stored in the same folder, you need to include only the workbook name in the external reference. However, when the source and destination workbooks are located in different folders, the workbook reference must

Tip

When you use the point-and-click method to build formulas with external references, Excel enters all of the required punctuation, including quotation marks.

include the file's complete location (also called the path). For example, if the destination file is stored in C:\TicketSales and the source file is stored in C:\TicketSales\Domestic Sales, the complete reference in the destination file would be:

```
='C:\TicketSales\Domestic Sales\[New Mexico.xlsx]Summary'!B6
```

The single quotation marks start at the beginning of the path and end immediately before the exclamation mark.

Understanding When to Link Workbooks | InSight

Linking workbooks is useful in many instances. The following are several examples of when to use linked workbooks:

- Separate workbooks have the same purpose and structure. For example, you can use related workbooks for different stores, branch offices, or departments with the same products or expenditure types and reporting periods (weekly, monthly, quarterly).
- A large worksheet has become unwieldy to use. You can break the large worksheet into smaller workbooks for each quarter, division, or product.
- A summary worksheet consolidates information from different workbook files. The linked workbooks enable you to more quickly and accurately summarize the information, and you know the summary worksheet contains the most current information if the information is later updated.
- Source workbooks you receive from another person or group are continually updated. With linked workbooks, you can replace an outdated source workbook and the destination workbook will then reflect the latest information without you having to modify the formulas.

Navigating and Arranging Multiple Workbooks

You'll combine the three state worksheets into one regional summary. You'll open all the workbooks you need to reference. Then, you'll switch between them to make each Summary worksheet the active sheet in preparation for creating the external references.

To open and switch between the workbooks needed to create the regional summary:

▶ **1.** If you took a break after the previous session, make sure the New Mexico workbook is open and the Summary worksheet is active.

▶ **2.** Open the **TravelTotals** workbook located in the **Tutorial.06\Tutorial** folder included with your Data Files, and then save the workbook as **Totals 2010** in the same folder.

▶ **3.** Enter your name and the current date in the Documentation sheet, and then make the **Summary** worksheet active.

▶ **4.** Open the **Utah** and **Colorado** workbooks located in the **Tutorial.06\Tutorial** folder included with your Data Files. Each open workbook has a button on the taskbar, but only one workbook is active.

▶ **5.** Click the **View** tab on the Ribbon, and then, in the Window group, click the **Switch Windows** button to open a list of all the workbooks currently open.

▶ **6.** Click **Utah** to make that the active workbook, and then make the **Summary** sheet active.

▶ **7.** In the Window group on the View tab, click the **Switch Windows** button, click **Colorado** to switch to the Colorado workbook, and then make the **Summary** worksheet active.

▶ **8.** Make the **Totals 2010** workbook the active workbook.

You'll need to move between open workbooks when you create the external reference formulas in the Totals 2010 workbook. Although you can use the Switch Windows button in the Window group on the View tab to change which workbook is active, you might find it easier to click the taskbar button for the workbook you want to make active.

Reference Window | **Arranging Workbooks**

- In the Window group on the View tab, click the Arrange All button.
- Select the desired option for arranging the workbook: Tiled, Horizontal, Vertical, or Cascade.
- When arranging multiple workbooks, uncheck the Windows of active workbook option unless you are arranging worksheets within one workbook.
- Click the OK button.

You might also want to display all the open workbooks on your screen at the same time. This way, you can easily click among the open workbooks to create links without having to continually change the active workbook. You can choose to arrange multiple open workbooks in one of four layouts:

- **Tiled** divides the open workbooks evenly on the screen.
- **Horizontal** divides the open workbooks into horizontal bands.
- **Vertical** divides the open workbooks into vertical bands.
- **Cascade** layers the open workbooks on the screen.

Currently, four workbooks are open but only one is visible. You'll arrange the workbooks using the tiled arrangement.

To tile the open workbooks:

▶ **1.** In the Window group on the View tab, click the **Arrange All** button. The Arrange Windows dialog box opens so you can select the layout arrangement you want.

▶ **2.** Click the **Tiled** option button, if necessary. The Tiled option arranges the four Global Travel workbooks evenly on the screen.

▶ **3.** Click the **OK** button. The four open workbooks appear in a tiled layout. See Figure 6-11. Totals 2010 is the active workbook (you might have a different workbook active). In the tiled layout, the active workbook has darker text in the title bar and includes scroll bars.

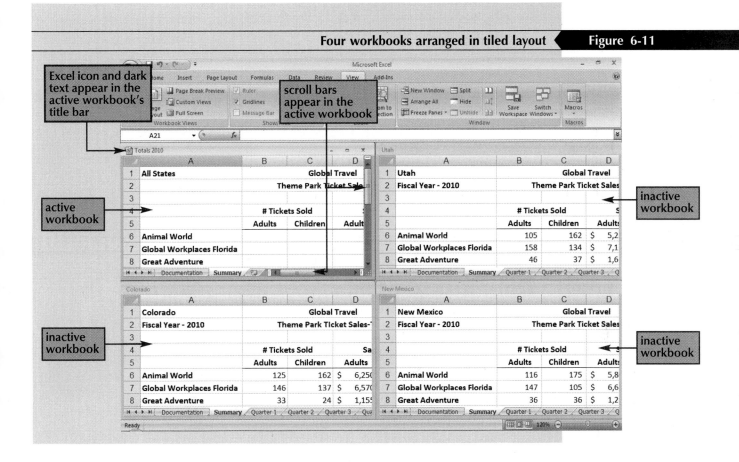

Four workbooks arranged in tiled layout   Figure 6-11

Creating External Reference Formulas

You need to enter the external reference formulas in the Totals 2010 workbook to create a set of linked workbooks and be able to summarize the states' totals into one workbook for Alvin. The process for entering a formula with an external reference is the same as entering any other formula using references within the same worksheet or workbook. You can enter the formulas by typing them or using the point-and-click method. In most situations, you will use the point-and-click method to switch between the source files and destination files so that Excel enters the references to the workbook, worksheet, and cell using the correct syntax.

You'll start by creating the formula that adds the total number of adult tickets to Animal World sold in New Mexico, Utah, and Colorado. You cannot use the SUM function with 3-D references here because you are referencing multiple workbooks.

To create the external reference formula to total adult tickets for Animal World:

▶ **1.** In the Summary worksheet in the Totals 2010 workbook, click cell **B6**, and then type **=** to begin the formula.

▶ **2.** Click anywhere in the **New Mexico** workbook, and then, in the Summary worksheet, click cell **B6**. The external reference to cell B6 in the Summary worksheet of the New Mexico workbook—'[New Mexico.xlsx]Summary'!$B$6—is added to the formula in the Totals 2010 workbook. See Figure 6-12.

Figure 6-12 External reference entered in formula

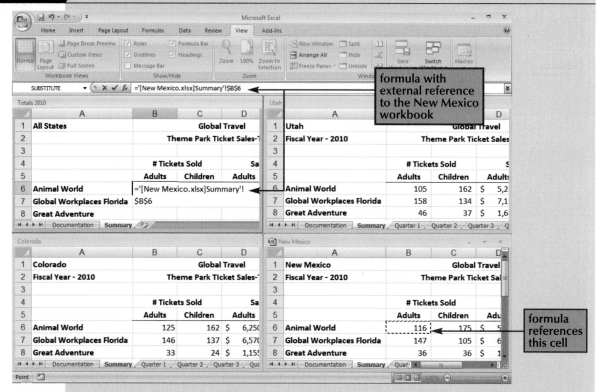

> 3. Type **+**. The Totals 2010 workbook becomes active and you can continue entering the formula. You need to create an external reference to the Utah workbook.

> 4. Click anywhere in the **Utah** workbook, click cell **B6** in the Summary worksheet, and then type **+**. The formula in the Totals 2010 workbook includes the external reference to the cell that has the total number of adult tickets to Animal World sold in Utah. The formula links two state workbooks to the Totals 2010 workbook.
>
>   Next, you'll create the external reference to the Colorado workbook.

> 5. Click anywhere in the **Colorado** workbook, click cell **B6** in the Summary worksheet, and then press the **Enter** key. The formula with three external references is entered in the Summary sheet in the Totals 2010 workbook.

> 6. In the Totals 2010 workbook, in the Summary sheet, click cell **B6**. The complete formula appears in the formula bar and the formula results appear in cell B6, showing that 346 adult tickets to Animal World were sold in the three states: 116 in New Mexico, 105 in Utah, and 125 in Colorado. See Figure 6-13.

> **Complete formula with external references** | **Figure 6-13**

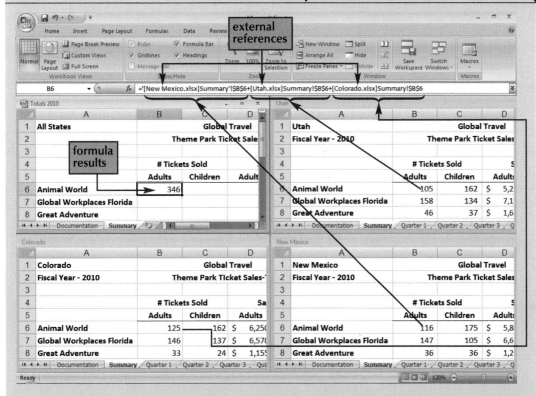

Trouble? If 346 doesn't appear in cell B6 in the Summary sheet in the Totals 2010 workbook, you might have clicked an incorrect cell for an external reference in the formula. Repeat Steps 1 through 6 to correct the formula.

You'll use the same process to enter the external reference formula for cell C6, which is the number of children's tickets to Animal World sold in the three states. Then you'll do the same to create the formulas to calculate the total sales from all three states.

To create the remaining external reference formulas:

▶ **1.** In the Totals 2010 workbook, in the Summary worksheet, click cell **C6**, and then type **=** to begin the formula.

▶ **2.** Click the **New Mexico** workbook, click cell **C6** in the Summary worksheet, and then type **+**. The formula in the Totals 2010 includes the external reference to cell C6 in the Summary worksheet in the New Mexico workbook.

▶ **3.** Click the **Utah** workbook, click cell **C6** in the Summary worksheet, and then type **+**. The formula includes an external reference to cell C6 in the Summary worksheet in the Utah workbook.

▶ **4.** Click the **Colorado** workbook, click cell **C6** in the Summary worksheet, and then press the **Enter** key. The external reference formula is complete.

▶ **5.** In the Totals 2010 workbook, click cell **C6** in the Summary sheet. Cell C6 displays 499, the total children's tickets sold to Animal World, and the following formula appears in the formula bar: =‘[New Mexico.xlsx]Summary’!$C$6+ [Utah.xlsx]Summary!$C$6+[Colorado.xlsx]Summary!$C$6.

Next, you'll enter the external reference formulas in cells D6 and E6 to add the total sales from adult and children's tickets to Animal World.

▶ 6. Use the same procedure in Steps 1 through 4 to enter the formula in cell **D6** in the Summary worksheet in the Totals 2010 workbook. The formula results displayed in cell D6 are 17300—the total sales from adult tickets to Animal World in New Mexico, Utah, and Colorado.

▶ 7. Use the same procedure in Steps 1 through 4 to enter the formula in cell **E6** in the Summary worksheet in the Totals 2010 workbook. The formula results displayed in cell E6 are 18962—the total sales from children's tickets to Animal World in New Mexico, Utah, and Colorado.

You need to enter the remaining formulas for the six other theme parks (rows 7 to 12). Rather than creating the rest of the external reference formulas manually, you can copy the formulas in row 6 to rows 7 through 12. The formulas created using the point-and-click method contain absolute references. Before you copy the formula to other cells, you need to change the formulas to mixed references because the rows in the formula need to change.

To edit the external reference formulas to use mixed references:

▶ 1. Maximize the Totals 2010 workbook. The Totals 2010 workbook fills the program window. The other workbooks are still open but are not visible.

▶ 2. In the Summary worksheet, double-click cell **B6** to enter editing mode and display the formula in the cell.

▶ 3. Click in the first absolute reference in the formula, and then press the **F4** key twice to change the absolute reference $B$6 to the mixed reference $B6.

▶ 4. Edit the other two absolute references in the formula to be mixed references with absolute column references and relative row references.

▶ 5. Press the **Enter** key. The formula is updated to include mixed references, but the formula results aren't affected. Cell B6 still displays 346, which is correct.

▶ 6. Edit the formulas in cells C6, D6, and E6 to change the absolute references to the mixed references $C6, $D6, and $E6, respectively. The formulas are updated, but the cells in the range C6:D6 still correctly display 499, 17300, and 18962, respectively.

> **Tip**
>
> You can also create the mixed reference by deleting the $ from the row references in the formula.

With the formulas corrected to include mixed references, you can now copy the external reference formulas in cells B6:E6 to the other rows.

To copy the formulas to rows 7 through 12 and total the column values:

▶ 1. Select the range **B6:E6**, and then drag the fill handle to select the range **B7:E12**. The formulas are copied to the rest of the range B7:E12 and the formula results appear in the cells. The Auto Fill Options button appears in the lower-right corner of the selected range.

Next, you'll enter the SUM function to total the values in each column.

▶ 2. In cell B13, enter the SUM function to add the range **B6:B12**. A total of 2035 adult tickets were sold for all theme parks.

▶ 3. Copy the formula in cell B13 to the range **C13:E13**. The totals are 1855, 81889, and 55704, respectively.

▶ 4. Format cells D6:E13 with the **Accounting** number format with no decimal place.

▶ **5.** Format the range B12:E12 with a bottom border, and then click cell **A1** to deselect the range. See Figure 6-14.

Completed formulas in the Summary worksheet in the Totals 2010 workbook | Figure 6-14

	A	B	C	D	E
1	All States		Global Travel		
2			Theme Park Ticket Sales-Total		
3					
4		# Tickets Sold		Sales ($)	
5		Adults	Children	Adults	Children
6	Animal World	346	499	$ 17,300	$ 18,962
7	Global Workplaces Florida	451	376	$ 20,295	$ 12,032
8	Great Adventure	115	97	$ 4,025	$ 2,134
9	Sea Aquarium Orlando	202	100	$ 7,000	$ 2,200
10	Marvin Lakes Tampa	431	428	$ 12,068	$ 8,560
11	City Studios	283	149	$ 11,886	$ 3,576
12	Topec	207	206	$ 9,315	$ 8,240
13	Total	2035	1855	$ 81,889	$ 55,704

Alvin is pleased; the regional summary results match the executive team's expectations.

Managing Linked Workbooks | InSight

As you work with a linked workbook, you might need to replace a source file or change where you stored the source and destination files. However, replacing or moving a file can affect the linked workbook. Keep in mind the following guidelines to manage your linked workbooks. If you rename a source file, the destination workbook won't be able to find it. A dialog box opens, indicating "This workbook contains one or more links that cannot be updated." You click the Continue button to open the workbook with the most recent values, or you click the Change Source button in the Edit Links dialog box to specify the new name of that linked source file.

If you move a source file to a different folder, the link breaks between the destination and source files. Click the Change Source button in the Edit Links dialog box to specify the new location of the linked workbook.

If you receive a replacement source file, you can replace the original source file with the replacement file with no additional corrections.

If you receive a destination workbook but the source files are not included, Excel will not be able to find the source files, and a dialog box opens with the message "This workbook contains one or more links that cannot be updated." Click the Continue button to open the workbook with the most recent values, or click the Break button in the Edit Links dialog box to replace the external references with current values.

If you change the name of a destination file, you can open the destination file using a new name without making any corrections.

Updating Linked Workbooks

Rhohit calls Alvin to tell him of an incorrect value in the New Mexico workbook. The Animal World children's sales amount for Quarter 4 should be $2,786 not $1,786, which is currently in the file. Alvin asks you to change the value in the New Mexico workbook. How will a change to a value in any of the source workbooks affect the destination workbook?

When workbooks are linked, it is important that the data in the destination file accurately reflects the contents of the source file. When data in the source file changes, you want the destination file to reflect the changes. If both the source and destination files are open when you make a change, the destination file is updated automatically. If the destination file is closed when you make a change in the source file, you choose whether to update the link to display the current values when you open the destination file or continue to display the older values from the destination file.

You have both the source and destination files open. You will increase the value of Animal World children's sales for Quarter 4 in the New Mexico workbook by $1,000. This change will increase the amount in the Summary worksheet of the New Mexico workbook and the regional total in the Totals 2010 workbook.

To change the value in the source workbook with the destination file open:

▶ 1. Switch to the **New Mexico** workbook, and then make the **Quarter 4** worksheet active. You'll update the value of the Animal World children's dollar amount in this worksheet.

▶ 2. In cell E6, enter **2786**. The Animal World children's sales are updated.

▶ 3. Switch to the **Summary** worksheet in the New Mexico workbook, and then verify that the total Animal World children's sales is now $7,650.

Next, you'll check the regional total.

▶ 4. Switch to the **Totals 2010** workbook, and then, in the Summary worksheet, verify that the value in cell E6 is $19,962 and the total dollar amount from sales of children's tickets is $56,704, reflecting the new value you entered in the New Mexico workbook. Because both the destination and source files are open, Excel updated the destination file automatically.

▶ 5. Save the New Mexico and Totals 2010 workbooks, and then close the Utah, Colorado, and Totals 2010 workbooks. The New Mexico workbook remains open.

Opening Destination Workbooks with Source Workbooks Closed

When you save a workbook that contains external reference formulas, such as Totals 2010, Excel stores the most recent results of those formulas in the destination file. Source files, such as the New Mexico, Colorado, and Utah workbooks, are often updated while the destination file is closed. In that case, the values in the destination file are not updated at the same time the source files are updated. When you open the destination file again it contains the old values in the cells containing external reference formulas. Therefore, some of the values in the edited source workbooks are different from the values in the destination workbook. How do you update the destination workbook?

When you open a workbook with external reference formulas (the destination file), as part of the Excel security system that attempts to protect against malicious software, links to other workbooks cannot be updated without your permission. As a result, a Security Warning appears in the Message Bar immediately below the Ribbon, notifying you that the automatic update of links has been disabled. If you "trust" the provider of the source file(s), you can choose to "Enable this content," which allows the external reference formulas to function and updates the links in the destination workbook. If you do not "trust" the provider of the source files or do not want the destination file updated at that time, do not select "Enable this content." The old values in the destination workbook are displayed and the links to the source files remain disabled.

Tip

To change the default behavior of disabling automatic links, click the Office Button, click the Excel Options button, and then click Advanced. In the General section, uncheck the Ask to update automatic links check box, and then click the OK button.

Rhohit informs Alvin that the New Mexico workbook needs a second correction. Great Adventure adult sales in Quarter 4 are $435 not $385, which is the value currently in the New Mexico workbook. You will increase the amount of the Great Adventure adult sales in Quarter 4 by $50. As a result, sales in the Summary sheet of the New Mexico workbook and the regional total in the Totals 2010 workbook will both increase by $50.

Alvin asks you to open the New Mexico workbook, correct the value in the cell, and then save the workbook. You'll edit the source file, the New Mexico workbook, while the destination file is closed.

To update the source workbook with the destination file closed:

1. In the New Mexico workbook, make the **Quarter 4** worksheet active.

2. In cell D8, enter **435**. The total sales for adults in Quarter 4 increases to $7,241.

3. Switch to the **Summary** worksheet. The total sales for 2010 in cell D8 is $1,310 and total adult sales is $26,375. See Figure 6-15.

Summary worksheet with revised Quarter 4 sales for Great Adventure — **Figure 6-15**

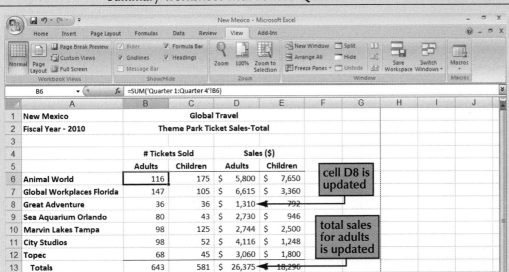

4. Save and close the New Mexico workbook.

Now you'll open the destination file (the regional workbook) to see if the total is automatically updated.

5. Open the **Totals 2010** workbook, and then switch to the **Summary** worksheet. The value in cell D8 has *not* changed; it still is $4,025. A Security Warning message appears in the Message Bar, indicating that automatic update of links has been disabled. See Figure 6-16.

Tip

When the destination file is open and the source files are closed, the complete file path is included as part of the external reference formula that appears in the formula bar.

Security Warning in the Message Bar — **Figure 6-16**

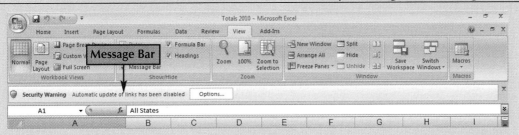

You want the current values in the source files to appear in the destination workbook.

▶ **6.** Click the **Options** button in the Message Bar. The Microsoft Office Security Options dialog box opens. See Figure 6-17.

Figure 6-17 | **Microsoft Office Security Options dialog box**

▶ **7.** Click the **Enable this content** option button, and then click the **OK** button. The values in the destination file are updated. The sales in cell D8 of the Totals 2010 workbook increase to $4,075 and the total in cell D13 increases to $81,939.

▶ **8.** Save the workbook.

Managing Links

After the fiscal year audit is completed and there are no more revisions to the source workbooks, Alvin will archive the summary workbook as part of his year-end backup process, and he'll move the files to an off-site storage location. He will make a copy of the Totals 2010 workbook and name it *Audited 2010*. Using the copy, he will break the links using the Break Links command in the Edit Links dialog box, which converts all external reference formulas to their most recent values.

To save a copy of the Totals 2010 workbook and open the Edit Links dialog box:

▶ **1.** Click the **Office Button** , and then click **Save As**. The Save As dialog box opens.

▶ **2.** Change the filename to **Audited 2010**, make sure the save location is the **Tutorial.06\ Tutorial** folder included with your Data Files, and then click the **Save** button. The Totals 2010 workbook closes and the Audited 2010 workbook remains open.

▶ **3.** Click the **Data** tab on the Ribbon, and then, in the Connections group, click the **Edit Links** button. The Edit Links dialog box opens. See Figure 6-18.

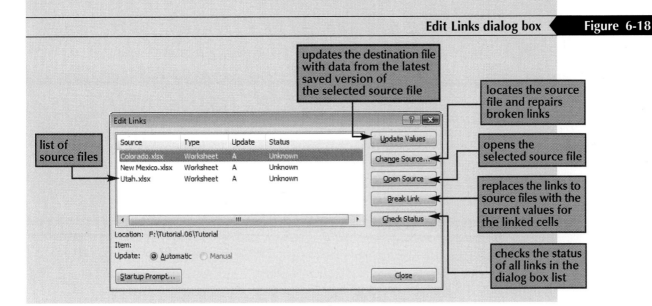

Edit Links dialog box | Figure 6-18

The Edit Links dialog box lists all of the files the destination workbook is linked to so that you can update, change, open, or remove the links. You can see that the destination workbook, Audited 2010, has links to the Colorado, New Mexico, and Utah workbooks. The dialog box shows the following information about each link:

- **Source**. The file the link points to. The Audited 2010 workbook contains three links pointing to the workbooks New Mexico.xlsx, Colorado.xlsx, and Utah.xlsx.
- **Type**. The type of each source file. In this case, the type is an Excel worksheet but it could also be a Word document, PowerPoint presentation, or some other type of file.
- **Update**. The way values are updated from the source file. The letter *A* indicates the link is updated automatically when you open the workbook or when both the source and destination files are open simultaneously. The letter *M* indicates the link must be updated manually by the user. You can set a link to update manually when you want to see the older data values before updating to the new data. Click the Update Values button in the Edit Links dialog box if the Update option is set to *M* and you want to see the new data values.
- **Status**. Whether Excel successfully accessed the link and updated the values from the source document (Status is OK), or Excel has not attempted to update the links in this session (Status is Unknown). The status of the three links in the Audited 2010 workbook is Unknown.

You'll break the links so the Audited 2010 workbook contains only the updated values (and is no longer affected by changes in the source files). Then you'll save the Audited 2010 workbook for Alvin to archive. This allows Alvin to store a "snapshot" of the data at the end of the fiscal year.

To convert all external reference formulas to their current values:

▶ **1.** Click the **Break Link** button. A dialog box opens, alerting you that breaking links in the workbook permanently converts formulas and external references to their existing values.

▶ **2.** Click the **Break Links** button. No links appear in the Edit Links dialog box.

▶ **3.** Click the **Close** button. The Audited 2010 workbook now contains values instead of formulas with external references.

Tip

When you use the Break Link button, you cannot undo that action. To restore the links, you must reenter the external reference formulas.

> You'll examine the worksheet to see how the links (external reference formulas) were converted to values.
>
> ► **4.** Click cell **B6**. The value 346 appears in the cell and the formula bar; the external reference formula was replaced with the data value. All cells in the range B6:E12 contain values rather than external reference formulas.
>
> ► **5.** Save and close the Audited 2010 workbook.

You have two workbooks. The Totals 2010 workbook has external reference formulas, and the Audited 2010 workbook has current values. The Audited 2010 workbook will be stored in Global Travel's off-site storage.

Creating an Excel Workspace

Alvin has four workbooks containing data for the ticket sales. Usually, he'll need to access only one workbook at a time, but occasionally he'll want to access all of the workbooks. If Alvin could open all the workbooks at once, he would save time, and, more important, not have to remember all the filenames and folder locations.

Tip

Because the workspace file contains only the location and name of each file, not the actual workbooks and worksheets, you cannot copy only the workspace file to another computer. Instead, you need to also copy the workbook files.

To open multiple workbooks at one time, you need to create a workspace. A **workspace** is an Excel file that saves information about all of the currently opened workbooks, such as their locations, window sizes, zoom magnifications, and other settings. The workspace does not contain the workbooks themselves—only information about them. To use that set of workbooks, you can open the workspace file. Excel then opens the workbooks and settings in the same configuration they were in when you saved the workspace file. Even if a workbook is included in a workspace file, you can still open that workbook separately.

You will create a workspace file for Alvin that includes the four workbooks in a cascade layout, which arranges the open workbooks so that they overlap each other with all the title bars visible. Alvin prefers this layout, because he can see more of the active workbook.

To create the Theme Parks workspace file:

► **1.** Open the **Colorado**, **New Mexico**, **Utah**, and **Totals 2010** workbooks located in the **Tutorial.06\Tutorial** folder included with your Data Files. Four workbooks are open.

► **2.** Make sure the **Summary** worksheet is the active worksheet in each workbook.

► **3.** Switch to the **Totals 2010** workbook.

► **4.** Click the **View** tab on the Ribbon, and then, in the Window group, click the **Arrange All** button. The Arrange Windows dialog box opens.

► **5.** Click the **Cascade** option button, and then click the **OK** button. The four workbooks overlap each other, with the title bars visible. See Figure 6-19.

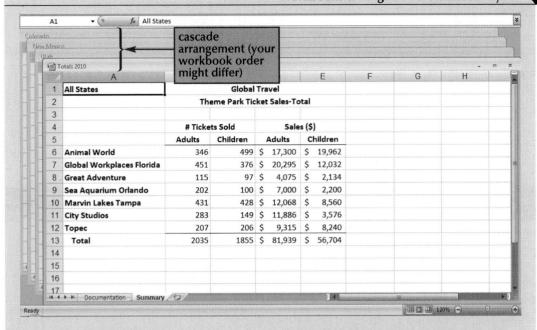

Workbooks arranged in the cascade layout ◀ Figure 6-19

▶ **6.** In the Window group on the View tab, click the **Save Workspace** button. The Save Workspace dialog box opens and functions similarly to the Save As dialog box.

▶ **7.** Type **Theme Parks** in the File name box, verify that **Workspaces** is selected in the Save as type box, verify that the save location is the **Tutorial.06\Tutorial** folder, and then click the **Save** button. A dialog box might open, prompting you to save your changes to the open workbook files, if you haven't already done so.

▶ **8.** If prompted to save changes, click the **Yes** button. The Theme Parks workspace file is saved. The workspace file has the file extension .xlw.

You will test the workspace file you created to make sure it opens all four Global Travel workbooks.

To test the Theme Parks workspace file:

▶ **1.** Close all four workbooks.

▶ **2.** Click the **Office Button** , and then click **Open**. The Open dialog box opens, displaying the Tutorial.06\Tutorial folder. The icon for the Theme Parks workspace file is different from the Excel workbook file icon.

▶ **3.** Click **Theme Parks** in the list of files, and then click the **Open** button. The four travel workbooks open and are arranged in a cascade layout, the same layout in which you saved them. You can then work with the workbooks as usual

▶ **4.** Click the **Colorado** workbook title bar to bring it to the front of the cascaded workbooks. Colorado is now the active workbook.

The workspace file provides a quick way to open a series of workbooks in a specific display. Because it doesn't actually contain the workbooks, you must close each workbook separately, saving as needed.

▶ **5.** Close the New Mexico, Utah, Colorado, and Totals 2010 workbooks without saving any changes.

In this session, you worked with multiple worksheets and workbooks, summarizing data and linking workbooks. This ensures that the data in the summary workbook is accurate and remains updated with the latest data in the source files.

Review | **Session 6.2 Quick Check**

1. What is the external reference to the range A1:A10 in the Sales Info worksheet in the Product Report workbook located in the Reports folder on drive D?
2. What is a source file?
3. What is a destination file?
4. Name two ways to update a link in a workbook.
5. How would you determine to what workbooks a destination file is linked?
6. What is a workspace file?
7. Explain how workspace files can help you organize your work.

Session 6.3

Creating a Hyperlink

Alvin has written an executive memo summarizing the results for 2010. He wants to give members of the executive team at Global Travel easy access to the memo by including a hyperlink from his workbook to the memo.

Inserting a Hyperlink

You can insert a hyperlink directly in a workbook file. A **hyperlink** is a link in a file, such as a workbook, to information within that file or another file. The hyperlinks are usually represented by colored words with underlines or images. When you click a hyperlink, the computer switches to the file or portion of the file referenced by the hyperlink. Although hyperlinks are most often found on Web pages, they can also be placed in a worksheet and used to quickly jump to a specific cell or range within the active work-sheet, another worksheet, or another workbook. Hyperlinks can also be used to jump to other files, such as a Word document or a PowerPoint presentation, or sites on the Web.

To use a hyperlink, you click the text inside the cell that contains the link. If you click white space in the cell or any text that flows into an adjacent cell, the hyperlink does not work.

Inserting a Hyperlink | Reference Window

- Select the text, graphic, or cell in which you want to insert the hyperlink.
- In the Links group on the Insert tab, click the Hyperlink button.
- To link to a file or Web page, click Existing File or Web Page in the Link to list, and then select the file or Web page from the Look in box.
- To link to a location in the current workbook, click Place in This Document in the Link to list, and then select the worksheet, cell, or range in the current workbook.
- To link to a new document, click Create New Document in the Link to list, and then specify the filename and path of the new document.
- To link to an e-mail address, click E-mail Address in the Link to list, and then enter the e-mail address of the recipient and a subject line for the e-mail message.
- Click the OK button.

Alvin wrote a memo summarizing the sales results for New Mexico, Utah, and Colorado in 2010. He wants the Totals 2010 workbook to include a link to this memo that points to the Word document Sales 2010.docx located in the Tutorial.06\Tutorial folder included with your Data Files.

To insert a hyperlink into the Totals 2010 workbook:

▶ 1. Open the Totals 2010 workbook located in the **Tutorial.06\Tutorial** folder included with your Data Files.

▶ 2. Switch to the **Documentation** worksheet, and then click cell **A12**. You want to create the hyperlink in this cell.

▶ 3. Click the **Insert** tab on the Ribbon, and then, in the Links group, click the **Hyperlink** button. The Insert Hyperlink dialog box opens with the Existing File or Web Page button selected in the Link to bar and the Current Folder displayed in the Look in area. You use this dialog box to define the hyperlink. See Figure 6-20.

Insert Hyperlink dialog box ◀ **Figure 6-20**

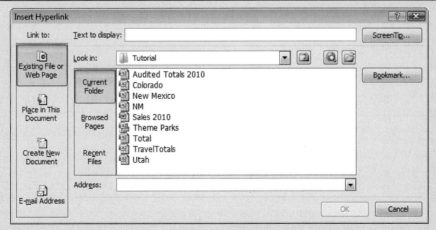

Trouble? If either the Existing File or Web Page option or the Current Folder option is not selected, select it before continuing.

▶ 4. Click the **Text to display** box, and then type **Click here to read Executive Memo**. This is the hyperlink text that will appear in cell A12 in the Documentation sheet.

▶ 5. Click the **Sales 2010** Word document in the list of files, and then click the **OK** button. As shown in Figure 6-21, the hyperlink text is in underlined blue font, indicating that the text within the cell is a hyperlink.

Figure 6-21 **Hyperlink to the Sales 2010 document**

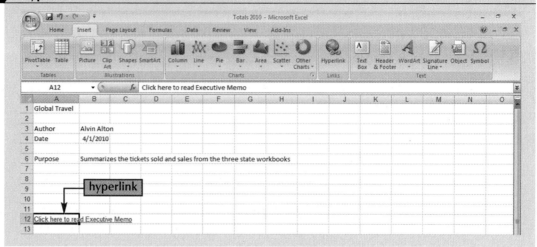

You will test the hyperlink that you just created to ensure it works correctly. To use a hyperlink, you click the text inside the cell that contains the link.

To jump to the hyperlink:

▶ **1.** Point to cell **A12** until you see 🖑, and then click the hyperlink. The Sales 2010 document opens in Word.

Trouble? If the hyperlink doesn't work, you might have clicked the text that overflows cell A12. Point to the text within cell A12, and then click the hyperlink.

▶ **2.** Click the **Close** button ⊠ on the Word title bar to close the document and exit Word. The Documentation sheet in the Totals 2010 workbook is active. The color of the hyperlink in cell A12 changed to indicate that you have used the link.

Editing a Hyperlink

ScreenTips, which appear whenever you place the pointer over a hyperlink, provide additional information about the target of the link. The default ScreenTip is the folder location and filename of the file you will link to. Alvin doesn't think that this is very helpful. He wants you to change the ScreenTip for the link you just created to be more descriptive. You can insert a ScreenTip when you create a hyperlink. However, because you've already created this hyperlink, you'll edit the hyperlink to change the ScreenTip.

To edit the hyperlink:

▶ **1.** In the Documentation worksheet, right-click cell **A12**, and then click **Edit Hyperlink** on the shortcut menu. The Edit Hyperlink dialog box opens; it has the same layout and information as the Insert Hyperlink dialog box.

▶ **2.** Click the **ScreenTip** button. The Set Hyperlink ScreenTip dialog box opens.

▶ **3.** Type **Click to view sales analysis for 2010** in the ScreenTip text box, and then click the **OK** button.

▶ **4.** Click the **OK** button to close the Edit Hyperlink dialog box.

▶ **5.** Point to cell **A12**, confirm that the ScreenTip *Click to view sales analysis for 2010* appears just below the cell, and then save and close the Totals 2010 workbook.

Tip

You can keep the text of a hyperlink but remove the functioning link by clicking Remove Hyperlink on the shortcut menu.

Alvin agrees that the ScreenTip is a useful addition to the hyperlink. If you want to remove a hyperlink, right-click the cell containing the hyperlink and then click Clear Contents on the shortcut menu to delete the hyperlink and text.

Creating Templates

The three state workbooks for 2010 have the same format. Alvin wants to use this workbook format for data collection and analysis for next year. One approach to accomplish this goal is to open one of the state workbooks, save it with a new name, and then replace the 2010 values with blank cells. Alvin is reluctant to use that approach because he might forget to change the filename and inadvertently overwrite the previous year's figures with blank cells when he saves the workbook. A better alternative is to have an Excel workbook that Alvin can open with the labels, formats, and formulas already built into it. Such a workbook is called a **template**. You use the template workbook as a model from which you create new workbooks.

When you use a template to create a new workbook, a copy of the template opens that includes text (row and column labels), formatting, and formulas from the template. Any changes or additions you make to the new workbook do not affect the template file. The original template retains its formatting and formulas, and the next time you open a workbook based on the template, those original settings will still be present.

There are several advantages to creating and using templates:

- Templates save you time entering formulas and formatting when you need to create several workbooks with similar features.
- Templates help you standardize the appearance and content of workbooks.
- Templates prevent you from accidentally saving new data in an old file if you use the Save command instead of the Save As command when basing a new workbook on an existing workbook.

Using Excel Templates | InSight

Excel has many templates available. Some are automatically installed on your hard disk when you install Excel, and others are available from the Microsoft Office Online Web site. In fact, the blank Book1 workbook that opens when you start Excel is based on the **default template**. The default template contains no text or formulas, but it includes all the formatting available in every new workbook: General number format applied to numbers, Calibri 11-point font, labels aligned to the left side of a cell, values and the formula results aligned to the right side of a cell, column width set to 8.43 characters, three worksheets inserted in the workbook, and so forth.

You can also download templates from the Microsoft Office Online Web site. These templates provide commonly used worksheet formats, saving you from "reinventing the wheel." Some of the task-specific templates available from the Microsoft Office Online Web site include the following:

- **Family Budget**. This template builds projections and actual expenditures for items such as housing, transportation, and insurance.
- **Inventory List**. This template tracks the cost and quantity reorder levels of inventory.
- **Team Roster**. This template lists each player's name, phone number, e-mail address, and so forth.
- **Time sheet**. This template creates an online time card to track employees' work hours.

If you need to create the same type of workbook repeatedly, it's a good idea to use a template to both save time and to ensure consistency in the design and content of the workbooks you create.

Creating a Workbook Based on an Existing Template

To see how templates work, you'll create a new workbook based on one of the Excel templates provided by Microsoft.

Reference Window | **Creating a Workbook Based on a Template**

- Click the Office Button, and then click New.
- In the Templates pane, click a template category for the type of workbook you want to create.
- In the center pane, click the template you want to use, and then click the Download button.
- Click the Continue button to let Microsoft verify your software.
- Save the workbook with a new filename.

You'll download the Time card template. **Note:** You need an Internet connection to complete the following set of steps; if you don't have an Internet connection, you should read but not complete the steps involving creating and using the online template.

To create a workbook based on a Microsoft Office Online template:

▶ **1.** Click the **Office Button** 🔘, and then click **New**. The New Workbook dialog box opens. The left pane lists the Microsoft Office Online template categories.

▶ **2.** Click **Time sheets**. A gallery of Time sheet templates appears in the center pane. The right pane shows a preview of the selected template.

▶ **3.** Scroll down the center pane until you see Time card, and then click the **Time card** thumbnail image. A preview of the worksheet based on the template appears in the right pane. See Figure 6-22.

Figure 6-22 ▶ **Preview of the Time card template**

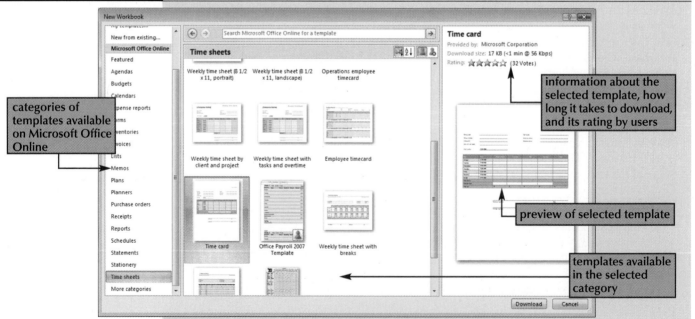

categories of templates available on Microsoft Office Online

information about the selected template, how long it takes to download, and its rating by users

preview of selected template

templates available in the selected category

4. Click the **Download** button. The Microsoft Office Genuine Advantage dialog box opens. Before you can access the templates on Microsoft Office Online, Microsoft verifies that you have an authentic copy of the software.

5. Click the **Continue** button to verify the copy of Microsoft Office on your computer. The Time card template opens. See Figure 6-23.

Workbook created from the Time card template   Figure 6-23

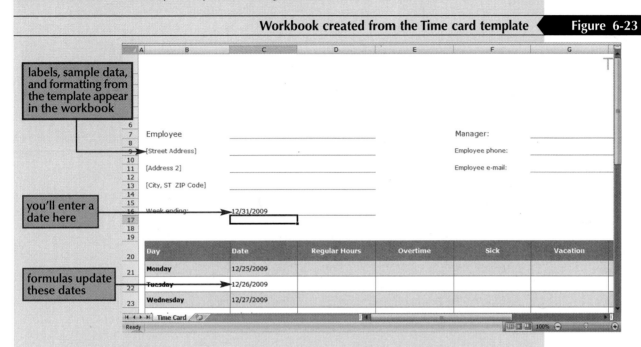

Trouble? If the Microsoft Office Genuine Advantage dialog box indicates that the software installed on your computer is not genuine, then Microsoft was not able to validate your software. Click the Resolve Later button, and ask your instructor or technical support person for help.

The workbook based on the Time card template shows the name *Time card1* in the title bar, not *Time card*. Just as a blank workbook that you open is named sequentially, *Book1*, *Book2*, and so forth, a workbook based on a specific template always displays the name of the template followed by a sequential number. Any changes or additions to data, formatting, or formulas you make in this workbook affect only the new workbook you are creating and not the template (in this case, the Time card template). If you want to save your changes, you must save the workbook in the same way as you would save any new workbook.

Look at the labels and formatting already included in the Time Card worksheet. Some cells have descriptive labels, others are blank so you can enter data in them, and still other cells contain formulas where calculations for total hours worked each day and pay category will be automatically displayed as data is entered.

You'll enter data for Ed Hoot, the student assisting Alvin, in the worksheet based on the Time card template.

To enter data in the workbook based on the Time card template:

1. In cell C7, enter **Ed Hoot**.

2. In cell C16, enter **3/21/2010**. The dates in cells C21:C27 are automatically updated to reflect the week you specify.

▶ 3. In cell D21, enter **8**. This is the total regular hours Ed worked on Monday. Totals appear in cells H21, D28, and H28 because formulas are already entered into these cells. Cell H21 shows 8 hours worked that day, cell D28 shows 8 regular hours worked that week, and cell H28 shows 8 hours total worked that week.

▶ 4. In cell D22, enter **8** as the total regular hours Ed worked on Tuesday, and then, in cell E22, enter **2** as the total overtime hours Ed worked on Tuesday. The totals are updated to show 10 hours worked that day, 16 regular hours worked that week, 2 overtime hours worked that week, and 18 total hours worked that week.

Next, you'll enter the regular hourly pay rate.

▶ 5. In cell D29, enter **10**. The Total pay amounts in cells D30 and H30 are updated to show $160 total pay.

Next, you'll enter the overtime hourly pay rate.

▶ 6. In cell E29, enter **15**. The Total pay amounts are updated to show $160 total pay for regular hours, $30 total pay for overtime hours, and $190 total pay for the week ending 3/21/2010.

▶ 7. Save the workbook as **Hoot Time Card** in the **Tutorial.06\Tutorial** folder included with your Data Files. The Hoot Time Card workbook, like any other workbook, is saved with the .xlsx file extension. It does not overwrite the template file.

▶ 8. Close the workbook.

Each day Ed Hoot works at Global Travel, he or his supervisor can open the Hoot Time Card workbook just like any other workbook and enter his hours worked for the day. The total hours and pay are automatically updated. You can see how useful templates with formulas to produce a weekly time card that is fully formatted.

Having completed the New Mexico workbook according to Alvin's specifications, you have the basis for a template that can be used for similar projects. Instead of using one of the Excel templates, you can use the New Mexico workbook to create your own template file. Then, Alvin can create new workbooks based on that template and distribute them to the accountants preparing the state workbooks.

Creating a Custom Workbook Template

A **custom template** is a workbook template you create that is ready to run with the formulas for all calculations included as well as all formatting. Usually, the template is set up so a user enters the data and sees results immediately. A template can use any Excel feature, including formulas, charts, data validation, cell protection, macros, and so forth. In other words, a template includes everything but the data.

To create a template from an existing workbook, you need to be sure that all the formulas work as intended, the numbers and text are entered correctly, and the worksheet is formatted appropriately. Next, you need to remove any values and text that will change in each workbook created from the custom template. Be careful not to delete the formulas. Finally, you need to save the workbook using the Excel template file format. You can store template files in any folder, although if you store the file in the Templates folder, your custom templates are available when you click Templates in the New Workbook dialog box. If you don't save the template to the Templates folder, you can save it to another location.

Tip

You might find it helpful to replace variable data values with spaces, and apply a background color to cells in which you want data entered to differentiate them from other cells in the worksheet.

Creating a Custom Template | Reference Window

- Prepare the workbook: enter values, text, and formulas as needed; apply formatting; and replace data values with zeros or blank cells.
- Click the Office Button, and then click Save As.
- In the File name box, enter the template name.
- Click the Save as type button, and then click Excel Template.
- Save the file in the Templates folder or select an alternative folder location.
- Click the Save button.

Alvin wants you to use the New Mexico workbook as the basis for creating a custom template. You'll reopen the workbook and clear the data values in the worksheets, leaving all of the formulas intact. After completing these modifications, you will save the workbook as a template.

To replace the data values in the New Mexico workbook:

1. Open the **New Mexico** workbook located in the **Tutorial.06\Tutorial** folder included with your Data Files.

2. Group the **Quarter 1** through **Quarter 4** worksheets. All the worksheets are grouped except the Summary and Documentation worksheets.

3. Select the range **B6:E12**. This range includes the specific ticket and sales data for each theme park. You want to delete these values.

4. Click the **Home** tab on the Ribbon, in the Editing Group click the **Clear** button ⌫ ▾, and then click **Clear Contents**. The data values are cleared from the selected range in each of the quarterly worksheets, but the formulas and formatting remain intact. The cleared cells are blank. The range B13:E13 displays dashes, representing zeros, where there are formulas.

   You'll apply a color to the range where you want users to enter data, the range B6:E12.

5. In the Font group on the Home tab, click the **Fill Color button arrow** ⌫ ▾, and then click **Orange** (the third color in the Standard Colors section of the Fill Color gallery). The selected range has an orange fill to indicate where to enter quarterly data for the number of tickets sold and the sales amount.

6. In cell A1, enter **=Summary!A1**. This formula inserts the contents of cell A1 in the Summary worksheet into cell A1 in the quarterly worksheets. The text "New Mexico" is still displayed because that's the text currently in cell A1 in the Summary worksheet.

7. Switch to the **Summary** worksheet. The quarterly worksheets are ungrouped, and dashes, representing zeros, appear in the cells in the range B6:E13, which contain formulas.

8. In cell A1, enter **Enter state name here**, and then, in cell A2, enter **Enter Fiscal Year – yyyy**. This text will remind users to enter the correct state name and year. See Figure 6-24.

Figure 6-24 | **Worksheet with formatting and formulas but no data**

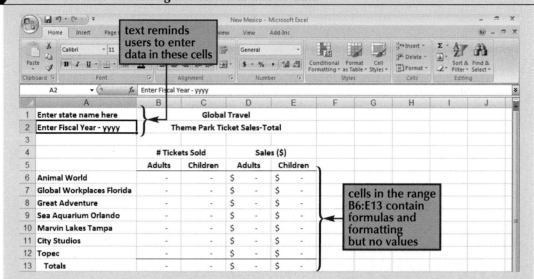

9. Switch to the **Documentation** worksheet, delete your name and the date from the range **B3:B4**, enter **Theme park ticket sales** in cell B6, and then click cell **A1**. The Documentation sheet is updated to reflect the purpose of the workbook.

The workbook is ready to save in template format. It no longer contains any specific data, but the formulas and formatting will still be in effect when new data is entered.

To save the workbook as a template:

1. Click the **Office Button** , and then click **Save As**. The Save As dialog box opens.

2. Type **Travel Template** in the File name box.

3. Click the **Save as type** button, and then click **Excel Template**. The Address bar displays the Templates folder, which is where custom template files are often stored. Excel, by default, looks for template files in this folder. However, you can store templates in other folders as well. Because you might not have access to the Templates folder, you will save the template file with your other Data Files.

4. Navigate to the **Tutorial.06\Tutorial** folder included with your Data Files, and then click the **Save** button.

5. Close the Travel Template workbook template.

Alvin will use the Travel Template file to create the workbooks to track next year's sales for each state and then distribute the workbooks via e-mail to each accountant. By basing these new workbooks on the template file, he has a standard workbook with identical formatting and formulas for each accountant to use. He also avoids the risk of accidentally changing the workbook containing the 2010 data when preparing for 2011. All template files have the .xltx extension. This extension differentiates template files from workbook files, which have the .xlsx extension. After you have saved a workbook in a template format, you can make the template accessible to other users.

Creating a New Workbook from a Template

After you have saved a template in the Templates folder, you open the New Workbook dialog box and go to the My Templates folder to select the template you want to use. If you don't save the template to the Templates folder, the New from existing button enables you to create a new workbook from a template, much like creating a workbook based on a template found in the Templates folder.

You will use the latter approach to create a workbook from the Travel Template file because you saved the template in your Tutorial.06\Tutorial folder. Alvin asks you to test the process of creating the workbook before the state workbooks are distributed to the accountants.

To create a new workbook based on the Travel Template template:

▶ 1. Click the **Office Button** , and then click **New**. The New Workbook dialog box opens.

▶ 2. Click **New from existing** in the Templates pane. The New from Existing Workbook dialog box opens, with All Excel Files displayed. This dialog box differs from the Open dialog box in two ways. First, instead of opening the actual workbook, it opens a copy of it. Second, when you save the workbook, it adds a number to the end of the filename and opens the Save As dialog box, which makes it very difficult to overwrite the original file.

▶ 3. Click **Travel Template** in the **Tutorial.06\Tutorial** folder included with your Data Files, and then click the **Create New** button. A copy of the Travel Template workbook opens named *Travel Template1* to indicate this is the first copy of the Travel Template workbook created during the current Excel session.

▶ 4. Click the **Summary** sheet tab, and then, in cell **A1**, enter **New Mexico** and in cell **A2**, enter **Fiscal Year - 2011**.

▶ 5. Switch to the **Quarter 1** worksheet. The text "New Mexico" appears in cell A1, and the text "Fiscal Year - 2011" appears in cell A2.

You'll enter test data in the data area (which has an orange background fill color).

▶ 6. Click cell **B6**, type **120**, click cell **C6**, type **150**, click **D6**, type **3000**, click **E6**, type **2850**, and then press the **Enter** key. The range B13:E13 shows the totals of each column because these cells contain formulas to sum each column.

▶ 7. Click cell **B7**, type **180**, click cell **C7**, type **200**, click **D7**, type **3500**, click **E7**, type **3150**, and then press the **Enter** key. The range B13:E13 is updated because these cells contain formulas to sum each column. See Figure 6-25.

> **Tip**
>
> The worksheet that is active when you create, save, and close a template workbook is the active worksheet when you create a new workbook based on the template. In this case, the Documentation sheet is active.

Figure 6-25 | New workbook based on Travel Template

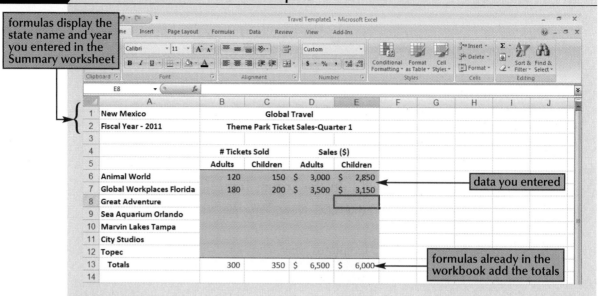

8. Switch to the **Summary** worksheet. Totals appear in the ranges B6:E7 and B13:E13 as a result of the formulas in this worksheet. See Figure 6-26.

Figure 6-26 | Summary worksheet after data is entered

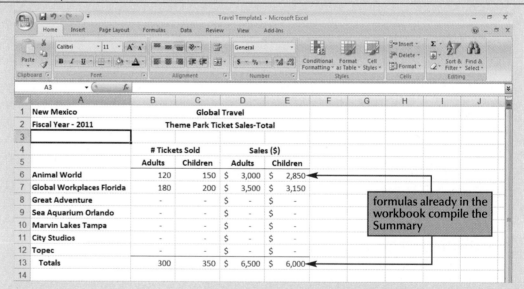

9. Save the workbook as **New Mexico 2011** in the **Tutorial.06\Tutorial** folder included with your Data Files. The copy of the template is saved as a workbook with the .xlsx extension. The original template file is not changed.

10. Close the workbook.

Alvin asks you to add data to the Quarter 2, Quarter 3, and Quarter 4 worksheets to verify that the Summary worksheet is correctly adding numbers from the four worksheets.

To test the New Mexico 2011 workbook:

▶ 1. Open the **New Mexico 2011** workbook located in the **Tutorial.06\Tutorial** folder included with your Data Files.

▶ 2. Group the **Quarter 2**, **Quarter 3**, and **Quarter 4** worksheets. You'll enter test values in the range B6:C6 so that each quarterly worksheet contains data.

▶ 3. In cell B6, enter **120**, and then, in cell C6, enter **150**.

▶ 4. Switch to the **Summary** worksheet. The total in cell B6 is 480 and the total in cell C6 is 600. The formulas in the Summary worksheet correctly add values from all the quarterly worksheets. So, Alvin knows that the template workbook is functioning as intended.

▶ 5. Save and close the workbook.

Alvin will use the custom template to create and distribute new state workbooks to each accountant for the next fiscal year.

Saving a Workbook as a Web Page

Alvin wants you to store the summary of the annual company-wide Theme Park Ticket Sales report you helped him create on the company's intranet which is a computer network, based on Internet technology, that is designed to meet the internal needs for sharing information within an organization.

You can convert Excel workbooks, worksheets, or ranges into Web pages that can be placed on the Web to be viewed by others. Excel allows you to create a Web page where users can scroll through the contents of an Excel workbook and switch between worksheets, but cannot make any changes to the data or formatting displayed on the Web page. When you save a worksheet as a Web page, Excel converts the contents of the worksheet into **HTML** (Hypertext Markup Language), which is a language used to write Web pages.

You can save an Excel workbook, a worksheet, or an item in a worksheet as a Web page and make it available to viewers via the Internet or an intranet. Alvin wants to make the company-wide results available to the executive team, so he needs you to create a Web page of the Totals 2010 Summary worksheet.

You use the Save As dialog box to create a Web page based on a workbook, a single worksheet, or a range within a worksheet. When you save a workbook as a Web page, you can save the workbook in one of two formats. The Web Page format saves the worksheet as an HTML file and creates a folder that stores the supporting files, such as a file for each graphic and worksheet that is included on the Web page. The Single File Web Page format saves all the elements of the Web page including text and graphics into a single file in the MHTML (Multipurpose Internet Mail Extension HTML) format.

Accessing Workbooks on the Web Interactively | InSight

In Excel 2007, if you want to publish interactive versions of your workbook or items from the worksheet as a Web page with spreadsheet functionality, you need to use a component of Microsoft Office Share-Point Server called Excel Services. This component lets users access all or part of the workbook in browsers interactively. Users can sort and filter an Excel table, use PivotTables for data analysis, and perform what-if analysis from a Web browser. To learn more, search the Excel Help system for "publish a workbook to Excel Services."

Reference Window | **Saving a Workbook, Worksheet, or Range as a Web Page**

- Click the Office Button, and then click Save As.
- Click the Save as type button, and then click Web Page or Single File Web Page.
- Click the Publish button.
- Click the Choose arrow, and select which portion of the workbook you want to publish as a Web page.
- Click the Change button to change the title of the Web page.
- Click the Browse button to change the filename and location for the Web page.
- Check or clear the AutoRepublish every time this workbook is saved check box.
- Check or clear the Open published web page in browser check box.
- Click the Publish button.

First, you will create and test the Web page on your hard drive. You will open the Save As dialog box, and then choose the Web Page file format, because it is the standard format the company uses for its Web pages, to create the Web page for the regional 2010 results.

After previewing your work offline, Alvin will "publish" the Web page by putting all of the files (both HTML files and graphic files) on the Web server that hosts the Global Travel site.

To start creating the Web page:

1. Open the **Totals 2010** workbook located in the **Tutorial.06\Tutorial** folder included with your Data Files.

2. Click the **Office button** 🔘, and then click **Save As**. The Save As dialog box opens.

3. Click the **Save as type** button, and then click **Web Page**. The area below the Save as type box expands to display several Web-based options. See Figure 6-27.

Figure 6-27 ▶ **Expanded Save As dialog box**

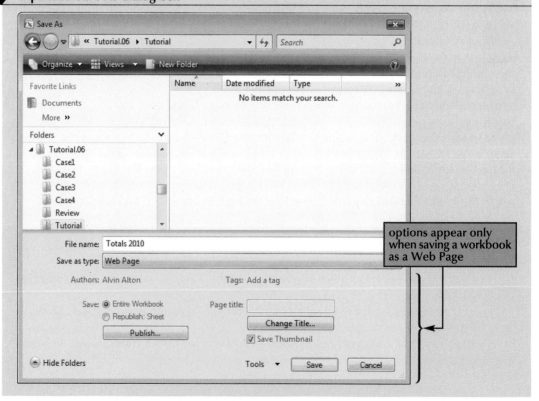

options appear only when saving a workbook as a Web Page

Setting the Page Title

Web pages usually have a page title that appears in the title bar of the Web browser. If a page title is not entered, the browser will display the page's file path and filename. Alvin wants the Web page title to clearly indicate to the executive team the purpose of the report. You'll enter a descriptive page title.

To specify the page title:

▶ **1.** Click the **Change Title** button. The Set Page Title dialog box opens.

▶ **2.** Type **Global Travel Theme Park Ticket Sales - 2010** in the Page title text box, and then click the **OK** button. The page title you just typed appears in the Page title box at the bottom of the Save As dialog box.

The next step in setting up the page for publishing on the Web is to choose which elements of the workbook to include in the Web page.

Setting the Web Page Options

You can specify which elements to include as part of the Web page. You can select the entire workbook, a specific worksheet in the workbook, a range of cells, or previously published items (which are items already on the Web server) that you are modifying. In this case, Alvin wants to include only the contents of the Summary worksheet.

To select the Summary worksheet for the Web page:

▶ **1.** In the Save As dialog box, click the **Publish** button. The Publish as Web Page dialog box opens. See Figure 6-28.

Publish as Web Page dialog box ◀ **Figure 6-28**

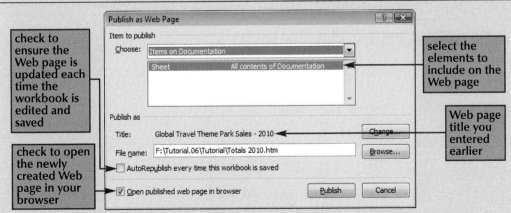

You'll specify the Summary worksheet as the item to include on the Web page.

▶ **2.** Click the **Choose** arrow, and then click **Items on Summary**. Items on Summary appears in the Choose box and the Summary worksheet is the active sheet in the workbook behind the dialog box.

In the Publish as section of the Publish as Web Page dialog box, you can also change the Web page title, browse to find the folder where you want to publish the Web page and assign or change the filename, enable automatic republishing of the Web page every time a change is saved to the workbook so the Web page always matches the source workbook, and immediately view the Web page in a browser.

The default filename for a Web page is based on the workbook's filename, which, in this case, is *Totals 2010.htm*. Alvin wants the name to conform to the company style. For consistency in naming company-related Web pages, he will name the file *Web Totals 2010.htm*. The extension .htm refers to an HTML file. You will change the filename.

To specify a filename for the Web page:

▶ **1.** Click the **Browse** button. The Publish As dialog box opens.

▶ **2.** Verify that the **Tutorial.06\Tutorial** folder is selected, and then type **Web Totals 2010** in the File name box.

▶ **3.** Click the **OK** button. The filename appears in the Publish as Web Page dialog box.

▶ **4.** Make sure the **Open published web page in browser** check box is checked so the Web page will open in a browser as soon as you complete these steps.

▶ **5.** Click the **Publish** button. Excel creates the Web page based on the contents of the Summary worksheet and opens the page in your browser. You don't need an Internet connection to see the Web page, because the HTML file is stored locally on your computer. The page title *Global Travel Theme Park Sales - 2010* appears in the browser's title bar, tab, and as a heading above the information from the worksheet. See Figure 6-29.

Figure 6-29	Web page based on the Summary worksheet

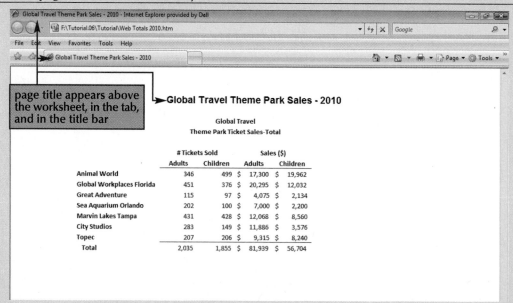

▶ **6.** Close your Web browser, and then close the Totals 2010 workbook without saving.

The Web page provides a concise summary of the Global Travel ticket sales. Alvin will complete the process by uploading the Web page you created to the company's intranet later on.

Session 6.3 Quick Check | Review

1. How do you insert a hyperlink into a worksheet cell?
2. True or False? A hyperlink in a worksheet cell can be used to jump to another worksheet in the same workbook.
3. What is a template?
4. What is an advantage of using a custom template rather than simply using the original workbook file to create a new workbook?
5. How do you save a file as a template?
6. What are the two different types of Web page file formats available?

Tutorial Summary | Review

In this tutorial, you worked with multiple worksheets and workbooks. You learned how to create a worksheet group and then edit multiple worksheets at once. You consolidated information in multiple worksheets using 3-D references. You also set up grouped worksheets for printing. You linked workbooks using external references. You created an Excel workspace file and explored the advantages of using workspace files when you need to work with multiple workbooks that are related to one project or goal. You added a hyperlink to a worksheet. You learned about Excel templates and created a custom template from an existing worksheet. Finally, you converted a worksheet into a Web page.

Key Terms

3-D reference
custom template
default template
destination file
external reference
HTML (Hypertext Markup
    Language)

hyperlink
link
ScreenTip
source file

template
worksheet group
workspace

Practice	**Review Assignments**

Practice the skills you learned in the tutorial using the same case scenario.

Data Files needed for the Review Assignments: OR.xlsx, Idaho.xlsx, Washington.xlsx, NW Totals 2010.xlsx, NW Travel.xltx

Elaine Dennerson, accountant for Global Travel in Oregon, needs your help. Global Travel has added Oregon to the Northwest territory, which already includes Washington and Idaho. She asks you to complete the Summary worksheet in the Oregon workbook and enter the formulas in the regional workbook, NW Totals 2010, to summarize the Northwest states' totals into one workbook.

Complete the following:

1. Open the **OR** workbook located in the Tutorial.06\Review folder included with your Data Files, and then save the workbook as **Oregon** in the same folder.

2. In the Documentation sheet, enter your name and the current date, and then review the worksheets in the workbook.

3. Create a worksheet group that contains the Qtr 1 through Qtr 4 worksheets.

4. In the worksheet group, insert formulas to total each column. Format each worksheet to match other state quarterly workbooks. Bold the range A1:B2;A6:A13;B4:E5. Merge and center the ranges B1:E1, B2:E2, B4:C4, and D4:E4. Format the range A6:A12 in italic. Add a top and double bottom border to the range B13:E13. Add a fill color to the range B1:E2 using the Orange theme color. Apply the Accounting number format with no decimal places to the range D6:E13. Ungroup the worksheets.

5. Make a copy of the Qtr 1 worksheet, name it **Summary**, and place it immediately after the Documentation worksheet. Remove the data from the range B6:E12. Change the heading in cell B2 to **Theme Park Ticket Sales-Total**. In cell A2, enter the label **Fiscal Year – 2010**.

6. In worksheets Qtr 1 through Qtr 4, enter formulas to reference the labels in cells A1 and A2 of the Summary worksheet.

7. In the Summary worksheet, create 3-D reference formulas to calculate annual totals for theme park tickets sold and sales.

8. Prepare all worksheets except the Documentation sheet for printing. Display the name of the workbook and the name of the worksheet on separate lines in the right section of the header. Display your name and the date on separate lines in the right section of the footer. Preview the worksheets.

9. Ungroup the worksheets and save the workbook.

10. Open the regional **NW Totals 2010** workbook located in the Tutorial.06\Review folder included with your Data Files, and then enter the external reference formulas in the NW Totals 2010 workbook to create a set of linked workbooks to summarize the states' totals into one workbook.

11. In the NW Totals 2010 workbook, switch to the Documentation sheet. In the range A10:A12, enter the name of each state. Create hyperlinks from each state label to the corresponding workbook (Idaho, Oregon, and Washington). Test each hyperlink.

12. Create a workspace with the following four workbooks in a tiled layout: Idaho, Oregon, Washington, and NW Totals 2010. Make the Summary worksheet in each workbook the active worksheet, and make the NW Totals 2010 workbook the active workbook. Save the workspace as **NW Workspace**.

13. Create a new workbook based on the **NW Travel** template, which is located in the Tutorial.06\Review folder included with your Data Files. Save the workbook as **Oregon 2011** in the same folder. In the Summary worksheet, enter **Oregon** in cell A1 and **Fiscal Year – 2011** in cell A2. In the Qtr 1 worksheet, enter **1000** in each cell of the range B6:C12. In the Qtr 2 worksheet, enter **2000** in each cell of the range B6:C12. Confirm that the values entered in this step were correctly totaled in the Summary worksheet. Save the Oregon 2011 workbook.

14. Create a Web page of the entire Oregon workbook, which you created in Steps 2 through 9. Add a title. Include all worksheets in the workbook. Use the Web Page format and name the Web page as **Web Oregon 2010**.

15. Close all the workbooks. Submit the finished workbooks to your instructor, either in printed or electronic form, as requested.

| Apply | **Case Problem 1** |

Use the skills you learned to summarize quarterly sales data for a coffee retailer.

Data File needed for this Case Problem: Cafe.xlsx

Java Café   Java Café currently has three stores in the Southwest: Tempe, Arizona; Las Cruces, New Mexico; and Austin, Texas. Jayne Mitchell manages the three stores and uses Excel to summarize sales data from these stores. She asks you to total the sales by product group and store for each quarter and then format each worksheet. Jayne also needs you to add another worksheet to calculate Summary sales for the stores and product groups.

Complete the following:

1. Open the **Cafe** workbook located in the Tutorial.06\Case1 folder included with your Data Files, and then save the workbook as **Java Cafe** in the same folder.

2. In the Documentation sheet, enter your name and the current date, and then switch to the Quarter 1 worksheet.

3. For each quarter, calculate the total sales for each product group and store, and then improve the formatting of the quarterly worksheets using the formatting of your choice.

4. Insert a new worksheet between the Documentation and Quarter 1 worksheets. Rename this as worksheet **Summary Sales**. Its appearance should be identical to the quarterly worksheets.

5. In the range B5:E7 of the Summary Sales worksheet, insert the formulas that add the sales in the corresponding cells of the four quarterly worksheets. Calculate the totals for each product group and store.

6. Set up the Summary Sales and four quarterly worksheets for printing. Each worksheet should be centered horizontally with the name of the worksheet centered in the header, and your name and the date placed on separate lines in the right section of the footer.

7. Save the Java Cafe workbook, and then remove the sales data, but not the formulas, from each of the quarterly worksheets.

8. Return to cell A1 of the Documentation sheet, and then save the workbook as an Excel template with the name **Java Template** in the Tutorial.06\Case1 folder included with your Data Files.

9. Use the Java Template template you created to create a new workbook. Name the workbook as **Java Cafe 2011**. In the range B5:E7 of all four quarterly worksheets, enter **1**. Save the workbook.

10. Create a Web page of the **Java Cafe** workbook in the Web Page format with the file-name **Web Java**. Add an appropriate title. Include all worksheets in the workbook. Preview the file in your Web browser, and then close it.

11. Close the workbook. Submit the finished workbooks to your instructor, either in printed or electronic form, as requested.

| Create | **Case Problem 2** |

Create linked work-books to summarize sales data for a car dealership.

Data Files needed for this Case Problem: Carson.xlsx, Reno.xlsx, Vegas.xlsx

Ute Auto Sales & Services Hardy Ute is founder and operator of Ute Auto Sales & Services with dealerships in Las Vegas, Reno, and Carson City, Nevada. His dealerships sell new and used cars, SUVs, minivans, and trucks as well as service customers' vehicles. To analyze sales and service at each of his three dealerships, Hardy asks his staff to prepare a regular report. Hardy wants the report to show the unit and dollar sales of new and used vehicles by type. In addition, he wants to see if his service business is bringing in the revenue that he anticipates.

Complete the following:

1. Open the **Carson** workbook located in the Tutorial.06\Case2 folder included with your Data Files, and then save the workbook as **UTE Carson City** in the same folder.

2. In the Documentation sheet, enter your name and the current date, and then switch to the Quarter 1 worksheet.

3. For each quarter, calculate the totals in the range B10:G10, and then improve the formatting of the quarterly worksheets using the formatting of your choice.

4. Insert a new worksheet between the Documentation and Quarter 1 worksheets. Rename this worksheet **Summary**. Format the worksheet identically to any of the quarterly worksheets except leave the range B6:G9 blank.

5. In the range B6:G9 of the Summary worksheet, insert the formulas that add the sales in the corresponding cells of the four quarterly worksheets.

6. Prepare the five sales worksheets for printing. Page setup should include the following: centered horizontally, the name of the worksheet centered in the header, and your name and the date placed on separate lines in the right section of the footer.

7. Save your changes to the workbook and close the workbook.

8. Open the **Reno** workbook located in the Tutorial.06\Case2 folder included with your Data Files, and then save the workbook as **UTE Reno**. Repeat Steps 2 through 7 for this workbook.

9. Open the **Vegas** workbook located in the Tutorial.06\Case2 folder, and then save the workbook as **UTE Vegas**. Repeat Steps 2 through 7 for this workbook.

10. Create a new workbook and use Figure 6-30 as a guide as you summarize the three dealerships' workbooks. Save the workbook as **UTE Summary**.

Figure 6-30

	A	B	C	D	E	F	G
1				Ute Auto Sales & Services			
2				Sales - All Dealers			
3							
4			New		Pre-owned		Service
5		Units	Sales ($)	Units	Sales ($)	Units	Sales ($)
6	Cars	733	$ 14,940,828	203	$ 1,476,397	5405	$ 1,058,958
7	SUVs	288	$ 7,979,268	76	$ 478,632	1798	$ 492,525
8	Vans	166	$ 3,928,990	87	$ 750,758	1007	$ 328,662
9	Trucks	113	$ 1,639,386	64	$ 341,907	691	$ 117,874
10	Totals	1300	$ 28,488,472	430	$ 3,047,694	8901	$ 1,998,019

11. Use the Web Page format to create a Web page based on the Summary worksheet in the UTE Summary workbook. Change the page title to **UTE Auto Sales & Services**. Open the Web page using your browser. Name the file **UTE Web Page**.

12. Use the UTE Carson City workbook to create an Excel template with the name **UTE Template** in the Tutorial.06\Case2 folder included with your Data Files. Add appropriate formatting of your choice.

13. Create a new workbook using the UTE Template. Add appropriate test data for Quarter 1. Save the workbook as **Carson City 2011** in the Tutorial.06\Case2 folder included with your Data Files.

14. Close the workbook. Submit the finished workbooks to your instructor, either in printed or electronic form, as requested.

| Create | **Case Problem 3** |

Create linked workbooks to summarize sales data for a specialty soft drink producer.

Data File needed for this Case Problem: InBurger.xlsx

Infusion Blend Micki Goldstein, a sales representative for a specialty soft drink producer, Infusion Blend, has Florida as her territory where she is based out of Tampa. Her job takes her around the state where she meets and presents her product offerings to store managers from major supermarket chains to the small mom-and-pop corner markets. Although she does not personally make the deliveries, she often works closely with the delivery staff to assure quality service to her customers.

Micki must report her sales progress to her regional manager in Atlanta, Georgia. These reports include the overall sales volume, the types of products sold, locations, and stores into which the products were delivered. For the larger markets, she must prepare a separate workbook for each chain store.

Complete the following:

1. Open the **InBurger** workbook located in the Tutorial.06\Case3 folder included with your Data Files, and then save the workbook as **InBurger 2010** in the same folder.

2. In the Documentation sheet, enter your name and the current date, and then switch to the January worksheet.

3. For each month (January through December), enter formulas to calculate the total sales for each product and store, and then improve the formatting of the monthly worksheets using the formatting of your choice.

4. Insert a new worksheet between the Documentation and January worksheets. Rename this worksheet **YTD Summary**. Format this worksheet identically to the monthly worksheets except leave the range B6:G11 blank.

5. Use 3-D reference formulas to add the cases sold from January through December. For example, in cell B6, the product Popgo sold in the Elteron store equals 1335 cases.

6. Insert formulas that add the total cases sold by product in column G and total cases sold by store in row 12. Calculate the Summary total for all products.

⊕ **EXPLORE**

7. Insert a new worksheet following the Documentation worksheet. Rename this worksheet as **Annual Recap**. Using Figure 6-31 as a guide, create three separate summaries on this worksheet: by Products, Store, and Month.

   a. Insert formulas that add the total cases sold of each product in the range C7:C12 (column G in the monthly worksheets). Calculate totals for all products.

   b. Insert formulas that add the total cases sold at each store in the range G7:G11 (row 12 in the monthly worksheets). Calculate totals for all stores.

   c. Insert formulas that add the total cases sold each month in the range K7:K18 (cell G12 in each worksheet). Calculate totals for all months.

Figure 6-31

	A	B	C	D	E	F	G	H	I	J	K	L
1						In Burger's Sales by Store and Product						
2							Cases Sold					
3												
4												
5			Breakdown by Products				Breakdown by Store				Breakdown by Month	
6		Products	Cases Sold	Percent		Store	Cases Sold	Percent		Store	Cases Sold	Percent
7		Popgo	7,065	31%		Elteron	4,700	20%		January	8,975	39%
8		Diet Popgo	4,760	21%		Mesa	4,600	20%		February	7,120	31%
9		Mt. Spring	3,360	15%		Franklin	4,700	20%		March	3,905	17%
10		Red Burst	1,675	7%		Grant	4,625	20%		April	2,980	13%
11		Dr Selsa	3,135	14%		Grover	4,355	19%		May	0	0%
12		Sun Maid	2,985	13%		Totals	22,980			June	0	0%
13		Totals	22,980							July	0	0%
14										August	0	0%
15										September	0	0%
16										October	0	0%
17										November	0	0%
18										December	0	0%
19										Totals	22,980	

8. Insert formulas in columns D, H, and L to calculate the percentage of products, stores, and months, respectively.

9. Results for the month of May are shown in Figure 6-32. Enter this data into the May worksheet.

Figure 6-32

	A	B	C	D	E	F	G
1	In Burger's Sales by Store and Product						
2	Cases Sold						
3							
4		Stores					
5	Products	Elteron	Mesa	Franklin	Grant	Grover	Totals
6	Popgo	515	545	560	670	510	2,800
7	Diet Popgo	435	445	435	430	410	2,155
8	Mt. Spring	235	275	240	240	205	1,195
9	Red Burst	125	125	150	150	325	875
10	Dr Selsa	160	145	150	160	125	740
11	Sun Maid	325	240	175	245	225	1,210
12	Totals	1,795	1,775	1,710	1,895	1,800	8,975

10. In the Documentation sheet, in the range A8:A19, type the months **January** through **December**. Create hyperlinks from each cell to its corresponding worksheet. Test the hyperlinks.

11. Save and close the workbook. Submit the finished workbook to your instructor, either in printed or electronic form, as requested.

Challenge | Case Problem 4

Explore using worksheet groups, 3-D references, external references, workspaces, and templates to summarize data for a pharmaceutical manufacturer.

Data Files needed for this Case Problem: Europe.xlsx, North America.xlsx, South America.xlsx, PlutoTemplate.xltx

Pluto Pharmaceuticals Pluto Pharmaceuticals is a multinational manufacturer of healthcare products. The chief financial analyst, Kevin Cross, asks you to prepare the first quarter revenue summary for three global regions based on workbooks from the regions of North America, South America, and Europe. Each workbook has monthly worksheets displaying forecasted and actual revenues of the major product groups for the first quarter. Kevin wants you to calculate the difference between forecasted and actual sales (Difference) and the percent change between forecasted and actual sales (% Change). He also wants you to summarize each workbook, reporting the quarterly forecasted and actual totals for revenues in a new worksheet. After you have added this information to each workbook, Kevin wants you to consolidate the information from the three regional workbooks, reporting in a single workbook the summarized information for each region.

Complete the following:

1. Open the **Europe**, **North America**, and **South America** regional revenue workbooks located in the Tutorial.06\Case4 folder included with your Data Files. Save the Europe workbook as **PlutoEU**, the North America workbook as **PlutoNA**, and the South America workbook as **PlutoSA** in the same folder. In the Documentation sheet in each regional revenue workbook, enter your name and the date.

2. Each regional workbook contains a Documentation sheet, a first quarter summary worksheet, and three monthly worksheets. Complete the monthly worksheets in each region's workbook by doing the following:

   - Calculate the difference for each product group: Actual–Forecast.
   - Calculate the % change for each product group: Difference/Forecast.
   - Calculate the total revenue for the Forecast, Actual, and Difference columns, and then calculate the total % Change.
   - Format the numbers to improve the appearance of the worksheets.

3. In each workbook, complete the Quarter 1 worksheet by first summarizing the forecasted and actual totals for product groups for the first three months of the year, then calculating the difference and the % change, and, finally, summarizing the forecasted, actual, difference, and % change values for the quarter. (*Hint:* The Total Revenue % change (cell E10) is not the sum of the column; it is the percent change between the forecasted and actual totals.) Use Figure 6-33 as a guide as you complete the worksheet.

Figure 6-33

	A	B	C	D	E
1		Pluto Pharmaceuticals-North America			
2		Revenue - Quarter 1			
3					
4	Product Group	Forecast	Actual	Difference	% Change
5	Healthcare	$ 2,295,600	$ 2,363,891	$ 68,291	3.0%
6	Consumer Healthcare	$ 340,500	$ 363,536	$ 23,036	6.8%
7	Animal Healthcare	$ 2,079,100	$ 2,101,693	$ 22,593	1.1%
8	Prescription Medicine	$ 522,300	$ 526,672	$ 4,372	0.8%
9	Over-the-Counter Medicine	$ 1,006,200	$ 976,096	$ (30,104)	-3.0%
10	Total Revenue	$ 6,243,700	$ 6,331,888	$ 88,188	1.4%

4. Format the Quarter 1 sheet for each regional workbook with the same formatting used for the monthly worksheets, and then save the workbooks.

5. Create a new workbook, and save it as **Pluto Summary** in the Tutorial.06\Case4 folder included with your Data Files. Rename the Sheet1 worksheet as **Documentation**, and in column A enter the same labels used in the Documentation sheets in the other workbooks. In column B, enter **Corporate** as the region, enter your name as the author and the current date as the date created, and then enter **To report on revenue for all regions** as the purpose. Format the Documentation sheet to match the Documentation worksheet formatting in the PlutoNA, PlutoSA, and PlutoEU workbooks.

6. Switch to the Sheet2 worksheet, and then use Figure 6-34 as a guide to enter the text shown. Enter formulas to total the forecasted and actual revenue for each product group. Compute the difference and % change for each product group. Include the totals for the Forecast, Actual, and Difference columns, and calculate the % Change for the total revenue for the quarter. Rename the worksheet as **Quarter 1**.

Figure 6-34

	A	B	C	D	E
1	Pluto Pharmaceuticals-Corporate				
2	Revenue - Quarter 1				
3					
4	Product Group	Forecast	Actual	Difference	% Change
5	Healthcare	$ 5,670,800	$ 5,913,673	$ 242,873	4.3%
6	Consumer Healthcare	$ 1,210,500	$ 1,250,000	$ 39,500	3.3%
7	Animal Healthcare	$ 4,632,300	$ 4,662,070	$ 29,770	0.6%
8	Prescription Medicine	$ 1,432,900	$ 1,507,357	$ 74,457	5.2%
9	Over-the-Counter Medicine	$ 2,707,600	$ 2,657,288	$ (50,312)	-1.9%
10	**Total Revenue**	$ 15,654,100	$ 15,990,388	$ 336,288	2.1%

⊕ **EXPLORE**   7. Insert a bar chart that compares the actual and forecast sales by product group. The chart is similar to Figure 6-35. Place the chart beneath the data you entered in the Quarter 1 worksheet. Change the axis so the sales are displayed in millions of dollars.

Figure 6-35

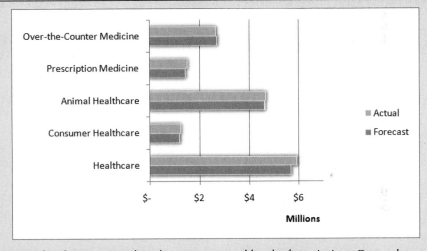

8. Prepare the three regional and corporate workbooks for printing. On each page, include the worksheet name in the center section of the header and your name in the left section of the footer.

9. Create a workspace that opens with the Quarter 1 worksheet active in each workbook using a horizontal layout for the four workbooks, and then save it as **Quarter1 Files** in the Tutorial.06\Case4 folder included with your Data Files.

10. Open the **Pluto Summary** workbook located in the Tutorial.06\Case4 folder included with your Data Files, and then save the workbook as **Pluto Yearend** in the same folder. For year-end backup, break the links in the Pluto Yearend workbook.

⊕ **EXPLORE**   11. You receive a new source file to substitute for the original source file. The new source file has a different name.

a. Open the **Pluto Summary** workbook, and then save the workbook as **Pluto Summary Test**. Close the workbook.

    b. Open the **PlutoNA** workbook, and then save the workbook as **PlutoNorth**. In the PlutoNorth workbook in the March worksheet, change the actual healthcare revenue in cell C5 to **$863,298**. Save and close the PlutoNorth workbook.

    c. Open the **Pluto Summary Test** workbook, and change the link to the source workbook from PlutoNA to **PlutoNorth**. (*Hint:* Use the Edit Links dialog box.) Save and close the Pluto Summary Test workbook.

⊕ **EXPLORE** 12. Update the source program but not the destination file.

    a. Open the **PlutoEU** workbook, and then save the workbook as **PlutoEurope**.

    b. Open the **Pluto Summary Test** workbook, and change the link to the source workbook from PlutoEU to **PlutoEurope**. Note the actual total revenue in the Quarter 1 worksheet (cell C10). Close the Pluto Summary Test workbook.

    c. In the PlutoEurope workbook, switch to the March worksheet and change the actual animal healthcare revenue in cell C7 to **$275,569**. Save and close the PlutoEurope workbook.

    d. Open the **Pluto Summary Test** workbook but keep the automatic update of the links disabled. How does this affect the Quarter 1 total actual revenue (cell C10) in the Pluto Summary Test workbook (compare the current value to the value you noted in Step b)?

    e. Use the Edit Links dialog box to update the Pluto Summary Test workbook. How does this affect the Quarter 1 total actual revenue (cell C10) in the Pluto Summary Test workbook (compare the current value to the value you noted in Step d)?

⊕ **EXPLORE** 13. Modify the template named **PlutoTemplate** located in the Tutorial.06\Case4 folder. Make the following two changes to the template, and then save the modified template as **PlutoTemplateRevised**.

    a. Instead of column E displaying #DIV/0! in all sheets, change the formula in column E to display 0% when no values are entered in column B (Forecast).

    b. Apply a fill color of your choice to the range B5:C9 in the monthly worksheets to identify where to enter data.

14. Create a new workbook from the modified PlutoTemplateRevised template. Enter **$500,000** in the range B5:B9 of each monthly worksheet. Enter **$550,000** in the range C5:C9 of each monthly worksheet. Save the workbook as **Pluto2011**.

15. Save and close all the workbooks. Submit the finished workbooks to your instructor, either in printed or electronic form, as requested.

Research | Internet Assignments

Use the Internet to find and work with data related to the topics presented in this tutorial.

The purpose of the Internet Assignments is to challenge you to find information on the Internet that you can use to work effectively with this software. The actual assignments are updated and maintained on the Course Technology Web site. Log on to the Internet and use your Web browser to go to the Student Online Companion for New Perspectives Office 2007 at **www.course.com/np/office2007**. Then navigate to the Internet Assignments for this tutorial.

Assess | **SAM Assessment and Training**

If you have a SAM user profile, you may have access to hands-on instruction, practice, and assessment of the skills covered in this tutorial. Log in to your SAM account (**http://sam2007.course.com**) to launch any assigned training activities or exams that relate to the skills covered in this tutorial.

Review | **Quick Check Answers**

Session 6.1

1. A worksheet group is a collection of two or more worksheets that have been selected.
2. To select an adjacent group of worksheets, click the first sheet tab, press and hold the Shift key, and then click the sheet tab of the last worksheet in the range. To select a nonadjacent group of worksheets, click the sheet tab of one of the worksheets in the group, press and hold the Ctrl key, and then click the sheet tabs of the remaining worksheets in the group. Deselect a worksheet group by either clicking the sheet tab of a worksheet not in the group or right-clicking one of the sheet tabs in the group and clicking Ungroup Sheets on the shortcut menu.
3. ='Quarter 2'!A10
4. 'Summary 1:Summary 3'!A10
5. the maximum value found in cell B1 of all worksheets from Sheet1 to Sheet4
6. MAX(Sheet1:Sheet5!B1); if Sheet5 were positioned before Sheet4, then MAX(Sheet1:Sheet4!B1) includes Sheet5.
7. Select a worksheet group that consists of all sheets in the workbook, click the Page Layout tab, and then select the page layout specification that you want to apply to all worksheets in the group.

Session 6.2

1. 'D:\Reports\[Product Report]Sales Info'!A1:A10
2. The source file is the file that contains the data values you want to link to.
3. The destination file receives the value(s) from the source file.
4. If both the destination and source files are open, Excel will update the link automatically when you update a value in the source file; when you open the destination file, click the Options button in the Message Bar, click the Enable this content option button, and then click the OK button.
5. In the Connections group on the Data tab, click the Edit Links button to open the Edit Links dialog box. The linked workbooks are listed in the dialog box.
6. A workspace file is a file containing information about all opened workbooks, including their locations, window sizes, and screen positions.
7. By opening a workspace file, you open all workbooks defined in the workspace. Using a workspace helps you organize projects that might involve several workbooks.

Session 6.3

1. Click the cell in which you want to insert the hyperlink, and then in the Links group on the Insert tab, click the Hyperlink button. Type the hyperlink text in the Insert Hyperlink dialog box.

2. True

3. A template is a workbook that contains specific content and formatting that you can use as a model for other similar workbooks.

4. A user can modify the contents of a workbook based on a template without changing the template file itself. The next time a new workbook is created based on a template, the workbook opens with all the original properties intact. If you use the workbook file to create a new workbook, you first must delete the values from cells that you want to change and then use the Save As dialog box to assign a new filename to the workbook.

5. Click the Office Button, click Save As, click the Save as type button, click Template, type a filename for the template, and then click the Save button.

6. Web Page; Single File Web Page

Ending Data Files

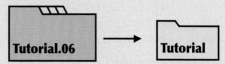

Tutorial.06 →

Tutorial

Audited 2010.xlsx
Colorado.xlsx
Hoot Time Card.xlsx
New Mexico.xlsx
New Mexico 2011.xlsx
Sales 2010.docx
Theme Parks.xlw
Totals 2010.xlsx
Travel Template.xltx
Utah.xlsx
Web Totals 2010.htm

Review

Idaho.xlsx
NW Totals 2010.xlsx
NW Travel.xltx
NW Workspace.xlw
Oregon.xlsx
Oregon 2011.xlsx
Washington.xlsx
Web Oregon 2010.htm
☐ **Web Oregon 2010_files**

Case1

Java Cafe.xlsx
Java Cafe 2011.xlsx
Java Template.xltx
Web Java.htm

Case2

Carson City 2011.xlsx
UTE Carson City.xlsx
UTE Reno.xlsx
UTE Summary.xlsx
UTE Template.xltx
UTE Vegas.xlsx
UTE Web Page.htm

Case3

InBurger 2010.xlsx

Case4

Pluto 2011.xlsx
Pluto Summary.xlsx
Pluto Summary Test.xlsx
Pluto Yearend.xlsx
PlutoEU.xlsx
PlutoEurope.xlsx
PlutoNA.xlsx
PlutoNorth.xlsx
PlutoSA.xlxs
PlutoTemplateRevised.xltx
Quarter1 Files.xlw

Using Advanced Functions, Conditional Formatting, and Filtering

Reviewing Employee Data

Case | Talent Tracs

Rita Corvales founded Talent Tracs, a software development company for the music and entertainment industry located in Austin, Texas. Talent Tracs sells EasyTracs, a software program that matches venues with artists and then schedules the performances. As the company's reputation grew, the business expanded rapidly. Today, Talent Tracs has nearly 100 employees, ranging from software developers to online customer relations staff. Rita uses Excel to track basic employee information such as each employee's name, gender, birth date, hire date, health plan, job status, pay type (hourly or salaried), pay grade, and annual salary.

Rita needs to review and manage the information about her company's employees on a regular basis. For example, she needs to track employee enrollment and costs in the benefit programs offered by the company. She also wants to calculate each employee's life insurance premium and how much the company contributes to each employee's 401(k) retirement account and health plan. And Rita needs to calculate the amount Talent Tracs spends on bonuses, which are based on employee pay grades and performance.

To provide Rita with the information she needs, you'll use a variety of Excel functions, filters, and conditional formatting.

Starting Data Files

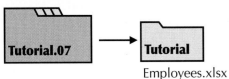

Tutorial.07 → Tutorial

Employees.xlsx

Review

Tracs.xlsx

Case1

Modem.xlsx

Case2

Leave.xlsx

Case3

M-Fresh.xlsx

Case4

Rock Island.xlsx

Session 7.1

Working with Logical Functions

The Talent Tracs compensation package includes salary, bonuses, and benefits. Right now, Rita wants to focus on three types of benefits: life insurance, retirement savings, and healthcare. Employees can choose to purchase additional supplemental life insurance coverage equal to their annual base salary times the insurance premium rate. The 401(k) retirement savings plan matches eligible employees' contributions, dollar for dollar, up to 3 percent of their salary. Employees can select a PPO or HMO health plan for families or individuals, or they can opt out of the health plan by providing evidence of other health-care coverage.

Rita created a workbook that contains descriptive data for employees and their benefits. You will open this workbook now and review the employee information.

To open the Employees workbook:

▶ 1. Open the **Employees** workbook located in the **Tutorial.07\Tutorial** folder included with your Data Files, and then save the workbook as **Talent Tracs** in the same folder.

▶ 2. In the Documentation worksheet, enter your name and the current date.

▶ 3. Switch to the **Employee Data** worksheet. See Figure 7-1.

| Figure 7-1 | Employee Data worksheet |

M91 | fx =DATEDIF([Hire Date],$AE$2,"y")

	A	B	C	D	E	F	G	H	I	J	K	L	M	N
1	ID	Last Name	Hire Date	Birth Date	Sex	Location	Job Status	Add Life Ins	Pay Grade	Pay Type	Annual Salary	Health Plan	Years Service	
2	1024	Hovey	8/28/2008	9/6/1966	M	Austin	FT	Y	3	S	$ 85,000	HMOF	1	
3	1025	Overton	5/24/2004	2/15/1986	F	Home	FT	N	2	S	$ 40,000	HMOF	6	
4	1026	Fetherston	4/24/2009	9/24/1968	M	New Orleans	FT	Y	2	S	$ 37,244	HMOF	1	
5	1027	Lebrun	7/18/2008	8/9/1959	F	Austin	FT	N	3	S	$ 80,000	None	1	
6	1028	Hanson	8/21/2009	7/15/1950	M	Austin	FT	Y	3	S	$ 65,000	None	0	
7	1029	Philo	3/5/2009	5/2/1958	M	New Orleans	FT	Y	3	S	$125,000	PPOI	1	
8	1030	Stolt	3/1/2007	12/7/1977	M	New Orleans	FT	N	3	S	$ 95,000	HMOI	3	
9	1031	Akhalaghi	12/8/2009	12/4/1961	M	Austin	FT	N	2	S	$ 36,000	None	0	
10	1032	Vankeuren	8/11/2005	1/10/1959	F	Austin	PT	N	1	H	$ 33,508	PPOF	4	
11	1033	Mccorkle	6/12/2003	1/30/1942	F	Nashville	FT	N	1	H	$ 21,840	None	7	
12	1034	Nightingale	5/4/2006	8/27/1989	M	Nashville	FT	N	1	H	$ 25,792	PPOF	4	
13	1035	Croasdale	12/18/2009	1/6/1968	F	Austin	FT	N	1	H	$ 32,011	PPOI	0	
14	1036	Lambrechts	5/4/2005	4/28/1958	F	Nashville	FT	Y	1	H	$ 23,920	HMOF	5	
15	1037	Palmer	11/26/1998	10/4/1971	F	Austin	FT	Y	1	H	$ 32,011	None	11	
16	1038	Tetreault	2/22/2002	1/4/1960	F	Nashville	FT	Y	1	H	$ 21,840	PPOI	8	
17	1039	Cugini	12/4/2009	1/16/1970	F	Austin	FT	Y	2	S	$ 55,000	PPOF	0	
18	1040	Dash	10/12/2009	12/2/1985	M	Nashville	FT	Y	2	S	$ 65,000	HMOF	0	
19	1041	Donnelly	12/4/2009	5/9/1959	F	New Orleans	FT	Y	3	S	$125,000	HMOF	0	

Documentation | **Employee Data** | Employee Summary | Lookup Tables

Ready | 120%

The Employee Data worksheet contains an Excel table of employee data. Rita entered each employee's ID, last name, hire date, birth date, gender, location, job status (FT for full-time, PT for part-time, or CN for paid consultant), additional life insurance coverage (Y for Yes, N for No), pay grade (1, 2, or 3), and pay type (S for Salaried, H for Hourly). The worksheet also includes the employee's annual salary, the type of health plan the employee selected (HMOF for HMO-Family, HMOI for HMO-Individual, PPOF for PPO-Family, PPOI for PPO-Individual, or None), and the number of years the employee has worked at Talent Tracs (Years Service). Rita stores the employees' additional personal information, including home address, phone numbers, Social Security numbers, and so forth, in another workbook.

Creating Fields in a Table | InSight

Keep the following guidelines in mind when creating fields in an Excel table:

- **Create fields that require the least maintenance.** For example, fields such as Hire Date and Birth Date require no maintenance because their values do not change, unlike fields such as Age and Years of Service, whose values change each year. If you need to track information such as the specific age or years of service, a best practice is to use calculations to determine these values based on values in the Hire Date and Birth Date fields.
- **Store the smallest unit of data possible in a field.** For example, use three separate fields for City, State, and Zip Code rather than one field. Using separate fields for each unit of data enables you to sort or filter each field. If you want to display data from two or more fields in one column, you can use a formula to reference the City, State, and Zip Code fields. For example, you can use the concatenation operator (the ampersand) to combine the city, state, and zip code in one cell as follows: =C2 & D2 & E2.
- **Apply a text format to fields with numerical text data.** For example, formatting fields such as Zip Code and Social Security Number as text ensures that leading zeros are stored as part of the data. Otherwise, the zip code 02892 is stored as a number and displayed as 2892, which is not the intended result.

Rita formatted the data as an Excel table to take advantage of the additional analysis and organization tools available for Excel tables. Rita asks you to replace the default name for the Excel table with a more descriptive name.

To rename the Excel table:

▶ 1. Make sure cell **A1** (the first cell in the Excel table) is the active cell, and then click the **Table Tools Design** tab on the Ribbon.

▶ 2. In the Properties group, select **Table1** in the Table Name box, type **Employee**, and then press the **Enter** key. The Excel table is now named *Employee*.

Next, you'll insert formulas that calculate each employee's additional life insurance premium (if any), 401(k) cost, health plan cost, and bonus amount. After you calculate those values, Rita wants you to summarize that information in the Employee Summary worksheet, so she can quickly see the impact of the compensation and benefits package on the company.

Whenever you enter a formula into an empty table column, Excel automatically fills the rest of that table column with the formula. This is referred to as a **calculated column**. If you need to modify the formula in a calculated column, you edit the formula in one cell of the column and the formulas in that table column are also modified. If you edit a cell in a calculated column so it is no longer consistent with the other formulas in the column (such as replacing a formula with a value), a green triangle appears in the upper-left corner of the cell, making the inconsistency easy to see. After a calculated column contains an inconsistency, any other edits you make to that column are no longer automatically applied to the rest of the cells in that column because Excel does not overwrite custom values.

> **Tip**
>
> Calculated columns work only in Excel tables. To achieve the same results in a range of data, you must copy and paste the formula or use the AutoFill feature.

You'll start by calculating the additional life insurance premiums. This amount depends on whether an employee has elected additional life insurance coverage. So, you'll need to enter a formula that includes the IF function to determine the amount of the premium.

Using the IF Function

In many situations, the value you store in a cell depends on certain conditions. Consider the following examples:

- An employee's gross pay depends on whether that employee worked overtime.
- An income tax rate depends on the taxpayer's adjusted taxable income.
- A shipping charge depends on the size of an order.

To evaluate these types of conditions in Excel, you use the IF function. Recall that the IF function is a logical function that evaluates a condition (a logical test), and then returns one value if the condition is true and another value if the condition is false. The IF function has the following syntax:

```
IF(logical_test, value_if_true, [value_if_false])
```

In this function, *logical_test* is a condition such as A5="Yes" that is either true or false, *value_if_true* is the value displayed in the cell if the logical test is true, and *value_if_false* is the value displayed in the cell if the logical test is not true. Although the *value_if_false* argument is optional, you should usually include it so the IF function covers both possibilities.

You use the IF function to create a conditional statement such as =IF(A5="Yes",C5+B5,B5–C5). The first argument, the *logical_test* A5="Yes", is always performed first and has a result that is either true or false. If the *logical_test* is true, the *value_if_true*, C5+B5, is calculated next and its value is displayed in the cell. If the *logical_test* is false, the *value_if_false*, B5–C5, is calculated next and its value is displayed in the cell. The IF function results in only one value—either the *value_if_true* or the *value_if_false*; the other is ignored.

Talent Tracs employees can purchase additional life insurance coverage equal to the employee's annual salary multiplied by the premium rate (.001). Rita created the flowchart shown in Figure 7-2, which illustrates the logic for calculating an employee's additional life insurance premium. The flowchart shows that if the employee elected additional life insurance (Add Life Ins = "Y" is True), then the premium is calculated using the formula Salary*.001. If the employee did not elect additional life insurance (Add Life Ins = "Y" is False), then the premium is 0.

Flowchart with logic for the additional life insurance premium ◀ **Figure 7-2**

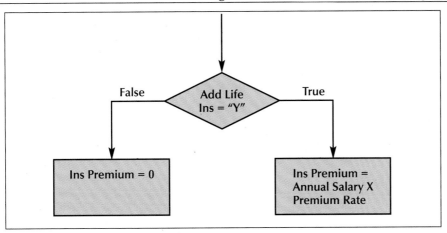

You will add a column in the Employee table to display the life insurance premium. Then, you'll enter a formula with an IF function to calculate the life insurance premium employees will pay if they select additional life insurance coverage.

To calculate the life insurance premium using an IF function:

▶ **1.** In cell N1, enter **Life Ins Premium**. The Excel table expands to include this column and applies the table formatting to all the rows in the new column.

▶ **2.** Make sure cell **N2** is the active cell, and then, on the formula bar, click the **Insert Function** button f_x. The Insert Function dialog box opens.

▶ **3.** Click **Logical** in the Or select a category list, click **IF** in the Select a function box, and then click the **OK** button. The Function Arguments dialog box for the IF function opens. You will use this dialog box to enter the values for the IF function arguments.

▶ **4.** In the Logical_test argument box, type **H2="Y"** and then press the **Tab** key. This sets the logical test to evaluate whether the employee wants additional life insurance, indicated by Y for Yes or N for No in cell H2. *TRUE* appears to the right of the Logical_test argument box, indicating the result for the employee in row 2 is true. That is, the employee wants additional life insurance.

> **Tip**
>
> Testing for text values is not case-sensitive. So the conditions H2="Y" and H2="y" return the same value.

▶ **5.** In the Value_if_true argument box, type **K2*0.001**. This argument specifies that if the condition is true (the employee wants additional life insurance), the result of the employee's current salary (listed in cell K2) is multiplied by 0.1% and appears in cell N2. The value to the right of the Value_if_true argument box is 85, which is the premium the employee in row 2 will pay for additional life insurance if the condition is true.

▶ **6.** In the Value_if_false argument box, type **0**. This argument specifies that if the condition is false (the employee does not want additional life insurance), 0 appears in cell N2. The value to the right of the Value_if_false argument box is 0, which is the value that appears in cell N2 if the condition is false. See Figure 7-3.

Figure 7-3 Function Arguments dialog box for IF function

Figure 7-3 Function Arguments dialog box for IF function

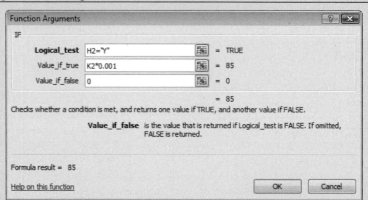

Tip

Click the top portion of the column header in an Excel table (not the worksheet column heading) to select the column data but not the header; double-click to select the entire column including the column header.

7. Click the **OK** button. The formula =IF(H2="Y",K2*0.001,0) appears in the formula bar, and the value 85 appears in cell N2 because the condition is true. The results are automatically copied to all rows in column N of the table.

8. Point to the top of cell **N1** until the pointer changes to ↓, and then click to select the range N2:N101. The data in the Life Ins Premium column is selected, but not the column header.

9. Format the selected range N2:N101 with the **Accounting** number format with **2** decimal places. The Life Ins Premium column shows the premiums employees will pay for additional life insurance, formatted as currency. See Figure 7-4.

Figure 7-4 Life Ins Premium column added to the Employee table

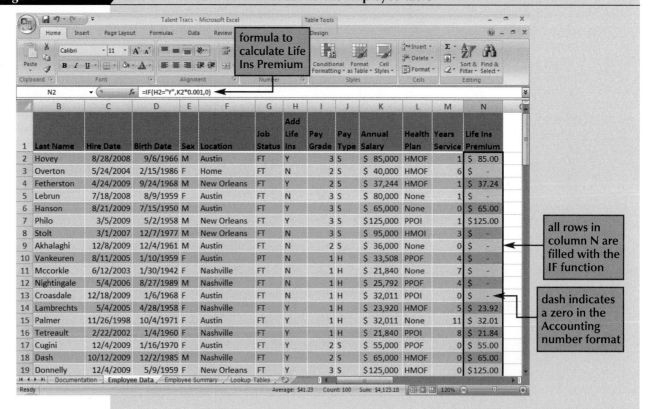

Using the And Function

Employees are eligible for the 401(k) benefit if they are full-time (FT in Job Status) *and* have worked for the company for one or more years (1 or greater in Years Service). As long as *both* conditions are true, the company contributes an amount equal to 3 percent of the employee's salary to the employee's 401(k). If neither condition is true or if only one condition is true, the employee is not eligible for the 401(k) benefit and the company's contribution is 0. Rita outlined these eligibility conditions in the flowchart shown in Figure 7-5.

Flowchart illustrating logic for the 401(k) benefit   **Figure 7-5**

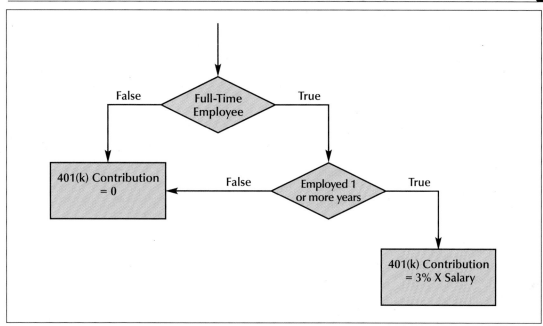

The IF function evaluates a single condition; however, you often need to test two or more conditions and determine whether *all* conditions are true. You can do this with the AND function. The **AND function** is a logical function that returns a TRUE value if all the logical conditions are true and a FALSE value if any or all of the logical conditions are false. The syntax of the AND function is as follows:

```
AND(logical1 [,logical2]...)
```

In this function, *logical1* and *logical2* are conditions that can be either true or false. If all of the logical conditions are true, the AND function returns the logical value TRUE; otherwise, the function returns the logical value FALSE. You can include up to 255 logical conditions in the AND function, but keep in mind that *all* the logical conditions listed in the AND function must be true for the AND function to return a TRUE value.

To calculate the contribution amount for each employee to the 401(k) plan, you need to use the AND function along with the IF function. You use the AND function to test whether each employee in the Employee table fulfills the eligibility requirements, as shown in the following formula:

```
=AND(G2="FT",M2>=1)
```

This formula tests whether the value in cell G2 (the job status for the first employee) is equal to FT (the abbreviation for full-time) and whether the value in cell M2 (the years of service for the first employee) is greater than or equal to 1 (indicating one or more years of employment at Talent Tracs). Therefore, if the employee is a full-time employee (G2="FT") *and* has worked one or more years at Talent Tracs (M2>=1), the AND function returns the value TRUE; otherwise, the AND function returns the value FALSE.

The AND function, however, does not calculate how much Talent Tracs will contribute to the employee's 401(k) plan. To determine whether an employee is eligible *and* to calculate the amount of the 401(k) contribution, you need to insert the AND function within an IF function, as shown in the following formula:

```
=IF(AND(G2="FT",M2>=1),K2*0.03,0)
```

The first argument of the IF function, =IF(AND(G2="FT",M2>=1), uses the AND function to determine if the employee is eligible for a 401(k) contribution. If the employee is eligible, the logical test AND(G2="FT",M2>=1) returns the logical value TRUE and the formula in the value_if_true argument of the IF function multiplies the employee's annual salary by 0.03 (K2*0.03). If one or both conditions are false, the logical test AND(G2="FT",M2>=1) returns the logical value FALSE, and the IF function displays the value 0.

You'll insert a new column in the Employee table, and then enter the formula to calculate the 401(k) contribution using structured references.

Using Structured References with Excel Tables

When you create a formula that references all or parts of an Excel table, you can replace the specific cell or range address with a **structured reference**, the actual table name or column header. The table name is Table1, Table2, and so forth unless you entered a more descriptive table name, as you did for the Employee table. Column headers provide a description of the data entered in each column. Structured references make it easier to create formulas that use portions or all of an Excel table because the names or headers are usually simpler to identify than cell addresses. For example, in the Employee table, the table name *Employee* refers to the range A2:N101, which is the range of data in the table excluding the header row and Total row. When you want to reference an entire column of data in a table, you create a column qualifier, which has the following syntax:

Tip

If you are not sure of a table's name, click in the table, click the Table Tools Design tab on the Ribbon, and then check the Table Name box in the Properties group.

```
Tablename[qualifier]
```

The *Tablename* is the name entered in the Table Name box in the Properties group on the Table Tools Design tab. The *qualifier* is the column header enclosed in square brackets. For example, the structured reference *Employee[Annual Salary]* references the annual salary data in the range K2:K101 of the Employee table. You use structured references in formulas, as shown in the following formula:

```
=SUM(Employee[Annual Salary])
```

This formula adds the annual salary data in the range K2:K101 of the Employee table. In this case, *[Annual Salary]* is the column qualifier.

When you create a calculated column, as you did to calculate life insurance premiums in the Employee table, you can use structured references to create the formula. A formula that includes a structured reference can be fully qualified or unqualified. In a fully qualified structured reference, the table name precedes the column qualifier. In an unqualified structured reference, only the column qualifier appears in the reference. For example, you could have used either of the following formulas with structured references to calculate Life Ins Premium in the calculated column you added to the Employee table (the first formula is unqualified, and the second is fully qualified):

```
=IF([Add Life Ins]="Y",[Annual Salary]*001,0)
=IF(Employee[Add Life Ins]="Y",Employee[Annual Salary]*.001,0)
```

If you are creating a calculated column or formula within an Excel table, you can use the unqualified structured reference in the formula. If you use a structured reference outside the table or in another worksheet to reference an Excel table or portion of the table, you need to use a fully qualified reference.

In addition to referencing a specific column in a table by its column header, you can also reference other portions of a table, such as the header row or Total row. Figure 7-6 lists the special item qualifiers needed to reference these table portions in the formula.

Special item qualifiers for structured references | **Figure 7-6**

Qualifier	References	Example of Structured Reference
#All	The entire table, including column headers, data, and Total row if displayed	=Employee[#All]
#Data	The data in the table	=Employee[#Data]
#Headers	The header row in the table	=Employee[#Headers]
#Totals	The Total row in the table; if the Total row is hidden, then an error is returned	=Employee[#Totals]
#ThisRow	The current row in the specified column of the table	=Employee[[#ThisRow],[Column Header]]

You'll use structured references to calculate the 401(k) contributions for Talent Tracs.

To enter a formula with IF and AND functions to calculate 401(k) contributions:

▶ **1.** In cell O1, enter **401(k)** as the column header. The Excel table expands to include the new column, and cell O2 is the active cell.

▶ **2.** In cell O2, type **=I**. A list of valid function names opens scrolled to the I entries.

▶ **3.** Double-click **IF**. The first part of the formula with the IF function, =IF(, appears in the cell and the formula bar with the insertion point placed directly after the opening parenthesis so you can continue typing the formula. The syntax of the IF function appears in a ScreenTip below cell O2. See Figure 7-7.

Tip

You can also insert the selected function in the list by pressing the Tab key.

IF function ScreenTip | **Figure 7-7**

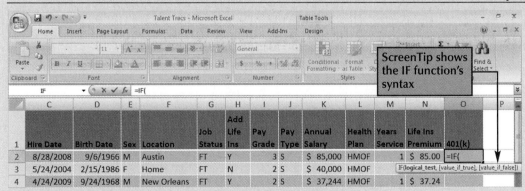

Next, you'll enter the AND function as the logical test for the IF function.

▶ **4.** Type **A** to open the function list scrolled to the A entries, and then double-click **AND**. The first part of the AND function is added to the formula, and =IF(AND(appears in the cell and the formula bar. The syntax of the AND function appears in a ScreenTip below cell O2.

Trouble? If a function other than the AND function appears in cell O2, you probably double-clicked a different function name. Press the Backspace key to delete the incorrect function name and redisplay the list of function names. When you see the AND function, double-click the name.

You'll enter the logical conditions for the AND function using structured references.

▶ **5.** Type **[** to display a list of all the column headers in the Employee table. You want to enter the Job Status column for the first logical condition. See Figure 7-8.

Figure 7-8 **List of column qualifiers**

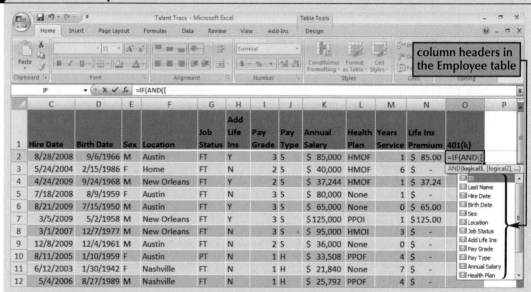

▶ **6.** Double-click **Job Status**, and then type **]** to enter the structured reference for column G, which is the Job Status column. A blue box surrounds the Job Status data and [Job Status] is colored blue in the formula =IF(AND([Job Status] in the cell. This is the first part of the logical condition for the AND function, which is job status is full-time.

▶ **7.** Type **="FT",** (including the comma) to complete the first logical condition. The first logical condition states that the content in the Job Status cell must equal FT.

▶ **8.** Type **[** to begin the second logical condition, double-click **Years Service** in the list, and then type **]**. The structured reference for cell O2, which is years of service for the first employee, is entered in the formula. A green box surrounds the Years Service data and the structured reference is colored green in the formula.

▶ **9.** Type **>=1),** to complete the second logical condition. The second logical condition states that the content in the Years Service cell must be greater than or equal to 1. The complete logical expression for the IF function, =IF(AND([Job Status]="FT",[Years Service]>=1), appears in the cell and the formula bar. The ScreenTip shows the syntax of the IF function again, because you are ready to enter the value_if_true argument and the value_if_false argument.

▶ **10.** Type **[** to open the list of column headers, double-click **Annual Salary**, and then type **]*0.03,** to complete the value_if_true argument using a structured reference. The Annual Salary data appears in a purple box, and the structured reference in the formula is purple. If the employee is eligible for the 401(k) contribution, as determined by the AND function, then the amount in the Annual Salary cell for the employee is multiplied by 3%.

You'll complete the formula by entering the value_if_false argument.

▶ **11.** Type **0)** for the value_if_false argument, and then press the **Enter** key. The formula is entered in cell O2 and copied to the rest of the 401(k) column in the table. If the employee is not eligible for the 401(k) contribution, as determined by the AND function, then 0 is entered in the 401(k) cell. In this case, cell O2 displays the value 2550, which is the result of multiplying the employee's annual salary of $85,000 by 3 percent, because the employee in row 2 meets both conditions of the logical test (job status is full-time and years of service is 1 year). See Figure 7-9.

Formula using IF and AND functions to calculate 401(k)   Figure 7-9

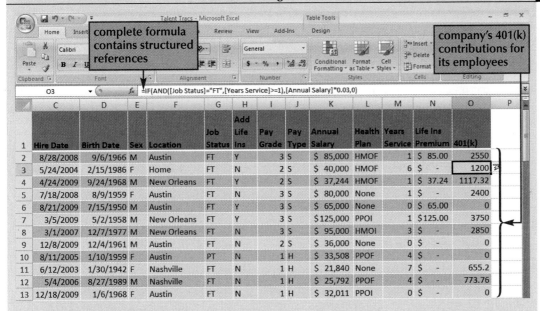

Trouble? If a dialog box opens, indicating that your formula contains an error, you might have omitted a comma, a square bracket, or a parenthesis. Edit the formula as needed to ensure the complete formula is =IF(AND([Job Status]="FT",[Years Service]>=1),[Annual Salary]*0.03,0), and then press the Enter key.

▶ **12.** Point to the top of cell **O1** until the pointer changes to ⬇, click to select the 401(k) data values, and then format the range using the **Accounting** number format with **2** decimal places.

InSight	Using the DATEDIF Function

The column Years Service was calculated using the DATEDIF function. The **DATEDIF function** calculates the difference between two dates and shows the result in months, days, or years. The DATEDIF function has the following syntax:

DATEDIF(*Date1*,*Date2*,*Interval*)

In this function, *Date1* is the earliest date, *Date2* is the latest date, and *Interval* is the unit of time the DATEDIF function will use in the result. You specify the *Interval* with one of the following interval codes:

Interval Code	Meaning	Description
"m"	Months	The number of complete months between Date1 and Date2
"d"	Days	The number of complete days between Date1 and Date2
"y"	Years	The number of complete years between Date1 and Date2

Thus, the formula to calculate years of service at Talent Tracs in complete years is:

=DATEDIF(C2,$AE$2,"y")

The earliest date is located in cell C2, the Hire Date. The latest date is in cell $AE$2, which shows the date used to compare against the Hire Date, the Years Service as of a cut-off date. The Interval is "y" to indicate you want to display the number of complete years between these two dates.

Note that the DATEDIF function is undocumented in Excel, but it has been available since Excel 97. If you want to learn more about this function, use your favorite search engine to search the Web for *DATEDIF function in Excel*.

Creating Nested IF Functions

The IF function tests for only two outcomes. However, many situations involve a series of outcomes. For example, Talent Tracs pays three levels of employee bonuses. Each bonus is based on the employee's pay grade, which is a system Talent Tracs uses to group jobs based on difficulty and responsibility. Talent Tracs has three pay grade codes (1, 2, and 3). Pay grade 1 has a starting bonus of $2,500, pay grade 2 has a starting bonus of $5,000, and pay grade 3 has a starting bonus of $7,500. Supervisors can increase or decrease these amounts based on the employee's performance. The IF function can choose between only two outcomes; it cannot choose between three outcomes. However, you can nest IF functions to allow for three or more outcomes. A **nested IF function** is when one IF function is placed inside another IF function to test an additional condition. You can nest more than one IF function. In this case, you need to nest three IF functions to calculate the different series of outcomes for the employee bonuses.

Rita created a flowchart to illustrate the logic for determining bonus awards, shown in Figure 7-10. She used different colors to identify each nested IF function. The flowchart shows that if the employee has a pay grade equal to 1, then the bonus equals $2,500 and the IF function is finished (the green portion of the flowchart). If the pay grade is not equal to 1, then the second IF function (shown in blue) is evaluated. If the employee has a pay grade equal to 2, then the bonus equals $5,000 and the IF function is finished. If the pay grade is not equal to 2, then the third IF function (shown in gray) is evaluated. If the employee has a pay grade equal to 3, then the bonus equals $7,500 and the IF function is finished. If the pay grade is not equal to 3, then the message "Invalid pay grade" (shown in dark yellow) is entered in the cell.

Flowchart illustrating the logic to determine the bonus amount ◄ **Figure 7-10**

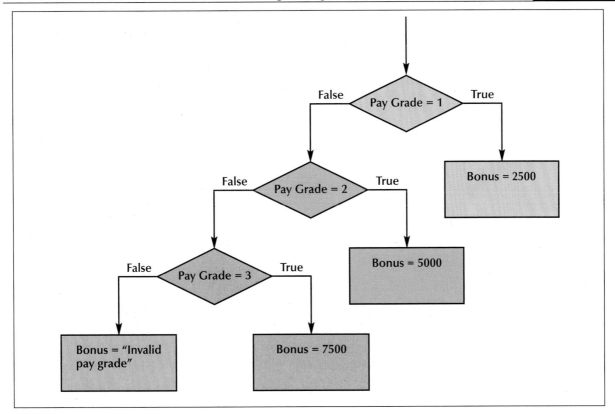

Next, you need to convert Rita's flowchart into a formula. The complete formula is as follows:

```
=IF([Pay Grade]=1,2500,IF([Pay Grade]=2,5000, IF([Pay Grade]=3,
7500,"Invalid pay grade")))
```

The first IF function (shown in green in the flowchart and the formula) tests whether the value in the current Pay Grade cell is equal to 1. If the condition ([Pay Grade]=1) is true, the formula enters 2500 in the Bonus cell. The second IF function (shown in blue in the flowchart and the formula) is executed only if Pay Grade is equal to 1 is false. If the value in the current Pay Grade cell is equal to 2, then the formula returns 5000 in the Bonus cell. The third IF function (shown in gray in the flowchart and the formula) is executed only if [Pay Grade]=2 is false. If the value in the current Pay Grade cell is equal to 3, then the formula returns 7500 in the Bonus cell. If the current value of Pay Grade is not equal to 3, then the message "Invalid pay grade" is entered in the Bonus cell (shown in dark yellow in the flowchart and the formula).

Next, you'll add a column to the Employee table to track the bonus and enter the formula to calculate the bonus amount. Rita mentions that the bonus amounts for each pay grade are not yet final. To make the bonus calculation more flexible, she stored the three bonus amounts (2500, 5000, 7500) in cells Y2, Y3, and Y4 of the Employee Data worksheet. You will reference these cells as you build the formula to calculate the employee bonus. This approach enables you to quickly update the calculated bonus amounts, by changing the values in cells Y2, Y3, and Y4, without having to edit the bonus formula.

To enter nested IFs to calculate employee bonuses:

▶ **1.** In cell P1, enter **Bonus**. A new column with the column header Bonus is added to the Employee table, and cell P2 is the active cell.

▶ **2.** In cell P2, type **=I**, and then double-click **IF**. The beginning of the formula =IF(appears in the cell and formula bar. The syntax of the IF function appears in a ScreenTip below cell P2.

▶ **3.** Type **[** to open a list of all the column headers in the Employee table, double-click **Pay Grade**, type **]** to complete the column qualifier, and then type **=1,$Y$2,** to complete the first logical condition. This condition states that if the logical condition [Pay Grade]=1 is true, then the value stored in cell Y2 (which contains the 2500 bonus) is displayed.

Next, you'll nest a second IF function inside the first IF function.

▶ **4.** Type **IF** and then press the **Tab** key to select the IF function.

▶ **5.** Type **[p**, press the **Tab** key to enter Pay Grade for the structured reference, type **]** to complete the column qualifier, and then type **=2,$Y$3,** to enter the rest of the first nested IF function. The partial formula IF([Pay Grade]=1,$Y$2,IF([Pay Grade]=2,$Y$3 appears in the cell. The second IF function, IF([Pay Grade]=2,$Y$3, is complete and is executed if the logical condition [Pay Grade]=1 is false. If the condition [Pay Grade]=2 is true, the value stored in cell Y3 (which contains 5000) is displayed.

Next, you'll enter a third IF function inside the second IF function.

▶ **6.** Type **IF([Pay Grade]=3, $Y$4,"Invalid pay grade")))**. The formula is complete. The third IF function is executed only if an employee's pay grade is neither 1 nor 2. If the condition [Pay Grade]=3 is true, the value stored in cell Y4 is displayed. If the Pay Grade cell is not equal to 3, then the message "Invalid pay grade" is displayed in the cell instead of the bonus amount.

▶ **7.** Press the **Enter** key. The value 7500 appears in the cell because this employee has a pay grade of 3. The bonus formula is automatically copied to all other rows in the Bonus column. The references to cells Y2, Y3, and Y4 are absolute references and do not change as you move from cell to cell in the Bonus column.

Trouble? If a dialog box opens, indicating that the name you typed is invalid, you might have omitted a square bracket around [Pay Grade] or made a typing error. Click the OK button. The section of the formula that appears to have a problem is highlighted in the formula bar. Compare the formula you typed to =IF([Pay Grade]=1,$Y$2,IF([Pay Grade]=2,$Y$3, IF([Pay Grade]=3,$Y$4,"Invalid pay grade"))) and edit the formula as needed to correct the problem.

▶ **8.** Format the Bonus values in the **Accounting** number format with no decimals. See Figure 7-11.

Tip

You can type an apostrophe to the left of the = sign to convert the formula to text, and then make the corrections to the text, saving you from retyping a long formula. After you correct the formula, delete the apostrophe to test the formula again.

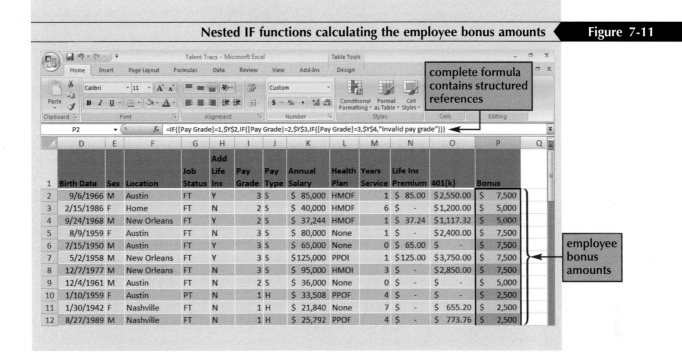

Nested IF functions calculating the employee bonus amounts | Figure 7-11

Checking Formulas for Matching Parentheses | InSight

You should verify that you enclosed the correct argument, function, or term within the parentheses of the formula you are creating. This is especially important when you develop a complex formula that includes many parentheses, because it's easy to lose track of how many closing parenthesis marks you need, particularly at the end of a complex formula. Excel color-codes the parentheses so you can quickly determine whether you have complete pairs of them. You can also verify that the formula includes matching pairs of parentheses by selecting the cell with the formula and then clicking in the formula bar. Press the right arrow key to move the insertion point through the formula one character at a time. When the insertion point moves across one parenthesis, its pair is also highlighted briefly. This color coding helps you make sure that all parentheses in a formula are part of a pair (opening and closing parentheses), which helps to ensure the accuracy of the formula and the results it produces.

You'll scroll the Bonus column to verify that all the bonus amounts were assigned correctly.

To check for invalid pay grade messages in the Employee table:

▶ **1.** Scroll the Bonus column. Cell P31 displays the message, "Invalid pay grade." Rita tells you the correct pay grade for this employee is 3.

▶ **2.** In cell I31 (row 31 of the Pay Grade column), enter **3**. The invalid pay grade code entry is removed and the correct bonus amount, $7,500, is displayed.

▶ **3.** AutoFit the column width of the Bonus column.

The executive team increased the bonus for employees in pay grade 1 from $2,500 to $2,750. Rita asks you to update the bonus amount for pay grade 1 so the employee bonuses will be current.

To update the Bonus amount for pay grade 1:

▶ **1.** In cell Y2, enter **2750**.

▶ **2.** Scroll to the Bonus column and observe that all employees with a pay grade equal to 1 now show a bonus amount equal to $2,750.

Exploring the OR Function

The **OR function** is a logical function that returns a TRUE value if any of the logical conditions are true and a FALSE value if all the logical conditions are false. The syntax of the OR function is as follows:

```
OR(logical1 [,logical2,]...)
```

In this function, *logical1* and *logical2* are conditions that can be either true or false. If any of the logical conditions are true, the OR function returns the logical value TRUE; otherwise, the function returns the logical value FALSE. You can include up to 255 logical conditions in the OR function. However, keep in mind that *if any* logical condition listed in the OR function is true, the OR function returns a TRUE value.

Talent Tracs' executive team is considering changing the criteria to determine which employees receive a bonus. They are considering excluding employees who have worked at Talent Tracs for less than one year or employees who earn more than $100,000 and have other compensation packages.

The OR function can be nested within the IF function to determine employees who are not eligible for a bonus under the proposed criteria and assign a 0 bonus for those employees. The modified formula to calculate the bonus is as follows:

```
=IF(OR([Years Service]<1,[Annual Salary]>100000),0, IF([Pay Grade]=
1,$T$1,IF([Pay Grade]=2,$T$2, IF([Pay Grade]=3,$T$3,"Invalid pay
grade"))))
```

This formula uses the OR function to test whether the current cell for Years Service is less than 1 and also whether the current cell for Annual Salary is greater than 100,000 (shown in red). If either condition or both conditions are true, the OR function returns a TRUE value and 0 is entered in the Bonus cell. If both conditions are false, the OR function returns a FALSE value and determines the bonus for the employee using the nested IF functions you just entered to calculate bonuses based on the pay grade (shown in blue).

In this session, you used the IF and AND functions to calculate the additional life insurance premium and 401(k) benefits for Talent Tracss' employees. You also used nested IF functions to calculate the employee bonuses. Next, Rita needs to calculate health plan costs and the employee recognition award for each employee. She also wants to ensure the validity of data entered into the Employee table and then summarize the results in the Employee Summary worksheet. You'll complete these tasks in the next sessions.

Session 7.1 Quick Check | Review

1. What changes occur in an Excel table's appearance and size after you enter the new column header *Phone*?

2. What term describes the following behavior in Excel: Whenever you enter a formula in an empty column of an Excel table, Excel automatically fills the column with the same formula.

3. An Excel worksheet stores the cost per meal in cell C5, the number of attendees in cell C6, and the total cost of meals in cell C7. What IF function would you enter in cell C7 to calculate the total cost of meals (cost per meal times the number of attendees) with a minimum cost of $10,000?

4. True or False? The AND function is a logical function that returns a TRUE value if any of the logical conditions are true and a FALSE value if all of the logical conditions are false.

5. Write the formula that displays the label *Outstanding* if the amount owed (cell J5) is above 0 and the transaction date (cell D5) is before 3/15/2008, but otherwise leaves the cell blank.

6. When you create a formula that references all or part of an Excel table, you can replace the specific cell or range address with the actual table name or column header name. What are these references called?

7. What are you creating when you include one IF function inside another IF function?

Session 7.2

Using Lookup Tables and Functions

At Talent Tracs, all employees are eligible for the company's health plan. Employees can choose one of four health plans: an HMO for individuals (HMOI), an HMO for families (HMOF), a PPO for individuals (PPOI), and a PPO for families (PPOF). Each health plan has a different monthly premium, and Talent Tracs pays the entire amount. If an employee shows evidence of coverage elsewhere, there is no health plan cost. Figure 7-12 shows the HealthPlanRates table that Rita created with the cost per employee for the different available health plans.

HealthPlanRates table ◄ **Figure 7-12**

	A	B	C	D
1				
2				
3		Plan	Monthly Premium	
4		HMOF	$ 1,500	
5		HMOI	$ 875	
6		PPOF	$ 1,650	
7		PPOI	$ 950	
8		None	$ -	
9				

Rita created a flowchart to explain the logic for determining health plan costs, as shown in Figure 7-13. The flowchart shows that if the employee chooses the HMO for Family health plan (Health Plan=HMOF), then Talent Tracs pays $1500 per month (Health Plan Cost=1500) and the IF function is finished. If the employee chooses the HMO for Individual health plan (Health Plan=HMOI), then Talent Tracs pays $875 per month (Health Plan Cost=875) and the IF function is finished. If the employee chooses the PPO for Family health plan (Health Plan=PPOF), then Talent Tracs pays $1650 per month (Health Plan Cost=1650) and the IF function is finished. If the employee chooses the PPO for Individual health plan (Health Plan=PPOI), then Talent Tracs pays $950 per month (Health Plan Cost=950) and the IF function is finished. If the employee chooses none of the health plans (Health Plan=None), then Talent Tracs pays $0 per month (Health Plan Cost=0), and the IF function is finished.

Figure 7-13 ▷ **Flowchart illustrating the logic of calculating health plan costs**

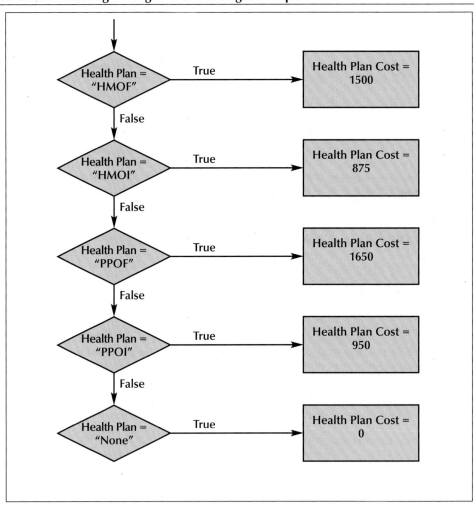

You could calculate these health plan costs using several nested IF functions. However, an easier approach is to use a lookup table. A **lookup table** is a table that organizes data you want to retrieve into different categories, such as each health plan code. The categories for the lookup table, called **compare values**, are located in the table's first column or row. To retrieve a particular value from the table, a **lookup value** (the value you are trying to find) needs to match the compare values. When the lookup value matches a particular compare value, a value from an appropriate column (or row) in the lookup table is returned to the cell in which the lookup formula is entered or used as part of a more complex formula.

You can use the HealthPlanRates table shown in Figure 7-12 that Rita created in the Lookup Tables worksheet as a lookup table. For example, the health plan cost for each eligible employee is based on the plan the employee selected. The lookup value is the employee's health plan code, which is entered in column L of the Employee table. The compare values come from the first column of the HealthPlanRates table, which is in the range B4:C8 in the Lookup Tables worksheet. To retrieve the monthly cost for an employee, Excel moves down the first column in the lookup table (HealthPlanRates) until it finds the health plan code that matches (is equal to) the lookup value. Then, it moves to the second column in the lookup table to locate the monthly cost, which is displayed in the cell where the lookup formula is entered or used as part of a calculation.

To retrieve correct values from the lookup table, you use either the VLOOKUP or HLOOKUP function. VLOOKUP and HLOOKUP functions search a lookup table and, based on what you entered, retrieve the appropriate value from that table. The **VLOOKUP** (vertical lookup) **function** searches vertically down the lookup table and is used when the compare values are stored in the first column of the lookup table. The **HLOOKUP** (horizontal lookup) **function** searches horizontally across the lookup table and is used when the compare values are stored in the first row of the lookup table.

The HealthPlanRates table's compare values are in the first column, so you will use the VLOOKUP function. The HLOOKUP function works similarly. The VLOOKUP function has the following syntax:

```
VLOOKUP(lookup_value, table_array, col_index_num, [range_lookup])
```

In this function, *lookup_value* is the value you want to use to search the first column of the lookup table; *table_array* is the cell reference of the lookup table or its table name, *col_index_num* is the number of the column in the lookup table that contains the value you want to return, and *range_lookup* indicates whether the compare values are a range of values (sometimes referred to as an approximate match) or an exact match. When you use a range of values (such as in a tax rate table), you set the *range_lookup* value to TRUE; when you want the *lookup_value* to exactly match a value in the first column of the *table_array* (such as in the HealthPlanRates table), you set the *range_lookup* value to FALSE. The *range_lookup* argument is optional; if you don't include a *range_lookup* value, the value is considered TRUE (an approximate match).

Looking Up an Exact Match

You'll use the VLOOKUP function to calculate the annual health plan cost for Talent Tracs. You'll use the VLOOKUP function because you want to search the values in the first column of the lookup table. You can use range references or structured references when you create the formula for the annual health plan cost for an employee from the HealthPlanRates table shown earlier in Figure 7-12, as follows (the first formula uses range references, and the second formula uses structured references):

```
=VLOOKUP(L2,'Lookup Tables'!$B$4:$C$8,2,FALSE)*12
=VLOOKUP([HealthPlan],HealthPlanRates,2,FALSE)*12
```

The formula uses the VLOOKUP function to search for the code in the Health Plan column (column L) of the Employee table in the first column of the lookup table (the HealthPlanRates table in the range B4:C8 in the Lookup Tables worksheet), and then return the value in the second column of the HealthPlanRates lookup table, which shows the monthly cost. This value is then multiplied by 12 to return the annual cost. The formula uses FALSE as the *range_lookup* argument because you want the lookup value to exactly match a value in the first column of the HealthPlanRates table.

To use the VLOOKUP function in the Employee table to find an exact match in the HealthPlanRates table:

▶ 1. If you took a break after the previous session, make sure the Talent Tracs workbook is open and the Employee Data worksheet is active.

▶ 2. In cell Q1, enter **Health Cost**. The table expands to include the new column and the table's formatting is applied to all rows in the new column.

▶ 3. Make sure cell **Q2** is the active cell, and then click the **Insert Function** button 𝑓𝑥 on the formula bar. The Insert Function dialog box opens.

▶ 4. Click the **Or select a category** arrow, click **Lookup & Reference**, and then double-click **VLOOKUP** at the bottom of the function list. The Function Arguments dialog box opens.

▶ 5. Drag the Function Arguments dialog box below row 2 to make it easier to see the column headers.

▶ 6. In the Lookup_value argument box, enter **L2**. The *lookup_value* is the employee's health plan code, which is located in column L.

Next, you'll enter the *table_array* argument, which is equal to the range containing the HealthPlanRates table located in the Lookup Tables worksheet.

▶ 7. Click the Table_array argument **Collapse** button 🔣 to shrink the dialog box to show only the Table_array argument box, switch to the **Lookup Tables** worksheet, select the range **B4:C8** (the HealthPlanRates table), and then click the **Expand** button 🔳 to return the dialog box to its full size. The table name *HealthPlan-Rates* appears in the Table_array argument box. If the HealthPlanRates data was entered in a range of cells instead of an Excel table, the table_array would be *'Lookup Tables'!B4:B8*, and you would need to change the range to absolute references *'Lookup Tables'!$B$4:$B$8* so the formula would copy correctly to other cells.

Tip

If you see *#NAME?* or *#VALUE!* as the result of a VLOOKUP formula, you might have entered a letter for the col_index_num instead of a number.

▶ 8. In the Col_index_num argument box, enter **2**. The number 2 indicates the monthly cost is stored in the second column of the HealthPlanRates lookup table. When entering the col_index_num value, be sure to enter the number that corresponds to the column's position within the lookup table, rather than its column letter.

▶ 9. In the Range_lookup argument box, enter **FALSE**. This sets the function to find an exact match in the lookup table. See Figure 7-14.

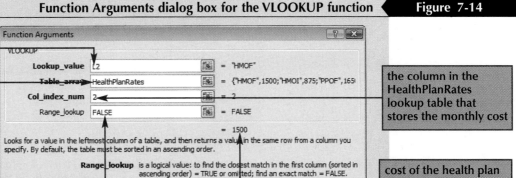

Function Arguments dialog box for the VLOOKUP function ◄ **Figure 7-14**

health plan code for the employee in row 2

table that contains the data you want to look up

indicates you want to find an exact match

the column in the HealthPlanRates lookup table that stores the monthly cost

cost of the health plan for the employee in row 2 of the Employee table

▶ **10.** Click the **OK** button. The dialog box closes and the result 1500 appears in cell Q2. The formula *VLOOKUP(L2,HealthPlanRates,2,FALSE)* appears in the formula bar. The remaining rows in the Health Cost column are filled with the VLOOKUP function. If a value in column L does not match a value in the first column of the HealthPlanRates table, there is not an exact match and #N/A appears in the cell, as you'll see shortly.

▶ **11.** Format the Health Cost values in the **Accounting** number format with no decimal places. Recall that a dash indicates a 0 in the Accounting number format. See Figure 7-15.

Employee table with health plan costs calculated ◄ **Figure 7-15**

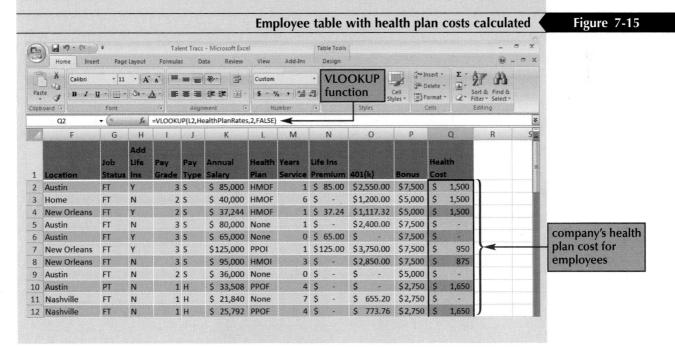

company's health plan cost for employees

The health plan costs in the Employee table are monthly amounts rather than annual. You need to modify the formula in the Health Cost column to reflect the annual amounts. Because the formula is in a calculated table column, you need to make the change in only one cell and the change will automatically be copied to all the cells in the column.

> **To modify the VLOOKUP function in the calculated column:**
>
> ▶ **1.** Double-click cell **Q2** to enter editing mode and display the formula in the cell.
>
> ▶ **2.** Click at the end of the formula, type ***12** to multiply the monthly amount by 12, and then press the **Enter** key. The amount in cell Q2 changes to $18,000 and all the other cells in the column are updated with the revised formula and display the annual cost.

Looking Up an Approximate Match

The previous table lookup used the HealthPlanRates table to return a value only if Excel found an exact match in the first column of the lookup table. The categories in the first column or row of a lookup table can also represent a range of values. As part of Talent Tracs 10-year anniversary, management plans to give employee recognition awards based on the number of years individuals have worked for Talent Tracs. Rita developed the criteria shown in Figure 7-16 to summarize how the company plans to distribute the recognition award.

Figure 7-16 ▶ **Recognition award distribution based on years of service**

Years of Service	Award
>=0 years and < 1 year	0
>=1 year and <3 years	100
>=3 years and <5 years	200
>=5 years and <7 years	300
7 years or more	500

In the recognition awards table, you are not looking for an *exact match* for the lookup value. Instead, you need to use an *approximate match* lookup, which determines whether the lookup value falls within a range of values. You want to use the table lookup to determine what service range an employee falls into and then return the recognition award based on the appropriate row. To accomplish this, you must rearrange the first column of the lookup table so each compare value (row) in the table represents the low end of the category range. Rita followed this format when she created the Recognition lookup table as shown in Figure 7-17.

Figure 7-17 ▶ **Recognition award table converted to a lookup table**

	F	G	H	I
1				
2				
3		Years of Service	Recognition Award	
4		0	$ -	
5		1	$ 100	
6		3	$ 200	
7		5	$ 300	
8		7	$ 500	
9				

To determine whether a lookup value falls within a range of values in the revised lookup table, Excel searches the first column of the table until it locates the largest value that is still less than the lookup value. Then, Excel moves across the table to retrieve the appropriate row. For example, an employee working at Talent Tracs for six years would receive a $300 employee recognition award.

Setting Up an Approximate Match Lookup Table | InSight

When a lookup table is used with a range of values, the compare values must be sorted in alphabetical order if they are text, and low-to-high order if they are numbers. When the compare values are arranged in a different order, Excel cannot retrieve the correct results. In this case, the VLOOKUP function seems incorrect, but the real problem is how the lookup table is organized. The setup of the lookup table in an approximate match is critical for a VLOOKUP formula to work as intended.

Consider the following example, in which an instructor uses Excel to calculate grades. The instructor assigns final grades based on the grading policy shown below, on the left. To set up the lookup table correctly, the leftmost column in the lookup table must represent the lower end of the range for each category *and* the lookup table must be sorted in ascending order based on the value in the first column. Otherwise, Excel cannot retrieve the correct result. Following this structure, the lookup table for the instructor's grading policy would be arranged as shown below, on the right.

Grading Policy

Score	Grade
90–100	A
80–89	B
70–79	C
60–69	D
0–59	F

Lookup Table

Score	Grade
0	F
60	D
70	C
80	B
90	A

If a VLOOKUP or HLOOKUP function with an approximate match doesn't return the values you expected, first confirm that you entered the formula correctly. Then, verify that the lookup table has the proper arrangement.

You'll create the formula in the Employee table to determine the recognition award for each employee. You will use an approximate match VLOOKUP formula because the years of service in the lookup table has a range of values.

To insert an approximate match VLOOKUP formula:

▶ **1.** In cell R1, enter **Award**. A new column is added to the table.

▶ **2.** In cell R2, type **=V** and then double-click **VLOOKUP**. The start of the formula =VLOOKUP(appears in the cell and formula bar.

▶ **3.** Type **[** to open a list of all the column headers in the Employee table, scroll down and double-click **Years Service**, and then type **]**, to complete the entry for the first argument of the VLOOKUP function.

▶ **4.** Type **R** and then double-click **Recognition** to enter the second argument, the lookup table. *Recognition* is the name of the Excel table in the range G4:H8 in the Lookup Tables worksheet.

▶ **5.** Type **,2)** to complete the VLOOKUP formula. The number 2 indicates the column number in the Recognition lookup table where the award amount is stored. You did not enter the optional fourth argument in the VLOOKUP formula; Excel assumes the value to be TRUE and uses an approximate match table lookup.

Tip

You can also enter a column header in a formula by starting to type the name of the column header until it is highlighted in the list, and then pressing the Tab key.

6. Press the **Enter** key. Each cell in the calculated column Award is filled. The employee in row 2 has 1 year of service and will receive a recognition award of $100. The employee in row 3 has 6 years of service and will receive an award of $300. This second employee is a good illustration of the approximate match lookup, because 6 is not equal to a value in the first column of the lookup table. Instead, it falls within two values in the table. See Figure 7-18.

| Figure 7-18 | Recognition award column |

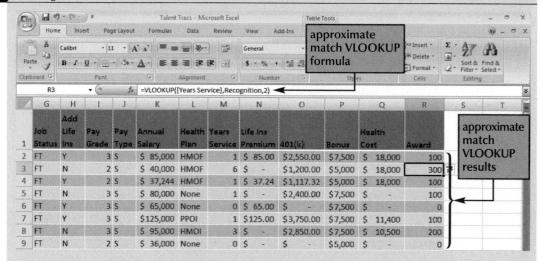

7. Format the Award values in the **Accounting** number format with no decimals places, and then AutoFit the column width.

Checking for Data Entry Errors

Rita believes the current data in the Employee table is accurate, but she is concerned that invalid data could be entered into the table. She wants to use conditional formatting and the IFERROR function to help reduce data entry errors.

| Reference Window | **Highlighting Duplicate Records with a Custom Format** |

- Select the column you want to search for duplicates.
- In the Styles group on the Home tab, click the Conditional Formatting button, point to Highlight Cells Rules, and then click Duplicate Values.
- Click the values with arrow, and then click Custom Format.
- In the Format Cells dialog box, set the formatting you want to use.
- Click the OK button in each dialog box.

Highlighting Duplicate Values with Conditional Formatting

Conditional formatting changes a cell's formatting when its contents match a specified condition. You've already used conditional formatting to add data bars that indicate the relative values in a range and to add highlights to cells based on their values for emphasis. Now you'll use conditional formatting to highlight duplicate values in a column of data. Duplicate value highlighting helps verify that columns of data have unique entries, such as the employee ID column in the Employee table. Rita wants you to change the background color of records that have duplicate employee IDs to red. This alert will help Rita ensure that each employee is entered in the table only once.

To highlight duplicate records in the Employee table:

1. Scroll to column A, point to the top of cell **A1** until the pointer changes to ⬇, and then click the top of cell **A1** just below the column header. Rows 2 through 101 in the ID column are selected.

2. Click the **Home** tab on the Ribbon, and then, in the Styles group, click the **Conditional Formatting** button.

3. Point to **Highlight Cells Rules**, and then click **Duplicate Values**. The Duplicate Values dialog box opens.

4. Click the **values with** arrow to display a list of formatting options, and then click **Custom Format** to create a format that is not in the list. The Format Cells dialog box opens. You'll change the background fill color to red.

5. Click the **Fill** tab, and then, in the Background Color palette, click **Red** (the second color in the last row).

6. Click the **OK** button in the Format Cells dialog box, and then click the **OK** button in the Duplicate Values dialog box. Any duplicate values in the ID column are in a red cell.

7. Scroll the table to see if any duplicate values are found.

No duplicate records are found in the Employee table. You need to test the conditional format to make sure it works as intended. As you build a formula, you should test all situations to verify how the formula performs in each case. In this case, you should test the column both with duplicate values and without duplicate values. You'll intentionally change the ID of the last record from 1123 to 1024, which is the ID of the first employee, to confirm the duplicate IDs are formatted in red cells. Then, you will return the ID to its original value and confirm that the duplicate highlighting is removed.

To test that the duplicate value conditional format works correctly:

1. Click in the **Name** box, type **A101**, and then press the **Enter** key. The active cell moves to the last record in the Employee table.

2. In cell A101, enter **1024**. The ID changes from 1123 to 1024 and red fills this cell because it has a duplicate ID. See Figure 7-19.

Duplicate record highlighted | Figure 7-19

	A	B	C	D	E	F	G	H	I	J	K	L	M	N
99	1121	Winters	2/14/2002	3/1/1953	F	Nashville	FT	N	1	H	$ 33,800	PPOF	8	$ -
100	1122	Wang	8/24/1998	8/11/1966	F	Austin	FT	N	1	H	$ 35,048	PPOI	11	$ -
101	1024	Harrison	6/19/2009	11/25/1963	M	Austin	FT	N	2	S	$ 41,000	PPOF	1	$ -
102														
103														

duplicate value highlighted in red

▶ **3.** Press the **Ctrl+Home** keys to move to the top of the table. Cell A2 also has a red background fill because it has the same ID you entered in cell A101. Excel identified the duplicate records.

| InSight | **Using a Formula to Conditionally Format Cells** |

Sometimes you might find that the built-in conditional formatting rules do not fit your needs. In these cases, you can create a conditional formatting rule based on a formula that uses a logical expression to describe the condition you want. For example, you can create a formula that uses conditional formatting to compare cells in different columns or to highlight an entire row.

When you create the formula, keep in mind the following guidelines:

- The formula must start with an equal sign.
- The formula must be in the form of a logical test that results in a true or false value.
- In most cases, the formula should use relative references and point to the first row of data in the table. If the formula references a cell or range outside the table, use an absolute reference.
- After you create the formula, enter test values to ensure the conditional formatting works in all situations that you intended.

For example, to use conditional formatting to highlight whether the Hire Date entered in column C is less than the Birth Date entered in column D (which would indicate a data entry error), you need to enter a formula that applies conditional formatting that compares cells in different columns of a table. Do the following:

1. Select the range you want to format (in this case, the Hire Date column).
2. Click the Conditional Formatting button in the Styles group on the Home tab, and then click New Rule.
3. In the Select a Rule Type box, click the "Use a formula to determine which cells to format" rule.
4. In the Format values where this formula is true box, enter the appropriate formula (in this case, =C2<D2).
5. Click the Format button to open the Format Cells dialog box, and select the formatting you want to apply.
6. Click the OK button in each dialog box.

Another example is to highlight the entire row if an employee has 10 or more years of service. In this case, you would select the range of data, such as A2:R101, and enter =M$2>10 in the Format values where this formula is true box. The other steps remain the same.

The red background fill makes the text difficult to read. Rita asks you to use yellow as the fill color to better contrast with the black text. After you apply a conditional format, you can modify it from the Conditional Formatting Rules Manager dialog box.

Using the Conditional Formatting Rules Manager

Each time you create a conditional format, you are defining a conditional formatting rule. A **rule** specifies the type of condition (such as formatting cells greater than a specified value), the type of formatting when that condition occurs (such as light red fill with dark red text), and the cell or range the formatting is applied to. You can edit existing conditional formatting rules from the Conditional Formatting Rules Manager dialog box. You'll use this dialog box to edit the rule that specifies the formatting applied to duplicate values in the ID column of the Employee table.

To change the duplicate values background fill color to yellow:

▶ **1.** In the Styles group on the Home tab, click the **Conditional Formatting** button, and then click **Manage Rules**. The Conditional Formatting Rules Manager dialog box opens, listing all the formatting rules for the current selection, which, in this case, is the Employee table.

▶ **2.** Verify that the Show formatting rules for box displays **This Table**. All the rules currently in effect in the Employee table are displayed. You can add new rules and edit or delete existing rules. You also can control which formatting rules are displayed in the dialog box, such as all rules in a specific worksheet or table. See Figure 7-20.

Conditional Formatting Rules Manager dialog box ◀ Figure 7-20

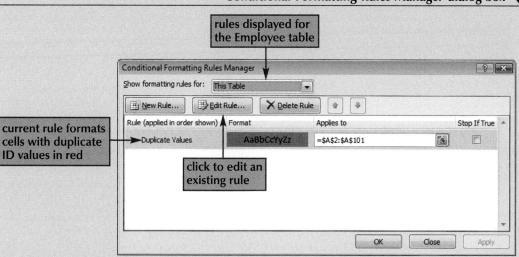

You want to change the Duplicate Values rule to use a yellow background fill color for duplicate entries in the ID column.

▶ **3.** Click **Duplicate Values** in the Rule list to select the rule, and then click the **Edit Rule** button. The Edit Formatting Rule dialog box opens. See Figure 7-21.

Edit Formatting Rule dialog box ◀ Figure 7-21

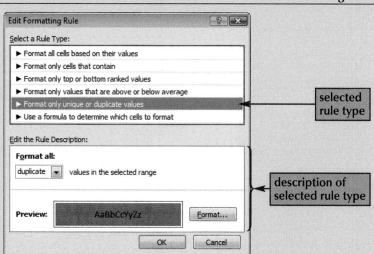

▶ **4.** Click the **Format** button. The Format Cells dialog box opens.

▶ **5.** Click the **Fill** tab, if necessary, and then click **Yellow** in the Background Color palette (the fourth color in the last row).

6. Click the **OK** button in each dialog box. The duplicate records in the table are now formatted with a yellow background color. See Figure 7-22.

Figure 7-22 | **Revised conditional format for duplicate records**

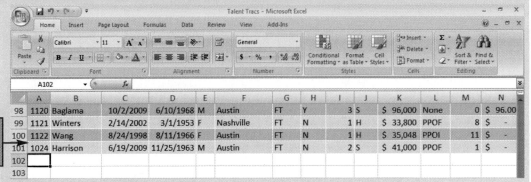

background color of duplicate value is yellow

The cell text is easier to read on the yellow background. You can filter the duplicate records by color. This enables you to view only records that are duplicates, because they are in the yellow background.

To filter duplicate records by color:

1. Click the **Data** tab on the Ribbon, and then, in the Sort & Filter group, click the **Filter** button. Filter arrows appear on the column headers.

2. Click the **ID** filter arrow to open the Filter menu, and then point to **Filter by Color** to display the Filter by Cell Color palette.

3. Click the **yellow** color. The filter is applied and only records with a yellow cell color (duplicate records) are displayed.

You'll redisplay all records.

4. Click the **ID** filter arrow to open the Filter menu, and then click **Clear Filter From "ID"**. The filter is removed and all of the records are displayed.

5. In the Sort & Filter group on the Data tab, click the **Filter** button to remove the filter arrows from the column headers.

Tip

You can also sort records by color. Click the filter arrow to open the Filter menu, and then click Sort by Color.

You'll correct the duplicate ID in cell A101 by entering the employee's actual ID number.

To correct the duplicate ID:

1. In cell A101, enter **1123**. The employee's ID is updated and the conditional formatting is removed because the value in the ID column is no longer a duplicate. However, the conditional formatting is still active. This rule will apply to any new records that Rita adds to the Employee table, which will help her to ensure that each employee has only one record in the table.

2. Scroll to the top of the Employee table, and verify that the conditional formatting no longer appears in cell A2.

3. Click cell **A1**.

The Duplicate Values rule enables you to verify that each entry in the ID column is unique, but it doesn't ensure that each unique value is accurate. Excel uses error values to help you find incorrectly entered data.

Using the IFERROR Function

Only five codes are used for the Health Plan column—PPOI, PPOF, HMOI, HMOF, and None. Rita wants to make sure that only these five valid codes are entered in the Health Plan column because the formula in the Health Cost column requires a valid health plan code. For instance, entering an inaccurate health plan code for an employee, such as HMOG instead of HMOF, would result in the error value (#N/A) in the Health Cost cell because the VLOOKUP function cannot find the invalid code in the HealthPlanRates lookup table.

Error values such as #DIV/0!, #N/A, and #VALUE! indicate that some element in a formula or a cell referenced in a formula is preventing Excel from returning a calculated value. An error value begins with a number sign (#) followed by an error name, which indicates the type of error. Figure 7-23 describes common error values you might see in workbooks.

Excel error values　　**Figure 7-23**

Error Value	Description of Error
#DIV/0!	The formula or function contains a number divided by 0.
#NAME?	Excel doesn't recognize text in the formula or function, such as when the function name is misspelled.
#N/A	A value is not available to a function or formula, which can occur when an invalid value is specified in the LOOKUP function.
#NULL!	A formula or function requires two cell ranges to intersect, but they don't.
#NUM!	Invalid numbers are used in a formula or function, such as text entered in a function that requires a number.
#REF!	A cell reference used in a formula or function is no longer valid, which can occur when a cell used by the function was deleted from the worksheet.
#VALUE!	The wrong type of argument is used in a function or formula, which can occur when you supply a range of values to a function that requires a single value.

These error value messages are not particularly meaningful or helpful, so Rita wants you to display a more descriptive message when Excel detects an error value. If a record includes an invalid health plan code, #N/A appears in the corresponding Health Cost cell because the VLOOKUP function doesn't find a value in the first column of the lookup table and cannot return a value. The IFERROR function enables you to display a more descriptive message that helps users fix the problem rather than adding confusion, as error values often do. The **IFERROR function** can determine if a cell contains an error value and display the message you choose rather than the default error value. The IFERROR function has the following syntax:

```
IFERROR(expression,valueIfError)
```

In this function, *expression* is the formula you want to check for an error and *valueIfError* is the message you want displayed if Excel detects an error in the formula you are checking. If Excel does not detect an error, the result of the *expression* is displayed.

The IFERROR function enables you to easily find and handle formula errors. For example, you can enter the following formula to determine whether an invalid code was entered in the Health Plan column of the Employee table:

```
=IFERROR(VLOOKUP(L2,HealthPlanRates,2,False)*12,"Invalid code")
```

Based on this formula, if the value in cell L2 is HMOF, the result of the VLOOKUP formula is $1,500 (a value from the HealthPlanRates table), and then the first argument in the IFERROR function (shown in blue) is executed. On the other hand, if cell L2 has an invalid Health Plan code, such as HMOG, the VLOOKUP function returns the error value #N/A, and then the second argument in the IFERROR function (shown in red) is executed, and the message "Invalid code" is displayed. You will scan the Health Cost column to verify that all employees have been assigned a health cost to determine if the formula calculating the health costs is working correctly.

To check for an error value in the Health Cost column:

▶ **1.** Scroll to row 54 of the Health Cost column to see the error value #N/A in cell Q54. See Figure 7-24.

Figure 7-24 ▶ **Error value in Health Cost column**

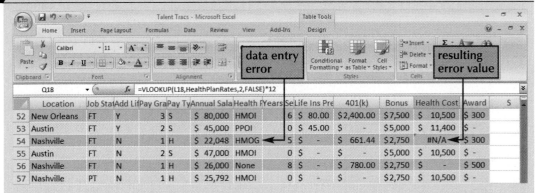

▶ **2.** In row 54 in the Health Plan column, observe that the Health Plan code is HMOG, which is an invalid code.

Rita asks you to modify the formulas in the Health Cost column to display a more descriptive error message. She wants the message "Invalid code" to appear rather than the error value. The IFERROR function will check for errors in the formula, and display the error message you create rather than the error value if it finds an error.

You'll nest the VLOOKUP function within the IFERROR function to display the message "Invalid code" in the Health Cost column if Excel detects an error value.

To nest the VLOOKUP function within the IFERROR function:

▶ **1.** Double-click cell **Q54** to enter editing mode. The formula =VLOOKUP(L54, HealthPlanRates,2,FALSE)*12 appears in the cell and the formula bar.

   You'll nest this formula within the IFERROR function.

▶ **2.** Click to the right of **=** (the equal sign), and then type **IFERROR(** to begin entering the IFERROR function. The first argument in the IFERROR function is the formula you want to use if no error value is found; this is the VLOOKUP formula already entered in the cell.

▶ **3.** Move the insertion point to the right of the VLOOKUP formula, and then type **,"Invalid code")** to add the text you want to display if an error is found.

▶ **4.** Press the **Enter** key, and then click cell **Q54**. The error message "Invalid code" appears in cell Q54, and the revised formula is automatically copied to all cells in the column. See Figure 7-25.

Invalid code message in the Health Cost column ◄ | Figure 7-25

Formula bar: `=IFERROR(VLOOKUP(L54,HealthPlanRates,2,FALSE)*12,"Invalid code")`

Callouts: **invalid code**, **completed IFERROR function**, **descriptive error message**

	Location	Job Stat	Add Lif	Pay Gra	Pay Ty	Annual Sala	Health F	Years	Se	Life Ins Pre	401(k)	Bonus	Health Cost	Award	S
52	New Orleans	FT	Y	3	S	$ 80,000	HMOI	6	$ 80.00	$2,400.00	$7,500	$ 10,500	$ 300	
53	Austin	FT	Y	2	S	$ 45,000	PPOI	0	$ 45.00	$ -	$5,000	$ 11,400	$ -	
54	Nashville	FT	N	1	H	$ 22,048	HMOG	5	$ -	$ 661.44	$2,750	Invalid code	$ 300	
55	Austin	FT	N	2	S	$ 47,000	HMOI	0	$ -	$ -	$5,000	$ 10,500	$ -	
56	Nashville	FT	N	1	H	$ 26,000	None	8	$ -	$ 780.00	$2,750	$ -	$ 500	
57	Nashville	PT	N	1	H	$ 25,792	HMOI	0	$ -	$ -	$2,750	$ 10,500	$ -	

▶ 5. In cell L54 (Health Plan), enter **HMOF**. You entered a valid Health Plan code, so the Health Cost value $18,000 appears in cell Q54.

▶ 6. Scroll to the top of the table, click cell **Q2**, and observe in the formula bar that the IFERROR formula was copied to this cell.

Tip

You can change a formula in any row of an Excel table (it doesn't have to be the first row) and all values in the column will be updated with the new formula.

Summarizing Data Conditionally

The COUNT function tallies the number of data values in a range, the SUM function adds the values in a range, and the AVERAGE function calculates the average of the values in a range. However, sometimes you need to calculate a conditional count, sum, or average using only those cells that meet a particular condition. In those cases, you need to use the COUNTIF, SUMIF, and AVERAGEIF functions. Rita wants you to create a report that shows the number, total, and average salaries for employees in Austin, New Orleans, and Nashville as well as for employees who work from home.

Using the COUNTIF Function

You can calculate the number of cells in a range that match criteria you specify using the **COUNTIF function**, which is sometimes referred to as a **conditional count**. The COUNTIF function has the following syntax:

`COUNTIF(range, criteria)`

In this function, *range* is the range of cells you want to count and *criteria* is an expression that defines which cells to count. Rita wants to know how many employees are located in Austin. You can use the COUNTIF function to find this answer, because you want a conditional count (a count of employees who meet a specified criterion; in this case, "employees located in Austin"). The location information is stored in column F of the Employee table. To count the number of employees in Austin, you can use either one of the following formulas (the first uses cell references, and the second uses fully qualified structured references):

```
=COUNTIF('Employee Data'!F2:F101,"Austin")
=COUNTIF(Employee[Location],"Austin")
```

With either formula, Excel counts all the cells in the Location column of the Employee table that contain the text "Austin". Because Austin is a text string, you must enclose it within quotation marks. Numeric criteria are not enclosed in quotes. You will enter this formula using the COUNTIF function in the Employee Summary worksheet.

Tip

You can use structured references or cell and range addresses to reference cells within an Excel table. If an Excel table has not been created for a range of data, you must use cell and range addresses.

To use the COUNTIF function to count employees located in Austin:

▶ 1. Switch to the **Employee Summary** worksheet. You will enter a formula using worksheet and range references to calculate the number of employees who work in Austin.

▶ 2. Click cell **C4**, type **=COU**, and then double-click **COUNTIF**. The beginning of the formula, =COUNTIF(, appears in the cell and the formula bar.

▶ 3. Type **'Employee Data'!F2:F101,** to enter the range to search. In this case, 'Employee Data'!F2:F101 refers to all data values in the range F2:F101 (Location column) of the Employee Data worksheet.

▶ 4. Type **B4)** to finish the formula. Cell B4, which contains the value Austin, is the criteria. The formula =COUNTIF('Employee Data'!F2:F101,B4) appears in the cell and the formula bar.

▶ 5. Press the **Enter** key. The value 57 appears in cell C4, indicating the company has 57 employees in Austin.

You will enter a similar formula using structured references to calculate the number of employees who work from home.

To use structured references to enter the COUNTIF function:

▶ 1. In cell C5, type **=COU**, and then double-click **COUNTIF**. The beginning of the formula, =COUNTIF(, appears in the cell and the formula bar.

▶ 2. Type **E** and then double-click **Employee**.

▶ 3. Type **[** to open the list of column headers, double-click **Location**, and then type **],** to complete the first argument of the COUNTIF function. In this formula, the structured reference Employee [Location] refers to the data values in the Location column (F2:F101) of the Employee table.

▶ 4. Type **B5)**. Cell B5 stores the value Home, which is the criterion. The formula =COUNTIF(Employee[Location],B5) appears in the cell and formula bar.

▶ 5. Press the **Enter** key. The formula results indicate that 7 employees work from home.

Next, you'll copy the formula in cell C5 to cells C6 and C7.

To copy the COUNTIF function:

▶ 1. Copy the formula in cell **C5** and then paste the formula in cells **C6** and **C7** to calculate the number of employees for Nashville (cell B6) and New Orleans (cell B7). The formula results show that Talent Tracs has 21 employees working in Nashville and 15 employees working in New Orleans.

▶ 2. In cell C8, enter a formula with the SUM function to calculate the total number of employees working at Talent Tracs. The formula results show that Talent Tracs has a total of 100 employees.

Using the SUMIF Function

The SUMIF function is similar to the COUNTIF function. You can add the values in a range that meet criteria you specify using the **SUMIF function**, which is also called a **conditional sum**. The syntax of the SUMIF function is:

```
SUMIF(range,criteria[,sum_range])
```

In this formula, *range* is the range of cells that you want to filter before calculating a sum, *criteria* is the condition used in the range to filter the table, and *sum_range* is the range of cells that you want to add. The *sum_range* argument is optional; if you omit it, Excel will add the values specified in the *range* argument. For example, if you want to add the salaries for all employees with salaries greater than $50,000, you do not use the optional third argument.

Rita wants to know the total salaries paid to employees at each location. She can use the SUMIF function to do this, because she wants to conditionally add salaries of employees at a specified location. Each employee's location is recorded in column F of the Employee Data worksheet, and the salary data is stored in column K. The formula to calculate this value is as follows (the first uses cell references, and the second uses fully qualified structured references):

```
=SUMIF('Employee Data'!F2:F101,"Austin",'Employee Data'!K2:K101)
=SUMIF(Employee[Location],"Austin",Employee[Annual Salary])
```

This formula states that employees whose location is "Austin" will have their salary values added to the total. You will insert this formula using the SUMIF function into the Employee Summary worksheet.

To use the SUMIF function:

▶ 1. In cell D4, enter **=SUMIF('Employee Data'!F2:F101,B4,'Employee Data'!K2:K101)**. The value $3,969,426—the total salaries paid to employees in Austin—appears in cell D4. The first argument specifies to use the range F2:F101 from the Employee Data worksheet (Location column) to filter the employee data. The second argument specifies that the criterion is equal to the value in cell B4 (Austin). The third argument indicates that the Annual Salary column, the range K2:K101 in the Employee Data worksheet, is used to add the filtered rows.

You will enter the formula to calculate the total salaries for employees working from home using structured references.

▶ 2. In cell D5, enter **=SUMIF(Employee[Location],B5,Employee[Annual Salary])**. Talent Tracs pays $236,313 per year to employees working from home. The first argument uses the structured reference Employee[Location] to specify you want to use the cells in the Location column to filter the employee data. The second argument specifies that the criterion is equal to the value in cell B5 (Home). The third argument uses the structured reference Employee[Annual Salary] to indicate that the Annual Salary column will be used to add the filtered rows.

▶ 3. Copy the SUMIF formula in cell D5 to the range **D6:D7**. The total salaries per year for employees working in Nashville (from cell B6) is $587,833. The total salaries per year for employees working in New Orleans (from cell B7) is $1,570,994.

▶ 4. In cell D8, use the SUM function to calculate the total of all salaries. The total salaries of all Talent Tracs employees is $6,364,566.

> **5.** If necessary, format the range D4:D8 in the **Accounting** number format with no decimal places.

Using the AVERAGEIF Function

The AVERAGEIF function works in the same way as the SUMIF function. You use the **AVERAGEIF function** to calculate the average of values in a range that meet criteria you specify. The syntax of the AVERAGEIF function is:

```
AVERAGEIF(range,criteria[,average_range])
```

In this function, *range* is the range of cells that you want to filter before calculating the average, *criteria* is the condition used in the range to filter the table, and *average_range* is the range of cells that you want to average. The *average_range* argument is optional; if you omit it, Excel will average the values specified in the *range* argument.

Rita wants to know the average salaries paid to employees at each location. Each employee's location is recorded in column F of the Employee Data worksheet, and the salary data is stored in column K. The formula to calculate this value is as follows (the first formula uses cell references, and the second uses fully qualified structured references):

```
=AVERAGEIF('Employee Data'!F2:F101,"Austin",'Employee Data'!K2:K101)
=AVERAGEIF(Employee[Location],"Austin",Employee[Annual Salary])
```

This formula states that any employee whose location is "Austin" will have his or her salary included in the average. You will enter this formula using the AVERAGEIF function into the Employee Summary worksheet.

To use the AVERAGEIF function:

> **1.** In cell E4, enter **=AVERAGEIF(Employee[Location],B4,Employee[Annual Salary])**. The value 69,639—the average salary paid to employees in Austin—appears in the cell. The first argument indicates that you want to use the cells in the Location column to filter the employee data. The second argument specifies that the criterion to filter the location column is equal to the value in cell D4 (Austin). The third argument indicates that the Annual Salary column will be used to average the filtered rows.
>
> You will enter the formula to calculate the average salaries for employees working at Home, Nashville, and New Orleans.

> **2.** Copy the formula in cell E4 to the range **E5:E7**. Talent Tracs pays an average of $33,759 to employees working at home, $27,992 to employees working in Nashville, and $104,733 to employees working in New Orleans.
>
> Next, you will calculate the average salary at Talent Tracs by dividing the total salaries at Talent Tracs by the number of employees at the company.

> **3.** In cell E8, enter **=D8/C8**. The average salary for all employees is $63,646.

> **4.** If necessary, format the range E4:E8 in the **Accounting** number format with no decimal places.

> **5.** Add a bottom border to the range C7:E7. See Figure 7-26.

Salary analysis of employees by location | **Figure 7-26**

As Rita enters new employees or edits the location or annual salary values of current employees, the values in the Employee Summary worksheet will be automatically updated because the formulas reference the Employee table.

Summarizing Data Using the COUNTIFS, SUMIFS, and AVERAGEIFS Functions

The COUNTIFS, SUMIFS, and AVERAGEIFS functions are similar to the COUNTIF, SUMIF, and AVERAGEIF functions except with the latter functions you can specify only one condition to summarize the data, whereas the former functions enable you to summarize the data using several conditions.

The **COUNTIFS function** counts the number of cells within a range that meet multiple criteria. Its syntax is as follows:

```
COUNTIFS(criteria_range1,criteria1[,criteria_range2,criteria2...])
```

In this function, *criteria_range1, criteria_range2*, represents up to 127 ranges (columns of data) in which to evaluate the associated criteria, and *criteria1, criteria2* and up to 127 criteria in the form of a number, expression, cell reference, or text define which cells will be counted. Criteria can be expressed as a number such as 50 to find a number equal to 50, ">10000" to find an amount greater than 10000, "FT" to find a text value equal to FT, or B4 to find the value equal to the value stored in cell B4. Each cell in a range is counted only if all of the corresponding criteria specified in the COUNTIFS function are true.

For example, to count the number of full-time employees (FT) who are female (F) and earn more than $50,000, you can use the following function:

```
=COUNTIFS(Employee[Job Status],"FT",Employee[SEX],"F",Employee
[Annual Salary],">50000")
```

This function counts the full-time employees using the argument combination Employee [Job Status],"FT", that are female using the arguments Employee[Sex],"F", and have a salary greater than 50,000 using the arguments Employee[Annual Salary],">50000".

The SUMIFS and AVERAGEIFS functions have a slightly different syntax. The **SUMIFS function** adds values in a range that meet multiple criteria using the following syntax:

```
SUMIFS(sum_range,criteria_range1,criteria1[,criteria_range2,
criteria2...])
```

In the SUMIFS function, *sum_range* is the range you want to add; *criteria_range1*, *criteria_range2*, represent up to 127 ranges (columns of data) in which to evaluate the associated criteria; and *criteria1*, *criteria2* and so on up to 127 criteria in the form of a number, expression, cell reference, or text define which cells will be added.

For example, to calculate the total salary paid to full-time (FT) employees hired after 2007 who are living in Austin, you can use the following SUMIFS function:

```
=SUMIFS(Employee[Annual Salary],Employee[Location],"Austin",
Employee[Hire Date],">=1/1/2008",Employee[Job Status],"FT")
```

This function adds the salaries (Employee[Annual Salary]) of employees located in Austin using the argument combination Employee[Location],"Austin", having a hire date on or later than 1/1/2008 using the arguments Employee[Hire Date],">=1/1/2008", and are full-time employees using arguments Employee [Job Status],"FT".

The **AVERAGEIFS function** calculates the average of values within a range of cells that meet multiple conditions. Its syntax is as follows:

```
AVERAGEIFS(average_range,criteria_range1,criteria1[,criteria_range2,
criteria2...])
```

In this function, *average_range* is the range to average; *criteria_range1, criteria_range2*, represent up to 127 ranges in which to evaluate the associated criteria; and *criteria1, criteria2* and so on up to 127 criteria in the form of a number, expression, cell reference, or text define which cells will be averaged.

For example, to calculate the average salary paid to males (M) who have worked at Talent Tracs for more than 5 years, you can use the following AVERAGEIFS function:

```
=AVERAGEIFS(Employee[Annual Salary],Employee[Sex],"M", Employee[Years
Service],">5")
```

This function averages the salaries (Employee[Annual Salary]) of male employees using the arguments Employee[Sex],"M", having more than 5 years of service using the arguments Employee[Years Service],">5".

In this session, you used the VLOOKUP function to calculate the health plan cost and employee recognition award. You used conditional formatting to identify duplicate employee IDs and the IFERROR function to help you correct errors. You used functions and features that deal with conditional situations. In the next session, you will use advanced filtering techniques to find potential candidates for a new full-time position and Database functions to prepare a report on the number of employees in each health plan who are classified as salaried and hourly.

Review | **Session 7.2 Quick Check**

1. Explain the difference between an exact match and approximate match table lookup.
2. A customers table includes name, street address, city, state abbreviation, and zip code. A second table includes state abbreviations and state names from all 50 states. You need to add a new column to the customers table with the state name. What is the most appropriate function to use to display the state name in this new column?
3. Would you apply the duplicate value conditional formatting rule to a table column of last names? Why or why not?

4. In cell D5, the error value #DIV/0! is displayed when you divide by 0. Use the IFERROR function with the formula =C5/C25 so instead of the error value #DIV/0!, you display the message "Dividing by 0" in the cell.

5. Explain what the formula =COUNTIF(Employee[SEX],"F") calculates.

6. Explain what the formula =AVERAGEIF(Employee[Pay Type],"H",(Employee[Salary])) calculates.

7. If you receive a worksheet that includes conditional formatting, which dialog box would you use to find out the criteria for the formatting?

Session 7.3

Using Advanced Filtering

Talent Tracs is growing rapidly and management plans to hire additional full-time employees. Rita wants to give first preference to part-time employees and consultants currently working for the company. She asks you to create a list of individuals who meet the following criteria:

- Consultants who have worked for Talents Tracs for more than three years earning less than $55,000

  or

- Part-time employees who have worked for Talent Tracs for two or more years

You need to use advanced filtering features to retrieve the list of individuals Rita wants. Advanced filtering enables you to perform OR conditions across multiple fields, such as the criteria Rita wants you to use to find eligible candidates within the company for the new full-time positions. You can also use advanced filtering to create complex criteria using functions and formulas. For example, if Rita wants to find all female salaried employees whose salary falls below the median salary for all employees, she could use advanced filtering.

Advanced filtering, similar to filtering, displays a subset of the rows in a table or range of data. The primary difference is that you specify criteria in a range outside the data you want to filter. So, before you can use advanced filters, you need to create a criteria range. The **criteria range** is an area in a worksheet, separate from the range of data or Excel table, used to specify the criteria for the data to be displayed after the filter is applied to the table. The criteria range consists of a header row that lists one or more field names from the table's header row and at least one row of the specific filtering criteria for each field. A criteria range must include at least two rows. The first row must contain field names (column headers). All other rows consist of the criteria. Figure 7-27 shows the criteria range you will create to display the eligible candidates within the company for the new full-time positions.

| Figure 7-27 | Criteria range above Excel table |

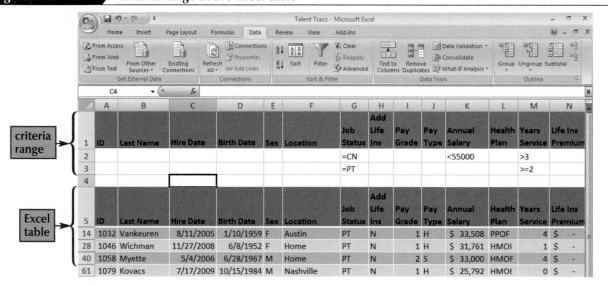

To create a criteria range, you need to specify the condition for each criterion. Text, numeric, and date conditions each use different syntax. Figure 7-28 lists the type of condition, corresponding syntax, and an example for each criterion. For example, to develop a criteria range to filter employees whose annual salaries (numeric data) are greater than (condition) 50,000, the top row of the criteria range contains the column header from the Employee table, Annual Salary, and the second row contains the criterion >50000.

| Figure 7-28 | Types of conditions |

Condition	Text Data		Numeric Data		Date Data	
	Syntax	Sample Last Name	Syntax	Sample Annual Salary	Syntax	Sample Hire Date
Exact match	="=text string"	="=Stolt"	value	50000	mm/dd/yyyy	1/3/2010
Begins with	text string	S	does not apply		does not apply	
Greater than	>text string	>S	>value	>50000	>mm/dd/yyyy	>12/31/2009
Greater than or equal to	>=text string	>=S	>=value	>=50000	>= mm/dd/yyyy	>=1/1/2010
Less than	< text string	<S	<value	<50000	<mm/dd/yyyy	<1/1/2010
Less than or equal to	<= text string	<=S	<=value	<=50000	<=mm/dd/yyyy	<=12/31/2009
Between (beginning and ending points must be in separate cells)	>=beginning text string	>=Sa	>= beginning value	>=50000	> beginning mm/dd/yyyy	>=4/1/2010
	<=ending text string	<=Sm	<= ending value	<=60000	< ending mm/dd/yyyy	<=4/30/2010

Understanding Criteria Ranges

The criteria range specifies which records from the Excel table will be included in the filtered data. The following examples illustrate multiple criteria conditions. Criteria placed on the same row are considered connected with the logical operator AND. That means all criteria in the same row must be met before a record is included in the filtered table. Figure 7-29 shows an AND criteria range to retrieve all employees from Nashville who are earning more than $55,000.

Example of AND criteria range | Figure 7-29

	F	G	H	I	J	K
1	Location	Job Status	Add Life Ins	Pay Grade	Pay Type	Annual Salary
2	="=Nashville"					>55000
3						

Specifying the equality comparison operator (exact match) for a text string in the criteria range, as in the Location field in Figure 7-29, is not intuitive. When you type a formula in a cell, the equal sign indicates that a formula follows. If you want to indicate the equality comparison operator within the criteria range, you must type the criteria using the following syntax:

`="=entry"`

In this syntax, *entry* is the text or value you want to find.

Criteria placed on separate rows are treated as the logical operator OR. That means records that meet all the criteria on either row in the criteria range will be displayed. Figure 7-30 shows the criteria range to retrieve female employees or employees who are working in Austin.

Example of OR criteria range | Figure 7-30

	E	F	G	H	I	J
1	Sex	Location	Job Status	Add Life Ins	Pay Grade	Pay Type
2	="=F"					
3		="=Austin"				
4						

To specify criteria between a range of values in the same field, you use the same field name repeated in separate cells within the same row to match a range of values (BETWEEN criteria). Figure 7-31 shows the criteria range to retrieve all employees who were hired between 1/1/2005 and 12/31/2008.

Example of BETWEEN criteria range | Figure 7-31

	B	C	D	E	F	G
1	Hire Date	Hire Date	Birth Date	Sex	Location	Job Status
2	>=1/1/2005	<=12/31/2008				
3						

You can also set up criteria to find records that begin with a group of characters. Figure 7-32 shows the criteria range that retrieves all records with a location that begin with *Home*. This criteria range would retrieve Talent Tracs employees working in Homewood, Illinois, along with those working from Home. If you want more precise results, you need to use the exact match criteria. The exact match criteria would be entered as ="=Home" and only employees working from Home would be retrieved.

| Figure 7-32 | Example of BEGINS WITH criteria range |

	F	G	H	I	J	K
1	Location	Job Status	Add Life Ins	Pay Grade	Pay Type	Annual Salary
2	Home					
3						

Tip

Because the field names in the criteria range must exactly match the field names in the Excel table or range except for capitalization, you should copy and paste the field names instead of retyping them.

Creating a Criteria Range

Typically, you place a criteria range above the Excel table to keep it separate from the table. If you place a criteria range next to the Excel table, the criteria might be hidden when the advanced filtering cause rows to be hidden. You can also place a criteria range in a separate worksheet, particularly if you need to enter several criteria ranges in different cells to perform calculations based on various sets of filtered records.

You will place the criteria range in rows 1 to 4 of the Employee Data worksheet to make it easier to locate.

To create the criteria range to find eligible candidates for full-time positions:

▶ 1. Switch to the **Employee Data** worksheet, and then click cell **A1**.

You'll insert four blank rows above the Excel table in which to place the criteria range.

▶ 2. Select rows **1** through **4**, right-click the selected row headings, and then click **Insert** on the shortcut menu. Four rows are added at the top of the worksheet.

Next, you'll copy the column headers from the Excel table into row 1.

▶ 3. Point to the left side of cell **A5** until the pointer changes to ➡, and then click the mouse button. The column headers in row 5 are selected.

▶ 4. Click the **Home** tab on the Ribbon, if necessary, and then, in the Clipboard group, click the **Copy** button 🖹 . The field names are copied to the Clipboard.

▶ 5. Click cell **A1**, and then, in the Clipboard group on the Home tab, click the **Paste** button. The field names for the criteria range appear in row 1.

In row 2, you will enter an AND criteria range with the criteria for consultants (code CN) who earn less than $55,000 and have worked at Talent Tracs for more than three years.

▶ 6. In cell G2, enter **="=CN"**. The condition =CN is displayed, which specifies the criteria to retrieve all consultants, employees with Pay Status code equal to CN.

▶ 7. In cell K2, enter **<55000**. This condition specifies the criteria to retrieve all employees who have salaries less than $55,000.

▶ 8. In cell M2, enter **>3**. This condition specifies the criteria to retrieve all employees with more than three years of service.

The criteria in row 2 selects all employees who are consultants and who earn less than $55,000 and have more than three years service at Talent Tracs. Next, you will enter the criteria for part-time employees working more than two years.

▶ 9. In cell **G3**, enter **="=PT"**; and then, in cell **M3**, enter **>=2**. The criteria in row 3 selects all employees who are part-time (Job Status is equal to PT) and who have two or more years service at Talent Tracs (Years Service is greater than or equal to 2). See Figure 7-33.

Criteria range ◀ **Figure 7-33**

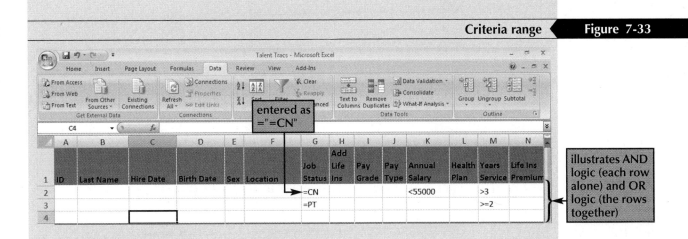

illustrates AND logic (each row alone) and OR logic (the rows together)

Now that the criteria range is established, you can use the Advanced Filter command to filter the Employee table. You can filter the records in their current location by hiding rows that don't match your criteria, as you have done with the Filter command. Or, you can copy the records that match your criteria to another location in the worksheet. Rita wants you to filter the records in their current location.

To filter the Employee table in its current location:

▶ **1.** Click any cell in the Employee table to make the table active.

▶ **2.** Click the **Data** tab on the Ribbon, and then, in the Sort & Filter group, click the **Advanced** button. The Advanced Filter dialog box opens.

▶ **3.** Make sure the **Filter the list, in-place** option button is selected and the range **$A$5:$R$105** appears in the List range box. The range $A$5:$R$105 is the current location of the Employee table, which is the table you want to filter.

   Trouble? If the List range displays $A$5:$L$105, you need to edit the range to $A$5:$R$105 to include the entire table.

▶ **4.** Type **$A$1:$R$3** in the Criteria range box. This is the range in which you entered the criteria range. See Figure 7-34.

Advanced Filter dialog box ◀ **Figure 7-34**

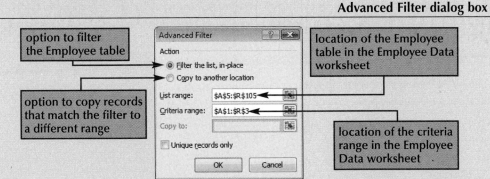

option to filter the Employee table

option to copy records that match the filter to a different range

location of the Employee table in the Employee Data worksheet

location of the criteria range in the Employee Data worksheet

▶ **5.** Click the **OK** button, and then scroll to the top of the worksheet. The list is filtered in its current location, and nine employee records match the criteria, as indicated in the status bar. See Figure 7-35.

Figure 7-35

Filtered Employee table

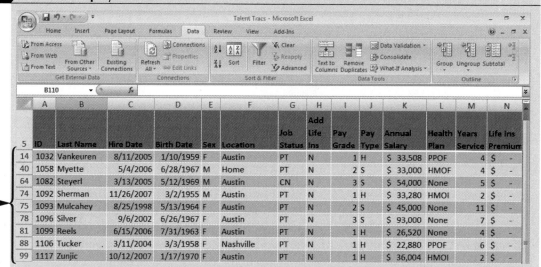

nine employees are eligible to apply for the full-time positions

ID	Last Name	Hire Date	Birth Date	Sex	Location	Job Status	Add Life Ins	Pay Grade	Pay Type	Annual Salary	Health Plan	Years Service	Life Ins Premium
14	1032	Vankeuren	8/11/2005	1/10/1959	F	Austin	PT	N	1	H	$ 33,508	PPOF	4	$ -
40	1058	Myette	5/4/2006	6/28/1967	M	Home	PT	N	2	S	$ 33,000	HMOF	4	$ -
64	1082	Steyerl	3/13/2005	5/12/1969	M	Austin	CN	N	3	S	$ 54,000	None	5	$ -
74	1092	Sherman	11/26/2007	3/2/1955	M	Austin	PT	N	1	H	$ 33,280	HMOI	2	$ -
75	1093	Mulcahey	8/25/1998	5/13/1964	F	Austin	PT	N	2	S	$ 45,000	None	11	$ -
78	1096	Silver	9/6/2002	6/26/1967	F	Austin	PT	N	3	S	$ 93,000	None	7	$ -
81	1099	Reels	6/15/2006	7/31/1963	F	Austin	PT	N	1	H	$ 26,520	None	4	$ -
88	1106	Tucker	3/11/2004	3/3/1958	F	Nashville	PT	N	1	H	$ 22,880	PPOF	6	$ -
99	1117	Zunjic	10/12/2007	1/17/1970	F	Austin	PT	N	1	H	$ 36,004	HMOI	2	$ -

Trouble? If no records appear in the filtered table, the list range or criteria range might be incorrect. Click the Clear button in the Sort & Filter group on the Data tab, and then repeat Steps 1 through 5, making sure the list range is $A$5:$R$105 and the criteria range is $A$1:$R$3 in the Advanced Filter dialog box.

After providing the list of eligible employees to Rita, you remove the filter to display all the records in the Employee table.

To show all the records in the Employee table:

▸ **1.** In the Sort & Filter group on the Data tab, click the **Clear** button. All the records in the Employee table reappear.

InSight | **Copying Filtered Records to a New Location**

The Advanced Filtering command does more than filter data in a range or an Excel table. You can also copy data in a table to another worksheet location. If you want to filter the data and then copy the filtered data to a different location, you select the Copy to another location option button in the Action section of the Advanced Filter dialog box and specify the first cell of the range where you want to copy the filtered records in the Copy to box. Excel copies the filtered records to the location beginning at the cell you specified in the Copy to box. All cells below this cell will be cleared when the Advanced Filter is applied.

The Advanced Filtering command offers many advantages, allowing you to copy the following:

- All the columns from the original table in their current order to another worksheet location.
- A subset of columns from the original table to another worksheet location.
- A subset or all the columns from the original table and change the sequence of columns in the new worksheet location.
- A unique list of values from the original table into another worksheet location. For example, you can obtain a unique list of customer names from a table of invoices where customer names are repeated many times.

Using Database Functions to Summarize Data

Functions that perform summary data analysis (SUM, AVERAGE, COUNT, and so on) on a table of values based on criteria that you set are called the **Database functions**, or **Dfunctions**. Figure 7-36 lists the Database functions. Although the SUMIF, AVERAGEIF and COUNTIF functions, the Total row feature of an Excel table, and PivotTables often can achieve the same results as Database functions and are considered simpler to use, some situations call for Database functions. For example, the type of summary analysis, the placement of the summary results, or the complexity of the criteria might require that you use Database functions.

Database functions ◄ **Figure 7-36**

Function Name	Description
DAVERAGE	Returns the average of the values that meet specified criteria
DCOUNT	Returns the number of cells containing numbers that meet specified criteria
DCOUNTA	Returns the number of nonblank cells that meets specified criteria
DMAX	Returns the maximum value in search column that meets specified criteria
DMIN	Returns the minimum value in search column that meets specified criteria
DSTDEV	Returns the estimate of standard deviation based on a sample of entries that meet the specified criteria
DSUM	Returns the sum of the values in the summary column that meets specified criteria

Rita wants you to provide a report summarizing the number of salaried and hourly workers by health plan. Rita's request combines the HMOF and HMOI codes into one group on the report and the PPOF and PPOI codes into another group. You must set up a criteria range to retrieve the appropriate records for each calculation. As a result, a Dfunction becomes a good approach for solving Rita's request.

Dfunctions use a criteria range to specify the records to summarize. In a Dfunction, the criteria range is used as one of the arguments of the function. Any Dfunction has the following general syntax:

`DfunctionName(table range, column to summarize, criteria range)`

In this syntax, *table range* refers to the cells where the data to summarize is located, including the column header, *column to summarize* is the column name of the field you want to summarize, and *criteria range* is the range where the criteria that determines which records are used in the calculation is specified.

You will use Dfunctions to complete the Employee Summary worksheet, summarizing the number of salaried and hourly employees covered by HMO and PPO health plans. First, you will set up a separate criteria range for each cell in the report, excluding totals for rows and columns. Although the criteria range often includes all fields from the table, even those that are not needed to select records, you do not have to include all field names from the table when setting up a criteria range. In setting up the criteria range to use with the Database functions, you will use only the fields needed to specify the criteria.

You will create six criteria ranges to complete the Health Plan Count report.

To establish criteria ranges for the Health Plan Count report:

▶ **1.** Switch to the **Employee Summary** worksheet. The column headers for the criteria range have already been copied from the Employee Data worksheet.

You'll set up the criteria for salaried employees who have selected HMOs, PPOs, and No Plan.

2. In cell G15, enter **HMO**, and then, in cell H15, enter **S**. You entered *begins with* criteria (HMO) to find all HMOs (HMOI and HMOF). The code for salaried employees is S and because only S or H codes are used in the Pay Type column, you used the *begins with* criteria to find salaried employees. The criteria range for salaried employees electing either HMO plan is complete.

3. In cell J15, enter **PPO** as the *begins with* criteria to find all PPOs (PPOI and PPOF), and then, in cell K15, enter the *begins with* criteria **S** to find salaried employees. The criteria range for salaried employees electing either PPO plan is complete.

4. In cell M15, enter the *begins with* criteria **None**, and then, in cell N15, enter the *begins with* criteria **S** to find salaried employees. The criteria range for salaried employees with no plan is complete.

You'll set up the criteria for Hourly HMOs, Hourly PPOs, and Hourly No Plan.

5. In cell G20, enter the *begins with* criteria **HMO** to find all HMOs (HMOI and HMOF), and then, in cell H20, enter the *begins with* criteria **H** to find hourly employees. The criteria range for hourly employees electing an HMO plan is complete.

6. In cell J20, enter the *begins with* criteria **PPO** to find all PPOs (PPOI and PPOF), and then, in cell K20, enter the *begins with* criteria **H** to find hourly employees. The criteria range for hourly employees electing a PPO plan is complete.

7. In cell M20, enter the *begins with* criteria **None**, and then, in cell N20, enter the *begins with* criteria **H** to find hourly employees. The criteria range for hourly employees with no plan is complete. See Figure 7-37.

Figure 7-37	Criteria range for report

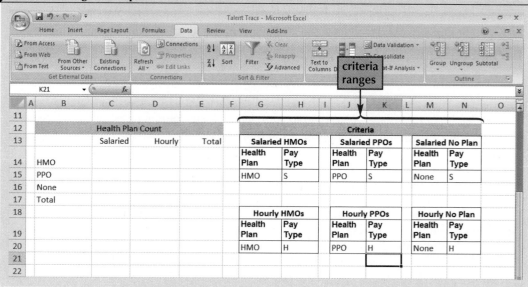

The criteria ranges are complete, so you can enter the formulas to finish the Health Plan Count report for Rita. You will enter the DCOUNT function six times. In each function, the first two arguments are identical. The third argument, the criteria range, is different for each function so that you can count a different subset of employees each time.

To enter the first DCOUNT function:

▶ 1. In cell C14, type **=D** and double-click **DCOUNT**. The beginning of the formula, =DCOUNT(, appears in the cell and the formula bar.

▶ 2. Type **Em** and then press the **Tab** key to enter Employee in the first argument. Employee references only the data in the Employee table.

▶ 3. Type **[#** to open the list of special Item qualifiers, press the **Tab** key to enter #All, and then type **],** to complete the first argument, Employee[#All],. The special qualifier [#All] indicates you want to reference the column headers as well as the data.

▶ 4. Type **"ID",** to specify the field in the Employee table that you want to count. The second argument, ID, shows the column whose cells will be counted. The field name must be within quotation marks.

▶ 5. Type **G14:H15)** to complete the formula. The third argument G14:H15 references the criteria range that determines which cells in the ID column to count.

▶ 6. Press the **Enter** key, and then click cell **C14**. There are 32 salaried employees electing either HMO plan. The formula =DCOUNT(Employee[#All],"ID",G14:H15) appears in the formula bar.

You'll repeat this process to finish the Health Plan Count report. The DCOUNT function is the same for each of the remaining counts, except the third argument reflects the appropriate criteria range that you entered in the Employee Summary worksheet.

To enter the remaining DCOUNT functions for the Health Plan Count report:

▶ 1. In cell C15, enter **=DCOUNT(Employee[#All],"ID",J14:K15)**. This DCOUNT function calculates the number of salaried employees electing either PPO plan. The formula is identical to the first DCOUNT function you entered except the criteria range J14:K15 specifies the criteria to retrieve salaried employees electing either PPO plan. There are 15 in this category.

▶ 2. In cell C16, enter **=DCOUNT(Employee[#All],"ID",M14:N15)**. This DCOUNT function calculates the number of salaried employees with no health plan. Again, the formula is identical to the other DCOUNT functions you entered except the criteria range M14:N15 specifies the criteria to retrieve salaried employees with no health plan. There are 18 employees in this category.

▶ 3. In cell D14, enter **=DCOUNT(Employee[#All],"ID",G19:H20)** to calculate the number of hourly HMO employees. The formula is identical to the other DCOUNT functions you entered except the criteria range G19:H20 specifies the criteria to retrieve hourly employees electing either HMO plan. There are 13 in this category.

▶ 4. In cell D15, enter **=DCOUNT(Employee[#All],"ID",J19:K20)** to calculate the number of hourly PPO employees. The criteria range references the criteria range J19:K20, which retrieves hourly workers electing either PPO plan. There are 14 employees in this category.

▶ 5. In cell D16, enter **=DCOUNT(Employee[#All],"ID",M19:N20)** to calculate the number of hourly employees with no plan. The criteria range references the range M19:N20, which retrieves hourly workers with no health plan. There are 8 in this category.

▶ 6. In cells C17 and D17, enter the SUM function to calculate totals for each column.

▶ 7. In the range E14:E17, use the SUM function to total each row.

> **8.** Add a bottom border to the range C16:E16, and then click cell **C18** to deselect the report. See Figure 7-38.

Figure 7-38 **Health Plan Count report**

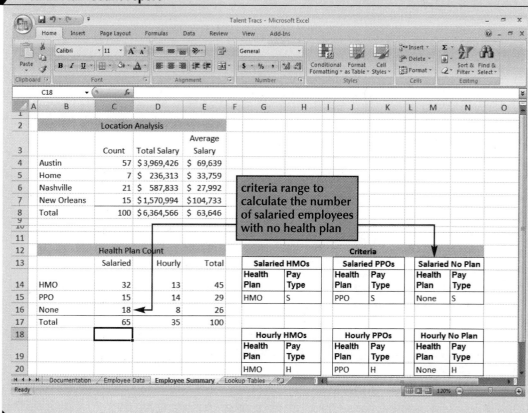

> **9.** Save the workbook, and then close it.

The Health Plan Count report provides Rita with useful information as she goes into a meeting to plan Talent Tracs' healthcare coverage for future years.

Session 7.3 Quick Check | Review

1. Describe in words the following criteria range:

   Sex   Salary Class
   ="=M" ="=H"

2. Create a criteria range to retrieve employees located in either Austin or New Orleans. The column name is Location.

3. Describe in words the following criteria range:

   Annual Salary   Annual Salary
   <25000
                 >=100000

4. After an Advanced Filter command has filtered records, how do you redisplay all the records in the table?

5. Explain the function: =DSUM(Employee[#All],"Annual Salary",T1:U2)

   The following criteria range appears in the range T1:U2:
   Sex   Hire Date
   M   >=1/1/2010

6. Why would you use the structured reference Employee[#All] in Quick Check 5 instead of Employee?

7. Rewrite the DSUM function in Quick Check 5 using range addresses instead of structured references. The employee data is found in the Employee Data worksheet in the range A5:R105. The DSUM function is entered in the Employee Summary worksheet.

Tutorial Summary | Review

In this tutorial, you used the Logical functions IF, AND, and OR, and you nested one IF function inside another IF function. You used the VLOOKUP function to look up data in a table. You used conditional formatting and the IFERROR function to locate and fix data entry errors. You also used the COUNTIF, SUMIF, and AVERAGEIF functions to calculate counts, sums, and averages based on search criteria. You filtered a table using more advanced filtering criteria. Finally, you used Database functions to summarize a table based on specified criteria.

Key Terms

AND function	criteria range	nested IF function
AVERAGEIF function	Database function	OR function
AVERAGEIFS function	DATEDIF function	rule
calculated column	Dfunction	structured reference
compare value	error value	SUMIF function
conditional count	HLOOKUP function	SUMIFS function
conditional sum	IFERROR function	VLOOKUP function
COUNTIF function	lookup table	
COUNTIFS function	lookup value	

Practice	**Review Assignments**

Practice the skills you learned by using the Employee Data worksheet to test alternative calculations.

Data File needed for the Review Assignments: Tracs.xlsx

Rita suggests you try some alternative calculations for bonuses and benefits. Complete the following:

1. Open the **Tracs** workbook located in the Tutorial.07\Review folder included with your Data Files, save the workbook as **Tracs Employees** in the same folder, and then, in the Documentation sheet, enter the date and your name.

2. In the Employee Data worksheet, rename the Excel table as **EmpData**.

3. Employees who want additional coverage (Add Life Ins) pay 0.1% premium rate times annual salary. For employees who do not elect additional coverage, enter 0 in the life Ins Premium column. The life insurance premiums are entered in cell Z9. Calculate the life insurance premiums using an IF function and include a reference to cell Z9 to obtain the life insurance rate.

4. All full-time (Job Status) employees over the age of 30 (Age in column N) are eligible for the 401(k) benefit. Use the IF and AND functions to calculate the 401(k) benefit as 3% of annual salary. If the employee is not eligible, enter 0. In the formula you create, include a reference to cell Z10 to obtain the 401(k) matching percent rate (3%).

5. Calculate Bonus assuming it is available to all employees with 1 or more years of service (Years Service). Employees with pay grade 1 receive $3,000 (cell Z6), pay grade 2 receive $6,000 (cell Z7), and pay grade 3 receive $8,000 (cell Z8). For employees not eligible for a bonus, display the label **NE**. For pay grades not equal to 1, 2, or 3, display the message **Invalid pay grade**. Use nested IF functions to calculate the bonus.

6. Change the format color of the duplicate value conditional formatting rule to Green (sixth color in the last row of the color palette) using the Conditional Formatting Rules Manager dialog box.

7. Calculate the health plan cost using the HLOOKUP function to do an exact match lookup. The layout of Health Plan Rates data ($B$2:$F$3) in the Lookup Tables worksheet has been revised to work with the HLOOKUP function. Use the range address reference in the HLOOKUP function to reference Health Plan Rates data.

8. Modify the calculation of the recognition award (Award) to incorporate the IFERROR function. Display the message **Invalid hire date**.

9. Change the hire date in cell C12 from 3/1/2007 to **#/1//2007** (note that you are entering a date with an intentional error). Insert a comment in cell S12 describing what appears in row 12 of the Years Service, Bonus, and Award columns. After entering the comment, change the date in cell C12 to **3/1/2007**.

10. Complete the criteria range located in the range A1:S3 of the Employee Data worksheet so you can use advanced filtering to display all part-time (PT) employees working in Austin as well as full-time (FT) employees working at home and earning $40,000 or more.

11. Use the COUNTIF count and AVERAGEIF functions to complete the Gender Summary report in the range B4:D5 of the Reports worksheet.

12. Use the Database function to calculate the average salary by Sex (F or M) and Pay Type (S or H). Enter the criteria in the ranges J12:K12, M12:N12, J17:K17, and M17:N17 in the Reports worksheet, and then use the DAVERAGE function to complete the report found in the range B11:D13 of the Reports worksheet.

13. Save and close the workbook. Submit the finished workbook to your instructor, either in printed or electronic form, as requested.

Apply	**Case Problem 1**

Apply the skills you learned to analyze and summarize monthly sales data for a computer supply store.

Data File needed for this Case Problem: Modem.xlsx

PC-Market Distribution   Linda Klaussen works for PC-Market Distribution, a computer supply store. She needs your help in designing an Excel workbook to enter purchase order information. She has already entered the product information on PC-Market's line of modems. She wants you to insert a lookup function to look up data from the product table. The company also supports three shipping options that vary in price. She wants the purchase order worksheet to be able to calculate the total cost of the order, including the type of shipping the customer requests. She also wants to use advanced filtering to copy data on all modems under $50 to a new worksheet to review prices of the inexpensive items. Finally, she wants to calculate average prices for each category of modems using a Database function.

Complete the following:

1. Open the **Modem** workbook located in the Tutorial.07\Case1 folder included with your Data Files, save the workbook as **PC Modem** in the same folder, and then, in the Documentation worksheet, enter the date and your name.

2. In the Purchase Order worksheet, Product ID numbers will be entered in cell B5. Create three lookup functions: the first to display the product type in cell C7, the second to display the model name in cell C8, and the third to display the price in cell C9. Product information is displayed in the Product List worksheet.

3. If an incorrect product ID number is entered in cell B5, then cells C7, C8, and C9 will display the #N/A error value. Linda wants these cells to display the message **Product ID not found** if the ID entered is not found.

4. Enter one of three shipping options offered by PC-Market (Standard, Express, Overnight) in cell B15. Set up an area in the range D40:E42 to store Standard shipping costs $9.50, Express shipping costs $14.50, and Overnight shipping costs $18.50. Use IF functions to display the costs of the shipping in cell C17. If an invalid shipping option is entered in cell B15, then **Invalid Shipping option** should appear in cell C17. If the Shipping option, cell B15, is blank, then cell C17 should be blank. (*Hint:* The IF functions should reference the cells in the range D40:E42.)

5. Display the total cost of the product (price times quantity) plus shipping in cell C19. If the cell equals an error value (#Value!), display the message **Check Product ID, Quantity, or Shipping option**.

6. Test the worksheet using a product ID number of **1050**, quantity **2**, and the **Express** shipping option.

7. On the Product List worksheet use advanced filtering to display all 56K Desktop modems (Type) with a price under $50 or Modem Card (Type) over $200. Make sure the values in all the columns are visible. Make a copy of the Product List worksheet, rename the copied worksheet **Q7 Advanced Filter** and then return to the Product List worksheet. Display all the records.

8. In the Summary worksheet, use appropriate functions to determine the average modem price and count for each modem type.

9. Save and close the workbook. Submit the finished workbook to your instructor, either in printed or electronic form, as requested.

Apply | Case Problem 2

Apply the skills you learned by creating a worksheet that tracks the amount of vacation time and family leave to which an employee is entitled.

Data File needed for this Case Problems: Leave.xlsx

Town of Baltic Administrative Office   Alan Welton, HR Generalist, at the Town of Baltic Administrative Office in Baltic, Indiana, has a workbook that tracks the amount of vacation time and family leave used by each employee in the town. Alan needs to calculate how much vacation and family leave each employee is eligible for. Then, he can subtract the amount they have already used from that amount. He also wants to calculate the total number of vacation and family leave days used by all employees, as well as the total number of days remaining. The eligibility requirements for the different vacation and family leave plans are as follows:

For vacation:
- 15 days for full-time employees who have worked 4 or more years
- 10 days for full-time employees who have worked 2 years but less than 4 years
- 5 days for full-time employees who have worked 1 year but less than 2 years
- 0 days for everyone else

For family leave:
- 5 days for full-time employees who have worked 1 or more years
- 3 days for full-time employees who have worked less than 1 year or for part-time employees who have worked more than 1.5 years
- 0 days for everyone else

Use these eligibility requirements to calculate the available vacation and family leave time for each employee.

Complete the following:

1. Open the workbook **Leave** located in the Tutorial.07\Case2 folder included with your Data Files, save the workbook as **Baltic Leave** in the same folder, and then enter the date and your name in the Documentation worksheet.

2. In the LeaveData worksheet, create an Excel table from the range A5:J107, name the Excel table as **Leave**, and then remove the filter arrows. Set the column width for columns B through J to **10**.

3. Calculate Years Employed in column D. Use Date Hired and current date (assume 7/1/2010, which is stored in cell Z6) and express length of time employed in years. Use the formula (current date – date hired)/365.

4. In column E, enter a formula using nested IF and AND functions to determine the number of vacation days (based on the vacation rules described previously) each employee is eligible for based on the employee's job status in column B and on the Length of Time Employed in column D.

5. Subtract the amount of vacation used from the available vacation time, displaying the remaining vacation time in column G for all employees.

⊕ EXPLORE   6. In column H, enter a formula to determine each employee's total family leave time (based on the family leave rules described previously). (*Hint*: Use nested IF, AND, and OR functions.)

7. To determine the remaining family time, subtract the used portion of the family leave from their total family leave and display the results in column J.

8. In the Leave Summary worksheet, use a function to calculate the total number of employees eligible for the different vacation leave plan. (*Hint*: An employee who is eligible for the 15-day vacation leave will have the value 15 in column E of the Leave Data worksheet.)

9. Enter formulas in the Vacation Leave Summary report to calculate the total number of vacation days and days remaining for each vacation plan.

10. Calculate the total number of employees, total days, and days remaining in row 8 of the report you started in Step 9.

11. Use advanced filtering to display all full-time employees with five remaining family leave days as well as all part-time employees with three remaining family leave days. Make a copy of the Leave Data worksheet, rename the copied worksheet **Q11 Advanced Filter**, and then return to the Leave Data worksheet. Clear the filter.

12. Save and close the workbook. Submit the finished workbook to your instructor, either in printed or electronic form, as requested.

| Challenge | **Case Problem 3** |

Create reports for a water company based on different billing plans.

Data File needed for this Case Problem: M-Fresh.xlsx

M-Fresh Water Company A small independent water company in Miami, Oklahoma, M-Fresh Water Company provides water to its commercial customers throughout the region, delivering the supply of water through pipelines, on-demand storage tanks, and bottles. Customers of M-Fresh Water range from government offices to nonprofit organizations to commercial retail shops and markets. Town regulations indicate that the latter group of commercial customers is taxed on their usage, whereas nonprofit and government offices are not. Furthermore, M-Fresh Water will, from time to time, choose to waive a water bill based on its charitable giving policy.

Dawes Cado is in charge of the billing system that must take into account these business rules and ensure accurate and on-time billing, which is completed each quarter. Complete the following:

1. Open the **M-Fresh** workbook located in the Tutorial.07\Case3 folder included with your Data Files, save the workbook as **Water Bills** in the same folder, and then enter the date and your name in the Documentation worksheet.

2. In the Quarterly Data worksheet, create an Excel table for the range A1:G73. Name the table as **WaterData**. Remove the filter arrows. Format the Gal Used data in the Comma Style number format with no decimal places. Add the following three columns to the table: **Water Bill**, **Tax**, and **Total Bill**.

3. Calculate the Water Bill based on the following rules:
   - If a customer's bill is waived, place 0 in the Water Bill column.
   - Gal Used (gallons used) must be greater than 25,000 gallons during the quarter; otherwise, the water bill is 0.
   - For all other accounts, the billing rate varies based on the type of customer. The billing rate is $3, $2, or $1.50 per *thousand* gallons used depending on the type of customer (see the Billing Rate worksheet). For example, a commercial customer using 75,000 gallons has a water bill of $225(75×$3), whereas a government customer using 100,000 gallons pays $150(100×$1.50). A commercial customer using 15,000 gallons has a water bill of 0.

4. Calculate Tax based on the following rule: If a customer is taxable, then multiply the water bill times 3.5%; otherwise, the tax is 0. (Tax rate is stored in cell T1.)

5. Calculate the Total Bill amount using the following formula: *Water Bill + Tax*.
6. Improve the formatting of the number fields, and then insert totals for GalUsed (average) and Total bill (sum). Make a copy of the Quarterly Data worksheet, rename the copied worksheet **Q2-6** and then return to the Quarterly Data worksheet.
7. Use conditional formatting to highlight the top 15% of customers based on the total bill. Use appropriate formatting. Filter the bills so only the top 15% are displayed. Sort the largest first. Make a copy of the Quarterly Data worksheet, rename the copied worksheet **Q7** and then return to the Quarterly Data worksheet. Display all records.
8. Insert a new worksheet and then create the Water Usage and Billing By Type of Customer report (shown in Figure 7-39). Rename the worksheet as **Q8 Billing Summary**. Use conditional IF functions to prepare the report.

Figure 7-39

	A	B	C	D	E	F
1						
2						
3						
4		Customer Type	Nbr Customers	Avg Gals Used	Total Billed	
5		Commercial	37	322,437	$ 37,043.12	
6		Non-profit	11	87,661	$ 224.18	
7		Government	24	774,532	$ 27,901.44	
8		Total	72	437,267	$ 65,168.74	
9						
10						

EXPLORE

9. Make a copy of the Quarterly Data worksheet, rename the copied worksheet **Q9-10**. Management is considering eliminating the 25,000 gallon cutoff and bill waivers. In the Quarterly Data worksheet use advanced filtering to copy all data for waived customers or customers using 25,000 gallons or less to row 101 in the Q9-10 worksheet.

EXPLORE

10. Use the data you retrieved from Step 9 to calculate the lost revenue from waived bills and customers with water usage below 25,000. Assume for the purposes of the analysis that all water usage (25,000 gallon cutoff no longer exists) will be billed. Prepare a report.

EXPLORE

11. You want to know how many businesses are either churches, schools, or clinics. Use the COUNTIF function to complete the report in a new worksheet named **Q11 Type Institution**. (*Hint:* Use Help to research using the wildcard characters as part of your criteria.)

12. Save and close the workbook. Submit the finished workbook to your instructor, either in printed or electronic form, as requested.

Create	**Case Problem 4**

Create a worksheet that compiles and summarizes reports for a newspaper.

Data File needed for this Case Problem: Rock Island.xlsx

Rock Island Home Sales Tim Derkson, reporter for Rock Island Times, in Rock Island, Illinois, is compiling a quarterly real estate sales analysis for his newspaper. He obtained data on home sales from the local real estate association and county records. He asked you to help design a worksheet that will display summary information on the home sales in Rock Island. Tim has already set up and formatted a workbook, but he wants you to insert the correct formulas. Tim stored the housing data in the Home Data worksheet. He wants to use the Home Summary worksheet to search for information about the homes.

Complete the following:

1. Open the **Rock Island** workbook located in the Tutorial.07\Case4 folder included with your Data Files, save the workbook as **Home Sales** in the same folder, and then, in the Documentation worksheet, enter the date and your name.

2. In the Home Sales Data worksheet, create an Excel table in the range A6:K123. Remove the filter arrows. Name the Excel table as **SalesData**.

3. Using the Date Sold and Date Listed columns, add a calculated column named **Days on Market**, which is the difference between these two dates. (*Hint:* You might need to format this column in the General number format.)

⊕ EXPLORE
4. Use conditional formatting to highlight records where the sales price was above the asking price. Add appropriate formatting. (*Hint:* Create a new rule using the formula rule type and build a conditional statement to compare first data row between the two columns of interest.) Make a copy of the Home Sales Data worksheet, rename the copied worksheet **Q3-4**, and then return to the Home Sales Data worksheet.

5. Insert a new worksheet, and then rename it as **Q5-6 Sales Summary**. Create a report on Overall Home Sales based on Sales Price, using Figure 7-40 as a guide.

Figure 7-40

	A	B	C	D	E	F	G
1				Rock Island Home Sales			
2				Overall Data			
3							
4			Number Sold	Average Sales Price	Highest Sales Price	Lowest Sales Price	
5			117	$ 100,461.54	$ 215,000	$ 51,000	
6							

⊕ EXPLORE
6. Below the report, create a report on Home Sales based on Sales Price and broken down by Type of Home. Figure 7-41 shows the output. Use conditional IF functions for Number Sold and Average Sales Price and database functions (DMAX and DMIN) to calculate the highest and lowest price.

Figure 7-41

7		By Type of Home			
8					
9	**Type**	**Number Sold**	**Average Sales Price**	**Highest Sales Price**	**Lowest Sales Price**
10	Condo	23	$ 90,347.83	$ 182,500	$ 53,000
11	Ranch	46	$ 91,842.39	$ 193,500	$ 51,000
12	Victorian	48	$ 113,567.71	$ 215,000	$ 51,750
13					

7. In the Home Sales Data worksheet use Advanced Filtering to display all homes that were:

- On the market more than 150 days and 25 or more years old

OR

- Have more than 2 bedrooms and 1.5 or more bathrooms

Sort the filtered data by Days on Market in descending order. Make a copy of the Home Sales Data worksheet, rename the copied worksheet **Q7 Advanced Filter** and then return to the Home Sales Data worksheet. Display all records.

⊕ EXPLORE 8. Insert a new worksheet. Rename the worksheet as **Q8-9 DaysOnMarket**. Create a PivotTable to create a report with the information in Figure 7-42.

Figure 7-42

4		Values	
5	**Days**	**Number Sold**	**Avg Sales Price**
6	1-100	31	$ 94,451.61
7	101-200	27	$ 106,879.63
8	201-300	37	$ 103,939.19
9	301-400	22	$ 95,204.55
10	**Grand Total**	**117**	**$ 100,461.54**

⊕ EXPLORE 9. In a separate section of the same Q8-9 DaysOnMarket worksheet, use Database functions and complete the criteria ranges to create the report shown in Figure 7-43, which provides the same information as the report you created in Step 8.

Figure 7-43

15	**Days**	**Number Sold**	**Avg Sales Price**
16	1-100	31	$ 94,451.61
17	101-200	27	$ 106,879.63
18	201-300	37	$ 103,939.19
19	301-400	22	$ 95,204.55
20	**Total**	**117**	**$ 100,461.54**

10. Display the Total row in the SalesData table. In this row, display a count of homes sold, average taxes, average asking price, average sales price, and average days on market. Make a copy of the Home Sales Data worksheet, rename the copied worksheet **Q10-11 Home Sales Data** and then return to the Home Sales worksheet.

⊕ EXPLORE
11. In the Q10-11 Home Sales Data worksheet, split the Home Sales Data worksheet so the top section shows all the Home Data table. The bottom section is the last one or two rows on your screen, which displays the Total row. (*Hint:* Use Excel Help to find information on how to split the window.)

12. Save and close the workbook. Submit the finished workbook to your instructor, either in printed or electronic form, as requested.

Research | **Internet Assignments**

Use the Internet to find and work with data related to the topics presented in this tutorial.

The purpose of the Internet Assignments is to challenge you to find information on the Internet that you can use to work effectively with this software. The actual assignments are updated and maintained on the Course Technology Web site. Log on to the Internet and use your Web browser to go to the Student Online Companion for New Perspectives Office 2007 at **www.course.com/np/office2007**. Then navigate to the Internet Assignments for this tutorial.

Assess | **SAM Assessment and Training**

If you have a SAM user profile, you may have access to hands-on instruction, practice, and assessment of the skills covered in this tutorial. Log in to your SAM account (**http://sam2007.course.com**) to launch any assigned training activities or exams that relate to the skills covered in this tutorial.

Review | **Quick Check Answers**

Session 7.1

1. The table style is applied to all rows in the new column; the range of the Excel table expands to include the new column (Phone). All features that apply to other columns in the table apply to the Phone column, too.
2. calculated column
3. In cell C7, enter = IF(C5*C6 > 10000,C5*C6,10000).
4. False
5. =IF(AND(J5>0,D5<3/15/2008),"Outstanding","")
6. structured references
7. nested IF

Session 7.2

1. An exact match compares the lookup value to the compare value. They must be equal for a value to be returned from the lookup table. An approximate match also compares the lookup value to the compare value. The two values do not have to be equal, just fall within a range of values for Excel to return a value from the lookup table.
2. VLOOKUP function
3. No, duplicate last names do not mean the data in the Last Name column is a duplicate.
4. =IFERROR(C5/C25,"Dividing by 0")
5. counts the number of females in the Employee table

6. Calculate the average salary for all hourly employees.
7. Conditional Formatting Rules Manager dialog box

Session 7.3

1. retrieve all male employees classified as hourly
2. Location
   ="=Austin"
   ="=New Orleans"
3. retrieve employees earning less than 25,000 or 100,000 or more in annual salary
4. Clear command
5. sum the annual salaries of all males hired on 1/1/2010 or later
6. The structured reference to Employee includes only the data in an Excel table, whereas Employee[#ALL] includes the header and total row. The DSUM function's first argument must reference the header row.
7. =DSUM('Employee Data'!A5:R105,"Annual Salary",T1:U2)

Ending Data Files

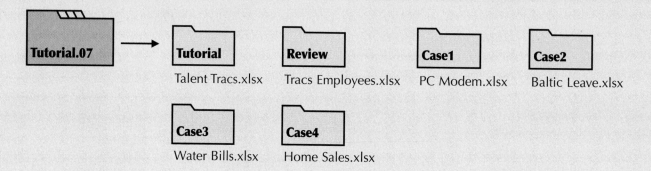

Tutorial.07 → Tutorial   Review   Case1   Case2

Talent Tracs.xlsx   Tracs Employees.xlsx   PC Modem.xlsx   Baltic Leave.xlsx

Case3   Case4

Water Bills.xlsx   Home Sales.xlsx

Developing an Excel Application

Creating an Invoice

Case | Eugene Community Theatre

Ellen Jefferson, business manager for the Eugene Community Theatre in Eugene, Oregon, is automating several processes for the theatre's business office. Each year, the theatre mails a brochure to patrons and other interested individuals showcasing the upcoming seasons' offerings. Then, theatre-goers make their selections and mail in the order form. Ellen wants to automate the process of invoicing, capturing the order, calculating the charges, and printing an invoice. She also wants the invoice system to reflect specific requests for tickets (number, series, and location in theatre).

Many of these tasks can be accomplished in Excel. But without validating data entry, protecting cells with formulas from accidental deletion, and reducing repetitious keystrokes and mouse clicks, Ellen realizes too many opportunities for errors exist. In addition, the theatre, as a nonprofit organization, relies on numerous volunteers who have varying degrees of computer experience and skill. To accommodate these varying skill levels and reduce potential errors, Ellen wants to create a custom interface for this project that does not rely exclusively on the Ribbon, galleries, and so forth. You'll help Ellen create a unique Excel application that can resolve these issues and help ensure accurate data entry.

Starting Data Files

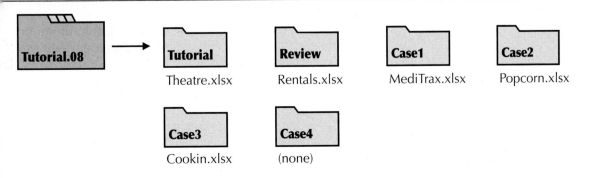

Tutorial.08 → Tutorial — Theatre.xlsx

Review — Rentals.xlsx

Case1 — MediTrax.xlsx

Case2 — Popcorn.xlsx

Case3 — Cookin.xlsx

Case4 — (none)

Session 8.1

Planning an Excel Application

An **Excel application** is a spreadsheet written or tailored to meet the user's specific needs. Applications typically include the following:

• Reports and/or charts designed to aid understanding and produce insights
• A way to enter and edit data, often controlling the type of values that can be entered and where data can be entered
• An interface that assists the user, ranging from buttons for executing specific tasks to customizing the entire Excel interface with custom tabs, menus, and toolbars
• Clearly written instructions and documentation

Ellen sketched the application she wants you to create, which is shown in Figure 8-1. She wants to be able to easily print the invoice and transfer the invoice items to another worksheet. In addition, she wants volunteers to be able to enter data for a season ticket in a specific area of the worksheet reserved for input. The application would use this data to automatically generate and print the invoice. To keep the process simple, she also wants users to be able to click buttons to print a single invoice, print the entire worksheet, and transfer the data from one worksheet to another.

| Figure 8-1 | Ellen's sketch of the Excel application for invoicing |

Application planning includes designing how the worksheet(s) will be organized. You can include different sections for each function, depending on the complexity of the project. For example, you could include separate sections to:

• Enter and edit data (even setting what types of values can be entered and where a user can enter data)
• Store data after it has been entered
• Use formulas to manipulate and perform calculations on data
• Prepare outputs, such as reports and charts

An application's interface helps others use it. For example, you can have separate sections for inputting data and displaying outputs. You can create special buttons for performing specific tasks. You can also change the entire Excel interface by adding custom menus, toolbars, and commands.

An application often includes internal documentation in a Documentation worksheet as well as comments to explain cell contents and provide instructions. It can also include a set of clearly written instructions. All of these help you and others use the workbook correctly and accurately.

You'll open the workbook Ellen created and complete the application.

To open and review the Theatre workbook:

▶ **1.** Open the **Theatre** workbook located in the **Tutorial.08\Tutorial** folder included with your Data Files, and then save the workbook as **Community Theatre** in the same folder.

▶ **2.** In the Documentation sheet, enter the current date and your name.

▶ **3.** Review the contents of the workbook, and then switch to the **Invoice** worksheet. See Figure 8-2.

Initial Invoice worksheet ◀ **Figure 8-2**

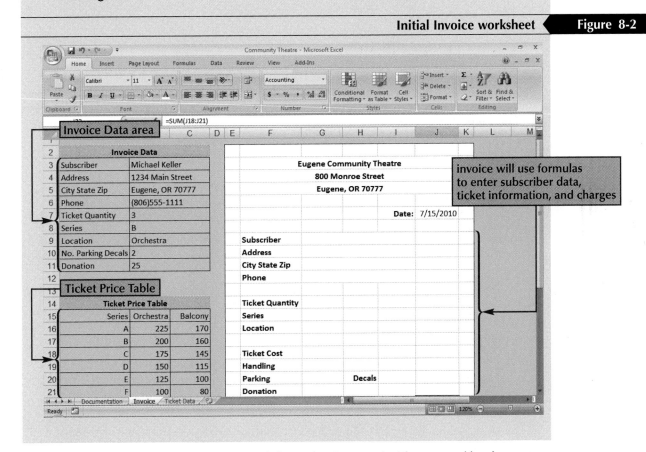

In addition to the Documentation worksheet, the Community Theatre workbook includes two other worksheets: Invoice and Ticket Data.

The Invoice worksheet contains input, output, and transfer data sections. The input section is divided into the following three areas:

Tip

Larger and more complex applications often place the input and output sections in separate worksheets.

- Invoice Data contains items that change for each request, such as the subscriber name, address, phone number, ticket quantity, series, location of seats, and so forth.
- Ticket Price Table contains the pricing table for all tickets for the upcoming season.
- Invoice Constants contains charges for items that will not change during the upcoming theatre season, such as the cost for parking ($15/decal) and the handling charge ($8/invoice).

The output section contains formulas and labels used to generate the invoice based on data in the input section. The invoice in the output section will be printed. The transfer data section gathers selected data from the invoice in one area before the data is transferred to the Ticket Data worksheet for storage. The transfer data section makes it simpler to move the data to the Ticket Data worksheet.

Naming Cells and Ranges

In the Invoice worksheet, the range B3:B11 contains the data values for each request for season tickets. As you can see, this range includes many variables. It will be simpler to remember where different data is stored by assigning a descriptive name to each cell or range rather than using its cell address. For example, the name *Customer* is easier to remember than cell B3. Assigning names to cells or ranges makes building an application more intuitive and easier to document. Ellen asks you to name the cells in the input section.

Creating Defined Names

So far, you have referred to a cell or range by its cell and range address except when you entered formulas within an Excel table. Cell and range references do not indicate what data is stored in those cells. Instead, you can assign a meaningful, descriptive name to a cell or range. A **defined name** (often called simply a **name**) is a word or string of characters associated with a single cell or a range. For example, if the range D1:D100 contains sales data for 100 transactions, you can define the name *Sales* to refer to the range of sales data.

You can use a defined name to quickly navigate within a workbook to the cell with defined name. You can also create more descriptive formulas by using defined names in formulas instead of cell or range references. For example, the defined name *Sales* can replace the range reference D1:D100 in a formula to calculate average sales, as follows (the first formula uses a range reference, the second formula uses a defined name):

```
=AVERAGE(D1:D100)
=AVERAGE(Sales)
```

When you define a name for a cell or range, keep in mind the following rules:

- The name must begin with a letter or _ (an underscore).
- The name can include letters and numbers as well as periods and underscores, but not other symbols or spaces. To distinguish multiword names, use an underscore between the words or capitalize the first letter of each word. For example, the names *Net_Income* or *NetIncome* are valid, but *Net Income* and *Net-Income* are not.
- The name cannot be a valid cell address (such as *FY2010*), function name, or reserved word (such as *Print_Area*).
- The name can include as many as 255 characters, although short, meaningful names of 5 to 15 characters are more practical.
- The name is not case-sensitive. For example, *Sales* and *SALES* are the same name and refer to the same cell or range.

Saving Time with Defined Names | InSight

Defined names have several advantages over cell references, especially as a worksheet becomes longer and more complex. Some advantages include:

- Names, such as *TaxRate* and *TotalSales*, are more descriptive than cell references, making it easier to remember a cell or range's content.
- Names can be used in formulas, making it easier for users to understand the calculations being performed. For example, =*GrossPay–Deductions* is more understandable than =*C15–C16*.
- When you move a named cell or range within a worksheet, its name moves with it. Any formulas that contain the name automatically reference the new location.
- In a formula, a named cell or range is the same as using the cell or range's absolute reference. So, if you move a formula that includes a defined name, the reference remains pointed to the correct cell or range.

By using defined names, you'll often save time and have a better understanding of what a formula is calculating.

Creating a Name for a Cell or Range | Reference Window

- Select the cell or range to which you want to assign a name.
- Click in the Name box on the formula bar, type the name, and then press the Enter key (or in the Defined Names group on the Formulas tab, click the Define Name button, type a name in the Name box, and then click the OK button).

or

- Select the range with labels and blank cells in the top row or first column to which you want to assign a name.
- In the Defined Names group on the Formulas tab, click the Create from Selection button.
- Specify whether to create the ranges based on the top row, bottom row, left column, or right column in the list.
- Click the OK button.

The fastest way to create a defined name is to use the Name box. You'll use the Name box to define names for the cells that contain the handling costs and the parking fee. Then, you'll define a name for the Ticket Price Table, which you will use in a formula later in the tutorial.

To use the Name box to name the invoice constants and the Ticket Price Table:

1. Click cell **B24** to make it active, and then click the **Name box**. The cell reference for the active cell, B24, is selected in the Name box.

2. Type **HandlingCost**, and then press the **Enter** key. Cell B24 remains active, and the name *HandlingCost* appears in the Name box instead of the cell reference.

   Trouble? If the label *HandlingCost* appears in cell B24, you probably did not click the Name box before typing the name. On the Quick Access Toolbar, click the Undo button, and then repeat Steps 1 and 2.

3. Click cell **B25** to make it active, click the **Name box** to select the cell reference, type **ParkingFee**, and then press the **Enter** key. Cell B25 remains active, and the name *ParkingFee* appears in the Name box instead of the cell reference. See Figure 8-3.

Figure 8-3 — Defined name for cell B25

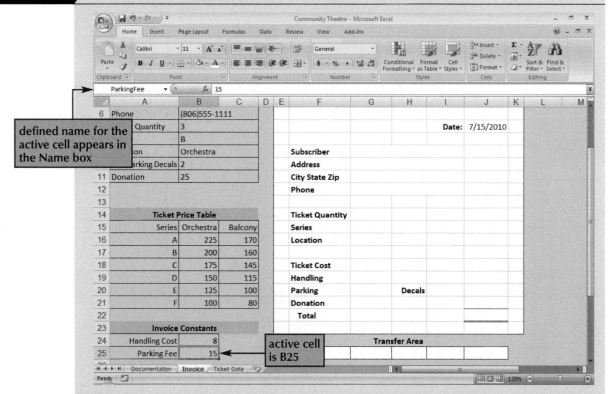

> **4.** Select the range **A16:C21**. The cell reference for the active cell in the range appears in the Name box.

> **5.** Click the **Name box**, type **TicketPrices**, and then press the **Enter** key. The name *TicketPrices* is assigned to the range A16:C21.

> **6.** Select the range **F25:J25**, click the **Name box**, type **TransferArea**, and then press the **Enter** key. The name *TransferArea* is assigned to the range F25:J25.

The Name box, as the title implies, displays all of the names in a workbook. You can select a name in the Name box to quickly select the cell or range referenced by the name. You'll view the defined names you added to the workbook.

To select cells and ranges with the Name box:

> **1.** Click the **Name box** arrow to open a list of defined names in the workbook. Four names appear in the list: *HandlingCost*, *ParkingFee*, *TicketPrices*, and *TransferArea*.

> **2.** Click **ParkingFee**. The active cell moves to cell B25.

> **3.** Click the **Name box** arrow, and then click **TicketPrices**. The range A16:C21 is selected in the worksheet, and cell A16 is the active cell.

Ellen wants to define names to each cell in the Invoice Data area. You can quickly define names without typing them if the data is organized in a tabular format with labels in the first or last column or top or bottom row. The names are based on the row or column labels. Any blanks or parentheses in the row or column labels are changed to an underscore (_) in the defined name.

You will create names for the Invoice Data area, using the labels in the range A3:A11.

To create defined names by selection for the Invoice Data area:

▶ **1.** Select the range **A3:B11**. In this range, column A contains the labels you want to use as the defined names and column B contains the cells you want to name.

▶ **2.** Click the **Formulas** tab on the Ribbon, and then, in the Defined Names group, click the **Create from Selection** button. The Create Names from Selection dialog box opens. See Figure 8-4.

Create Names from Selection dialog box ◀ Figure 8-4

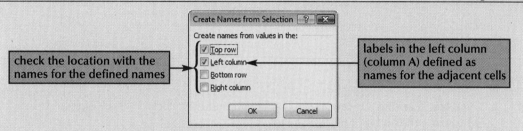

check the location with the names for the defined names

labels in the left column (column A) defined as names for the adjacent cells

▶ **3.** Click the **Top row** check box to remove the check mark, and then verify that the **Left column** check box contains a check mark. The labels in the left column will be used to create the defined names.

▶ **4.** Click the **OK** button. Each cell in the range B3:B11 is named based on its label in column A.

Although you can use the Name box to verify the names were created, the Name Manager dialog box lists all of the names currently defined in the workbook, including Excel table names. You can also use the Name Manager dialog box to a create new names, edit or delete existing names, and filter the list of names.

To use the Name Manager dialog box to edit and delete defined names:

▶ **1.** In the Defined Names group on the Formulas tab, click the **Name Manager** button. The Name Manager dialog box opens, listing the nine defined names based on the labels in the range A3:A11 in the Invoice Data area as well as the four names you defined with the Name box. See Figure 8-5.

Tip

The Name Manager dialog box also lists Excel table names.

Figure 8-5 | **Name Manager dialog box**

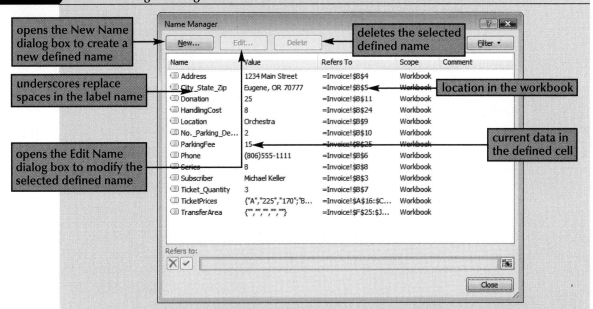

The name *No._Parking_Decals* is too long, so you'll change it to *Decals*.

▶ **2.** Click **No._Parking_Decals** in the Name list, and then click the **Edit** button. The Edit Name dialog box opens. See Figure 8-6.

Figure 8-6 | **Edit Name dialog box**

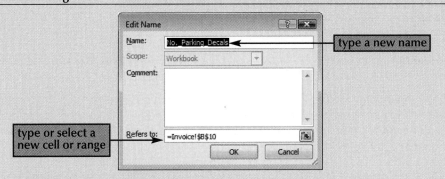

▶ **3.** In the Name box, type **Decals**, and then click the **OK** button. The edited name appears in the list.

Ellen decides the name *TransferArea* is not needed.

▶ **4.** Click **TransferArea**, and then click the **Delete** button. A dialog box opens, confirming that you want to delete the selected name.

▶ **5.** Click the **OK** button. The name is removed from the list.

▶ **6.** Click the **Close** button. The Name Manager dialog box closes.

When a workbook contains many defined names, it can be helpful to list all of the defined names and their corresponding cell addresses as part of the workbook's documentation. You can generate a list of names using the Paste Names command.

To create a list of defined names in the Documentation worksheet:

▶ 1. Switch to the **Documentation** worksheet.

▶ 2. Click in cell **A12**, type **Defined Names**, and then press the **Enter** key. The heading for the list of defined names appears in cell A12, and cell A13 is the active cell.

▶ 3. In the Defined Names group on the Formulas tab, click the **Use in Formula** button. The list includes all the defined names in the workbook followed by the Paste Names command.

▶ 4. Click **Paste Names**. The Paste Name dialog box opens. You can paste any selected name, or you can paste the entire list of names.

▶ 5. Click the **Paste List** button. The defined names and their associated cell references are pasted into the range A13:B24.

▶ 6. Adjust the column widths of columns A and B to display all the defined names data, if necessary, and then deselect the range. See Figure 8-7.

Defined names in the Community Theatre workbook ◀ Figure 8-7

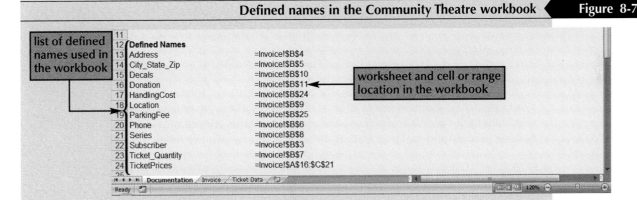

▶ 7. Switch to the **Invoice** worksheet.

If you edit a defined name or add a new defined name, the list of defined names and their addresses in the Documentation worksheet is not updated. You must paste the list again to update the names and locations. Usually, it is a good idea to wait until the workbook is complete before pasting defined names in the Documentation worksheet.

Entering Formulas with Defined Names

Ellen already entered the TODAY function in cell J7 to ensure the current date always appears on the invoice. You'll enter the remaining formulas needed to generate the invoice. You'll start by entering formulas to display the subscriber's name and address in the invoice. Ellen entered sample subscriber data in the input section of the Invoice worksheet so you can test the formulas as you enter them.

To enter formulas to display the subscriber's name and address:

▶ 1. In cell G9, enter **=B3**. Michael Keller, the subscriber's name in the sample data, appears in the cell.

▶ 2. In cell G10, enter **=B4**. The subscriber's address, 1234 Main Street, appears in the cell.

▶ **3.** Click cell **G10**. The formula =B4 appears in the formula bar.

You entered these formulas using cell addresses rather than defined names. Although you defined names for cells B3 and B4, the names do not automatically replace the cell addresses in the formula. Because defined names make formulas simpler to enter and understand, you will use the named cells and ranges as you enter the remaining formulas.

As you type a defined name in a formula, the Formula AutoComplete box lists items that match the letters you typed. You can type the entire name, double-click the name in the Formula AutoComplete box, or press the Tab key to enter the selected name.

To type defined names in formulas:

▶ **1.** In cell G11, enter **=City_State_Zip**.

▶ **2.** Click cell **G11**. The data from cell B5 appears in the cell, and the formula with the defined name, =City_State_Zip, appears in the formula bar.

▶ **3.** In cell G12, enter **=Phone**, and then click cell **G12**. The sample data from cell B6 appears in the cell, the formula with the defined name, =Phone, appears in the formula bar.

You can also use the point-and-click method to create a formula with defined names. When you click a cell or select a range, Excel substitutes the defined name for the cell reference in the formula. You'll use this method to enter formulas that display the ticket quantity, series, and theatre location from the input area in the invoice.

To enter formulas with defined names using the point-and-click method:

▶ **1.** Click cell **I14**, type **=**, and then click cell **B7**. The formula uses the defined name *Ticket_Quantity* rather than the cell reference B7.

▶ **2.** Press the **Enter** key. The number 3, indicating the number of tickets the subscriber ordered, appears in cell I14.

▶ **3.** In cell I15, type **=**, and then click cell **B8**. The formula uses the defined name *Series* rather than the cell reference B8.

▶ **4.** Press the **Enter** key. The letter B, indicating the series the subscriber selected, appears in cell I15.

Next, you'll move the subscriber's preferred location to the invoice.

5. In cell I16, type **=**, click **B9**, and then click the **Enter** button ☑ on the formula bar. Orchestra, the location the subscriber selected, appears in cell I16, and the formula with the defined name, =Location, appears in the formula bar. See Figure 8-8.

Formula with a defined name ◄ **Figure 8-8**

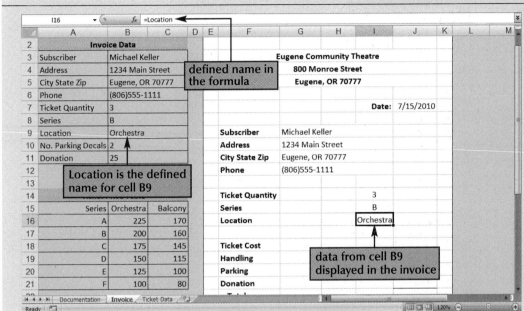

Next, you will enter the formula to calculate the ticket cost to the subscriber. You need to combine two VLOOKUP functions within an IF function to create the formula to calculate ticket costs. The VLOOKUP functions will find the ticket price. The lookup value is the Series the subscriber selects (A, B, C, D, E, or F). Recall that the lookup value searches the first column of the lookup table to find the appropriate row. In this case, the lookup table is the Ticket Price Table (the range you earlier named *TicketPrices*) which has two columns of ticket prices. Column 2 of the table lists the prices for the Orchestra and column 3 of the table lists the prices for the Balcony. The column used to return the ticket prices depends on the Location the subscriber selected. You need to use an IF function to determine whether to search the second or third column for the ticket price.

To enter the formula to determine ticket cost:

▶ 1. In cell J18, enter **=IF(Location="Orchestra",VLOOKUP(Series,TicketPrices, 2,FALSE),VLOOKUP(Series,TicketPrices,3,FALSE))*Ticket_Quantity**. The ticket cost based on the sample subscriber data is $600. The first argument of the IF function, *Location="Orchestra",* determines which VLOOKUP formula to use—the one returning a value from column 2 (Orchestra) in the TicketPrices table or the one returning a value from column 3 (Balcony) in the TicketPrices table. The second argument, *VLOOKUP(Series,TicketPrices,2,FALSE),* uses the VLOOKUP function to find a ticket price for a seat in the Orchestra. The first argument of the VLOOKUP function, *Series,* is the defined name that stores the Series code (A, B, C, and so on) used to look up a value in the second argument, *TicketPrices* (range A16:C21). The third argument, *2,* returns a ticket price from the second column (Orchestra) of the TicketPrices table. The fourth argument, *FALSE,* indicates an exact match lookup. The second VLOOKUP function is identical except the third argument has a value of 3, which returns a ticket price from the third column (Balcony) of the TicketPrices table. The final part of the formula, **Ticket_Quantity,* multiplies the ticket price by the number of tickets to calculate the ticket cost.

Trouble? If #Name? or #Value? appears in the cell J18, you might have entered the formula incorrectly. Click cell J18, compare the formula you entered with the formula in Step 1, and then edit the formula in the formula bar as needed. Also, make sure the references in your defined names are correct (see Figure 8-7).

▶ 2. Click cell **J18**, and then click the **Expand Formula Bar** button ⌄ on the right side of the formula bar. The entire formula is visible in the expanded formula bar. The IF function determines which column in the TicketPrices range to use to return the ticket price. If Location in the invoice data area is Orchestra, then the condition Location="Orchestra" is TRUE and the VLOOKUP function returns a ticket price from column 2. If the subscriber requests the Balcony location, then the VLOOKUP function searches column 3 for the ticket price. The price for one ticket, as determined by the IF and VLOOKUP functions, is multiplied by the ticket quantity to calculate the total ticket cost for this transaction. See Figure 8-9.

Figure 8-9	Formula to calculate the ticket cost

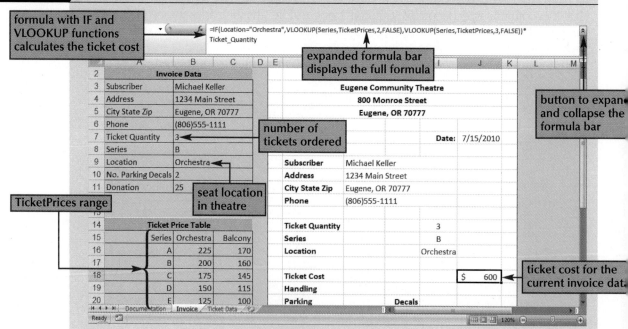

▶ **3.** Click the **Collapse Formula Bar** button ⊼ on the formula bar. The formula bar returns to its usual height.

You'll enter the remaining formulas needed to complete the invoice.

To enter the remaining formulas in the invoice:

▶ **1.** In cell J19, enter **=HandlingCost**. The handling cost is $8, which is the amount in cell B24 in the Invoice Constants area.

▶ **2.** In cell I20, enter **=Decals**. The number of parking decals ordered is 2, which is the number listed in cell B10 in the Invoice Data area.

▶ **3.** In cell J20, enter **=Decals*ParkingFee**. The parking cost is $30, which is the number of decals listed in cell B10 multiplied by the parking fee in cell B25. You can see how the defined names make entering this calculation faster and the formula easier to understand.

▶ **4.** In cell J21, enter **=Donation**. The donation amount is $25, which is listed in cell B11.

▶ **5.** In cell J22, enter **=SUM(J18:J21)**. The SUM function adds all the costs to determine the total invoice amount of $663. See Figure 8-10.

Invoice with all formulas entered ◀ Figure 8-10

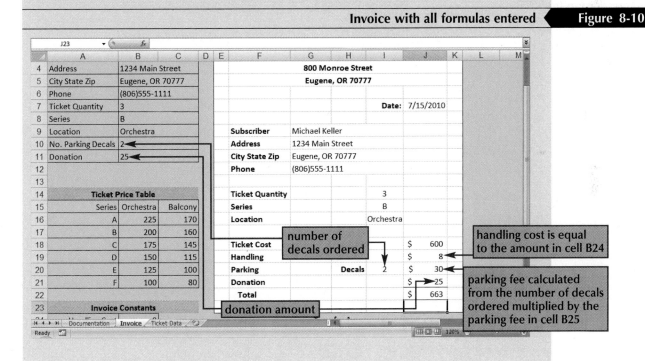

Adding Defined Names to Existing Formulas

Sometimes, you might name cells after creating formulas in the worksheet. Other times, you might not use the defined names when you create formulas (as with the first two formulas you created in the invoice for the subscriber name and address). Recall that defined names are not automatically substituted for the cell addressess in a formula. However, you can replace cell addresses in existing formulas with their defined names to make the formulas more understandable.

Tip

If a formula uses a defined name that doesn't exist, #NAME? appears in the cell. Verify the defined name is spelled correctly and that the name wasn't deleted from the worksheet.

Reference Window | **Adding Defined Names to Existing Formulas**

- In the Defined Names group on the Formulas tab, click the Define Name button arrow, and then click Apply Names (if the cell reference and defined name definition are in the same worksheet).
- In the Apply Names dialog box, select the names you want to apply, and then click the OK button.

or

- Edit the formula by selecting the cell reference and typing the defined name (or clicking the appropriate cell).

You'll change the two formulas you created to display the subscriber name and address in the invoice to use defined names instead of cell references.

To add defined names to existing formulas in the invoice:

▶ 1. In the Defined Names group on the Formulas tab, click the **Define Name** button arrow, and then click **Apply Names**. The Apply Names dialog box appears. See Figure 8-11.

Figure 8-11 | **Apply Names dialog box**

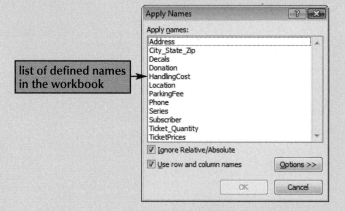

list of defined names in the workbook

You want to select only the two names you need for the existing formulas with cell references.

▶ 2. If any name is selected in the Apply names list, click that name to deselect it.

Now that no names are selected in the Apply names list, you will select the names you want to apply to the formulas.

▶ 3. In the Apply names list, click **Address** and **Subscriber**. The two names are selected.

▶ 4. Click the **OK** button. The two selected names are applied to the formulas.

▶ 5. Click cell **G9** and verify that the formula changed to =Subscriber, and then click cell **G10** and verify that the formula changed to =Address.

Ellen wants to store the following items in the Ticket Data worksheet: subscriber name, transaction date, ticket quantity, ticket cost, and total amount owed from the invoice. Displaying these data items in the Transfer Area enables you to copy and paste all the items to the Ticket Data worksheet at once. You'll enter formulas to display the appropriate items in this section of the worksheet.

To enter formulas to display data in the Transfer Area:

▶ **1.** In cell F25, enter **=Subscriber**. The formula displays the subscriber name in this cell.

▶ **2.** In cell G25, enter **=J7**. The formula displays the current date.

▶ **3.** In cell H25, enter **=I14**. The formula displays the number of tickets.

▶ **4.** In cell I25, enter **=J18**. The formula displays the ticket cost.

▶ **5.** In cell J25, enter **=J22**. The formula displays the total cost.

The worksheet contains all the formulas to create the invoice based on the subscriber information. Because Ellen relies on volunteers to enter season ticket requests into the worksheet and print invoices, she wants to be sure the values entered are correct. You will continue to work on Ellen's application by creating validation checks, which are designed to prevent users from inserting incorrect data values. You will also protect cells so that volunteers cannot accidentally overwrite or delete the formulas. You'll do both of these tasks in the next session.

Session 8.1 Quick Check | Review

1. What is a defined name? Give two advantages of using names in workbooks.
2. Describe three ways to create a name.
3. Which of the following is a valid defined name?
    a. Annual_Total
    b. 3rdQtr
    c. Annual total
4. How can you quickly select a cell or range using its name?
5. In the Report workbook, the Expenses name refers to a list of expenses stored in the range D2:D100. Currently the total expenses are calculated with the formula =SUM(D2:D100). Change this formula to use the defined name.
6. True or False? If you define names for a range referenced in an existing formula, you cannot change the formula to use the new name.

Session 8.2

Validating Data Entry

To ensure that correct data is entered and stored in a worksheet, you can use **data validation** to create a set of rules that determine what users can enter in a specific cell or range. Each **validation rule** defines criteria for the data that can be stored in a cell or range. You can specify the type of data allowed (for example, whole numbers, decimals, dates, time, text, and so forth) as well as a list or range of acceptable values (for example, the condition codes *Excellent*, *Good*, *Fair*, and *Poor*, or integers between 1 and 100).

You can also add messages for the user to that cell or range. An **input message** appears when the cell becomes active and can be used to specify the type of data the user should enter in that cell. An **error alert message** appears if a user tries to enter a value in the cell that does not meet the validation rule.

Reference Window | **Validating Data**

- In the Data Tools group on the Data tab, click the Data Validation button.
- Click the Settings tab.
- Click the Allow arrow, click the type of data allowed in the cell, and then enter the validation criteria for that data.
- Click the Input Message tab, and then enter a title and text for the input message.
- Click the Error Alert tab, and then, if necessary, click the Show error alert after invalid data is entered check box to insert a check mark.
- Select an alert style, and then enter the title and text for the error alert message.
- Click the OK button.

Specifying a Data Type and Acceptable Values

Ellen wants you to add three validation rules to the workbook to help ensure that volunteers enter the correct values in the designated range of the Invoice worksheet. These three rules are:

- The Ticket Quantity value in cell B7 should be between 1 and 19. In previous years, 19 was the maximum number of tickets purchased in any invoice transaction.
- The Series value in cell B8 is one of the following: A, B, C, D, E, or F.
- The Location value in cell B9 is either Orchestra or Balcony.

These validation rules will help ensure that the invoice is completed accurately.

Each of these rules specifies the type of values allowed and the validation criteria used when entering a value in a cell. For example, the first rule allows a range of numbers, the second and third rules allow only the values in a list. When you create a data validation rule, you specify what types of values you want to allow as well as the validation criteria. Figure 8-12 describes the types of values you can allow.

Tip

Each cell can have only one validation rule. Creating a second validation rule for a cell replaces the existing rule.

Figure 8-12 | **Allow options for the validation criteria**

Value Type	Cell Accepts
Any value	Any number, text, or date; removes any existing data validation.
Whole number	Integers only; you can specify the range of acceptable integers.
Decimal	Any type of number; you can specify the range of acceptable numbers.
List	Any value in a range or entered in the Data Validation dialog box separated by commas.
Date	Dates only; you can specify the range of acceptable dates.
Time	Times only; you can specify the range of acceptable times.
Text length	Text limited to a specified number of characters.
Custom	Values based on the results of a logical formula.

You will define the validation rule for the number of season tickets.

To specify a whole number range validation rule for the number of tickets:

▶ **1.** If you took a break after the previous session, make sure the Community Theatre workbook is open and the Invoice worksheet is active.

▶ **2.** Click cell **B7**. This is the first cell for which you will enter a validation rule.

▶ **3.** Click the **Data** tab on the Ribbon, and then, in the Data Tools group, click the **Data Validation** button. The Data Validation dialog box opens. It contains three tabs: Settings, Input Message, and Error Alert. You use the Settings tab to enter the validation rule for the active cell.

Cell B7, the number of tickets, requires an integer that is greater than 0 and less than 20.

▶ **4.** On the Settings tab, click the **Allow** arrow, and then click **Whole number**. This option specifies that the number must be an integer. The Data Validation dialog box expands to display the options specific to whole numbers. The Ignore blank check box is checked, which means the validation rule is not applied when the cell is empty. If you uncheck the option, users are required to make an entry in the cell.

▶ **5.** If necessary, click the **Data** arrow, and then click **between**. The dialog box reflects the selected criteria.

▶ **6.** Click the **Minimum** box, and then type **1** to specify the smallest value a user can enter.

▶ **7.** Press the **Tab** key to move to the Maximum box, and then type **19** to specify the largest value a user can enter. See Figure 8-13.

Settings tab in the Data Validation dialog box ◀ **Figure 8-13**

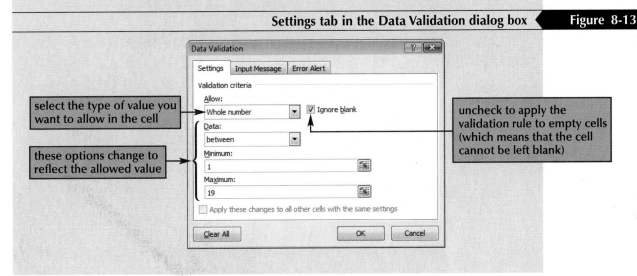

select the type of value you want to allow in the cell

these options change to reflect the allowed value

uncheck to apply the validation rule to empty cells (which means that the cell cannot be left blank)

Validating Existing Data | InSight

Validation rules come into play only during data entry. If you add validation rules to a workbook that already contains data with erroneous values, Excel does not determine if any existing data is invalid. Instead, you can use the Circle Invalid Data command to help identify invalid data that is already in the workbook. (You'll learn about the Circle Invalid Data command later in this tutorial.)

Specifying an Input Message

One way to reduce the chance of a data-entry error is to display an input message when a user makes the cell active. An input message provides additional information about the type of data allowed for that cell. Input messages appear as ScreenTips next to the cell when the cell is selected. You can add an input message to a cell even if you don't set up a rule to validate the data in that cell.

Before a user enters values into the input section of the workbook, Ellen wants them to see the acceptable data values that can be entered in the cell. You will create an input message for cell B7, where users enter the ticket quantity. The input message will help minimize the chance of a volunteer entering an incorrect value.

To create an input message for the ticket quantity cell:

▶ **1.** In the Data Validation dialog box, click the **Input Message** tab. You enter the input message title and text on this tab.

▶ **2.** Verify that the **Show input message when cell is selected** check box contains a check mark. If you uncheck this option, you cannot enter a new input message and any existing input message will not be displayed.

▶ **3.** Click in the **Title** box, and then type **Number of Tickets**. This title will appear in bold at the top of the ScreenTip above the text of the input message.

▶ **4.** Press the **Tab** key to move the insertion point to the Input message box, and then type **Enter the number of tickets purchased**. This text will appear in the Screen-Tip when the cell becomes active. See Figure 8-14.

| Figure 8-14 | Input Message tab in the Data Validation dialog box |

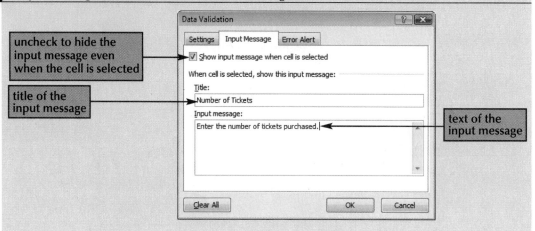

Specifying an Error Alert Style and Message

Ellen wants to display an error alert message if a volunteer enters data that violates the validation rule. The three error alert styles are Stop, Warning, and Information. The style of the error alert determines what happens after a user attempts to make an invalid entry. The Stop alert prevents the entry from being stored in the cell. The Warning alert prevents the entry from being stored in the cell, unless the user overrides the rejection and decides to continue using the data. The Information alert accepts the data value entered, but allows the user to choose to cancel the data entry.

Although ticket quantities between 1 and 19 are the norm for the theatre, occasionally a subscriber wants to purchase 20 or more tickets, and those entries should be allowed. To account for this possibility, you will create a Warning error alert that appears when a user enters a value greater than 20 or less than 1 for the number of tickets purchased. The user can verify the number entered. If the entry is correct, the user can accept the entry. If the entry is incorrect, the user can reenter a correct number.

You'll enter the Warning error alert message for the ticket quantity cell.

To create the Warning error alert message for the ticket quantity cell:

▶ **1.** In the Data Validation dialog box, click the **Error Alert** tab. You use this tab to select the type of error alert and enter the message you want to appear.

▶ **2.** Make sure that the **Show error alert after invalid data is entered** check box is checked. If unchecked, the error alert won't appear when an invalid value is entered in the cell.

▶ **3.** Click the **Style** arrow, and then click **Warning**. This style allows the user to accept the invalid value, return to the cell and reenter a valid value, or cancel the data entry and restore the previous value to the cell.

▶ **4.** Click in the **Title** box, and then type **Number of Tickets Invalid?**. This text will appear as the title of the error alert message box.

▶ **5.** Press the **Tab** key to move the insertion point to the Error message box, and then type **You have entered a value less than 1 or greater than 19. Check the number you entered. If it is correct, click Yes. If it is incorrect, click No. If you are not sure, click Cancel.** (including the period). See Figure 8-15.

Tip

You might hide the input and error alert messages when only experienced users will enter data in the workbook. Because the messages are not deleted, you can show them again if a new user will enter data in the workbook.

Error Alert tab in the Data Validation dialog box ◀ **Figure 8-15**

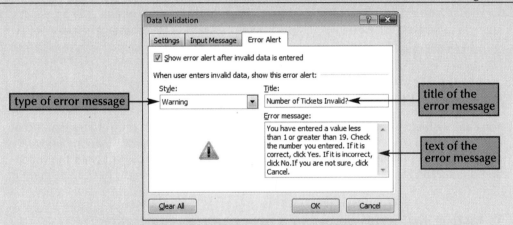

▶ **6.** Click the **OK** button. The input message appears below cell B7. See Figure 8-16.

Input message for cell B7 ◀ **Figure 8-16**

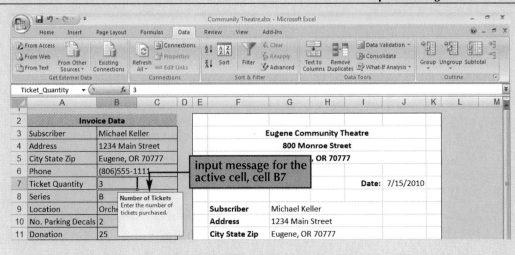

InSight | **Using Formulas to Define Complex Validation Criteria**

The built-in data validation rules are adequate for most simple needs. Sometimes, however, those rules just don't fit your specific worksheet. In those cases, you need to create a custom validation rule that includes a formula. To create a custom validation rule, open the Data Validation dialog box. On the Settings tab, click the Allow arrow, and then click Custom. You can then create the data validation formula.

The formula you specify must be in the form of a condition that returns either True or False. If True is returned, the data entered is considered valid and accepted. If False is returned, the entry is considered invalid and an error alert message is displayed. Consider the following two data validation examples.

The first example uses data validation to prevent the entry of dates that fall on Saturday or Sunday. The WEEKDAY function returns a number (1 to 7) for the date entered in the cell, and then you create a formula to display an error alert if values of 1 (Sunday) or 7 (Saturday) are detected. Assuming the date is entered in cell B2, the following formula returns False if either Saturday or Sunday is entered in cell B2:

`=AND(WEEKDAY(B2)<>1,WEEKDAY(B2)<>7)`

The second example uses data validation to ensure all product codes begin with the letter C. To prevent any letter except a C as the first character entered in cell A2, you would use the LEFT function to extract the first character in the cell. The following formula returns True if the first character entered in cell A2 begins with a C; otherwise, an error alert message is displayed:

`=LEFT(A2,1) = "C"`

Creating a List Validation Rule

You can use the data validation feature to restrict a cell to accept only entries that are on a list you create. You can create the list of valid entries in the Data Validation dialog box, or you can use a list of valid entries in a single column or row. You will enter the validation rule for the Series being requested, which is one of six values (A, B, C, D, E, and F).

To restrict the Series values to a list of entries you create:

▶ **1.** Click cell **B8**. Users will enter the series data in this cell.

▶ **2.** In the Data Tools group on the Data tab, click the **Data Validation** button to open the Data Validation dialog box, and then click the **Settings** tab.

▶ **3.** Click the **Allow** arrow, and then click **List**. The dialog box expands to display the Source box. You can enter values directly in the Source box separated by commas, or you can select a range of valid entries in the worksheet.

▶ **4.** Click the **Collapse** button 🔳 next to the Source box so you can see the entire worksheet.

▶ **5.** Select the range **A16:A21**, which lists the valid six entry values in a row, and then click the **Expand** button 🔳. The Data Validation dialog box returns to its full size. Next, you'll enter an input message.

▶ **6.** Click the **Input Message** tab, click in the **Title** box, and then type **Series** to enter the title of the input message.

▶ **7.** Click in the Input message box, and then type **Click the arrow and select one of the choices listed.** to enter the text of the input message.

▶ **8.** Click the **Error Alert** tab, and then verify that **Stop** appears in the Style box. You want to prevent a user from entering a value that is not included in the list of values you specified.

▶ **9.** In the Title text box, type **Invalid Series**, and then in the Error message box, type **An invalid series has been entered. Click Retry. Press the Esc key, and click the arrow to the right of cell B8. Select A, B, C, D, E, or F.** (including the period). This is the title and text for the error alert message.

▶ **10.** Click the **OK** button. An arrow appears to the right of cell B8 and the input message appears in a ScreenTip.

You need to enter a third data validation rule for cell B9, which indicates the subscriber's choice of location. You will create another list validation rule that allows a user to select either Orchestra or Balcony. You will also create an error alert message.

To create a drop-down list for the Location field:

▶ **1.** Click cell **B9**, and then, in the Data Tools group on the Data tab, click the **Data Validation** button. The Data Validation dialog box opens.

▶ **2.** Click the **Settings** tab, select **List** in the Allow box, and then set the Source box for the range **B15:C15**. This range contain the two values you want to allow users to select for the location.

▶ **3.** Click the **Input Message** tab, type **Location** in the Title box, and then type **Click the arrow and select Orchestra or Balcony** in the Input message box.

▶ **4.** Click the **Error Alert** tab, verify that **Stop** is in the Style box, type **Invalid Location** in the Title box, and then type **An invalid location has been entered. Click Retry, press Esc, and click the arrow to the right of cell B9. Select Orchestra or Balcony.** (including the period) in the Error message box.

▶ **5.** Click the **OK** button. The data validation rule is complete.

You will test the validation feature you've just created by entering incorrect values that violate the validation rules.

To test the data validation rules:

▶ **1.** Click cell **B7**. The input message appears in a ScreenTip, indicating the type of data allowed in the cell. You will enter an invalid value to test the validation rule for the Ticket Quantity field.

▶ **2.** Type **30**, and then press the **Tab** key. The Number of Tickets Invalid? message box opens, informing you that the value you entered might be incorrect. The entry 30 is incorrect; you'll enter a valid number.

▶ **3.** Click the **No** button, type **3** in cell B7, and then press the **Enter** key. The data is entered in cell B7. Cell B8 is the active cell and the input message for Series appears.

You will select a value for the Series using the list.

▶ **4.** Click the arrow to the right of cell B8, and then click **C**. The value is accepted.

The only way an error occurs in cells that have a list validation is if an incorrect entry is *typed* in the cell. You'll try that method.

▶ **5.** In cell B8, enter **G**. The Invalid Series message box opens.

> **6.** Click the **Retry** button to close the message box, press the **Esc** key to clear the current value from the cell, and then click the arrow to the right of cell B8 and select **B**. The value is accepted.
>
> Next, you will enter the Location value. You should use the arrow to select an option but you'll intentionally type an invalid entry.
>
> **7.** In cell B9, enter **Mezzanine**. The Invalid Location message box opens, indicating that the Location must be Orchestra or Balcony.
>
> **8.** Click the **Retry** button, press the **Esc** key, click the arrow to the right of cell B9, and then click **Orchestra**. The value is accepted. The three validation rules you entered work as you intended.

Drawing Circles Around Invalid Data

Data validation prevents users from entering invalid data into a cell. It does not verify data that was already entered into a worksheet before the validation criteria were applied. To ensure the entire workbook contains valid data, you need to also verify any data previously entered in the workbook. You can use the Circle Invalid Data command to find and mark cells that contain invalid data. Red circles appear around any data that does not meet the validation criteria, making it simple to scan a worksheet for errors. After you correct the data in a cell, the circle disappears.

To display circles around invalid data, you must perform the following steps:

1. Apply validation rules to existing data.
2. In the Data Tools group on the Data tab, click the Data Validation button arrow, and then click Circle Invalid Data. Red circles appear around cells that contain invalid data.
3. To remove the circle from a single cell, enter valid data in the cell.
4. To hide all circles, in the Data Tools group on the Data tab, click the Data Validation button arow, and then click Clear Validation Circles.

To ensure an error-free workbook, you should use the Circle Invalid Data command to verify data entered before you set up the validation criteria or to verify data in a workbook you inherited from someone else, such as a coworker.

Protecting a Worksheet and Workbook

Another way to reduce data-entry errors is to limit access to certain parts of the workbook. When you **protect** a workbook, you limit the ability users have to make changes to the file. For example, you can prevent users from changing formulas in a worksheet, or you can keep users from deleting worksheets or inserting new ones. You can even keep users from viewing the formulas used in the workbook.

To further help the volunteers work error-free, Ellen wants to protect the contents of the Invoice and Ticket Data worksheets. She wants users to have access only to the range B3:B11, where new season request data are entered. She wants to prevent users from editing the contents of any cells in the Ticket Data worksheet.

Locking and Unlocking Cells

Every cell in a workbook has a **locked property** that determines whether changes can be made to that cell. The locked property has no impact as long as the worksheet is unprotected. However, after you protect a worksheet, the locked property controls whether the cell can be edited. You unlock a cell by turning off the locked property. By default, the locked property is turned on for each cell, and worksheet protection is turned off.

So, unless you unlock cells in a worksheet *before* protecting the worksheet, all of the cells in the worksheet will be locked, and you won't be able to make any changes in the worksheet. Usually, you will want to protect the worksheet, but leave some cells unlocked. For example, you might want to lock cells that contain formulas and formatting so they cannot be changed, but unlock cells in which you want to enter data.

To protect some—but not all—cells in a worksheet, you first turn off the locked property of cells in which data can be entered. Then, you protect the worksheet to activate the locked property for the remaining cells.

In the Invoice worksheet, you want users to be able to enter data in the range B3:B11 but not any other cell in the worksheet. To do this, you must unlock the cells in the range B3:B11.

To unlock the cells in the range B3:B11:

1. In the Invoice worksheet, select the range **B3:B11**. You want to unlock the cells in this range before you protect the worksheet.

2. Click the **Home** tab on the Ribbon, and then, in the Font group, click the **Dialog Box Launcher**. The Format Cells dialog box opens with the Font tab active.

3. Click the **Protection** tab, and then click the **Locked** check box to remove the check mark.

4. Click the **OK** button, and then click cell **A1** to deselect the highlighted cells. The cells in the range B3:B11 are unlocked.

Protecting a Worksheet

When you set up worksheet protection, you specify which actions are still available to users in the protected worksheet. For example, you can choose to allow users to insert new rows or columns or to delete rows and columns. You can limit the user to selecting only unlocked cells or allow the user to select any cell in the worksheet. These choices remain active as long as the worksheet is protected.

A protected worksheet can always be unprotected. You can also add a password to the protected worksheet that users must enter in order to turn off the protection. If you are concerned that users will turn off protection and make changes to formulas you should use a password; otherwise, it's probably best to not specify a password.

> **Tip**
>
> You can password-protect ranges of cells by selecting the ranges and clicking the Allow Users to Edit Ranges button in the Changes group on the Review tab. Specify a name for the selected cells and provide a password to protect the values in the range. Range passwords become active only when the worksheet is protected.

Protecting a Worksheet | Reference Window

- Select the cell or range you want to unlock.
- In the Font group on the Home tab, click the Dialog Box Launcher.
- In the Format Cells dialog box, click the Protection tab, click the Locked check box to remove the check mark, and then click the OK button.
- In the Changes group on the Review tab, click the Protect Sheet button.
- Enter a password (optional).
- Select all of the actions you want to allow users to take when the worksheet is protected.
- Click the OK button.

Ellen wants to protect the Invoice and Ticket Data worksheets, but she doesn't want a password specified. You will enable worksheet protection that will allow users to select any cell in those worksheets, but enter data only in the unlocked cells.

To protect the Invoice and Ticket Data worksheets:

▶ **1.** Click the **Review** tab on the Ribbon, and then, in the Changes group, click the **Protect Sheet** button. The Protect Sheet dialog box opens, as shown in Figure 8-17.

Figure 8-17   **Protect Sheet dialog box**

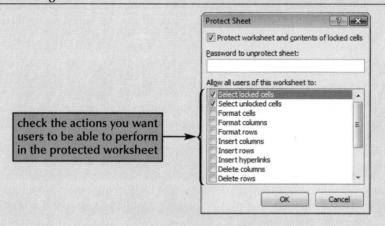

check the actions you want users to be able to perform in the protected worksheet

---

Tip

Keep passwords in a safe place. Remember, passwords are case sensitive. If you forget the password, it is very difficult to remove the worksheet protection.

You will leave the Password box blank because you do not want to use a password. By default, users can select locked and unlocked cells, which are all cells in the worksheet, but they can enter or edit values only in unlocked cells. Ellen wants the volunteers to be able to perform these actions.

▶ **2.** Click the **OK** button. The Protect Sheet dialog box closes.

You'll test the protection by trying to edit a locked cell and then an unlocked cell in the Invoice worksheet.

▶ **3.** Click cell **I14**, and then type **8**. As soon as you press any key, a dialog box opens, indicating that the cell is protected and cannot be modified.

▶ **4.** Click the **OK** button.

▶ **5.** Click cell **B7**, type **8**, and then press the **Enter** key. The ticket quantity is updated because you allowed editing in the range B3:B11. A user can enter and edit values in these cells. Although users can select any cell in the worksheet, they cannot make an entry in any other cell.

▶ **6.** On the Quick Access Toolbar, click the **Undo** button 🔄 to return the Ticket Quantity to 3.

Next, you will protect all of the cells in the Ticket Data worksheet.

▶ **7.** Switch to the **Ticket Data** worksheet.

▶ **8.** In the Changes group on the Review tab, click the **Protect Sheet** button to open the Protect Sheet dialog box, and then click the **OK** button to accept the default set of user actions.

You will test to see what would happen if someone tried to edit one of the cells in the Ticket Data worksheet.

▶ **9.** Click cell **A2** and type **B**. A dialog box opens, indicating that the cell is protected and cannot be modified. All the cells in this worksheet are protected because no cells have been unlocked.

▶ **10.** Click the **OK** button to close the dialog box.

Protecting a Workbook

The contents of the Invoice and Ticket Data worksheets, with the exception of the range B3:B11 in the Invoice worksheet, cannot be changed. However, worksheet protection applies only to the contents of the worksheet, not to the worksheet itself. So, a theatre volunteer could inadvertently rename or delete the protected worksheet. To keep the worksheets themselves from being modified, you need to protect the workbook.

You can protect both the structure and the windows of the workbook. Protecting the structure prohibits users from renaming, deleting, hiding, or inserting worksheets. Protecting the windows prohibits users from moving, resizing, closing, or hiding parts of the Excel window. The default is to protect only the structure of the workbook, not the windows used to display it. You can also add a password; however, the same guideline is true here as for protecting worksheets. Add a password only if you are concerned that others might unprotect the workbook and modify it. If you add a password, keep in mind that it is case sensitive and you cannot unprotect the workbook without it.

Protecting a Workbook | Reference Window

- In the Changes group on the Review tab, click the Protect Workbook button.
- Click the check boxes to indicate whether you want to protect the workbook's structure, windows, or both.
- Enter a password (optional).
- Click the OK button.

Ellen doesn't want users to be able to change the structure of the workbook, so you will set protection for the workbook structure, but not the window.

To protect a workbook:

▶ **1.** In the Changes group on the Review tab, click the **Protect Workbook** button. The Protect Structure and Windows dialog box opens. You can choose to protect the structure, protect the windows, or both. See Figure 8-18.

Protect Structure and Windows dialog box ◀ **Figure 8-18**

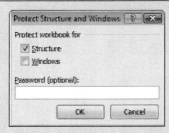

▶ **2.** Make sure the **Structure** check box is checked, the Windows check box is unchecked, and the Password box is blank.

▶ **3.** Click the **OK** button to protect the workbook without specifying a password.

▶ **4.** Right-click the **Ticket Data** sheet tab, on the shortcut menu, notice that the Insert, Delete, Rename, Move or Copy, Tab Color, Hide, and Unhide commands are gray, indicating that the options that modify the worksheets are no longer available for the Ticket Data worksheet.

▶ **5.** Press the **Esc** key to close the shortcut menu.

Unprotecting a Worksheet

Ellen is pleased with the different levels of protection that can be applied to the worksheet. At this point, you still have a lot of editing to do in the Invoice worksheet, so you'll turn off worksheet protection in that worksheet. Later, when you've completed your modifications, Ellen can turn worksheet protection back on.

To turn off worksheet protection for the Invoice worksheet:

▶ **1.** Switch to the **Invoice** worksheet.

▶ **2.** In the Changes group on the Review tab, click the **Unprotect Sheet** button. Worksheet protection is removed from the Invoice worksheet. The button changes back to the Protect Sheet button. If you had assigned a password when you protected the worksheet, you would have had to enter the password to remove worksheet protection.

> **Tip**
>
> You can also remove workbook protection; in the Changes group on the Review tab, click the Unprotect Workbook button.

Adding Worksheet Comments

Providing documentation is important for a successful application. In addition to including a documentation sheet that provides an overview of the workbook, you used defined names instead of cell addresses to make it easier to write and understand formulas and then you pasted a list of these names in the worksheet for you and others to see. You also used input messages to assist with data validation. Another source of documentation you can use in a workbook is comments. A **comment** is a text box that is attached to a specific cell in a worksheet. Comments are often used in workbooks to: (a) explain the contents of a particular cell, such as a complex formula, (b) provide instructions to users, and (c) share ideas and notes from several users collaborating on a project.

Reference Window | **Inserting a Comment**

- Click the cell to which you want to attach a comment.
- Right-click the cell, and then click Insert Comment on the shortcut menu (or in the Comments group on the Review tab, click the New Comment button).
- Type the comment into the comment box.

Ellen wants you to insert a brief note about entering data from the order form into the input section in cell A2 and a note explaining how the IF and VLOOKUP functions are used to determine the cost of theatre tickets in cell J18.

To insert comments in cells A2 and J18:

▶ **1.** In the Invoice worksheet, right-click cell **A2**, and then click **Insert Comment** on the shortcut menu. A text box opens to the right of cell A2. The user name for your installation of Excel appears in bold at the top of the box. A small red triangle appears in the upper-right corner of the cell.

▶ **2.** Type **Enter all data from the order form into cells B3 through B12** in the text box. An arrow points from the text box to cell A2 which contains the comment. Selection handles appear around the text box, which you can use to resize the box; you can drag the text box by its hatched border to move the comment to a new location in the worksheet. See Figure 8-19.

Comment added to cell A2 ◀ **Figure 8-19**

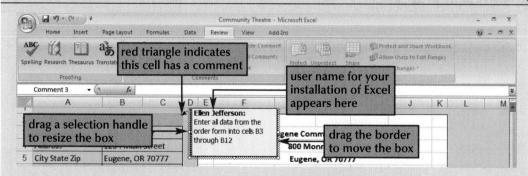

▶ **3.** Click cell **B12** to hide the comment. The comment disappears. A small red triangle remains in the upper-right corner of cell A2 to indicate this cell contains a comment.

The comment in cell A2 should reference the range B3:B11. You'll edit the comment.

▶ **4.** Click cell **A2**, and then, in the Comments group on the Review tab, click the **Edit Comment** button. The text box appears with the insertion point at the end of the comment text.

▶ **5.** In the text box, change B12 to **B11**.

▶ **6.** Click any cell to hide the text box, and then point to cell **A2** to view the edited comment.

Next, you'll add a comment to cell J18.

▶ **7.** Click cell **J18**, and then, in the Comments group on the Review tab, click the **New Comment** button. A comment box opens to the right of cell J18.

▶ **8.** Type **This IF function determines whether to use a VLOOKUP function referencing column 2 or 3 of the Ticket Price table** in the text box.

▶ **9.** Drag the lower-right selection handle down to increase the size of the text box to fit the comment.

▶ **10.** Click cell **I17** to hide the comment. A small red triangle remains in the upper-right corner of cell J18 to indicate it contains a comment.

▶ **11.** Point to cell **J18** to see the comment.

Ellen decides that the volunteers don't need to know how the ticket cost is calcuated. You'll delete the comment in cell J18.

Tip

To keep an active cell's comment on screen, in the Comments group on the Review tab, click the Show/ Hide Comment button. Click the button again to hide the active cell's comment. To show or hide all the comments in a worksheet, click the Show All Comments button.

▶ **12.** Click cell **J18**, and then, in the Comments group on the Review tab, click the **Delete** button. The comment is deleted, and the red triangle in the upper-right corner of cell J18 is removed.

In this session, you used data validation to help ensure that all values entered in the Invoice worksheet are accurate. You created validation rules that included input messages and error alert messages. You learned how to protect and unprotect both the worksheet and the workbook. In addition, you learned how to use comments to add notes to specific cells in the workbook. In the next session, you'll automate some of the steps in the application by recording macros.

Review | **Session 8.2 Quick Check**

1. How do you turn on data validation for a specified cell?
2. How do you specify an input message for a cell?
3. Describe the three types of error alert messages Excel can display when a user violates a validation rule.
4. What is a locked cell?
5. What is the difference between worksheet protection and workbook protection?
6. Can you rename a protected worksheet? Explain why or why not.
7. What are the steps for editing a comment?

Session 8.3

Working with Macros

Ellen needs to print the entire Invoice worksheet, which includes the input area, transfer area, and invoice, for her paper files. In addition, she needs to print only the invoice to send to the season subscriber. Each printout has different custom headers and footers. In addition, data from the invoice needs to be transferred to the Ticket Data worksheet. Ellen wants to simplify these tasks so volunteers don't need to repeat the same actions for each subscriber order and also to reduce the possibility of errors being introduced during the repetitive process.

You can automate any task you perform repeatedly with a macro. A **macro** is a series of stored commands that can be run whenever you need to perform the task. For example, you can create a macro to print a worksheet, insert a set of dates and values, or import data from a text file and store it in Excel. Macros perform repetitive tasks more quickly than you can. And, after the macro is created, you can be assured that no mistakes will occur from performing the same task over and over again.

To create and run macros, you need to use the Developer tab. By default, this tab is not displayed on the Ribbon, so you'll display it. The Developer tab has three groups: one for code, one for controls, and one for XML. You'll use the Code group when working with macros.

To display the Developer tab on the Ribbon:

▶ **1.** If you took a break after the previous session, make sure the Community Theatre workbook is open and the Invoice worksheet is active.

▶ **2.** Look for the **Developer** tab on the Ribbon. If you see the Developer tab, continue with Step 5. If you do not see the Developer tab, continue with Step 3.

3. Click the **Office Button** , and then click the **Excel Options** button. The Excel Options dialog box opens with the Popular options displayed. See Figure 8-20.

Popular category in the Excel Options dialog box   **Figure 8-20**

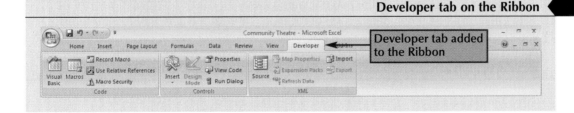

4. In the Top options for working with Excel section, click the **Show Developer tab in the Ribbon** check box to insert a check mark, and then click the **OK** button. The Developer tab appears on the Ribbon.

5. Click the **Developer** tab. See Figure 8-21.

Developer tab on the Ribbon   **Figure 8-21**

Protecting Against Macro Viruses

In recent years, viruses have been attached as macros to files created in Excel and other Office programs. When unsuspecting users opened these infected workbooks, Excel automatically ran the attached virus-infected macro. **Macro viruses** are a type of virus that uses a program's own macro programming language to distribute the virus. Most macro viruses are not harmful and do not affect data in any way. For example, one macro virus changed the title bar text from *Microsoft Excel* to *Microsofa Excel*. Occasionally, macro viruses are destructive and can modify or delete files that may not be recoverable. Because it is possible for a macro to contain a virus, Microsoft Office 2007 provides several options from which you can choose to set a security level you feel comfortable with.

Macro Security Settings

The **macro security settings** control what Excel will do about macros in a workbook when you open that workbook. For example, one user may choose to run macros only if they are "digitally signed" by a developer who is on a list of trusted sources. Another user might want to disable all macros in workbooks and see a notification when a workbook contains macros. The user can then elect to enable the macros. Excel has four macro security settings, as described in Figure 8-22.

Figure 8-22	Macro security settings

Setting	Description
Disable all macros without notification	All macros in all workbooks are disabled and no security alerts about macros are displayed. Use this setting if you don't want macros to run.
Disable a macro with notification	All macros in all workbooks are disabled, but security alerts appear when the workbook contains a macro. Use this default setting to choose on a case-by-case basis whether to run a macro.
Disable all macros except digitally signed macros	The same as the *Disable a macro with notification* setting except any macro signed by a trusted publisher runs if you have already trusted the publisher. Otherwise, security alerts appear when a workbook contains a macro.
Enable all macros	All macros in all workbooks run. Use this setting temporarily in such cases as when developing an application that contains macros. This setting is not recommended for regular use.

You set macro security in the Trust Center using the Security dialog box. The **Trust Center** is a central location for all the security settings in Office 2007. By default, all potentially dangerous content, such as macros and workbooks with external links, is blocked without warning. If content is blocked, the Message Bar (also called the trust bar), located under the Ribbon, appears, notifying you that some content was disabled. You can click the Message Bar to open a dialog box with all of the disabled content and options for enabling or disabling that content.

In Office 2007 you can define a set of locations (file path) where you can place files you consider trustworthy. This feature is known as *Trusted Locations*. Any workbook opened from a trusted location is considered "safe" and content such as macros will work without having to respond to additional security questions to use the workbook.

Setting Macro Security in Excel | Reference Window

- In the Code group on the Developer tab, click the Macro Security button.
- Click the option button for the security setting you want.
- Click the OK button.

or

- Click the Office Button, and then click the Excel Options button.
- Click the Trust Center category, and then click the Trust Center Settings button.
- Click the Macro Settings category, and then select the option button for the security setting you want.
- Click the OK button.

Ellen wants some protection against macro viruses, so she suggests you set the security level to *Disable all macros with notification*. When you open a file with macros, the macros will be disabled and a security alert will appear, allowing you to activate the macros if you believe the workbook comes from a trusted source.

To set the macro security level:

▶ **1.** In the Code group on the Developer tab, click the **Macro Security** button. The Trust Center dialog box opens with the Macro Settings category displayed.

▶ **2.** In the Macro Settings section, click the **Disable all macros with notification** option button if it is not selected. See Figure 8-23.

Macro Settings in the Trust Center dialog box ◄ Figure 8-23

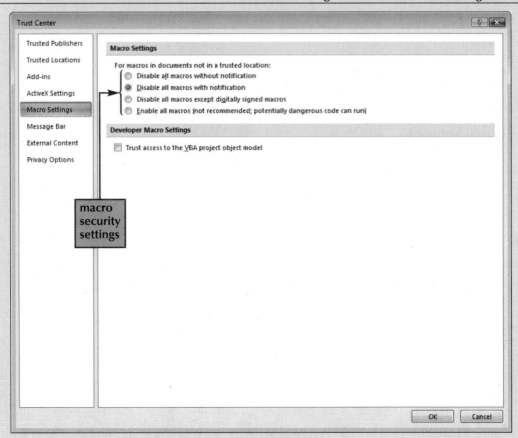

▶ **3.** Click the **OK** button.

Each time you open a workbook that contains a macro that the Trust Center detects, the macro is disabled and a Message Bar appears below the Ribbon with the Security Warning that macros have been disabled. Click the Options button to open a security dialog box with the option to enable the macro or leave it disabled. If you developed the workbook or trust the person who sent you the workbook, click the Enable this content option button to run the macros in the workbook.

InSight	**Using Digital Signatures with Macros**

A **digital signature** is like a seal of approval. It's often used to identify the author of a workbook that contains macros. You add a digital signature as the last step before you distribute a file. Before you can add a digital signature to a workbook, you need to obtain a digital ID (also called a digital certificate) that proves your identity. Digital certificates are typically issued by a certificate authority. After you have a digital certificate, do the following to digitally sign a workbook:

1. Click the Office Button, point to Prepare, and then click Add a Digital Signature to open the Sign dialog box.
2. Click in the Purpose for signing this document box, and then type a reason why you are adding a digital signature to this workbook.
3. Click the Sign button. The invisible digital signature does not appear within the workbook, but users will see the Signatures button on the status bar.

By digitally signing a workbook that contains a macro you intend to publicly distribute, you assure others of two things: (1) the identity of the creator of the macro, and (2) the macro has not been altered since the digital signature was created.

When you open a digitally signed file, you can see who the author is and decide whether the information in the file is authentic and you trust that the macros in the workbook are safe to run.

The digital signature is removed any time a file is saved after the signature has been added to the file. Therefore, no one (including the original workbook author) can open a digitally signed file, make changes to the workbook, save the workbook, and then send the file to another user with the digital signature intact. The original author must digitally resign the modified workbook.

Recording a Macro

You can create an Excel macro in one of two ways: You can use the macro recorder to record keystrokes and mouse actions as you perform them, or you can enter a series of commands in the **Visual Basic for Applications (VBA)** programming language. The macro recorder can record only those actions you perform with the keyboard or mouse. The macro recorder is a good choice for creating simple macros. For more sophisticated macros, you might need to write VBA code directly in the Visual Basic Editor.

For Ellen's application, the tasks you need to perform can all be done with the keyboard and the mouse, so you will use the macro recorder to record the three macros. One macro will show the invoice in Print Preview, a second macro will show the entire Invoice worksheet in Print Preview, and a third macro will transfer data from the Invoice worksheet to the Ticket Data worksheet.

| InSight

Planning and Recording a Macro

Advance planning and practice help to ensure you create an error-free macro. First, decide what you want to accomplish. Then, consider the best way to achieve those results. Next, practice the keystrokes and mouse actions before you actually record the macro. This may seem like extra work, but it reduces the chance of error when you actually record the macro. As you set up the macro, consider the following:

- Choose a descriptive name that helps you recognize the macro's purpose.
- Weigh the benefits of selecting a shortcut key against its drawbacks. Although a shortcut key is an easy way to run a macro, you are limited to one-letter shortcuts, which can make it difficult to remember the purpose of each shortcut key. In addition, the macro shortcut keys will override the standard Office shortcuts for the workbook.
- Store the macro with the current workbook unless the macro can be used with other workbooks.
- Include a description that provides an overview of the macro and perhaps your name and contact information.

Ellen provides you with an outline of the actions needed for the macro to show the invoice in Print Preview. These are:

1. Set the print area (E2:J23).
2. Define the Page Layout setting with the custom heading I N V O I C E.
3. Display the invoice in Print Preview.
4. Close the Print Preview window.
5. Make cell B3 the active cell.

Each macro must have a unique name that begins with a letter. The macro name can be up to 255 characters, including letters, numbers, and the underscore symbol. The macro name cannot include spaces or special characters. It is helpful to use a descriptive name that describes the macro's purpose. You can assign a shortcut key to run the macro directly from the keyboard. You can also add a description of the macro. Finally, a macro needs to be stored somewhere. By default, the macro is stored in the current workbook, making the macro available in only that workbook when it is open. Another option is to store the macro in the **Personal Macro workbook**, a hidden workbook named *Personal.xlsb* that opens whenever you start Excel, making the macro available anytime you use Excel. The Personal Macro workbook stores commonly used macros that apply to many workbooks. It is most convenient for users on stand-alone computers. Finally, you can store the macro in a new workbook. Keep in mind, the new workbook must be open to use the macro. For example, an accountant might store a set of macros that help with end-of-the-month tasks in a separate workbook.

Recording a Macro

| Reference Window

- In the Code group on the Developer tab, click the Record Macro button.
- Enter a name for the macro, and specify the location to store the macro.
- Specify a shortcut key (optional).
- Enter a description of the macro (optional).
- Click the OK button to start the macro recorder.
- Perform the tasks you want to automate.
- Click the Stop Recording button.

For Ellen's application, you'll record a macro named *PrintPreviewInvoice*, assigned a keyboard shortcut, with a description, stored in the Community Theatre workbook. Macro shortcut keys are used to run a macro. Assigning a shortcut key overrides the default Office shortcut for the open workbook. Therefore, pressing the Ctrl+p keys runs the PrintPreviewInvoice macro, overriding the default Office 2007 shortcut for printing a selected area. Some people find macro shortcut keys a quick way to run a macro; others dislike them because they lose the original function of the shortcut key. It's a personal preference.

You'll start the macro recorder.

To start the macro recorder:

▶ **1.** In the Code group on the Developer tab, click the **Record Macro** button. The Record Macro dialog box opens. The Macro name box displays a default name for the macro that consists of the word *Macro* followed by a number that is one greater than the number of macros already recorded in the workbook during the current Excel session. See Figure 8-24.

| Figure 8-24 | Record Macro dialog box |

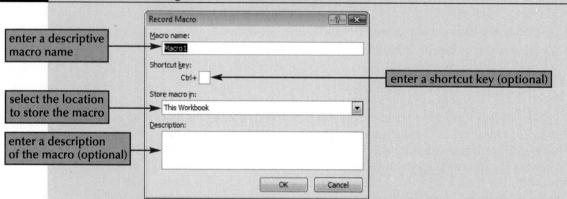

enter a descriptive macro name

select the location to store the macro

enter a description of the macro (optional)

enter a shortcut key (optional)

▶ **2.** In the Macro name box, type **PrintPreviewInvoice** to change the default name to a more descriptive one, and then press the **Tab** key.

▶ **3.** In the Shortcut key box, type **p** to set Ctrl+p as the shortcut to run the macro from the keyboard, and then press the **Tab** key.

▶ **4.** Verify that **This Workbook** appears in the Store macro in box to store the macro in the Community Theatre workbook, and then press the **Tab** key.

▶ **5.** In the Description box, type **Created 7/15/2010. Print Preview of invoice area: range E2:K23.** (including the period) to enter notes about the macro.

▶ **6.** Click the **OK** button. The workbook enters macro record mode. The Record Macro button in the Code group on the Developer tab changes to the Stop Recording button, which also appears on the status bar.

From this point on, every mouse click and keystroke you perform will be recorded and stored as part of the PrintPreviewInvoice macro. For that reason, it's very important to follow the instructions in the next steps precisely. Take your time as you perform each step, reading the entire step carefully first. After you finish recording the keystrokes, you click the Stop Recording button to turn off the macro recorder.

To record the PrintPreviewInvoice macro:

▶ 1. Click the **Page Layout** tab on the Ribbon.

▶ 2. Click cell **E2**, press and hold the **Shift** key, click cell **K23**, and then release the Shift key to select the range E2:K23. This range contains the invoice area.

▶ 3. In the Page Setup group, click the **Print Area** button, and then click **Set Print Area**. The invoice area is set as the print area. Next, you'll insert a custom header.

▶ 4. In the Page Setup group, click the **Dialog Box Launcher** to open the Page Setup dialog box, click the **Header/Footer** tab, click the **Custom Header** button to open the Header dialog box, click in the **Center section** box, type **I N V O I C E**, and then click the **OK** button.

▶ 5. Click the **Margins** tab, verify that the **Horizontally** check box is checked to center the invoice on the page.

▶ 6. Click the **Print Preview** button. The invoice appears in Print Preview. Next, you will close the Print Preview window and set cell B3 as the active cell.

▶ 7. Click the **Close Print Preview** button to return to Normal view. Although this step is not intuitive, you need to close Print Preview before you can continue recording the macro or stop recording the macro. When you run the macro, Excel will automatically stop at the point where the Print Preview window opens to give the user the option of printing or closing Print Preview without printing.

▶ 8. In the Invoice worksheet, click cell **B3**. You've completed all the steps in the Print-PreviewInvoice macro. You'll turn off the macro recorder.

▶ 9. Click the **Stop Recording** button 🔲 on the status bar. The button changes to the Record macro button.

Trouble? If you made a mistake while recording the macro, close the Community Theatre workbook without saving your changes. Reopen the workbook, and then repeat all the steps beginning with the "To start the macro recorder" steps.

Trouble? If you need to save your work before completing the tutorial, read pages EX 439–440 to learn how to save a workbook with macros.

> **Tip**
>
> You can also turn off the macro recorder by clicking the Stop Recording button in the Code group on the Developer tab.

Running a Macro

Next, you'll test the macro to ensure it works as intended. To run the macro you created, you can either use the shortcut key you specified or select the macro in the Macro dialog box and click the Run button.

Running a Macro | Reference Window

- Press the shortcut key assigned to the macro.

or

- In the Code group on the Developer tab, click the Macros button.
- Select the macro from the list of macros, and then click the Run button.

To run the PrintPreviewInvoice macro:

▶ **1.** Click the **Developer** tab on the Ribbon, and then, in the Code group, click the **Macros** button. The Macro dialog box opens, as shown in Figure 8-25. This dialog box lists all of the macros in the open workbooks. You can select a macro, and then run it, edit the macro with VBA, run the macro one step at a time so you can determine in which step an error occurs, or delete it.

Figure 8-25 ▶ **Macro dialog box**

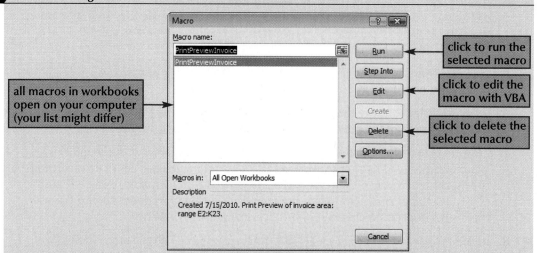

2. Verify that **PrintPreviewInvoice** is selected in the list, and then click the **Run** button. The PrintPreviewInvoice macro runs and the invoice appears in Print Preview. You can now print the invoice or close Print Preview without printing. Notice that the PrintPreviewInvoice macro did not run very quickly and caused some screen flicker. You will fix this later in the tutorial.

Trouble? If the PrintPreviewInvoice macro did not run properly, you might have made a mistake in the steps while recording the macro. Click the Close Print Preview button in the Preview group on the Print Preview tab. Click the Developer tab, and then, in the Code group, click the Macros button. Select the PrintPreviewInvoice macro and then click the Delete button. Click the OK button to confirm the deletion, and then repeat all the steps beginning with the "To start the macro recorder" steps.

▶ **3.** In the Preview group on the Print Preview tab, click the **Close Print Preview** button. The workbook returns to Normal view and cell B3 is the active cell. The macro works correctly. If you had printed the invoice, the Print Preview window would automatically close after the invoice printed.

Next, you will test the shortcut keys you used for the PrintPreviewInvoice macro.

▶ **4.** Press the **Ctrl+p** keys. The PrintPreviewInvoice macro runs. The invoice is displayed in the Print Preview window.

You will not print the invoice.

▶ **5.** In the Preview group, click the **Close Print Preview** button. The worksheet returns to Normal view and cell B3 is the active cell. As an alternative, you could select the Print command on the Print Preview tab to print the invoice. After printing the invoice, the worksheet would return to Normal view and cell B3 would be the active cell.

Trouble? If your macro doesn't end on its own, you need to end it. Press the Ctrl+Break keys to stop the macro from running.

How Edits Can Affect Macros | InSight

Be careful when making seemingly small changes to your workbook, as these can have a great impact on your macros. If a runtime error (an error that occurs while running a macro) appears when you run a macro that has worked in the past, some part of the macro code no longer makes sense to Excel. For example, simply adding a space to a worksheet name can affect a macro that references the worksheet. If you recorded a macro that referenced a worksheet named *TicketData* (no spaces in the name) that you later changed to *Ticket Data* (space added to the name), the macro no longer works because the TicketData worksheet no longer exists. You can record the macro again, or you could edit the macro in VBA changing *TicketData* to *Ticket Data*.

Next, you'll record the macro to print the entire worksheet. The steps will be similar to the first macro, except that you'll set the print area to A1:K25, display *OFFICE COPY* as the custom header, display Ellen's name and title in the left section of the custom footer, and scale the worksheet to fit on one page. For this macro, you'll use the Ctrl+s shortcut keys.

To record the PrintPreviewEntireSheet macro:

▶ **1.** On the status bar, click the **Record Macro** button ▦. The Record Macro dialog box opens.

▶ **2.** In the Macro name box, type **PrintPreviewEntireSheet** to enter a descriptive name, and then press the **Tab** key.

▶ **3.** In the Shortcut key box, type **s**, and then press the **Tab** key twice. The This Workbook option appears in the Store macro in box.

▶ **4.** In the Description box, type **Created 7/15/2010. Print Preview of entire worksheet area: range A1:K25**, and then click the **OK** button. The macro recorder is on.

▶ **5.** Click the **Page Layout** tab on the Ribbon.

▶ **6.** In the Invoice worksheet, select the range **A1:K25**, in the Page Setup group, click the **Print Area** button, and then click **Set Print Area**.

▶ **7.** In the Page Setup group, click the **Dialog Box Launcher** to open the Page Setup dialog box, click the **Header/Footer** tab, click the **Custom Header** button, select the text in the Center section box, type **O F F I C E   C O P Y**, and then click the **OK** button.

▶ **8.** Click the **Custom Footer** button, click in the **Left section** box, type **Ellen Jefferson, Business Manager**, and then click the **OK** button.

▶ **9.** Click the **Page** tab in the Page Setup dialog box, in the Scaling section, click the **Fit To** option button, and then confirm that **1** appears in both Fit to boxes.

▶ **10.** Click the **Print Preview** button to display the invoice in Print Preview.

▶ **11.** Click the **Close Print Preview** button, and then click cell **B3**.

▶ **12.** Click the **Stop Recording** button ▦ on the status bar. The button changes to the Record Macro button, and the macro recorder is turned off.

You'll use the shortcut key method to test both the PrintPreviewEntireSheet and PrintPreviewInvoice macros.

To test the PrintPreviewEntireSheet and PrintPreviewInvoice macros:

▶ **1.** Press the **Ctrl+s** keys. The PrintPreviewEntireSheet macro runs.

▶ **2.** In the Preview group on the Print Preview tab, click the **Close Print Preview** button. The worksheet returns to Normal view and cell B3 is the active cell. The PrintPreviewEntireSheet macro was successful.

Trouble? If the PrintPreviewEntireSheet macro did not run properly, you might have made a mistake in the steps while recording it. Click the Close Print Preview button in the Preview group on the Print Preview tab. Click the Developer tab, and then, in the Code group, click the Macros button. Select the PrintPreviewEntireSheet macro, and then click the Delete button to remove the macro. Click the OK button to confirm the deletion, and then repeat all the steps beginning with the "To record the PrintPreviewEntireSheet macro" to record and test the macro again.

Next, you'll run the PrintPreviewInvoice macro.

▶ **3.** Press the **Ctrl+p** keys. The PrintPreviewInvoice macro runs.

▶ **4.** In the Preview group on the Print Preview tab, click the **Close Print Preview** button.

Creating the TransferData Macro

You need to record one more macro. The data you entered earlier in the input section of the Invoice worksheet was never added to the Ticket Data worksheet. Ellen wants to add this data from the purchase of season tickets to the next available blank row in the Ticket Data worksheet. The macro that you'll create will fix that problem. The actions of this macro will be as follows:

- Switch to the Ticket Data worksheet.
- Turn off worksheet protection in the Ticket Data worksheet.
- Switch to the Invoice worksheet.
- Select and copy the Transfer Area to the Clipboard.
- Switch to the Ticket Data worksheet.
- Go to cell A1, and then go to last row in ticket data table.
- Turn on Relative References. The Relative Reference button controls how Excel records the act of selecting a range in the worksheet. By default, the macro will select the same cells regardless of which cell is first selected because the macro records a selection using absolute cell references. If you want a macro to select cells regardless of the position of the active cell when you run the macro, set the macro recorder to record relative cell references.
- Move down one row.
- Turn off Relative References.
- Paste values to the Ticket Data worksheet.
- Go to cell A1.
- Turn on worksheet protection.
- Switch to the Invoice worksheet, and go to cell A1.

Ellen wants you to name this new macro *TransferData*. You'll assign the Ctrl+t keys as the shortcut.

To record the TransferData macro:

1. Click the **Record Macro** button ▣ on the status bar to open the Record Macro dialog box, type **TransferData** in the Macro name box, type **t** in the Shortcut key box, type **Created 7/15/2010. Copy values in the transfer area in the Invoice worksheet to Ticket Data worksheet** in the Description box, and then click the **OK** button. The macro recorder is on.

2. Click the **Ticket Data** sheet tab, click the **Review** tab on the Ribbon, and then, in the Changes group, click the **Unprotect Sheet** button to turn off protection.

3. Click the **Invoice** sheet tab, and then select the range **F25:J25** in the Transfer Area.

4. Click the **Home** tab on the Ribbon, and then, in the Clipboard group, click the **Copy** button ▣.

5. Click the **Ticket Data** sheet tab, click cell **A1**, and then press the **End+↓** keys to go to the last row with values.

6. Click the **Developer** tab on the Ribbon, and then, in the Code group, click the **Use Relative References** button. Relative references are on so you don't always go to row 5 in the Ticket Data worksheet

7. Click the **↓** key to move to the first blank cell in the worksheet.

8. In the Code group on the Developer tab, click the **Use Relative References** button. The Use Relative References button is toggled off.

9. Click the **Home** tab on the Ribbon, in the Clipboard group, click the **Paste button arrow**, and then click **Paste Values**. This option pastes the values in the transfer area to the data area rather than the formulas entered in the transfer area.

   Trouble? If #REF! appears in row 6 of the Ticket Data worksheet, you clicked the Paste button instead of the Paste Values button. Stop recording the macro. Delete the macro and begin recording the macro again.

10. Click cell **A1**, click the **Review** tab on the Ribbon, click the **Protect Sheet** button, and then click the **OK** button.

11. Click the **Invoice** sheet tab, and then click cell **B3**.

12. Click the **Stop Recording** button ▣ on the status bar. The macro recorder turns off.

You've completed recording the TransferData macro. Next, you'll test whether it works. Ellen has a new season ticket request to add to the worksheet. You'll enter this data as you test the TransferData macro.

To test the TransferData macro:

1. Enter the following data into the range B3:B11, pressing the **Enter** key after each entry.

   Kate Holland
   186 Pinetop Drive
   Eugene, OR 70777
   (888) 555–1234
   2 tickets, D series, Balcony
   1 decal, 40 donation

You'll print preview the invoice, and then you'll use the macro to transfer the data.

▶ **2.** Press the **Ctrl+p** keys to display the invoice in Print Preview, and then in the Preview group on the Print Preview tab, click the **Close Print Preview** button.

▶ **3.** Press the **Ctrl+t** keys. The TransferData macro runs and the data transfers to the Ticket Data worksheet.

▶ **4.** Switch to the **Ticket Data** worksheet, verify the data for Kate Holland transferred, and then switch to the **Invoice** worksheet.

Fixing Macro Errors

If a macro does not work correctly, you can fix it. Sometimes, you'll find a mistake when you test a macro you just created. Other times, you might not discover that error until later. No matter when you find an error in a macro, you have the following options:

• Rerecord the macro using the same macro name.
• Delete the recorded macro, and then record the macro again.
• Run the macro one step at a time to locate the problem, and then use one of the previous methods to correct the problem.

You can delete or edit a macro by opening the Macro dialog box (shown earlier in Figure 8-25), selecting the macro from the list, and then clicking the appropriate button. To rerecord the macro, simply restart the macro recorder and enter the same macro name you used earlier. Excel overwrites the previous version of the macro.

Working with the Macro Editor

Ellen is concerned about the flickering screen activity that occurs when the PrintPreview-Invoice macro is running. She thinks that this might be disconcerting to some volunteers. Eric Dean, an Office application developer, says you can speed up the macro and eliminate the flicker using a simple VBA command.

Reference Window │ Editing a Macro

• In the Code group on the Developer tab, click the Macros button, select the macro in the Macro name list, and then click the Edit button (or in the Code group on the Developer tab, click the Visual Basic button).
• Use the Visual Basic Editor to edit the macro code.
• Click File on the menu bar, and then click Close and Return to Microsoft Excel.

To view the code of the PrintPreviewInvoice macro, you need to open the **Visual Basic Editor**, which is a separate application that works with Excel and all of the Office programs to edit and manage VBA code. You can access the Visual Basic Editor through the Macro dialog box.

To view the code for the PrintPreviewInvoice macro:

▶ **1.** Click the **Developer** tab on the Ribbon, and then, in the Code group, click the **Macros** button. The Macro dialog box opens.

▶ **2.** Click **PrintPreviewInvoice** in the Macro name list, and then click the **Edit** button. The Visual Basic Editor opens as a separate program, consisting of several windows. The Code window contains the VBA code generated by the macro recorder. See Figure 8-26.

Code window in the Visual Basic Editor ◀ **Figure 8-26**

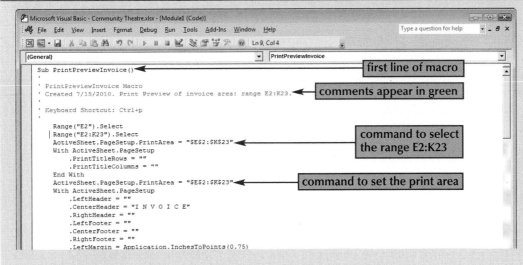

Trouble? The number of windows and their contents will differ, depending on how your computer is configured. At this point, you can ignore all other windows aside from the Code window.

▶ **3.** If the Code window is not maximized, click the **Maximize** button 🔲 on the Code window title bar.

Understanding the Structure of Macros

The VBA code in the Code window lists all of the actions you performed when recording the PrintPreviewInvoice macro. In VBA, macros are called **sub procedures**. Each sub procedure begins with the keyword *Sub* followed by the name of the sub procedure and a set of parentheses. In this example, the code begins with:

```
Sub PrintPreviewInvoice()
```

which provides the name of this sub procedure, *PrintPreviewInvoice*—the name you gave the macro. The parentheses are used to include any arguments in the procedure. These arguments pass information to the sub procedure and have roughly the same purpose as the arguments in an Excel function. If you write your own VBA code, sub procedure arguments are an important part of the programming process, but they are not used when you create macros with the macro recorder.

Following the Sub PrintPreviewInvoice() statement are comments about the macro, taken from the description you entered in the Record New Macro dialog box. Each line appears in green and is preceded by an apostrophe ('). The apostrophe indicates that the line is a comment and does not include any actions Excel needs to perform.

After the comments is the body of the macro, a listing of all of the commands performed by the PrintPreviewInvoice macro as written in the language of VBA. Your list of commands might look slightly different, depending on the exact actions you performed when recording the macro. Even though you might not know VBA, some of the commands are easy to interpret. Near the top of the PrintPreviewInvoice macro, you should see the command:

```
Range("E2:K23").Select
```

This command tells Excel to select the range E2:K23. The next command is:

```
ActiveSheet.PageSetup.PrintArea= $E$2:$K$23
```

This command sets the range E2:K23 as the print area. At the bottom of the macro is the statement:

```
End Sub
```

This statement indicates the end of the PrintPreviewInvoice sub procedure.

A Code window can contain several sub procedures, with each procedure separated from the others by the *Sub ProcedureName()* statement at the beginning, and the *End Sub* statement at the end. Sub procedures are organized into **modules**. As shown in Figure 8-26, all of the macros that have been recorded are stored in the Module1 module (your window may differ).

Writing a Macro Command

Eric wants you to insert two commands into the PrintPreviewInvoice sub procedure to hide the actions of the macro as it runs. The first command, which needs to be inserted directly after the *Sub PrintPreviewInvoice()* statement, is:

```
Application.ScreenUpdating = False
```

This command turns *off* Excel's screen updating, keeping any actions that run in the macro from being displayed on the screen. The second command, which needs to be inserted before the *End Sub* statement, is:

```
Application.ScreenUpdating = True
```

This command turns Excel's screen updating back on, enabling the user to see the final results of the macro after it has completed running.

You must enter these commands exactly. VBA will not be able to run a command if you mistype a word or omit part of the statement. The Visual Basic Editor provides tools to assist you in writing error-free code. As you type a command, the editor will provide pop-up windows and text to help you insert the correct code.

To insert the new commands into the macro:

▶ **1.** At the top the Code window, click the end of the Sub PrintPreviewInvoice () statement and then press the **Enter** key. A new blank line appears under the statement.

▶ **2.** Press the **Tab** key, and then type **Application.** (including the period, but no spaces). A list box opens with possible keywords you could type at this point in the command. You can either scroll down the list or continue typing the command yourself.

3. Type **ScreenUpdating =**. As you type the equal sign, another list box opens with two possible choices: True or False. This instruction eliminates the screen refreshing (updating) which causes the screen flickering.

4. Type **False** to turn off the screen updating feature of Excel, and then press the **Enter** key. Figure 8-27 shows the new command inserted into the sub procedure.

Command inserted in the PrintPreviewInvoice macro ◣ **Figure 8-27**

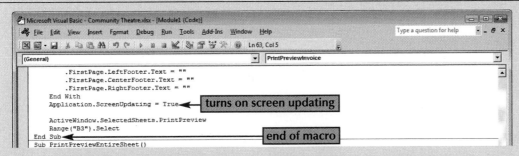

Next, you'll insert a command at the end of the sub procedure to turn screen updating back on.

5. Scroll down the Code window to view the end of the PrintPreviewInvoice sub procedure.

6. Click three lines above the End Sub statement at the end of the End With statement to position the insertion point, and then press the **Enter** key. A new blank line appears below the End With statement.

7. Type **Application.ScreenUpdating = True** and then press the **Enter** key. The command appears in the macro. See Figure 8-28.

Second command added to the PrintPreviewInvoice macro ◣ **Figure 8-28**

8. Click **File** on the menu bar, and then click **Close and Return to Microsoft Excel**. The Visual Basic Editor closes, and the Community Theatre workbook is redisplayed.

To return to the Visual Basic Editor, you can select a macro in the Macro dialog box and click the Edit button again, or you can click the Visual Basic button in the Code group on the Developer tab.

Eric suggests that you test the macro. You'll check to see whether the commands to turn off the screen updating feature make the macro run more smoothly.

To test the edited PrintPreviewInvoice macro:

1. Press the **Ctrl+p** keys. The PrintPreviewInvoice macro runs faster and without the flicker.

> **2.** In the Preview group on the Print Preview tab, click the **Close Print Preview** button. The worksheet returns to Normal view.

Ellen is pleased with the change you made to the macro. She thinks it runs more smoothly and will be less distracting to the theatre's volunteers.

Creating Macro Buttons

Another way to run a macro is to assign it to a button placed directly on the worksheet. Ellen wants you to add three macro buttons to the Invoice worksheet, one for each of the macros you've created. Macro buttons are often a better way to run macros than shortcut keys. Clicking a button (with a descriptive label) is often more intuitive and simpler for users than trying to remember different combinations of keystrokes.

Reference Window | **Creating a Macro Button**

- In the Controls group on the Developer tab, click the Insert button.
- In the Form Controls section, click the Button (Form Control) tool, click the worksheet where you want the macro button to be located, drag the pointer until the button is the size and shape you want, and then release the mouse button.
- In the Assign Macro dialog box, select the macro you want to assign to the button, and then, with the button still selected, type a new label.

You'll add the three macro buttons to the Invoice worksheet.

To insert a button on the worksheet:

> **1.** If necessary, scroll to the right so columns **L**, **M**, and **N** are completely visible.

> **2.** In the Controls group on the Developer tab, click the **Insert** button. The Form Controls appear, with a variety of objects that can be placed in the worksheet. You'll insert the Button form control. See Figure 8-29.

Figure 8-29 | **Form Controls**

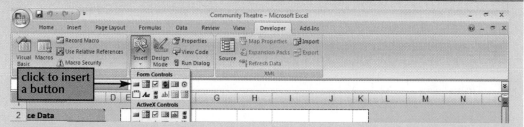

Trouble? If the Insert command is unavailable, the worksheet is protected. Click the Review tab on the Ribbon, in the Changes group, click the Unprotect Sheet button to unprotect the Invoice worksheet, and then repeat Step 2.

> **3.** In the Form Controls section, click the **Button (Form Control) tool** ▣, and then point to cell **L3**. The pointer changes to +.

> **4.** Click and drag the pointer over the range **L3:M4**, and then release the mouse button. A button appears on the worksheet, and the Assign Macro dialog box opens with the button's default name in the Macro name box. See Figure 8-30.

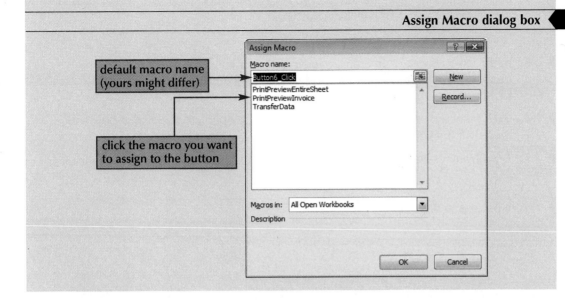

From the Assign Macro dialog box, you can assign a macro to the button. Ellen wants you to assign the PrintPreviewInvoice macro to this new button.

To assign a button to the PrintPreviewInvoice macro:

▶ 1. Click **PrintPreviewInvoice** in the list of macros, and then click the **OK** button. The PrintPreviewInvoice macro is assigned to the selected button.

You will change the default label on the button to a descriptive one that indicates which macro will run when the button is clicked.

▶ 2. With the selection handles still displayed around the button, select the label text, and then type **Preview Invoice** (do not press the Enter key). The new label replaces the default label.

Trouble? If no selection handles appear around the button, the button is not selected. Right-click the button, and then click Edit Text to place the insertion point within the button, and then repeat Step 2.

Trouble? If you pressed the Enter key after entering the label on the button, you created a new line in the button. Press the Backspace key to delete the line, and then continue with Step 3.

▶ 3. Click any cell in the worksheet to deselect the macro button.

At this point, if you click the Preview Invoice button, the PrintPreviewInvoice macro will run. Before you test the Preview Invoice button, you will add the other buttons.

To add the remaining macro buttons to the Invoice worksheet:

▶ 1. In the Controls group on the Developer tab, click the **Insert** button to display the Form Controls, and then click the **Button (Form Control)** tool ▄ .

▶ 2. Point to cell **L6**, click and drag the pointer over the range **L6:M7**, and then release the mouse button. The Assign Macro dialog box opens.

▶ 3. Select **PrintPreviewEntireSheet** in the Macro name list, and then click the **OK** button. The selected macro button appears in the Invoice worksheet.

▶ **4.** Select the label text in the button, type **Preview Worksheet** as the new label, and then click any cell to deselect the button.

Next, you'll insert the Transfer Data button.

▶ **5.** In the Controls group on the Developer tab, click the **Insert** button, click the **Button (Form Control)** tool ▦, and then drag the pointer over the range **L9:M10**.

▶ **6.** Click **TransferData** in the Macro name list in the Assign Macro dialog box, and then click the **OK** button.

▶ **7.** Type **Transfer Data** as the button label, and then click any cell in the worksheet to deselect the button. See Figure 8-31.

| Figure 8-31 | **Macro buttons in the Invoice worksheet** |

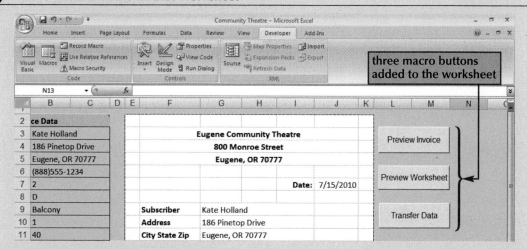

Trouble? If the macro buttons on your screen do not match the size and location of the buttons shown in the figure, right-click a button to select it, press the Esc key to close the shortcut menu, and then resize or reposition the button on the worksheet.

You have completed the application so you will reset worksheet protection.

▶ **8.** Click the **Review** tab on the Ribbon, in the Changes group click the **Protect Sheet** button to open the Protect Sheet dialog box, and then click the **OK** button to turn on worksheet protection.

> **Tip**
>
> To move or resize a macro button, right-click the button to select it, press the Esc key to close the shortcut menu, and then drag a selection handle to resize the button or drag the selection border to move the button.

Next, you will test the macro buttons to verify that they run the macros. Ellen received another subscriber order. You will use the new macro buttons as you enter this data.

To test the macro buttons:

▶ **1.** In the range **B3:B11**, enter the following subscriber order:

George Zidane
105 Central Ave.
Eugene, OR 70777
(808) 685–1111
3 tickets, E series, Balcony
2 parking decals, 30 donation

▶ **2.** Click the **Preview Invoice** button to display the current invoice in Print Preview, and then close Print Preview to return to the Invoice worksheet.

▶ **3.** Click the **Preview Worksheet** button to display the Invoice worksheet in Print Preview. The flickering occurs as this macro runs because you did not edit the code in the PrintPreviewEntireSheet macro.

▶ **4.** Close Print Preview without printing.

▶ **5.** Click the **Transfer Data** button to transfer data to the Ticket Data worksheet. Excel inserts the new transaction in the table.

▶ **6.** Switch to the **Ticket Data** worksheet, and verify the data was transferred. See Figure 8-32.

Ticket Data worksheet with new transaction record ◀ **Figure 8-32**

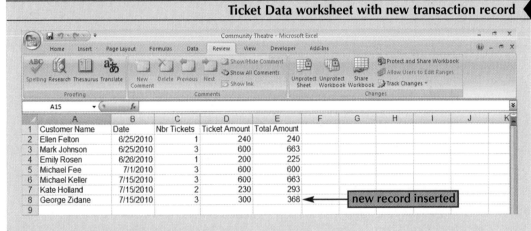

▶ **7.** Switch to the **Documentation** sheet.

Saving Workbooks with Macros

You've completed your work on the Excel application, so you will save and close the workbook and then exit Excel.

To save a workbook with a macro:

▶ **1.** On the Quick Access Toolbar, click the **Save** button 🔡. A dialog box opens, indicating that the workbook you are trying to save contains features that cannot be saved in a macro-free workbook. See Figure 8-33. The default Excel workbook (.xlsx file extension) does not allow macros to be stored as part of the file. If you click the Yes button, this workbook will be saved as a macro-free workbook, which means the macros you created will be lost.

Dialog box with macro warning ◀ **Figure 8-33**

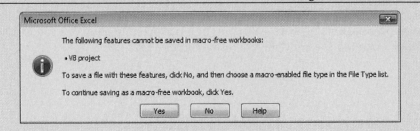

You want to include the macros in the file. To do this, you have to save the workbook as a new file; one that allows macros to be saved as part of the file.

▶ **2.** Click the **No** button. The Save As dialog box opens.

▶ **3.** In the File name box, type **Theatre With Macros** so you can easily determine which workbook contains macros.

The default Excel Workbook, which is a macro-free workbook, has the .xlsx file extension. You need to change this to a macro-enabled workbook, which has the .xlsm file extension.

▶ **4.** Click the **Save as type** button, and then click **Excel Macro-Enabled Workbook**.

▶ **5.** Click the **Save** button. The workbook is saved with the macros.

Minimize the Ribbon

Now that the application is complete, Ellen wants to provide more screen space for the input and output sections of the worksheet. You can minimize the Ribbon to make more space for the worksheet. When the Ribbon is minimized all that is displayed is the Quick Access Toolbar and the tab names. To access any command from the Ribbon, click the desired tab. The Ribbon expands to show all the groups and buttons on the tab.

To minimize the Ribbon:

▶ **1.** Double-click any tab on the Ribbon. The Ribbon is minimized. See Figure 8-34.

Figure 8-34 ▶ **Minimized Ribbon**

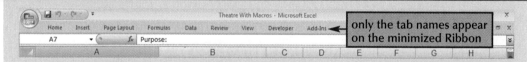

2. Click the **Home** tab to view all buttons and toolbars for this tab. You can click any other tabs on the Ribbon to display their options. After you click any button on the Ribbon or a cell in the worksheet, the Ribbon returns to its minimized state.

▶ **3.** Close the workbook.

Opening a Workbook with Macros

What happens when you open a file with macros, Excel checks the opening workbook to see if it contains a macro. The response you see is based on the security level set on the computer. Ellen has disabled all macros with notification. So, all macros are disabled upon opening the workbook, but a security alert provides her with the option to enable the macros so they can be run or open the workbook with the macros disabled. If you know a workbook contains macros that you or a coworker created, you can enable them. You'll open the Theatre With Macros workbook.

To open the Community Theatre workbook that contains macros:

▶ **1.** Open the **Theatre With Macros** workbook. The workbook opens, and a Message Bar appears below the Ribbon indicating the macros have been disabled. See Figure 8-35. Although the workbook is open you must complete one more step to use the macros.

Security alert appears when opening a workbook with macros | Figure 8-35

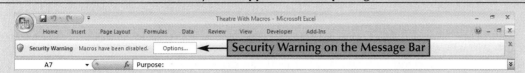

▶ **2.** In the Message Bar, click the **Options** button to open the Microsoft Office Security Options dialog box. See Figure 8-36.

Microsoft Office Security Options dialog box | Figure 8-36

▶ **3.** Click the **Enable this content** option button, and then click the **OK** button. The macros in the workbook are available for use. If you selected the recommended option, Help protect me from unknown content, the macros would remain disabled and unavailable during the current session. The other features of the workbook would still be available.

▶ **4.** Click the **Invoice** sheet tab. The Ribbon is still minimized. It will remain minimized in Excel on this computer until you maximize the Ribbon.

▶ **5.** Double-click any tab to maximize the Ribbon, and then close the workbook without saving the changes.

Finally, you'll remove the Developer tab from the Ribbon.

▶ **6.** Click the **Office Button** (⊞), and then click the **Excel Options** button to open the Excel Options dialog box.

▶ **7.** In the Popular section, click the **Show Developer tab in the Ribbon** check box to remove the check mark, and then click the **OK** button. The Developer tab is hidden from the Ribbon.

Ellen is pleased with the ease of the interface for the community theatre workbook. The workbook protection and macros will streamline the data entry process for the theatre volunteers.

Review | **Session 8.3 Quick Check**

1. Discuss two ways of creating a macro.
2. How do you identify a comment in the Visual Basic code?
3. What are the three places in which you can store a macro?
4. What are the steps you follow to delete a macro?
5. What are the steps you follow to edit a macro?
6. How do you insert a macro button into your worksheet?

Review | **Tutorial Summary**

In this tutorial, you learned how to create data validation rules that help guide users as they input data into a worksheet. You learned how to define names to make formulas easier to understand. You also learned how to protect the contents of worksheets, the worksheets themselves, and workbooks. Finally, you learned how to automate a series of actions by creating macros.

Key Terms

comment	locked property	protect worksheet
data validation	macro	sub procedure
defined name	macro security settings	Trust Center
digital signature	maco virus	validation rule
error alert message	module	Visual Basic Editor
Excel application	name	Visual Basic for Applications
input message	Personal Macro workbook	(VBA)

| Practice | | **Review Assignments** |

Practice the skills you learned in the tutorial to create a workbook with macros for a car rental company.

Data File needed for the Review Assignments: Rentals.xlsx

Ellen's student intern, Mark, did such a good job helping her with the Community Theatre application that she recommended him to a friend who has a similar project. Ellen's friend needs to create an invoice system for his new car rental company, Eugene Discount Car Rental.

Complete the following:

1. Open the **Rentals** workbook located in the Tutorial.08\Review folder included with your Data Files, and then save the workbook as **Discount Rental** in the same folder.
2. Enter the current date and your name in the Documentation sheet.
3. In the Customer worksheet, define names for cells using the following information:

Cell	Defined Name	Cell	Defined Name
B4	**Customer**	H9	**ChargePerDay**
B5	**TypeCar**	H10	**ChargePerMile**
B6	**DaysRented**	A12:C16	**RentalRates**
B7	**MilesDriven**	B19	**SalesTaxRate**

4. Create the validation rules for cells B5, B6, and B7 shown in Figure 8-37.

Figure 8-37

Cell	Settings	Input Message	Error Alert
B5	List Source (A12:A16)	Enter an appropriate title and message	Style: Stop Title: Invalid Type Message: Enter an appropriate message
B6	Integers >0 and <30	Enter an appropriate title and message	Style: Warning Title: Warning Days Rented Message: Enter an appropriate message
B7	Integers >0 and <=5000	Enter an appropriate title and message	Style: Warning Title: Warning Miles Message: Enter an appropriate message

5. Enter the following formulas, using the defined names you created in Step 3, to calculate the Rental Bill:
   - Cell F6 is equal to the value in cell B4.
   - Cell F7 is equal to the value in cell B5.
   - Cell F9 is equal to the value in cell B6.
   - Cell F10 is equal to the value in cell B7.
   - Cell H9 is equal to charge per day, which depends on the type of car entered in cell B5 and the rate table. (*Hint:* Use the VLOOKUP function.)
   - Cell H10 is equal to the charge per mile, which depends on the type of car rented in cell B5 and the rate table. (*Hint:* Use the VLOOKUP function.)
   - Cell F12 is equal to the Rental Amount, which equals the days rented multiplied by the charge per day plus the miles driven multiplied by the charge per mile.
   - Cell F13 is equal to Sales Tax Rate times Rental Amount.
   - Cell F14 is equal to Rental Amount plus Sales Tax.
   - Use the IFERROR function in cells H9, H10, F12, F13, and F14 to test for an error value. If an error value is found, display a blank; otherwise, use the appropriate formula.

6. Test the worksheet using the data: **Myles Fast**, **Intermediate**, **4**, **450**.

7. Protect the worksheet so a user can enter data only in the range B4:B7. Do not use a password to enable protection. Save the workbook.

   Note: In the following steps, you'll be creating two macros. Save your workbook before recording each macro. That way, if you make a mistake in recording the macro, you can close the workbook without saving the changes, and then reopen the workbook and try again. Be sure to read the list of tasks before you begin recording them.

8. Remove worksheet protection from the Customer worksheet.

9. Create a macro named **PrintPreviewBill** with the shortcut key **Ctrl+p** that displays only the bill portion of the worksheet in the range E3:H15 in Print Preview, centers the bill horizontally on the page and shows your name in the right footer of the printout. Create a macro button, assign the PrintPreviewBill macro to the button, and then change the default label to **Preview Bill**.

10. Create a macro named **ClearInputs** with the shortcut key **Ctrl+c** that clears the data in the rental inputs section of the worksheet (range B4:B7). Create a macro button, assign the ClearInputs macro to the button, and then change the label to **Clear**.

11. Turn protection on in the Customer worksheet.

12. Test the macro using the data: **Eddie Elders**, **Intermediate**, **3** days, **2000** miles.

13. Use the Preview Bill macro button to preview the customer bill for Ed Elders.

14. Use the Clear macro button to remove the rental data.

15. In the Documentation worksheet, use the Paste List command to document the defined names and their locations.

16. Save the workbook with the name **Rentals With Macros** in the macro-enabled workbook format, and then close it. Submit the finished workbook to your instructor, either in printed or electronic form, as requested.

Apply | Case Problem 1

Apply the skills you learned to create, edit, and run macros to produce monthly reports.

Data File needed for this Case Problem: MediTrax.xlsx

MediTrax Controls   MediTrax Controls, a U.S. subsidiary of a European multinational corporation, is testing an HVAC system designed to eliminate large temperature variances in its medical storage rooms. Lisa Goodman is a product tester for MediTrax, and each week, she records 25 temperature readings, five samples each day, in an Excel workbook. At the end of the month, Lisa sends the results to the parent company's Quality Department. Because many repetitive steps occur in developing the output requested by the parent company, Lisa asks you to create a macro to speed the creation of the report and reduce chances for error.

Complete the following:

1. Open the **MediTrax** workbook located in the Tutorial.08\Case1 folder included with your Data Files, and then save the workbook as **MediTrax Controls** in the same folder.

2. In the Documentation sheet, enter your name and the current date, and then review all the worksheets in the workbook. Make Week 1 the active worksheet.

3. Create a macro to convert the worksheet to the one shown in Figure 8-38. Name the macro **ConvertData** and assign the shortcut key **Ctrl+d** to run the macro. The macro performs the following steps:
   a. Formats the dates in the Date column using the date format type (3/14/2001).
   b. Formats the times in the Time column so they are displayed in 24-hour notation (format type 13:30).
   c. Types the title **Celsius** in cell D1.
   d. Converts the Fahrenheit temperatures to Celsius by entering the following formula in cell D2 and then copying down the column: **=5/9*(C2–32)**
   e. Formats the cells in column D using the Number format to 1 decimal place.
   f. Bolds the column heading and resizes the column to fully display "Fahrenheit."
   g. Places the label **Average** in cell A27, computes the average Celsius temperature for the week in cell D27 and bolds the row.
   h. Makes cell F1 the active cell.
   i. Uses Print Preview to view the results centered horizontally on the page with the worksheet name in the center header and your name in the right footer.
   j. Closes Print Preview.
   k. Stops recording the macro.

Figure 8-38

	A	B	C	D
1	Date	Time	Fahrenheit	Celsius
2	4/1/2010	1:05	60.5	15.8
3	4/1/2010	2:02	64.5	18.1
4	4/1/2010	6:42	63.8	17.7
5	4/1/2010	14:45	61.1	16.2
6	4/1/2010	21:12	60.2	15.7
7	4/2/2010	1:33	61.2	16.2
8	4/2/2010	2:25	62.9	17.2
9	4/2/2010	6:12	64.4	18.0
10	4/2/2010	15:35	62.3	16.8
11	4/2/2010	20:32	61.9	16.6
12	4/3/2010	1:56	63.9	17.7
13	4/3/2010	2:51	60.6	15.9
14	4/3/2010	6:55	62.6	17.0
15	4/3/2010	14:30	64.5	18.1
16	4/3/2010	22:18	63.2	17.3
17	4/4/2010	1:32	62.6	17.0
18	4/4/2010	2:58	62.7	17.1
19	4/4/2010	7:05	62.4	16.9
20	4/4/2010	14:12	63.5	17.5
21	4/4/2010	21:45	62.6	17.0
22	4/5/2010	1:22	64.8	18.2
23	4/5/2010	2:18	62.4	16.9
24	4/5/2010	6:50	61.9	16.6
25	4/5/2010	13:59	63.4	17.4
26	4/5/2010	22:03	64.2	17.9
27	Average			17.1
28				

Documentation | **Week 1** | Week 2 | Week 3

Ready   120%

4. Switch to the Week 2 worksheet and test the macro using the shortcut key.
5. Edit the macro so screen updating is turned off while the macro is running and turned on when the macro ends.
6. Switch to the Week 3 worksheet and test the revised macro using the shortcut key.
7. Save the workbook as **MTC With Macros** as an Excel Macro-Enabled workbook, and then close it. Submit the finished workbook to your instructor, either in printed or electronic form, as requested.

| Apply | | **Case Problem 2** |

Apply the skills you've learned to define data validation rules, name cells, set worksheet protection, and create macros in a profit analysis workbook.

Data File needed for this Case Problem: Popcorn.xlsx

Seattle Popcorn   Seattle Popcorn is a small company located in Tacoma, Washington, that produces gourmet popcorn distributed in the Northwest. Steve Wilkes has developed a workbook that will allow him to perform a profit analysis for the company. Using this workbook, he wants to create formulas to determine the break-even point for the company—the sales volume needed so that revenues will match the anticipated monthly expenses. Three factors determine the break-even point: the sales price of each unit of Seattle Popcorn, the variable manufacturing cost to the company for each unit, and the fixed expenses (salaries, rent, insurance, and so on) that the company must pay each month. Steve wants to be able to explore a range of possible values for each of these factors, as follows:

- The sales price of each unit of Seattle Popcorn can vary from $5 to $15 (in whole numbers).

- The variable manufacturing cost of each unit can vary from $5 to $15 (in whole numbers).

- The fixed monthly expense for the company can vary from $15,000 to $30,000 (in whole numbers).

Figure 8-39 shows a preview of the application you'll create for Steve.

Figure 8-39

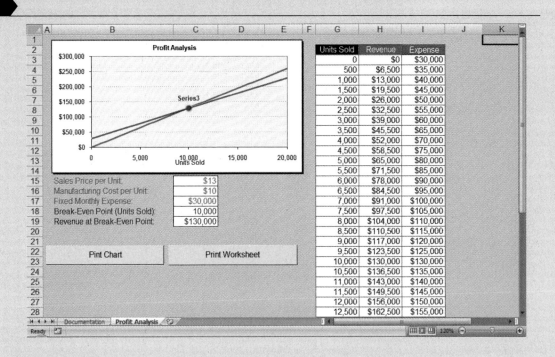

Complete the following:

1. Open the **Popcorn** workbook located in the Tutorial.08\Case2 folder included with your Data Files, and then save the workbook as **Seattle Popcorn** in the same folder. Enter the date and your name in the Documentation sheet.

2. Switch to the Profit Analysis worksheet, and then define the following names: in cell C15 **PricePerUnit**, in cell C16 **CostPerUnit**, and in cell C17 **MonthlyExpenses**.

3. In the range H3:H43, enter a formula using defined names to calculate the revenue, which is determined by the units sold multiplied by the price per unit. In the range I3:I43, enter a formula using defined names to calculate the expenses, which are determined by the units sold multiplied by the cost per unit plus the fixed monthly expense.

4. In cell C18, enter a formula to calculate the break-even point, which is determined by the fixed monthly expense divided by the difference between the price per unit and the cost per unit. Use the IFERROR function to display a blank cell instead of an error value.

5. In cell C19, enter a formula to calculate the revenue at the break-even point, which is determined by the break-even point multiplied by the sale price per unit. Use the IFERROR function to display a blank cell instead of an error value.

6. Create the validation rules for cells C15, C16, and C17, as shown in Figure 8-40.

Figure 8-40

Cell	Settings	Input Message	Error Alert
C15	Integers from 5 to 15	Enter an appropriate title and message	Title: Sales Price Warning Style: Warning Message: Enter an appropriate message
C16	Integers from 5 to 15	Enter an appropriate title and message	Title: Cost Warning Style: Warning Message: Enter an appropriate message
C17	Integers from 15000 to 30000	Enter an appropriate title and message	Title: Fixed Monthly Expense Warning Style: Warning Message: Enter an appropriate message

7. Protect the worksheet so the user can enter data only in cells C15, C16, and C17. Everything else in the worksheet should remain locked.

8. Enter the following values in the worksheet to determine how many units Seattle Popcorn must sell each month in order to break even:
   - Sales Price per Unit = **$13**
   - Manufacturing Cost per Unit = **$10**
   - Fixed Monthly Expense = **$30,000**

   Note: In the following steps, you'll create two macros. Save your workbook before recording each macro. That way, if you make a mistake while recording the macro, you can close the workbook without saving the changes, and then reopen it and try again. Also, read the list of tasks before you begin recording them.

9. Create a macro named **PrintChart** with the shortcut key **Ctrl+a** that performs the following tasks:
   a. Print Preview the chart and input/output area (range A1:E20) in landscape orientation, centered horizontally on the page, and with the text **Break-even Analysis** in the center header, and your name and date in the right footer.
   b. Closes Print Preview and then makes cell A1 the active cell.

10. Test the PrintChart macro by pressing the Ctrl+a keys. If the macro doesn't work, close the workbook without saving your changes, reopen the workbook, and record the macro again.

11. Create a button in the range A22:B23, assign the PrintChart macro to the button, and change the default label to a more descriptive one.

12. Edit the PrintChart macro so screen updating is turned off while the macro is running and turned on when the macro ends.

13. Run the PrintChart macro again to test the button and verify that screen updating is turned off while the macro is running and on when the macro ends.

14. Create a macro named **PrintWorksheet** with shortcut key **Ctrl+b** that performs the following tasks:
    a. Print Preview the entire worksheet on one page with text **Profit Analysis** in the center header and your name and date in the right footer.
    b. Closes Print Preview, and then makes cell A1 the active cell.

15. Test the PrintWorksheet macro by pressing the Crtl+b keys. If the macro doesn't work, close the workbook without saving your changes, reopen the workbook, and record the macro again.

16. Create a button in the range C22:E23, assign the PrintWorksheet macro to the button, and then change the default label to a more descriptive one.

17. Edit the macro so screen updating is turned off while the macro is running and turned on when the macro ends.

18. Run the PrintWorksheet macro again to test the button and verify that screen updating is turned off while the macro is running and on when the macro ends.

19. Save the workbook as **SP With Macros**, and then close it. Submit the finished workbook to your instructor, either in printed or electronic form, as requested.

Apply	**Case Problem 3**

Apply the skills you learned to design an Excel workbook for use as a data entry form.

Data File needed for this Case Problem: Cookin.xlsx

Cookin Good   Cookin Good is a company that sells specialized home cooking products. The company employs individuals to organize "Cookin Good Parties" in which the company's products are sold. Cleo Benard is responsible for entering sales data from various Cookin Good Parties. She wants to design an Excel workbook to act as a data entry form. She has already created the workbook, but she needs your help in setting up data validation rules, creating a table lookup, and writing the macros to enter the data.

Complete the following:

1. Open the **Cookin** workbook located in the Tutorial.08\Case3 folder included with your Data Files, save the workbook as **Cookin Good** in the same folder. Enter your name and the date in the Documentation sheet, and then switch to the Sales Form worksheet.

2. Create appropriate defined names for each cell in the range C3:C8. Assign the name **ProductInfo** to the range E4:G15.

3. In the Sales Form worksheet, create the following validation rules:
   a. Cell C3 for which the criteria allows only one of five regions (represented by the numbers 1, 2, 3, 4, and 5) to be entered. Enter an appropriate input message and error alert.
   b. Cell C4 for which the criteria provides the list of 12 products (found in range E4:E15). Enter an appropriate input message and error alert.
   c. Cell C7 for which the criteria allows only positive numbers to be entered as the number of units sold. Enter an appropriate input message and error alert.

4. Use a Lookup function to have the product name and price automatically entered into the sales form when the ProductID is entered. (*Hint:* Cells should be blank if an error value appears in a cell.)

5. Enter a formula that automatically calculates the total sale for the order, which is determined by the number of units sold multiplied by the price of the product.

6. Prevent users from selecting any cell in the Sales Form worksheet other than cells C3, C4, and C7, and then protect all of the worksheets in the workbook, except for the Documentation sheet.

7. Test the data entry form by entering the following new record: Region = **1**, Product ID = **CW**, Units Sold = **5**.

8. Save the workbook, and then create a macro named **AddData** with the shortcut key **Ctrl+d** that performs the following tasks:
    a. In the Sales Form worksheet, copy the values in the range C3:C8. (*Hint:* You'll paste later in the macro.)
    b. Switch from the Sales Form worksheet to the Sales Record worksheet. Click cell A1.
    c. Turn on Relative References. Use the arrow keys to locate the last used row in the table.
    d. Use an arrow key to move to the next row. Turn off Relative References.
    e. Paste the copied values from Step A into the blank row. (*Hint:* Use the Paste Special command to paste transposed values, Values option, Transpose check box.)
    f. Switch to the Sales Table worksheet, click inside the PivotTable and refresh the contents of the PivotTable to include the new data.
    g. Switch to the Sales Form and clear the values in cells C3, C4, and C7 of the Sales Form worksheet. Make C3 the active cell.
    h. Stop Recording.

9. Create a button in the range C11:C12 on the Sales Form worksheet and assign the AddData macro to the button. Change the button label to **Transfer Sales Data**.

10. Test the data entry form and AddData macro by entering the following new records:

Region	Product ID	Units Sold
3	HR	7
4	OEG	3

11. Create a macro named **ViewTable** with the **Ctrl+t** shortcut key that displays the contents of the Sales Table worksheet.

12. Create a macro named **ViewChart** with the **Ctrl+c** shortcut key that displays the Sales Chart worksheet.

13. Create a macro named **ViewForm** with the **Ctrl+f** shortcut key that displays the Sales Form worksheet. Test each macro using its shortcut keys.

14. In the Documentation sheet, create three macro buttons to view the Sales Table (Step 11), the Sales Chart (Step 12), and the Sales Form (Step 13). Insert the macro buttons below row 9. Change the labels on the buttons to be more descriptive.

⊕ EXPLORE

15. Sales Table displays the Total product sales in each region. Change the display so the values in the cell are percentage of the total (Field Setting). You can return the original value by choosing Normal.

16. Save the workbook as **CG With Macros**, and then close it. Submit the finished workbook to your instructor, either in printed or electronic form, as requested.

Create | **Case Problem 4**

Go beyond what you've learned to define names, apply worksheet protection, and create macros to prepare an invoice.

There are no Data Files needed for this Case Problem.

Alia's Senior Living Supplies Alia Moh for years had been touched by the needs of the senior population she was serving, thinking that if people had just a little help, they might not end up at her hospital. Ultimately, she left her job at a local hospital in Chicago to establish Alia's Senior Living Supplies, which supplies products and services designed for seniors. Products offered by Alia on her Web site range from safety step ladders, doorknob grippers, skid resistant surfaces, to wheelchair ponchos.

Finding these uniquely designed products a great help in their day-to-day lives, a large following of clients regularly purchase from Alia. To be sure her company stays in business, Alia must assure timely receipt of payments from her growing client base. She wants a billing/invoicing system to expedite that work. Figure 8-41 shows the finished application she asks you to create.

Figure 8-41

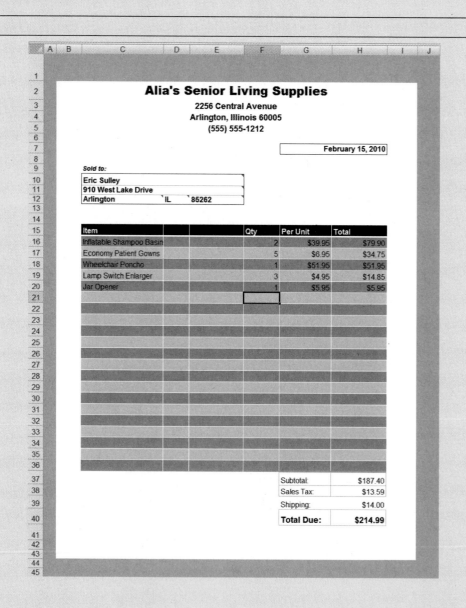

Complete the following:

1. Open a new workbook, and save it as **AliasSupplies** in the Tutorial.08\Case4 folder included with your Data Files.

2. Rename the first sheet **Documentation** and then enter the company name, your name, the current date, and a purpose statement. Rename the second sheet **Invoice**. Rename the third sheet **Product Pricing And Shipping**.

3. Review Figures 8-42 and 8-43, and the steps below before you begin to enter the tables, labels, and formulas to build the invoice. First, enter the data for Product Pricing (shown in Figure 8-42) and Shipping costs (shown in Figure 8-43) in the Product Pricing And Shipping worksheet. Next, follow Steps a through n and Figure 8-41 to build the invoice. Use defined names and structured referencing to assist in creating formulas.

   a. Current date in cell G7 (merged with H7).

   b. Insert comments as a reminder as to what data is to be entered in cells C10, C11, C12, D12, and E12.

   c. Adjust the column widths so column A is 2.57; column B is 6.14; column C is 20.86; Column D is 6.14; column E is 13.57; column F is 8.71; column G is 12.71; column H is 13.71; and column I is 7.29.

   d. Insert the column headers in row 15.

   e. Create an Excel table in the range C15:H36. Remove the filter arrows and format cells G7 and the range G40:H40 as bold.

   f. Use defined names wherever appropriate.

   g. Item column (the range C16:C36): User looks up Item using a list. Use the Product Pricing table, shown in Figure 8-42, for the Item.

Figure 8-42

	A	B
1	**Product Pricing**	
2		
3	Adjustable Home Bed Rail	89.95
4	Bed Cane	81.95
5	Doorknob Gripper	4.95
6	Easy Grip Utensils	32.95
7	Economy Patient Gowns	6.95
8	Full-page Magnifier	4.99
9	Giant TV Remote	34.95
10	Inflatable Shampoo Basin	39.95
11	Jar Opener	5.95
12	Lamp Switch Enlarger	4.95
13	Medication Dispenser	135.95
14	No Rinse Shampoo	34.95
15	Tilting Overbed Table	114.95
16	Trolley Walker	139.95
17	Wheelchair Poncho	51.95

   h. Qty column: User enters the quantity ordered. Issue an error alert warning message if the quantity is above 50.

   i. Per Unit column: Based on a table lookup in the Product Pricing table based on value selected in Item column (refer to Figure 8-42).

   j. Total column: Qty × Per Unit.

   k. Subtotal (cell H37): Sum of Total column. Format this cell appropriately.

   l. Sales tax: 7.25% of subtotal in cell H38 if the customer state is IL; otherwise, sales tax is 0. Format this cell appropriately.

   m. Shipping costs: If subtotal is $200 or more, no shipping cost; otherwise, look up shipping cost (refer to Figure 8-43) based on the subtotal in cell H37. Format this cell appropriately.

Figure 8-43

Subtotal amount	Shipping cost
0–54.99	5.95
55–99.99	8.25
100–149.99	11.50
150–199.99	14.00

   n. Total Due = Subtotal + Sales Tax + Shipping. Format this cell appropriately.

4. Protect the worksheet so a user can enter data in cells C10, C11, C12, D12, E12, items (C16:C36), and Qty (F16:F36) but not in any other cells. Do not use a password.

5. Create a macro named **PrintInvoice** that prints the Invoice. Assign the **Ctrl+p** shortcut key to this macro. Center the worksheet horizontally and fit it on 1 printed page. The heading has the label **I N V O I C E**. Attach a button and place it on the worksheet (column K) that is assigned to the PrintInvoice macro. Assign a descriptive name to the macro button.

6. Create a macro named **ClearInputs** that deletes the values from cells C10, C11, C12, D12, E12, items in the range C16:C36, and quantities in the range F16:F36. Assign the **Ctrl+c** shortcut key to this macro. Attach a button and place it on the worksheet (column K) that is assigned to the ClearInputs macro. Assign a descriptive name to the macro button.

7. In the Documentation sheet, paste a list of defined names with location, and list of macro names, shortcut keys, and purpose.

8. Test the worksheet using the data in Figure 8-40.

9. Use the PrintInvoice macro button to print the bill for the data you entered in Step 8, and then use the ClearInputs macro button to remove the input data.

10. Save the workbook as **Alia With Macros**, and then close it. Submit the finished workbook to your instructor, either in printed or electronic form, as requested.

Research | **Internet Assignments**

Use the Internet to find and work with data related to the topics presented in this tutorial.

The purpose of the Internet Assignments is to challenge you to find information on the Internet that you can use to work effectively with this software. The actual assignments are updated and maintained on the Course Technology Web site. Log on to the Internet and use your Web browser to go to the Student Online Companion for New Perspectives Office 2007 at **www.course.com/np/office2007**. Then navigate to the Internet Assignments for this tutorial.

Assess | **SAM Assessment and Training**

If you have a SAM user profile, you may have access to hands-on instruction, practice, and assessment of the skills covered in this tutorial. Log in to your SAM account (**http://sam2007.course.com**) to launch any assigned training activities or exams that relate to the skills covered in this tutorial.

Review | **Quick Check Answers**

Session 8.1

1. A descriptive word or characters assigned to a cell or range. Defined names make interpreting formulas easier. If you move a cell or range with a defined name to a different location, any formula using that named range reflects the new location.
2. any three of the following: Name box, New Name dialog box, Create Names from Selection dialog box, and Name Manager dialog box
3. (a) Annual_Total
4. Click Name box arrow, and then click the defined name
5. =SUM(Expenses)
6. False

Session 8.2

1. Select the cell, click the Data tab on the Ribbon, and then, in the Data Tools group, click the Data Validation button.
2. Select the cell, open the Data Validation dialog box, click the Input Message tab, and then enter the input message title and text.
3. The *Stop* alert prevents the user from storing the data in the cell; the *Warning* alert rejects the invalid data but allows the user to override the rejection; and the *Information* alert accepts the invalid data but allows the user to cancel the data entry.
4. A locked cell prohibits data entry when the worksheet is protected.
5. Worksheet protection controls the user's ability to edit cells within the worksheet. Workbook protection controls the user's ability to change the structure of the workbook (including worksheet names) and the format of the workbook window.
6. Yes, as long as the structure of the workbook is not protected.
7. Select the cell with a comment. In the Comments group on the Review tab, click the Edit Comment button, edit the comment in the text box, and then click any cell.

Session 8.3

1. Use the macro recorder to record the exact keystrokes and commands you want the macro to run, or write the macro code directly in the Visual Basic Editor with VBA macro language.
2. A line that begins with an apostrophe is treated as a comment; the line of a comment is green.
3. You can store a macro in the current workbook, in a new workbook, or in the Personal Macro workbook, which is available whenever you use Excel.
4. Click Developer tab, in the Code group click Macros to open the Macros dialog box, select the macro from the list of macros, and then click the Delete button.
5. Click the Developer tab on the Ribbon, in the Code group, click the Macros button to open the Macro dialog box, select the macro from the list of macros, and then click the Edit button.
6. If the worksheet is protected, unprotect the worksheet. In the Controls group on the Developer tab, click the Insert button to display the Form Controls toolbar. Click the Button (Form Control) tool, and then draw the button image on the worksheet. Assign a macro and label to the button.

Ending Data Files

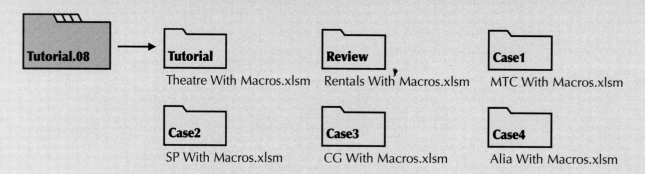

Tutorial.08 → Tutorial
Theatre With Macros.xlsm

Review
Rentals With Macros.xlsm

Case1
MTC With Macros.xlsm

Case2
SP With Macros.xlsm

Case3
CG With Macros.xlsm

Case4
Alia With Macros.xlsm

Reality Check

Excel can be a useful program for tracking information about many everyday activities, such as

- Organizations you belong to/participate in
- Collections
- Hobbies
- Community work
- Social events
- Sports records and statistics

In this exercise, you need to select an area that fits your interests and create an application in Excel to track information related to your area of interest, using the Excel skills and features presented in Tutorials 5 through 8.

Note: Please be sure *not* to include any personal information of a sensitive nature in any worksheets you create to submit to your instructor. Later, you can update the worksheets with such information for your own personal use.

1. Plan the organization of your workbook—what information related to your area of interest do you want to track; what fields do you need to enter; how will you organize the data; what calculations will you need to perform; how do you want to format the information, and so on.
2. Create a Documentation worksheet that includes your name, the date, and the purpose of your workbook. Format it appropriately.
3. Set up multiple worksheets to record your data on (for example, a budget for each event could be a separate worksheet). Use a worksheet group to enter labels and other nonvariable text, formatting, and formulas in the worksheets.
4. Apply validity checks to improve the accuracy of data entry.
5. Create a summary worksheet that consolidates the information from these worksheets.
6. Create an Excel table to track data. Enter an appropriate table name, column headers, and formulas. Format the table attractively. Add records to the table. Insert a Total row in the table with an appropriate summary calculation (SUM, COUNT, etc.).
7. Add a calculated column to the table with an appropriate function (such as an IF function, an AND function, and so on).
8. In a worksheet with a range of data, define names for cells and ranges. Convert the existing formulas in that worksheet to use the defined names.
9. Paste a list of defined names as documentation in the Documentation sheet.
10. Check for duplicate values using conditional formatting.
11. Check for data entry errors using the IFERROR function.
12. Sort the data as needed.
13. Use a filter to answer a specific question about the data. Add a comment to explain how the data was filtered and what question it answers.
14. Create an advanced filter using a criteria range, such as a filter to determine which events have food costs less than $100.

15. Use a PivotTable to analyze data in the workbook. Format, filter, and sort the PivotTable appropriately. Add a comment to explain what you learned from the PivotTable.

16. Plan and record an appropriate macro. Assign the macro to a button. Save the workbook in macro enabled format.

17. Prepare the workbook for printing. Include headers and footers that indicate the filename of your workbook, the workbook's author, and the date on which the workbook is printed. If a printed worksheet will extend across several pages, repeat appropriate print titles across all of the pages and include page numbers and the total number of pages on each printed page.

18. Save the workbook. Submit the completed workbook to your instructor, in printed or electronic form, as requested.

Objectives

Developing a Financial Analysis

Working with Financial Tools and Functions

Case | Bent Cycling

Diane Cross is the owner of Bent Cycling, a small company in Longmont, Colorado, that designs and manufactures custom-made recumbent bicycles. Recumbents or "bents" are bicycles in which the rider sits in a reclined position with the pedals placed forward rather than below the feet. Interest in recumbents has increased in the past few years as more cyclists discover the higher speeds and reduced lower back strain associated with recumbent riding. This interest has carried over to Diane's company. By properly marketing Bent Cycling's products, market analysts believe her company could double its annual revenue in five years. However, to do that would require completely rebuilding the company's workshop and design facility. That expansion requires a major investment of time and money and poses some financial risk. Diane wants to use Excel to explore the different financing options available to her and to determine the profitability of such a venture. She knows that Excel supports a wealth of financial functions for just this kind of task, but needs your help in using them.

Starting Data Files

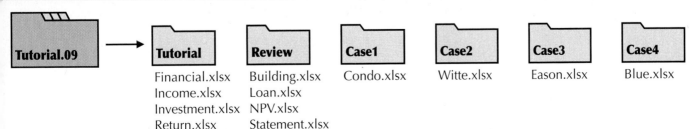

Tutorial.09 →	Tutorial	Review	Case1	Case2	Case3	Case4
	Financial.xlsx	Building.xlsx	Condo.xlsx	Witte.xlsx	Eason.xlsx	Blue.xlsx
	Income.xlsx	Loan.xlsx				
	Investment.xlsx	NPV.xlsx				
	Return.xlsx	Statement.xlsx				

Session 9.1

Evaluating Investment Options

Diane has been meeting with the head of the manufacturing department, a civil engineer, and an industrial architect for the past few months to design Bent Cycling's new workshop and design facility. She wants the workshop to accommodate the increased demand for the company's cycles and incorporate the latest manufacturing techniques to deliver a quality product for the consumer. The final recommendation of her team comes with a hefty price tag: The new workshop will cost the company $1.2 million. The company does not have that much available in ready capital, so Diane will have to look for other sources to finance the company's expansion.

Diane asks you to create a financial analysis of the situation. She wants to know what options are available to finance the expansion and how much each option will cost. Diane has already created Excel workbooks containing many of the worksheets you'll need to do the analysis.

To open Diane's workbook:

▶ **1.** Open the **Investment** workbook located in the **Tutorial.09\Tutorial** folder included with your Data Files, and then save the workbook as **Investment Analysis** in the same folder.

▶ **2.** In the Documentation sheet, enter your name in cell B3 and the date in cell B4.

▶ **3.** Switch to the **Investment Analysis** worksheet.

Diane informs you that Bent Cycling has $400,000 in cash reserves. Because this amount is not large enough to finance the proposed expansion, Diane proposes two alternatives: (1) Continue to save money until her company can afford to build the new workshop and design facility, or (2) borrow the money and start building immediately. Bent Cycling started as a small company and is still a minor player in the market, making specialized bikes for the discriminating consumer. For much of its history, Diane has tried to finance the company without going deeply into debt. So, she first wants to examine whether the company can save enough money from its cash receipts to finance the proposed expansion in the near future. To answer that question, you'll use the following five financial functions used to calculate the impact of investing money into interest-bearing accounts:

• **FV function**, which calculates the future value of an investment or loan
• **PV function**, which calculates the present value of an investment or loan
• **RATE function**, which calculates the interest rate charged or received during each payment period
• **NPER function**, which calculates the number of payment periods in an investment or loan
• **PMT function**, which calculates the amount paid into an investment or loan during each payment period

Refer to Figure 3-33 for a description of the five financial functions for evaluating investments and loans. In each case, the financial function returns the value of one financial variable in terms of the values of the other four.

Working with Loans and Investments | Reference Window

- To calculate the present value of a loan or investment, use the PV function.
- To calculate the future value of a loan or an investment, use the FV function.
- To calculate the size of the monthly or quarterly payments required to pay off a loan or meet an investment goal, use the PMT function.
- To calculate the number of monthly or quarterly payments required to pay off a loan or meet an investment goal, use the NPER function.
- To calculate the interest of a loan or investment, use the RATE function.

Calculating a Periodic Payment with the PMT Function

Currently, the $400,000 is invested in a money market fund that pays 5.3% annual interest, compounded monthly. (For a discussion of compounded interest, refer to Tutorial 3.) Diane wants to know how much the company would have to add to this fund each month so that the value of the fund reaches $1,200,000 18 months from now. In other words, Diane wants to know the periodic payment, or PMT value, needed to reach her goal. To perform this calculation, you use the PMT function, which has the following syntax:

```
=PMT(rate, nper, pv, [fv=0] [type=0])
```

In this function, *rate* is the interest rate per period, *nper* is the number of payment periods, *pv* is the present value of the investment or loan, and *fv* is the future value of the loan or investment. The *fv* argument is optional. If you don't include an *fv* value, Excel assumes a future value of 0. The PMT function, like the other Excel financial functions dealing with loans and investments, also includes an optional *type* argument. The *type* argument specifies whether payments are made at the end of each period (*type*=0) or at the beginning (*type*=1). The default is *type*=0, which is what you'll use for Diane's investments in the money market fund.

The interest rate and the payment period must use the same time unit. For example, if the interest rate is compounded monthly, the payment period must also be in months. Because the money market fund Diane uses has an annual interest rate of 5.3%, compounded monthly, you need to convert the annual interest rate to a monthly rate, which is $\frac{1}{12}$ of 5.3%, or approximately 0.442% or 0.00442. Diane plans to invest the money for 18 months, so the value of the *nper* argument is 18 because each month represents a payment period.

The PMT function, like the other four Excel financial functions, can be used with either investments or loans. The difference between a loan and an investment is based on cash flow. **Cash flow** is the movement of cash assets into or out of an account. As shown in Figure 9-1, a **positive cash flow**, or **cash inflow**, occurs whenever money is flowing *into* the account; a **negative cash flow**, or **cash outflow**, occurs when money is flowing *out of* the account.

Figure 9-1	Cash flow

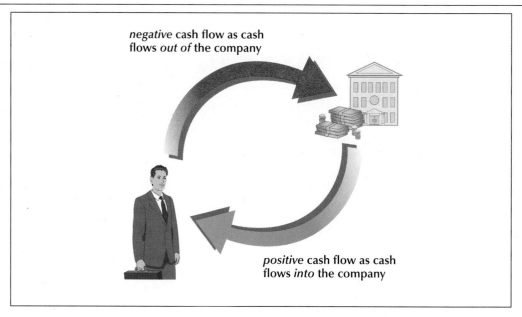

negative cash flow as cash flows *out of* the company

positive cash flow as cash flows *into* the company

Consider Diane's plan to invest in a money market fund. Bent Cycling starts out with $400,000, which Diane takes *out* of the company and places into the fund. This represents a negative cash flow because money is leaving the company. After 18 months and additional monthly payments, Diane takes money out of the fund and moves it back *into* the company to fund the expansion. This represents a positive cash flow because now the money is flowing back into Bent Cycling.

Cash flow has nothing to do with who owns the money. Bent Cycling still owns the $400,000 even when the money is transferred to the money market fund. Cash flow is solely concerned with the direction of the money as it moves in and out of the company. Thus, the value of the *pv* (present value) argument for Diane's investment is –$400,000 to indicate a negative cash flow as the money leaves the company to go into the money market fund. At the end of 18 months, Diane wants to retrieve $1,200,000 from the fund and put it back into the company, so the value of the *fv* (future value) argument is $1,200,000 to indicate a positive cash flow.

Based on this information, the PMT function to calculate the monthly payment Bent Cycling must make to increase the value of the money market fund from $400,000 to $1,200,000 in 18 months is the following:

```
=PMT(5.3%/12, 18, -400000, 1200000)
```

This formula returns the currency value –$41,032.54, indicating that the company must invest a little more than $41,000 each month to meet its savings goal of $1,200,000 after 18 months. The value returned by the PMT function is negative in this case because it represents the amount of money flowing out of the company into the fund each month.

It is good practice, however, not to enter values directly into a function. In most instances, you should reference worksheet cells in which the values are entered so the values are easily visible. You'll enter the PMT function into Diane's workbook to calculate the monthly payment the company needs to make to reach its savings goal.

> **Tip**
>
> The financial functions automatically format calculated values as currency with negative cash flows appearing in a red font enclosed within parentheses.

To calculate the monthly payment to the money market fund:

▶ **1.** In cell A5, enter **Monthly Payment (PMT)**, and then format the cell using the **20% – Accent3** cell style.

▶ **2.** In cell B5, enter **–400,000**, which is the amount of the initial investment. You inserted a negative sign before the value to indicate a cash outflow from the company into the money market fund.

▶ **3.** In cell C5, enter **1,200,000**, which is the investment goal: what you want the future value of the investment to be.

▶ **4.** In cell D5, enter **5.3%** for the annual interest rate, and then, in cell E5, enter **12**.

▶ **5.** In cell F5, enter the formula **=D5/E5** to calculate the interest rate per month.

▶ **6.** In cell G5, enter **18**, which is the number of months that Diane will transfer money into the fund.

▶ **7.** In cell H5, enter the formula **=G5/E5** to calculate the number of years that the money will be invested.

▶ **8.** In cell I5, enter the formula **=PMT(F5, G5, B5, C5)** to calculate the monthly payment (PMT). Excel returns the negative currency value, ($41,032.54).

You'll apply formatting to make the data you've just entered easier to read.

▶ **9.** Click cell **I5**, and then, in the Number group on the Home tab, click the **Decrease Decimal** button ⇥.0 twice to display the monthly payment value to the nearest dollar.

▶ **10.** In the Clipboard group on the Home tab, click the **Format Painter** button 🖌 to copy the formatting from cell I5, and then select the range **B5:C5** to format these cells the same way.

▶ **11.** Format cell **F5** as a percentage with two decimal places, and then click cell **I5**. See Figure 9-2.

Monthly payment for the investment | **Figure 9-2**

You tell Diane that Bent Cycling needs to divert a little more than $41,000 per month from cash receipts into the money market fund to reach a savings goal of $1,200,000 in the next year and a half.

Calculating a Future Value with the FV Function

The $41,000 per month is more than Bent Cycling can afford. The company can place at most $30,000 into the money market fund each month. Diane asks you to calculate how much the fund would be worth in 18 months if the company puts $30,000 a month into the fund. To calculate the future value of the fund, you use the FV function, which has the following syntax:

```
=FV(rate, nper, pmt, [pv=0] [type=0])
```

In this function, the *rate*, *nper*, *pmt*, and *type* arguments still represent the interest rate per period, number of payments, payment each period, and when the payment is due (beginning or end of the period). The *pv* argument is optional and represents the present value of the investment. The *type* argument is also optional and, as with the PMT function, indicates when payments are made into the loan or investment. For the Bent Cycling investment, these function argument values are:

```
=FV(5.3%/12, 18, -30000, -400000)
```

As with the PMT function, the interest rate is 5.3% divided by 12, the total number of payments is 18, the amount invested each month is –30,000 (a negative cash flow), and the present value is 400,000, also a negative cash flow because it represents money that has already been invested in the fund. You'll use the FV function to calculate the future value of the money market fund under this investment strategy.

To calculate the future value of an investment:

► **1.** Select the range **A5:I5**. You want to copy this formatting to the next row.

► **2.** In the Clipboard group on the Home tab, click the **Format Painter** button 🖋, and then click cell **A6**. The formatting is pasted to the range A6:I6.

► **3.** In cell A6, enter **Investment Goal (FV)**.

► **4.** Copy the initial investment value in cell B5 to cell B6.

► **5.** Copy the rate and payment period formulas and values in the range D5:H5 to the range D6:H6.

► **6.** In cell I6, enter **–30,000**, which is the monthly payment Bent Cycling can afford.

► **7.** In cell C6, enter the formula **=FV(F6, G6, I6, B6)**. Excel returns the value $993,780, which is the value of the fund after 18 months (cell G6) of depositing $30,000 each month (cell I6) at a 0.44% monthly interest rate (cell F6). The value is positive, indicating a positive cash flow from the fund back to the company. See Figure 9-3.

Future value of the investment ◄ Figure 9-3

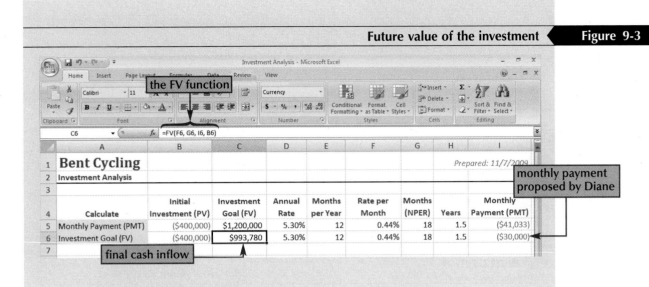

You tell Diane that by limiting the monthly deposit to $30,000, the money market fund would grow to less than $1,000,000 in the next year and a half.

Calculating the Length of an Investment with the NPER Function

After checking with the contractor, Diane concludes that the expansion cannot be done for less than $1,200,000 and certainly not for less than $1,000,000. She asks you to determine how long it would take to save $1,200,000 with a monthly deposit of $30,000. To calculate the amount of time needed to save the $1,200,000, you must determine the number of payments that have to be made into the fund. This is done with the NPER function, which uses the following syntax:

```
=NPER(rate, pmt, pv, [fv=0] [type=0])
```

The arguments in this function have the same meaning as with the financial functions you've used already. The *fv* argument is optional, and has a default value of 0. For the Bent Cycling investment, you use the following formula:

```
=NPER(5.3%/12, -30000, -400000, 1200000)
```

Again, the interest rate per month is 5.3%/12, the monthly cash outflow is −30,000, the initial value invested in the fund is also a cash outflow of −400,000, and the future value, or savings goal, is a cash inflow of 1,200,000. The important point to remember about the NPER function is that it returns the number of payment periods, not necessarily the number of years. Recall that the financial functions are based on the time interval in which interest is compounded. So, if you are making periodic monthly payments and the interest is compounded monthly, then the number of periods is also in months, not years.

To calculate the number of payments in the investment:

► **1.** Select the range **A6:I6**. You will copy the formats from this range to the next row.

► **2.** In the Clipboard group on the Home tab, click the **Format Painter** button ![Format Painter icon], and then click cell **A7** to paste the selected formatting to the range A7:I7.

► **3.** In cell A7, enter **Months (NPER)**.

Tip

If the NPER function returns the error value #NUM!, the loan cannot be paid back in any length of time. This happens when the monthly payments are too small to cover even the monthly interest charges, making it impossible to gain any ground repaying the loan.

▶ **4.** Copy the values and formulas in the range B5:F5 to the range B7:F7. Copy the values and formulas in the range H6:I6 to the range H7:I7.

▶ **5.** In cell G7, enter the formula **=NPER(F7, I7, B7, C7)**. Excel returns the value 23.932, which indicates that at the current interest rate (cell F7) with a monthly payment of $30,000 (cell I7), the number of months required to meet the investment goal (cell C7) would be almost 24 months, or 2 years. See Figure 9-4.

Figure 9-4 **Number of payments in the investment**

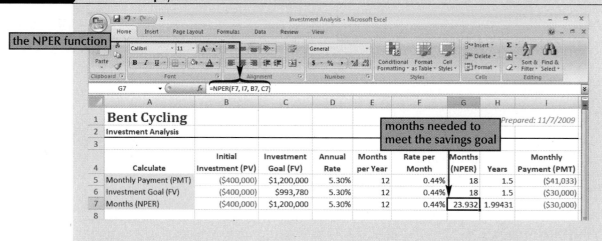

You report the results to Diane, telling her that it will take about two years to save $1,200,000 with monthly payments of $30,000. Diane is concerned that this would be too long to wait to begin the expansion. With increasing interest in recumbents, Diane does not want to lose this window of opportunity by waiting too long to upgrade the company's production facilities.

Calculating the Present Value of an Investment with the PV Function

Diane wonders whether Bent Cycling could reach its savings goal within the required 18 months by increasing the amount of the initial $400,000 investment. How much would the company have to place into the account to reach its savings goal of $1,200,000 in 18 months? To answer that question, you need to determine the investment's present value by using the PV function, which has the following syntax:

```
=PV(rate, nper, pmt, [fv=0] [type=0])
```

In this function, *rate* is the interest per period, *nper* is the number of payments, *pmt* is the payment made each period, and *fv* is the future value. For the Bent Cycling project, the argument values would be:

```
=PV(5.3%/12, 18, -30000, 1200000)
```

This calculates the present value of the investment, assuming a 5.3% interest compounded monthly for 18 payments of $30,000 to reach a future value of $1,200,000.

To calculate the present value of the investment:

▶ **1.** In cell A8, enter **Initial Investment (PV)**.

2. Copy the values and formulas from the range **C7:F7** to the range **C8:F8**, and then copy the values and formulas from the range **G6:I6** into the range **G8:I8**.

3. In cell B8, enter the formula **=PV(F8, G8, I8, C8)**. The formula returns the value −$590,493.18, which is how much Diane needs in the account today to reach $1,200,000 in savings after 18 months of investing $30,000 per month at 5.3% annual interest.

4. Click cell **B8**, and then, in the Number group on the Home tab, click the **Decrease Decimal** button 🔘 twice to display the currency value to the nearest dollar. See Figure 9-5.

Present value of the investment | Figure 9-5

You tell Diane that she would have to increase the amount currently invested in the fund from $400,000 to $590,000 to reach her savings goal. The company doesn't have another $190,000 in ready cash assets to invest, so this is not a reasonable option for Diane.

Calculating the Interest Rate of an Investment with the RATE Function

With the interest rate offered by the money market fund, Bent Cycling cannot save enough money in the next 18 months to finance the expansion. Diane wonders what interest rate would be needed to reach her savings goal. To answer that question, you'll use the RATE function, which has the following syntax:

```
=RATE(nper, pmt, pv, [fv=0] [type=0])
```

The function arguments should be familiar: nper is the number of payments, pmt is the amount of each payment, pv is the investment's present value, and fv is the investment's future value. To calculate the interest rate for the Bent Cycling investment, you use the following formula with the RATE function:

```
=RATE(18, -30000, -400000, 1200000)
```

The value returned by the rate function is based on 18 payments of $30,000 each with an initial investment of $400,000 that results in a future value of $1,200,000. Note that the value returned by the RATE function is the interest rate per period, *not* the interest rate per year.

Tip

To calculate the annual rate, you must multiply the value returned by the RATE function by the number of payments per year. For monthly payments, you multiply the rate value by 12.

To calculate the interest rate of an investment:

▶ **1.** In cell A9, enter the text **Rate per Month (RATE)**.

▶ **2.** Copy the values and formulas in the range B7:C7 to the range B9:C9; in cell E9, enter the value **12**; and then copy the values and formulas in the range G8:I8 to the range G9:I9.

▶ **3.** In cell F9, enter the formula **=RATE(G9, I9, B9, C9)**, which uses the worksheet cells for the number of payments (cell G9), the monthly payments (cell I9), the present value (cell B9), and the future value (cell C9). The function returns the value 2%, which represents the monthly interest rate. This value is rounded, so you'll show the percentage to two decimal places.

▶ **4.** In the Number group on the Home tab, click the **Increase Decimal** button twice to display the value as 1.91%.

▶ **5.** In cell D9, enter the formula **=F9*E9**, which multiplies the monthly interest rate by 12 months to calculate the annual interest rate of 0.229533.

▶ **6.** Format the value in cell D9 as a percentage with two decimal places. The value 22.95% represents the annual interest rate required to meet Diane's savings goal.

You will highlight the calculated values in the different rows to make them easier to locate and read.

▶ **7.** Select the nonadjacent range **I5;C6;G7;B8;F9**, apply the **Accent3** cell style, and then click cell **A3** to deselect the range. See Figure 9-6.

Figure 9-6	Interest rate of the investment

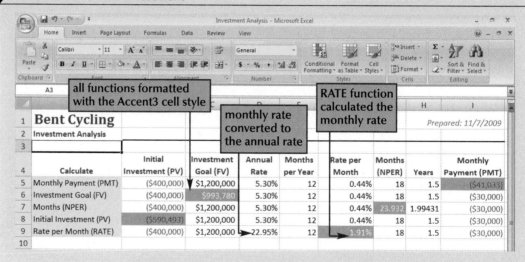

Based on your calculations, Diane needs an investment vehicle with an annual interest rate of 22.95% compounded monthly. Because no such investment opportunity is available at present, Diane decides that the company will borrow the money to fund the expansion.

Working with Loans and Mortgages

Diane asks you to determine how much it will cost Bent Cycling to borrow the entire $1,200,000 rather than dipping into its cash reserves. A local bank is willing to lend the entire amount at 9.5% annual interest compounded quarterly. Diane wants to pay back the loan in five years. She needs you to calculate how much each quarterly payment would be to repay the loan within the specified time.

Calculating a Loan Payment

The functions to work with loans are the same ones you used to work with investments. The only difference is the direction of the cash flow. When you borrow money, the money you receive represents a positive cash flow. As you repay the loan, each payment represents a negative cash flow as you are sending money back to the lending institution. Thus, to calculate the quarterly payment for the loan, you use the same PMT function you used to calculate the value of periodic deposits into an investment. Because the interest is compounded quarterly, the value of the *rate* argument is 9.5% divided by 4, or 2.375%. The value of the *nper* argument is 20, which is the total of quarterly payments for the 5-year period. The value of the *pv* argument is $1,200,000, the present value of the loan. The value is positive because it represents cash flowing to the company. The value of the *fv* argument is 0 because the company will repay the loan in full, making the future value of the loan 0 (that is, the company will not owe the bank anything at the end of the transaction). Using these values, the complete PMT function is:

```
=PMT(9.5%/4, 20, 1200000)
```

Note that this formula doesn't include a value for the optional *fv* argument. When omitted, Excel assumes a future value of 0, which is what you want for this calculation. You'll enter this function into the Loan Schedule worksheet.

To calculate the periodic payment for the loan:

▶ **1.** Switch to the **Loan Schedule** worksheet, and then, in cell A5, enter **$1,200,000**. The loan amount is entered as a positive cash flow because the money is flowing from the bank to Bent Cycling.

▶ **2.** In cell B5, enter **9.5%**, which is the annual interest rate. In cell C5, enter the value **4**, which is the number of quarters in the year.

▶ **3.** In cell D5, enter the formula **=B5/C5**, which divides the annual interest by 4 to calculate the quarterly interest rate of 0.02375, and then format cell D5 as a percentage with two decimal places. The quarterly interest rate is 2.38%.

▶ **4.** In cell E5, enter the value **20**, which is the number of quarterly payments needed to repay the loan.

▶ **5.** In cell F5, enter the formula **=E5/C5**, which divides the number of quarterly payments by 4 to calculate the number of years needed to repay the loan.

▶ **6.** In cell G5, enter the formula **=PMT(D5, E5, A5)**, and then decrease the decimal twice to format the value to the nearest dollar. The quarterly payment to repay a $1,200,000 loan (cell A5) in 20 quarters (cell E5) at a quarterly interest rate of 2.38% (cell D5) is $76,071. This value is negative because it represents a negative cash flow as money is being repaid from the company back to the bank. See Figure 9-7.

Figure 9-7 **Quarterly loan payment**

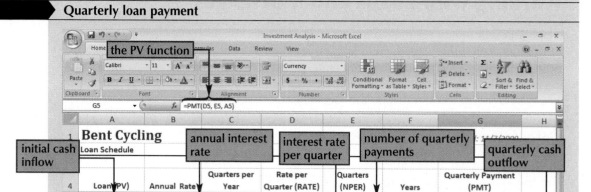

	Loan (PV)	Annual Rate	Quarters per Year	Rate per Quarter (RATE)	Quarters (NPER)	Years	Quarterly Payment (PMT)
5	$1,200,000	9.50%	4	2.38%	20	5	($76,071)

- the PV function
- initial cash inflow
- annual interest rate
- interest rate per quarter
- number of quarterly payments
- quarterly cash outflow

Based on these calculations, Bent Cycling could repay the loan in full with quarterly payments of $76,071 over the next five years. This is about $25,000 per month, which Diane believes the company can afford. After consulting with the management team, she tentatively approves the conditions of the loan, but she wants some more information.

Creating an Amortization Schedule

Diane wants to know how much of the $76,071 is being used to pay interest on the loan and how much is being used to repay the *principal*, which is the amount of the loan that is still unpaid. When paying off loans, the initial payments mostly pay the interest. As more and more of the loan is repaid, the percentage of each payment used for interest decreases (because less of the loan is left to charge interest upon) until the last few payments are used almost entirely for paying off the principal. Figure 9-8 shows a typical relationship between the amount paid toward interest and the amount paid toward the principal plotted against the number of payments.

Figure 9-8 **Interest and principal payments**

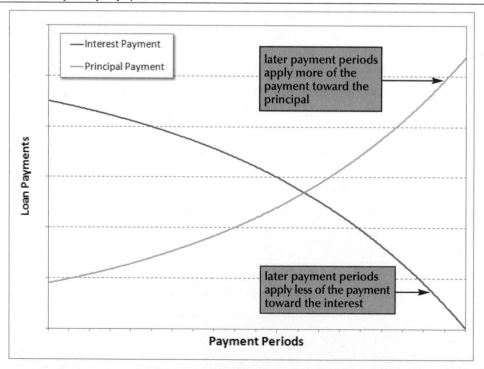

- later payment periods apply more of the payment toward the principal
- later payment periods apply less of the payment toward the interest

To calculate these values in Excel, you can use the IPMT and PPMT functions. The IPMT function returns the amount of a particular payment that is used to pay the interest on the loan and has the following syntax:

`=IPMT(rate, per, nper, pv, [fv=0] [,type=0])`

In this function, the *rate*, *nper*, *pv*, *fv*, and *type* arguments have the same meaning as they do for the PMT function. The *per* argument contains the period for which you want to calculate the interest due. For example, to calculate how much interest is due in the fifth payment of the $1,200,000 loan that Diane is contemplating, you enter the formula:

`=IPMT(9.5%/4, 5, 20, 1200000)`

Excel returns the value −$23,817.23, which means that about $24,000 in interest is paid to the bank in the fifth payment. Once again, the value of the *fv* argument was omitted because we assume that the loan is paid off in full.

The PPMT function, which calculates the amount used to pay off the principal, is similar. It has the following syntax:

`=PPMT(rate, per, nper, pv, [fv=0] [,type=0])`

Thus, to calculate the amount of the principal that is paid off with the fifth payment, you enter the formula:

`=PPMT(9.5%/4, 5, 20, 1200000)`

The formula returns the value −$52,253.34, which means the amount owed to the bank is reduced by about $52,000 after the fifth payment on the loan. The sum of the interest payment and the principal payment is −$76,070.78, which is the same value returned by the PMT function earlier. The total amount paid to the bank each month doesn't change, only how that amount is divided between paying the interest and paying off the principal.

Like the other financial functions already discussed, Excel automatically formats the value returned by the IPMT and PPMT functions in a currency format with negative values displayed in a red font and surrounded by parentheses.

Creating an Amortization Schedule | Reference Window

- To calculate the amount of interest due in a specified payment period from a loan, use the IPMT function.
- To calculate the amount of a loan payment used to pay off the principal of the loan, use the PPMT function.

One use of the IPMT and PPMT functions is to create an **amortization schedule**, which provides details about each loan payment, specifying how much of the payment is devoted toward interest and how much toward repaying the principal. Diane wants you to create an amortization schedule for the proposed loan. She's already created the structure of the schedule. You'll complete the table by entering the formulas to calculate the monthly payments on the loan's interest and principal.

To complete the amortization schedule:

▶ 1. Click cell **C9**, type **$1,200,000**, and then press the **Tab** key. Column C lists the amount of the principal remaining on the loan. The initial value in cell C9 is the amount of the loan.

In cell D9, you'll enter the amount of interest due during the first payment period. Because you'll copy this formula throughout the amortization schedule, it will use a combination of absolute and relative references. The absolute references all need to refer to the original conditions of the loan that remain unchanged throughout the entire amortization schedule. These are cells $D$5 (the interest rate per quarter), $E$5 (the total number of quarterly payments), and $A$5 (the present value of the loan). The relative reference needs to point to the number of the current payment period, listed in cell B9, because you want this value to change when you copy the formula to the remaining rows of the amortization schedule.

▶ 2. In cell D9, enter the formula **=IPMT($D$5, B9, $E$5, $A$5)**, and then press the **Tab** key. The formula returns the value ($28,500), indicating a negative cash flow in which $28,500 is spent on interest during the first period of the loan.

In cell E9, you'll calculate the amount of the payment that is directed toward reducing the principal. Again, you'll reference the conditions of the loan using absolute references and the payment period using a relative reference.

▶ 3. In cell E9, enter the formula **=PPMT($D$5, B9, $E$5, $A$5)**, and then press the **Tab** key. The formula returns the value ($47,571), indicating a negative cash flow, reducing the amount due on the loan by over $47,500 after the first quarterly payment.

▶ 4. In cell F9, enter the formula **=D9+E9** to calculate the total payment for the first period of the loan. The formula returns the value ($76,071), which matches the quarterly payment value shown in cell G5. See Figure 9-9.

| Figure 9-9 | Amortization schedule with the initial payment |

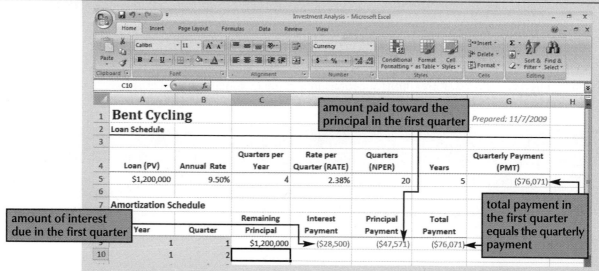

In the next quarter, the amount of the remaining principal is equal to the remaining principal from the previous quarter reduced by the amount paid toward the principal in the previous quarter.

▶ 5. In cell C10, enter the formula **=C9+E9**, and then press the **Tab** key. The formula returns the value $1,152,429, which is the amount of the principal remaining at the start of the second quarter of the loan.

▶ **6.** Copy the range **D9:F9** and paste the formulas into the range **D10:F10** to calculate the interest, principal, and total payment for the second period. Excel displays an interest payment value of ($27,370), a principal payment of ($48,700), and a total payment of ($76,071). The amount of interest due on the second period declined from the first period because the remaining principal is less. As a result, more of the total payment for this quarter can be used to reduce the amount of the remaining principal.

You will copy the formulas in the range C10:F10 into the rest of the rows of the amortization schedule to calculate the remaining principal, interest due, principal payment, and total payment for each of the 18 periods of the loan.

▶ **7.** Select the range **C10:F10**, and then drag the fill handle down to select the range **C10:F28**.

▶ **8.** Click the **Auto Fill Options** button 🔡, and then click the **Fill Without Formatting** option button. Excel enters the formulas without overwriting the existing formatting in the worksheet. See Figure 9-10.

Figure 9-10 **Complete amortization schedule**

	A	B	C	D	E	F	G	H
9	1	1	$1,200,000	($28,500)	($47,571)	($76,071)		
10	1	2	$1,152,429	($27,370)	($48,700)	($76,071)		
11	1	3	$1,103,729	($26,214)	($49,857)	($76,071)		
12	1	4	$1,053,872	($25,029)	($51,041)	($76,071)		
13	2	5	$1,002,831	($23,817)	($52,253)	($76,071)		
14	2	6	$950,578	($22,576)	($53,494)	($76,071)		
15	2	7	$897,083	($21,306)	($54,765)	($76,071)		
16	2	8	$842,318	($20,005)	($56,066)	($76,071)		
17	3	9	$786,253	($18,674)	($57,397)	($76,071)		
18	3	10	$728,856	($17,310)	($58,760)	($76,071)		
19	3	11	$670,096	($15,915)	($60,156)	($76,071)		
20	3	12	$609,940	($14,486)	($61,585)	($76,071)		
21	4	13	$548,355	($13,023)	($63,047)	($76,071)		
22	4	14	$485,308	($11,526)	($64,545)	($76,071)		
23	4	15	$420,764	($9,993)	($66,077)	($76,071)		
24	4	16	$354,686	($8,424)	($67,647)	($76,071)		
25	5	17	$287,039	($6,817)	($69,253)	($76,071)		
26	5	18	$217,786	($5,172)	($70,898)	($76,071)		
27	5	19	$146,888	($3,489)	($72,582)	($76,071)		
28	5	20	$74,306	($1,765)	($74,306)	($76,071)		
29								

amount of remaining principal equals the final principal payment

Auto Fill Options button

Documentation Investment Analysis Loan Schedule

Ready Average: $124,243 Count: 76 Sum: $9,442,435 120%

Tip

A whole table of red values enclosed in parentheses can be hard to read. Amortization schedules often format all entries as positive values, and then label the columns to indicate the values represent negative cash flows.

In the last quarterly payment at the end of the fifth year of the loan, only $1,765 of the $76,071 payment is used to pay the interest on the loan. The rest, $74,306, is used to pay the principal. The last principal payment is equal to the amount of the remaining principal. This is to be expected because the loan must be repaid completely.

Calculating Yearly Interest and Principal Payments

Diane appreciates seeing the breakdown of the quarterly payments in the amortization table. However, budgeting for the company is done annually, not quarterly. She also wants to know how much this proposed loan will cost the company in interest payments and principal payments during each of the next five years. This will help her estimate costs and make projections about taxes the company may owe during that time.

One way of calculating totals from several payment periods is to use the Analysis Tool-Pak add-in. The add-in contains two functions: CUMIPMT and CUMPRINC, which calculate the total interest and principal payments between two periods. You'll learn more about installing and activating add-ins in the next tutorial.

The CUMIPMT function has the following syntax:

```
=CUMIPMT(rate, nper, pv, start, end, type)
```

In this function, *rate* is the interest rate per period, *nper* is the total number of payment periods, *pv* is the present value of the loan, *start* is the starting payment period for the interval you want to sum, *end* is the ending payment period, and *type* defines whether the payments are made at the beginning or end of each period. This function has no *fv* argument, so the assumption is that loans are always completely paid off and that the *type* argument is not optional as it is with the financial functions you used earlier. If you want to calculate the total interest payments of the loan in the first year, or first four quarters, you enter the following formula:

```
=CUMIPMT(9.5%/4, 20, 1200000, 1, 4, 0)
```

Excel returns the value –$107,113.22, which is the total interest payments made during the first through fourth periods of the loan. To calculate the total payments made toward the principal, you use the CUMPRINC function, which has the following syntax:

```
=CUMPRINC(rate, nper, pv, start, end, type)
```

In this function, the *rate, nper, pv, start, end,* and *type* arguments are the same as with the CUMIPMT function. So, to calculate the total amount paid toward the principal during the first four quarters of the loan, you enter the following formula:

```
=CUMPRINC(9.5%/4, 20, 1200000, 1, 4, 0)
```

Excel returns the value –$197,169.08. Note that unlike the other financial functions, the CUMIPMT and CUMPRINC functions do not automatically format the returned values as cash flows.

The CUMIPMT and CUMPRINC functions require that the Analysis ToolPak add-in is installed and activated. Because Diane plans to share this workbook with several users, she does not want to make that a requirement before people can view the analysis of the proposed loan. Another approach that doesn't require the use of an add-in is to simply add the appropriate cells from the amortization schedule you created. You can calculate this sum using the Subtotal command located in the Outline group on the Data tab, but Diane wants this information in a separate table. To place calculations in a separate table, you use the SUMIF function.

The SUMIF function adds a range of data matching a specified criterion. The syntax of the SUMIF function is:

```
=SUMIF(range, criteria, [sum_range])
```

where *range* is the cells to be evaluated by the criteria, *criteria* is a value or text expression that the cells in *range* must match, and *sum_range* are the actual cells to add if their corresponding cells in *range* match the criteria. The *sum_range* argument is optional. If you don't include it, Excel will add the values specified in the *range* argument.

Figure 9-11 shows a simple example of using the SUMIF function to add values. In this example, only values whose corresponding cell in the range A2:A10 equals "A" are added. The total of those cells is 28, which is the sum of the values in cells B2, B5, B6, and B9.

SUMIF function   **Figure 9-11**

SUMIF function adds only cells whose criteria value equals "A"

You'll use this SUMIF function to calculate the yearly interest and principal payment totals in the table that Diane set up in the Loan Schedule worksheet.

To calculate the total yearly payments:

▶ 1. Click cell **B32**, and then, on the formula bar, click the **Insert Function** button ▣. The Insert Function dialog box opens. You'll search for the SUMIF function.

▶ 2. In the Search for a function box, type **SUMIF**, click the **Go** button, and then, in the Select a function box, double-click **SUMIF**. The Function Arguments dialog box opens.

▶ 3. With the Range box active, select the range **A9:A28**. This range contains the year values for each of the 20 periodic payments. Because you will copy this formula to other cells in the table, you need to use an absolute reference rather than a relative reference.

▶ 4. In the Range box, select the range reference **A9:A28**, and then press the **F4** key. The range reference changes to $A$9:$A$28.

   The next argument in the list is the Criteria argument. For cell B32, you want to add the interest payments for the first year—the year with the value *1*. Rather than entering the value, you'll reference cell B31, which already contains a 1, so you can copy this formula to other cells. Because different columns refer to different years, you'll enter a relative reference.

▶ 5. Press the **Tab** key to move the insertion point to the Criteria box, type **B31**, and then press the **Tab** key. The insertion point moves to the Sum_range box.

   The final argument is the Sum_range argument. For this argument, you want to add the interest payments found within the range D9:D28.

▶ **6.** Select the range **D9:D28**. Excel inserts the range reference D9:D28 into the Sum_range box.

▶ **7.** In the Sum_range box, select the range reference **D9:D28**, and then press the **F4** key. The range reference changes to the absolute reference $D$9:$D$28. See Figure 9-12.

| Figure 9-12 | Function Arguments dialog box for the SUMIF function |

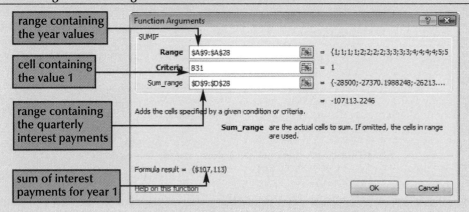

range containing the year values

cell containing the value 1

range containing the quarterly interest payments

sum of interest payments for year 1

▶ **8.** Click the **OK** button. The value ($107,113) appears in cell B32. The total amount of interest paid during the first year of the loan is more than $107,000.

Next, you'll calculate the total principal payments for Year 1.

▶ **9.** In cell B33, enter the formula **=SUMIF($A$9:$A$28, B31, $E$9:$E$28)**. This formula is the same as the one you entered in cell B32, except that now the totals added are from the range $E$9:$E$28, which contains the principal payments. The value ($197,169) appears in cell B33. This is the amount by which the principal will be reduced during Year 1 of the loan.

Next, you'll calculate the total of the interest and principal payments.

▶ **10.** In cell B34, enter the formula **=B32+B33**. The resulting value ($304,282) is the total amount Bent Cycling will pay on the loan in the first year.

You'll copy the formulas from the range B32:B34 into the cells for the remaining four years of the loan. Because you used absolute references for the list of year numbers and the interest and principal payments and a relative reference for the year number, the pasted formulas will correctly calculate these values in the other four years.

▶ **11.** Copy the range **B32:B34** and paste it into the range **C32:F34**. The total payments for each year is $304,282, even though the amount paid on interest steadily declines from Year 2 through Year 5. Review the formulas in the range C32:F34 to see how the SUMIF function calculated the interest and principal payments for each year.

Finally, you'll calculate the total spent on interest and principal payments through the five years of the loan.

▶ **12.** Select the range **G32:G34**, in the Editing group on the Home tab, click the **Sum** button Σ, and then click cell **A30** to deselect the range. See Figure 9-13.

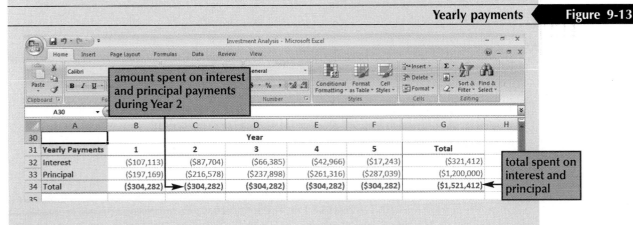

Yearly payments | **Figure 9-13**

▶ **13.** Save and close the workbook.

Notice that the total paid on the principal in cell G33 is $1,200,000, which is expected given that the loan is completely repaid at the end of the five years. However, the total spent on the loan is $1,521,412, which means that Bent Cycling will pay $321,412 in interest to finance the expansion. Whether this is a wise investment depends on how much extra revenue the company can generate by the proposed building project. In the next session, you'll make projections about the company's future earnings assuming that they do finance the expansion.

Tips on Financial Functions | InSight

Financial functions are one of the most important tools in Excel. To properly use financial functions, keep in mind the following:

- Place all important financial variables at or near the top of a worksheet in plain view. For example, place the interest rate you use in calculations in a well-labeled worksheet cell.
- Use range names with the financial variables to make it easier to apply them in formulas and functions.
- Be aware of cash flow issues. Most Excel financial functions require a particular direction to the cash flow to return the correct value. Using the wrong sign will turn the calculation of a loan payment into an investment deposit or vice versa.
- Never place argument values directly into a financial formula. Instead, place these values in worksheet cells where they can be viewed and easily changed.
- Make sure the arguments in a financial function are measured in the same unit of time. For example, when using the PMT function to calculate monthly loan payments, the interest rate and the number of payments should be based on the interest rate per month and the total months to pay off the loan.

Session 9.1 Quick Check | Review

1. Explain the difference between positive and negative cash flow. If you borrow $100 from a bank, is that a positive or negative cash flow? Justify your answer.
2. Use Excel to calculate how much a savings account would be worth if the initial balance is $500 and you deposit $50 per month for 10 years at 5.8% annual interest compounded monthly.

3. You want a savings account to grow from $1000 to $3000 within two years. Assume the bank provides a 5.2% annual interest rate compounded monthly. Calculate how much you have to deposit each month to meet your savings goal.

4. You want to take out a loan for $200,000 at 7% interest compounded monthly. If you can afford to make monthly payments of only $1500 on the loan, how many months will it take you to pay off the loan completely?

5. Rerun your calculations from the previous question assuming that you can afford only a $1000 monthly payment. What value does Excel return? How do you explain the result?

6. You take out a loan for $200,000. The loan must be repaid in 10 years with quarterly payments of $7200. Under those terms, what is the annual interest rate of the loan?

7. You take out a 10-year loan for $150,000 at 6.3% interest compounded monthly. What is the monthly payment? How much of the first payment is used for interest and how much is used to pay off the principal?

8. The range A2:A100 contains the last names of contributors to a charitable fund. The range B2:B100 contains the value of each contribution. What formula calculates the total contributions made by people with the last name "Harris"?

Session 9.2

Projecting Future Income and Expenses

Diane has reviewed the costs associated with the proposed loan and is concerned Bent Cycling will pay more than $320,000 in interest payments by the time the loan is repaid. She wants to know how this additional expense will affect the company's income over the next five years. To provide her with an answer, you'll complete an income statement to project the company's future income. An **income statement**, also known as a **profit and loss statement**, shows how much money a business makes or loses over a specified period of time. Income statements are often created monthly, semiannually, or annually. Diane is interested only in annual projections. She already created the layout for the projected income statement in an Excel workbook that you'll use as a starting point for your analysis.

To open the income statement workbook:

▶ 1. Open the **Income** workbook located in the **Tutorial.09\Tutorial** folder included with your Data Files, and then save the workbook as **Income Projection** in the same folder.

▶ 2. In the Documentation sheet, enter your name in cell B3 and the date in cell B4.

▶ 3. Switch to the **Income Statement** worksheet.

The Income Statement worksheet contains columns for income and expense projections over the next five years. The statement is divided into five sections. The first section displays the gross profit the company is anticipated to make during each of the next five years. The second section displays the company's annual general expenses. The third section displays the company's annual operating profit, which is the difference between the gross profit and total general expenses and depreciation of tangible assets. The fourth section projects the company's annual earnings before taxes. The fifth and last section projects the company's net income, which is the income it generates after all expenses and taxes have been accounted for. To begin completing this income statement, you'll examine different ways of projecting the company's gross profit over the next five years.

Linear and Growth Trends

Diane has already projected $3,200,000 in revenue for the first year of the company's next five years. She believes that with growing interest in recumbents and the company's expansion of its production facilities, the company's Year 1 revenue will double by the end of Year 5. She's unsure what will happen between Years 1 and 5. She sees two possibilities: (1) revenues will grow by a constant amount from year to year, or (2) revenues will grow by a constant percentage each year.

Diane's first possibility, in which the values change by a constant amount, is an example of a **linear trend**. When plotted, a linear trend appears as a straight line. The second possibility is an example of a **growth trend**, in which the values change not by a constant amount but by a constant percentage. For example, each value might be 15% higher or 1.15 times greater than the previous value in the series. When plotted, a growth trend appears as a curve with the greatest increases occurring near the end of the series. Figure 9-14 shows an example of these two trends. The growth trend lags substantially behind the linear trend in the early stages but reaches the same stopping value.

Tip

Growth trend calculations are also called *exponential growth trends* or *exponential trends* in the fields of economics and statistics.

Comparison of linear and growth trends ◄ **Figure 9-14**

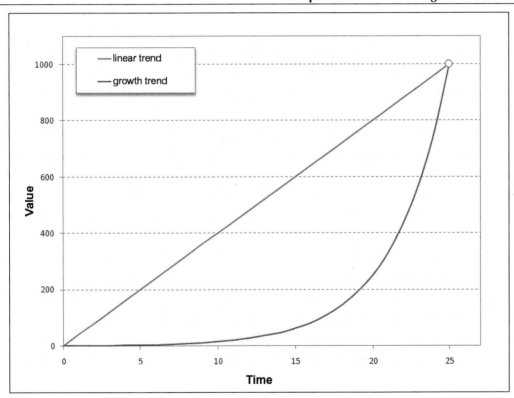

Interpolating a Trend

If you know the beginning and ending values in a series and the series trend, you can fill in the missing values through **interpolation**. In this case, you know that the initial projection for revenue is $3,200,000 and the final projection in Year 5 is double that, or $6,400,000. You'll fill in the remaining values by interpolation based on a linear trend.

To project the company's future revenue based on a linear trend:

▶ 1. In cell B7, enter **3,200,000**, which is the projected revenue for the first of the next five years. In cell F7, enter **6,400,000**, which is a doubling of the company's revenue by the end of the five-year period.

▶ 2. Select the range **B7:F7**. In the Editing group on the Home tab, click the **Fill** button ▣▾, and then click **Series**. The Series dialog box opens.

▶ 3. Verify that the **Rows** option button and the **Linear** option button are selected, and then click the **Trend** check box to insert a check mark.

▶ 4. Click the **OK** button.

Excel interpolates a linear trend for the revenue figures, projecting an increase of $800,000 per year from Year 1 through Year 5. Next, you'll interpolate the revenue figures based on a growth trend. To interpolate the growth trend correctly, you must remove the Year 2 through Year 4 values, leaving those cells blank.

▶ 5. Delete the values in the range **C7:E7**.

▶ 6. Select the range **B7:F7**, click the **Fill** button in the Editing group, and then click **Series**. The Series dialog box opens.

▶ 7. In the Type section, click the **Growth** option button, click the **Trend** check box to insert a check mark, and then click the **OK** button. Excel fills in the Year 1 through Year 5 revenue projections based on a growth trend. See Figure 9-15.

Tip

To interpolate a series, the cells between the first and last cells in the series must be blank.

| Figure 9-15 | Projected revenues based on a growth trend |

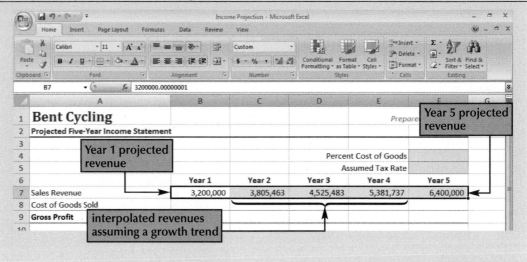

Under the growth trend projections, the largest increases in revenue occur near the end of the five-year period. For example, the revenue grows by more than $600,000 from Year 1 to Year 2, but by more than $1,000,000 from Year 4 to Year 5. If you were to calculate the percentage change in revenue from year to year under the growth trend projection, rather than the absolute change in dollars, you would find that the revenue is projected to increase by 19% each year. Diane thinks that the projections based on a growth trend are more likely and asks you to use those figures in your income statement calculations.

The next part of the income statement displays the **cost of goods sold** in which costs are directly related to production. Bent Cycling needs to purchase basic parts and raw materials to manufacture recumbents. The more recumbents the company builds, the more parts and materials it must purchase, increasing the cost to the company. The difference between the company's sales revenue and the cost of goods sold is the company's **gross profit**.

Based on past experience, Diane knows that for every dollar of sales revenue the company makes selling its product, it has to spend 72 cents to cover the cost of production. In other words, the cost of goods is about 72% of the revenue generated. You can use this information to project the cost of goods sold for each of the next five years.

To project the cost of goods sold:

▶ **1.** In cell F4, enter **72%**. This is the cost of goods percentage.

▶ **2.** In cell B8, enter the formula **=B7*$F$4**. This formula multiplies projected sales revenue by the cost of goods percentage to calculate the projected cost of goods sold, which is 2,304,000 for Year 1.

▶ **3.** In cell B9, enter the formula **=B7–B8**. This formula subtracts the cost of goods sold from the sales revenue to project a gross profit of 896,000 for Year 1.

▶ **4.** Format the value in cell B9 using the Accounting number format with no decimal places.

▶ **5.** Copy the range **B8:B9** to the range **C8:F9** to project the cost of goods sold and gross profit for each of the next five years. See Figure 9-16.

Projected gross profit   Figure 9-16

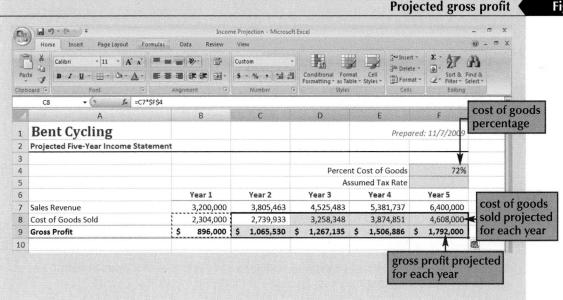

Reference Window | **Interpolating and Extrapolating**

To interpolate a series of values between starting and ending values:
- Select the range with the first cell containing the starting value, blank cells for middle values, and the last cell containing the ending value.
- In the Editing group on the Home tab, click the Fill button, and then click Series.
- Specify whether the series is organized in rows or columns and the type of series to interpolate. Check the Trend check box.
- Click the OK button to insert the interpolated series into the middle cells.

To extrapolate a series from a starting value:
- Select a range with the first cell containing the starting value followed by blank cells to store the extrapolated values.
- In the Editing group on the Home tab, click the Fill button, and then click Series.
- Select whether the series is organized in rows or columns. Select the type of series to extrapolate into the blank cells. Enter the step value in the Step value box.
- Click the OK button to insert the extrapolated series into the blank cells.

Extrapolating a Trend

The next section of the income statement contains the projected general expenses for the company. These are expenses not directly related to production. For example, Bent Cycling has to purchase insurance, provide for general maintenance and utilities, and pay for advertising regardless of the number of bikes it actually sells. Diane has projected values for Year 1 that she wants you to enter into the worksheet.

To enter the Year 1 general expenses:

▶ 1. In cell B11, enter **7,000**. In cell B12, enter **21,000**. In cell B13, enter **2,000**. In cell B14, enter **4,800**. In cell B15, enter **7,600**. In cell B16, enter **2,400**.

▶ 2. In cell B17, enter **=SUM(B11:B16)** to calculate the total general expenses for Year 1, which is 44,800.

▶ 3. Use the Format Painter to copy the formatting from cell **B9** to cell **B17**, displaying the total general expenses in the Accounting number format with no decimal places.

Diane does not have an expectation for the Year 5 expenses, but she estimates that with the proposed expansion the expenses will increase by about 15% per year. This is equivalent to multiplying the expense values by 1.15 each year. To calculate a series of values from a starting point without a defined ending point, you have to **extrapolate** the values. As with interpolation, you can extrapolate a series of values from the Series dialog box. You'll extrapolate each expense category over the next five years, assuming a growth trend in which the expenses increase by 15% each year.

To extrapolate the Year 1 expenses through the next four years:

▶ 1. Select the range **B11:F16**.

▶ 2. In the Editing group on the Home tab, click the **Fill** button 🔽, and then click **Series**. The Series dialog box opens.

▶ 3. Click the **Rows** option button because you want to create a series of values in the rows of the selected range.

4. Click the **Growth** option button, enter **1.15** in the Step value box, and then click the **OK** button. Excel extrapolates the expense values from Year 1 into the Year 2 through Year 5 columns.

5. Copy the formula in cell **B17** into the range **C17:F17** to project the total general expenses for the company for each year.

6. In cell B19, enter the formula **=B9-B17** to calculate an initial estimate of the yearly earnings, which is equal to the gross profit minus the total general expenses. This value is 851,200 for Year 1.

7. Copy the formula in cell **B19** into the range **C19:F19**. See Figure 9-17.

Tip

When you extrapolate a series, the Step value represents the amount that each value is increased or multiplied as the series is extended. You do not have to specify a stopping value.

Total general expenses and earnings ◀ **Figure 9-17**

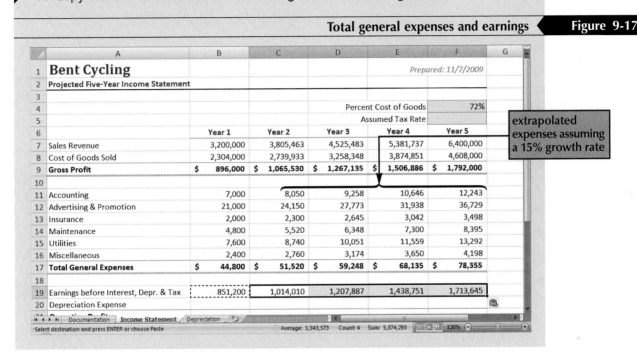

You calculated an initial estimate for the company's earnings over the next five years. The remaining parts of the income statement estimate the company's yearly taxes, because the effect of taxes must also be included in any projection of future income. First, you'll consider the effect of depreciation on the company's reported income.

Working with Depreciation

The financial status of a company includes information about the company's tangible possessions. Bent Cycling owns items such as equipment, land, buildings, and delivery trucks. These combined assets are known as **tangible assets** because they are long-lasting assets not intended for sale. Not all materials are tangible assets. For example, assets such as the raw materials the company uses to manufacture bikes are not considered tangible assets because they are used in the production process and are sold directly or indirectly to the consumer in the form of a finished project.

To calculate Bent Cycling's tax liability, you subtract any expenses the company incurs from the revenue it generates. However, the cost of the building project is neither an income nor an expense. It's an investment in a tangible asset that will be used for many years to generate revenue for the company. Tax rules allow the original cost of the investment to be subtracted from the company's reported income, reducing the company's tax liability. In many cases, however, the entire cost of the investment is not reported at once.

Tip

To project a trend that decreases rather than increases, use a step value of less than 0 for a linear trend and between 0 and 1 for a growth trend.

Instead, the original cost is allocated over the years in which the product is used. For example, instead of deducting the entire $1,200,000 from the company reported income, the company might only be able to deduct $100,000 per year for the next 12 years from its reported income.

This process of allocating the original cost of the investment over the years of use is known as **depreciation**. Different types of tangible assets have different rules for depreciation. However, in general, to calculate the depreciation of an asset, you need to know the following about the asset:

- The asset's original cost
- The asset's useful life
- The asset's **salvage value** (the value at the end of the asset's useful life)
- The rate at which the asset is depreciated over time

You already know the cost of the new workshop and design facility is $1,200,000. Given how quickly technology changes in bicycle design and manufacturing, Diane puts the useful life of the new facility and its equipment at 15 years. After 15 years, she assumes the company will require another substantial upgrade of its facilities. When that day comes, Diane estimates the salvage value of the old workshop to be one-third of its current value, or $400,000. You'll enter this information in the Depreciation worksheet.

To insert the depreciation parameters:

▶ **1.** Switch to the **Depreciation** worksheet.

▶ **2.** In cell B4, enter **$1,200,000**. This is the asset's initial value.

▶ **3.** In cell B5, enter **$400,000**. This is the asset's estimated salvage value.

▶ **4.** In cell B6, enter **15**. This is the projected useful life of the asset in years.

The only thing remaining is to determine how quickly the new facility depreciates from its original cost of $1,200,000 to $400,000. Excel has several financial functions to model this action.

Reference Window | **Calculating Depreciation**

- To calculate a straight-line depreciation, use the SLN function.
- To calculate a declining balance depreciation, use the DB function.
- To calculate a sum-of-years' digit depreciation, use the SYD function.
- To calculate a double-declining balance depreciation, use the DDB function.
- To calculate a variable depreciation, use the VBD function.

Straight-Line Depreciation

With **straight-line depreciation**, the asset depreciates by equal amounts each year of its lifetime until it reaches the salvage value. You can calculate this annual depreciation by dividing the total depreciation of the asset by the number of years the asset is used. Based on Diane's numbers, the new workshop will depreciate $800,000 in 15 years, which is a straight-line depreciation of $53,333.33 per year. If you don't want to do this calculation manually, you can use the SLN function to calculate the yearly straight-line depreciation. The SLN function has the following syntax:

```
=SLN(cost, salvage, life)
```

In this function, *cost* is the initial cost or value of the asset, *salvage* is the salvage value of the asset at the end of its useful life, and *life* is the number of years the asset will be used. To calculate the annual straight-line depreciation for Bent Cycling's new workshop, you enter the formula:

=SLN(1200000, 400000, 15)

Excel returns the value $53,333.33. You'll enter this function to calculate the annual depreciation of the new workshop, the cumulative depreciation that will take place over the next five years, and the depreciated value of the workshop for each of the next five years.

To calculate the straight-line depreciation of the workshop:

1. In cell B10, enter the formula **=SLN($B$4,$B$5,$B$6)** to calculate the straight-line depreciation for Year 1. You used absolute references so the cells won't change when you copy the formula. Excel returns the value $53,333, which is the annual depreciation of this asset.

2. Copy the formula in cell **B10** to the range **C10:F10**. Because this is a straight-line depreciation, the asset depreciates the same amount each year.

3. In cell B11, enter the formula **=B10**, which displays the depreciation for the first year.

4. In cell C11, enter the formula **=C10+B11** to calculate the cumulative depreciation of the asset through the first two years.

5. Copy the formula in cell **C11** to the range **D11:F11** to calculate the cumulative depreciation of the asset over all five of the years. At the end of Year 5, the asset will have depreciated $266,667.

6. In cell B12, enter the formula **=$B$4–B11**, and then copy the formula in cell **B12** to the range **C12:F12** to calculate the depreciated value of the asset at the end of each of the five years by subtracting the value of the cumulative depreciation from the asset's original cost. See Figure 9-18.

Straight-line depreciation of the workshop | **Figure 9-18**

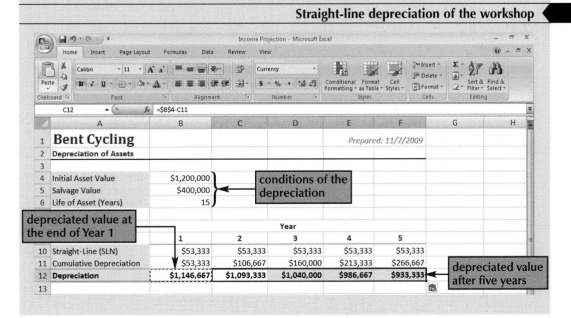

Tip

You can estimate straight-line depreciation by using AutoFill to interpolate the linear trend using the initial value of the asset as the starting value and the salvage value as the stopping value.

Based on a straight-line depreciation, the new workshop's depreciated value will be more than $930,000 at the end of Year 5. In other words, about 78% of the original cost of the new facility could still be depreciated after the fifth year.

Declining Balance Depreciation

Another way to calculate depreciation is to use **declining balance depreciation**, in which the asset depreciates by a constant percentage each year rather than a constant amount. The depreciation value is highest early in its lifetime, so that is also when the highest declines occur. As the asset loses value, the depreciation amounts steadily decrease, though the percentage decrease remains the same. Figure 9-19 compares the straight-line and declining balance depreciation for an asset over a 20-year lifetime.

Figure 9-19	Straight-line and declining balance depreciation

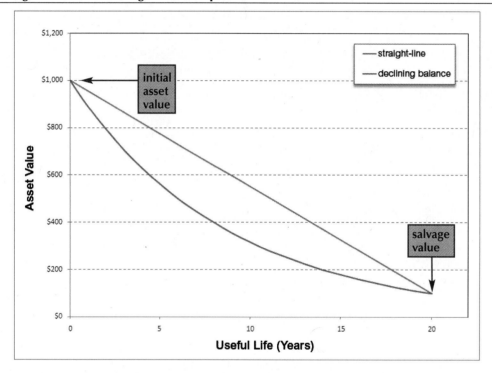

As is clear from Figure 9-19, depreciation under the declining balance model occurs more quickly than under the straight-line model. The DB function to calculate the declining balance depreciation has the following syntax:

```
=DB(cost, salvage, life, period [month])
```

In this function, *cost*, *salvage*, and *life* are again the initial cost, salvage cost, and lifetime of the asset, and *period* is the period for which you want to calculate the depreciation. If you are calculating depreciation on a yearly basis, then the *period* argument would contain the year value of the depreciation. For example, to calculate the depreciation of the new workshop during the third year of its use, you enter the following formula:

```
=DB(1200000, 400000, 15, 3)
```

The formula returns the value $237,882, indicating that the asset will depreciate by almost $240,000 during the third year of its use. The DB function also supports an optional *month* argument, which is needed when the asset is used for only part of the first year. For example, if you are depreciating an asset for only two months of the first year, you would set the value of the *month* parameter to 2.

Diane also wants you to calculate a depreciation schedule based on the declining balance assumption.

To calculate declining balance depreciation:

▶ 1. In cell B14, enter the formula **=DB($B$4, $B$5, $B$6, B9)** to calculate the declining balance depreciation for Year 1. The formula returns $85,200, indicating the new workshop will depreciate by more than $85,000 within its first year of operation. Note that you use the cell reference B9 to reference the year value.

▶ 2. Copy the formula in cell **B14** to the range **C14:F14** to calculate the depreciation for each of the remaining four years. The amount of depreciation decreases each year under the declining balance schedule.

▶ 3. Copy the range **B11:F12** and paste to the range **B15:F16** to calculate the cumulative depreciation and depreciation value.

▶ 4. Click cell **A9** to deselect the range. Figure 9-20 shows the depreciation, cumulative depreciation, and depreciated value for Years 1 through 5.

Estimating the declining balance depreciation | Figure 9-20

	A	B	C	D	E	F	G	H
1	**Bent Cycling**				*Prepared: 11/7/2009*			
2	Depreciation of Assets							
3								
4	Initial Asset Value	$1,200,000						
5	Salvage Value	$400,000						
6	Life of Asset (Years)	15						
7								
8				Year				
9		1	2	3	4	5		
10	Straight-Line (SLN)	$53,333	$53,333	$53,333	$53,333	$53,333		
11	Cumulative Depreciation	$53,333	$106,667	$160,000	$213,333	$266,667		
12	Depreciation	$1,146,667	$1,093,333	$1,040,000	$986,667	$933,333		
13								
14	Declining Balance (DB)	$85,200	$79,151	$73,531	$68,310	$63,460		
15	Cumulative Depreciation	$85,200	$164,351	$237,882	$306,192	$369,653		
16	Depreciation	$1,114,800	$1,035,649	$962,118	$893,808	$830,347		
17								

Based on a declining balance depreciation, the depreciated value of the new workshop declines to a little more than $830,000 after five years. Although the amount of depreciation changes from year to year, you can verify that the asset decreases at a constant 7.1% rate from one year to another. If you use these figures in the projected income statement, you would be assuming that the workshop depreciates more quickly than under the straight-line depreciation method.

Other Depreciation Options

There are other ways to estimate depreciation besides straight-line and declining balance. Excel supports five functions to calculate depreciation under different assumptions. Figure 9-21 summarizes all of the Excel depreciation functions.

Figure 9-21 | **Excel depreciation functions**

Function	Description
SLN(cost, salvage, life)	Returns the straight-line depreciation in which the asset declines by a constant amount each year, where *cost* is the initial cost of the asset, *salvage* is the salvage value, and *life* is the useful lifetime of the asset.
DB(cost, salvage, life, period [month])	Returns the declining balance depreciation in which the asset declines by a constant percentage each year, where *period* is the year of the depreciation and *month* is an optional argument that defines the number of months that assets were owned during Year 1.
SYD(cost, salvage, life, period)	Returns the sum-of-years' digit depreciation that results in a more accelerated depreciation than straight-line depreciation, but less than declining balance depreciation.
DDB(cost, salvage, life, period [factor=2])	Returns the double declining balance depreciation that doubles the depreciation under the straight-line method and applies that accelerated rate to the original asset value minus the cumulative depreciation. The *factor* argument specifies the factor by which the straight-line depreciation is multiplied. If no *factor* is specified, a factor of 2 (for doubling) is assumed.
VDB(cost, salvage, life, start, end, [factor=2] [no_switch=FALSE])	Returns a variable declining depreciation for any specified period using any specified depreciation method, where *start* is the starting period of the depreciation, *end* is the ending period, *factor* is the rate at which the depreciation declines, and *no_switch* specifies whether to switch to the straight-line method when the depreciation falls below the estimate given by the declining balance method.

InSight | **Choosing a Depreciation Schedule**

Which method of depreciation is the most appropriate? The answer depends on the type of asset being depreciated. Tax laws allow different depreciation methods for different kinds of assets and different situations. In general, you want to choose the depreciation method that most accurately describes the financial status of the company. In tax statements, depreciation appears as an expense that is subtracted from the company's earnings. So, if you accelerate the depreciation of an asset in the early years of use, you might be underestimating the company's profits, making it appear that the company is less profitable than it actually is. On the other hand, depreciating an asset slowly could make it appear that the company is more profitable than it really is. For this reason, the choice of a depreciation method is best left to a tax accountant, fully aware of the financial issues and the tax laws involved in depreciating an asset.

Now that you have an estimate of the depreciation of the proposed building project, you can add this information to the income statement. Diane's main concern is to get a general picture of the depreciation of the proposed expansion and its impact on the company's income over the next five years. Diane suggests that you use the straight-line depreciation method.

To include depreciation in the income statement:

▶ **1.** Switch to the **Income Statement** worksheet.

▶ **2.** Click cell **B20**, and type **=** to begin the formula. You want to use the value in cell B10 of the Depreciation worksheet.

▶ **3.** Click the **Depreciation** sheet tab, click cell **B10**, and then press the **Enter** key to enter the formula =Depreciation!B10. The depreciation expense for Year 1 is 53,333.

▶ **4.** Copy cell **B20**, and then paste the formula into the range **C20:F20**. The depreciation expense for each of the five years is entered in the income statement.

▶ **5.** In cell B21, enter the formula **=B19–B20**. This formula calculates the operating profit for the company, which is the company's initial earnings estimate reduced by the amount of the depreciation of its assets during the year.

▶ **6.** Copy the formula in cell **B21** to the range **C21:F21** to calculate the operating profit for each of the five years, and then use the Format Painter to copy the format from the range **B17:F17** to the range **B21:F21**. The projected operating profit of the company is $797,867 in Year 1 of the proposed expansion, rising to $1,660,311 at the end of the fifth year. See Figure 9-22.

Depreciation and operating profit for Years 1 through 5   **Figure 9-22**

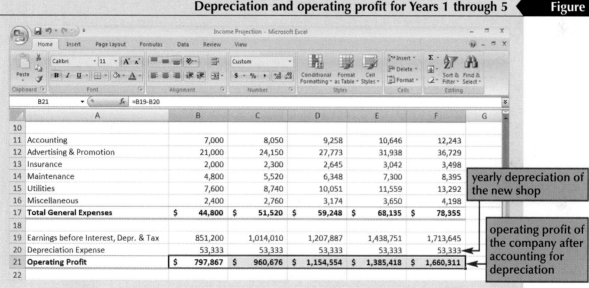

The next part of the income statement details the company's expense from the interest payments on the $1,200,000 loan. You calculated these values at the end of the previous session in the Loan Analysis worksheet. You'll enter the yearly interest payments now.

To deduct the interest payment from the operating profit:

▶ **1.** In cell B23, enter **107,113**. In cell C23, enter **87,704**. In cell D23, enter **66,385**. In cell E23, enter **42,966**. In cell F23, enter **17,243**.

The next row of the table displays the taxable income, which is calculated by deducting the interest payments from the operating profit.

▶ **2.** In cell B24, enter the formula **=B21–B23**. Excel returns $690,754, which is the taxable income for the company at the end of Year 1.

3. Copy the formula in cell **B24** to the range **C24:F24**. The taxable income at the end of Year 5 is $1,643,068.

4. Use the Format Painter to copy the format from the range **B21:F21** to the range **B24:F24**.

To conclude the income statement, you enter the amount of taxes the company will pay during each of the next five years and subtract this amount from the taxable income. The final row of the income statement displays the company's **net income**, which is the company's income after all expenses and taxes have been paid. Diane is most interested in this value because it provides a measure of the company's bottom line.

Approximately one-third of the company's taxable income is paid toward taxes. So, for the purposes of this projected income statement, you'll assume a 33% tax rate for each of the five years.

To calculate the taxes and net income:

1. In cell F5, enter **33%**. This is the tax rate you'll use to calculate the taxes.

2. In cell B26, enter the formula **=B24*$F$5** to multiply the earnings before taxes in Year 1 by the tax rate. The estimated tax is 227,949, indicating that the company can expect to pay almost $230,000 in taxes during Year 1.

3. Copy cell **B26**, and then paste the formula into the range **C26:F26**. At the end of the fifth year, the company's tax burden is estimated to be $542,213.

In the final row of the income statement, you'll calculate the net income.

4. In cell B27, enter the formula **=B24–B26** to calculate the net income by subtracting the estimated tax from the earnings before taxes.

5. Copy the formula from cell **B27** into the range **C27:F27**, use the Format Painter to copy the format from the range **B24:F24** to the range **B27:F27**, and then click cell **A28** to deselect the range. See Figure 9-23.

Figure 9-23   **Final income statement**

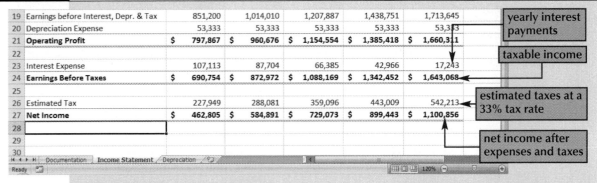

19	Earnings before Interest, Depr. & Tax	851,200	1,014,010	1,207,887	1,438,751	1,713,645	yearly interest payments
20	Depreciation Expense	53,333	53,333	53,333	53,333	53,333	
21	Operating Profit	$ 797,867	$ 960,676	$ 1,154,554	$ 1,385,418	$ 1,660,311	
22							taxable income
23	Interest Expense	107,113	87,704	66,385	42,966	17,243	
24	Earnings Before Taxes	$ 690,754	$ 872,972	$ 1,088,169	$ 1,342,452	$ 1,643,068	
25							estimated taxes at a 33% tax rate
26	Estimated Tax	227,949	288,081	359,096	443,009	542,213	
27	Net Income	$ 462,805	$ 584,891	$ 729,073	$ 899,443	$ 1,100,856	
28							net income after expenses and taxes
29							
30							

Documentation / Income Statement / Depreciation

Ready   120%

6. Save and close the workbook.

You report to Diane that if the company's revenues grow at the rate she projected and if her estimate of expenses is accurate, the company's net income will rise from $462,805 in Year 1 to $1,100,856 at the end of Year 5. This represents about a 138% increase in net income over the five-year period. Of course, this rough estimate will no doubt change as Diane revises the estimates of the company's sales revenue, expenses, and tax liability; but it gives Diane a starting point when considering the future income of her company.

As Diane continues to explore the feasibility of the building project, she still wonders whether it represents a good financial investment and how it would relate to other ways of investing the company's money. You'll explore this question in the next session using another set of financial functions.

Session 9.2 Quick Check | Review

1. The first value in a linear trend is 1000. The fifth value is 4000. What are the values of the second, third, and fourth items?
2. Repeat Question 1, assuming a growth trend.
3. The first value in a series is 1000. Extrapolate the next four values assuming a linear trend of 500.
4. Repeat Question 3, assuming a growth trend in which the next four values increase by 15% each time.
5. A new business buys $25,000 worth of computer equipment. If the useful life of the equipment is 5 years with a salvage value of $2000, how much will the equipment depreciate per year, assuming a straight-line depreciation?
6. Repeat Question 5 assuming a declining balance depreciation and calculate how much the equipment depreciates in the first year.
7. Repeat Question 5 assuming double-declining balance depreciation with a factor of 2, once again calculating how much the equipment depreciates in the first year.

Session 9.3

Working with the Payback Period

Diane has had some time to work with the income projections you generated in the last session. She has also estimated the additional cash revenue that will be generated by the expansion. She's placed this information in an Excel workbook.

To open the workbook:

▶ 1. Open the **Return** workbook located in the **Tutorial.09\Tutorial** folder included with your Data Files, and then save the workbook as **Return Analysis** in the same folder.

▶ 2. In the Documentation sheet, enter your name in cell B3 and the date in cell B4.

▶ 3. Switch to the **Return on Building Project** worksheet.

The Return on Building Project worksheet lists the yearly revenue that Diane's analysts predict will be generated by the expansion. Based on their projections, the company will generate an additional $150,000 in cash revenue during the first year, $250,000 during the second year, $400,000 during the third year, $550,000 during the fourth year, and $750,000 during the fifth year. This information doesn't tell Diane whether the initial investment is worth the total return. What if she took the $1,200,000 and used it a different way? How does the return on her investment from building the new workshop compare to the return she would get investing the money elsewhere?

One simple measure of the return from an investment is the **payback period**, which is the length of time required for an investment to recover its initial cost. For example, if the $1,200,000 building project brought in $300,000 per year in cash, it would take four years to pay back the cost of the initial investment. Diane has already given you an estimate of the cash receipts that will be generated by the building project. You can use the cumulative cash flow values to determine when the $1,200,000 investment will pay for itself.

To determine the payback period:

▶ **1.** In cell B7, enter the formula **=B6+A6**. Excel returns the value ($1,050,000). After the first year, more than $1,000,000 of the $1,200,000 initial investment in the building project still needs to be repaid.

▶ **2.** In cell C7, enter the formula **=C6+B7**. Excel returns the value ($800,000), indicating that at the end of the second year, more than $800,000 of the initial investment remains to be paid.

▶ **3.** Copy the formula in cell **C7** into the range **D7:F7** to calculate the remaining cumulative net cash flow values. See Figure 9-24.

Tip

You can also calculate cumulative totals using a combination of absolute and relative references by entering the formula =SUM($A$6:B6) into cell B7 and copying to the range C7:F7.

Figure 9-24 ▶ **Payback period calculated**

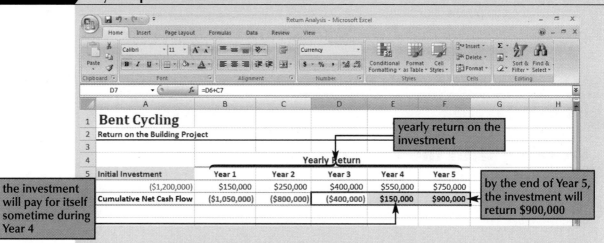

Based on these calculations, the accumulative additional revenues will pay back the $1,200,000 investment sometime during the fourth year (when the value of the cumulative net cash flow changes from negative to positive). By the end of the fifth year, the company will have shown a total profit of $900,000 from the $1,200,000 initial investment.

Calculating Net Present Value

The payback period is a quick method of determining the value of an investment. The major drawback to the payback period is that it does not take into account the time value of money. To understand why, you must explore how time affects financial decisions.

The Time Value of Money

The **time value of money** is based on the assumption that money received today is worth more than the same amount received later. One reason for this is that you can invest the money you receive today and earn interest on the investment. The time value of money can be expressed by what represents a fair exchange between current dollars and future dollars. You can do this in Excel using the PV, or present value, function. For example, to determine how much you would have to invest today at a 5% annual interest rate to receive $100 two years from now, you enter the following formula:

=PV(5%, 2, 0, 100)

The formula returns the value −$90.70, a negative cash flow which indicates that spending $90.70 today is a fair exchange for receiving $100 two years from now. The interest rate in this formula, also known as the **rate of return** or **discount rate**, defines the time value of money for the investment. A higher discount rate means that future dollars are discounted even more in comparison to current dollars. If you choose a rate of return of 10% to express the time value of money, $100 two years from now would be worth only $82.64 today.

For a series of cash payments, you repeat the PV function to calculate the present value of each payment. The sum total of those present values is the value of the entire transaction in today's dollars. Figure 9-25 shows a worksheet in which an investor receives $100 each year for five years. If the discount rate is 5%, then the present value of this investment in today's dollars is −$432.95. Spending $432.95 today is a fair exchange for receiving $100 per year for the next five years.

> ### Tip
>
> You can also use the FV, or future value, function to estimate how much a dollar amount today is worth in future dollars. The formula =FV(5%, 2, 0, −100) returns the value $110.25, a positive cash flow indicating that spending $100 today with a discount rate of 5% is worth receiving $110.25 two years from now.

Present value of a series of cash flows ◀ **Figure 9-25**

	A	B	C
1	Interest Rate	5%	
2			
3	Year	Cash Receipts	Present Value
4	1	$100.00	=PV($B$1,A4,0,B4)
5	2	$100.00	=PV($B$1,A5,0,B5)
6	3	$100.00	=PV($B$1,A6,0,B6)
7	4	$100.00	=PV($B$1,A7,0,B7)
8	5	$100.00	=PV($B$1,A8,0,B8)
9			
10		Total PV	=SUM(C4:C8)

PV function used to calculate the present value of a series of cash flows

	A	B	C
1	Interest Rate	5%	
2			
3	Year	Cash Receipts	Present Value
4	1	$100.00	($95.24)
5	2	$100.00	($90.70)
6	3	$100.00	($86.38)
7	4	$100.00	($82.27)
8	5	$100.00	($78.35)
9			
10		Total PV	($432.95)

total present value of $500 received in increments of $100 per year is $432.95 if the interest rate is 5%

This method of calculating the present value allows you to compare the returns from two investments to determine which is more valuable. Figure 9-26 shows two scenarios, one in which larger cash payments are weighted toward the end of the five-year period and the other in which larger cash payments are provided earlier. Both investments return $500, but the total present value of the first scenario is −$412.10, whereas the present value of the second is −$454.31. In other words, you should be willing to spend about $42 more on the second investment, making it the more valued investment. The difference between the two is that in the second investment, the larger cash returns occur earlier when the money is worth more. In the first investment, the same cash payments are given later at a point in which their value has been discounted.

Figure 9-26

Comparison of two series of cash flows

	A	B	C	D	E	F	G
1	Interest Rate	5%					
2							
3	Scenario 1: Increasing Cash Flows				Scenario 2: Decreasing Cash Flows		
4	Year	Cash Receipts	Present Value		Year	Cash Receipts	Present Value
5	1	$25.00	($23.81)		1	$250.00	($238.10)
6	2	$50.00	($45.35)		2	$100.00	($90.70)
7	3	$75.00	($64.79)		3	$75.00	($64.79)
8	4	$100.00	($82.27)		4	$50.00	($41.14)
9	5	$250.00	($195.88)		5	$25.00	($19.59)
10							
11		Total PV	($412.10)			Total PV	($454.31)

Scenario 1: large payments occur later   Scenario 2: large payments occur earlier

Scenario 2 is worth $42 more than Scenario 1 because the larger
receipts are received earlier in dollars of greater value

A transaction can involve both negative and positive cash flows. Figure 9-27 shows a transaction in which the investor receives $250 in Year 1, $150 in Year 2, and $100 in Year 3, but has to pay $150 in Year 4 and $400 in Year 5. This would seem to be a bad deal because the investor spends $550 while receiving only $500; but that ignores the time value of money. The investment pays off early while the payments are due at a later date to be paid in dollars of lesser value. The total present value of the entire transaction is –$23.72. If the rate of return were 10%, the present value of the transaction would be –$75.55. With that rate, it would be a fair exchange to spend $75.55 today to take part in the transaction over the next five years.

Figure 9-27

Transaction with positive and negative cash flows

	A	B	C
1	Interest Rate	5%	
2			
3	Year	Cash Receipts	Present Value
4	1	$250.00	($238.10)
5	2	$150.00	($136.05)
6	3	$100.00	($86.38)
7	4	($150.00)	$123.41
8	5	($400.00)	$313.41
9			
10		Total PV	($23.72)

	A	B	C
1	Interest Rate	10%	
2			
3	Year	Cash Receipts	Present Value
4	1	$250.00	($227.27)
5	2	$150.00	($123.97)
6	3	$100.00	($75.13)
7	4	($150.00)	$102.45
8	5	($400.00)	$248.37
9			
10		Total PV	($75.55)

present value with an interest of 5%   present value with an interest of 10%

despite the total cash flow, both investments are profitable because the cash receipts are received
earlier in dollars of greater value and the payments are made later in dollars of lesser value

Reference Window | **Determining the Return from an Investment**

- To calculate the net present value when the initial investment is made immediately, use the NPV function with the discount rate and the series of cash returns from the investment. Subtract the cost of the initial investment from the value returned by the NPV function.
- To calculate the net present value when the initial investment is made at the end of the first payment period, use the NPV function with the discount rate and the series of cash returns from the investment. Include the initial cost of the investment as the first value in the series.
- To calculate the internal rate of return, use the IRR function with the cost of the initial investment as the first cash flow value in the series. For investments in which there are several positive and negative cash flow values, include a guess to aid Excel in arriving at a reasonable internal rate of return value.

Using the NPV Function

Another way to calculate the present value of a series of cash flows is with the NPV function. The syntax of the NPV function is:

```
=NPV(rate, value1 [value2, value3, ...])
```

In this function, *rate* is the rate of return and *value1*, *value2*, *value3*, and so on are the values of future cash flows in the investment. The NPV function assumes that all cash flows occur at the end of evenly spaced periods, such as at the end of each fiscal year. For example, to calculate the present value of receiving $100 per year for five years assuming a 5% rate, you enter the following formula:

```
=NPV(5%, 100, 100, 100, 100, 100)
```

This formula returns the value $432.95, which is the same amount shown in Figure 9-25 except that the NPV function returns a positive rather than a negative value. This is because the PV function calculated how much you should invest at a given interest rate (a negative cash flow) to receive a series of future payments, whereas the NPV function calculates the value of those payments in today's dollars based on your chosen rate of return.

The NPV function is used in calculating the **net present value** of a transaction, which is the current value of all of the cash inflows and outflows in the investment adjusted by the time value of money. A positive net present value indicates that an investment makes money, a negative net present value indicates a losing investment, and a 0 net present value indicates a fair exchange between the cost of the investment and the expected return.

For example, if you were offered the previous transaction for the price of $400, would it be a profitable exchange? To correctly answer that question, you have to know when you're paying the $400. The NPV function assumes that the initial payment is made at the end of the first period, such as at the end of the first year of the transaction. So to calculate the net present value of the previous transaction, you enter the following formula:

```
=NPV(5%, -400, 100, 100, 100, 100, 100)
```

The formula returns a net present value of $31.38, indicating a profit of $31.38 from the investment. You could also make the initial payment immediately. If that is the case, the $400 you invest would not be discounted at all and you would subtract 400 from the value returned from discounting the other cash flows. The formula is as follows:

```
=NPV(5%, 100, 100, 100, 100, 100)-400
```

This formula returns the value $32.95. The net present value is higher with an immediate payment because you're paying for the transaction using current dollars rather than discounted dollars. In financial applications, the calculation of net present value usually follows this second formula, making the assumption that the initial payment is made immediately. This tutorial follows that convention unless stated otherwise.

InSight | **Understanding Net Present Value and the NPV Function**

One common source of confusion is that the NPV function in Excel does not correspond to the financial definition of net present value. Excel's NPV function only calculates the present value of a series of cash flows and assumes the initial payment occurs at the end of the first period, not immediately. To calculate the net present value based on the accepted financial definition, don't include the initial payment in the NPV function, only the other receipts. The initial payment is then subtracted from whatever value is returned by the NPV function. The only exception is if the initial payment occurs at the end of the first payment period. In that case, you can use the NPV function with the initial payments and all of the subsequent receipts. This design of the NPV function extends back to the first spreadsheet program, VisiCalc. VisiCalc's formulation of the NPV function was adopted by Lotus, which became the first spreadsheet program to enjoy widespread adoption in the business community. Excel adopted the Lotus formulation to be compatible with that popular application.

Choosing a Rate of Return

You can use the NPV function to determine how valuable Diane's proposed expansion is to the company. The initial cost of the investment is $1,200,000. The return on the investment is indicated by the Year 1 through Year 5 yearly return values shown earlier in Figure 9-24. The only information you don't have is the rate of return. Choosing an appropriate rate of return is tied in with the concept of **risk**—the possibility that the entire transaction will fail, resulting in a loss of the initial investment. Investments with higher risks generally should have higher rates of return. If Diane took the $1,200,000 and invested it in a money market fund (a low-risk venture), she would not demand a high rate of return; on the other hand, taking the $1,200,000 and using it to fund an expansion of the company's facilities merits a higher rate of return.

Determining the appropriate rate of return for a given investment is a complex process. After discussing the issue with financial analysts, Diane has settled on a rate of return of 12%. This means that Diane wants this venture to return at least as much cash over the next five years as she would get if she had invested the $1,200,000 in an account that paid 12% annual interest. Under that rate of return, you'll calculate the net present value of the proposed expansion project.

To calculate the net present value:

1. In cell A9, enter **Return on Investment**, and then format the cell using the **Heading 4** cell style.

2. In cell A10, enter **Desired Rate of Return**. In cell A11, enter **Net Present Value**. Apply the **20% – Accent3** cell style to the range A10:A11.

3. In cell B10, enter **12%**.

4. Click cell **B11**, click the **Insert Function** button on the formula bar to open the Insert Function dialog box, type **NPV** in the Search for a function box, click the **Go** button, and then double-click **NPV** in the Select a function box. The Function Arguments dialog box opens.

5. With the Rate box active, click cell **B10** to insert Diane's rate of return, and then press the **Tab** key.

6. With the Value1 box active, select the range **B6:F6** containing the projected cash flows from the investment. See Figure 9-28.

Function Arguments for the NPV function ◄ Figure 9-28

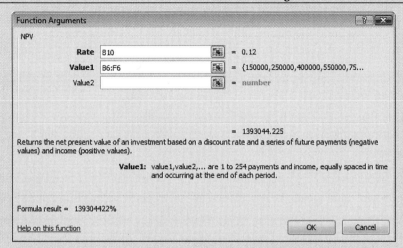

7. Click the **OK** button to enter the formula =NPV(B10, B6:F6) into cell B11. The cell displays the value $1,393,044.22. This is the present value of all of the yearly returns from the building project.

You need to edit this formula to subtract the startup cost from the present value of the investment. Because the startup cost is represented in this worksheet as a negative cash flow, you *add* it to the present value of the investment.

8. Double-click cell **B11** to enter editing mode, change the formula to **=NPV(B10, B6:F6)+A6**, and then press the **Enter** key. The value $193,044.22 appears in the cell.

9. Reduce the number of digits to the right of the decimal point, changing the displayed value to $193,044. See Figure 9-29.

Net present value of building project ◄ Figure 9-29

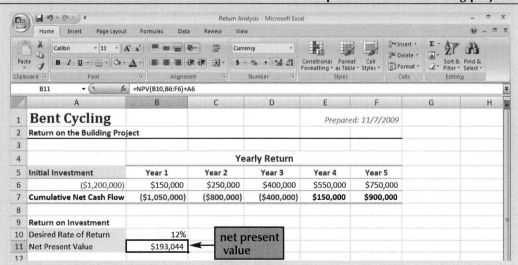

You report to Diane that with a rate of return of 12%, the net present value of the $1,200,000 building project is almost $200,000 in current dollars. In other words, if all of her assumptions are correct, investing $1,200,000 in the expansion is worth almost $200,000 more than investing the same amount in an account paying 12% annual interest. The proposed expansion appears to be profitable under those terms.

Calculating the Internal Rate of Return

To calculate the net present value, you picked an appropriate rate of return. In any financial analysis, it is a good idea to try other values to see how they impact your conclusions. Diane asks you to rerun the calculation using different rates of return.

To view the impact of different rates of return:

▶ **1.** Change the value in cell B10 to **9%**, which decreases the desired rate of return. The net present value increases to $333,990. At a rate of return of 9% per year, the proposed project shows a positive cash flow value of more than $330,000.

What happens if Diane wants a higher rate of return from the building project?

▶ **2.** Change the value in cell B10 to **15%**. The net present value drops to $69,824.

▶ **3.** Change the value in cell B10 to **20%**. The net present value drops to –$103,260.

▶ **4.** Change the value in cell B10 back to **12%**.

At higher rates of return, the net present value of the investment goes down. That's not surprising when you realize the expansion is being compared with investments that offer higher and higher return values. Compared with an investment that offered a 20% interest rate, the expansion would actually show a negative cash flow value, indicating that it is worth less than an investment that offers 20% annual interest. As you increase the desired rate of return, at some point the net present value is equal to 0. See Figure 9-30.

| Figure 9-30 | Plot of the net present value for different rates of return |

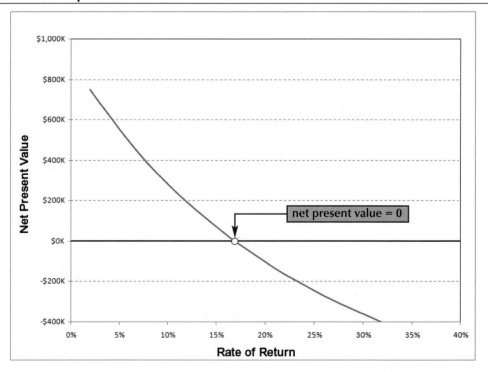

The point at which the net present value of an investment equals 0 is the **internal rate of return (IRR)**. At rates of return beyond that, the net present value is negative, meaning that the expansion is no longer a good investment compared with the desired rate of return.

Using the IRR Function

The internal rate of return is another measure of the value of an investment. Investments with higher IRRs are usually preferred to those with lower IRRs. The IRR function calculates the internal rate of return, and has the following syntax:

```
=IRR(values, [guess=0.1])
```

In this function, *values* are the cash flow values for which you want to calculate the IRR and *guess* is an optional argument in which you guess the IRR value. A guess is needed for a financial transaction in which there are multiple possible values for the IRR. In those situations, the guess assists Excel in locating the final value for the IRR. Without the guess, Excel might not be able to calculate the IRR. If you don't include a guess, Excel will use an initial guess of 10% for the IRR and proceed from there to derive the answer. (Case Problem 2 explores how to use the guess argument in the IRR function and shows why it is sometimes necessary.)

The list of *values* in the IRR function must include at least one positive cash flow and one negative cash flow and the order of the values must reflect the time order of the cash flows. As with the NPV function, the IRR function assumes that the cash flows occur at evenly spaced intervals.

Figure 9-31 demonstrates how to calculate the IRR for a transaction in which an initial investment of $400 results in five yearly payments of $100. The internal rate of return for this transaction is 7.93%. You would choose this investment over another investment that pays off at a lower rate of return.

Tip

An investment might have several different possible internal rates of return when it switches between cash inflows and cash outflows several times during the course of the investment.

Internal rate of return calculation ◀ **Figure 9-31**

	A	B	C
1	Year	Cash Flows	
2	0	($400.00)	
3	1	$100.00	
4	2	$100.00	
5	3	$100.00	
6	4	$100.00	
7	5	$100.00	
8			
9	Internal Rate of Return	=IRR(B2:B7)	
10			

	A	B	C
1	Year	Cash Flows	
2	0	($400.00)	
3	1	$100.00	
4	2	$100.00	
5	3	$100.00	
6	4	$100.00	
7	5	$100.00	
8			
9	Internal Rate of Return	7.93%	
10			

IRR function calculates the internal rate of return for a series of cash flows

IRR of the investment is 7.93%

You'll calculate the internal rate of return for the proposed workshop.

To calculate the IRR for the proposed workshop:

▶ **1.** In cell A12, enter **Internal Rate of Return**, and then copy the formatting from cell A11 to cell A12.

▶ **2.** In cell B12, enter the formula **=IRR(A6:F6)** to calculate the IRR based on yearly returns of the investment, and then format the cell as a percentage with two decimal places. The IRR is 16.89%. See Figure 9-32.

| Figure 9-32 | IRR of the proposed expansion |

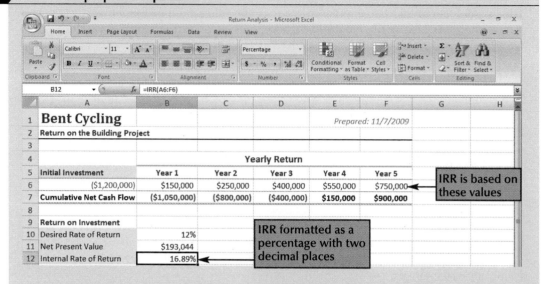

Notice that the IRR function requires you to include the initial cost of the investment, ($1,200,000), as part of the list of cash flows. This differs from the NPV function, in which you subtract the cost of the investment from the investment present value.

3. Save and close the workbook.

You report to Diane that the internal rate of return of the expansion is 16.89%. This value gives her a basis of comparison with other investment options open to her, assuming the estimated returns generated by the project are accurate.

Using the NPV and IRR Functions to Compare Investments

Both the internal rate of return and the net present value provide a measure of the return given by an investment. Figure 9-33 summarizes how to use the results of these functions to aid in decision making. In general, you want to accept investments that have positive net present values or internal rates of return higher than a specified rate, r. In comparing two investments, a commonly used guideline is to accept the investment with the higher net present value or the higher internal rate of return. Other proposals will cross Diane's desk in the coming months; this provides a basis for comparison right now.

| Figure 9-33 | NPV and the IRR comparison |

	Choosing to accept an investment at a given rate of return (r)	Comparing investment A to investment B
NPV	If NPV > 0, accept If NPV < 0, reject If NPV = 0, gather more information	If NPV(A) > NPV(B), accept A If NPV(A) < NPV(B), accept B If NPV(A) = NPV(B), gather more information
IRR	If IRR > r, accept If IRR < r, reject If IRR = r, gather more information	If IRR(A) > IRR(B), accept A If IRR(A) < IRR(B), accept B If IRR(A) = IRR(B), gather more information

Exploring other Financial Functions

Both the NPV and IRR functions assume the cash flows occur at evenly spaced intervals. For cash flows that appear at unevenly spaced intervals, you use the XNPV and XIRR functions. Both of these functions are available in the Analysis ToolPak add-in, which must be installed and activated before you can use the functions. The XNPV function syntax is:

=XNPV(*rate, values, dates*)

In this function, *rate* is the desired rate of return, *values* is the list of cash flows, and *dates* are the dates associated with each cash flow. The series of values must contain at least one positive and one negative value. The cash flow values are discounted starting after the first date in the list, with the first value not discounted at all. Figure 9-34 shows an investment in which the initial payment on September 1 is $300 repaid in eight deposits spaced at irregular intervals over the next two years. The value of this investment is $18.17 compared with an investment that has a 5% rate of return.

Net present value calculated over irregular time intervals | **Figure 9-34**

	A	B	C
1	Rate of Return	5%	
2			
3	Date	Cash Flow	
4	September 1, 2009	($300.00)	
5	December 3, 2009	$20.00	
6	February 24, 2010	$20.00	
7	June 1, 2010	$25.00	
8	September 5, 2010	$50.00	
9	December 10, 2010	$50.00	
10	March 4, 2011	$50.00	
11	June 15, 2011	$50.00	
12	September 14, 2011	$75.00	
13			
14	XNPV	=XNPV(B1,B4:B12,A4:A12)	
15			

	A	B	C
1	Rate of Return	5%	
2			
3	Date	Cash Flow	
4	September 1, 2009	($300.00)	
5	December 3, 2009	$20.00	
6	February 24, 2010	$20.00	
7	June 1, 2010	$25.00	
8	September 5, 2010	$50.00	
9	December 10, 2010	$50.00	
10	March 4, 2011	$50.00	
11	June 15, 2011	$50.00	
12	September 14, 2011	$75.00	
13			
14	XNPV	$18.17	
15			

The XIRR function does the same thing in calculating the internal rate of return for a series of unevenly spaced payments. The syntax of the XIRR function is:

=XIRR(*values, dates, [guess = 0.1]*)

In this function, again *values* is the list of cash flow values, *dates* are the dates of each cash flow, and *guess* is an optional argument used to help Excel arrive at an answer. Figure 9-35 shows the internal rate of return for the transaction described previously. The IRR of this investment is 9.69%.

| Figure 9-35 | IRR calculated over irregular time intervals |

For the expansion, all of the cash flow values are projected at regular intervals, at the end of each fiscal year, so you do not need to use either the XNPV or the XIRR function.

Auditing a Workbook

Diane prepared a workbook summarizing the proposed expansion. Somewhere in the process of creating the workbook, several errors have crept in. She wants you to examine the workbook, resolve any errors, and return the completed workbook to her.

To open the workbook:

1. Open the **Financial** workbook located in the **Tutorial.09\Tutorial** folder included with your Data Files, and then save the workbook as **Financial Report** in the same folder.

2. In the Documentation sheet, enter your name and the date.

3. Review the contents of the workbook.

The Financial Report workbook contains several worksheets projecting the financial future of the company under the proposed expansion. Some of these worksheets you've already seen in a slightly different form. Two new worksheets are the Cash Flow Schedule and Balance Sheet worksheets.

The Cash Flow Schedule worksheet is used to project the yearly cash flow of the company. One purpose of this worksheet is to forecast the ability of a company to pay its bills. A company could show a positive net income on its income statement but still not be able to pay its bills if a lot of the wealth of the company is tied up in noncash assets. So, although the income statement you just created for Diane earlier was useful, Diane needs more information.

The Balance Sheet worksheet projects the company's expected assets, liabilities, and equity over the next five years. In general, a **balance sheet** shows what the company owns and how its assets are financed. With the income statement, the schedule of cash flows, and the balance sheet, Diane has three of the most important financial reports that can tell her of the health of her company under the proposed expansion. She collected the information in the three worksheets and placed them in the Summary worksheet.

However, you might have noticed that cells throughout the workbook display the #NAME? error value. Diane wants you to track down and correct the source of this error. The challenge is that all of the worksheets are interconnected. A formula in one worksheet might be based on several values scattered in several other worksheets. It's not immediately clear which cell or cells is the source of the error. To find the source of the error, you can use the auditing tools to examine the interrelationships of formulas and values throughout the workbook.

Tracing an Error

When Excel cannot return a value from a formula, it will display an error value in the cell. An error value begins with the number sign (#) followed by an error name. The error name indicates the type of error encountered by Excel, explaining the reason why it was unable to return a value. (Refer to Figure 7-23 for a list of error names that might appear in a workbook.) The #NAME? error value indicates a mistyped function name. But, where is it?

To trace the source of an error value, you need to understand how formulas in the worksheet cells are interconnected. The formula in the active cell might have several **precedent cells** whose values are used to calculate the active cell's value. For example, if the active cell is cell C15 and contains the formula =C13+C14, then cells C13 and C14 are precedent cells for cell C15. The active cell itself may be used as a precedent cell for other cells in the worksheet, called **dependent cells** because their value depends on the value of other cells. In the preceding example, cell C15 is a dependent cell, depending on the values in cells C13 and C14. In an interconnected workbook like the one you received from Diane, a single cell can be both a precedent and a dependent cell.

You might have already noticed worksheet cells that contain green triangles in the upper-left corner of the cell. These **error indicators** are another way Excel points out an error or potential error. Not all errors are the result of Excel being unable to return a value. For example, if a cell contains a formula that is markedly different from adjacent cells, Excel might flag that cell with an error indicator, notifying you of the possibility that you might have entered an incorrect formula.

Error values will propagate throughout a workbook. When you notice an error value, you need to trace it back to its source. When a workbook has many error values, as Diane's workbook does, you might wonder where to start. Usually, when a workbook has several error values, they all can be traced to the same source. First, select a cell containing an error value and locate its precedents. If any of those precedents display an error value, locate that cell's precedent cells, and so on. Eventually, you'll reach an error value that has no precedents. That cell is the source of the error values in the dependent cells. After you correct the error, you might find that you removed all of the error values throughout the workbook. If error values still exist, select another cell containing an error value and repeat the process until you have fixed the workbook.

> **Tip**
>
> After you select a cell with an error indicator, you can click the Error Alert button to display additional information about the possible error and determine whether further action is necessary.

Tracing Error Values | Reference Window

- Select the cell containing an error value.
- In the Formula Auditing group on the Formulas tab, click the Error Checking button arrow and then click Trace Error.
- Follow the tracer arrows to a precedent cell containing an error value.
- If the tracer arrow is connected to a worksheet icon, double-click the tracer arrow and open the cell references in the worksheet.
- Continue to trace the error value to succeeding precedent cells. When you locate a cell containing an error value that has no precedent cells with errors, you have located the source of the error.

The process of tracing the precedents of an error value is greatly simplified by using the auditing tools. You'll use this process to locate the source of the error in the Financial Report workbook.

To trace an error value in the Financial Report workbook:

▶ **1.** Switch to the **Summary** worksheet. You'll start tracing the error with cell F18.

▶ **2.** Click cell **F18**.

▶ **3.** In the Formula Auditing group on the Formulas tab, click the **Error Checking button arrow**, and then click **Trace Error**. See Figure 9-36.

| Figure 9-36 | Tracing an error value |

		Year 1	Year 2	Year 3	Year 4	Year 5
11	Cash Flows	Year 1	Year 2	Year 3	Year 4	Year 5
12	Total Cash Inflows	#NAME?	1,013,562	1,206,852	1,436,958	1,710,883
13	Total Cash Outflows	#NAME?	580,047	654,007	740,634	842,344
14	Net Cash Flow	#NAME?	$ 433,514	$ 552,846	$ 696,324	$ 868,540
15						
16	Balance Sheet	Year 1	Year 2	Year 3	Year 4	Year 5
17	Total Current and Noncurrent Assets	#NAME?	#NAME?	#NAME?	#NAME?	#NAME?
18	Total Liabilities and Equity	#NAME?	#NAME?	#NAME?	#NAME?	#NAME?
19						
20						

icon indicates that the precedent cell is located on a different worksheet

tracer arrow

Documentation | **Summary** | Income Statement

Ready 120%

Tip

To keep track of the original tracer arrows, print the worksheet with the tracer arrows displayed before you edit the formulas.

Excel displays a tracer arrow pointing toward cell F18 from a worksheet icon. The **tracer arrow** provides a visual clue to the relationship between two cells by pointing from the precedent cell to the dependent cell. In this case, the tracer arrow points from a worksheet icon to cell F18. This tells you that the precedent for cell F18 lies in another worksheet. You can jump to that cell by double-clicking the tracer arrow.

To trace the error to its source:

▶ **1.** Double-click the **tracer arrow** that connects the worksheet icon to cell F18. The Go To dialog box opens, listing the reference to cell G19 in the Balance Sheet worksheet.

▶ **2.** In the Go to box, click the cell reference, and then click the **OK** button. Cell G19 in the Balance Sheet worksheet is now the active cell. Notice that the #NAME? error values appear throughout this worksheet, too.

▶ **3.** In the Formula Auditing group, click the **Error Checking button arrow**, and then click **Trace Error** to show the tracer arrows on this worksheet. The tracer arrows go through several cells, once again stopping at a worksheet icon. See Figure 9-37.

| Figure 9-37 | Error value traced across the worksheet |

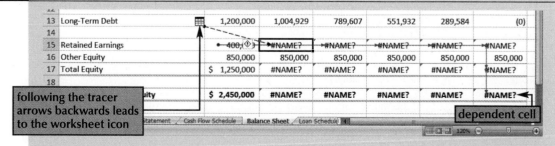

13	Long-Term Debt	1,200,000	1,004,929	789,607	551,932	289,584	(0)
14							
15	Retained Earnings	400,	#NAME?	#NAME?	#NAME?	#NAME?	#NAME?
16	Other Equity	850,000	850,000	850,000	850,000	850,000	850,000
17	Total Equity	$ 1,250,000	#NAME?	#NAME?	#NAME?	#NAME?	#NAME?
18							
	uity	$ 2,450,000	#NAME?	#NAME?	#NAME?	#NAME?	#NAME?

following the tracer arrows backwards leads to the worksheet icon

dependent cell

tatement | Cash Flow Schedule | **Balance Sheet** | Loan Schedule

120%

The tracer arrows give a visual picture of how the formulas in the Balance Sheet worksheet are interconnected. Examining the arrows, you can see that cell G19 is dependent on the value in cell G17; cell G17 in turn depends on the value in cell G15, which is dependent on cell F15 and then cells E15, D15, and C15. The value in cell C15 is dependent on the values in cell B15 and a cell in another worksheet. Notice that Excel displays red tracer arrows for dependent cells that themselves have error values and blue tracer arrows for cells without error values. This makes it easier for you to locate the cells containing errors.

▶ 4. Double-click the **tracer arrow** that connects the worksheet icon to cell C15 to open the Go To dialog box, click the reference to cell B27 in the Income Statement worksheet, and then click the **OK** button. Cell B27 in the Income Statement worksheet becomes active.

▶ 5. Click the **Error Checking button arrow**, and then click **Trace Error** to trace the source of the error in cell B17. As shown in Figure 9-38, the source of this error ends at cell B17.

Source of the error value ◀ **Figure 9-38**

10					
11 Accounting	7,000	8,120	9,419	10,926	12,674
12 Advertising & Promotion	21,000	24,360	28,258	32,779	38,023
13 Insurance	2,000	2,320	2,691	3,122	3,621
14 Maintenance	4,800	5,568	6,459	7,492	8,691
15 Utilities	7,600	8,816	10,227	11,863	13,761
16 Miscellaneous	2,400	2,784	3,229	3,746	4,346
17 **Total General Expenses**	#NAME?	$ 51,968	$ 60,283	$ 69,928	$ 81,117
18					
19 Earnings before Interest, Depr. & Tax	#NAME?	1,013,562	1,206,852	1,436,958	1,710,883
20 Depreciation Expense	105,600	96,307	87,832	80,103	73,054
21 **Operating Profit**	#NAME?	$ 917,254	$ 1,119,020	$ 1,356,855	$ 1,637,829
22					
23 Interest Expense	112,835	92,584	70,231	45,558	18,322
24 **Earnings Before Taxes**	#NAME?	$ 824,670	$ 1,048,789	$ 1,311,298	$ 1,619,507
25					
26 Estimated Tax	#NAME?	272,141	346,100	432,728	534,437
27 **Net Income**	#NAME?	$ 552,529	$ 702,689	$ 878,569	$ 1,085,070
28					

this error value has no precedence cells containing errors

Summary | Income Statement | Cash Flow Schedule | Balance Sheet | Loan Schedule
Ready — 120%

When you examine the formula in cell B17, the source of the error is immediately clear. The previous user had entered the formula =SUMM(B11:B16) rather than =SUM(B11:B16). Excel, not recognizing the function name *SUMM*, returned the #NAME? error value.

▶ 6. Change the value in cell B17 to **=SUM(B11:B16)**, and then press the **Enter** key. When you change the formula, the #NAME? error values disappear from the worksheet. Also, the color of the tracer arrows change from red to blue because they no longer point to cells containing errors.

▶ 7. In the Formula Auditing group on the Formulas tab, click the **Remove Arrows** button to remove all of the tracer arrows from the worksheet.

Trouble? If the tracer arrows disappeared from your workbook, Excel automatically removed them. Continue with Step 8.

▶ 8. Verify that the #NAME? error values disappeared from all of the cells in the workbook, and then switch to the **Summary** worksheet.

Tip

Tracer arrows disappear when you change the formula to which the arrows point, insert or delete columns and rows, or delete or move cells. To restore the tracer arrows, use the auditing tools to retrace the formulas in the workbook.

Using tracer arrows, you quickly located the source of the #NAME? error values, even though it was located in a different worksheet and required you to navigate through several layers of precedent cells. You can use the auditing tools to track any cell formula. To trace the precedents of the active cell, click the Trace Precedents button in the Formula Auditing group on the Formulas tab. If you want to discover the cells that are dependent upon the active cell, click the Trace Dependents button.

Evaluating a Formula

The Summary worksheet contains another error. Cells F17 and F18 show Bent Cycling's total assets, liabilities, and equity in Year 5. This information is drawn from the Balance Sheet worksheet. One of the features of a balance sheet is that the value of the total assets must match the value of the total liabilities and equity. Checking that these two totals match is a basic step in auditing any financial report. However, the total assets value in cell F17 is $5,133,798, whereas the total liabilities and equity in cell F18 is $4,892,809. Because the values differ, an error must be somewhere in the workbook. You could try to trace this error using the tracer arrows to trace the precedents of cells F17 and F18.

However, one drawback to using tracer arrows is that they can clutter the worksheet with too much information. Sometimes, you want to trace only a single formula to its roots. Another way to explore the relationship between cells in the workbook is by evaluating formulas. To evaluate a formula, you select the cell and then click the Evaluate Formula button in the Formula Auditing group on the Formulas tab, which opens a dialog box that displays the formula. From this dialog box, you can display the value of different parts of the formula or "drill down" through the cell references in the formula to discover the source of the formula's value. You'll use this auditing tool to evaluate the formula in cell F17 of the Summary worksheet.

To evaluate the formula in cell F17 of the Summary worksheet:

▶ **1.** Click cell **F17**, and then, in the Formula Auditing group on the Formulas tab, click the **Evaluate Formula** button. The Evaluate Formula dialog box opens. See Figure 9-39.

Figure 9-39 ▶ **Evaluate Formula dialog box**

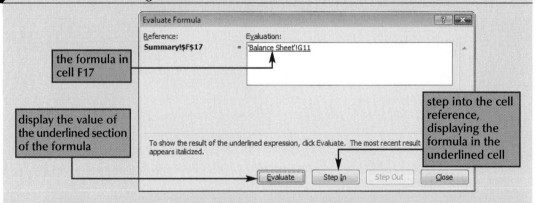

The dialog box displays the cell's formula with any cell references underlined. You can either click the Evaluate button to display the value of the underlined section of the formula, or you can click the Step In button to display the formula contained in the cell reference.

▶ **2.** Click the **Step In** button. Excel opens cell G11 in the Balance Sheet worksheet, displaying the formula =G7+G9, which is the formula stored in that cell. Cell G7, which contains the total current assets for the company in Year 5, is underlined. You'll use the Evaluate button to display the value of this cell.

3. Click the **Evaluate** button to display the value stored in cell G7. The Evaluate Formula dialog box displays 4135705.18729347+G9. Cell G9, which contains the depreciated value of the company's plant and equipment for Year 5, is underlined. It's possible that the source of the error lies in this cell's value. You'll continue to step into the formula to find out where the value for this cell comes from.

4. Click the **Step In** button. The dialog box displays the formula =Depreciation!C12. This indicates that the depreciated value of the company's plant and equipment in Year 5 comes from cell C12 in the Depreciation worksheet.

5. Click the **Step In** button again. Excel jumps to the Depreciation worksheet and selects cell C12. See Figure 9-40.

Drilling down through a formula   **Figure 9-40**

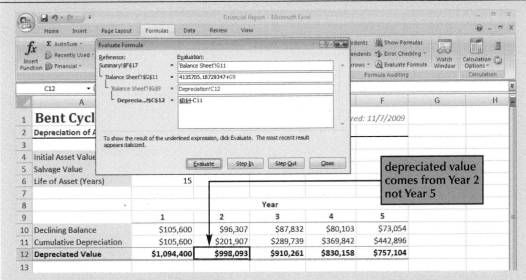

At this point, you discuss the issue with Diane. She tells you that the depreciated value should be based on the Year 5 value in cell F12, not the Year 2 value in cell C12. This is probably the source of the error. She asks you to make the correction to the formula in the Balance Sheet worksheet.

6. Click the **Step Out** button to move back up in the hierarchy of functions, returning to cell G9 in the Balance Sheet worksheet, and then click the **Close** button to close the dialog box.

7. In the Balance Sheet worksheet, in cell G9, change the formula to **=Depreciation!F12**.

8. Switch to the **Summary** worksheet, and then confirm that the values in cells F17 and F18 match. You've discovered the source of the error and now the Year 5 values for assets, liabilities, and equity are in balance.

Using the Watch Window

In a workbook that involves dozens of worksheets with interconnected formulas, you may often want to be able to view the impact of changing a value in one worksheet on cell values in other worksheets. Of course, you can always move back and forth between worksheets, but that can be time consuming and clumsy if the workbook contains many worksheets and the values you want to follow are spread across several of them.

For example, Diane is still interested in looking at some of the underlying assumptions in the building project. Recall that when you worked on the income statement, you assumed a 33% income tax rate. Diane knows that few things are more unpredictable than future tax rates, and wants to know what would happen to the building proposal if the government decided to increase taxes in the next five years. Rather than jumping back and forth between different sheets in the workbook, you can create a **Watch Window** that displays the net present value and internal rate of return as you edit the income tax rate value.

To use the Watch Window:

▶ **1.** Switch to the **Income Statement** worksheet.

▶ **2.** In the Formula Auditing group on the Formulas tab, click the **Watch Window** button. The Watch Window dialog box opens.

▶ **3.** Click the **Add Watch** button to open the Add Watch dialog box, click cell **F9** in the Summary worksheet, and then click the **Add** button.

The information in cell F9 is added to the Watch Window.

▶ **4.** Click the **Add Watch** button, click cell **F14** in the Summary worksheet, and then click the **Add** button.

▶ **5.** Click the **Add Watch** button, click cell **F17** in the Summary worksheet, and then click the **Add** button.

The Watch Window displays the net income, net cash flow, and total asset values for Year 5 in the Summary worksheet. At this point, you can change values at any point in the workbook and view the impact of that change in the Watch Window.

▶ **6.** In cell F5, change the value of the assumed tax rate from 33% to **39%**. In the Watch Window, you instantly see that increasing the tax rate to 39% decreases the net income at the end of Year 5 to $987,899. The net cash flow for that year also drops to $771,369. Finally, the total assets of the company in Year 5 drop to $4,566,587. See Figure 9-41.

Figure 9-41	Watch Window

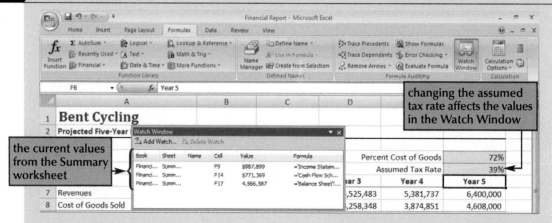

▶ **7.** In cell F5, change the assumed tax rate value back to **33%**, and then close the Watch Window dialog box.

▶ **8.** Save and close the workbook.

You report to Diane that if income taxes increase six percentage points to 39%, the net income for the company at the end of Year 5 will drop from the current estimate of $1,085,070 to $987,899—a decline of almost $100,000. Net cash flow will also drop from the current Year 5 estimate of $868,540 to $771,369. So the company will have less cash assets at the end of the fifth year of the project. Whether this will affect the overall profitability of the proposed expansion will require further study.

1. Why is the payback period not always appropriate for determining the value of an investment?
2. If the rate of return is 5%, is $95 today worth more, less, or the same as $100 a year from now?
3. You receive the following payments: $50 a year from now, $75 in two years, and $100 in three years. What is the present value of this investment? Assume a 6% rate of return.
4. You spend $350 on an investment that pays $75 a year for the next six years. If you make the payment immediately, what is the net present value of your investment? Assume a 6% rate of return.
5. Repeat Question 4, assuming that you pay $350 a year from now and the $75 payments start a year after that.
6. Calculate the internal rate of return for the investment in Question 4. If you have another investment available to you that pays a 7.3% rate of return, should you take it?
7. If an investment pays back at irregular time intervals, what Excel functions can you use to evaluate the return of those investments?
8. A cell displays the #REF! error value. Suggest a possible source of this error.

Tutorial Summary | Review

In this tutorial, you learned how to use Excel's financial tools to analyze the financial aspects of a proposed expansion. In the first session, you explored different options for financing the expansion through the use of the PV, PMT, FV, NPER, and RATE functions. You also learned how to create an amortization schedule to track payments made on principal and interest throughout the history of a loan. In the second session, you examined some of the Excel tools to project future values through interpolation and extrapolation. You also explored the concept of depreciation of assets and looked at the library of built-in Excel functions to calculate depreciation. The third session covered functions to calculate the return from investments of using the net present value and internal rate of return functions. The tutorial concluded with an overview of the auditing tools used to track formulas and trace errors.

Key Terms

amortization schedule	FV function	positive cash flow
balance sheet	gross profit	precedent cell
cash flow	growth trend	profit and loss statement
cash inflow	income statement	PV function
cash outflow	internal rate of return (IRR)	RATE function
cost of goods sold	interpolate	rate of return
declining balance	linear trend	risk
depreciation	negative cash flow	salvage value
dependent cell	net income	straight-line depreciation
depreciation	net present value	tangible asset
discount rate	NPER function	time value of money
error indicator	payback period	tracer arrow
extrapolate	PMT function	Watch Window

Practice	**Review Assignments**

Practice the skills you learned in the tutorial using the same case scenario.

Data Files needed for the Review Assignments: Building.xlsx, Loan.xlsx, NVP.xlsx, Statement.xlsx

Diane has been examining another building proposal for Bent Cycling. Rather than building a new workshop and design facility, the company will substantially upgrade its existing facilities. The cost of the remodeling is estimated to be $950,000. Diane wants you to redo your analysis for this new proposal, reporting on the financial aspects of the proposed remodeling, taking into account the cost of the loan and the yearly depreciation of the new equipment. She already created the workbooks to do this analysis. You need to complete the workbooks by adding the appropriate financial functions and formulas and correcting any errors you find.

Complete the following:

1. Open the **Building**, **Loan**, **NPV**, and **Statement** workbooks located in the Tutorial.09\Review folder, and then save them in the same folder as **Building Project**, **Loan Schedule**, **NPV and IRR**, and **Income Statement**, respectively. In the Documentation sheet of each workbook, enter your name and the date.

2. To pay for the remodeling, the company will take out a five-year loan at 7.5% interest, compounded monthly. Enter the terms of the loan in the Loan Analysis worksheet in the Loan Schedule workbook.

   a. In the range A5:F5, enter the conditions of the loan. Use formulas to calculate the rate per month and the number of payment periods in the loan.

   b. In cell G5, calculate the total monthly payment on the loan based on the loan conditions already entered into the worksheet. Assume the loan will be completely paid off at the end of the last period.

   c. Complete the amortization schedule at the bottom of the worksheet. Column D contains the interest payment for each month, column E contains the principal payment, and column F contains the total payment. Column C contains the remaining principal at the start of each month. The initial principal remaining is $950,000. The subsequent remaining principal values should be reduced by the principal payment made in the previous month.

   d. In the range B9:F10, use the SUMIF function to calculate the total interest and principal payments for each of the five years. Also, calculate the total payments per year and over all five years.

3. Save and close the Loan Schedule workbook.

4. The Income Statement workbook contains a five-year projection of the income statements for the company. Project the revenue and extrapolate the expense values in the Income Statement worksheet.

   a. Project the revenue in Years 2 through 4 by interpolating the increase in revenue between Year 1 ($3,200,000) and Year 5 ($4,800,000) assuming a growth trend.

   b. Extrapolate the expense values in the range B12:B17 through the range C12:F17 assuming a growth trend in which expenses rise by 12% per year.

5. Diane estimates that the new equipment and features of the remodeled workshop will depreciate from $950,000 to a salvage value one-fifth of that in 10 years' time. Complete the depreciation schedule in the Depreciation worksheet.

   a. In the range B4:B6, enter the conditions of the depreciation.

b. In the range B10:F10, calculate the yearly depreciation of the asset assuming a straight-line depreciation. In the range B11:F11, calculate the cumulative depreciation. In the range B12:F12, calculate the asset's depreciated value each year.

c. Repeat Step b in the range B14:F16 assuming a declining balance depreciation schedule.

6. In the Income Statement worksheet, apply the yearly depreciation you calculated in the Depreciation worksheet under the declining balance schedule to the cells in the range B21:F21. In the range B24:F24, insert the interest expense values you calculated for each year in the Loan Schedule workbook.

7. Save and close the Income Statement workbook.

8. The NPV and IRR workbook contains the yearly return that Diane expects the remodeling to generate. In the Return on Investment worksheet, analyze the return on the remodeling project.

a. The range B6:F6 contains the yearly cash receipts generated by the building project. In the range B7:F7, calculate the cumulative net cash flow from these receipts. In what year will the building project pay for itself?

b. Diane wants this investment to be comparable to what she would receive from an investment returning 10% annual interest. In cell B10, enter **10%**. In cell B11, calculate the net present value of the remodeling investment. How does it compare in current dollars to what Diane could have received by investing the $950,000 in an account paying 10% annual interest?

c. In cell B12, calculate the internal rate of return for this investment.

9. Save and close the NPV and IRR workbook.

10. The Building Project workbook contains projections for future income statements, cash flow schedules, and balance sheets. Several cells display the #DIV/0! error value. Starting with cell E5 in the Balance Sheet worksheet, trace the error to its source and then correct it.

11. Save and close the Building Project workbook. Submit the finished workbooks to your instructor, either in printed or electronic form, as requested.

Apply	**Case Problem 1**

Use the skills you learned to calculate the return from investing in real estate.

Data File needed for this Case Problem: Condo.xlsx

E-Park Real Estate Greg Baer is the owner of E-Park Real Estate, a small real-estate company in Estes Park, Colorado. Greg is examining the finances involved with purchasing a large condo outside of the village. E-Park Real Estate will hold onto the condominium for the next 10 years, receiving yearly income from rentals that will cover the expenses and will eventually pay back the cost of the initial investment. Greg wants you to calculate the return from this investment. He already created a worksheet containing the relevant financial data. You need to complete the worksheet by adding the formulas to project the value of the investment over the next 10 years.

Complete the following:

1. Open the **Condo** workbook located in the Tutorial.09\Case1 folder, and then save the workbook as **Condo Investment** in the same folder. In the Documentation sheet, enter your name in cell B3 and the date in cell B4.

The Investment Analysis worksheet contains a projected income statement and a cash flow statement. Greg entered the initial conditions of the investment. The cost of the condo is $325,000. For tax purposes, Greg plans to depreciate the condo completely over the 10-year period of the investment. At the end of the 10-year period, he plans to sell the condo for $450,000. Greg assumes a 34% tax rate on rental income and also on the income resulting from the sale of the condo in Year 10. You need to complete the worksheet by adding the formulas to project the value of the investment over the next 10 years.

2. In the range C11:L11, enter the yearly rental income for the condo, assuming that the income grows at a linear trend from $42,000 in Year 1 to $56,000 in Year 10. In cell L12, enter the revenue that Greg will generate by selling the condo at the end of Year 10. In the range C13:L13, calculate the total revenue generated by the rental and sale of the condo from Year 1 through Year 10.

3. In the range C17:L17, insert the annual property tax paid on the condo, assuming that $2000 is paid in Year 1 and the tax increases following a linear trend to a value of $4000 in Year 10. In the range C18:L18, insert the annual miscellaneous expenses, starting from a Year 1 value of $1500 and assuming that expenses increase following a linear trend to a Year 10 value of $6000. Enter both the property tax and the miscellaneous expenses as negative cash flows. In the range C19:L19, calculate the total expenses for each year.

4. In the range C21:L21, calculate the initial earnings estimate by subtracting the total yearly expenses from the total yearly revenue.

5. In the range C22:L22, calculate the annual depreciation of the condo from Year 1 to Year 10. Assume a straight-line depreciation and use the initial cost, useful life, and salvage values entered at the top of the worksheet.

6. In the range C23:L23, calculate the taxable income by subtracting the yearly depreciation from the yearly initial earnings estimate.

7. In the range C25:L25, calculate the tax due on rental income for each of the 10 years. In cell L26, enter the tax due on the sale of the condo at the end of Year 10. The tax due is equal to the difference between the sales price and the salvage value, multiplied by the tax rate. In the range C27:L27, calculate the total tax due for each of the 10 years in the investment.

8. In the range C29:L29, calculate the net income for each of the 10 years of the investment. The net income is equal to the taxable income minus the total tax due from the tax on the rental income and the tax on the condo sale.

The cash flow schedule at the bottom of the worksheet calculates the yearly cash receipts that Greg expects to receive from owning the condo. Greg already entered all of the formulas to generate the cash flow schedule. The range B37:L37 contains the cumulative cash flow from the condo through the 10 years that Greg will own it. Based on his financial projections, how long will Greg have to wait until the yearly cash receipts generated from the condo cover the original purchase price?

9. Greg wants his investment to have a rate of return of at least 7%. Enter this value in cell F4.

10. In cell F5, calculate the net present value of the investment using the cash flow values in the cell range C35:L35 as the yearly returns from the condo investment and cell B4 as the initial cost of the investment. Assume that initial expenditure on the condo occurs immediately.

11. In cell F6, calculate the internal rate of return in the investment using the cash flow values from the range B35:L35. Based on your analysis, will purchasing the condo provide a greater return than a different investment offer with 7% annual interest? If the tax rate increases from 34% to 38%, will this still be the case?

12. Save and close the workbook. Submit the finished workbook to your instructor, either in printed or electronic form, as requested.

Apply	Case Problem 2

Use the skills you learned to calculate the profitability of a proposed limestone quarry.

Data File needed for this Case Problem: Witte.xlsx

Witte Limestone   Sheila Dawson is a manager at Witte Limestone, a firm specializing in the excavation and processing of limestone. Sheila is currently working on a proposal for excavating a new limestone quarry outside of the town of New Berlin, Wisconsin. According to the most recent estimates, the area has enough limestone to support a quarry for the next 20 years. There will be a substantial startup cost as well as substantial costs at the end of the quarry's useful lifetime. Current environment regulations require the company to restore the area to its original condition when the quarry work is finished. Sheila asks you to determine the profitability of the investment in the New Berlin quarry.

Complete the following:

1. Open the **Witte** workbook located in the Tutorial.09\Case2 folder, and then save the workbook as **Witte Limestone** in the same folder. In the Documentation sheet, enter your name in cell B3 and the date in cell B4.

2. The initial cost to set up the quarry is $3,500,000. Enter this value as a negative cash flow in cell B5 of the Investment Analysis worksheet.

3. Sheila estimates the quarry will generate $150,000 in cash during its first year of operation, with the yearly cash flow increasing to $900,000 by the end of Year 5. Interpolate the Year 1 through Year 5 cash flow values, assuming that the increase in cash follows a growth trend.

4. From Year 5 to Year 10, Sheila estimates the yearly cash flow will increase from $900,000 to $950,000. Interpolate the cash flow figures, assuming a linear trend in the increase in cash. From Year 10 to Year 15, Sheila estimates the yearly cash flow will decrease from $950,000 to $750,000. Interpolate the yearly cash flow figures once again assuming a linear trend in the decline.

5. From Year 15 to Year 20, the yearly cash flow from the quarry will decline from $750,000 down to $50,000. Interpolate the yearly cash flow figures assuming a growth trend in the decline in net cash.

6. In Year 21, the quarry will close and the company will spend an estimated $10,000,000 to restore the area to its original pristine condition. Enter this value in cell B26 as a negative cash flow.

7. Calculate the total cash flow of the project by entering **Total** in cell A27 and the sum of the values in the range B5:B26 in cell B27. Format the range A27:B27 with the Total cell style. Based on this estimate, will the quarry pay back the cost of the initial investment and the environmental cleanup?

8. Create a chart of the net cash flow values from the range A6:B25 using the Scatter with Straight Lines chart type. Place the new chart on a chart sheet named **Cash Flow Chart**. Remove the legend from the chart. Add the chart title **Yearly Cash Returns from the New Berlin Quarry** above the chart. Add the title **Year** to the horizontal axis and the title **Yearly Net Cash Flow per Year** to the vertical axis.

⊕ **EXPLORE**

9. The company wants a rate of return on this investment of at least 11%. In the Investment Analysis worksheet, estimate the internal rate of return for the entire investment from Year 0 through Year 21 by first inserting guesses on the IRR in cells D5 and D6. Enter the value **1%** in cell D5 and the value **10%** in cell D6. In cell E5, calculate the IRR of the investment, using the guess from cell D5. In cell E6, calculate the IRR of the investment using the guess from cell D6. Format the calculated IRRs so that they display the internal rate of return to two decimal places. Does your analysis confirm that the investment will have a return rate high enough for the company to proceed?

10. Calculate the net present value of the quarry project for different discount rates. Enter the values 1% through 20% in increments of 1% in the range D9:D28. In the range E9:E28, calculate the net present value of the investment assuming the discount rates in column D and that the initial investment in the quarry will occur immediately. For what discount rates is the NPV positive? For what discount rates is the NPV negative? Using your calculations, can you determine whether the investment will be worthwhile if the desired rate of return is 11%? Compare your answer with your answer in Step 7. What accounts for the apparent discrepancy between the two answers?

⊕ **EXPLORE**

11. Create a chart of the net present values from the range D9:E28 using the Scatter with Smooth Lines chart type. Place the new chart on a chart sheet named **NPV Chart**. Remove the legend from the chart. Add the chart title **Net Present Values** above the chart. Add the title **Rate of Return** to the horizontal axis and the title **Net Present Value** to the vertical axis. Does the chart explain the results you noticed in Step 8?

12. The startup date for the quarry might be delayed because of local community action over environmental concerns about the quarry. Recalculate the net present values for each of the discount rates in E9:E28 by inserting new net present value calculations in the range F9:F28, assuming that the initial investment occurs not immediately but in a year. Assuming a discount rate of 11%, how much will the delay cost the company in current dollars?

13. Save and close the workbook. Submit the finished workbook to your instructor, either in printed or electronic form, as requested.

Challenge | Case Problem 3

Explore how to use functions to analyze the affordability of a home mortgage.

Data File needed for this Case Problem: Eason.xlsx

Eason Financial Services   Jesse Buchmann is a finance officer at Eason Financial Services in Meridian, Idaho. One of her jobs is to work with potential clients who are looking for home mortgages. The first question her clients usually ask is, "How large of a mortgage can I qualify for?" To answer that question, Jesse needs to know two things: the client's monthly take-home pay and the monthly debt they're currently carrying. To qualify for a mortgage, the monthly mortgage payment should be no more than 28% of the client's take-home pay. However, some clients also have debts they have to repay each month, such as student loans, car payments, or credit card debt; a second rule is that the total debt amount (including their mortgage payment) should be no more than 36% of their net income.

Jesse wants a quick-and-easy way to determine whether a client qualifies for a loan under those two conditions. She asks you to help develop an Excel workbook into which she can enter the key information about her client's financial status and desired mortgage, and have an answer that tells her whether the client will qualify for the home loan.

Jesse's already done a lot of the work formatting her worksheet and she has already entered the financial data and loan conditions for her client Tony Bocelli. Tony is interested in getting a home loan for $215,000. Does he qualify? Jesse wants you to finish the job by entering all of the necessary formulas and functions.

Complete the following:

1. Open the **Eason** workbook located in the Tutorial.09\Case3 folder, and then save the workbook as **Eason Financial Services** in the same folder. In the Documentation sheet, enter your name and the date. Switch to the Loan Calculator worksheet.

2. Each month, Tony and his wife make $5400 in take-home pay, $1200 from other wages, and $150 from investments. Enter these values in the range E8:E10 as positive cash flows. Then, in cell E12, calculate the total monthly revenue for Tony Bocelli and his family.

3. The family has to pay $250 in car payments and $150 in student loans each month. In the Loan Calculator worksheet, enter these values in the cell range J8:J9 as negative cash flows. In cell J12, calculate their total monthly debt.

EXPLORE
4. In cell E19, calculate 28% of the family's monthly revenue. This value represents the most they can expect to spend on a home each month under the income qualification test.

EXPLORE
5. In cell E23, calculate 36% of the family's monthly revenue and reduce that value by their current monthly debt. This value represents the most they can spend on a home each month under the debt qualification test.

EXPLORE
6. In cell E25, display the minimum of the two qualification tests. This value represents the most they can spend on a home without violating either of the two qualification tests.

7. In cell J17, insert a reference to the value in Step 6. The range J18:J20 contains other monthly expenses that will come with owning a house, such as the monthly property tax assessment and home insurance costs. Estimate the tax escrow at $100 per month, the homeowner's insurance at $75 per month, and the miscellaneous expenses at $125. Enter these values as negative cash flows. In cell J21, calculate the amount left for paying the mortgage after accounting for these other expenses. This value represents the most that Tony can spend per month on the mortgage.

8. In the range E30:E33, enter the conditions of the home loan being offered by Eason Financial Services. Currently, the annual interest rate for home loans is 6.5% compounded monthly. Enter this information into the appropriate cells in the worksheet. Tony is interested in a 20-year loan. Enter that value and calculate the total number of monthly payments that will occur in 20 years. Enter the size of those monthly payments in cell E34 by referencing the value in cell J21. Change the sign of the monthly payment so that it appears as a negative cash flow.

9. The maximum loan that Tony can handle under these loan conditions can be determined using the PV function, which returns the present value of this proposed loan. Using the loan values you specified in Step 8 and the PV function, calculate the maximum loan that Tony can afford, displaying that value in cell H30.

10. In the Amortization Table worksheet, complete the amortization table using the loan values from the Loan Calculator worksheet.

11. Use your worksheet to test other loan possibilities for Jesse and her client. What size loan can Tony qualify for if the duration of the loan is reduced, so that he has to pay it all back in 15 years rather than 20 years? If he pays off all of his current debts, can Tony qualify for a 20-year loan for $215,000? Some borrowers allow clients to have loans as long as the monthly income ratio does not exceed 40%. If Tony pays off all of his debt, what is the largest 20-year loan he can qualify for under that more lenient test?

12. Save the workbook. Submit the finished workbook to your instructor, either in printed or electronic form, as requested.

Create | **Case Problem 4**

Create a workbook to analyze the profitability of a new car wash.

Data File needed for this Case Problem: Blue.xlsx

Blue Marlin Gas   Yasmin Arizmendi is the business manager for Blue Marlin Gas, a gas station and convenience store in Hartford, Michigan. Yasmin is looking at some capital improvements, such as adding a drive-through car wash to the station. He wants to perform an investment analysis to determine whether the capital improvement will pay off for the company. He has asked for your help in creating the workbook to determine what kind of return he can expect on his investment.

Complete the following:

1. Open the **Blue** workbook located in the Tutorial.09\Case4 folder, and then save the workbook as **Blue Marlin** in the same folder. In the Documentation sheet, enter your name and the date.

2. Create a worksheet to analyze Yasmin's investment in the new car wash. The cost to install a drive-through car wash is $250,000. Yasmin determines that the useful life of the equipment is 15 years with a salvage value of $35,000. Enter this information into the worksheet.

3. Yasmin expects the car wash to generate $62,000 in revenue during the first year and $90,000 in Year 15. The income should increase following a linear trend in the intervening years. The cost of operating the car wash will be $8000 in Year 1 and then increasing each year following a linear trend up to $25,000 in Year 15. Calculate his initial earnings (income minus expenses) for each of the 15 years.

4. Yasmin wants to use a straight-line depreciation on the car wash equipment when he calculates his taxes. Calculate the depreciation for each year and subtract that amount from his initial earnings estimate. This value is the company's taxable income on the operation of the car wash.

5. Assume a 33% tax rate and subtract the taxes due from the taxable income. The resulting value is the company's net income. Do this calculation for each of the 15 years.

6. Calculate the yearly cash flow from the new car wash. The cash inflow is equal to the net income plus the depreciation value you calculated in Step 4. The cash outflow will only consist of the taxes that you calculated in Step 5. Perform this calculation for each of the 15 years. Calculate the net cash flow by subtracting the cash outflow from the cash inflow for each of the 15 years the car wash is in operation.

7. Using the yearly net cash flow figures you calculated in Step 6, calculate the net present value of the investment in the new car wash over its 15-year history. Yasmin wants the investment to show at least a 7% rate of return. Assume that the initial investment of $250,000 in building the car wash occurs immediately.

8. Calculate the internal rate of return for the investment.
9. Prepare a summary of your findings, indicating whether the investment in the car wash will generate the kind of return Yasmin is looking for.
10. Save and close the workbook. Submit the finished workbook to your instructor, either in printed or electronic form, as requested.

Research | **Internet Assignments**

Use the Internet to find and work with data related to the topics presented in this tutorial.

The purpose of the Internet Assignments is to challenge you to find information on the Internet that you can use to work effectively with this software. The actual assignments are updated and maintained on the Course Technology Web site. Log on to the Internet and use your Web browser to go to the Student Online Companion for New Perspectives Office 2007 at **www.course.com/np/office2007**. Then navigate to the Internet Assignments for this tutorial.

Assess | **SAM Assessment and Training**

If you have a SAM user profile, you may have access to hands-on instruction, practice, and assessment of the skills covered in this tutorial. Log in to your SAM account (**http://sam2007.course.com**) to launch any assigned training activities or exams that relate to the skills covered in this tutorial.

Review | **Quick Check Answers**

Session 9.1

1. Positive cash flow is money flowing to you or your company. Negative cash flow is money flowing away from you or your company. Borrowing $100 from a bank is a positive cash flow because the money is flowing to you.
2. Enter the formula =FV(5.8%/12,10*12,−50,500), which returns the value $7,213.86.
3. Enter the formula =PMT(5.2%/12,2*12,1000,3000), which returns the negative cash flow value ($162.84).
4. Enter the formula =NPER(7%/12,−1500,200000), which returns the value 258.59315. It will take you 259 months to pay off the loan.
5. If you change the monthly payment to −1000, Excel returns the value #NUM!, indicating that you cannot pay off the loan at this low of a monthly payment.
6. Enter the formula =RATE(4*10,−7200,200000)*4, which returns the value 7.65%.
7. To calculate the monthly payment, enter the formula =PMT(6.3%/12,10*12,150000), which returns the negative cash flow value ($1,688.00). The amount of interest paid in the first month is calculated with the formula =IPMT(6.3%/12,1,10*12,150000), which returns the value ($787.50). The principal payment in the first month is calculated with the formula =PPMT(6.3%/12,1,10*12,150000), which returns the value ($900.50).
8. =SUMIF(A2:A100,"Harris",B2:B100)

Session 9.2

1. 1750, 2500, 3250
2. 1414.2136, 2000, 2828.4271
3. 1500, 2000, 2500, 3000
4. 1150, 1322.5, 1520.875, 1749.006
5. Enter the formula =SLN(25000, 2000, 5), which returns the value $4600.00.
6. Enter the formula =DB(25000, 2000, 5, 1), which returns the value $9925.00.
7. Enter the formula =DDB(25000, 2000, 5, 1), which returns the value $10,000.

Session 9.3

1. Payback periods do not take into account the time value of money.
2. Use the formula =PV(5%,1,0,100) to calculate the present value of $100 a year from now. Excel returns the negative cash flow value ($95.24), indicating that $100 a year from now is a fair exchange for $95.24 today. In other words, $100 a year from now is worth more than $95 today by 24 cents.
3. Enter the Excel formula =NPV(6%,50,75,100), which returns the value $197.88.
4. Enter the formula =NPV(6%, 75, 75, 75, 75, 75, 75)−350, which returns the value $18.80.
5. Enter the formula =NPV(6%, −350, 75, 75, 75, 75, 75, 75). Excel returns the value $17.74.
6. Enter the formula =IRR(*range*), where *range* is a cell range containing the values: −350, 75, 75, 75, 75, 75, 75. Excel returns the value 7.69%. You should take this investment over one offering a 7.3% internal rate of return.
7. The XNPV and XIRR functions available on the Analysis Toolpak add-in.
8. The formula points to a worksheet cell that has been deleted.

Ending Data Files

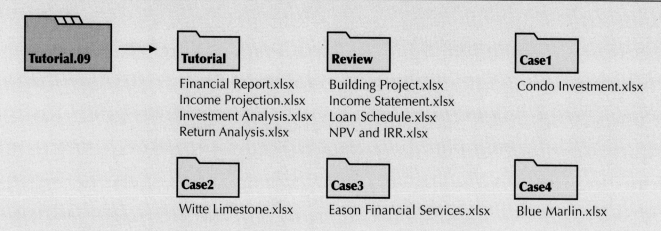

Tutorial.09 →

Tutorial
Financial Report.xlsx
Income Projection.xlsx
Investment Analysis.xlsx
Return Analysis.xlsx

Review
Building Project.xlsx
Income Statement.xlsx
Loan Schedule.xlsx
NPV and IRR.xlsx

Case1
Condo Investment.xlsx

Case2
Witte Limestone.xlsx

Case3
Eason Financial Services.xlsx

Case4
Blue Marlin.xlsx

Performing What-If Analyses

Analyzing the Cost-Volume-Profit Relationship

Case | Creative Ventures

Creative Ventures is a toy company in Fernwood, Illinois, founded by Todd and Brent Kendall. A few years ago, they created the HoverDisk, a toy that has attracted much attention and enthusiasm. Todd and Brent want to expand their market and need to perform a cost-volume-profit analysis to determine how much they can charge for the product and still break even (or show a specific level of profit). They also need to perform a price analysis to determine the optimal price for the product to maximize the company's net income. They asked you to help design an Excel workbook to answer these questions.

Starting Data Files

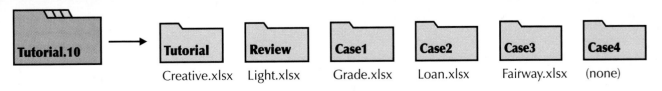

Tutorial.10 →	Tutorial	Review	Case1	Case2	Case3	Case4
	Creative.xlsx	Light.xlsx	Grade.xlsx	Loan.xlsx	Fairway.xlsx	(none)

Session 10.1

Understanding Cost-Volume-Profit Relationships

Todd and Brent Kendall have been very busy as Creative Ventures expands well beyond their expectations. Their talent lies in designing toys, not in the financial aspects of the business. As sales of their most popular toy, the HoverDisk, increase, they are unsure of what is a reasonable price for the product. To help determine this, you need to quantify the different factors that affect the product's profitability. For example, how many disks does the company need to sell to break even? If Creative Ventures increases sales by 2000 units annually, how much additional revenue will be generated, and how much additional overhead will be required to meet the increased production? What price should be charged for the HoverDisk? At what point will the price hurt sales and reduce revenue? You can use cost-volume-profit analysis to find answers to questions like these.

Cost-volume-profit (**CVP**) **analysis** expresses the relationship between a company's expenses, its volume of business, and the resulting profit or net income. CVP analysis is an important business decision-making tool because it predicts the effect of cutting overhead or raising prices on net income. Before applying a CVP analysis to Todd and Brent's data, you should understand the types of expenses that will be part of your CVP calculations.

Comparing Types of Expenses

The first component of CVP analysis is cost, or expense. There are three types of expenses: variable, fixed, and mixed. **Variable expenses** change in proportion to the amount of business a company does. For example, Creative Ventures has to spend more money on raw materials if it increases the number of HoverDisks produced. In addition, as the sales volume increases, the costs associated with production also increases. Each HoverDisk costs the company $8.50 in raw materials and $5.25 in other production costs, for a total cost of $13.75 per disk. The total variable expenses for the company are equal to the cost per disk multiplied by the total number of disks produced. The line graph in Figure 10-1 plots the total variable expenses based on the production volume. As you can see from this graph, it will cost Creative Ventures almost $200,000 to produce 15,000 disks.

Creative Ventures sells HoverDisks for $28.50. You can deduct the variable expenses ($13.75) from the sales price ($28.50) to determine the company's profit of $14.75 on each sale. That might seem like a lot, but that profit has to cover the company's fixed expenses. A **fixed expense** is an expense that must be paid regardless of sales volume. For example, Creative Ventures has to pay salaries and benefits for its employees as well as insurance, maintenance fees, and taxes. The company has almost $300,000 in fixed expenses, which must be paid even if the company doesn't sell a single disk.

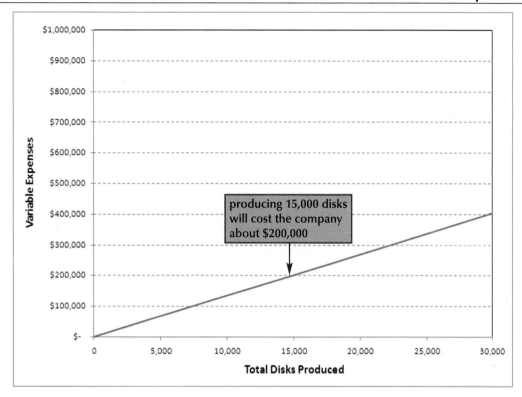

You can estimate Creative Ventures' total expenses by adding the variable and fixed expenses. The graph in Figure 10-2 shows the company's total expenses for a given number of disks produced each year.

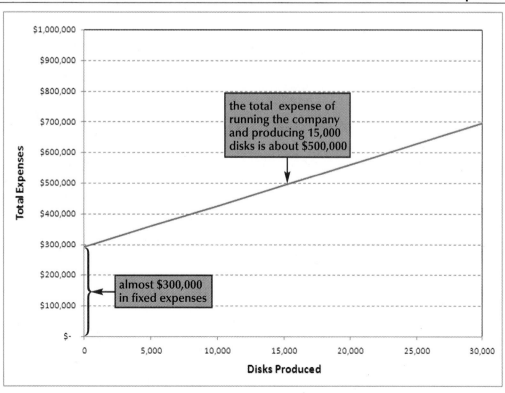

If the company produces 15,000 disks, its total expense would be almost $500,000, of which about $300,000 represents fixed expenses and about $200,000 represents variable expenses.

A third type of expense is a **mixed expense**, which is part variable and part fixed. At this point, you will not consider any mixed expenses in your calculations.

Determining the Break-Even Point

Creative Ventures is selling most of what it produces, so the company should bring in more revenue as it increases production. Figure 10-3 shows the increase in revenue in relation to the increase in sales volume. Selling 15,000 disks at $28.50 brings in about $400,000 of revenue. As shown in Figure 10-2, total expenses for 15,000 disks are almost $500,000, which means a net loss to the company of around $100,000. This leads to the first question Brent and Todd want you to answer: How many disks must the company sell to match its total expenses? The point where revenue equals expenses is called the **break-even point**. For this reason, CVP analysis is sometimes called **break-even analysis**. The more disks the company sells above the break-even point, the greater the profit for the company, but sales volume below the break-even point means the company is losing money.

| Figure 10-3 | Chart of revenue |

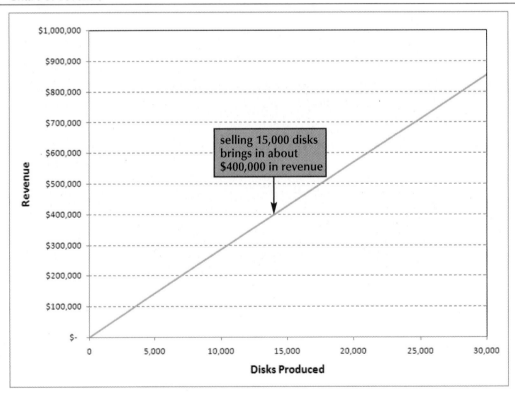

You can present a break-even analysis by charting revenue and total expenses versus sales volume. The point at which the two lines cross is the break-even point. This type of chart is called a **cost-volume-profit (CVP) chart**. A CVP chart is a quick way of presenting the relationship between expenses and revenue. Figure 10-4 shows a typical CVP chart.

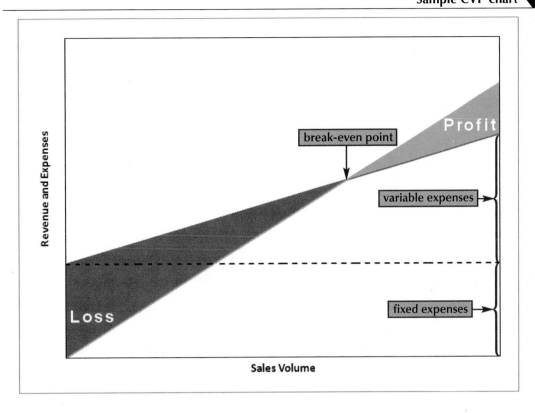

Working with What-If Analysis and Goal Seek

Todd and Brent have given you an income statement that contains the projected income and expense amounts for the current year based on the actual amounts from the previous year. You'll use these figures as the basis for your CVP analysis.

To open the income statement workbook:

▶ **1.** Open the **Creative** workbook located in the **Tutorial.10\Tutorial** folder included with your Data Files, and then save the workbook as **Creative Ventures** in the same folder.

▶ **2.** In the Documentation sheet, enter your name in cell B3 and the current date in cell B4.

▶ **3.** Switch to the **Income Statement** worksheet and review its contents and formulas. See Figure 10-5, which shows the entire income statement.

Figure 10-5 ▶ **Creative Ventures income statement**

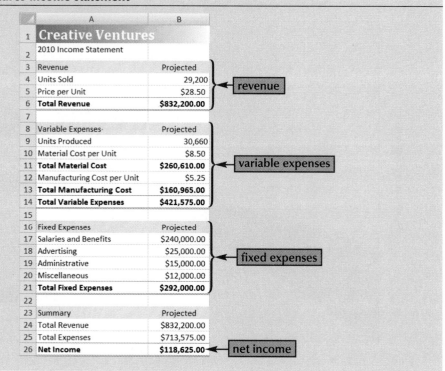

The Income Statement worksheet contains projected revenue, variable expenses, and fixed expenses based on the previous year's sales of the HoverDisk. Todd and Brent expect to sell 29,200 disks at a price of $28.50 per disk, generating $832,200 in revenue. They plan to produce 5% more disks than they expect to sell to create a reasonable inventory. This means the company will produce 30,660 disks at a cost of $421,575. The fixed expenses are projected to be $292,000. The net income from the sale of the disks is projected to be $118,625.

Performing a What-If Analysis

Todd and Brent want you to perform a what-if analysis to investigate what would happen to the company's net income if certain factors are changed. The toy industry is competitive, and Todd and Brent want to explore the impact on the company's net income if sales declined to 25,000 units or lower. To examine this scenario, you can edit the worksheet by changing the projected values.

To calculate the net income for different sales volumes:

▶ **1.** Click cell **B4** and change the expected sales from 29,200 units to **25,000**.

▶ **2.** Scroll down the worksheet and note the net income under this scenario. If sales drop to 25,000 units, the net income will be cut in half, falling to $59,562.50.

▶ **3.** Change the value in cell B4 to **20,000**. If sales drop to this level, the company will show a net loss of $10,750.

▶ **4.** Change the value in cell B4 back to **29,200**. The net income returns to $118,625.

You show Todd and Brent your calculations. They wonder exactly how many disks they must sell to break even, assuming no other factors change in the projections. You could find this value by inserting different values in cell B4, hunting for a units sold value resulting in a net income of zero. A faster approach is to use Goal Seek.

Using Goal Seek

In the what-if analysis you just performed, you change an input value—Units Sold—to see how it affected a calculated item. **Goal Seek** takes the opposite approach by specifying a value for a calculated item and then returning the input value needed to reach that goal. Figure 10-6 illustrates the difference between what-if analysis and Goal Seek.

What-if analysis and Goal Seek ◀ **Figure 10-6**

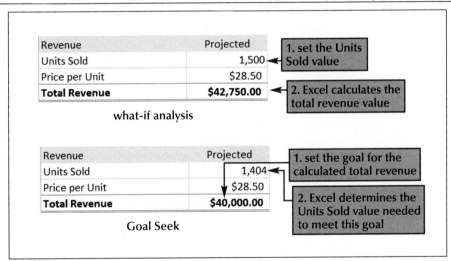

In this example, Creative Ventures produces each disk at a price of $28.50. A what-if analysis might ask *what* would be the total revenue *if* the company sold 1,500 disks. The input value is the number of disks sold and the result is the total revenue, which, in this case, is $42,750. Goal Seek might determine how many disks the company needs to sell to meet the specified goal of $40,000 in revenue. In this case, selling 1,404 disks would result in slightly more than $40,000 of revenue.

Reference Window | **Performing What-If Analysis and Goal Seek**

To perform what-if analysis:
- Change the value of a worksheet cell (the input cell).
- Observe its impact on one or more calculated cells (the result cells).

To perform Goal Seek:
- In the Data Tools group on the Data tab, click the What-If Analysis button, and then click Goal Seek.
- In the Set cell box, select the result cell, and then, in the To value box, specify its value (goal).
- In the By changing cell box, specify the input cell.
- Click the OK button. The value of the input cell changes to set the value of the result cell.

You'll use Goal Seek to determine the number of disks that Creative Ventures must sell to break even.

To use Goal Seek to determine the break-even point:

▶ 1. Click the **Data** tab on the Ribbon.

▶ 2. In the Data Tools group, click the **What-If Analysis** button, and then click **Goal Seek**. The Goal Seek dialog box opens.

▶ 3. Click the **Set cell** box if it is not already active, and then click cell **B26** in the worksheet (you might need to scroll to see the cell).

▶ 4. Press the **Tab** key to move the insertion point to the To value box, and then type **0**, which indicates that you want to set the value of cell B26 (the net income cell) to 0.

▶ 5. Press the **Tab** key to move the insertion point to the By changing cell box, and then click cell **B4**. The absolute reference $B$4 is entered, which indicates that you want to set the total income value to 0 by changing the value in cell B4 (the units sold cell). See Figure 10-7.

Figure 10-7 | **Goal Seek dialog box**

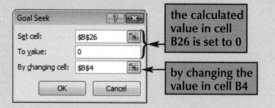

▶ **6.** Click the **OK** button. The Goal Seek dialog box closes, and the Goal Seek Status dialog box opens, indicating that Goal Seek found a solution.

▶ **7.** Click the **OK** button. The value 20,764 appears in cell B4. See Figure 10-8.

Annual sales required to break even ◀ Figure 10-8

	A	B
1	**Creative Ventures**	
2	2010 Income Statement	
3	Revenue	Projected
4	Units Sold	20,764
5	Price per Unit	$28.50
6	**Total Revenue**	**$591,786.67**
7		
8	Variable Expenses	Projected
9	Units Produced	21,803
10	Material Cost per Unit	$8.50
11	**Total Material Cost**	**$185,322.67**
12	Manufacturing Cost per Unit	$5.25
13	**Total Manufacturing Cost**	**$114,464.00**
14	**Total Variable Expenses**	**$299,786.67**
15		
16	Fixed Expenses	Projected
17	Salaries and Benefits	$240,000.00
18	Advertising	$25,000.00
19	Administrative	$15,000.00
20	Miscellaneous	$12,000.00
21	**Total Fixed Expenses**	**$292,000.00**
22		
23	Summary	Projected
24	Total Revenue	$591,786.67
25	Total Expenses	$591,786.67
26	**Net Income**	**$0.00**

yearly sales of 20,764 units

resulting net income is $0

▶ **8.** Click cell **B4**. Observe the formula bar and note that the exact value in the cell is 20764.44444. There is no integer units sold value that will result exactly in $0 net income.

▶ **9.** Change the value in cell B4 back to **29,200**.

Based on the results from Goal Seek, the company needs to sell about 20,764 Hover-Disks each year to cover expenses. Todd and Brent want to compare this value to the results obtained from other assumptions of sales volume. For example, what would the company's net income be if sales increased to 30,000 units or 35,000 units or 40,000 units? How many units will the company need to sell to reach a net income of $200,000? You could continue to perform what-if analyses and run the Goal Seek command to answer these questions, but a more efficient approach is to use a data table.

Working with One-Variable Data Tables

A **data table** organizes the results of several what-if analyses within a single table. Two important elements are involved in creating a data table: input cells and result cells. **Input cells** are the cells containing values you want to modify in a what-if analysis. **Result cells** are the cells containing the values that you want to examine. For example, you changed the value in cell B4 (the input cell) to examine what would happen if Creative Ventures' sales volume decreased. The result of that change was reflected in the company's net income in cell B26 (the result cell).

Exploring One-Variable Data Tables

Excel supports two kinds of data tables: one-variable data tables and two-variable data tables. In a **one-variable data table**, you specify one input cell and any number of result cells. The range of possible values for the input cell is entered in the first row or column of the data table, and the corresponding values of the result cells appear in the accompanying rows or columns. One-variable data tables are particularly useful in business to explore how altering one value can impact several result cells. For example, Figure 10-9 shows a one-variable data table created to determine the impact of different interest rates on the monthly payment and total cost of a mortgage.

Figure 10-9 ▸ **Sample one-variable data table**

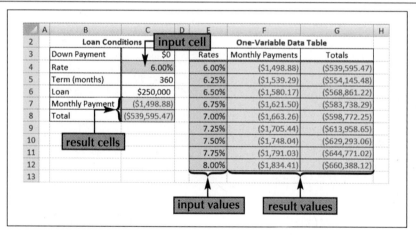

In this example, the interest rate in cell C4 is the input cell, and the values in the range E4:E12 are **input values**, that is, possible values for the input cell. Cells C7 and C8 are the result cells, and the values in the range F4:G12 are the **result values**. The results from nine different what-if analyses appear in this single table. For example, you can quickly see that a 7% interest rate results in a $1,663.26 monthly payment and a total mortgage cost of $598,772.25. You can also observe how quickly the total payments rise with an increasing interest rate. When the annual interest rate increases two percentage points from 6% to 8%, the total cost of the mortgages increases about $120,000.

| Reference Window

Creating a One-Variable Data Table

- Insert a formula that references the input cell in the upper-left cell of the table.
- Insert input values in either the first row or first column of the table.
- For input values in the first row, insert formulas referencing result cells in the table's first column; for input values in the first column, insert formulas referencing result cells in the table's first row.
- Select the table (excluding any row or column headings). In the Data Tools group on the Data tab, click the What-If Analysis button, and then click Data Table.
- If the input values are in the first row, enter the cell reference to the input cell in the Row input cell box; if the input values are in the first column, enter the cell reference to the input cell in the Column input cell box.
- Click the OK button.

Creating a Data Table

You need to create a data table for the Creative Ventures income statement. You'll create a one-variable data table to examine the impact of changing sales volume on the company's revenue, total expenses, and net income. To set up a data table, you first insert references to the input and result cells. The input and result values can be arranged in rows or columns. You should always clearly label the row or column containing the input and result values.

You'll create the data table.

To set up the one-variable data table:

1. In cell E2, enter **Cost-Volume-Profit Analysis**. In cell E3, enter **Units Sold**. In cell F3, enter **Revenue**. In cell G3, enter **Expenses**. In cell H3, enter **Net Income**.

2. Merge and center the range E2:H2 and format the text using the **20% - Accent3** cell style.

    Next, you'll enter the references to the input cell and the two result cells.

3. In cell E4, enter the formula **=B4**. In cell F4, enter the formula **=B24**. In cell G4, enter the formula **=B25**. In cell H4, enter the formula **=B26**.

    Finally, you'll enter the input values you want to appear in the data table. Todd suggests that you insert sales volumes of 15,000 units sold up to 40,000 units sold in increments of 5,000 units.

4. In cell E5, enter **15,000**. In cell E6, enter **20,000**.

5. Select the range **E5:E6**, and then drag the fill handle down to cell **E10**. Excel completes the series, displaying Units Sold values up to 40,000.

6. Click cell **E11** to deselect the range. See Figure 10-10.

Figure 10-10 **Input and result cells and input values**

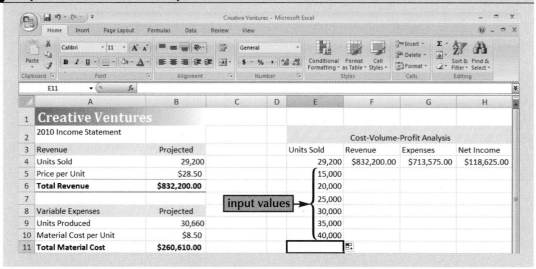

You are ready to fill the table with the result values. To do this, you select the range that contains the data table (excluding the column headings), and then you open the Data Table dialog box, specifying the input cell based on whether the input values are arranged in rows or columns. Because your input values are in a column, you'll use the Column input cell option. If you had oriented the table so that the input values were in a single row, you would use the Row input cell option.

To complete the one-variable data table:

▶ **1.** Select the range **E4:H10**. This is the range of the data table.

▶ **2.** In the Data Tools group on the Data tab, click the **What-If Analysis** button, and then click **Data Table**. The Data Table dialog box opens.

▶ **3.** Press the **Tab** key to move the insertion point to the Column input cell box, and then click cell **B4** in the worksheet. See Figure 10-11.

Figure 10-11 **Data Table dialog box**

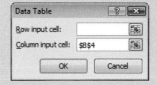

Tip

Use matching fill colors and styles between the input cells and input values and result cells and result values so others can quickly see which cells in the worksheet the data table is based on.

▶ **4.** Click the **OK** button. The data table displays the expenses and revenues for each of the input values in the range E5:E10.

▶ **5.** Select the range **F4:H4**, right-click the selected range, click the **Format Painter** button 🖌 on the Mini toolbar, and then select the range **F5:H10** to apply the copied formats.

▶ **6.** Click cell **E11** to deselect the range. See Figure 10-12.

Completed data table | Figure 10-12

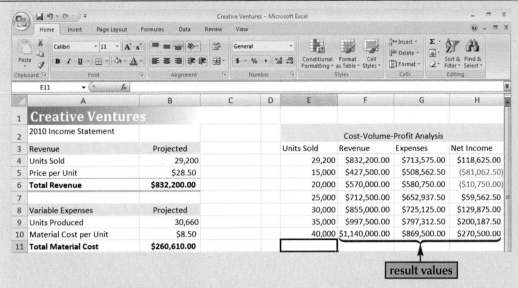

The data table shows the results of several what-if analyses simultaneously. For example, if annual sales increase to 35,000 units, the company's revenue will be more than $997,000, but the total expenses will be more than $797,000, making a net income of more than $200,000.

Charting a One-Variable Data Table

You could give Todd and Brent a copy of the data table you have created, but the results might be clearer if you include a CVP chart along with the table. The chart will give Todd and Brent a better picture of the relationship between sales volume, revenue, and total expenses. To create the CVP chart, you'll use a scatter chart to chart the revenue and total expenses against the total number of units sold.

To create the CVP chart:

▶ 1. Select the range **E3:G10**. This range contains the data you want to chart.

▶ 2. Click the **Insert** tab on the Ribbon. In the Charts group, click the **Scatter** button, and then click the **Scatter with Smooth Lines** chart type (the left chart in the second row).

▶ 3. In the Location group on the Chart Tools Design tab, click the **Move Chart** button. The Move Chart dialog box opens.

▶ 4. Click the **New sheet** option button, type **CVP Chart** in the New sheet box, and then click the **OK** button. The CVP Chart sheet is added to the workbook.

▶ 5. Drag the **CVP Chart** sheet after the Income Statement worksheet.

▶ 6. Click the **Chart Tools Layout** tab. You'll use the tools on this tab to edit the chart.

▶ 7. Add the chart title **Cost-Volume-Profit Analysis** above the chart, add a primary vertical axis title rotated with the text **Revenue and Expenses**, and then add a primary horizontal axis title below the axis with the text **Units Sold**.

▶ 8. Change the font size of both axis titles to **14** points.

▶ 9. Format the values on the vertical axis as Currency with no decimal places. Format the values on the horizontal axis using the Number style with no decimal places. See Figure 10-13.

Figure 10-13 Completed CVP chart

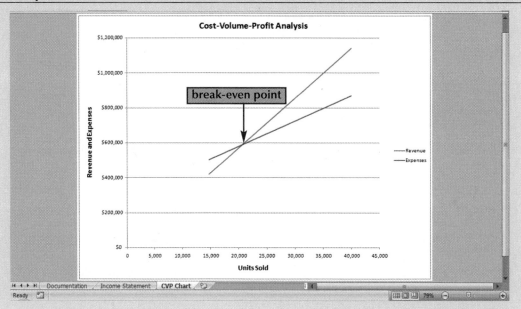

Excel plots each of the points in the data table, connecting them with a line. The blue line represents revenue; the red line represents expenses. The break-even point occurs at a sales volume of about 20,000 units. The data table and CVP chart give a comprehensive picture of the impact of sales volume on total expenses and revenue.

Todd and Brent are considering lowering the price of HoverDisks to be more competitive with other toy manufacturers. You'll perform another what-if analysis using a sales price of $23.50. Because data tables are dynamic, changes in the worksheet are automatically reflected in the data table values.

To view the impact of changing the price:

▶ **1.** Switch to the **Income Statement** worksheet.

▶ **2.** Change the value in cell B5 from $28.50 to **$23.50**. See Figure 10-14.

Figure 10-14 Data table for the $23.50 price

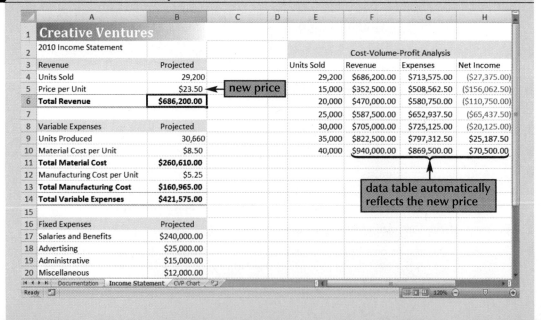

▶ **3.** Switch to the **CVP Chart** sheet and view the results of the change you made in the price. The break-even point, where the Revenue and Expenses lines intersect, has moved to the right, indicating that Creative Ventures would have to sell about 32,000 units to break even at this new price.

▶ **4.** Return to the **Income Statement** worksheet and change the value in cell B5 back to **$28.50**.

Working with Two-Variable Data Tables

Todd and Brent are concerned the company might not be able to sell 32,000 units even at the $23.50 price and wonder what the break-even point would be at other prices. They want you to perform several more what-if analyses for multiple combinations of sales price and units sold, determining under which combinations the company would show a profit. They ask you to calculate the net income for prices ranging from $20 to $40 in increments of $5 and for units sold from 15,000 units per year up to 40,000 units in increments of 5,000 units.

Rather than repeatedly change the input values for the one-variable data table, you can analyze all of these combinations simultaneously with a two-variable data table. As the name implies, a **two-variable data table** uses two input cells, but unlike a one-variable data table, only the value of a single result cell can be displayed. Two variable data tables are often used to explore the impact of changing two values on a single result. Figure 10-15 shows an example of a two-variable data table that examines the impact of the interest rate and the length of the mortgage on the monthly payment.

Sample two-variable data table   **Figure 10-15**

In this example, the two input cells are cell C4, the interest rate, and cell C5, the number of months before the loan is repaid. The first column of the data table displays a range of interest values for the first input cell and the first row of the data table shows a range of possible terms for the second input cell. The result cell in this what-if analysis is cell C7—the monthly payment. Result values are displayed in the two-variable data table at the intersection of each input value. For example, a 240-month loan at 7.25% interest would require a monthly payment of $1,975.94 (cell H10). The advantage of this data table is that it quickly shows the results of 36 what-if analyses on different loan conditions.

Reference Window | **Creating a Two-Variable Data Table**

- Insert a formula that references the result cell in the upper-left cell of the table.
- Insert input values in the first row and first column of the table.
- Select the table (excluding any row or column headings)..
- In the Data Tools group on the Data tab, click the What-If Analysis button, and then click Data Table.
- Enter the cell reference corresponding to the input values in the first row in the Row input cell box; enter the cell reference to the input values in the first column in the Column input cell box.
- Click the OK button.

Creating a Two-Variable Data Table

For Creative Ventures, you'll create a two-variable data table that examines the impact of sales price and the yearly sales volume on net income. You'll start by entering the labels and input values for the table.

To set up the two-variable data table:

1. In cell E12, enter **Net Income Analysis**, and then merge and center the range E12:J12.

2. In cell F13, enter **Price per Unit**, merge and center the range F13:J13, and then format the merged cell using the **20% - Accent3** cell style.

3. In the range E15:E20, enter the values 15,000 through 40,000 in increments of 5,000.

4. In the range F14:J14, enter the values $20 to $40 in increments of $5.

5. Click cell **E14** to deselect the range. See Figure 10-16.

Figure 10-16 **Structure for the two-variable data table**

11	$260,610.00							
12	$5.25				Net Income Analysis			
13	$160,965.00				Price per Unit			
14	$421,575.00			$20	$25	$30	$35	$40
15			15,000					
16	Projected		20,000					
17	$240,000.00		25,000					
18	$25,000.00		30,000					
19	$15,000.00		35,000					
20	$12,000.00		40,000					
21	$292,000.00							
22								
23	Projected							
24	$832,200.00							
25	$713,575.00							
26	$118,625.00							
27								

Documentation Income Statement CVP Chart

Ready   120%

In two-variable data tables, the reference to the result cell is placed in the upper-left corner of the table at the intersection of the two sets of input values. In this case, you'll enter a formula in cell E14 that references the company's net income. Because placing a value in this location on the table might confuse some users, you'll format the cell to hide the value, displaying instead the text "Units Sold."

To insert the reference to the result cell:

▶ **1.** In cell E14, enter the formula **=B26**. The formula returns the value $118,625.00, which is the current projected net income.

▶ **2.** Right-click cell **E14**, and then click **Format Cells** on the shortcut menu. The Format Cells dialog box opens.

▶ **3.** Click the **Number** tab if it is not selected, click **Custom** in the Category box, and then type **"Units Sold"** in the Type box. See Figure 10-17.

Tip

Another way to hide the reference to the result cell is to apply the same fill color to the cell text and background.

Custom format to display a text label ◀ **Figure 10-17**

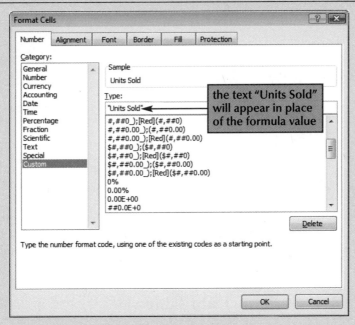

▶ **4.** Click the **OK** button. The text *Units Sold* appears in cell E14, even though the cell's underlying contents is the formula =B26, which results in the value $118,625.

▶ **5.** Format cell E14 with the **20% - Accent3** cell style.

With the table set up, you can use the Data Table command to display the net income for each combination of price and units sold. When creating a two-variable data table, you must identify the row input cell and the column input cell. The **row input cell** is the cell on which you base values placed in the first row of the data table. The first row of your data table contains the unit price, so the row input cell is cell B5—the current unit price of the HoverDisk. Similarly, the **column input cell** is the cell on which values placed in the first column of the data table are based. In this case, cell B4, the number of disks sold by the company, is the column input cell. You'll complete the two-variable table by identifying the two input cells.

To complete the two-variable data table:

▶ 1. Select the range **E14:J20**. This range includes input values for both the row and the column input cell as well as the hidden reference to the result cell in cell E14.

▶ 2. In the Data Tools group on the Data tab, click the **What-If Analysis** button, and then click **Data Table**. The Data Table dialog box opens.

▶ 3. Type **B5** in the Row input cell box, type **B4** in the Column input cell box, and then click the **OK** button. The data table values are filled in.

▶ 4. Use the Format Painter to copy the format from cell H10 into the range F15:J20.

▶ 5. Click cell **E13** to deselect the range. See Figure 10-18.

Figure 10-18	Completed two-variable data table

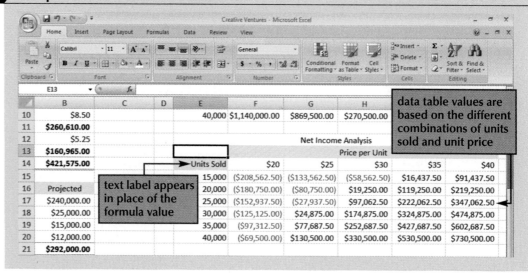

Based on the results shown in Figure 10-18, you inform Todd and Brent that if the unit price drops to $20 per disk, none of the sales volume figures would show a net profit. On the other hand, the company will show a profit for all of the sales volume figures if the price is set at $35.

Charting a Two-Variable Data Table

You will chart the data from the two-variable data table. The chart will plot net income versus sales volume with the data from each unit price displayed on a different line.

To begin creating the chart of the two-variable data table:

▶ 1. Select the range **E15:J20**. You'll plot this range on a scatter chart. You did not select the unit prices in row 14 because Excel will interpret these values as data values to be charted, not as labels.

▶ 2. Click the **Insert** tab on the Ribbon, click the **Scatter** button in the Charts group, and then click the **Scatter with Straight Lines** chart type (the chart in the third row).

▶ 3. In the Data group on the Chart Tools Design tab, click the **Switch Row/Column** button to plot the data values based on a column rather than a row layout.

4. In the Location group on the Chart Tools Design tab, click the **Move Chart** button to open the Move Chart dialog box.

5. Move the chart to a new chart sheet named **Net Income Chart**, and then drag the **Net Income Chart** sheet tab to the end of the workbook.

6. Click the **Chart Tools Layout** tab on the Ribbon, and then insert the title **Net Income Analysis** above the chart.

7. Insert the primary vertical axis title with the rotated title **Net Income**, insert the primary horizontal axis title below the axis as **Units Sold**, and then set the font size of both axis titles to **16** points. See Figure 10-19.

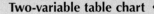

Two-variable table chart ◄ **Figure 10-19**

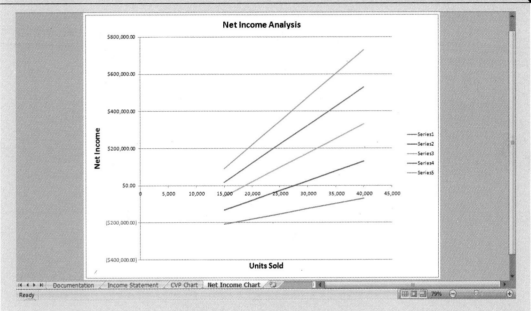

The chart shows a different trend line for each of the five possible values for unit price. However, the prices are not listed in the chart and Excel uses the generic series names Series1, Series2, Series3, Series4, and Series5. To use the unit prices rather than the generic names in the chart, you have to edit the property of each series.

To edit the chart series names:

1. Click the **Chart Tools Design** tab on the Ribbon, and then, in the Data group, click the **Select Data** button. The Select Data Source dialog box opens.

2. Click **Series1** in the Legend Entries (Series) box, and then click the **Edit** button. The Edit Series dialog box opens with the Series name box active.

3. Click the **Income Statement** sheet tab, click cell **F14** to insert the reference in the Series name box, and then click the **OK** button. The Select Data Source dialog box reappears, and the Series1 name changes to $20.

4. Repeat the process in Steps 2 and 3 to rename the four remaining chart series. For Series2, use the value in cell **G14**. For Series3, use the value in cell **H14**. For Series4, use the value in cell **I14**. For Series5, use the value in cell **J14**. See Figure 10-20.

Figure 10-20 Select Data Source dialog box

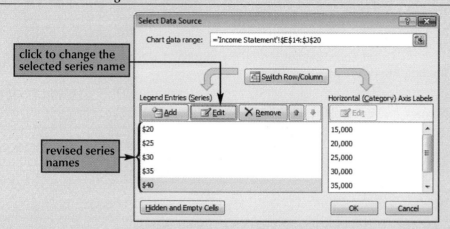

5. Click the **OK** button. The legend shows the renamed series.

   The default line colors do not reflect the increasing value of the unit price. You'll change the line color to different shades of green with the light shade applied to the highest unit price values.

6. In the Chart Styles group on the Chart Tools Design tab, click the **More** button to open the Chart Styles gallery, and then click **Style 13** (the fifth style in the second row) to change the line colors to shades of green. See Figure 10-21.

Figure 10-21 Final chart of net income values

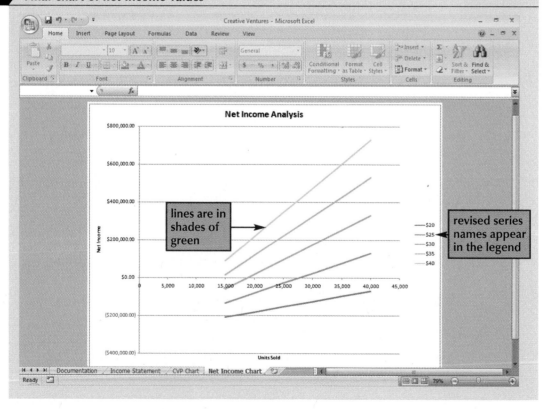

Todd and Brent can use the chart to quickly see how different unit prices will affect the relationship between sales volume and net income. A value of 0 on the vertical axis represents the break-even point. The $20 line doesn't cross 0 in the chart, indicating that you cannot make a profit by charging $20 per disk unless the company has a much higher sales volume than Todd and Brent have specified. On the other hand, at $40 per disk, Creative Ventures will always show a profit (albeit a small one) with even as little as 15,000 units sold per year.

Data Tables and Arrays | InSight

If you examine the cells in the two-variable data table you just created, you can see that every cell displays a different value even though it has the same formula: {=TABLE(B5, B4)}. This formula is an **array formula**, which is a formula that performs multiple calculations in a single step, returning either a single value to one cell or multiple values to several cells. Array formulas are always enclosed within curly braces.

One example of an array formula that returns a single value is {=SUM(B1:B10*C1:C10)}. This formula multiplies each cell in the range B1:B10 by the matching cell in the same row of the range C1:C10. The sum of those 10 products is then calculated and returned. To create this array formula, enter the formula =SUM(B1:B10*C1:C10) and press the Ctrl+Shift+Enter keys. Excel treats the formula as an array formula, adding the curly braces for you.

The **TABLE function** is an array function that returns multiple values to multiple cells. Other such functions include the TREND, MINVERSE, MMULT, and TRANSPOSE functions. To calculate multiple cell values, select the range and type the array formula, pressing the Ctrl+Shift+Enter keys to enter the formula. Excel applies the array formula to all of the selected cells.

Array formulas are a powerful but underused feature of Excel. Used properly, they help you perform complex calculations within a single formula. To learn more about array formulas and the functions that support them, refer to Microsoft Office Excel Help.

So far, you've shown Todd and Brent some of the factors that affect the company's profitability. They now have a better idea how much they can charge for the HoverDisk and what impact sales volume has on Creative Ventures' profitability. However, data tables limit you to working with at most two input cells. Some situations require that you examine the impact of more than two factors on an outcome. You'll look at tools to do that kind of what-if analysis in the next session.

Session 10.1 Quick Check | Review

1. Describe the difference between a what-if analysis and Goal Seek.
2. Name the three components of the Goal Seek command.
3. What is a data table? What is an input cell? What is a result cell?
4. What is a one-variable data table? What is a two-variable data table?
5. How many result cells can you display with a one-variable data table? How many result cells can be displayed with a two-variable data table?
6. Cell E5 contains the formula =B10. You want to display, not the formula's value, but the text string "Profits." What custom format would you use?
7. What is an array formula?

Session 10.2

Using Scenario Manager

Todd and Brent reviewed the what-if analyses you completed in the previous session. They now want to change other values in the income statement to see the impact on the company's revenue, expenses, and net income. They have four situations they want you to investigate, labeled Status Quo, Expanded Operations, Reduced Operations, and Sale. Figure 10-22 shows the values of the input cells for these four situations and the result cells they want you to calculate.

Figure 10-22	New what-if scenarios					
Cell Type	**Revenue and Expense Categories**	**Status Quo**	**Expanded Operations**	**Reduced Operations**	**Sale**
Input Cells	Units Sold (B4)	29,200	35,000	20,000	40,000
	Unit Price (B5)	$28.50	$28.50	$28.50	$20.00
	Salaries and Benefits (B17)	$240,000	$300,000	$200,000	$200,000
	Advertising (B18)	$25,000	$40,000	$15,000	$15,000
	Administrative (B19)	$15,000	$25,000	$10,000	$10,000
	Miscellaneous (B20)	$12,000	$20,000	$10,000	$10,000
Result Cells (to be calculated)	Total Revenue (B24)				
	Total Expenses (B25)				
	Net Income (B26)				

The Status Quo situation assumes that everything remains the same for the upcoming year. All of the fixed expenses, units sold, and unit price are unchanged. The Expanded Operations situation assumes that the company will expand its production and marketing of HoverDisks. Under this proposal, the company will hire additional workers, expand its advertising budget, and spend more on administrative and miscellaneous expenses with the hoped-for result that sales of HoverDisks will increase. The Reduced Operations situation decreases the amount spent for fixed expenses and assumes a decline in sales. The Sale situation assumes the unit price for HoverDisk will drop from $28.50 to $20 per unit. To cover the loss in revenue, the company will also reduce its fixed expenses.

You cannot generate such a report using a data table because you need six input cells and three result cells. To perform a what-if analysis with more than two input cells, you create scenarios. A **scenario** is a defined set of input values used to perform a what-if analysis. Rather than entering and reentering these values, you can define the scenario once and then reload the scenario whenever you want to view the results. **Scenario Manager** enables you to create as many scenarios as you want, easily switching between the different scenarios to display the results of several what-if analyses.

Before using Scenario Manager, you should assign range names to all the input and result cells that you intend to use in the analysis. As you'll see later in this tutorial, the range names automatically appear in the reports generated by Scenario Manager. Though not a requirement, range names make it easier for you to work with scenarios and for other people to understand the scenario reports.

To create names for the income statement values:

▶ 1. If you took a break after the previous session, open the Creative Ventures workbook located in the Tutorial.10\Tutorial folder included with your Data Files.

▶ 2. Switch to the **Income Statement** worksheet, and then select the nonadjacent range **A4:B5;A17:B20;A24:B26**. You'll define names for each of these cells.

3. Click the **Formulas** tab on the Ribbon, and then, in the Defined Names group, click the **Create from Selection** button. The Create Names from Selection dialog box opens.

4. Verify that the **Left column** check box contains a check mark, and then click the **OK** button. The selected cells in column B are named using the labels in the corresponding cells in column A.

5. Click cell **A1** to deselect the range.

Now that you have named cells in the worksheet, you are ready to start defining the scenarios using Scenario Manager.

Defining a Scenario | Reference Window

- Enter the data values in the worksheet for the scenario.
- In the Data Tools group on the Data tab, click the What-If Analysis button, and then click Scenario Manager.
- Click the Add button in the Scenario Manager dialog box.
- In the Scenario name box, type a name for the scenario.
- In the Changing cells box, specify the input or changing cells.
- Click the OK button.
- In the Scenario Values dialog box, specify values for each of the input cells, clicking the Add button after each.
- Click the OK button.

Defining a Scenario

To create the first scenario, you open Scenario Manager and enter a name for the scenario. You'll start by creating the Status Quo scenario whose values match those currently entered in the workbook.

To add the Status Quo scenario:

1. Click the **Data** tab on the Ribbon, in the Data Tools group, click the **What-If Analysis** button, and then click **Scenario Manager**. The Scenario Manager dialog box opens. No scenarios are defined yet. You'll add the first scenario.

2. Click the **Add** button. The Add Scenario dialog box opens.

3. In the Scenario name box, type **Status Quo**, and then press the **Tab** key. The range in the Changing cells box is selected.

Next, you need to specify the input cells for this scenario. Scenario Manager refers to input cells as **changing cells** because these worksheet cells contain values that are changed under the scenario. Changing cells can be located anywhere in the worksheet. You can type the range names or locations of changing cells, but it's faster and more accurate to select them with the mouse. To select nonadjacent changing cells, press and hold the Ctrl key as you click each cell. The changing cells for each of the four scenarios are:

- Cell B4: Units Sold
- Cell B5: Price per Unit
- Cell B17: Salaries and Benefits
- Cell B18: Advertising
- Cell B19: Administrative
- Cell B20: Miscellaneous

To specify the changing cells:

▶ **1.** Select the nonadjacent range **B4:B5;B17:B20**. The range appears in the Changing cells box. These are the input cells.

▶ **2.** Press the **Tab** key to select the default text in the Comment box, and then type **Scenario assuming current values**. See Figure 10-23.

Figure 10-23	Add Scenario dialog box for the Status Quo scenario

Tip

If the changing cells in the scenario are unlocked and the worksheet is protected, users can show the scenario but not edit it.

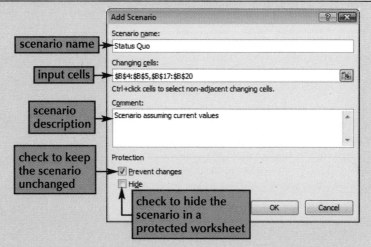

▶ **3.** Click the **OK** button. The Scenario Values dialog box opens, so you can specify values for each of the input cells you entered in the Changing cells box in the Add Scenario dialog box. Because the Status Quo scenario values are the current values in the workbook, you can accept the values displayed in the Scenario Values dialog box. See Figure 10-24.

Figure 10-24	Input values for the Status Quo scenario

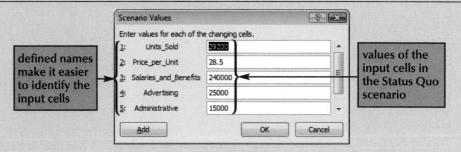

▶ **4.** Click the **OK** button. The Scenario Manager dialog box reopens. This time it displays the Status Quo scenario in the Scenarios box.

Next, you'll add the remaining three scenarios that Todd and Brent are interested in.

To add the remaining scenarios:

▶ **1.** Click the **Add** button. The Add Scenario dialog box opens. You need to enter the scenario name.

▶ **2.** In the Scenario name box, type **Expanded Operations**, and then press the **Tab** key. The nonadjacent range you selected for the Status Quo scenario is selected in the Changing cells box. You want to use the same set of changing cells, so you won't make any edits to the range. You will modify the scenario comment.

▶ **3.** Press the **Tab** key to select the text in the Comment box, type **Scenario assuming expanded operations**, and then click the **OK** button. The Scenario Values dialog box opens. This scenario uses different values for the changing cells, which you'll enter now.

▶ **4.** Enter the following values for the Expanded Operations scenario, pressing the **Tab** key to move from one input box to another.

Units_Sold	**35,000**
Price_per_Unit	**28.50**
Salaries_and_Benefits	**300,000**
Advertising	**40,000**
Administrative	**25,000**
Miscellaneous	**20,000**

Trouble? If you press the Enter key instead of the Tab key, the Scenario Manager dialog box reopens. Make sure that the Expanded Operations scenario is selected in the Scenarios box, click the Edit button, and then click the OK button to return to the Scenario Values dialog box. Enter the remaining values in the scenario, being sure to press the Tab key to move to the next input box.

▶ **5.** Click the **Add** button. The Add Scenario dialog box opens. You'll create the third scenario now. As with the second scenario, you need to enter a new name and comment. The changing cells are the same.

▶ **6.** Type **Reduced Operations** in the Scenario name box, press the **Tab** key twice, type **Scenario assuming reduced operations** in the Comment box, and then click the **OK** button.

▶ **7.** Enter the following values for the Reduced Operations scenario in the Scenario Values dialog box, pressing the **Tab** key to move between input boxes.

Units_Sold	**20,000**
Price_per_Unit	**28.50**
Salaries_and_Benefits	**200,000**
Advertising	**15,000**
Administrative	**10,000**
Miscellaneous	**10,000**

▶ **8.** Click the **Add** button to open the Add Scenario dialog box and create the fourth scenario.

▶ **9.** Type **Sale** in the Scenario name box, press the **Tab** key twice, type **Scenario assuming a sale of HoverDisks** in the Comment box, and then click the **OK** button.

▶ **10.** Enter the following values for the Sale scenario in the Scenario Values dialog box, pressing the **Tab** key to move between input boxes.

Units_Sold	**40,000**
Price_per_Unit	**20**
Salaries_and_Benefits	**200,000**
Advertising	**15,000**
Administrative	**10,000**
Miscellaneous	**10,000**

▶ **11.** Click the **OK** button. The Scenario Manager dialog box lists all four of the scenarios you created. See Figure 10-25.

Figure 10-25 ▶ **Scenario Manager dialog box**

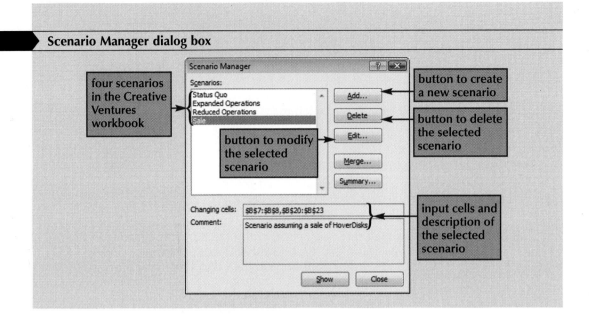

Viewing Scenarios

Now, you can view the effect of each of the four scenarios on the company's income statement by selecting the scenario in the Scenario Manager dialog box. You switch from one scenario to another by clicking the Show button in the Scenario Manager dialog box. You do not have to close the dialog box to switch between scenarios.

You'll start by viewing the Expanded Operations scenario.

To view the effect of the Expanded Operations scenario:

▶ **1.** In the Scenarios box in the Scenario Manager dialog box, click **Expanded Operations**. The scenario is selected, and its changing cells and comment appear in the bottom of the Scenario Manager dialog box.

▶ **2.** Click the **Show** button. The values in the Income Statement worksheet are changed to reflect the scenario.

▶ **3.** Click the **Close** button. The Scenario Manager dialog box closes, and you can view the income statement for Creative Ventures assuming expanded operations with increased fixed expenses. See Figure 10-26, which shows the entire income statement.

Tip

You can also view a scenario by double-clicking its name in the Scenarios box in the Scenario Manager dialog box.

Income statement for the Expanded Operations scenario ◀ **Figure 10-26**

	A	B
1	**Creative Ventures**	
2	2010 Income Statement	
3	Revenue	Projected
4	Units Sold	35,000
5	Price per Unit	$28.50
6	**Total Revenue**	**$997,500.00**
7		
8	Variable Expenses	Projected
9	Units Produced	36,750
10	Material Cost per Unit	$8.50
11	**Total Material Cost**	**$312,375.00**
12	Manufacturing Cost per Unit	$5.25
13	**Total Manufacturing Cost**	**$192,937.50**
14	**Total Variable Expenses**	**$505,312.50**
15		
16	Fixed Expenses	Projected
17	Salaries and Benefits	$300,000.00
18	Advertising	$40,000.00
19	Administrative	$25,000.00
20	Miscellaneous	$20,000.00
21	**Total Fixed Expenses**	**$385,000.00**
22		
23	Summary	Projected
24	Total Revenue	$997,500.00
25	Total Expenses	$890,312.50
26	**Net Income**	**$107,187.50**

Trouble? If the values in your income statement do not match those in the figure, you might have entered the values for the scenario incorrectly. You'll learn how to edit a scenario shortly.

Excel automatically changes the values of the six input cells to match the scenario. Under the Expanded Operations scenario, the company's net income drops from the current value of $118,625 to $107,187.50. Even though sales of the HoverDisk increase under the Expanded Operations scenario, the increased sales do not offset the additional money spent on fixed expenses. You'll review the other scenarios you created.

To view the effect of the remaining scenarios:

▶ 1. In the Data Tools group on the Data tab, click the **What-If Analysis** button, and then click **Scenario Manager**. The Scenario Manager dialog box opens.

▶ 2. Double-click **Reduced Operations** in the Scenarios box to update the worksheet, and then click the **Close** button to close the Scenario Manager dialog box. Under the Reduced Operations scenario, the net income value shown in cell B26 decreases to $46,250.

▶ 3. Repeat Step 1 to reopen the Scenario Manager dialog box.

Double-click **Sale** in the Scenarios box to update the worksheet, and then click the **Close** button to close the Scenario Manager dialog box. Under the Sale scenario with the reduced unit price of each disk, the company would show a net loss of $12,500. Figure 10-27 shows the complete income statements for the Reduced Operations and Sale scenarios you created.

Figure 10-27 ▸ **Income statements for the Reduced Operation and Sale scenarios**

	A	B
1	**Creative Ventures**	
2	2010 Income Statement	
3	Revenue	Projected
4	Units Sold	20,000
5	Price per Unit	$28.50
6	**Total Revenue**	**$570,000.00**
7		
8	Variable Expenses	Projected
9	Units Produced	21,000
10	Material Cost per Unit	$8.50
11	**Total Material Cost**	**$178,500.00**
12	Manufacturing Cost per Unit	$5.25
13	**Total Manufacturing Cost**	**$110,250.00**
14	**Total Variable Expenses**	**$288,750.00**
15		
16	Fixed Expenses	Projected
17	Salaries and Benefits	$200,000.00
18	Advertising	$15,000.00
19	Administrative	$10,000.00
20	Miscellaneous	$10,000.00
21	**Total Fixed Expenses**	**$235,000.00**
22		
23	Summary	Projected
24	Total Revenue	$570,000.00
25	Total Expenses	$523,750.00
26	**Net Income**	**$46,250.00**

Reduced Operations

	A	B
1	**Creative Ventures**	
2	2010 Income Statement	
3	Revenue	Projected
4	Units Sold	40,000
5	Price per Unit	$20.00
6	**Total Revenue**	**$800,000.00**
7		
8	Variable Expenses	Projected
9	Units Produced	42,000
10	Material Cost per Unit	$8.50
11	**Total Material Cost**	**$357,000.00**
12	Manufacturing Cost per Unit	$5.25
13	**Total Manufacturing Cost**	**$220,500.00**
14	**Total Variable Expenses**	**$577,500.00**
15		
16	Fixed Expenses	Projected
17	Salaries and Benefits	$200,000.00
18	Advertising	$15,000.00
19	Administrative	$10,000.00
20	Miscellaneous	$10,000.00
21	**Total Fixed Expenses**	**$235,000.00**
22		
23	Summary	Projected
24	Total Revenue	$800,000.00
25	Total Expenses	$812,500.00
26	**Net Income**	**($12,500.00)**

Sale

You can draw several conclusions from the four scenarios. Both the Status Quo and the Expanded Operations scenarios result in net income values of more than $100,000, but the Reduced Operations scenario predicts a much smaller net income value. The Sale scenario projects a net loss for the company. Todd and Brent assumed that they would be able to successfully cut costs in the Sale scenario, but apparently the cost cutting wasn't enough to make a profit.

Editing a Scenario

Todd and Brent use your scenario results report to reevaluate their budget strategy. They ask you to modify the Reduced Operations scenario to show the sales volume increasing to 22,000 units per year, and to increase the value for Salaries and Benefits from $200,000 to $220,000.

After you create a scenario, you can easily make changes like these. This enables you to examine variations of a given set of assumptions. The scenario results will automatically update to reflect the new information.

To edit the Reduced Operations scenario:

▸ 1. In the Data Tools group on the Data tab, click the **What-If Analysis** button, and then click **Scenario Manager**. The Scenario Manager dialog box opens.

▸ 2. Click **Reduced Operations** in the Scenarios box, and then click the **Edit** button. The Edit Scenario dialog box opens. You don't need to make any changes in this dialog box.

▸ 3. Click the **OK** button. The Scenario Values dialog box opens. You'll change values in some of these cells.

▶ 4. Change the value of Units_Sold from 20,000 to **22,000**, and then change the value of Salaries_and_Benefits from 200,000 to **220,000**.

▶ 5. Click the **OK** button. The Scenario Manager dialog box reopens.

▶ 6. Click the **Show** button. The Income Statement worksheet updates to reflect the revised scenario.

▶ 7. Click the **Close** button. The Scenario Manager dialog box closes. The income statement reflects the edited Reduced Operations scenario. Revising the input values in this scenario results in an increase in the net income from $46,250 to $54,375. See Figure 10-28, which shows the entire income statement.

Income statement with the revised Reduced Operations scenario ◀ **Figure 10-28**

	A	B
1	**Creative Ventures**	
2	2010 Income Statement	
3	Revenue	Projected
4	Units Sold	22,000
5	Price per Unit	$28.50
6	**Total Revenue**	**$627,000.00**
7		
8	Variable Expenses	Projected
9	Units Produced	23,100
10	Material Cost per Unit	$8.50
11	**Total Material Cost**	**$196,350.00**
12	Manufacturing Cost per Unit	$5.25
13	**Total Manufacturing Cost**	**$121,275.00**
14	**Total Variable Expenses**	**$317,625.00**
15		
16	Fixed Expenses	Projected
17	Salaries and Benefits	$220,000.00
18	Advertising	$15,000.00
19	Administrative	$10,000.00
20	Miscellaneous	$10,000.00
21	**Total Fixed Expenses**	**$255,000.00**
22		
23	Summary	Projected
24	Total Revenue	$627,000.00
25	Total Expenses	$572,625.00
26	**Net Income**	**$54,375.00**

▶ 8. In the Data Tools group on the Data tab, click the **What-If Analysis** button, and then click **Scenario Manager** to open the Scenario Manager dialog box.

▶ 9. Click **Status Quo** in the Scenarios box, and then click the **Show** button. The income statement returns to the original values. You'll leave the Scenario Manager dialog box open.

Creating a Scenario Summary Report

Although scenarios can help you make important business decisions, you might find switching between scenarios time-consuming. It would perhaps be better to present Todd and Brent with a single table containing the results from all of the scenarios. You can do this with a **scenario summary report** that lists the values for the changing cells and result cells under each scenario. The report's tabular layout makes it simpler to compare the results of each scenario, and the automatic formatting makes it useful for reports and meetings.

Reference Window | **Creating a Scenario Report**

- In the Data Tools group on the Data tab, click the What-If Analysis button, and then click Scenario Manager.
- Click the Summary button.
- Click the Scenario summary option button to create a scenario summary report (or click the Scenario PivotTable report option to create a PivotTable describing the scenarios).
- Select the results cells to display in the report.
- Click the OK button.

To create a scenario summary report, you must identify the result cells. Todd and Brent are interested in the following result cells: cell B24 (Total Revenue), cell B25 (Total Expenses), and cell B26 (Net Income).

You'll display these values, along with the values of the input cells, in your report.

To create the scenario summary report:

1. Click the **Summary** button in the Scenario Manager dialog box. The Scenario Summary dialog box opens, allowing you to create a scenario summary report or a Scenario PivotTable report. You want to create a summary.

2. Verify that the **Scenario summary** option button is selected.

   Next, you'll enter the range references for the result cells to display in the report.

3. With the Result cells box active, select the range **B24:B26**.

4. Click the **OK** button. The Scenario Summary report is inserted in the workbook.

5. Move the **Scenario Summary** report to the end of the workbook. See Figure 10-29.

Tip

If you want to concentrate on only a few key cells, the scenario summary report has outline tools so you can hide and expand different parts of the report.

Figure 10-29 Scenario summary report

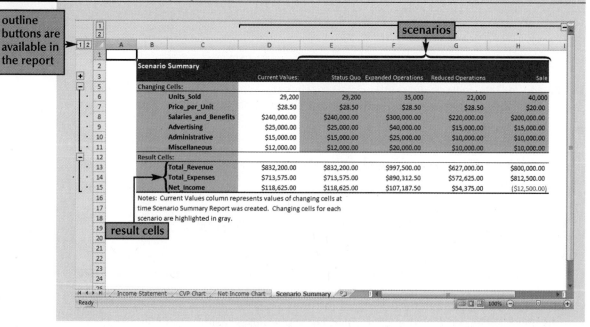

The scenario summary report displays the values of the input cells and result cells under each scenario. Each scenario is listed by name, and the current worksheet values are also displayed. Note that the report uses the range names you defined earlier to identify the changing and result cells. The range names make the report simpler to interpret.

Creating a Scenario PivotTable Report

Another way to display the results of scenarios is with a PivotTable report. As the name implies, a **Scenario PivotTable report** displays the results from each scenario as a pivot field in a PivotTable. You'll create a Scenario PivotTable report.

To create the scenario PivotTable report:

▶ **1.** Return to the **Income Statement** worksheet, in the Data Tools group on the Data tab, click the **What-If Analysis** button, and then click **Scenario Manager**. The Scenario Manager dialog box opens.

▶ **2.** Click the **Summary** button to open the Scenario Summary dialog box, and then click the **Scenario PivotTable report** option button.

▶ **3.** Click the **OK** button. The Scenario PivotTable sheet is inserted in the workbook and contains the scenario values in PivotTable form.

▶ **4.** Move the **Scenario PivotTable** sheet to the end of the workbook. See Figure 10-30.

Scenario PivotTable report ◀ Figure 10-30

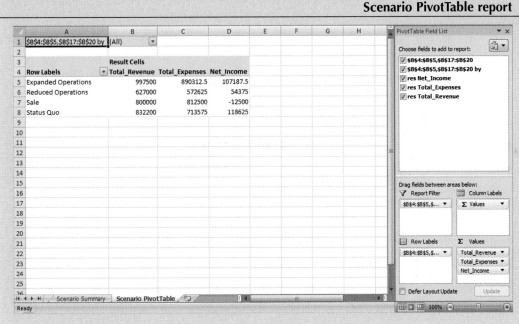

You'll edit the table to make it easier to read, but not filter it, and then generate a PivotChart of revenue, expenses, and net income under each scenario.

To edit the PivotTable report:

▶ **1.** In the Values box of the PivotTable Field List, click the **Total Revenue** button, and then click **Value Field Settings**. The Value Field Settings dialog box opens.

▶ **2.** Click the **Number Format** button to open the Format Cells dialog box, click the **Number** tab (if necessary), click **Currency** in the Category box, and then click the last entry **($1,234,10)** in the Negative numbers list box to display negative currency values in a red font enclosed in parentheses.

▶ **3.** Click the **OK** button in the Format Cells dialog box, and then click the **OK** button in the Value Field Settings dialog box. The number format is applied to the Total_ Revenue cells.

> **4.** Repeat Steps 1 through 3 for the **Total_Expenses** and the **Net_Income** buttons in the Values box to apply the same number format. There is no need to filter this PivotTable.

> **5.** In the Report Filter box, click the **$B$4:$B$5,$..** button, and then click **Remove Field**. The field is removed from the PivotTable.

> **6.** In cell A1, enter **Scenario PivotTable**, and then format the text using the **Title** cell style. See Figure 10-31.

| Figure 10-31 | Scenario PivotTable report |

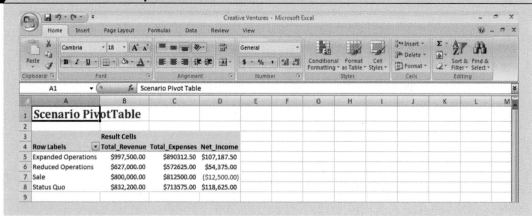

Finally, you'll display the results of this table in a PivotChart.

To create the PivotChart:

> **1.** Click cell **A4** to select the PivotTable, click the **PivotTable Tools Options** tab on the Ribbon, and then click the **PivotChart** button in the Tools group. The Insert Chart dialog box opens.

> **2.** Click the **Clustered Column** chart type (the first chart type in the Column section), and then click the **OK** button.

> **3.** Move and resize the embedded chart so that it covers the range A10:F26 on the worksheet, and then click cell **C1** to deselect the PivotTable and PivotChart. See Figure 10-32.

| Figure 10-32 | Scenario PivotChart |

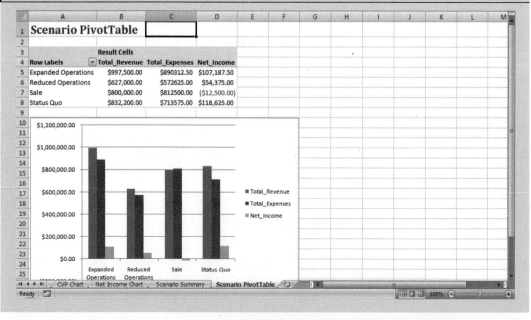

Based on the findings, Todd and Brent can expect a net income for the company of $54,000 to $118,000 per year. Also, it is not recommended that they pursue the Sale scenario because of the risk of substantially reduced profits.

Merging Scenarios | InSight

In a business, you will often have several workbooks that track the same set of figures and evaluate the same set of scenarios. You can merge scenarios from multiple workbooks into a single workbook. To merge scenarios from several workbooks:

1. Open all of the workbooks containing the scenarios you want to merge.
2. Switch to the worksheet in the active workbook where you want to merge the scenarios.
3. Open the Scenario Manager dialog box, and then click the Merge button.
4. Click the workbook containing the scenario in the Book box, and then click the worksheet in which the scenario appears in the Sheet box.
5. Click the OK button to merge the scenario from the selected workbook and worksheet in the active sheet.
6. Repeat these steps to merge scenarios from additional workbooks and worksheets.

The scenarios merge into the active sheet. Note that it's easier to merge scenarios if all of the what-if analyses on the different worksheets and workbooks are identical. All of the changing cells from the merged scenario must correspond to changing cells in the active workbook and worksheet.

Session 10.2 Quick Check | Review

1. What is an advantage of scenarios over data tables?
2. What should you do before creating a scenario report to make the entries on the report easier to interpret?
3. What are changing cells?
4. What are result cells? Where do you define result cells in Scenario Manager?
5. How do you display a scenario in the active worksheet?
6. How do you create a scenario PivotTable report?

Session 10.3

Understanding Price Elasticity of Demand

Any analysis of the relationship between cost, sales volume, and profit needs to take into account the impact of price on demand. In the scenarios you analyzed in the last session, Todd and Brent understood that demand for HoverDisks would go down as they raised the price and would increase as the price fell. This relationship between sales price and demand affects revenue. By raising the price, they might generate more revenue, but at a certain point higher prices will generate less revenue as customers stop buying HoverDisks. On the other hand, lower prices might actually increase revenue if enough new customers are attracted to their product, but at a certain point the price will be so low that there will simply not be enough customers to make the product profitable. This means that the point of maximum revenue occurs somewhere between the lowest sales price and the highest sales price, as illustrated by the charts in Figure 10-33.

| Figure 10-33 | Demand and revenue as functions of price |

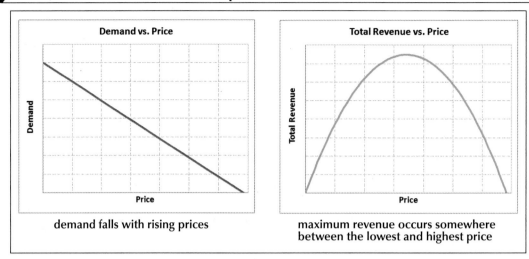

To find the point of maximum revenue, you must specify how changes in price alter demand. For example, Todd and Brent might assume that if they increase the price of Hover-Disks by 10%, demand will drop by 15%. The response of one variable to another is called **elasticity**. The effect that price has on demand is called the **price elasticity of demand**. One way of measuring the price elasticity of demand is to calculate the absolute value of the change in demand divided by the change in price. The formula is:

$$e = \left| \frac{\text{\% change in demand}}{\text{\% change in price}} \right|$$

In this formula, e is the value of the price elasticity of demand. For example, if demand decreases by 15%, then for every 10% increase in price, the price elasticity of demand would be:

$$e = \left| \frac{-15\%}{10\%} \right| = |-1.5| = 1.5$$

Note that elasticity measures are always expressed in terms of absolute value because it is assumed that demand will never increase with increased price.

Based on the value of e, we can make some general statements about the product being sold. When $e<1$, the price elasticity of demand is **relatively inelastic**, which means that large changes in price will cause relatively little changes in demand. For example, if $e=0.1$, then increasing the price of an item by 10% decreases demand by only 1%. If $e=0$, then changes in price have *no* impact on demand. This situation is referred to as **perfectly inelastic** and occurs when the item being sold is rare or essential, such as a life-saving drug for which people are willing to spend whatever necessary to procure it.

When $e>1$, the price elasticity of demand is **relatively elastic**, indicating that demand is very responsive to changes in price. If $e=2.0$, then increasing the price of an object by 10% decreases demand by 20%. As the value of e increases, the result is that any change in price causes a huge change in demand, resulting in a **perfectly elastic** relationship between price and demand. This can occur when consumers have to choose between two products that are exactly equal in all respects. Then, raising the price of one would cause a huge decrease in demand (because consumers will opt for the cheaper though identical product). For example, if neighboring gas stations are competing for business selling the same quality of gas, the station that raises its price might see demand for its product drop considerably because motorists will simply purchase the less expensive gas at the nearby station.

Finally, if $e=1$, then the elasticity is referred to as **unit elastic** because any change in price is met by an equal and opposite change in demand.

Estimating Net Income Through Trial and Error

Todd and Brent want you to add another what-if analysis to the workbook, one that includes the price elasticity of demand as a factor in calculating sales volume. First, you have to determine the value of e.

Determining a value for the price elasticity of demand involves a shrewd examination of the market, the product itself, and the desires of consumers. A review of historical trends and relations between demand and price for similar products can also be helpful. The relationship between price and demand for a novelty item such as Creative Ventures' HoverDisk is relatively elastic because the product is of interest to the public, but the novelty will quickly wear off if the price is set too high. Todd and Brent settle on a value of 1.2 for e. In other words, for every 10% increase in the price of HoverDisks, they expect that the demand will decrease by 12%.

Because you are dealing with percentage increases and decreases, you need to work from an established baseline. You'll use the current projections from the income statement, which indicates that 29,200 HoverDisks can be sold at a price of $28.50 per disk. So, if the price increased 10%, or $2.85, to $31.35, but the demand decreased by 12%, or 3,504 units, the sales volume would be 25,696 disks per year. If the price of HoverDisk increased to $31.35, Todd and Brent would expect to only sell about 25,700 units.

The general formula for determining the demand for a product based on the price is:

$$New\, Demand = Old\, Demand \times \left[1 + e * \left(1 - \frac{New\, Price}{Old\, Price}\right)\right]$$

In this formula, *Old Demand* is the current demand for the product, *e* is the price elasticity of demand, *New Price* is the proposed price for the product, *Old Price* is the current price of the product, and *New Demand* is the demand for the product at its new price. You'll add this formula to the workbook to project the revenue, expenses, and net income that would result from raising the price of HoverDisks by 10%.

To project the effect of raising the price of HoverDisks:

▶ 1. If you took a break at the end of the previous session, make sure the Creative Ventures workbook located in the Tutorial.10\Tutorial folder included with your Data Files is open.

▶ 2. Switch to the **Income Statement** worksheet, select the range **A3:B26**, and move it down to the range **A6:B29**.

You need to add a new column to the workbook for revenue and expenses calculations on the price elasticity model.

▶ 3. Copy the range **B6:B29**, paste it into the range **C6:C29**, and then, in cells C6, C11, C19, and C26, enter **New Price**.

▶ 4. In cell A3, enter **Price Elasticity of Demand**. In cell B3, enter **1.2**. Format cell A3 using the **20% - Accent3** cell style.

In the new column, you'll make the Units Sold value a calculated item based on the elasticity value and the ratio of the new price to the old price. You'll use the general formula described above with the Old Demand value from cell B7, the elasticity value from cell B3, the New Price value from cell C8 and the Old Price value from cell B8. The New Demand value will be placed in cell C7.

▶ 5. In cell C7, enter the formula **=B7*(1+B3*(1–C8/B8))**. The formula returns the value 29,200, which is what we would expect if the new sales price remained unchanged at $28.50.

> **6.** In cell C8, enter the new sales price of **$31.35**. As discussed earlier, the demand for disks at this price drops to 25,696. Review the income statement under this new price. See Figure 10-34.

| Figure 10-34 | Price elasticity of demand to calculate net income |

units sold is calculated based on the value of the sales price and the price elasticity of demand

	A	B	C	D	E	F	G	H
1	**Creative Ventures**		for every 10% increase in price, sales volume drops by 12%			Cost-Volume-Profit Analysis		
2	2010 Income Statement							
3	Price Elasticity of Demand	1.2			Units Sold	Revenue	Expenses	Net Income
4					29,200	$832,200.00	$713,575.00	$118,625.00
5					15,000	$427,500.00	$508,562.50	($81,062.50)
6	Revenue	Projected	New Price		20,000	$570,000.00	$580,750.00	($10,750.00)
7	Units Sold	29,200	25,696		25,000	$712,500.00	$652,937.50	$59,562.50
8	Price per Unit	$28.50	$31.35		30,000	$855,000.00	$725,125.00	$129,875.00
9	Total Revenue	$832,200.00	$805,569.60		35,000	$997,500.00	$797,312.50	$200,187.50
10					40,000	$1,140,000.00	$869,500.00	$270,500.00
11	Variable Expenses	Projected	New Price					
12	Units Produced	30,660	26,981				Net Income Analysis	
13	Material Cost per Unit	$8.50	$8.50					Price per Unit
14	Total Material Cost	$260,610.00	$229,336.80		Units Sold	$20	$25	$30
15	Manufacturing Cost per Unit	$5.25	$5.25		15,000	($208,562.50)	($133,562.50)	($58,562.50)
16	Total Manufacturing Cost	$160,965.00	$141,649.20		20,000	($180,750.00)	($80,750.00)	$19,250.00
17	Total Variable Expenses	$421,575.00	$370,986.00		25,000	($152,937.50)	($27,937.50)	$97,062.50
18					30,000	($125,125.00)	$24,875.00	$174,875.00
19	Fixed Expenses	Projected	New Price		35,000	($97,312.50)	$77,687.50	$252,687.50
20	Salaries and Benefits	$240,000.00	$240,000.00		40,000	($69,500.00)	$130,500.00	$330,500.00

From these calculations, the total revenue under this new price drops by about $27,000 from $832,200 to $805,569.60. However, variable expenses also decrease under this plan because the company will not be manufacturing as many disks as before. The result is that the net income to the company actually increases by almost $24,000 from $118,625 under the current price to $142,583.60 under the new price. If Todd and Brent's assumptions are correct regarding the relationship between price and demand for the HoverDisk, they can actually increase the company's net income by increasing the sales price even if they sell fewer disks. You'll examine the effect of other prices on net income. Can the company make even greater profit if it increases the price further?

To calculate net income for other prices:

> **1.** Change the value in cell C8 from $31.35 to **$35.00**. At this price, the net income to the company increases even more to $144,098.16.

> **2.** Change the value in cell C8 to **$40.00**. At this price, the company sells about 15,000 disks per year and the net income drops to $92,998.16. At that high price, the company sells so few disks that it's no longer profitable even with the higher price per disk.

> **3.** Change the value in cell C8 to **$32.00**. At $32 per disk, the company's projected net income is $145,250.79—the largest value you've achieved yet.

Clearly, increasing the price doesn't always mean increasing the profit. Todd and Brent want to find the best price for the HoverDisks: one that results in the maximum net income for the company. You could continue entering different price values, zeroing in on the one value that produces the highest net income. This process, known as **trial and error**, can be very time-consuming if you have a large range of possible values. In this case, you've already determined that you cannot increase the price of the HoverDisk past

$40 without continuing to lose money, but it's not immediately clear what the best price below $40 would be. To determine the answer to that question, you can use Solver.

Finding an Optimal Solution Using Solver

Solver is a program that searches for the optimal solution of a problem involving several variables. For example, Solver can find the curve or line that best fits a set of data or to minimize production costs for a product or service. You'll use Solver to determine the unit price that maximizes net income from the sales of HoverDisks.

Installing and Activating Solver

Solver is an **add-in**, a customized program that adds commands and features to Microsoft Office programs such as Excel. Because Solver is an "added" feature of Excel, it might not be installed on your computer. Before attempting to run Solver, you should check to see whether it is installed and activated on your version of Excel.

Activating Solver | Reference Window

- Check whether Solver is already installed and activated. If it is, Solver will appear in Analysis group on the Data tab.
- Click the Office Button, and then click the Excel Options button.
- Click Add-Ins in the left pane, and then click the arrow next to the Manage box and click Excel Add-ins.
- Click the Go button to open the Add-Ins dialog box.
- Click the Solver Add-in check box, and then click the OK button. Follow the remaining prompts to install Solver, if it is not already installed.

You'll check whether Solver is already installed and activated on your computer. You can determine this by looking at the Data tab on the Ribbon. If Solver does not appear as a command on the Data tab, the program either needs to be installed or activated. If you are working on a network, you might need your instructor or network administrator to install Solver for you. If you are working on a stand-alone PC, you might have to install the program yourself using the Microsoft Office 2007 installation CD. However, Solver might be installed, just not activated. You will test for this possibility first. If not, then you'll need to install and activate the add-in.

To install and activate Solver:

▶ **1.** Click the **Data** tab on the Ribbon, and then look to see if the Solver button appears in the Analysis group at the right side of the tab, as shown in Figure 10-35. If you see the Solver button, Solver is installed and activated, and you should read but not perform the rest of the steps in this section. If you don't see the Solver button, Solver might not be installed or activated, and you should continue with Step 2.

Solver button in the Analysis group on the Data tab ◀ **Figure 10-35**

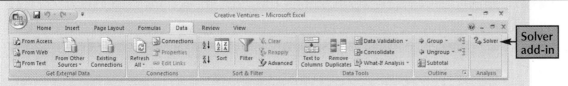

> **2.** Click the **Office Button** ⊞, and then click the **Excel Options** button. The Excel Options dialog box opens.

> **3.** In the list on the left side of the dialog box, click **Add-Ins**. Information about all of the add-ins currently installed on your computer appears in the right pane of the dialog box.

> **4.** If necessary, click the arrow next to the Manage box, and then click **Excel Add-ins**.

> **5.** Click the **Go** button. The Add-Ins dialog box opens and displays a list of all of the installed add-ins. A check box appears before each add-in name that has been activated and is ready for use.

> **6.** Click the **Solver Add-in** check box to insert a check mark. See Figure 10-36.

Figure 10-36	Add-Ins dialog box

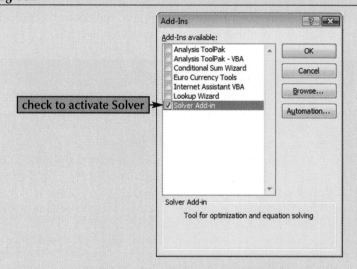

check to activate Solver ▶

> **7.** Click the **OK** button. If Solver was installed, but not activated, the Add-Ins dialog box closes, and the Solver button is added to the Data tab. Read, but do not perform, Step 8. If Solver has not been installed yet, a dialog box opens, stating that you cannot run the add-in because it is not installed. Continue with Step 8 to install Solver.

> **8.** Click the **Yes** button to install Solver. If you are prompted, insert the Microsoft Office installation CD in the computer's CD drive, and then click the **OK** button. The Solver button appears in the Analysis group on the Data tab.

Solver is only one of a collection of Excel add-ins. Other add-ins provide the ability to perform statistical analyses, calculate conditional sums, or connect easily to the Internet. You can also create your own add-in using the Visual Basic for Applications (VBA) macro language. The process of activating and installing add-ins follows the same process you used to install and activate the Solver add-in.

Setting Up Solver to Find a Solution

To use Solver, there are three items, or **Solver parameters**, that you must specify: the target cell, the adjustable (or changing) cells, and the constraints on the problem. The **target cell** is a cell that you want to maximize, minimize, or change to a specific value. In this case, the company's net income is your target cell, whose value you want to maximize.

An **adjustable cell** is a cell that Excel changes to produce the desired result in the target cell. In this case, the adjustable cell is the sales price of each HoverDisk. Finally, a **constraint** is a limit that is placed on the problem's solution. For example, Creative Ventures might have a physical limit on the number of HoverDisks it can produce in a given year (no matter how profitable it would be to produce extra disks), so this would be a constraint that Solver would have to include in finding the maximum net income.

Setting Solver Parameters | Reference Window

- In the Analysis group on the Data tab, click the Solver button.
- In the Set Target Cell box, specify the target cell.
- Click the Max, Min, or Value of option buttons to maximize, minimize, or set the target cell to a specified value.
- In the By Changing Cells input box, specify the changing cells.

You'll set up the Solver parameters.

To define the target cell and changing cells:

▶ **1.** In the Analysis group on the Data tab, click the **Solver** button. The Solver Parameters dialog box opens.

▶ **2.** With the Set Target Cell box active, click cell **C29** on the Income Statement worksheet. The absolute reference to the cell appears in the Set Target Cell box.

▶ **3.** Verify that the **Max** option button is selected. This sets cell C29 to its maximum possible value.

Next, you specify the cell or cells that you want to change to locate the maximum possible net income. In this case, the only changing cell is cell C8, which contains the unit price.

▶ **4.** Click the **By Changing Cells** box, and then click cell **C8** in the Income Statement worksheet. The absolute reference to cell C8 appears in the input box. See Figure 10-37.

Solver Parameters dialog box ◀ **Figure 10-37**

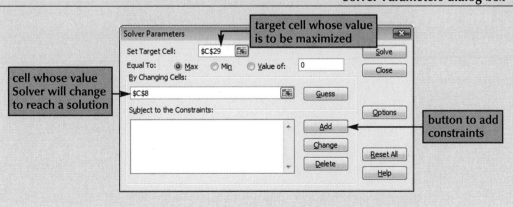

Reference Window | **Setting Constraints on the Solver Solution**

- In the Solver Parameters dialog box, click the Add button.
- Enter the cell reference of the cell or cells containing the constraint.
- Specify the nature of the constraint (<=, =, >=, int, or bin).
- Enter the constraint value in the Constraint box.
- Click the OK button to add the constraint and return to the Solver dialog box.
- Repeat for each constraint you want to add.

Next, you'll add constraints, or limits, for the solution. Constraints are important because they confine the solution within a reasonable set of limits that you define. Solver supports five possible constraints. The <=, >=, and = constraints are used when you want to set a cell's value to always be less than or equal to, greater than or equal to, or equal to a specified value. You can also use an integer or int constraint, which forces a cell value to always be a whole number. Finally, you can apply a binary or bin constraint that forces a cell value to always be either 0 or 1.

Todd and Brent know that the company can't produce more than 35,000 disks per year, even if it were more profitable to do so. They also know that to keep their staff, they have to produce at least 15,000 disks each year. You'll add a >= and a <= constraint to ensure that the production always falls between those two limits, even if it means accepting less profit. You do not have to add an = constraint, integer constraint, or binary constraint to the Solver model.

Tip

You can apply the same constraint to a range of cells. Select the cell range in the Cell Reference box of the Add Constraint dialog box and then specify the constraint you want applied to each cell in the range.

To add constraints to Solver:

► **1.** Click the **Add** button to open the Add Constraint dialog box.

► **2.** With the Cell Reference box active, click cell **C12**. This is the number of units the company will produce annually.

► **3.** Press the **Tab** key, click the arrow, and then click **>=** in the center box.

► **4.** Type **15000** in the Constraint box. See Figure 10-38.

Figure 10-38 | Add Constraint dialog box

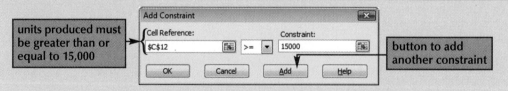

units produced must be greater than or equal to 15,000

button to add another constraint

► **5.** Click the **Add** button. The constraint is saved and the Add Constraint dialog box is cleared so you can enter another constraint.

► **6.** With the Cell Reference box active, click cell **C12**, press the **Tab** key, and then verify that <= is selected in the center box.

► **7.** Press the **Tab** key, and then type **35000** in the Constraint box. The constraint is that the units produced must be less than or equal to 35,000.

You do not need to enter any more constraints at this time.

8. Click the **OK** button to return to the Solver Parameters dialog box. See Figure 10-39.

Completed Solver Parameters dialog box ◆ **Figure 10-39**

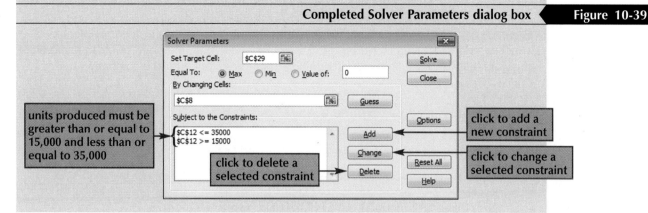

units produced must be greater than or equal to 15,000 and less than or equal to 35,000

click to add a new constraint

click to delete a selected constraint

click to change a selected constraint

Now that you've specified all of the parameters for the model, you can run Solver to determine what unit price will result in the maximum net income to the company.

To calculate the maximum net income:

1. In the Solver Parameters dialog box, click the **Solve** button to run Solver. The status bar shows Solver rapidly "trying out" solutions. In a moment, the Solver Results dialog box opens, and indicates that Solver has found a solution that satisfies the constraints. See Figure 10-40.

Solver Results dialog box and solution ◆ **Figure 10-40**

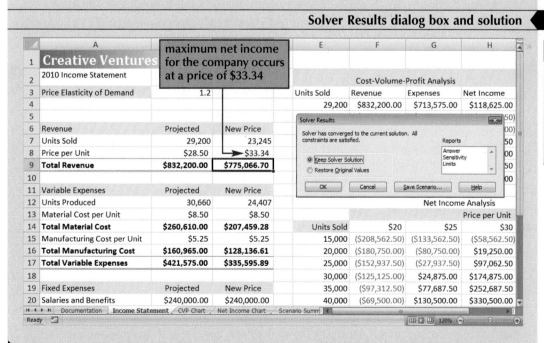

maximum net income for the company occurs at a price of $33.34

Tip

You can click the Save Scenario button in the Solver Results dialog box to save the Solver solution as a scenario, which you review using the Scenario Manager.

2. In the Solver Results dialog box, verify that the **Keep Solver Solution** option button is selected, and then click the **OK** button. The Solver solution is saved with the workbook.

Based on the result returned by Solver, Creative Ventures will maximize its net income by selling HoverDisks for $33.34 each. Under this plan, the company will sell 23,245 units yearly for a net income of $147,470.81. This assumes that the price elasticity of demand for their product is equal to 1.2. However, it's quite possible that Todd and Brent's assumptions are inaccurate and that the elasticity value is considerably higher, which would mean a greater drop-off in sales if they increase the price. You can explore this possibility and use Solver to determine a new "best" price for the company.

To rerun Solver to determine a new "best" price:

▶ 1. Change the value in cell B3 from 1.2 to **1.8**. This elasticity value assumes that a 10% increase in the sales price causes demand to fall 18%.

   If the elasticity value is 1.8 rather than 1.2, Creative Ventures will sell only 20,267 HoverDisks per year at $33.34 per disk. The net income under the scenario also drops by about $56,000 from $147,470.81 down to $91,174.96. If Todd and Brent's estimate of elasticity is incorrect, it will cost the company a lot in lost revenue. You'll use Solver to determine the best price with the new elasticity value.

▶ 2. In the Analysis group on the Data tab, click the **Solver** button to open the Solver Parameters dialog box.

▶ 3. Click the **Solve** button to run Solver. The Solver Results dialog box opens.

▶ 4. Click the **OK** button to keep the Solver solution.

If the elasticity value is as high as 1.8, then the "best" price for HoverDisks is $29.39, which is fairly close to the current price of $28.50. The maximum net income would be $120,070.79. It's clear that knowing the correct value for *e* is important in ensuring a company remains profitable, which is why companies invest so much on market analysis.

InSight | Understanding the Iterative Process

Solver arrives at optimal solutions through an **iterative procedure,** in which Solver starts with an initial solution (usually the current values from the worksheet) and uses that as a basis to calculate a new set of values. If those values improve the value of the target cell, the new values are used as a basis to generate the next set of values. If they don't improve the solution, Solver tries a different set of values. Each step, or iteration, in this process improves the solution until Solver reaches the point where the new solutions are not significantly better than the solution from the previous step. At that point, Solver will stop and indicate that it has found an answer.

What does "significantly better" mean? The default convergence value is 0.001, which means that if the change in the target cell between the new solution and the previous solution is less than or equal to 0.001, Solver will consider that it has converged to the solution and stop the iterative process.

Solver will also stop if it is not making progress toward a solution. The default length of time that Solver will spend on the iterative process is 100 seconds or 100 total iterations (whichever comes first). If 100 seconds or 100 iterations have passed and Solver has not found a solution, it will report this fact. At that point, you can have Solver continue the iterative process or stop the process without finding a solution. If Solver is taking too long to find a solution, you can halt the program at any time by pressing the Esc key. If you want to see the iterative process in action, click the Show Iteration Results check box in the Solver dialog box, and Excel will pause after each iteration and show the intermediate solution.

Creating a Solver Answer Report

How do you evaluate the solution that Solver produced? Solver can create three different reports—an answer report, a sensitivity report, and a limits report. The **answer report** may be the most useful of the three because it summarizes the results of a successful solution by displaying information about the target cell, changing cells, and constraints. This report includes the original and final values for the target and changing cells, as well as the constraint formulas. The **sensitivity report** and **limits report** are often used in science and engineering environments when the user wants to investigate the mathematical aspects of the Solver solution. These reports allow you to quantify the reliability of the solution. You cannot use these reports when your problem contains integer constraints.

As part of your cost-volume-profit analysis, you will create an answer report, which will provide information on the process used to determine the optimal price for their product. To make sure that the answer report includes information on the entire process, you'll set the quantities back to their original values, and then you will solve the problem again.

To generate an answer report:

▶ 1. Change the value in cell B3 to **1.2**. Change the value of cell C8 to **$28.50**.

▶ 2. In the Analysis group on the Data tab, click the **Solver** button to open the Solver Parameters dialog box, and then click the **Solve** button to run Solver.

You'll create an answer report.

▶ 3. In the Reports box, click **Answer**, and then verify that the **Keep Solver Solution** option button is selected. See Figure 10-41.

Solver Results dialog box for an answer report ◀ **Figure 10-41**

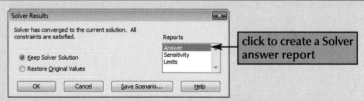

▶ 4. Click the **OK** button to accept the solution and generate the answer report in a separate sheet called "Answer Report 1." The first answer report for a problem is named Answer Report 1, the second report is named Answer Report 2, and so on.

▶ 5. Drag the **Answer Report 1** worksheet to the end of the workbook and then rename the sheet **Optimal Price Report**. See Figure 10-42.

Figure 10-42 ▶ **Answer report created by Solver**

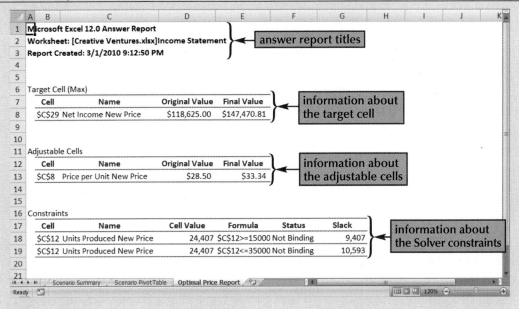

The answer report is divided into four sections. The first section includes titles, which indicate that this is an Excel answer report created from the Income Statement worksheet in the Creative Ventures workbook created on the day and at the time specified. The second section displays information about the target cell, its location, the cell label, and the cell's original value and final values. The third section displays information about the changing cells, which the report calls adjustable cells. This section of the report shows the location, column and row label, original value, and final value of each cell.

The fourth section of the report displays information about the constraints. In addition to the location, name, and value of each constraint, this section shows the constraint formulas. The second column from the right shows the status of each constraint. The status of both of the constraints is listed as "Not Binding." A **not binding constraint** is a constraint that was not a limiting factor in arriving at the solution. The other possibility is a **binding constraint** in which Solver was forced to include the constraint as part of the final solution. For example, if it turned out that the maximum net income occurred when the number of units produced was equal to 35,000 (one of the constraints in your Solver model), then this would be a binding constraint.

The last column on the right shows the slack for each constraint. The **slack** is the difference between the value in the cell and the value at the limit of the constraint. The slack for the first constraint is 9,407 because that is the difference between the final cell value, 24,407, and the first constraining value 15,000. The slack is useful in indicating how close the optimal price value is near to a constraining point. In this case, the slack for both constraints is large, so the constraints do not have any impact on the solution. Binding constraints always show a slack of 0.

InSight | **Choosing a What-If Analysis Tool**

Part of performing an effective what-if analysis lies in knowing which tool to use. Data tables are best used when you want to perform several what-if analyses involving one or two input cells. For more than one or two input cells, you must create a scenario. Data tables and scenarios can give you a quick snapshot of possible outcomes, but they can't easily provide a single solution or "best outcome." If you need to maximize or minimize a value, you must use Solver. You can also use Solver to set a calculated cell to a specific value. However, if you don't need to specify any constraints on your solution, it is generally quicker and easier to use Goal Seek.

Saving and Loading Solver Models

Todd and Brent are pleased with your solution and the answer report. Now they are look-ing at ways to reduce the cost of producing HoverDisks. Until they have a final proposal in place, they want to know what unit price results in the highest revenue for the com-pany, but not necessarily the highest net income.

They want your workbook to have two Solver models: one that maximizes net income and another that maximizes revenue. Rather than reentering the Solver parameters for each model, you can save the parameters into cells in the worksheet. Then, if you want to rerun a particular problem, you can reload the parameters from the worksheet cells with-out having to reformulate the problem. You decide to store the parameters for both mod-els in empty cells in the Income Statement worksheet.

Saving and Loading a Solver Model | Reference Window

To save a Solver model:
- Open the Solver dialog box.
- Click the Options button and then click the Save Model button.
- Select the range to contain the parameters of the Solver model, and then click the OK button.

To load a Solver model:
- Open the Solver dialog box.
- Click the Options button and then click the Load Model button.
- Select the range within the current worksheet containing the Solver parameters, and then click the OK button.

You'll start by saving the current Solver model. This command is available in the Solver Options dialog box.

To save the current model:

▶ **1.** Switch to the **Income Statement** worksheet, and then, in the Analysis group on the Data tab, click the **Solver** button. The Solver Parameters dialog box opens.

▶ **2.** Click the **Options** button. The Solver Options dialog box opens. From this dialog box, you can control how Solver operates and the method it uses to arrive at a solution. You can also use the Solver Options dialog box to save and load Solver models. See Figure 10-43.

Solver Options dialog box ◀ **Figure 10-43**

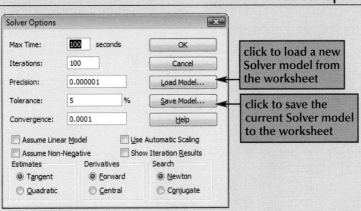

▶ **3.** Click the **Save Model** button. The Save Model dialog box opens, and a range in the worksheet to place the model information is suggested in the Select Model Area box. See Figure 10-44.

Figure 10-44 **Save Model dialog box**

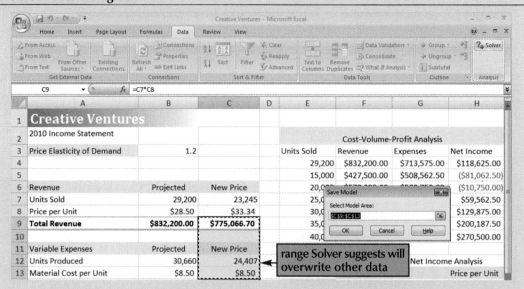

Trouble? If the suggested area on your worksheet differs from that shown in the figure, don't worry. Next, you will specify a new area in which the Solver parameters should be written.

Sometimes, the selected area will contain cells that you do not want overwritten, which is the case with the worksheet shown in Figure 10-44. You want to select a blank area of the worksheet that doesn't contain data, such as an area below the Summary section of the worksheet.

▶ 4. Scroll down the worksheet, click cell **A32** to select the upper-left corner of the range in which you want to save the model, and then click the **OK** button. Information about the Solver parameters is entered into the worksheet in the range A32:A36.

▶ 5. Click the **Cancel** button in the Solver Options dialog box, and then click the **Close** button in the Solver Parameters dialog box. Both dialog boxes close.

▶ 6. In cell A31, enter **Maximum Net Income Model**, and then format the text using the **20% - Accent3** cell style. See Figure 10-45.

Figure 10-45 **Saved Solver model parameters**

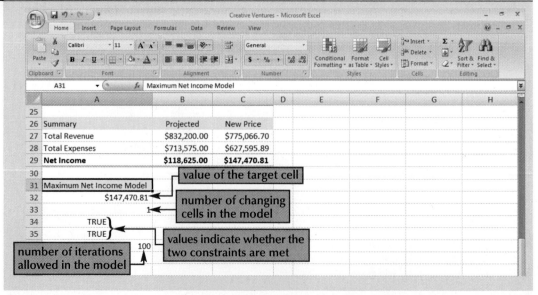

The first parameter in cell A32 displays the value $147,470.81, which is the value of the target cell under this model. The second parameter in cell A33 displays the value 1, indicating the number of changing cells in the model. The next two cells display the value TRUE. Those cells correspond to the constraints in the model. The fact that they both display the value TRUE indicates that all of the values in the worksheet must satisfy the constraints. If, at a later date, you change some of the values in this worksheet, violating one of those constraints, the Solver parameter cells will display the value FALSE. The cells can act as a visual check that all of the model's conditions are still being met as the worksheet is modified. The final parameter cell, cell A36, contains technical details about how Excel will run Solver. You'll learn about some of the technical details later in this tutorial.

Now that you've saved this model, you can create a second model to determine the optimal price that maximizes revenue for the company. This model will be the same as the model to maximize net income except that the target cell will be cell C9 rather than C29.

To calculate the price to maximize the company's revenue:

▶ **1.** In the Analysis group on the Data tab, click the **Solver** button. The Solver Parameters dialog box opens.

▶ **2.** With the Set Target Cell box active, click cell **C9** in the Income Statement worksheet. The target cell changes to cell C9.

▶ **3.** Click the **Solve** button, and then when the Solver Results dialog box opens, click the **OK** button to accept the Solver solution. See Figure 10-46.

Price that results in maximum revenue   **Figure 10-46**

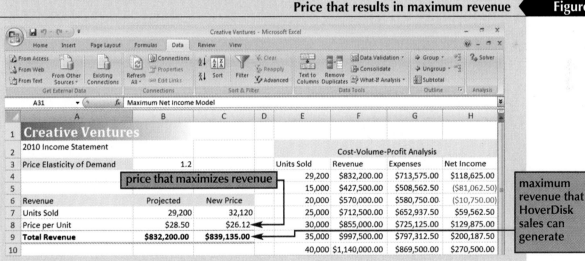

You inform Todd and Brent that the maximum revenue that the company can generate is $839,135 based on a sales volume of 32,120 units per year at $26.12 per unit. You will save this new Solver model to the worksheet and then reload the model that maximizes net income.

To save the maximum revenue model:

▶ **1.** In cell A38, enter **Maximum Revenue Model**, and then format the text using the **20% - Accent3** cell style.

▶ **2.** In the Analysis group on the Data tab, click the **Solver** button to open the Solver Parameters dialog box, click the **Options** button to open the Solver Options dialog box, and then click the **Save Model** button. The Save Model dialog box opens, with the suggested range selected in the Select Model Area box.

▶ **3.** Click cell **A39** in the Income Statement worksheet, and then click the **OK** button. Excel pastes the Solver parameters into the range A39:A43.

Next, you'll reload the previous Solver model.

▶ **4.** In the Solver Options dialog box, click the **Load Model** button. The Load Model dialog box opens so you can select the model you want to load.

▶ **5.** Select the range **A32:A36** and then click the **OK** button in the Load Model dialog box. A dialog box opens to confirm that you want to reset the previous Solver cell selections.

▶ **6.** Click the **OK** button. The Solver Options dialog box reappears.

▶ **7.** Click the **OK** button to return to the Solver Parameters dialog box, and then click the **Solve** button to rerun the Solver model to maximize net income. The Solver Results dialog box opens, indicating that Solver has found a solution that satisfies all the constraints.

▶ **8.** Click the **OK** button to accept the Solver solution with the unit price value of $33.34.

▶ **9.** Save and close the Creative Ventures workbook.

By saving Solver model parameters to cells on the worksheet, you can create dozens of models that you can load and apply to your analysis as new data is entered.

| InSight | | **Linear and Nonlinear Models** |

Solver models are divided into two classes: those that use linear functions and those that use nonlinear functions. A **linear function** is a function that can be written as the sum of terms, with each term multiplied by a constant value. For example, the function

$$w = 14 + 25x - 37y + 108z$$

is linear because it is written as a sum of the variables x, y, and z, with each variable multiplied by a constant. A **nonlinear function** is any function that cannot be written in this form. For example, the function

$$w = \frac{1}{\sin(x)\cos(y)\tan(z)}$$

is nonlinear because the value of w cannot be written as a sum of x, y, and z. The distinction between linear and nonlinear is important when running Solver. Solver can quickly and easily solve linear functions. If a problem is nonlinear, you could run into several difficulties. Solver can display different solutions depending on your worksheet's initial values or might even fail to find a solution. For this reason, if you are using Solver with a nonlinear problem, you should try several different starting values in your worksheet and then choose the solution that produces the optimal value for the target cell.

You've completed your work analyzing the cost-volume-profit relationship for Creative Ventures' HoverDisk. Your analysis explored the relationship between unit price, sales volume, and profit. By using Solver, you were able to provide Todd and Brent with several pricing options for the upcoming year. They'll study your work and get back to you with any questions or problems.

Session 10.3 Quick Check | Review

1. What is an add-in?
2. What are three options of the target cell using Solver?
3. What are the five types of constraints you can put on a cell in a Solver model?
4. Define the following terms: *not binding constraint, binding constraint, slack.*
5. How would you create several Solver models on a single worksheet?
6. What is an iterative procedure?
7. What is a linear function?

Tutorial Summary | Review

In this tutorial, you explored how to perform what-if analyses in a cost-volume-profit problem. In the first session, you examined how to create one-variable and two-variable data tables to return the results of several what-if analyses at once. You also used Goal Seek to calculate the value of a target cell based on the value of a single changing cell. The second session expanded the what-if analysis to include scenarios in which several possible values are assigned to changing cells to view their impact on several result cells. The final session explored the financial concept of elasticity and showed how to use Solver to determine a sales price to maximize profits. You also learned how to store and load Solver models, allowing several Solver models to be associated with a single worksheet.

Key Terms

add-in
adjustable cell
answer report
array formula
binding constraint
break-even analysis
break-even point
changing cell
column input cell
constraint
cost-volume-profit (CVP)
    analysis
cost-volume-profit
    (CVP) chart
data table
elasticity
fixed expense

Goal Seek
input cell
input value
iterative procedure
limits report
linear function
mixed expense
nonlinear function
not binding constraint
one-variable data table
perfectly elastic
perfectly inelastic
price elasticity of demand
relatively elastic
relatively inelastic
result cell

result value
row input cell
scenario
Scenario Manager
Scenario PivotTable report
scenario summary report
sensitivity report
slack
Solver
Solver parameter
TABLE function
target cell
trial and error
two-variable data table
unit elastic
variable expense

| Practice | **Review Assignments** |

Practice the skills you learned in the tutorial using the same case scenario.

Data File needed for the Review Assignments: Light.xlsx

Creative Ventures has another product that it has been selling in the last year called a Light Styk. Todd and Brent have used last year's sales data to project next year's income statement. They want you to repeat the analysis you did for the HoverDisk by analyzing the cost-volume-profit relationship of the Light Styk product. They also want you to determine the price for Light Styks that maximizes the company's net income.

Complete the following:

1. Open the **Light** workbook located in the Tutorial.10\Review folder included with your Data Files, and then save the workbook as **Light Styks** in the same folder. In the Documentation sheet, enter your name in cell B3 and the current date in cell B4.
2. In the Income Statement worksheet, create a one-variable data table to calculate the revenue, expenses, and net income for sales volume ranging from 0 units sold up to 30,000 units sold in increments of 5000 units. Format the table so that it is easy to read.
3. Use the data table you created in Step 2 to create a scatter chart with straight lines displaying the revenue and total expenses plotted against units sold. Store the chart in a chart sheet named CVP Chart. Based on the chart, project the break-even point for the company's sale of Light Styks. Add appropriate titles to the chart and chart axes.
4. Create a two-variable data table that calculates net income based on different units sold and sales price values. Assume that the units sold values range from 0 to 30,000 units in increments of 5000 units and that the possible sales price values are $10, $12, $14, and $16. Format the table so that it is easy to read and interpret.
5. Plot the results of the two-variable data in a scatter chart with straight lines. Save the chart in a chart sheet named **Net Income Chart**. Edit the chart series so that the series names, $10, $12, $14, and $16, are displayed in the legend for each chart. Add appropriate titles to the chart and chart axes. Based on the results of the chart, estimate the amount of units that must be sold for each price for the company to break even.
6. Create range names for the values in the nonadjacent range B7:B8;B12:B16;B20: B22;B26:B28 based on the corresponding labels in column A.
7. Todd and Brent want to study the four scenarios shown in Figure 10-47. Add these scenarios to the Light Styks workbook.

Figure 10-47

Changing Cells	Status Quo	Expanded	Reduced	Sale
Units Sold (B7)	14,000	18,000	10,000	20,000
Price per Unit (B8)	$11.95	$11.95	$11.95	$9.95
Advertising (B20)	$15,000	$30,000	$10,000	$10,000
Administrative (B21)	$10,000	$15,000	$5,000	$5,000
Miscellaneous (B22)	$5,000	$10,000	$5,000	$5,000

8. Create a scenario summary report on the four scenarios you created, reporting their effect on total revenue, total expenses, and net income.

9. Create a Scenario PivotTable based on the four scenarios. Format the values in the PivotTable as currency.

10. Create a Scenario PivotChart based on the four scenarios. Place the PivotChart in a chart sheet named **Scenario PivotChart**. Add an appropriate chart title and axes titles.

11. Todd and Brent want to calculate the optimal price for their Light Styks product, assuming a price elasticity of demand value of 1.2. With the Status Quo scenario displayed in the worksheet, copy the values in the range B6:B28 into the range C6:C28. Change the label in cells C6, C11, C19, and C25 to **Optimal Price**.

12. In cell C7, project the units sold based on the sales price by entering the formula **=B7*(1+B4*(1–C8/B8))**. Verify that with the price of $11.95 in cell C8, the units sold value in C7 is 14,000.

13. Use Solver to calculate the sales price that results in the maximum net income subject to the following constraints: units produced (cell C12) must be less than or equal to 30,000 and greater than or equal to 5,000.

14. Save the Solver Answer report to a worksheet named **Net Income Answer Report**.

15. In cell A30 of the Income Statement worksheet, enter **Maximum Net Income** and then format the cell using the 20% - Accent3 cell style. Save the parameters of the Solver model to the range A31:A35.

16. Save and close the workbook. Submit the finished workbook to your instructor, either in printed or electronic form, as requested.

Challenge | Case Problem 1

Expand on the skills you've learned to help an instructor create a grading curve.

Data File needed for this Case Problem: Grade.xlsx

High Desert University   Karen Reynolds teaches Calculus at High Desert University at Tempe, Arizona, in which 220 students are distributed in dozens of sections and discussion groups. She wants to use Excel to determine appropriate cutoff points for her grading curve. Generally, she wants to set the cutoff points so that the following distribution of grades is observed in the student body:

F	2%
D	10%
C	35%
B	35%
A	18%

Professor Reynolds has put forward five possible grading curves shown in Figure 10-48. For example, in Grading Curve 1, she will assign As to test scores from 80 to 100. She wants you to evaluate each one and determine which one results in a distribution of grades closest to her proposed distribution. After you choose which of the five scenarios fits the data the best, she wants you to use Solver to determine whether there is a grading curve that is even closer than any of her proposed scenarios to the desired distribution of grades.

Figure 10-48

Scenario	F	D	C	B	A
Grading Curve 1	0 – 19	20 – 39	40 – 59	60 – 79	80 – 100
Grading Curve 2	0 – 29	30 – 49	50 – 69	70 – 89	90 – 100
Grading Curve 3	0 – 49	50 – 64	65 – 79	80 – 94	95 – 100
Grading Curve 4	0 – 39	40 – 59	60 – 74	75 – 84	85 – 100
Grading Curve 5	0 – 59	60 – 69	70 – 79	80 – 89	90 – 100

Complete the following:

1. Open the **Grade** workbook located in the Tutorial.10\Case1 folder included with your Data Files, and then save the workbook as **Grade Curve** in the same folder. In the Documentation sheet, enter your name in cell B3 and the current date in cell B4.
2. The Test Score worksheet contains a table of individual student scores and a table for the grading curve. In the Test Score worksheet, the range F4:G8 is the lower and upper ranges for each letter grade. Complete the upper range values in the range G4:G7 by inserting formulas so that the upper range for each letter grade is one point lower than the lower range of the next letter grade.
3. In cell D4, enter the VLOOKUP function to return the letter grade for the first student in the list. (*Hint*: The lookup value is the student's final score, the table array is the cell range $F$4:$H$8, the column index number is 3, and the lookup should find the closest match in the first column of the lookup table.) Copy the formula in cell D4 into the range D5:D223 to calculate the grades for the rest of the students' scores.
4. In cell I4, use the COUNTIF function to count the total number of letter grades in the range $D$4:$D$223 equal to "F". Copy your formula into the range I5:I8 to count the total number of the other letter grades assigned under the current grading scale. In cell I9, calculate the total number of all letter grades, verifying that the total equals 220.
5. In the range J4:J8, calculate the percent of each letter grade assigned to the student body. In cell J9, calculate the total percentage of all letter grades, verifying that the total percentage is 100%.
6. In range L4:L8, use the ABS function to calculate the absolute value of the difference between the observed percentage of each letter grade and Professor Reynolds' optimal percentage. In cell L9, calculate the total value of these absolute differences.

⊕ EXPLORE

7. Assign the range names **LowF** through **LowA** for the values in the range F4:F8. Assign the range names **HighF** through **HighA** for the values in the range G4:G8. Assign the range names **PercentF** through **PercentA** for the values in the range J4:J8. Assign the range name **DifferenceFromCurve** to the value in cell L9.
8. Enter the five grading curve scenarios shown in Figure 10-48 into scenarios named **Grading Curve 1** through **Grading Curve 5**. Use the range F4:F8 as your changing cells and the range J4:J8;L9 as your result cells. Create a scenario summary report evaluating the results from each of the five scenarios.
9. The closeness of each grading curve to Professor Reynolds' optimal grading curve is expressed in the value of cell L9. If there was perfect correspondence, the value of cell L9 would be 0. Pick the grading curve that has the lowest value for cell L9 and show that grading curve in the Test Score worksheet.

⊕ EXPLORE   10. Using those scenario values as a starting point, create a Solver model to minimize the value in cell L9 by changing the values in the range F5:F8, subject to the following constraint that all of the values in the range F5:F8 must be integers.

⊕ EXPLORE   11. Store the grading curve returned by Solver as a new scenario named **Optimal Grading Curve**. Create a second scenario summary report displaying this grading curve along with the five others you've investigated.

⊕ EXPLORE   12. The results that Solver returned for a problem of this type can be sensitive to the initial values. Investigate this issue by displaying the grading curve from the Grading Curve 1 scenario and then rerunning Solver with those initial values. What solution does Solver find and how does it compare with the one you discovered in Step 10?

13. Restore the grading curve values from the Optimal Grading Curve scenario.

14. Save and close the workbook. Submit the finished workbook to your instructor, either in printed or electronic form, as requested.

Apply | **Case Problem 2**

Use the skills you've learned to create a data table describing the conditions of a home loan.

Data File needed for this Case Problem: Loan.xlsx

Mortgage Analysis   Kevin Webber is considering taking out a second mortgage for an addition on his home. He decides to use Excel to analyze several possibilities for the loan, including the size of the loan, the interest rate, and the number of years required to pay back the loan. He's asked for your help in developing a two-variable data table and scenarios to examine how varying these factors affect the required monthly payment and the total cost of the loan.

Complete the following:

1. Open the **Loan** workbook located in the Tutorial.10\Case2 folder included with your Data Files, and then save the workbook as **Loan Table** in the same folder. In the Documentation sheet, enter your name in cell B3 and the current date in cell B4.

2. In the Mortgage worksheet, define names for the values in the range B3:B8 based on the name values in the left column.

3. Enter **Monthly Payment** in cell D1. Enter **Years** in cell E2, and then merge and center the range E2:I2. Enter the values 10 through 30 in increments of 5 in the range E3:I3. Enter the values 5.5% through 7.0% in increments of 0.1% in the range D4:D19.

4. In cell D3, enter a reference to the value in cell B7. Format the cell to display the text string **Interest Rate**.

5. Create a two-variable data table in the range D3:I19 using cells B5 and B4 as the column and row input cells, respectively.

6. Format the resulting two-variable data table so that the result values appear as currency and the row and column labels appear on a light yellow background. Add gridlines to the table.

7. Format the sheet so that it prints in landscape orientation on a single page with your name, the filename, and the date in the right footer.

8. Add scenarios to the worksheet to display all combinations of the loan assuming that the number of years required for payment is 30; the interest rate is 5.5%, 6.0%, or 6.5%; and the amount of the loan is $100,000, $125,000, or $150,000. (*Hint*: There will be nine scenarios.)

9. Create a scenario summary report that displays the value of the monthly payment and total cost of the loan for each of the scenarios you created.

10. Format the scenario summary report so that it prints in landscape orientation on a single page with your name, the filename, and the date in the right footer.

11. Save and close the workbook. Submit the finished workbook to your instructor, either in printed or electronic form, as requested.

| Challenge | Case Problem 3 |

Explore how to use Solver to aid in the scheduling of conference center rooms.

Data File needed for this Case Problem: Fairway.xlsx

Fairway Convention Center Patrick Ross is the resource manager at the Fairway Convention Center in Atlanta, Georgia. One of his tasks is to determine who reserves which of the 10 conference rooms. To best match the individual with the room, Patrick asks applicants to list their room preferences from 1 (the most desirable) to 10 (the least desirable). Patrick then tries to allocate the rooms so that the sum of the preference scores is minimized. If an applicant requires a particular room, Patrick can reserve that room for the applicant. Knowing that this type of problem might be appropriate for Solver, Patrick requests your help in setting up a Solver solution for one of his scheduling problems.

Complete the following:

1. Open the **Fairway** workbook located in the Tutorial.10\Case3 folder included with your Data Files, and then save the workbook as **Fairway Convention Center** in the same folder. In the Documentation sheet, enter your name in cell B3 and the current date in cell B4. Switch to the Rooms worksheet.

   The Rooms sheet has two tables. The first table indicates each applicant's preference for the 10 conference rooms. The second table indicates the assignment of the room to the applicant. A value of 1 in the table indicates that the conference room has been assigned to an applicant. A value of 0 indicates that the room has not been assigned. Only one conference room can be assigned to each applicant and each applicant can only reserve one room; thus, each row and column of the table will have one cell containing the value 1 and the rest of the cells will contain the value 0. Cells N18:N27 display the preference score for each applicant's assigned conference room. Cell B29 displays the sum of the 10 preference scores. This is the value you seek to minimize for Patrick.

2. Start Solver and indicate that the target cell, cell B31, should be set to its minimal value by changing the values in the range B18:K27.

✛ EXPLORE

3. Add the following constraints to the problem:

   • The values in the range B18:K27 must be binary.

   • The values in the range B29:K29 must all equal 1 (indicating that each room has a single occupant).

   • The values in the range M18:M27 must all equal 1 (indicating that each applicant receives a single room).

   • The values in the range N18:N27 must be less than or equal to 6 (indicating that each applicant will receive no worse than their sixth-best choice).

   • William Conklin needs the larger space that can be found only in the Canyon Room. Constrain the value of cell D23 so that it equals 1 and that all of the other cells in row 23 and column D of the Room Assignments table are equal to 0.

   • Laura Ward needs to use the Oak View Room. Constrain the value of cell I26 so that it equals 1 and that all of the other cells in row 26 and column I of the Room Assignments table are equal to 0.

EXPLORE

4. Run Solver (it might take a while for Solver to arrive at a solution). Verify that all of the constraints have been satisfied.

5. Enter the text Room Assignment Model in cell A33 displayed on a yellow background. Save your Solver model to the range A34:A50.

6. Format the page layout of the Rooms worksheet, limiting the print area to the range A1:N32. Format the worksheet so that it prints on a single page in landscape orientation. Add your name, the date, and the filename to the lower-right footer of the printout.

7. Save and close the workbook. Submit the finished workbook to your instructor, either in printed or electronic form, as requested.

| Create | **Case Problem 4** |

Create an Excel workbook to analyze the cost-volume-profit relationship of a new robotic product.

There are no Data Files needed for this Case Problem.

NewGen Robotics Wesley Lee is a marketing manager at NewGen Robotics of Greenville, Oregon. The company is introducing a new line of household robots capable of performing basic vacuuming and cleanup tasks. Wesley needs you to examine a projected income statement for the company's operations and calculate the break-even point for the product and determine the optimal price point. Figure 10-49 shows the projected income statement for the company.

Figure 10-49

Revenue	
Units Sold	102,391
Price per Unit	$399.95
Variable Expenses	
Material Cost per Unit	$175.50
Manufacturing Cost per Unit	$143.25
Fixed Expenses	
Salaries and Benefits	$3,450,000
Advertising	$775,000
Administrative	$520,000
Miscellaneous	$500,000

Complete the following:

1. Create a workbook named **NewGen Robotics** located in the Tutorial.10\Case4 folder included with your Data Files. Add a Documentation sheet describing the workbook.

2. Complete an income statement based on the values from Figure 10-49. Assume that the company produces enough cleaning robots to have a 1% surplus over units sold.

3. Based on your income statement, calculate the number of units the company would have to sell at its current price to break even.

4. Use a one-variable data table to calculate the total revenue, expenses, and net income if the company sells from 50,000 to 200,000 units in increments of 25,000. Create a CVP chart based on your results.

5. Use a two-variable data table to calculate the net income for units sold from 50,000 to 200,000 units in increments of 25,000 and sales prices of $300 up to $500 in increments of $50. Plot your results.

6. Create scenarios based on the possibilities displayed in Figure 10-50. Report the net income, revenue, and total expenses for each scenario in a scenario summary report.

Figure 10-50

Changing Values	Status Quo	Scenario 1	Scenario 2	Scenario 3
Units Sold	102,391	75,000	125,000	150,000
Price per Unit	$399.95	$415.00	$380.00	$375.00
Salaries and Benefits	$3,450,000	$3,200,000	$3,600,000	$3,900,000
Advertising	$775,000	$700,000	$850,000	$1,000,000
Administrative	$520,000	$450,000	$650,000	$800,000
Miscellaneous	$500,000	$450,000	$550,000	$700,000

7. Wesley assumes that for their product the price elasticity of demand is 1.8 (for every 10% increase in sales price, they expect to see sales drop by 18%). Using the values from the Status Quo scenario as a basis, run Solver to calculate the optimal price for the company's product to maximize net income. Assume that the company must manufacture at least 25,000 units but no more than 250,000.

8. Because this is a new market, the company is willing to build the market for cleaning robots in exchange for losing money. Use Solver to calculate the sales price the company can charge for its product in order to lose no more than $1,000,000 in net income. Assume an initial value of $300 for the product and a price elasticity of demand of 1.8. What is the sales price under this scenario and how many units would the company sell?

9. Save and close the workbook. Submit the finished workbook to your instructor, either in printed or electronic form, as requested.

Research | Internet Assignments

Use the Internet to find and work with data related to the topics presented in this tutorial.

The purpose of the Internet Assignments is to challenge you to find information on the Internet that you can use to work effectively with this software. The actual assignments are updated and maintained on the Course Technology Web site. Log on to the Internet and use your Web browser to go to the Student Online Companion for New Perspectives Office 2007 at **www.course.com/np/office2007**. Then navigate to the Internet Assignments for this tutorial.

Assess | SAM Assessment and Training

If you have a SAM user profile, you may have access to hands-on instruction, practice, and assessment of the skills covered in this tutorial. Log in to your SAM account (**http://sam2007.course.com**) to launch any assigned training activities or exams that relate to the skills covered in this tutorial.

Review | **Quick Check Answers**

Session 10.1

1. In a what-if analysis, you change the input cell to observe the value in the result cell. With Goal Seek, you define a value that you want to obtain for the result cell and then you determine what value is required in the input cell.

2. The Set cell input box, in which you specify the cell containing the value you want to set; the To value input box, in which you specify the value for the Set cell; and the By changing cell input box, in which you specify which cell in the worksheet to change to achieve the desired result.

3. A data table is a table that shows the outcomes of several what-if analyses. The input cell is a cell in the table containing a value you're interested in changing to examine its impact in the what-if analysis. The result cell is the result you're interested in viewing based on the changing value of the input cell.

4. A one-variable data table is a data table with a single column or row of input values and multiple results. A two-variable data table is a data table with two input values and a single result.

5. There is no limit to the number of results cells with a one-variable data table. There is only one result cell for a two-variable data table.

6. Enter the custom format, "Profits".

7. An array formula is a formula that acts upon a value array, returning either a single value or an array of values.

Session 10.2

1. Scenarios enable you to perform what-if analyses using several input and result cells.

2. Assign range names to the input and result cells.

3. Changing cells are cells that contain values you change under the different scenarios.

4. Result cells display the output values of interest in the different scenarios. You define the result cells when creating scenario summary reports.

5. Open the Scenario Manager dialog box and then select the scenario to view from the Scenarios list box. Click the Show button to display the scenario in the active worksheet.

6. Click the Summary button in the Scenario Manager dialog box, click the Scenario PivotTable Report option button, select the result cells you want to display in the PivotTable, and click the OK button to generate the PivotTable report.

Session 10.3

1. An add-in is a customized program that adds commands and features to Microsoft Office programs such as Excel.

2. Maximize it, minimize it, or set it to a specific value.

3. Set the cell equal to a value, make it less than or equal to a value, make it greater than or equal to a value, constrain it to be an integer, or constrain it to be a binary value (0 or 1).

4. A not binding constraint is a constraint that is not a limiting factor in the Solver solution. A binding constraint is a limiting factor in the Solver solution. Slack is the difference between the value of a constraining cell and the limiting value of the constraint.

5. Save the Solver models to different cells in the worksheet and then load each one you want to run using the Solver parameters saved in those cells.

6. An iterative procedure starts with an initial solution and uses it as a basis to calculate a series of solutions. Each step, or iteration, improves the solution until the point is reached where one solution is no longer significantly better than the previous solution.

7. A linear function is a function that can be written as the sum of a series of terms, with each term multiplied by a constant value.

Ending Data Files

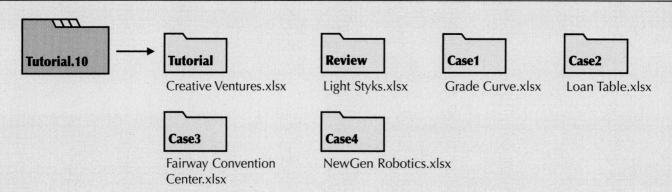

Tutorial.10 → Tutorial
Creative Ventures.xlsx

Review
Light Styks.xlsx

Case1
Grade Curve.xlsx

Case2
Loan Table.xlsx

Case3
Fairway Convention
Center.xlsx

Case4
NewGen Robotics.xlsx

Objectives

Connecting to External Data

Importing Financial Data from Several Sources

Case | Union Financial

Union Financial is a brokerage firm based in Moline, Illinois. The company has provided financial planning and investment services to corporations and people in the area for the past 25 years. As part of its investment services business, the company advises clients on their investment portfolios, so it needs to have access to current stock market information. Like all brokerage firms, Union Financial is connected to many financial and investment information services. The investment counselors at the company need current financial data and reports, but they also must examine information on long-term trends in the market.

Some of this information comes from Excel workbooks, but other information is stored in specialized financial packages and statistical programs. In addition, the company maintains a database with detailed financial information about a variety of stocks, bonds, and funds. Company employees also use the Internet to receive up-to-the-minute market reports. Because much of the information that the counselors need comes from outside the company, they must retrieve information to analyze it and make decisions.

Carol Hill is an investment counselor at Union Financial. She wants you to help her manage the different types of data available as she works on the Horizons Fund, one of the company's most important stock portfolios. Because Carol prefers to work with financial data using Excel, she wants you to retrieve sample data from different sources and include them in a workbook.

Starting Data Files

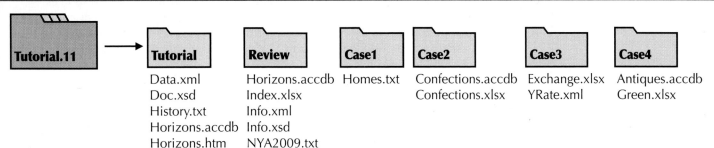

Tutorial.11 →	Tutorial	Review	Case1	Case2	Case3	Case4
	Data.xml	Horizons.accdb	Homes.txt	Confections.accdb	Exchange.xlsx	Antiques.accdb
	Doc.xsd	Index.xlsx		Confections.xlsx	YRate.xml	Green.xlsx
	History.txt	Info.xml				
	Horizons.accdb	Info.xsd				
	Horizons.htm	NYA2009.txt				
		Summary.htm				

Session 11.1

Examining Data Sources

In her job as an investment counselor at Union Financial, Carol helps her clients plan their investment strategies. To do her job well, Carol needs to look at the market from a variety of angles. She examines long-term trends so that her clients understand the benefits of creating long-term investment strategies. She also tracks market performance in recent months to analyze current trends. Finally, she assesses the daily mood of the market by regularly viewing up-to-the-minute reports.

The information that Carol needs comes from many sources. As shown in Figure 11-1, long-term and historical stock information from the company's old record keeping system has been retrieved from financial software packages and placed in text files that all counselors can use. Union Financial stores its current market information in databases, which is where Carol finds information on recent trends. Carol can also access current market reports electronically from the Internet.

| Figure 11-1 | Carol's data sources |

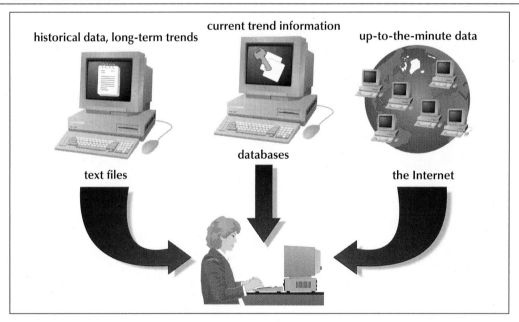

Carol is responsible for tracking the performance of the Horizons Fund, one of the company's investment vehicles. The Horizons Fund is composed of several stocks on the New York Stock Exchange (NYSE), and it is one of Union Financial's oldest and most successful funds. Carol asks you to develop a single Excel workbook that summarizes essential information about the Horizons Fund. She wants the workbook to connect to sources describing (1) how the fund has performed over the past few years, (2) more recent information on the fund's performance in the last year as well as the last few days, and (3) up-to-the-minute reports on the fund's current status. To that end, Carol has laid out the strategy for the workbook that she wants you to create, shown in Figure 11-2.

Carol's plan for the Horizons Fund workbook | **Figure 11-2**

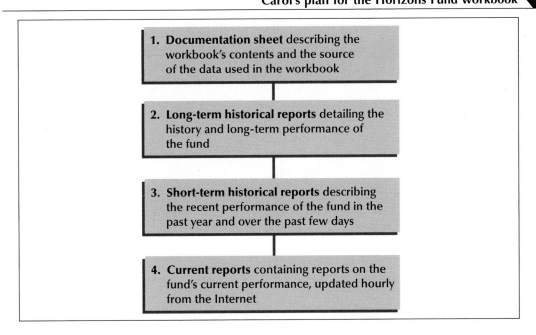

1. **Documentation sheet** describing the workbook's contents and the source of the data used in the workbook

2. **Long-term historical reports** detailing the history and long-term performance of the fund

3. **Short-term historical reports** describing the recent performance of the fund in the past year and over the past few days

4. **Current reports** containing reports on the fund's current performance, updated hourly from the Internet

After you provide these three types of report-related information in her Excel workbook, Carol will use Excel tools to analyze the data.

To gather data from three sources, you need to connect the workbook to external data files. First, you'll create a connection to the Horizons Fund's historical data. The daily values for the fund over the previous three years are stored in a text file. You'll import this text file into Excel.

Working with Text Files

A **text file** contains only text and numbers without any formulas, graphics, special fonts, or formatted text. Text files are one of the simplest and most widely used methods of storing data because most software programs can save and retrieve data in a text file format. For example, Excel can open a text file in a worksheet, where you can format it as you would any data. Excel can also save a workbook as a text file, preserving only the data values without any of its formats. In addition, many types of computers can read text files. So, although text files contain only raw, unformatted data, they are very useful when you want to share data across software programs and computer systems. There are several types of text file formats, which you'll learn about in the next section.

Reference Window | **Connecting to a Text File**

- In the Get External Data group on the Data tab, click the From Text button.
- In the first step of the Text Import Wizard, choose how the data is organized, and then specify the row in which to start the import.
- In the second step, set the column breaks by clicking a location in the Data preview window to insert a column break, double-clicking a column break to delete it, and dragging a column break to move it to a new location.
- In the third step, specify the data format for each column by clicking the column, and then selecting the appropriate data format option button, or skip import columns by clicking the column in the Data preview window then clicking the Do not import option button.
- Click the Finish button.
- Specify where to insert the imported text, and then click the OK button to import the text file into the worksheet.

Understanding Text File Formats

Because a text file doesn't contain formatting codes to give it structure, a program needs another way to understand the file contents. If a text file contains only numbers, how does the importing program know where one group of values ends and another begins? You have to know how that data is organized within the file. One way to structure a text file is to use a **delimiter**, which is a symbol—usually a space, a comma, or a tab—that separates one column of data from another. Text that is separated by a delimiter is called **delimited text**. Figure 11-3 shows three examples of the same stock market data delimited by spaces, commas, and tabs.

Figure 11-3 | **Examples of delimited text**

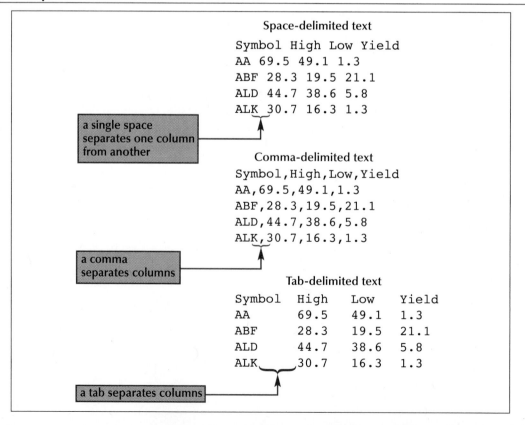

```
                            Space-delimited text
                         Symbol High Low Yield
                         AA 69.5 49.1 1.3
                         ABF 28.3 19.5 21.1
                         ALD 44.7 38.6 5.8
                         ALK 30.7 16.3 1.3
```
a single space separates one column from another

```
                            Comma-delimited text
                         Symbol,High,Low,Yield
                         AA,69.5,49.1,1.3
                         ABF,28.3,19.5,21.1
                         ALD,44.7,38.6,5.8
                         ALK,30.7,16.3,1.3
```
a comma separates columns

```
                            Tab-delimited text
                         Symbol    High    Low    Yield
                         AA        69.5    49.1   1.3
                         ABF       28.3    19.5   21.1
                         ALD       44.7    38.6   5.8
                         ALK       30.7    16.3   1.3
```
a tab separates columns

Each example contains four columns of data: Symbol, High, Low, and Yield. In the first example, a space separates the columns. The second example shows the same data, except that a comma separates each data column. In the third example, a tab separates the columns. Columns in delimited text files are not always vertically aligned as they would be in a spreadsheet, but this is not a problem for a program that recognizes the delimiter. A tab delimiter is often the best way to separate text columns because tab-delimited text can include spaces or commas within each column.

Another way to organize text is with a **fixed-width text file** in which each column starts at the same location in the file. For example, the first column starts at the first space in the file, the second column starts at the tenth space, and so forth. Figure 11-4 shows columns arranged in a fixed-width format. In this example, all the columns line up visually because each one must start at the same location.

Example of fixed-width text ◀ **Figure 11-4**

```
Symbol   High   Low    Yield
AA       69.5   49.1   1.3
ABF      28.3   19.5   21.1
ALD      44.7   38.6   5.8
ALK      30.7   16.3   1.3
```

each column entry begins at the same point in the text file

Starting the Text Import Wizard

When you use Excel to connect to a text file, the Text Import Wizard determines whether the data is in a fixed-width format or a delimited format—and if it's delimited, what delimiter is used. You can also tell Excel how to interpret the text file.

The text file that Carol wants you to import into Excel is stored in the file named History.txt. The .txt filename extension identifies it as a text file. (Other common text file-name extensions are .dat, .prn, and .csv.) Neither you nor Carol knows anything about the file's structure, but you can easily determine that using the Text Import Wizard. You'll begin by creating a connection to the text file.

To connect to the History text file:

▶ 1. Create a new workbook, and then save the workbook as **Horizons Fund** in the **Tutorial.11\ Tutorial** folder included with your Data Files.

▶ 2. With cell A1 selected in the Sheet1 worksheet, click the **Data** tab on the Ribbon, and then, in the Get External Data group, click the **From Text** button.

▶ 3. Locate and select the **History** text file located in the **Tutorial.11\Tutorial** folder included with your Data Files, and then click the **Import** button. The Text Import Wizard opens. In the Original data type section, the Fixed width option button is already selected, indicating that the Text Import Wizard has determined the data is arranged in a fixed-width format. See Figure 11-5.

Tip

You can also open a text file using the Open dialog box. When Excel detects the data in the text file, the Text Import Wizard opens.

Figure 11-5 Text Import Wizard – Step 1 of 3

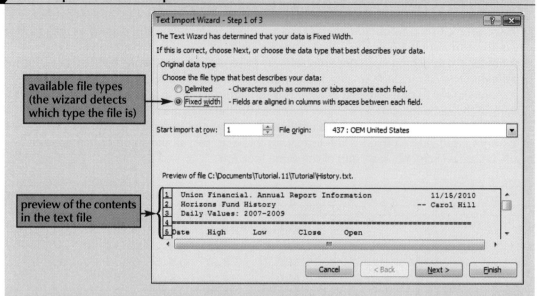

> **4.** Scroll the preview box to view the data in the text file. The data list begins at row 6 (or row 5 if you include the column titles).

Specifying the Starting Row

The text file has five columns of data—Date, High, Low, Close, and Open—corresponding to the date, the fund's high and low values on that date, and the fund's opening and closing values. The first several lines of the file contain titles and a description of the contents of the text file. Because you're only interested in the data, you'll skip these lines.

By default, the Text Import Wizard starts importing text with the first row of the file. You will have the Text Import Wizard skip the first four lines of the file by specifying row 5, which contains the labels for each column of numbers, as the starting row.

To specify row 5 as the starting row:

> **1.** Click the **Start import at row** up arrow to change the value to **5**.

> **2.** Click the **Next** button to display the second step of the Text Import Wizard.

> **3.** Scroll the preview box to display data from the text file starting with the column titles. See Figure 11-6.

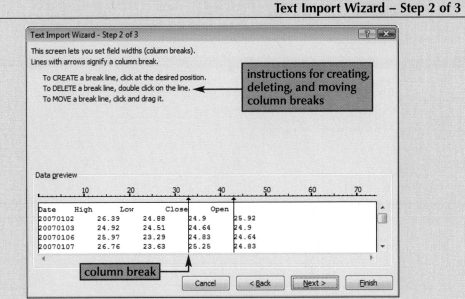

Text Import Wizard – Step 2 of 3 | Figure 11-6

Editing Column Breaks

To correctly import a fixed-width text file, the Text Import Wizard needs to know where each column begins and ends. The point at which one column ends and another begins is called a **column break**. In a delimited file, the delimiter determines the column breaks, whereas in a fixed-width file, the wizard guesses the locations of the column breaks. Sometimes, the wizard incorrectly defines the number and location of columns, so you should always check the Data preview box and edit the columns, if necessary. Figure 11-6 shows the columns the wizard proposes for your text file. Unfortunately, the wizard inserted column breaks between the Close and Open columns, but nowhere else. You need to revise the column breaks.

You insert a new column break by clicking the position in the Data preview window where you want the break to appear. If a break is in the wrong location, click and drag it to a new location in the Data preview box. You can delete an extra column break by double-clicking it. You'll modify the column breaks for the History text file.

To edit the column breaks in the History text file:

1. Click the space between the Date and High columns to insert a column break. Be sure that the break does not intersect the column titles or any of the values in the two columns.

   Trouble? If the column break you just created intersects any text, drag the line away from the text or values it intersects.

2. Click the space between the High and Low columns to insert a break in that location. Again, make sure that the column break does not intersect any text.

3. Drag the column break in the Close column between the Low and Close columns, taking care not to intersect any text or values in those columns.

4. Drag the column break in the Open column between the Close and Open columns. See Figure 11-7.

Figure 11-7 **Revised column breaks**

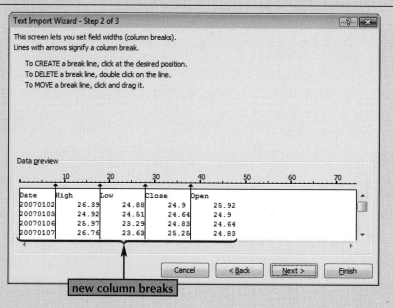

5. Click the **Next** button to display the third step of the Text Import Wizard. See Figure 11-8.

Figure 11-8 **Text Import Wizard – Step 3 of 3**

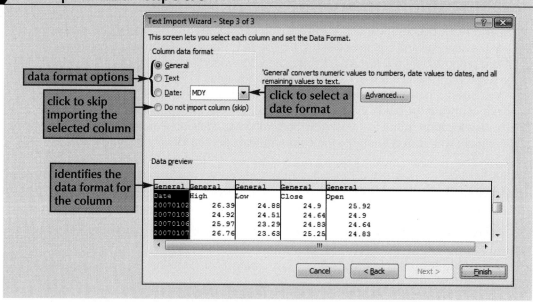

Formatting and Trimming Incoming Data

The third and final step of the Text Import Wizard allows you to format the data in each column. Unless you specify a format, the General format style is applied to all columns. To specify a format, select a column from the Data preview box and click the appropriate data format option button. You can also indicate which columns you do not want to import. Eliminating columns is useful when you want to import only a few items from a large text file containing many columns.

The Date column in the text file displays the year first, followed by the month and the day with no separators. This is not a common date format, so you want to make sure that the Text Import Wizard correctly interprets these values by applying a date format to these values, rather than leaving the General format style.

To reduce the amount of data in the workbook, you will not import Horizons Fund's daily opening value, which is the same as the closing value from the previous day. You'll import only the date and the high, low, and closing values of the fund for each day.

To specify a date format and remove the Open column:

1. Verify that the first column is selected in the preview box, and then, in the Column data format section, click the **Date** option button. The first column heading changes from General to MDY.

   Trouble? If the first column is not selected, click anywhere within the column to select it.

2. Click the **Date button arrow** to display a list of date formats, and then click **YMD**. The column heading for the first column changes to YMD, indicating the values in this column will be interpreted as dates formatted with the year followed by the month and day.

   Next, you'll omit the Open column from the text import because the opening values are the same as the closing values from the previous day.

3. In the preview box, click anywhere within the **Open** column to select it, and then click the **Do not import column (skip)** option button. The column heading for the Open column changes from General to Skip Column, indicating the data from this column will not be imported.

4. Click the **Finish** button. The Import Data dialog box opens so you can specify the location of the imported data.

5. Click cell **A4** in the Sheet1 worksheet, and then click the **OK** button.

> **Tip**
> If you're importing international data from a text file, click the Advanced button in Step 3 of the Text Import Wizard to specify a different character for the decimal point and thousands separator.

The data appears in the worksheet in the range A4:D769. Next, you'll add a descriptive title to the worksheet and format the column headings.

To title and format the worksheet:

1. In cell A1, enter **Horizons Fund History**, and then format the title using the **Title** cell style.

2. In cell A2, enter **2007 – 2009**, format the text with the **Heading 1** cell style, and then remove the bottom border from cell A2.

3. Bold and center the headings in the range A4:D4, and then increase the width of column A to **13** characters.

4. Click cell **B5**, and then press **Ctrl+Shift+End** to select the range B5:D769.

5. Apply the **Number** format to the selected data, and then click cell **A3** to deselect the range.

6. Rename the worksheet as **Fund History**. See Figure 11-9.

Figure 11-9 ▷ **Fund History worksheet**

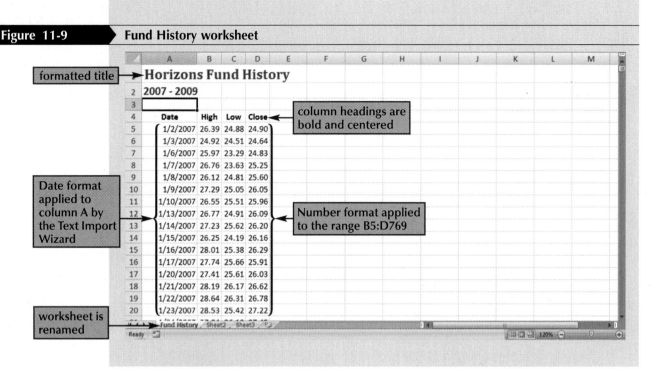

formatted title →

column headings are bold and centered ◀

Date format applied to column A by the Text Import Wizard →

Number format applied to the range B5:D769 ◀

worksheet is renamed →

	A	B	C	D	E
1	**Horizons Fund History**				
2	2007 - 2009				
3					
4	**Date**	**High**	**Low**	**Close**	
5	1/2/2007	26.39	24.88	24.90	
6	1/3/2007	24.92	24.51	24.64	
7	1/6/2007	25.97	23.29	24.83	
8	1/7/2007	26.76	23.63	25.25	
9	1/8/2007	26.12	24.81	25.60	
10	1/9/2007	27.29	25.05	26.05	
11	1/10/2007	26.55	25.51	25.96	
12	1/13/2007	26.77	24.91	26.09	
13	1/14/2007	27.23	25.62	26.20	
14	1/15/2007	26.25	24.19	26.16	
15	1/16/2007	28.01	25.38	26.29	
16	1/17/2007	27.74	25.66	25.91	
17	1/20/2007	27.41	25.61	26.03	
18	1/21/2007	28.19	26.17	26.62	
19	1/22/2007	28.64	26.31	26.78	
20	1/23/2007	28.53	25.42	27.22	

Fund History / Sheet2 / Sheet3

In addition to the fund values themselves, Carol asks you to include a high-low-close chart in the workbook displaying the fund's recent history. You will select a Stock chart type designed to compare the high, low, and closing prices of a stock.

To create a high-low-close chart for the fund data:

▶ 1. Click cell **A4**, and then press the **Ctrl+Shift+End** keys to select the range A4:D769. Scroll to the top of the worksheet without deselecting the range.

▶ 2. Click the **Insert** tab on the Ribbon, and then, in the Charts group, click the **Other Charts** button.

▶ 3. Click the **High-Low-Close** stock chart type (the first stock chart listed in the Chart gallery). The High-Low-Close chart is embedded in the Fund History worksheet.

▶ 4. Move the chart so that its upper-left corner covers cell E4, and then hold down the **Shift** key as you drag a corner of the chart to cover the range **E4:M20**.

▶ 5. Add the chart title **Horizons Fund** above the chart, add the horizontal axis title **Date**, add rotated vertical axis title **Fund Value**, and then remove the legend.

▶ 6. Click cell **A3** to deselect the chart. See Figure 11-10.

Tip

When you hold down the Shift key as you resize a chart or drawing object, the image is resized proportionally.

Formatted chart on the worksheet ◄ **Figure 11-10**

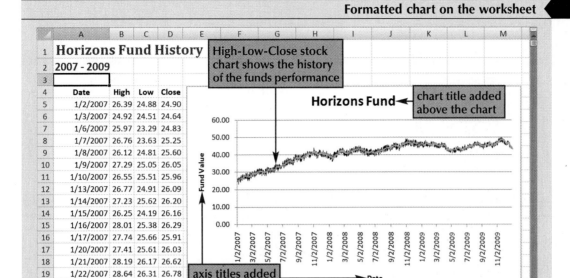

Carol wants to know what happens to the workbook if data is added or edited in the History text file. Will the workbook always show the most current data? To answer that question, you have to examine how data connections are created and controlled within Excel.

Working with Connections and Data Ranges

When you imported the fund history data, you also created a connection between the Fund History workbook and the History text file. A **connection** is a defined method of retrieving data from an external file. In this case, the method involves importing the data columns from the History text file. All of the connections used in the current workbook are listed in the Workbook Connections dialog box.

You'll open the Workbook Connections dialog box to examine the connections currently established in the Horizons Fund workbook.

To view the list of workbook connections:

► 1. Click the **Data** tab on the Ribbon, and then, in the Connections group, click the **Connections** button. The Workbook Connections dialog box opens. Currently only a single connection is listed—the connection you just created to the History text file.

► 2. Click **Click here to see where the selected connections are used**. The Workbook Connections dialog box shows where the connection to the History text file is used. See Figure 11-11.

Tip

To delete a connection to its data source, select the connection in the list in the Workbook Connections dialog box, and then click the Remove button.

Figure 11-11 ▶ **Workbook Connections dialog box**

Tip

To apply a connection to a new location, click the Existing Connections button in the Get External Data group on the Data tab. Open the connection you want to apply, and specify the new location in the workbook.

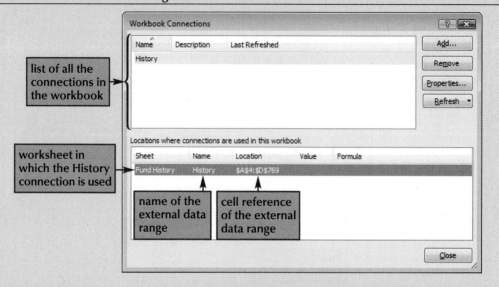

3. Click the **Close** button to close the dialog box.

External Data Ranges

The same connection might be used in several locations in the workbook, freeing Excel from having to establish a connection to the same file every time the data is imported. Each location in which a connection is applied is called an **external data range**. Excel gives each external data range a name. You can change this name by editing the properties of the external data range.

Reference Window | **Editing the Properties of an External Data Range**

- Click any cell in the range containing the external data.
- In the Connections group on the Data tab, click the Properties button.
- To define a name for the data range, enter the name in the Name box.
- To specify how the external data is refreshed in the workbook, check the appropriate check boxes in the External Data Range Properties dialog box.
- Click the Close button.

The external data range in the range A4:D769 of the Fund History worksheet is named *History*—the same name given to the connection. This is the only external data range in the workbook at the moment. Because you'll soon add more connections and external data ranges to this workbook, Carol wants you to use a more descriptive title for the data range.

To edit the properties of an external data range:

1. Click cell **A4** to select one cell within the History external data range.

2. In the Connections group on the Data tab, click the **Properties** button. The External Data Range Properties dialog box opens.

▶ 3. Type **Horizons Fund History: 2007 – 2009** in the Name box, and then click the **OK** button.

▶ 4. In the Connections group on the Data tab, click the **Connections** button.

▶ 5. With the History connection selected in the Workbook Connections list, click **Click here to see where the selected connections are used**. The name of this location is now "Horizons Fund History: 2007 – 2009," as you entered in Step 3.

▶ 6. Click the **Close** button to close the Workbook Connections dialog box.

Refreshing an External Data Range

In addition to setting the name of an external data range, you can also define how Excel updates, or **refreshes**, the data. You can:

- Keep a report current by having Excel refresh the connection when the workbook is opened or at specific intervals when the workbook is in use.
- Require the user to enter a password before data is refreshed, preventing other users from updating the data without permission.
- Remove the connection to the external data range, freezing the data so that it cannot be refreshed.
- Refresh the connection in the background, so you can work on other portions of the workbook as you wait for the data to be retrieved; this is helpful if you are retrieving large amounts of data.
- Define whether the refreshed data retains the formatting and layout you've already defined for the location or replaces the current format and layout.
- Define whether Excel inserts or overwrites cells when new rows are added to the data range.

Refreshing External Data | Reference Window

To manually refresh a data range:
- In the Connections group on the Data tab, click the Refresh All button arrow.
- Click Refresh to refresh the currently selected data range or click Refresh All to refresh all of the connections in the workbook.

To automatically refresh a data range:
- Select any cell in the data range, and then, in the Connections group on the Data tab, click the Properties button.
- Click the Refresh every check box and then enter a minutes value to refresh the data range at regular intervals.
- Click the Refresh data when opening the file check box to refresh the data when the user opens the workbook.

To manually refresh a connection:
- In the Connections group on the Data tab, click the Connections button.
- Select the connection in the Workbook Connections list, and then click the Refresh button.

To automatically refresh a connection:
- In the Connections group on the Data tab, click the Connections button.
- Click the Properties button.
- Click the Usage tab in the Connection Properties dialog box, and then select the Refresh options.

The History text file is periodically updated as recent fund values are transferred from current documents into historic documents. Carol wants the workbook to always display the most current values from the History text file, so she asks you to ensure that the connection to the file is updated whenever the workbook is opened. You can define how Excel refreshes this data by editing the properties of the connection or the properties of the external data range. The advantage of editing the connection is that your choices are applied to all of the external data ranges that use that connection. Because the History connection is only used in one location, it doesn't matter which you choose. You'll edit the property of the external data range rather than the connection.

To define how external data is refreshed:

▶ 1. Verify that cell **A4** is still selected, and then, in the Connections group on the Data tab, click the **Properties** button. The External Data Range Properties dialog box opens.

▶ 2. Click the **Refresh data when opening the file** check box to insert a check mark.

▶ 3. Click the **Prompt for file name on refresh** check box to remove the check mark. Now, Carol will not be prompted for the filename each time the data is refreshed.

▶ 4. Click the **Adjust column width** check box to remove the check mark, because you've already set the column widths. See Figure 11-12.

| Figure 11-12 | External Data Range Properties dialog box |

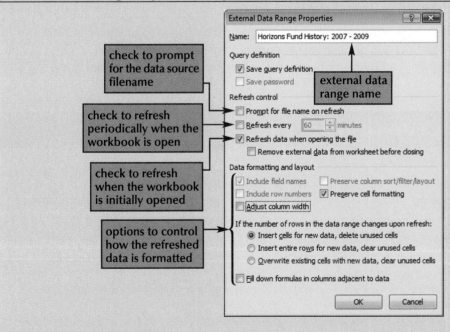

▶ 5. Click the **OK** button.

When you selected the Refresh data when opening the file check box, the Remove external data from worksheet before closing check box became available. This option allows Excel to remove the data you have retrieved from the workbook before closing the workbook. This makes the size of the workbook relatively small when the workbook is not in use. When you reopen the workbook, Excel automatically retrieves the data and restores it to its proper place.

Carol discovered an error in the History text file. The first value in the High column is incorrectly entered as 26.39. The correct value is 26.59. She asks you to fix the error and verify that the workbook will be automatically updated to reflect the edit.

To edit the text file and refresh external data:

▶ **1.** Save and close the Horizons Fund workbook.

▶ **2.** In Notepad or another text editor, open the **History** text file located in the **Tutorial.11\Tutorial** folder included with your Data Files.

▶ **3.** Change the High value in the first row from 26.39 to **26.59**. See Figure 11-13.

History text file in Notepad  Figure 11-13

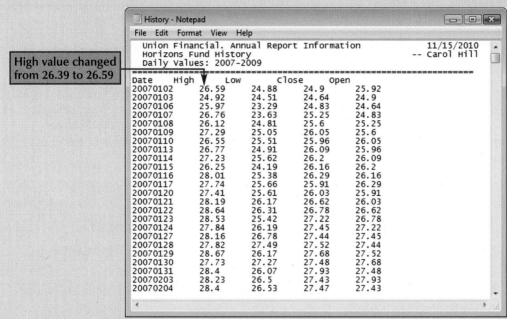

▶ **4.** Save and close the file, and then close the text editor.

▶ **5.** In Excel, open the **Horizons Fund** workbook located in the **Tutorial.11\Tutorial** folder included with your Data Files.

A security warning appears in the Message Bar above the workbook window, indicating that the data connections have been disabled. The value in cell B5 has not yet been updated and still displays the value 26.39. Disabling the connection is a security feature, similar to the macro security features you studied in Tutorial 8, designed to prevent users from inadvertently opening workbooks infected with connections to invalid data sources.

▶ **6.** Click the **Options** button in the Security Warning box, and then click the **Enable this content** option button.

▶ **7.** Click the **OK** button. Excel refreshes the connection to the History text file. The value in cell B5 changes from 26.39 to 26.59.

After opening the workbook, you can refresh external data manually by clicking the Refresh All button in the Connections group on the Data tab. The Refresh All button provides two options: Refresh All refreshes all of the external data ranges in the workbook, or Refresh refreshes only the current data range.

Defining a Trusted Location

Carol is concerned about Excel automatically disabling external data and forcing the user to enable it before the data can be refreshed. She wants this process to be seamless and asks you to override Excel so that it always enables her data sources. You do this by defining the location of Carol's data sources as a **trusted location** so that Excel will always refresh the connection to this data source without prompting.

Reference Window | **Defining a Trusted Location**

- Click the Office Button, and then click the Excel Options button.
- Click Trust Center in the Excel Options list, and then click the Trust Center Settings button.
- Click Trusted Locations in the Trust Center list, and then click the Add new location button.
- Click the Browse button to locate the trusted location, specify whether to include subfolders.
- Click the OK button in each dialog box.

As with the macros you created in Tutorial 8, defining a trusted location is done through the Trust Center. You'll define all of the subfolders in the Tutorial.11 folder as trusted locations.

To set up a trusted location:

▶ 1. Click the **Office Button** 🔘 , and then click the **Excel Options** button.

▶ 2. Click **Trust Center** in the Excel Options list, and then click the **Trust Center Settings** button. The Trust Center dialog box opens.

▶ 3. Click **Trusted Locations** in the Trust Center list to display the list of locations that are trusted by Microsoft Office.

▶ 4. If your data files are located on a network folder, click the **Allow Trusted Locations on my network** check box.

▶ 5. Click the **Add new location** button. The Microsoft Office Trusted Location dialog box opens.

▶ 6. Click the **Browse** button, and then navigate to the **Tutorial.11** folder included with your Data Files.

▶ 7. Double-click the **Tutorial.11** folder icon to open it, and then click the **OK** button to return to the Microsoft Office Trusted Location dialog box.

▶ 8. Click the **Subfolders of this location are also trusted** check box to insert a check mark. This option allows all of the subfolders in the Tutorial.11 folder to be trusted.

▶ 9. Type **Data sources for Tutorial 11** in the Description box. See Figure 11-14.

Microsoft Office Trusted Location dialog box ◄ Figure 11-14

path to trusted location (yours might differ)

check to trust all subfolders in the folder specified in the Path box

text to describe the trusted folder

10. Click the **OK** button in each of the three dialog boxes to return to the Excel workbook.

You'll test that Excel trusts your data source and will refresh the data from the History text file without prompting.

11. Close the Horizons Fund workbook, saving your changes, and then reopen the workbook. Verify that you are not prompted to enable the data connections in the workbook when you reopen it.

Moving a Workbook with Data Connections to a New Location | InSight

When other users copy your Excel projects to their own computers, path names to external data sources might change and become unusable. To fix this problem, those users have to modify the properties of the connections you've established in the workbook. When you move or copy a workbook that is connected to external data, change the path to the external data or let other users know how to change the path. To update the connection, you modify the path on the Definition tab in the Connection Properties dialog box. To open this dialog box, click the Connections button in the Connections group on the Data tab, select the connection, and then click the Properties button. With the definition established for the connection, other users can access and refresh the data from the external data source.

You've completed your work setting up the connection to the History text file. In the process, you've worked with connections, external data ranges, and trusted locations. In the next session, you'll learn about databases and how to connect an Excel workbook to a database.

Session 11.1 Quick Check | Review

1. What is the difference between a fixed-width and a delimited text file?
2. Name three delimiters that can be used to separate data in a delimited text file.
3. How do you insert column breaks when importing a text file using the Text Import Wizard?

4. What is the relationship between a connection and an external data range?
5. Name two ways in which Excel automatically refreshes a connection.
6. What is a trusted location?

Session 11.2

Introducing Databases and Queries

As in many financial firms, much of the information Union Financial analysts work with is stored in databases. A **database** is a file that stores a collection of related data. You use a database program to add, retrieve, and create reports describing that data. Many database programs are available, including Microsoft Office Access, dBASE, Paradox, Oracle, and FoxPro. Excel can retrieve data from most database programs. At Union Financial, information on the stocks in the Horizons Fund is stored in the Horizons database, which was created using Access. Before establishing a connection to the information in this database, you need to understand how databases are organized.

Understanding Tables, Fields, and Records

Databases store information in the form of tables. A **table** is a collection of data arranged in rows and columns. Figure 11-15 shows the Company table, which Carol created in the Horizons database. Each column of the table, called a field, stores information about a specific characteristic of a person, place, or thing. In this example, the middle field, called the Company field, stores the names of the companies whose stock is part of the Horizons portfolio. Each row of the table, called a record, displays a collection of characteristics of a particular person, place, or thing. The first record in the Company table displays stock information for the Aluminum Company of America, which has the ticker symbol AA and belongs to the group of industrial stocks. To simplify the workbook, Carol included only a selection of 15 stocks in her sample database.

Figure 11-15	Database table

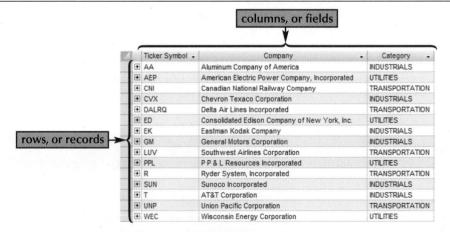

Ticker Symbol	Company	Category
AA	Aluminum Company of America	INDUSTRIALS
AEP	American Electric Power Company, Incorporated	UTILITIES
CNI	Canadian National Railway Company	TRANSPORTATION
CVX	Chevron Texaco Corporation	INDUSTRIALS
DALRQ	Delta Air Lines Incorporated	TRANSPORTATION
ED	Consolidated Edison Company of New York, Inc.	UTILITIES
EK	Eastman Kodak Company	INDUSTRIALS
GM	General Motors Corporation	INDUSTRIALS
LUV	Southwest Airlines Company	TRANSPORTATION
PPL	P P & L Resources Incorporated	UTILITIES
R	Ryder System, Incorporated	TRANSPORTATION
SUN	Sunoco Incorporated	INDUSTRIALS
T	AT&T Corporation	INDUSTRIALS
UNP	Union Pacific Corporation	TRANSPORTATION
WEC	Wisconsin Energy Corporation	UTILITIES

The Horizons database has four tables: Company, Long Term Performance, Recent Performance, and Stock Info. Figure 11-16 describes the contents of each table.

Horizons Fund database tables ◄ **Figure 11-16**

Table Name	Description
Company	Includes data about each company in the fund and the percentage of the fund that is allocated to purchasing stocks for that company
Long Term Performance	Summarizes the performance over the last 52 weeks for each stock, recording the high and low values over that period of time, and its volatility
Recent Performance	Daily high, low, closing, and volume values for each stock in the portfolio over the last five days
Stock Info	Description of each stock, including the yield, dividend amount and date, earnings per share, and number of outstanding shares

With several tables in a database, you need some way of relating information in one table to information in another. You relate tables by using **common fields**, which are fields that appear in more than one table. As shown in Figure 11-17, both the Company table and the Stock Info table contain the Ticker Symbol field, so Ticker Symbol is a common field in this database.

Combining tables based on a common field ◄ **Figure 11-17**

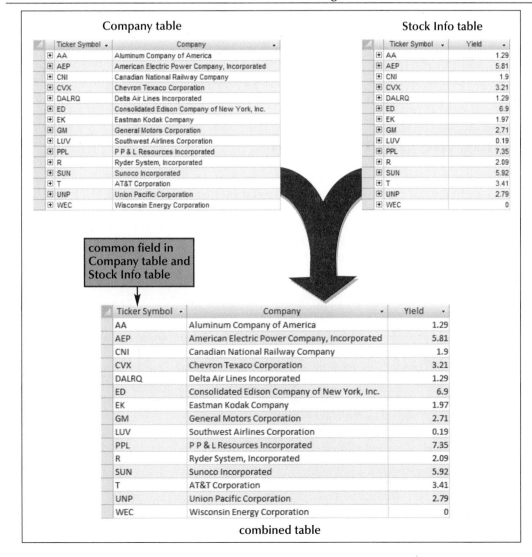

combined table

In retrieving information from two tables, such as the Company table and the Stock Info table, the value of the ticker symbol in one table is matched with the value of the ticker symbol in the other table, displaying information about both the company and the stock itself. Without common fields, you cannot match the company information from one table with the yield information from the other.

Queries

A large database can contain dozens or hundreds of tables, and each table can have several fields and thousands of records, so you need a way to choose only the information that you most want to see. When you want to look at only specific information from a database, you create a query. A **query** is a question you ask about the data in the database. In response to the query, the database displays the records and fields that meet the requirements of that question. A query might ask, "What are the names of all the stocks in the portfolio, and what are their corresponding ticker symbols?" To answer this question, you submit the query to the database in a form that the database can read. The database then extracts the relevant information, displaying the stock names alongside their ticker symbols.

A query might extract only specific records. In this case, the query contains **criteria**, which are conditions that limit the number of records in the results. Excel then extracts only those records that match the specified conditions. For example, you might want to know the names and ticker symbols of only the top five performing stocks from the past three months. In submitting the query to the database, you include criteria to limit the results to only the top five performing stocks from that time period in the portfolio. In a query, you can also specify how you want the data to appear. If you want the names and ticker symbols of the top five performing stocks arranged alphabetically by ticker symbol, you include that in the query definition.

Using the Query Wizard

Carol wants the workbook to list the stocks in the Horizons Fund and describe their performance in the last year. According to the worksheet plan (refer to Figure 11-2), you can extract this information from the Horizons database. Excel supports two ways of importing database data. One way is to create a connection to the database and retrieve all of the information from a single table. However, if you want to retrieve data from multiple tables, you use the Query Wizard.

| Reference Window | **Running Microsoft Query to Connect to an Access Database** |

- In the Get External Data group on the Data tab, click the From Other Sources button, and then click From Microsoft Query.
- In the Choose Data Source dialog box, specify MS Access Database as the data source, select a database file, and then click the OK button.
- In the first step of the wizard, select the columns from the different tables to include in your query, and then click the Next button.
- In the second step of the wizard, filter the data by selecting the columns to filter, specifying the nature of the filter in the Only include rows where list boxes, and then click the Next button.
- In the third step of the wizard, specify the sort order for the data values in the query, and then click the Next button.
- In the last step of the wizard, specify whether to return the query data to Excel, view or edit the data in Microsoft Query, or save the written query to a permanent file for use later.

The **Query Wizard** is an application included with Microsoft Office to write database queries. Like the Text Import Wizard you used in the previous session, the Query Wizard contains a collection of dialog boxes that step you through the entire query-writing process. The first step in the Query Wizard is to create a data source. A **data source** is any file that contains the data you want to retrieve. Data sources can be databases, text files, or other Excel workbooks. In this tutorial, you'll use the Query Wizard only with databases because Excel supports newer and better tools to deal with those other types of data sources.

To start the Query Wizard:

▶ **1.** If you took a break at the end of the previous session, make sure the Horizons Fund workbook located in the Tutorial.11\Tutorial folder is open.

▶ **2.** Switch to the **Sheet2** worksheet.

▶ **3.** Click the **Data** tab on the Ribbon, if necessary.

▶ **4.** In the Get External Data group, click the **From Other Sources** button, and then click **From Microsoft Query**. The Choose Data Source dialog box opens. See Figure 11-18.

Choose Data Source dialog box   **Figure 11-18**

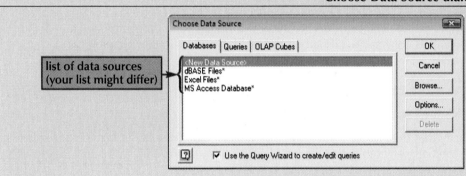

Connecting to a Data Source

The Choose Data Source dialog box lists several data sources from which you can retrieve data. You can define your own data source by clicking <New Data Source> in the list of databases. In this case, because you're trying to connect to a Microsoft Access database, you'll use the MS Access Database data source.

To connect to an Access data source:

▶ **1.** Click **MS Access Database*** in the list of data sources.

▶ **2.** Verify that the **Use the Query Wizard to create/edit queries** check box is checked, and then click the **OK** button. The Select Database dialog box opens.

▶ **3.** Navigate to the **Tutorial.11\Tutorial** folder included with your Data Files, and then click the **Horizons** database.

Trouble? Microsoft Query does not support the use of network folders. If your data source is located on a network folder, you must map the folder to a drive letter. You can map the network folder to a drive letter by clicking the Network button on the Select Database dialog box to open the Map Network Drive dialog box.

▶ **4.** Click the **OK** button. Excel connects to the data source, the Horizons database, and then opens the Query Wizard – Choose Columns dialog box. See Figure 11-19.

| Figure 11-19 | ▶ Query Wizard – Choose Columns dialog box |

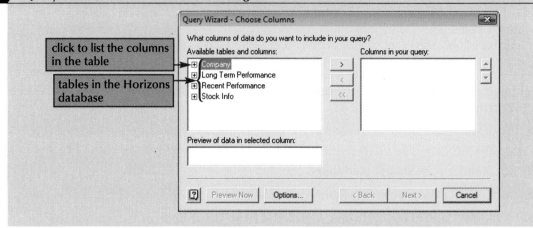

Choosing Tables and Columns

The next step in retrieving data from the Horizons database is to choose the table and fields (columns) to include in the query. The Query Wizard lets you preview the structure of the database and its contents. You'll start by examining the fields in the Company table.

To view a list of fields in the Company table:

▶ **1.** Click the **Expand** button ⊞ for the Company table.

▶ **2.** Verify that the Available tables and columns list box displays the columns (or fields) in the Company table. See Figure 11-20.

| Figure 11-20 | ▶ Columns in the Company table |

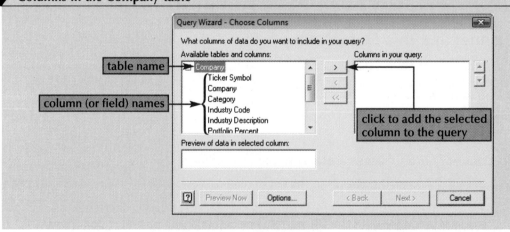

Carol wants to include the ticker symbol, the company, and the portfolio percent from the Company table in the query. The portfolio percent is the percentage of the portfolio that is invested in each particular stock. Carol also wants to include the Year High and Year Low fields from the Long Term Performance table so that she can tell what the high and low points in the previous year have been for each stock in the portfolio. Because the two tables share Ticker Symbol as a common field, you'll select data from both tables with the Query Wizard.

To select the columns to import into Excel:

▶ 1. Click **Ticker Symbol** in the Available tables and columns list box, and then click the **Select Field** button ⬚ ▷ . The Ticker Symbol column moves to the Columns in your query list box, indicating that it will be included in the query.

   You'll continue to select other columns for your query by double-clicking the column names.

▶ 2. In the Available tables and columns list box, double-click the **Company** column name (not the Company table name) and then double-click **Portfolio Percent**. These columns now appear in the Columns in your query list box.

▶ 3. Click the **Expand** button ⊞ for the Long Term Performance table name to display the list of columns within that table.

▶ 4. Double-click the **Year High** and **Year Low** column names. The five fields that Carol wants to include in the query are selected. See Figure 11-21.

Columns selected for the query | Figure 11-21

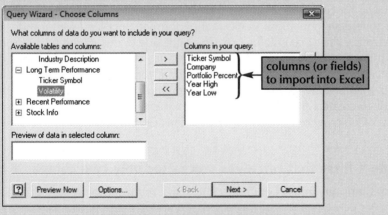

You can preview the contents of each field in the table by selecting the field (in either the left or right pane of the Query Wizard – Choose Columns dialog box), and then clicking the Preview Now button. You will preview the contents of the Company field to see the types of entries it contains.

To preview the contents of the Company field:

▶ 1. Click **Company** in the Columns in your query list box.

▶ 2. Click the **Preview Now** button. Some of the values in this column appear in the Preview of data in selected column box. See Figure 11-22. You can scroll to see more of the values.

| Figure 11-22 | Completed Query Wizard – Choose Columns dialog box |

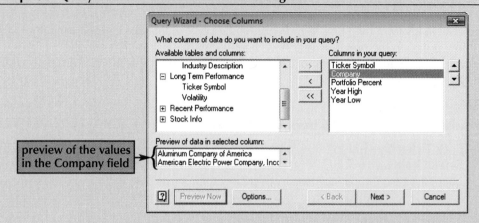

preview of the values in the Company field

3. Click the **Next** button to go to the next step in the Query Wizard.

Filtering and Sorting Data

Now that you've selected the five columns for the Portfolio worksheet, you must determine whether to retrieve all of the records in the tables or only records that satisfy particular criteria. Carol wants you to retrieve information on all the stocks. However, she might occasionally want information on only some of the stocks. To achieve this goal, you can filter the data. When you filter data, you specify which records you want to retrieve using specific criteria. In this query, you can filter the data to remove particular stocks or to retrieve only those stocks that perform at a certain level. You do so using the Query Wizard - Filter Data dialog box. The right side of this dialog box includes two columns of list boxes. The column on the left specifies the type of comparison you want to make in the filter, such as "equals," "greater than," or "less than." In the column on the right, you enter a value for the comparison. You'll use the Query Wizard – Filter Data dialog box to create a filter that retrieves stock information only for stocks from the Eastman Kodak Company or from Southwest Airlines Corporation.

To create a filter that retrieves stocks for only two companies:

1. Click **Company** in the Column to filter box. You want to retrieve the Eastman Kodak stock.

2. Click the **arrow** button in the first row of the left column, and then click **equals**.

3. Click the **arrow** button in the first row of the right column, and then click **Eastman Kodak Company**.

   Next, you'll add a second set of conditions so that the query includes either the Eastman Kodak Company or Southwest Airlines Corporation.

4. Click the **Or** option button. You have completed the first row and indicated that you want to include another filter. The second row becomes available.

5. Click the **arrow** button in the second row of the left column, and then click **equals**.

▶ **6.** Click the **arrow** button in the right column of the second row, and then click **Southwest Airlines Corporation**. See Figure 11-23.

query will filter records to display only Eastman Kodak Company or Southwest Airlines Corporation

The filter you created retrieves only those records for Eastman Kodak or Southwest Airlines. The Query Wizard will not retrieve stock information for other companies in the Horizons Fund. Although only three rows of criteria are shown in the Query Wizard – Filter Data dialog box, the dialog box expands to provide additional rows as you specify requirements for your filter. Because Carol wants information on all the companies in the portfolio, you'll remove the data filters you just created.

To remove the filter from the query:

▶ **1.** Click the **equals arrow** button in the second row, and then click the blank space at the top of the list (you might have to scroll up).

▶ **2.** Repeat Step 1 for the box in the first row. The filters are removed from the query.

▶ **3.** Click the **Next** button to continue to the next step of the Query Wizard.

So far, you've identified the fields you want to retrieve, and you've had a chance to filter records to narrow the selection. In the last part of writing a query, you sort the data in either ascending or descending order. Carol wants to display the portfolio information starting with the stocks in which the Horizons Fund has the largest capital investment and proceeding down to the stocks with the smallest capital investment. The Portfolio Percent field tells you how much of the fund is invested in each stock, so you'll sort the data by the values in that field in descending order (from highest percentage to lowest).

To sort the data in the query:

▶ **1.** Click the **Sort by arrow** button, and then click **Portfolio Percent**.

▶ **2.** Click the **Descending** option button. See Figure 11-24.

Figure 11-24 ▶ **Query Wizard – Sort Order dialog box**

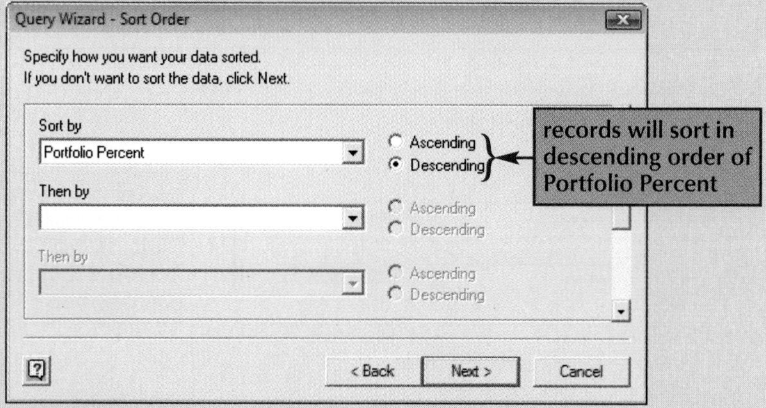

records will sort in descending order of Portfolio Percent

▶ **3.** Click the **Next** button to go to the final Query Wizard dialog box. See Figure 11-25.

Figure 11-25 ▶ **Query Wizard – Finish dialog box**

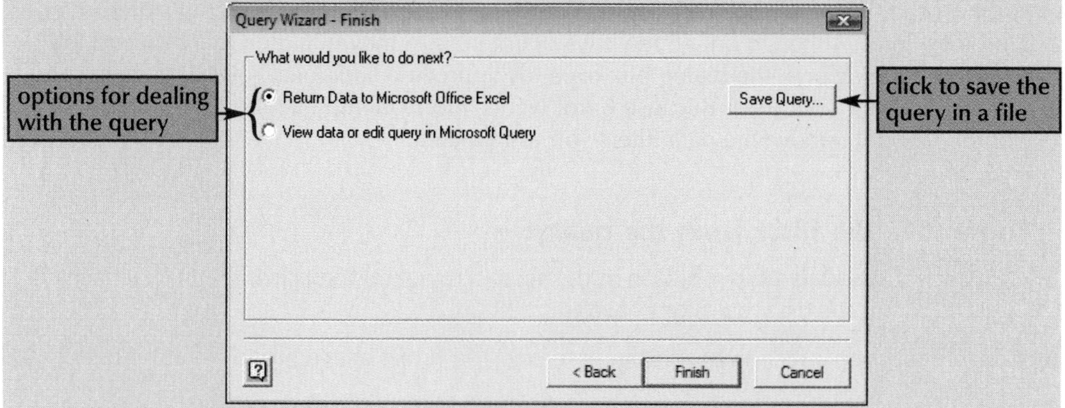

options for dealing with the query

click to save the query in a file

Saving a Query

You have finished defining the query. Before you run the query and produce the information Carol requested, you will save your query. When you save a query, you are placing the query choices you've made into a file. You can open the file later and run the query, saving you the trouble of redefining it. You can also share the query with others who might want to extract the same information from the data source. You can store query files in any folder you choose. The default folder for queries is the Queries folder located on your computer's hard disk. Saving the query file to this folder has some advantages. If you are running Excel on a network, you can make the query file accessible to other network users. Also, query files in this folder appear on the Queries tab of the Choose Data Source dialog box (refer to Figure 11-18), giving you quick access to saved queries. In this case, however, you'll save the query with your other Data Files because you might not have access to your Queries folder. After saving a query as a file, you return to the final dialog box of the Query Wizard, where you can import the data from the database into your workbook.

You will save your query with the name "Horizons Portfolio" because it displays a list of stocks in the Horizons Fund. Query files have the .dqy file extension.

To save the query:

▶ **1.** Click the **Save Query** button in the Query Wizard – Finish dialog box. The Save As dialog box opens and displays the contents of the Queries folder.

▶ **2.** Navigate to the **Tutorial.11\Tutorial** folder included with your Data Files, and then save the query as **Horizons Portfolio** in the same folder. The query file is saved and you return to the final step of the Query Wizard.

Now that you saved your query, you have two options. You can return (import) the data into the Excel workbook or you can display the results of the query in Microsoft Query, where you can further edit the data and the query definition. Microsoft Query is an Office program that includes several tools that allow you to create even more complex queries. Because you don't need to refine the query, you don't need to open it in Microsoft Query. Instead, you'll import the data into the Horizons Fund workbook.

To import the query data into Excel:

▶ **1.** Make sure the **Return Data to Microsoft Office Excel** option button is selected, and then click the **Finish** button. The Import Data dialog box opens, in which you can select where you want to place the imported data.

▶ **2.** Click cell **A3** in the Sheet2 worksheet.

▶ **3.** Verify that the **Table** option button is selected so that the data is stored as an Excel table, and then click the **OK** button. The data from the query is imported into the worksheet. Next, you can format the Sheet2 worksheet.

▶ **4.** In cell A1, enter **Horizons Fund Portfolio**, and then format it using the **Title** cell style.

▶ **5.** Format the data in the range C4:C18 using the **Percentage** format, and then format the data in the range D4:E18 using the **Number** format.

▶ **6.** Click cell **A2** to deselect the range, rename the worksheet as **Portfolio**, and then move it to the beginning of the workbook. See Figure 11-26.

Formatted Portfolio worksheet ◢ **Figure 11-26**

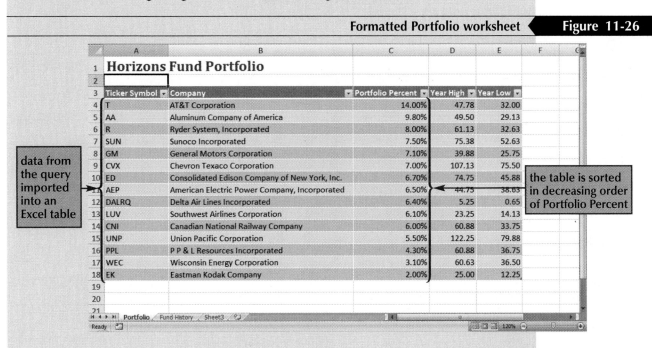

The contents of the portfolio show that 14% of the fund is invested in the AT&T Corporation and that the value of that stock has ranged from a high of 47.78 points to a low of 32 points. The table is sorted in descending order by the percentage of each stock in the portfolio, making the most heavily invested stocks the first in the list. This worksheet will help Carol understand the financial makeup of the Horizons fund.

As with the connection to the History text file, Carol wants to refresh the connection to the Horizons database whenever the workbook is opened.

To edit the properties of the connection to the Horizons database:

▶ **1.** Click any cell in the Excel table, click the **Data** tab on the Ribbon, and then, in the Connections group, click the **Connections** button. The Workbook Connections dialog box lists the two connections—History and Horizons Portfolio—active in the workbook.

▶ **2.** Click **Horizons Portfolio** in the list, and then click the **Properties** button. The Connection Properties dialog box opens.

▶ **3.** Type **Portfolio data imported from the Horizons database using Microsoft Query** in the Description box.

▶ **4.** Click the **Refresh data when opening the file** check box. See Figure 11-27.

| Figure 11-27 | Connection Properties dialog box |

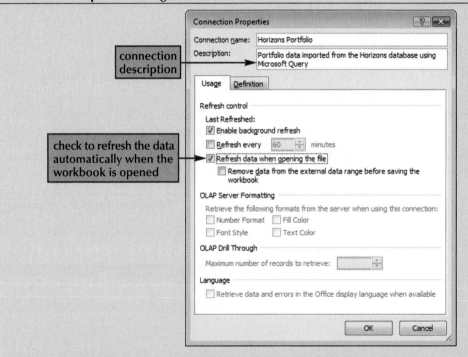

▶ **5.** Click the **OK** button to close the Connection Properties dialog box, and then click the **Close** button to close the Workbook Connections dialog box.

Tip

To detach an Excel table from its data source, select a cell in the table, click the Table Tools Design tab, and then, in the External Table Data group, click the Unlink button.

The external data range for the Horizons Portfolio connection covers the Excel table in the range A3:E18 of the Portfolio worksheet. You can edit the properties of this table by clicking any cell in the table and then clicking the Properties button in the Connections group on the Data tab. Carol is pleased with the layout format and does not want you to make any changes. However, she wants you to add a new field to the table that indicates the category of each stock (industrial, transportation, or utility). To make this change, you'll have to edit the properties of the query you just created.

Editing a Query

By editing the query, you can add new columns to your worksheet, change the sort order options, or specify a filter. Carol wants you to add the Category field to the query and to change the sort order so that the Excel table is sorted by stock category first and then within each stock category by descending order of the Portfolio Percent field.

Editing a Database Query	Reference Window

- In the Connections group on the Data tab, click the Connections button.
- Select the connection used by the database query, and then click the Properties button.
- Click the Definition tab in the Connection Properties dialog box, and then click the Edit Query button.
- Change the query definition using the dialog boxes provided by the Query Wizard.

You edit a query by editing the definition of the connection. When you edit the connection, Excel recognizes that the Query Wizard was used to define the parameters of the connection and restarts the Query Wizard. You can then walk through the steps of the wizard, modifying the query definition as you go.

To edit the query:

▶ 1. In the Connections group on the Data tab, click the **Connections** button. The Workbook Connections dialog box opens.

▶ 2. Click the **Horizons Portfolio** connection, and then click the **Properties** button. The Connection Properties dialog box opens.

▶ 3. Click the **Definition** tab. From this tab, you can view the current definition of the Horizons Portfolio query. You can also edit the query, changing its definition.

▶ 4. Click the **Edit Query** button. The Query Wizard – Choose Columns dialog box opens.

▶ 5. Click the **Expand** button ⊞ for the Company table, and then double-click the **Category** field. Category is added to the list of columns in the query. See Figure 11-28.

Tip

If you know the SQL query language, you can edit the definition directly from within the Connection Properties dialog box, bypassing the Query Wizard.

Category field added to the query	Figure 11-28

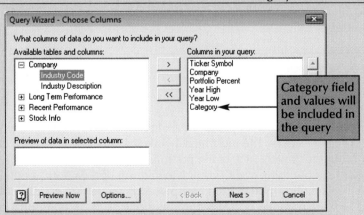

▶ 6. Click the **Next** button twice to go to the Query Wizard – Sort Order dialog box.

▶ 7. Click the **Sort by arrow** button, click **Category**, and then click the **Ascending** option button.

▶ **8.** Click the **Then by arrow** button, click **Portfolio Percent**, and then click the **Descending** option button. See Figure 11-29.

Figure 11-29 **Sort order of the query modified**

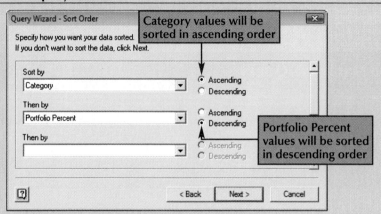

▶ **9.** Click the **Next** button, and then click the **Finish** button to close the Query Wizard.

▶ **10.** Click the **OK** button, and then click the **Close** button to return to the Portfolio worksheet. See Figure 11-30.

Figure 11-30 **Revised portfolio table**

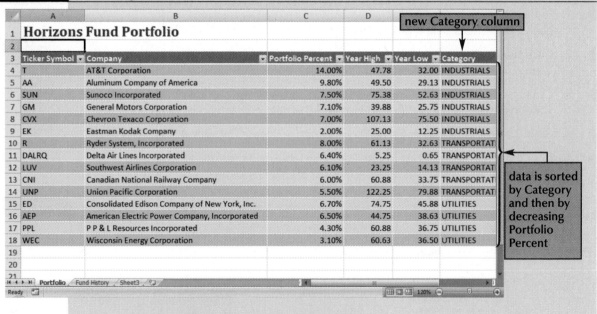

The fund is composed of 15 stocks—with six industrial stocks, five transportation stocks, and four utility stocks. The most heavily invested stocks within each category are AT&T, an industrial stock with 14% of the portfolio; Ryder System, Inc., a transportation stock with 8% of the portfolio; and Consolidated Edison of New York, a utilities stock with 6.7% of the portfolio. Though it's not displayed in the table, you can quickly calculate that 47.2% of the portfolio is invested in industrials, 32% in transportation, and 20.6% in utilities.

Relational Databases and SQL | InSight

Databases such as those created in Access are examples of relational databases in which data is organized as a collection of tables with rows and columns. Relationships are also defined between the tables so that the data can be stored in smaller, more manageable chunks. Relational databases reduce data redundancy and increase data integrity.

One way to interact with a relational database is with a query language. The most popular query language is Structured Query Language (SQL). SQL consists of a series of statements that you use to define exactly how to extract data from the relational database.

Microsoft Query supports SQL. In fact, the Query Wizard puts a friendly interface on the process of writing the SQL statement for you. You can view the SQL statement that the Query Wizard generates by viewing the definition of the connection for the query.

Importing Data into PivotTables and PivotCharts

The Recent Performance table in the Horizons database contains a record of the last five days of stock market activity for each of the 15 stocks in the Horizons Fund. Figure 11-31 shows the contents of the Recent Performance table.

Recent Performance table | **Figure 11-31**

Ticker Symbol	Date	Volume	High	Low	Closing
AA	09/06/2010	364300	38.75	38	38.25
AA	09/07/2010	412300	38.625	37.125	37.25
AA	09/08/2010	650100	37.25	36	36.75
AA	09/09/2010	891200	39.25	36.75	37.625
AA	09/10/2010	459500	38	36.625	36.625
AEP	09/06/2010	134100	41.625	41.125	41.25
AEP	09/07/2010	1481100	41.625	40.75	41.125
AEP	09/08/2010	1761000	40.875	40.5	40.625
AEP	09/09/2010	459300	41.375	40.75	41.375
AEP	09/10/2010	494100	41.75	41.25	41.75
CNI	09/06/2010	339900	47.75	47	47.75
CNI	09/07/2010	297900	47.25	46.75	47
CNI	09/08/2010	120800	46.875	46	46.25
CNI	09/09/2010	58100	46.625	46	46.625
CNI	09/10/2010	161500	46.875	46.375	46.625
CVX	09/06/2010	590600	75.5	73	75.5
CVX	09/07/2010	796700	76.5	74.625	75.375
CVX	09/08/2010	1140000	76	72.75	73.875
CVX	09/09/2010	964000	73.875	71	72
CVX	09/10/2010	1310000	73	71.625	72.5
DALRQ	09/06/2010	331300	0.9	0.67	0.75
DALRQ	09/07/2010	92600	1.01	0.72	0.91

Record: 1 of 75 ▸ ▸ No Filter Search

Carol wants to connect the Horizons Fund workbook to this data, creating a chart and table that show the recent activity of each stock. You could create 15 charts and tables, one for each stock in the fund; however, this approach would result in a cumbersome workbook that would be difficult to manage. Besides, Carol wants to create similar workbooks for other databases that contain records of hundreds of stocks and funds.

Another option is to create a PivotTable and PivotChart that display market values from the past five days. Recall that PivotTables are interactive tables in which you can group and summarize data values. You can use this interactivity to select and display values from only one stock at a time, adding only a single table and chart to the workbook rather than 15. A second advantage of a PivotTable and PivotChart is that the data used in the table and chart can be stored in an external data source. As the user interacts with the table and chart, the needed data is retrieved from the data source, freeing your workbook from having to store data that is not immediately required.

All of the five-day stock data you need for the report is stored in the Recent Performance table, so your first step is to establish a connection to the table. Because you'll be working with only this one table and not several tables from the Horizons database, you don't have to use the Query Wizard and can import the table's contents directly. As you establish the connection, you can use the Connection Properties dialog box to provide a name and description of the connection. Always document your connections to external data so that users can see what the data is used for and where it came from.

To import data into a PivotTable and PivotChart:

▶ **1.** Rename the **Sheet3** worksheet as **Recent Performance**, and then move the worksheet between the Portfolio and Fund History worksheets.

▶ **2.** In cell A1, enter **Horizons Fund Recent History**, and then format the text using the **Title** cell style.

▶ **3.** In cell A2, enter **5-Day Stock Report**, format the text using the **Heading 1** cell style, and then remove the border from cell A2.

▶ **4.** Click cell **A6**, click the **Data** tab on the Ribbon, and then, in the Get External Data group, click the **From Access** button. The Select Data Source dialog box opens.

▶ **5.** Select the **Horizons** database file located in the **Tutorial.11\Tutorial** folder included with your Data Files, and then click the **Open** button. The Select Table dialog box opens.

▶ **6.** Click **Recent Performance** in the list of tables, and then click the **OK** button. The Import Data dialog box opens. Before importing the recent performance data, you'll change the properties of this connection.

▶ **7.** Click the **Properties** button to open the Connection Properties dialog box, and then type **Horizons Fund Recent History** in the Connection name box.

▶ **8.** Type **Retrieves data from the Recent Performance table in the Horizons database** in the Description box, and then click the **Refresh data when opening the file** check box so that Excel refreshes the data in this connection whenever the workbook is opened. See Figure 11-32.

Connection properties of the recent performance data | Figure 11-32

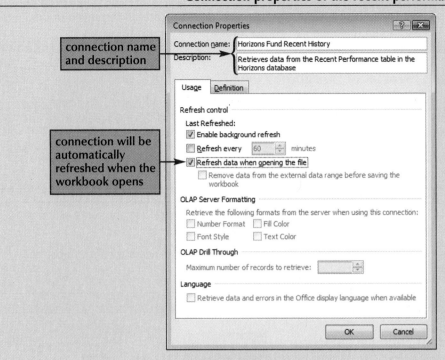

connection name and description

connection will be automatically refreshed when the workbook opens

9. Click the **OK** button to return to the Import Data dialog box.

10. Click the **PivotChart and PivotTable Report** option button, and then click the **OK** button. An empty PivotTable and PivotChart are added to the Recent Performance worksheet. See Figure 11-33.

PivotTable and PivotChart added to the worksheet | Figure 11-33

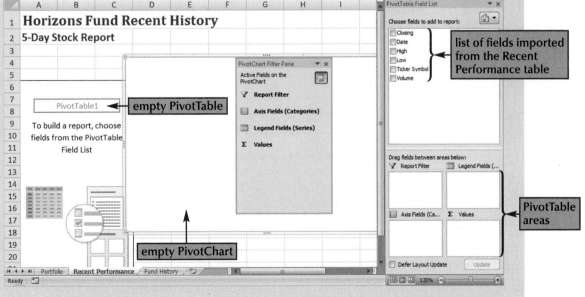

list of fields imported from the Recent Performance table

empty PivotTable

empty PivotChart

PivotTable areas

When Excel imports external data into a PivotTable or PivotChart, the initial table and chart are empty because you have not defined yet where to place the different fields from the data source. The fields of the Recent Performance table are all displayed in the Pivot-Table Field List. You'll create the PivotTable for Carol.

To set the PivotTable layout:

▶ 1. Drag the **Ticker Symbol** field from the Field List to the Report Filter area. The Ticker Symbol field is the report filter, allowing you to display stocks from one company—or ticker symbol—at a time.

▶ 2. Drag the **Date** field to the Axis Fields area. The Date field from the five-day data will appear as an axis or category field in the PivotTable.

▶ 3. Drag the **High**, **Low**, and **Closing** fields into the Values area in that order. The High, Low, and Closing fields will be the values displayed in the table and chart. You won't use the Volume field in this table or chart.

▶ 4. Close the PivotChart Filter Pane so that you can better view the PivotTable and PivotChart. See Figure 11-34.

Figure 11-34 Importing the PivotTable and PivotChart data

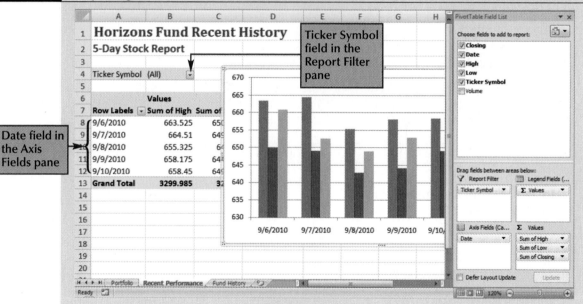

The Data area labels read "Sum of" before the name of each field. This label is misleading because only one value appears for these items for each stock on each day, so the PivotTable shows a "sum" of only one record. The table will display individual volume and stock values, so you can change the labels to avoid confusing others who might interpret them as the sum of many values. You can also specify the format for these values.

To change the labels and format the data values in the PivotTable:

▶ 1. Click the **Sum of High** button in the Values area, and then click **Value Field Settings**. The Value Field Settings dialog box opens.

▶ 2. Type **High Value** in the Custom Name box.

3. Click the **Number Format** button to open the Number tab in the Format Cells dialog box, and then click **Number** in the Category list. You'll use this default number format.

4. Click the **OK** button in each dialog box.

5. Repeat Steps 1 through 4 for the Sum of Low and Sum of Closing entries in the Values pane, renaming Sum of Low as **Low Value** and Sum of Closing as **Closing Value**.

6. Close the PivotTable Field List pane to display more of the worksheet containing the PivotTable and PivotChart.

   Because you do not need to include grand totals, you can remove them from the PivotTable.

7. Click cell **A4** to select the PivotTable, and then click the **PivotTable Tools Design** tab on the Ribbon.

8. In the Layout group, click the **Grand Totals** button, and then click **Off for Rows and Columns**. See Figure 11-35.

Formatted PivotTable data ◀ Figure 11-35

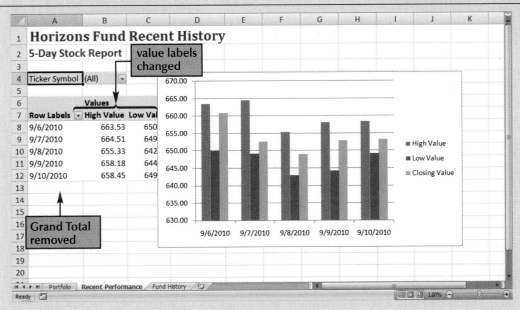

Finally, you need to format the PivotChart. Carol wants you to resize the chart smaller and move it closer to the PivotTable. She also wants you to change the chart type from a column chart to a line chart. Finally, she wants you to add an appropriate title to the chart.

To format the PivotChart:

1. Move and resize the PivotChart so that it covers the range **E4:K19**.

2. Insert the chart title **Recent Performance** above the chart, and change the font size of the title to **12** points.

3. Change the chart type from Column to **Line**.

4. Click cell **A3** to deselect the PivotTable and PivotChart. See Figure 11-36.

| Figure 11-36 | Formatted PivotChart |

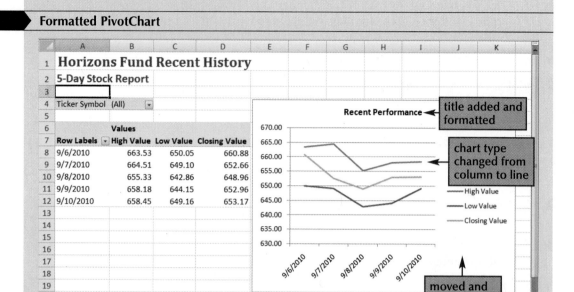

The line chart gives you a quick view of each stock's low, high, and closing values. By default, the PivotTable and PivotChart show the sum of these values over all of the stocks in the portfolio. Those values are not very useful. However, by clicking the Ticker Symbol arrow button, you can quickly view the daily values from the last five days for any individual stock in the portfolio.

To view the recent performance of the General Motors stock:

1. Click the **Ticker Symbol arrow** button in cell B4 of the PivotTable.

2. Click **GM** in the list of ticker symbols, and then click the **OK** button. See Figure 11-37.

| Figure 11-37 | Recent performance of the GM stock |

Tip

You can connect a new PivotTable to an external data source by clicking the PivotTable button in the Tables group on the Insert tab and then choosing a connection in the Create PivotTable dialog box.

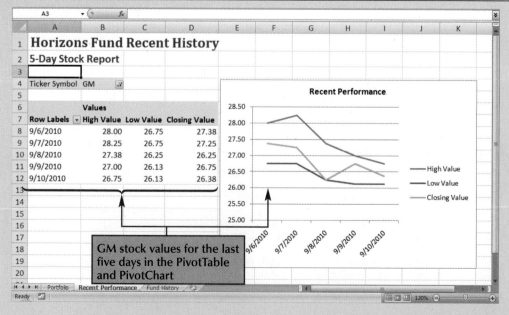

▶ **3.** Click the **Ticker Symbol arrow** button and select other stocks, verifying that you can view the five-day history for any stock from the Recent Performance table.

Working with Connection Files | InSight

Connection information is stored within the workbook, allowing users to interact with their connections as they design their Excel project. For more extensive projects, you can store connections in an external file such as an Office Data Connection (ODC) file or a Universal Data Connection (UDC) file. It's a good idea to use connection files when you want to share information about a connection with other users, use the same connection in multiple workbooks, or create a library of connection files for use with large database structures.

To manually save a connection to an ODC file, use the Export Connection File button on the Definition tab of the Connection Properties dialog box to specify the name and location of your Office Data Connection file. The default location for ODC files is the My Data Sources subfolder of the Documents folder (or My Document folder in Windows XP). ODC files are added to the My Data Sources whenever you create a connection to an Access database table. UDC files are not created within Excel. To create a UDC file, you can use Microsoft's InfoPath program for creating and designing XML-based data entry forms for businesses.

To access a connection file, click the Existing Connections button in the Get External Data group on the Data tab to select the connection file from your workbook, your network, or your computer.

In this session, you explored how to connect an Excel workbook to an Access database. You used the Query Wizard to retrieve data from several database tables and connected directly to the Access database when you wanted only one table. From the database, you created an Excel table, PivotTable, and PivotChart for Carol's report. Carol is pleased with your progress and wants to look for more sources of data that she can use in the Horizons Fund workbook.

Session 11.2 Quick Check | Review

1. Define the following terms: (a) database, (b) table, (c) field, (d) record, (e) common field.
2. What is a query?
3. How do you edit a query?
4. How do you create a PivotTable and PivotChart based on an external data source?
5. What is the advantage of using external data in a PivotTable rather than importing data into the workbook and creating a PivotTable from the imported data?
6. What is SQL?
7. List two places that connection information can be stored.

Session 11.3

Creating a Web Query

Union Financial has another data source that Carol accesses on a regular basis—the company Web site. The Web site includes pages that describe the various funds the company supports. The Horizons Fund Web page shown in Figure 11-38 provides descriptive information about the fund, such as the fund's manager and its inception date.

Figure 11-38	Horizons Fund Web page

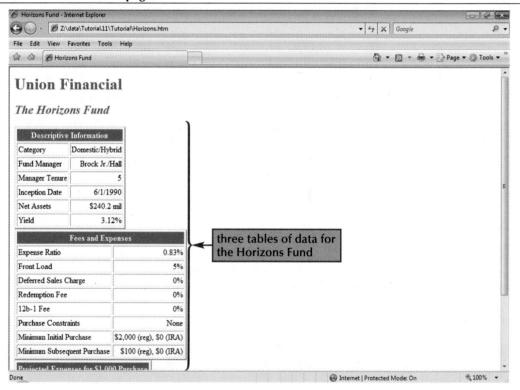

You could copy and paste the data from the Web page into your workbook, but Carol wants to create a connection between the Web page and her workbook so that her workbook always matches the material on the company's Web site. A **Web query** specifies how data should be retrieved from the Web page and indicates exactly which parts of the Web page should be included and which parts should be excluded.

To create a Web query, you need to know the URL of the resource you're accessing. The **Uniform Resource Locator (URL)** is the address of the resource (usually a Web page). A copy of the Horizons Fund's information Web page has been made available to you with the filename Horizons.htm. If you store the file on a Web server, the URL will probably have the form:

`http://server/path/filename`

In this URL, *server* is the name of the computer or Web server storing the page, *path* is the path to the folder on the server in which the page is stored, and *filename* is the name of the Web page file. For Carol's company, the URL for the Horizons HTML file is:

`http://www.ufcompany.com/docs/History.htm`

When a file is stored locally and not on a Web server, the general form of a URL is:

`file:///`*drive*`:/`*path*`/`*filename*

In this URL, *drive* is the drive letter of the disk containing the file, *path* is the full path name of the folder containing the file, and *filename* is the filename of the Web page. For example, if the Data Files are on drive Z and Horizons.htm is located in the Tutorial.11\ Tutorial folder, the URL is:

`file:///Z:/Tutorial.11/Tutorial/Horizons.htm`

If you don't include the "file:" prefix for the URL, your computer will attempt to locate the file on the World Wide Web and not in a folder stored locally on your computer. If you don't want to enter this long string of text, you can also enter the path to the folder and Web page file in the more standard form:

`Z:\Tutorial.11\Tutorial.Horizons.htm`

The Web query will replace this text with the URL form.

Working with Web Queries | Reference Window

To create a Web query:
- In the Get External Data group on the Data tab, click the From Web button.
- Enter the URL of the Web site or the folder path to a local file in the Address box of the New Web Query dialog box.
- Click the selection arrows for the parts of the Web page you want to retrieve.
- Click the Import button.

To set the Web query format options:
- Open the Connection Properties dialog box for the query.
- Click the Edit Query button on the Definition tab.
- Click the Options button and select the format options in the Web Query Options dialog box.

To save a Web query:
- Open the Connection Properties dialog box for the query.
- Click the Edit Query button on the Definition tab.
- Click the Save Query button in the Edit Web Query dialog box and specify the filename and location of the Web query file.

You'll create a connection to the Horizons HTML file from Carol's workbook.

To create a Web query to import the contents of the Horizons Web page:

1. If you took a break at the end of the previous session, make sure the Horizons Fund workbook located in the **Tutorial.11\Tutorial** folder is open.

2. Insert a new worksheet named **Horizons Fund** at the beginning of the workbook.

3. In cell A1, enter **The Horizons Fund**, and then format the text using the **Title** cell style.

4. In cell A2, enter **Summary**, format the text using the **Heading1** cell style, and then remove the border from cell A2.

5. Click cell **A4**, click the **Data** tab on the Ribbon, and then, in the Get External Group, click the **From Web** button. The New Web Query dialog box opens.

6. Enter the path to the Horizons.htm file in the Address box, and then press the **Enter** key. For example, if the file is located in the Documents\Data\Tutorial.11\Tutorial folder of drive E, enter E:\Documents\Data\Tutorial.11\Tutorial\Horizons.htm. The contents of the Web page appear in the dialog box. See Figure 11-39.

Figure 11-39 New Web Query dialog box

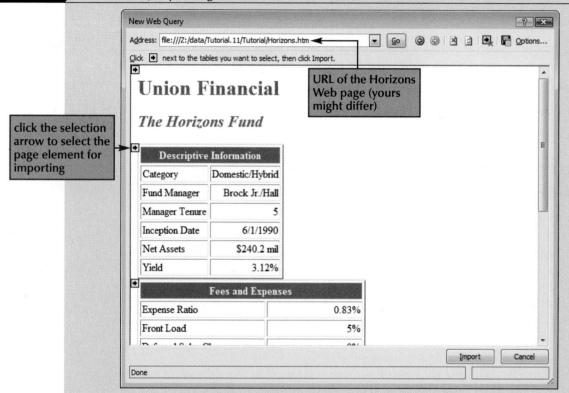

Trouble? If you're not sure of the path to the Horizons.htm file, open the file with your Web browser and copy the path from your Web browser's Address box into the Address box of the New Web Query dialog box. If you're not sure how to enter the URL of the Horizons Web page, ask your instructor or technical resource person.

7. Click the **selection arrow** ➡ next to the Descriptive Information table to select the table, and then scroll down and click the **selection arrows** ➡ for the Fees and Expenses table and the Projected Expenses for $1,000 Purchase table. The selection arrows change from arrows to check marks to indicate that these sections of the Web page have been selected for import.

8. Click the **Import** button. The Import Data dialog box opens.

9. Verify that the data will be placed starting in cell A4 of the existing worksheet, and then click the **OK** button. The Web content is imported into the Horizons Fund worksheet. See Figure 11-40.

Horizons Web page imported into the workbook ◄ **Figure 11-40**

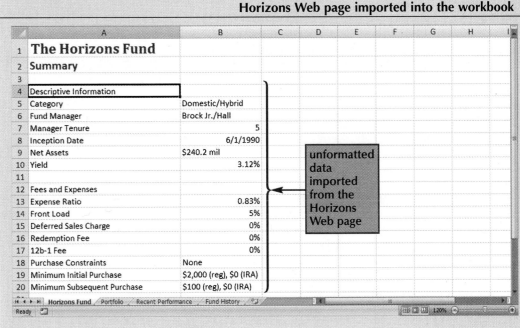

	A	B	C	D	E	F	G	H
1	**The Horizons Fund**							
2	**Summary**							
3								
4	Descriptive Information							
5	Category	Domestic/Hybrid						
6	Fund Manager	Brock Jr./Hall						
7	Manager Tenure	5						
8	Inception Date	6/1/1990						
9	Net Assets	$240.2 mil						
10	Yield	3.12%						
11								
12	Fees and Expenses							
13	Expense Ratio	0.83%						
14	Front Load	5%						
15	Deferred Sales Charge	0%						
16	Redemption Fee	0%						
17	12b-1 Fee	0%						
18	Purchase Constraints	None						
19	Minimum Initial Purchase	$2,000 (reg), $0 (IRA)						
20	Minimum Subsequent Purchase	$100 (reg), $0 (IRA)						

unformatted data imported from the Horizons Web page

Horizons Fund / Portfolio / Recent Performance / Fund History

Ready

The text from the Web query has been placed into the Horizons Fund Web page as unformatted text. If you format this text, the formatting is preserved when Excel refreshes the data later. Another option is to retrieve both the Web page data and the styles used on the Web page.

Formatting a Web Query

Carol wants the text on this page to resemble the Web page. You can retrieve the Web page format using None (the default, which imports the text but not the formatting), Rich text formatting only, or Full HTML formatting. **Rich Text Format** (**RTF**) is a file format that allows for text formatting styles including boldface, italic, and color, but not advanced features such as hyperlinks or complicated table structures. The Full HTML formatting option retrieves all simple as well as advanced HTML formatting features, including hyperlinks. Full HTML formatting results in imported data that most closely resembles the appearance of the Web page. You will format the Web query you just created to use full HTML formatting by modifying the properties of the connection.

To format the Web query:

▶ **1.** In the Connections group on the Data tab, click the **Connections** button.

▶ **2.** Click **Connection** in the list of workbook connections, and then click the **Properties** button.

▶ **3.** Type **Horizons Fund Web Page** in the Connection name box. Type **Retrieves summary information from the Horizons Fund Web page** in the Description box. Click the **Refresh data when opening the file** check box.

Next, you need to change the definition of this Web query so that it retrieves the HTML formatting along with the Web page text.

▶ **4.** Click the **Definition** tab, and then click the **Edit Query** button. The contents of the Horizons HTML file appears in the Edit Web Query dialog box.

5. Click the **Options** button on the Edit Web Query toolbar. The Web Query Options dialog box opens.

6. Click the **Full HTML formatting** option button, and then click the **OK** button.

7. Click the **Import** button, click the **OK** button, and then click the **Close** button to return to the workbook. The worksheet is updated, reflecting the full HTML formatting of the original Web page. See Figure 11-41.

Figure 11-41	Formatted Horizons Fund sheet

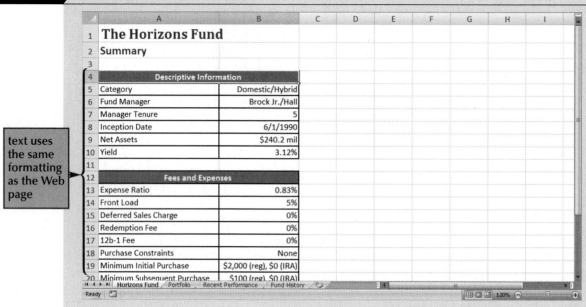

text uses the same formatting as the Web page

	A	B
1	**The Horizons Fund**	
2	**Summary**	
3		
4	**Descriptive Information**	
5	Category	Domestic/Hybrid
6	Fund Manager	Brock Jr./Hall
7	Manager Tenure	5
8	Inception Date	6/1/1990
9	Net Assets	$240.2 mil
10	Yield	3.12%
11		
12	**Fees and Expenses**	
13	Expense Ratio	0.83%
14	Front Load	5%
15	Deferred Sales Charge	0%
16	Redemption Fee	0%
17	12b-1 Fee	0%
18	Purchase Constraints	None
19	Minimum Initial Purchase	$2,000 (reg), $0 (IRA)
20	Minimum Subsequent Purchase	$100 (reg), $0 (IRA)

Horizons Fund / Portfolio / Recent Performance / Fund History

Ready

120%

Saving a Web Query

Carol has other Excel workbooks in which she wants to place this information. Rather than copying the worksheet into those workbooks, she wants you to save the Web query connection to a permanent file that she can quickly load into any other workbook.

To save a Web query:

1. In the Connections group on the Data tab, click the **Connections** button. The Workbook Connections dialog box opens.

2. Click **Horizons Fund Web Page** in the list of workbook connections, and then click the **Properties** button. The Connection Properties dialog box opens.

3. Click the **Definition** tab, and then click the **Edit Query** button. The Edit Web Query dialog box opens.

4. Click the **Save Query** button 🖳 on the Edit Web Query toolbar. The contents of the Microsoft\Queries folder appear in the Edit Web Query dialog box. This is the default folder in which all queries are placed. In this case, you'll save the query file in the Tutorial.11\Tutorial folder.

5. Navigate to the **Tutorial.11\Tutorial** folder included with your Data Files, type **Horizons Web Query** in the File name box, and then click the **Save** button to save the Web query.

6. Click the **Import** button, click the **OK** button, and then click the **Close** button to return to the workbook.

Tip

Web query files are simple text files, so you can view and edit their contents in Notepad. If you understand the Web query language, you can create sophisticated programs to retrieve and process Web data.

With the Web query saved to a file, Carol can load the connection file in any Office program. For example, she can retrieve the contents of the Horizons Web page and display it in a Word document. Microsoft also supports a library of built-in Web queries. You'll explore one of these next.

Importing Data from the World Wide Web

As you've seen, the files of Union Financial contain long-range historical data in text files and more recent data in databases and on the company's Web site, but sometimes Carol needs information that is even more current. In fact, she often needs to know how the stocks in the Horizons Fund portfolio are doing at this very moment. She can get that kind of information from the World Wide Web, where up-to-the-minute stock values are posted for online traders and brokers.

Carol wants to use a Web query that retrieves that online data and imports it into her Excel workbook. To access data from the Web, Excel provides several Web query files. These files are similar to the query file you just created and saved, except that they define how to retrieve data from a page on the World Wide Web.

Retrieving Multiple Stock Quotes

Carol's sample database includes 15 stocks, and she wants to be able to view current information on all of them. One of the Web query files that Excel supplies is the MSN MoneyCentral Investor Stock Quotes query. It allows you to enter up to 20 **ticker symbols** (abbreviations for the stock names used by the market), and then it retrieves current market values of those stocks and places the information into a table in the workbook. You will begin by creating a new worksheet for the current stock values, and then opening the query file for the MSN MoneyCentral Stock Quotes query.

To retrieve current stock quotes:

1. Insert a new worksheet named **Current Values** to the right of the Portfolio worksheet.

2. In cell A1, enter **Horizons Fund Stocks**, and then format the text using the **Title** cell style.

Tip

To list your connection file in the Existing Connections dialog box, place it in your My Data Sources folder.

3. In cell A2, enter **Current Quotes**, format the text using the **Heading 1** cell style, and then remove the border from cell A2, making it the active cell.

4. Click cell **A4**, and then, in the Get External Data group on the Data tab, click the **Existing Connections** button. The Existing Connections dialog box opens, listing all of the connections accessible to the workbook. See Figure 11-42.

Figure 11-42 | **Existing Connections dialog box**

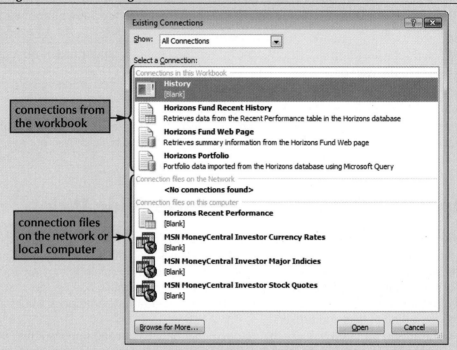

5. Click **MSN MoneyCentral Investor Stock Quotes**, and then click the **Open** button. The Import Data dialog box opens.

6. Verify that Excel will place the data in cell A4 of the current worksheet, and then click the **OK** button. The Enter Parameter Value dialog box opens.

   Some of the built-in queries include parameters that you can enter to specify exactly what information is imported. In this case, you have to specify the stock values to be imported by entering their ticker symbols. This information is found in the Portfolio worksheet.

7. Click the **Portfolio** sheet tab, and then select the range **A4:A18**. The range reference =Portfolio!$A$4:$A$18 appears in the dialog box. See Figure 11-43.

Enter Parameter Value dialog box ◀ Figure 11-43

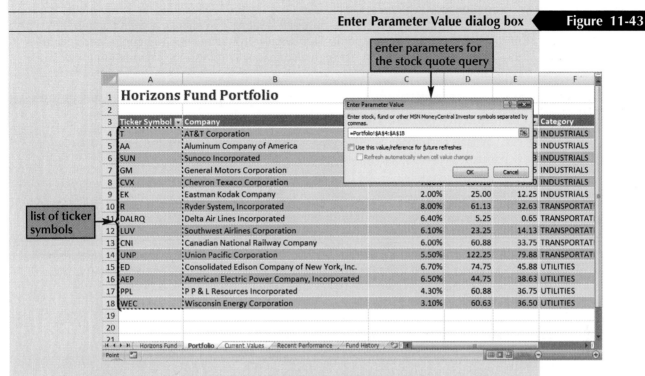

enter parameters for
the stock quote query

list of ticker
symbols

▶ **8.** Click the **Use this value/reference for future refreshes** check box to insert a
check mark. Excel will always use the ticker symbols from the Portfolio worksheet.

▶ **9.** Click the **OK** button. Excel retrieves the most current stock information on the 15
stocks in the Horizons Fund portfolio and displays that data in the Current Values
worksheet. See Figure 11-44.

Stock quotes imported from the Web ◀ Figure 11-44

	A	B	C	D	E	F	G
1	**Horizons Fund Stocks**						
2	**Current Quotes**						
3							
4	**Stock Quotes Provided by MSN Money**						
5	Click here to visit MSN Money						
6				Last	Previous Close	High	Low
7	AT&T Inc.		Chart	News	41.14	40.39	41.22	40.39
8	Alcoa Inc.		Chart	News	39.04	39.29	39.25	38.65
9	Sunoco, Inc.		Chart	News	73.46	73.24	73.89	71.87
10	GENERAL MOTORS		Chart	News	31.74	31.97	32.11	31.3
11	Chevron Corporation		Chart	News	80.73	80.15	80.93	79.61
12	Eastman Kodak Company		Chart	News	24.06	24.03	24.37	23.72
13	Ryder System, Inc.		Chart	News	53.63	52.53	53.67	52.41
14	DELTA AIR LINES INC		Chart	News	0.02	0.05	0.04	0.01
15	Southwest Airlines Co.		Chart	News	14.42	14.22	14.45	14.26
	CANADIAN NATIONAL RAILWAY		Chart	News	53.39	53.4	53.85	53.24
16	COMPANY						

Trouble? If some of the ticker symbols are no longer listed on the stock exchange
due to the changing nature of the stock market, your screen will look different
from Figure 11-44.

Based on the Web query results, Carol has a good idea of how the stocks in the database are doing at the moment. Because stock values can change a great deal from the time she first opens the workbook, Carol wants this connection to be refreshed regularly throughout her Excel session. She can also manually refresh the information in her workbook at any time.

To manually refresh the Web query:

▶ **1.** In the Connections group on the Data tab, click the **Refresh All button arrow**. A menu of refresh commands opens.

▶ **2.** Click **Refresh**. Excel refreshes the stock values on the Current Values worksheet.

Trouble? If you don't have access to the Internet, you cannot refresh the data in the Web query. Continue with the tutorial.

Another way to ensure current stock results is to have Excel periodically refresh the stock quotes for you by editing the properties of the connection to the Web site. Carol wants the data refreshed every 10 minutes while the workbook is open.

To periodically update the stock quotes:

▶ **1.** In the Connections group on the Data tab, click the **Connections** button. The Workbook Connections dialog box opens.

▶ **2.** Click the **MSN MoneyCentral Investor Stock Quotes** connection, and then click the **Properties** button. The Connection Properties dialog box opens.

▶ **3.** Enter **Retrieves current quotes for stocks in the Horizons Fund** in the Description box.

▶ **4.** Click the **Refresh data when opening the file** check box to insert a check mark. Excel will update the stock values automatically when opening the workbook.

▶ **5.** Click the **Refresh every** check box to insert a check mark, and then type **10** in the minutes box. Excel will update the stock values every 10 minutes while the workbook is open.

▶ **6.** Click the **OK** button in the Connection Properties dialog box, and then click the **Close** button in the Workbook Connections dialog box to return to the workbook.

The workbook will now retrieve stock values every 10 minutes from the MSN Money-Central Web page. These stock values are at least 20 minutes old because you are using a free service. If you need real-time stock reports, you must pay for that capability.

Using Hyperlinks

Carol notices that some of the text in the Web query results in the Current Values worksheet is underlined in blue. This text is a hyperlink to documents that contain additional information about the stocks in the portfolio. Clicking a hyperlink in a worksheet activates the computer's Web browser to display the Web page associated with that entry. Carol can click a hyperlink when she wants more detailed information about a particular stock. She can even use a hyperlink to access the home page of each company listed in the fund. You will try the hyperlink associated with AT&T.

To activate a hyperlink to external data:

▶ **1.** Point to the **AT&T Inc.** hyperlink in cell A7. The URL appears in a ScreenTip.

Trouble? If the AT&T hyperlink does not appear in your workbook, point to a different hyperlink and continue with the remaining steps.

▶ **2.** Click the link. Your default Web browser starts, and displays a Web page describing the current financial status of AT&T stock. See Figure 11-45.

Web page for AT&T stock ◀ Figure 11-45

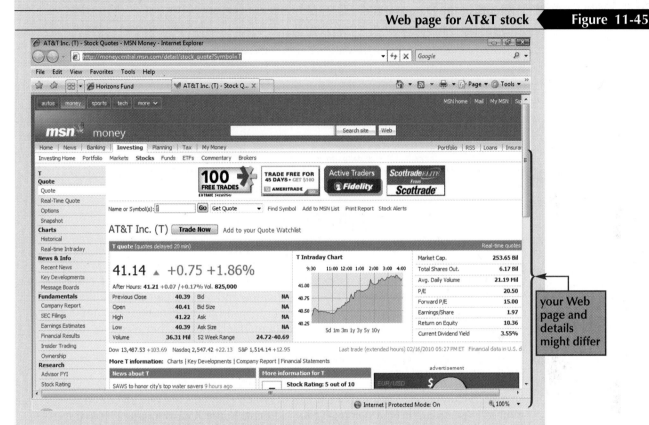

Trouble? If you are using a Web browser other than Internet Explorer, such as Firefox, your screen will look different from Figure 11-45. The numeric values of the Web page you retrieve will be different because the values change rapidly over time. If the links do not open any Web pages, ask your instructor or technical support person for help.

▶ **3.** Review the Web page, and then close your Web browser and return to the Horizons Fund workbook.

The Web page you opened contains additional information about the stock, along with links to other pages on the Web with even more information. Thus, the Horizons Fund portfolio workbook contains important information in its own right, but it also acts as a gateway to additional data resources.

Importing Data from XML

The final data source you'll examine for Carol's workbook involves XML. **Extensible Markup Language** (**XML**) is a language that structures data in text files that can be read by a wide variety of programs. In recent years, XML has been widely used in database programs, Web programming, and word processing. Office 2007 files are now stored in an XML-based file format called **Office Open XML Format**. Union Financial is working toward converting much of its data into XML documents that can be read and processed by a wide range of XML-based programs.

One of the programmers at Carol's company has created an XML document that contains information on the Excel workbook you've been using. Figure 11-46 shows the contents of the XML document, named Data.xml.

Figure 11-46 ▶ **Contents of the Data.xml file**

```
<?xml version="1.0" encoding="UTF-8" standalone="yes"?>
<document xmlns:xsi="http://www.w3.org/2001/XMLSchema-instance"
          xsi:noNamespaceSchemaLocation="Doc.xsd">

    <title>Union Financial</title>
    <subtitle>Horizons Fund Report</subtitle>
    <date>2010-11-15</date>
    <author>Carol Hill</author>
    <filename>Horizons.xlsx</filename>
    <notes>1) Horizon Fund information comes from the Web page, Horizons.htm</notes>
    <notes>2) Portfolio data comes from the Access database, Horizons.accdb</notes>
    <notes>3) Current Values data comes from the NYSE Web site</notes>
    <notes>4) Recent Results data comes from the Access database, Horizons.accdb</notes>
    <notes>5) Fund History data comes from the History.txt file</notes>

</document>
```

opening tag → notes element ← closing tag

Data in an XML document is contained within **elements**. Elements are roughly analogous to the fields used in databases. The name of each element is contained within an **opening tag**, which also marks the beginning of the data value. A **closing tag** marks the end of the data value. In Figure 11-46, the opening and closing tags are highlighted in red to make it easier to differentiate the element tags from the data they contain. For example, the following code contains the data marked by the author element. In this case, the value is the text string *Carol Hill*.

```
<author>Carol Hill</author>
```

An XML document is structured like a tree in which elements are placed within one another, descending from a common **root element**. In the XML document shown in Figure 11-46, the root element is called document and contains six elements named title, subtitle, date, author, filename, and notes. To better understand the structure of an XML document, a **data map** can be created that displays the layout of the elements in a schematic diagram. Figure 11-47 shows a data map for the structure of the Data.xml file.

Figure 11-47 ▶ **Data map of the Data.xml document**

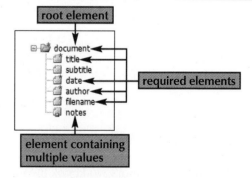

root element

required elements

element containing multiple values

One of the advantages of XML is that the XML author defines what constitutes a valid document, indicating which elements are required and which are optional. The document author can also indicate what type of values each element can contain. Documents that fail to meet these rules can be rejected by an XML program as invalid, thus ensuring data integrity. Information about the requirements for a valid XML document is also displayed in the data map. Required elements are shown with a red star. The required elements in the Data.xml file are document, title, date, author, and filename. An element containing other elements is displayed using a folder icon, whereas an element that only contains data is displayed with a document icon. In the Data.xml file, only the document element contains other elements. Finally, an element can allow for multiple values. This is indicated with a document icon containing an arrow. Only the notes element in the Data.xml file allows for multiple values, with each note specifying a different piece of information about the data sources for Carol's workbook.

The rules about which elements are required and which are not and which elements support multiple values and which only allow for a single value are stored in a second document called a **schema**. Schemas are not required in XML, but they are useful in ensuring that any data inserted into an XML document follows predefined rules for both content and structure. Carol has created a schema for the Data.xml file, which she stored in a text file named Doc.xsd. Like the data file, schema files are also stored as simple text documents.

When you connect to an XML document, Excel creates a data map of the document's structure and contents. If a schema is present, Excel uses it to create the data map; otherwise, it creates the map based on the contents of the XML document. After the data map is created, you can use it to place XML elements anywhere within the workbook.

Loading an XML Data Map

The commands to access the data map of an XML document are part of Excel's developer tools. To work with an XML data map, you must show the Developer tab on the Ribbon. If the XML document has a schema file attached to it, you can load a data map without actually importing the data into the Excel workbook.

Loading an XML Data Map		Reference Window

- In the XML group on the Developer tab, click the Source button.
- In the XML Source pane, click the XML Maps button.
- Locate and select the XML document file.
- Click the Rename button within the XML Maps dialog box to define a name for the map.

To see how you can load a data map without importing the data, you'll load the data map for Carol's Data.xml file.

To load the data map for the Data.xml file:

▶ 1. If the Developer tab is not on the Ribbon, click the **Office Button** 🔘, and then click the **Excel Options** button. Click **Popular** in the Excel Options dialog box, click the **Show Developer tab in the Ribbon** check box to insert a check mark, and then click the **OK** button.

▶ 2. Click the **Developer** tab on the Ribbon, and then, in the XML group, click the **Source** button. The XML pane opens at the right side of the workbook window. From this pane, you can load the data map for the Data.xml file.

▶ 3. Click the **XML Maps** button at the bottom of the XML Source pane. The XML Maps dialog box opens.

▶ 4. Click the **Add** button to add an XML data map to the workbook. The Select XML Source dialog box opens.

▶ **5.** Click the **Data** file located in the **Tutorial.11\Tutorial** folder included with your Data Files, and then click the **Open** button. The document map for the Data.xml file is added to the list of XML maps in the current workbook and assigned the default name, document_map. You can rename this data map to something more descriptive.

▶ **6.** Click the **Rename** button, type **Horizons Fund XML Data**, and then press the **Enter** key. Resize the **Name** column to display the entire name. See Figure 11-48.

Figure 11-48 ▶ **XML Maps dialog box**

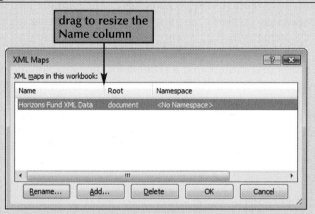

▶ **7.** Click the **OK** button. The Horizons Fund XML Data map is loaded into Excel and appears in the XML Source pane. See Figure 11-49.

Figure 11-49 ▶ **Data map in the XML Source pane**

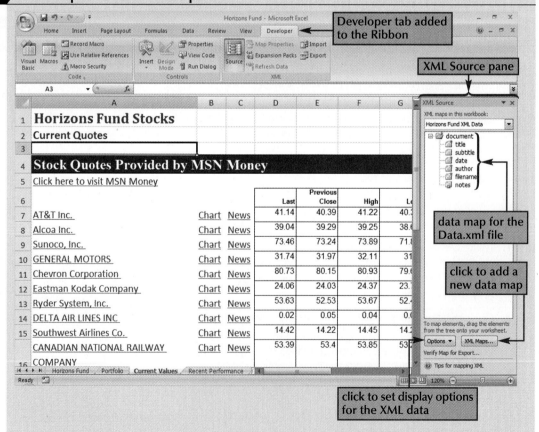

Binding XML Elements to a Worksheet

One of the advantages of using XML as a data source is that it allows you to attach, or **bind**, elements to specific cells in the workbook, providing you with greater freedom in designing a worksheet layout. To bind an element to a cell, you drag the element name from the XML map and drop it into the cell. After you drop the element, you can place the element name above or to the right of the cell (if those locations are available). If a Header Options button appears next to a cell, you can click the button to define where you want to place an element's name (if you want it displayed at all). The Header Options button does not appear for elements you place in the leftmost column of the worksheet because no room is available to place the element name to the left or above the element data.

Next, you'll bind the elements of the Data.xml file to cells in a Documentation sheet.

To place elements from the data map into the workbook:

▶ **1.** Insert a new worksheet named **Documentation** at the beginning of the workbook.

▶ **2.** In the XML Source pane, click **title** in the Horizons Fund XML Data map and drag it to cell A1 in the Documentation worksheet.

No data appears in the cell because you have not actually imported the contents of the Data.xml file. You've only defined where you want to place the contents of the title element.

▶ **3.** Drag **subtitle** from the data map to cell A2 of the Documentation sheet.

▶ **4.** Drag **author** from the data map to cell B4. When you drop the author element into cell B4, the Header Options button ▥ appears to the right of cell B4. You can select the Header Options button to determine where to place the author element name.

▶ **5.** Click the **Header Options** button ▥ , and then click the **Place XML Heading to the Left** option button.

▶ **6.** Repeat Steps 4 and 5 for the date and filename elements, placing those elements in cells B5 and B6.

▶ **7.** Drag the **notes** element from the data map to cell B8. Because this element can contain multiple values, Excel places it into the cell as an Excel table. The element name is placed above the table in cell B8. See Figure 11-50.

> ### Tip
>
> To map an XML document directly into an Excel table, click the From Other Sources button in the Get External Data group on the Data tab, and then click From XML Data Import.

Completed layout of the XML elements from the data map ◀ **Figure 11-50**

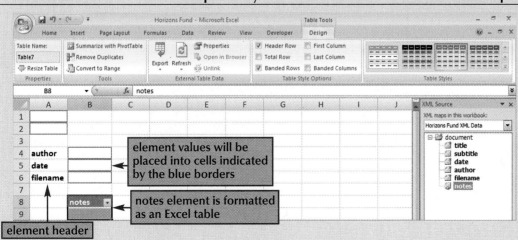

By using XML and the data map, you placed the elements in specific locations in the Documentation sheet. Because these cells are now bound with elements from the XML file, you can import the XML data directly into the worksheet cells.

Importing XML Data

To retrieve the XML data, you refresh the connection to the data source. Excel will automatically place the data in the correct worksheet cells. You can also complete the Documentation sheet by formatting its contents. Formatting the worksheet does not affect Excel's ability to retrieve and display the data from the XML document.

To import data from the Data.xml file:

1. Click the **Data** tab on the Ribbon, and then, in the Connections group, click the **Connections** button. The connection you made to the Data.xml file is listed as Data in the Workbook Connections dialog box.

2. Verify that **Data** is selected in the list of workbook connections, click the **Refresh button arrow**, and then click **Refresh**. Excel refreshes the connection to the Data.xml file, importing the data into the Documentation sheet. You should also provide descriptive information about the connection you've established to the Data.xml file.

3. Click the **Properties** button to open the Connection Properties dialog box, type **Horizons Fund Report** in the Connection name box, and then type **Retrieves information about the Horizons Fund Report from the Data.xml file** in the Description box.

4. Click the **OK** button, and then the **Close** button.

5. Format cell A1 with the **Title** cell style, format cell A2 with the **Heading 4** cell style, and then click cell **A3**. See Figure 11-51.

Figure 11-51 | **Binding XML data to cells in the Documentation sheet**

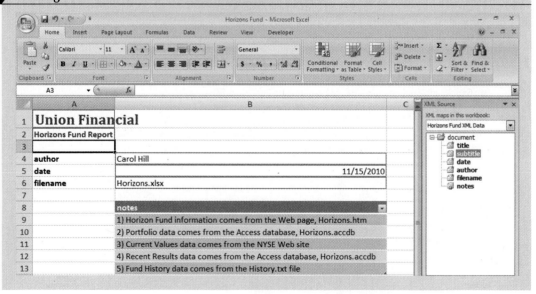

As with database and Web page queries, you can automatically update the XML data in this workbook to reflect changes to the source XML document. You'll change the values in the Data.xml file to include information about the source of the data for the Documentation sheet and add your name as the document author.

To modify the Data.xml data file:

▶ 1. Use your text editor to open the **Data** file located in the **Tutorial.11\Tutorial** folder included with your Data Files.

▶ 2. Delete the text **Carol Hill** from between the <author> and </author> tags and type your name.

▶ 3. Directly below the fifth notes element, insert the following text: **<notes>6) Documentation sheet data comes from the Data.xml file</notes>**

▶ 4. Save and close the file.

▶ 5. Return to the **Documentation** sheet in the Horizons Fund workbook.

▶ 6. Click cell **A1** to select an element from the data map, click the **Data** tab on the Ribbon, in the Connections group click the **Refresh All button arrow**, and then click **Refresh** to refresh the data in the Documentation sheet.

▶ 7. Close the XML Source pane to free up space in the workbook window. See Figure 11-52.

Completed Documentation sheet | **Figure 11-52**

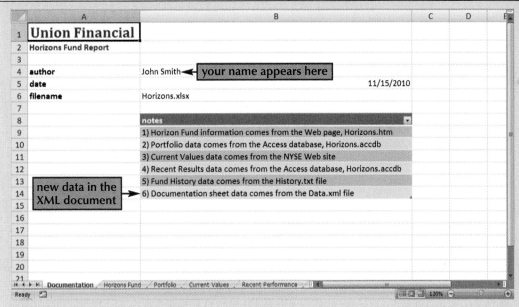

▶ 8. Save and close the **Horizons Fund** workbook.

You can also use a data map to export data from your worksheet to an XML document. After cells have been mapped to XML elements, save the worksheet as an XML document. The contents of the cells will be placed into elements in the XML file.

The Horizons Fund workbook is complete. By tapping into a variety of data sources, you've created a file that Carol can use to get current information on the fund as well as examine long-term and short-term data to look for important trends. She expects to find many ways to incorporate this new information into her daily work as an investment counselor at Union Financial.

InSight	**Excel and the Office Open XML Format**

In Office 2007, Microsoft continues to move its file from binary formats to formats based on the XML language. Changing the file formats gives developers access to a wealth of tools for working with XML files. The new formats improve file and data management, data recovery, and interoperability with line-of-business systems. Any program that supports XML can access and work with data in the new file format. The program does not need to be part of Microsoft Office.

The Office Open XML format stores the XML code in a compressed file, not as a text file. However, you can open an Office file using compression programs such as WinZip to view the underlying XML files. A single Excel workbook might consist of several XML files, including a file to contain the workbook data and another file to contain the document's schema. The schema file allows developers to ensure the data integrity of Excel data. You can extract the compressed XML files as text files and then view or manipulate the contents of the workbook from outside of Excel.

Understanding Real-Time Data Acquisition

For Carol's workbook, you imported data from four sources: simple text files, databases, Web pages, and XML documents. Scientists and researchers have a fifth possible data source: **real-time data** values from measuring devices and scientific equipment. A scientist might connect a computer to a temperature sensor, for example, and import temperature values at one-minute intervals directly into a workbook. If you want to use real-time data acquisition, you usually need to purchase an add-in to work with Excel and the device. To facilitate importing data from an external device, Excel provides the RTD function. The syntax of the RTD function is

`RTD(ProgID, server, topic1 [, topic2] [, topic3] ...)`

In this function, *ProgID* is the program ID of the add-in that has been installed on the computer to retrieve the real-time data, *server* is the name of the server where the add-in is run (leave the server parameter blank if the add-in is being run on your computer), and *topic1*, *topic2*, and so forth are names assigned to the real-time data values. You can insert up to 28 different topics. After you insert the RTD function into a cell, the value of the cell displays the latest value retrieved from the measuring device. You can also write a VBA macro to run the RTD function in a range of cells, recording the last several values from the measuring device.

By using the RTD function along with an add-in program, the scientist or researcher can save hours of data entry time, and concentrate on analysis.

Session 11.3 Quick Check | Review

1. Describe how to import data from a Web page into a workbook.
2. What are the three options for retaining the format styles found within an imported Web page?
3. How would you import the most current stock market data into a workbook?
4. How current are the stock market quotes retrieved from Excel's built-in Web queries?
5. What is XML?
6. What is an XML data map?
7. What Excel function would you use to retrieve real-time data from a measuring device connected to your computer?

Tutorial Summary | Review

In this tutorial, you learned how to create a connected workbook in which much of the data and content of the workbook came from outside sources. You began with importing a simple text file, and learned about the different text file formats and ways of delimiting one column of data from another. After importing data from the text file, you examined how connections operate within Excel. You learned how to set connection properties and how to control when connections are refreshed. You also examined how Excel manages data security using the concept of trusted locations.

The second session explored how to integrate databases with Excel. You learned about the structure of databases and database tables and how to access a database using the Query Wizard. After examining how to save a query for future use in other programs, you applied a query to a PivotTable and PivotChart. You also explored how to edit a query and refresh data from a query whenever a workbook is opened.

The final session explored ways of retrieving data from the Web through the use of Web queries. You created a Web query for a sample Web page, and examined some of the built-in Web queries supplied with Excel, which can be used to retrieve data from pages on the World Wide Web. You also used a Web query to create hyperlinks to sites on the Web containing financial data. Finally, you learned about the general structure of XML documents and how to bind elements of an XML document with specific cells in the workbook. The tutorial concluded with a brief discussion of real-time data acquisition.

Key Terms

bind	element	Rich Text Format (RTF)
closing tag	Extensible Markup	root element
column break	Language (XML)	schema
common field	external data range	table
connection	fixed-width text file	text file
criteria	Office Open XML Format	ticker symbol
data map	opening tag	trusted location
data source	query	Uniform Resource
database	Query Wizard	Locator (URL)
delimited text	real-time data	Web query
delimiter	refresh	

Practice the skills you learned in the tutorial using the same case scenario.

Data Files needed for the Review Assignments: Index.xlsx, NYA2009.txt, Horizons.accdb, Summary.htm, Info.xml, Info.xsd

Carol wants you to create a new workbook that analyzes the performance of the stocks in the Horizons database by the three NYSE categories: the industrials, the transportation stocks, and the utilities. She has a text file that contains the daily indexes of these sub-groups for the year 2009 that she wants you to import into a workbook. Then, she wants you to create a table of yield and price/earnings, or P/E ratio values, for the stocks in the Horizons database, sorted by category. Your next task is to create a table and chart that displays the average closing values of the industrial, transportation, and utility stocks in the Horizons Fund over the past five days. Carol wants the data in a PivotTable in which she can click a Category list box and view the corresponding table and chart for that category (industrial, transportation, or utility). She also wants a worksheet that displays a table of current Dow Jones stock quote data retrieved from the Web. Finally, she wants to import data about the workbook from an XML file, binding the XML data to cells in the workbook.

Complete the following:

1. Open the **Index** workbook located in the Tutorial.11\Review folder included with your Data Files, and then save the workbook as **Index Report** in the same folder.
2. In cell A3 of the Historical Data worksheet, establish a connection to the **NYA2009** text file located in the Tutorial.11\Review folder included with your Data Files. Choose the Fixed-Width file type option, and skip the first three lines of the text file. Import the Date, Composite, Industrial, Transport, and Utility columns. Adjust the column breaks as needed. Import the Date column in YMD format. Do not import the Finance column.
3. Resize the columns to completely display all of the data. Format the values in the Composite, Industrial, Transport, and Utility columns using the Number format.
4. Set the properties of the external data range containing the imported text to refresh the connection whenever the workbook is opened.
5. Go to the Yield and PE Ratios worksheet and select cell A3. Use the Query Wizard to import the following fields from the **Horizons** database located in the Tutorial.11\Review folder included with your Data Files, and then sort the data from the query in ascending order by the values of the Category field:
   • Ticker Symbol, Company, and Category fields from the Company table
   • Yield and P/E Ratio fields from the Stock Info table
6. Save the query as a permanent file named **Index Query** in the Tutorial.11\Review folder.
7. Import the results of the query into the Yield and PE Values worksheet as an Excel table starting in cell A3.
8. Set the connection properties of the query so that it is refreshed whenever the workbook is opened. Add the description **Retrieves yield and pe ratios from the Horizons database** to the connection.
9. Click cell A5 in the Five-Day Averages worksheet. Use the Query Wizard to import the Category field from the Company table and the Date and Closing fields from the Recent Performance table. Import the data from this query into cell A5 as a PivotChart and PivotTable Report.

10. Format the PivotTable so that the Category field is displayed as the Report Filter, the Date field is displayed as an axis field, and the Closing field is displayed as a Pivot-Table value. Edit the field settings of the Closing field so that it summarizes the values using the average rather than the sum. Display the average values using the Number format. Remove the Grand Total row from the PivotTable.

11. Move and resize the PivotChart so that it covers the range C3:I17. Change the chart type to a line chart and remove the legend from the chart. Change the text of the chart title to Five-Day Averages in a 12-point font. Display the values from the Utilities category.

12. Name this connection **Five Day Averages** with the description **Retrieves five days of closing values from the Horizons database**. Set the connection to refresh whenever the workbook is opened.

13. In the Summary worksheet, create a Web query that accesses the **Summary** file located in the Tutorial.11\Review folder included with your Data Files. Retrieve only the four tables located at the bottom of the page and preserve their formats using Rich text formatting. Place the imported data into cell A3.

14. Name the Web query connection you just created **NYSE Summary Web page** with the description **Retrieves financial tables from the Summary.htm file**. Set the connection to refresh when the workbook is opened.

15. In the Dow Jones worksheet, use the MSN MoneyCentral Major Indices query to import current index values. Place the imported data into the worksheet starting at cell A3. (*Note*: The MSN MoneyCentral Major Indices query might display invalid ticker symbols in some of the cells.)

16. Edit the properties of the connection to the MSN MoneyCentral Web site so that it refreshes every 10 minutes and when the workbook is opened. Name the connection **Current Index Values** and add the description **Retrieves current financial indices using the MSN MoneyCentral Web Query**.

17. Use a text editor to open the **Info.xml** file located in the Tutorial.11\Review folder included with your Data Files. Substitute your name for Carol Hill as the document author. Also add the following line directly below the last notes tag, and then close the file, saving your changes:
    <notes>6) Documentation data comes from the Info.xml file</notes>

18. In the Index Report workbook, add a data map to the workbook based on the contents of the Info.xml file.

19. In the Documentation sheet, bind the title element to cell A1, the subtitle element to cell A2, the author, date, and filename elements in the range B4:B6, and the notes element to cell B8. Display the headings for the date, author, and filename elements to the left of the element values. Format cell A1 using the Title cell style. Format cell A2 using the Heading 4 cell style.

20. Refresh the connections in the Documentation worksheet to display the text from the Info.xml file. Edit the properties of the Info connection, changing the name to **Document Information** and adding the description **Retrieves document titles from the Info.xml file**.

21. Save and close the workbook. Submit the finished workbook to your instructor, either in printed or electronic form, as requested.

| Apply | | **Case Problem 1** |

Use the skills you learned to import home sales data from a delimited text file.

Data File needed for this Case Problem: Homes.txt

Kroft Realty   Tim Kroft is the owner of Kroft Realty, a large and popular real estate agency in Ames, Iowa. One of Tim's tasks is to create tables of comparable sales prices for homes listed in the area. Tim downloads a file containing the most recent sales listings that includes details such as the price, age, and size of the home and its location within the city of Ames. Tim wants your help in importing the data from this text file into Excel and then using that data to create a PivotTable. The text file uses a delimited format in which one column is separated from another using the forward slash (/) character.

Complete the following:

1. Use Excel to open the **Homes** text file located in the Tutorial.11\Case1 folder included with your Data Files.
2. When the Text Import Wizard starts, select the Delimited text input option and choose to start the text import in the fifth row of the file.
3. In the second step of the wizard, choose the forward slash character, /, as the delimiter.
4. Do not import the Offer Pending and Annual Tax columns. Use the General format for all of the columns in the file except the Age column. Import the contents of the Age column as text.
5. After importing the data, save the workbook as **Home Sales Analysis** in the Tutorial.11\Case1 folder included with your Data Files.
6. Resize the columns to fit the data. Rename the worksheet as **Home Listings**.
7. Add a new worksheet named **Home Summary** to the end of the workbook. In the Home Summary worksheet, create a PivotTable using the data on the Home Listings sheet to show the average sales price of each home. Format the sales data as currency with no decimal places. Display Square Feet as a row label in the table, Age as a column label, and NE Sector as a report filter.
8. Insert a Documentation sheet at the beginning of the workbook containing your name, the current date, the purpose of the workbook, and a description of the data source used in the analysis.
9. Save and close the workbook. Submit the finished workbook to your instructor, either in printed or electronic form, as requested.

| Apply | | **Case Problem 2** |

Use the skills you learned to query and summarize data for an online candy company.

Data Files needed for this Case Problem: Confections.accdb, Confections.xlsx

Kate's Confections   Kate Amundsen is the owner of Kate's Confections, an online company that sells delicious candies and chocolates. Kate has been storing her orders in an Access database and wants to import its data into an Excel worksheet. For this project, she has created a smaller version of the complete database, containing only a subset of all the orders. The database, named Confections.accdb, contains five tables named Customers, Orders, Products, Customers_Orders, and Orders_Products. The Customers table lists the names and contact information for customers who have ordered items from Kate's Confections over the past several weeks. The Orders table lists each order and the date it was submitted. The Products table lists some of the products sold by Kate's Confections. The Customers_Orders table matches each order with the customer who ordered it. Finally, the Orders_Products table matches each order with the products on the order.

Kate wants your help in importing this data. She wants you to display the data from the Customers and Products table in separate worksheets in an Excel workbook. She also wants you to create a PivotTable that displays details on each order.

Complete the following:

1. Open the **Confections** workbook located in the Tutorial.11\Case2 folder included with your Data Files, and then save the workbook as **Kate's Confections** in the same folder.
2. In the Documentation sheet, enter your name in cell B3 and the current date in cell B4.
3. Insert a new worksheet named **Customers** at the end of the workbook. In cell A1, enter **Kate's Confections** and format the text with the Title cell style. In cell A2, enter **Customer List** and format the text with the Heading 4 cell style.
4. Create a connection to the Customers table of the **Confections** database located in the Tutorial.11\Case2 folder included with your Data Files. Place the data as an Excel table starting in cell A4 of the Customers worksheet.
5. Edit the properties of the connection you just created. Name the connection **Customer List** and add the description **Data retrieved from the Customer table in the Confections database**. Refresh the connection whenever the workbook is opened.
6. Create a worksheet at the end of the workbook named **Products**. Enter the title **Kate's Confections** in cell A1 and the subtitle **Product List** in cell A2. Format cells A1 and A2 as you did for the title and subtitle in the Customers worksheet.
7. Establish a connection to the Products table of the **Confections** database located in the Tutorial.11\Case2 folder included with your Data Files, importing the data as an Excel table starting in cell A4. Format the Price values in column C using the Currency format.
8. Edit the properties of the connection, naming the connection **Product List** and entering the description **Data retrieved from the Products table in the Confections database**. Refresh the connection whenever the workbook is opened.
9. Insert a worksheet at the end of the workbook named **Product Orders**. Enter the title **Kate's Confections** in cell A1 and the subtitle **Product Orders** in cell A2. Format cells A1 and A2 as you did for the previous two worksheets.
10. Use the Query Wizard to create a query based on the tables in the Confections database. The query should extract the following fields:
    • Name from the Customers table
    • CID and OID from the Customers_Orders table
    • Date from the Orders table
    • PID from the Orders_Products table
    • Product and Price from the Products table.
11. Save the query as a permanent file named **Order Query** in the Tutorial.11\Case2 folder.
12. Import the data from the query into cell A5 of the Product Orders sheet as a Pivot-Table Report.
13. Place the Name, Date, and Product fields as row labels in the PivotTable. Display the sum of the Price field in the Values section of the table. Format the Sum of Price values using the Currency format.
14. Name this connection **Product Orders** with the description **Retrieves product orders from Kate's Confections customers recorded in the Confections database**. Refresh the connection whenever the workbook opens.

⊕ **EXPLORE**   15. Kate wants to save the connections you've created as Office Data Connection (ODC) files for use in other projects. To save the connections as permanent files, open the Connection Properties dialog box for each of the three connections you've created and click the Export Connection File button on the Definition tab. Name the ODC files **Customer List**, **Product List**, and **Product Orders** and save them to the Tutorial.11\Case2 folder.

16. Save and close the workbook. Submit the finished workbook to your instructor, either in printed or electronic form, as requested.

⊕ **EXPLORE**   17. Test the connection files you created in Step 15 by opening a new blank workbook. Click the Connections button in the Connections group on the Data tab, and then click the Add button. Click the Browse for More button to locate and select the three connection files you created in Step 15.

18. Click the Existing Connections button in the Get External Data group on the Data tab and verify that the three connections you added to this workbook are listed. Select the Customer List connection and click the Open button. Confirm that you can insert the data from this connection into your workbook as an Excel table.

19. Close the blank workbook without saving; you do not need to submit this workbook to your instructor.

| Challenge | **Case Problem 3** |

Explore how to import data for a financial consultant tracking currency exchange rates.

Data Files needed for this Case Problem: Exchange.xlsx, YRate.xml

Brooks and Beckman   Henry Sanchez is a financial consultant at Brooks and Beckman. He is developing an Excel workbook that will allow him to calculate money values in different currencies, based on the current exchange rate. He has already created the part of the workbook that performs the actual calculations, but he needs your help in determining the current exchange rate between U.S. dollars and foreign currencies. Henry is paying particular attention to the exchange rate between U.S. dollars and Japanese yen. Therefore, he also wants to insert the contents of an XML document that has the last 120 days of exchange rate information into the workbook. One of the built-in Web queries offered by Excel links to a Web page that displays current exchange rates. You'll use this query to complete Henry's workbook.

Complete the following:

1. Open the **Exchange** workbook located in the Tutorial.11\Case3 folder included with your Data Files, and then save the workbook as **Exchange Rate Calculator** in the same folder.

2. In the Documentation sheet, enter your name in cell B3 and the current date in cell B4.

3. Insert a new worksheet named **Exchange Rates** at the end of the workbook.

⊕ **EXPLORE**   4. Create a connection to the built-in Web query MSN MoneyCentral Investor Currency Rates. Place the data in cell A1 of the Exchange Rates worksheet.

5. Modify the properties of the MSN MoneyCentral connection so that currency rate data is refreshed whenever the workbook is opened and every 10 minutes thereafter.

6. Assign the range name **currency_names** to the names of the currency exchanges in column A of the Exchange Rates worksheet. Assign the range name **currency_rates** to the three columns of currency data in the Exchange Rates worksheet. Do not include the column headings in either of these ranges.

⊕ EXPLORE   7. Increase the width of column A to 60 characters. Modify the properties of the connection so that Excel does *not* adjust the column width of the worksheet when it refreshes the data.

⊕ EXPLORE   8. In cell C3 of the Calculator worksheet, insert a data validation rule that only allows values from a list. The source of the list is the range of values returned by the currency_names range reference.

⊕ EXPLORE   9. In cell C5, use the VLOOKUP function to retrieve the exchange rates between a selected currency and U.S. dollars. (*Hint*: The lookup value is the currency value in cell C3, the lookup table is the table of currency rates referenced by the currency_rates range reference. Use the second column of the table and instruct Excel to return only exact matches.) Multiply the lookup value by the value in cell C4.

10. Repeat Steps 8 and 9 for the exchange rate calculator in cells C8 and C10. However, in the calculator, use the third column from the lookup table to return the exchange rate.

11. Determine the current value of 15,000 yen in U.S. dollars by entering **15,000** in cell C4 and then choosing the Japanese Yen currency exchange rate from the list box in cell C3.

12. Determine the current value of $75 in Japanese yen by entering **75** in cell C9 and then choosing the Japanese Yen currency exchange rate from the list box in cell C8.

13. Insert a new worksheet named **Japanese Yen Recent History** at the end of the workbook.

⊕ EXPLORE   14. Create a connection to the YRate.xml file located in the Tutorial.11\Case3 folder included with your Data Files. (*Hint*: Use the From XML Data Import options listed for the From Other Sources button in the Get External Data group on the Data tab.) Import the data from this file as an Excel table.

15. Create a line chart in the Japanese Yen Recent History worksheet based on the exchange rate data you imported. Add the title **Value of Yen per U.S. $** above the chart. Remove the chart legend.

16. Edit the properties of the connection you just created, changing the name of the connection to **Recent values of the Yen**.

17. Save and close the workbook. Submit the finished workbook to your instructor, either in printed or electronic form, as requested.

Create | **Case Problem 4**

Use your creativity to create a sales report for an antiques reseller with data imported from an Access database.

Data Files needed for this Case Problem: Antiques.accdb, Green.xlsx

Green Cove Antiques   Green Cove Antiques, located in Burlington, Vermont, is an online reseller of antiques and fine arts. Karl Umhoefer is a sales manager at the store. One of his jobs is to maintain reports on customer orders to help the company notice trends in sales and product interest. The customer order data is stored in an Access database, which contains five tables: Products, Customer, Orders, Item, and Staff. Each table shares a common field with at least one other table in the database. The Products table stores information about products in the company's catalog. The Customer table records personal information about people who have bought products from Green Cove Antiques. The Orders table contains information about each order, including the date, who placed the order, and who recorded the transaction. The Item table records the items purchased in each order. Finally, the Staff table contains information about the sales personnel who take the orders. Karl asks you to help him extract this information and place it into an Excel workbook.

Complete the following:

1. Open the **Green** workbook located in the Tutorial.11\Case4 folder included with your Data Files, and then save the workbook as **Green Cove Antiques** in the same folder.

2. In the Documentation sheet, enter your name in cell B3 and the current date in cell B4.

3. Create a worksheet named **Staff** containing an Excel table listing the sales staff at Green Cove Antiques. Connect to the STAFF table in the **Antiques** database located in the Tutorial.11\Case4 folder included with your Data Files. Name this connection **Green Cove Staff** and refresh the connection when the workbook opens.

4. Insert a worksheet named **Products** containing an Excel table listing the products in the company database. Display the price of each item in currency format. Connect to the PRODUCTS table in the Antiques database located in the Tutorial.11\Case4 folder included with your Data Files. Name this connection **Green Cove Products** and refresh the connection when the workbook is opened.

5. Create a worksheet named **Customers** containing an Excel table listing the customers. Connect to the CUSTOMER table in the Antiques database located in the Tutorial.11\Case4 folder included with your Data Files. Name this connection **Customer List** and refresh the connection when the workbook opens.

6. Create a worksheet named **Orders**. Use the Query Wizard to import the following fields from the different tables in the Antiques database:
   - LAST_NAME, FIRST_NAME, and COMPANY from the CUSTOMER table
   - QUANTITY from the ITEM table
   - DATE from the ORDERS table
   - SELLER, TYPE, DESCRIPTION, and ITEM PRICE from the PRODUCTS table

7. Save the query in a permanent file named **Orders Query** in the Tutorial.11\Case4 folder.

8. Import the data into cell A1 of the Orders worksheet as an Excel table. Name this connection **Customer Orders** and refresh it whenever the workbook is opened.

9. Add a new column to the table you created in the previous step that calculates the total price of each order (equal to the item price multiplied by the quantity). Use SALES as the heading text for the new column. Format its values and the values of the ITEM PRICE column as Currency. Add a Total row to the table that calculates the total income from all of the orders in the database.

10. Add a worksheet named **Sales Types** at the end of the workbook. Use the Query Wizard to import the following fields from the tables in the Antiques database:
    - QUANTITY and ITEM_ID# from the ITEM table
    - ORDER_ID# from the ORDERS table
    - TYPE from the PRODUCTS table
    - STAFF_ID# and LAST_NAME from the STAFF table

11. Save the definition of this query as a permanent file named **Sales Types Query** in the Tutorial.11\Case4 folder included with your Data Files. Import the query data into cell A1 of the Sales Types worksheet as a PivotTable Report. Rename the connection for this query as **Sales Types** and refresh the query whenever the workbook is opened.

12. Display the quantity of each order broken down by the staff person's last name and the type of product sold.

13. Save and close the workbook. Submit the finished workbook to your instructor, either in printed or electronic form, as requested.

Research | **Internet Assignments**

Use the Internet to find and work with data related to the topics presented in this tutorial.

The purpose of the Internet Assignments is to challenge you to find information on the Internet that you can use to work effectively with this software. The actual assignments are updated and maintained on the Course Technology Web site. Log on to the Internet and use your Web browser to go to the Student Online Companion for New Perspectives Office 2007 at **www.course.com/np/office2007**. Then navigate to the Internet Assignments for this tutorial.

Assess | **SAM Assessment and Training**

If you have a SAM user profile, you may have access to hands-on instruction, practice, and assessment of the skills covered in this tutorial. Log in to your SAM account (**http://sam2007.course.com**) to launch any assigned training activities or exams that relate to the skills covered in this tutorial.

Review | **Quick Check Answers**

Session 11.1

1. A fixed-width text file places all columns in the same location in the file; a delimited text file uses a special character to separate columns.
2. space, comma, tab
3. Click the location in the Data preview window of the Text Import Wizard to indicate where you want the column break to appear.
4. The connection establishes the method by which data is retrieved from an external source into an Excel workbook; the external data range is the actual location in the workbook where the data is placed.
5. A connection is either refreshed manually by the user clicking the Refresh button on the Data tab or automatically either when the workbook is initially opened or periodically as the user works in the document.
6. A trusted location is a file location that Excel trusts as being free of security risks, allowing it to open files from that location without prompting the user for permission.

Session 11.2

1. (a) a program that stores and retrieves large amounts of data and creates reports describing the data; (b) a collection of data stored in rows and columns; (c) a column of the table that stores information about a specific characteristic for a particular person, place, or thing; (d) a row of the table that displays a collection of characteristics for a particular person, place, or thing; (e) a field that is shared by two or more tables and used to combine information from those tables
2. a method of extracting information from a database that satisfies certain conditions by selecting specific fields, filtering the data to match a condition, and sorting the data in a specified order
3. Click the Connections button in the Connections group on the Data tab. Select the connection from the list of connections in the workbook and click the Properties button. Click the Definition tab and then click the Edit Query button.
4. Set up the connection to the external data source and then select the PivotTable Report and PivotChart option button when importing the data into the workbook.

5. It reduces the size of the workbook because Excel does not have to store the data when the workbook is not in use.

6. SQL stands for Structured Query Language and is a standard database language for writing queries to extract data from relational databases.

7. Connections are either stored as part of the Excel workbook and are available for use only within that workbook or as external files and, thus, are potentially available for use with any Office program.

Session 11.3

1. Click the From Web button in the Get External Data group on the Data tab. Enter the URL for the Web page in the New Web Query dialog box. Click the yellow arrows of the sections of the Web page that you want to import.

2. None, Rich text formatting, and Full HTML formatting

3. Click the Existing Sources button in the Get External Data group on the Data tab. Choose one of the built-in MSN financial queries from the list of connections.

4. 20 minutes old

5. XML stands for Extensible Markup Language and is a language used for storing data in text files through the use of tags that mark the beginning and end of elements within the document.

6. An XML map shows the structure of an XML document and can be used in Excel to place elements of the XML document at specified cells in the workbook.

7. The RTD or real-time-data function

Ending Data Files

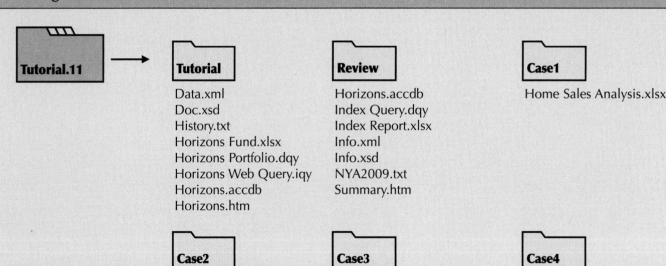

Tutorial.11 →

Tutorial
Data.xml
Doc.xsd
History.txt
Horizons Fund.xlsx
Horizons Portfolio.dqy
Horizons Web Query.iqy
Horizons.accdb
Horizons.htm

Review
Horizons.accdb
Index Query.dqy
Index Report.xlsx
Info.xml
Info.xsd
NYA2009.txt
Summary.htm

Case1
Home Sales Analysis.xlsx

Case2
Confections.accdb
Customer List.odc
Kate's Confections.xlsx
Order Query.dqy
Product List.odc
Product Orders.odc

Case3
Exchange Rate Calculator.xlsx
YRate.xml

Case4
Antiques.accdb
Green Cove Antiques.xlsx
Orders Query.dqy
Sales Types Query.dqy

Objectives

Session 12.1
- Create a macro using the macro recorder
- Work with the Project Explorer and Properties window of the VBA Editor
- Edit a sub procedure
- Run a sub procedure

Session 12.2
- Work with VBA objects, properties, and methods
- Create an input box to retrieve information from the user

Session 12.3
- Create and run If-Then control structures
- Work with comparison and logical operators
- Create message boxes
- Customize the Quick Access Toolbar
- Customize Excel

Expanding Excel with Visual Basic for Applications

Analyzing Weather Data

Case | Center for Atmospheric Science

David Faducci is a researcher at the Midwest Center for Atmospheric Science in Council Bluffs, Iowa. One of his areas of research involves tornadoes. He has collected data on the yearly occurrence of tornadoes in the United States from 1950 to 1999 to analyze the relationship between tornadoes and climate change. One of the questions that interests David is whether tornadoes were occurring at a faster rate in the last 25 years of the twentieth century. To investigate this question, David has compiled statistics on the rate of tornado occurrence and created charts that display the annual numbers of tornadoes in the country.

The research has revealed some interesting results. He is planning to use this information in a kiosk to be run in the public entrance at the center. He wants visitors to be able to interact with the data, choosing which charts or tables of statistics to display. Because David doesn't expect visitors to know how to use Excel, he wants the workbook to contain custom dialog boxes, macro buttons, and menus more suited to his users.

You'll help David complete the project.

Starting Data Files

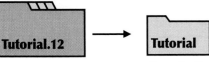

Tutorial.12 →	Tutorial	Review	Case1	Case2	Case3	Case4
	Sample Report.xlsx Tornado.xlsm	Storm.xlsm	Pixal.xlsm Regions.xlsx	Quality.xlsm	Batting.xlsm	(none)

Session 12.1

Developing an Excel Application

Historically, the intensity of tornadoes was classified according to the Fujita Tornado Scale, which rates tornadoes from F0 (a gale-force tornado capable of minor damage) up through F6 (an inconceivably strong tornado capable of widespread destruction). David stored information on the yearly occurrence of tornadoes classified as F0, F1, and F2 or higher. He has also created charts and statistical tables based on his data. You'll open and review David's workbook.

To open and review David's workbook:

▶ **1.** Open the **Tornado** workbook located in the **Tutorial.12\Tutorial** folder included with your Data Files, and then save it as a macro-enabled workbook named **Tornado Analysis** in the same folder.

 Trouble? If a security warning opens, click the Options button and then click the Enable this content option button.

▶ **2.** In the **Documentation** worksheet, enter your name and the current date.

▶ **3.** Review the **Report**, **Time Chart**, **Histogram**, **Statistics**, and **Raw Data** worksheets.

Besides the Documentation sheet, the Tornado Analysis workbook contains five worksheets: Report, Time Chart, Histogram, Statistics, and Raw Data. The Report worksheet contains macro buttons that David wants to use to display analyses of his tornado data. The Time Chart worksheet contains a line chart showing the yearly occurrence of tornadoes over a 50-year period. The Histogram worksheet contains a chart showing the distribution of the annual occurrence of tornadoes divided into two 25-year periods. The Statistics worksheet contains statistics that describe the annual occurrence of tornadoes from 1950 to 1974 and 1975 to 1999. Finally, the Raw Data worksheet contains a table of the actual data that David collected for this report.

Because this workbook will be used by the general public, David wants it to be easy for non-Excel users to operate. He wants to create an Excel application—a workbook that has customized buttons and toolbars for users to work with instead of Excel commands. As a first step, he created the Report worksheet shown in Figure 12-1. The worksheet contains five macro buttons. The first four macro buttons are labeled Statistics, Time Chart, Histogram, and Table. David wants you to create macros for these buttons to display the corresponding worksheets in the workbook. The fifth button, Specify a Tornado Type, will be used to select display charts and statistics on a different tornado type. In addition, each of the remaining worksheets in the workbook contains a macro button, Return to Report Tab, which David wants to use to return to the Report worksheet.

David's proposed application ◀ **Figure 12-1**

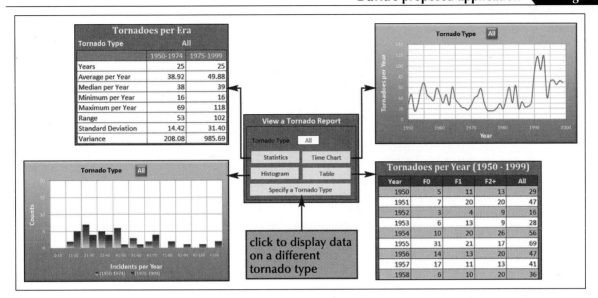

The fastest way to create macros is to use the Excel macro recorder. After recording a macro, you can edit it to make it more suitable for David's needs. The first macro you'll record will display the contents of the Statistics worksheet. You already saved the workbook with macro capability enabled, in preparation for recording macros.

To record the Statistics macro:

▶ 1. If the Excel Developer tab is not on the Ribbon, click the **Office Button** 🔘, click the **Excel Options** button, click **Popular** in the Excel Options dialog box (if necessary), click the **Show Developer** tab in the **Ribbon** check box to insert a check mark, and then click the **OK** button.

▶ 2. Click the **Developer** tab on the Ribbon, and then click the **Record Macro** button in the Code group. The Record Macro dialog box opens.

▶ 3. Type **Statistics** in the Macro name box, and make sure **This Workbook** is selected in the Store macro in box. The Statistics macro will be used only in this workbook.

▶ 4. Type **This macro displays the contents of the Statistics worksheet.** in the Description box.

▶ 5. Click the **OK** button. The dialog box closes, and you can begin to record the macro.

▶ 6. Click the **Statistics** sheet tab, and then press the **Ctrl+Home** keys to select cell A1.

▶ 7. In the Code group on the Developer tab, click the **Stop Recording** button.

You'll run the macro to verify that it works correctly.

To test the Statistics macro:

▶ 1. Click cell **C2** in the Statistics worksheet to make it the active cell, and then switch to the **Report** worksheet.

▶ 2. In the Code group on the Developer tab, click the **Macros** button. The Macro dialog box opens.

▶ 3. Click **Statistics** in the Macro name box, if necessary, and then click the **Run** button. The Statistics worksheet becomes active and cell A1 is selected.

Trouble? If the Statistics macro does not make the Statistics worksheet active and select cell A1, open the Macro dialog box, click Statistics in the Macro name box, and then click the Delete button to delete the macro. Repeat the previous set of steps to record the macro again, and then repeat this set of steps to test the macro.

▶ 4. When you are sure that the macro runs correctly, save the workbook.

Working with the Visual Basic Editor

Tip

You can quickly switch to the Visual Basic Editor by pressing the Alt+F11 keys.

Recall that Excel macros are written in a programming language called Visual Basic for Applications (VBA). VBA is the common language used by all Microsoft Office programs. So after you learn how to use VBA in Excel, you can also use VBA to write and edit macros in other Office products. To edit the Statistics macro, you need to use the Visual Basic Editor.

You'll start the Visual Basic Editor and examine the macro.

To start the Visual Basic Editor:

▶ 1. In the Code group on the Developer tab, click the **Macros** button.

▶ 2. Click **Statistics** in the Macro name box, if necessary, and then click the **Edit** button. The Visual Basic Editor opens. See Figure 12-2.

Figure 12-2	Visual Basic Editor

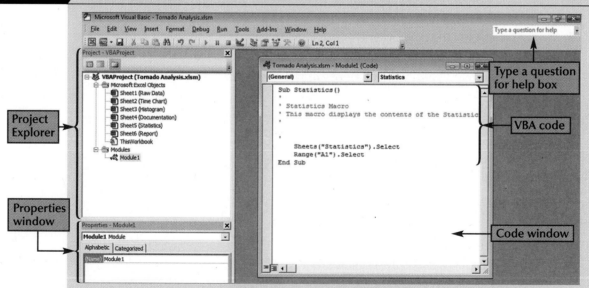

Trouble? If your Visual Basic Editor window does not look like the one shown in Figure 12-2, it might be set up differently on your computer. You'll change the appearance of the Editor shortly.

The Visual Basic Editor usually displays three windows: the Project Explorer window, the Properties window, and the Code window. You can use these windows to examine the structure and content of workbooks as well as macros. You might see other windows, depending on how the Editor was installed on your system. You'll close these windows and then reopen them one at a time.

To clear the Visual Basic Editor:

► **1.** Close each open window within the Visual Basic Editor, including the Project Explorer and Properties windows.

Examining Project Explorer

One important use of the Visual Basic Editor is to manage your projects. A **project** is a collection of macros, worksheets, data-entry forms, and other items that make up the customized application you're trying to create. **Project Explorer** is the window in the Visual Basic Editor that displays a hierarchical list of all currently open projects and their contents.

The Project Explorer window is **dockable**, meaning that you can drag it to the edge of the screen, and the window stays on top of other windows. Docking a window is useful when you want the contents of that window to always remain in view, but the drawback is that the window takes up screen space. The alternative is to let the window float free within the Visual Basic Editor. You can resize or minimize a floating window as you would other windows. You'll display Project Explorer, and float the window to make it easier to view the other windows you'll open.

To view and undock Project Explorer:

► **1.** Click **View** on the menu bar, and then click **Project Explorer**. The Project Explorer window opens with Project – VBAProject in its title bar.

► **2.** Right-click the **title bar** of the Project Explorer window, and then click **Dockable** to remove the Dockable check mark. Figure 12-3 shows the contents of the floating Project Explorer window.

Undocked Project Explorer window | Figure 12-3

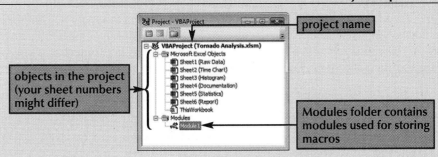

Trouble? If the shortcut menu does not appear when you right-click the title bar, Project Explorer is already undocked. Continue with Step 3.

► **3.** If the Project Explorer window fills the Visual Basic Editor window, click the **Restore Window** button 🔲 to resize the Project Explorer window.

Like Windows Explorer, Project Explorer allows you to view your project components hierarchically. At the top of the hierarchy is the project itself. Each project is identified by a project icon 🐝 , followed by the project name and the filename in parentheses. The default project name given to new projects is "VBAProject." You might see other projects listed in Project Explorer, including projects for Excel add-ins such as Solver. Within each project are various items called objects. An **object** is any element within the Excel working environment such as a worksheet, cell, workbook, or even Excel itself. As shown in Figure 12-3, some of the objects listed for the Tornado Analysis workbook include each worksheet and "ThisWorkbook," which refers to the Tornado Analysis workbook itself. To help you manage and organize projects, you can rename a project with a meaningful and easily recognized name. You can also enter a description of the project, so you can recall its purpose or goal and provide others a clear understanding of the project. You can rename a project in the Project Explorer window.

You'll change the default project name, "VBAProject," to a more informative name for other users and enter a description of the project in the Project Properties dialog box.

To rename the project and add a description:

▶ 1. If necessary, click the **title bar** of the Project Explorer window to make it the active window.

▶ 2. Click **Tools** on the menu bar, and then click **VBAProject Properties**. The VBAProject – Project Properties dialog box opens.

   Because project names cannot include spaces, you can use an underscore (_) to separate the words in the name.

▶ 3. On the General tab, type **Tornado_Analysis** in the Project Name box, and then press the **Tab** key.

▶ 4. In the Project Description box, type **Application to review tornado annual occurrence data**.

▶ 5. Click the **OK** button. Project Explorer displays the new project name.

Using the Properties Window

When you entered the name and description of your project, you were actually modifying two of its properties. A **property** is an attribute of an object that defines one of its characteristics, such as its name, size, color, or location on the screen. All objects have properties. You can view a list of properties for any object in the **Properties window**. You'll display the Properties window for the Tornado_Analysis project.

To view the Properties window:

▶ 1. Click **Tornado_Analysis (Tornado Analysis.xlsm)** in Project Explorer.

▶ 2. Click **View** on the menu bar, and then click **Properties Window**. The Properties window opens.

▶ 3. Right-click the **title bar** of the Properties window, and then uncheck **Dockable** on the shortcut menu. The Properties window floats in the Visual Basic Editor. See Figure 12-4.

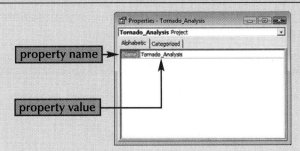

> **Trouble?** If you don't see a shortcut menu when you right-click the title bar, the Properties window is already undocked, and you can continue with the tutorial.

The Properties window displays each property's name in the left column and its value in the right column. To view the list of properties in alphabetical order and by category, you can click the Alphabetic and Categorized tabs at the top of the window. Figure 12-4 lists only one property, the Name property, which has the value Tornado_Analysis.

You'll change the name of the Raw Data worksheet in the Tornado Analysis workbook to "Table." You could do this in Excel, but changing the name from within VBA will give you practice with Project Explorer and the Properties window.

To rename the Raw Data worksheet in the Project Explorer window:

▶ 1. Click **Sheet1 (Raw Data)** in the Project Explorer window. The Properties window shows a list of properties associated with the Raw Data worksheet.

▶ 2. In the Properties window, click the **Alphabetic** tab, if necessary, to show its contents. The Properties window has two columns. The left column contains the name of the property and the right column contains the property value.

▶ 3. Locate and click the **Name** property in the list of properties in the first column (it is located directly above the ScrollArea property), and then press the **Tab** key to select the property value, Raw Data.

▶ 4. Type **Table** as the new name, and then press the **Enter** key. The name of the worksheet displayed in the Project Explorer window changes to Table. When you return to the Tornado Analysis workbook in Excel, you'll find that the worksheet name has changed there as well.

Many properties can be listed in the Properties window. The meaning of some of them is clear (such as the Name property), whereas others might require further explanation. You can use Visual Basic online Help to obtain more information about a particular property in the Properties window. In general, if you are not sure what a VBA button, command, or object does, or the meaning of an element in the VBA programming language, you can enter a description of the item in the Type a question for Help box to view documentation on it. You'll use online Help now to learn more about one of the properties of the Main Menu worksheet.

To view information about the ScrollArea property:

▶ **1.** Type **ScrollArea** in the Type a question for help box located in the upper-right corner of the Visual Basic Editor window, and then press the **Enter** key. The Excel Help window opens.

▶ **2.** Click **ScrollArea Property** in the search results list. The Help topic for ScrollArea property opens in the Help window.

▶ **3.** Read the topic, and then close the Excel Help window.

Naming Modules

When you viewed the project in Project Explorer, you might have noticed the Modules folder at the bottom of the object list. A **module** is a collection of VBA macros. A project might contain several modules, with each one containing macros that accomplish a common set of tasks. For example, you might group all the macros that handle printing tasks in one module and the macros that format worksheets in another. When you recorded the Statistics macro, the Visual Basic Editor placed the macro in a new module with the default name Module1. A good practice is to rename the module with a descriptive name that describes the type of macros it will contain.

You'll rename Module1 as "Sheet_Macros" because the macros in this module will be used to display different worksheets in the workbook.

To rename the macro module:

▶ **1.** Click **Module1** in Project Explorer. The Module is selected.

▶ **2.** Click the Properties window **title bar** to make the window active.

▶ **3.** Double-click **Module1** in the (Name) row to select it, type **Sheet_Macros**, and then press the **Enter** key. The name of the module in the Project Explorer window and the Properties window changes to Sheet_Macros. See Figure 12-5.

Figure 12-5 ▶ **Renamed project module**

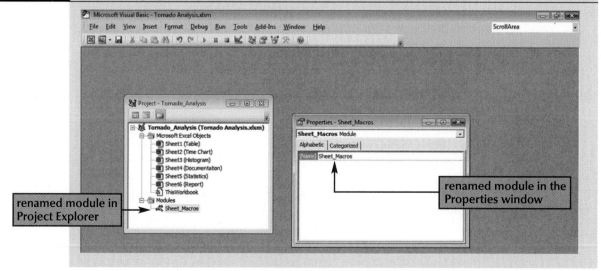

Viewing the Code Window

When you want to view the contents of the macros in your project modules, you use the Code window. The **Code window** displays the VBA macro code associated with any item in Project Explorer. You saw the Code window when you first opened the Visual Basic Editor. You'll reopen it now.

Tip

To open the Code window to the contents of a specific module, select the module in the Project Explorer window and then press the F7 key.

To view the Code window:

▶ **1.** Click **View** on the menu bar, and then click **Code**. The Code window opens, floating in the Visual Basic Editor. The Code window displays the lines of VBA code that make up your Statistics macro. See Figure 12-6.

Floating Code window ◀ **Figure 12-6**

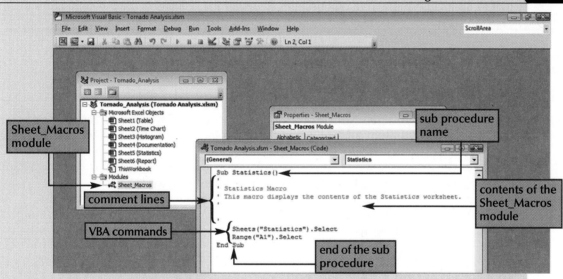

Working with Sub Procedures

The macro you recorded earlier is a special example of a procedure. Visual Basic supports three kinds of procedures: sub procedures, function procedures, and property procedures. A **sub procedure** performs an action on your project or workbook, such as formatting a cell or displaying a chart. You created a sub procedure when you recorded the Statistics macro. A **function procedure** returns a value. Function procedures are often used to create custom functions that can be entered in worksheet cells. A **property procedure** is used to create custom properties for the objects in your project.

Because your project deals with displaying different worksheets within the Tornado Analysis workbook, you'll create only sub procedures.

Introducing Sub Procedures

To create a sub procedure without using the macro recorder, you need to understand the basics of VBA syntax. **Syntax** refers to the set of rules that specify how you must enter certain commands so that VBA interprets them correctly, much like the grammatical syntax rules that make our sentences understandable to others. If you use improper syntax, Excel cannot run the macro.

All sub procedures follow the general syntax:

```
Sub Procedure_Name(parameters)
    VBA commands and comments
End Sub
```

Procedure_Name is the name of the macro, and *parameters* are values passed to the sub procedure that control the operation of the procedure.

Review the code generated by the macro recorder when it created the Statistics macro shown in Figure 12-6. The Statistics macro has the sub procedure name *Statistics*. Although the Statistics sub procedure has no parameter values, the parentheses are required anyway. After the name of the sub procedure, the description you entered in the Record Macro dialog box appears as a comment. A **comment** is a statement that describes the behavior or purpose of a procedure, but does not perform any action. Comments must begin with an apostrophe ('). The Editor displays comments in a green font to distinguish them from other statements. After the comments are the commands to select the Statistics worksheet and to select cell A1 on that worksheet. The End Sub line signals the end of the Statistics sub procedure. If you want more information about sub procedures or about any of the commands in the Statistics macro, use online Help.

> **Tip**
>
> Use comment lines to explain the purpose of the macro and how it works without affecting the code.

Creating a Sub Procedure Using Copy and Paste

The Statistics sub procedure you created displays the Statistics worksheet, but you need additional procedures to display other worksheets in the workbook. You could use the macro recorder to create these other sub procedures, but because the code will be very similar to the Statistics sub procedure, you can simply copy it. You'll start by creating a sub procedure called *Time_Chart* that displays the Time Chart worksheet.

You can enter new sub procedures into the Code window either by typing the VBA commands directly or by using the Insert Procedure command. You'll use the Insert Procedure command to help you create the new procedure.

To begin creating a new procedure:

▶ **1.** If necessary, click the **title bar** of the Code window to activate it.

▶ **2.** Click **Insert** on the menu bar and then click **Procedure**. The Add Procedure dialog box opens. You'll enter the name and type of procedure you're creating.

▶ **3.** Type **Time_Chart** in the Name box to assign a title to the sub procedure. See Figure 12-7.

Figure 12-7 ▶ **Add Procedure dialog box**

> **Tip**
>
> Use descriptive names for sub procedures. Procedure names can be up to 255 characters in length and cannot contain spaces.

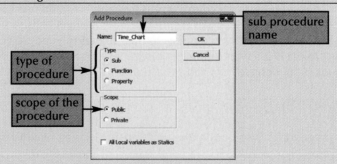

▶ **4.** Click the **Sub** and **Public** option buttons to select them, if necessary, and then click the **OK** button. The Code window displays the beginning and ending lines of the new sub procedure. A horizontal line separates the new procedure from the Statistics sub procedure. See Figure 12-8.

New sub procedure inserted ◀ **Figure 12-8**

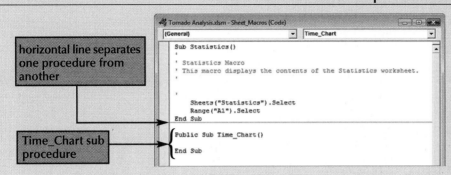

horizontal line separates one procedure from another

Time_Chart sub procedure

The new sub procedure starts with the term *Public*, which means that the sub procedure is available to other modules in the project. The Statistics sub procedure is also public, even though the text *Public* is not shown. All procedures are considered public unless prefixed with the term *Private*. In some cases, you'll want to hide procedures in one module from other modules to avoid conflicts in procedure names.

Next, you'll copy the VBA code from the Statistics sub procedure into the Time_Chart sub procedure. If you had not already recorded the Statistics macro, you would have to enter the codes manually. You add, delete, and replace text in the Code window the same way you do in any text editor.

To copy and paste the VBA code from the Statistics sub procedure:

▶ 1. If necessary, scroll up the Code window until you can see the entire Statistics sub procedure.

▶ 2. Position the insertion point to the left of the apostrophe for the first comment line located directly below the Sub Statistics() line of code.

▶ 3. Select all the comment lines and VBA commands, beginning with the first apostrophe and ending with the Range("A1"). Select line. Do not select either the Sub Statistics() or the End Sub line.

▶ 4. On the Standard toolbar, click the **Copy** button 🖹. The selected code is copied.

▶ 5. Scroll down the Code window, if necessary, and then click the blank line below the Time_Chart sub procedure name.

▶ 6. On the Standard toolbar, click the **Paste** button 🖹. The code you copied from the Statistics sub procedure is pasted into the Time_Chart sub procedure.

You need to edit the pasted code. You'll replace all occurrences of *Statistics* with *Time Chart*. You could do this by selecting the text and typing the new text. But it is faster and more efficient to use the Replace command to replace all the occurrences at once.

To replace text in the Time_Chart sub procedure:

▶ 1. Click **Edit** on the menu bar, and then click **Replace**. The Replace dialog box opens.

▶ 2. Type **Statistics** in the Find What box, and then press the **Tab** key.

▶ 3. Type **Time Chart** in the Replace With box.

▶ 4. In the Search section, click the **Current Procedure** option button. This option specifies that text is replaced only within the current procedure (in this case, the Time_Chart procedure).

Tip

To replace text throughout the current procedure, current module (across several procedures), or current project (across several modules), click the corresponding option button in the Replace dialog box.

5. Click the **Replace All** button. A dialog box indicates that three occurrences of the Statistics text were replaced.

6. Click the **OK** button, and then click the **Cancel** button to close the Replace dialog box. The Time_Chart sub procedure is edited. See Figure 12-9.

Figure 12-9 ▶ **Edited Time_Chart sub procedure**

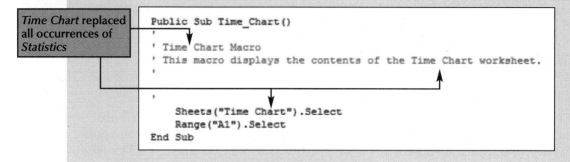

Time Chart replaced all occurrences of Statistics

```
Public Sub Time_Chart()
'
' Time Chart Macro
' This macro displays the contents of the Time Chart worksheet.
'

'
    Sheets("Time Chart").Select
    Range("A1").Select
End Sub
```

Running a Sub Procedure

You need to test the new procedure you created in the Tornado Analysis workbook. Because you replaced the name *Statistics* with *Time Chart*, the procedure should display the contents of the Time Chart worksheet when you run it. You could test this macro by running it from the workbook or from within the Visual Basic Editor. You'll run the Time_Chart procedure in the Visual Basic Editor to verify that it opens the Time Chart worksheet.

To run the Time_Chart sub procedure:

1. With the insertion point still within the Time_Chart sub procedure, click **Run** on the menu bar and then click **Run Sub/UserForm**. The Visual Basic Editor runs the current sub procedure selected in the Code window, which, in this case, is the Time_Chart sub procedure.

   Trouble? If the Visual Basic Editor displays an error message, you probably made a mistake while creating the Time_Chart sub procedure. Click the End button in the dialog box, check your code against the code in the figures, correct any errors that you find, and then repeat Step 1.

   Because you can't see the Tornado Analysis workbook, you need to return to the workbook to make sure that running the sub procedure actually selected the Time Chart worksheet.

2. Switch to Excel and the Tornado Analysis workbook. The Time Chart worksheet is the active sheet in the workbook and cell A1 is selected on the sheet.

3. Save the workbook, and then return to the Visual Basic Editor.

You'll use the same process to create macros that display the remaining worksheets in the Tornado Analysis workbook. You'll copy and edit the sub procedure to display the contents of the Histogram, Table, and Report worksheets.

To create the remaining sub procedures:

1. With the Code window active in the Visual Basic Editor, click **Insert** on the menu bar, and then click **Procedure**. The Add Procedure dialog box opens.

Tip

To step through your sub procedure one line at a time, click in the sub procedure code, and then repeatedly press the F8 key. To run the entire sub procedure, press the F5 key.

2. Type **Histogram** in the Name box, verify that the **Sub** and **Public** option buttons are selected, and then click the **OK** button.

   Because the selected lines of code are still on the Clipboard, you can paste them recopying the code from the Statistics sub procedure.

3. On the Standard toolbar, click the **Paste** button 🖺.

4. Click **Edit** on the menu bar, and then click **Replace**. The Replace dialog box opens.

5. Type **Statistics** in the Find What box, type **Histogram** in the Replace With box, verify that the **Current Procedure** option button is selected, and then click the **Replace All** button.

6. Click the **OK** button to confirm that three occurrences of the word *Statistics* were replaced, and then click the **Cancel** button to close the Replace dialog box.

7. Repeat Steps 1 through 6 to create a sub procedure named **Table**, replacing all occurrences of the word *Statistics* with *Table*.

8. Repeat Steps 1 through 6 to create a sub procedure named **Report**, replacing all occurrences of the word *Statistics* with *Report*.

   Trouble? If you made a mistake in creating these sub procedures, click the Undo button on the Standard toolbar to reverse the action.

You've created five sub procedures to display each of the worksheets in the Tornado Analysis workbook. You'll return to Excel and assign those macros to macro buttons in the workbook. You do not need to save the code within the VBA Editor because macro code is part of the Excel workbook. When you save the workbook, you are also saving the macro code.

To assign the sub procedures to macro buttons:

1. Click **File** on the menu bar, and then click **Close and Return to Microsoft Excel**. The Visual Basic Editor closes and you return to the Tornado Analysis workbook.

2. Switch to the **Report** worksheet, right-click the **Statistics** macro button, and then click **Assign Macro** on the shortcut menu. The Assign Macro dialog box opens.

3. Click **Statistics** in the list of macro names, and then click the **OK** button to assign the macro to the button.

4. Repeat Steps 2 and 3 for the **Time Chart**, **Histogram**, and **Table** macro buttons, assigning the appropriate macros to them.

5. Click the **Statistics** macro button and verify that the Statistics worksheet opens.

   Trouble? If the worksheet doesn't open, the macro button might be selected (indicated by selection handles around the button). If the button is selected, click any cell to deselect the macro button, and then click the button again.

6. In the Statistics worksheet, right-click the **Return to Report Tab** macro button, click **Assign Macro** on the shortcut menu, and then double-click **Report** to assign that macro to the button.

7. Click the **Return to Report Tab** macro button and verify that the Report worksheet opens.

8. Repeat Steps 5 through 7 to test the **Time Chart**, **Histogram**, and **Table** macro buttons and assign the **Report** macro to the Return to Report Tab macro button on each worksheet.

9. Test that you can move through the workbook using only the macro buttons, and then save and close the workbook.

InSight	Learning to Use VBA

The best way to learn VBA is by doing. Start with the macro recorder to generate VBA code. The code is guaranteed to be free of syntax errors, so you can identify the key elements of the VBA language. However, the macro recorder does not write the most efficient code and records commands and actions you might not want or need in a finished project. Experienced programmers might use the macro recorder as a starting point, but quickly edit the generated code to remove the extraneous material. As you learn more about VBA, you'll likely rely on the macro recorder less often.

The next source of information for a new programmer is the VBA Editor online Help. The online Help contains descriptions of all of the VBA commands and operations. The Help windows also include code samples you can often apply to your own projects.

After becoming familiar with the VBA Editor online Help, write some code. The interactive tools guide you to use the correct syntax by identifying syntax errors as you type them rather than after the program is run. You often learn more from overcoming mistakes than by reading a hundred programming manuals.

Finally, examine what other programmers are doing. In many cases, program code is password-protected, but not always. You can learn from other's techniques and the Web is a great source of VBA code samples. However, if you do use code from another programmer, be sure to obtain permission first and to cite the programmer's work in any publication.

So far, you have created macros that allow users to easily move between sheets in the workbook and assigned them to macro buttons. In the next session, you'll create a sub procedure to display information on different tornado types. In the process, you'll learn how to write and interpret VBA sub procedures.

Review	Session 12.1 Quick Check

1. Describe what you use each of the following VBA elements for: (a) Project Explorer, (b) Properties window, (c) Code window
2. Define the following terms: *project, object, property, module, syntax*
3. How can you get help on a property listed in the Properties window?
4. What are the three types of procedures in VBA?
5. Write the general syntax of a sub procedure.
6. Why would a project contain several modules?

Session 12.2

Introducing Visual Basic for Applications

The next macro you need to create for David's application will allow users to view statistics on different tornado types. First, you need to learn a little more about the VBA programming language. The following discussion provides an overview of some of the concepts involved in writing a VBA program. You'll use a sample workbook as you explore the syntax of the Visual Basic for Applications language.

To open the sample workbook:

1. Open the **Sample Report** workbook located in the **Tutorial.12\Tutorial** folder included with your Data Files.

2. Review the contents of the **Yearly Counts**, **Incidents**, and **Statistics** worksheets. Each worksheet describes the prevalence of tornadoes in the latter half of the twentieth century. You have already seen a variation of these pages in the Tornado Analysis workbook.

3. Switch to the **Yearly Counts** worksheet, and then click cell **A1**, if necessary, to make it the active cell.

4. Press the **Alt+F11** keys to open the Visual Basic Editor.

Using the Immediate Window to Learn VBA

As you work in VBA, you might want to see the effects of a single command rather than an entire sub procedure. You can run single command lines in the Visual Basic Editor **Immediate window**. As you enter a command in the Immediate window, its effects are immediately applied to the workbook, making it an ideal way to learn VBA syntax and debug programs that fail to run correctly. You'll open the Immediate window, and then use it to interactively explore the different elements of the VBA programming language.

To open the Immediate window:

1. Click **View** on the menu bar, and then click **Immediate Window**. The Immediate window opens.

2. If the Immediate window is docked at the bottom of the screen, right-click the **Immediate** window, and then click the **Dockable** check mark to undock the window. See Figure 12-10.

> **Tip**
>
> Another way to open the Immediate window is by pressing the Ctrl+G keys in the Visual Basic Editor.

Immediate window in the Visual Basic Editor | **Figure 12-10**

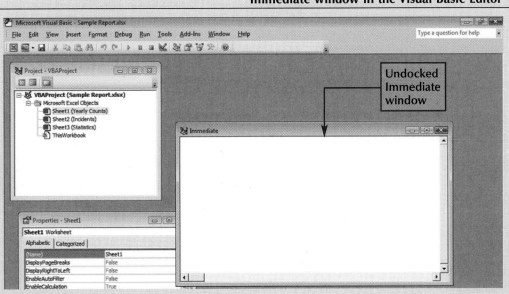

Trouble? If the Immediate window displays command lines, you need to delete them. Drag to select the lines in the Immediate window, and then press the Delete key. The window is blank.

Referring to Objects

VBA is an **object-oriented programming language**, in which tasks are performed by manipulating objects. Almost anything in Excel, from a single cell, to an entire worksheet, to the Excel application itself, is considered an **Excel object**. You can perform any task on these objects that you can perform in Excel, such as creating charts, moving worksheets, or entering formulas into cells. Figure 12-11 describes some of the important Excel objects you'll use to create VBA programs.

Figure 12-11 ▶ **VBA objects in Excel**

Excel Object	Description
Range	A cell range in a worksheet
Name	A range name in a workbook
Chart	A chart in a workbook (either embedded within a worksheet or stored as a chart sheet)
ChartObject	A chart embedded within a worksheet
Worksheet	A worksheet in a workbook
Workbook	An Excel workbook
VBAProject	A VBA project
Application	The Excel application itself

Objects are often grouped into collections, which are themselves objects, called **collection objects**. For example, a sheet in a workbook is an object, but the collection of all the sheets in a workbook is also an object. To refer to a specific object in a collection, use the following syntax:

```
object_collection(id)
```

In this syntax, *object_collection* is the name of the object collection and *id* is either a name or ID number that identifies an object in the collection. For example, the object collection Sheets refers to all of the sheets in a particular workbook. The VBA code that references the Statistics worksheet is *Sheets("Statistics")* where *Sheets* is the object collection and *"Statistics"* is the name of a specific member in the collection. You could also use the object reference *Sheets(5)* because the Statistics worksheet is the fifth object in the collection of worksheets. The id number is not a location in the workbook. For example, the Statistics worksheet is the fifth worksheet in the collection, but it might be placed anywhere within the workbook. Figure 12-12 provides other examples of VBA code that use object collections.

Figure 12-12 ▶ **Object collection examples**

Object Collection	Description
Range("A1:B10")	The collection of cells in the range A1:B10
Names("F1Data")	The F1Data range name
ChartObjects(3)	The third embedded chart in a worksheet
Charts(3)	The third chart sheet in a workbook
Sheets("Statistics")	The Statistics worksheet
Workbooks("Tornado Analysis")	The Tornado Analysis workbook
Windows(2)	The second open Excel workbook window

VBA organizes objects and object collections in a hierarchy with the Excel application at the top and the individual cells of a workbook at the bottom. This hierarchy is often referred to as the **Excel Object Model**. Figure 12-13 shows a small portion of the hierarchy that the Excel Object Model follows. You can view the complete listing of the hierarchy using the online Help in the Visual Basic Editor.

A portion of the Excel Object Model ◀ **Figure 12-13**

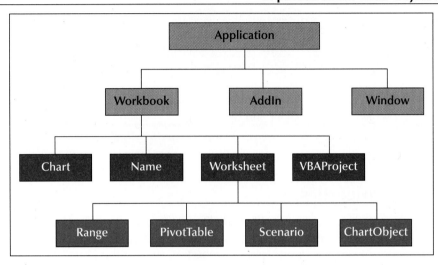

Sometimes you'll refer to an object by indicating its place within the Excel Object Model. The general syntax for expressing an object's location within this hierarchy is:

```
object1.object2.object3
```

In this syntax, *object1* is an object at the upper level of the hierarchy, *object2* is next in line, and *object3* is at the lower level in the hierarchy, and so forth. For example, the complete object reference to cell A1 in the Statistics worksheet of the Tornado workbook within the Excel application is:

```
Application.Workbooks("Tornado").Sheets("Statistics").Range("A1")
```

This object reference starts at the top level in the Excel Object Model (the Excel application) and drills down to a specific cell in a worksheet (cell A1). If you don't include the complete object hierarchy, the object is assumed to be based in the active application, workbook, and worksheet. For example, the following object reference refers to cell A1 of the Statistics worksheet, and the workbook is assumed to be the active workbook:

```
Sheets("Statistics").Range("A1")
```

Similarly, the following object reference refers to cell A1 of the active sheet in the active workbook:

```
Range("A1")
```

To help you work with the hierarchy of objects in the Excel Object Model, VBA provides special object names to refer directly to certain objects. For example, ActiveSheet refers to the worksheet currently displayed in the workbook. Figure 12-14 describes some of these special object names.

Figure 12-14 ▷ **Special object names**

Object Name	Description
ActiveCell	The currently selected cell
ActiveChart	The currently selected chart
ActiveSheet	The currently selected sheet
ActiveWindow	The currently selected window
ActiveWorkbook	The current workbook
ThisCell	The cell from which a custom function is being run
ThisWorkbook	The workbook containing the macro code that is currently running

Tip

The ActiveWorkbook is the workbook selected when the macro is running, whereas the ThisWorkbook object refers to the workbook in which the macro code has been stored.

As far as VBA is concerned, the following two lines are equivalent because they both reference cell A1 of the active sheet and workbook:

```
Range("A1")
ActiveWorkbook.ActiveSheet.Range("A1")
```

Modifying Properties

The VBA language alters objects by either modifying the object's properties or applying a method to the object. Properties are the attributes that characterize the object. For example, a worksheet cell supports several properties, such as the value or formula contained in the cell, the formatting applied to the cell's appearance, or the text of the comment that might be attached to the cell. Figure 12-15 describes some Excel objects and the properties associated with them. Note that some properties are themselves objects.

Figure 12-15 ▷ **Objects and their properties**

Object	Property	Description
Range	Address	The cell reference of the range
	Comment	A comment attached to the cell
	Formula	The formula entered into the cell
	Value	The value of the cell
Name	RefersTo	The cell(s) that a range name refers to
	Value	The value of the cell referred to by the range name
Worksheet	Name	The name of the worksheet
	Visible	Whether the worksheet is visible or hidden
Chart	ChartTitle	The text of the chart's title
	ChartType	The type of the chart
	HasLegend	Whether the chart has a legend
Workbook	HasPassword	Whether the workbook has a password
	Name	The name of the workbook
	Path	The folder and drive in which the workbook is stored
	Saved	Whether the workbook has been saved

This list is only a small sample of the vast number of objects and properties available in VBA programs. Literally, everything contained in Excel can be expressed in terms of an object or a property.

To change the property of an object, you enter the following statement:

```
object.property=expression
```

In this statement, *object* is the object name, *property* is the name of the property, and *expression* is a value that you want to assign to the property. For example, to change the value of cell A2 in the active sheet to 395, you would use the following command:

```
Range("A2").Value=395
```

Figure 12-16 shows other examples of VBA statements that use this syntax. The third example changes the Name property of the Raw Data worksheet object to *Table*. You did this in the previous session when you changed the name of the worksheet in the Properties window. This example shows how you would write the command to do the same thing in VBA.

Tip

Property values containing text strings and formulas must be placed within quotation marks; property values containing numeric values or Boolean values (true or false) do not.

Examples of changing a property's value | **Figure 12-16**

VBA Code	Description
ActiveCell.Value=23	Changes the value of the active cell to 23
Range("A5").Formula="SUM(A1:A4)"	Changes the formula of cell A1 to add the values in the range A1:A4
Range("A5").Font.Italic=true	Displays the text of cell A5 in an italic font
Worksheets("Raw Data").Name="Table"	Changes the name of the Raw Data worksheet to *Table*
ActiveWorkbook.Password="weather"	Changes the password of the current workbook to *weather*
Application.StatusBar="Running macro"	Changes the status bar text to *Running macro*
Application.StatusBar=false	Resets the status bar text to its default value
Application.ScreenUpdating=false	Turns off screen updating within Excel
Application.ScreenUpdating=true	Turns on screen updating within Excel

You can also use an object property statement to turn a property on or off. The following VBA command hides the Documentation worksheet from the user by setting the sheet's Visible property to false; to make the worksheet visible again, you switch the value to true:

```
Sheets("Documentation").Visible=false
```

You'll work with objects and properties as you write VBA commands to modify the contents of the Sample Report workbook. You'll write a VBA command in the Immediate window to change the value of a worksheet cell. When you type a VBA command in the Immediate window (and, as you'll see later, in the Code window), ScreenTips describe how to correctly enter the command.

To modify cell F6 in the active worksheet with an object property statement:

▶ **1.** With the insertion point in the Immediate window, type **Range(** to begin the command. A ScreenTip indicates that to complete the Range object, you need to enter one or two cell addresses. See Figure 12-17.

Command in the Immediate window | **Figure 12-17**

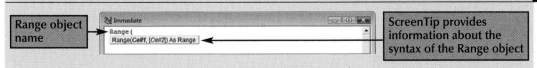

Range object name

Immediate

Range (
Range(*Cell1*, [*Cell2*]) As Range

ScreenTip provides information about the syntax of the Range object

▶ **2.** Type **"F6").** (including the period) to continue entering the command. A list of properties and methods associated with the Range object opens. (You'll learn about methods shortly.) From this list, you can select the appropriate property for the object. See Figure 12-18.

| Figure 12-18 | List of properties and methods |

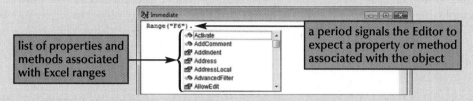

▶ **3.** Scroll down the list, and then double-click **Value**. The text string Value is inserted into the command.

▶ **4.** Type **=49** to complete the command line, and then press the **Enter** key. The command Range("F6").Value=49 is entered into the Immediate window. See Figure 12-19.

| Figure 12-19 | Completed VBA command to set a cell value |

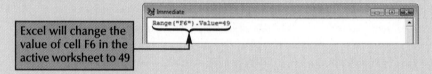

When you pressed the Enter key, the Editor ran the command, changing the value of cell F6 in the active worksheet to 49. To verify this change, you'll return to the Sample Report workbook.

▶ **5.** Press the **Alt+Tab** keys to return to the Sample Report workbook, and then verify that the value in cell F6 is 49. The original value in the cell was 29. You'll change it back with another VBA command.

▶ **6.** Press the **Alt+Tab** keys to return to the Visual Basic Editor, type **Range("F6"). Value=29** in the Immediate window, and then press the **Enter** key. The completed command is entered in the Immediate window and runs.

▶ **7.** Press the **Alt+Tab** keys to return to the Sample Report workbook, verify that the value in cell F6 is 29, and then press the **Alt+Tab** keys to return to the Visual Basic Editor.

Tip

To save time when running similar commands, press the Up Arrow key to go to the previous command, edit it, and then press the Enter key to run the revised command.

You cannot use the Undo button on the Quick Access Toolbar in the Excel workbook to return cell F6 to its original value. The Undo and Redo buttons record the keystrokes and commands you made within the Excel window. They do not record the effect of VBA commands, which are applied to the objects found in the workbook.

Applying Methods

Next, you'll apply a method to an object. A **method** is an action that can be performed on an object, such as closing a workbook or printing the contents of a worksheet. The syntax to apply a method is:

```
object.method
```

In this statement, *object* is the name of the object and *method* is the name of the VBA method. One method you can apply to a worksheet is to select it. The following command selects the Statistics worksheet in the active workbook:

```
Sheets("Statistics").Select
```

Figure 12-20 describes methods associated with different VBA objects.

Objects and their methods ◄ **Figure 12-20**

Object	Method	Description
Range	Clear	Clears all formulas and values in the range
	Copy	Copies the values in the range to the Clipboard
	Merge	Merges the cells in the range
Worksheet	Delete	Deletes the worksheet
	Select	Selects (and displays) the worksheet
Workbook	Close	Closes the workbook
	Protect	Protects the workbook
	Save	Saves the workbook
Chart	Copy	Copies the chart to the Clipboard
	Select	Selects the chart
	Delete	Deletes the chart
Charts	Select	Selects the chart sheets in the workbook
Worksheets	Select	Selects the worksheets in the workbook

You'll apply the Select method to the Statistics worksheet.

To apply the Select method to the Statistics worksheet:

▶ **1.** Press the **Enter** key to move the insertion point to a new line in the Immediate window, type **Sheets("Statistics").Select**, and then press the **Enter** key. The Statistics worksheet is active.

You can also use the Select method with a worksheet cell to select it, making it the active cell.

▶ **2.** Type **Range("D13").Select** in the Immediate window, and then press the **Enter** key. Cell D13 is the active cell in the worksheet.

▶ **3.** Press the **Alt+Tab** keys to return to the Sample Report workbook, and then verify that the Statistics worksheet is the active sheet and cell D13 is the active cell.

Methods often have parameters that govern how they are applied. A workbook object has the SaveAs method for saving the workbook to a file, but to run the SaveAs method you need to supply a filename. The following syntax is used to apply parameter values to a method:

```
object.method parameter1:=value1 parameter2:=value2...
```

In this syntax, *object* is the name of an object, *method* is a method that can be applied to that object, *parameter1* and *parameter2* are the names of parameters associated with the method, and *value1* and *value2* are the values assigned to those parameters. To save the active workbook using the filename Budget.xlsx, you would run the following VBA command:

```
ActiveWorkbook.SaveAs Filename:="Budget.xlsx"
```

Figure 12-21 describes other ways of applying methods with parameter values to an object.

Figure 12-21 | Applying a method with parameters

VBA Code	Description
Range("A1").Copy Destination:=Range("A5")	Copies the contents of cell A1 into cell A5
Range("A1").AddComment Text:="Total Assets"	Adds the comment *Total Assets* to cell A1
Sheets("Sheet 1").Move After:=Sheets("Sheet 3")	Moves the Sheet 1 worksheet after Sheet 3
ActiveWorkbook.SaveAs Filename:="Tornado Analysis"	Saves the active workbook as *Tornado Analysis*
ActiveWorkbook.Protect Password:="tornado"	Protects the current workbook using the password *tornado*
Workbooks.Open Filename:="Budget.xlsx"	Opens the Budget.xlsx file, adding it to the collection of open workbooks

You'll write a VBA command to move the Statistics worksheet directly before the Yearly Counts worksheet. You'll apply the Move method and set the Before parameter, which defines before which sheet in the workbook to place the worksheet.

To apply the Move method with the Before parameter:

▶ 1. Press the **Alt+Tab** keys to return to the Visual Basic Editor, click in the **Immediate** window, press the **Enter** key, type **Sheets("Statistics").Move Before:= Sheets("Yearly Counts")**, and then press the **Enter** key. See Figure 12-22.

Figure 12-22 | Method with a parameter

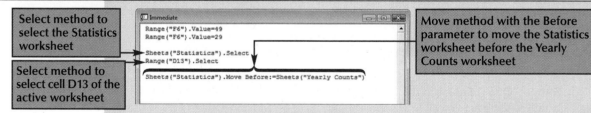

Select method to select the Statistics worksheet

Select method to select cell D13 of the active worksheet

Move method with the Before parameter to move the Statistics worksheet before the Yearly Counts worksheet

Trouble? If the Immediate window displays an error message, you might have entered the code incorrectly. Close the dialog box and then compare your code to the code shown in Figure 12-22, editing it as needed.

▶ 2. Press the **Alt+Tab** keys to switch to the Sample Report workbook, and then verify that the Statistics worksheet is before the Yearly Counts worksheet at the front of the workbook.

▶ 3. Press the **Alt+Tab** keys to return to the Visual Basic Editor.

Another way of entering an object method is to use the following syntax, which requires that the parameter values be entered in a specific order as determined by the syntax for the method that is being applied:

```
object.method(value1, value2, ...)
```

However, you must know exactly what parameters are required for the method and in what order they need to be entered. For example, to save the active workbook in the Budget.xlsx file, you could run the following VBA command:

```
ActiveWorkbook.SaveAs("Budget.xlsx")
```

The SaveAs method has only one required parameter value, the filename. The filename must be entered before the other parameters, which are optional.

Working with Variables and Values

So far, you've written code for tasks that are more easily accomplished within Excel. The power of VBA really begins when you start using variables. A **variable** is a named element in a program that can be used to store and retrieve information. Every variable is identified by a unique **variable name**. For example, you could declare a variable named *tornado_type* and use it to store the type of tornado data displayed in the Tornado Analysis workbook. Variables are case-sensitive. For example, VBA distinguishes between a variable named *WBook* and one named *wbook*.

Declaring a Variable

To declare a variable, you use the following command:

```
Dim variable
```

In this command, *variable* is the variable name, and "Dim" stands for "dimensioning" a variable (which means to allocate storage space for it). You can also define exactly what type of data can be stored in a variable with the following command:

```
Dim variable as type
```

In this command, *type* is the data type. For example, the following command declares a variable named SheetName that will contain text strings:

```
Dim SheetName as String
```

It is not strictly required to specify a data type in Visual Basic. If no data type is specified, Excel determines the data type by what you store in the variable. You are also not strictly required to declare variables because Excel automatically creates the variable when you first attempt to store data in it. However, good programming practice is to declare variables and their data types as a way of catching errors that might creep into the code.

VBA supports a wide range of data types. For example, it supports several data types for numeric values, including the Integer data type for whole numbers and the Single data type for decimal values. In David's project, you'll only use the String data type. You can learn more about data types using the VBA online Help.

> **Tip**
>
> Declare all variables and their data types at the start of sub procedures to document exactly what variables are used in running the procedure and what type of data each variable stores.

Assigning a Value to a Variable

After you declare a variable, you store data in it using the following command:

```
variable=expression
```

In this command, *expression* is the initial value or text string that is assigned to the variable. For example, the following command stores the text string "Budget" in the variable SheetName. If you have not declared the SheetName variable beforehand, this command creates the variable for you.

```
SheetName="Budget"
```

Variables can also store objects such as worksheets, workbooks, or cell ranges. The following syntax stores an object in a variable:

```
Set variable = object
```

In this statement, *object* is an object in Excel. So, the command that stores the Statistics worksheet in the ReportSheet variable is as follows:

```
Set ReportSheet=Sheets("Statistics")
```

You can use a VBA property or method with the ReportSheet variable in the same way you would use it with the object itself. For example, the following command uses the ReportSheet variable to select the Statistics worksheet:

```
ReportSheet.Select
```

Figure 12-23 shows VBA statements in which variables are assigned values or are used to store objects.

| Figure 12-23 | Value of a VBA variable |

VBA Code	Description
Year=2010	Stores the value 2010 in the Year variable
Type="F2"	Stores the text string *F2* in the Type variable
Type=Range("A2").Value	Stores in the Type variable the value entered in cell A2 of the active worksheet
Set WSheet=Sheets("Statistics")	Stores the Statistics worksheet in the WSheet variable
Set WBook=Workbooks("Tornado Analysis")	Stores the Tornado Analysis workbook in the WBook variable

You can use variables to create general procedures that apply to several objects. For example, to select a worksheet, you could create a variable named *SheetName* that contains the name of a sheet you want to select. The general sub procedure might look as follows:

```
Sub SelectSheet()
    Dim SheetName
    SheetName="Statistics"
    Sheets(SheetName).Select
    Range("A1").Select
End Sub
```

Tip

You can display the value of a variable by typing ?*variable* in the Immediate window and pressing the Enter key, where *variable* is the variable name.

Later in this session, you'll learn how to set variable values with user input as the program is running to create a general program, but this code shows how the variable is used within the procedure.

You'll return to the Sample Report workbook and enter code to change the name of a worksheet to the value stored in the SheetName variable. Because of how memory is allocated in the Immediate window, you cannot run the Dim statement to declare the variable. Instead, you assign a value to the SheetName variable, which creates the variable without declaring it.

To create and apply a variable:

▶ **1.** Within the Immediate window, press the **Enter** key, type **SheetName= Range("B4").Value**, and then press the **Enter** key. Excel creates the SheetName variable, giving it the value entered into cell B4 of the active worksheet.

▶ **2.** Type **ActiveSheet.Name=SheetName**, and then press the **Enter** key. Excel uses the Name property of the ActiveSheet object to change the sheet's name to the value stored in the SheetName variable. See Figure 12-24.

Variable used in VBA | **Figure 12-24**

SheetName variable stores the value of cell B4

name of the active worksheet changes to the value of the SheetName variable

```
Range ("F6") .Value=49
Range ("F6") .Value=29

Sheets ("Statistics") .Select
Range ("D13") .Select

Sheets ("Statistics") .Move Before:=Sheets ("Yearly Counts")

SheetName=Range ("B4") .Value
ActiveSheet.Name=SheetName
```

▶ **3.** Press the **Alt+Tab** keys to switch to the Sample Report workbook, and then verify that the name of the Statistics worksheet (the active sheet) changed to *Tornadoes per Era*, which is the value in cell B4 of that sheet.

▶ **4.** Close the Sample Report workbook without saving.

Creating a Sub Procedure to Switch Tornado Types

You'll use the basic concepts of the VBA programming language you just reviewed to create a sub procedure in which you can display the atmospheric data for different tornado types in David's workbook. To create a program to display data on different tornado types, you first must understand how David organized the data in the Tornado Analysis workbook. David assigned names to the values he collected and stored in the Table worksheet. All of the charts and statistics displayed in the Tornado Analysis workbook are based on defined names rather than cell references. Figure 12-25 lists all of the defined names in the Tornado Analysis workbook.

Defined names in the Tornado Analysis workbook | **Figure 12-25**

Defined Name	Definition	Refers to
AllData	=Table!$F$7:$F$56	All tornado data regardless of type
F0Data	=Table!$C$7:$C$56	Data on the occurrence of F0 tornadoes
F1Data	=Table!$D$7:$D$56	Data on the occurrence of F1 tornadoes
F2Data	=Table!$E$7:$E$56	Data on the occurrence of F2+ tornadoes
TornadoData	=AllData	Data from the currently selected tornado type
TornadoAll	=Table!$F$6	A cell containing the text "All"
TornadoF0	=Table!$C$6	A cell containing the text "F0"
TornadoF1	=Table!$D$6	A cell containing the text "F1"
TornadoF2	=Table!$E$6	A cell containing the text "F2+"
Tornado	=TornadoAll	The name of the selected tornado type

Range C6:F6 in the Table worksheet contains the names of the different tornado types in David's workbook. Each of these cells has been assigned a name. For example, the TornadoF1 name points to cell D6, which displays the text *F1*. The type of tornado displayed in the workbook's charts and statistics is assigned the range name *Tornado*. The current definition of the Tornado range name is "=TornadoAll," which means that it points to the TornadoAll range (cell F6 in the Table worksheet). Similarly, AllData, F0Data, F1Data, and F2Data point to the data values detailing the number of occurrences per year of each type, and AllData points to the sample values of the current tornado type.

If David wants to switch from one tornado type to another, he simply changes the definition of the Tornado and TornadoData names. For example, to display data about F1 tornadoes, he changes the definition of the Tornado name from "=TornadoAll" to "=TornadoF1" and changes the definition of the TornadoData name from "=AllData" to "=F1Data". All of the charts and statistics are updated and display data on F1 tornadoes.

Writing a Sub Procedure

David wants to automate this process because other users might not be familiar with names or know how to use them. Instead of using the Name Manager dialog box, he wants to have Excel prompt the user for the tornado type to display and then have Excel automatically switch to the type indicated by the user. You can create such a dialog box using VBA. First, you'll write a sub procedure to display data on F1 tornadoes. To do that, you'll use some of the objects, properties, and methods you used with the Sample Report workbook.

Range names are stored in the Names object collection. To modify the definition of a particular range name, you use either the Value property or the RefersTo property. The command to change the definition of the Tornado range name to point to "=TornadoF1" is:

```
Names("Tornado").Value="=TornadoF1"
```

The command to change the definition of the TornadoData range name is:

```
Names("TornadoData").Value="=F1Data"
```

Both commands assume that the Names collection is contained within the currently active workbook.

To write the Change_Type sub procedure:

1. Open the **Tornado Analysis** workbook you stored in the **Tutorial.12\Tutorial** folder included with your Data Files, enabling the macros in the workbook if necessary.

2. Press the **Alt+F11** keys to open the Visual Basic Editor, and then close the Immediate window.

3. Go to the Code window, click **Insert** on the menu bar, and then click **Procedure**. The Add Procedure dialog box opens.

4. Type **Change_Type** in the Name box, and then click the **OK** button. The Visual Basic Editor inserts a new sub procedure in the Code window named *Change_Type*. The insertion point is placed below the Public Sub Change_Type() line.

   Next, you'll enter a command to change the value of the Tornado range name from "=TornadoAll" to "=TornadoF1".

5. Press the **Tab** key, type **Names("Tornado").Value = "=TornadoF1"**, and then press the **Enter** key.

Tip

Indenting command lines makes the code easier to read by emphasizing the structure of the sub procedure.

6. Type **Names("TornadoData").Value = "=F1Data"** into the next line of the sub procedure, and then press the ↓ key to go to the next line. See Figure 12-26.

Change_Type() sub procedure 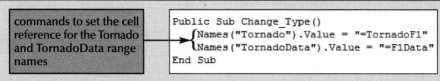 **Figure 12-26**

commands to set the cell reference for the Tornado and TornadoData range names

```
Public Sub Change_Type()
    Names("Tornado").Value = "=TornadoF1"
    Names("TornadoData").Value = "=F1Data"
End Sub
```

Trouble? If you have problems running this macro, you might have mistyped the code. Review the code to make sure you included the equal sign in "=TornadoF1", as shown in Figure 12-26.

Next, you'll test the Change_Type sub procedure by running the procedure from within the Visual Basic Editor.

To test the Change_Type sub procedure:

1. With the insertion point within the Change_Type sub procedure, click **Run** on the menu bar, and then click **Run Sub/UserForm**.

2. Press the **Alt+Tab** keys to switch to the Tornado Analysis workbook, switch to the **Report** worksheet, and then verify that the tornado type in cell C6 is *F1*.

3. Switch to each of the other worksheets in the workbook, verifying that the layout of the charts and tables changed to reflect the new data source. Figure 12-27 shows the revised appearance of the histogram chart.

Histogram of the yearly occurrence of F1 tornadoes 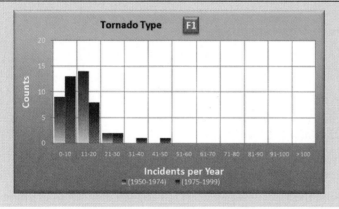 **Figure 12-27**

InSight | **Common Sources of Program Errors**

When you write VBA programs, you can encounter three types of errors: syntax errors, run-time errors, and logical errors. Syntax errors occur when a line of VBA code is entered improperly. The Visual Basic Editor catches such errors before you get a chance to run the program and usually provides ScreenTips to help you fix the error.

Run-time errors occur when the program is executing. At that point, the code has no known syntax errors, but something in the code keeps it from running successfully. For example, Excel does not recognize a mistyped worksheet name as a programming error, but the code will fail when it cannot locate the sheet object the program references. You can use the debugging tools in Excel to run the program up to a certain spot in the code. By running only part of the code, you can quickly locate the command line that is causing the program to fail. After you identify the command, you can use Excel online Help to determine the reason for the error.

Logical errors can be the most difficult to resolve. With these errors, the program is free of syntax errors and it runs without failing, but the results are incorrect. To fix a logical error, run the program one line at a time, confirming the correctness of each operation until you find the command that results in an incorrect value or operation. If you still cannot find the source of the error, consider a different approach to solving the problem. VBA often provides several different ways of performing the same task.

Creating a Variable

What if you want to change the program so that it displays data from F2 tornadoes? You could edit the code, changing "TornadoF1" and "F1Data" to "TornadoF2" and "F2Data," but a more general approach is to create a variable that stores the tornado type you want to display in the workbook. You'll create such a variable named *T_Type*, setting its initial value to the text string *F2*.

To create the T_Type variable:

1. Press the **Alt+Tab** keys to switch to the Visual Basic Editor.

2. Click at the end of the Public Sub Change_Type() line, and then press the **Enter** key to insert a new line at the top of the procedure.

3. Press the **Tab** key, type **Dim T_Type As String**, and then press the **Enter** key to insert a new line.

4. Type **T_Type = "F2"** and press the **Enter** key.

Next, you'll use the T_Type variable to change the cell references of the two range names. Currently, the tornado type name has the reference "=TornadoF1". You'll replace this value with the expression "=Tornado" & T_Type. The ampersand symbol (&) is used to combine two text strings into a single text string. Because T_Type variable has a value of "F2", the value of "=Tornado" & T_Type is "=TornadoF2". Similarly, the reference for the second range name changes from "=F1Data" to "=" & T_Type & "Data". In this case, you'll use the ampersand symbol twice to connect three text strings.

Tip

All VBA commands are read on a single line of code. To break a line to make your code easier to read, type a space followed by the underscore character, _, at the end of the line.

To edit range reference names:

1. In the next line of the sub procedure, change "=TornadoF1" to **"=Tornado" & T_Type** and then press the ↓ key.

2. Change "=F1Data" to **"=" & T_Type & "Data"**. See Figure 12-28.

VBA variable ◀ Figure 12-28

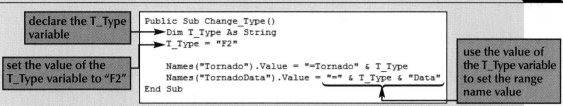

declare the T_Type variable

set the value of the T_Type variable to "F2"

use the value of the T_Type variable to set the range name value

```
Public Sub Change_Type()
    Dim T_Type As String
    T_Type = "F2"

    Names("Tornado").Value = "=Tornado" & T_Type
    Names("TornadoData").Value = "=" & T_Type & "Data"
End Sub
```

Next, you'll test the program to confirm that it switches from displaying information on F1 type tornadoes to F2 type tornadoes.

▶ **3.** With the insertion point within the Change_Type sub procedure, click **Run** on the menu bar and then click **Run Sub/UserForm**. The program runs.

▶ **4.** Press the **Alt+Tab** keys to switch to the Tornado Analysis workbook, and then verify that the workbook displays data on F2-type tornadoes in all of the charts and tables.

Trouble? If you receive an error message, check your code against the code shown in Figure 12-28. Pay close attention to the use of upper- and lowercase letters and verify that you have closed all quotation marks.

Retrieving Information from the User

The macro works, but you want to prompt users for the value of the T_Type variable rather than entering it directly into the VBA code. You can do this using the InputBox method, which has the following syntax:

```
variable = InputBox(Prompt, Title)
```

In this command, *variable* is a variable whose value is set based on whatever the user enters into the input box, *Prompt* is the message you want to appear in the input box, and *Title* is the text that appears in the title bar of the input box. For example, the following VBA code produces the input box shown in Figure 12-29, storing the result from the input box in a variable named *user*:

```
user = InputBox("Enter your username", "Log In")
```

InputBox function ◀ Figure 12-29

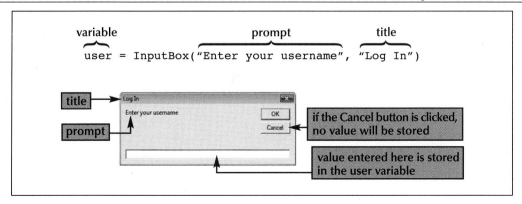

variable   prompt   title

```
user = InputBox("Enter your username", "Log In")
```

title

prompt

if the Cancel button is clicked, no value will be stored

value entered here is stored in the user variable

You'll use an input box to prompt the user for the value of the T_Type variable.

To create the input box:

▶ **1.** Press the **Alt+Tab** keys to switch to the Visual Basic Editor.

▶ **2.** Change the second line of the Change_Type() sub procedure from T_Type = "F2" to **T_Type = InputBox("Enter F0, F1, F2, or All", "Tornado Type")**. See Figure 12-30.

Figure 12-30	Input box command

> use an input box to set the value of the T_Type variable

```
Public Sub Change_Type()
    Dim T_Type As String
    T_Type = InputBox("Enter F0, F1, F2, or All", "Tornado Type")

    Names("Tornado").Value = "=Tornado" & T_Type
    Names("TornadoData").Value = "=" & T_Type & "Data"
End Sub
```

▶ **3.** Close the Visual Basic Editor, and return to the Report worksheet of the Tornado Analysis workbook.

Next, you'll apply the Change_Type macro to the Specify a Tornado Type macro button on the Report worksheet, and then run the macro, changing the type from F2 to F0.

To test the Change_Type macro:

▶ **1.** On the Report worksheet, right-click the **Specify a Tornado Type** button, and then click **Assign Macro** on the shortcut menu.

▶ **2.** Select **Change_Type** in the Macro name box, and then click the **OK** button.

▶ **3.** Click outside the macro button to deselect it, and then click the **Specify a Tornado Type** button. The Tornado Type dialog box opens.

▶ **4.** Type **F0**. See Figure 12-31.

Figure 12-31	Tornado Type input box

> value in cell C6 will change to the value entered here

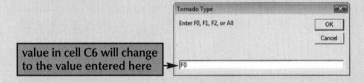

▶ **5.** Click the **OK** button. The value in cell C6 changes from F2+ to F0.

▶ **6.** View the other worksheets, verifying that the charts and tables changed to display data on F0 tornadoes, and then save the workbook.

Using VBA, you created a macro that makes it easier to view data on different tornado types. In the next session, you'll create procedures called control structures that "make decisions" based on the type of information the user enters.

Good Coding Practices | InSight

As you write VBA programs, good coding practices will help you avoid bugs and errors that cause the program to return wrong values or to not run at all. Keep in mind these general tips:

- Add comment lines to programs to document exactly what the program is doing at each step in the process and why.
- Declare all variables at the top of the sub procedure with comments describing the purpose of each variable. Use descriptive variable names.
- Assign data types to all of your variables.
- Indent the code to make it easier to read.
- Write code in lowercase text. If the spelling is correct, the Visual Basic Editor automatically capitalizes the letters to fit the syntax.
- Use the macro recorder to generate code samples and use the list boxes and ScreenTips to ensure good syntax.
- Use the Immediate window to test specific command lines before committing them to a sub procedure.
- Use the Visual Basic Editor debugging tools to track down errors in your code. You can step through your procedures one line at a time. You can create Watch windows to follow the changing values of your variables as the code is run. You can also use the Immediate window to halt the program at any command line and check the status of the program.

Session 12.2 Quick Check | Review

1. Define the following terms: *object-oriented programming language, collection object, method, parameter,* and *variable*
2. What VBA command would you enter to change the name of the Histogram worksheet to *Histogram Chart*? (*Hint*: The object name is Sheets("Histogram"), and the name of the worksheet is contained in the Name property.)
3. What VBA command would you enter to select the Histogram worksheet?
4. What VBA command would you enter to store the name of the active worksheet in a variable named *SheetName*?
5. What VBA command would you enter to change the text of the Excel status bar to *Program Running*?
6. What VBA command would you enter to turn off screen updating in Excel?
7. What VBA command would you enter to display an input box containing the prompt "Enter your last name," the text "Log In" in the title bar, and then save whatever the user entered into a variable named *Lastname*?

Session 12.3

Working with Conditional Statements

David has been testing the macro buttons in the Tornado Analysis workbook, and found that the Change_Type macro does not accept any entry other than F0, F1, F2, and All, without a resulting error. Once, David mistakenly typed *F3* in the input box you created and then pressed the OK button, resulting in the error value shown in Figure 12-32. Later, he mistakenly typed F3 again but clicked the Cancel button. However, an error value still resulted.

Figure 12-32 ▶ **Report worksheet after specifying an incorrect type**

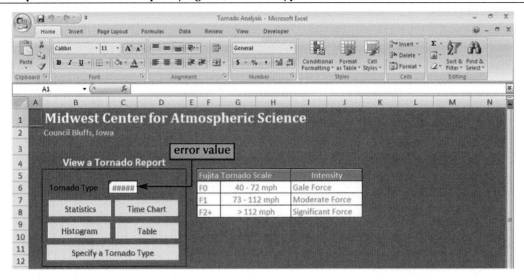

The error value means that Excel cannot find the range name used in the formula. When David entered F3 in the input box, the Change_Type macro attempted to assign the Tornado and TornadoData range names to the cell references "=TornadoF3" and "=F3Data." However, because the workbook does not contain these range names, an error value appeared for formulas that use either the Tornado or TornadoData range name. Similarly, when David clicked the Cancel button, no value was assigned to the T_Type variable, so the definitions of Tornado and TornadoData range names again had improper values.

Because other people will be using this workbook, David is concerned that those who are not familiar with Excel might be confused if this happens to them. He wants you to modify the Change_Type macro to handle this problem. To do this, you have to create a control structure. A **control structure** is a series of commands that evaluates conditions in your program and then directs Excel to perform certain actions based on the status of those conditions. Figure 12-33 shows the kind of control structure that David has in mind for the Change_Type macro.

Figure 12-33 ▶ **Control structure for the Change_Type macro**

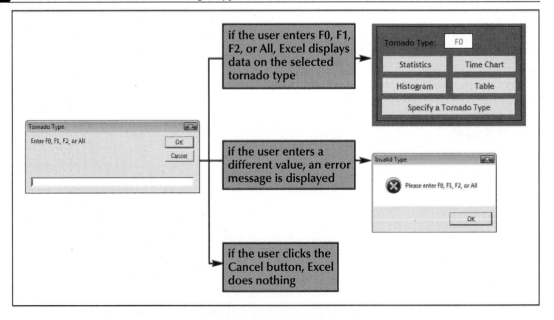

In this control structure, if the user enters F0, F1, F2, or All, Excel displays information on the selected tornado type. However, if the user enters a different text string, the program displays a message indicating the acceptable entries. If the user clicks the Cancel button instead of entering a tornado type, the input box closes without doing anything, and the user returns to the Report worksheet.

Using the If Statement

The most basic way to run a VBA command in response to a particular condition is the If statement. In this type of control structure, if a certain condition is met, such as the user entering F0, F1, F2, or All, the program executes a specified command. The If statement has the following syntax:

```
If Condition Then Command
```

In this statement, *Condition* is a VBA expression that is either true or false, and *Command* is a command that the macro will run if *Condition* is true. For example, the following statement sets the value of cell B10 to "Loan Approved" if the Savings variable has a value greater than 20,000:

```
If Savings > 20000 Then Range("B10").Value = "Loan Approved"
```

Using the If-Then-Else Control Structure

When the condition of the If statement is not true, the macro does nothing. In order for the macro to run an alternate command when the condition is false, you need to use an If-Then-Else statement. In an **If-Then-Else control structure**, one set of commands is run if the condition is true and a different set of commands is run if the condition is false. The syntax for the If-Then-Else control structure is as follows:

```
If Condition Then
    Commands if Condition is true
Else
    Commands if Condition is false
End If
```

In this control structure, *Condition* is a VBA expression that is either true or false. If the condition is true, then the first set of commands is run; otherwise, the second set of commands is run. Figure 12-34 shows an example of an If-Then-Else control structure. This macro has two possible outcomes based on whether the user has more than $20,000 in savings. If the value of the Savings variable is greater than 20,000, Excel displays "Loan Approved" in cell B10; otherwise, it displays "Loan Denied."

Sample If-Then-Else control structure ◀ **Figure 12-34**

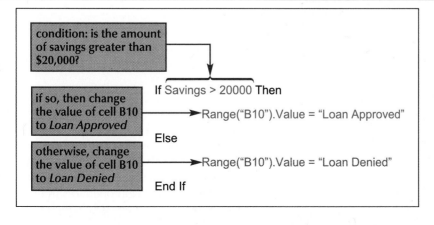

If a control structure has several conditions, you need to use an **If-Then-ElseIf control structure** to run commands in response to each condition. The syntax for this control structure in VBA is as follows:

```
If Condition1 Then
    Commands if Condition1 is true
ElseIf Condition2 Then
    Commands if Condition2 is true
ElseIf Condition3 Then
    Commands if Condition3 is true
Else
    Commands if none of the conditions are true
End If
```

In this control structure, *Condition1*, *Condition2*, *Condition3*, and so forth are expressions that represent distinct conditions. You can specify an unlimited number of conditions. Visual Basic analyzes the conditions in sequence, bypassing any remaining conditions when it finds a condition that is true. You should use conditions that are mutually exclusive.

Figure 12-35 shows an example of VBA code using multiple conditions in a control structure that evaluates whether a user qualifies for a loan. This example presents three conditions: (1) The person applying for the loan could have more than $20,000 in savings. (2) The person could have between $15,000 and $20,000. (3) The person could have less than $15,000. Based on which condition is true, the text *Loan Approved*, *Loan Pending*, or *Loan Denied* is entered into cell B10.

Tip

The If-Then-ElseIf control structure can be unwieldy with many conditions. To test several conditions in a macro, use the VBA Select Case statement instead.

| Figure 12-35 | Sample If-Then-ElseIf control structure |

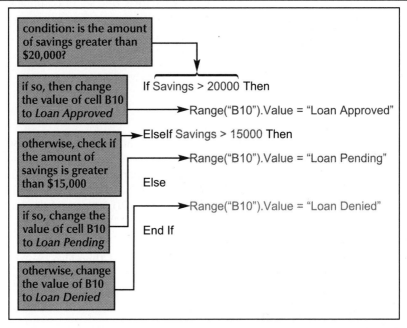

Using Comparison and Logical Operators

To determine whether the expression used in the condition is true or false, the expression needs to contain a comparison operator. Recall that a comparison operator is a symbol used to compare one value with another, such as <, >, =, <=, >=, and <>. Figures 12-34 and 12-35 used > in the expression that determined whether the value of the Savings variable was greater than 20,000. You'll use these comparison operators frequently in VBA control structures. Another common comparison operator is *is*, which tests whether one object is the same as another.

As you write conditions for control structures, you'll also use logical operators. **Logical operators** combine expressions within a condition. The most common logical operators are the And and Or operators. The And operator requires both expressions to be true before the procedure acts on them, whereas the Or operator requires only one of the expressions to be true. Figure 12-36 shows a condition that uses the And logical operator. In this example, the text *Loan Approved* is placed in cell B10 only if the Savings variable has a value greater than 20,000 and the Credit variable has the value "Good." Otherwise, the value placed in cell B10 is *Loan Denied*.

Condition with the And logical operator ◄ **Figure 12-36**

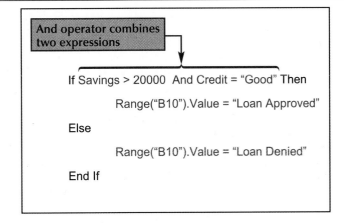

Figure 12-37 shows a similar condition that uses the Or logical operator. In this example, the loan is approved if either the Savings variable is greater than 20,000 or the value of the equity in a home mortgage is greater than 10,000.

Condition using the Or logical operator ◄ **Figure 12-37**

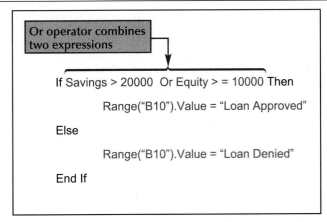

VBA supports other control structures as well. These include the For-Next control structure, which allows you to repeat a series of commands a set number of times, and the Do-While control structure, which repeats a series of commands as long as a particular condition is true.

InSight | **Using the NOT Logical Operator and Function**

Every VBA logical operator is matched by a logical function. You can simplify your program code by inserting logical tests within the worksheet and then referencing those worksheet values in your program. One advantage of using logical functions is that the worksheet will then display the logical conditions under which the program is being run. For example, the Not operator, which reverses the logical value of an expression, could be used in the following statement in the VBA code:

```
If Not(Savings>2000) Then
```

This statement tests whether the value of the Savings variable is not greater than 2000.

To perform the same type of test in your worksheet, you could use the NOT function. The syntax of the NOT function is:

```
=NOT(logical)
```

In this function, *logical* is an expression that can be true or false. The NOT function returns the value FALSE if the *logical* expression is true, and it returns the value TRUE if the *logical* expression is false. The NOT function is helpful when you want to make sure that an expression does not result in a specific value, text, or date.

For example, consider the following formula with the NOT() function, in which cell A1 contains the value of the Savings variable:

```
=NOT(A1>2000)
```

The logical expression in this NOT function looks at the value in cell A1, which is the amount of savings, and then evaluates if the value is greater than 2000. If the value is greater than 2000, the logical expression is true. The NOT function then reverses that value and returns FALSE, indicating that the savings value is not greater than 2000.

To add this NOT function to a cell in a worksheet, you could perform the following steps:

1. In cell B2, enter **Cash assets available?** to enter a descriptive label for the NOT function.
2. Click cell **B3** to make it the active cell, and then on the formula bar, click the **Insert Function** button [fx] . The Insert Function dialog box opens.
3. Click the **OR select a category** arrow, and then click **Logical**. The Logical functions are listed in the Select a function box.
4. In the Select a function box, click **NOT**, and then click the **OK** button. The Function Arguments dialog box opens.
5. In the Logical box, enter **A1>2000**. This logical expression evaluates whether the value in cell A1 is greater than 2000.
6. Click the **OK** button. The NOT function is entered in cell B3. If the value in cell A1 is greater than 2000, FALSE appears in cell B3. If the value in cell A1 is less than 2000, TRUE appears in cell B3.

Your program could then access the logical value stored in the cell using the object reference Range("B3").

Using the If-Then-ElseIf Control Structure

You are ready to write the control structure to make the Change_Type macro work under all possible conditions. The three possible conditions you must account for in the macro and how they relate to the value of the T_Type variable are:

- The user enters a valid tornado type (the T_Type variable is equal to F0, F1, F2, or All).
- The user enters an invalid tornado type.
- The user clicks the Cancel button (the T_Type variable has no value).

Because you have three conditions, you must use an If-Then-ElseIf control structure. Also, because the first condition (the user enters a valid type) has four valid answers, it will contain several expressions linked with the Or operator.

Be careful of case distinctions. You want the control structure to work for both upper-case and lowercase letters so that it treats entries such as f0 and F0 the same way. To do this, you'll use VBA's UCase() function to convert the text the user enters in the input box into uppercase letters. Then, you can test only uppercase letters.

You'll start editing the Change_Type macro to specify the conditions necessary for the macro to work properly. The first line you'll add to the sub procedure will convert the text string entered by the user into all uppercase letters. You'll then enter the first condition to test whether the user has entered F0, F1, F2, or All.

To enter the first condition of the If-Then-ElseIf control structure:

▶ **1.** If you took a break at the end of the previous session, open the Tornado Analysis workbook located in the Tutorial.12\Tutorial folder, and go to the Visual Basic Editor.

▶ **2.** In the Change_Type sub procedure, click at the end of the line containing the InputBox function, and then press the **Enter** key to insert a new blank line.

▶ **3.** Type **T_Type = UCase(T_Type)**, press the ↓ key, and then press the **Enter** key. This command converts any text string entered in the T_Type variable into upper-case letters.

Next, you'll enter the condition that checks whether the T_Type variable is equal to F0, F1, F2, or All.

▶ **4.** Type **If T_Type = "F0" or T_Type = "F1" or T_Type = "F2" or T_Type = "ALL" Then**, and then press the ↓ key.

▶ **5.** Use the **Tab** key to indent the next two lines of code setting the value of the Tornado and TornadoData range names.

After the If statement, the next two lines set the reference values for the Tornado and TornadoData range names. However, these definitions apply only if the user enters F0, F1, F2, or All. Therefore, in the next part of the control structure, you need to account for the two remaining possibilities: The user enters an invalid tornado type in the input box, or the user clicks the Cancel button and does not enter any value. First, you'll enter a condition that determines whether a value is entered into the input box, and, if so, display an error message if an incorrect type is entered.

Tip

You can nest If statements to handle complicated conditions. Be sure that each If statement is matched with an End If statement.

To enter the second condition of the If-Then-ElseIf control structure:

▶ **1.** Click at the beginning of the End Sub line, press the **Enter** key, and then press the ↑ key to move the insertion point to the new blank line.

▶ **2.** Press the **Tab** key, type **ElseIf T_Type <> "" Then**, and then press the **Enter** key. This is the second condition. If the user did not enter F0, F1, F2, or ALL, the condition tests whether the T_Type variable "is not equal to" nothing. In other words, as long as something is entered in the input box, this condition will be true. To indicate no value, you use a set of quotation marks.

▶ **3.** Next, you'll enter a comment statement as a placeholder for the error message, which you will create later in this tutorial.

▶ **4.** Press the **Tab** key, type **'Display an error message**, and then press the **Enter** key. You'll replace this VBA comment with a command to create a message box later.

The only remaining possibility is that the user has entered nothing at all, which occurs when the user clicks the Cancel button in the input box. In this case, you want the macro to do nothing, so you'll simply end the If-Then-ElseIf structure without entering any commands for this condition.

To complete the control structure:

▶ **1.** Press the **Backspace** key to move the insertion point back toward the left margin.

▶ **2.** Type **EndIf**, and then press the **Enter** key. The control structure is complete. See Figure 12-38.

Figure 12-38	Change_Type sub procedure

```
Public Sub Change_Type()
    Dim T_Type As String
    T_Type = InputBox("Enter F0, F1, F2, or All", "Tornado Type")
    T_Type = UCase(T_Type)

    If T_Type = "F0" Or T_Type = "F1" Or T_Type = "F2" Or T_Type = "ALL" Then
        Names("Tornado").Value = "=Tornado" & T_Type
        Names("TornadoData").Value = "=" & T_Type & "Data"
    ElseIf T_Type <> "" Then
        'Display an error message
    End If

End Sub
```

run these commands if T_Type contains a valid value

run this command if T_Type doesn't have a valid value

do nothing if T_Type has no value

Next, you'll test the Change_Type macro and verify that no errors are generated when you click the Cancel button in the input box.

To test the Cancel button:

▶ **1.** Press the **Alt+Tab** keys to switch to the Tornado Analysis workbook, and then switch to the **Report** worksheet.

2. Click the **Specify a Tornado Type** macro button. The Tornado Type dialog box opens.

3. Click the **Cancel** button. At this point, the Tornado Type dialog box closes and nothing changes in the workbook.

Trouble? If an error message opens or ### appears in cell C6 in the Report worksheet, the code probably contains a typing error. Press the Alt+Tab keys to switch to the Visual Basic Editor, compare your code with the code shown in Figure 12-38, make any necessary changes to the code, and then repeat Steps 1 through 3.

Tip

To hide a macro's actions as it runs, insert the command *Application. ScreenUpdating = false* at the beginning of the sub procedure. Insert *Application. ScreenUpdating = true* at the end of the program to display the results.

Creating a Message Box

To create a message box, you use the MsgBox function, which is similar to the InputBox function you used in the previous session, except the MsgBox function does not contain a text box for the user to enter values. You use a message box for situations where you simply want to send the user a message. The MsgBox function has the following syntax:

```
MsgBox Prompt, Buttons, Title
```

As in the InputBox function, *Prompt* is the message in the dialog box, and *Title* is the text that appears in the title bar. The *Buttons* parameter specifies the kind of buttons that appear in the message box, as well as the style of the message box itself. You can choose several options for the Buttons parameter, a few of which are shown in Figure 12-39.

Button parameters   **Figure 12-39**

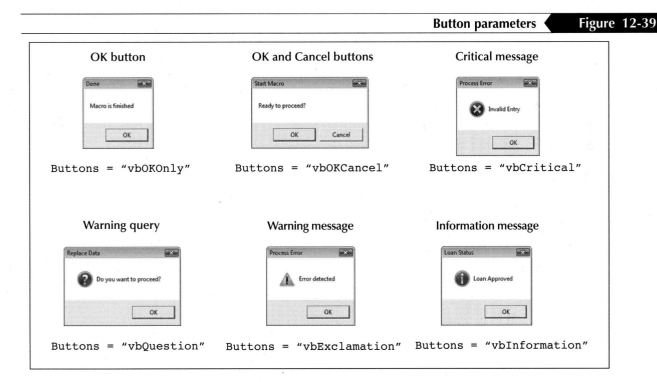

Some button styles merely inform, some ask a question, and others provide an alert to a problem. You don't have to learn the names of these different buttons and message styles; the Visual Basic Editor will display a description box as you enter the MsgBox function.

You'll use the MsgBox function in the Change_Type macro. Because the message box will be reporting a user error, you'll use the vbCritical button style, which indicates an invalid entry.

To create the message box with the vbCritical button style:

▶ 1. Press the **Alt+Tab** keys to switch to the Visual Basic Editor and the Change_Type sub procedure in the Code window.

▶ 2. Select the **'Display an error message** comment line you entered as a placeholder, and then press the **Delete** key, leaving a blank line in its place.

▶ 3. Press the **Tab** key to indent the line of code, if necessary, and then type **MsgBox "Please enter F0, F1, F2, or All",** to begin the MsgBox function. After you type the comma, a list of the possible values for the Buttons parameter appears.

▶ 4. Double-click **vbCritical** in the list.

▶ 5. Type **, "Invalid Type"** and then press the ↓ key. The macro is completed. See Figure 12-40.

Figure 12-40	Complete macro with the message box command

```
Public Sub Change_Type()
    Dim T_Type As String
    T_Type = InputBox("Enter F0, F1, F2, or All", "Tornado Type")
    T_Type = UCase(T_Type)

    If T_Type = "F0" Or T_Type = "F1" Or T_Type = "F2" Or T_Type = "ALL" Then
        Names("Tornado").Value = "=Tornado" & T_Type
        Names("TornadoData").Value = "=" & T_Type & "Data"
    ElseIf T_Type <> "" Then
        MsgBox "Please enter F0, F1, F2, or All", vbCritical, "Invalid Type"
    End If

End Sub
```

MsgBox function

Trouble? If an error message opens, the command you entered probably contains a typing error. Compare the command in your Code window to the code shown in Figure 12-40, and make any necessary corrections to the MsgBox command.

▶ 6. Close the Visual Basic Editor and return to the Tornado Analysis workbook.

Next, you'll verify that the macro identifies errors by intentionally entering an invalid value in the input box.

▶ 7. In the Report worksheet, click the **Specify a Tornado Type** macro button. The Tornado Type dialog box opens.

▶ 8. Type **F3** in the input box, and then click the **OK** button. The Invalid Type message box opens.

▶ 9. Click the **OK** button to close the dialog box and return to the workbook.

▶ 10. Test that the macro works properly by changing the tornado type displayed in the workbook to **F0, F1, F2,** and **All**.

Trouble? If the macro does not work, your code probably contains a typing error. Return to the Visual Basic Editor and compare the complete Change_Type macro code in your Code window with the code shown in Figure 12-40. Make any necessary corrections to the code, and then repeat Steps 6 through 10.

Tip

To display the message box prompt on more than one line, enter the text as "*line1*" & vbCrLf & "*line2*", where *line1* is the text of the first line and *line2* is the text of the second line.

Customized Dialog Boxes and VBA | InSight

The simplest way to create a dialog box in VBA is with the InputBox() and MsgBox() methods. However, both dialog boxes are limited in the amount of information they can present to and receive from the user. If these dialog boxes do not meet your needs, you can create custom dialog boxes, known as user forms. You create user forms in the Visual Basic Editor by clicking User-Form on the Insert menu. You can then insert controls on a blank form to create a custom dialog box. User forms support a wide range of controls, including input boxes, option buttons, check boxes, and list boxes. Information entered into these controls can be retrieved and stored in variables used in your VBA programs. After designing a custom dialog box, you can display it using the *userform*.Show command where *userform* is the name of the user form. See the VBA Editor online Help for more information and tutorials on creating custom dialog boxes.

Customizing the Quick Access Toolbar

David is pleased with how easy it is to switch between one tornado type and another in the Tornado Analysis workbook and how the Change_Type macro prevents users from entering invalid data. He noticed that whenever he wants to switch between the Statistics, Time Chart, and Histogram worksheets or choose a different tornado type, he must return to the Report worksheet. David wants users to be able to move among these worksheets in a single step.

You could copy all of the macro buttons on the Report worksheet to each of the other sheets in the workbook, but David thinks this will make the other sheets too cluttered. Instead, he wants you to create a toolbar for the macros that is accessible from any sheet in the workbook.

Adding Commands to the Quick Access Toolbar

You cannot customize the Ribbon, which is the main tool used for selecting and running Excel commands. You can, however, customize the Quick Access Toolbar. By default, three commands appear on the toolbar: the Save command, the Undo command, and the Redo command. You can add or remove commands and macros from the Quick Access Toolbar.

When you customize the Quick Access Toolbar, you can apply the changes to your installation of Excel to affect all workbooks, or you can assign them to a specific workbook, which enables you to create a custom Quick Access Toolbar for each workbook.

Customizing the Quick Access Toolbar | Reference Window

- Click the Office Button, and then click Excel Options.
- Click Customize in the Excel Options list.
- Click the Customize Quick Access Toolbar arrow, and select whether to customize the toolbar for all documents or a specific workbook.
- To add a command to the Quick Access Toolbar, click the command in the left list box, and then click the Add button.
- To remove a command from the Quick Access Toolbar, click the command in the right list box, and then click the Remove button.
- Click the OK button.

David wants you to add all of the macro commands you've created for his project to the Quick Access Toolbar in the Tornado Analysis workbook. He doesn't want these changes to appear in other workbooks.

To add macros to the Quick Access Toolbar:

▶ 1. Click the **Office Button** , and then click the **Excel Options** button. The Excel Options dialog box opens.

▶ 2. Click **Customize** in the list of Excel options. The right pane shows the Customize the Quick Access Toolbar options.

▶ 3. Click the **Choose commands from** arrow, and then click **Macros**. A list of all the macros in the current workbook, other workbooks, or add-ins installed in Excel appears in the left box.

▶ 4. Click the **Customize Quick Access Toolbar** arrow, and then click **For Tornado Analysis.xlsm**. Only the Quick Access Toolbar in the Tornado Analysis workbook will be customized.

▶ 5. Click **Change_Type** in the list of macros, and then click the **Add** button. The macro will be added to the Quick Access Toolbar. See Figure 12-41.

Figure 12-41   **Excel Options dialog box**

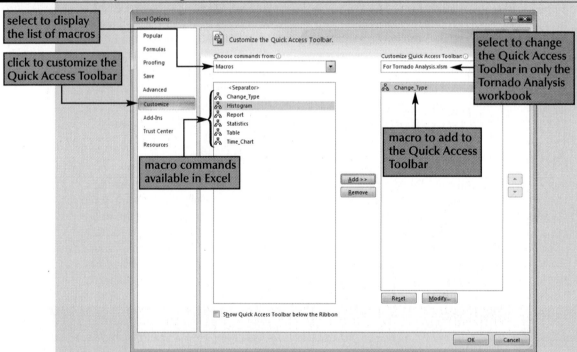

▶ 6. Add the macro commands **Histogram**, **Report**, **Statistics**, **Table**, and **Time_Chart** to the Quick Access Toolbar. Be sure not to add the HISTOGRAM macro, which is from the Data Analysis ToolPak, to the Quick Access Toolbar.

▶ 7. Click the **OK** button. The Excel Options dialog box closes, and six macro buttons appear on the Quick Access Toolbar. See Figure 12-42.

Figure 12-42   **Customized Quick Access Toolbar**

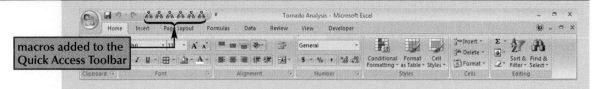

Excel uses the same symbol for each macro button in the Quick Access Toolbar. However, each button's ScreenTip displays the macro name. To test the customized Quick Access Toolbar, you click the macro buttons.

To test the Quick Access Toolbar macro buttons:

▶ **1.** On the Quick Access Toolbar, point to the second macro button and verify that the ScreenTip *Histogram* appears.

▶ **2.** On the Quick Access Toolbar, click the **Histogram** macro button. The Histogram worksheet is active.

▶ **3.** On the Quick Access Toolbar, point to the last macro button and verify that the ScreenTip *Time_Chart* appears.

▶ **4.** On the Quick Access Toolbar, click the **Time_Chart** macro button. The Time Chart worksheet is active.

▶ **5.** On the Quick Access Toolbar, click the **Report** macro button (the third macro button). The Report worksheet is active.

Customizing a Quick Access Toolbar Button

The macro buttons on the Quick Access Toolbar each use the same icon, making it difficult to distinguish between them. David asks you to use different icons for each macro button. You'll modify the buttons so each has a distinct image. You'll also enter ScreenTip text that is more descriptive than the name of the macro command.

To modify the appearance of the macro buttons:

▶ **1.** Click the **Office Button** , click the **Excel Options** button to open the Excel Options dialog box, and then click **Customize**. The Excel Options dialog box shows the Customize the Quick Access Toolbar options.

▶ **2.** Click the **Customize Quick Access Toolbar** arrow, and then click **For Tornado Analysis.xlsm**. The commands on the Quick Access Toolbar in the Tornado Analysis workbook appear in the right box.

▶ **3.** Click **Change_Type**, and then click the **Modify** button. The Modify Button dialog box opens with a gallery of button images.

▶ **4.** Scroll to the bottom of the button image gallery, and then click the **Cloud** icon . This is the image you'll use for the Change_Type macro button.

▶ **5.** Select **Change_Type** in the Display name box, and then type **Select a Tornado Type**. This is the descriptive text for the SceenTip. See Figure 12-43.

Modify Button dialog box ◣ **Figure 12-43**

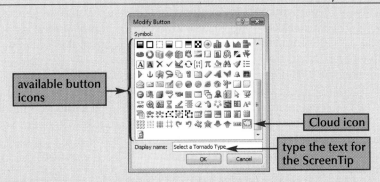

available button icons

Cloud icon

type the text for the ScreenTip

6. Click the **OK** button. The button image and descriptive text of the Change_Type macro command changes.

7. Repeat Steps 3 through 6 for the other five macro commands. For the Histogram command, use the **Column Chart** icon 🔳 and the display name **Display a Histogram**. For the Report command, use the **Book** icon 📖 and the display name **Display the Report Sheet**. For the Statistics command, use the **Pi** icon π and the display name **Display Statistics on Tornadoes**. For the Table command, use the **Table** icon 🔲 and the display name **Display Tornado Data**. Ffor the Time_ Chart command, use the **Line Chart** icon 📈 and the display name **Display a Time Chart**. Figure 12-44 shows the list of edited macro buttons.

Figure 12-44	New button images for the macro commands

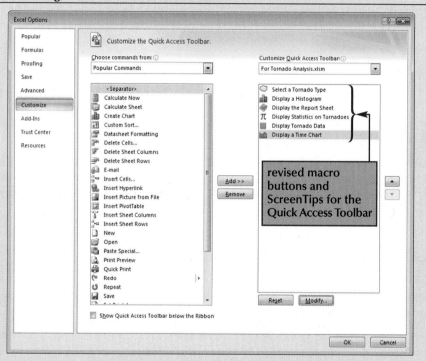

8. Click the **OK** button. The six macro buttons on the Quick Access Toolbar have new icons.

9. For each macro button on the Quick Access Toolbar, verify that the ScreenTip shows the descriptive text and the button makes the correct worksheet active.

Customizing Excel Screen Elements

When David displays the workbook in the kiosk, he does not want other elements of Excel to distract users. He asks you to modify the Excel workbook and worksheet window to display only the Tornado Analysis workbook, the Ribbon, the Quick Access Toolbar, and a few other Excel screen elements.

Excel screen elements fall into three general categories with elements that are: (1) part of the Excel program, (2) part of the Excel workbook window, and (3) part of the Excel worksheet. The difference is important. For example, screen elements you hide that are part of the workbook window are hidden in all Excel workbooks you open. Screen elements that are part of the worksheet are hidden in only that worksheet and do not affect other worksheets and workbooks. Figure 12-45 lists the screen elements you can hide and the category to which they belong.

Modifiable screen elements ◀ **Figure 12-45**

Displayed in the	Screen Element
Excel window	Formula bar
	ScreenTips
	Chart element names on hover
Workbook	Horizontal scroll bar
	Vertical scroll bar
	Sheet tabs
Worksheet	Row and column headers
	Gridlines

You use the Excel Options dialog box to specify which screen elements to show and hide. You'll group the worksheets before hiding the row and column headers so that the headers will be hidden in all the worksheets.

To hide the row and column headers in the worksheets:

▶ **1.** Click the **Documentation** sheet tab, hold down the **Shift** key, click the **Table** sheet tab, and then release the Shift key. All of the sheets in the workbook are selected.

▶ **2.** Click the **Office Button** 🔘 , click the **Excel Options** button to open the Excel Options dialog box, and then click **Advanced** in the list of Excel options.

▶ **3.** Scroll down to the Display options for this worksheet section, and verify that **Multiple Selected** appears in the Display options for this worksheet box.

▶ **4.** Click the **Show row and column headers** check box to remove the check mark. See Figure 12-46.

Advanced Excel options ◀ **Figure 12-46**

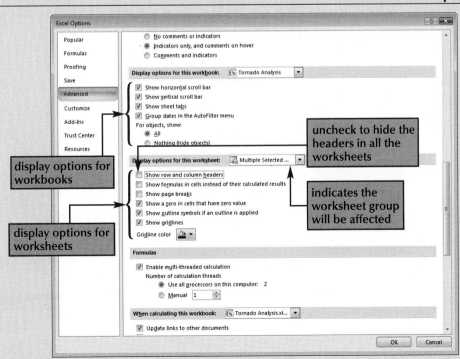

▶ **5.** Click the **OK** button. Scroll through the workbook and verify that the row and column headings are hidden on each worksheet.

Next, David wants you to hide the sheet tabs, which are part of the display options for the entire workbook. He also wants you to remove the formula bar, which is a display option for the Excel program, and then minimize the Ribbon.

To edit the workbook and Excel display options and minimize the Ribbon:

▶ **1.** Click the **Office Button** 🔘, click the **Excel Options** button to open the Excel Options dialog box, and then click **Advanced** in the list of Excel options.

▶ **2.** Scroll down to the Display options for this workbook section, and then verify that **Tornado Analysis** appears in the Display options for this workbook box.

▶ **3.** Click the **Show sheet tabs** check box to remove the check mark.

▶ **4.** Scroll down to the Display section, click the **Show formula bar** check box to remove the check mark, and then click the **OK** button. The sheet tabs are hidden in the workbook and the formula bar is hidden for all workbooks.

▶ **5.** Double-click the active Ribbon tab to minimize the Ribbon. See Figure 12-47.

| Figure 12-47 | Tornado Analysis workbook with display elements hidden |

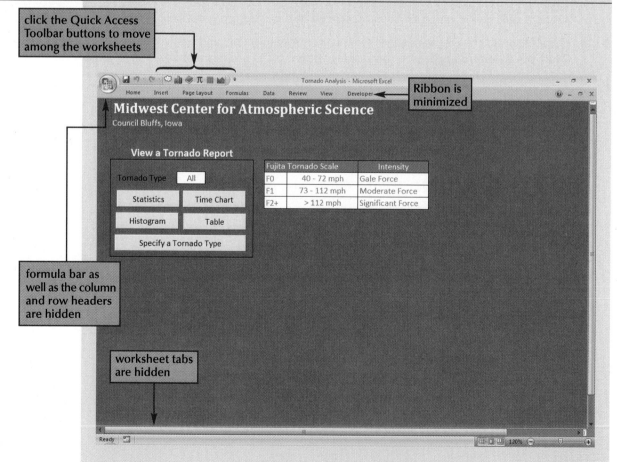

click the Quick Access Toolbar buttons to move among the worksheets

Ribbon is minimized

formula bar as well as the column and row headers are hidden

worksheet tabs are hidden

Hiding the formula bar affects every Excel workbook. David wants you to redisplay the formula bar so he can use it in other workbooks.

▶ **6.** Click the **Office Button** 🔘 , click the **Excel Options** button, click **Advanced** in the list of Excel options, scroll down to the Display section, click the **Show formula bar** check box to insert a check mark, and then click the **OK** button. The formula bar reappears in all workbooks.

▶ **7.** On the Quick Access Toolbar, click the **Report** button 🔷 to switch to the Report worksheet.

The Excel Options dialog box provides many customization options for controlling how Excel operates on your computer. For example, you can change the default font setting, which is 11-point Calibri. Or, you can change the default number of worksheets in new workbooks from three to another number. Figure 12-48 lists other features you can customize.

Excel customization options ◀ **Figure 12-48**

Customization Option	Location in Excel Options dialog box
Turn on and off Formula AutoComplete	Formulas options
Select the default file format for saving workbooks	Save options
Set the length of time in minutes to create an AutoRecover file	Save options
Set the default location for Excel workbook files	Save options
Set the number of recent documents to show in the Office menu	Advanced options, Display section
Show all workbook windows as separate icons on the Windows taskbar	Advanced options, Display section
Automatically format percent values in the Percent style	Advanced options, Editing options section
Turn on or off AutoComplete for cell values	Advanced options, Editing options section

Using the Save As PDF Add-In

One of David's colleagues asked for a copy of the Histogram worksheet for all types of tornadoes in PDF format. **PDF** (**Portable Document Format**) is a file format developed by Adobe Systems that supports all of the elements of a printed document but in an electronic format that is easily shared. To display a PDF file, you need only the free Adobe Acrobat Reader. Many documents are available in PDF because of the format's popularity.

You'll download and install an add-in from the Microsoft Web site to add Save As PDF capability to Microsoft Office programs. Recall that an add-in is a special program that expands another program's capabilities. The Web is constantly changing. You might find differences between the Web pages described here and the ones you see on your screen. If you cannot locate and download the Save As PDF add-in based on the instructions provided at the Web site, contact your instructor or technical support person. If you don't have Internet access, you can read but not complete the next set of steps.

To download the Save As PDF add-in from the Microsoft Web site:

▶ **1.** Use your Web browser to open the Microsoft Web page at the address **www.microsoft.com/downloads**.

▶ **2.** Click the **Search** box at the top of the page, and then click **Office** to search for material within the Office section of the Microsoft Web site.

▶ **3.** Type **Save As PDF add-in** in the box directly to the left of the list box, and then press the **Enter** key. The Microsoft Web site returns a list of Web pages that match the search description.

▶ **4.** Click the **2007 Microsoft Office Add-in: Microsoft Save as PDF or XPS** link.

▶ **5.** If you are prompted to validate your copy of Microsoft Office before you can download the file, click the **Continue** button and follow the instructions to install Office Genuine Advantage.

▶ **6.** Click the **Download** button to begin downloading the SaveAsPDFandXPS.exe file to your computer. Click the **OK** button.

▶ **7.** Click the **Run** button to run the file to install the Save As PDF add-in.

   Trouble? If you or your instructor prefers that you save a copy of the file on your computer, click the Save button instead of the Run button, and then run the file from the location to which you downloaded it.

▶ **8.** Follow the on-screen instructions to install the add-in file.

   Trouble? If you are prompted to exit Excel to install the add-in, save your changes to the Tornado Analysis workbook, and then reopen the workbook after the installation is complete.

After you install the Save As PDF add-in, you can use it to publish any or all of the sheets in an Excel workbook as pages in a PDF document. Before you publish the Histogram worksheet as a PDF, David wants you to format the worksheet in landscape orientation, add a header and footer, and set the page margins.

To format the Histogram worksheet:

▶ **1.** On the Quick Access Toolbar, click the **Display a Histogram** button to switch to the Histogram worksheet.

▶ **2.** Double-click the **Page Layout** tab to redisplay the Ribbon, click the **Orientation** button in the Page Setup group, and then click **Landscape**.

▶ **3.** Click the **Page Layout** button 🔲 on the status bar, and then zoom the worksheet to **90%**.

▶ **4.** Click the center heading box, and then type **An Analysis of the Prevalence of Tornadoes from 1950 to 1999**.

▶ **5.** In the Navigation group on the Design tab, click the **Go to Footer** button, and then type **your name** in the center footer box.

▶ **6.** Click cell **A1** to deselect the footer box.

Tip
You can specify your own margin sizes by clicking the Margins button and then clicking Custom Margins.

▶ **7.** In the Page Setup group on the Page Layout tab, click the **Margins** button, and then click **Narrow**. The Histogram worksheet is formatted.

▶ **8.** Click the **Normal** button ▦ on the status bar to return the Histogram worksheet to Normal view.

The command to publish this worksheet as a PDF is listed with the Save commands on the Office menu.

To publish the Histogram worksheet as a PDF:

▶ **1.** Click the **Office Button** , point to **Save As**, and then click **PDF or XPS**. The Publish as PDF or XPS dialog box opens.

▶ **2.** Type **Tornado History (1950 – 1999)** in the File name box, verify that **PDF** appears in the Save as type box, and then click the **Publish** button. The worksheet publishes as a PDF file, and opens in Adobe Reader. See Figure 12-49.

Tornado History PDF document ◀ **Figure 12-49**

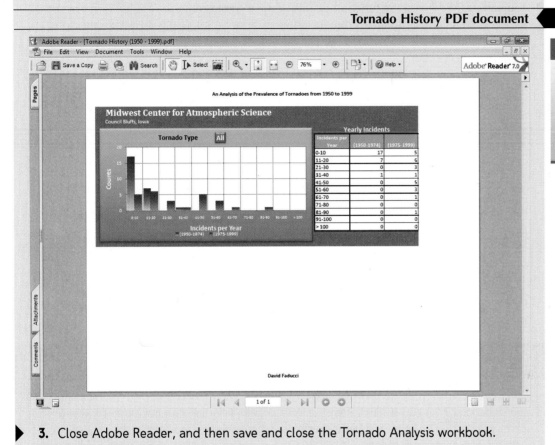

Tip

To publish multiple worksheet pages, click the Options button in the Publish as PDF or XPS dialog box and select the page range for your PDF document.

▶ **3.** Close Adobe Reader, and then save and close the Tornado Analysis workbook.

Introducing Custom Functions

All of the programming you've done for David's project involved creating sub procedures that performed actions in the Tornado Analysis workbook. David could also use a function procedure that returns a value rather than performing an action. Function procedures have the following syntax:

```
Function function_name(parameters)
    VBA commands
    function_name = expression
End Function
```

In this code, *function_name* is the name of the custom function, and *parameters* is a list of parameters (separated by commas) required by the function. Note that *function_name* is listed twice: once in the Function statement that starts the function procedure and again in the last statement of the function procedure in which a value is assigned to the function. It is this last value that is returned by Visual Basic to Excel.

The following TaxesDue function has two parameters—income and taxrate—and returns the amount of taxes due by multiplying the income value by the taxrate value (taxrate is assumed to be a percentage).

```
Function TaxesDue(income, taxrate)
    TaxesDue = income * taxrate
End Function
```

You can run the TaxesDue function just like any of the Excel built-in functions. For example, to calculate the taxes due for an income of $45,000 at a 33% tax rate, you enter the formula =TaxesDue(45000, 33%) and Excel returns the value 14850 or $14,850.

The following is a slightly more complex custom function that uses an If-Then structure to apply one of two tax rates, depending on whether the value of the income parameter is less than 30,000:

```
Function TaxesDue(income, lowtax, hightax)
    If income < 30000 Then
        TaxesDue = income * lowtax
    Else
        TaxesDue = income * hightax
    End If
End Function
```

Tip

Use built-in functions in sub procedures with the WorksheetFunction object. To calculate the sum of the cell range A1:A100, enter the VBA command WorksheetFunction. Sum(range("A1:A100")).

Running this function, the formula =TaxesDue(45000, 20%, 33%) would return a value of 14,850 (using the higher tax rate), whereas the formula =TaxesDue(25000, 20%, 33%) would return a value of 5,000 (using the lower tax rate).

David does not need to create custom functions for his report, but he might for future projects. You've completed the tasks that David requested, making the Tornado Analysis workbook an application that others can use easily and efficiently.

InSight | **Turning a Workbook into an Add-In**

After you become more familiar with VBA, you might want to store favorite macros and custom functions in an add-in file, making them available to other workbooks. To convert an Excel workbook into an add-in file, save the workbook in the Excel Add-In. If you need to support earlier versions of Excel, save it in the Excel 97-2003 Add-In file format. Add-in files are not displayed in the Excel workbook window; their contents can be viewed only from within the Visual Basic Editor.

To load a customized add-in, go to the Add-Ins options in the Excel Options dialog box, and then click the Go button to manage your Excel add-ins. Within the Add-Ins dialog box, click the Browse button to locate and select the add-in file. The selected add-in will be available to everything you run in Excel.

Review | **Session 12.3 Quick Check**

1. What is a control structure, and why might you need one in your VBA procedure?
2. Define the terms *comparison operator* and *logical operator*.
3. What is the syntax of the If-Then-Else control structure?
4. What control structure would you use if you had multiple conditions from which to choose?
5. What is the syntax of the MsgBox function?

6. What command would you enter to display a message box with the following elements: the text *File Status* in the title bar, the message *File Saved*, and an OK button in the dialog box?
7. Where can you store a custom menu in Excel?
8. What is the difference between a sub procedure and a function procedure?

Tutorial Summary | Review

In this tutorial, you learned how to expand Excel capabilities by using the Visual Basic for Applications programming language and by customizing built-in features. In the first session, you explored the Visual Basic Editor, the main tool you can use to create and edit Excel macros. You learned how macros are expressed as VBA sub procedures, and how to create, edit, and run those sub procedures. You also learned how to assign a sub procedure to a macro button in the workbook.

The second session introduced the basic terms and concepts of the VBA programming language. You learned how Excel features can be expressed in terms of objects, properties, and methods. You interpreted the programming code created by the macro recorder in the first session and edited a sub procedure generated by the macro recorder. You also learned how to write a macro to receive direct input from the user.

The third session introduced control structures, specifically the If-Then-Else structure. Using a control structure, you added program code to "capture" user input errors. You also created a message box to notify users of input mistakes. You then customized the Quick Access Toolbar. You also changed Excel display options to hide and display different features of Excel, Excel workbooks, and Excel worksheets. Finally, you installed and used the Save As PDF add-in and reviewed techniques to create custom functions.

Key Terms

Code window
collection object
comment
control structure
dockable
Excel object
Excel Object Model
function procedure
If-Then-Else control
    structure

If-Then-ElseIf control
    structure
Immediate window
logical operator
method
module
object
object-oriented program-
    ming language
PDF (Portable Document
    Format)

project
Project Explorer
Properties window
property
property procedure
sub procedure
syntax
variable
variable name

Practice	**Review Assignments**

Practice the skills you learned in the tutorial using the same case scenario.

Data File needed for the Review Assignments: Storm.xlsm

David has a new version of his workbook for which he wants you to create macros. In this version, he moved all charts to chart sheets. He also added a new chart describing the number of tornadoes occurring each decade. Finally, he expanded the scope of the report, including information on F3, F4, and F5 type tornadoes. As with the first workbook, David wants you to create macros to move between the different sheets in the workbook and to select among the different tornado types to display. He wants these macros to be run from either macro buttons on the chart sheets and worksheets or from the Quick Access Toolbar.

Complete the following:

1. Open the **Storm** workbook located in the Tutorial.12\Review folder included with your Data Files, and then save the file as a macro-enabled workbook named **Storm Report** in the same folder. In the Documentation worksheet, enter your name and the current date.

2. Use the macro recorder to record the action of going to the Yearly Chart sheet by clicking the Yearly Chart sheet tab. Name the macro **Yearly_Chart**.

3. Open the Visual Basic Editor and change the name of the project associated with the Storm Report workbook to **Storm_Report_Project**. Rename Module 1 as **Storm_Report_Module**.

4. Using the Yearly_Chart sub procedure as a guide, create four more sub procedures. In the Decades_Chart sub procedure, display the contents of the Decades Chart sheet. In the Comparison_Chart sub procedure, display the Comparison Chart sheet. In the Stat_Sheet sub procedure, display the contents of the Statistics worksheet and select cell B6 on the worksheet. Finally, in the Report_Sheet worksheet, display the Report worksheet and select cell C6 on the sheet.

5. Create a sub procedure named **Change_Type** that does the following:
   - Declare a variable named **Tornado** and a variable named **PromptTxt** both of the String data type.
   - Set the value of the PromptTxt variable to **"Please enter F0, F1, F2, F3, F4, F5, or All"**.
   - Set the value of the Tornado variable based on the value returned from an input box. The prompt of the input box should be equal to the value of the PromptTxt variable. The title of the input box should be **Tornado Type**.
   - Change the value of the Tornado variable to uppercase letters.
   - Create an If-Then-ElseIf control structure that first tests whether the Tornado variable equals F0, F1, F2, F3, F4, F5, or ALL. If it does, then change the value of the TornadoLabel range name to "=*Tornado*Label", where *Tornado* is the value of the Tornado variable, and change the references of the TornadoData range name to "=*Tornado*Data"; else if the Tornado variable does not equal an empty text string, display a critical message box with a prompt equal to the value of the PromptTxt variable and the title, **Invalid Type**.

6. In the Storm Report workbook, assign the sub procedures you created to the appropriate macro buttons in the workbook. Test each macro to verify that it works correctly.

7. Customize the Quick Access Toolbar, adding buttons for the six macros in the workbook. For each button, choose an appropriate image and add a descriptive ScreenTip.

8. Hide the row and column headings and gridlines on the Report worksheet.

9. Hide the gridlines on the Statistics worksheet.

10. Hide the sheet tabs on the Storm Report workbook.

11. Publish the Yearly chart for F0 tornadoes as a PDF file named **F0 Tornadoes by Year**. Set the margin size to Narrow and the page orientation to Landscape.

12. Save and close workbook. Submit the finished workbook and the PDF file to your instructor, either in printed or electronic form, as requested.

Apply	**Case Problem 1**

Use the skills you learned to create an Excel application that retrieves sales data from another workbook.

Data Files needed for this Case Problem: Pixal.xlsm, Regions.xlsx

Pixal Printing, Inc. Francis York is a sales manager at Pixal Printing, Inc., and tracks sales figures from 20 sales regions. She has placed sales data for these regions over the last 12 months in a workbook named *Regions*. The information for each region is stored in a separate worksheet named after the region (Region 1, Region 2, and so on).

Because navigating 20 worksheets in a file is cumbersome, Francis created a second workbook to display summary information on a single region. Currently, the workbook displays information on Region 1. All of the sales values in the workbook are linked to source data in the Regions workbook. If Francis wants to display information on a different region, she has to use the Find and Replace command to replace the text in a selected range with the text of the region she wants to view. The updated formulas then display information on the new region.

Francis wants to automate this process. She added a list box that displays 20 region names. She wants to be able to select a region from the list and have Excel automatically perform the Find and Replace command, replacing the current region with data from the region selected in the list box. To do this, you'll need to use the Replace method of the Range object, which has the following syntax:

```
Range.Replace OldText, NewText
```

In this code, *Range* is a cell range, *OldText* is text within that range to be replaced, and *NewText* is the new text you want to substitute for the old text.

Complete the following:

1. Open the **Pixal** workbook located in the Tutorial.12\Case1 folder included with your Data Files, and then save it as a macro-enabled workbook named **Pixal Sales Report** in the same folder. In the Documentation worksheet, enter your name and the current date.

All of the data values in the range E3:F19 are formulas linked to the cells in the Regions workbook. For example, cell F3 is linked to cell B2 in the Regions1 worksheet. The list of regions that Francis can choose from is contained in the list box in cell C4.

2. In the Sales worksheet, assign a new macro named **Retrieve_Sales** to the Go macro button. (*Hint*: Click the New button in the Assign Macro dialog box to create the sub procedure and open the Visual Basic Editor.) Within the Retrieve_Sales sub procedure, add the commands outlined in Steps 3 through 8.

3. Declare the following variables:
   - **OldRegion** with the String data type. Set OldRegion equal to the value of cell E2.
   - **NewRegion** with the String data type. Set it equal to the value of cell C4.

✛ EXPLORE

4. Change the text of the status bar to **Retrieving data on *NewRegion***, where *NewRegion* is the value of the NewRegion variable. Turn off screen updating to hide the action running the Replace method. (*Hint*: Also refer to Figure 12-16 for code samples to modify the status bar text and turn screen updating on and off.)

✛ EXPLORE

5. Use the Replace method of the Range object to replace all occurrences of *OldRegion* with *NewRegion* in the range E2:F19, where *OldRegion* is the value of the OldRegion variable and *NewRegion* is the value of the NewRegion variable.

6. Turn screen updating back on.

7. Reset the text of the status bar to its default value.

8. Close the Visual Basic Editor and return to the Pixal Sales Report workbook.

9. Hide the gridlines on the Sales worksheet.

10. Select Region 10 from the list in cell C4, and then click the Go button. The workbook displays information on sales from Region 10.

11. Save and close the workbook. Submit the finished workbook to your instructor, either in printed or electronic form, as requested.

| Apply | **Case Problem 2** |

Use the skills you learned to create an Excel application that enters data into a quality control chart.

Data File needed for this Case Problem: Quality.xlsm

Steel Crafters Uwe Vandenbloom is the quality control manager for Steel Crafters of Port Buren, Washington. His job is to monitor the quality of steel ingots produced by the company's machine presses. Each ingot must be manufactured with a tensile strength with a certain range of values. A press that is starting to show the effects of overuse and wear will begin to produce ingots out of the specified tolerance. To save money, malfunctioning presses are taken offline and fixed or replaced.

Uwe wants to use Excel to enter press samples to determine whether the machine is working properly or "in-control." To help decide whether a manufacturing process is in-control, engineers create quality control charts that display the sample values. Upper- and lower-control limits are displayed on the chart. Values outside of the control limits indicate a process that is out-of-control and might need to be shut down.

Uwe created a workbook to generate the quality control chart and calculate the upper- and lower-control limits. He's entered sample data in the QC Data sheet and created a quality control chart based on the data in the QA Chart sheet. He's asked you to automate the process with a macro so he can enter sample values in the worksheet with an input box. The macro should place the value from the input box in the correct cell and then update the quality control chart. The macro should also report any quality control failures with a message box. Eventually, Uwe will replace the input box with a process in which the data values are retrieved directly from the machinery, but this is a good first step.

Complete the following:

1. Open the **Quality** workbook located in the Tutorial.12\Case2 folder included with your Data Files, and then save it as a macro-enabled workbook named **Quality Control Report** in the same folder. In the Documentation worksheet, enter your name and the current date.

2. In the QC Chart sheet, add a new observation to the sample by doing the following:

   a. Turn on the macro recorder with the Use Relative References button *not* selected and create a macro named **Add_Data** and the macro description **Adds an observation to the quality control chart**.

    b. Click the QC Data sheet tab, select the range A3:E3, and then, in the Cells group on the Home tab, click the Insert button to insert new cells, shifting the existing cells down one row.

    c. In cell A3, enter **26**, and then in cell B3, enter **60**.

    d. Copy the range C4:E4 and paste it into the range C3:E3.

    e. Click the QC Chart sheet tab to return to the chart sheet, and then turn off the macro recorder.

EXPLORE

3. Go to the Add_Data sub procedure in the Visual Basic Editor. Below the comments at the top of the sub procedure, enter the following statements:

    a. Declare the **new_obs** variable. This variable will store the observation number of the quality control sample. Set the data type of the variable to Integer because it will store only whole numbers.

    b. Declare the **new_data** variable. This variable will store the actual quality control values. Set the data type of the variable to Single because it will store decimal values.

    c. Set the value of the new_obs variable equal to the value of cell A3 in the QC Data worksheet plus 1. (*Hint*: Use an object reference that includes the object hierarchy from the Sheets collection to the range object.)

    d. Set the value of the new_data variable equal to the numeric value returned from an input box. The input box prompt should read **Enter tensile strength value** and the input box title should be **Add Data**.

4. Turn off screen updating for Excel.

5. Within the code generated by the macro recorder, replace the text string "26" with the new_obs variable. Replace the text string "60" with the new_data variable. (*Hint*: Replace the values including the quotation marks with the variable names for the new_obs and new_data variables.)

6. At the bottom of the sub procedure, directly above the End Sub statement, declare two variables named **lcl** and **ucl**. These variables will store the lower- and upper-control limit values used in the quality control chart. Set the data type of both variables to Single.

7. Set the value of the lcl variable equal to the value of cell D3 in the QC Data worksheet. Set the value of the ucl variable equal to the value of cell E3 in the QC Data worksheet.

8. If the value of the new_data variable is less than the lcl variable, display a critical message box with the message **Value below control limits**. The message box title should read **Out of Control**.

9. If the value of the new_data variable is greater than the ucl variable, display a critical message box with the message **Value above control limits**. Again, the title of the message box should read **Out of Control**.

10. Turn screen updating back on.

11. Return to the Quality Control Report workbook and assign the New_Data macro to the corresponding macro button on the QC Chart sheet.

12. Use the Add New Data macro button to add the following sample values to the quality control chart: 65, 57, 50, 47, and 55. Verify that the new data is added to the control chart and to the QC Data worksheet. Also verify that the sample values 65 and 47 are reported by the macro as being out of control.

13. Return to the QC Chart sheet, if necessary. Use the macro recorder to record another macro named **Remove_Data** with the description **Removes the last data sample from the chart**. With the macro recording running, do the following:

    a. Click the QC Data sheet tab.

b. Select the range A3:E3, and then, in the Cells group on the Home tab, click the Delete button, deleting the cells and shifting the other cells up one row.

c. Click the QC Chart sheet tab to return to the control chart and turn off the macro recorder.

14. Edit the code for the Remove_Data sub procedure, adding a line at the top of the procedure to turn off screen updating and another line at the end of the procedure to turn screen updating back on.

15. Return to the workbook and assign the Remove_Data macro to the Remove Last Value macro button on the chart sheet.

16. Test the Remove_Data macro by removing the last two values from the Quality Control chart.

17. Save and close the workbook. Submit the finished workbook to your instructor, either in printed or electronic form, as requested.

| Challenge | **Case Problem 3** |

Explore how to use Visual Basic for Applications to create a custom function.

Data File needed for this Case Problem: Batting.xlsm

Stats, Inc. Hiroshi Suzuki works at Stats, Inc., a repository of sports facts and statistics. One of Hiroshi's jobs is to maintain an Excel workbook of baseball batting statistics. Two statistics that Hiroshi needs to calculate on a regular basis are batting average and slugging percentage. The following formula calculates the batting average:

```
BA = Hits / AB
```

In this formula, *BA* is the batting average, *Hits* is the total number of hits by the player, and *AB* is the total number of at bats. The following formula calculates the slugging percentage:

```
SLG = (Hits + Doubles + 2 * Triples + 3 * Home Runs) / AB
```

In this formula, *SLG* is the slugging percentage, *Hits* is the total number of hits, *Doubles* is the total number of doubles, *Triples* is the total number of triples, *Home Runs* is the total home runs, and *AB* is the total number of at bats.

Hiroshi wants to use VBA to calculate these kinds of values rather than always entering the formulas. He asks you to create two custom functions named *BA* and *SLG*. The BA function will have two parameters: hits and ab. The SLG function will have five parameters: hits, doubles, triples, homeruns, and ab.

Complete the following:

1. Open the **Batting** workbook located in the Tutorial.12\Case3 folder included with your Data Files, and then save it as a macro-enabled workbook named **Batting Statistics** in the same folder. In the Documentation worksheet, enter your name and the current date. Review the Stats worksheet contents; the values in the columns will be used to calculate the values of the batting average and slugging percentage statistics.

2. Go to the Visual Basic Editor and change the name of the project for the Batting Statistics workbook from VBAProject to **Baseball_Stats**.

3. Insert a new module into the Baseball_Stats project named **Functions**. Open the Functions module in the Code window.

 EXPLORE

4. Use the Insert menu to insert a function procedure named **BA**. Add the following parameters to the BA() function: hits and ab.

EXPLORE 5. Insert a line in the function procedure to return the value of the BA() function. The value should be equal to the value of the hits parameter divided by the value of the ab parameter.

EXPLORE 6. Insert another function procedure into the Code window with the name **SLG**. The SLG() function should have the following parameters: hits, doubles, triples, homeruns, and ab.

EXPLORE 7. Add a line to the SLG() function procedure to return the value of the SLG statistic.

8. Close the Visual Basic Editor and return to the Batting Statistics workbook.

9. Select cell J5 in the Stats worksheet. Click the Insert Function button in the Function Library group on the Formulas tab. In the User Defined category of functions, select the BA function. Calculate the batting average for the first place in the list.

10. Click cell K5 and use the SLG function to calculate the slugging percentage for the first place.

11. Fill the formulas from the range J5:K5 into the range J6:K44.

12. Sort the baseball statistics in the table in descending order of slugging percentage.

13. Format the page layout of the Stats sheet to print in portrait orientation with narrow margins.

14. Publish the Stats worksheet to a PDF file named **Baseball Report**.

15. Save and close the workbook. Submit the finished workbook and the PDF file to your instructor, either in printed or electronic form, as requested.

Create | **Case Problem 4**

Test your knowledge of VBA by creating an accounting program.

There are no Data Files needed for this Case Problem.

The Brass Broker Linda Greenwood has a small at-home business called The Brass Broker, in which she purchases brass instruments from online auctions, reconditions them, and resells them at a profit. Linda wants to create an Excel workbook to track her purchases and resales from the online auctions she participates in. The workbook will essentially be an interactive checking account. She will enter the cost of the purchases she makes or the income from her resales in one worksheet. Another worksheet will contain a running list of the transactions, including the cost of the purchase or the income it generated, the item purchased, the date, and the current balance in her auction account.

Linda wants to automate this process in Excel so that she enters the data in a form in one worksheet and the data is automatically transferred to the list in another sheet. She also wants the application to check her running balance, displaying an error message if she attempts to make a purchase for which there are insufficient funds in the auction account. You'll help her by designing a VBA program to create this interactive checking account.

Complete the following:

1. Create a macro-enabled workbook named **The Brass Broker** and save it in the Tutorial.12\Case4 folder included with your Data Files. Add a Documentation sheet to the workbook containing a title, your name, the date, and a brief statement describing the purpose of the workbook.

2. Create a worksheet named **Auction Account** that contains a range of columns with the following labels: the date, the transaction description (purchase or sale), the item being purchased or sold, the transaction amount (enter purchases as negative cash flows and sales as positive cash flows), the starting balance (before the transaction), and the ending balance (after the transaction).

3. Enter the information shown in Figure 12-50 as the starting point for the auction account. The most recent transactions are at the top of the table. Use a formula to calculate the starting and ending balances (aside from the initial starting balance of $321).

Figure 12-50

Date	Description	Item	Amount	Starting Balance	Ending Balance
3/31/2010	Purchase	New Bb Brass Band Trumpet	−$131	$541	$410
3/24/2010	Sale	Dolnet Alto Saxophone	$75	$466	$541
3/22/2010	Sale	Bach TR300 Trumpet	$179	$287	$466
3/21/2010	Purchase	Brass Bugle Army Horn	−$34	$321	$287

4. Create a worksheet named **Transaction** that contains cells in which you'll enter the details of new transactions. The worksheet should contain places to enter the date of the transaction, the transaction type, the item being sold or purchased, and the cost or income from the transaction.

5. Write a macro named **Insert_Transaction** to copy the transaction data from the Transaction worksheet and insert it at the top of the list of transactions in the Auction Account. (*Hint*: You can use the macro recorder to record the steps to copy sample data from the Transaction sheet to the Auction Account sheet.) The macro should include the following:

- An If statement that verifies that there is enough money in the auction account to cover the transaction. If there is not enough money, the macro should prevent the transaction from being entered into the auction account and notify the user with a message box, indicating how much money is in the account.

- If the transaction is covered by the account, copy the values from the Transaction worksheet into the Auction Account worksheet. After the values have been copied, use a message box to notify the user of a successful transaction along with the current account balance. Replace the values in the Transaction worksheet with blanks.

6. Test the macro by entering the data shown in Figure 12-51 in the order shown. Sales are entered as positive values and purchases are entered as negative values.

Figure 12-51

Date	Description	Item	Amount
4/2/2010	Purchase	Bach Trumpet with Mouth Piece	–$143
4/4/2010	Sale	King 1130 Flugabone	$189
4/7/2010	Purchase	Schiller Lightweight Trumpet	–$313

7. Add any final formatting to your workbook to give it a professional look.
8. Save and close the workbook. Submit the finished workbook to your instructor, either in printed or electronic form, as requested.

Research | Internet Assignments

Use the Internet to find and work with data related to the topics presented in this tutorial.

The purpose of the Internet Assignments is to challenge you to find information on the Internet that you can use to work effectively with this software. The actual assignments are updated and maintained on the Course Technology Web site. Log on to the Internet and use your Web browser to go to the Student Online Companion for New Perspectives Office 2007 at **www.course.com/np/office2007**. Then navigate to the Internet Assignments for this tutorial.

Assess | SAM Assessment and Training

If you have a SAM user profile, you may have access to hands-on instruction, practice, and assessment of the skills covered in this tutorial. Log in to your SAM account (**http://sam2007.course.com**) to launch any assigned training activities or exams that relate to the skills covered in this tutorial.

Review | Quick Check Answers

Session 12.1

1. (a) Project Explorer gives a hierarchical view of the objects in a VBA project. (b) The Properties window gives you a view of the properties of the individual objects. (c) The Code window displays the VBA code for a project's macros.
2. A *project* is a collection of macros, worksheets, forms for data entry, and other items that make up the custom application you're creating. An *object* is an element of an application, such as a worksheet, cell, chart, form, or report. A *property* is an attribute of an object that defines one of its characteristics, such as its name, size, color, or location on the screen. A *module* is a collection of macros or procedures. *Syntax* is the set of rules specifying how you must enter certain commands (in a VBA application).
3. Open the online VBA Help window and search for information on the property.
4. sub procedures, function procedures, and property procedures
5. Sub *Procedure_Name* (*parameters*)
   Visual Basic commands and comments
   End Sub
6. A project might contain several modules as a way to organize macros based on their content and purpose.

Session 12.2

1. An *object-oriented programming language* is a programming language that performs tasks by manipulating objects. A *collection object* is an object that is composed of a group of other objects. *Method* is an action that can be performed on an object. *Parameter* is data sent to a method, procedure, or function that is used in the operation of the method, procedure, or function. *Variable* is a named element in a program that can be used to store and retrieve information.
2. Sheets("Histogram").Name = "Histogram Chart"
3. Sheets("Histogram").Select
4. SheetName = ActiveSheet.Name
5. Application.StatusBar = "Program Running"
6. Application.ScreenUpdating = false
7. LastName = InputBox("Enter your last name", "Log In")

Session 12.3

1. A control structure is a series of commands that evaluates conditions in your program and then directs the program to perform certain actions based on the status of those conditions. Control structures are necessary for macros that need to perform different actions for different conditions.
2. A comparison operator is a word or symbol that is used to compare values or expressions within a condition. A logical operator is used to combine conditions within an expression.
3. If *condition* Then
       VBA commands if the condition is true
   Else
       VBA commands if the condition is false
   End If.
4. If-Then-ElseIf control structure
5. MsgBox *Prompt, Button, Title*
6. MsgBox "Filed Saved", vbOKOnly, "File Status"
7. within the Quick Access Toolbar
8. A sub procedure performs an action; a function procedure returns a value.

Ending Data Files

Tutorial.12 →

Tutorial
Tornado Analysis.xlsm
Tornado History (1950 – 1999).pdf

Review
F0 Tornadoes by Year.pdf
Storm Report.xlsm

Case1
Pixal Sales Report.xlsm
Regions.xlsx

Case2
Quality Control Report.xlsm

Case3
Baseball Report.pdf
Batting Statistics.xlsm

Case4
The Brass Broker.xlsm

Reality Check

Excel is a powerful program for analyzing financial data, projecting future income and expenses, and organizing information from a wide variety of sources. With Excel's support for Visual Basic for Applications, experienced users and programmers can expand Excel's capability to accommodate a wide range of problems and challenges. To explore the ways you can use Excel's capabilities to assist you in the business world, talk to instructors, colleagues, and business leaders about getting access to some real-world financial data, particularly accounting data in which you can perform a financial analysis. Obtain the following:

- A balance sheet
- An income statement
- A cash flow report
- Sales data of a product or service that indicates the level of sales volume for a given price or fee

In this exercise, you'll use Excel to create a workbook that will contain information of your choice, using the Excel skills and features presented in Tutorials 9 through 12. Use the following steps as a guide to completing your workbook.

Note: Please be sure *not* to include any personal information of a sensitive nature in the files you create to be submitted to your instructor for this exercise. Later, you can update your data in Excel with such information for your personal use.

1. Place the financial data in external data files. Be ready to consolidate several sources of data from text files and databases to Web queries and other Excel workbooks.
2. Create a new workbook to contain the business information you intend to collect. Use the first worksheet to document the scope and purpose of your workbook, including a listing of all data sources you intend to use.
3. Create connections to the financial data you have accumulated.
4. On the next several sheets, use the connections you created to import and display the data. Format the data so it is easy to read and interpret. If you have collected financial reports from a company, examine how the reports interrelate. Replace the data values with formulas whenever possible.
5. Perform a what-if analysis on your financial data. Determine what would happen to the company's balance sheets, cash flow, or net income if certain key variables were changed.
6. Create a worksheet that contains either a one-variable or a two-variable table. Use the data table to explore the financial impact of several what-if analyses.
7. Extrapolate the company's income and expenses three years into the future assuming first a linear trend and then a growth trend. Discuss with your colleagues and advisors what would constitute a realistic trend line.
8. Create charts and tables that clearly explain your projections and assumptions.
9. Investigate the sales data you collected. Assuming different values for price elasticity, calculate the company's break-even point. Investigate market information to determine which value for price elasticity is the most appropriate for the sale item.

10. Under your assumed value for price elasticity, calculate the price that would result in maximum revenue. Calculate the price that would result in maximum net income. Save both Solver models in your workbook.

11. Insert a Web page that documents your conclusions and methods.

12. Create VBA sub procedures to automate the process of displaying the different charts and tables of your report. Insert a worksheet at the beginning of your workbook that contains macro buttons users can click to quickly navigate the workbook, displaying the chief items of interest.

13. Modify the Quick Access Toolbar for the workbook so you can run the macros from either the toolbar or the worksheet.

14. Save and close the workbook, and then submit the completed workbook to your instructor, in printed or electronic form, as requested.

Creating a Grading Workbook

Objectives

- Create a connection to a text file
- Create range names
- Apply data validation based on a list of values
- Use the VLOOKUP function to retrieve data from a list
- Use the SUMPRODUCT function to calculate the sum from multiplying two lists of numbers
- Use the COUNTIF function to count totals corresponding to a query
- Display data values using data bars
- Display an array of data values with freeze panes
- Save a workbook as a template file

Case | High Plains School

Fran Lewis teaches math and science at High Plains School in Lane, Kansas. She's been asked to develop a grading workbook for the staff at the school. The workbook needs to allow teachers to submit final grades based on a weighted average of homework, projects, quizzes, and exams. The workbook should also contain sheets for entering absences and tardiness as well as any special notes about student performance and behavior. The school uses a special database system in which homework, quiz, and exam scores are entered automatically during class. The scores are then exported to text files. The workbook needs to be able to connect to these text files and extract the student scores.

Fran already developed a prototype workbook that contains the formatting and some of the text needed for the final workbook. You'll complete the workbook for Fran and then save it as a template file that other staff members can use.

Complete the following:

1. Open the **Grading** workbook located in the **AddCases** folder, and then save the workbook as **Grading Sheet** in the same folder. In the Documentation sheet, enter your name and the current date.

2. In the Class Summary worksheet, which will show basic information about a course, enter **Algebra II** for the course title, **Fran Lewis** for the instructor, and **IV** for the quarter. Assign the following weights to the grading components: Homework (20%), Quizzes (40%), and Exams (40%).

3. Assign the range name **Grade_Scale** to the range B13:C26 with the entire workbook as its scope because the grading scale is set by the school.

4. In the Student List worksheet, which will list students in the class and their grades, create a connection to the student list stored in the tab-delimited **Student List** text file located in the **AddCases** folder. Import the data starting at the seventh row. Set the properties of the import so that Excel does not adjust the column widths. Place the imported data in the range B6:C25.

Starting Data Files

AddCases

Exam Grades.txt
Grading.xlsx
Homework Grades.txt
Quiz Grades.txt
Student List.txt

5. Assign the range name **Student_List** to the range B6:B25. Set the scope of the range name to the entire workbook.

6. In the Student Notes worksheet, which will store notes about a student's progress and behavior, add data validation to the range B5:B40, confining entries to the list of students from the Student_List range. In the Resolved? column, confine entries to either Yes or No.

7. Add the following notes to the worksheet:

Boyd, Jason	**3/1/2010**	**Missing homework**	**Yes**
Jared, Lynn	**3/3/2010**	**Talking in class, disruptive behavior**	**No**

8. In the Attendance worksheet, which will store attendance records, confine the entries in the Student column to the student names from the Student_List range. Limit the entries in the Attendance Issue column to either Absent or Tardy. Limit the entries in the Excused? column to either Yes or No.

9. Add the following attendance issues to the worksheet:

Trout, Jay	**3/2/2010**	**Absent**	**Yes**
Trout, Jay	**3/3/2010**	**Absent**	**Yes**
Benjamin, Andrea	**3/4/2010**	**Tardy**	**No**

10. In the Homework worksheet, which will record homework scores, in the range A9:A28, insert a reference to each of the student names in the Student List worksheet.

11. Create a connection to the homework scores from the **Homework Grades** text file located in the **AddCases** folder. Import the data starting at row 6, excluding the first column. Set the import properties so that Excel does not adjust the column width when importing the data. Import the data into the range B9:O28.

12. Freeze the worksheet at cell B9.

13. Repeat Steps 10 through 12 for the Quizzes worksheet. Import the grades from the **Quiz Grades** text file, placing the imported data into the range B9:E28.

14. Repeat Steps 10 through 12 for the Exams worksheet. Import the grades from the **Exam Grades** text file located in the **AddCases** folder, placing the imported data into the range B9:C28.

15. In the Grades worksheet, which will calculate each student's final grade, in the range B6:D6, insert references to the three component percentages in the Class Summary worksheet in the range C9:C11. In cell E6, calculate the total of the percentages.

16. In the range A7:A26, insert a reference to each student name in the Student List worksheet.

17. In cell B7, create a formula to calculate the first student's percentage score on homework by adding all of the values in that student's row in the Homework worksheet and then dividing the sum by the total number of homework points in row 7 of the Homework worksheet. Fill the formula into the rest of the column to calculate each student's homework percentage.

18. Repeat Step 17 to calculate each student's quiz percentage and exam percentage.

19. In cell E7, use the SUMPRODUCT function to calculate the weighted percentage of each component score multiplied by the weight assigned to that component. Copy the formula into the rest of the column to calculate each student's final overall grade percentage.

20. In cell F7, calculate the student's final grade using the VLOOKUP function with grades taken from the Grade_Scale range. Use an approximate match to the scores from the Grade_Scale range.

21. In the Student List worksheet, insert references to the Grades worksheet to display each student's final score and grade.

22. In the Class Summary worksheet, in the range D14:D26, use the COUNTIF function with the grades from the Student List worksheet to calculate the total number of each grade in the class.

23. Add tan data bars to the values in the range D14:D26 to indicate the frequency of each grade in the class.

24. Save the workbook.

25. Delete the class data from the range C4:C6;C9:C11 in the Class Summary worksheet. Delete the student name data from the range B6:C25 in the Student List worksheet, but do not delete the query. Delete the student notes data and the attendance data from the Student Notes and Attendance worksheets.

26. In the Homework worksheet, delete the homework descriptions in row 5, the homework points in row 7, and the homework scores in the range B9:O28. Do not delete the query associated with the homework data.

27. Repeat Step 26 for the quiz and exam data in the Quizzes and Exams worksheets.

28. Save the workbook as a template file named **Grading Template** in the **AddCases** folder. Do not have Excel automatically refresh the external data before saving the workbook nor when the workbook is opened.

29. Submit the finished workbooks to your instructor, either in printed or electronic form, as requested.

Ending Data Files

AddCases

Exam Grades.txt
Grading Sheet.xlsx
Grading Template.xltx
Homework Grades.txt
Quiz Grades.txt
Student List.txt

Additional Case 2

Objectives

- Calculate revenue assuming price elasticity of demand
- Format a scatter plot chart
- Add new data series to a chart
- Use Solver to determine an optimal price point
- Add constraints to a Solver model
- Save a Solver model
- Add headers and footers to a page layout
- Publish a worksheet as a PDF file

Calculating the Optimal Price Point

Case | StarDust Scopes

Kevin Falk is the owner of StarDust Scopes, a small company in Chandler, Arizona, that specializes in manufacturing telescopes, binoculars, and spotting scopes. Kevin is trying to determine a sales price for the StarDust 8 telescope to maximize the company's revenues. The sales price must take into account several limiting factors. Telescopes tend to be considered luxury items, so increasing the price too much will greatly decrease sales. By decreasing the sales price, Kevin believes he can sell more scopes and maximize the company's revenue. But, to meet the increased demand, Kevin must have enough parts in inventory to cover production. He asks you to determine the optimal sales price for his product under these conditions. He wants you to present this information clearly and concisely in an Excel chart. Because this report will be presented to the company's board of directors, he also needs the analysis published as a PDF file.

Complete the following:

1. Open the **StarDust** workbook located in the **AddCases** folder included with the Data Files, and then save the workbook as **StarDust Scopes** to the same folder. In the Documentation sheet, enter your name and the current date.

2. Based on the past year's sales, Kevin estimates that the company can sell 2,700 scopes at a price of $1,800 per telescope. In the Price Point Analysis worksheet, enter these values in the range D5:D6, and then calculate the revenue from the sales in cell D7. Format the values appropriately.

3. Kevin assumes a price elasticity of demand for sale of the telescope of 1.6. In other words, for every 10% increase in price, sales will decline by 16%. Enter the elasticity value in cell D10. Enter the sales price of **$1,800** in cell D12. Calculate the estimated units sold assuming elasticity in cell D11 and use the INT function to truncate the value to limit the units sold to an integer. (*Hint*: Use the formula from Tutorial 10 to calculate the units sold value.)

4. Enter **Price Elasticity Curve** in cell B15, and then enter the column labels **Price** and **Revenue** in cells B16 and C16. Insert a reference to the values of cells D12 and D13 in the range B17:C17.

Starting Data Files

AddCases

StarDust.xlsx

5. In the range B18:C38, complete a one-variable data table for price values ranging from $500 up to $2,500 in increments of $100. Format the text and data values in the one-variable data table appropriately.

6. Create a scatter plot with smooth lines of the data in the range B18:C38. The plot will show how changing the sales price of the StarDust telescope affects revenue. Edit the scatter plot as follows:

   - Resize the chart to cover the range D16:H36.
   - Change the name of the data series from Series1 to **Price Elasticity Curve**. (*Hint*: Use the Select Data button in the Data group on the Chart Tools Design tab.)
   - Move the chart legend to the bottom of the chart.
   - Change the color of the scatter plot line to an Olive Green.
   - Set the range of horizontal axis to $500 up to $2,500.
   - Set the range of the vertical axis to $3,000,000 up to $5,500,000. Display the vertical axis values in units of 1 million. Do not show the display units label on the chart. Edit the axis number format to display the axis values in the form "$n.n mil" where *n.n* is the revenue value in millions of dollars.
   - Add **Price** as the horizontal axis title and **Revenue** as the vertical axis title. Rotate the vertical axis title.

7. Add the data values from the range D6:D7 to the plot as a single point in a new data series. (*Hint*: Use the Select Data button in the Data group on the Chart Tools Design tab to select and add the data). Name this series **Current Price Point**. Edit the series as follows:

   - Do not display a line for the point. (*Hint*: You can select the data series with the Selection list box in the Current Selection group on the Chart Tools Layout tab.)
   - Change the marker to a dark tan circle that is 7 points in size.

   The location of the Current Price Point on the Price Elasticity Curve shows that Kevin could actually increase the company's revenue by decreasing the price of the telescope.

8. Use Solver to find the maximum revenue in cell D13 by changing the value of cell D12. Constrain cell D12 to integer values greater than or equal to $500.

9. Enter **Optimal Price Point** in cell I15. Enter **Price** in cell I16. Enter **Revenue** in cell I17. Copy the values (not the formulas) from the range D12:D13 into the range J16:J17, and format them appropriately.

10. Add the values from the range J16:J17 as a new data series into the chart. Name the series **Optimal Price Point**. Format the data series to have no lines, but a 7-point blue circle.

11. Enter **Solver Model Parameters** in cell I19. Save the parameters of the current Solver model into the range I20:I24. Format the cells appropriately.

12. In the range I6:I12, calculate the number of parts Kevin would need to order to create the number of units produced and sold indicated in cell D11. Kevin can make only as many scopes for which he has parts.

13. In the range J6:J12, calculate the number of parts remaining after completing the orders indicated by the optimal price point. Does Kevin have enough parts to fill the order? Format all negative values in the range in a red font enclosed in parentheses.

14. Edit the Solver model to include the constraint that you cannot produce more tele- scopes than allowed by the amount of available parts. Change the price value in cell D12 back to **$1,800** and rerun the model.

15. Enter **Optimal Price Point w/ Inventory** in cell I26. Enter **Price** in cell I27. Enter **Revenue** in cell I28. Copy the values (not the formulas) from the range D12:D13 into the range J27:J28, and format them appropriately.

16. Add the values from the range J27:J28 as a new data series into the chart. Name the series **Optimal Price Point w/ Inventory**. Format the data series to have no lines, but displayed with a 7-point red circle.

17. Add the title **Price Point Analysis** to the chart.

18. Add a drop shadow to the chart.

19. Enter **Solver Model Parameters** in cell I30. Save the parameters of the current Solver model into the range I31:I36. Format the cells appropriately.

20. Change the page orientation of the Price Point Analysis worksheet to landscape and scale it to fit on a single page.

21. Center the header, **Price Point Analysis**, on the printed page. Add a right footer con- taining your name, the date, and the name of the workbook on separate lines.

22. Save the workbook, and then publish the Price Point Analysis worksheet as a PDF file named **Price Point Analysis** in the **AddCases folder**.

23. Save and close all files. Submit the finished files to your instructor, either in printed or electronic form, as requested.

Ending Data Files

AddCases

Price Point Analysis.pdf
StarDust Scopes.xlsx

Objectives

- Import data from an XML document
- Use the IF and VLOOKUP functions
- Load an XML map
- Map XML elements to worksheet cells
- Export a worksheet to an XML document
- Record a macro and assign it to a macro button
- Edit a VBA sub procedure
- Unlock worksheet cells and protect a worksheet

Creating an Interactive Order Form

Case | The Mustard Hut

Helen Jankowski works at The Mustard Hut, a novelty shop in Sanford, Maine, that sells a wide variety of mustards ranging from common American deli mustards like brown Dijon and classic yellow to exotic mustards like maple walnut. The company is starting to transfer its order data and inventory reports to XML files. Helen wants to use an Excel application to easily enter customer orders and then export the order data into an XML document. Because this application will be used by other employees, she wants to make it as easy to use as possible. She wants to include macros to help simplify the process. She wants the finished product to export data to a single XML document by clicking a macro button on the workbook. Helen has already created the initial workbook that you'll complete.

Complete the following:

1. Open the macro-enabled **Mustard** workbook located in the **AddCases** folder, and then save it as a macro-enabled workbook named **Mustard Hut** in the same folder. In the Documentation sheet, enter your name and the current date.
2. In the Mustard Products worksheet, enter a list of products sold by the Mustard Hut, which is stored in an XML document. Create a connection to the **Product List.xml** document located in the **AddCases** folder and insert the contents of the file as an XML table into the worksheet starting at cell B5.
3. Name the XML table **Product_List**. (*Hint:* Enter the name in the Table Name box in the Properties group on the Table Tools Design tab.) Assign the range name **Item_IDs** to the item ID values in the first column of the Product_List table. Format the item price values as currency.
4. In the Order Form worksheet, all customer orders should be based on products in the Product_List table. In the range B17:B22, add a data validation check to ensure that item IDs come from the list of values in the Item_IDs range.

Starting Data Files

Mustard Orders.xsd
Mustard.xlsm
Product List.xml

5. In cell C17, insert an IF function that tests whether the value in cell B17 is equal to an empty text string (""). If so, display an empty text string; otherwise, use the VLOOKUP function to look up the name of the item corresponding to the item ID in cell B17 in the Product_List table. Specify an exact match. Copy the formula in cell C17 to the range C18:C22.

6. In cell D17, insert an IF function that tests whether the value in cell B17 is equal to an empty text string. If so, display an empty text string; otherwise, use the VLOOKUP function to look up the price of the item in the Product_List table. Again, specify an exact match and copy the formula in cell D17 to the range D18:D22.

7. In cell F17, insert an IF function that tests whether the value in cell B17 is equal to an empty text string. If so, display an empty text string; otherwise, multiply the item price in cell D17 by the quantity in cell E17. Copy the formula in cell F17 to the range F18:F22.

8. In cell F24, calculate the total charges from the range F17:F22.

9. The Mustard Hut gives a 3% discount for sales over $100. Insert an IF function in cell F25 that calculates the discount (if any) for the order. In cell F26, calculate the cost of the order minus the discount.

10. There is a 5% sales tax on all orders. Calculate the sales tax in cell F28. Calculate the total cost of the order (charge after discount plus the sales tax) in cell F30.

11. Test the worksheet by inserting the following sample customer order:

Customer	**Paul Nichols**
Date	**3/10/2010**
Order No.	**17871**
Shipping Address	**1500 Palm Drive**
	Clearwater, FL 33755
Customer Order	**EX004** (2 items), **HVM015** (1 item), **HVM018** (2 items), **FM013** (2 items), **FM010** (2 items), **HD011** (3 items)

12. Verify that the subtotal value is $101.25, the discount value is $3.04, the cost after discount is $98.21, the 5% sales tax is $4.91, and the total cost of the order is $103.12.

13. To export this order to an XML document, you must map each value in the order sheet to an element in the XML file. Load the XML map based on the file **Mustard Orders.xsd** located in the **AddCases** folder.

14. Drag each element from the data map into the corresponding cell in the Order Form worksheet. You do not have to display any element headers because they already appear in the worksheet. Because the customer_order element contains the table of order items, drag the customer_order element to cell B16. You do not have to match any of the item elements within the customer_order element to cells in the worksheet.

15. Start the macro recorder. Name the macro **Export_Order** and add the description **This macro exports the customer order to the Order.xml file.**

16. Click the Export button in the XML group on the Developer tab. Export the contents of the document to a new XML file named **Order** located in the **AddCases** folder. Stop the macro recorder.

17. View the code for the Export_Order sub procedure in the Visual Basic Editor. The Export method has a single parameter named *URL* that indicates the path and file-name for the exported document. You need only the filename, not the path for this project. Edit the text string with the URL for the Order.xml file; delete the path to file, leaving only the filename "Order.xml." Close the Editor and return to the Mustard Hut workbook.

18. Using Notepad or another text editor, open the **Order.xml** file located in the **AddCases** folder. Verify that the XML document contains the order details you entered in Step 11, and then save the file as **Initial Order.xml** in the **AddCases** folder.

19. In the Order Form worksheet in the Mustard Hut workbook, add a form control button with the label **Export to XML** directly below the Customer Order table. Assign the Export_Order macro to the button.

20. Start the macro recorder. Name the macro **Erase_Order** and add the description, **This macro erases the current customer order.**

21. Select the nonadjacent range C5:C7; C10:C13; B17:B22; E17:E22, press the Delete key to clear the contents of the order, click cell C5, and then stop the macro recorder.

22. Add a second form control button with the label **Erase Order** below the Customer Order table. Assign the Erase_Order macro to the button.

23. Enter the following customer order to your worksheet:

Customer	**Jane Reynolds**
Date	**3/11/2010**
Order No.	**17872**
Shipping Address	**31 West Lincoln**
	Laurel, MD 20707
Customer Order	**FM015** (2 items), **FM013** (1 item)

24. Click the Export to XML button to export the order, and then click the Erase Order button to erase the order.

25. Select the range C5:C7; C10:C13; B17:B22; E17:E22, and change the protection properties of the selected cells to unlocked.

26. Protect the worksheet, allowing users to select only unlocked cells. Do not specify a password for the protected worksheet.

27. Save and close the workbook. Submit the finished files to your instructor, either in printed or electronic form, as requested.

Ending Data Files

AddCases

Initial Order.xml
Mustard Hut.xlsm
Mustard Orders.xsd
Order.xml
Product List.xml

Additional Case 4

- Create a connection to an Access database
- Insert a PivotTable
- Add fields to a PivotTable
- Group PivotTable row and column labels
- Format PivotTable data
- Create and format a 3-D chart
- Modify the properties of a connection
- Save a worksheet to a Web page

Analyzing Housing Prices

Case | Premier Realty

Janice Carson works at Premier Realty in Loveland, Colorado, analyzing the housing market. Janice wants to use Excel to create a report that describes the average price of houses in different sectors of the city. She wants to compare homes in the northeast sector against homes in other sectors and she wants to break down the data by the age of the home and the size of the home in square feet. The company keeps daily records of home sales and prices in an Access database. Janice asks you to retrieve the data from the database and put it in a PivotTable and PivotChart. She also wants to save the final version of the worksheet as a Web page that can then be posted on the company's intranet to be viewed by her colleagues. Janice has not done any work on this project, so you'll have to create the workbook yourself.

Complete the following:

1. Create a workbook named **Home Prices** in the **AddCases** folder. In a Documentation sheet, enter the name of the company, your name, the current date, and a purpose statement.
2. Create a worksheet named **Home Price Analysis**. Add a title to the worksheet and a subtitle indicating that this worksheet will contain an analysis of home prices in the Loveland area.
3. Insert a PivotTable based on a connection to the **Loveland Homes** database in the **AddCases** folder.
4. The NE Sector field indicates whether a home is located in the northeast sector of the city. Use this field as a report filter.
5. Display the Square Feet field as a row label, grouped into the following categories: Less than 1200 sq. ft., 1200 – 2000 sq. ft., and Greater than 2000 sq. ft. Name the row labels **Home Size**.
6. Display the Age field as a column label grouped into the following categories: 1 to 10 years, 11 to 20 years, and Greater than 20 years. Name the column labels **Home Age**.
7. Display the average price of the homes in the Loveland area. Format the values as currency.

Starting Data Files

Loveland Homes.accdb

8. Create a 3-D column chart of the data from the PivotTable. Format the chart as follows:
    - Remove the chart legend.
    - Add the chart title **Home Price Analysis**.
    - Rotate the chart 210° in the x-direction, 20° in the y-direction, and with a perspective value of 25°.

9. Apply an appropriate built-in PivotTable style to the PivotTable.

10. Apply an appropriate built-in chart style to the PivotChart.

11. Edit the properties of the connection to the Loveland Homes database so that the data is refreshed whenever the workbook is opened. Change the name of the connection to **Loveland Housing Prices** and add the description **Data from the Loveland Homes Access database containing housing prices in the Loveland area.**

12. Export the ODC connection file to the **Loveland Homes Connection.odc** file in the **AddCases** folder so Janice can use this connection again in another Office file.

13. Delete any unused worksheets, and then save the workbook.

14. Save the contents of the Home Price Analysis worksheet as a Web page. Change the page title to **Loveland Housing Prices**. Have Excel automatically republish this Web page every time the workbook is saved.

15. Save and close the workbook.

16. View the Loveland Housing Prices Web page in a Web browser, print the Web page, and then close the browser.

17. Submit the finished files to your instructor, either in printed or electronic form, as requested.

Ending Data Files

AddCases

Home Prices.xlsx
Loveland Homes Connection.odc
Loveland Homes.accdb
Loveland Housing Prices.htm
Loveland Housing Prices_files\filelist.xml
Loveland Housing Prices_files\Home Prices_6116_image001.png
Loveland Housing Prices_files\Home Prices_6116_image001.gif

Objectives

- Open a workbook in Compatibility Mode
- Use the LEN function to determine the number of characters in a cell
- Use the LEFT function to extract a series of characters from a text string
- Use the Paste Values command
- Use the PROPER function to convert the case of a text string
- Use the Concatenation operator to join several text strings into one text string
- Use the Text to Columns command to separate multiple pieces of data in one column into separate columns
- USE the UPPER function to convert text to uppercase
- Use the SUBSTITUTE function to replace characters in a text string
- Use a special format for phone number
- Create custom formats for numbers and dates

Working with Text Functions and Creating Custom Formats

Cleaning Data in a Spreadsheet

Case | Zeus Engineering

Growth in the town of Bayville has strained the capacity of local roads. Traffic increases have created delays, vehicular hazards, and pedestrian safety concerns. To address these issues, the town has contracted Zeus Engineering to develop a Transportation Improvement Program (TIP).

Myron Londale, traffic analyst at Zeus Engineering, will analyze data on private homes and commercial buildings located along the route being analyzed. He received the data from the Bayville Assessor's office, which transferred the data to Excel. Before Myron begins his analysis, he needs to "clean" the data, and has asked for your help.

Starting Data Files

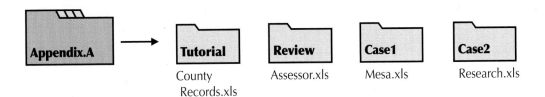

Appendix.A → Tutorial
County Records.xls

Review
Assessor.xls

Case1
Mesa.xls

Case2
Research.xls

Opening and Saving Workbooks Created in Earlier Versions of Excel

The workbook Myron received from the Bayville Assessor's office was created in an earlier version of Excel. When you open a workbook that was created in an earlier version of Excel, Excel 2007 opens the workbook in **Compatibility Mode**. The words *[Compatibility Mode]* appear in the title bar, indicating the file is not in the latest Excel format. You can work in Compatibility Mode, which keeps the workbook in the older file format and makes the workbook accessible for users who do not have the current version of Excel installed. However, to have access to all the latest features and tools in Excel 2007, the workbook must be converted to the current file format, which has the file extension .xlsx. This is the file format you have used to save all workbooks in this book.

Myron wants to use Excel tables to manage and analyze the data. Because tables are a new feature in Excel 2007, Myron asks you to open the current workbook and convert it to the current file format. You can tell when a workbook has been saved in the current file format, because its file extension changes from .xls to .xlsx.

To save the County Records workbook in the Excel 2007 file format:

▶ **1.** Open the **County Records** workbook located in the **Appendix.A\Tutorial** folder included with your Data Files. The workbook opens in Compatibility Mode, because the workbook was created in an earlier version of Excel. See Figure A-1.

Figure A-1 ▶ | **Workbook in Compatibility Mode**

title bar shows that the workbook was created in an earlier version of Excel

▶ **2.** Click the **Office Button** , and then click **Save As**. The Save As dialog box opens.

▶ **3.** Type **Bayville County** in the File name box.

The Save as type box shows that the current file format is Excel 97-2003 Workbook, which is the earlier file format. You'll change this to the latest file format.

▶ **4.** Click the **Save as type** button, and then click **Excel Workbook**. This is the file format for Excel 2007.

▶ **5.** Click the **Save** button. The workbook is saved with the new name and file type.

The workbook remains in Compatibility Mode, as you can see from the title bar. You can continue to work in Compatibility Mode, or you can close and then reopen the workbook in the new file format.

To open the Bayville County workbook in the Excel 2007 file format:

▶ **1.** Close the Bayville County workbook.

▶ **2.** Open the **Bayville County** workbook. The words *[Compatibly Mode]* no longer appear on the title bar, indicating the workbook is in the Excel 2007 file format.

▶ **3.** In the Documentation sheet, enter your name and the current date.

The Data worksheet contains data obtained from the county assessor's office. Myron wants you to convert this data to an Excel table.

To create an Excel table from the county records:

▶ **1.** Switch to the **Data** worksheet.

▶ **2.** Click the **Insert** tab on the Ribbon, and then, in the Tables group, click the **Table** button. The Create Table dialog box opens with the data in the range A1:H51 selected.

▶ **3.** Click the **OK** button to create the Excel table.

▶ **4.** In the Properties group on the Table Tools Design tab, type **TIPData** in the Table Name box to rename the table.

▶ **5.** Click the **Data** tab on the Ribbon, and then in the Sort & Filter group, click the **Filter** button. The filter arrows are removed from the column headers.

▶ **6.** Click any cell in the Excel table.

Using Text Functions

If you receive a workbook from a coworker or obtain data from other software packages, you often have to edit (sometimes referred to as *clean* or *scrub*) and manipulate the data before it is ready to use. Many Text functions help users edit and correct the text values in their workbooks. Text values, also referred to as a *text string* or *string*, contain one or more characters and can include spaces, symbols, and numbers as well as uppercase and lowercase letters. For example, Text functions are used to return the number of characters, remove extra spaces, and change the case of text strings. Figure A-2 reviews some of the common Text functions available in Excel.

Text functions ◀ **Figure A-2**

Function	Syntax	Description	Example
LEFT	LEFT(text,nbr chars)	Returns a specified number of characters at the left of the string	=LEFT("Michael",3) returns Mic
RIGHT	RIGHT(text,nbr chars)	Returns a specified number of characters at the right of the string	=RIGHT("Michael",3) returns ael
MID	MID(text,start nbr, nbr chars)	Returns a specified number of characters from a string, starting at a position you specify	=MID("Net Income"),5,3) returns Inc
UPPER	UPPER(text)	Converts all lowercase characters in a string to uppercase	=UPPER("kim") returns KIM
LOWER	LOWER(text)	Converts all uppercase characters in a string to lowercase	=LOWER("KIM") returns kim
PROPER	PROPER(text)	Capitalizes first letter of each word in a string	=PROPER("JASON BAKER") returns Jason Baker
LEN	LEN(text)	Returns the number of characters in a string	=LEN("Judith Tinker") returns 13
SEARCH	SEARCH(find_text, within_text, start_nbr)	Returns the number of the character at which the find_text is first found reading from left to right	=SEARCH("Main", "1234 Main St",1) returns 6
TEXT	TEXT((value, format_text_code)	Formats numbers within text using a specific number format	="Total Revenue" & TEXT(SUM(D5:D75),"$#,0.00")
TRIM	TRIM(text)	Remove all spaces from a string except for single spaces between words	=TRIM(" Mary Eck") returns Mary Eck

The Zip column includes zip codes in both 5-digit and 10-digit formats. Myron wants only the 5-digit component of the zip code. You will use the LEN and LEFT functions to convert all of the zip codes to the shorter format.

Using the LEN function

First, you need to determine how many characters are in each cell of the Zip column. The **LEN function** returns the number of characters (length) of the specified string. The syntax for the LEN function is:

LEN(*text*)

In this function, *text* is a string constant or cell address containing a text string. For example, cell D4 stores the text value *Narragansett, ri* so the formula =LEN(D4) returns the value 16, the number of characters, including spaces, in *Narragansett, ri*.

The LEN function will be nested inside an IF function to test whether the length of the zip code is equal to 10. If the length is equal to 10, you will use the LEFT function to display the first 5 digits of the zip code; otherwise, the entire contents of the cell will be displayed.

Using the LEFT Function

The **LEFT function** returns a specified number of characters from the beginning of the string. The syntax for the LEFT function is:

LEFT(*text, number of characters*)

In this function, *text* is a string constant or cell address, and *number of characters* indicates the number of characters from the beginning of the string that you want to return. For example, to extract the 5-digit zip code from the zip code 92975-0999 stored in cell G3, you use the following LEFT function to return 92975:

=LEFT(G3,5)

You can use the IF function to display a 5-digit zip code. The IF function uses the LEN function to test whether the zip code has 10 digits. If true (the zip code is 10 digits), the LEFT function displays the first 5 digits in the cell. If false (the code is not 10 digits), all the digits in the cell are displayed. You'll enter the following formula to display the first five digits from the Zip column:

=IF(LEN([Zip]) = 10, LEFT([Zip],5),[Zip])

You'll insert a new column to the left of the Phone column in which to display the results.

To extract the 5-digit zip code from the Zip column:

▶ **1.** Click cell **F2**. You'll insert the table column to the left of this column.

▶ **2.** Click the **Home** tab on Ribbon, in the Cells group, click the **Insert button arrow**, and then click **Insert Table Columns to the Left**. A new column named *Column1* is inserted with the same formatting as the column to its left. The new column is formatted in the Text number format, which is the same format as the Zip column (column E).

   You cannot enter a formula in a cell formatted as Text. You'll convert the new column to General number format.

▶ **3.** Select the range **F2:F51**, and then, in the Number group on the Home tab, click the **Number Format** box arrow and click **General**.

   Now, you can insert the formula in cell F2.

▶ **4.** Click cell **F2**, type **=I** and then double-click **IF** to start the formula.

▶ **5.** Type **L** and then double-click **LEN**. The LEN function is nested in the IF function.

6. Type **[** to begin the column specifier, double-click **Zip**, and then type **])** to complete the LEN function.

7. Type **=10,** to complete the first argument of the IF function. The logical test *LEN([Zip])=10* tests whether the number of characters in the current cell of the Zip column equals 10.

8. Type **L** and double-click **LEFT** to begin the second argument of the IF function.

9. Type **[** to begin the column specifier, double-click **Zip**, and then type **],5),** to complete the second argument. If LEN([Zip])=10 is true, LEFT([ZIP],5) displays the first five characters from the value in the cell.

10. Type **[** to begin the column specifier, double-click **Zip**, and then type **])** to enter the third argument. If LEN([Zip])=10 is false, [Zip] displays all the characters from the value in the cell. The complete formula =IF(LEN([Zip])=10,LEFT([Zip],5),[Zip]) appears in the cell and formula bar.

11. Press the **Enter** key. Each cell in column F displays the 5-digit zip code. See Figure A-3.

Table column displays 5-digit zip codes | **Figure A-3**

You now have two columns with zip codes (column E and F). You need to keep only the column that displays the 5-digit zip code. However, the data in column F is dependent on column E. If you delete column E, column F displays the error value #REF!. Therefore, before you delete column E, you need to convert the data in column F, which is based on a formula, to values. The easiest way to do that is to copy and paste the formula results, but not the actual formula, to a new column using the Paste Values command. Then, you can delete columns E and F.

To convert the 5-digit zip code formula results to values:

1. Click cell **G2**, in the Cells group on the Home tab, click the **Insert button arrow**, and then click **Insert Table Columns to the Left**. A new column named Column 2 is inserted to the left of the Phone column.

2. Select the range **F2:F51**, which contains the formula results you want to convert to values.

3. In the Clipboard group on the Home tab, click the **Copy** button.

4. Click cell **G2**, in the Clipboard group, click the **Paste button arrow**, and then click **Paste Values**. The values from Column 1 are pasted into Column 2.

5. Press the **Esc** key, and then click cell **F2**. The formula appears in the formula bar and the formula results appear in the cell.

6. Click cell **G2**. Both the formula bar and the cell display values because you pasted the range using the Paste Values command.

You no longer need columns E and F, so you will delete them.

7. Select columns E and F, right-click the selected columns, and then click **Delete**. The two columns are removed.

8. In cell E1, enter **Zip**. Column E, which stores the 5-digit zip code values, now has a descriptive column header.

Using the Proper Function

Myron wants to capitalize the first letter of each name in the First Name and Last Name columns. The **PROPER function** converts the first letter of each word in a text string to uppercase, capitalizes any letter in a text string that does not follow another letter, and changes all other letters to lowercase. The syntax of the PROPER function is:

PROPER(text)

In this function *text* is a string constant or contents of a cell. For example, the following formula changes the word *BOOTH* to *Booth*:

=PROPER("BOOTH")

Joining Text Using the Concatenation Operator

Myron wants to combine the First Name and Last Name columns into one column named Owner. You need to use the concatenation operator (&, an ampersand) to do this. **Concatenation** describes what happens when you join the contents of two or more cells. The syntax of the concatenation operator is as follows:

Value1 & Value2 [& Value3 ...]

where & (the ampersand) operator joins (or concatenates) two or more string constants, cells, or expressions to produce a single string. For example, if cell B2 contains the last name *Eaton* and cell C2 contains the first name *Graham*, and you want to combine these cells' contents to display the full name in cell D2, you can use the following formula to join the contents of the two cells (last name and first name):

=B2 & C2

However, this formula returns *EatonGraham* in cell D2. To include a comma and a space between the two names, you must change the formula to the following:

=B2 & ", " & C2

This formula uses two concatenation operators and a string constant (a comma and a space enclosed in quotation marks) to display *Eaton, Graham*.

You need to combine the PROPER function and the concatenation operator as shown in the following formula:

=PROPER(B2) & ", " & PROPER(C2)

This formula capitalizes the first letter in the First Name and Last Name columns and combines them into one column named *Owner*.

To enter the formula to change the names to standard capitalization and combine them in one column:

▶ **1.** Click cell **D2**, in the Cells group on the Home tab, click the **Insert button arrow**, and then click **Insert Table Columns to the Left**. A new column named *Column1* is inserted to the left of the City State column.

▶ **2.** In cell D2, type **=PR**, and then double-click **PROPER**. The beginning of the formula, =PROPER(, appears in the cell and the formula bar.

▶ **3.** Type **[** to begin the column specifier, double-click **Last Name**, and then type **])** to complete the PROPER function that converts the last name to upper and lowercase letters.

▶ **4.** Type **& ", "** to join the contents of cell D2 with a comma and space.

▶ **5.** Type **& PR** and then double-click **PROPER** to begin the second PROPER function.

▶ **6.** Type **[** to begin the column specifier, double-click **First Name**, and then type **])** to complete the second PROPER function. The complete formula =PROPER([Last Name]) & ", " & PROPER([First Name]) appears in the cell and the formula bar.

▶ **7.** Press the **Enter** key. Each cell in column D displays the owner's name in the form *Last name, First name* with the first letter of each name capitalized. See Figure A-4.

Owner's names displayed in one column | **Figure A-4**

formula displays the owners' names in one column

D3   fx =PROPER([Last Name])&"," &PROPER([First Name])

	A	B	C	D	E	F	G	Acq
1	Parcel ID	First Name	Last Name	Column1	City State	Zip	Phone	Acq
2	11371432	GRAHAM	EATON	Eaton, Graham	Carolina, ri	02975	4.018E+09	5/3/2001	433500
3	12627149	ROXANA	UHLIG	Uhlig, Roxana	Carolina, ri	02975	4.018E+09	3/8/1990	342000
4	135-15-509	DOLORES	FORRESTER	Forrester, Dolores	Narragansett, r	02895	2.025E+09	######	206200
5	14000828	ELIZABETH	WHITNEY	Whitney, Elizabeth	Narragansett, r	02895	4.014E+09		
6	16410001	CHARLES	BULLOCK	Bullock, Charles	Carolina, ri	02975	4.019E+09		
7	17732304	LINDA	COULAHAN	Coulahan, Linda	Narragansett, r	02895	2.075E+09		
8	19869177	ROBERT	BURNS	Burns, Robert	Carolina, ri	02975	9.784E+09		
9	204-11-401	CYNTHIA	BEROUNSKY	Berounsky, Cynthia	Narragansett, r	02895	5.085E+09	######	500000
10	22502215	BARBARA	RICHMOND	Richmond, Barbara	Wakefield, ri	02079	4.018E+09	######	413900
11	23980026	CHARLES	DEVINE	Devine, Charles	Wakefield, ri	02082	9.415E+09	######	559500

names listed last name, first name with proper capitalization

Now that the owners' names data is stored in column D, you no longer need the data in column B (Last Name) and column C (First Name). Because the results in column D are based on a formula, you need to convert the formula in column D to values before you delete columns B and C.

To paste the formula results as values and delete the original data:

▶ **1.** Click cell **E2**, in the Cells group on the Home tab, click the **Insert button arrow**, and then click **Insert Table Columns to the Left**. A new column named *Column2* is added to the table.

▶ **2.** Select the range **D2:D51**. You want to copy this range and paste the values to Column2.

▶ **3.** In the Clipboard group on the Home tab, click the **Copy** button.

▶ **4.** Click cell **E2**, in the Clipboard group, click the **Paste button arrow**, and then click **Paste Values**.

▶ **5.** Press the **Esc** key, and then AutoFit column E so you can see the owners' full names.

▶ **6.** In cell E1, enter **Owner** as the column header.

▶ **7.** Select columns **B**, **C**, and **D**, right-click the selected columns, and then click **Delete** on the shortcut menu. The three columns are deleted. Column B, the Owner column, remains in the Excel table.

Using the Text to Columns Command

Myron wants you to split the city and state data into different columns. When multiple data is stored in one cell, you can separate each piece of data into a separate column using the Text to Columns command. You select what **delimits**, or separates, the data, such as a tab, a semicolon, a comma, or a space.

To split the city and state data into separate columns:

1. Click cell **D2**, in the Cells group on the Home tab, click the **Insert button arrow**, and then click **Insert Table Columns to the Left**. A new column named *Column1* is inserted to the left of the Zip column.

2. Select the range **C2:C51**. These cells contain the values you want to split.

3. Click the **Data** tab on the Ribbon, and then, in the Data Tools group, click the **Text to Columns** button. The Convert Text to Columns Wizard - Step 1 of 3 dialog box opens. You select how the data is organized in this step—delimited or a fixed width.

4. In the Original data type area, verify that the **Delimited** option button is selected, and then click the **Next** button. The Convert Text to Columns Wizard - Step 2 of 3 dialog box opens. You select the delimiter character in this step.

5. Click any check box with a check mark in the Delimiters section to remove the check mark, and then click the **Comma** check box. The data in the City State column is separated by a comma. The Data preview box shows the City and State data in separate columns. See Figure A-5.

Figure A-5 **Convert Text to Columns Wizard - Step 2 of 3 dialog box**

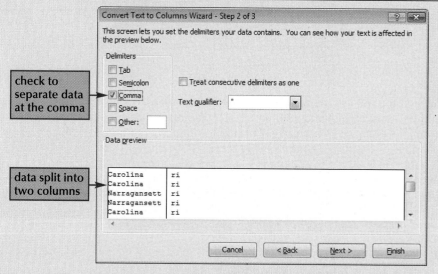

6. Click the **Next** button. The Convert Text to Columns Wizard - Step 3 of 3 dialog box opens so you can set the data format for each column. The Data preview box shows that each column is set to the General number format. You'll leave this format.

7. Click the **Finish** button. The cities remain in column C and the states move to column D.

8. In cell C1, enter **City**. In cell D1, enter **State**. See Figure A-6.

City and state in separate columns ◄ **Figure A-6**

City data remains in column C

State data moved to column D

Using the UPPER Function to Convert Case

The state abbreviations in column D are all lowercase. Myron wants to capitalize them. The **UPPER function** converts all letters of each word in a text string to uppercase. The syntax of the UPPER function is:

UPPER(text)

In this function, *text* is a string constant or contents of a cell. For example, the following formula returns RI:

=UPPER("ri")

You'll enter the UPPER function now.

Tip

You can convert cell contents to all lowercase by using the LOWER function.

To enter the UPPER function to capitalize the state abbreviations:

1. Click cell **E2**, and then click the **Home** tab on Ribbon.

2. In the Cells group, click the **Insert button arrow**, and then click **Insert Table Columns to the Left**. A new column named *Column1* is inserted to the left of the Zip column.

3. In cell E2, type **=U**, and then double-click **UPPER**. The beginning of the formula, =UPPER(, appears in the cell and the formula bar.

4. Type **[** to begin the column specifier, double-click **State**, and then type**])**. The formula =UPPER([STATE]) appears in the formula bar.

5. Press the **Enter** key. The state abbreviation appears in all uppercase in column E. See Figure A-7.

UPPER function converts the state abbreviations to uppercase ◄ **Figure A-7**

UPPER function formula converts cell contents to uppercase

state abbreviations are capitalized

You need to keep only the data in column E. Because the results of column E are based on a formula, you again need to convert the formula in column E to values before you delete columns D and E.

To paste the state abbreviations as values:

▶ 1. Click cell **F2**. In the Cells group on the Home tab, click the **Insert button arrow**, and then click **Insert Table Columns to the Left**. A new column named Column2 is inserted to the left of column E.

▶ 2. Select the range **E2:E51**. You want to copy and paste these values to Column2.

▶ 3. In the Clipboard group on the Home tab, click the **Copy** button 📋.

▶ 4. Click cell **F2**, in the Clipboard group, click the **Paste button arrow**, and then click **Paste Values**.

▶ 5. Select columns **D** and **E**, right-click the selected columns, and then click **Delete** on the shortcut menu. The two columns are deleted. Column D remains in the Excel table.

▶ 6. In cell D1, enter **State**. The column is renamed with a more descriptive header.

Using the SUBSTITUTE Function

The entries in Parcel ID, column A, are inconsistent. Sometimes they are an 8-digit value, other times hyphens separate the components of the Parcel (Book No., Map No., and Parcel No.). Myron wants you to remove the hyphens from the Parcel ID. The **SUBSTITUTE function** replaces existing text with new text in a text string. The SUBSTITUTE function has the following syntax:

SUBSTITUTE (*text,old_text,new_text,instance_num*)

In this function, *text* is a string constant or reference to a cell containing text you want to replace, *old_text* is the existing text you want to replace, *new_text* is the text you want to replace *old_text* with, and *instance_num* specifies which occurrence of *old_text* you want to replace. If you omit *instance_num*, every instance of *old_text* is replaced. For example, the following formula returns 16445890:

=SUBSTITUTE("164-45-890","-","").

You'll enter the formula to remove the hyphens from the Parcel ID data.

To remove hyphens from the Parcel ID data:

▶ 1. Click cell **B2**. In the Cells group on the Home tab, click the **Insert button arrow**, and then click **Insert Table Columns to the Left**. A new column named Column1 is inserted to the left of the Owner column.

▶ 2. Click the **Insert Function** button 𝑓ₓ on the formula bar. The Insert Function dialog box opens.

▶ 3. Click the **Or select a category** arrow, click **Text** to display the Text functions, and then double-click **SUBSTITUTE** in the Select a function box. The Function Arguments dialog box opens.

▶ 4. In the Text argument box, type **A2**. The text in cell A2 is displayed.

▶ 5. In the Old_text argument box, type **"-"**. The hyphen is the text you want to remove.

▶ 6. In the New_text argument box, type **""**. You want to replace the old text with nothing. You do not need to enter anything in the Instance_num argument box because you want to replace every instance of a hyphen.

7. Click the **OK** button. All of the Parcel IDs are changed to 8-digit numbers. The hyphens were replaced with an empty string (a blank or nothing). See Figure A-8.

SUBSTITUTE function removed hyphens from the Parcel IDs ◄ **Figure A-8**

After you convert the formula in column B to values, you can delete columns A and B.

To paste the Parcel ID column as values:

1. Click cell **C2**. In the Cells group on the Home tab, click the **Insert button arrow**, and then click **Insert Table Columns to the Left**. A new column named *Column2* is inserted to the left of the Owner column.

2. Select the range **B2:B51**. You want to copy this range and paste the values in Column2.

3. In the Clipboard group on the Home tab, click the **Copy** button.

4. Click cell **C2**. In the Clipboard group, click the **Paste button arrow**, and click **Paste Values**.

5. Select columns **A** and **B**, right-click the selected columns, and then click **Delete** on the shortcut menu. The two columns are deleted. Column A, the Parcel ID column, remains in the Excel table.

6. In cell A1, enter **Parcel ID**.

7. AutoFit the Parcel ID, Owner, State, City, Zip, Phone, Acquired, and Market Value columns.

You have cleaned all of the data in the worksheet. Myron can more easily work with the data in this arrangement.

Adding Special and Custom Formatting

Now that the data in the workbook is clean, Myron wants you to apply the following formatting to the data:

- Display the phone number using the common format of area code in parentheses and a hyphen between the prefix and the last four digits.
- Display the market values in thousands, so that a value such as 456600 is displayed as 457.
- Display the acquired date with the name of the month followed by the year (for example, 6/12/2005 is displayed as June, 2005).

These formatting changes will make the data easier to understand and use.

Using Special Formats

Four commonly used formats, referred to as Special formats, are available. They include two zip code formats (5-digit and 10-digit), a phone number format (with area code in parentheses and hyphen between the prefix and the last four digits), and a social security number format. Using these Special formats allows you to type a number without punctuation, yet still display that number in its common format.

To format the phone number with the Phone Number format:

▶ **1.** Select the range **F2:F51**.

▶ **2.** In the Numbers group on the Home tab, click the **Dialog Box Launcher**. The Format Cells dialog box opens with the Number tab active.

▶ **3.** In the Category list, click **Special**. Four special formats appear in the Type list: Zip Code, Zip Code + 4, Phone Number, and Social Security Number.

▶ **4.** In the Type list, click **Phone Number**, and then click the **OK** button. The phone numbers are formatted in a standard phone number format.

Creating Custom Formats

Excel supplies a generous collection of formats and styles to improve the appearance and readability of your documents. However, sometimes you still will not be able to find formats and styles to accommodate a specific requirement. In these cases, you can create your own formats, called **custom formats**. Custom formats use **format codes**, a series of symbols, to describe exactly how Excel should display a number, date, time, or text string. You can use format codes to display text strings and spaces, and determine how many decimal places to display in a cell.

Working with Numeric Format Codes

Each number is composed of digits. In displaying these digits, Excel makes special note of **insignificant zeros**, which are zeros whose omission from the number does not change the number's value. For example, the number 0.1 is displayed in the General number format but changes to 0.10 when the cell is formatted as a number. To format a value, Excel uses the **placeholders** shown in Figure A-9 to represent individual digits.

Description of digit placeholders ◀ **Figure A-9**

Placeholder	Description
#	Displays only significant digits; insignificant zeros are omitted.
0 (zero)	Displays significant digits as well as insignificant zeros.
?	Replaces insignificant zeros with spaces on either side of the decimal point so that decimal points align when formatted with a fixed-width font, such as Courier.

A custom format can use combinations of these placeholders. For example, the custom format #.00 displays the value 8.9 as 8.90. If a value has more digits than placeholders in the custom format, Excel rounds the value to match the number of placeholders. Thus, the value 8.938 formatted with the custom format #.## is displayed as 8.94. Figure A-10 shows how the same series of numbers appear with different custom number formats.

Examples of digit placeholders ◀ **Figure A-10**

| Value in Cell | Custom Formats | | | |
	#.##	0.00	?.??	#.#0
0.57	.57	0.57	.57	.57
123.4	123.4	123.40	123.4	123.40
3.45	3.45	3.45	3.45	3.45
7.891	7.89	7.89	7.89	7.89
5.248	5.25	5.25	5.25	5.25

In addition to digit placeholders, number formats also include separators, such as the decimal point separator (.), the thousands separator (,), and the fraction separator (/). The thousands separator can be used to separate the number in groups of one thousand, but it can also be used to scale a number by a multiple of one thousand.

The fraction separator displays decimal values as fractions. The general syntax is *placeholder/placeholder*, where *placeholder* is one or more of the custom format placeholders discussed above. Excel displays the fraction that best approximates the decimal value. You can also specify the denominator for the fraction to convert the decimals to halves, quarters, and so forth. Figure A-11 provides examples of the thousands separator and the fraction separator.

Examples of thousands separator and fraction separator ◀ **Figure A-11**

Value in Cell	Custom Format	Appearance
12000	#,###	12,000
12000	#,	12
12200000	0.0,,	12.2
5.4	# #/#	5 2/5

All of the numeric format codes can be combined in a single custom format, providing you with great control over data's appearance. If you don't specify a numeric code for data values, Excel uses the General format code, which applies a general numeric format to the data values. The General format hides all insignificant zeros.

Myron wants you to display the market value of the properties to the nearest thousand. You will create the custom format #.###, to display the market values to the nearest thousands.

To create a custom format for the market values to the nearest thousands:

1. Select the range **H2:H51**.

2. In the Number group on the Home tab, click the **Dialog Box Launcher**. The Format Cells dialog box opens with the Number tab active.

   You will enter a custom format to display the numbers to the nearest thousand.

3. Click **Custom** in the Category box.

4. In the Type box, double-click **General** to select it, and then type **#,###,** as the custom format code. See Figure A-12.

Figure A-12   Custom category on the Number tab

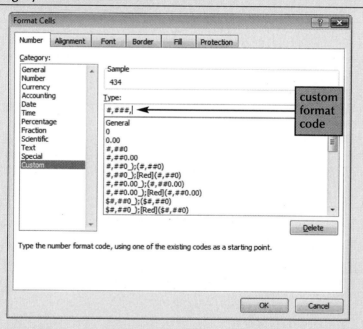

5. Click the **OK** button. The market values are displayed to the nearest thousand.

   Next, you'll enter a comment in cell H1 to explain how the values are displayed.

6. Right-click cell **H1**, and then click **Insert Comment** on the shortcut menu. A comment box appears next to the cell.

7. Type **market values are rounded to nearest thousand**, and then click any cell to close the comment box.

8. Point to cell **H1**. The comment appears.

Formatting Dates

When you have dates, times, or both in a workbook, you can use a predefined date and time format to display this information in a readable format. Although the predefined time and date formats are usually fine, you can also create your own custom date formats. Figure A-13 describes the format codes used for dates and times.

Date and Time format codes ◄ **Figure A-13**

Symbol	To Display
m	Months as 1 through 12
mm	Months as 01 through 12
mmm	Months as Jan through Dec
mmmm	Months as January through December
d	Days as 1 through 31
dd	Days as 01 through 31
ddd	Days as Sun through Sat
dddd	Days as Sunday through Saturday
yy	Years as 00 through 99
yyyy	Years as 1900 through 9999
h	Hours as 1 through 24
mm	Minutes as 01 through 60 (when immediately following h, mm signifies minutes; otherwise, months)
ss	Seconds as 01 through 60

Myron wants the date values in the Acquired column to show the name of the month followed by the year (for example, July, 2010). You need to apply the custom format code *mmmm, yyyy* to do this.

To apply a custom date format to the Acquisition dates:

▶ 1. Select the range **G2:G51**.

▶ 2. In the Number group on the Home tab, click the **Dialog Box Launcher**. The Format Cells dialog box opens with the Number tab active.

▶ 3. Click **Custom** in the Category box.

▶ 4. In the Type box, select the current format, and then type **mmmm, yyyy**. The Sample box shows an example of the custom format you entered.

▶ 5. Click the **OK** button, and then click cell **A1** to deselect the range. See Figure A-14.

Final formatted workbook ◄ **Figure A-14**

▶ 6. Save the workbook.

Any custom format you create is stored in the workbook, and you can apply the custom format to any other cell or range in the workbook. However, you can use a custom format only in the workbook in which it was created. If you want to use the custom formats you created for the Bayville County workbook in another workbook, you need to reenter them.

InSight

Storing Dates and Time in Excel

Excel stores dates and times as a number representing the number of days since January 0, 1900 plus a fractional portion of a 24-hour day. This is called a **serial date**, or serial date-time.

Dates The integer portion of the number is the number of days since January 0, 1900. For example, the date 1/1/2010 is stored as 40,179, because 40,179 days have passed since January 0, 1900. The number 1 is the serial date for 1/1/1900.

Times The decimal portion of the number is the fraction of a 24-hour day that has passed. For example, 6:00 AM is stored as 0.25, which is 25% of a 24-hour day. Similarly, 6 PM is stored as 0.75, which is 75% of a 24-hour day.

Any date and time can be stored as the sum of the date and the time. For example, 3 PM on 1/1/2010 is stored in Excel as 40,179.625.

As an experiment, enter 1/1/2010 in cell A1 of a new worksheet. Change the format in the cell to General. The value appears as 40179. Change the format to a Short Date format to see the value displayed as 1/1/2010.

Using the Compatibility Checker

Myron needs to travel to Seattle while continuing to work on this project. Although all of the desktop computers at Zeus Engineering have Excel 2007 installed, Myron's notebook computer hasn't yet been upgraded. Myron asks you to make a copy of the current workbook, converting it to a format Excel 2003 can read. When you save an Excel 2007 formatted workbook to an earlier format, the **Compatibility Checker** alerts you to any features that are not supported by earlier versions of Excel.

To convert an Excel 2007 workbook to an earlier Excel file format:

▶ 1. Click the **Office Button** , and then click **Save As**. The Save As dialog box opens.

▶ 2. In the File Name box, change the filename to **Bayville County 2003**.

▶ 3. Click the **Save as type** button, and then click **Excel 97-2003 Workbook**. This is the earlier Excel file format you want to use.

▶ 4. Click the **Save** button. The Microsoft Office Excel – Compatibility Checker dialog box opens, alerting you to features not supported by earlier versions of Excel. See Figure A-15.

Figure A-15 | **Compatibility Checker**

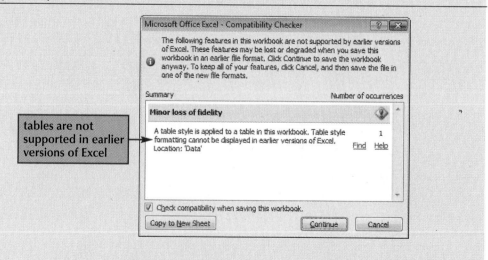

tables are not supported in earlier versions of Excel

5. Read the message, and then click the **Continue** button. The workbook is saved in the earlier file format with the file extension .xls.

6. Close the workbook.

The workbook data is clean and formatted in the best way for Myron. He'll analyze this data as he comes up with a proposal to address Bayville's traffic concerns.

Appendix Summary | Review

In this appendix, you used a variety of Text functions, the concatenation operator, and the Text to Column command. You created a custom format to round numbers to the nearest thousands. Finally, you created a custom format code to display dates as a month and year.

Key Terms

Compatibility Checker

Compatibility Mode

concatenation

custom format

delimit

format code

insignificant zero

LEFT function

LEN function

placeholder

PROPER function

serial date (or serial date-
    time)

SUBSTITUTE function

UPPER function

Practice	**Review Assignments**

Practice the skills you learned in the appendix using the same case scenario.

Data File needed for the Review Assignments: Assessor.xls

As part of the Transportation Improvement Program (TIP) study, Myron Londale, traffic analyst at Zeus Engineering, obtained a second workbook from the Bayville Assessor's Office containing data on private homes and commercial buildings located along the route being reviewed. The assessor's office was able to transfer the data requested by Zeus Engineering to Excel. Before Myron begins his analysis, he asks you to clean and format the data.

Complete the following:

1. Open the **Assessor** workbook located in the Appendix.A\Review folder included with your Data Files, and then save the workbook in the Excel 2007 format as **Owners** in the same folder.
2. Insert a new worksheet. Enter your name, the date, and a purpose statement in the worksheet, and then rename the worksheet as **Documentation**.
3. Create an Excel table for the data in the range A1:G5.
4. Use the Text to Columns command to split the Owner column into two columns named **Last Name** and **First Name**. Insert a blank column to the left of column C to store the first name and leave the last name in column B.
5. In cell I1, enter the column header **Status**. In the Status column, use the IF and LEFT functions to display the word **Discard** if the address is a PO Box; otherwise, leave the cell blank.
6. In cell J1, enter the column header **Twn**. In cell J2, enter a formula to convert the data in the Town column to proper case.
7. In cell K1, enter the column header **St**. In column K, enter a formula to convert the data in the State column to uppercase.
8. In cell L1, enter the column header **Town State**. In column L, combine the town and state data into one column using the format *town, state*.
9. Format the data in the SSN column (column A) with the special Social Security number format.
10. Save and close the workbook. Submit the finished workbook to your instructor, either in printed or electronic form, as requested.

Apply	**Case Problem 1**

Apply the skills you learned to clean and format membership data.

Data File needed for this Case Problem: Mesa.xls

Mesa Senior Center Elliot Turner, director of the Mesa Senior Center, has begun compiling a list of its members. He's asked you to clean and format the data in the worksheet before he continues working on the project.

Complete the following:

1. Open the **Mesa** workbook located in the Appendix.A\Case1 folder included with your Data Files, and then save the workbook as **Senior Center** in the same folder.
2. Insert a new worksheet. Enter your name and the date in the worksheet, and then rename the worksheet as **Documentation**.

3. In the Members worksheet, apply the special Social Security Number format to the data in the SSN column.

4. Split the Name data into two columns. Store the first name in column B and the last name in column C. Change the column headers to **First Name** (column B) and **Last Name** (column C).

5. Insert two columns to the left of the City column. In column D, apply the proper case to the first name data, and change the column header to **F Name**. In column E, apply the proper case to the last name data, and change the column header to **L Name**.

6. In the Member Since column, apply a custom format that displays only the year.

7. Split the CSZ column into three columns named **City**, **State**, and **Zip**.

8. Sort the data by City and then within City by L Name.

9. Name column J as **UniqueID**. Instead of using Social Security numbers as the unique identifier, the senior center is considering using an ID of the first three letters of the last name (L Name) followed by the first letter of first name (F Name). If the last name is fewer than three characters, the letter Z replaces each missing character. Use the LEN and LEFT functions and the concatenation operator to display the proposed Unique ID.

10. Save the workbook. Submit the finished workbook to your instructor, either in printed or electronic form, as requested.

Apply | **Case Problem 2**

Apply the skills you learned to calculate overhead allocation.

Data File needed for this Case Problem: Research.xls

Steuben Institute   Every two weeks Elli Pjster processes payroll information for employees whose salaries are paid fully or partially from research grants. She downloads an Excel workbook from the Institute's Research and Grant Accounting system to calculate overhead. The overhead rate varies depending on the research grant. Overhead is calculated by multiplying the employee salary by the overhead rate of the grant that funds the employee. She asks you to clean and format the data in the worksheet.

Complete the following:

1. Open the **Research** workbook located in the Appendix.A\Case2 folder included with your Data Files, and then save the workbook in the Excel 2007 file format as **Grants** in the same folder.

2. Insert a new worksheet, enter the company name, your name, the date, and a purpose statement in the worksheet, and then rename the worksheet as **Documentation**.

3. In the Pay Period worksheet, create an Excel table for the data in the range A1:C51. Hide the filter arrows.

4. Split the data in column A into separate columns for the first name and the last name. Change the column headers to **First Name** and **Last Name**. AutoFit the two columns, and then sort the table by the Last Name data.

EXPLORE

5. Use the MID function to extract the grant number from the ChartString column and display it in column E. Name the new column **Grant Nbr**. The Grant Nbr is a four-digit number that begins in position ten of the ChartString column. (*Hint:* Research the MID function in the Help system.)

6. In the column to the right of the Grant Nbr column (column F), enter a VLOOKUP function to find the grant number in the lookup table in the Overhead Rates worksheet and display the grant name from column 2. Name the column header in cell F1 **Grant Name**. AutoFit the column.

7. In column G enter the formula to calculate overhead, which is the Overhead Rate located in the third column of the Overhead Rates worksheet multiplied by Salary. You need to use a VLOOKUP function to find the correct overhead rate for the grant. Name the column **Overhead**.

8. Format the Salary and Overhead columns in the Accounting number format with two decimals place.

9. Save and close the workbook. Submit the finished workbook to your instructor, either in printed or electronic form, as requested.

Ending Data Files

Appendix.A → Tutorial
Bayville County.xlsx
Bayville County 2003.xls

Review
Owners.xlsx

Case1
Senior Center.xlsx

Case2
Grants.xlsx

Objectives

- Learn about methods of integration using Office programs
- Link an Excel worksheet to a Word document
- Update a linked object
- Embed an object
- Modify an embedded object

Integrating Excel with Other Windows Programs

Creating Integrated Documents

Case | Metro Zoo

Marvin Hall is the director of Metro Zoo. Each year, he sends out a financial report to the zoo's supporters and contributors. Marvin stores the financial data in an Excel workbook, and he uses Word to create a letter that includes data from Excel. Marvin wants to be able to copy the Excel data and insert it directly into the Word document. He also wants to tie the two documents together, so that if he updates the financial information in the Excel workbook, the report in the Word document will be automatically updated as well.

Marvin asks you to help him integrate his Excel data into his Word document and link the files, so that the data in the report is automatically updated each time Marvin modifies the workbook.

Starting Data Files

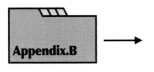

Appendix.B →

Tutorial
MZoo.xlsx
Zoo Letter.docx

Review
Sales Memo.docx
State Sales.xlsx

Case1
Event.docx
Quote.xlsx

Case2
Request.docx
Usage.xlsx

Methods of Integration

Excel is part of a suite of programs called Microsoft Office. In addition to Excel, the Office programs include Word, a word-processing program; Access, a database management program; PowerPoint, a presentation and slide show program; Outlook, a personal information manager; and Publisher, a program for creating desktop publishing projects. All of these programs share a common interface and can read each other's file formats.

Occasionally, you will create a file that relies on data from more than one program. This type of file is called a **compound file**. The **source file** (or files) supplies the data to be shared. The **destination file** (or files) displays the data from the source file (or files). Compound files are easy to create in Office because of the tight integration of the Office programs. At Metro Zoo, Marvin needs to create a letter using Word that incorporates information from an Excel workbook that contains financial data as well as a chart.

There are three ways to insert data from one program into another program: copying and pasting, linking, and embedding. Each of these techniques can be used to create a compound file. Figure B-1 describes each of these methods, and provides examples of when each method is appropriate.

Figure B-1	Integration methods

Method	Description	Use When
Copying and pasting	Inserts an object into a file	You want to exchange the data between the two files only once, and it doesn't matter if the data changes.
Linking	Displays an object in the destination file but doesn't store it there—only the location of the source file is stored in the destination file	You want to use the same data in more than one file, and you need to ensure that the data will be current and identical in each file. Any changes you make to the source file will be reflected in the destination file(s).
Embedding	Displays and stores an object in the destination file	You want the source data to become a permanent part of the destination file, or the source data will no longer be available to the destination file. Any changes you make to either the destination file or the source file do not affect the other.

Copying and Pasting Data

You can copy text, values, cells and ranges, or even charts and graphics from one program and paste it in another program using the Windows copy and paste features. The item being copied and pasted is referred to as an **object**. When you paste an object from the source file into the destination file, you are inserting the object so that it is part of the destination file. The **pasted object** is static, having no connection to the source file. If you want to change the pasted object, you must do so in the destination file. For example, a range of cells pasted into a Word document can be edited only within the Word document. Any changes made in the original Excel workbook have no impact on the Word document. For this reason, pasting is used only for one-time exchanges of information.

Object Linking and Embedding

If you want to create a live connection between two files, so that changes in the source file are automatically reflected in the destination file, you must use object linking and embedding. **Object linking and embedding (OLE)** refers to the technology that allows you to copy and paste objects, such as graphic files, cell and ranges, or charts, so that information about the program that created the object is included with the object itself.

The objects are inserted into the destination file as either linked objects or embedded objects. A **linked object** is actually a separate file that is linked to the source file. If you make a change to the source file, the destination file can automatically reflect the change. On the other hand, an **embedded object** is stored in the destination file (Word, in this example) and is no longer part of the source file. In the case of Office programs, embedded objects include their Ribbon, tabs, and buttons. This means you can edit an Excel worksheet or chart embedded in a Word document using Excel tools and commands to modify the worksheet or chart content. Because embedded objects have no link to the source file, changes made to the embedded object are not reflected in the source file.

Thus, the main difference between linked and embedded objects lies in where the data is stored and how the data is updated after being inserted into the destination file. Figure B-2 illustrates the difference between linking and embedding.

Embedding contrasted with linking ◄ **Figure B-2**

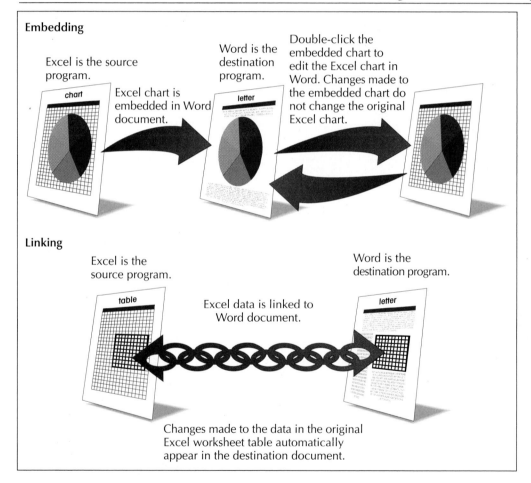

Embedding

Excel is the source program.

Excel chart is embedded in Word document.

Word is the destination program.

Double-click the embedded chart to edit the Excel chart in Word. Changes made to the embedded chart do not change the original Excel chart.

Linking

Excel is the source program.

Excel data is linked to Word document.

Word is the destination program.

Changes made to the data in the original Excel worksheet table automatically appear in the destination document.

Linking Excel and Word Files

Marvin asks you to insert the financial data stored in a workbook into a letter he has been writing to Metro Zoo's supporters. He is still working on the details of the financial report, and he might need to edit some of the values in the workbook. Rather than pasting the data each time he modifies the report, Marvin wants you to create a link between his Excel workbook and his Word document, so that any changes he makes to the workbook are automatically reflected in the letter. You will open both files and link the Excel data to the Word document.

To open Marvin's two files:

© **1.** Open the **MZoo** Excel workbook located in the **Appendix.B\Tutorial** folder included with your Data Files, and then save the workbook as **Metro Zoo** in the same folder.

© **2.** In the Documentation sheet, enter your name and the current date.

© **3.** Open the **Zoo Letter** Word document located in the **Appendix.B\Tutorial** folder included with your Data Files, and then save the document as **Metro Zoo Ltr** in the same folder.

© **4.** Return to the **Metro Zoo** workbook, and then switch to the **Financial Summary** worksheet.

The financial data Marvin wants to display in his letter is stored in the range A2:D17 of the Financial Summary worksheet. To transfer that data, you'll copy the range in the workbook and then paste the data as a link in the Word document.

To copy and paste a link:

© **1.** Select the range **A2:D17**.

© **2.** In the Clipboard group on the Home tab, click the **Copy** button 🖹.

© **3.** Return to the **Metro Zoo Ltr** document, and then click the paragraph mark below the letter's second paragraph (below the sentence that reads "Below are Metro Zoo's revenues and expenses for the past two years"). See Figure B-3.

| **Figure B-3** | **Metro Letter document** |

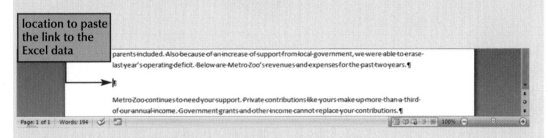

location to paste the link to the Excel data

Trouble? If your document does not show paragraph marks at the end of each paragraph, you need to show the nonprinting characters. In the Paragraph group on the Home tab, click the Show/Hide button.

© **4.** In the Clipboard group on the Home tab, click the **Paste button arrow**, and then click **Paste Special**. The Paste Special dialog box opens. The Paste link option enables you to paste data in several different formats. The default format is to insert the data as a Word table using HTML (Hypertext Markup Language). You could also paste the data as a graphic image, unformatted text, or an embedded worksheet object. See Figure B-4.

Paste Special dialog box ◄ **Figure B-4**

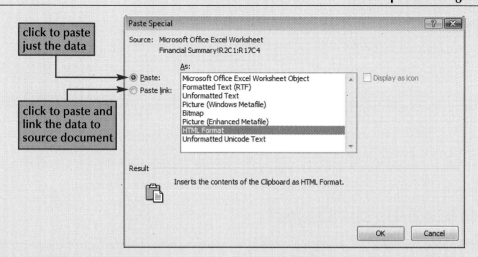

click to paste just the data

click to paste and link the data to source document

5. Click the **Paste link** option button, and then click **Microsoft Office Excel Worksheet Object**.

6. Click the **OK** button. Word places a link (the location of the source file) to the Excel object within the Word document so the financial data is linked to the Excel workbook. A representation of the financial data is displayed in the Word document, as shown in Figure B-5.

Financial data pasted into the Metro Zoo Ltr document ◄ **Figure B-5**

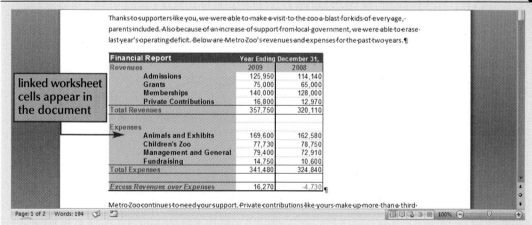

linked worksheet cells appear in the document

> **Tip**
>
> You can edit and format this table using any of the Word formatting features.

Updating a Linked Object

When an object is linked, the linked objects are updated automatically. This means that Word updates the linked information every time you open the Word document or any time the Excel source file changes while the Word document is open.

Marvin finished reviewing the financial summary in the Metro Zoo workbook. He finds a data-entry error in the report. A $2500 overstatement of a government grant to Metro Zoo was entered in error. You need to correct the total amounts of grants. You can update the linked data without having to paste the data again.

To update the linked data:

© 1. Return to the **Metro Zoo** workbook, and then press the **Esc** key to deselect the range A2:D17.

© 2. In cell C5 enter **72500**. The correct value for the government grants is inserted.

© 3. Switch to the **Metro Zoo Ltr** document to verify that the value of the grant changed, reflecting the current value in the Metro Zoo workbook.

   Trouble? If the link doesn't update automatically, right-click the table and click Update Link on the shortcut menu.

Tip

You can also double-click the Excel object in Word to return to Excel and edit the Excel worksheet. The linked object in Word is automatically updated.

Embedding an Object

Marvin also wants the letter to include the pie chart in the Metro Zoo workbook that details the source of Metro Zoo's revenue. Marvin is confident that the financial summary is correct and requires no further edits. Therefore, you don't need to create a link between Marvin's letter and the workbook's chart. Instead, Marvin wants to embed the chart in the letter. Then, he will be able to use the Excel chart-editing tools directly from the Word document, if he chooses to modify the chart's appearance before printing the letter. You will embed the Revenue chart in the document.

To embed an Excel chart in a Word document:

© 1. Switch to the **Metro Zoo** workbook, and then click the **Revenues** chart to select it.

© 2. In the Clipboard group on the Home tab, click the **Copy** button 📋.

© 3. Switch to the **Metro Zoo Ltr** document, and then click the paragraph mark above the letter's next to last paragraph (above the sentence that reads "If you would like to learn more about the Metro Zoo...").

© 4. In the Clipboard group on the Home tab, click the **Paste button arrow**, and then click **Paste Special**. The Paste Special dialog box opens, displaying two format options for charts in the As box. You can choose to paste the chart as an Excel chart object; or you can choose to paste the chart as a graphic object. Marvin wants to be able to use the Excel chart-editing tools, so you'll choose the first option.

© 5. Verify that the **Paste** option button is selected, click **Microsoft Office Excel Chart Object**, and then click the **OK** button. Excel places a copy of the chart as an embedded object into the letter. See Figure B-6.

Figure B-6 ▶ **Chart embedded in the Metro Zoo Letter document**

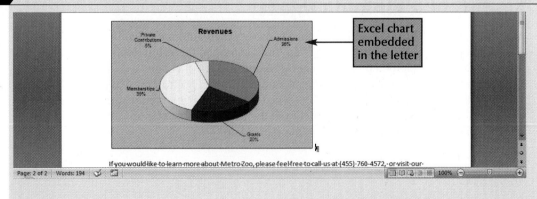

Modifying an Embedded Object

Embedded objects such as the chart become part of the Word document after they are inserted; they are no longer linked to the source file. For example, if you change the chart in the source file, the embedded object in Word does not change. Conversely, if you change the embedded object in Word, the source file is not modified.

After viewing the contents of the chart, Marvin wants you to change the chart's title from "Revenues" to "Revenues for 2009." You can do this by editing the chart within Word. Recall that when you make changes to an embedded object, those changes will not be reflected in the object in the source file. You will change the title of the chart that is embedded in the letter.

To edit the embedded chart:

© **1.** Double-click the embedded chart in the Metro Zoo Letter document, and then click any-where within the chart. The hatch-marked border appears around the chart, and the embedded object appears in an Excel workbook window, as shown in Figure B-7. Also, notice that the Ribbon shows the Excel tabs and buttons.

Embedded chart selected for editing ◄ **Figure B-7**

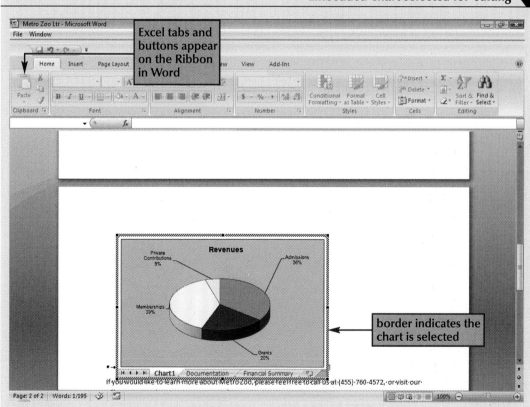

You can edit the object using the Excel chart-editing tools within Word.

© **2.** Click the **Title object** and change the title to **Revenues for 2009**. The chart title is updated.

© **3.** Click outside the chart to deselect it. See Figure B-8.

Figure B-8 Embedded chart updated with new chart title

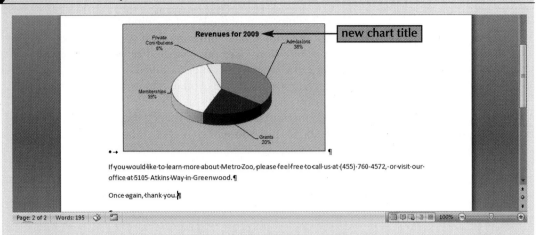

Your work on both the Metro Zoo workbook and the Metro Zoo Letter document are complete. You can save your changes and then exit the programs.

© **4.** Save and close the Metro Zoo Ltr document, and then exit Word.

© **5.** Return to the **Metro Zoo** workbook, and verify that the revenue chart title remains *Revenues*. The title was not updated to *Revenues for 2009* because you edited the embedded chart, which is not linked to the Excel workbook.

© **6.** Save and close the Metro Zoo workbook, and then exit Excel.

You may have noticed in Figure B-8 that the embedded object included not just the chart sheet for the revenue statement, but also the other worksheets in the workbook. You could have selected one of the other worksheets in the workbook and displayed that information in place of the chart. This highlights one disadvantage of embedded objects: They tend to greatly increase the size of the destination file. The Metro Zoo Letter document now contains both the original letter and the Metro Zoo workbook. For this reason, you should embed objects only when file size is not an issue.

In this appendix, you examined the different methods for sharing data between Office programs. You learned how to copy data from Excel to Word using pasting and linking. You saw how changes to the data in an Excel workbook are updated automatically in a linked Word document. You also learned how to embed an Excel chart within a Word document, making Excel tools available in Word.

Key Terms

compound file
destination file
embedded object
linked object

object
object linking and
    embedding (OLE)

pasted object
source file

| Practice | **Review Assignments** |

Practice the skills you learned in the appendix.

Data Files needed for the Review Assignments: State Sales.xlsx, Sales Memo.docx

Happy Morning Farms   Cassie Meyers is product manager for a line of breakfast cereals at Happy Morning Farms. Cassie is waiting for one number to complete her sales report for next week's Operations Management Team (OMT) meeting. As she is working on the report, she receives an urgent call from the Chicago sales representative, asking her to come to Chicago immediately to deal with a customer problem that requires management attention. Cassie plans to complete her sales report while she is in Chicago. After she finishes the report, she will e-mail it to John Styles, a colleague, who will represent her at the meeting.

Complete the following:

1. Open the **State Sales** workbook located in the Appendix.B\Review folder included with your Data Files, and then save the workbook as **State Sales Embed** in the same folder.
2. In the Documentation sheet, enter the date and your name, and then switch to the Sales Data worksheet.
3. Open the **Sales Memo** document located in the Appendix.B\Review folder, and then save the document as **Sales Memo Embed** in the same folder.
4. Return to the State Sales Embed workbook, and then copy the range A1:C24 in the Sales Data worksheet.
5. Return to the Sales Memo Embed document, and embed the worksheet data you copied at the end of the memo.
6. Save the Sales Memo Embed document. Close the State Sales Embed workbook.
7. Update the Word document by entering the Iowa sales for this month, which are $42.1 (omit the 000). Do not open the Excel workbook.
8. Save and close the Sales Memo Embed document.
9. Open the **State Sales** workbook located in the Appendix.B\Review folder included with your Data Files, and then save the workbook as **State Sales Link** in the same folder.
10. In the Documentation sheet, enter the date and your name, and then switch to the Sales Data worksheet.
11. Open the **St Memo** document located in the Appendix.B\Review folder, and then save the document as **Sales Memo Link** in the same folder.
12. Return to the State Sales Link workbook, and then copy the range A1:C24 in the Sales Data worksheet.
13. Return to the Sales Memo Link document, and then paste the selected range as a link at the end of the memo. Save the Word document.
14. Update the State Sales Link workbook by entering the Iowa sales for this month, which are $42.1 (omit the 000).
15. Save and close the Sales Memo Link document.
16. Open both the **State Sales Embed** and **State Sales Link** workbooks. Scroll to cell C10, sales for Iowa, in each worksheet. Using the results in these cells, explain the differences between object linking and embedding.
17. Close all files. Submit the finished workbooks and documents to your instructor, either in printed or electronic form, as requested.

| Apply | | Case Problem 1 |

Apply the skills you learned by inserting Excel objects into a Word document.

Data Files needed for this Case Problem: Quote.xlsx, Event.docx

Kirk Harbor Inn   Ellen Felton is events coordinator at Kirk Harbor Inn, which is located on Cape Cod. She schedules weddings, conferences, engagements, and so forth at this water-front Victorian inn. She constantly is sending quotes to potential clients and asks you to assist her in linking the workbook she developed to the letter she sends to potential clients.

Complete the following:

1. Open the **Quote** workbook located in the Appendix.B\Case1 folder included with your Data Files, and then save the workbook as **Harbor Quote** in the same folder.
2. In the Documentation sheet, enter the date and your name, and then switch to the Quote worksheet.
3. Open the **Event** document located in the Appendix.B\Case1 folder, and then save the document as **Event Planner** in the same folder.
4. Return to the Harbor Quote workbook, and then copy the range B2:H20 in the Quote worksheet.
5. Return to the Event Planner document, and then paste the selected range as a link below the sentence "Here are the details."
6. Ellen's client requests two changes: move the wedding to the Salon room and change the number of guests to 160. Make these changes in the Harbor Quote workbook, and then verify that the Harbor Quote document is updated. (*Hint*: You might need to right-click the mouse and click Update Link.)
7. Save and close the Harbor Quote and Event Planner files. Submit the finished workbook and document to your instructor, either in printed or electronic form, as requested.

| Apply | | Case Problem 2 |

Apply the skills you learned by inserting Excel objects into a Word document.

Data Files needed for this Case Problem: Usage.xlsx, Request.docx

Bright Light   Peter Skinner is writing a letter to the state government to report on the Shelter and meal programs used at Bright Light. He has data in an Excel workbook and needs to incorporate the data into the letter he is composing in Word. Because the report will also include projections for the upcoming year, which he might modify, Peter wants to create a link between the information in the Excel workbook and the Word document. He also wants to embed in the Word document a chart that he has created in his workbook. He asked you to help link the two files.

Complete the following:

1. Open the **Usage** workbook located in the Appendix.B\Case2 folder included with your Data Files, and then save the workbook as **Bright Usage** in the same folder.
2. In the Documentation sheet, enter the date and your name, and then switch to the Shelter Usage worksheet.
3. Open the **Request** document located in the Appendix.B\Case2 folder, and then save the document as **Bright Request** in the same folder.
4. Return to the Bright Usage workbook, and then copy the range A2:G9 in the Shelter Usage worksheet.
5. Return to the Bright Request document, and then paste the selected range as a link below the first paragraph of Peter's letter. (*Hint*: If necessary, display the paragraph marks in the Word document.)

6. Peter discovered that the number of client days in the domestic abuse shelter in December 2010 was actually 75, not 72. Make this change in the Bright Usage workbook, and then verify that the Bright Request document is automatically updated. (*Hint*: If necessary, use the Update Link command on the shortcut menu to see the change.)

⊕ EXPLORE

7. Copy the Projected Usage chart from the Shelter Usage worksheet, and then embed the chart below the second paragraph in Peter's letter (do not link the chart).

8. Edit the embedded chart, changing the background color of the plot area from yellow to white.

9. Save and close the Bright Request and Bright Usage files. Submit the finished workbook and document to your instructor, either in printed or electronic form, as requested.

Ending Data Files

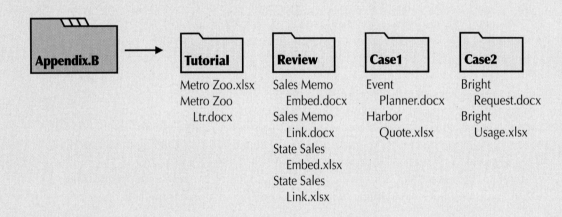

Appendix.B →

Tutorial
Metro Zoo.xlsx
Metro Zoo
    Ltr.docx

Review
Sales Memo
    Embed.docx
Sales Memo
    Link.docx
State Sales
    Embed.xlsx
State Sales
    Link.xlsx

Case1
Event
    Planner.docx
Harbor
    Quote.xlsx

Case2
Bright
    Request.docx
Bright
    Usage.xlsx

Objectives

- Split the workbook window into panes
- Create a shared workbook
- Review edits to a shared workbook
- Merge two workbooks into one
- Inspect a document for hidden data
- Encrypt a workbook
- Digitally sign a finished workbook

Creating a Shared Workbook

Collaborating on a Financial Report

Case | DataSafe

DataSafe, a company based in Mobile, Alabama, specializes in data storage and recovery. Each year the company publishes a financial report for its stockholders. Jennifer Inwe and her team in the financial department are responsible for creating and publishing this year's report.

In the process of developing this report, different employees will review and edit the workbook's content, which will go through several drafts and revisions. Jennifer asks you to help manage this collaborative process of development from initial draft to final form. Jennifer is aware that the final version of the workbook should be error-free. You'll be the first reviewer and then send the workbook to other employees to review. The finished report will be distributed to the rest of the company and presented to the stockholders in time for the annual meeting.

Starting Data Files

Appendix.C →

Tutorial
Financial.xlsx
Group.xlsx
Linde Edits.xlsx
Merge.xlsx

Review
Projected.xlsx
SL Comments.xlsx
Stockholders.xlsx
Team.xlsx

Case1
Covey.xlsx
Kao.xlsx
Roper.xlsx

Case2
Mailing.xlsx
Student.xlsx

Splitting the Workbook Window into Panes

Jennifer entered the first draft of the financial report into a workbook, which contains four worksheets that describe DataSafe's financial status over the prior three years as well as the Documentation sheet. Jennifer suspects the Balance Sheet worksheet contains a mistake, because the total assets do not match the total liabilities and shareholders equity for one of the three years in the report. She wants you to find the source of the error.

Reference Window	Splitting the Workbook Window into Panes

- Drag the split box located at the top of the vertical scroll bar or at the right edge of the horizontal scroll bar into the workbook window, releasing the mouse button at the row or column where you want to split the workbook window into two panes (or in the Window group on the View tab, click the Split button to split the workbook window into four panes).
- To unsplit the workbook window, double-click the split bar that separates the workbook window into two panes (or in the Window group on the View tab, click the Split button).

The Balance Sheet worksheet is so long, it doesn't fit into the workbook window unless you greatly reduce the magnification. Another approach is to split the window into two panes, which you can scroll independently.

Tip

You can split a worksheet into two horizontal panes by dragging the split box located at the lower-right corner of the window to the left. You can also use both split boxes, dividing the workbook window into four panes.

To open Jennifer's workbook and split the Balance Sheet worksheet into two panes:

1. Open the **Financial** workbook located in the **Appendix.C\Tutorial** folder included with your Data Files, and then save the workbook as **Financial Report** in the same folder.

2. In the Documentation sheet, enter your name and the current date.

3. Switch to the **Balance Sheet** worksheet and point to the split box at the top of the vertical scroll bar. The pointer changes to ⬍.

4. Drag the split box down to row 10. As you drag, a thick gray bar appears across the worksheet.

5. Release the mouse button. The worksheet window separates into two vertical panes, indicated by the solid split bar across the window.

6. Scroll the top pane down until row 26 is the last row displayed in the top pane, and then scroll the bottom pane down until row 44 is the first row displayed in the bottom pane. See Figure C-1.

Balance Sheet split into two panes — Figure C-1

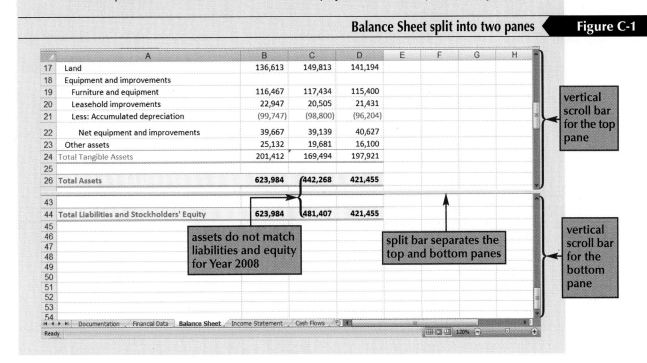

By splitting this long worksheet into two panes you can view the Total Assets row and the Total Liabilities and Stockholders' Equity row at one time. The values in cells C26 and C44 do not match, indicating an error in the Balance Sheet worksheet for the 2008 figures, because assets must always match liabilities and stockholders' equity.

To unsplit the workbook window:

1. Click the **View** tab on the Ribbon, and then, in the Window group, click the **Split** button to remove the split bar.

2. Scroll down the worksheet to display row 26.

The small green triangle in the upper-left corner of cell C24 indicates this cell might be the source of the error. You'll view the error message for this cell.

To view the error message for cell C24:

▶ 1. Click cell **C24**, click the **Formulas** tab on the Ribbon, and then, in the Formula Auditing group, click the **Error Checking** button. The Error Checking dialog box opens. See Figure C-2.

Figure C-2 ▶ Error Checking dialog box

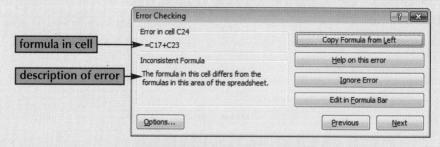

The formula differs from the formulas in cells B24 and D24, which calculate the total tangible assets for 2009 and 2007. You'll correct this error by copying the formula from the left side of the cell, which is cell B24 in this case.

▶ 2. Click the **Copy Formula from Left** button. The formula from cell B24 is copied to cell C24. The error check is complete for the entire sheet and no other errors are present.

▶ 3. Click the **OK** button.

▶ 4. Double-click the split box above the vertical scroll bar. The workbook window splits into two horizontal panes.

▶ 5. Scroll the panes until you can see rows 26 and 44, and then verify that 481,407 appears in cells C26 and C44.

▶ 6. Double-click the split bar separating the top and bottom panes to remove it.

Jennifer wants to distribute the workbook to the other members of the Finance department to get their input. She asks you to include a comment that asks whether the report should be expanded to included data from the previous five years.

To insert Jennifer's comment:

▶ 1. Switch to the **Financial Data** worksheet, and then click cell **A5**.

▶ 2. Click the **Review** tab on the Ribbon, and then, in the Comments group, click the **New Comment** button.

▶ 3. Type **Should we extend the scope of the report to include the previous five years of data?** in the comment box.

▶ 4. Click cell **A6**, and then, in the Comments group on the Review tab, click the **Show All Comments** button to display the comment.

Sharing a Workbook

To enable several users to view and modify a workbook while you have it open, you must share the workbook. A **shared workbook** can be edited simultaneously by more than one user when it is placed on a shared network folder, accessible to several users. Or, the shared workbook can be edited sequentially by users who edit the file in turns.

In a shared workbook, you can enter numbers and text, edit cells, move data, insert new rows and columns, and perform the other usual editing tasks. However, you cannot delete worksheets and ranges, insert ranges, merge and split cells, edit charts, or use the drawing tools. In general, you can do anything in the workbook that does not drastically change the layout or content to such an extent that Excel no longer can reconcile your edits with the edits from other users.

Tip

You cannot share a workbook with an Excel table or an XML data map; the Excel table must be converted to a range and the XML data map must be removed before sharing the workbook.

Setting Privacy Options

By default, Excel does not enable workbook sharing to prevent malicious software from opening and sharing personal information and sensitive data with the outside world. Before you can share a workbook, you must reset the privacy options. You set the privacy options for each workbook you wish to share, not the entire Excel program.

To enable sharing for the Financial Report workbook:

▶ **1.** Click the **Office Button** 🔘 , and then click the **Excel Options** button. The Excel Options dialog box opens.

▶ **2.** Click **Trust Center** in the Excel Options list, and then click the **Trust Center Settings** button.

▶ **3.** Click **Privacy Options** from the Trust Center list, and then, in the Document-specific settings section, uncheck the **Remove personal information from file properties on save** check box.

▶ **4.** Click the **OK** button in each dialog box to return to the workbook.

Sharing a Workbook

You can begin sharing the Financial Report workbook with other users. You'll first share the workbook immediately, making it possible for several users to access and edit the same data simultaneously.

To begin sharing the workbook:

Tip

You can add a password to a shared workbook so only approved users can edit it by clicking the Protect Shared Workbook button in the Changes group on the Review tab.

▶ **1.** In the Changes group on the Review tab, click the **Share Workbook** button. The Share Workbook dialog box opens with the Editing tab active.

▶ **2.** Click the **Allow changes by more than one user at the same time** check box to insert a check mark. This allows others to access and edit this workbook.

▶ **3.** Click the **OK** button. A dialog box indicates the workbook must be saved, which changes its status to shared.

▶ **4.** Click the **OK** button. The workbook is saved and [*Shared*] appears on the title bar next to the workbook name.

Jennifer notifies the finance group that the workbook is available on a network folder for review and editing. She will monitor their access to the workbook by opening the Share Workbook dialog box. As shown in Figure C-3, Alberto has also opened the workbook.

Figure C-3	**Share Workbook dialog box**

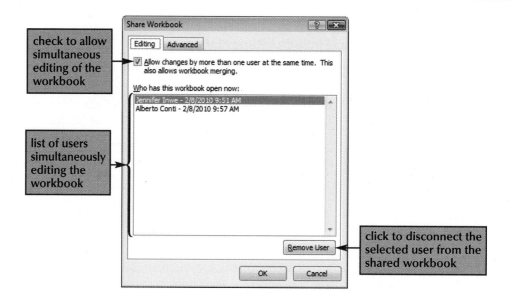

check to allow simultaneous editing of the workbook

list of users simultaneously editing the workbook

click to disconnect the selected user from the shared workbook

Resolving Conflicts

When each person makes changes to different cells, Excel integrates them into the shared workbook and notifies users of the change. Consider the situation shown in Figure C-4, in which Jennifer and Alberto are working on the same document. Alberto changes the value in cell B7, and then saves the workbook. When Jennifer saves the shared workbook, any changes made by other users appear as comments attached to the edited cells. Excel will remove these comments automatically when Jennifer reopens the workbook at a later date.

Two users edit a shared workbook | Figure C-4

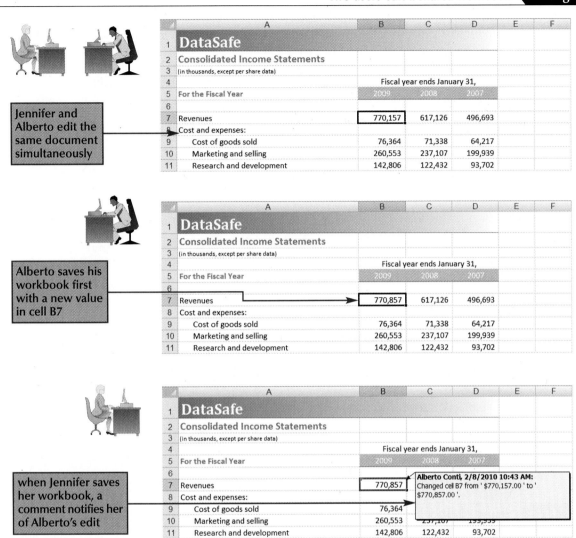

Conflicts occur when users try to save different changes to the same cell. Consider what happens when Jennifer and Alberto make different edits to cell B7. Alberto saves his workbook first. When Jennifer saves her workbook, the Resolve Conflicts dialog box opens, notifying her of the conflict in the value of cell B7, as shown in Figure C-5. From this dialog box, Jennifer can choose which edit to accept. She can repeat this process for each conflict.

Resolve Conflicts dialog box | Figure C-5

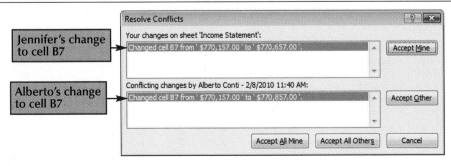

All users have equal authority to resolve conflicts. The last user to save the document sees the Resolve Conflicts dialog box. Rejected edits are stored in a **tracking log** so any user can review and retrieve them. This feature is particularly useful when a large group is editing a workbook and more control over the final content is needed. In the financial report for DataSafe, Jennifer will review the tracking log before signing off on the final report.

To close the Financial Report workbook:

▶ **1.** In the Documentation sheet, click cell **A1**.

▶ **2.** Save and close the Financial Report workbook.

Tracking Changes to a Workbook

Alberto Conti, Thomas Uecker, and Mai Le of the finance group have reviewed the Financial Report workbook and added comments and edits. You'll open the shared workbook and help Jennifer resolve the different changes made to the report.

To open and review the shared workbook:

▶ **1.** Open the **Group** workbook located in the **Appendix.C\Tutorial** folder included with your Data Files, and then save the workbook as **Group Edit** in the same folder.

▶ **2.** In the Documentation sheet, enter your name and the current date.

▶ **3.** Click the **Review** tab, and then, in the Comments group, click the **Next** button. The next, or in this case the first, comment is selected. It contains the responses to Jennifer's query about whether to expand the report to five years. Alberto and Mai suggest leaving the report as is, whereas Tom prefers the five-year report. See Figure C-6.

Figure C-6 ▶ **Shared workbook with user's comments**

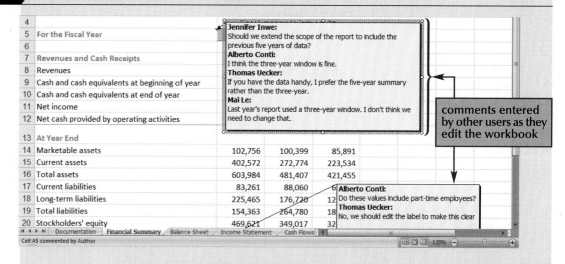

4. In the Comments group on the Review tab, click the **Next** button. The cell A22 comment is selected in which Alberto asks whether the number of employees reported in the worksheet includes part-time employees. Thomas responds that it doesn't and suggests changing the label.

5. In the Comments group, continue to click the **Next** button and review comments until a dialog box indicates you reached the end of the workbook.

6. Click the **Cancel** button to end reviewing the comments, and then click cell **A1** in the Financial Summary worksheet.

Because you have reviewed all of the comments in the workbook, Jennifer wants you to delete them.

To delete the comments:

1. In the Comments group on the Review tab, click the **Next** button to go to the first comment in the workbook.

2. In the Comments group on the Review tab, click the **Delete** button. The comment in cell A5 is deleted.

3. Repeat Steps 1 and 2 for the remaining comments in the workbook until you have deleted all of the comments.

4. Click cell **A1** in the Financial Summary worksheet to return to the beginning of the report.

Reviewing Changes and the Tracking Log

The tracking log, by default, stores all edits made to the workbook during the previous 30 days. However, inserted or deleted worksheets and style changes are not tracked. To review the tracked edits, you can use the Track Changes feature to highlight each edit. When Track Changes is enabled, the edits appear in a comment box next to the cell that describes the change, who made it, and when.

Reviewing Edits in a Shared Workbook | Reference Window

- In the Changes group on the Review tab, click the Track Changes button, and then click Highlight Changes.
- Specify when, who, and where, and click the Highlight changes on screen check box.
- To view the tracking log, click the List changes on a new sheet check box.
- Click the OK button. Point to the highlighted cells to see the edits, and view the tracking log on the History worksheet.

You'll use Track Changes to highlight the edits to the Group Edit workbook.

To highlight and review the changes to the shared workbook:

1. In the Changes group on the Review tab, click the **Track Changes** button, and then click **Highlight Changes**. The Highlight Changes dialog box opens. You'll review all the changes made by everyone but yourself.

2. Click the **When** arrow, and then click **All**.

3. Click the **Who** arrow, and then click **Everyone but Me**. The Who check box is automatically checked.

4. Verify that the **Highlight changes on screen** check box is checked and the **List changes on a new sheet** check box is unchecked. See Figure C-7.

Figure C-7 **Highlight Changes dialog box**

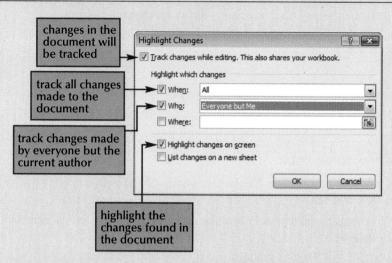

5. Click the **OK** button. Each cell that has been changed is displayed with a colored border.

6. In the Financial Summary worksheet, point to cell **A14**. A comment box opens with a description of the change made to the cell, including the change's author and the date and time when the change occurred. See Figure C-8.

Figure C-8 **Highlighted change**

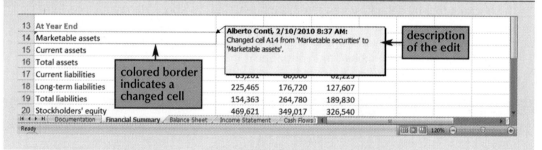

Examining all the sheets in a workbook to find the highlighted changes can be time-consuming, especially in workbooks with many worksheets. The tracking log provides a faster method to review the changes.

To show the contents of the tracking log:

1. In the Changes group on the Review tab, click the **Track Changes** button, and then click **Highlight Changes**. The Highlight Changes dialog box opens.

2. Click the **List changes on a new sheet** check box to insert a check mark, and then click the **OK** button. The History worksheet is created, detailing the history of the six changes made to the workbook in chronological order along with who made the change, where it was made, and what kind of change it was. See Figure C-9.

History worksheet with the tracking log Figure C-9

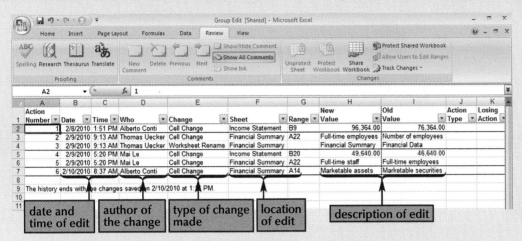

From the History worksheet, Jennifer sees that five edits change cell values, and one edit, made by Thomas Uecker, renamed the second worksheet from Financial Data to Financial Summary. Alberto Conti made the last edit at 8:37 AM. The History sheet exists only for the current Excel session. It is automatically deleted when the workbook is closed or you start rejecting or accepting the changes from the tracking log.

Accepting and Rejecting Changes

Jennifer wants to keep some changes but not others. You can accept or reject changes with commands on the Review tab. As with tracking changes, you specify which changes you want to examine for accepting and rejecting. The changes are reviewed in chronological order, just as they appeared in the tracking log.

Accepting and Rejecting Changes to a Workbook | Reference Window

- In the Changes group on the Review tab, click the Track Changes button, and then click Accept/Reject Changes.
- Specify when, who, and where changes are to be reviewed, and then click the OK button.
- Proceed through the list of changes, clicking the Accept, Reject, Accept All, Reject All, or Close buttons.

To accept or reject changes:

▶ **1.** In the Changes group on the Review tab, click the **Track Changes** button, and then click **Accept/Reject Changes**. The Select Changes to Accept or Reject dialog box opens. You'll use the default settings shown in Figure C-10.

Figure C-10 | **Select Changes to Accept or Reject dialog box**

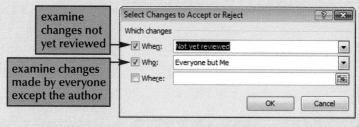

Tip

You can accept or reject all changes to the workbook at one time by clicking the Accept All or Reject All button.

examine changes not yet reviewed

examine changes made by everyone except the author

▶ **2.** Verify that your dialog box matches the one shown in Figure C-10, and then click the **OK** button. The first change is in cell B9 of the Income Statement worksheet. Alberto Conti changed the value from 76,364 to 96,364. See Figure C-11.

Figure C-11 | **Accept or Reject Changes dialog box**

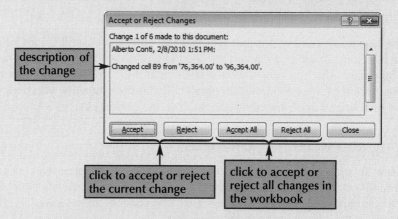

description of the change

click to accept or reject the current change

click to accept or reject all changes in the workbook

▶ **3.** Click the **Accept** button to accept this edit. The next change is in the Financial Summary worksheet in cell A22, which contains two conflicting edits. See Figure C-12.

Figure C-12 | **Multiple edits for the same cell**

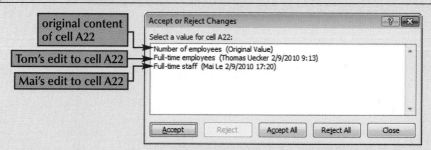

original content of cell A22

Tom's edit to cell A22

Mai's edit to cell A22

▶ **4.** In the Select a value for cell A22 box, click **Full-time employees**, and then click the **Accept** button. This accepts Tom's edit, rejecting the original text and Mai's subsequent edit.

▶ **5.** Click the **Accept** button to accept Tom's edit to rename the second worksheet from Financial Data to Financial Summary.

▶ **6.** Click the **Accept** button to accept Mai's edit of the value of cell B20 in the Income Statement worksheet from 46,640 to 49,640.

▶ **7.** Click the **Reject** button to reject Alberto's edit to cell A14 of the Financial Summary worksheet, which returns to *Marketable securities*.

▶ **8.** Save and close the Group Edit workbook.

Merge and Compare Workbooks

Jennifer's supervisor, Steve Linde, is at a conference and cannot access the shared file on the company network. Instead, he edited a copy of the workbook and e-mailed it to Jennifer. Jennifer wants to merge her workbook with Steve's to create a single workbook that combines the edits from both files. The following conditions must be met to merge two workbooks:

- The two workbooks must be copies of a common file, which must also be a shared workbook.
- The two workbooks must have different filenames.
- The two workbooks must either have the same password or not be password-protected.
- The Track Changes feature must be turned on for both workbooks.
- The tracking log must be kept from the time the two workbooks are made from the original common file.

The Compare and Merge Workbooks button does not appear on the Ribbon. You must add it to the Quick Access Toolbar.

Merging Workbooks | Reference Window

- Customize the Quick Access Toolbar to display the Compare and Merge Workbooks button.
- Open the workbook into which you want to merge the workbooks.
- Click the Compare and Merge Workbooks button on the Quick Access Toolbar.
- Select the workbook that you want to merge into the current document, and then click the OK button.

To add the Merge and Compare button to the Quick Access Toolbar:

▶ **1.** On the Quick Access Toolbar, click the **Customize Quick Access Toolbar** button, and then click **More Commands**.

▶ **2.** Click **Commands Not in the Ribbon** from the Choose commands list box to display a list of all of the Excel commands which are not displayed on any of the Ribbon tabs.

▶ **3.** Click **Compare and Merge Workbooks** from the list of commands and then click the **Add** button. The Compare and Merge Workbooks command button is added to the commands on the Quick Access Toolbar.

▶ **4.** Click the **OK** button.

Now you can merge Jennifer's workbook with Steve's. First, you open the workbook into which you want to merge the two files—in this case, Jennifer's workbook. Then, you use the Compare and Merge command to open the other workbook—in this case, Steve's workbook. One advantage of merging workbooks is that each user works on a separate copy, protecting the original from mistakes until the workbooks are merged.

To merge Jennifer's workbook with Steve's workbook:

▶ **1.** Open the **Merge** workbook located in the **Appendix.C\Tutorial** folder included with your Data Files, and then save it as **Merged Report** in the same folder.

▶ **2.** In the Documentation sheet, enter your name and the current date.

▶ **3.** On the Quick Access Toolbar, click the **Compare and Merge** button 🔘.

▶ **4.** Click the **Linde Edits** workbook located in the **Appendix.C\Tutorial** folder included with your Data Files, and then click the **OK** button. The two workbooks are merged.

▶ **5.** Switch to the **Financial Summary** worksheet. Steve inserted a comment indicating that he thinks the workbook is in good shape.

▶ **6.** Click cell **A2**, click the **Review** tab, and then, in the Comments group, click the **Delete** button to delete Steve's comment.

Next, you'll review the edits in the two workbooks. You've already reviewed the changes in Jennifer's workbook, so you'll review only the changes that Steve made.

To review Steve's changes in the merged workbook:

▶ **1.** In the Changes group on the Review tab, click the **Track Changes** button, and then click **Accept/Reject Changes**. The Select Changes to Accept or Reject dialog box opens.

▶ **2.** In the Who box, select **Steve Linde** to review only the changes Steve made, and then click the **OK** button. Steve made four changes. The first is in cell A2 of the Financial Summary worksheet where he changed the subtitle to *Select Three-Year Financial Data*.

▶ **3.** Click the **Accept** button to accept the change. Jennifer tells you to accept all of Steve's edits.

▶ **4.** Click the **Accept All** button, and then save the workbook.

Preparing a Final Workbook Version

Jennifer is ready to release the financial report for wider dissemination in the company. First, she'll send the workbook to department heads. She doesn't want the department heads to edit the workbook, so you will remove the sharing features.

To create the final workbook version:

▶ **1.** Save the workbook as **Financial Report Final Draft** in the **Appendix.C\Tutorial** folder included with your Data Files.

▶ **2.** In the Changes group on the Review tab, click the **Share Workbook** button. The Share Workbooks dialog box opens.

▶ **3.** Uncheck the **Allow changes by more than one user at the same time** check box, and click the **OK** button.

▶ **4.** Click the **Yes** button to confirm that you want to remove the workbook from shared use.

Setting Document Properties

The Documentation sheet includes a description of the final workbook, its contents, and purpose. But, the worksheet is not easily accessible outside of Excel. Instead, you can modify the workbook's **document properties**, or **metadata**, which are the descriptive details about a file, including its author, title, and subject. The five types of document properties are:

- Standard properties, which are properties associated with all Office files and include the author, title, and subject.

- Automatically updated properties, which are properties usually associated with the file itself, such as the file size or date the file was last edited. You cannot modify the automatically updated properties.

- Custom properties, which are properties you define and create designed specifically for your workbook.

- Organization properties, which are properties created for organizations using the Document Information Panel available with Microsoft InfoPath.

- Document library properties, which are properties associated with documents in a document library on a Web site or in a public network folder. You can create a document library with Microsoft SharePoint, a group of services that support document collaboration and information sharing.

   One advantage is that users can access document properties without opening the workbook, making it easier to find key files. For example, in a network folder with hundreds of files, Jennifer's colleagues can quickly locate workbooks she authored or on a specific topic, such as the stockholders meeting. You'll add document properties that describe the workbook.

To add document properties to the workbook:

▶ **1.** Click the **Office Button** 🔘 , point to **Prepare**, and then click **Properties**. The Document Properties pane opens between the Ribbon and the formula bar. It contains input boxes for the most common properties.

▶ **2.** Type your name in the Author box, type **DataSafe Financial Report** in the Title box, type **Finance** in the Subject box, type **stockholders; yearly meeting** in the Keywords box, type **Financial Statements** in the Category box, and then type **Final Draft** in the Status box.

   Trouble? If prompted to turn on AutoComplete, you can click the Yes or No button, depending on whether you want Excel to remember your previous entries.

▶ **3.** Type **Final draft of the 2010 financial report to be presented at the Stockholders' Meeting on March 3 in Atlanta, GA.** in the Comments box. See Figure C-13.

Figure C-13 ▶ Document Properties pane

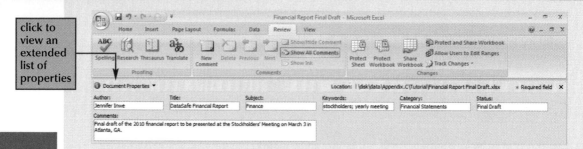

click to view an extended list of properties

Tip

You can insert multiple values for a document property by typing a semi-colon between the property values.

Jennifer needs to identify the department that created this workbook. You'll create a custom document property for the department name.

▶ **4.** Click the **Document Properties** button, and then click **Advanced Properties**. The Financial Report Final Draft Properties dialog box opens.

▶ **5.** Click the **Custom** tab, and then click **Department** in the Name box. The data type is correctly set as Text.

▶ **6.** Type **Finance** in the Value box, and then click the **Add** button. The Department property is added to the Properties box. See Figure C-14.

Figure C-14 ▶ Custom document properties

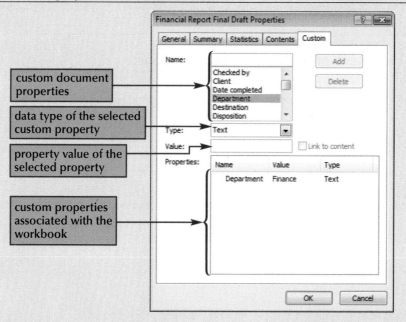

custom document properties

data type of the selected custom property

property value of the selected property

custom properties associated with the workbook

▶ **7.** Click the **OK** button to close the dialog box, and then click the **Close** button ☒ in the Document Properties pane to close it. After you save and close the workbook, its properties are available to other programs, including the Windows operating system.

Inspecting a Document

Before distributing the workbook, Jennifer wants to be sure it doesn't contain sensitive or personal information. Personal information can come from comments and annotations, document properties and metadata attached to the workbook, custom XML data stored within the XML code for the workbook file, headers and footers, hidden worksheets and cells, cells whose display styles rendered them invisible to the user, and server information inserted by saving a workbook on the Document Workspace site or within a Document Library. To determine whether a workbook contains sensitive or personal information, you can use the **Document Inspector** which searches the workbook, locating data and text that fit these categories. You can then remove any personal information, if necessary, with the Document Inspector.

To use the Document Inspector:

1. Click the **Office Button** 🪟 , point to **Prepare**, and then click **Inspect Document**. The Document Inspector opens with a list of the different categories of content to be inspected. By default, all categories are inspected.

   Trouble? If a dialog box opens asking whether you want to inspect or save the document, click the Yes button.

2. Leave all of the check boxes checked, and then click the **Inspect** button. The inspection results appear in the dialog box. See Figure C-15.

Document Inspector results ◄ **Figure C-15**

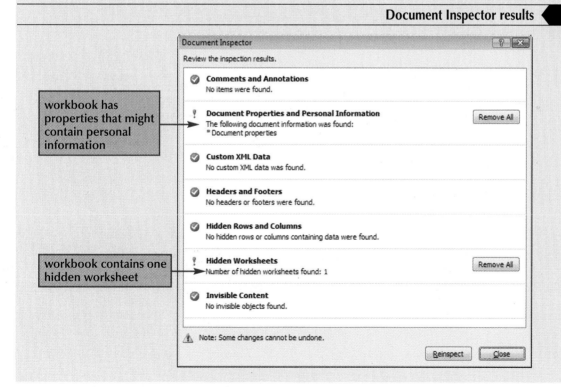

workbook has properties that might contain personal information

workbook contains one hidden worksheet

The Document Inspector indicates two instances where personal or sensitive information might appear in the workbook. The first are the document properties; you just entered that information and want it to appear in the workbook. The Document Inspector has found a worksheet hidden in the workbook. **Hidden worksheets** are removed from the user's view often to conceal source data and documentation that is useful to the author but is distracting or confusing to other users. Before Jennifer distributes the workbook, you must find out what the hidden sheet contains.

To show and hide the worksheet:

▶ **1.** Click the **Close** button to close the Document Inspector dialog box.

▶ **2.** Right-click any sheet tab in the workbook, and click **Unhide** on the shortcut menu. The Unhide dialog box opens, displaying a list of all of the hidden sheets in the workbook. In this case, the only hidden sheet is the Notes on the Report worksheet.

▶ **3.** With the sheet name selected, click the **OK** button. The Notes on the Report worksheet appears between the Documentation and Financial Summary worksheets. The worksheet contains Jennifer's to-do list for the project, which is not relevant for her colleagues.

▶ **4.** Right-click the **Notes on the Report** sheet tab, and then click **Hide** on the shortcut menu. The worksheet is again hidden from view.

Jennifer asks you to delete the Notes on the Report worksheet before she distributes the workbook. Rather than unhiding the worksheet again and then deleting it, you'll delete it using the Document Inspector.

To remove the hidden worksheet with the Document Inspector:

▶ **1.** Click the **Office Button** 🪟 , point to **Prepare**, click **Inspect Document** to open the Document Inspector, click the **Inspect** button, and then click the **Yes** button. The Document Inspector again reports the existence of the document properties and the hidden worksheet.

▶ **2.** In the Hidden Worksheets section, click the **Remove All** button. The hidden worksheet is deleted from the workbook.

▶ **3.** Click the **Close** button to close the Document Inspector, and then save the workbook.

> ### Tip
>
> Use caution when you remove information and data from a workbook with the Document Inspector, because you cannot undo the removal.

| InSight | | **Using the Document Inspector to Detect Viruses** |

The Document Inspector, in addition to ensuring that no personal or inappropriate information is included in the final version of a workbook, can be used to verify that the workbook has not been corrupted by a malicious program. A workbook virus might be signaled by a hidden worksheet or hidden code attached to the XML code in the file.

Encrypting a Workbook

When a workbook is free of errors and invalid hidden data, you can encrypt the workbook to help secure its contents. **Encryption** is the process by which a file is encoded so that it cannot be opened without the proper password. Jennifer wants to encrypt the workbook before sending it to the department heads to ensure that only authorized users can view the data. You've already used passwords to prevent users from editing a worksheet or the entire workbook; this is different. Jennifer wants to prevent users from even opening the file. Jennifer does not want the details of DataSafe's 2009 financial report to be made public, so only a few key people will know the password to view the document's contents. Passwords can be up to 255 characters in length and can include numbers, symbols, and upper- and lowercase letters.

To encrypt the workbook:

▶ 1. Save the workbook as **Financial Report Final Draft Encrypted** in the **Appendix.C\Tutorial** folder included with your Data Files.

▶ 2. Click the **Office Button**, point to **Prepare**, and then click **Encrypt Document**. The Encrypt Document dialog box opens.

▶ 3. Type **datasafe** (in all lowercase letters) in the Password box, and then click the **OK** button.

▶ 4. Type **datasafe** in the Reenter password box, and then click the **OK** button.

▶ 5. Save and close the workbook, and then reopen the workbook. The Password dialog box opens, preventing the workbook from opening without the password.

▶ 6. Type **datasafe** in the Password box, and then click the **OK** button. The workbook opens.

Trouble? If the workbook doesn't open, you might have mistyped the password. Repeat Step 6. If the workbook still doesn't open, you might have mistyped the password in Steps 3 and 4. There is no simple way to recover a mistyped password from an encrypted document. Open the Financial Report Final Draft workbook, and then repeat Steps 1 through 6 to recreate the encrypted version of the workbook.

Marking a Workbook as Final

Jennifer wants the department heads to know that the workbook they receive is the final version of the report. She can do this by marking the workbook as final, which makes the workbook read-only, preventing any additional changes to it. A final workbook has the editing, typing, and proofing commands disabled or turned off. The user can only view the contents of the file, not change it. Also, the status document property value changes to Final.

To mark the financial report workbook as final:

▶ 1. Click the **Office Button**, point to **Prepare**, and then click **Mark as Final**. A dialog box indicates that the workbook will be marked as final and then saved.

▶ 2. Click the **OK** button in each dialog box. A marked-as-final workbook is displayed with [*Read-Only*] in the title bar, indicating the file can be read but not edited. The icon in the status bar changes to 📝.

▶ 3. Click a blank cell in the active worksheet to confirm that you cannot edit the workbook.

The Mark as Final command lets you inform others that this is the final version of the workbook. Despite its name, marking a workbook as final is not a security feature. Anyone can remove the Mark as Final status from the workbook by reapplying the Mark as Final command to deselect it. To ensure a workbook cannot be edited, password-protect the workbook using the Protect Workbook button in the Changes group on the Review tab.

Providing a Digital Signature

Another way to monitor access to a workbook is with digital signatures. A **digital signature** is an electronic version of a written signature and provides a way to authenticate a workbook. Digital signatures cannot be forged. Also, a workbook signed with a digital signature cannot be altered without removing the signature, ensuring that the workbook received is the one that the user intended to send. With a digital signature, other users know that the workbook comes from a trusted source, has not been altered since originally signed, and its origin is accepted by all parties and can't be repudiated by the signer.

To add a digital signature, you need a **digital ID** or **digital certificate**, which authenticates the source of the signature. If you do not have a digital certificate, you can get one from a third-party source or you can create your own. The third-party source, also known as a **certificate authority (CA)**, is a trusted entity that issues certificates as a service for companies and individuals. The CA may be a commercial service that requires payment. If you create your own certificate, it authenticates the file only for that computer and not for other users on other computers.

Reference Window | **Adding a Digital Signature to a Workbook**

- Click the Office Button, point to Prepare, and then click Add a Digital Signature.
- If requested, specify whether to create a third-party digital ID or a local digital ID. Provide descriptive information for the digital ID.
- If no digital IDs are made, specify whether to create a third-party digital ID or a local digital ID. Provide descriptive information for the digital ID, and then click the Create button.
- Enter a purpose for the digital signature, click the Sign button, and then click the OK button.

DataSafe uses digital signatures to monitor and authenticate files as they travel between departments. Jennifer does not have a third-party digital certificate, so you'll create one as you add the digital signature.

To add a digital signature:

▶ 1. Click the **Office Button** 🔘 , point to **Prepare**, and then click **Add a Digital Signature**. The Get a Digital ID dialog box opens.

   Trouble? If a dialog box opens, describing digital signatures, click the OK button.

▶ 2. Click the **Create your own digital ID** option button, and then click the **OK** button. The Create a Digital ID dialog box opens.

3. Type your name in the Name box, type your e-mail address in the E-mail address box, type the name of your school or organization in the Organization box, and then type your city or location in the Location box. See Figure C-16.

Create a Digital ID dialog box | **Figure C-16**

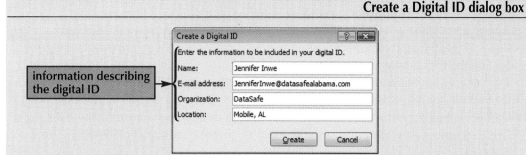

information describing the digital ID

Create a Digital ID

Enter the information to be included in your digital ID.

Name: Jennifer Inwe
E-mail address: JenniferInwe@datasafealabama.com
Organization: DataSafe
Location: Mobile, AL

Create   Cancel

4. Click the **Create** button. A dialog box prompts you to enter a purpose for the digital signature.

5. Type **Authenticating the final version of the DataSafe financial report**, click the **Sign** button, and then click the **OK** button. The Signatures pane opens, listing the valid signatures applied to the file and the digital certificate icon appears in the status bar. See Figure C-17.

Digitally signed workbook | **Figure C-17**

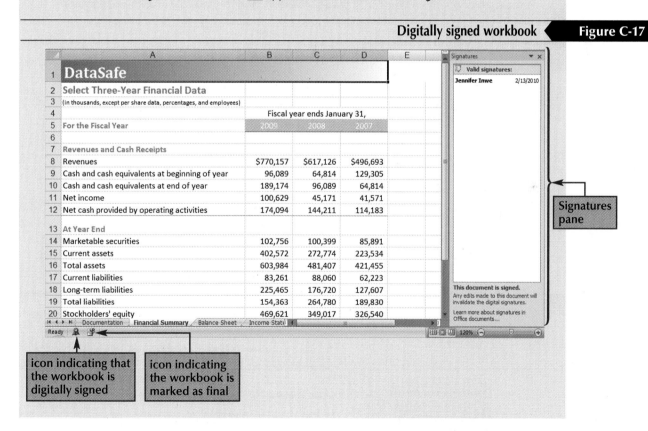

	A	B	C	D	E
1	**DataSafe**				
2	**Select Three-Year Financial Data**				
3	(in thousands, except per share data, percentages, and employees)				
4		Fiscal year ends January 31,			
5	For the Fiscal Year	2009	2008	2007	
6					
7	**Revenues and Cash Receipts**				
8	Revenues	$770,157	$617,126	$496,693	
9	Cash and cash equivalents at beginning of year	96,089	64,814	129,305	
10	Cash and cash equivalents at end of year	189,174	96,089	64,814	
11	Net income	100,629	45,171	41,571	
12	Net cash provided by operating activities	174,094	144,211	114,183	
13	At Year End				
14	Marketable securities	102,756	100,399	85,891	
15	Current assets	402,572	272,774	223,534	
16	Total assets	603,984	481,407	421,455	
17	Current liabilities	83,261	88,060	62,223	
18	Long-term liabilities	225,465	176,720	127,607	
19	Total liabilities	154,363	264,780	189,830	
20	Stockholders' equity	469,621	349,017	326,540	

Signatures

Valid signatures:

Jennifer Inwe   2/13/2010

Signatures pane

This document is signed.
Any edits made to this document will invalidate the digital signatures.
Learn more about signatures in Office documents...

Documentation | Financial Summary | Balance Sheet | Income Stat...

Ready

icon indicating that the workbook is digitally signed

icon indicating the workbook is marked as final

If any edits are made to the digitally signed workbook document or if the marked as final status is changed, the digital signature will be displayed in a red font and marked as invalid, providing another protection against unapproved edits.

Excel and Information Rights Management

You can also control access to a workbook with **Information Rights Management (IRM)**, a service installed with Office to safeguard digital information from unauthorized use. To use IRM, the Windows Rights Management Services (RMS) Client Service Pack must be installed on your computer. The RMS client comes preinstalled with Windows Vista Premium, Business, and Ultimate, but not with Windows Vista Basic. The IRM service helps you:

- Prevent unauthorized recipients from forwarding, copying, editing, printing, faxing, or pasting the file content
- Prevent copying of unauthorized file with the Windows Print Screen feature
- Restrict file content wherever it is sent
- Set file expiration so the file cannot be viewed or accessed after the expiration date
- Enforce corporate policies to govern the use and dissemination of content within the company

An RMS administrator sets IRM policies to define who can access information and what level of editing each user is allowed. With IRM installed and activated, Jennifer could specify who could access her files and what they could do (or not do) with them. When IRM is active, click the Office Button, point to Prepare, and then click Restrict Permission. A dialog box opens so you can set who to restrict and the level of restriction. For more information, refer to Excel Help.

Ensuring Backward-Compatibility in a Workbook

Most DataSafe employees are using Excel 2007, but a few still use an earlier version. Because earlier versions of Excel cannot open Excel 2007 files, you'll create a copy of Jennifer's workbook that is compatible with earlier Excel versions. Jennifer wants you to ensure that no critical features or content in the financial report are lost. You'll use the Compatibility Checker to flag any content, formatting, or element in the workbook that cannot be transferred to earlier versions of Excel.

To run the Compatibility Checker on Jennifer's workbook:

1. Click the **Office Button** (icon), point to **Prepare**, and then click **Run Compatibility Checker**. The Compatibility Checker dialog box opens, indicating minor issues with formatting styles that will be lost when the workbook is saved for earlier versions of Excel. See Figure C-18.

Figure C-18 ▶ Compatibility Checker dialog box

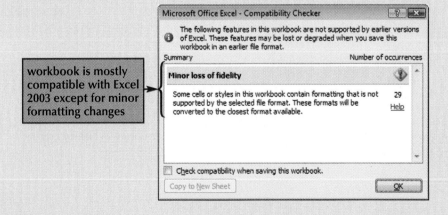

workbook is mostly compatible with Excel 2003 except for minor formatting changes

▶ **2.** Click the **OK** button. You'll save the financial report workbook in the Excel 97-2003 file format.

▶ **3.** Click the **Office Button** 🔵 , and then click **Save As**. The Save As dialog box opens.

▶ **4.** Save the workbook in the **Appendix.C\Tutorial** folder included with your Data Files, with the filename **Financial Report Excel 2003**, and in the file type **Excel 97-2003 Workbook**.

▶ **5.** Click the **Save** button. Saving a workbook in an earlier file format is considered an edit, so a dialog box notifies you that Excel will remove the digital signature.

▶ **6.** Click the **Yes** button to continue with saving the file, and then click the **No** button if prompted to convert the file to an Office Open XML (Excel 2007) format. Excel performs a last compatibility check, again finding that there will be minor differences in the format styles.

▶ **7.** Click the **Continue** button to save the Excel 2003 version of the workbook.

Jennifer asks you to restore the digital signature and then resave the workbook.

▶ **8.** Click the **Office Button** 🔵 , point to **Prepare**, and then click **Add a Digital Signature**.

▶ **9.** Click the **OK** button, click the **Sign** button, and then click the **OK** button. The digital signature is restored to the workbook.

▶ **10.** Save and close the workbook.

Improving the Collaborative Process | InSight

The collaborative tools in Excel make it simpler for groups to share the work of writing, editing, and finishing a financial report. No tool, however useful, can overcome problems associated with colleagues who cannot work together effectively. Keep in mind the following to improve the collaborative process:

- Project goals should be stated in advance with all team members clearly understanding what is expected of them. Team members should feel comfortable requesting clarification of those goals at any time in the process.
- Identify the strengths and weaknesses of each team member and adjust the project accordingly.
- Start work on the project at the earliest possible date.
- Constantly monitor the progress of the project, staying up to date on what has been done and what needs to be done. Communicate the status of the project with progress reports to each team member.
- Make it easy for team members to suggest new ideas and voice objections.
- Finish your tasks on time and meet your project goals.
- Treat each team member with respect. Do not allow personal grudges or differences to influence the successful completion of the project.

By successfully managing the group dynamic, you can make Excel's collaborative tools even more effective and useful.

Jennifer has two versions of the workbook: one for users of Excel 2007 and one for users of Excel 2003. Both workbooks are digitally signed, marked as final, and encrypted against unauthorized access. Jennifer will distribute the workbooks to the department heads for review and then use their feedback to prepare the final report for the annual stockholders' meeting.

Appendix Summary | Review

In this appendix, you learned how to review and edit a document in a workgroup environment. You learned how to share a workbook with several users, allowing for simultaneous and sequential editing. You accepted and rejected edits made to a workbook by a team of colleagues. You merged different edited versions of a common workbook into one file. Then, you created a final draft of the workbook by inserting document properties, encrypting the workbook to prevent unauthorized access, marking the workbook as final, and adding a digital signature to authenticate the workbook. Finally, you used the Compatibility Checker to ensure that Excel 2007 workbooks were backward-compatible with earlier versions of Excel.

Key Terms

certificate authority (CA)
digital certificate
digital ID
digital signature
Document Inspector

document properties
encryption
hidden worksheet
Information Rights
    Management (IRM)

metadata
shared workbook
tracking log

...actice the skills you ...arned in the appendix ...ing the same case ...enario.

Data Files needed for the Review Assignments: Projected.xlsx, Team.xlsx, Stockholders.xlsx, SL Comments.xlsx

Jennifer needs to provide a projected income statement and project cash flow schedule of the upcoming year for the stockholders' meeting. She created the initial workbook, but wants your help in sending it out for review and then reconciling the edits made by her colleagues. After Jennifer has a final draft, she wants you to add document properties, encrypt the workbook, marking it as final, and add a digital signature. She also wants you to create a copy of the workbook for employees who are using an earlier version of Excel.

Complete the following:

1. Open the **Projected** workbook located in the Appendix.C\Review folder included with your Data Files, and save the workbook as **Projected Statements** in the same folder. In the Documentation sheet, enter your name and the current date.
2. In the Projected Income worksheet, add the following comment to cell B7: **Do you think that $840,000 is a reasonable estimate for next year's revenue?**
3. Share the workbook, enabling changes by more than one user at a time. Save and close the Projected Statements workbook.
4. Open the **Team** workbook located in the Appendix.C\Review folder, and then save the workbook as **Team Edits** in the same folder. In the Documentation sheet, enter your name and the current date.
5. In the Income Projections worksheet, delete the comments that were added to cell B7.
6. Review the changes in the workbook by everyone but you, accepting them or rejecting the changes as follows:
   - Accept Alberto Conti's recommended projection for the 2010 net revenue in cell B7 of the Income Projections worksheet.
   - Accept the rest of Alberto Conti's edits.
   - Accept Tom Uecker's edit of cell B19 in the Income Projections worksheet.
   - Reject Mai Le's edit of cell B13 in the Income Projections worksheet.
   - Reject both of Tom Uecker's edits to cell A2 in the Cash Flow Projections and Income Projections worksheets.
7. Save and close the workbook. Open the **Stockholders** workbook located in the Appendix.C\Review folder, and then save the workbook as **Stockholders Report** in the same folder. In the Documentation sheet, enter your name and the current date.
8. Merge the contents of the **SL Comments** workbook with the current workbook. Delete Steve's comment on the Cash Flow Projections worksheet. Accept all of Steve's edits to the workbook, and then save the workbook.
9. Save the workbook as **Stockholders Report Final** in the Appendix.C\Review folder. Remove the workbook from shared use.
10. Add the following document properties to the workbook: your name as the author, **Financial Projections** as the title, **Stockholders' Report** as the subject, **projections**; **stockholders'** as document keywords, **Conference Reports** as the category, and **Final Draft** as the status.
11. Enter the following document comment: **Financial projections for the 2010 Stockholders' Conference**.
12. Create the Department custom property and enter **Finance** for the property.
13. Use the Document Inspector to determine whether Jennifer left any notes hidden in a cell or column. If so, remove the hidden row or column from the workbook.

14. Encrypt the document using the password **datasafe**.
15. Mark the document as final.
16. Digitally sign the document using a digital certificate supplied by your instructor or one you create. Save the workbook.
17. Save the workbook as **Stockholders Report Final for Excel 2003** in the Excel 97-2003 Workbook file format. Confirm that there are no major compatibility issues, and then reapply the digital signature to this version of the workbook.
18. Save and close the workbook. Submit the finished workbooks to your instructor, either in printed or electronic form, as requested.

| Apply | Case Problem 1 |

Use the skills you learned to merge data from several workbooks and prepare the final budget analysis for a city government.

Data Files needed for this Case Problem: Covey.xlsx, Roper.xlsx, Kao.xlsx

City of Covey Pines   Dale Jaffa, an assistant to the treasurer of the town of Covey Pines, Iowa, is helping to prepare the annual budget forecast. He e-mailed his budget workbook to different department heads to get their budget projections. Norma Roper is responsible for budgeted and actual expenses in the general fund. Mary Kao is responsible for budgeted and actual expenses for special funds. Dale received their workbooks and needs to merge them into one workbook that he can prepare for final distribution to other city leaders.

Complete the following:

1. Open the **Covey** workbook located in the Appendix.C\Case1 folder, and then save the workbook as **Covey Pines Budget** in the same folder. In the Documentation sheet, enter your name and the current date.
2. Merge the workbook with both the Roper and Kao workbooks located in the Appendix.C\Case1 folder.
3. Remove the workbook from shared use.
4. Add the following document properties to the workbook: your name as the author, **Covey Pines Budget** as the title, **Annual Budget Forecast** as the subject, **budget**, **general fund**, and **special funds** as keywords, **budget** as the category, and **proposed** as the status.
5. Insert the document comment: **Proposed 2010 – 2011 budget for the general fund and special funds**.

⊕ EXPLORE
6. Insert the Date Completed document property using the current date for the property value. Set the type of the document property to Date.
7. Split the Budget worksheet into two panes at row 9. Scroll the lower pane to show row 18 at the top of the pane.
8. Inspect the workbook for hidden data or content, and then remove any hidden comments or annotations. Save the workbook.
9. Save an encrypted version of the workbook as **Covey Pines Budget Encrypted**. Use the encryption password **coveypines** (in all lowercase letters). Close the workbook.
10. Submit the finished workbooks to your instructor, either in printed or electronic form, as requested.

| **Case Problem 2**

...e the skills you ...rned to share a mail-...g list workbook and ...concile edits made by ...veral users.

Data Files needed for this Case Problem: Mailing.xlsx, Student.xlsx

Templeton University Foundation   Tim Stoddard is in charge of fund raising for the Templeton University Foundation (TUF) of Madison, Wisconsin. As TUF's spring fund raising drive approaches, Tim needs to compile a mailing list of past contributors. He created a workbook with names and addresses, and wants several student assistants to review the workbook and fix any errors they find. Tim asks you to set up the shared workbook and reconcile the edits made by his assistants. When he has a final draft of the workbook, Tim will send it to TUF members who are creating the form letters and mailing labels.

Complete the following:

1. Open the **Mailing** workbook located in the Appendix.C\Case2 folder included with your Data Files, and then save the workbook as **Mailing List Shared** in the same folder. In the Documentation sheet, enter your name and the current date.

⊕**EXPLORE**

2. Share the workbook, making it available for editing. (*Hint*: Excel cannot share the document because of the Excel table in the Mailing List worksheet. Convert the table to a range, and then share the workbook.)

3. Open the **Student** workbook located in the Appendix.C\Case2 folder, and then save the workbook as **Student Edits** in the same folder. In the Documentation sheet, enter your name and the current date.

4. Display the tracking log for all edits made to the workbook except yours. Print the History worksheet with the tracking log in landscape orientation scaled to fit on a single page.

5. Review the changes made by Tim's student assistants. Accept all of their edits except for Sandy Lopez's edit of cell B54 in the Mailing List worksheet. In cell B16, accept Alvaro Sanchez's edit over those made by Sandy Lopez and Gary Weiss.

6. Remove the workbook from shared use.

7. Add the following document properties to the workbook: your name as the author, **Templeton University Foundation** as the title, **Mailing List** as the subject, **fund raising** as the keyword and the category, **final** as the status. Also enter the comment property, **Mailing list for 2010 appeal**.

⊕**EXPLORE**

8. In the advanced document properties, add the Checked by property four times with the values **Sandy Lopez; Alvaro Sanchez; Gary Weiss**.

9. Inspect the document for hidden or personal data. If you find a hidden worksheet, print it in portrait orientation on two pages and then remove it from the workbook.

10. Create a local digital ID for the workbook, using your name for the Name element, your e-mail for the E-mail address, your school or organization for the Organization element, and your city or location for the Location element.

11. Enter **To ensure the integrity of the mailing list** as the purpose of the digital signature, and then sign the workbook.

12. Save and close the workbook. Submit the finished workbooks to your instructor,

Ending Data Files

Appendix.C →

Tutorial
Financial Report.xlsx
Financial Report Excel
    2003.xls
Financial Report Final
    Draft.xlsx
Financial Report Final
    Draft Encrypted.xlsx
Group Edit.xlsx
Merged Report.xlsx

Review
Projected
    Statements.xlsx
Stockholders
    Report.xlsx
Stockholders Report
    Final.xlsx
Stockholders Report
    Final for Excel
    2003.xls
Team Edits.xlsx

Case1
Covey Pines
    Budget.xlsx
Covey Pines Budget
    Encrypted.xlsx

Case2
Mailing List
    Shared.xlsx
Student Edits.xls

Objectives

- Create a custom cell style
- Create a custom table style
- Create a conditional format to highlight cells
- Create a color scale conditional format
- Create an icon set conditional format
- Insert and modify a SmartArt graphic
- Modify the image properties of a picture
- Create and save a theme

Working with Enhanced Formatting Tools

Formatting a Chemistry Report

Case | Online Interactive Chemistry

Dr. Charles Scott is an award-winning high school chemistry teacher with 30 years teaching experience. In recent years, he's turned his attention to creating a collection of interactive chemistry tutorials called *Online Interactive Chemistry,* or *OIC*. Charles knows from his classroom experience and discussions with other professionals that Excel is a useful tool for recording and analyzing chemistry experiments. He wants to create a series of Excel chemistry workbooks to allow students to work with chemical concepts, perform what-if analysis, and generate reports.

The first set of workbooks he wants to create is based on the chemical properties described in the periodic table. Rather than provide students with raw data values, he wants the periodic table to present these values graphically with custom symbols and colors. You'll help him develop the first prototypes for his project.

Starting Data Files

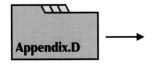

Appendix.D →

Tutorial

Dalton.jpg
Democritus.jpg
Mendeleev.jpg
Periodic.xlsx

Review

Elements.xlsx
Table1.jpg
Table2.jpg
Table3.jpg
Table4.jpg

Case1

Big.xlsx
Water.jpg

Case2

FPS.xlsx

Creating a Custom Cell Style

Charles created a sample workbook that, in addition to the Documentation sheet, contains four worksheets. The Element Families worksheet contains the periodic table with each element labeled according to its element family. The Ionization Energy worksheet contains the periodic table listing each element's ionization energy. The Radioactive Elements worksheet contains the periodic table identifying radioactive elements. The Element Data worksheet contains the raw data about each element from which the other worksheets draw their information.

To open and review the periodic table workbook:

▶ **1.** Open the **Periodic** workbook located in the **Appendix.D\Tutorial** folder included with your Data Files, and then save the workbook as **Periodic Table**. In the Documentation sheet, enter your name and the current date.

▶ **2.** Review the workbook contents, reducing the zoom percentage to see the entire periodic tables in the worksheets.

Charles wants you to use custom styles to create a unifying look for the workbook. To create a custom cell style, you select a cell with the formatting you want to use in the new style. When you save the cell formatting as style, you select which formatting elements to include in the final cell style definition. The new cell style then appears in the Cell Style gallery, ready to be applied to other worksheet cells and shared with other workbooks.

Reference Window	**Creating a Cell Style**

- Select a cell with the formatting you want to use in the custom cell style.
- In the Styles group on the Home tab, click the Cell Styles button, and then click New Cell Style.
- In the Style name box, enter a name for the style, and then check the style elements that you want to be part of the custom style.
- Click the Format button, and select any other formatting options you want to include in the custom style.
- Click the OK button in each dialog box to add the custom cell style to the Cell Styles gallery.

You'll create a custom cell style named *PTitle* that formats the title in a large bold font centered over a double bottom border.

To create and apply the PTitle cell style:

▶ **1.** Switch to the **Element Families** worksheet, and then click cell **B4**.

▶ **2.** In the Styles group on the Home tab, click the **Cell Styles** button to open the Cell Styles gallery, and then click **New Cell Style**. The Style dialog box opens.

▶ **3.** In the Style name box, type **PTitle**.

4. Click the **Number**, **Fill**, and **Protection** check boxes to remove the check marks, leaving the Alignment, Font, and Border style elements checked. The checked elements are included in the custom style. See Figure D-1.

Figure D-1 — Style dialog box

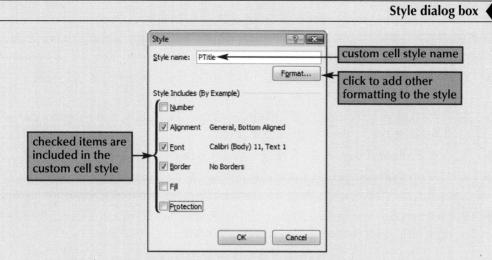

5. Click the **Format** button. The Format Cells dialog box opens.
6. Click the **Alignment** tab, and then click **Center** in the Horizontal list box.
7. Click the **Font** tab, click **Bold** in the Font style box, and then click **20** in the Size box.
8. Click the **Border** tab, click the **double line** in the Style box, and then click the **bottom border** of the Border preview box.
9. Click the **OK** button in each dialog box to return to the workbook. The PTitle cell style appears in the Cell Styles gallery ready to be applied to the active cell, which is cell B4, in this case.
10. In the Styles group on the Home tab, click the **Cell Styles** button to open the Cell Styles gallery, in the Custom section, click **PTitle**, and then click cell **A1** to deselect the cell with the formatted title. See Figure D-2.

Tip

Apply the Normal cell style to a cell before formatting the cell you want to use to create a custom cell style to ensure that the new style has only the formatting options you intended.

Figure D-2 — PTitle cell style applied

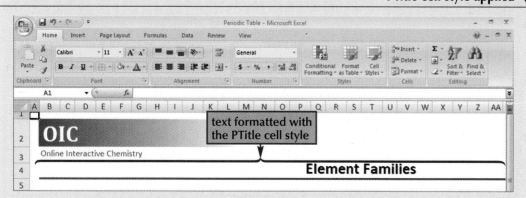

11. Select the **Ionization Energy**, **Radioactive Elements**, and **Element Data** worksheets to create a worksheet group, click cell **B4**, apply the **PTitle** cell style, and then switch to the **Element Families** worksheet. Cell B4 in the four worksheets is formatted with the PTitle cell style.

After you have defined and applied a cell style, you can modify it. Modifying a cell style affects any cell with that style. In a large workbook, you can use styles to make global changes to the workbook's appearance without having to select and reformat individual cells. Charles wants you to modify the PTitle cell style, changing the font color to a dark olive green.

To modify the PTitle cell style:

▶ **1.** In the Styles group on the Home tab, click the **Cell Styles** button. The Cell Styles gallery opens.

▶ **2.** In the Custom section, right-click **PTitle**, and then click **Modify** on the shortcut menu. The Style dialog box for the PTitle cell style opens.

▶ **3.** Click the **Format** button. The Format Cells dialog box opens.

▶ **4.** Click the **Font** tab, click the **Color** box, and then, in the Theme Colors section of the palette, click **Olive Green, Accent3, Darker 50%** (the seventh color in the last row).

▶ **5.** Click the **OK** button in each dialog box. The PTable Title cell style is updated, and the font color in cell B4 of each worksheet is dark olive green.

The PTtitle style is part of the Periodic Table workbook, but not other workbooks. You can copy styles from one workbook to another to create workbooks with a common look and feel. To copy a style, click the Cell Styles button in the Styles group on the Home tab, click Merge Styles, and then select the workbook with the cell styles to copy to the active workbook.

Creating a Custom Table Style

Charles wants you to format the tabular data in the Element Data worksheet. The data is already formatted with cell styles, but Charles wants you to use a table style.

To apply a table style to the data in the Element Data worksheet:

▶ **1.** Switch to the **Element Data** worksheet, click cell **B6**, and then press the **Ctrl+Shift+End** keys. The entire range of worksheet data is selected.

▶ **2.** In the Styles group on the Home tab, click the **Format as Table** button to open the Table Style gallery, and then, in the Medium section, click **Table Style Medium 4** (the fourth table style in the first row). The Format As Table dialog box opens.

▶ **3.** Confirm that the range **$B$6:$I$124** is selected as the data for your table, check the **My table has headers** check box if necessary, and then click the **OK** button. The table style is applied to the selected data.

▶ **4.** In the Table Style Options group on the Table Tools Design tab, click the **First Column** check box to insert a check mark. The first column of the table (in column B) is formatted with bold.

5. Click cell **A1** to deselect the table. See Figure D-3.

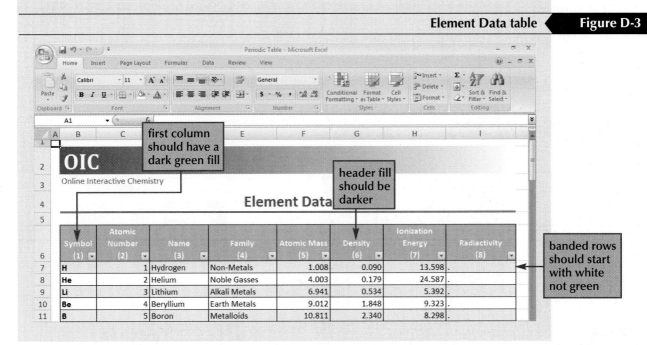

As you did with cell styles, you can create custom table styles. A table style has parts that correspond to different elements of the table structure. To create a table style, you must specify the format for each element. Each table style has 13 elements, including the header row, first and last columns, first and last rows, and the stripes used in banded rows or columns. Any element left unformatted in a custom table style uses its default style.

Charles wants the table headers to be darker green, the banded rows fill color to start with white not light green, and the first column filled with dark green fill. You'll modify the table style to create this custom style and then apply it.

To modify and apply the custom table style:

1. In the Styles group on the Home tab, click the **Format as Table** button, and then click **New Table Style**. The New Table Quick Style dialog box opens. The Table Element list box shows the 13 table elements you can format. The Preview box shows the formatted table.

2. In the Name box, type **ElemTable**.

3. Click **Header Row** in the Table Element box, and then click the **Format** button. The Format Cells dialog box opens.

4. Click the **Fill** tab, and then, in the Background Color palette, click **dark green** (the seventh color in the sixth row).

5. Click the **Font** tab, click the **Color** box, and then click **White, Background 1** (the first color in the first row).

6. Click the **OK** button to return to the New Table Quick Style dialog box.

7. Click **First Row Stripe** in the Table Element box, verify that **1** is entered in the Stripe Size box, and then click the **Format** button.

8. Click the **Fill** tab, click **white** (the first color in the first row) in the Background Color palette, and then click the **OK** button.

Tip

You can create banded rows covering more than one row with a color by increasing the value of the Stripe Size.

▶ **9.** Click **Second Row Stripe** in the Table Element box, click the **Format** button, click **light green** (the seventh color in the second row) in the Background Color palette on the Fill tab, and then click the **OK** button.

▶ **10.** Click **First Column** in the Table Element box, click the **Format** button, and then click **dark green** (the seventh color in the sixth row) in the Background Color palette on the Fill tab.

▶ **11.** Click the **Font** tab, click the **Color** box, click **White, Background 1** (the first color in the first row), and then click the **OK** button. See Figure D-4.

Tip

You can create a new table style by copying an existing table style and then editing table elements as needed.

Figure D-4 ▶ **Modify Table Quick Style dialog box**

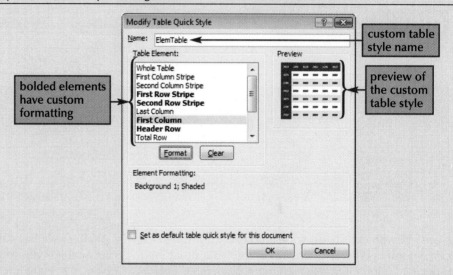

▶ **12.** Click the **OK** button. The ElemTable style is added to the Table Styles gallery.

▶ **13.** Click **B6** to select the table, in the Styles group on the Home tab, click the **Format as Table** button to open the Table Styles gallery, and then, in the Custom section, click **ElemTable**. The table is formatted with the custom table style.

Charles wants to use this custom table style in other workbooks. To make a table style available to every workbook you open, create the custom table style in a blank workbook, and then save the workbook as an Excel Template named *book.xltx* in the xlStart folder.

Working with Conditional Formats

Charles wants to present the information in the three periodic table worksheets in a visually interesting and informative way. The periodic table in the Element Families worksheet lists each element along with its atomic number and family. All of this information is stored in the Element Data worksheet.

Highlighting Cells

Charles added a legend to the worksheet indicating how he wants the different cells colored. Although you could edit the fill colors of selected cells to match the legend, it is more efficient to highlight the cells using conditional formats. Charles defined a name for the periodic table cells, which you can use with the highlight cells rules to quickly format them.

To highlight an element family:

1. Switch to the **Element Families** worksheet, press the **F5** key to open the Go To dialog box, and then double-click **Family_Data** in the Go to box. All of the cells in the periodic table containing the element names are selected.

2. In the Styles group on the Home tab, click the **Conditional Formatting** button, point to **Highlight Cells Rules**, and then click **Equal To**. The Equal To dialog box opens. Instead of typing text, you'll use the element family entry from the legend.

3. Click cell **H6**, click the **with** box, and then click **Custom Format**. The Format Cells dialog box opens.

4. Click the **Fill** tab, click **light orange** (the last color in the second row) in the Background Color palette, and then click the **OK** button to return to the Equal To dialog box and apply the highlighting rule to the table. See Figure D-5.

Non-Metals family highlighted ◄ **Figure D-5**

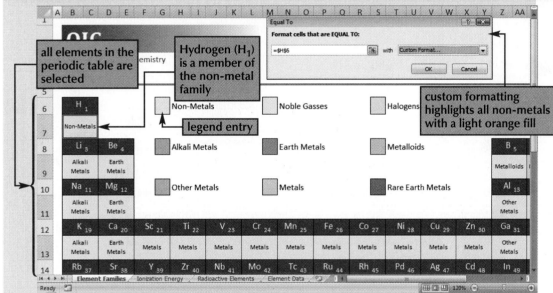

5. Click the **OK** button to accept the highlighting rule, click cell **A1** to deselect the range, and then scroll the worksheet to verify that the only cells with a light orange fill are Hydrogen (H_1), Carbon (C_6), Nitrogen (N_7), Phosphorus (P_{15}), Sulfur (S_{16}), and Selenium (Se_{34}). All of the other cells retain a white background color.

To highlight the other eight element families, you'll repeat this process for the remaining entries in the legend.

To highlight the remaining element families:

1. Press the **F5** key to open the Go To dialog box, and then double-click **Family_Data** in the Go to box to select all of the elements in the periodic table.

2. In the Styles group on the Home tab, click the **Conditional Formatting** button, point to **Highlight Cells Rules**, and then click **Equal To**. The Equal To dialog box opens.

▶ **3.** Click cell **N6**, click the **with** box, and then click **Custom Format**. The Format Cells dialog box opens.

▶ **4.** Click the **Fill** tab, click **light blue** (the ninth color in the second row) in the Background Color palette, and then click the **OK** button in each dialog box.

▶ **5.** Repeat Steps 2 through 4 for the remaining legend entries, using the following cell references and colors:

Halogens	cell T6	light purple (eighth color in the second row)
Alkali Metals	cell H8	blue (fifth color in the fourth row)
Earth Metals	cell N8	rose (sixth color in the fourth row)
Metalloids	cell T8	medium orange (last color in the fourth row)
Other Metals	cell H10	gray (first color in the fourth row)
Metals	cell N10	tan (third color in the second row)
Rare Earth Metals	cell T10	medium tan (third color in the fourth row)

▶ **6.** Click cell **A1** to deselect the range, and then zoom out to view the entire table. See Figure D-6.

Tip

You can clear all conditional formatting rules from a range or the entire worksheet by clicking the Conditional Formatting button in the Styles group on the Home tab, and then clicking Clear Rules.

| **Figure D-6** | **All element families highlighted** |

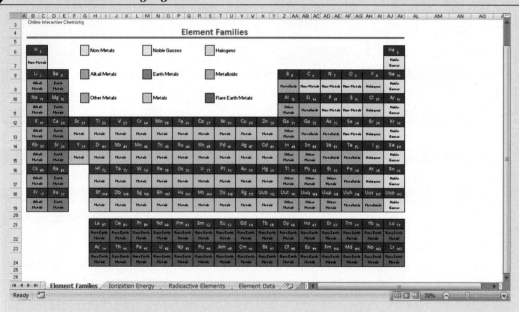

Charles wants you to hide the element family names. Instead of changing the font color to match the background color to hide the text, you'll apply a custom format that prevents Excel from displaying a cell's value.

To hide the element family names:

▶ 1. Click the **Name box arrow**, and then click **Family_Data** to select all of the elements in the periodic table.

▶ 2. In the Number group on the Home tab, click the **Dialog Box Launcher**. The Format Cells dialog box appears with the Number tab displayed.

▶ 3. In the Category box, click **Custom**, type **;;;** in the Type box, and then click the **OK** button.

▶ 4. Click cell **A1** to deselect the range. All of the family names in the periodic table are hidden.

Modifying a Conditional Format Rule

Charles wants you to change the color of the Metals family elements to a dark red fill color. You can do this by editing the properties of the conditional format rule applied to those cells.

To modify a conditional format rule:

▶ 1. In the Styles group on the Home tab, click the **Conditional Formatting** button, and then click **Manage Rules**. The Conditional Formatting Rules Manager dialog box opens.

▶ 2. Click the **Show formatting rules** box, and then click **This Worksheet** to display all of the formatting rules for the current worksheet.

▶ 3. Click **Cell Value = $N$10** in the Rule list to select the highlighting rule for the Metals family elements, and then click the **Edit Rule** button. The Edit Formatting Rule dialog box opens.

▶ 4. Click the **Format** button to open the Format Cells dialog box, click the **Fill** tab, and then click **dark red** (the sixth color in the fifth row) in the Background Color palette.

▶ 5. Click the **OK** button in each dialog box to return to the worksheet.

▶ 6. Click cell **M10** to select the Metals legend entry, click the **Fill Color button arrow** in the Font group on the Home tab, and then, in the Theme Colors section, click **Red, Accent 2, Darker 25%**. See Figure D-7.

> **Tip**
>
> To delete a rule, select the rule in the Rule list, and then click the Delete Rule button.

Final periodic table of element families | **Figure D-7**

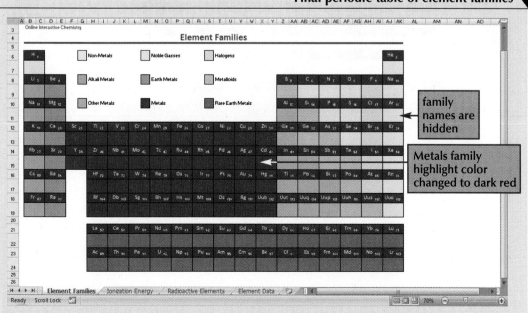

family names are hidden

Metals family highlight color changed to dark red

Working with Color Scales

Ionization energy is the energy required to remove an electron from an element, which indicates the element's ability to form bonds with atoms from other elements. The higher the ionization energy, the more difficult it is for the element to bond. For example, noble gasses (Helium, Argon, Neon, Krypton, etc.) have the highest ionization energy and are the most difficult to bond with other elements.

To illustrate this concept clearly in the Ionization periodic table, Charles wants to base the fill color of each element on its ionization energy. The color shade should grow increasingly darker as the ionization energy increases so that elements with the lowest ionization energy have the lightest fill and elements with the highest ionization energy have the darkest fill. You can do this by applying a **color scale**, which is a conditional format that bases the color shade of a cell on its value.

To apply a color scale:

▶ 1. Switch to the **Ionization Energy** worksheet, click the **Name box arrow**, and then click **Ionization_Data** to select the cells with the ionization data values.

▶ 2. In the Styles group on the Home tab, click the **Conditional Formatting** button, point to **Color Scales**, and then click **Green – Yellow – Red Color Scale** (the first color scale in the first row). The color scale is applied to the ionization data values.

▶ 3. Click cell **A1** to deselect the range, and then zoom the worksheet to view the entire table. See Figure D-8.

Figure D-8 ▶ **Color scale added to the ionization energy data values**

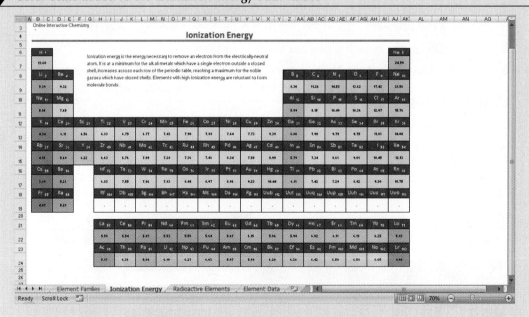

The color scale displays cells with the highest values in dark green, the lowest values in dark red, and the middle values in orange and yellow. The cells that remain white are unstable synthetic elements that do not exist long enough to have their ionization energies determined, and Charles entered a period (.) for these values, which cannot be placed on a color scale.

Charles doesn't think the default color scale presents the data clearly and wants all the cells to be orange, growing increasingly darker for higher ionization values.

To modify the color scale:

▶ **1.** In the Styles group on the Home tab, click the **Conditional Formatting** button, and then click **Manage Rules**. The Conditional Formatting Rules Manager dialog box opens.

▶ **2.** Click the **Show formatting rules for** box, and then click **This Worksheet** to display all of the formatting rules for the current worksheet.

▶ **3.** Click **Graded Color Scale** in the Rule list, and then click the **Edit Rule** button. The Edit Formatting Rule dialog box opens, showing the three colors used in the color scale and a Preview box with the color gradation.

▶ **4.** Click the **Minimum Color** box to open a color palette, and then, in the Theme Colors section, click **Orange, Accent 6, Lighter 80%**.

▶ **5.** Click the **Midpoint Color** box to open a color palette, and then, in the Theme Colors section, click **Orange, Accent 6, Lighter 40%**.

▶ **6.** Click the **Maximum Color** box to open a color palette, and then, in the Theme Colors section, click **Orange, Accent 6, Darker 50%**. See Figure D-9.

Edit Formatting Rule dialog box ◀ **Figure D-9**

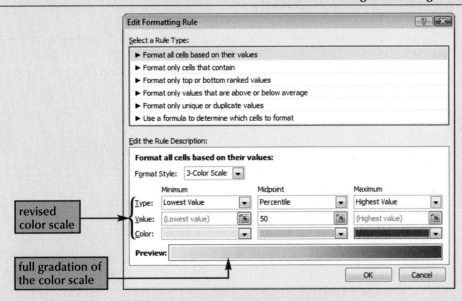

7. Click the **OK** button in each dialog box to return to the worksheet. See Figure D-10.

Edit Formatting Rule dialog box

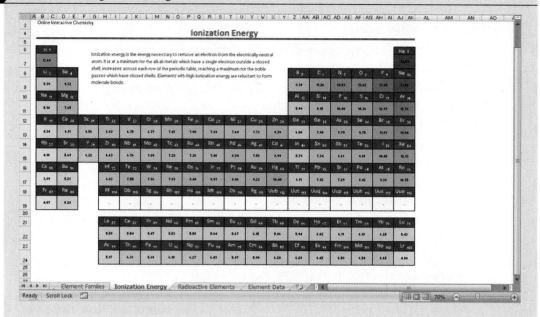

The revised color scale more clearly shows how the ionization energies generally increase as you move across the table to the right, and the highest values occur for elements of the Noble Gasses family. You'll add a legend to the worksheet to make this clear.

To add a color scale legend:

1. Zoom the worksheet to **120%** and scroll to the top of the worksheet.

2. Select the range **G10:X10**, and then, in the Alignment group on the Home tab, click the **Merge & Center** button ⊞ .

3. Right-click the merged cell, click **Format Cells** on the shortcut menu to open the Format Cells dialog box, click the **Fill** tab, and then click the **Fill Effects** button to open the Fill Effects dialog box.

4. In the Colors section, click the **Color 1** box, click **Orange, Accent 6, Lighter 80%** in the Theme Colors section of the color palette, click the **Color 2** box, and then click **Orange, Accent 6, Darker 50%** in the Theme Colors section of the color palette.

5. In the Shading Styles section, click the **Vertical** option button, and then, in the Variants section, click the first color variant in the first row, in which the color shades darken from left to right. See Figure D-11.

Fill Effects dialog box ◄ **Figure D-11**

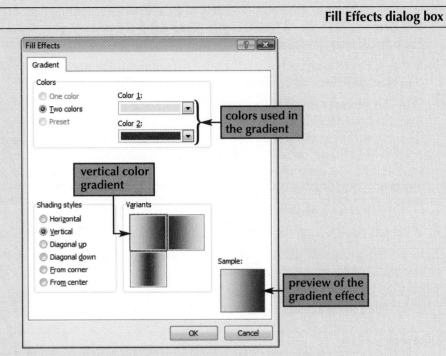

6. Click the **OK** button in each dialog box to return to the worksheet.

7. In cell G11, enter **lower energy** and then top-align the text. In cell X11, enter **higher energy** and then right-align and top-align the text.

8. Click cell **A1**. See Figure D-12.

Color scale legend ◄ **Figure D-12**

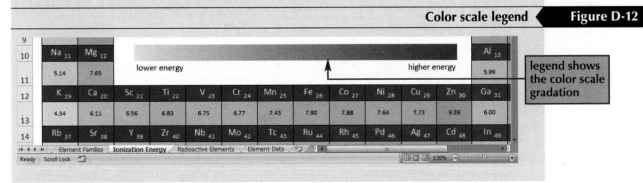

Working with Icon Sets

The Radioactive Elements worksheet lists elements that are considered radioactive. Radioactive elements have the value 1; non-radioactive elements have a period (.) as their value. Charles wants the values replaced with a red circle indicating a radioactive element. You'll add a conditional format called an **icon set**, which displays a symbol based on a cell's value.

To apply and modify an icon set:

1. Switch to the **Radioactive Elements** worksheet, click the **Name box arrow**, and then click **Radioactivity_Data** to select the cells with the radioactive data values.

2. In the Styles group on the Home tab, click the **Conditional Formatting** button, point to **Icon Sets**, and then click **3 Traffic Lights (Rimmed)**, the third icon set in the left column. The periodic table has green traffic lights in all cells with the value 1.

3. In the Styles group on the Home tab, click the **Conditional Formatting** button, and then click **Manage Rules**. The Conditional Formatting Rules Manager opens.

4. Click **This Worksheet** in the Show formatting rules box, click **Icon Set** in the Rule list, and then click the **Edit Rule** button. The Edit Formatting Rule dialog box opens. According to the rule description, the green traffic light icon appears in cells with a value greater than or equal to 67%. The yellow traffic light icon appears in cells with a value greater than or equal to 33%. The red traffic light icon appears in all other cells in the range. In this case, you want to display a red traffic light icon for cells with a value equal to 1.

5. Click the **Reverse Icon Order** check box. The red icon is first and the green icon is last.

6. In the red icon row, click the **Type** box, click **Number**, and then type **1** in the Value box.

7. In the yellow icon row, click the **Type** box, and then click **Number**. This makes the value consistent although it has no effect in this case.

8. Click the **Show Icon Only** check box to hide the cell values. Figure D-13 shows the completed Edit Formatting Rule dialog box.

Figure D-13	**Edited icon set rule**

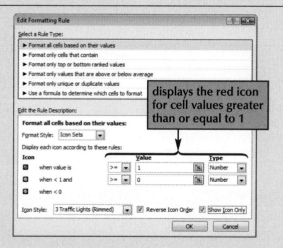

9. Click the **OK** button in each dialog box to return to the worksheet. The red traffic light icon appears in 22 elements in the periodic table. The periods in non-radioactive elements still show periods because the icon set rule applies only to number value.

Charles wants you add a legend to this table, making it clear that the red traffic light icon identifies the radioactive elements. You'll create the legend by editing the conditional format rule you used in the table to include the legend text. This ensures that if you change the icon style in the icon set rule, both the periodic table and the legend are automatically updated.

Tip

When possible, use one conditional format rule for the legend and the cell values so any edits you make affect both.

To create a legend for the icon set:

▶ 1. In cell J10, enter **1** and then center and middle align the value.

▶ 2. In the Styles group on the Home tab, click the **Conditional Formatting** button, and then click **Manage Rules**. The Conditional Formatting Rules Manager opens.

▶ 3. Click **This Worksheet** in the Show formatting rules box, click after = in the Applies to box, click cell **J10** in the worksheet to insert an absolute reference to the legend cell, and then type **,** (a comma). The range =$J$10,$H$24:$AK$24,$H$22:$AK$2... appears in the Applies to box.

▶ 4. Click the **OK** button. The red traffic light icon appears in cell J10, matching the icon for radioactive elements in the periodic table.

▶ 5. In cell K10, enter **Radioactive Element** and then middle-align the text.

▶ 6. Click cell **A1**, and then zoom the worksheet to view the entire periodic table. See Figure D-14.

Final radioactive element table | **Figure D-14**

legend shows icon used in the table

Conditional Formatting with Formulas

All of the conditional formats you used so far are based on the cell's value. You can also base the format on a function of the cell's value. For example, you can highlight cells with dates that fall on a weekend differently from cells with data that fall on a weekday. To highlight a cell based on a formula, click the Conditional Formatting button in the Styles group on the Home tab, click New Rule to open the New Formatting Rule dialog box, and then, in the Select a Rule Type box, click Use a formula to determine which cells to format. In the Edit the Rule Description section of the dialog box, enter a formula that begins with an equal sign and uses a logical function that returns a true or false value. If the formula's value is true, the conditional format is applied; if the value is false, the format is not applied. For example, the following formulas will format the cell only if the value in cell A3 is less than the value in cell A4 (the first formula uses the IF function, the second formula is a briefer format of the first formula):

```
=IF(A3<A4, true, false)
=A3<A4
```

Conditional formatting formulas can use relative, absolute, and mixed references. When applying a conditional format formula to a range of cells, write the formula for the active cell in the selected range. Excel will modify the references to match the new location of each cell in the range.

You can use formulas when defining conditional formatting rules for data bars, color scales, and icon sets. Enter the formula as a function of the selected cell using a logical function. For example, to display an icon in comparison to the average value in the range A1:A10, in the rule description select Formula in the Type box, and enter the following formula:

```
=AVERAGE(A1:A10)
```

As with highlight cells formulas, Excel will adjust the relative references as the format is copied across the selected range.

Working with SmartArt Graphics and Pictures

Charles wants you to create a logo for Online Interactive Chemistry based on the idea he sketched in Figure D-15. You'll create this logo as a **SmartArt graphic**, which is a professionally designed business diagram, such as a flow chart, organization chart, or production cycle chart. They can also be used to create graphic logos.

Figure D-15 ▶ **Charles' proposed logo**

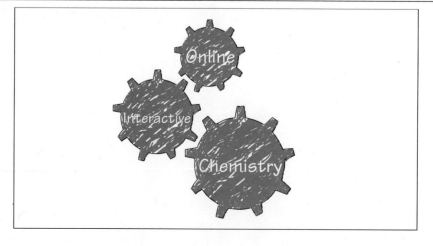

You'll insert the SmartArt graphic in the Documentation sheet.

To insert a SmartArt graphic:

▶ 1. Switch to the **Documentation** worksheet, click the **Insert** tab on the Ribbon, and then, in the Illustrations group, click the **SmartArt** button. The Choose a SmartArt Graphic dialog box opens.

▶ 2. Click the **Cycle** in the type list, and then click **Gear** (the last graphic in the last row) as the layout. See Figure D-16.

Choose a SmartArt Graphic dialog box ◀ **Figure D-16**

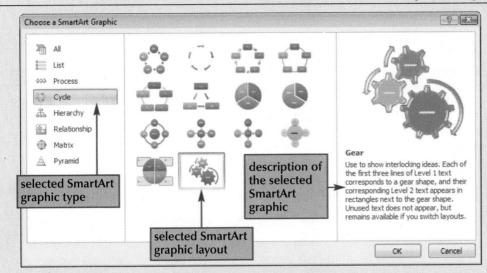

▶ 3. Click the **OK** button. The gear SmartArt graphic is inserted in the Documentation worksheet. See Figure D-17.

SmartArt graphic inserted in worksheet ◀ **Figure D-17**

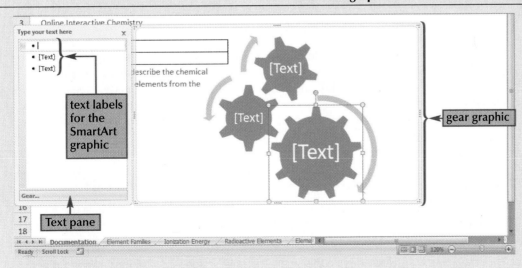

Inserting Text Labels

You enter or edit text for each element of the SmartArt graphic in the Text pane. Most SmartArt graphics support several levels of text. The gear graphic has three rows of text by default. The first level of text will appear in the largest gear, in the lower-right of the graphic. As you type the text, the font size changes so that the labels fit within the graphic elements. Font sizes also increase or decrease as needed when the SmartArt graphic is resized. The Text pane uses the following rules for editing the SmartArt graphic text:

- Press the Enter key to add a new row of text to the Text pane and a new element to the SmartArt graphic.
- Press the Tab key to demote the text to the next lower level.
- Press the Backspace key to promote the text to the next higher level.
- Hold the shift as you press the Enter key to insert text on a new line at the same level.
- Press the up and down arrow keys to between the entries in the Text pane without inserting new text.

Charles wants you to insert the label *Online Interactive Chemistry* in the gears. Because the most prominent and largest graphic element is listed first in the Text pane but appears in the last gear graphic, you'll enter the label text in reverse order so that it reads correctly on the screen.

To enter text into the SmartArt graphic:

▶ **1.** With the first entry selected in the Text pane, type **Chemistry**, and press the ↓ key.

Trouble? If you do not see the Text pane, it is closed and you must open it. In the Create Graphic group on the SmartArt Tools Design tab, click the Text Pane button, and then repeat Step 1.

▶ **2.** Type **Interactive** for the second text label, and then press the ↓ key.

▶ **3.** Type **Online** for the third text label, and then click cell **A1** to deselect the graphic.

Working with SmartArt Quick Styles

Charles wants the SmartArt graphic to have a 3-D or "chiseled" look and the gear color to match the olive green color used elsewhere in the workbook. **Quick Styles** are a collection of styles you can use to quickly and easily format a SmartArt graphic's appearance. With Quick Styles you can change the color and outline style of the graphic. You can also rotate the graphic elements to give them a 3-D look. You'll use a Quick Style to format the gear SmartArt graphic.

To apply a Quick Style to the gear graphic and change its color:

▶ **1.** In the SmartArt Styles group on the SmartArt Tools Design tab, click the **More** button, and then, in the 3-D section of the gallery, click **Inset** (the second style in the first row, second column). The style is applied to the gear graphic.

▶ **2.** In the SmartArt Styles group on the SmartArt Tools Design tab, click the **Change Colors** button, and then, in the Accent 3 section, click **Gradient Loop – Accent 3**. The graphic color changes to shades of olive green.

3. Click cell **A1** to deselect the graphic. The formatted SmartArt image is shown in Figure D-18.

Reformatted SmartArt graphic ◄ **Figure D-18**

Charles has graphic images of three famous chemists from history: Democritus, the Greek philosopher who first proposed that all matter is composed of atoms; John Dalton, the English chemist and physicist who proposed a modern interpretation of the atomic theory; and Dmitri Mendeleev, the Russian chemist who was the primary creator of the first periodic table of elements. Charles wants you to insert these images into the three gears of the logo.

Tip

You can restore a SmartArt graphic to its original appearance by clicking the Reset Graphic button in the Reset group on the SmartArt Tools Design tab.

To fill the gear elements of the logo with images:

1. Click the **Chemistry** gear in the SmartArt graphic. A solid selection box appears around the selected element.

Trouble? If the selection box is dotted, only the Chemistry label is selected. Click the gear element but not its label to select the entire gear element.

2. Click the **SmartArt Tools Format** tab, click the **Shape Fill button arrow** in the Shape Styles group, and then click **Picture**. The Insert Picture dialog box opens.

3. Click the **Mendeleev** image file located in the **Appendix.D\Tutorial** folder included with your Data Files, and then click the **Insert** button. The fill style of the Chemistry gear displays a portion of the Mendeleev image, and the Chemistry label is difficult to read.

4. Click the **Home** tab, the Font group, click the **Bold** button **B**, click the **Font Color button arrow** **A ▼**, and then click **Yellow** in the Standard Colors section. The Chemistry label changes to bold yellow.

5. Click the **Interactive** gear in the SmartArt graphic, repeat Steps 2 and 3 to fill the background with the **Dalton** image file located in the **Appendix.D\Tutorial** folder, and then repeat Step 4 to change the Interactive label to bold yellow.

6. Click the **Online** gear in the SmartArt graphic, repeat Steps 2 and 3 to fill the background with the **Democritus** image file located in the **Appendix.D\Tutorial** folder, and then repeat Step 4 to change the Online label to bold yellow.

▶ **7.** Click cell **A1** to deselect the graphic. See Figure D-19.

Figure D-19 ▷ **Pictures used for background fill**

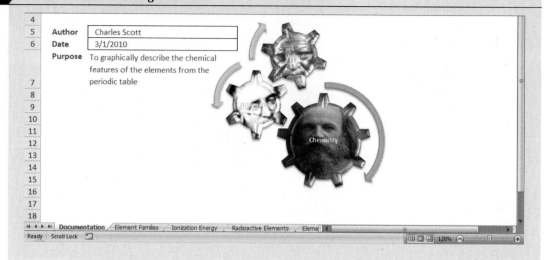

Editing a Picture

Imaging tools enable you to modify the appearance of pictures in a workbook. You can recolor pictures and change the picture's contrast and brightness level. For pictures inserted into a workbook as separate graphic objects (as opposed to fills), you can change the picture's shape, add a graphical border, and apply special effects such as rotating the picture in three dimensions and adding a drop shadow.

Reference Window | **Editing a Picture**

- Select the picture image to display the Picture Tools Format tab on the Ribbon.
- To change the color tint, brightness, or contrast of the picture, click the Recolor, Brightness, or Contrast button in the Adjust group.
- To apply a style to the picture, select an effect in the Styles gallery in the Picture Styles group.
- To change the picture's shape, add a graphical border, or add a special effect, click the Picture Shape, Picture Border, or Picture Effects button in the Pictures Styles group.
- To crop or resize the picture, click the Crop or Size button in the Size group.
- To restore the picture to its original appearance, click the Reset Picture button in the Adjust group.

Charles wants you to recolor the graphic images to make them darker, which would make the labels more readable. He wants you to give the Mendeleev image a green tint, the Dalton image a red tint, and the Democritus image a blue tint, and then increase the contrast to make the labels stand out.

To edit the pictures:

1. Click the **Mendeleev** image in the Chemistry gear to select it.

2. Click the **Picture Tools Format** tab, click the **Recolor** button in the Adjust group, and then, in the Dark Variation section of the Recolor gallery, click **Accent color 3 Dark** (the fourth color). The picture color changes.

3. In the Adjust group on the Picture Tools Format tab, click the **Brightness** button, and then click **–20%**. The green tint applied to the Mendeleev picture darkens.

4. Click the **Dalton** image in the Interactive gear to select it, repeat Step 2 to apply the **Accent color 2 Dark** (the third color) in the Dark Variation section of the Recolor gallery, and then repeat Step 3 to set the brightness to **–30%**.

5. Click the **Democritus** image in the Online gear to select it, repeat Step 2 to apply the **Accent color 1 Dark** (the second color) in the Dark Variation section of the Recolor gallery, and then repeat Step 3 to set brightness to **–10%**.

6. Click cell **A1** to deselect the SmartArt graphic. See Figure D-20.

Adjusted pictures | **Figure D-20**

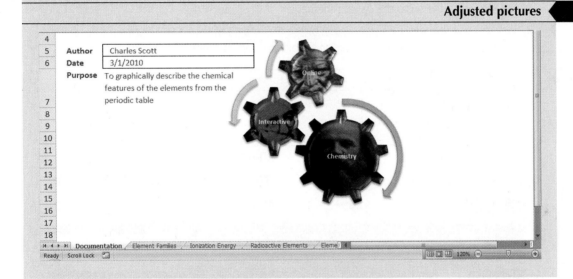

Choosing a Graphic Image Type | InSight

Excel supports most graphic file formats, so you have a choice of formats for the pictures you import into workbooks. The most common picture format is the **Joint Photographic Experts Group format**, commonly known as **JPEG**. JPEGs are produced by most digital cameras and can support up to 16.7 million colors (which is more colors than the human eye can distinguish). JPEGs can also be compressed to save file space without greatly affecting image quality.

Another popular format found on the Web is the **Graphics Interchange Format**, or **GIF**. GIFs are limited to 256 colors but can support animation and transparent colors. Excel does not support animated GIFs, so if you import an animated GIF, the animation will not play in the workbook.

For better quality photos, use the **Tag Image File Format**, or **TIFF**. Although photo quality is higher with TIFFs, the image files tend to be much larger as well, increasing the workbook's size. Finally, you can import logos and formatted documents in **Encapsulated PostScript**, or **EPS**. Written in the PostScript language, EPS files provide perhaps the highest quality format for clip art files, but require access to a PostScript printer to view the results; otherwise EPS files are not viewable.

Working with Themes

The Periodic Table workbook uses a constant design theme. For example, the various shades of olive green provide the workbook's visual effects and the text is either Cambria or Calibri font. Charles wants you to look at other design themes.

Applying a Theme

As discussed in Tutorial 2, Office supports a library of built-in themes. If a workbook uses only theme colors and fonts, you can switch between themes without editing the styles of individual cells and ranges. You'll change the theme to see its impact on the workbook's appearance.

To apply a different theme:

▶ **1.** Click the **Page Layout** tab on the Ribbon, click the **Themes** button in the Themes group to open the Themes gallery, and then click **Aspect**. The workbook's theme changes from the default Office theme to the Aspect theme.

▶ **2.** View each worksheet in the workbook to see the impact of the Aspect theme on the workbook. The fonts and colors changed to reflect the Aspect theme. See Figure D-21.

Figure D-21 ▶ **Element Families worksheet under the Aspect theme**

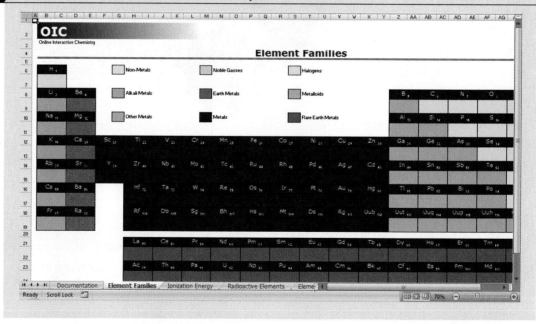

Creating and Saving a Theme

If the built-in themes do not meet your needs, you can create a custom theme by selecting different fonts, colors, and effects. You can choose from a list of built-in theme fonts, colors, and effects, or you can create your own collection. After the custom theme is complete, you can save it as a permanent file to format other workbooks. You can save theme files in the default theme folders on your computer or in another folder you choose. Files stored in the default theme folders appear in the Themes gallery, which is not the case when you save the theme file elsewhere. All theme files have the .thmx file extension.

Word and PowerPoint use the same file format for theme files, so you can share custom themes you create in Excel with other Office files. Charles could create a consistent look and feel for all of his Office files by designing a theme with the fonts, colors, and effects he wants. If Charles later modifies and resaves the custom theme file, the changes will be automatically reflected in every Excel, PowerPoint, and Word document that uses the theme.

Creating and Saving a Theme | Reference Window

- In the Themes group on the Page Layout tab, click the Themes button arrow, and then click a theme to apply.
- In the Themes group on the Page Layout tab, click the Font button arrow, the Colors button arrow, or the Effects button arrow, and then click the theme fonts, colors, or effects you want to use in the custom theme.
- In the Themes group on the Page Layout tab, click the Themes button arrow, and then click Save Current Theme.
- Type a filename in the File name box, and then click the Save button.

Charles likes the Aspect theme's effects, but not its fonts or colors. You'll change the font to Arial and the colors to Metro. Then, you'll save the current theme as *OIC* in the Appendix.D\Tutorial folder included with your Data Files.

To modify the Aspect theme and save the custom theme:

▶ **1.** In the Themes group on the Page Layout tab, click the **Fonts** button to open the Built-In Fonts menu, and then click **Office Classic 2**. All of the text in the workbook changes to Arial.

▶ **2.** In the Themes group on the Page Layout tab, click the **Colors** button to open the Built-In Colors menu, and then click **Metro**. Figure D-22 shows the appearance of the Element Families worksheet under your choices for theme font and theme color.

Custom theme applied to the Element Families worksheet ◄ **Figure D-22**

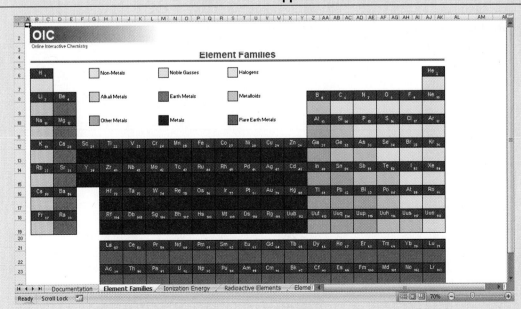

▶ **3.** View all of the worksheets in the workbook with the custom theme.

▶ **4.** In the Themes group on the Page Layout tab, click the **Themes** button, and then click **Save Current Theme**. The Save Current Theme dialog box opens, displaying the default Office theme folders.

▶ **5.** Save the custom theme with the filename **OIC** in the **Appendix.D\Tutorial** folder included with your Data Files.

▶ **6.** Save and close the Periodic Table workbook.

The Periodic Table workbook is complete. Charles is pleased with design and graphic elements you added. He plans to produce other workbooks for students to use in their explorations of chemistry concepts. When he is ready to create new workbooks, he will contact you.

Review | **Appendix Summary**

In this appendix, you learned about advanced formatting and graphic tools you can use in workbooks. You created custom cell styles and table styles that can be saved to use with other workbooks. You used conditional formats to highlight cell values, create a color scale, and show an icon set. Graphic images and pictures add value and visual interest to a workbook, so you created a logo using a SmartArt graphic, and then inserted and modified pictures in the graphic. Finally, you created a new theme to apply a consistent design to the entire workbook, and then saved the theme to reuse in other workbooks and Office files.

Key Terms

color scale	icon set	Tag Image File Format (TIFF)
Encapsulated PostScript (EPS)	Joint Photographic Experts Group format (JPEG)	
Graphics Interchange Format (GIF)	SmartArt graphic	
	Quick Style	

Practice | **Review Assignments**

ractice the skills you arned in the appendix ing the same case enario.

Data Files needed for the Review Assignments: Elements.xlsx, Table1.jpg, Table2.jpg, Table3.jpg, Table4.jpg

Charles created another workbook of chemistry information based on the periodic table. This workbook contains charts of the periodic table describing the orbital group of each element, each element's melting and boiling point, and a list of the elements present in the human body. He wants you to add graphical elements to the workbook and create a unified design theme.

Complete the following:

1. Open the **Elements** workbook located in the Appendix.D\Review folder included with your Data Files, and then save the workbook as **Elements Table** in the same folder. In the Documentation sheet, enter your name and the current date.

2. Create a new cell style named **ETitle** that uses the following formatting:
   - Font size of 18 point bold with the Olive Green, Accent 3, Darker 50% theme color
   - Text centered horizontally
   - Single thick bottom border in Olive Green, Accent 3, Darker 50% theme color

3. Apply the ETitle cell style to cell B4 in the last five worksheets of the workbook.

4. In the Data worksheet, create a custom table style named **ETable** that uses the following formatting, and then apply it to the Element Data table:
   - A header row with white text on a dark olive background (use the theme color) and a double bottom border.
   - Banded rows five stripes high. The first set of stripes has a light green background fill (using the theme colors). The next set of stripes has a white background.

5. Switch to the Sub-Orbital Blocks worksheet, which indicates to which of four electron sub-orbital group each element belongs S, D, P, and F. The range name Sub_Orbital_Blocks_Data references all of the data in the table and the entries in the legend. Create the following conditional formatting rules to highlight the values in this range:
   - Highlight cells that contain the S character with a medium orange fill color (the tenth theme color).
   - Highlight cells that contain the D character with a medium turquoise fill color (the ninth theme color).
   - Highlight cells that contain the P character with a medium lavender fill color (the eighth theme color).
   - Highlight cells that contain the F character with a medium olive green fill color (the seventh theme color).
   - Hide the cell text of all values in the selected range.

6. Go to the Melting Point worksheet, which contains the melting points of the elements from the periodic table. Display the values from this table using a color scale ranging from a light red theme color for the lowest melting points to a dark red theme color for the highest melting points. Use the Melting_Point_Data range name to quickly select the data values from the table. Use a gradient fill in cell H9 to indicate the range of colors used in the table.

7. Go to the Boiling Point worksheet and repeat Step 6, using the orange theme color to indicate low to high boiling points.

8. Go to the Human Body worksheet and create a conditional formatting rule that displays a green circle with a white check mark for all cells in the table and legend in place of the value 1. Use the Human_Body_Data range name to select the appropriate cells in the worksheet.

9. Go to the Documentation sheet and then insert the Picture Caption List SmartArt graphic (the second layout in the List type of SmartArt graphics). Add the text labels **Sub-Orbital Blocks**, **Melting Point**, **Boiling Point**, and **Human Body** to the four blocks in the list.

10. Change the Quick Style of the graphic to the Brick Scene style from the 3-D section of the Quick Style gallery.

11. Insert the graphic image files **Table1.jpg**, **Table2.jpg**, **Table3.jpg**, and **Table4.jpg** located in the Appendix.D\Review folder into the four blocks from the SmartArt graphic. Display the Table1 picture using the Accent color 1 Light tint variation, Table2 using the Accent 2 color 2 Light tint variation, Table3 with the Accent color 3 Light variation, and Table4 with the Accent color 4 Light variation.

12. Create a custom theme for the workbook using the Module color theme combined with fonts from the Foundry Theme. Save the custom theme with the filename **ETheme** in the Appendix.D\Review folder.

13. Save and close the workbook. Submit the finished workbook and theme file to your instructor, either in printed or electronic form, as requested.

Apply	**Case Problem 1**

Use the skills you learned to format an attendance report for a southern water park.

Data Files needed for this Case Problem: Big.xlsx, Water.jpg

Big Wave Water Park Robert Tru is an operations manager at Big Wave Water Park, a popular indoor/outdoor water park located outside of Greenville, South Carolina. He is preparing an annual report that contains the daily attendance figures at the park and that compares the total annual attendance to previous years. He wants you to format the workbook.

Complete the following:

1. Open the **Big** workbook located in the Appendix.D\Case1 folder included with your Data Files, and then save the workbook as **Big Wave** in the same folder. In the Documentation sheet, enter your name and the current date.

2. In the 2010 Attendance worksheet, create a color scale for the daily attendance figures in the range C7:AG18 that displays days of lowest attendance with a light blue fill and days of highest attendance with dark blue fill.

3. Add a conditional format to the daily attendance figures that highlights the day of highest attendance with a white background and a solid black border.

4. Add a color scale to the monthly totals in the range AH7:AH18 that displays the months of lowest attendance with a light aqua fill and the months of highest attendance with a dark aqua fill.

5. Add a conditional format to the monthly attendance figures that highlights the month of highest attendance with a white background and a solid black border.

6. In the Yearly Attendance sheet, replace the values in the change column with an icon set that displays a green up arrow for years the attendance increased compared to the previous year, a yellow horizontal arrow when the attendance was unchanged, and a red down arrow for years the attendance decreased. Center the arrows in the cells.

7. Format the contents with a new table style named **attendance**. The header row should be displayed in a white font on a dark blue background and a double bottom border. The contents of the table should be displayed in banded rows, starting with a light blue fill color on the first row and alternating with rows with a white fill color.

⊕ EXPLORE

8. Insert the picture file **Water.jpg** located in the Appendix.D\Case1 folder next to the yearly attendance table. Make the following edits to the picture:
   - Change the picture size to 2.67 inches high by 4 inches wide.
   - Recolor the picture with an Accent color 1 Light tint.
   - Apply the Drop Shadow Rectangle picture style to the graphic.
9. Save and close the workbook. Submit the finished workbook to your instructor, either in printed or electronic form, as requested.

Challenge | **Case Problem 2**

Expand on the skills you learned to create a Gantt Chart for a video production company.

Data File needed for this Case Problem: FPS.xlsx

FPS Productions Linda Thomas owns FPS Productions, a video production company located in St. Charles, Missouri, that specializes in creating short videos for local businesses and government agencies. The company just received a contract to create a promotional video for the St. Charles Civic Center. The video must be ready for distribution in four weeks. To keep the project on schedule, Linda wants to create a Gantt chart (a graphical representation of a project with each phase represented as a horizontal bar with vertical lines often superimposed to indicate the current date to show the progress of the project versus time). Linda asks you to create the Gantt chart.

Complete the following:

1. Open the **FPS** workbook located in the Appendix.D\Case2 folder included with your Data Files, and then save the workbook as **FPS Productions** in the same folder. In the Documentation sheet, enter your name and the current date.
2. In the Production Schedule worksheet, you'll create the Gantt chart. Linda already entered the start and stop dates of the eight tasks involved producing the video. In the range B7:B14, calculate the percentage of each task that has been completed given the task's start and stop dates and the current date in cell E5. (*Hint*: The percentage equals the number of days from the current date to the task's start date divided by the length of days for the project.)

⊕ EXPLORE

3. Replace the percentages in the range B7:B14 with the 5 Quarters icon set. Modify the icon set to display the full circle when the cell's value is greater than or equal to 1, the three-quarter circle when the cell's value is from 0.75 up to 1, the half circle when the cell's value is 0.5 up to 0.75, the quarter circle when the value is 0.25 up to 0.5, and an empty circle when the cell's value is less than 0.25.

⊕ EXPLORE

4. Create a conditional formatting rule that places a red right border in the Gantt Chart cells that fall on the current date as specified in cell E5. To create the rule, select the range F7:AG14 and create a highlight rule for the cells in the range using a formula. The formula should test whether the value in the cell F$4 (a date from the Gantt chart) is equal to the value in cell $E$5 (the current date). If the function returns the value true, the cell should display a red right border.

⊕ EXPLORE   5. Create another conditional rule that highlights the cells in the Gantt chart corresponding to the dates in which task is performed. To create this rule, add a second highlight rule for the cells in the range F7:AG14 using another formula. The formula should test whether the value in cell F$4 is greater than or equal to the value in cell $D7 (the start date) and whether the value in cell F$4 is less than or equal to the value in cell $E7 (the stop date). If the formula returns a value of true, the cell should have a horizontal gradient fill starting with a white color at the top and a purple color at the bottom. (*Hint*: Use the IF function and the AND function in the formula.)

6. In the Production Tasks worksheet, insert the Continuous Block Process SmartArt graphic, and then type the eight task names from the Production Schedule worksheet into eight blocks on the SmartArt graphic.

7. Format the SmartArt graphic by setting its size to 3.75 inches high by 7 inches wide, changing its color to Colored Fill – Accent 4, and changing its style to the Cartoon Quick Style.

8. Save and close the workbook. Submit the finished workbook to your instructor, either in printed or electronic form, as requested.

Ending Data Files

Appendix.D → **Tutorial**
OIC.thmx
Periodic Table.xlsx

Review
Elements Table.xlsx
ETheme.thmx

Case1
Big Wave.xlsx

Case2
FPS Productions.xlsx

Glossary/Index

Note: Boldface entries include definitions.

Special Characters

Task Reference

TASK	PAGE #	RECOMMENDED METHOD
3-D reference, use	EX 290	*See* Reference Window: Entering a Function That contains a 3-D Reference
Absolute reference, change to relative	EX 119	*See* Reference Window: Entering Relative, Absolute, and Mixed References
Access database, retrieve data from	EX 606	Click From Access button in Get External Data group on Data tab, locate and select Access database file, select database table, click OK, specify where and how to import table data, click OK
Action, redo	EX 38	Click 🔁
Action, undo	EX 38	Click 🔙
Amortization schedule, create	EX 469	*See* Reference Window: Creating an Amortization Schedule
AutoFill, copy formulas	EX 132	*See* Reference Window: Copying Formulas and Formats with AutoFill
AutoFill, create series	EX 135	*See* Reference Window: Creating a Series with AutoFill
Background color, apply	EX 61	Select range, in Font group on Home tab click 🔲 ▾, click color
Border, create	EX 71	Select range, in Font group on Home tab click 🔲 ▾, click border
Cell, clear contents of	EX 20	Right-click cell, click Clear Contents
Cell, edit	EX 37	Double-click cell, enter changes
Cell or range name, create	EX 397	*See* Reference Window: Creating a Name for a Cell or Range
Cell or range, select by name	EX 398	Click Name box arrow, click defined name
Cell reference, change	EX 119	*See* Reference Window: Entering Relative, Absolute, and Mixed References
Cell style, create	EX D2	*See* Reference Window: Creating a Cell Style
Cell value, hide	EX D9	Select cell, open Format Cells dialog box, click Number tab, click Custom category, type ;;; in Type box, click OK
Cells, delete	EX 20	Select range, click Delete button in Cells group on Home tab
Cells, insert	EX 19	*See* Reference Window: Inserting a Column or Row
Cells, lock or unlock	EX 415	Select cell or range, in Font group on the Home tab, click Dialog Box Launcher, click Protection tab, check or uncheck Locked check box, click OK
Cells, merge and center	EX 70	Select adjacent cells, in Alignment group on Home tab click 🔲
Cells, reference in other worksheets	EX 288	Enter reference in the following format: =SheetName!CellRange
Chart, add data label	EX 174	Click chart, in Labels group on Chart Tools Layout tab click Data Labels button, select options
Chart, add data series	EX 195	*See* Reference Window: Adding a Data Series to a Chart
Chart, add gridline	EX 193	Click chart, in Axes group on Chart Tools Layout tab click Gridlines button
Chart, change location	EX 167	Select chart, in Location group on Chart Tools Design tab click Move Chart button
Chart, change to 3D	EX 177	Select chart, in Type group on Chart Tools Design tab click Change Chart Type button, select 3D chart type
Chart, format data marker	EX 185	Click data marker, in Current Selection group on Chart Tools Layout tab click Format Selection
Chart, move	EX 167	Select chart, drag to new location
Chart, resize	EX 167	Select chart, drag resizing handle

TASK	PAGE #	RECOMMENDED METHOD
Chart, select	EX 167	Move pointer over a blank area of the chart, and then click
Chart, update	EX 179	Enter new values for chart's data source
Chart axis title, add or edit	EX 184	Select chart, in Labels group on Chart Tools Layout tab click Axis Titles button
Chart title, edit	EX 171	Double-click chart title, edit text of title
Code window, view	EX 647	In Visual Basic Editor, click View, click Code
Color scale, apply	EX D10	Click Conditional Formatting button in Styles group on Home tab, point to Color Scales, click scale type
Column, change width	EX 16	*See* Reference Window: Changing the Column Width or Row Height
Column, insert	EX 19	*See* Reference Window: Inserting a Column or Row
Column, select	EX 19	Click column heading; to select a range of columns, click the first column heading in the range, hold down Shift and click the last column heading
Column breaks in imported text file, edit	EX 578	*See* Reference Window: Connecting to a Text File
Combination chart, create	EX 197	*See* Reference Window: Creating a Combination Chart
Comment, delete	EX 420	Click cell with comment, in Comments group on Review tab, click Delete button
Comment, insert	EX 418	*See* Reference Window: Inserting a Comment
Comment, show or hide	EX 419	Click cell with comment, in the Comments group on the Review tab, click the Show/Hide Comment button
Comments, show or hide all	EX 419	In the Comments group on the Review tab, click the Show All Comments button
Compressed files, extract	FM 18	Right-click compressed folder, click Extract All, select location, click Extract
Compressed folder, create	FM 17	Right-click a blank area of a folder window, point to New, click Compressed (zipped) Folder
Conditional format, apply	EX 87	*See* Reference Window: Applying Conditional Formats (Data Bars and Highlights)
Conditional formatting rule, modify	EX D9	Click Conditional Formatting button in Styles group on Home tab, click Manage Rules, click Show formatting rules box, click This Worksheet, click rule, click Edit Rule, change formats as desired, click OK in each dialog box
Conditional Formatting Rules Manager, use	EX 363	In the Styles group on the Home tab, click the Conditional Formatting button, click Manage Rules
Connection, edit	EX 602	Click Connections button in Connections group on Data tab, select connection to edit, click Properties, make edits, click OK, click Close
Connections, view list of	EX 585	Click Connections button in Connections group on Data tab, click connection, click link
Criteria filters, specify complex criteria	EX 239	Click filter arrow, point to Number Filters, Text Filters, or Date Filters, specify filter criteria, click OK as needed
Cumulative interest, calculate	EX 472	Use the CUMIPMT function: =CUMIPMT(*rate*, *nper*, *pv*, *start*, *end*, *type*)
Cumulative principal, calculate	EX 472	Use the CUMPRINC function: =CUMPRINC(*rate*, *nper*, *pv*, *start*, *end*, *type*)

TASK	PAGE #	RECOMMENDED METHOD
Custom formats, create	EX A13	In the Number group on the Home tab, click the Dialog Box Launcher, on Number tab, click Custom in the Category box, enter format codes in the Type box, click OK

Custom VBA function, create	EX 691	All VBA custom functions have basic structure:
		Function *function_name* (*parameters*)
		   VBA commands
		   function_name = expression
		End Function

Data, create error alert message	EX 408	*See* Reference Window: Validating Data
Data, create input message	EX 408	*See* Reference Window: Validating Data
Data, create validation rule	EX 408	*See* Reference Window: Validating Data
Data series, add to chart	EX 195	*See* Reference Window: Adding a Data Series to a Chart
Database query, create	EX 594	*See* Reference Window: Running Microsoft Query to Connect to an Access Database
Date, insert current	EX 145	Insert TODAY() or NOW() function
Dates, fill in using AutoFill	EX 135	*See* Reference Window: Creating a Series with AutoFill
Depreciation, calculate	EX 482	*See* Reference Window: Calculating Depreciation
Developer tab, display or hide on the Ribbon	EX 420	Click 🔘, click Excel Options button, check or uncheck the Show Developer tab in the Ribbon check box, click OK
Digital signature, add to workbook	EX C20	*See* Reference Window: Adding a Digital Signature to a Workbook
Document Inspector, run	EX C17	Click 🔘, point to Prepare, click Inspect Document, click Inspect
Duplicate records, highlight	EX 361	In the Styles group on the Home tab, click Conditional Formatting button, point to Highlight Cells Rules, click Duplicate Values
Embedded object, create	EX B5	Copy selection, place insertion point where you want to place the object, in the Clipboard group on the Home tab, click the Paste button arrow, click Paste Special, click Paste option button, select object type, click OK
Embedded object, edit	EX B6	Double-click the embedded object, make edits, deselect object
Error message, view	EX C4	Click Error Checking button in Formula Auditing group on Formulas tab, edit formula as needed, click OK
Error value, trace	EX 501	*See* Reference Window: Tracing Error Values
Excel, start	EX 3	Click 🪟, click All Programs, click Microsoft Office, click Microsoft Office Excel 2007
Excel screen elements, customize	EX 686	Click 🔘, click Excel Options, click Advanced, select options in Display options for this worksheet section, click OK
Excel table, add record	EX 225	*See* Reference Window: Adding a Record to an Excel table
Excel table, create	EX 222	On Insert tab, in Tables group, click Table button, verify range of data, click OK
Excel table, format	EX 224	In Table Style Options group on Table Tools Design tab, click an option
Excel table, rename	EX 224	Click in table, in Properties group on Table Tools Design tab, select name in Table Name box, type name
External data, refresh	EX 587	*See* Reference Window: Refreshing External Data
External data range, set properties	EX 586	*See* Reference Window: Editing the Properties of an External Data Range

TASK	PAGE #	RECOMMENDED METHOD
External reference formula, create	EX 299	Click cell in destination file, type=, click cell in source file, complete formula as usual
File, close	OFF 21	Click 🔘, click Close
File, copy	FM 14	*See* Reference Window: Copying a File or Folder
File, delete	FM 16	Right-click the file, click Delete
File, move	FM 12	*See* Reference Window: Moving a File or Folder
File, open	OFF 22	*See* Reference Window: Opening an Existing File or Creating a New File
File, print	OFF 27	*See* Reference Window: Printing a File
File, rename	FM 16	Right-click the file, click Rename, type the new name, press Enter
File, save	OFF 18	*See* Reference Window: Saving a File
Files, compress	FM 17	Drag files into a compressed folder
Filter, clear from column	EX 237	Click column filter arrow, click Clear Filter command
Filter, clear from entire table	EX 240	In Sort & Filter group on Data tab, click the Clear button
Filter, select multiple items in a column	EX 238	Click filter arrow, check two or more items, click OK
Filter, use multiple columns	EX 236	Filter for one column, then repeat to filter for additional columns
Filter, use one column	EX 233	Click the column's filter arrow, check item to filter by, click OK
Filter arrows, display or hide	EX 233	In Sort & Filter group on Data tab, click Filter button
Filter by color, apply	EX 364	Click filter arrow, point to Filter by Color, click a color in the palette
Financial data, retrieve	EX 617	Click Existing Connections button in Get External Data group on Data tab, select MSN MoneyCentral Investor query, click Open, specify location, click OK
Folder, copy	FM 14	*See* Reference Window: Copying a File or Folder
Folder, create	FM 11	*See* Reference Window: Creating a Folder
Folder, move	FM 12	*See* Reference Window: Moving a File or Folder
Folder, rename	FM 16	Right-click the folder, click Rename, type the new name, press Enter
Folder or drive contents, view in Windows Explorer	FM 7–8	Click ▷
Font, change color	EX 61	In Font group on Home tab, click 🅰 ▾, click color
Font, change size	EX 60	In Font group on Home tab, click Font Size arrow, click point size
Font, change style	EX 60	In Font group on Home tab, click **B**, click *I*, or click U̲
Font, change typeface	EX 59	In Font group on Home tab, click Font arrow, click font
Format, apply Accounting Style, Percent Style, or Comma Style	EX 65–66	In Number group on Home tab, click $, click %, or click ,
Format, copy using Format Painter	EX 75	Select range, in Clipboard group on Home tab click 🖌, click range
Format, decrease decimal places	EX 66	In Number group on Home tab, click 🔢
Format, find and replace	EX 38	In Editing group on Home tab, click Find & Select, click Replace
Format, increase decimal places	EX 66	In Number group on Home tab, click 🔢
Format Cells dialog box, open	EX 72	In Number group on Home tab, click Dialog Box Launcher
Formula, copy	EX 24	*See* Reference Window: Moving or Copying a Cell or Range
Formula, copy using the fill handle	EX 132	*See* Reference Window: Copying Formulas and Formats with AutoFill

TASK	PAGE #	RECOMMENDED METHOD
Formula, enter	EX 29	*See* Reference Window: Entering a Formula
Formula, evaluate	EX 504	Select cell with formula, click Evaluate Formula button in Formula Auditing group on Formulas tab
Formula, reference another worksheet	EX 288	*See* Reference Window: Entering a Formula That References Another Worksheet
Formula results, copy and paste as values	EX A8	Copy range with formula results, click first cell in paste location, in the Clipboard group on the Home tab, click the Paste button arrow, click Paste Values
Formulas, add names to existing	EX 406	*See* Reference Window: Adding Defined Names to Existing Formulas
Formulas, view	EX 44	Click 🖩 , press Ctrl+`
Function, insert	EX 123	*See* Reference Window: Inserting a Function
Future value, calculate	EX 462	Use the FV function: =FV(*rate*, *nper*, *pmt*, [*pv*=0] [*type*=0])
Goal Seek, perform	EX 527	Click What-If Analysis button in Data Tools group on Data tab, click Goal Seek, enter parameters, click OK
Header/footer, create	EX 99	In Page Layout view, click header or footer section, type text or click button in Header & Footer Elements group on Design tab
Help task pane, use	OFF 24	*See* Reference Window: Getting Help
Hyperlink, create	EX 311	*See* Reference Window: Inserting a Hyperlink
Hyperlink, edit	EX 312	Right-click cell with hyperlink, click Edit Hyperlink, make edits in Edit Hyperlink dialog box, click OK
Icon set, apply	EX D14	Click Conditional Formatting button in Styles group on Home tab, point to Icon Sets, click icon set type
Immediate window, open	EX 653	In Visual Basic Editor, click View, click Immediate Window
Input box, create with VBA code	EX 671	Use VBA command: *variable*=InputBox(*Prompt*, *Title*)
Input message, create	EX 408	*See* Reference Window: Validating Data
Interest rate of investment, calculate	EX 465	Use the RATE function: =RATE(*nper*, *pmt*, *pv*, [*fv*=0] [*type*=0])
Internal rate of return, calculate	EX 492	*See* Reference Window: Determining the Return from an Investment
Internal rate of return at irregular intervals, calculate	EX 499	Use the XIRR function: =XIRR(*values*, *dates* [*guess*=0.1])
Invalid data, circle	EX 414	In the Data Tools group on the Data tab, click the Data Validation button arrow, click Circle Invalid Data
Length of investment, calculate	EX 463	Use the NPER function: =NPER(*rate*, *pmt*, *pv*, [*fv*=0] [*type*=0])
Linked object, edit	EX B5	Edit as usual in source file, or double-click the linked object in the destination file, make edits, deselect object
Linked object, paste to another file	EX B4	Copy selection, place insertion point where you want to place the link, in the Clipboard group on the Home tab, click the Paste button arrow, click Paste Special, click Paste link option button, select object type, click OK
Linked workbooks, update	EX 304	Click in source file and edit as usual
Links, manage	EX 306	In the Connections group on the Data tab, click the Edit Links button, select desired option, click OK
Macro, edit	EX 432	*See* Reference Window: Editing a Macro
Macro, record	EX 425	*See* Reference Window: Recording a Macro
Macro, run	EX 427	*See* Reference Window: Running a Macro

TASK	PAGE #	RECOMMENDED METHOD
Macro, set security level for	EX 423	*See* Reference Window: Setting Macro Security in Excel
Macro, view code	EX 432	*See* Reference Window: Editing a Macro
Macro button, create	EX 436	*See* Reference Window: Creating a Macro Button
Macro button, move	EX 438	Right-click the button, press Esc, drag the button by its selection border to a new location
Macro button, resize	EX 438	Right-click the button, press Esc, drag a selection handle
Message box, create with VBA code	EX 681	MsgBox *Prompt, Buttons, Title*
Module, rename	EX 646	Select module in Project Explorer, type new module name in (Name) row of Properties Window
Monthly loan payment, calculate	EX 459	Use the PMT function: =PMT(*rate, nper, pv,* [*fv*=0] [*type*=0])
Name, add to existing formulas	EX 406	*See* Reference Window: Adding Defined Names to Existing Formulas
Name, create for cell or range	EX 397	*See* Reference Window: Creating a Name for a Cell or Range
Net present value, calculate	EX 492	*See* Reference Window: Determining the Return from an Investment
Net present value at irregular intervals, calculate	EX 499	Use the XNPV function: =XNPV(*rate, values, dates*)
Office program, start	OFF 3	*See* Reference Window: Starting Office Programs
One-variable data table, create	EX 527	*See* Reference Window: Creating a One-Variable Data Table
Page, change orientation	EX 96	Click Page Layout tab, click Orientation button in Page Setup group, choose orientation type
Page break, set	EX 97	*See* Reference Window: Setting and Removing Page Breaks
Page break preview, switch to	EX 96	Click 🖾
PDF, save worksheet as	EX 689	Install Save as PDF add-in, click 🔘, point to Save As, click PDF or XPS, enter filename, click Publish
Picture, edit	EX D20	*See* Reference Window: Editing a Picture
Pie chart, 3D, rotate	EX 177	Select chart, in Background group on Chart Tools Layout tab, click 3-D Rotation button
Pie chart, create	EX 165	Select data values to chart, click Insert tab, click Pie button in Charts group, select a chart to sub-type
PivotChart, create	EX 269	In the Tools group on the PivotTable Tools Options tab, click the PivotChart button, complete the Insert Chart dialog box, click OK
PivotTable, create	EX 248	*See* Reference Window: Creating a PivotTable
PivotTable, rearrange	EX 255	Drag field buttons in the PivotTable Field List
PivotTable, refresh	EX 264	In the Data group on the PivotTable Tools Options tab, click the Refresh button
PivotTable field, remove	EX 263	In PivotTable Field List, uncheck items in the field area
PivotTable fields, filter	EX 258	Click the field arrow button in the PivotTable for the data you want to filter, then check and uncheck items
PivotTable items, group	EX 267	In the Group group on the PivotTable Tools Options tab, click the Group Field button, select options in the Grouping dialog box, click OK
PivotTable report layout, change	EX 255	In the Layout group on the PivotTable Tools Design tab, click the Report Layout button, click a layout
PivotTable style, apply	EX 253	In the PivotTable Styles group on the PivotTable Tools Design tab, click

TASK	PAGE #	RECOMMENDED METHOD
		More button, click a style
PivotTable value fields, format	EX 254	Click cell in PivotTable, in the Active Field group on the PivotTable Tools Options tab, click Field Settings button, click Number Format button, select format, click OK
Present value of investement, calculate	EX 464	Use the PV function: =PV(*rate*, *nper*, *pmt*, [*fv*=0] [*type*=0])
Print area, define	EX 96	Select range, click Page Layout tab, click Print Area button in Page Setup group, click Set Print Area
Program, Office, exit	OFF 28	Click ▣ on the title bar
Programs, Office, open	OFF 3	*See* Reference Window: Starting Office Programs
Project Explorer, view	EX 643	In Visual Basic Editor, click View, click Project Explorer
Project property, change	EX 645	In Project Explorer window, open Properties window, select property on appropriate tab, enter new value
Properties Window, view	EX 644	In Visual Basic Editor, click View, click Properties Window
Query, edit	EX 603	*See* Reference Window: Editing a Database Query
Query, save	EX 600	In the last step of Query Wizard, click Save Query, specify filename and location
Query Wizard, start	EX 595	Click From Other Sources button in Get External Data group on Data tab, click From Microsoft Query
Quick Access Toolbar, customize	EX 683	*See* Reference Window: Customizing the Quick Access Toolbar
Range, copy	EX 24	*See* Reference Window: Moving or Copying a Cell or Range
Range, move	EX 24	*See* Reference Window: Moving or Copying a Cell or Range
Range, select adjacent	EX 22	*See* Reference Window: Selecting Cell Ranges
Range, select nonadjacent	EX 22	*See* Reference Window: Selecting Cell Ranges
Real-Time data, acquire	EX 628	Use the RTD function: =RTD(*ProgID*, *server*, *topic1* [, *topic2*] …)
Record, delete from Excel table	EX 227	Select the record, in Cells group on Home tab, click Delete button arrow, and then click Delete Table Rows
Records, find and replace in Excel table	EX 226	Click in table, in Editing group on Home tab, click the Find & Select button, use Find and Replace dialog box as usual
Relative reference, change to absolute	EX 119	*See* Reference Window: Entering Relative, Absolute, and Mixed References
Report filter, add to a PivotTable	EX 257	In the PivotTable Field List, drag a field button to the Report Filter box
Report filter, modify	EX 257	Click the report filter arrow, click filter items
Ribbon, minimize or maximize	EX 440	Double-click any tab
Row, change height	EX 16	*See* Reference Window: Changing the Column Width or Row Height
Row, delete from Excel table	EX 27	*See* Reference Window: Inserting or Deleting a Cell Range
Row, hide	EX 95	In Cells group on Home tab, click Format button, point to Hide & Unhide, click Hide Rows
Row, insert	EX 19	*See* Reference Window: Inserting a Column or Row
Row, select	EX 19	Click row heading; to select a range of rows, click the first row heading in the range, hold down Shift and click the last row in the range
Row, unhide	EX 95	Select rows above and below hidden rows, in Cells group on Home tab click Format button, point to Hide & Unhide, click Unhide Rows

TASK	PAGE #	RECOMMENDED METHOD
Row to start import, specify	EX 578	*See* Reference Window: Connecting to a Text File
Rows, repeat in printout	EX 98	Click Page Layout tab, click Print Titles button in Page Setup group, click Rows to repeat at top
Row(s) and column(s), freeze	EX 221	Click cell below and to right of row(s) and column(s) to freeze. On View tab, in Window group, click Freeze Panes button, click option
Row(s) and column(s), unfreeze	EX 221	On View tab, in Window group, click Freeze Panes button, click Unfreeze Panes
Scenario, define	EX 539	*See* Reference Window: Defining a Scenario
Scenario, edit	EX 544	Click What-If Analysis button in Data Tools group on Data tab, click Scenario Manager, select scenario, click Edit, make edits, click Close
Scenario, view	EX 542	Click What-If Analysis button in Data Tools group on Data tab, click Scenario Manager, select scenario, click Show
Scenario PivotTable report, create	EX 546	*See* Reference Window: Creating a Scenario Report
Scenario summary report, create	EX 546	*See* Reference Window: Creating a Scenario Report
Shape, insert	EX 200	Click Insert tab, click Shapes button in Illustrations group, click desired shape, drag pointer to create shape
Shared workbook, accepting and rejecting changes	EX C11	*See* Reference Window: Accepting and Rejecting Changes to a Workbook
Shared workbook, review edits	EX C9	*See* Reference Window: Reviewing Edits in a Shared Workbook
SmartArt graphic, insert	EX D17	Click SmartArt button in Illustrations group on Insert tab, click a type, click a graphic, click OK
Solver, create Answer Report	EX 559	Run Solver, click Answer button in Reports box, click Keep Solver Solution option button, click OK
Solver, install and activate	EX 553	*See* Reference Window: Activating Solver
Solver, run	EX 555	Click Solver button in Analysis group on Data tab, click Solve
Solver, set constraints	EX 556	*See* Reference Window: Setting Constraints on the Solver Solution
Solver, set parameters	EX 555	*See* Reference Window: Setting Solver Parameters
Solver model, load	EX 561	*See* Reference Window: Saving and Loading a Solver Model
Solver model, save	EX 561	*See* Reference Window: Saving and Loading a Solver Model
Sort, create a custom list	EX 231	*See* Reference Window: Creating a Custom List
Sort, multiple columns	EX 229	*See* Reference Window: Sorting Data Using Multiple Sort Fields
Sort, one column	EX 228	Click ⬆ or ⬇
Special formats, use	EX A12	In the Number group on the Home tab, click the Dialog Box Launcher, on Number tab, click Special in the Category box, select a format, click OK
Spelling, check in worksheet	EX 40	Click Review tab, click Spelling in Proofing group
Style, apply	EX 77	*See* Reference Window: Applying Styles
Sub procedure, insert	EX 648	Open Code window, click Insert, click Procedure, enter procedure name, type, and scope, click OK
Sub procedure, run	EX 650	Click in sub procedure in the Visual Basic Editor, click Run, click Run Sub/User Form
Sub procedure, syntax	EX 648	Sub *Procedure_Name(parameters)* *VBA commands and comments* End Sub

TASK	PAGE #	RECOMMENDED METHOD
Subtotal Outline view, use	EX 245	Click an outline button to show or hide the selected outline level
Subtotals, insert	EX 243	*See* Reference Window: Calculating Subtotals for a Range of Data
Subtotals, remove	EX 246	In Outline group on the Data tab, click Subtotal button, click Remove All button, click OK
Sum, create conditional	EX 472	Use the SUMIF function: =SUMIF(*range*, *criteria*, [*sum_range*])
Sum function, apply	EX 33	Click cell, in Editing group on Home tab, click Σ
Table style, modify	EX D5	Click Format as Table button in Styles group on Home tab, click New Table Style, type name, format elements as desired, click OK
Template, create custom	EX 317	*See* Reference Window: Creating a Custom Template
Text, align within a cell	EX 68	In Alignment group on Home tab, click ▤, click ▤, or click ▤
Text, enter into cell	EX 10	Click the cell, type text entry, press Enter
Text, enter multiple lines in a cell	EX 12	*See* Reference Window: Entering Multiple Lines of Text Within a Cell
Text, increase or decrease indent of	EX 68	In Alignment group on Home tab, click ▤ or ▤
Text file, connect to	EX 578	*See* Reference Window: Connecting to a Text File
Theme, create and save	EX D23	*See* Reference Window: Creating and Saving a Theme
Total row, add or remove from Excel table	EX 240	In Table Style Options group on the Table Tools Design tab, check or uncheck Total Row check box
Total row, select summary statistics	EX 240	Click arrow button in Total row cell, click summary function
Tracking log, view	EX C9	*See* Reference Window: Reviewing Edits in a Shared Workbook
Trend, extrapolate	EX 480	*See* Reference Window: Interpolating and Extrapolating
Trend, interpolate	EX 480	*See* Reference Window: Interpolating and Extrapolating
Trusted location, define	EX 590	*See* Reference Window: Defining a Trusted Location
Two-variable data table, create	EX 532	*See* Reference Window: Creating a Two-Variable Data Table
Validation circles, clear all	EX 414	In the Data Tools group on the Data tab, click the Data Validation button, click Clear Validation Circles
Validation circles, clear from a cell	EX 414	Enter valid data
Validation circles, create	EX 414	In the Data Tools group on the Data tab, click the Data Validation button, click Circle Invalid Data
Validation rule, create	EX 408	*See* Reference Window: Validating Data
Variable, declare	EX 665	Use VBA command: Dim *variable* as *type*
Variable, store object in	EX 666	Use VBA command: Set *variable=object*
Variable, store value in	EX 665	Use VBA command: *variable=expression*
VBA, insert a command	EX 434	Open the Visual Basic Editor, display the macro in the Code window, click at the end of a VBA command, press Enter, type the new command
VBA code, view	EX 432	*See* Reference Window: Editing a Macro
VBA object, apply method	EX 661	Use VBA command: *object.method*
VBA object, set property	EX 657	Use VBA command: *object.property = expression*
VBA object collection, reference	EX 654	Use reference: *object_collection(id)*
Visual Basic Editor, open or close	EX 432	*See* Reference Window: Editing a Macro
Visual Basic Editor, start	EX 642	Click Macros button in Code group on Developer tab, click a macro name, click Edit

TASK	PAGE #	RECOMMENDED METHOD
Watch Window, use	EX 505	Click Watch Window button in Formula Auditing group on Formulas tab, click Add Watch, click a cell, click Add
Web page, create from a workbook, worksheet, or range	EX 326	*See* Reference Window: Saving a Workbook, Worksheet, or Range as a Web Page
Web query, create	EX 613	*See* Reference Window: Working with Web Queries
Web query, refresh automatically	EX 620	In Connections group on Data tab, click Connections button, click connection, click Properties, click Refresh data when opening the file check box, click Refresh every check box, enter time, click OK, click Close
Web query, refresh manually	EX 620	In Connections group on Data tab, click Refresh All button arrow, click Refresh
Web query, save	EX 613	*See* Reference Window: Working with Web Queries
Web query, set format options	EX 613	*See* Reference Window: Working with Web Queries
What-if analysis, perform	EX 522	Change value in input cell, observe impact on result cells
Window, close	OFF 6	Click [X] or click [X]
Window, maximize	OFF 7	Click [□] or click [□]
Window, minimize	OFF 7	Click [—] or click [—]
Window, restore	OFF 7	Click [⯗] or click [⯗]
Windows Explorer, start	FM 7	Click 🟢, click All Programs, click Accessories, click Windows Explorer
Workbook, check backward compatibility	EX C22	Click 🔘, point to Prepare, click Run Compatibility Checker, click OK
Workbook, create from template	EX 314	*See* Reference Window: Creating a Workbook Based on a Template
Workbook, encrypt	EX C19	Click 🔘, point to Prepare, click Encrypt Document, type password, click OK, type password again, click OK
Workbook, mark as final	EX C19	Click 🔘, point to Prepare, click Mark as Final, click OK in each dialog box
Workbook, preview	EX 43	Click 🔘, click Print, click Print Preview
Workbook, print	EX 43	Click 🔘, click Print, click Print, click OK
Workbook, protect	EX 417	*See* Reference Window: Protecting a Workbook
Workbook, save	EX 21	On Quick Access Toolbar, click 💾
Workbook, save as a Web page	EX 326	*See* Reference Window: Saving a Workbook, Worksheet, or Range as a Web Page
Workbook, save earlier version in Excel 2007 file format	EX A2	In Save As dialog box, select save location, enter filename, click the Save as type button, click Excel Workbook, click Save
Workbook, save in earlier Excel file format	EX A17	In Save As dialog box, change filename, select save location, click the Save as type button, click Excel 97-2003 Workbook, click Save
Workbook, save with macros	EX 440	In Save As dialog box, select save location, enter filename, click the Save as type button, click Excel Macro-Enabled Workbook, click Save
Workbook, share	EX C5	Click Share Workbook button in Changes group on Review tab, check Allow changes by more than one user at the same time check box, click OK, click OK
Workbook properties, set	EX C15	Click 🔘, point to Prepare, click Properties, enter values for document properties, click Close

TASK	PAGE #	RECOMMENDED METHOD
Workbook window, split and unsplit	EX C2	*See* Reference Window: Splitting the Workbook Window into Panes
Workbooks, arrange	EX 298	*See* Reference Window: Arranging Workbooks
Workbooks, link	EX 296	Enter a formula in the following form: =[WorkbookName]WorksheetName!CellRange
Workbooks, merge	EX C13	*See* Reference Window: Merging Workbooks
Workbooks, switch	EX 297	In the Window group on the View tab, click the Switch Windows button, click the workbook to make active
Worksheet, add background image	EX 63	Click Page Layout tab, click Background button in Page Setup group, click image file, click Insert
Worksheet, delete	EX 35	Right-click sheet tab, click Delete
Worksheet, hide	EX C18	Right-click sheet tab, click Hide
Worksheet, insert	EX 35	Click 🗐
Worksheet, move	EX 36	Drag sheet tab to new location
Worksheet, protect	EX 415	*See* Reference Window: Protecting a Worksheet
Worksheet, rename	EX 36	Double-click sheet tab, type new name, press Enter
Worksheet, unhide	EX C18	Right-click any sheet tab, click Unhide, select hidden worksheet, click OK
Worksheet, unprotect	EX 418	Make worksheet active, in Changes group on the Review tab, click the Unprotect Sheet button
Worksheet group, print	EX 293	Select worksheet group, set up worksheets and print as usual
Worksheets, copy to another workbook	EX 287	*See* Reference Window: Copying Worksheets to Another Workbook
Worksheets, group or ungroup	EX 283	*See* Reference Window: Grouping and Ungrouping Worksheets
Worksheets, move between	EX 7	Click sheet tab; or click a tab scrolling button and then click the sheet tab
Workspace, create	EX 309	Open and arrange workbooks as desired, in the Window group on the View tab, click the Save Workspace button, type a filename, select save location, click Save
Workspace, zoom	OFF 8	*See* Reference Window: Zooming the Workspace
XML data, bind to cells	EX 625	Drag XML element from XML Source pane, drop into cell, click Header Options button to display element name next to bound cell
XML data, import	EX 626	Bind XML elements to worksheet cells, refresh connection to XML data file
XML data map, load	EX 623	*See* Reference Window: Loading an XML Data Map
XML Source pane, display	EX 623	Click Source button in XML group on Developer tab